THE LIFE AND WORK
OF
CARL ROGERS

HOWARD KIRSCHENBAUM

PCCS Books

Ross-on-Wye

First published in 2007

PCCS BOOKS
2 Cropper Row
Alton Road
Ross-on-Wye
Herefordshire
HR9 5LA
UK
Tel +44 (0)1989 763900
contact@pccs-books.co.uk
www.pccs-books.co.uk

© Howard Kirschenbaum, 2007

Howard Kirschenbaum asserts his right to be
identified as the author of this work in accordance
with the Copyright, Designs and Patents Act 1988.

The Life and Work of Carl Rogers

British Library Cataloguing in Publication Data.
A catalogue record for this book is available from the British Library.

ISBN 978 1 898059 98 1 (Cloth)
ISBN 978 1 898059 93 6 (Printed Paper Case)

Cover design by Old Dog Graphics
Printed by Cromwell Books, Trowbridge, UK

CONTENTS

PREFACE

In recent years, when friends heard I was working on Carl Rogers' biography, they would ask, "Didn't you do that twenty-five years ago?" Implicit in the question was a wonder about why a biography would need to be updated. Rogers died in 1987. What more was there to say?

Actually there are five answers to this question—five ways in which the present volume is substantially different from *On Becoming Carl Rogers* which was published by Delacorte Press in 1979. These differences tell something about the subject and the author.

First is that Rogers lived another ten years after 1977, which was when the earlier chronicle ended. This decade, when Rogers was seventy-five to eighty-five years old, turned out to be one of the most important periods in his career. It was during this time that Rogers extended his person-centered approach to helping relationships into the resolution of inter-group and international conflict. Through the Carl Rogers Peace Project and other venues he and his colleagues conducted important experiments in cross-cultural communication and peacekeeping, work for which he was nominated for the Nobel Peace Prize. This work was not and is not widely known. Not only is it important in its own right, it puts Rogers' historical contributions to psychology, psychotherapy and group work into a wider social and political context. Comprehending his last ten years is essential to understanding the life and work of Carl Rogers.

Secondly, we know much more about Carl Rogers now than we did before he died. By "we," I certainly include myself, but also many of Rogers' friends and associates. As open as Rogers was in many respects, there were some important areas of his life and career that he kept confidential, but which are revealed in his private papers donated to the Library of Congress and other papers residing in the University of California at Santa Barbara Library. His relationships with the Central Intelligence Agency, women, alcohol, and the paranormal and spirituality, among other areas, are described in these documents, as well as interviews I conducted with close associates and relatives after Rogers' death. They reveal a more complex and some would say more interesting character than even those familiar with Rogers would have imagined.

I have no doubt that Rogers wanted these stories to be told eventually. He said as much to me, telling me that he was glad I intended to update his biography after his death and that he was leaving papers for me to see that he was not comfortable coming to light during his lifetime.[1] And he did leave his papers for future researchers to peruse.[2] Natalie Rogers, his daughter and often his close colleague, had difficulty understanding why her father would preserve letters and documents that were sometimes unflattering, compromising or controversial, that might give posterity a less positive image of the man, that might tarnish his greatness in the eyes of his admirers and give ammunition to his detractors.[3] In fact, one critical biographer of Rogers did take some of these letters out of context to present a distorted and sensationalized portrait of the man.[4] That "outing" of Rogers alone justifies a fuller, more balanced, more nuanced understanding of Rogers' character.

More importantly, Rogers *wanted* us to know him in all his complexity. I am not surprised that he left these private records for posterity. Throughout his life Rogers had a deep desire to *be known*, to be close to others. Yet as much as he shared himself with others—in his writings, in therapy, in encounter groups, in relationships—there were still important parts of himself that he kept private. Throughout his professional life he discouraged "Rogerians"; he did not want people to idolize or emulate him. He wanted them to trust themselves, to find their own voice. I believe he left *all* his papers behind for two reasons: to try one last time to share himself with us and to remind us that he was not perfect, that it would be an error to put him on a pedestal, that we need to find our own way.

A third way this edition is different from the earlier one is that we now have over a quarter century's perspective with which to understand Rogers' contributions to psychology, the helping professions and society. Some of his historical contributions were already clear in the 1970s, but much was in flux. Would the encounter group movement, for example, or Rogers' concept of "the fully functioning person" and "the person of tomorrow" prove to be seminal or faddish, prescient or ephemeral? Would Rogers' contributions to psychotherapy be of historic interest only or would they survive and influence future generations of research and practice? While some of these questions remain outstanding, it is now possible to appreciate Rogers' work with greater historical perspective. The new, last chapter of this volume, in particular, devotes itself to an examination of what the last several decades of research and development in psychotherapy and the person-centered approach have revealed about Rogers' legacy.

Fourth, my own relationship to the subject has matured over the past three decades. When I first approached Rogers, requesting his cooperation on writing his biography, I was a doctoral student in my mid-twenties. Although I certainly was enamored with the man and his ideas, I was never a person-centered purist. I had already developed a professional identity in other areas. Over the next seven years of researching and writing the biography, in my own thought and practice I integrated Rogers' model with other counseling and educational approaches. I was never awed by Rogers personally. So I had a good deal of independence from my subject. (In fact, years later, a few weeks before Rogers died, he asked me to co-edit with him a collection of his writings, telling me, "I ask you because, more than any of my colleagues here, you have a greater distance from my work.")[5] On the other hand, because I needed his cooperation and he did not know me from Adam, I initially offered and he accepted that, in return for his cooperation on the biography (extensive interviews, access to his files, addresses of current and former colleagues, etc.) he would have final say over whether the biography would be published. I was convinced that this would not affect my work and that he would like the final product. As it turned out, after I sent him the first few chapters for factual corrections he voluntarily released me from this agreement, characteristically telling me that he had come to trust me, that he didn't want our agreement to discourage me from being critical, and that I should put more of myself in the book. This I did, as best as I knew how to do at the time. Yet looking back almost thirty years, I recognize that I was still a relative youngster in the 1970s. Since then my own understanding of Carl Rogers, counseling and psychotherapy, education, the human condition—in a word, *life*—has matured. I would hope that the current edition will reflect a wiser, more balanced perspective toward my subject.

Finally, this edition is fully referenced, which the previous one was not. Actually I did have citations and references for most of the previous edition, but the publisher and I agreed not to include them in the biography. We concluded, mistakenly I think, that the book would sell better as a popular biography if it did not appear too scholarly. In retrospect, I think that decision backfired and took away from the book's credibility and gravitas, perhaps making it seem more of an authorized biography rather than an independent and objective, sometimes critical, sometimes affectionate portrait of the man and his work. Hence the current edition includes ample endnotes and references. Hopefully, the tiny numbers in the text denoting endnotes will not distract the reader who has no interest in the source of the particular anecdote, quotation, fact or idea. At the same time, students and scholars who wish to identify or locate sources and reference materials should find this information helpful. More information on my sources, together with acknowledgements, appear at the end of the book.

In his last book, Carl Rogers wrote, "Writing is my way of communicating with a world to which, in a very real sense, I feel I do not quite belong. I wish very much to be understood, but I don't expect to be."[6] That feeling of not quite belonging, which began in his childhood, remained throughout his life. Yet, in the end, I believe it *is* possible to know Carl Rogers. It is my hope that this volume will help fulfill his wish to be understood.

Howard Kirschenbaum
Rochester, New York
December 2006

CHAPTER 1

Childhood and Youth
1902–1919

Carl Rogers was a product of midwestern America. Born at a time when most leading psychologists and psychotherapists were Europeans or European emigrants to America, Carl Rogers' roots go far back in United States history.

His fraternal grandmother, Betsy Ferris, was descended from Ticknors, who emigrated from Kent, England to Massachusetts in 1633, and eventually settled around Glens Falls, New York.[1] His fraternal grandfather, Alexander Hamilton Rogers, was also descended from English emigrants who settled in the Glens Falls area around 1800. In two generations the Rogers family firmly established themselves in the community, several becoming lawyers and judges, others farmers and business people. Alexander and Betsy married before the Civil War and left Glens Falls, traveling along the recently completed Erie Canal, which opened the Northwest Territories to new settlers, and then through the Great Lakes. They eventually stopped in Milwaukee, where Alexander became a conductor on the Milwaukee Railroad on the run from Milwaukee to Prairie du Chien on the western border of Wisconsin.[2] Still later they moved to Wauwatosa, Wisconsin, where they raised five sons. There is still a Rogers Avenue in Wauwatosa; their house, the Damon House, is a historical landmark. Alexander's second son, Walter Alexander Rogers, was born there in 1868.

Carl Rogers' mother was also descended from early American settlers. Matthew Cushing, baptized in England in 1589, crossed the Atlantic on the ship "Diligent" in 1638 with 133 passengers and settled in Hingham, Massachusetts. "The immediate occasion of their departure seems to have been trouble in ecclesiastical matters."[3] The *Genealogy of the Cushing Family*, compiled

1

by James S. Cushing in 1877, describes again a family that made many contributions to the community and to the new country.[4] Like the Rogers, a branch of the Cushings moved west along the Erie Canal and settled in Wisconsin. In Delafield, Wisconsin, there stands a memorial to three Cushing brothers killed in the Civil War. After the war one of the Cushing family purchased a farm in Brookfield, about six miles from Wauwatosa. There Julia Margaret Cushing, one of three daughters, was born, also in 1868.

Walter Rogers and Julia Cushing knew each other as children. The Cushings had moved into town, a block away from the Rogers, so they met at various school, church, and social occasions. On New Year's Day the five brothers would dress up and "go calling" on the three sisters.

Walter attended the University of Wisconsin where he was president of the campus Y.M.C.A. and remained for a year of graduate work to become a civil engineer.[5] At the University he resumed his acquaintance with Julia Cushing who attended college there for two or three years.[6] They must have found much in common: they were the same age, they came from the same home town and from similar farming and religious backgrounds, and they attended the same college. They were married in Wauwatosa on July 1, 1891. As the local paper announced, "After the wedding, Mr. and Mrs. Rogers left for their home in Livingston, Montana."[7]

Walter was often away from home, supervising the construction of track, bridges, and tunnels for different railroads across the country. Thus they spent the beginning of their marriage in western Montana, where Walter was supervising several construction projects. A short time later they moved back to Elgin, Illinois, near Chicago. Their first three children, Lester, Margaret, and Ross, were born there in 1893, 1895, and 1899, respectively. In 1901 Rogers and a partner went into business for themselves, forming the Bates and Rogers Construction Corporation with headquarters in Chicago. Around that time they rented a bigger house a few miles away, at 237 Clinton Avenue in the new "suburb" of Oak Park, about eight miles west of Chicago.[8] Here their fourth child, Carl Ransom Rogers, was born on January 8, 1902. Two more sons, Walter and John, came later, in 1907 and 1908.

Suburban Childhood

Carl was a rather sickly child—slight, shy, prone to tears, often the target of jokes and teasing by his older brothers. With his father away from home on business trips, he developed much warmer feelings for his mother. The baby of the family for over five years, he received considerable attention from her and the older children, who taught him to read at about age four. He seemed to take easily to the world of books and before long was reading many of the thick volumes on the family's bookshelves, especially a book of Bible stories called *The Story of the Bible from Genesis to Revelation Told in Simple Language Adapted to All Ages, but Especially to the Young,*[9] which he read from beginning to end many times, to the approval of his religion-minded parents.

Business continued to improve for Walter Rogers, so that when Carl was almost five the family moved about a mile away to a new house at 547 North Euclid Avenue, on the north side of Oak Park.[10] The Village of Oak Park had been incorporated the year Carl was born. Proudly described by its residents as "the place where the saloons end and the churches begin,"[11] Oak Park had ordinances to protect its adult citizens from uncensored movies, boxing matches, information on venereal disease and birth control, all forms of gambling, and all consumption of alcohol. Similar restrictions protected Oak Park's children under eighteen from buying cigarettes, playing billiards, driving a car, owning a cap gun, or being out of the house after the 8 or 9 p.m. winter and summer curfew unless accompanied by a parent or responsible adult.[12] It was an upper-middle-class community of doctors, lawyers, bankers, businessmen and other professionals. Among its residents were Frank Lloyd Wright, Dr. Clarence Hemingway (Ernest's father), Edgar Rice Borroughs (creator of the Tarzan books), and Charles MacArthur (co-author of the play "The Front Page").[13]

In this prosperous, protected setting, Walter designed and supervised the building of their new house. It was a light brick, center-hall Colonial home, with six or more bedrooms, a covered front porch spanning the whole front side, and a glassed-in sun porch on the rear.[14] The corner lot ran clear through the block to the other street and had a barn for the horses and buggies, a pen for chickens and turkeys, Julia Rogers' large vegetable and flower garden, and a sandbox for the younger children. Although the move was exciting for Carl, it marked the first in a series which would repeatedly interrupt the friendships he had barely begun to establish. But he quickly made new playmates in the neighborhood and soon was quite happy in the new house.

Possibly because of his fragile health, Carl did not begin school until the age of six years and nine months. He attended the Oliver Wendell Holmes School which Ernest Hemingway, who lived three blocks away and was two years older than Carl, and the children of Frank Lloyd Wright also attended at the time. The children used to call Hemingway "Dirty Ernie" because he swore.[15]

On his first day in school Carl was placed in Miss Ely's first-grade class. She seemed like a very stern teacher to the little boy, and he was relieved when Miss Ely alerted the principal, Miss Hood, that he was too far advanced for the first-grade reader. Helen Elliott, one of Carl's classmates then, later recalled how, on the second day of school, a small boy was ushered into her second-grade classroom and asked to read to the class from the second-grade reader.[16] His performance was so fluent that he also read to the third and fourth grades that day; but it was decided that the second grade would be far enough along for Carl to begin

3

school. He found Miss Littler, the second-grade teacher, to be nice and soon felt very fondly toward her.

With Miss Littler's and subsequent teachers' encouragement, his love for reading increased. Father Rogers also encouraged this at first. Carl's sister Margaret recalled how "Father would get these exciting Indian stories. The Indians were just coming over the hill and we'd be breathless ... then father would close the book and say, 'It's time to go to bed.'"[17] Carl remembered similar excitement when his father read to them about man-eating lions approaching the corral or the establishment of Fort Dearborn which later became Chicago.[18] Consequently Carl devoured all the books he could get his hands on, mostly novels and adventure stories—tales of Indians, wars, pioneers, and pirates—and he came to love more and more the fantasy world created through his reading. James Fenimore Cooper was a great favorite. One history book he loved and read through many times was *The Sinking of the Albemarle.*[19] This told of the exploits of Willie B. Cushing, one of his mother's family, who became a Civil War hero when he took a small boat with a torpedo on it and, with a small crew, went up one of the coastal rivers and blew up the Confederate ironclad *Albemarle,* which at that point was sinking many Union ships. When no other books were available, he would read the encyclopedia or even the dictionary, occasionally trying to gain sex information through these sources. Like most parents then, his own never provided such information; the subject was taboo.

In addition to being an avid reader of adventure stories, Carl seemed to have a talent for creating stories himself. When he was in the second grade, one of his stories—a fantasy about leaves talking to each other and finally falling off the trees—was posted for visitors to see. A few years later he would keep his younger brothers, Walter and John, entertained for hours with war and adventure stories that he would make up on the spot.

Although his parents were both college educated, and although his father was partly responsible for his love of adventure stories, they soon began to frown upon his reading habits and his fantasy world. They were somewhat anti-intellectual and very practical people. Bible reading, of course, was to be encouraged, as were technical and how-to books, but when there were chores to be done, reading and storytelling for their own sake were considered unproductive, self-indulgent, and practically sinful. One of his mother's frequent reprovals was, "There you are again with your nose in a book," and many were the times when he would be embarrassingly startled out of his dream world to remember, "Oh, gosh, I was supposed to do this or that and I never once thought of it."[20] (Years later, as a college professor, it took him some time to overcome feelings of guilt when he read in the morning.) Once, in the third or fourth grade, Carl wandered off from recess and walked home thinking school was over. He had to get a note from their housekeeper Mrs. Robinson and returned to school feeling humiliated.[21] Brother John remembered a sign on Carl's dresser, in large print, reading, DO IT NOW!—an antidote for his forgetfulness.[22]

In the family Carl's tendency toward dreaminess was the source of many jokes and barbs. It was a teasing family, and, as he later recalled, the teasing could be vicious at times. "You just took digs at everybody and everybody took digs at you."[23] Thus he was dubbed with many nicknames, like "Mr. Absent-Minded Professor" and "Mr. Mooney," the latter after a somewhat spaced-out comic strip character of the time. Margaret remembered how "those boys nearly tore each other limb from limb in their arguing, but after they were over with it they were good friends again. That was the sort of fellowship we had. It was really rough at times but you stood your own ground or you knuckled under, but then you were friends afterward." Years later, after Carl described his family in an autobiographical essay,[24] Walter, John, and Margaret Rogers all insisted that Carl had exaggerated the negative quality of the teasing. They saw it mostly as being in good fun, and John and Margaret seemed almost offended that Carl would characterize the family in this way. On the other hand, they all agreed that Carl was the most sensitive of the children. Walter said the "teasing bothered [Carl] a helluva lot more than anyone else."[25] John referred to "Carl's thin skin" and maintained the teasing "wasn't all that bad." Carl, in turn, insisted that the teasing was decidedly negative and often mean, as when the brothers mercilessly teased their shy sister on one of her rare dates and just about destroyed "any interest she had in boys." When the date arrived, instead of calling their dog "Here, Sheppy," Carl called the dog by saying, "Here, Charlie" (or whatever the date's name was). "I meant 'Here, Sheppy.' I was after the dog; but I was calling *his* [the date's] name. But it was just an example of the fact that we'd been talking about nothing else for the previous hour, kidding about him and so on … Oh my God, we just made her so miserable … that's probably one of the reasons she never got married."[26]

Whatever the reality of the teasing, the picture emerges of Carl as a vulnerable child, tender and easily hurt, yet feisty and even sarcastic in his own way, since this was necessary to survive in the family repartee. While his siblings apparently took the teasing for granted, it left a deep imprint on Carl's psyche; even sixty years later he could be deeply hurt by his brother Lester's teasing.[27]

Walter and Julia Rogers were both committed Christians. His family had been Congregational, hers Baptist. Both took their religion seriously, but Julia was more conservative and traditional, Walter a bit more flexible and open-minded. When the family might have attended the more orthodox Third Congregational Church in Oak Park, Walter chose the more progressive First Congregational Church whose pastor William E. Barton (brother of Red Cross founder Clara Barton) "made it clear that the old theology of original sin and damnation had no place in forward thinking Oak Park."[28] Although Rogers' parents "felt he was much too radical" and "he and the church and the doctrines were very suspect,"[29] perhaps they attended the First Church because its congregation comprised the leading members of the community.[30] On Sundays the family all climbed into the larger of their two horse-drawn buggies (the smaller one was for shopping), and Walter drove the family to church. In the cold Illinois winters they piled on layers of blankets to keep warm. When they got their first automobile, an Argo electric model with isinglass curtains, a charcoal-burning foot warmer in the back seat helped provide additional heat in the uncovered car as they drove the several miles to church.[31] Later father Rogers served as Chairman of the Board of Trustees of the First Congregational Church in Glen Ellyn, Illinois, where they dedicated "the Rogers chapel" out of gratitude for his generous help in their building program.

A daily religious ritual of the Rogers was morning prayers. The family sat in a circle with each member reading a verse from the Bible and Walter or Julia offering an original prayer. Carl later wrote, "My mother was a person with strong religious convictions, whose views became increasingly fundamentalist as she matured. Two of her biblical phrases, often used in family prayers, stick in my mind and give the feeling of her religion: 'Come out from among them and be ye separate'; 'All our righteousness is as filthy rags in Thy sight, oh Lord.' (The first expressed her conviction of superiority, that we were of the 'elect' and should not mingle with those who were not so favored; the second her conviction of inferiority, that at our best we were unspeakably sinful.) My father was involved too in the family prayers, church attendance and the like, but in a less emotional way. They were both devoted and loving parents, giving a great deal of time and energy to creating a family life which would 'hold' the children in the way in which they should go. They were masters of the art of subtle and loving control. I do not remember ever being given a direct command on an important subject, yet such was the unity of our family that it was understood by all that … 'Other persons behave in dubious ways which we do not approve of in our family. Many of them play cards, go to movies, smoke, dance, drink, and engage in other activities, some unmentionable. So the best thing to do is to be tolerant of them, since they may not know better, but to keep away from any close communication with them, and to live your life within the family.' … For some reason, swearing was not quite so strictly tabooed—perhaps because father would, on occasion, vent his anger in that way."[32]

Along with religion, another value of the family was the Protestant work ethic. There was little that good hard work would not cure, and the children were all expected to do their share of the chores. One of Carl's responsibilities was feeding and caring for the chickens out behind the house. This was the traditional "business enterprise" of the Rogers children, and while in elementary school Carl took over the job of selling eggs to his mother and the neighbors. His parents encouraged this type of activity. He would be near home, away from possibly bad influences, and engaged in productive work. He had to make out bills, keep records, and do most everything required of a small businessman. If he did not submit a bill to his mother for the eggs he sold her, he simply would not get paid. When the children were youngsters, father Rogers would empty his pockets when he came home and have them put the pennies, nickels, and other coins in similar piles; or he would have them put his canceled checks in numerical order. Carl later wrote, "With regard to money, I feel my parents were very wise. We had an allowance. If we earned money, that was our money; we were encouraged to have separate enterprises … So we got the notion of earning money very early in the game and that you could do things with earned money."[33]

Both father and mother encouraged that kind of practical knowledge wherever they could. Walter would often take his children on trips with him to broaden their experience in the real world; then he would urge them to keep a journal and describe what they had seen. In 1914, for example, he took the family to British Columbia, where Lester and Ross were working on one of his construction sites, the Connaught Tunnel.[34] They were in Winnipeg the day the First World War began, and Carl swam in a hot spring pool in Banff, Alberta, in a July Fourth snowstorm. Aside from their educational value, John thought there was another reason his father took the children on trips. "Since he was away so much of the time during World War I, this gave him an opportunity to further enjoy his children. If he couldn't stay home, he'd try to take someone with him when possible."

Julia Rogers was quite capable of managing the household in Walter's absence. Daughter Margaret recalled how her mother once put a revolver in the kitchen table drawer to be ready in case a workman made trouble when she was home alone. "Mother could do all sorts of repairs around the house. It was she more than father who taught us to use tools … [She had] firm hands. They could make your bottom sting when she thought the occasion demanded a spanking … they were creative hands. She could paint beautiful pictures which all of us treasure."[35]

Helen Elliott, his classmate since the second grade, lived a block away from Carl in Oak Park. Along with several other boys and girls from the neighborhood, they walked or rode their bicycles to school together and would often play together on the block, riding or playing tag, "pom-pom-pull-away," "three old cat," and other games. But Carl was expected home right after school and so did not develop as deep friendships with the others as he might have. Helen remembered him then as a "shy, sensitive, and unsocial boy, who preferred to live in his books and his dream world rather than encounter the rough-tumble of the play yard or enter into competitive sports. He went directly home after school and while we lingered to bat the ball in a softball game, he was feeding his chickens or selling eggs to the neighbors."[36] He recalled having "one fairly close friend, the girl next door," but beyond that, the other children were only acquaintances.[37]

Living in a world of books as he did, he was an excellent student, always getting among the highest grades in the class. He was the pet of several teachers, anxious to do well and please them. They encouraged his reading and intellectual curiosity in ways his parents did not. He had another crush on his fifth-grade teacher, Miss Kuntz, and one of his first minor acts of personal independence was to stay after school frequently, helping her with tasks around the classroom. He once cheated on a test that year, so scared was he of failing. Other than being something of a teacher's pet, he did nothing to alienate his fellow students; but neither did they know him very well or particularly like him. He had only one fist fight in elementary school and later wrote of it, "I was frightened to death but did my best in what ended as pretty much of a draw."[38] Walter and John, on the other hand, were often getting into fights with their classmates. John recalled how "Carl would come on us fighting and stop it. Walt would say, 'The kid started it.' Carl would ask why. I would say, 'Walt was the reason.' After a series of these came the nicknames: John, the Kid; Carl, the Lad; Walt, the Reason. So we were The Kid, The Lad and The Reason."

As Carl grew up his father was prospering. Beyond bridges, tunnels and railroads Bates and Rogers expanded into all kinds of construction work, especially hydroelectric power plants and dams and, with the coming of the automobile, concrete roads across the country.[39] When Carl was in the eighth grade, his father had to leave on a trip to several construction sites in the South and the East. Carl was invited to go along and allowed to miss school for two or three weeks with the understanding that he would write a report about his "educational trip," including Chicago, New Orleans, and Norfolk, Virginia. At some point it began to occur to him that his father was trying to interest him in the construction business. Later he realized that this was not necessarily the main motive, as his brothers Lester and Ross were already interested in that business; nor was it entirely "educational." It was more that his father was concerned with his withdrawn, dreamy, and impractical nature and wanted to interest him in something outside himself and his books, something in the "real" world. The trip failed in that regard, but Carl did come the closest he had ever been to his father, from whom he usually felt somewhat remote, and toward whom his attitude was more respectful than affectionate. This trip afforded them the chance to enjoy themselves together and contributed to a feeling of camaraderie that Carl had not experienced before. By contrast Carl's younger brother Walter always felt very close to his father. "Once, when I was isolated in bed for three months with the scarlet fever, the old gent would come home each night and come up and read to me for an hour at a time … He was a sweet man … he loved his grandchildren," Walter recalled many years later, and the fondness was apparent in his eyes as he said it.[40] Margaret, too, the only daughter, remembered her father with the greatest fondness and admiration. Nothing Carl wrote or said about his parents, to my knowledge, ever conveyed a feeling of fondness or affection.

The parents were stern disciplinarians, but also tenderhearted and warm. Son Walter admitted his father "could be a bastard at times, but he could also be

8

very understanding."[41] Although the parents exercised tight control over their children's behavior, there was still much fun and laughter in their home. Margaret remembered, "One time my brother Ross who just loved horses—and I didn't care a bit about them—encouraged me to ride this old horse that had been on the construction jobs and was farmed out to pasture at home. Well, I did, and I got scared and screamed and Ross came and ... well, anyway, I didn't ride again. But the next morning my verse at worship was that in Proverbs which said, 'A horse is a vain thing for safety.' Of course that broke the family up."

Realizing that perhaps they could hold the family together more if their children's social events took place at home, Walter and Julia also tried hard to make their home a comfortable place for their children's friends. They installed a tennis court out back. Carl's oldest brother Lester often invited friends to the Euclid Avenue house, and Carl remembered many parties with the older children laughing, singing popular songs, playing approved-of games like pin-the-tail-on-the-donkey, and thoroughly enjoying themselves. There was also a good deal of music in their home. Red Seal records of operas and classical music were often played, and although he did not keep up with it in later years, Carl learned to play the piano quite well. The parents' concern was to keep the children from the contaminating influences of suburban living. When Carl was just beginning high school, his parents went even further in this direction. They moved the whole family to a 300-acre farm, about twenty-five miles west of Chicago.

Youth on a Farm

Although he grew up in a town, Walter Rogers always had a love of farming. By 1914 he was well established and could think about taking on the expensive and time-consuming avocation of gentleman farmer. He bought a farm near Glen Ellyn, Illinois, in the only rolling area immediately west of Chicago. For the summers of 1914 and 1915 and weekends during the fall, the family lived out there in a large barracks his construction crew had erected—"The Shanty," as they called it. Although Julia did not relish the idea of getting tied down to a farm, both parents agreed the farm environment was better for their children, since it was away from all the corrupting influences of city and suburbs. Julia continued to teach the boys how to use tools and to garden. They loved it and seemed to thrive on the farm. Things were working out so well that Walter soon began building a substantial new home there. Just before Christmas 1915 the family sold their house in Oak Park and moved to the farm to live year round. John remembered his father explaining the move to friends by saying it was a good place to raise his four lively boys who were still at home.

It is widely known that Carl Rogers grew up on a farm,[42] but not so widely known that the farm was approached through brick entrance walls and iron gates and that the farm house was actually a brick manor house with slate roof, tile floors, dark wood paneled dining room, many fireplaces, eight bedrooms and five baths, *porte cochere*, and a clay tennis court behind the house. Nor does one readily imagine the scale of the farm operation with its extensive fields; substantial horse barn; wagon barn; large cow barn with tall silos and about twenty-eight cows; sheep barn with some fifty sheep; piggery with twenty pigs (some easily 200 pounds); poultry houses for ducks, geese, hens, and turkeys; greenhouse; garage; about eighty-foot windmill with water tower, and at least two farm houses for the farm superintendent, caretakers, chauffeur and other employees and their families.[43]

After a family meeting and vote they named the farm-estate "Warwood," the first three letters being Walter Alexander Rogers' initials and the last four acknowledging the wooded areas around the farm. "When we made the move … to Warwood mother gave up more than any of us—and more than I realized until years later," Margaret wrote.[44] Carl, too, paid a price in social relationships. He had just started high school in Oak Park, so when the family moved at Christmas time he transferred to the high school in Downers Grove. Whatever friendships he had begun to develop in Oak Park had to be discontinued; nor was there much of a chance for new ones in Downers Grove. Each morning he and his brother Ross would go three miles by horse and buggy or car, over rough roads, to Lisle and then take the train five miles to Downers Grove. In order to get home in time for chores and supper, they had to leave right after classes. As if this weren't enough to prevent him from developing his own friendships, after a year and a half at Downers Grove, a change in the train schedule forced him to transfer again, and so he completed his last two years of high school in Naperville.

In Carl's case, then, his parents' desire to keep the children close to home seemed to be working very well. He spent his high school years socially isolated from his peers. He never brought friends to Warwood.[45] Since dancing was not allowed for the Rogers, and that was what the young people mostly did at parties, he had practically no social life. He had only one "date." This was a result of his having been elected junior class president, which he attributed to his good grades and his not belonging to any of the class cliques—an ironic compensation for having no close friends. As class president he had to attend the one social event of the year, a dinner to which it was necessary to bring a girl. Later he remembered "the agony I went through in inviting an auburn-haired lass whom I had admired from a distance. Fortunately for me, she accepted. If she had not, I don't know what I would have done."[46]

And so he turned back to his own family for the companionship he needed. Lester, the oldest brother, was in his twenties and away from home when the Rogers moved to the farm. Carl had always admired and respected him, but they were too many years apart to be real friends. During the war, when Lester scored the highest grade of any soldier ever tested at Camp Grant on the Army's Alpha

Intelligence Test, Carl was so proud that he clipped the newspaper article and kept it all his life. Margaret was also considerably older than Carl and not a likely friend for a young boy. Her attitude toward him had always been more maternal than chummy. Ross, only three years older, was perhaps the most likely companion in the family, but the two brothers never got along very well.[47] While Ross may have been jealous of Carl, who had supplanted him as the "baby" of the family years before, Carl was definitely jealous of Ross, believed that his parents favored Ross, and for a while got attached to the notion that he, Carl, had been adopted. "One Christmas," recalled brother John, "the folks gave Ross and Carl a set of boxing gloves. While Mother was getting dinner ready and Father was someplace else, they decided they'd try out the gloves. Soon it got to be a pretty hot fight, and Walt and I hid behind chairs to keep out of the way. They stopped after a while in about a draw, but the gloves got a real good initiation."[48]

Given Carl's jealous and competitive relationship with Ross, the brother closest in age to him, his brother Walter, five and a half years younger, became his closest comrade and conspirator. John, a year and a half younger still, usually tagged along, getting teased in the typical family fashion. Fighting in the house was absolutely forbidden. The parents' response to it was characteristic of their non-coddling, practical child-rearing: "'Go outdoors and beat your brains out if you want, but don't come screaming to me when you get hurt.' By the time we got outside," Walt recalled, "we had usually cooled off anyway."

Carl loved to play in the woods behind the farm and the stream that ran through the farm, learning the names of the animals, birds, trees, and shrubs. To him the eighty acres of woods and underbrush were a veritable forest, a wilderness that shielded an Indian behind every tree. All the fantasy tales from his reading came alive, and he led his brothers in many an adventure, expedition, or battle against their imaginary foes. "Carl was the guy who dreamed up all the fancy stuff to do," Walter remembered. "He was a great one for reliving the life of the pioneers in the woods. One time he had us out shooting some pigeons; then we built a big brush fire, encased the pigeons and potatoes in wet clay and threw them in the ashes—which, according to Carl, was the proper procedure … We'd go around finding big hornets' nests. We'd throw rocks at them, and when they swarmed out, we'd run like hell." Or, as John recalled, Carl and Walter would try to straddle and ride the young heifers, only to be ignominiously thrown off. They wrote a family newspaper chronicling life on the farm, including, for example, the death of one of the chickens with a headline reading, "Mrs. Pecked-One Has Been Murdered Abruptly for Family Food."[49]

It wasn't all fun by any means. There was always work to do on the farm, and the children were expected to do their share, and then some.[50] Using a hatchet Carl helped clear out the underbrush in the woodlot. While attending high school he would be up at five o'clock or earlier to milk a dozen cows every

11

morning and again at night. As a result his hands and arms were continually stiff, prickly, and "asleep" during much of the school day. In the winter for a time he had also to care for the furnace—shake the grates, shovel in the coal, regulate the damper. During the summers he often drove the milk truck to town and one summer was in charge of all the pigs on the farm. Also during the summer he often rode the cultivator all day long. He was assigned a section of the farm very distant from the house. This portion of land was entirely in his care, with the decisions and action about repairing the equipment, caring for the team, figuring on the soil and weather conditions left solely in his hands. It was a lonesome task.

The farm work, however, helped him overcome his early childhood sickliness, and he developed a strong, wiry, and sturdy frame. Although he was not much of an athlete, he enjoyed playing softball when he could and was fairly good at tennis. From then on, with only a few exceptions, his health was excellent and his capacity for long hours of untiring work rarely diminished. Another important result of his responsibilities on the farm was that he developed a lifelong love of the outdoors, of working with his body and hands, and of watching and helping natural things grow. Years later, when I interviewed Carl, Margaret, and Walter Rogers, Carl showed me his begonias, Walter gave me a tour through his greenhouse filled with numerous kinds of cacti, and Margaret proudly conducted me through her garden. The farm apparently had a similar effect on all of them. When he went away to college, Carl would write, "Oh! how I long to be home and feel the cool breeze brush my hot forehead as I work outdoors. I can hardly keep myself at work."[51]

When he was about thirteen he developed another hobby that was very important to him and to his later development. At the time, Gene Stratton-Porter's books—*Freckles, Girl of the Limberlost, Moths of the Limberlost* and others—were very popular. These books described the world of nature, especially the large night-flying moths, and were a combination of technical and fictional writing. Carl had read the whole series. "So I was in a responsive mood when I discovered in the woods close to home, against the dark fissured bark of a black oak tree, two lovely luna moths, just emerged from their cocoons. These beautiful pale green creatures, large as a small bird, with long 'swallowtail' wings spotted with purple, would have intrigued anyone. They fascinated me. I began my first 'independent study project,' as it would be termed today. I obtained books on moths. I found and raised their caterpillars. I hatched the eggs and raised caterpillars through their whole series of moults, into the cocoons, until the 12-month cycle was complete and they emerged again as moths—Polyphemus, Cecropia, Prometheus, or one of the dozens of other varieties I came to know. I even 'tied out' a female moth on the roof to attract males—a very successful experiment—and was continually busy getting leaves of the special sorts which the caterpillars demanded as food. In my own very small and specialized field I became something of a biologist."[52]

His reputation as a biologist soon spread. Neighbors would often call, saying, "We've got a big bug over here, do you want it?" And he would go over to see if it was a new variety to include in his carefully mounted collection. This was the first serious, spontaneous interest that was entirely his own and that was tied to the world of reality. The interest lasted until he left for college and marked the beginning of a scientific inclination toward careful observation, collection, and organization of objective data. Bird watching, which had many of these characteristics, was another hobby of his.

Having thus commenced his scientific career at age thirteen, Carl soon developed a second and related interest, this time in the field of agriculture. Because Walter Rogers wanted to run the farm in the most modern way, he frequently had experts from the university out to advise him, the foreman, and the herdsman about the best methods. Carl often listened to these experts but, at first, had little interest in the subject. Then he began to read many of his father's books, magazines, and catalogues on farming. Just as he had learned to play chess by reading the *Encyclopedia Britannica*, it was rather typical of him then that he would become interested in farming through books, rather than through face-to-face contact with the adults on the farm or the consultants who were called in. Later he recalled, "I can remember reading these books— particularly the heavy scientific one by Morrison on *Feeds and Feeding*. The descriptions of all the scientific experiments on feeding, on milk and egg production, on the use of different fertilizers, different varieties of seed, of soil, etc., gave me a thorough-going feeling for the essential elements of science. The design of a suitable experiment, the rationale of control groups, the control of all variables but one, the statistical analysis of the results—all of these concepts were unknowingly absorbed through my reading at the age of 13 to 16."[53]

"He practically memorized Morrison's *Feeds and Feeding*," Walter said. After a while he sent away to some of the seed companies for several varieties of oats, barley, and corn and planted these in some informal experimental plots to see what might happen. The plants grew and so did his interest in farming. Soon Walter and John joined him in the venture and their father gave them a couple of acres to use as they liked. The farm foreman prepared the ground for them in the spring, but they did the planting and set up some good experiments using various types of seeds, soils, and fertilizers. The "Rogers Bros." even sold some of their produce, as well as poultry and eggs, to the local market and declared dividends at the end of the year.[54] Unfortunately the whole experiment ended prematurely, when Walter, Sr. and the foreman decided they needed those few acres after all and wanted to combine the smaller plot into a larger adjoining field. Compared to the satisfaction he and his brothers were getting, his father's reasons seemed weak to Carl. He protested vigorously, argued, reasoned, wept, and finally lost one of the biggest fights he could ever remember with his father. It was at about this time, age thirteen, that he began to question the thinking of his parents. "I never rebelled in behavior very much, not until much later. But in a sense I did feel that nobody was going to dominate me."[55] "I took defeat very hard. I expected that if I wanted something I would get it!"[56]

Although Carl lost the battle over the farm plot, there were plenty of other projects to keep him and his brothers engaged and many opportunities to demonstrate he could master tasks himself. "Father sold the sheep on the farm but there were, as I recall, eleven lambs which were too young to sell and he gave them to myself, Walter, and John. We raised them on bottles for as long as necessary and then fed them, pastured them, cared for them, and so forth. It never would have occurred to me to ask any of the farm workers how to go about this. Instead, I wrote and got Government bulletins about the care of sheep. When it came time to butcher one of the lambs again I would have scorned any practical advice. I read up on how to butcher a lamb from a Government bulletin and did so. I did everything 'by the book.' And I realize as I look back that I certainly avoided asking advice whenever possible."[57]

Brother John added, "Carl neglected to tell of the technique used in butchering the lamb. He read that in a slaughter house a man swung a heavy mallet to stun the animal, then another would stick it with a knife, then hang it up to skin it and dress it out. Since we didn't have such a mallet, he elected to use our Louisville Slugger baseball bat. Well, the first crack wasn't hard enough; the second was. Walt and I were his helpers until Walt started to turn green and left for the house. So Carl and I were the two who butchered the lamb. Walt later went on to become a leading O.B. and gynecologist in Pasadena." Aside from lambs, Carl also had personal experience killing chickens, turkeys, geese, ducks, hogs and calves for food.[58]

Carl soon realized he wanted to become a farmer. Beyond loving the outdoor work, he had been stimulated by the possibilities of scientific agriculture. His agricultural readings had challenged his intelligence and, like his father, he now looked forward to running the farm in the most modern manner. To do that, of course, he would have to go to college to learn all the latest developments in farming and farm management.

High School and Beyond

High school seemed rather dull compared to his own educational pursuits on the farm or experiences like in the summer of 1917 when his father's company was building Camp Grant near Rockford, Illinois for the U.S. Army—a virtual city for 43,000 people[59]—and Carl spent a few weeks there delivering messages by horseback between different parts of the camp under construction.[60] But like many bright students he did not let the perceived irrelevance of his formal education prevent him from working hard at it. His parents held Lester's and

Ross's achievements up as models to the three younger boys. Walter considered Carl the most competitive member of the family. "He's never been satisfied unless he was number one. If he didn't come home with all A's he was depressed."

That Rogers felt depressed when he failed to achieve all A's is noteworthy. Not disappointed, but *depressed*. While this was not offered as a clinical judgment, it calls attention to some contradictory aspects of Rogers' childhood. On the one hand he grew up in a secure, prosperous home, was indulged in many ways, felt entitled, expected he would get what he wanted. Yet at the same time, he wasn't coddled, was expected to work hard, was teased by his siblings, and felt like he had to compete to win their respect. In many ways he was quite confident and secure, but in other ways he felt vulnerable and insecure. His family may have thought their teasing was all in good fun, but he took it seriously, as he did the religious messages about sinfulness. He couldn't ask for help because it would confirm all the negative evaluations he'd internalized from his family. Rather he had to prove himself—to show his parents and brothers *and himself* that he *wasn't* absentminded, that he *could* do practical things, that he could do them independently, that he was as good as others, that he was good, period.

And he was. He brought home his A's, and soon he, too, was being held up as one of the models for Walter and John to emulate. He did his best in English and science. The course he liked best was taught by Miss Graham, "a spinsterish teacher of English at Naperville High School. Though she was a strict disciplinarian and rarely if ever smiled, she had a true scholarly interest in her work. I somehow felt that she would understand what I wrote, so for themes in English I wrote personal accounts as well as rebellious papers on 'Shakespeare as an over-rated author'[61] … She helped me realize that it was alright to be original and unique."[62]

In his senior year he competed in the Seventh Annual Oratorical Contest for the W.M. Givler Prize in the high school auditorium. Three boys and three girls competed, while five university professors served as judges. Reflecting on the recently ended World War, Carl spoke on "Two Battles of the Marne," while opponents declaimed on "Lincoln in 1917—What Would He Have Done?" and "The Death Penalty."[63]

On the day of his high school graduation Carl was given his first diary, in which he wrote:

> I don't think I shall use this book as I am supposed to. Some days I have so much to write about and then for days and days I'll have nothing to write at all so I will write when I please and put down the date. Besides, when I write, I want to write enough to look at. I am not like Mrs. Bryant, who when William Cullen Bryant was born wrote in her diary Nov.—Stormy. N.E. wind churned. Seven in the evening a son born … She must have had an ultra practical mind.[64]

15

Just after Carl's graduation Walter Rogers was going to take the family to Estes Park, Colorado. At the last minute he was called to Philadelphia to finalize plans with the government about some construction work in Panama City. So the trip west became a trip east, and Carl saw the sights of Philadelphia, Atlantic City, New York City, and Washington, DC. On trips like this, Walter Rogers "was always getting special treatment from railroad people," such as riding on a private railroad car with the president of the Erie Railroad.[65] By now the Rogers were quite prosperous, but, in spite of this it was expected that Carl would work during the summer to help put himself through college. Thus he spent the summer of 1919 in Kenmare, North Dakota, working in one of the chain of lumberyards owned by his three uncles. He worked a full day at the yard, unloading lumber, filling customers' orders, shoveling coal, unloading bricks, and learning the ins and outs of the lumber business, which impressed him no more than the construction business had. He also lived and slept there, being the only one on the premises after work hours were over. "I get pretty lonesome," he wrote in his diary, "but I have a fine time with my new books."[66]

With forty-three dollars of a fifty-dollar graduation present from his parents he had bought a set of chessmen, a kit of toilet articles and, typically, twenty-two books, including works by Carlyle, Hugo, Dickens, Ruskin, Stevenson, Emerson, Scott, Poe, Dumas, and many others. After hours, as he had often done as a boy, he compensated for his lack of social contacts by losing himself in the world of literature. He wrote in his diary:

> I have come to love my books a great deal. Dickens, with his humor and his indignation at oppression of any kind, and his wonderful characters, is a very good friend. Mark Twain with his chuckles can always knock out my homesickness. I listen to Scott's tales with a wide open mouth. I have somber discussions with Emerson and Van Dyke, but one author has utterly captured me in his spell, and his name is Victor Hugo. He speaks nothing in whole chapters, and then suddenly volumes spring forth in sentences. Far far back he begins, picking up each separate thread of each separate life and I grow almost weary watching him trace each one. Then suddenly, several of them cross and he certainly makes the most of every dramatic situation. Then at last at the crisis every loose fact comes together with a flash that almost blinded me and the whole beautiful story stands complete. I came to the crisis of the story Mon. night and this is how it affected me:
>
> In three hours I read 300 pages. I knew nothing of time or external things. When at last I reached the apex of the story and laid down the book I could not remember what day it was, or what I had been doing. It was 15 minutes before I knew what I had been doing, etc. For three hours he had utterly fascinated me. Les Miserables is one of the most wonderful bugle notes of truth that I have ever read as well as the most fascinating story. Hugo is a wonder.

I have had lots of time to think this summer and I feel that I have come much closer to God, tho there are thousands of things that still perplex and baffle me.[67]

Carl's summer was symbolic of his childhood and youth. While he was developing a rich inner life of intellect and emotion, he remained socially and emotionally isolated. After work, "I didn't smoke or drink or have soda pop or go to the movies or contact girls." Instead he went to his room and read and wrote in his diary. There was little communication with others and certainly no sharing of his inner thoughts and feelings. In his family such sharing would not have felt safe. They would not understand; worse yet, they would dismiss or ridicule him. Later he reflected, "I must have had a lot of hunger for human contact but didn't really know it." But at that time he took for granted that one simply could not be in intimate relationship with others. "Anything that was important was private and concerned things nobody else could understand. I certainly couldn't confide in anybody else—that never occurred to me."[68]

Yet, on the way home, he had a contrary experience on a short visit in Minot, North Dakota, with one of the men from the lumberyard and his wife who were newlyweds. "I think perhaps it was … the first time in my life I realized that loving someone could be *fun* … I think it was the first time I had ever had any direct experience of *romance*. They clearly enjoyed each other—were thrilled to be together. I don't believe it was the sexual overtones of their relationship (which must have been present) but the open expression of romantic, loving feelings which captivated me. I no longer remember their names, but I remember *them* and the way they unknowingly enriched my life."[69] It would not be until he left home for college that he would experience deep and intimate relationships himself.

Back home again, shortly before leaving for college, Carl reflected on the previous two months. His major learning was not about relationships, but about his vocation. "As I look back over the summer," he wrote, "I feel that I have really gained a great deal in many ways … I have learned to love farm life better thru absence and I fully intend to be a farmer."[70]

CHAPTER 2

College Years
1919–1924

In September of 1919 Rogers packed his bags, said good-bye to his family, and traveled the 120 miles to Madison, Wisconsin. There he joined almost 2,400 first-year students, the largest freshman class yet enrolled at the University of Wisconsin.[1] Although his major was scientific agriculture, and Wisconsin had an excellent school of agriculture, this was not the main reason for his choice of college. The Rogers family had always gone to the University of Wisconsin. Both parents and his older brothers and sister had studied there; there simply was never any question that Carl would study there, too.[2] Consistent with the Rogers' tradition of "sticking together," he moved into the campus Young Men's Christian Association and roomed with his brother Ross, who was student president of the campus Y.M.C.A. chapter. During his sophomore year, he roomed with a cousin.

From Agriculture to Religion

Although he did well in his subjects, the first two and a half years at Wisconsin had little permanent impact on him academically. Among several autobiographical essays and interviews, Rogers made only one reference to the classroom for this entire period: "One of the things I remember best was the vehement statement of an agronomy professor in regard to the learning and use of facts. He stressed the futility of an encyclopedic knowledge for its own sake, with the injunction, 'Don't be a damned ammunition wagon; be a rifle!'"[3]

Of far greater importance were Rogers' extracurricular experiences during these years. With his religious background and his eagerness to meet people and make friends, it was natural that he would join the "Ag-Triangle," a group of agricultural students meeting under the auspices of the Y.M.C.A. Professor George Humphrey was the adult leader of the group of twenty-five or so young men. Rogers saw him as a well-intentioned man, but rather weak. Whether or not Humphrey knew what he was doing in leaving everything up to the group, his was an example of facilitative leadership which Rogers was to advocate years later. Left to their own devices, the group set up its own curriculum, organized social and educational activities, conducted business in parliamentary fashion, discussed topics deeply, and became a very closely-knit group.[4]

The Ag-Triangle was an extremely important experience for Rogers. Having come from a cloistered background, never having had real friendships outside his family, here he was able to interact on a deep and trusting level with many other young men from different backgrounds. In February, writing in his journal, he summed up his first semester in glowing terms: "As I look back, it seems to me that it has been the best and richest five months I have ever had. I have learned more from the hearts and lives of men. I have made the first friend I have ever had and hosts and hosts of fine acquaintances."[5]

Another outcome of the Ag-Triangle experience was a lasting understanding and appreciation of parliamentary rules. During Rogers' career he would serve as president and chairman of many professional organizations. The skill he developed in the Y.M.C.A. group in using parliamentary procedure always proved useful to him, and he never felt fearful later about chairing any type of parliamentary assembly.[6] He assumed leadership roles in the Ag-Triangle and became a Boys' Club leader, organizing and directing activities for boys both in Madison and at summer camp in Sturgeon Bay.

It was not for religious or social reasons, however, that Rogers' parents were putting him through college. He had come to the University to learn to be a successful farmer in what was rapidly becoming a modern industry. But once away from home, surrounded by new people and fresh ideas, presented with many new alternatives for his life's direction, he began to realize that becoming a farmer was not a foregone conclusion and that many other possibilities were before him. His growing uncertainty and ambivalence were reflected in an October entry in his journal. "This whole year," he wrote, "everything that has happened during vacation and in school has impressed on me the wonderful opportunities before me, and I sometimes wonder—well, anyway, I'm going to be a good farmer first, because that's the work I love and am fitted for, and if a bigger better job comes, I hope and pray that I'll have the sense to take it and the guts to make good."[7]

But agriculture could not contain Rogers' imagination. Over the course of his childhood and youth—nurtured by a combination of social isolation, teasing, fantasy, reading, creative writing, and scientific experiments—Carl had developed an emotional and intellectual depth, a sense of being different, a contradictory set of feelings that included humility and inadequacy along with confidence and entitlement, and a yearning to demonstrate his potential. Now stimulated by intellectual and religious discussions among young men of different backgrounds, he sought a path with great emotional commitment and intellectual challenge. By November of his freshman year his life's work was clearly an open question. Again in his journal:

> I have just come from a fine Fellowship meeting. "Dad" Wolfe spoke on "Selecting a Life Work." Oh, it's wonderful to feel that God will really lead me to my life work, and I know He will, for never has He deserted me. Just the same, tho, it is an awesome thing to think that a wrong decision will wreck my life, but oh, how I'll try and keep my life in tune with God, so that He can guide me. I have plenty of ambition, in fact I sometimes think I'm too ambitious, but if I can only keep that terrible swelling force within me in the right path, I know all will be well. The most wonderful promise in the Bible for me is: Ask, and it shall be given you; seek and ye shall find; knock and it shall be opened unto you. Lord, I ask Thy guidance; I am seeking the kingdom of Heaven; and the door at which I knock Thou alone knowest beside myself. Lord help me to see in the right spirit that I may obtain. Amen.[8]

As the year drew to a close, religion came to consume an increasing amount of his emotional and intellectual energy. As Brian Thorne described Rogers' transition in this period, "The dogmatic and moralistic Christianity of Rogers' home environment now gave way to an altogether more passionate and personal involvement, based on a changing perception of the nature of Christ. A vibrantly human Jesus offered the possibility of a new intimacy and with it a sense of personal freedom that would have been inconceivable in the context of the evangelical fundamentalism with which Rogers had grown up."[9] Thus, under "Plans for 1920" Rogers wrote, "I intend to live closer to God, to form a more intimate friendship with Him and to spend more time and effort in communion with Him. I spend time cultivating my friends and count it time well spent. How much better should I count the time spent when I am cultivating God's friendship … I intend to earnestly seek and follow the great trial which God has staked out for my life."[10]

Then, at the turn of the year, Rogers traveled to Iowa to attend the Des Moines Convention, a series of meetings organized by the International Y.M.C.A. devoted to educating and inspiring young people to spreading the Christian gospel throughout the world. The Des Moines Convention was a turning point for eighteen-year-old Carl Rogers:

A Great Flame! That to me was the Des Moines Convention. A great consuming flame which for a few great moments burned away all dross and showed the world and also my soul, not as they look but as they are! A great lifting hand which bore us up, up, up, until the world was below us, a great field white for the harvest, a great multitude of starving faces, looking for the Christ love, a great pot of molten metal, dross on top but pure gold underneath.

And the cry is "Men! give us men!" Men to reap the white fields, men to let the Christ love shine thru their lives, men to sweep the dross from the pot and help shake the gold.

We cannot always live on the mountain top and see that view, but we can never forget once we have seen it. This is what I wrote after Sherwood Eddy's third great speech:

"During Eddy's morning speech I almost made up my mind to go into Christian work and during his afternoon speech I made my final decision. God help me keep it! All my previous dreams seem cheap now, for I have volunteered for the biggest, the greatest work on the globe. I have found what I never found before, the peace of God which passeth all understanding. I never dreamed that simply enlisting for Christ could make me feel so right with the world. It is wonderful."[11]

Despite this and other occasional moments of certainty, his decision to make Christianity his life's work was not yet absolute. For two or three years he wavered, but he began to guide his life more and more in the direction of the ministry. He helped organize campus religious conferences, traveled to meetings in other states, shifted his major from agriculture to history—an area he felt would better prepare him for the ministry—and continued to lead his group in the Boys' Club. At one Y.M.C.A. conference he attended at Lake Geneva, Wisconsin, in June 1921, his religious vision was extended beyond the theological, and he began seriously to consider the need for "Christianizing industrial, political, social and international relationships."[12] He also joined the college debating team, which considerably bolstered his confidence in speaking before groups. By the end of his sophomore year his decision was becoming increasingly firm. "I am more positive than ever I will go into Christian work, and feel quite convinced that it will be the ministry, whether rural or not I do not know."[13]

In the summer of 1921 he was the leader of a barracks of eight high school counselors and one hundred poor boys from Milwaukee who spent the summer at a cherry pickers' camp at Sturgeon Bay, Wisconsin. The boys, mostly of Italian descent, ordinarily would not have had the chance to spend the summer in the country. The camp enabled them to work at picking cherries for part of the day to pay their expenses, while during the rest of the day they had a more typical Y.M.C.A. camp program. Rogers took his leadership position very seriously. He felt responsible not only for their recreational lives, but also for their moral

21

development. On one occasion there was a theft in the camp and a boy everyone suspected of being the thief. "We got him alone behind one of the buildings and talked with him and threatened him and prayed over him … whether he fessed up or not I don't remember, but we were trying to use all the leverage at our disposal, including the divine."[14]

Because of his considerable involvement in Christian youth work, Rogers met many leaders in the evangelical movement. When international religious leaders like John R. Mott and Sherwood Eddy came to campus, Rogers got to organize their itinerary and show them around. Sherwood Eddy even asked Rogers to prepare a prayer to deliver to a university audience.[15] Not only was he influenced by their ideas, Rogers in turn impressed these leaders with his sincerity, intelligence, and leadership ability. Nevertheless he was amazed and even wept upon learning in December of 1921 that he had been chosen to be one of ten United States youth delegates to the World Student Christian Federation's Conference in Peking, China, that coming April.[16] At the time and thereafter, he thought his parents' ability to finance the trip was a significant factor in his selection, but this was not the case. The selection was made by Ray Sowers, then State Secretary for the Y.M.C.A., who was later to become a well-known Wisconsin educator.

Fifty years later Sowers himself recalled how "I immediately thought of the many able and promising leaders in the twenty student Y.M.C.A.s in the state, but I could think of none who would be more representative of Wisconsin youth than two brothers, Ross and Carl Rogers, at Wisconsin University in Madison. Ross, the elder brother, had been president of the University Y.M.C.A. and was recognized as an outstanding leader on campus. Carl while younger showed equal promise. I discussed the matter with Fred Wolfe and the Dean of the Law School who was then serving as the faculty advisor for the Y.M.C.A. We all agreed that either of these two students would make an excellent choice, but because Ross would be leaving the campus at the end of the year and Carl would remain on campus for several years, we decided to nominate Carl … Next came the matter of financing the trip. While the Rogers family was in better than moderate financial circumstances and could have afforded the expense, we felt that the members would feel more that Carl would be their representative if they assumed responsibility for raising a major proportion of the expenses. We therefore set out to secure the funds by popular subscription … and in short order the money was raised from students and faculty interested in the project."[17]

Although the April conference would last only a week, the trip would involve six months away from home, including travel in many countries and meetings and speaking engagements throughout China and the Orient. The trip would mean missing the last semester of his junior year, but this loss seemed insignificant compared to the experience ahead. "Why? Why?" he asked himself. "That is the question of my life. Surely God wants me for some great task, something that he is saving for me alone. I feel as David must have felt when he was anointed by Samuel, and may it be true of me, as it was of David; 'and the Spirit of the Lord was upon him from that day forward.' Surely God's hand is visible in this last and greatest opportunity and responsibility that has come upon me. May I be big enough to meet it ... I am 20 years old today."[18]

Trip to China

On February 15, 1922, Rogers left Wheaton, Illinois, near his farm home, on the Overland Limited, to begin the trip that five months later he would call "the greatest experience of my life."[19] On the eve of his departure he wondered "how much the trip will change me and whether the Carl Rogers that comes back will be more than a speaking acquaintance of the Carl Rogers that is going out."[20]

The Carl Rogers who came back *was* considerably changed. One of those changes resulted from almost missing his train on the trip from Chicago to San Francisco, when the train stopped frequently for passengers to have their meals in restaurants along the way. At one meal Rogers must have been daydreaming, as everyone had left the restaurant and the train was leaving before he noticed. Fortunately a porter also noticed that one passenger was missing, so he left the door open and the step down which enabled Rogers to jump on the moving train as it left the station. This incident, which might have resulted in his missing the boat for China, left Rogers with a lifelong fear of missing trains and later airplanes.[21]

Most of the changes Rogers experienced on the trip were more profound than this one, and we are fortunate in having detailed records of the six-month trip to help shed light on his evolution. In addition to an enormous correspondence that he carried on during the journey ("Part of the morning I wrote letters, but I had finished most of the seventeen the evening before")[22] Rogers faithfully kept a journal, which he called his "China Diary." Written on a portable typewriter he must have carried throughout the trip, the voluminous correspondence and the eighty-six-page, single-spaced *China Diary* show that, as early as age twenty, Rogers had an intense drive to communicate his observations and reflections, to reach out to the world through his writing.

His need to communicate in writing can hardly be separated from his drive to work, to produce—a strong part of his upbringing. On three different days, just after leaving Illinois, he noted: "I read for about an hour and a half after I got on board, finishing about 110 pages of Prof. Ross' book on 'The Changing Chinese,'" "I was the last one to bed and the first one up, and have finished about 150 pages of a book on Japan, as well as having looked at the scenery a lot, and read several descriptive pamphlets on the scenery we are passing through," and "This morning I read 130 pages of a book on China before 11 o'clock."[23]

Beyond reporting "the facts," his pride in his own productivity is evident. He maintained this throughout his life. Forty-eight years later he circulated a two-page paper called "A Day in My Life," in response to numerous inquiries as to how "an old man spends his time." After describing a staggering array of activities for the day, he concluded, with obvious irony, "As you can see, it is a very boring life."[24]

Two other qualities that always contributed to Rogers' productivity were evident on the trip: his generally excellent health and his very high energy level. As the boat left San Francisco in a heavy gale, ninety percent of the passengers became so seasick that they did not even come to the dining room for supper. Rogers was among the other ten percent. While others in the various delegations occasionally became ill due to variations in dietary and climatic conditions throughout the Orient, he was in perfect health the whole time. He sampled all the new foods possible, slept in unlikely places, and traveled by train and boat thousands of miles throughout Hawaii, Japan, Korea, China, Hong Kong, and the Philippines. His health and energy were again revealed on the return trip when he was worried that he might miss his only chance to climb Mt. Fujiyama, the highest mountain in Japan. So, anxious to cram every new experience possible into his trip, while most of his companions were asleep he spent all night climbing the 12,368 foot "Fuji," arriving at the top just in time to see the sunrise.

One of the major changes Rogers went through during the trip was the liberalizing of his religious views. Until that point his exposure to religious orientations other than his own had been very limited. At home his mother had been the chief source of his spiritual guidance. The students he met at Wisconsin reflected a similar Midwestern, rural, conservative, religious background. His influences at the Des Moines Convention, where he had first decided upon a religious life, were also highly evangelical and traditional.

Imagine, then, young Rogers' experience on the three-week voyage across the Pacific, when he had a chance to hear, question, debate and discuss numerous religious questions with students, scholars and religious leaders from all parts of the country and from all types of background and experience. Five days into the voyage he wrote, "We have had many discussions already on lots of the doubtful points, and I am thankful beyond words that we are with a group of leaders who are all forward-looking, young-minded people, who are still building up their own faiths, not dogmatists who are sure that their own interpretation is the only one. The more we talk and think, the more I am finding it possible to define what I myself believe, and what I consider non-essential."[25]

The next day "we got started on a discussion of whether a man had to believe in the deity of Christ to be a Christian, and that led to 'What is a Christian?' and we sat at the table thrashing things out and trying to thrash them out until ten o'clock. That is the beauty of this life on shipboard, that when we get into a profitable discussion, none of us have to quit, so that we either keep on until we are worn out or else have arrived somewhere."[26] By the return voyage home he was able to write:

> Naturally all these friendships, and this eye-opening trip, and the time to think that I have had on shipboard, etc., have tremendously changed me. Most of all perhaps, I have changed to the only logical viewpoint—that I want to know what is true, regardless of whether that leaves me a Christian or no. Since taking that attitude (and it has been a gradual step, starting before I left home) I have found the most wonderful new riches in the life of Christ and in the Bible as a whole. It is a tremendous relief to quit worrying about whether you believe what you are supposed to believe, and begin actually studying Christ to find whether he is a personality worth giving your life to. I know that for myself that method of approach has led me to a far deeper and a far more enthusiastic allegiance to Him. For the first time in my life, I find myself anxious to tell people what I believe about Him, and about His wonderful Kingdom that he came to establish. I don't wonder that His early disciples simply couldn't keep from telling the "good news."[27]

For Rogers' family back in Illinois, it was hardly good news that they were receiving in his letters. His brother Walter found the letters from China fascinating and was puzzled by his parents' reaction. "Mother was very depressed by the contents."[28] Beginning with the ocean voyage and continuing on throughout the trip, his letters revealed that his religious views were becoming increasingly different from theirs. To even entertain the idea that Christ was not a deity but a man was unthinkable for Julia and Walter Rogers. Yet this is what their son had come to believe, writing home that "Jesus himself was a man who came nearer to God than any other man in history."[29] Most of Rogers' family regarded his new ideas as "queer" and "unsafe," and he was sorely grieved that they had not shared the experiences that had helped change his thinking.

Moving away from the family's views, fortunately, did not involve much of the internal conflict, guilt, and rebellion that often accompany achieving independence from one's parents. The transcontinental and transpacific mails were so slow in 1922 that his parents' reaction to one of his letters might not arrive for two months after his own letter was written. By then two months more of living had ensued, and whatever imminent changes he had discussed in the earlier correspondence were all but solidified. By the time he returned home in August there was an intellectual and emotional gap between him and most of the family that would never be bridged. The next few years were not without their conflicts and heated discussions in the Rogers home; but "from the date of this trip, my goals, values, aims, and philosophy have been my own."[30]

The Peking conference itself was an exciting week of forums, committee meetings, general sessions, speeches, debates, and informal meetings and discussions among the 200 foreign and 600 Chinese delegates. As Rogers described it in his first published article, on the front page of the Y.M.C.A.'s *Intercollegian,* "From the Orient, and from the Occident, from Czecho-Slovakia and Poland, from Burma and Ceylon, from white and black and yellow races, students came together at Tsing Hua College, for the purpose of understanding one another, of comparing and discussing their problems and their opportunities, and in the hope of binding together in a real and vital fellowship the Christian students of the world."[31]

This was the first such gathering to take place since the New York conference in 1913, with the First World War intervening, and one of the liveliest topics of debate was the position of the world's Christian youth regarding war and pacifism. The Indians and Australians argued that Christianity and pacifism were inseparable. The Europeans disagreed, arguing that some wars could be justified. One student of the latter persuasion tried to gloss over the differences in the room by saying that, after all, the group had a spiritual unity which transcended their differences. To which Rogers noted in his journal: "How can he say that we have a spiritual unity that goes deeper than our differences, when he knows that if we all believed the same as he does, we would be shooting each other tomorrow if our governments ordered us to?"[32]

Rogers participated actively in all the General Sessions and served on two subcommittees, deliberating over the membership composition of the World Federation, the attitude the student Christian movement should take toward members of other religions, how to present Christ to students, the goals and purposes of the international Christian youth movement, and whether, in fact, it really was a youth movement or one controlled by adults. His faith was strengthened as he saw a common bond, Christianity, able to keep people working together for common goals. "In spite of differences of race and nationality," he wrote, "in spite of sore spots in the relations of many countries, never, even in the hottest committee discussions, have I seen any of the delegates show anything but the finest kind of spirit … it has been an education for a narrow, provincial middle westerner like myself to find what splendid men may be hidden behind different labels of nationality, or wrapped up in packages of different color. I have made a good many friends during this period, and that alone has made the conference worth while."[33]

After the conference Rogers spent almost three months traveling through China, first as part of an international delegation that included Rogers and a student from Germany, France, England, China, and another country. Later he accompanied Professor Kenneth Latorette, a former missionary to and expert on China and Japan and later the leading scholar on the history of Christian missions around the world.[34] Visiting Hankow, Nanking, Shanghai, Canton, Foochow, and numerous other towns and cities unfamiliar to most Westerners, he took in the sights and snapped photographs like many tourists, but he also had unique experiences unavailable to most travelers. In each city Y.M.C.A. representatives or local missionaries offered the visitors their best hospitality, which included introducing them to local friends and officials and giving them specially guided tours of the area.

Thus Rogers was able to see the inside of an old Chinese prison ("the filthiest, lousiest hole that I ever care to see ... The poor wretches just kow-towed and groveled on the ground when they saw us. I suppose they thought we could do something to help them"); talk politics with the military governor of the Philippines, General Wood ("If the American people knew all that he told us, I think that there would be a considerable reaction"); ride through the streets of Yokohama in a rickshaw ("It is a queer feeling to ride behind a human draft animal. It is something that I am afraid I would never get used to. I couldn't help but think of the fact that he was a man, not an animal, and that he had a home, no doubt, and possibly a family"); spend a good deal of time traveling through China with an African-American and a Native-American ("there have been groups of people who nearly ruin their eyesight staring at us"); hear hair-raising stories of brutality from an escapee of a Russian prison camp that had not been informed that the war was over ("The whole dinner seemed like a dream ... Think of eating dinner in a Chinese house, in Peking, talking to two of our late enemies, the Austrians, and hearing about men suffering up in Russia who didn't even know that the war was over").[35]

He was able also to visit a children's hospital in the Philippines ("We saw there poor little kiddies whose legs and arms were simply bones with the skin hanging on in folds and flaps. I have seen lots of sights, but this was honestly the worst I have ever seen. There was one little girl eight years old, who weighed 25 pounds. Her case was complicated by tuberculosis. I wish that I could forget some of the things I saw there"); and see countless examples of fantastic poverty and squalor ("I wouldn't advise you to look very long at this beggar we are passing—I'm afraid that you might not sleep very well. Can the ragged, warped, deformed thing, holding out his hand and making a pitiful moaning sound, be made in the image of God?")[36]

More and more he began to juxtapose his religious beliefs with the social and economic realities around him. Visiting a Chinese silk factory, he saw six- and seven-year-old girls, some of whom had just had their feet bound—causing permanently deformed feet, yet according to the tradition, more feminine— working over tubs of steaming water all day long.

Somehow silk will never look quite the same to me [he wrote]. It has lost considerable of its luster ... Anyone who could see those tiny little kids (some of the poor little tykes were just having their feet bound and stood first on one foot and then on the other to ease the pain)—anyone who could see those little kids, and say that such things were all right, is not a Christian, by my definition. I

27

don't care if he believes the whole Bible from beginning to end … These kids came to work at four thirty in the morning, and go home at a quarter to eight at night … Think of kids seven years old working fourteen hours and a quarter every day! I don't know how it makes other people feel, but it makes me see red, and I wish I had a gun. I no longer wonder that people turn Bolshevik. I consider it mighty fortunate that I have all my life seen the other side of the question, for even with that, it sometimes seems as if the best thing to do were to send the whole system to _____, where it came from [sic].[37]

One of the Hankow mills which declared a 40% dividend besides putting a large sum in the sinking fund … had not twelve-hour days for women and children, but a fourteen-hour day! God knows that we have given them splendid examples in our own history. The U.S. Steel Corporation, the Standard Oil, the packers, the Colorado Fuel and Iron—goodness knows that they have done [worse] things than have yet been attempted in China, and I suppose that we can't blame heathen China too harshly for following Christian America and England.[38]

Nor did he attempt to avoid his own responsibility. At Nagasaki, before returning to San Francisco, he witnessed a human conveyor belt made up of women passing twenty- to twenty-five-pound baskets of coal up from the dock into the hold of the ships. "If you want to know what people mean by a 'sense of guilt' I think you ought to stand as I did for a couple of hours and watch those women slave away in the blazing sun, grimy and dirty, without a chance to rest even for a moment, and then meditate on the fact that you are partly responsible for those conditions. Those women are submitting to those conditions, and slaving their lives out, simply to get you across the ocean, and yet you go calmly ahead and let them do it, without a thought for anything but your own comfort. That to my mind, is a good example of the fact that we are each one of us responsible to a certain extent for the unchristian conditions that we find around us."[39]

Although neither he nor anyone else would have used the term then, his views were developing an "existential" slant in religion and morality. A person is a Christian not on the basis of words or beliefs, but on actions. He came to believe that good works were more important than ritual or doctrine in Christianity. One must take responsibility for one's actions. References to being "chosen" to do God's work or God's "leading" him were replaced in his letters and diary by indications that he, Carl Rogers, was going to have to do the choosing; the responsibility was his own.

Thus his views on many religious, political, social, and economic questions changed considerably as a result of his trip to the Orient.[40] Years later, Rogers said, "I went to that conference as a naïve, religious, Christian, Midwestern, parochial boy brought up quite narrowly in every respect—patriotic, nationalistic and so forth. To be faced with an international conference of really very good minds, diverse opinions, a lot of discussion about war, about social issues, about international problems, seeing a new culture, seeing many cultures at the conference, and one culture closely—it was just an absolutely mind-boggling experience, and I evidently was very open to it."[41] Although he never actually became a pacifist, he did seriously consider joining the Fellowship of Reconciliation, an ecumenical, pacifist–activist organization whose members often made sacrifices, including going to jail, for their principles of peace and justice. The social conscience he developed on the China trip lasted throughout his career. For example, thirteen years later, in the depths of the Great Depression, when prominent in the social-work field, he would criticize the profession for being "reluctant to face the fact that by and large the interest of social workers favoring the welfare of each individual and the more equitable distribution of wealth and income, is more or less opposed to the interest of the business and taxpayers groups."[42] He also maintained sympathy for the peace movement throughout his life and was outspoken in his opposition to the Vietnam War. He devoted a significant portion of his final years to international conflict resolution and peacemaking.

Another important consequence of the China trip for him was a significant increase in his self-confidence. At the Peking conference, the shy Midwesterner was selected by his delegation to represent the Christian youth of the United States before the World Federation. Throughout China and the Orient he gave dozens of formal speeches and informal talks to groups of hundreds of students and adults. He debated religion, politics, and economics with men much older and more experienced than he. He impressed many adult missionary workers[43] and was offered a job on the Y.M.C.A. staff in India, which he declined in order to continue his education.[44] He even did some personal counseling with students in trouble.[45]

In reading the *China Diary*, Rogers' first lengthy, though unpublished manuscript, one is struck immediately by his literary style. Especially when describing agriculture and nature, which he did frequently, there is omnipresent both an artist's and scientist's interest in detail. For example, in China he wrote,

As we got higher, the whole Foochow basin lay in a panorama below us—the long island, with a silver strip of river on each side—the bevy of dusky winged junks coming upriver on the incoming tide—the little clustered villages scattered over the plain, with a few wisps of smoke hanging over each one—the clean little rice paddies, cut here and there with little threadlike canals—and off to the right, the close packed city of Foochow, with a crowd of anchored junks at the river bank. Frame all this flat basin with an irregular ring of mountains, extending range behind range as far as you can see, and hang a wine red sun just over the westernmost range, so that it lights up the clouds and the mountains with a strong tinge of red, and you have some faint idea of the view that we had from old Kushan.[46]

While Rogers' narrative was filled with many extensive descriptions of nature and of social conditions, there were only a few passing references to Chinese, Buddhist or Confucian religion, culture or traditional architecture—for example, "This afternoon we went to see the Forbidden City and the Temple of Heaven, two sights that one *must* see when he is in Peking. They were very interesting and impressive, but as usual the sights we saw going and coming were of more interest to me than any old temple."[47] That Rogers had little interest then in understanding Oriental culture reflects both his youth and the traditional, Christian missionary view that such customs were at best quaint and at worst heathen practices, the sooner replaced by morally and spiritually superior Christianity the better, as this was the only route to salvation. While the *China Diary* has many examples of Rogers' questioning Christian dogma and practice and a growing respect for individuals of different races and cultures, it nevertheless demonstrates a lack of interest and respect for the cultures themselves beyond that of the superficial tourist. In this sense he was typical of the period.[48]

Rogers concluded his "China Diary" with a description of his nighttime climb up Mt. Fujiyama, on the eve of his return to America. While he might have mentioned the religious significance of the pilgrimage for the Japanese, he focused instead on the excitement of the physical challenge and the wonder of nature. Only many years later did he describe it as "clearly a religious experience for me."[49]

About nine or nine thirty we got above the timber line, and from there on the trip was wonderful. All the clouds and mist had cleared away, and the stars seemed so close you could almost reach up and touch them ... We stopped every now and then at the rest houses along the way, and about ten thirty stopped for a meal, and laid down to sleep until ... a little before twelve ... The climb was getting steeper and steeper, and the rarity of the air was beginning to bother the other two fellows ... A slender silver crescent of moon began to show up about twelve thirty, adding to the light of the stars, and making our pathway considerably plainer. At three o'clock we stopped at the sixth of the nine stations. Phelps had told me that we should be at the eighth station by four o'clock if we wanted to see the sunrise from the top, so that at three thirty, I got the bunch started again, but their pace was entirely too slow. I wanted to get to the top, so I took a few sandwiches from the pack that the guide was carrying, and started out at my own pace. It was very cold now, and we had to keep moving to keep the sweat from freezing. The east was just beginning to show a few streaks of light, and I knew that I would have to hurry. When I was a little above the eighth station, the view in the east became so wonderful that I watched it for some time. The country around the foot of the mountain, as far as one could see in every direction, was covered with a thick blanket of billowing white clouds, looking for all the world like a great expanse of foaming ocean breakers, frozen silent in mid-air.

On the eastern edge of this expanse, there was a great glowing light coming up from beneath that colored the sky all colors of the rainbow. There was a perfect prismatic scheme of colors, blue, fading into purple, green, yellow and red. It was one of the most beautiful sights I have ever seen, looking across that snowfield of clouds. In a little while the light became brilliant, and more brilliant, and then—Hurrah! the SUN. I wish you could have heard the shout that came from the many pilgrims at various stages of the climb, when the sun finally shoved its white-hot brim up thru those soft clouds. And I shouted too, and waved my cap. We had seen a tremendous event.[50]

A Semester Break

Fired with enthusiasm, filled with great goals and plans, and bolstered by an enhanced self-confidence, Rogers returned to the United States in August 1922. Shortly after his return he began to suffer from abdominal pains which had troubled him, from time to time, since age fifteen. The problem turned out to be a duodenal ulcer, which became so serious that it demanded five weeks in Chicago's Presbyterian Hospital and a half-year away from college to recuperate. Interestingly, three of the six Rogers children suffered from ulcers at some time during their lives, a fact which Rogers attributed to a "gently suppressive" atmosphere at home, in which emotional displays were inappropriate and hard work was the solution to all obstacles and frustrations.[51] "It'll get well before you're married," was a typical response of their parents to many of the children's complaints.[52] Even during his period of recuperation he was expected to do his full share of physical work around the farm. He also worked in a local lumberyard for two months, driving back and forth between work and home in his first car, a second-hand Model T Ford, for which he had paid eighty-five dollars.[53] On one occasion the car was wedged in a tight parking space at the lumber yard. Rather than ask for help he lifted the back end by himself, moved it over a few inches, and strained his back.[54]

While working at the lumberyard he took a correspondence course in introductory psychology from the University of Wisconsin. It was his first formal introduction to the subject and, using William James as the text, he found it rather dull. "The only portion of the course I remember is that I got into an argument by mail with my instructor as to whether dogs could reason. It was his claim that only human beings could reason. I was quite able to prove to my own satisfaction that my dog, Shep, was definitely able to solve difficult problems by reasoning."[55]

There was a good deal of tension at home, which Rogers ascribed to his mother's "increasingly fundamentalist views" and her inability to accept the changes in him. Brother Walter thought differently. He saw both his mother

31

and father becoming increasingly more accepting of new ideas as they grew older and as the children left home. All the tension of that transition seemed to center around Carl. For example, Carl was the first to dance and the first to join a fraternity, so he had to contend with his parents' resistance. But having lived through it with Carl, the parents found it easier to accept such behavior in the younger children. In fact, once it was clear the dancing battle was lost, they invited a dance instructor to Warwood to teach Walter and John. If the children were going to dance, they were going to do it right, and under parental supervision.[56]

Walter thought Carl and his mother very similar temperamentally. "Carl found disagreement with her to be very uncomfortable, and vice versa." Yet, "Carl would go out of his way to do battle .... he would argue vehemently with our parents. Vigorous arguments over interpretation of scripture ... Both Carl and Mother are somewhat Billy Graham types at heart. This is where the fireworks occurred." Why couldn't he leave well enough alone and go his own way when he disagreed, as Walter learned to do? "I think he felt the need of Mother's approval; he felt closer to her than Father. It was a serious attempt on his part to communicate."[57] When the barriers to communication proved too great, he more or less gave up. When he finally left home, he did not keep up with his parents as much as the other children did. They did not offer him as much help as they did the others, nor did he accept as much of the help that was offered. Only later in life was Carl able to communicate better with his mother, after his own sense of identity was long established and his listening and helping skills were well developed.

History Major

Back at the University, stimulated by all he had seen, heard, and done in the Orient, he plunged into scholastic work with a new relish. While in China, he had received word that he had been elected to Phi Beta Kappa, the national academic honor society—an accomplishment under any circumstances, but especially so for a junior in college then. Against his parents' wishes, he now joined the Alpha Kappa Lambda fraternity, noted for its scholastic excellence, and lived at the fraternity house during his junior year. Again, he relished feeling close to his friends in the fraternity.[58]

In classes he was very impressed by Wisconsin historians Carl Russell Fish, George Sellery, and Eugene Byrne and developed a great respect for scholarship and historical research. Unlike many students, he used the term paper as a vehicle for exploring his own interests. In one paper, "The Soul of a Troubadour," he showed how St. Francis of Assisi placed far greater emphasis on doing good works and following the example of Christ than on a mystical union with God.

In "The Pacifism of Wyclif" and "The Development of Luther's Idea of Authority in Religion, 1518–19," he explored two other themes which were important to him. Throughout the former paper he seemed to sympathize with Wyclif's views on war, writing:

> A summary of his principles ... put into modern language, will show this: It is wrong to kill, either through hate or fear. War cannot be reconciled with love, the central principle of Jesus' teaching. It is impossible for love to be the motive of war. The best defense is not a military offense, but a resistance of love and patience and suffering to force. To deny the foregoing principle is to admit that Christianity is not practicable—that force is stronger than love, evil stronger than good. The virtues of which war is the mother are the virtues of the hangman. Conquerors have not title to their conquests unless they rule justly. The approval of the church does not make war right. Indeed, it is worse for the church to approve war than for any other organization ... The above summary, as far as its ideas are concerned, might be the brief of a pamphlet published last week or last month in London, or New York, or Chicago, by some "dangerous" group of radicals. It is most interestingly modern in its outlook and in its underlying thought.[59]

Throughout most of his professional life, a basic tenet of Rogers was the importance of the individual's trusting his or her own experience—for example, the client directing the course of therapy, not the authoritative therapist, or the student setting and following his or her own learning goals. Concluding the Luther paper in 1923 he wrote, "Fortunately for later generations, he ... dared to set the authority of his own reason and his own clear conscience above any other, be it Church, or Pope, or a rigid interpretation of the Bible. As Dr. McGiffert says, 'He really substituted for all external authorities the enlightened conscience of the individual Christian. The Bible he read for himself and admitted the claim of no council or body of men to read it for him. This, in principle, though he never fully realized it, and seldom acted upon it, meant the right of private judgment in religious things, and in it lay the promise of a new age.'"[60]

Later Rogers reflected that "I'm sure I was working out a personal problem with authority and coming to be my own source."[61] He was also learning to gather data from other scholars to help him clarify and support his own thinking and to set this down for others to see. This skill would play an important part in his later professional writings; at this point they merely impressed his instructors. On the Luther paper, which would become his bachelor's thesis, Dean Sellery wrote "Ex/First rate work" and on the Wyclif essay "Excellent/High grade work." On a paper on "Benjamin Franklin and the Treaty of 1783," the professor wrote, "Do not use first person 'we', 'us' in a paper"—ironically anticipating an issue which would return years later as a controversial aspect of Rogers' professional writing style.

Years later Rogers expressed his amazement that the dean of the College of Letters and Sciences would agree to sponsor his undergraduate thesis. "I remember meeting with him in his office and discussing ideas, and the fact that he had some respect for my ideas came across and really touched me. Again, I was thinking, 'Who, me? He really thinks my ideas have some merit?'"[62]

During these later years at the University Rogers also resumed his involvement with intercollegiate debating. "I found it both surprising and thrilling," he wrote, "to realize that I could tackle a subject on which I knew nothing—in this case the compulsory arbitration of labor disputes—put in eight solid hours a day working at it over a period of weeks—and come out reasonably 'well informed.' It somehow gave me a feeling of confidence in my own ability to tackle a new intellectual problem and to master it."[63]

For Rogers, then, the second half of his undergraduate career was very different from the first. Earlier his courses had not interested him much. His real learning and important involvements came through extracurricular religious and social activities. The last two years continued to offer extracurricular involvements,[64] but now academic life became important to the young man, desiring as he did to learn as much as possible in order to become a more effective agent in Christian work. Ray Sowers, the Y.M.C.A. leader, remembered how "on two or three occasions when I would be at the University, Carl would indicate that he felt a bit frustrated at times, because he found so few of his classmates with whom he could share 'the long thoughts of youth'—their concerns and occupations were primarily transient and trivial … Because of these encounters with Carl, I gained the impression that he was well on his way to a level of perception and maturity which had great promise for the future."[65]

Rogers also had a business going which had great promise for the future, if he cared to develop it. When he returned from China he had brought with him a variety of Chinese jewelry and handicrafts which his friends and relatives very much treasured. Mrs. Taylor, wife of the dean of the Peking Union Medical School, with whom he stayed during the Peking conference, had offered to shop for him on a commission basis. So he sent her twenty-five dollars with a small order for various Chinese crafts. The duty came to another twenty-five and, to his surprise, he had no difficulty selling the lot for a hundred dollars. Seeing the chance to help pay his way through school (his parents were supplying half of the cost), he began ordering more items in larger quantities. There were strings of beads and other jewelry made of all kinds of material—ivory, agate, cornelian, carved olive bits, glass, crackled glass, and so on. He also sold finely embroidered Chinese linen, and napkins, bridge sets, Mandarin rugs, *cloisonné* bowls and vases, and a whole range of Chinese handicrafts—some twenty items in all.

The Christmas season of his senior year was his most daring venture. He had sent an extremely large order to China, and when it didn't arrive he became frantic. Finally the goods came, around December first. He practically dropped all his studies and spent his time classifying, pricing, and labeling his products and selling them. For weeks he banked from one hundred to four hundred dollars per day, half of it profit. In all, he earned several thousand dollars profit from his brief importing career, enough to help pay his way through the last year of college and the first year of graduate school.[66]

Carl and Helen

During his freshman year at the University, Rogers had several dates with Helen Elliott, one of his childhood playmates, the girl from Oak Park who had seen him read before her second-grade class. Since the Rogers and Elliotts lived a block apart in Oak Park, Carl and Helen had known each other throughout grammar school. When the Rogers moved to the country, they did not see one another for four years. "She was my first date in college, largely because I was too shy to date a stranger."[67] "My father unexpectedly arrived in Madison and called Ross and told him we were both invited to have dinner with him at the University Club, and why didn't we bring a couple of girls. Ross had a girlfriend. I was not due back from class until about 5:30 or so, and dinner was soon after, so Ross thought it over; he knew that I knew Helen and knew that she was at Wisconsin, so he called her and asked her if she could join us for dinner. And I believe that's how my first date with her came about."[68]

Meeting again at the University, Rogers found Helen "tall, graceful and very attractive."[69] Later, as he did date a few other girls, he came to appreciate Helen's "gentleness, her straightforwardness, her thoughtfulness—not a brilliant academic glow, but a willingness to think openly about real issues, while I was caught up in the desire to appear scholarly. I can remember being ashamed of her sometimes in social groups because she seemed lacking in general and academic information."[70]

As each exposed the other to new interests, their friendship deepened. On hikes and picnics Carl showed Helen the world of nature that he loved. He would cook breakfast for her on the shore of Lake Monona, with an old frying pan over an open fire.[71] She taught him to dance and derive some enjoyment from social events. He began writing to her in the summer of 1920, and they continued to date throughout the following year at Wisconsin. Busy with his school work, Boys' Club, and religious activities, he confined his dating almost exclusively to Helen, while she continued to date several others. At the end of their sophomore year he noted, "tho I haven't been such a fool as to fall in love, I must say that I like Helen very well. I hope, surely hope she will change her present plans and decide to come back next year, because I'd like to carry the thing a bit further."[72]

Helen did not return the next year, but "the thing" did go a bit further. In November he wrote, "I have found a small portion of myself missing; it seems that a piece, at least, of my heart is in the slender hand of a certain young lady named Helen. It is a great life, I imagine, if you follow Emerson's advice, and 'give all to love.' I think I will try it someday."[73]

Helen had been an art student at the University. She had considerable talent in painting and design—a talent she continued to cultivate throughout her life. After two years at Wisconsin she transferred to the Chicago Academy of Fine Arts to learn to be a fashion artist and thus earn a living. It was a two-year course of study, and she lived at home in Oak Park during that time. Except for vacations and occasional weekends, Carl and Helen's courtships had to be carried on through correspondence. In December of his junior year he wrote in his journal:

> I am making a particular effort these days to keep any thought of Helen out of my mind as much as possible, and get my work done. I appreciate, I think, that my life is mine to forge out, and I've got to forge it out now while it's hot, into the kind of a weapon I plan to make it. I'm bound that that is going to be my main business and everything else is incidental, as far as I can make it so ... But while uttering these noble sentiments, I may add that if I don't get a letter from Helen tomorrow, I'll be as dejected as I was when I didn't get one today. Goldarn that little cuss without any clothes that goes around with a bow and arrow![74]

By January, at about the time he discovered he would be going to China, he also had discovered the full extent of his feelings for Helen: "She is a splendid girl, fine looking, with a beautiful face that is a good deal more than pretty—she has a great fund of common sense, that priceless article—she is bright, rather deep thinking than witty—she is neat and has excellent taste in everything—she is a good housekeeper—she is a fine Christian girl ... In short, I love her, and I love her very deeply, tho not with as fine and deep a love as I hope we may have some day, when I am sure it is mutual."[75]

He proposed to her before leaving for China. She put him off. She was quite fond of Carl, but she was also a practical person. It seemed fairly certain that Carl was heading toward religious work and probably the ministry. She did not feel cut out to be a minister's wife; feeling neither as spiritually or intellectually inclined as she imagined the role called for. Yet she liked him a lot and was undecided. So she asked that they postpone a decision until after his return from the Orient.

Having always been a shy person, Carl had little confidence about his relationships with women in general and Helen in particular. While he knew he loved her, he hardly dared hope that the feeling was mutual.[76] They corresponded heavily throughout his trip. For Helen the correspondence was a help to understanding and appreciating Carl as never before.[77] He, not knowing this, sometimes wondered if he had been wise to tell her of his feelings. "Since then there have been times when I felt sure she loved me, and times when I have felt she only cared for me as for any other friend. The real truth, I think, lies somewhere in between."[78] In words that he might have used years later to describe the therapeutic relationship, he added, "It is a wonderful experience, this exploring, with fear and trembling, the depths of another personality. It is wonderful what unexpected riches we sometimes find."[79]

During the period of recuperation after his hospitalization, Carl lived at home and was therefore able to see Helen quite frequently, although it meant a twenty-five mile drive, each way, over terrible roads. During this time the love became mutual. In late fall he wrote in his journal, "Two weeks ago last night, Oct. 29th, the world changed. The most wonderful miracle in the universe took place—for Helen told me that she loved me."[80] Love, in that era of courtship, went hand in hand with marriage; they were engaged that night. In later years Carl described that evening and the feelings that went with his realization of their mutual love as one of the peak experiences of his life.[81]

For the next two years, Carl and Helen saw each other as frequently as possible. Although distance often kept them apart, the telephone was considered too expensive a means of communication; but a two-cent stamp was sufficient to carry their love long distance. From 1922 to 1924 he wrote her 169 letters and she sent 85 to him.[82] Their love continued to deepen, as he described in his journal three months after the engagement. "There have been times when we have been together—like last Wednesday night—when it has just seemed to both of us that we have loved each other with an intensity that simply couldn't be measured—when mind and soul and body are just flooded in a mighty tide of love. And then there are often times when we have opened the secret chambers of our personalities to each other, and oh, the treasures I've found hidden in those inner sanctuaries! And there are other times when our love means simply the satisfying companionship of two lovers who understand each other. But in all its aspects and variations, it is growing more beautiful, more precious each day. And she is, too."[83]

During the half year at home, after his hospitalization, he wrote, "At home, there is continually, whether spoken or unspoken, the clash of different types of personalities—liberal vs. conservative—and it has been a joyous relief to have a lover who is as deeply sympathetic as Helen. I have at times stood in great need of just such a safety valve."[84]

Their correspondence shows what a safety valve she was. He explored his feelings and ideas with her on far-ranging topics, from the tensions at home to the world situation. Some excerpts from his letters illustrate vividly many of the significant themes in his life at that time.

The moving away from his parents. Referring to a letter from his mother he wrote, "Her letter sounded tired, and she said she had been in bed Tues., Wed., and Thurs. And the thing that worries me is that the letter I wrote her about Walt probably arrived Monday. Cause and effect? Je ne sais pas. I don't know whether I feel more like crying or more like swearing about it. I wrote that letter so carefully I thought it couldn't possibly hurt anyone's feelings, and all I did was to beg that they should try and see things from Walt's point of view, because if they didn't he would be apt to drift away from them. He and I are so much alike I know how he feels. And then in order to meet one of Mother's pet answers— that she's sorry she hasn't brought us up more as we think we ought to be brought up—I added that nothing I said was any criticism of our bringing up. It was because all of us, Walt included, have been brought up to be *men,* that we do try and stand on our own feet intellectually as well as in other ways. I was fool enough to think that the letter might clear things up a bit. I might have known better. Towards the close of her letter Mother says, 'Thank you for your letter regarding Walt—Am sorry you feel as you do about your early life and home.' That is all. But she couldn't have slapped much harder … Oh well, what does it all matter? I'm an ass to think I can change things at home, or that I can ever do anything to make father and mother anything but unhappy. And I certainly have no reason to bother you with all of it, but I have no apology to make. I had to talk to somebody. It's lots of fun to be a black sheep."

His self-concept. After quoting a letter of recommendation to graduate school, which described him as "one of a very small group of the most promising men I know in the present student generation who are headed for the ministry" and "To unusual qualities of mental keenness and fearlessness, he adds still rarer qualities of heart and spirit that, in my judgment, qualify him unusually for religious leadership in the coming generation," Carl told Helen how the writer "quite outdid himself in trying to make them believe I was somebody. And like all pats on the back, it makes one feel for a little while that possibly he is good for something. Even tho he may know better."

His fun-loving, robust side. At the fraternity initiation, "they had a bunch of crazy stunts, tests for us to pass through, etc. Some of them were dandy, and in one of them I had a corking time. It was a blind-folded boxing match between two of us pledges. After a few seconds of fighting I got what proved to be a brilliant hunch. I slipped past my real opponent and started pummeling one of the active members who was helping to form the ring to keep us in. Before they could shove me back into the ring I had given several of them some dandy swats, pretending that I thought I was fighting my opponent. I sure did have fun during the two rounds."

His social and religious concerns. Just back from a campus Y.M.C.A. meeting, he wrote: "All their plans seemed so trivial … his deepest idea of change in Y policy was that we should fix up a parlor for members only and arrange for other privileges. Oh *Hell!!!* … And then at great length plans for the frosh mixers were discussed, and how we could entertain the frosh, and what we should do about the freshman banquet, etc. … The churches are split wide open on the questions of whether a man can think in modern terms and still be a Christian. Martial law is on in Oklahoma because a large body of Protestant 'Christians' [the Ku Klux Klan] believe that the only solution for the Catholic, Jewish and alien problem is to flog out of the state those other groups. Europe is breeding hell for future generations because France thinks that the way to insure peace is to throttle Germany until she pays her last cent. An editorial writer in the Trib condemns the latest modern language New Testament because the old St. James version is good enough. And yet with the thousand and one problems of our day begging for a Christian solution, we sit around and twiddle our thumbs and wonder whether an old Haresfoot act would be entertaining for the frosh, or whether we can't find some clever fellow who can put on a little act of his own."

His empirical side, his desire to find the truth. "And the one big thing both of us must do now is to bend every effort to finding out something about this old, old riddle of Life and what it is all about. There will be plenty of time for affirming things later on, but the preparation for that will be to question clear to the bottom every doubt we have. If there is a doubt about God let's follow it out into every ramification we can until we have settled whether, for us, God does or does not exist. If there is a question about prayer let's ferret the thing out until we know either that prayer has no value, or that it has some value in releasing latent power already within us, or that it supplies us with power from outside. If there is some doubt as to whether the principles of Jesus will work, let's observe in our own lives and in the lives of others, and in the history of nations and peoples, whether they do or do not work better than the methods he condemned."

Most of all, the letters reveal Carl's caring and loving side. Excerpts from two letters and a poem he wrote for Helen capture the flavor.

I'm so thankful I have a girl whom I can love in so many ways. It makes me gasp sometimes when the realization of what a sweetheart I have grips me. I like some girls because they are practical. I like some because with all their education they are still unselfish and thoughtful of others. I like some girls because they are capable of big things, full of semi-dormant possibilities. I like some girls because they are good looking and some because they are good sports. And I like some because they are strong minded and strong in character, not afraid of other opinions, nor afraid to express their own. And when with all that, one finds a girl who has the dearest gray eyes, and slender tapered hands which handle things just as the mind behind them handles problems—delicately, yet with the sureness and firmness that ought to go with an artist's touch—when one finds all that, I say, how can one do otherwise than say with all that is in him—*I love you.*

The poem is one of several he wrote during this period.

To A Gray-Eyed Goddess

In Sappho's time and Sophocles'
The gray-eyed goddess men sought to please
And lyrics, rhymes, and satires keen
They dedicated to fair Athene.

No lofty lyrics mine—yet deep
Within my heart of hearts, I keep
Love, and hope, and great desires,
The stuff, I think, for lyric fires.
And if from that heap a flickering light
Lifts a white arm to the night
And smoky threads of fragrance rise,
I dedicate them to your sweet gray eyes.

Finally:

> If you had a sweetheart that meant all the world to you, and that sweetheart had a birthday, what would you say? Would you try and tell her how deliciously sweet her kisses were, or would you try to describe that joyous dancing love-smile that lights her face when she is completely happy in the arms of her lover? Of course if you were a poet there would be no question about what to do. A dainty little lyric that would sing like my heart sings when I think of her, and the long cool hands of her, and above all in the precious, precious heart of her,— that would be the very thing—if one were a poet. For if you take the coolness and freshness of the April breeze—yes, and the occasional gray sky of April, too; and add the vigor and strength and upward-pushing courage of all that lives in April; and sweeten it with the breath of the woodsy mayflower and make it soft as the underside of a thrush's wing—there you have my sweetheart. Why you couldn't help being born in April, Dearest. It's the very month most like you.

A half century later when Helen Rogers loaned me these letters to read, she wrote, "When you read all the passion we poured forth in these letters, you won't believe that we never once went to bed together. I can hardly believe it myself. But that was how it was for us then—it simply *had* to be legal."[85] It was a different age then in many ways, as one last excerpt indicates. In this letter Rogers unknowingly predicted what much of their life together would be like.

> I had the most glorious time last night, although I thought my heart would bust for wanting you. You see I went to bed early, about 10:30, and a little after midnight I was awakened by singing. At first I couldn't imagine where it was but gradually realized that the Varsity Glee Club was serenading the Kappa Delts across the street. I've forgotten the first song, but the second was "The Bedouin

Love Song." I've always liked that as a poem, but when the words are sung to a haunting melody that carries in it the breath of the desert and the very heartbeats of love—well, they could have sung it over fifty times and I wouldn't have been satisfied ... I'm afraid the Bedouins went to my head last night ... May we always live as Arabs—never unwilling to fold up our tents—either material or spiritual—and move onward to new lands of promise if we feel the urge.

In his senior year Rogers applied to and was accepted at Union Theological Seminary in New York. He and Helen had every intention of going together. The families disapproved. Married people, they felt, ought to be settling down, with the man holding a steady job and the woman raising a family. The idea of four years of schooling after marriage was positively scandalous. Besides, Carl's graduate studies toward the ministry would be demanding enough, without adding to them the obligations and distractions of marriage. Both families thought highly of the match but advised the young couple to wait.

The couple, deeply in love, would not wait—at least, not for their parents' reasons. Helen was somewhat reluctant to give up the promising career as a commercial artist which she had begun six months before. But she finally agreed with Carl that since so much was likely to happen to him during his four years in New York, unless they could share these experiences together, they would very likely grow in different directions. Against their parents' advice, they were married on August 28, 1924, at Helen's sister and brother-in-law's home in River Forest, Illinois, commencing a marriage that would last for 55 years. For their honeymoon, they piled all their belongings into Carl's new Model A Ford coupe, purchased for $450, and drove east to New York City.[86]

41

CHAPTER 3

The New York City Years
1924–1928

Driving to New York City in their own car was a great adventure for the new couple. Before the wedding Carl had given Helen a book on sex and marriage—an avant-garde thing to do at the time. Nevertheless both partners were extremely naïve. "Whether in spite of or because of our lack of sophistication," Rogers later wrote, "we had a delightful honeymoon."[1]

Like today, the Morningside Heights area on Manhattan's Upper West Side was a center of university life when the Rogers arrived in 1924. Broadway separated Barnard College and Union Theological Seminary on the west from Columbia University on the east. Dormitories for married students were practically nonexistent then; but arriving just before classes began, they managed to find "the world's smallest apartment in New York" on the ground floor of the Cathedral Ayrcourt Apartments at 540 West 123rd Street.[2] Rogers' mother calculated the square footage as smaller than his bedroom at Warwood.[3] A large vacant lot of solid rock (now the site of the Jewish Theological Seminary) and Broadway separated them from Union, while six flights of stairs separated them from the roof of their apartment house, where they would dry their clothes and, later, the diapers.

For about four and a half dollars both of them could have a splendid evening on the town. They would begin with a full course dinner for a dollar apiece at their favorite French restaurant on Amsterdam Avenue and then ride the subway, for a nickel each, down to Times Square. On Monday nights they could get theater tickets at half price at Gray's Drug Store where, if they were lucky, they could get two of the cheapest seats for a dollar and seventy-five cents. A pound of their favorite peppermint patties, for fifty-nine cents, would top off the evening.[4]

The city proved to be an exciting place for them both. Helen found "the thrill of exploring the big city with its many cultural advantages of the theatre, the Art Museums, the bohemian area of the Village—as well as the intellectual stimulation of studying under such giants in education as Kilpatrick, Dewey, Fosdick, and McGiffert—had a very freeing quality for two young provincial Midwesterners."[5]

Union Theological Seminary

Rogers chose Union Theological Seminary because "it was the most liberal in the country and an intellectual leader in religious work."[6] It promoted the Social Gospel movement, which made love and justice in this world a central focus of religion. Union's religious humanism placed faith in science, reason and morality as keys to creating the kingdom of God on earth.

Rogers' parents had wholeheartedly opposed this decision, believing "their fundamentalist journals which told them that [Union] was the devil in disguise ... My father even tried to bribe me ... he told me that if I should happen to choose to go to Princeton Seminary, which was of course the outstanding Fundamentalist seminary at the time, then he would be able to pay my way." Rogers resented the offer and indignantly rejected it. "Instead, I took some competitive examinations and won a good scholarship at Union Seminary and we made our plans for going there. My parents were more generous in gifts to help us get underway [they gave the couple a $2,500 wedding gift], though it was still necessary for me to earn a considerable amount of money for our expenses."[7]

Rogers had a great deal of respect for Arthur Cushman McGiffert, then head of the Seminary. "He created an exciting philosophical climate at Union Seminary ... You were there to do your own thinking and there was no pressure toward an orthodoxy of any kind."[8] McGiffert was also "a remarkable teacher and a profound scholar. His course on 'Protestant Thought before Kant' and other similar courses introduced me to a new level of teaching excellence. As we heard him present the thinking of one philosopher or theologian, we in the class would become convinced that, 'Aha! This is the person with whom he really agrees.' The next week he would present someone else with equal conviction and persuasiveness."[9]

Rogers later wondered if McGiffert "could have done such a beautiful job of presenting others' points of view if he'd had any of his own";[10] but in the end his students had to think for themselves, which was of course what McGiffert intended. With experiences like this, Rogers found Union "a stimulating and exciting place. I made friends, found new ideas, and fell thoroughly in love with the whole experience."[11]

Helen sat in on many of Carl's classes, which enabled them to grow together. One was taught by the famous Harry Emerson Fosdick and gave them "a feeling for a modern and liberal religion."[12] In the courses and on their own they read many books together, attended shows, and discussed all the new ideas to which they were exposed.

Rogers' term papers that year reflected his increasingly liberal thinking. Had his parents read them, their worst fears would have been confirmed. In a paper he wrote for "Systematic Theology 1," he concluded that Christianity had primarily three dimensions: the person and life of Jesus of Nazareth, a lofty system of ethics, and an inherent tendency toward social improvement. "These are the three contributions which I would suggest as the most valuable Christianity has made. We could now question—do these things give a basis for hailing Christianity as in any sense the universal or final religion? By no means. Other religions have given to the world great personalities. Other religions have high ethical standards. Other religions and quasi-religions (e.g. Communism) have high social vision. It seems to me typically Western and very tragic that we have persisted in viewing Christianity as the one and only religion."[13]

In another paper, written for "Church History 9," he went so far as to say there was no such thing as Christianity. In an impressive *tour de force*, he compared Jesus, Peter, Paul, Marcion, Ignatius of Antioch, Augustine, Hildebrand, Francis of Assisi, Savonarola, John Huss, Erasmus, Martin Luther, and Ignatius Loyola on their attitudes toward public worship, prayer, doctrine, the Church, Jesus Christ, the Bible and religious authority, immortal life, the Spirit, and the Christian life. He showed how all these Christian leaders had widely divergent attitudes on almost all of the issues. Thus he concluded:

> The Christian religion has satisfied very different psychological needs in different men ... The important thing is not the religion but the man ... The third conclusion is closely linked with the first two, and forces itself upon me as I consider the data. It is this; there is no such thing as the religion of Christianity—the term is simply a name with which we cover a multitude of religions. No one religion can possibly cover the vast number of directly opposed ideas which we have uncovered. It is a confusion in terms to call it one religion. Let us rather seek among this jumble of religions for a faith which will enrich and vitalize our own lives.[14]

The first year at Union Seminary also reintroduced Rogers to the world of psychology. Harrison Elliot and Grace Loucks Elliot were on the Seminary faculty and very involved in working with individuals and in the group discussion approach, from a Christian perspective. Through them Rogers recognized for the first time that "working with individual persons in a helping relationship could be a professional enterprise."[15] But his major influence in psychology that year came through a young man who was to become a lifelong friend and an extremely important figure in his early professional career.

Goodwin Watson was only a few years older than Rogers and came from a similar Midwestern background with strong religious values. As a student at the University of Wisconsin, Watson had known Carl's older brother Ross when the latter was president of the campus Y.M.C.A. Watson moved to New York and became an Instructor in Religious Education at Union Theological Seminary. In 1925 he moved across the street to Teachers College, Columbia University, where he became an Instructor in Educational Psychology. Remaining at Teachers College until 1962, Watson had a long and distinguished career as an educational and social psychologist.[16]

In 1925 Rogers and Watson were not aware that their careers would parallel and interweave in so many ways. Their first meeting came when Watson crossed back over Broadway to teach a course at Union, with the psychiatrist Joseph Chassell, on "Working with Individuals." Union, Teachers College and the Columbia Graduate School had a very freewheeling exchange program then; faculty and students teaching or taking courses at the neighboring institution was not at all unusual. Watson and Chassell invited many prominent people in New York City to the class to discuss their interest in psychology and their particular type of work with individuals. Whereas a few years earlier, in his correspondence course, Rogers had found psychology to be a dull and lifeless field, now it seemed alive and exciting. The course proved to be a turning point in Rogers' career. "I began to see ... that one could do the kind of thing that I was drawn to, namely, helping people change—not that I would have put it in these terms at the time—but helping people to change, grow, develop, live more satisfying and better lives. That didn't have to be done in a church."[17]

But Rogers still was in a religious education program, and in the summer of 1925 Carl and Helen went to East Dorset, Vermont, where for several months Rogers assumed the position of pastor of a tiny church. This was a customary part of the seminarian's training at Union. Many rural churches could not afford a full-time minister, and in the winter months they often had to share one with several neighboring communities. Union arranged for its students to take over full-time summer pastoral responsibilities in these small churches. The communities were grateful, and the seminarians received important, practical experience.

Rogers' eleven sermons that summer were filled with the latest developments in modern religious thinking. This being the summer of the famous Scopes "Monkey Trial," in Dayton, Tennessee, in which William Jennings Bryan and Clarence Darrow battled over the teaching of the Darwinian theory of evolution in the public schools, Rogers chose to teach his little church something of the "higher criticism." In one sermon, "Three Stories of Creation," he showed how the Book of Genesis contained not one, but *two* stories of creation; therefore, why not recognize the Darwinian theory as a third story and acknowledge the meaning and beauty of all three?[18] On another occasion he preached, "I may doubt whether God spoke as directly to Moses as the naïve writer of the book supposed, but I cannot doubt that the message he gave is the message of the universe to every nation ..."[19] His sermons (as Jesus' were) were filled with rural and agricultural images and analogies that reflected his own background; but they were also full of his new learnings from psychology. "The psychologists tell us ..." and similar phrases were frequent.

"I worked very hard on my sermons," Rogers later wrote. "Each was a decidedly polished and scholarly product, not particularly appropriate for a small village. I found it absolutely impossible to make my sermons longer than 20 minutes, a fact which disturbed me but for which my congregation was doubtless thankful ...

> Helen and I were very much welcomed by the village. The town drunkard had given up his house for the summer in order that we might have it ... Helen taught the girls softball and other games that they had never known. I took the boys on hikes and inaugurated a number of activities such as a men's club. We were both involved in many new experiences.
>
> One of these new experiences was my first encounter with death. A parishioner died of cancer and I thought that I would have to console the family and conduct the funeral services. I was enormously relieved that a neighboring minister was invited to undertake the task and I was not called upon to meet this ultimate problem. I also recall my surprise that the dull son in the family (ten or twelve years of age) became hysterical and went racing around the house laughing at the top of his voice as his reaction to his mother's death.
>
> Up the road from our house lived a confirmed alcoholic who brought different women into his home at different times. Still further up the road was a woman who was completely psychotic, living with her very unstable son. All in all, this summer gave us a real acquaintance with the range of psychological and personal problems which exist in the ordinary community. It also gave me an increasing interest in understanding these problems, though at that time my understanding was very limited indeed.[20]

It was that summer that Carl and Helen decided to start a family. The morning after the first night they stopped using contraceptives, Helen announced she was pregnant. Carl thought that was silly, but in a few days the signs were unmistakable. Throughout their lives they often told this story to indicate how Helen was much better at trusting her intuition and feelings than Carl was.[21]

During his second year at Union, 1925–26, Rogers registered for several courses at Teachers College, the professional education school of Columbia

University, the fifth oldest higher education institution in the United States.[22] Building on his new interest in psychology he took his first course in clinical psychology with Leta Hollingworth and found it fascinating, especially because she seemed to him to be so interested in children and people in general.[23] He also had his first real exposure to progressive education, through the famous William Heard Kilpatrick. Originally a student of John Dewey, Kilpatrick was the greatest translator and popularizer of his teacher's philosophy. According to historian Lawrence Cremin,

> He was by all reports a master at working with classes numbering in the hundreds, managing to engage individuals to the point where both their ideas and their teaching techniques changed radically. And however much he personally detested indoctrination, he seems to have been extraordinarily effective in making disciples. In all he taught some 35,000 students from every state in the Union at a time when Teachers College was training a substantial percentage of the articulate leaders of American education.[24]

Consistent with this description, Rogers found Kilpatrick's "Philosophy of Education" course "very stimulating indeed—not only the lectures and question and answer periods, but also the small group discussions which were a part of the course."[25] Twenty years later, when students from across the nation would flock to Rogers' huge lecture courses on counseling and psychotherapy at the University of Chicago, his students would describe him in much the same way that he and Cremin described Kilpatrick.

Rogers was much influenced by Kilpatrick, Dewey and progressive education. During his two years at Union Seminary, in order to supplement the income from his scholarship and savings, he worked weekends as the director of religious education at the First Congregational Church in suburban Mt. Vernon, New York. The community was well educated and middle class and the church modern in its thinking. Average church attendance was about 300, average church school attendance a bit more than half of that. When Rogers took over as religious education director, he found the worship services dull and rather sterile. To involve the church school youngsters in the service and to make the service more gripping and personal, he introduced processionals, more organ music, robes for the Choir, and reports from the religious education classes on their projects. All of this helped; but in his reading for Union Seminary he noted some criticism of the type of worship service that aimed primarily at an emotional–psychological effect, instead of some sort of commitment to social action. He began to doubt the usefulness of the changes he had introduced.[26] On one of his examinations, for "Religious Education 22," he explored some of his new thoughts: "If however one holds the Dewey–Kilpatrick type of educational philosophy, then the meaning is: The work of the church is a type of social education, and the task of the workers is to enrich the experience of those within the group, and make sure that each experience leads out into richer fields ... Personally I hold the latter view, and I have done considerable thinking as to what it involves. In the first place it means helping people to solve the immediate problems which they are facing, in the best possible way. For the life of me, I cannot see that there can be any distinction as to the type of problems we help them solve. If their real problem is one of sex adjustment, we cannot turn them toward some problem about God, because that is 'religious.' It means that we regard all of life as our field of education ... In the second place this type of approach means that we will encourage a scientific facing of such problems as they bring. When it is realized that this means the facing of the current standards of morality, the belief in God and in religion itself, all as mere hypotheses, and the examination of the evidence for and against, we realize some of the radical ways in which this educational approach is bound to work out."[27]

Again the worship service at the Congregational Church changed its focus, and Rogers encouraged religious education classes to use the group problem-solving approach of the progressives. During the week the children would tackle real problems in their lives and in the community. On Sunday the worship service would be a time of sharing and reflection on these efforts, a time for renewal of faith in their ethical mission, and a time to build a sense of community which comes from group effort. Rogers thus anticipated by some forty years the changes in church services which would occur widely in the 1960s—primarily the renewed sense of celebration and of community sharing and involvement.

Even his recommendations for the training of religious education teachers showed the influence of the progressives. "Put not your trust in Teacher Training courses as they are presently offered," he wrote in May 1926. "By beginning with the immediate problems of the teachers, by sharing experiences between the new teachers and those who have been longer at it, and by developing further the interest which all have in certain common problems, I believe one will accomplish more actual education than through a formal course. Furthermore, the reading that is done when a person asks for help on a particular problem, is of much greater value than the very small amount of routine reading that is done for a standard Teacher Training Course."[28]

A fellow graduate student, Theodore Newcomb, began to think of Rogers as "an educational radical."[29] Although he did not turn again to education as a primary focus for several decades, it is apparent how deeply Rogers' own teaching style and his subsequent educational thinking were rooted in the progressive tradition.

While he developed his views on education, religion, and religious education, however, Rogers became increasingly perplexed by an unavoidable dilemma. If, as he stated above, religious education is primarily progressive social education, and if a scientific examination of all the foundations of religion is essential, then, he wrote,

It seems to me that the policy works itself into a hopeless tangle. In the first place, its scope becomes so wide that it includes almost exactly the territory of the modern school. When the question arises as to which is better equipped to handle this sort of education, it seems to me that the modern school has all the arguments, and that the only excuse for the continuation of the church school is that in many localities there is as yet no conception of modern education in the public schools. In the second place, I am inclined to wonder whether the thoroughly scientific attitude is compatible with the idea of religion. I am afraid that without some "Eternal Verity" which it was unwilling to question, there could be no such thing as religion …

It is impossible to make plain my position in such a short space and without more time to think it out, but as a summary of my appraisal of this educational approach to religious leadership I should say something like this. From the point of view of social progress, and ultimate human welfare, I should say that it represents a sound and valuable contribution. From the point of view of religion I should say that it was quite subversive of anything that might be called religion, and that it was a grave question as to whether it had any right to work under the aegis of religion.[30]

Rogers' instructor wrote on this paper, "This is a very clear analysis of the problem. Some day I'd be glad to talk with you further on your conclusions." But "some day" never came, and Rogers and several of his peers at Union Seminary were left with many distressing questions. The young men needed answers if they were to remain in their calling. The situation led to what Rogers later described as "an amusing but highly significant venture."

Knowing universities and graduate schools as I do now—knowing their rules and their rigidities—I am truly astonished at the freedom which was granted us at Union. A group of students, of which I was one, felt that ideas were being fed to us and that we were not having an opportunity to discuss the religious and philosophical issues which most deeply concerned us. We wanted to explore our own questions and doubts and find out where they led. We petitioned the administration that we be allowed to set up a seminar (for credit!) in which there would be no instructor and in which the curriculum would be composed of our own questions. The Seminary was understandably perplexed by this request but they granted our petition. The only restriction was that in the interest of the Seminary a young instructor was to sit in on the course but to take no part in it unless we wished him to be active. This seminar was deeply satisfying and clarifying. It moved me a long way toward a philosophy of life which was my own. The majority of the members of that group, in thinking their way through the questions that they had raised, thought their way right out of religious work. I was one. Theodore Newcomb was another. Various other members of the group have gone on in sociology and psychology. The whole seminar was very freewheeling. It took up profound philosophical, religious and social problems. My own reason for deciding at that time to leave the field of religious work was that although questions as to the meaning of life and the possibility of the constructive improvement of life for individuals were of deep interest to me, I could not work in a field where I would be required to believe in some specified religious doctrine. I realized that my own views had changed tremendously already and would very likely continue to change. It seemed to me that it would be a horrible thing to have to profess a set of beliefs in order to remain in one's profession. I wanted to find a field in which I could be sure my freedom of thought would not be limited."[31]

So, in the fall of 1926, Rogers again crossed Broadway to Teachers College, this time to stay. He scored highest in his group in the Thorndike intelligence test and the matriculation examination required of applicants.[32] Majoring in clinical and educational psychology, he was now able to continue his graduate work at Columbia.

His parents' worst fears had been proven true. From the liberal Union Theological Seminary, Rogers left the church never to return to any formalized religion. (It is a shame, though, that Walter and Julia Rogers did not live until 1967; for if they had, it might have been some small consolation to see their son receive the Distinguished Contribution Award from the American Pastoral Counselors Association.)

Personal Life

Their first child, David, was born on March 17, 1926, when Carl was finishing his work at Union. At about this time his ulcer began bothering him again, and they realized that expert medical attention was needed. Consequently Carl, Helen, and David traveled to Rochester, Minnesota, to the Mayo Clinic, where several of the Rogers had been treated and which had the family's highest confidence. A successful operation, a gastro-enterostomy, was performed. Helen rented a room for herself and David near the hospital; so, by running back and forth, she could look after both her recuperating husband and their three-month-old son. They received no help then, financial or otherwise, from Carl's family, a fact which, looking back on the episode, was puzzling to them, as finances were no problem to his parents and Carl's mother or sister could easily have come up from Chicago.[33] Carl's recent decision to leave Union Seminary probably was a factor in the family's remoteness, as well as his history of refusing their help when it *was* offered.

Still recovering from the operation, Carl and Helen left David with Helen's mother and went to the Y.M.C.A. Camp in Estes Park, Colorado. There they both conducted a short workshop-course on marital and sexual adjustment.

The group with whom they worked was very grateful for the chance to talk freely about their concerns in this area. It was a daring enough venture at that in 1926; but Carl and Helen also passed out a questionnaire to elicit some facts about the participants' sex lives and to generate topics for discussion. They were amazed to discover that the questionnaire, falling into hands outside the group, created quite a stir and almost lost the Y.M.C.A. the support of one of its major contributors.[34]

One reason the Rogers had felt competent to lead the course was the sexual awareness that had recently emerged in their own marriage. Many years later he described how he had become "very dimly aware that though our sexual relationship was great for me, it was not great for her. I realize, though, how little I understood the deeper meaning of her phrases: 'Oh, not tonight'; 'I'm too tired'; 'Let's wait 'till some other time.' There is no doubt the situation could have led to a crisis.

> At this point sheer luck gave us a break, though like most good luck, it needs to be used. In my graduate school, I learned that a psychiatrist, Dr. G.V. Hamilton, needed a few more young married men to complete a research study he was engaged in.[35] Probably there was some pay involved, which would account for my snatching the opportunity so promptly. (Actually the study was a more personalized forerunner of the Kinsey researches, and very well done, though never widely known.) I went to Dr. Hamilton's office for two or three lengthy interviews. He questioned so calmly and easily about every aspect of my sexual development and life, that I gradually found myself talking with almost equal ease. One thing I came to realize was that I just didn't *know* whether my wife had ever had an orgasm. She often seemed to enjoy our relationship, so I *assumed* I knew the answer. But the most important thing I learned was that the things in one's private life which cannot possibly be talked about, *can* be talked about, easily and freely.
>
> So then came the question, could I translate this into my personal life? I began the frightening process of talking—really talking—with Helen about our sexual relationship. It was frightening because every question, and every answer, made one or the other of us so vulnerable—to attack, to criticism, to ridicule, to rejection. But we weathered it! Each learned to understand much more deeply the other's desires, taboos, satisfactions, and dissatisfactions, in our sexual life. And while at first it led only to greater tenderness, and understanding, and improvement, gradually it led not only to orgasms for her, but to a full, continuing, satisfying and enriching sexual relationship—in which we could talk out new difficulties as they arose.[36]

Helen later wrote, "What I feel was the most fortunate for me was Carl's ability to be open and frank and truthful in facing all our problems, including our sex

51

life. We were able to establish a free communication with each other, never allowing misunderstandings or hurts to fester. It gave us a basis for growth and closeness which has lasted through the years. His ability to listen and be empathic was there in the very first years of our marriage."[37]

So was his sarcasm. Taking playful or not-so-playful digs at your family members was the communication milieu in which Rogers was raised. When he saw how one of his snide comments or little "jokes" could easily reduce Helen to tears, he worked hard to change his behavior and, with occasional lapses, generally succeeded.[38]

As parents they followed the Watsonian behaviorism which was popular then, including strict scheduling and little emotional or physical contact. "It was a period when you were supposed to let a child cry for four hours, if he was on a four-hour feeding schedule, no matter what his feelings were. We were influenced by that, though I'm glad to say we didn't always follow it ..." To break David of his thumb sucking, they put bad-tasting things on the thumb or covered the hand with an aluminum mitt. "Fortunately, Helen had enough common sense to make a good mother in spite of all this damaging psychological knowledge."[39] David was an active toddler, who was inclined to run out into Amsterdam Avenue, so Helen often had him "harnessed, like a puppy."[40] Helen, Gladys Watson and Rita Spence (wives of Goodwin Watson and Ralph Spence) often wheeled their baby carriages over to Riverside Park where they talked while the children played. The Rogers put David in an experimental nursery school at Teachers College at eighteen months— a rather modern idea which Helen had some guilt feelings about, but which they both thought would be good for him, and would also give them more freedom. Soon they also had a regular babysitter in Helen's mother who moved to New York City after her husband's death.

Columbia University

When Rogers transferred to Teachers College in 1926, Columbia University was the leading center in the country for the training of psychologists. Of the 616 members of the American Psychological Association with Ph.D. degrees in 1928 (the majority of the overall membership), 135 were graduates of Columbia, followed by 85 from Chicago and 56 from Harvard.[41] America's first major educational psychologist, E.L. Thorndike, was teaching at Columbia when Rogers arrived. Because of Thorndike's considerable reputation Rogers was eager to take a course with him. He found the lectures interesting, although he was not particularly interested in the subject, the testing of mathematical aptitude. The science of psychology was still in its infancy in the twenties, and the psychology department at "T.C." was dominated by a strong interest in testing.[42] Freud was generally regarded as a dirty word in academic circles.

Thorndike and his colleagues saw measurement as being fundamental to the growing science. Intelligence testing was relatively new and quite the rage, as was the creation of new tests and measures for any psychological phenomenon one wanted to study. Goodwin Watson, for his dissertation, had developed a *Measurement of Fair-Mindedness*. Rogers, too, for his dissertation, would develop a new psychological test.

Naturally he had to take his share of statistics courses. When he went to register for the first such course, however, he found it was offered at a very inconvenient hour. Always confident in his intellectual abilities, he decided he could probably bypass the introductory course, and managed to get permission to enroll in the second statistics course, with Professor Ruger. Here he found the lectures terribly abstruse and confusing, and for the first time knew the feeling of not being able to grasp the material. Although he worked hard on his own, he knew there was a strong likelihood of failing the final exam and the course. He did as best he could on the exam, but was quite certain he had failed. Figuring that under the circumstances he had nothing to lose, at the end of his examination blue book he wrote a scathing criticism of the course and the instructor's method of teaching. He passed, but never knew why.[43]

Testing also played a part in his second course in clinical psychology with Leta Hollingworth. "It was under her supervision that I first came in actual clinical contact with children—testing them, talking with them, dealing with them as fascinating objects of study, helping to make plans for their welfare."[44] He worked especially hard on his first "case" in this practicum, giving the boy many psychometric tests, interviewing him at length, and writing a long and eloquent analysis of the whole situation. Several years later the boy's father telephoned Rogers, explaining that his son was seeing another psychologist and that Rogers' original report would be very helpful. Rogers no longer had the actual report but, as with first love, could not forget his first client. He typed out another lengthy analysis, from memory, and sent it on, shortly thereafter receiving a thank-you note from the psychologist who was impressed, not only that Rogers remembered, but that he had been so perceptive in his observations.[45]

Leaving his studies at Union Seminary had created a financial problem, for he could no longer continue as religious education director in Mt. Vernon. Fortunately, just when he needed it, Rogers received an attractive job offer from Goodwin Watson, whom he later called his "brilliant young sponsor ... He was a very good teacher, but I particularly appreciated the fact that he was quite willing to let me go my own way in my graduate work and research."[46]

As Watson described Rogers' job, "The one in which Carl assisted me was entitled 'Orient and Occident: An Opinion Survey.' It was financed by the Institute of Pacific Relations and designed to explore attitudes of numerous American groups (students, businessmen, farmers, club-women, prisoners, etc.) on domestic and foreign issues relating to China and Japan. Our sampling techniques weren't very sophisticated but we got several thousand replies and tallied them by hand. This was rather typical of the exploitation commonly practiced when graduate students were available as cheap labor. Why was Carl selected? Bright young man, needed to earn money, hard-working, wholly trustworthy, friendly and cooperative."[47]

Rogers remembered how Watson "always had many irons in the fire, and he turned over to me almost complete responsibility for an extensive survey he had initiated. I employed a sizable group of research assistants, conducted the analysis of some very complex material, and organized and wrote the presentation, all under pressure of an unyielding and imminent deadline."[48]

Rogers' training at Teachers College strongly reinforced and advanced his belief in and understanding of the scientific method, which had existed for him ever since his early agricultural experiments. The training also instilled in him a definite respect for the concept of intelligence and for intelligence testing. Over the next decade of working intensively with children, he frequently used terms like "dull," "dull-normal," "average," and "superior" to describe the intelligence of children he had studied. Later on, when he abandoned psychological testing in his clinical work, he stopped using these terms. But even forty years later, describing a "revolutionary program for graduate education," he included "intelligence, perhaps more specifically defined as a high degree of ability in problem solving," as one of the three criteria for selection of students into the program.[49]

After a year of graduate study at Teachers College, in June Rogers received his Master of Arts degree in Psychology from Columbia University.[50] It is not clear when he made his decision to go on for his Ph.D. degree, but he did continue his graduate work without a pause.

Institute for Child Guidance

Late in 1926 Rogers applied for a Fellowship at the about-to-be-formed Institute for Child Guidance in New York City. In addition to providing a valuable internship experience that would enable him to complete his training as a psychologist and do much of the research on his doctoral dissertation, the Fellowship also carried a salary of $2,500—just enough to support his family. He won the appointment for the 1927–28 school year; but shortly before the year began, he received "an embarrassed letter from Dr. Frankwood Williams, the psychiatrist who headed the selection committee. He had just discovered that psychiatrists were to get $2,500. The Fellowships for psychologists were to be only $1,200. It was the financial rather than the professional insult which roused my dander. I wrote him a very strong letter, saying essentially that the Fellowship had been awarded, I had been informed of it, I had made all my personal plans on this basis, I needed the money to support my family. On the strength of my letter he made an exception and I received a $2,500 Fellowship."[51]

Throughout his career psychiatrists would often complain that Rogers, a psychologist, was encroaching on their territory. Thus he later commented, "It is interesting and symbolic that I started my professional training—through a fluke—on the same level with psychiatric residents."[52]

Just before beginning work at the Institute, Carl, Helen, and David spent the summer of 1927 in Willoughby, Ohio, where Rogers served both as camp counselor and psychologist at Camp Wawokeye, the summer camp for "problem boys" from the Cleveland Child Guidance Clinic. Theodore Newcomb, one of the members of the student-directed seminar at Union Seminary and later a famous social psychologist himself, was also a counselor at Camp Wawokeye that summer. Newcomb remembered how "One of their recurrent 'problems' was bed-wetting. I remember that all five of my charges, who slept with me in the same tent (on straw mattresses) were so afflicted. The camp had almost no money, and Carl decided to make a 'project' of building a rowboat, with some assistance from the boys. As it was nearly completed, the question arose of what name to give the boat. Although it eventually turned out to be properly seaworthy, as well as good-looking, it was still untested. I believe it was I who therefore proposed that we name it the S.S. Enuresis—and so it was. Carl, of course, was instantly dubbed 'Captain of the S.S. Enuresis.'"[53]

"Child guidance work was just coming into its own," wrote Rogers, "and an elaborate Institute for Child Guidance was established by the Commonwealth Fund in New York City in order to provide training for such clinical workers."[54] The facility was lavish and impressive, and the Institute employed a large and excellent staff. (When the Great Depression came a few years later, the Institute folded.) Dr. David Levy, chief of staff, introduced the Rorschach method to this country and was a pioneer in using play therapy with children.[55] Rogers found E.K. Wickman, the chief psychologist, "thoughtful, balanced, a good research worker, genuinely interested in discovering the truth" and always admired his "open-mindedness."[56] The well-known child psychiatrist Lawson Lowrey was director of the clinic staff and, along with Levy and Wickman, was helpful to Rogers.

As Rogers described the Institute in his dissertation, "The Institute for Child Guidance offers almost ideal facilities for carrying on any type of research among difficult children ... Problem-children in large numbers, widely varying in age, mentality, and behavior, are brought to the Institute for study. Harassed parents, baffled teachers, and perplexed social workers keep its offices filled with youngsters whose behavior is to be diagnosed and treated ... The child receives a complete study from the psychiatric, psychological, and physical angles. An exhaustive social history, obtained by competent workers, chronicles the child's behavior and family background as completely as it is possible to do so. This wealth of data about each child is of first importance in conducting research. The large staff of the Institute represents a wide variety of experience and training. They do not represent any one school of psychological thought." Professional roles tended to be fairly distinct, although Rogers was exposed to them all: "the social worker worked with the family, the psychologist did the testing, the psychiatrist interviewed the child. If there was treatment work for the parents, the social worker did that ... If there was remedial work—tutoring—to be done, the psychologist did that."[57]

At the Institute, Rogers had considerably more exposure to Freudian thinking than before. It was only eighteen years earlier, in 1909, that Sigmund Freud had first come to America to lecture at Clark University, after which Dr. A.A. Brill worked indefatigably to translate Freud's voluminous writings into English and to popularize his views. Just before the war Freud and the "new psychology" was *the* topic of discussion in Greenwich Village and among New York's intelligentsia,[58] but psychoanalysis caught on much more slowly in medical circles. Rogers characterized the Institute's philosophy as "an eclectic Freudianism," representing many "different shades of psychoanalytic thinking and other psychiatric and psychological views."[59] He had an initial interest in psychoanalysis and occasionally used some analytic techniques in his "remedial work" with children. But psychoanalysis proved too esoteric for this practical Midwesterner with a growing scientific bent, and his interest waned over the year. He later commented how, "[t]he fact that they could spin elaborate theories with no regard for using them in research really offended me."[60]

He had a variety of experiences at the Institute. Under the supervision of trained psychologists he made complete psychometric examinations of children, utilizing tests as different as the Stanford Binet Intelligence Test, Healy Picture Completion Test, Ferguson Form Boards, Porteus Maze, Gates Primary Reading, and Stanford Achievement. He helped conduct a psychological survey of a school. He took part in case conferences.[61] He was exposed to the many different points of view of the various psychologists, psychiatrists, psychoanalysts, and social workers who were invited to speak to the Institute's staff. "Alfred Adler lectured to us, for example, and shocked the whole staff by thinking that an elaborate case history was not necessary. I remember how misinformed I thought he must be, since we routinely took case histories 50 to 70 pages in length."[62] In recent decades Adler and Rogers' theories and methods have often been compared, and some commentators have noted similarities in their work; but clearly there was no direct influence on Rogers at the time.[63]

On another occasion, early in his stay at the Institute, he and the other interns were meeting in a seminar with staff member Dr. Marion Kenworthy. The interns wanted to make some changes in their program or, at least, discuss certain problems of concern to them. Kenworthy, instead of dealing with their questions, chose to interpret their behavior to them. It was natural, she said, that they would feel somewhat rebellious in a new situation, in having to deal with a woman, and so on. It was kindly but, as Rogers saw it, "a definite indication that we were small boys and we would get over it and she knew best, etc. Being on the receiving end of that kind of interpretation, which had some truth in it, showed me how demeaning and degrading it was. We might have been willing to give in a bit up to that point, but after that we wouldn't give in come hell or high water."[64]

"I also began to realize that I had real clinical skill, both in dealing with individuals and with colleagues. I remember one case conference with an uncooperative caseworker from outside, discussing a boy with whom I had been working. I was late because of a sleet storm that morning. When I arrived the conference was obviously stalemated because the outside worker was totally unsympathetic and uncooperative. I won her over by my explanation of the situation, though I was the youngest and least experienced member of the conference group. It was this boy who was the first individual with whom I carried on regular therapy (though when psychologists did it, it was called remedial work or some such name). I made real progress in helping him, though I was full of the psychoanalytic theories which I was trying out at the time."[65]

His year at the Institute was "extremely stimulating," but not without its conflicts. While Teachers College, where he was still taking courses, emphasized measurement and statistics, the Institute for Child Guidance emphasized emotions and personality dynamics. Having to resolve the tension between the two approaches—understanding the person from the outside through objective testing versus understanding the individual from the person's own perspective through sensitive interviewing—was very important in Rogers' growth and eventually led to some of his major contributions to psychology and psychotherapy. His resolution was to combine *both* the external and internal perspective, as he did in his doctoral dissertation, *Measuring Personality Adjustment in Children Nine to Thirteen Years of Age.*[66] Using and adapting many of the questions that psychologists and psychiatrists normally would ask children in clinical interviews, he constructed a paper-and-pencil test which helped reveal the child's attitude toward: (1) himself and his abilities, (2) his relationship to his companions, (3) his family, and (4) all of these, as revealed by the content of his daydreams and fantasies. (Years later Rogers commented, "It fascinated me that I put in a section on daydreaming. I must have been developing the test for myself as a child.")[67]

It is also interesting that one of the types of questions he asked children on the test foreshadowed his landmark research on psychotherapy and personality change some twenty years later. Some of the questions were constructed like this:

10. Anna is the most popular girl in the school. Everybody likes her.

Am I just like her?	Yes	☐	☐	☐	☐	☐	☐	☐	*No*
Do I wish to be just like her?	Yes	☐	☐	☐	☐	☐	☐	☐	*No* [68]

By checking the boxes closer to the Yes or No responses, children would indicate what Rogers later would call their "self concept" and "ideal concept," although he did not use these terms for some years.

In designing this instrument, Rogers was following the example of a contemporary leader in the study and treatment of juvenile delinquency, William Healy, M.D. Jon Snodgrass wrote that Healy, among other contributions, "established the first child guidance clinic and helped to build and sustain the child guidance movement; was one of the earlier advocates of the team approach in research and therapy; and worked to collect the 'child's own story,' meaning the individual's subjective viewpoint, as a source of diagnostic and research information."[69] Later Rogers wrote that he was fascinated by Healy's writings during his training,[70] so it is likely that his initial research approach was influenced by Healy.

Rogers gave the test to about 200 children from a school for child actors and actresses and from the public schools, the former tending to be more maladjusted.[71] There were separate test forms for boys and girls. He developed norms for scoring and measured the test's reliability and validity—in short, created an instrument which the Institute for Child Guidance found useful and practical and which Teachers College judged as being objective and scientific. The following excerpt from his dissertation is part of Rogers' "preliminary diagnosis" of Edward L., Anglo-Saxon, Age 9, Grade 4A, I.Q. 115, based solely on the boy's test responses. It presents a good picture of the nature of the test. The boy scored third highest in Rogers' sample on overall maladjustment, but as Rogers wrote,

No scores are necessary to show that Edward is a badly adjusted boy. His test is full to bursting with unusual and abnormal responses. His three wishes are to be stronger, brighter, and better looking, and this evidence of personal inadequacy is borne out by a great many bragging responses. He is evidently sensitive about his looks and feels he is not at all good-looking. He refuses to answer the question in response to which he would rate himself on his brightness. He is extremely anxious "to be a very great person, and to do great things that people will talk about."

Edward brags not only of his accomplishments, but also of his lack of them, especially when answering questions in the realm of social adjustment. He admits that he does not know how to play games, and says he has no wish to be different. He is not popular and he does not care. When asked how many friends he would like to have he replies, "None." ... On the other hand he says, "I just can't stand it if people don't like me."

A daydreaming tendency is indicated by his rather extravagant ambitions—to be a movie star, a cowboy, an aviator—and by his imaginary companions, preference for solitary play, etc. He gives considerable evidence of a tension in the family area. He likes his mother best, his youngest sister next, and his father comes third in his affections. However, he would prefer to go with his father to the circus.

The test gives a picture of a boy who feels very inferior personally, who seems almost completely isolated socially, who evidently indulges in a good deal of fantasy, and is not entirely happy at home. He seems to be a very serious case.[72]

This preliminary diagnosis made from the test was later confirmed in almost every respect by an extensive case study on the boy. The test proved to be a useful instrument. It was published in 1931 by Association Press, the Y.M.C.A. publishing house, along with a manual for its administration. Right away several clinics around the country began using it, as did many schools and private clinicians. By 1971 over 430,000 copies of the test had been sold, and for a number of years it continued to sell over 15,000 copies a year, not including the Australian, Portuguese, French, and Italian editions.[73] In a 1970 textbook, *The Psychological Assessment of Children*, author James Palmer suggested that Rogers' adjustment inventory was a significant contribution to the field and deserved even wider usage.[74]

Rogers had gathered most of the data on the test by 1928, shortly before leaving New York City. However, "in the excitement of a new job and all, I came very close to not finishing up my degree. Goodwin Watson jolted me on that finally … in late '29 or '30, I suppose … said if I was ever going to get my degree I better get the darn thing out of the way. I had all the data but I had never worked it up or written my thesis. So I finally did that while I was working in Rochester and got my Ph.D. in '31."[75]

Move to Rochester

In the spring of 1928 Rogers was looking for a job. Positions for psychologists were not plentiful, and at one point he felt he might have to accept a position at Culver Military Academy in Indiana. In mid-April, leaving David with Helen's mother, Carl and Helen drove to Rochester, New York, for an interview at the Rochester Society for the Prevention of Cruelty to Children.

Besides leaving David, they also left springtime and tulips behind in New York City. They encountered snow, slush, hazardous driving conditions, and even a frozen radiator when they stopped for the night on the way up. While Carl spent the day interviewing, Helen hunted around for a suitable apartment, should the job work out. David was two and extremely active; Helen was again pregnant, and they wanted an apartment with a roomy yard, big enough for the children to romp in and for a flower and vegetable garden.

He was offered the position, which involved working with delinquent and problem children—diagnosing their difficulties, making plans for their treatment, and perhaps conducting some "treatment interviews" with them. He was a bit depressed by the Children's Shelter or detention home where many of them would be staying while he worked with them; but all in all the job followed logically from his training and he thought he would like the work.[76] Rochester was a city with a population of over 300,000 then, the twenty-second largest city in the country.[77] Although the University of Rochester's River Campus had just been built with a gift from Eastman-Kodak founder George Eastman, it had not yet achieved a national reputation. Colleagues' warnings that he would be isolated from university life and from stimulating professional contacts did not deter him; nor did the $2,900 salary, low even in those days. Throughout his career Rogers tended to follow his instincts about job moves, operating on the assumption that if he were doing work he enjoyed, everything else would fall into place. He accepted the position.

Helen had mixed reports to give on her day. She had not succeeded in finding an apartment or house to rent, but she did find a house she wanted to buy. He went back with her to survey the situation. They had not come to Rochester prepared to buy a house, but the builder trusted them. With a twenty-five-dollar cash deposit and their names on the dotted line, they were the proud future owners of a brand-new, small, $8,500 Dutch Colonial home at 180 Eastland Avenue in a new subdivision in the growing suburb of Brighton. It had a big yard in the back, although Carl would have to plant the lawn and do the landscaping.[78]

It had been quite a weekend—a new job and a new house in the space of a few hours. Their parents and, in fact, many of their friends were appalled at the haste with which both decisions were made. Such impetuosity, however, was rather typical of them both. As Rogers described them, "Both of us have clear (though often intuitive rather than conscious) feelings as to what we want. When we examine something—a position, a home, a plan for a trip, a piece of furniture—it either 'clicks' or it does not. Our independent reactions are nearly always similar, and when we both feel that something is 'right' we have rarely been mistaken. When it does seem 'right' we make an immediate decision and move ahead. Neither of us has ever been troubled by backward looks, or by regrets. We have, in some significant psychological sense, always seemed to 'face forward.'"[79]

Although Rogers' parents disapproved of their taking on a big mortgage, they eventually offered to help; but he would have no part of it.[80] Rochester, New York, it would be—for the next twelve years—on their own.

CHAPTER 4

The Rochester Years
1928–1939

The early 1900s had seen enormous growth in the fields of psychology, psychiatry, and social work.

In psychology the two major thrusts were, first, testing and measurement and, second, experimental work in the laboratory, using animals to explore various theories of learning. Psychological testing usually played an important part in clinical work; psychotherapy, however, was not widely used. Clinical psychology, the treatment of people with problems, was just coming into its own, but was still a minor part, if any part at all, of most psychologists' work. In 1928, when the Rogers moved to Rochester, only 104 members of the American Psychological Association were engaged in clinical work. By 1931, the number had grown to 800.[1]

In psychiatry, in the late 1800s most M.D.s, psychiatrists, psychopathologists, alienists, and neurologists were still seeking organic causes for the various neuroses, psychoses, hysterias, and anxieties in humans. They used shock treatments, drugs, medications, and hypnosis as the primary means of treatment. Freud graduated from these practices and went on to revolutionize our thinking about the causes of psychological problems and the manner of treating them. His disciples in America and abroad often modified his theories and techniques, and various schools of analysis and therapy were formed. By the late 1920s to the 1930s, through the efforts of this small minority of the medical profession and others, psychoanalysis and psychotherapy had achieved a firm foothold in several metropolitan centers along the eastern seaboard of the United States.[2]

Along with psychology and psychiatry, the field of social work was achieving professional status and developing its techniques in a more rigorous fashion.[3] In the nineteenth century, social work had moved through several phases, emphasizing charity work, institutional care, and socioeconomic legislation. By the turn of the century the number of social agencies dealing with children's problems had proliferated dramatically in almost every large city. The courts, hospitals, orphanages, "shelters," "reform schools," foster homes, school systems, religious institutions, youth clubs, settlement houses, charity organizations, psychological and psychiatric clinics all had resources to offer the child in trouble. But the poor or troubled family rarely knew about all these available resources, let alone how to go about using them. A professional person was needed to serve as a liaison between the child or family in trouble and the helping agencies of the community. She (for it was predominantly women who entered this field) would need a background in sociology, economics, psychology, and child care, a knowledge of the new techniques of diagnosis, placement, and counseling, and considerable skill in working with people under stress. Thus the roles of "case worker" or "social case worker" and later "psychiatric social worker" came into prominence, and social work came to be viewed more widely than ever before as a legitimate new profession. In the first quarter of the century many colleges and universities instituted departments or schools of social work, and the beginnings of scientific research in the field were undertaken.

In many clinics and institutions, the three fields of psychology, psychiatry, and social work joined forces in diagnosing and treating individual problems. This was often the case with child guidance centers, which "provided a setting in which the so-called core mental health professions could interact and collaborate, learning about and from the skills and expertise of each other."[4] Before 1916 there had been only one such child guidance clinic in the United States; by 1927 there were 102.[5] Only 27 had full-time staffs.[6] One of these was in Rochester, New York, where Carl Rogers joined the Child Study Department of the Society for the Prevention of Cruelty to Children, thus situating himself at the confluence of three new professions, each in its infancy, each presenting opportunities for pioneering research on methods of helping children and their parents in trouble.

Society for the Prevention of Cruelty to Children

And troubled children there were. Each year an average of 600–700 children, mostly lower- to lower-middle-class whites, came or were sent to the Society for help.[7] They were referred by dozens of social agencies throughout the community: parents, the social worker, Children's Court, the schools, private charitable organizations, medical authorities, and the like. They represented every behavior and personality problem imaginable: enuresis, stealing, lying, extreme sex curiosity, sex perversions, sadism toward animals or younger children, extreme withdrawal or aggressiveness, incest, stammering, eating dirt and worms, and numerous other comparable problems.

To help these children were five departments within the Society. "Intake" made the initial contact with the child and filled out the required paperwork. The Medical Department gave each child a complete physical examination. When exploitation or neglect was part of the problem, the child would be seen and the case investigated by the Protective Department. Child Placing supervised the foster homes, adoptions, and the temporary placements of children. In almost every case the child also would visit the Child Study Department in which Rogers was a staff psychologist in 1928 and the director by 1929.

His first introduction to a given child might be no more than a few words or phrases on the referral card forwarded by Intake to the Child Study Department.

Stealing, truancy from school, sex play.

Boy has thrown knife at mother, threatens to kill her.

Child mentally retarded (?) and deaf; present foster mother finds him unmanageable.

Girl very promiscuous. Is she committable?

Needs vocational guidance.

Delinquency (purse-snatching).[8]

These descriptions conveyed little of the actual circumstances. From talking with the child and perhaps the parent, Rogers or his coworkers would soon understand more about the child's situation. Dick was one boy Rogers interviewed shortly after coming to Rochester. He later described him in a case study:

An eight-year-old boy backed into a corner of the schoolroom, face livid, eyes partly closed, hatred in every line of his body, hurled an eraser at his teacher and shouted, "You shut your mouth! You can't make me do it!"

This particular tantrum on Dick's part was caused by the teacher's request that he go to his seat. Other tantrums, equally violent, made him a very difficult problem in school. Dick's diagnosis of the situation given in one of his better moments was "Satan had my father. I have a temper just like him. It's better to have a temper—you need it. When the Devil comes around, I just have to get mad." Dick had other satanic afflictions. He had a mania for knives and slept with one under his pillow, often threatening what he would do with it. He had always had night terrors, which would waken him screaming with fright. He showed a deeply sadistic streak, enjoying cruelty to pets and small animals and continually poking, teasing, and pinching children at school.

Needless to say, there was ample home background to explain Dick's behavior. The mother, an attractive woman, had spent most of her childhood in an orphanage, and her adult years were given over to compensating for the boredom of the institution. Her promiscuity engendered a deep jealousy in Dick's father, and his fearful temper storms gave the boy the pattern for his behavior. The father's cruelty was known throughout the rural neighborhood, and his almost insane torture of some of the farm animals makes gruesome reading. More than once he threatened to kill his family, and his beatings terrorized the children. When he was sent to the penitentiary on a charge of rape, the mother became even more promiscuous and also more religious. She joined a revival mission, taught the children large portions of the Bible, and became a very earnest worker. The whole situation was so extremely unsatisfactory for the children that they were removed by court order.[9]

Another boy Rogers saw during his first years in Rochester was John. We will hear more of both Dick and John later.

John came from a slovenly home in which there was little or no discipline. At the time that he and his sister, aged seven and ten respectively, were removed from their mother because of her flagrant immorality, most of John's life had been spent in "running wild" in a very questionable neighborhood. The home situation had been such as to stimulate in the boy an overwhelming curiosity in regard to sex. The mother had lived with several men, and John had spent hours at the keyhole watching his mother and her latest companion, or the actions of the boarder and his sister. An atmosphere of filthy sex talk in the home added further elements to his fund of information, and even this was supplemented by spying on older boys and girls in the neighborhood. John early learned that his sex knowledge gave him a source of power and he was not slow in using it. He achieved a reputation among children of his own age, not only for his talk, but for his actions. He had persuaded several of the small girls in the neighborhood to engage in sex experiments with him. A complaint was lodged with the police when he initiated two other boys in various sex perversions. His language was a scandal in the neighborhood, so much so that even the firemen, with whom John loved to lounge about, chastised him on several occasions as an aid to public morals.

When seen in the clinic, it was felt that John was more saturated with an unwholesome and smutty attitude toward sex, and was more aggressive in sex matters, than any boy who had ever entered the department. Within a few moments after his introduction to the psychologist, he was inquiring whether that gentleman was married, and whether he slept with his wife![10]

What could be done to help these children? There sat the young clinical psychologist, confronted by real-life problems and responsibilities that went far beyond his training. The helping professions themselves were not much older than twenty-six-year-old Carl Rogers, who looked around him and saw that for every twenty books which explained the causes of behavior problems, there was only one that dealt with their treatment.[11] There were several other comparable clinics around the country, but each of these, too, was trying in its own way to develop effective techniques, and none had any definitive answers.

For Rogers, then, the Rochester years were a decade of experimentation. Will this work? Is it effective? These were the questions he asked himself and his staff, again and again, throughout the years.[12] The principle that guided his efforts was pragmatism, a quality nurtured by his childhood experiments with scientific agriculture. Any method of helping children was worthy of consideration if it seemed potentially effective. The theoretical base of a helping approach was far less important to him than the results the approach yielded. Whether a professional was a psychologist, psychiatrist, or social worker also mattered little if that person had insights or techniques which could be of help.

Diagnosis and Treatment Planning

Almost universally accepted at this time was the belief that the first step in helping problem children was to understand thoroughly the nature of the problem. Rogers was so convinced of the critical importance of diagnosis that, early in his stay in Rochester, he was wont to tell PTA and community groups that their clinic was "rather similar to a garage—you brought in a problem, received an expert diagnosis, and were advised how the difficulty could be corrected."[13]

Friendly questioning and a look at the child's records might reveal a great deal about the child and the family background; but the child's mental and emotional life might still remain mostly concealed. Given his Teachers College background, Rogers believed that psychological testing could reveal many of the hidden factors, and such tests were used as a matter of course in the Child Study Department. No one set of tests was administered; rather, depending on the particular child, tests were selected that would help elucidate his particular problems or situation. Intelligence tests were used most frequently, along with reading and mathematical achievement tests, mechanical aptitude tests, interest inventories and, beginning in 1931, when it was published, Rogers' own Personal Adjustment Inventory.

The more diagnoses he made, however, the more dissatisfied he became with the process. He wanted a consistent, organized, diagnostic approach—not one based on the personal intuition or guesswork of the psychologist or case worker. He also wanted an approach toward diagnosis that went beyond the ideological biases of various schools of thought. Freudians, for example, tended to give great weight to early childhood influences. Sociologically inclined workers gave greater weight to the neighborhood, school, and peer group. Other psychologists relied almost entirely on psychological testing. In an attempt to

65

cut across ideological boundaries and take into consideration all the factors that could significantly be influencing the child's present behavior, Rogers and his colleague Chester Bennett developed a new method of diagnosis—the "component factor method."[14]

They were not the first to recognize the many factors that contributed to children's behavior problems. William Healy, for example, wrote a well-known text identifying fifteen categories of causes for delinquency, broken down into hundreds of major and minor factors.[15] Rogers and Bennett's model was simpler. In the component factor method, eight factors influencing the child's development and present behavior were considered: heredity, physical factors, mentality, self-insight, family emotional tone, economic and cultural factors, social experience, education and supervision. On each factor, children were rated on a seven-point scale (minus three to plus three), based on how the child compared to seven standardized descriptions for that factor. The psychologist's ratings would be placed on a grid with an "x" to indicate how the child was rated on each factor at the time of diagnosis. Then an arrow would be drawn to indicate what degree of change would be realistic to expect, given the situation. A year or more later the actual changes which had occurred in the child's situation could be compared to the predicted results, on each of the eight factors.

The component factor method demonstrates the eclectic pragmatism that would often lead Rogers to develop his own approach to a particular subject or problem. His eight-factor method did not ignore Freudian or behavioral or sociological theories; it simply incorporated them. The method also shows Rogers' concern for science and the scientific method. He was not content with vague thinking about the causes of children's problems. He wanted every possible factor clearly spelled out, so that it could be considered, and so that one psychologist's ratings could be open to the scrutiny of other professionals who might want to double-check the work. Finally, the method illustrates Rogers' concern with evaluating the results of his work, a consistent priority for much his career. By using the factor chart again a year or more after the original ratings, workers could evaluate not only the validity of the original predictions, but also the effectiveness of the treatment. By averaging many individual cases on one chart, the results of treatment for large numbers of children could be determined, too, thereby assessing the effectiveness of an entire clinic.

Although its validity, reliability, and usefulness were clearly demonstrated, and although Rogers and Bennett publicized the method in several well-received speeches and a paper,[16] the component factor method never caught on. Whether clinical workers were reluctant to give up their biases about the primary causes of children's problems or whether they did not want to look at their actual, possibly disappointing results or whether they did not want to invest the time or energy that follow-up work required or whether the approach was too complicated to use, one may speculate. Nevertheless the method enabled Rogers and his colleagues to examine much more critically the work *they* were doing. Just how effective is our treatment? What degree of change is realistic to expect along the different factors? Why are our predictions consistently overly optimistic on this factor and overly pessimistic on that factor? What is the significance of this surprising trend we have just discovered? How do our results compare with those of other clinics? Important questions like these could be generated and sometimes answered by the component factor chart. "So far as diagnostic techniques are concerned," he wrote, "there is no best method; there are only methods which need testing and experiment and revision."[17] His own work in this area set a good example.

After Rogers had talked with the child and parent, the psychological examinations had been administered, the case records had been perused, and the diagnosis seemed complete, the original question remained: How can we be of help to this child?

The answer was not provided by the psychologist alone. Once the child had been seen by the Child Study Department, a case conference was called, with a representative of each agency that had an interest in the child present. Rogers had learned about the case conference system in New York City and then introduced it to Rochester, later calling it "one of the best things I did."[18] At one case conference, there might be the social worker, a foster parent, and a doctor. At another there might be a probation officer, the "cottage parent" from a reform school, and a member of the Society's Protective Department. In each case Rogers or one of the other psychologists from his department would conduct the conference, acting, as he described it, as "a catalytic agent ... to bring out the pertinent experience of each conference member, and also contribute the findings of the clinic in regard to the child's abilities and attitude and the significant patterns evident in his behavior ... Rightly managed, such sharing conferences became the best and most practical means of using and strengthening the cooperative relationships, with a wide group of agencies offering a range of treatment services."[19]

Years later Rogers noted that writing up these cases was "the experience which perhaps contributed most to my psychological writing [skill] ... Frequently these reports had to meet a deadline of a court hearing or agency decision. If they were to have any influence they had to be accurate, penetrating, comprehensive, persuasive in presenting the reasons for our recommendations, clear and interesting enough to read, and able to stand the test of time, since we would continue to be in contact with both the agency and the child, often for long periods."[20]

The goal of the case conference was to arrive at an effective treatment plan for the child. Generally treatment fell into one or more of three categories—changing the child's living situation, modifying the child's living situation, or direct therapy. Each of these approaches constituted a major portion of Rogers' work.

Environmental Treatment

The first two types of treatment were commonly thought of as "environmental" treatment or therapy. The more extreme of the two involved a major change in the child's living situation—to a foster home, from one foster home to another, to an institution, or a return to the child's own home. When Rogers introduced a research program to look more closely at the work they were doing in their clinic, one of the surprising findings was that one of the first steps in treatment for over half the children who came to them was to select a totally new environment for the child—a practice similar to that used in many other child guidance clinics at the time.[21]

Dick and John, whose cases are described above, were both boys for whom Rogers and the case conference arranged foster home care. The boys were sent to the "Thompson home," one of the best foster homes in Rochester according to Rogers, who liked to tell an anecdote that illustrated Mrs. Thompson's ability to accept the children's feelings without being manipulated herself.

> William, having "tried out" previous foster mothers so successfully that it had been necessary to move him several times, renewed his tactics in this home within the first few days of placement.
>
> "I'm tough!" he said, slapping his chest.
>
> "Are you?" answered mother. "I'm tough, too."
>
> William looked decidedly surprised and in a somewhat lower tone of voice asked, "How tough are you?"
>
> "I'm tough like you," confided the foster mother.
>
> "Well," said William in a subdued voice after a thoughtful pause, "I'm not so tough."[22]

How did Dick and John respond to foster home treatment? Rogers continued their case studies:

> After clinic study, a foster home was recommended—a home where the foster mother was strict and positive, and where Dick would be with other boys. It is interesting, in looking over the conference notes, to see that foster home placement was regarded as a forlorn hope, and it was the consensus of conference opinion that Dick would soon have to be institutionalized. His behavior was too extreme for lesser methods. To quote from the record, "Dick has an extremely disorganized personality. His temper tantrums have made him feared and disliked. He should be tried in a foster home before institutionalization is decided upon."
>
> Dick was placed in the Thompson home. At first he remained quiet, aloof, solitary. He seemed to be thinking and dreaming much of the time, which was

quite unlike his former self. The foster mother encouraged vigorous activity, and gradually Dick began to mingle with the other boys. He began to join more in the conversation and seemed more contented. Six weeks after placement he had his first temper tantrum. It occurred (poor Dick!) when Mr. Thompson asked him to take his cod-liver oil as usual with the other boys. Dick refused, began to scream and kick, and then let out a burst of oaths which were remarkable for an eight-year-old. Without any hesitation, Mr. Thompson washed his mouth with bitter aloes. Dick quieted immediately, became quite contrite, and ceased his tantrum. Since that time there have been no violent tantrums and a decreasing number of temper outbursts of any sort. Within ten months of placement the foster mother reported that he presented no problem at all.

At the present time (two and one-half years from date of placement) certain new difficulties are arising. Dick's mother—now on a salary with the revival mission and creating a scandal by her actions with the minister—visits Dick quite frequently and heaps presents on the boy as she coddles and kisses him. Dick is quite upset by her visits and by her talk of taking him to live with her. After these visits he becomes irritable and more inclined to temper spells. He also shows a tendency to lord it over the other boys because of his more numerous possessions. Were it not for this outside influence, Dick would be making a completely satisfactory adjustment. Temper tantrums, sadistic impulses, vicious tendencies—all have disappeared.[23]

Commenting on the case, Rogers wrote: "In Dick's case, as with some of the other boys, the greatest contribution made by the foster home is that of consistent control. Rewards and punishment follow with certainty on the heels of good and bad behavior. The child's universe comes to have a logic, a reasonableness, which was scarcely discernible in the riotous confusion and fear of the early home life."[24]

Returning to John, the seven-year-old with the incredible sophistication about sex. Rogers wrote,

The psychological tests showed that John, in spite of his alert manner, was a very dull boy, and this, combined with his attitude toward sex, made the outlook most unfavorable. It was felt that whether he was placed in a foster home or an institution, he was certain to "corrupt" the children with whom he came in contact. It was as a very dubious experiment, and because of his extreme youth, it was decided to place him in the Thompson home.

The fear of John's influence seemed justified the first day of placement. Mrs. Thompson had been forewarned as to John's behavior, but even she was scarcely prepared to hear a burst of obscenity directed toward the social worker as that individual started to drive away from the home. John was using his best means of gaining attention and he was highly satisfied to see the gaping astonishment on the faces of the other children. Mrs. Thompson immediately talked to John

69

alone and told him in a kindly, but firm manner that her boys did not speak like that and that if she ever heard such language again, she would wash his mouth with soap. This was the first and the last obscenity that John used as an attention-getting device. To be sure, when aroused, his swearing was extremely colorful, but this, too, gradually came under control. He did try other means of getting attention, as might have been expected. He began to tell "tall tales," which the foster mother met by replying with even wilder statements and then laughing away both as jokes. She refused to consider them as lies, and hence made it easy for John to give them up. She also gave him ample opportunity to gain attention in other ways; she asked him to perform little tasks for her; she praised him liberally when he brought home a good school paper; she told him of the improvement he was making.

In four months Mrs. Thompson was able to report that John was no longer swearing and was very proud of his progress along this line. She could also say that at no time had sex talk or sex practices constituted a problem with John. When his previous behavior is recalled, this seems nothing short of astounding.

A year after John's placement in the home, he was re-studied at the clinic. Without a knowledge of his past, it would have been impossible to recognize this jolly, healthy, eight-year-old, full of amusing stories about life at "home," as the grave problem of the previous year. He told of earning his spending money, of the fun they had at Christmas, of his responsibility for wiping the dishes, in a frank, spontaneous fashion that seemed to have nothing in common with the smirking, sophisticated attitude of his first clinic contact. Even the memory of his own home seemed to have become dimmed and uncertain. He told the interviewer confidentially that he had had "another home," but regarded Thompson's very definitely as his "real home." To cap the climax of the transformation, John spoke with genuine horror of a boy on their street who actually swore!

Three and a half years have slipped by and John's excellent record continues. Nearly eleven years old now, he has developed into an attractive, friendly boy, with a very winning smile. He is truthful and dependable, though he is full of life and has to be handled with a firm and consistent hand. He is in fourth grade, doing "D" work, which is all that could be expected of a boy of his mentality. He has developed an interest in nature study, and enjoys working with tools.[25]

This foster home, however, was not utopia. Rogers described how, on one occasion, "when the foster mother was very new in the work, two of the boys were found masturbating. The goddess of mental hygiene must have wept to see their punishment—two small boys, solemnly washing their hands for thirty minutes."[26] Nor was foster home placement successful in all cases. "If we could fully explain why Donald has failed to adjust while the other boys have successfully adjusted, we should have the solution to much of the mystery of human nature."[27]

Yet, he could not deny what he witnessed, time and time again, in the lives of hundreds of children. Extreme behavioral, psychological and emotional problems would often disappear or be reduced to a minimum in a healthy environment. The child has within him the drive, the need to grow and mature. To create an environment that supports growth is to allow the child to be healthy.

What constitutes this healthy, supportive environment? Rogers, thinking of the foster parent, listed four conditions, which are noteworthy in that they contain the roots of much of his later thinking. "It seems clear," he wrote, "that the suitability of a foster home for the care of problem children depends more upon certain types of attitudes than on any external factor. These attitudes might be summarized as follows:

> 1. An attitude of intelligent understanding. This involves the ability to look at the child's behavior as a natural result of his makeup and experience, rather than as an infraction of moral rules, or a deviation from adult convention. It also requires the creative imagination to understand the way the child feels and the motives for his acts ... 2. A consistency of viewpoint and discipline. This element of stability in management gives the child the comforting feeling of knowing where he stands with reference to some standard. The consistency of viewpoint seems more important than the actual type of discipline itself, since every clinic or child-placing agency can point to successful homes with very diverse views on discipline ... 3. An attitude of interested affection. It is the moderate type of affection which seems most helpful, not the glowing enthusiasm of the emotionally starved parent. "Fundamental interest and affection" is perhaps the best descriptive phrase. It is a primary factor in the child's security ... 4. Satisfaction in the child's developing abilities. Only if the foster parent finds this satisfaction will he wisely reward the youngster for achievement, and permit the child more and more freedom to grow in independence."[28]

The foster home was only one environmental change which Rogers and the Child Study Department used to help children. Institutional care was another, although it was employed much less frequently, especially during the Depression, when the delinquency rate throughout the country fell off dramatically. From his experiences with institutions and from the great amount of research he read on the subject, Rogers came to see that regimented, military-style institutions rarely lessened but usually exacerbated emotional problems which led to delinquency. On the other hand he was very impressed by a few institutions he visited or read about that provided individual treatment for the delinquent and dependent children. In his writing and his speeches before community groups, he advocated institutional structures that gave the young men and women significant choices to make as part of their re-education.

In addition to using methods of changing the child's environment, Rogers and his staff frequently recommended "treatment through modifying the environment." This often involved working with the parents to change parental attitudes (psychotherapeutic methods were sometimes used here). It also might mean working through the schools—perhaps recommending remedial work or a change in the child's program.

Another means of treatment through modifying the environment was the intelligent use of camps, groups, and clubs. After three summers in college as a leader at the Y.M.C.A. camp in Wisconsin and at Camp Wawokeye near Cleveland, Rogers knew that these activities could be an important, positive influence in the lives of children. Although it was not directly connected with his duties as director of the Child Study Department, he served as consultant for Camp Cory, a Y.M.C.A. camp, and helped organize a "farm camp," an effort by the Society for the Prevention of Cruelty to Children to provide a meaningful work experience for teenage boys during the Depression. He played a significant role in its direction and growth.

Those who are familiar with Carl Rogers' later contributions to the field of psychotherapy may be surprised to see how his earliest treatment efforts revolved primarily around environmental therapy—foster homes, institutions, schools, and camps. The importance of total treatment was underscored most strongly in his second published professional article, in 1931. "We Pay for the Smiths," coauthored with a coworker, Mitchell E. Rappaport, is an interesting, if depressing, case study of a welfare family with thirteen children—a family already in its third consecutive generation on Rochester's relief rolls and which had already cost the city well over $50,000. The authors' conclusion would probably bring a chuckle to B.F. Skinner, Rogers' latter-day sparring partner on many psychological and social questions. "Deep laid social ills," they wrote, "of the sort the Smiths represent will not be cured by new ways of relief giving, by an analysis of the emotional situation between worker and client, or by new systems of keeping case records. They call not only for refinement of method, but for bold, farsighted policies of social planning and social control."[29]

Although Rogers' own interests gradually moved toward intensive psychotherapy during his years in Rochester, he remained very much impressed with the power of environmental therapy, writing at the time, "The changing of parental attitudes, the manipulation of the school and social environment, the use, in serious situations, of a completely new and therapeutic environment outside of the home, have all been suggested as means of attacking the causes of problem behavior. There has been, in some quarters, a tendency to look down upon such methods of treatment as being in some way inferior to direct methods of psychotherapy, which deal with the child himself. This viewpoint is both unrealistic and unfortunate. We shall not be inclined to look down upon treatment involving the manipulation of the environment, if we recall the fundamental axiom upon which it is based, namely, that most children, if given a reasonably normal environment which meets their own emotional, intellectual, and social needs, have within themselves sufficient drive toward health to respond and make a comfortable adjustment to life."[30]

This "fundamental axiom" represents the basis of all Rogers' subsequent work after he left Rochester. Later on, some of his most important work went into supporting his theory that human beings, like animals and plants, have an innate "drive toward health," an "actualizing tendency," which can be nurtured by the right type of environment. Although at this stage of his career Rogers was more interested in the child's "adjustment" than his self-actualization, the basic premise was firmly in place that the person has within him or herself the resources to grow in healthy directions when suitable conditions are present. The basis of this "axiom" was dramatically illustrated by a small research study conducted by the Child Study Department. It involved a fifteen-month follow-up study on children for whom the case conference had recommended some kind of environmental treatment, usually a change of residence. Each child was rated as "adjusting" or "failed to adjust." Rogers and his staff found that "of the 89 cases where the court had followed the treatment plan mapped out by the clinic conference, one was a failure and was transferred from the recommended institution to another. Of the 6 cases where minor changes had been made in the plan, one was a failure. Of the 19 cases where the court had adopted some totally different residence plan than that suggested, 12, or 63 percent, were failures within the fifteen months."[31]

"As a mode of treatment," Rogers wrote in 1939, "the selection of a place of residence which will have a therapeutic effect does not necessarily appeal to the imagination. Such a choice has about it none of the mysterious elements or technical verbiage which make some types of therapy so alluring. It is nevertheless the only sound foundation for all the more subtle or more refined sorts of treatment which we shall proceed to consider."[32]

Treatment Interviews

For about one-fifth of the children who came to the Child Study Department, "treatment interviews" or "direct therapy" was conducted.[33] Rogers had come to Rochester with an open mind about psychotherapy. Although he had been exposed to psychoanalysis in New York, most of his own work was in the area of psychological testing and the analysis of case studies. With respect to psychotherapy he was quite willing to learn from his experiences in Rochester. Again the principle which guided his explorations into the various schools of therapy was pragmatism. Is this method effective? Will it work?

Unfortunately, as he looked for professional guidance on the subject, there was little help to be found in the literature. "A verbatim record of intensive psychotherapy with one child, giving in full all the conversation of both child and therapist, would be a new and valuable contribution to our thinking," he noted.[34] But no such account was available. Nor was there any substantial scientific research on the different approaches to or outcomes of psychotherapy. "In this realm where so much depends on the personal interactions and responses of worker and child," he wrote in 1939, "we find more the skills of an art than the technique of science. Nevertheless there is reason to hope that even these subtle relationships may be helpfully studied by scientific means and more accurately known and guided. As a preliminary to such a study we shall endeavor to describe and classify some of the methods used with children."[35]

He distinguished between those treatment interviews which used "deeper therapies" and those which did not. By deeper therapy he meant "those therapeutic methods which aim toward giving the child self-insight, or in which the emotional relationship between child and worker is a very strong one."[36] Among these he included psychoanalysis, interpretive therapy, and relationship therapy. Among the less-deep therapies were educational therapy, persuasion or suggestion, and release or expressive therapy. He tried out every one of these approaches. His Rochester years were a period of experimentation, during which he gradually came to develop his own ideas on the process of psychotherapy. This led eventually to Rogers' formulating a new school of therapy that would have a profound impact on the helping professions.

Education, Persuasion, and Release

Rogers sometimes used educational therapy, as with Philip, who was referred to the Society for the Prevention of Cruelty to Children by Children's Court. Rogers saw the boy[37] and wrote the following report.

> Philip was an overgrown Polish boy of 14 when he came to the clinic on a serious delinquency charge. He had broken into the house of his next-door neighbor in the middle of the night, had made his way to the room of the 18-year-old daughter, and had attempted to strike her over the head with a crude lead pipe blackjack. Fortunately the blackjack struck the head of the bed, the girl awoke and screamed, and Philip was captured. The situation as it revealed itself was plainly an acute personality problem. Philip was an inarticulate, shy boy of better than average mentality. He was much the youngest of four children and associated little with his older siblings. His father was dead, and his relationship with his mother was one of obedience rather than trust and confidence. He was not at all social, but did have two good friends, both of them very respectable boys. He was gifted along mechanical lines. Everyone knew him as a very quiet, very colorless, well-behaved boy. He had literally no sex information, and no sources of such information. As he became adolescent, he mulled over his perplexities about sex. The girl next door, whose bedroom window was visible from his own, became the object of his daydreams, and time

after time he concocted imaginary means of disrobing her in order to answer his fundamental questions regarding female anatomy. Finally he acted out one of these daydreams.

In treatment of Philip the whole aim was educational. Throughout a number of contacts with the boy very complete sex education was given, in as matter-of-fact a manner as possible. Male and female anatomy, intercourse, reproduction, the birth process, masturbation, boy and girl relationships were discussed with more than usual thoroughness. Because he was so inarticulate himself, this was a somewhat one-sided process. Later after a period of a few months, these topics were brought up again to make sure he had assimilated the information. This was practically the only type of treatment used, with the exception of some reassurance to the mother that her boy was not abnormal. It was not felt safe to interpret to the mother the full significance of her boy's actions, since she was herself too repressed.[38]

Because Philip found it difficult to verbalize his conflicts, this treatment was used without too precise a knowledge of the content of his fantasies or perplexities, save that they were sexual. It may well be that there were aspects of his problem which we did not know and which remained untreated. Three years have elapsed, however, and there has been reasonably satisfactory personal adjustment without further delinquent behavior.[39]

There were educational techniques other than information-giving. The therapist might also help children in difficult choice situations clarify the alternatives available and their likely consequences. From his experience Rogers concluded that the educational therapies could be helpful "where ignorance of facts is a source of mental conflict or emotional tension ... no matter how deep-seated the problem may seem.[40]

His experience also taught him the limitations of the educational approach. Deep-seated emotional problems would scarcely be touched by education. And even when ignorance of basic facts was an important part of the problem, emotional conflicts often interfered with the individual's ability to accept the facts. Rogers described an example of this in an interview he had with a parent (clearly reflecting the profession's painful ignorance regarding Down's Syndrome at the time).

A mother requests help with her child, a girl of 11, who is difficult to manage and has never been allowed to attend school. It needs little more than a glance at the child to recognize that she is the type of mental defective known as Mongolian, and a brief examination establishes her mental development as approximately that of a three-year-old. The obvious step for the clinician seems to be to educate the mother as to the nature of mongolism, to point out to her that there is no known cure or remedy for the condition, that she must face the tragic fact that her child can never develop much beyond this point, and that institutional care is the only sensible and kind procedure for the welfare of both child and parent. Recognizing that this information may be upsetting and disappointing to the parent, there would seem to be no difficulty in at least conveying the simple facts regarding the condition and the experiences of others with similar children. We find, however, that this mother, of at least average intelligence, is quite unable to digest this information. She insists that the child can read and write at the very moment that the youngster is making unintelligible sounds to indicate its wants, unable to formulate a complete sentence. She is sure that the child has shown great improvement in the past, then shifts to the notion that she will show great improvement in the future. In spite of the explanation of the nature of mongolism, she states that the child's condition is due to the refusal of the educational authorities to let her attend school. Finally she reveals that four other competent physicians and psychologists have examined the child in the last five years and have given her substantially the same diagnosis and suggestions as are being given to her now. Although she reports this, she seizes upon some minor circumstance or statement of each examination to fortify her own viewpoint. She leaves, having gained nothing from this attempt to "educate" her, nor, it would seem, from any of the four previous attempts.[41]

Another form of therapy was that of persuasion or suggestion or the therapist's use of personal influence. Although these techniques were widely used by therapists with varying orientations, Rogers observed that they were no longer being explicitly advocated as they had been in earlier treatises on psychotherapy.[42] Interestingly enough, one of the explicit proponents of this approach was Dr. Samuel Hartwell, whom Rogers had employed as the consulting psychiatrist for the Child Study Department when he became director. Hartwell argued that one of the psychiatrist's goals was to achieve a rapport with the child in which the child would become increasingly suggestible to the psychiatrist's guidance. At the deepest level of rapport, Hartwell wrote, "he is suggestible to the greatest possible degree. He considers things in the light of my emotional response to them rather than his own ... [The child] wants his psychiatrist to be his best friend. He wishes to please him more than he wishes to do anything else. Out of loyalty to his friend he is perfectly willing to alter his emotional life as far as it is possible for him."[43] On one occasion Hartwell encouraged a boy to join some group activities the child was afraid of by saying, "I want you to do it because you're my kid."[44]

Rogers had a great deal of respect for Hartwell. He envied Hartwell's ability to put a child on his lap and, in a fatherly way, establish an immediate rapport. While unquestionably friendly and sincere, Rogers was more emotionally reserved at this time in his life and would not have felt comfortable enough to do this.[45] He was also caught up in the techniques of interviewing, trying to decide the "right" thing to do. Hartwell "was himself and wanted a real relationship with the kid" and therefore was "definitely more therapeutic than I was at that time," Rogers commented years later.[46] But in spite of his respect for and admiration of Hartwell's fashion of relating to children, he was not impressed by the direct persuasion that Hartwell and others sometimes advocated and frequently used as a therapeutic technique. He acknowledged that suggestion could serve some good purpose. As with Hartwell's "kid," mentioned above, if the persuasion had "served to tide the boy over the initial difficulties of group adjustment, he would then find social contacts satisfying in themselves. In such instances personal influences may be likened to a hypodermic given as a temporary measure, either to inhibit or stimulate behavior of a certain type until the more lasting therapeutic influences can take place."[47]

This statement also suggests Rogers' misgivings about the use of persuasion and suggestion in therapy. The results were only temporary, wherever deep-seated emotional problems were present. Persuasion was based on the therapist's supplied motivation, not the child's. Once away from the therapist's influence, the original emotional conflicts would reassert themselves, and the original problem symptoms or new ones would emerge. Rogers' growing distaste for persuading or "pushing" the child in a given direction was illustrated by Louise Johnson, then a counselor at the University of Rochester. She recalled how, "I was working with a student whose problem was too complex for me to handle, so I, with her permission, approached Carl to ask him to see her. When I attempted to arrange an appointment with him for the student, he checked me saying, 'Let the student call me—and we can go on from there.'"[48]

One experience which helped confirm Rogers' pessimism about persuasive therapy involved a very intelligent, very insecure eleven-year-old boy being treated for his enuresis. After he was placed in a foster home which seemed to meet some of his deeper emotional needs, it was decided to attack the bed-wetting directly by means of hypnosis.[49] The treatment was carried out by Dr. Griffith Williams, who was an expert in hypnotic therapy, and Mr. Gordon Riley, a psychologist on the clinic staff. The hypnosis took place right in the Child Study Department and Rogers followed the case closely from the start.

> The boy was trained until he was able to go into a fairly deep trance and carry out post-hypnotic suggestions of a neutral sort. Then such suggestions were made as that he would ask the foster mother for a chamber to keep under his bed so that he could use it just before he retired. These suggestions were carried out post-hypnotically, but the enuresis continued in spite of more frequent use of toilet facilities brought about through suggestion. In later trances, as specific suggestions were made attacking the symptom more directly, such as suggesting that he would wake at intervals during the night, it became more difficult to gain the boy's cooperation, and finally it was impossible to induce a trance state at all.[50]

Rogers was deeply impressed by what he saw. Everything, so it seemed, was operating in their favor—the boy's initial cooperation, his successful adjustment in the foster home, the expertise of the psychologists—yet the treatment was a failure. To Rogers the case demonstrated "a clear picture of the limitations of hypnotic suggestion, and the limitations of conscious suggestion and persuasion seem very similar. When suggestion or persuasion cuts definitely across the deeper emotional purposes and needs," he concluded, "it can hardly be effective."[51]

The last of the "less-deep" therapies which Rogers employed during his Rochester years was "expressive therapy" or "release." He was more intrigued by the possibilities of this approach than by those already mentioned. To "talk out" one's feelings, to ventilate one's conflicts, to unburden oneself of concerns, anxieties and problems, Rogers felt, had considerable therapeutic value. "Such a catharsis," he wrote then, "even where the therapist is a listener only, has a constructive effect, since the child clarifies his feelings by verbalizing them."[52]

Since Rogers often worked with young children, sometimes preschoolers, one of the expressive therapies that greatly interested him was "expression through play techniques." Dr. David Levy, director of the Institute for Child Guidance where Rogers had worked in New York City, was a leader in this approach, which utilized clay, stuffed animals and other common toys, as well as dolls with amputatable legs, arms, heads, breasts, and other body parts. Children would begin playing with the toys, the therapist would observe and ask the child questions, and before long the child would be using the dolls and toys to express many important feelings and conflicts that would have been difficult, if not impossible, to get to with words alone. Rogers described one of his own experiences with play therapy.

> Freddie, a hyperactive eight-year-old, was regarded as a serious school problem … A series of interview contacts on a play basis assisted Freddie in dramatizing and acting out his feelings which he did not express with much freedom in words. To quote one such incident from the record,
>
>> "Examiner gave Freddie modeling clay. He made a figure. 'Who is it? Guess.'
>>
>> Examiner: 'Your father? Me?'
>>
>> 'No, it's the principal. He's got flat feet.' He made a fist on the figure. 'Gee, he's mad.' Vindictively he knocked off the head and the fist, jumped the figure around the table singing, 'Poor Mr. W (the principal)' and gradually annihilated it."[53]

Rogers did "a moderate amount of play therapy" with children.[54] Reared in an environment that discouraged the expression of feelings, he thought that the expressive therapies which encouraged catharsis, ventilation, and release were very promising. They could help children see themselves more clearly, accept themselves more easily, and, to some extent, cope with reality more effectively.

But Rogers noted that, in terms of coping with reality, the various types of expressive therapies had not yet found ways to help the child really work through the conflicts and make a satisfactory adjustment in the real world.[55] Thus he was sympathetic to the goals and methods of expressive therapy, but felt more work was needed to make it as effective as it might be. Actually one of his students would do just that years later.[56]

Psychoanalysis

Although Rogers had experimented with psychoanalytic theories in some of the therapy he had conducted at the Institute for Child Guidance, he never was very impressed by the psychoanalytic movement. He did recognize Freud's great contribution to psychology—his exposure of the powerful psychological dynamics operating within the individual, his and his followers' insights into repressions and defense mechanisms, his legitimizing the therapeutic interview as an accepted professional procedure.[57] But by nature and by training Rogers was a pragmatist and a psychologist. While he recognized Freud's historical importance, his whole nature and training were opposed to the elaborate theoretical superstructure and method of psychoanalysis which Freud had introduced.

For one thing, psychoanalysis was impractical. It took so much time and money that only a handful of those needing help could receive it through analysis. "One hundred analytic hours would be regarded by most Freudians as a minimum amount of time in which to complete the analysis of the child,"[58] he wrote. Meanwhile, in Rochester, he saw *hundreds* of children in need, every year. So he felt very impatient with analysis as a useful tool in his own work.

A second objection he had to psychoanalysis was that, with its emphasis on past and repressed material and events, it tended to ignore or to minimize the importance of the individual's present environment.[59] In Rochester he learned just the opposite. He knew of too many examples of intensive individual help which failed because the unhealthy environment the child was in simply could not support the growth taking place in the clinic or the therapist's office.

A third fault he found with analysis was that "unfortunately, psychoanalysts have not favored the investigation of their methods by evaluative research."[60] As a psychologist he had been taught and had come to believe in the importance of research and evaluation. As a pragmatist, he continued to ask himself, "Am I being effective? How can we improve if we don't see clearly what we are actually accomplishing?" As a scientist, he knew that careful research procedures were the only way to answer these questions honestly, minimizing the biases of the experimenter. Ironically, while psychiatrists and psychoanalysts have traditionally branded Rogers' theories and methods as "superficial," Rogers similarly felt condescending in his attitude toward psychoanalysis. This was in no small part due to the value he placed on careful process and outcome research, one of his own lasting contributions to the field of psychotherapy.

Another reason for his somewhat superior attitude toward analysis was theoretical. As a psychologist trained in the scientific method, he had learned that one quality of a good theory is that it attempts to explain phenomena in the least complicated way.[61] He saw psychoanalysis doing just the opposite. "The [psychoanalytic] interpretation," he wrote, "is not usually made on the simplest basis which will explain the facts but is made in terms of a preconceived ideology, frequently unverified, sometimes fantastic."[62]

Rogers also objected to the mystique he thought psychoanalysis created about mental illness and the way it tended to exaggerate common problems. He wrote in 1937 that "too often in psychoanalytic and psychiatric literature any negative experience, any confusion of thought, any tendency to daydream, or to feel inadequate to life is regarded as significant of abnormality."[63] The psychologist's personality tests, Rogers believed, "helped to bring reason back into the situation by pointing out the degree to which the average and presumably normal individual shows neurotic tendencies or other personality difficulties."[64] Later in his career he would go even further toward arguing that there is no qualitative difference between mentally "sick" and "healthy" people, the difference being essentially only quantitative, and that the same basic methods of helping could be used with the college student confused about his goals and the institutionalized schizophrenic.

Rogers' various objections to psychoanalysis at this point in his career did not constitute a campaign to discredit analysis or its practitioners, nor a rebellion or defensive attack on the older psychotherapeutic establishment. Unlike some of Freud's disciples, Rogers never had enough of an emotional or professional investment in psychoanalysis to openly rebel against it and thus form his own school of thought. In fact his reading of Freud was relatively shallow. He was always grateful that his thinking did not come from the teachings of one special mentor, nor out of the writings of one special person, nor out of endless philosophical debates on the merits of the various schools of therapy, or the nuances and changes in some "master's" thinking over the years. Rogers' ideas developed primarily from his own experiences—and from several other influences which shall be mentioned shortly.[65] It was only in organizing and communicating his learnings that he bothered to invest time and energy in expressing his misgivings about psychoanalysis. Since at this time his primary concern was with children, and he noted that "from a quantitative viewpoint, the treatment of children's problems through psychoanalysis is negligible,"[66] he did not expect his opinions on psychoanalysis to be particularly controversial. Only in his last two years in Rochester did he become embroiled in his first major controversy between psychology and psychiatry, and by then his views on the latter profession had been well established.

Given Rogers' views on psychoanalysis and, to some extent, psychiatry, the relationship between the psychologists and the consulting psychiatrist in the

Child Study Department was significant. As expressed in the 1933 brochure of the Society for the Prevention of Cruelty to Children, "When there are indications which might point toward mental disease or where further help is desired, the child, or the child and his parents, may be seen by a psychiatrist."[67] Rogers reflected the same role definitions in the 1937 Annual Report of his department, writing, "The psychiatrist is a physician trained in the prevention and treatment of abnormal mental conditions and insanity. He is especially helpful in dealing with the mentally disturbed individual, whether child or adult, and with any individual who shows symptoms indicative of neurological difficulty or mental disease ... The psychologist is trained to understand the normal child and the emotional, educational and behavior difficulties which such children present. He is skilled in the measurement of the child's developing mentality and personality traits. He is especially helpful in diagnosing and treating the behavior, personality, and educational problems of children who fall within the 'normal grouping' and are not definitely abnormal."[68]

Rogers wrote this for political reasons, so that the psychiatrists and psychoanalysts in the community would not feel their territory was being encroached upon. During that same year Rogers was writing his first book, in which no such vague, oversimplified distinctions as "normal," "definitely abnormal," "mental disease," "insanity," and "mentally disturbed individual" are ever used in this way. In reality the Child Study Department often violated the separation between the psychiatrist's and the psychologist's roles as delineated above. While theoretically the prevention and treatment of "insanity" was to be left to the psychiatrist, another annual report dramatically shows the opposite happening in the case of Arthur who is "diagnosed by his companions as just a bit 'goofy,' and while they stand in awe of his screaming, brick-throwing tantrums, they know nothing of the nightmares where he dreams of going insane ... Of the many elements in his treatment, those that were primarily environmental, such as a move to a new home and a transfer to another school, were left with the social agency. In addition, however, the boy needed skilled help in removing this basic fear, and this help was given through interviews with the psychologist in this department."[69]

This blurring of distinct roles was probably facilitated by the consulting psychiatrist with whom Rogers first worked when he came to Rochester. Rogers described him as "a rather weak person and for the most part we told him what we thought he should say and he said it, thus giving our recommendations more force and authority."[70] When Rogers became director and employed Samuel Hartwell as consulting psychiatrist, a man he really respected, the psychologists' freedom and scope of operation had already become a norm in the department. Still, Hartwell tried to persuade Rogers to take at least four to five years off to become a medical doctor and then a psychiatrist, so he could have more influence on the field. Rogers had neither the means nor the desire.[71] Yet the issue illustrates a commonly held notion about the differences between psychiatrists, clinical psychologists, and mental health counselors. It is widely thought that psychiatrists work with people whose problems are "deeper" or "more serious" and that clinical psychologists and mental health counselors, progressively, work with less serious cases. And non-mental health counselors, *even less* serious cases of social and emotional adjustment. Rogers felt that this distinction between the professions and the distinction between "normal" children's problems and "abnormal" children's problems were both spurious. However, the territorial prerogatives of the helping professions would come back to plague Rogers on several occasions during his long career and still remain a controversial issue almost a century later.

Interpretive Therapy

If Rogers favored any one deep, therapeutic approach when he came to Rochester, it was "interpretive therapy," the major goal of which is to help the child or parent achieve insight into his* own behavior and motives, past and present. Such insight then presumably enables the child or parent to give up any symptoms of distress, change problematic behavior, and cope realistically with the future.

Interpretive therapy works toward insight in a rather consistent way, wrote Rogers.[72] As rapport and trust are established, the child or parent feels increasingly free to tell (or in the case of young children in play therapy, to show) the therapist a great deal about himself. As the therapist begins to understand the individual's behavior and psychodynamics, and as she feels the individual is ready for self-understanding, the therapist begins to interpret the individual's behavior to him. If relevant, dreams can be interpreted. Where the relationship of the child or parent to the therapist seems significant, this, too, is subject to interpretation. As with one of Rogers' clients:

> Treatment took the form of getting John to go over the events of his early history until he understood their influence on him: his first five years living with his grandmother, who favored and spoiled him, moving to the separate home which his parents then established and the coming of his baby sister, the competition with his sister, his repeated patterns of tantrum behavior to gain his own way, which he could remember clearly as far back as the age of eight. As he went over this material during several interviews he was able to laugh at himself and to see how his childish patterns originated. The psychologist also interpreted this material to him in clearer terms. Another means used to help John attain insight

---

* To avoid the clumsy "he or she" or equivalent circumlocutions, yet to maintain equity, I have chosen to use the female pronouns throughout the book to refer to those in the helping role (therapist, teacher, parent, etc.) and the male pronouns to refer to the recipient of help (the client, student, child, etc.). When quoting Rogers or others, I have retained the original usage.

was to describe in concrete terms the dependency and egocentric tendencies of the child, and the ways in which those characteristics were changed in the mature adult, who is able to take responsibility for himself, whose interests are socialized, who is able to face reality. He was encouraged to analyze the ways in which he was mature, his reading interests, for example, and the many ways in which he was immature. From the time that treatment contacts began, the tantrums diminished greatly in number and severity until they were no longer a problem. John sometimes became upset by the dictatorial and unreasonable requests of his father, but in these instances his behavior represented a fairly normal reaction.[73]

Implicit in the interpretive approach is an optimistic view of human nature—that, basically, people want to be healthy, to grow toward psychological maturity. Because they are also frightened by growth and its risks, they may erect many defenses against seeing themselves and their situation clearly; but if they can be helped beyond these defenses, they will, as they achieve insight and self-understanding, choose a healthy course for themselves.

Although he never abandoned this optimistic view of humans underlying the therapeutic process, Rogers gradually did develop mixed feelings, and then increasingly negative feelings, about interpretive therapy. Sometimes it worked. Sometimes it only seemed to work. The interpretation was "accepted" by the child or parent who, at the time, also seemed to "feel" the interpretation to be true. Yet, weeks or months later, the child or parent would seem to "forget" or be unable to act upon his new insight. On other occasions, after interpreting a child's behavior to him, Rogers found he was unable to get the child to see him again.[74] Maybe there was more to therapy than having the child or parent accept and believe a valid interpretation. Rogers' weaning from interpretive therapy was very gradual. He often illustrated his process of disillusionment by relating three of his experiences in Rochester.

As described earlier, Rogers had been influenced by the work of William Healy, a leading authority on delinquent and problem behavior in children.[75] According to Rogers, Healy, who had a Freudian orientation, felt that delinquency was often associated with sexual conflict, and that if the real conflict were uncovered, the delinquent behavior would cease.[76] One or two years after coming to the Child Study Department, Rogers began working with a young pyromaniac. He held numerous treatment interviews with the boy in the detention home, tracing back the causes of the boy's behavior to his sexual impulses about masturbation, and gradually interpreting this understanding to him. The treatment was terminated and Rogers, feeling very proud of his skill in handling the case, was shortly thereafter amazed to find out that the boy, on probation, had been arrested again for setting fires.

Rogers was incredulous. Why had the therapy failed? Could Healy have been wrong about the causes of delinquency? Was he learning something that Healy did not know about therapeutic treatment? For Rogers this shock constituted a naïve but important realization. Authorities in his field could be wrong. There was new knowledge yet to be discovered.[77]

Shortly after he came to Rochester, Rogers was asked to lead a discussion group on interviewing techniques. As a catalyst for group discussion he brought in "a published account of an interview with a parent, approximately verbatim, in which the case worker was shrewd, insightful, clever, and led the interview quite quickly to the heart of the difficulty. I was happy to use it as an illustration of good interviewing techniques." Several years later he had a similar assignment and remembered this material. "I hunted it up again and reread it. I was appalled. Now it seemed to me to be a clever legalistic type of questioning by the interviewer which convicted this parent of her unconscious motives, and wrung from her an admission of her guilt. I now knew from my experience that such an interview would not be of any lasting help to the parent or the child. It made me realize that I was moving away from any approach which was coercive or pushing in clinical relationships, not for philosophical reasons, but because such approaches were never more than superficially effective."[78]

The third experience occurred a few years later, near the end of Rogers' time in Rochester. "I had learned to be more subtle and patient in interpreting a client's behavior to him, attempting to time it in a gentle fashion which would gain acceptance. I had been working with a highly intelligent mother whose boy was something of a hellion. The problem was clearly her early rejection of the boy, but over many interviews I could not help her to this insight. I drew her out, I gently pulled together the evidence she had given, trying to help her see the pattern. But we got nowhere. Finally I gave up. I told her that it seemed we had both tried, but we had failed, and that we might as well give up our contacts. She agreed. So we concluded the interview, shook hands, and she walked to the door of the office. Then she turned and asked, 'Do you ever take adults for counseling here?' When I replied in the affirmative, she said, 'Well, then, I would like some help.' She came to the chair she had left, and began to pour out her despair about her marriage, her troubled relationship with her husband, her sense of failure and confusion, all very different from the sterile 'case history' she had given before. Real therapy began then, and ultimately it was very successful.

"This incident was one of a number which helped me to experience the fact—only fully realized later—that it is the *client* who knows what hurts, what directions to go, what problems are crucial, what experiences have been deeply buried. It began to occur to me that unless I had a need to demonstrate my own cleverness and learning, I would do better to rely upon the client for the direction of movement in the process."[79]

Since psychoanalysis is one type of interpretive therapy, in which the interpretation of facts fits into a particular school of psychological thought, it is interesting that Freud himself, during the course of his career, went through a process very similar to Rogers, in recognizing the limitations of coercive or ill-timed interpretation. As Freud wrote in 1924,

> This answer of course involves a condemnation of that mode of procedure which consists in communicating to the patient the interpretation of the symptoms as soon as one perceived it oneself, or of that attitude which would account it a special triumph to hurl those "solutions" in his face at the first interview ... Such conduct brings both the man and the treatment into discredit and arouses the most violent opposition, whether the interpretations be correct or not; yes, and the truer they are actually the more violent is the resistance they arouse. Usually the therapeutic effect at the moment is nothing; the resulting horror of analysis, however, is ineradicable. Even in later stages of the analysis one must be careful not to communicate the meaning of a symptom or the interpretation of a wish until the patient is already close upon it, so that he has only a short step to take in order to grasp the explanation himself. In former years I often found that premature communication of interpretations brought the treatment to an untimely end, both on account of the resistances suddenly aroused thereby and also because of the relief resulting from the insight so obtained.[80]

Although Freud never went as far as Rogers, who eventually abandoned interpretation altogether, Nathaniel Raskin argued that Freud, too, even "with his fundamentally authoritative orientation found it necessary to reckon more and more with the attitudes of the patient and to depend less and less upon the will of the analyst, in order to make therapeutic progress."[81]

Otto Rank and Relationship Therapy

Around 1935–36 Rogers became familiar with the work of Otto Rank and his students Jessie Taft, Virginia Robinson and Frederick Allen, and he often acknowledged later that their work had a very important influence on his own professional growth.[82] Their direction in therapy, more than any other discussed so far, eventually became a part of his own, unique approach.

Rank was, for many years, one of Freud's closest associate-disciples. His break with Freud became evident in 1925 after the publication of Rank's *The Trauma of Birth*. He came to the United States in 1926 and, for a short time, joined the faculty of the Pennsylvania School of Social Work, where he continued to work out his own therapeutic approach, known as "will therapy." Rogers' first real exposure to will therapy came through a former member of his staff who was analyzed by Rank. She wrote Rogers a long letter describing her therapy in great detail. He was very impressed by her description. The next exposure to Rank's work came through several social workers connected with the Rochester

Society for the Prevention of Cruelty to Children. They had been trained at the Pennsylvania School of Social Work, and their use of Rankian methods kindled enough interest in Rogers and the other psychologists in the Child Study Department to invite Rank to Rochester to conduct a seminar for interested members of the helping professions in that city. He came in June 1936.[83]

One chronicler of Rank's career declared that this was the occasion when Rank "meets Carl Rogers and influences him to abandon Freudian technique for 'client-centered' and 'relationship' therapy."[84] That is quite an exaggeration. Rogers was already bored with Freud's ideology and had never adopted his technique, although he tried it out in his training a decade earlier. Nor was he particularly impressed with Rank's theoretical formulations.[85] Rank's substitution of birth for castration as the first trauma and source of anxiety, and the substitution of the breast for the penis as the first libido object, had little interest or significance for the practical Rogers. On the other hand Rogers was quite fascinated by Rank's description of his therapeutic approach. Nathaniel Raskin summarized some of the highlights of Rank's will therapy:

> The individual seeking help is not simply a battleground of impersonal forces such as id and superego, but has creative powers of his own, a will ... Because of the dangers involved in living and the fear in dying, all people experience a basic ambivalence, which may be viewed in various aspects. Thus, there is a conflict between will-to-health and will-to-illness, between self-determination and acceptance of fate, between being different and being like others, etc. This ambivalence is characteristic not just of neurotics, but is an integral part of life ...
>
> The aim of therapy, in light of the above, becomes acceptance by the individual of himself as unique and self-reliant, with all his ambivalences, and the freeing of the positive will through the elimination of the temporary blocking which consists of the concentration of creative energies on the ego. ... In order to achieve this goal, the patient rather than the therapist must become the central figure in the therapeutic process. The patient is his own therapist, he has within him forces of self-creation as well as self destruction, and the former can be brought into play if the therapist will play the role, not of authority, but of ego-helper or assistant ego ...
>
> The goals of therapy are achieved by the patient not through an explanation of the past, which he would resist if interpreted to him, and which, even if accepted by him, would serve to lessen his responsibility for his present adjustment, but rather through the experiencing of the present in the therapeutic situation ... The neurotic is hamstrung, not by any particular content of his past, but by the way he is utilizing material in the present; thus, his help must come through an understanding of present dynamics, rather than of past content ...
>
> The ending of therapy, the separation of patient from therapist, is a symbol of all separations in life, starting with the separation of fetus from womb in

birth, and if the patient can be made to understand the will conflict present here, the conflict over growth towards independence and self-reliance, and if he can exercise the separation as something which he wills himself, despite the pain of it, then it can symbolize the birth of the new individual.[86]

Unfortunately Rank was rather vague about what he actually *did* and did not do in therapy. "My technique," he wrote, "consists essentially in having no technique, but in utilizing as much as possible experience and understanding that are constantly converted into skill but never crystallized into technical rules which would be applicable ideologically."[87]

Although Rank often condemned the techniques of education and interpretation, many of his statements seemed to justify interpretation. Rank said, "I unmask all the reactions of the patient even if they apparently refer to the analyst, as projections of his own inner conflict and bring them back to his own ego." The therapeutic hour "is the place to show him how he tries to destroy the connection with this experience just as he does with the past … All the therapist can do is to take over with understanding the role falling to his lot, and to make clear to the patient the universal meaning of this experience (therapy) which comprehends in itself the whole man, yes, almost the whole of humanness. This explanation, however, can be given only in the individual terminology of the particular patient and not in a general ideology."[88]

Apparently the distinction is one between the past and present. While it is forbidden to interpret to the patient the meaning of past content (earlier experiences, dreams, etc.), it is permissible to interpret to the patient the meaning of his behavior in the therapeutic relationship.

Rogers, from his own experience, had already come to distrust therapist interpretation of past *or* present events, feeling that this interpretation led to only superficial understanding and behavior change by the child or parent. So Rank's interpretation of the dynamics of the therapeutic relationship did not appeal to him. In other areas, however, Rank's thinking did influence him—but only indirectly. Rank's seminar in Rochester lasted for only two or three days.[89] One searches Rogers' writings in vain for even a single quotation from Rank or even for more than three consecutive sentences on Rank's thinking. It was more through the influence of the social workers connected to his clinic and his reading of Rank's students Jessie Taft and Frederick Allen that Rogers came to incorporate Rankian views and methods into his own developing viewpoint.

After Rank's visit, Rogers employed the social worker Elizabeth Davis. Although she only stayed a year or two, Rogers' recalled, "I learned a great deal from her. She'd been trained in the Pennsylvania School of Social Work; that's why I employed her. And one of the things she taught me was to focus on the feelings that were being expressed and to respond to those feelings. It was this that led to the whole idea of reflection of feelings … I've always felt grateful to her."[90] Given this gratitude, it is odd that Rogers only acknowledged Elizabeth Davis publicly by name and made her specific influence explicit for the first time in his eighties.[91] Throughout most of his life, he credited Jessie Taft, who also reflected clients' feelings, and Frederick Allen as being his major influences in this period. Perhaps it was easier to credit Taft and Allen's influence in his writings because they had publications that could be cited, while Davis did not.

Taft and Allen, writing in English, were clearer than Rank and more explicit about what the therapist actually does. They also published several accounts of their therapy which provided detailed records of therapist and patient responses. Unlike Rank or Allen, Taft went so far as to abandon interpretation altogether, even interpretation of the dynamics of therapy. Rogers called Taft's book *The Dynamics of Therapy in a Controlled Relationship,* which was published in 1933 and which he first quoted in 1937, "a small masterpiece of writing and thinking."[92] Perhaps he called it "small" because it contained only about sixty pages of discussion on psychotherapy, with the bulk of the book consisting of a sixteen-session case and a thirty-one-session case of child therapy, with Taft and a visiting social worker conducting the therapy, respectively. Although these were not verbatim transcripts from recordings, nevertheless they provided detailed examples of the therapists' and children's interactions, along with occasional commentary by the author, thus providing a vivid picture of how the therapy was conducted. If one had to choose an individual who had the greatest influence on Rogers' evolving views during his Rochester years, it would be she, Dr. Jessie Taft.

Thus not so much Rank himself, but the Rankian school, contributed to and supported Rogers' own thinking. First, their emphasis on the patient's positive will as the source of growth in therapy was particularly attractive to Rogers. Referring to relationship therapy (Taft's term), in 1939 Rogers wrote, "its major value may be … the fresh viewpoint of non-interference and reliance upon the individual's own tendency toward growth which it has emphasized."[93] Stemming from this, the Rankian conception of the therapist, not as director of therapy, but as supporter and helper to the patient in his struggle toward health, was also very congenial to Rogers' thinking.

But perhaps most important was the Rankians' shift in emphasis from the analysis of past content to a focus on the patient's self-insight and self-acceptance within the therapeutic relationship. Of course, both of these elements—past content and the emotional dynamics of the therapy—were stressed in classical psychoanalysis. In analysis, however, working through the patient's resistances and transference in the therapeutic relationship were considered important primarily because this freed the patient to move ahead toward understanding his own psychological development—the *understanding* being the goal of the relationship. For the Rankians, the *therapeutic relationship itself* became the main goal. If the patient could develop the ability to live as a healthy individual in the therapeutic hour, they believed, this would be carried over into daily living.

Jessie Taft was particularly eloquent in describing the therapeutic hour as a microcosm of life itself.

> The reaction of each individual to limited or unlimited time betrays the deepest and most fundamental life pattern, his relation to the growth process itself, to beginnings and endings, to being born and to dying ... in accepting time, one accepts the self and life with their inevitable defects and limitations. This does not mean a passive resignation but a willingness to live, work and create as mortals within the confines of the finite ... one might fairly define relationship therapy as a process in which the individual finally learns to utilize the allotted hour from beginning to end without undue fear, resistance, resentment or greediness. When he can take it and also leave it without denying its value, without trying to escape it completely or keep it forever because of this very value, in so far he has learned to live, to accept this fragment of time in and for itself, and strange as it may seem, if he can live this hour he has in his grasp the secret of all hours, he has conquered life and time for the moment and in principle.[94]

It is difficult to provide one good example of relationship therapy, because there were many differences in the way Rank, Taft, Allen, and others in this tradition actually operated, once the door to the office was closed. The case of Edward, however, which Rogers once used to illustrate relationship therapy, contains elements common to most of the case reports published by the Rankian school and illustrates the aspects of relationship therapy that had significance to Rogers.

> As he became more secure in the visiting-teacher relationship, he began to express more and more open and violent aggression. The situation was intensified because of the visiting teacher's carrying on treatment simultaneously with another child in his room, Daniel Allen, who happened to have the same name as his younger brother. The climax of his expression of hostility toward the visiting teacher came in the third month of treatment:
>
> E. began making faces and guttural noises. "You're the dumbest cluck I ever saw," he said. V.T. said it must make him mad for other children to come to her office. He began a train of rapid talk—something about locking Daniel Allen in the gym at the 'Y'; then he went into pantomime, pretending to draw a gun, saying, "Stick 'em up." ... There were many noises and then, "I don't care if I yell—I'll get you fired, and then you can't bring other kids down." V.T. said, "It does make you mad for other kids to come down, doesn't it?" The play grew wilder, he picked up a box, saying, "I'll bump this over your head." There were many noises, twisting of his face, and then aiming at the wall, "Bing-bing, now you're dead." V.T. interpreted that she could see that he had pretended to kill her but that sometimes he liked her too ...
>
> In this excerpt from the interview we of course see E. expressing his inability to share the visiting teacher with other children just as in the home situation he

was unable to share the mother with his siblings. In an interview a few days later he was physically ill on discovering that the visiting teacher was married and was helped to express his rivalry and resentment that he had to share her interest with a father-person, just as he had to share his mother with his father. This interview occurred the day before the Christmas holidays. In the next interview after expressing these feelings he was able to work through to an expression of his positive feelings also.

V.T. talked with him about the times before the vacation, saying that he must have been very mad with her and that she knew how he felt. E. began fussing with the file and said, "The only one I like is only you; they've had a lot of sissies around here." V.T. accepted this ...[95]

Rogers' analysis of the critical elements in relationship therapy with parents is particularly interesting because all these elements would be a part of his own approach throughout his long career. "It applies only to those parents who have a desire to be helped ..." he wrote. "The relationship between the worker and the parent is the essential feature ... The worker endeavors to provide an atmosphere in which the parent can come freely to experience and realize his own attitudes. The worker creates this atmosphere by her acceptance of the parent, by her failure to criticize, by her refusal to impose on the parent any program or recommendations, and by her refusal to answer questions except when the parent genuinely desires an answer and is unable to answer for himself ... The effect of this relationship upon the parent may be characterized by the terms 'clarification of feelings' and 'acceptance of self'... It is typical of relationship therapy that it does not aim toward such clarification and insight primarily as a means to the end that the individual will change his attitudes or personality. Their stress is very frankly upon the individual's full realization and acceptance of himself. Any changes will come from normal growth in personality once the parent can accept himself and his limitations."[96]

While Rank called his approach "will therapy," Taft and Allen's approach was usually called "relationship therapy." In an interview many years later Rogers summed up these influences on his own thinking: "I became infected with Rankian ideas and began to realize the possibilities of the individual being self-directing. This certainly fit in with earlier ideas I had absorbed from Kilpatrick and John Dewey. I was clearly fascinated by Rankian ideas but didn't quite adopt his emphases for myself until I left Rochester. But the core idea did develop. I came to believe in the individual's capacity. I value the dignity and rights of the individual sufficiently that I do not want to impose my way upon him. Those two aspects of the core idea haven't changed since that time."[97]

To one who is familiar with Rogers' later work in "nondirective" and then "client-centered" therapy, it may now appear as if Taft, Allen, Rank, Virginia Robinson, and others in this school were the real founders of "Rogerian" therapy, and that Rogers was merely the one who was the best salesman for the approach and got most of the credit. As we shall see, however, as Rogers developed his own approach to psychotherapy in the years ahead, there were significant differences between his and the Rankians' methods.

The Clinical Treatment of the Problem Child

Carl Rogers spent twelve years in Rochester, the years of the Great Depression, learning a great deal about helping people while actually helping thousands of children and their parents. In addition to environmental therapy he had varying degrees of personal experience with all the deeper, direct therapies discussed above. From this experience, shortly after he left Rochester, a new approach to therapy would emerge. So would a book.

Before he left Rochester, Rogers wrote his first major book, *The Clinical Treatment of the Problem Child,* published in 1939.[98] Leonard Carmichael called the book "a progress report" on the field of child guidance.[99] It was also a progress report on Rogers' own growth, describing and presenting the pros and cons of all the types of environmental and direct therapy he had worked with in Rochester. Rogers would show chapters of the evolving book to colleagues at work and was taken aback when one of the staff commented, "Oh, but that's just what we're doing." Then he thought, "But no one has said what they are doing," hoping the book would be useful to others by being explicit about various approaches to helping troubled children and their families.[100]

In addition to cataloguing these approaches, the book contained the seeds of Rogers' future work as well. Of special interest in charting his growth are two sections of the book—his description of the therapist's role and his references to scientific research.

Having experienced a great deal and read and heard a great deal about the different approaches to therapy, Rogers asked the question: What, if anything, do all these therapeutic approaches have in common? The one point he saw where the different approaches did converge was in the attitude of the therapist. Whatever one's orientation, Rogers wrote, there were four qualifications required of all therapists. First was *objectivity.*

There is included in the concept a capacity for sympathy which will not be overdone, a genuinely receptive and interested attitude, a deep understanding which will find it impossible to pass moral judgments or be shocked and horrified. A person with this attitude differs on the one hand from the cold and impersonal detachment of the individual with Jovian tendencies, and differs quite as sharply from the deeply sympathetic and sentimental individual who becomes so wrapped up in the child's problems as to be quite incapable of helping. It is, to come back

91

to the first description of it, a degree of sympathetic "identification" with the child sufficient to bring about an understanding of the feelings and problems which are disturbing the youngsters.[101]

The second qualification of the therapist was a *respect for the individual.*

a deep-seated respect for the child's integrity ... a willingness to accept the child as he is, on his own level of adjustment, and to give him some freedom to work out his own solutions to his problems ... Frequently in environmental therapy the worker does select the treatment goal and arranges circumstances so as to develop the child in that direction. In psychotherapy the aim is to leave the major responsibilities in the hands of the child as an individual growing toward independence. The more this is and can be done, the more lasting and effective the treatment. It cannot be accomplished at all unless the therapist has the capacity to see the child as a separate individual, who has both a right and obligation to maintain his separateness.[102]

The third qualification was *an understanding of the self.* The therapist must have

a sound understanding of himself, of his outstanding emotional patterns, and of his own limitations and shortcomings. Unless there is this considerable degree of insight, he will not be able to recognize the situations in which he is likely to be warped and biased by his own prejudices and emotions ... the individual whose own life is reasonably well adjusted, and whose own emotional needs are in large measure satisfied, is capable of becoming a helpful counselor. Perhaps the outstanding quality of some of the lay and professional people who, without much expert knowledge, have acquired reputations as trusted advisers is the fact that they are "comfortable" people, with an acceptance of themselves and an adjustment to others which gives them freedom to be objective and helpful in regard to those in trouble.[103]

In these three qualifications of the therapist are the roots of "empathic understanding," "unconditional positive regard" and "congruence"—three concepts which would be among Rogers and his colleagues' most important contributions to the understanding of helping relationships. Finally, he included *psychological knowledge,* "a thorough basis of knowledge of human behavior and of its physical, social and psychological determinants," and added, "It might seem more logical to put this qualification first, but the experience of every clinic would bear out the viewpoint that a full knowledge of psychiatric and psychological information, with a brilliant intellect capable of applying this knowledge, is of itself no guarantee of therapeutic skill. The essential qualifications of the psychotherapist lie primarily, as we have pointed out, in the realm of attitudes, emotions, and insight, rather than in the realm of intellectual equipment."[104]

A second aspect of interest in *The Clinical Treatment of the Problem Child* is Rogers' concern with scientific research. Throughout the book he referred extensively to previous research on dealing with problem children. Equally important was his frequently repeated emphasis on the need for further research. This was not a widely accepted view. The science was in its infancy; its terms—like "mental illness," "neurosis," "insight"—were vague; and the techniques of therapy were in the early stages of development. Many therapists felt it was too soon for research. Others felt the time was right but despaired at the difficulty of the task. Still others, like Jessie Taft, believed that science could not be applied to therapy at all. To her the process was "purely individual, non-moral, non-scientific, non-intellectual—divorced from all hint of control."[105]

Rogers disagreed with all these viewpoints. "The psychologist cannot agree that this relationship, whatever its results, is a process which goes beyond intellectual understanding. If it is a process, it is possible to analyze and describe it. If it produces results, as I think most of us would agree it does, it will someday be possible—horrible thought—to measure them. The psychologist is not impressed by the claim that this is something purely individual, beyond the domain of science, some almost mystical process which simply occurs. Undoubtedly the psychologist will do his part in bringing the movement down to earth."[106] Indeed the next 20 years would justify Rogers' faith in the methods of science and bring him worldwide acclaim for his pioneering research on psychotherapy.

Professional Activities

For Rogers the Child Study Department proved to be a fascinating laboratory in which to experiment and learn. By no means, however, did he spend all his time in the laboratory. As he was learning himself, he began to teach others and, in so doing, gradually began to build a reputation.

Certainly in the Rochester area he came to be regarded as one of the major authorities in the community on children and youth and their problems. He was elected Chairman of Rochester's Conference on Youth Problems, became a member of the board of directors of Rochester's Council of Social Agencies, Harley School, and Memorial Scholarship Fund, and was elected President of the Rochester Psychological Society. He gave frequent talks before community groups and, as part of the departmental program which he established, he taught short courses to foster mothers, teachers in six different schools, an orphanage staff, a group of workers with boys, a staff of camp counselors, social workers, two groups at the Y.W.C.A., and the Mental Health Society of Utica. Both as

Director of the Child Study Department and as a private consultant, his advice was sought frequently by social agencies and institutions concerned with youth.[107]

In the summer of 1935 he was invited to return to New York City as a visiting lecturer at Teachers College, Columbia University. "I found this highly rewarding and ego strengthening," he recalled. "I was much surprised that the classes, even though enormous (150–300) seemed to respond to me very favorably and had good learning experiences. My approach at that time was to give a lecture but with ample opportunity for questions and discussion from the group. I particularly remember one course which was broken into thirds. I taught the first part, a much more experienced psychologist [Goodwin Watson] taught the second portion, and I was to teach the third portion of the course. When I returned for this last portion the class applauded loud and long when I came in. I was bowled over by the message that this contained, namely, that they were glad to see me back and really liked me better than the more experienced faculty member who had been teaching them. I began to realize not only that I loved to get people excited about new ideas and new approaches, but that they loved this too."[108]

His reputation soon spread beyond New York State. Out of his years in Rochester came the publication of a dozen articles, many of them involving original research in the child-guidance field, several of them coauthored with colleagues. Most of these articles were first read at various professional meetings. For example he presented "Three Surveys of Treatment Measures Used with Children" at the 1936 meeting of the American Association of Orthopsychiatry in Cleveland; "The Clinical Psychologist's Approach to Personality Problems" at the 1937 meeting of the National Council of Social Work in Indianapolis; and "Needed Emphases in the Training of Clinical Psychologists" at the 1939 meeting of the New York State Association of Applied Psychology at Cornell University. After the conference the papers would usually be published in the official journal of the organization.[109] In 1936 he wrote about social work and legislation and was asked by Governor Lehman's office to represent New York State at the sixty-third annual meeting of the National Conference on Social Work in Atlantic City.[110] Thus Rogers' face and name began to be visible at the conferences and in the journals of several helping professions. Publication of *The Clinical Treatment of the Problem Child* in 1939 also added to his growing reputation.

During his years in Rochester, Rogers often questioned just which helping profession he identified with the most. On a civil service application in 1934, for a position in Washington, DC as "senior social economist" in the Children's Bureau of the Department of Labor, he described his "seven and one-half years of progressive, responsible experience in the child welfare field."[111] Although half of his articles were published in the journals of the social work profession, and although he referred to the "worker" as often as to the "psychologist" in *The Clinical Treatment of the Problem Child*, he still tended to think of himself as a psychologist. But, he wrote, "The University of Rochester made it clear that the work I was doing was not psychology, and they had no interest in my teaching in the psychology department. I went to APA [American Psychological Association] meetings and found them full of papers on the learning processes of rats and laboratory experiments which seemed to me to have no relation to what I was doing. The psychiatric social workers, however, seemed to be talking my language, so I became active in the social work profession, moving up to local and even national offices."[112] Among other things, he was chairman of the Rochester chapter of the American Association of Social Workers, one of the organizers and first chairman of the New York State Council of the AASW, President of the Monroe County Mental Hygiene Society, and a member of the executive committee of the American Association of Social Workers. "Only when the American Association for Applied Psychology was formed did I become really active as a psychologist," he wrote.[113]

His movement between social work and psychology is also visible in the courses he began teaching for the University of Rochester in the mid-1930s. His name first appeared in the University's Extension Division bulletin for 1935–36, teaching "Children's Behavior Problems I and II," a six-credit course for the Sociology Department. The following year and thereafter these became two three-credit courses, "Children's Behavior Problems" and "Treatment of Children's Problems," listed as both sociology and education courses for the next several years. In 1937–38 he is listed in the University's College of Arts and Sciences bulletin, teaching "Clinical Psychology" for the Psychology Department, which he continued doing until he left Rochester.[114]

During 1937 and 1938 Rochester's Council of Social Agencies decided that a community guidance center was needed to coordinate the work of all the helping agencies in the community. Since the Child Study Department was already fulfilling a good deal of this function with children and parents, the Council felt that the Department should be the core of the new guidance center, with Rogers as the director. "At this point," Rogers wrote, "my psychiatric friends made a strong case to the Community Chest, to my board of directors, and to all who would listen, that such a clinic should be headed by a psychiatrist. So far as I know there was little criticism of the job I had done. The argument was simply that a psychiatrist was in charge of almost all similar clinics in other cities, and must be in charge here."[115] Undoubtedly behind this argument was also the feeling that, where depth psychotherapy was to be involved, psychiatrists and not psychologists were the professionals best suited to the task.

Judging from his later writings, tapes and films, people often picture Carl Rogers as a totally accepting, warm, and understanding person. While these characteristics certainly did describe him, they definitely did not comprise his entire repertoire of responses. Whenever Rogers' personal or professional interests were threatened, he was extremely tenacious about getting his own way, or in his own words, "capable of a dogged determination in getting work done or in winning a fight."[116] The fight over the directorship of Rochester's community guidance center was the first of many professional battles in his long career, a good many of them with the psychiatric profession. This particular battle encompassed a year of heated, often bitter, meetings, debates, and letters. In January 1939, however, Rogers became the first director of the Rochester Guidance Center.

Personal Life

David Rogers was two years old when Carl and Helen moved to Rochester in the summer of 1928, and their daughter, Natalie, was born that fall. The birth went well, but afterward Helen began hemorrhaging. As blood transfusions were not routinely available then, her life was in serious danger.[117] Fortunately the hemorrhaging soon ceased and she recovered quickly.

With the experience Rogers was getting in the clinic and sharing with Helen, their opinions about proper child rearing practices changed rapidly. As opposed to the strict Watsonian behaviorism they had tried to practice in New York City, Rogers was now telling parent groups how "the growing weight of evidence regarding the vital importance of deep emotional security and affection for the infant is rapidly changing our parent education programs. No longer do we find stress on rigid schedules, on the importance of definite rules, on the hospital-like method of caring for infants. Instead there is a wholesome stress on the infant's need of affection and cuddling, on the fact that such emotional security is as important as cod liver oil."[118]

Because of his active professional life, Helen had the far greater responsibility for rearing David and Natalie. Rogers credited her with being the better parent. "I would rate myself only fair as a father then … in those days I was more concerned with whether they were disturbing me, than whether what they were doing was in the direction of promoting their own growth."[119] His children had mixed feelings on this subject. Although Natalie recalled her father then as "shy and nondemonstrative. I have very little recollection of his cuddling or playing with us,"[120] she also said, "I think he's much too hard on himself that way … We had a lot of times together which kids don't have with their fathers."[121] In an autobiographical essay, David acknowledged, "I remember him as being shy, outdoorsy, gentle, but not around very often. I don't really remember many conversations with him."[122] Yet in an interview he thought his father exaggerated his preoccupation with work. "Dad wasn't away on trips very often, was home almost every night, was accessible, was always interested in how I was doing … I always felt secure that I could do what I wanted to, that he would be pleased and proud of me."[123] Carl's brother Walter also remembered many occasions when the Rogers spent weekends together. Walter, who was by now a physician, and his wife Elise lived in Rochester for six years during this period—for two of those years only two houses away from Carl and Helen. Walter and Elise joined them for Sunday drives in the country, family picnics, games, bridge, and even the building of a kayak together. They had always been close as boys, and this period united the brothers again as adults and cemented their lifelong friendship.[124] The truth, then, was probably a combination of these recollections. Rogers was a less involved, less demonstrative parent than he and the children might have wished, but still was a consistently present and supportive father.

Mostly through Helen's initiation and guidance there was lots of stimulation for the children at home. "Mother would have a table filled with art materials," David remembered, "and we'd all make mobiles or collages, and I remember everybody taking great pride and interest in what everybody else was doing. Nat was a good painter and, of course, Mom was superb. So I did sculpture. We all used to get very turned on by what we were doing. Mother gave very professional criticism." Natalie recalled how "Mother gave us the encouragement to create. Being somewhat critical by nature, her methods of teaching tended to be 'this is how you do it' rather than 'enjoy the process.' Nevertheless, my appetite was whetted and the creative act was encouraged and appreciated ... she took us to art museums and occasionally treated us to children's art classes ... Mother's sense of composition and color was noticeable in our home, in our clothes (she made most of mine), as well as in the pictures she painted."[125]

Something of their parenting style and of the atmosphere in which Carl Rogers was raised can be inferred from Natalie's recollections of their occasional trips back to Warwood. "I was terrified of my grandparents, particularly grandmother. Grandfather was kind of pleasant. He'd have a twenty-five or fifty-cent piece in our jeans for us and joke around and be kind of jovial and fun, but Grandma Rogers scared me to death. There was something about going into their fairly formal living room and the fact that they said prayers every morning and I didn't know what it was about, and I was worried that I was going to make a mistake. It felt like everything was good or evil there and I couldn't win; it had to be evil. I felt I could never possibly perform like I was supposed to, I didn't know what the ground rules were. And while it was kind of a big adventure to go to what seemed like a big estate, it had such a different feel to it, I was frightened ... One time Dave and I had taken a bath together and then were running around nude. We were really young and this is how we acted at home. Then I remember Aunty Meg catching us and just laying it on so heavy. 'What are you doing?' I don't remember what she said exactly, but this whole feeling came over me that there was something wrong with the two of us running around nude and having a good time—like our bodies were horrible. It was my first concept of sin. I felt like just going into the closet and hiding for a long time. It was terrible, just awful."

David and Natalie attended the Harley School, a private school in Rochester. It was essentially a college preparatory school, although in its elementary grades there was a good deal of emphasis on art, music and creativity. The choice reflected the value Carl and Helen put on academics and the arts, as well as their dissatisfaction with the public school the children would have attended. Natalie thought her parents "didn't have the kind of money that most of the parents who sent their kids to that private school had … they were certainly sacrificing, in the Depression years, in sending us to a private school." David felt somewhat ashamed of his father in that social context. "We lived in a smaller house than the other kids and Dad didn't have a typical business job. Plus he looked different. His collars were always sticking out from his shirt and none of the other fathers looked that way … I remember often being embarrassed by my rather shy father in the presence of hearty, hail-fellow-well-met fathers who were better dressed, were possessed of small talk, ran large businesses, and seemed 'in charge'… Later, at around 16 or 17, as I began to find out who he was and what he did, I felt so profoundly lucky compared to my contemporaries."[126]

Both children were extremely intelligent, a trait which their Columbia-trained, psychologist father must still have thought was quite important, as he had Gordon Riley and other colleagues test their intelligence annually for twelve years! Each year Rogers recorded the scores on a page headed "David—Psychological Tests" and the same for Natalie. David's IQ scores ranged between 138–166 and Natalie's from 126–156.[127]

As a girl Natalie experienced her father's achievement expectations less acutely than David. He recalled one time when he brought home a report card and was feeling pretty cocky about his grades. He was startled when his father got angry, pulled out a class roster (Rogers was on the board of directors of the school), and said, "Well, you think you're doing so well, let me just show you how you stacked up against your classmates." David remembered being so chagrined that he buckled down to work and got almost all A's for the rest of his educational career. The expectation was quite clear.

In fact, there were quite a few expectations like this. David felt, "You were expected to do well, to do things correctly, to be polite to your parents and others. My dad was just martinetish about that sort of thing. I remember one time going in and working at his desk on a pad—just a yellow pad—drawing pictures and so on. And I remember my dad calling me in and explaining very carefully how that was not *his* pad of paper, that it belonged to the University and that, if I wanted paper, then he would be glad to help me get some or I should buy it; but that it wasn't his pad. I thought of that many times, in terms of how far he carried that very, very exquisitely honest behavior.

"He was fairly meticulous. I remember him buying me a whole set of tools quite early on, and I think it was because he used to get fairly frustrated to find nicks in his chisels or his hammers where they shouldn't be. I don't ever remember him berating me about that; but he helped me build a bench and he got me my own set of tools, and they were *mine* and the others were *his*."

This was fairly typical of his style of discipline—calm, reasonable, and firm. Strong negative feelings were not permitted to ruffle the waters, neither between the parents nor between parent and child. Years later David said, "I never saw Dad get mad at Mom; and the reverse only once. Mom had made some pudding which was cooling in the sink. Dad washed his hands in the sink. Mom got mad and cried." Natalie said she "was never aware of any conflict between them. I never saw any anger between them and I still don't [in 1974]. They were affectionate with each other in front of us—physically demonstrative, warm and affectionate. But I never had any models for how to deal with anger ... As kids we were sent to our rooms to deal with our feelings ... There wasn't facilitation of open feelings in the family by anybody. The way to deal with it was to go to your room and cool off or go out for a walk or essentially keep it to yourself—not to work it through. When it wasn't interpersonal in the family, when there was a problem at school, etc., then I felt listened to and understood and so forth. But not on the crucial ground which is in the home ground. For example, I don't remember anybody ever talking out loud about the fact that Dave and I were competitive and jealous and envious. That would have helped a whole bunch. It was too early in his or their life to apply what they were learning to the family situation."

With this combination of reason and affection characterizing the children's upbringing, his father was, as David put it, "a very reluctant disciplinarian." David's uncle Walter recalled a time when "David did something that really bugged Carl. Carl took after him. Dave wasn't about to be caught. Carl laughed and said, 'Well, you know it's real good for kids to win every now and again.'"[128] "I never got spanked or got really berated for anything," said David. "There were a couple of times he got fairly sore at me, but they stand out as being such an unusual occurrence, such as when for the umpteenth time I'd ridden my bicycle over to some little girl's house and hadn't appeared for supper, and it had gotten dark, and I called and explained where I was and asked if he'd come get me in the car. It had happened enough times before, but he was clearly sore when he got there and said something that I remember was very crushing. He said, 'You just never know when to quit, and I hope you never take a drink because if you do you'll be a drunkard.' It was about the harshest thing he ever said to me."

Rogers was by no means the only authority figure in the family. David realized his mother was "a big, strong gal and, if I ever got really sassy, she would haul off and let me have it—very rarely—but I always felt she was perfectly able to handle a discipline situation all by herself." One such occasion was when, at age eight or nine, David went to Camp Cory, near Rochester, for two weeks. "I got there and I was just desperately homesick. And I cried and cried and my cabin mates were so pissed off at me. I remember one day I came in the cabin and they were all standing there with paddles, and they said if I didn't stop crying they were just going to beat the hell out of me, and I couldn't stop crying, so they proceeded to beat the hell out of me. I remember calling home repeatedly and saying, 'Come get me!' and finally mother came down that week. She took me out for the night and I wept most of the way. And then she came in the next morning and said that I really ought to finish camp, that if I really wanted to be a man I had to finish out the two weeks. And I remember crying all over again and saying that I didn't want to be a man—all I wanted to do was go home. But she took me back to camp. I think the second week was better."

One thing that was *not* part of the children's upbringing was religion. As Natalie recalled, "I grew up never hearing a single word about prayer. We never prayed. We never meditated. I never heard the word 'God.' I never was taken to church. I never was exposed to any religious ideas."[129] At the time Natalie simply took this for granted. Later on she was amazed that someone who was as steeped in religion as her father was when he was younger could have so completely banished this dimension from his life.

Many of the family's most memorable occasions during these years took place at Seneca Lake, about fifty miles from Rochester. Thirty years later, during the 1960s and 70s in the United States, a great number of young people returned to the country, to the land, often in communal living situations. Rogers, in his later years, was intrigued by this phenomenon and wrote and spoke frequently on the subject. This interest can be partly understood by a letter which Helen and Carl wrote in 1931 to several of their friends from Union Seminary and Teachers College who had decided to look for a summer place together.

Dear Gang:
We have found a marvelous piece of property—10 acres in all, of woods, bluffs and lake front on the east shore of Seneca Lake near the town of Valois ... It is very accessible yet it is isolated, it has both a glorious view and good bathing, it has woods and bluffs, and we think some flat land would be available for ball grounds, etc., and last but by no means least, it is within our reach financially ... On the property is a good house, one that could be made into a main building for the group. It has a kitchen and two other rooms downstairs ... and enough room for at least three bedrooms upstairs. ... It is well built ... cost $1400 to build in 1914 ... and in good repair. ... He will sell the house and one acre for $500, and will give us the other 9 acres for another $500. ... We would say the land is from 300 to 500 feet deep and stretches along the shore about 900 to 1100 feet. If you don't know about Seneca Lake, it is the largest and most beautiful, we think, of the Finger Lakes. It is 40 miles long and about 3 miles wide, and not heavily populated.[130]

In April 1932 the Rogers put down a $50 deposit, four other families joined them and the property was purchased, with a mortgage for about half the purchase price.[131] While the families were building their own cabins or having them built, they used the main house as the communal dining area and dormitory. Carl purchased all the materials needed for their own primitive cabin for $155 and the Rogers built the cabin themselves.

It was at Seneca Lake, on summer vacations and many spring and fall weekends, that the children got to know their father best. Natalie commented, "It's true he wasn't around during the day, some evenings and so on; but he doesn't give himself the credit for how big an influence he was in the summers and the whole spirit of working together, building together, doing projects together and the values of self-sufficiency and appreciating nature and learning how to do for yourself and the fun and excitement of that."

Both children felt as Natalie did, that "working on projects with him was the best way to communicate with him—not to sit down and talk." As David said, "a lot of my communication with Dad was doing things together. ... We'd be involved building a cabin or a bridge or sailing or something like that. ... how to be a carpenter, or the outside world, or what trees were what, or how to make a bow and arrow or a shack I learned from Dad—the motor-active kinds of things." Helen recalled one of these family projects. "Carl wanted a sailboat, so in the winter months which were long and snowy in Rochester, he designed and constructed 'The Snark'—a 12-foot flat-bottomed sturdy sailboat with centerboard, jib and mainsail. This was a project we both loved. I laid out the pattern for the sails on our living-room floor, cut and sewed the sail cloth, complete with grommets and binding and rope and together we built the neatest little craft that was ever launched on Seneca Lake (or, at least that was our conviction)."[132]

Unfortunately, when the Snark was first put into the water, its proud captain did not realize that the centerboard, which provides balance and better maneuverability, had not yet been attached. He stepped confidently from the dock, and, as his weight shifted from dock to boat, the Snark promptly tipped to one side and dumped Rogers headlong into the lake—an event that soon became a favorite family anecdote.[133]

For Natalie, the sailboat left another set of memories. "As I have thought about my girlhood," she wrote in her late forties, "the metaphor that comes to mind is that of being crew in a sailboat. That I enjoyed sailing in the boat with my father and/or my brother is a simple, joyful recollection. That being the crew for one or two men skippers while Mom was on the shore making lunch, has become a metaphor that has much significance in my development as a female. I was proud to be a good crew: I knew how to keep the boat ship-shape to the requirements of the captains ... As crew, I was pleasing the men in my life, getting their praise for doing what was expected of me. It was exciting to me to be a part of their action. I was aware that I didn't have to take full responsibility for the boat. I liked that feeling, of being protected from the full responsibility, yet being part of the excitement. I used to think, 'Too bad for you, Mom, you're not out here with the adventure of making the boat heel, or of racing towards home before the squall comes up.' I must have felt proud to be included with the men and somewhat disdainful of the woman left on shore, yet glad that she was there with the warm soup, when we got back.

"It doesn't take an analyst to see that I was part of an acculturation for my role as a woman ... Whether the metaphor is literally true in detail or not (I can hear my father and brother objecting), the truth for me is how I perceived my role ... Though I was appreciated and loved and included, the expectation seemed to be that I would not be capable of being captain of a ship. I would ask for a turn at the tiller with full knowledge that I could only be second best. They had the real understanding of how things worked ...

"As a model for being a wife and mother, my mother set very high standards. She was nurturing, supportive, always there to do things for us, feed us, take care of us. Although she had interests of her own, the message to me was definitely that 'children and husband come first, my own needs come last.' We prospered under this in many ways, but at what cost to her?"[134]

At one point during these years, with the primary child-rearing responsibility on her shoulders, Helen did begin to feel a bit "put upon," as she described it, "though not as put upon as many young women would feel today."[135] So she began attending some night school classes, while Carl took care of the children. She also continued her painting and became quite actively involved in a cause that proved to be an intense, lifelong interest of hers—the Planned Parenthood movement. She never experienced a serious, sex-role identity crisis; although the issue did surface in the final years of her life. She continued to assume the major responsibilities as parent and homemaker, and this clearly gave Rogers the added mobility to advance as fast as he did in his profession.

Rogers tended to characterize their Rochester years, which coincided with the years of the Great Depression, as times of scarcity. "We were poor during the depression—I remember trying to decide which bills we would not pay this month—but I was never unemployed and felt really fairly secure in a minimum way." In his oral history, he pointed out how the group had to take out a $450 mortgage for the Seneca Lake property and how he and Helen purchased all the materials to build their cabin.[136] This was not a fully accurate picture. They need not have scrimped and saved. Rogers' parents would have been glad to help them out, but Carl was loathe to ask, preferring to demonstrate his independence.

Still Rogers' father made unsolicited gifts. In October 1934, for Carl and Helen's tenth anniversary he gave them a half interest "in the 110 acre farm owned by me in DuPage County, Illinois [not Warwood] ... I wish you to accept this gift with the greatest good wishes from me ... With much affection, Sincerely yours, W.A. Rogers." The next year he wrote that he was giving them 235 acres adjoining the 110, saying he would operate it for them, pay taxes, insurance, and other expenses, but they could sell it or subdivide it as they liked at any time. In a subsequent letter, he explained, "My reason for doing this is ... in addition to wishing to be relieved of the ownership and care of this farm, I am also solicitous of making all of my children at least partially independent and giving them a place to live on if they choose to go to a farm." In 1939, Walter wrote to say he was transferring to Carl and Helen 10 shares of AT&T stock with a total value over $1,500 and this time signed it, "Lots of love to you all from us all. Pop."[137] While living frugally through the Depression, then, the Rogers were also amassing substantial savings, which would be available when they soon had occasion to purchase a new home.

Move to Ohio

In the summer of 1939 Bernard Covner was working as an intern in the Rochester Guidance Center. He recalled how, "having gotten an M.A. in June from Penn, I had not an ounce of *practical* experience. My first assignment from Rogers at the beginning of the summer was to do a work-up on a family of 12 children coming up for adoption. He sure was willing to take risks! ... During that summer, I decided to forfeit my scholarship at the University of Pennsylvania and not return. I told Rogers I was considering Ohio State and Iowa. He said both choices were good. I applied to both, was accepted at both. He made no attempt to influence me. I decided on Ohio State. *Then* he told me that he would join me there in January, having been appointed full professor ..."[138]

William Snyder, then a graduate student at Ohio State, remembered that "it was strongly implied that since Rogers had little academic experience, he would not threaten any of the academicians in the department."[139] Rogers thought, "I am sure the only reason I was considered was my book on *The Clinical Treatment of the Problem Child*, which I had squeezed out of vacations and brief leaves of absence."[140] "Clinical psychologists were very few in number; by writing the book, I suppose I demonstrated that here was a person with practical experience in the field who also could do a reasonably scholarly job of bringing together much of the evidence. Ohio State at that time was looking for a replacement for Henry Goddard, who was one of the first people in the clinical field, and they invited me to come there. And I came in the best mood that one can come for getting a job. I really didn't think I wanted the position. I had just finished setting up ... the Rochester Guidance Center ... and I felt I was obligated to stay there. So they offered me an associate professorship and could see that it was very much touch and go as to whether I would even be interested in their offer. Then they upped it to a full professorship ..."[141]

103

"I heartily recommend starting in the academic world at the top level," he once wrote. "I have often been grateful that I have never had to live through the frequently degrading competitive process of step by step promotion in university faculties, where individuals so frequently learn only one lesson—not to stick their necks out."[142]

Even with the full professorship offer he still wavered in his decision. Helen influenced him to accept it, saying, "Now look. You've always liked teaching, you've always thought you wanted to get into a university sometime; here's a good opportunity and you shouldn't be too bound by the Rochester situation." Rogers followed her prompting and subsequently felt that "the outcome of that has helped me to make other decisions, leaving places when everyone else would say that in the obvious light of common sense I should *not* leave."[143]

The news of the move was announced late in October 1939. The Rochester newspaper wrote, "Confessing yesterday that he felt some 'qualms' about leaving the Guidance Center in Rochester, … Dr. Rogers pointed out that the university post would afford a broader field in which to apply the knowledge and experience afforded by the Rochester experiment."[144]

"So," Helen wrote, "with many protests from our teenage son who was loath to leave Rochester, we moved to Columbus in a blizzard in December, 1939."[145]

CHAPTER 5

The Ohio State Years
1940–1944

The Rogers moved into a rented house on Weisheimer Road in Columbus. David told them it was a "crummy little house" and they had ruined his life by moving from Rochester.[1] Carl and Helen agreed with the first charge but not the second, and David quickly adjusted to Columbus. Regarding the living situation Helen recalled, "We knew we wished to build ourselves a home and we started as soon as possible. It was a great experience for me—choosing the lot and planning and supervising the house as it went up."[2] Their large lot, with many black walnut trees, was in a rural area on Rustic Bridge Road in Beechwold, on the outskirts of Columbus. They built what they considered a very beautiful home—stonework facing the first floor, stucco above that, a slate roof, and a red brick fireplace—at a cost of $14,000. "It was a lovely creation, and with my art training, I had a field day choosing colors and carpeting, making drapes, and so on. We moved in in January of 1941 … the brunt of the moving fell on my shoulders, as both Carl and Dave were down very sick with the flu. Natalie and I did it all."[3]

Although the Rogers lived outside the city, the children were able to attend the University's Laboratory School. This meant Carl or Helen chauffeured David and Natalie to and from school each day. Carl usually was able to drive them in the morning and then go on to his office. If he left the University in the late afternoon, he could also pick them up, or they would walk over to his office and read or do their homework while their father finished up his counseling, meetings, classes, or paperwork.

The New Professor

Rogers' contract called for a $5,100 salary for teaching three quarters of the year. His natural predilection for work was augmented by a desire to do well at his first full-time college teaching position. So, in addition to teaching a full load of courses in each of the *four* quarters of 1940, he supervised counselors-in-training both in the schools and in the campus Psychological Clinic, gave eighteen speeches and workshops for local, state, and national organizations, had seven articles accepted for publication, served as a consultant to the Kellogg Foundation and the Rochester, New York schools, served on several college and professional committees, carried on intensive counseling with seventeen students for a total of over one hundred interviews, and saw fifty-four additional students for one or two interviews on personal or vocational problems.[4] After the first year the number of individuals he personally counseled decreased, although he continued to accept enough cases so that he would be working with one to three students at all times.[5] With the decrease in counseling, however, came a rapidly growing number of graduate students working for advanced degrees under his supervision.

While he felt successful enough with the undergraduate students whom he taught in a standard course called Mental Hygiene, he derived his greatest satisfaction from his graduate seminars and supervision of counselors-in-training. After taking mostly laboratory and theory courses, the graduate students were extremely interested in the actual process of therapy. This mirrored Rogers' own growing interest in counseling and psychotherapy. Because of his pragmatic bent and his minimal interest in theory at the time, his courses emphasized the various therapeutic techniques employed in treatment interviews. This was rather unusual then, as most counseling programs emphasized psychological theory and diagnostic, rather than treatment, techniques.

In the winter quarter of 1940 he taught a seminar in clinical psychology called Techniques of Psychotherapy, covering the various direct treatment approaches he had described in the last section of *The Clinical Treatment of the Problem Child*. Thomas Gordon, then a student at Ohio State recalled how, "A new professor joined the department, and word quickly got around that he was a young clinical psychologist with a lot of experience treating maladjusted children and youth ... His first course at Ohio State attracted nearly every psychology graduate student plus many students from other departments. Even most of my upper-level graduate friends enrolled."[6]

Later, in the fall quarter that year, he set up a practicum in advanced clinical treatment. "Each student carried at least one case on intensive treatment, and many of the interviews were recorded phonographically. The two-hour session was devoted to a thorough-going analysis of the treatment procedures used in a particular case, and the ways in which they might have been improved."[7] To have one's case be the focus of a session, the student had to transcribe one complete interview and make copies for all members of the group so they could follow the transcription while listening to the recording, making comments and discussing the case.[8] Rogers later wrote, "I have been told that the practicum in counseling and psychotherapy which I established in 1940 was the first instance in which supervised therapy was carried on in a university setting—that neither Freud nor any other therapist had ever managed to make supervised experience in the therapeutic relationship a part of academic training. I am not certain that this statement is true. I do know, however, that I had no such brash thought in mind when I inaugurated this practicum. It simply seemed essential that if students were to study therapy, they must also carry it on, and should have the opportunity to analyze and discuss what they were doing."[9]

One of the students in this practicum, William Snyder, remembered that "Carl's classes were intensely popular. Harold Burtt would schedule them in the evenings and on Saturday morning and at all the most unpopular times and still they would be filled to overflowing. I remember, for instance, that there were two clinics, one on Wednesday afternoon and one on Saturday morning. Students usually took the Wednesday afternoon because no one wanted to be there at 8 a.m. on Saturday mornings … But when Rogers was in charge of the Saturday morning clinic, we all gladly got there before 8 a.m. and spent the morning in the most delightful work anyone can imagine. Then, voluntarily, we would go to lunch together and come back and spend the afternoon holding case conferences with him. This was above and beyond the requirements of the course, but everyone did it because it was such a stimulating situation to be in."[10]

It was stimulating for Rogers, too. In *The Clinical Treatment of the Problem Child* he had described the major approaches to psychotherapy and had given the pros and cons of each. But he had not argued for any one point of view, although his preference for the "expressive" and "relationship" therapies was easily discernible. But the graduate students at Ohio State wanted more than the pros and cons of the various schools. They wanted their professor to teach them to be good therapists, and that meant he would have to formulate his own concept of good therapy. Pressed by their questions and comments Rogers began to describe effective therapy in his own terms. As he described it to them, he wrote an article on "The Process of Therapy," which was published in the *Journal of Consulting Psychology* in September of 1940.[11]

The process of therapy which he began to explain and advocate, however, seemed not very original to him. That year he participated in a session on "Areas of Agreement in Psychotherapy" at the American Association of Orthopsychiatry, where many of the panelists, including Frederick Allen, Saul Rosenzweig, Joseph Chassell and especially Goodwin Watson, reflected and contributed to his own impression of the common understandings in the field.[12] So it seemed that what he was advocating to his students was what most modern therapists were already taking for granted. It was all rather obvious to him, certainly not controversial.

True, his students regarded his ideas as new, but he assumed this was because most of their experiences were in the classroom, and they had not had much contact with practicing clinicians.[13]

Fortunately he soon had the opportunity to put these assumptions to the test. He was invited to deliver a speech in December at the University of Minnesota, before the campus chapter of Psi Chi, the psychological honor society. Prominent psychologist Ernest Hilgard had addressed the same group in September and the famous psychotherapist Charlotte Buhler would do so in February. The chairman of the program was Theodore Sarbin, an Ohio State doctoral candidate living in Minnesota and working with E.G. Williamson and John Darley while finishing his dissertation. He wrote to Rogers shortly after Rogers' article on the process of therapy appeared, saying, "at the present time much discussion centers upon therapy and the clinical psychologist's role in therapy … it seems that you have thought this problem through. We would like to have you address this topic or a related topic."[14]

The counseling program then at the University of Minnesota had developed under the leadership of Edmund (E.G.) Williamson who had a clearly directive approach toward counseling. He believed firmly in psychological tests and the ability of the trained counselor to actively guide the student toward satisfying personal and vocational choices. This viewpoint tended to characterize the philosophy and practice at Minnesota, which was regarded as one of the leading centers for student personnel work at that time.[15] It was before this group that Rogers went to present his paper on "Newer Concepts in Psychotherapy."

"If we can see outworn and discarded techniques as the background out of which recent therapeutic approaches have developed," he told his audience, "we shall have a deeper understanding of present points of view and an increased ability to criticize them in a constructive fashion."[16] He went on to briefly describe and criticize the more traditional approaches to counseling and psychotherapy— ordering and forbidding, exhortation, suggestion, advice, and intellectualized interpretation. Of all the approaches he criticized, he was harshest when it came to the use of advice. To prove his point he quoted part of the record of an interview conducted by an advice-giving counselor.

My job was to dissuade him from continuing in pre-business and in having him accept a substitute program of general education. First I pointed out the standard of competition in the professional School of Business. This made no dent in his armor. He still maintained that his D+ average would come up to a C this year. Knowing his dislike of courses involving math, I showed him the courses as catalogued in the professional business curriculum: statistics, finance, money and banking, theoretical economics, insurance accounting and so on. (With silent apologies to my friends who teach these courses) I told the student that these courses were "highly theoretical and abstract" and considered "very dry."

On the other hand, courses in general education were practical and interesting; no economics or math prerequisites were necessary. I described some of the interesting features of the Orientation Courses. He finally agreed to think it over. I outlined this plan of action: (1) see the counselor in the general education unit for further information (I arranged an appointment); (2) discuss the matter with his folks; (3) secure transfer blanks from the Registrar's Office.[17]

Rogers did not realize at the time that the counselor in this interview was none other than the program chairman, Ted Sarbin. "That was embarrassing," recalled Rogers, "and I didn't blame him for being a little upset … later he pretty well forgave me [and] became a good psychologist in his own right."[18] But Sarbin had a different memory of the incident. At the time, he thought Rogers *knew* he was the author and regarded the incident as an example of Rogers' "characteristic tact" for not naming him.[19] In any case, having criticized the older methods, many of which his audience were still practicing, Rogers went on to describe the "newer practices" or "newer therapy," crediting its roots in the therapy of Rank as modified by Taft, Allen, and Robinson, in the neo-Freudian analysts—notably Karen Horney—and in the fields of play therapy and the more recent group therapy.

"The aim of this newer therapy," he said, "is not to solve one particular problem, but to assist the individual to grow, so that he can cope with the present problem and with later problems in a better integrated fashion … it relies much more heavily on the individual drive toward growth, health, and adjustment … In the second place, this newer therapy places greater stress on the emotional elements, the feeling aspects of the situation, than upon the intellectual aspects … In the third place, this newer therapy places greater stress upon the immediate situation than upon the individual's past … Finally this approach lays stress upon the therapeutic relationship itself as a growth experience."[20]

Rogers later said, "I was totally unprepared for the furor the talk aroused. I was criticized, I was praised, I was attacked, I was looked on with puzzlement."[21] Ted Sarbin recalled, indeed, "Carl's talk was not received sympathetically," although "Williamson's response to Carl's presentation was politely restrained, but he did cite some evaluation studies to show that testing and directed counseling were effective."[22] In any event, said Rogers, "By the end of my stay in Minneapolis it really struck me that perhaps I was saying something new that came from *me*; that I was not just summarizing the viewpoint of therapists in general." For this reason, he concluded, "It would seem quite absurd to suppose that one could name a day on which client-centered therapy was born. Yet I feel it is possible to name that day and it was December 11, 1940."[23]

Rogers scholar Brian Thorne doubted whether Rogers was as unprepared for his reception in Minneapolis as he claimed. "Rogers, it would seem, had gone to the foremost citadel of directive therapy and there began his paper with a powerful attack on the 'home team's' theories and practices. It is difficult to believe that he did not realize at some level that he was carrying out a revolutionary act. His later development shows him to have been a skilled political animal with a sure nose for the effective strategy … I have little doubt that he went to Minnesota in December 1940 knowing that he had something of a time bomb in his briefcase."[24]

In either case, naïvely entering the lion's den or knowingly provoking a reaction, the Minnesota experience convinced Rogers that he had a perspective worth developing. As a result, he recalled, "It was shortly after that that I decided I would work toward a book presenting my point of view—a point of view drawn in large measure from others, nourished by others, but still a point of view which was my own."[25]

Counseling and Psychotherapy

He began to write *Counseling and Psychotherapy: Newer Concepts in Practice* shortly thereafter; but given all his other responsibilities at Ohio State, he made little headway. Then after teaching a full load of courses for six consecutive quarters, he managed to take the next two quarters off-duty and so spend the summer and autumn of 1941 writing his second major book. It was soon ready for publication, but Houghton Mifflin, who had published *The Clinical Treatment of the Problem Child*, was not happy with his latest achievement. They did not see what college courses would use it, and when they asked the author if he knew what courses might adopt it, he could only mention two such courses—his own and one taught by an acquaintance at another university. The publisher thought he should have written the book to fit into already existing courses. They couldn't picture it selling the 2,000 copies necessary for them to break even financially. Only after Rogers threatened to take it to another publisher did they reluctantly agree to publish it.[26]

In spite of his stubbornness about getting the book published, Rogers still had his own doubts about its likelihood of success. While writing the manuscript, he had shown it to some of his graduate students and asked them whether they thought it was publishable and whether anyone would read it. William Snyder recalls Rogers' "deep humility about his book … To us, the mere asking of such questions was almost unbelievable. I perceived the book practically as the New Testament."[27] In addition, when Rogers heard that Frederick Allen, one of the major proponents of relationship therapy with children and one of Rogers' own influences, was also writing a book on therapy, he felt very discouraged. He doubted whether many people would pay attention to his own book, compared to one written by the older, more experienced, and more venerable Allen.[28] As it turned out, Allen's book had relatively little impact, while Rogers' book sold well over

100,000 copies, [29] an extremely high figure for a clothbound volume of highly technical interest.* It had a major, some would argue revolutionary, effect on the field of psychotherapy, and remained in print for most of the twentieth century.

In his preface, both speaking for the profession and describing his own growth, Rogers set the book in its historical context: "In the period of the 1920's the interest in the adjustment of the individual was primarily analytical and diagnostic. In social work it was the period of the flowering of the case history; in psychology there was a lush tropical growth of tests; in educational guidance both records and tests grew apace; in psychiatry multisyllabled diagnostic labels blossomed into elaborate diagnostic formulations. Never had so much been known about the individual. As time has gone on, however, these groups, and others with similar interests, have given more consideration to the dynamic processes through which adjustment is improved. The balance has definitely shifted from diagnosis to therapy, from understanding the individual to an interest in the processes through which he may find help."[30]

The Client

The book contained many innovations or contributions to the fields of counseling and psychotherapy. One of these might appear rather inconsequential on the surface: Rogers used the word "client."

For the first twelve years of his career he had never had any question about what to call the recipient of therapy. In Rochester, the recipients had been either children or parents. "Dr. Rogers, there's a parent waiting to see you," the receptionist might say. "Sorry, I have two children coming in for appointments this afternoon," the counselor could explain. At Ohio State "student" joined "child" and "parent" as an appropriate description to use in the clinic and in writing about counseling. But once he began to generalize about the therapeutic process and to describe it in terms which would cover the various forms of counseling and psychotherapy, he needed a broader term to describe the recipient of help. He chose the word "client," which he had first used in a 1940 article. Rogers was not the first to use the term in this context. For example, Jessie Taft used it occasionally in *The Dynamics of Therapy*, the book Rogers so admired.[31] Otto Rank had been using the term "as early as the mid-30s."[32] Percival Symonds had a chapter on "Counselor-Client Relationships" in his 1939 book *The Psychology of Parent-Child Relationships*.[33] However, the term became popular in the counseling field only after the publication of *Counseling and Psychotherapy* in 1942.

---

* None of the sales figures cited throughout this book include sales of foreign translations, which were substantial. *Counseling and Psychotherapy*, for example, by 1971 had been translated into Portuguese, French, Italian, German, and Japanese. Altogether, by 1979, there were over sixty foreign editions of Rogers' books.

111

His choice of the term, however, was not important because it solved a semantic problem—finding a single term to include all recipients of counseling and psychotherapy. Rather it was important in its connotation of a newer therapeutic relationship, in which the traditional word "patient" was no longer appropriate. Since psychiatry had grown out of the medical profession, it was natural that psychiatrists and psychoanalysts would view their clients as patients. The word, however, indicates much about the two roles in the relationship. A patient is usually regarded as a "sick" person. He expects the doctor to cure him, to do something *to* him, to assume much of the responsibility for his well-being. The assumption is that the doctor, because of her training, can know, even better than the patient, what is wrong with him and can prescribe the necessary method of treatment.

Rogers had long been dissatisfied with this approach to therapy and counseling. He often called it "counselor-centered therapy," [34] in which the therapist administers tests, asks questions, makes a diagnosis and suggests, directly or subtly, courses of action for the client to follow. He had difficulty controlling his old tendency toward sarcasm, when it came to describing this type of approach: "we find these counselors deciding with assurance such diverse issues as how to study history, how to get along with one's parents, how to solve the issue of racial discrimination, and what is the proper philosophy of life. From other records we know that such counselors decide issues of marital adjustment, questions of vocational choice, problems of discipline, and, in fact, all the puzzling questions which a perplexed individual can face. Obviously a generous portion of supernatural wisdom is required of the individual who takes such an attitude toward counseling. When the goal is more modest and the aim is to help the individual to free himself so that he can decide these issues in his own way, then the necessary attributes of the counselor are reduced to a human dimension." [35]

His experiences in Rochester had convinced him that counselor-centered therapy may tend to make the client more dependent, less able to solve new problems as they arise, while it simultaneously creates unproductive resistance in the client. He believed that the greater the responsibility the individual could take in guiding his own life, in and out of therapy, the more effective and long-lasting the therapy would be. If, as Taft had said, the therapeutic hour was a microcosm of life itself, then as the client learned to set and achieve his own goals within the hour, he also would be learning how to do it during all the other hours of life. In this context, the name "client" implied a locus of control. One consults a professional who has both knowledge and skill, but the locus of control remains with the client who will make his own decisions. Call a client a patient, and he is liable to act like one.

The new term also faced head-on the question of whether the person who seeks psychological help is to be regarded as being mentally ill, unfit, or sick. It was a common prejudice in the early years of therapy that individuals seeking psychological help were, at worst, crazy and, at best, flawed, subnormal in adjustment, inferior. Many employers, for example, would not consider hiring a person if they knew he had been or was seeing a psychiatrist. But after working intensely with hundreds of individuals, Rogers was finding less and less meaning in the traditional distinctions between sick and healthy people. Although his early work had given him the tendency to label people according to their intelligence (average, dull, superior, etc.) and their personality (neurotic, psychotic, normal, etc.), this early work in testing had also taught him that adjustment and maladjustment were arbitrary terms assigned to the distribution of test scores on a bell-shaped curve or continuum, meaning that all individuals are maladjusted to some degree. Many professionals and laymen thought (and still think) that therapy is for people with mental illness, while counseling is for basically healthy people with relatively transient problems. After counseling so many students whose "presenting problems" of vocational choice or poor study habits were soon revealed to be the symptoms of much deeper psychological conflict, Rogers no longer accepted these superficial labels and distinctions. He wanted a client to be able to come for psychological help—counseling or therapy—in much the same spirit that a client comes for legal counsel or consults an accountant or architect. Rogers always sat face-to-face with his clients, conveying this same egalitarian idea.

The word "client," then, symbolized a basic attitude toward the therapeutic relationship—one which gave considerable dignity to the client, which conceived of the counselor and client as equals working together to achieve the client's goals as he sees them. To describe this approach, Rogers introduced two terms: "client-centered" and "nondirective" counseling and therapy. Probably because he used the latter term much more frequently and even devoted a whole chapter of *Counseling and Psychotherapy* to contrasting "The Directive Versus the Non-Directive Approach," beginning in 1942, the phrases "nondirective counseling" and "nondirective therapy" became associated with the name of Carl Rogers.[36]

The Nondirective Method

But was it really his own contribution, this nondirective therapy? In his 1939 book, Rogers used Frederick Allen's 1935 description to describe the nondirective counselor's attitude toward the client:

> We are prepared to take people as we find them—willing, resistive, skeptical—
> and create a situation which from the beginning gives both parent and child the
> feeling that here is a place which imposes nothing beyond helping them to clarify
> what they are ready to do in their relation to us—where they can feel the interest
> is in them as people, not as problems, and where if they continue they are doing

so because there is some desire and not because of our decision. They become participants—not recipients of help from the very beginning.

From the beginning, our relation to parent and child is based on a respect for the integrity and capacity of that person—limited though at times it may be—and disguised as it frequently is by a sense of defeat and failure. We do not bring into our relation with them, except where our own human limitations prevent it, a preconceived conception of what they should be or how they should manage their relationships. We are anxious that this relation shall provide an opportunity for both parent and child to get a clearer understanding and acceptance of what they are, at that time, and what they are able to do, with the strengths they have, to deal more responsibly with a reality which is theirs and which no one, however well equipped, can assume for them.[37]

So much of Rogers' thinking and practice was steeped in earlier traditions, especially that of relationship therapy, he hardly knew himself what was original and what was not. To assess his unique contribution it is necessary to go beyond general descriptions like the above and to look more closely at what many psychologists and counselors, for almost a generation, came to view as "The Method" of nondirective counseling.

To Rogers, nondirective counseling was a clearly structured process that consisted of three major phases, often overlapping: (1) release, (2) insight, and (3) positive actions based on insight.[38] In a highly condensed fashion, his account of therapy with Johnny and his mother illustrates the three phases:

Johnny ... in his contacts, is made to feel free to express his attitudes toward his parents, toward other persons and elements in his environment, and toward the clinic and the therapist. He is free to vent his angers by bitter talk, by shooting toy soldiers, by criticizing the clinic equipment, or in any other way which gives free expression to his feeling. The only limitation is upon destructive action which has social consequences. He can hate the therapist, if he wishes, and can destroy a doll which represents him, but he cannot attack the therapist directly. All of John's attitudes are recognized and clarified. The therapist shows his understanding, but he does not criticize, does not approve, does not try to meet the boy's needs himself. If Johnny feels unloved, the worker may recognize this ("You feel that nobody cares about you at all") but he does not try to become a parent substitute. Gradually, as Johnny begins to see himself in a certain way— for example, as a boy who feels very much unloved, and who in return hates his parents and torments them, but turns to others who will give attention—he finds that he has more control over his actions. He begins to see that there are some limited things he could do about his own situation. Perhaps he puts these into words. Perhaps he merely surprises his mother by offering to help her in her housework. A slight, but deeply significant change, takes place.

In her interviews, the mother goes through a parallel experience. For the first time in her life she finds herself able to talk of hidden attitudes which she has never admitted to herself. She does not know how the therapist makes this possible, but the dropping-away of the necessity of defending all her actions is something which is vividly experienced. Gradually she can admit how much she prefers her other child to John. Suddenly it occurs to her, and she can face the thought, that this is one of the reasons why John likes to do mean things just to annoy her. Because of her new understandings, her tone of voice changes when dealing with the boy at home, her discipline loses its slightly sadistic quality, and when John offers to help with the dishes, she is able to respond with a thoroughly sincere expression of her gratitude, and of her affection for him. Freed from the necessity of always being "right," she decides to discard some of the rigid methods she has devised for controlling him and to put their relationship on a more realistic and comfortable basis—a relationship in which each may express annoyance at the other, but in which there is also room for real affection. In her case, as in John's, a release of feeling leads to self-understanding, and this in turn leads to actions directed toward a more satisfying goal—a more genuine, more mature parent-child relationship.[39]

In the first phase, that of "release," the client unburdens himself about his problems and concerns. This process, initially, has a cathartic value; it is psychologically, emotionally, and even physically freeing to express pent-up feelings. If rightly handled by the therapist, the release of feelings can move the therapy rapidly forward. Correct handling consists essentially of two specific techniques—"simple acceptance" and "reflection of feelings." Simple acceptance might be an "I see," "Yes," "M-hm," or anything, verbal or nonverbal, to let the client know he is being heard, followed attentively, understood, and still accepted. This helps him continue to reveal himself and explore the issues he has been discussing. Reflection of feelings is a more difficult skill for the therapist to learn. It requires a deep concentration on what the client is saying and then a restatement of what the client has communicated, particularly the essential *feeling element* in what has been said. For example there is the student who wanted Rogers to solve his problem for him—whether or not to tell his parents that he was failing in his college work.

STUDENT: Oh, I don't know if they're going to sort of condemn me. I think so, because that's what they've done in the past. They've said, "It's your fault. You don't have enough will power, you're not interested." That's the experience I've had in the past. I've been sort of telling them that I improved in this respect. I was—I was all right the first quarter. Well, I wasn't entirely all right, but I just got worse. (*Pause.*)

ROGERS: You feel that they'll be unsympathetic and they'll condemn you for your failures.

STUDENT: Well, my—I'm pretty sure my father will. My mother might not. He hasn't been—he doesn't experience these things; he just doesn't know what it's like. "Lack of ambition" is what he'd say. *(Pause.)*

ROGERS: You feel that he could never understand you?

STUDENT: No, I don't think he is—is capable of that, because I don't get along with him, don't at all!

ROGERS: You dislike him a good deal?

STUDENT: Yes, I did feel bitter toward him for a while and I've gone out of that stage, and now I don't feel bitter against him but I—I'm sort of ashamed. I think that that's it more than anything else, an experience of shame that he is my father ...[40]

Reflection of feelings communicates to the client that whatever his feelings and behavior are or have been, no matter how troubling or frightening or socially disapproved of, he is understood and still accepted as a worthy human being by the therapist. This kind of acceptance enabled Mike, a teenage boy, to share his feelings about his stepfather, while talking to Rogers, for the first time, before a large audience of high school counselors:

ROGERS: But, uh, part of what really makes for difficulty is the fact that your relationship with your stepfather is not completely rosy.

MIKE: M-hm. Let's just put it this way: I hate him and he hates me, and it's that way.

ROGERS: *You really* hate him and you feel he really hates you.

MIKE: Well *(thinking about it),* I don't know if he hates me or not, but I know one thing. I don't like him whatsoever.

ROGERS: M-hm. You can't speak for sure about his feelings, cause only he knows exactly what those are; but as far as you're concerned ...

MIKE: He knows how I feel about him.

ROGERS: You don't have any use for him.

MIKE: Not whatsoever ... And that's been for about eight years now.

ROGERS: So, for about eight years, you've lived with a person whom you have no respect for and really hate.

MIKE: Oh, I respect him ...

ROGERS: *(simultaneously)* Oh, I got that wrong.

MIKE: ... I don't have to but I do. But I don't love him. I hate him. I can't stand him.

ROGERS: There are certain things you respect him for, but that doesn't alter the fact that you definitely hate him and don't love him.

MIKE: That's the truth. I respect anybody if they have bravery and courage and he does. And though I respect him—I don't like him.[41]

Rogers often used the expression "clarification" of feelings along with "reflection." The two previous examples illustrate this, when the student says, "Well, my … I'm pretty sure my father will. My mother might not." and Mike says, "Oh, I respect him … But I don't love him." In both cases, the young men, in responding to the therapist's reflection, modify more explicitly their previous expression of their feelings. In the process they become a bit clearer about and see more vividly what their own feelings are. It is as though they are looking into a psychological mirror which the therapist holds up for them to view themselves. They might have some previous understanding of their feelings, but the mirror helps them see more clearly, and in an accepting context.

The potency of this method is apparent in a brief but moving exchange between Ernest (E) and Virginia Axline, his teacher-therapist (T), one of Rogers' students at Ohio State. Ernest is six years old, very insecure because of earlier events in his young life, and unable for psychological reasons to take food orally. He must be fed intravenously. He cannot even swallow water without regurgitating it. Ernest and his teacher, on the first day of school, are watching the other children gleefully drinking from the water fountain, the "bubbler," which obviously fascinates them all.

E. It looks like fun.

T. You think it would be fun to drink from it, too.

E. (*Nods agreement*) But I can't.

T. *You* don't think you could drink it.

E. It looks like fun.

T. You don't think you could drink it, but still you would like to.

E. I'd like to try.

T. You want to try it.

E. I used to take a drink from one of those things when I was in the hospital. I don't drink now.

T. You remember what fun it was (E. *grins and goes over to the drinking fountain.*)

E. It might not stay down.

T. *You* think it might not stay down, but you still want to try. (E. *nods his head. He takes the handle and turns it up too high and jumps back.*)

E. It's a lot of water.

T. It looks like a lot of water to you.

E. I'll drown myself. (*He takes a drink, glances at the teacher, grins broadly.*) It stayed down!

T. Yes. It stayed down. (*He drinks again.*)

E. It stays down. (*He seems quite delighted.*) [42]

What was significant to Rogers in this dialogue was how the teacher showed "an accepting, non-argumentative, non-coercive attitude, being just as ready to accept his discouraged and fearful attitudes as his courageous ones. Untrained workers are prone to persuade—'I'm sure you can take a drink'—or to be supportive—'I'll help you and then it won't be so hard'—or to bring pressure to bear—'You want to be a big boy like the others, don't you.' It takes restraint and a therapeutic point of view to let the child know that he is accepted for what he is, not for what he is not."[43]

Clients often try to express the usefulness of this approach for them. An adolescent girl once told Rogers, "You're like a balance wheel … It's almost as if I were talking to myself, but with someone listening and trying to think on it … What you do is let a person talk and put in comments that keep it going instead of stewing in a circle … You're someone to blow off steam to and to talk to so I can make up my mind."[44]

Not only does reflection and clarification of feelings help the client see himself more objectively, it also helps him accept himself as he is, which gives him a firmer foundation on which to grow. Implicit in the process is the growing attitude in the client who feels, in effect, "Well, I'm saying all these terrible things about myself and showing myself to be a deeply troubled, confused, perhaps even despicable person; yet here this other person is listening to me, understanding what I'm trying to say, doesn't seem shocked by anything I say, doesn't approve or disapprove, but gives me the feeling that I'm not so bad or abnormal or crazy. Well, then maybe it's true. Maybe I'm not such a bad, unhealthy person. Maybe I have more value than I give myself credit for. Maybe I shouldn't put myself down all the time and believe all the negative things people tell me about myself. Maybe if I stay with this, I'll learn more about myself and more about how to solve my problems."

Thus the therapist, through her attitude of acceptance and her skill in reflecting and clarifying feelings enables the client to move naturally into the second phase of therapy, that of "insight." As he accepts himself more easily and recognizes his feelings and the facts about himself more clearly, the client soon begins to make connections between the separate feelings and facts. "To see new relationships of cause and effect, to gain new understanding of the meaning which behavior symptoms have had, to understand the patterning of one's behavior—such learnings constitute insight," wrote Rogers.[45] For example, "one graduate student says with feeling, 'I'm really just a spoiled brat, but I do want to be normal. I wouldn't let anyone else say that of me, but it's true.' A husband says, 'I know now why I feel mean toward my wife when she's sick, even though I don't want to feel that way. It's because my mother predicted when I married her that I'd always be saddled with a sick wife.'"[46] "A mother gradually recognizes her own responsibility for the poor relationship with her son. As her counselor described it, "One of the things that she brought up was that he seems to want attention, but that the methods he uses get negative attention. After we had talked a little bit about that she said, 'Perhaps what would do him most good would be for him to have some affection and love and consideration entirely apart from any correcting. Now, I guess we've been so busy correcting him that we haven't had time to do anything else.'"[47]

How does insight develop? What does the therapist do to promote it? Rogers wrote, "The primary technique which leads to insight on the part of the client is one that demands the utmost in self-restraint on the counselor's part, rather than the utmost in action … The primary technique is to encourage the expression of attitudes and feelings … until insightful understanding appears spontaneously … To recognize that insight is an experience which is achieved, not an experience which can be imposed, is an important step in progress for the counselor."[48]

As the client gains increasing insight into his patterns of feeling and behavior, he gradually begins to enter the third major phase of therapy, that of "positive actions resulting from insight." A small, scared boy takes a drink from a water fountain. A man brings flowers to his sick wife whom he has resented. A mother changes her way of disciplining her son. The actions may be small ones, but terribly important as symbolic, self-initiated first steps in a lifelong process of psychological growth. "In actual counseling practice," Rogers wrote, "such positive steps are almost invariable concomitants of insight."[49]

At this point, therapy begins moving rapidly toward its conclusion. With the new positive actions the client takes outside the therapy comes further insight which, in turn, leads to still newer, more independent action. There comes a time when he begins to wonder aloud whether he isn't about ready to end the interviews. The therapist, by reflecting and clarifying these feelings, allows the client to work through his ambivalence about ending therapy. When the client feels ready, he terminates the relationship. However, "it is not expected that his problems will all be solved through counseling, nor is this assumed to be a desirable goal. Satisfying living consists, not in a life without problems, but in life with a unified purpose and a basic self-confidence which gives satisfaction in the continual attack upon problems."[50] Rogers emphasized this point. Describing the ending of therapy with a teenage girl, he wrote, "She has not achieved complete insight into her behavior, nor has this ever been the goal of counseling. She has achieved what might be called a 'working insight,' sufficient to enable her to meet her present problems, and to make continued growth inevitable."[51]

This was nondirective counseling. "Release," "catharsis," "acceptance," "reflection and clarification of feelings," "insight"—all these terms have become a routine part of most psychologists' vocabularies, as well as those of many laypersons. But what, if anything, was new with Rogers? As he pointed out himself, release or catharsis had long been used as a therapeutic tool[52]—for example, in Greek drama, in the confessional of the Catholic church, later in psychoanalysis, and still later in the field of play therapy from which he had learned a great deal. Neither did he introduce the concept of acceptance, nor the technique of recognizing, reflecting, and clarifying feelings, nor the practice of refraining from directing the client in his life. All these had been used often by the Rankian school and by other individual therapists of different schools. Insight too, was a widely used word in psychiatry, psychoanalysis and psychology, although it had many different meanings attached to it. It was not by introducing new concepts, then, that Rogers made his initial mark on the field of counseling and psychotherapy. What, then?

I would suggest that Rogers' contribution lay not in the uniqueness of any particular concept or technique, but in his extreme and systematic approach to therapy. In effect he took many of the newer concepts and practices in therapy and built them into an organized system which was more extreme than any of his recent predecessors or contemporaries.[53] To appreciate his radical approach, one might make some comparisons between Rogers and his teachers in the Rankian school. The following is an excerpt from the third interview that Jessie Taft conducted with a child named Helen.

Helen is drawing a picture of a lady holding an umbrella: "That's you," she says laughingly.
"Helen, were you mad at me last week?"
"No."
"Weren't you mad just a little? I should have been in your place—because I wouldn't let you take the crayons home."
"I wasn't mad. I like to come here to draw."[54]

Later in the same interview, Helen reiterates, "I like to come," and Taft responds, "Yes, I know you do, but you may feel differently some day."

Or, as Taft describes the social worker's fourth interview with a boy named Jackie:

He goes over to the steam pipes which he had found hot before, and shows extreme caution and fear. Can hardly bring himself to touch the pipe which burned him. Finally does so after much effort and finds it cold.
"You decided to stay home on Thursday, didn't you, Jack?"
"Yes." No further comment. "It's hot here."[55]

Again with Jackie:

> He runs out quickly to see if the broom is there. When he comes back the story
> has grown. "We took the broom away from her and chased her. She was going to
> chase us, but we chased her."
> "And that's what you'll be doing to me some day. I see I have to look out."[56]

Clearly Dr. Taft is trying to help the children express their feelings and is communicating that feelings of anger, of avoidance, and of the eventual desire to end the relationship are all acceptable. However, she is also responding to feelings which the children probably hold but have not yet verbalized or which she expects the children will come to hold in the future. In Rogers' view, while the reflection of unexpressed feelings might sometimes prove helpful, it is a highly dangerous technique which usually sidetracks the interview—either because the therapist cannot really know what the client is feeling and might perceive it incorrectly, or because even when the therapist is correct in reflecting the unexpressed feeling, the client often becomes resistant, since he is not yet emotionally ready to recognize the feeling on his own.[57] In recognizing and reflecting unexpressed feelings, the therapist attempts to hasten the process of therapy, but, in fact, often retards it by driving the client into a stance of defensiveness. The therapist, said Rogers, should avoid "the verbal recognition of repressed attitudes which the client has not yet been able to express."[58]

None of Rogers' predecessors had gone to this extreme. How would therapy move forward if the therapist refrained totally from introducing new data in the form of questions, comments, or reflections of feeling designed to delve beyond the surface and let the client see his previously hidden feelings? Rogers was not troubled by this. When the client was ready to acknowledge his deeper feelings, he would. Probing is more than likely to produce resistance. Provide total acceptance and the accurate reflection of feelings, and the therapy will move forward on its own. Speaking with increasing authority, he often reminded his readers that "in this type of situation, insight and self-understanding come bubbling through spontaneously. Unless one has thus watched insight develop, it is difficult to believe that individuals can recognize themselves and their patterns so effectively."[59]

But what about interpretation? Could this not hasten insight? The therapist has spent years studying the dynamics of personality. Does she throw all this knowledge out the window and merely reflect the client's feelings? Admittedly even Freud recognized that interpretation could produce resistance rather than insight, if it were ill-timed; but still he advocated interpretation, as long as it was well-timed and offered in a way likely to be accepted by the patient. Here, again, Rogers went to the extreme, advocating that the counselor refrain entirely from any interpretation. He wrote, "The counselor will do well to refrain ... from giving interpretations of the client's behavior, the elements of which are based,

121

not on the client's expressed feelings, but on the counselor's judgment of the situation."[60] Even if the interpretation were accurate and accepted, it would still be more valuable to allow the client to achieve it on his own, thought Rogers.

He did make one exception. "When the interpretation is based entirely upon statements which the client has made, and when the interpretation is merely a clarification of what the client has already perceived for himself, this type of approach can be successful."[61] An example of this comes in an interview Rogers conducted with a teenage girl, Barbara, who is explaining,

> "Before all this, I believed in controlling oneself, in complete mastery of my mind and feeling." Counselor discussed this, saying that what she was gradually learning was that there was no such thing as complete control of mind and feeling; that it was rather hard for her to recognize that the part she was shutting out was a part of herself. She said, "You know that motto, 'Be yourself.' I used to hear that, and I couldn't understand it. I didn't think that I wanted to be myself, or that I knew what it meant to be yourself. I guess I have acted that way so long that I don't quite know how to be myself."[62]

The counselor's interpretation inserts no new ideas or attitudes into the therapy. In effect, it is not an interpretation at all, but a reflection and clarification of several attitudes Barbara has expressed earlier. Thus Rogers' position remains an extreme one: no interpretations, unless the client has already achieved the insight on his or her own.

In both encouraging release and furthering insight, then, Rogers' client-centered therapist was more nondirective than any other writer had ever advocated and illustrated. What about the third phase of therapy—the positive actions which result from insight? Surely the therapist takes some more active stand here—suggesting alternatives, pointing out possible consequences of certain actions, asking clarifying questions that would help the client think through his situation and choices. Surely she does more than continue to accept, reflect and clarify feelings. On the contrary, Rogers maintained his extreme position, writing that "social behavior originates in a genuine desire to be social ... mature behavior grows out of the desire to be grown up ... affectionate behavior can come only from feelings of affection. We cannot *make* people social, or mature, or affectionate. We can, however, help parent and child to see themselves more clearly, to explore their own purposes more deeply, and to make a more clear-cut conscious choice as to the direction they wish to take and the behavior which is in accord with their own deepest purposes."[63]

But even when a person knows his deepest purposes, does that necessarily mean he will act on them? Just because people know what is right or know what they want does not mean they are going to act accordingly, does it? Yes, said Rogers. If the insight is real insight and not insight imposed by the therapist, then positive actions based on the insight are almost inevitable. They may not be fully mature actions, but they are first steps which are highly significant for the client.

Still, all this assumes that we operate rationally, that we can behave in more mature ways simply because we know it would be better for us. Even Rogers admitted that the neurotic person will often cling to his symptoms and, "because he is unhappy and threatened by others or by circumstance, he cannot consider clearly or objectively the alternative courses of action which may offer less in the way of immediate gratification, but more in long-term satisfactions. Like Hamlet he finds that the situation 'puzzles the will | And makes us rather bear those ills we have | Than fly to others that we know not of.'"[64]

Why should a client give up the security and satisfactions that his neuroses have provided for so long? Why take that leap into the unknown? Again because of insight. "When the neurotic sees clearly the choice between his present satisfactions and the satisfactions of adult behavior, he tends to prefer the latter."[65] Why? Here Rogers borrowed a concept from the Rankians, and mentioned, only in passing, a type of "creative will," which acts upon the situation in a similar way to "the choice exercised by the child who decides to forego the immediate ice-cream cone in order to save his nickels for the prized roller skates. He chooses the course which gives him the greater satisfaction, even though that satisfaction is delayed."[66] And so the client makes his own positive choices as he more clearly sees himself and his situation. (A decade later Rogers' would use the concept of the "actualizing tendency" to explain the human motivation toward growth and change.)

With each chapter of *Counseling and Psychotherapy* the system in Rogers' therapy emerged with cumulative clarity. With all his ambivalences, the client wants to grow, wants to mature, wants to face his problems and work them through. Accept and clarify his initial expressions of feeling, and a fuller, deeper expression of feelings will follow. Accept and clarify these and insight will spontaneously occur. Accept and clarify these insights, and the client will begin to take positive actions in his life, based on his insight. Accept and clarify the meaning the client sees in his positive actions, and at some point, when he feels enough self-acceptance, self-understanding, and confidence in his ability to continue to deal with his own problems, he will end the relationship.

"Clinically," Rogers wrote, "we know that sometimes this process is relatively shallow, involving primarily a fresh reorientation to an immediate problem, and in other instances so deep as to involve a complete reorientation of personality. It is recognizably the same process whether it involves a girl who is unhappy in a dormitory, and is able in three interviews to see something of her childishness and dependence, and to take steps in a mature direction, or whether it involves a young man who is on the edge of a schizophrenic break, and who in thirty interviews works out deep insights in relation to his desire for his father's death, and his possessive and incestuous impulses toward his mother, and who not only takes new steps but rebuilds his whole personality in the process. Whether shallow or deep, it is basically the same."[67]

With this assertion, both implicit and explicit throughout the book, *Counseling and Psychotherapy* made still another radical contribution to the helping professions. It blurred the boundary between counseling and psychotherapy. Before Rogers, it was assumed that "counseling" applied to milder problems of adjustment or career guidance, while "psychotherapy" was needed for more deep-seated psychological problems. *Counseling and Psychotherapy* suggested that not only the same term, *client*, but the same nondirective method of helping could be applied to all problems along the adjustment continuum. Therefore, someone trained in the practice of counseling could work with clients with anything from academic to vocational to social adjustment to mental health problems. This then-radical proposition has been debated ever since—by professionals, state legislatures and insurance companies. Psychiatrists, psychologists, psychotherapists, psychoanalysts, psychiatric nurses, social workers, mental health counselors, community counselors, school counselors, pastoral counselors, music and art therapists, and other helping professionals have struggled vigorously to extend or protect their prerogatives to be certified, licensed, credentialed, regulated or unregulated practitioners of counseling and psychotherapy. While the debate is far from settled, Rogers redrew the battle lines in 1942 by making the case that the counseling profession deserved a level of parity with other psychological helping professions. Henceforth, as the very title *Counseling and Psychotherapy* implied, Rogers used the two terms more or less interchangeably (as I do in this volume).

The First Research

It was incredibly simple, yet profound in its ramifications. For several years Rogers had been saying that psychotherapy was not an intuitive art, but a scientific endeavor which could be described and measured. Now he had described it in terms and with examples so concrete that any therapeutic interview could be evaluated in terms of his nondirective model. In fact he and his students began doing just that, measuring various aspects of therapy.[68] In the chapter blatantly titled "The Directive Versus the Non-Directive Approach," Rogers described the first pieces of data they had gathered when the two types of therapists were studied. In one chart he listed the techniques most frequently used by the directive and nondirective groups of counselors. Typical directive counselor techniques were: asking highly specific questions, explaining, discussing, giving information, indicating topics of conversation, proposing client activities, and so on. The most frequent nondirective counselor techniques were: recognizing the client's feelings or attitudes, and recognizing or interpreting feelings or attitudes expressed by general demeanor, specific behavior, or earlier statements. Although each group sometimes used techniques more typical of the other, Rogers pointed out, "the fundamental contrast is emphasis, the directive group stressing those techniques which control the interview and move the client toward a counselor chosen goal, the nondirective group stressing those means which cause the client to be more conscious of his own attitudes and feeling, with a consequent increase in insight and self-understanding."[69]

In a sentence which undoubtedly made many therapists distinctly uncomfortable, he pointed out how, in one small study, "the directive counselors used on the average almost six times as many words as the nondirective."[70] He also pointed out how their studies showed that "most counselors are far more directive than they suppose."[71]

Although this initial research proved nothing about the relative effectiveness of the two types of therapy, it did serve to focus attention, more specifically than ever before, on the methods used in therapy. Vague concepts like "accepting" and "directiveness" were given concrete meaning in therapists' specific behaviors. The therapist responses could then be correlated with the subsequent client responses. The research of one student, William Snyder, enabled Rogers to write that the therapist's asking questions, giving information and advice, persuading and pointing out, neither encouraged release nor led to real insight by the client.[72] Simple acceptance and the recognition and clarification of feelings did. By classifying almost 10,000 counselor and client responses, in thirteen interviews with six clients and four different counselors, Snyder showed how acceptance by the counselor was followed by insight by the client, with a marked degree of regularity.

As rudimentary as these first research efforts were, they provided another level of credibility to *Counseling and Psychotherapy*. Here was an author willing to put some of his assumptions to a test. At a time when empirical, quantitative research on psychotherapy was virtually unheard of, Rogers and his students' early studies represented a significant innovation in the field. Thus Germain Lietaer credited Rogers with being "the founder of process research ... I mean he was the first who made tape recordings and then transcripts and then did lots of studies on it ... Until then process was a black box. If there was any research at all, it was mainly outcome research."[73] Rogers pioneered the study of *the process* of psychotherapy, and in the coming years would take both process *and* outcome research to another level.

Rogers, then, had introduced a new model of therapy—new not in concepts or techniques, but in its collection of already existing ideas and practices organized into a clear, consistent, and extreme system of thought and practice. He had supported his new model with page after page of examples based on his own experience, with forceful polemical writing and with the smallest beginnings of empirical research. Still, I wonder whether *Counseling and Psychotherapy* would have received nearly the attention it did were it not for still another innovation— "The Case of Herbert Bryan."

Recording Therapy—The Case of Herbert Bryan

In 1940 complete transcripts of actual therapy cases were not available. Jessie Taft presented two complete child therapy cases in her 1933 book which so influenced Rogers, but these were compiled from the therapist's or observer's notes and were therefore incomplete and subject to the observer's conscious or unconscious selection bias.[74] In 1929 Earl F. Zinn became the first person to actually record psychotherapy using a system developed by the Dictaphone Corporation employing wax cylinders. Later as assistant professor of psychiatry at the Yale University Medical School, he recorded a number of psychoanalytic interviews with different patients and in 1935 completed the extraordinary feat of recording a complete psychoanalysis of some 425 hours; but although transcribed, it was never published or made widely available.[75] Few people knew of its existence. Beginning in 1930 Harold Lasswell also experimented with recording psychoanalysis, and Percival Symonds made recordings of counseling interviews around 1938 but did not publish them, or only published excerpts. Apparently Rogers was unaware of these other pioneers and wrote in *The Clinical Treatment of the Problem Child* in 1939 that "a verbatim record of intensive psychotherapy with one child, giving in full all the conversation of both child and therapist, would be a new and valuable contribution."[76]

In Rochester he thought he might try to make that contribution himself. In 1938 Virginia Lewis of the Rochester Guidance Center staff was conducting some interviews in the clinic, and Rogers and the others set up some borrowed recording equipment—a conventional mandrel-type Dictaphone—in the office next door, concealing the microphone in the lamp by the counselor's desk. They recorded the first interview, then eagerly gathered around the phonograph to hear what they expected would be a landmark in the history of psychotherapy. What they did hear was an excellent reproduction of streetcar rumblings, automobile traffic, and street noise, and Rogers abandoned the whole idea for the time being.[77]

In 1940 Bernard Covner, one of Rogers' graduate students at Ohio State, reminded him of what he had written in *Problem Child* and informed him that he was a radio ham with some skills in electronics. Covner went out and priced the needed equipment, but Rogers did not follow up initially. "Then one day Rogers called me at home, saying that the department's budget had $150 left that had to be spent that day, and since I knew of purchasable equipment he would like to see it."[78] They purchased the phonographic recording equipment that day, along with a year's supply of phonograph discs and styli. Thanks to Rogers' colleague Frank Robinson, Ohio State already had observation rooms that were used to observe undergraduate seniors help freshman with study skills and counsel them on personal and social adjustment problems.[79] The students' voices could be heard but there was no means for recording them until now. The

University installed microphone cable lines from three interviewing rooms to a secret recording room.[80] Covner obtained from his father's store enough old drapes and rugs to sound-treat the recording rooms, and then set up the whole operation.[81] They were in business. The 78-rpm discs were set up on two recording machines, so while one record was being turned or removed, the other machine could begin recording, without missing a word. This had to be done about every three minutes. Meanwhile it was necessary to continually clean off the shavings which the stylus cut into the recording discs.

Within a few months about eight hundred record faces, or fifty hours of actual interviewing, were recorded in this manner and then laboriously transcribed. At first they disguised the presence of the microphone and neither informed the clients nor requested their consent, fearing that clients might not give their permission and assuming that clients' knowledge of the recording would alter the session dynamics. (This was long before universities developed institutional review boards for the protection of human subjects of research.) Soon they recognized the ethical problems in this approach and obtained the clients' informed consent for doing the recordings and publishing the transcripts, with clients' names changed.[82] They were pleased to discover that most clients readily gave their permission for the recordings and that the session dynamics did not appear to be altered even when the microphone was visible in the counseling room.

The recordings and transcripts served several valuable purposes. First, they proved to be excellent case studies for Rogers' practicum with graduate students in training. Second, the recordings and transcripts enabled Rogers and his students to study certain therapeutic concepts in much more detail than before. For example, disagreeing with classical psychoanalysts, Rogers wrote, "In fact, study of our recordings has led us to new concepts of resistance in therapy. We have come to feel that resistance to the therapist is entirely due to too much probing, or too rapid interpretation on the part of the counselor and that it is neither a desirable nor a constructive part of therapy."[83] With their recordings he and his students could identify just when resistance first appeared, what the counselor had said to encourage it, and whether she increased or lessened the resistance in subsequent responses. For example, a boy is talking about his mother:

> Boy: She is a social worker, by the way. She drives everybody nuts talking about her clients all the time.
>
> Counselor: You feel that perhaps she pays more attention to them than to you?
>
> Boy: Well, I—ah—more or less. Oh, I don't know—it doesn't bother me or anything like that.[84]

Without the precise phonographic record, such an exchange would be unlikely to have been reported by the counselor. Third, the recordings furnished rich data for scientific research studies on psychotherapy, including many dissertations under Rogers' sponsorship. Finally, the verbatim transcripts of interviews could be used in articles and books as concrete examples of psychotherapy as actually practiced. In this last area Rogers made an historical contribution.

From among the 800 record sides came the last 170 pages of *Counseling and Psychotherapy*—"The Case of Herbert Bryan"—eight full interviews with a young man, constituting the first complete series of therapeutic interviews ever to be fully recorded, transcribed, and published. Never before had the field of psychotherapy had the opportunity to follow, word for word, complete with "U-hm's" and pauses, the full course of a therapy, from the first words the client uttered to the final good-byes. Never before had any therapist been willing and able to subject himself to that degree to the minute scrutiny of the entire profession, to hold himself up as an example to be praised, ridiculed or emulated. Never before had such a valuable tool, one which could furnish the raw data for innumerable scientific studies on psychotherapy, been placed so dramatically before the psychological community.

In the transcript of the case, before each counselor response, Rogers wrote the letter C and then a number. Thus, the counselor's first statement was prefixed with a C1 and his very last ("O.K. And good luck to you") with a C614. Likewise, an S, the traditional designation for the subject in an experiment, and a number preceded each client response. In this way Rogers, in commenting upon the interviews as they evolved, could refer to precise statements of the two parties.

One has to read several of these interviews—both the transcript and Rogers' running commentary on it—to appreciate fully the cumulative impact of this type of presentation upon the reader. Several of Rogers' comments on the first interview convey some of the flavor of "The Case of Herbert Bryan."

C1. The counselor by this very broad kind of opening question makes it easy for the client to discuss his problem in any way he wishes. Note that S1, 2, and 3 are all in response to this one question.

C4. Here is a moderately directive question limiting the client to a specified area for discussion. It might have been better for the counselor simply to recognize the material expressed, in some such statement as, "You've noticed a real change in these symptoms?"

C7. This counselor response is definitely helpful in bringing progress. It must already be evident to the counselor that these are psychological, not organic, sufferings. The usual reaction is to question, in some way, their validity. Any such implication would have thrown the client on the defensive and made him intent on proving that his pain was real. The counselor's recognition that he is describing real pain helps Mr. Bryan to feel that he is genuinely understood, and makes it possible for him to go ahead and tell of times when he is not suffering (S8).

C11, C12. Good instances of entirely non-directive responses which simply recognize the feeling being expressed, make conversation easy, and enable the client to continue to explore his attitudes.

C26. Why did the counselor interrupt here? This seems to be a quite unnecessary directive question breaking into the flow of feeling. It leads to brief client responses ending in a pause (S28), which the counselor has to break with another rather directive question. This in turn leads to a repetition of the symptoms originally described (S29), and it is only following this that a fresh start in recognition of feeling is made. This is a minor example of the way in which clumsy handling by the counselor can delay progress.

C40. This direct question is in line with the client's feeling, and in the rapid give and take of the interview we cannot expect perfection. Nevertheless, it is plain that a better response on the part of the counselor would have been, "You like to write, but this blocking keeps you from it." It often seems difficult to catch and bring into the open the ambivalent impulses.

C43, S43, C44. Adequate recognition of attitudes brings the flow of feeling around again to the same point which was poorly recognized at C18, C19. The phonographic recordings indicate that this frequently occurs. If the client expresses some attitude which has significance for him, and this is misunderstood or inadequately recognized by the counselor, the same attitude is likely to be expressed again later. Adequate recognition, on the other hand, tends to lead to further and deeper expression.

C46. Here the counselor makes a more complete and satisfactory attempt to define the type of help which the client can expect from counseling.

S46, S47. Is it because the counselor's remarks sound almost as though he were bringing the interview to a close that Mr. Bryan is able to reveal this highly significant feeling? Or is it merely that having revealed his superficial symptoms, he is now ready to recognize that they are to some extent symptoms that he wants? At any rate, in this one interview, he has gone through three levels of expression of his problems. At first they are described as pain, suffering, maladjustment. Then (S35) they are described as conflicting forces within himself. Now they are recognized as symptoms to which he can cling, in spite of his desire to change. This is actually the beginning of insight, a clearer degree of self-understanding.

C48. Fortunately the counselor recognizes and states clearly the ambivalent feeling which is being expressed. This enables the client further to express his feeling in what are the most significant items of this first interview. They show clear progress in exploration at more than a superficial level.

C53. Here, again, the counselor must have been tempted to agree or disagree. He wisely does neither, but merely clarifies the attitude that is being expressed.

C57. Here is the second blunder of the hour. The counselor departs from sound recognition of feeling. Instead of some such response as "You feel that someone else must start the ball rolling," he asks a direct question which goes deep into the client's situation. If Mr. Bryan were fully aware of why his "negative" side was in power, he would have little need of help. The counselor draws nothing but a confused and somewhat defensive answer (S57), and follows it with another direct question which endeavors to tie the client down to a specific situation, that of dancing (C58). The client makes a partial response, and then definitely retreats into a long philosophical statement (S59) which has no direct relation to his problems and is as far as possible from being specific ... This indicates how easily the course of constructive therapy can be diverted by errors which may not be recognized as errors at the time.

C79. The first portion of this conversation is helpful in that it defines the client's responsibility for the direction of the counseling interviews. In the last portion the counselor returns to the same direct question which delayed therapy before (C57) and unwisely tries to give this problem as a "homework assignment." This would seem to be the third blunder in the interview.

S79, S80, S81, S82. The client is determined to answer the counselor's questions at once. To some extent this represents insight. To some extent it is almost certainly an attempt to prolong the interview. The counselor has definitely to call a halt (C85).[85]

The "Case of Herbert Bryan" was a fitting summary for *Counseling and Psychotherapy*. The eight interviews with Herbert Bryan made all the preceding chapters come dramatically alive in what amounted to a "supervised internship" for all the counselors and psychologists reading along. What therapist could read these interviews, with Rogers' comments, and remain aloof? Vicariously each reader became the counselor of Herbert Bryan, wondering, "Now how would *I* respond at this point?" In fact Rogers advocated just that—that readers cover up the counselor's response, while reading, and formulate their own response before reading further. In critiquing the anonymous counselor in the case of Herbert Bryan, then, Rogers was critiquing all counselors; for all counselors, more or less frequently, do what this one counselor got praised or blamed by Rogers for doing.

Thus Rogers became the conscience of counselors and therapists across the country. In his nondirective approach every single statement or reaction of the therapist could be judged according to a set of criteria. Although there was hardly anything in his approach which could be described as his invention, nevertheless the extremity of his views, the clarity of his writing, and the concreteness of his examples—especially the case of Herbert Bryan—made Rogers, almost overnight, the foremost proponent of the "newer concepts in practice" in psychotherapy. Even personally he became the symbol of the nondirective counselor, for most readers soon realized that it was Rogers himself who was the counselor of Herbert Bryan. At the very end of the eighth interview, this exchange took place:

S598. You're sort of a pioneer in this, aren't you? Is this largely your own technique?

C599. Oh—I don't know. It seems to work, at any rate.

S599. I haven't kept up so much with the latest psychoanalytic techniques.

C600. Well, there certainly are many others. I think that a good many different people have been working toward somewhat the same point of view.

S600. Well, perhaps some day I can bring you a copy of my novel.

C601. (*Laugh*.) Right. I'd be delighted to get it. Well, now, you're feeling pretty confident in your ability to handle this. I would like to leave the notion of further contacts up to you …[86]

Implementing the Method

Readers of transcripts and, even more so, listeners and viewers of tapes and films where Rogers is the counselor often comment upon how deeply he seems to understand and accept the client and how sincerely and creatively he manages to communicate this understanding and acceptance to the client, as he reflects and clarifies feelings. Unfortunately not all counselors have this degree of acceptance, understanding, and skill. Consequently, while attempting to employ the deceptively simple method of reflecting feelings, many counselors unintentionally acted out a grotesque parody of the client-centered approach. Movements are often condemned because of the first people who jump on the bandwagon. One hears many anecdotes like the following:

> I once went to a Rogerian counselor. I started talking about my problems and all he did was repeat back, word for word, everything I said. I couldn't figure out who was the crazy one, him or me. I said, "I know that; that's what I just told you. " So he said, "You know that. That's what you just told me." After a while, I really started getting angry. So then he tells me I'm getting angry …

Certainly the nondirective approach is easy to satirize. Arthur Combs, then one of Rogers' doctoral students, recalls how "We became so nondirective that, if you had asked me in those days, 'What time is it?' I probably would have replied, 'You're wondering what time it is.'"[87] The best known satire of all, a favorite of Rogers' critics, originated some time in the early forties and goes something like this:

> It seems a client came into Dr. Rogers' office, on the thirty-fourth floor, and said, "Dr. Rogers, I've been feeling awfully depressed lately." "Oh, you've been feeling very depressed lately?"
>
> "Yes, I've even seriously been considering suicide."

"You feel you might like to kill yourself?"

"Yes, in fact, I'm going to walk over to the window here."

"U-hm. You're walking over to the window there."

"Yes, I'm opening up the window, Dr. Rogers."

"I see. You're opening the window."

"I'm about to jump."

"U-hm. You're about to jump."

"Here I goooo. . . ." *(He jumps.)*

"There you go."

A loud crash is heard below. Dr. Rogers walks over to the office window, looks down, and says, "SPLAT!"

Of course Rogers never lost any patients in this manner. His experience taught him that adequate recognition of self-destructive attitudes mitigated a client's desire to do himself harm. He also believed that definite limits preventing physical violence should be a part of therapy. As he told one interviewer years later, when she began to ask him about the often-repeated anecdote, "I *know* the story. My answer, for once and for all time, is that I would not have let him jump out the window."[88]

Nevertheless there was one passage in *Counseling and Psychotherapy* which probably helped the suicide anecdote to spread. It was his reference to "Jessie Taft's story of a little girl who persisted in hanging farther and farther out of the window to test out the situation to the utmost. Dr. Taft was rightly reluctant to put a limit to this activity, which did not directly affect the rights of others. When she made it plain that the responsibility rested with the child and that she might fall if she wanted to, the youngster became cautious."[89]

Even had this paragraph not appeared, the anecdote, no doubt, would have been created and repeated anyway. For, as in all satire, the anecdote merely carried the reality to an absurd extreme, and the reality here was Rogers' great emphasis on *technique* in nondirective therapy. Technique was the thing. Just as free association was the primary technique for the classical psychoanalyst, reflection of feelings was the primary technique to Rogers, the key to the whole process, the source of all growth in nondirective therapy. Thus, when Rogers' graduate students would meet in their practicum and listen to the phonographic recordings, Rogers would lift the needle after each client response and ask the students how they would respond at that point.[90] Then he would offer his own response, not as the definitive answer, but as his own judgment. And so they would spend hour upon hour sharpening their technique. Art Combs said, "we all thought it's the method that made the difference, so we were *practicing* the method."[91] Likewise, the initial research he sponsored centered almost exclusively on counselor techniques.

With this kind of emphasis it should not be surprising that counselors came to think of counseling merely as the reflection of feelings. If one could learn this simple technique, he or she could be a counselor, or so it seemed. True, Rogers also wrote that the counselor "creates a bond characterized by warmth, interest, responsiveness …" is "sensitive to human relationships," and has a "deep-seated respect for the child's integrity";[92] but these attitudinal elements were easily overlooked because of the preoccupation with technique. And the technique was not as easy as it seemed. Again, one has almost to hear tapes of Rogers counseling clients to appreciate the subtle yet profound difference between reflections of feeling which convey genuine acceptance and a sincere desire to understand as opposed to those reflections of feelings which come off as rote, distant, and superfluous responses. Rogers' comments were almost always tentative, conveying, "Have I understood you? Do I have it just the way you feel it, neither more nor less? Do you feel I'm really with you?" He was also very imaginative in the way he reflected feelings, as shown by how he put a tense young student at ease during a first interview, while also conveying understanding and acceptance:

> ROGERS: And you do feel, I take it, that this thing bothers you most in a social situation?
> STUDENT: Yes, whenever I'm with people.
> ROGERS: You wouldn't be bothered if you were a hermit?
> STUDENT: *(Laugh.) No,* but I don't want to be.
> ROGERS: I understand.[93]

Or in interviewing a teenage boy, for the first time, before a large group of counselors:

> MIKE: Well, my outlook on life isn't dim, but it's not the shiniest thing in the world either.
> ROGERS: It's about 15 watt, maybe, or something? Right?
> MIKE: Well, maybe 75.
> ROGERS: *(Surprised.)* Oh, 75 … [94]

Or in working with a woman who was describing her growing overdependence on her mother:

> WOMAN: I accepted what she did for me and I just took it for granted, and it made me more reliant on her, really.
> ROGERS: You stood on her two feet.[95]

He found many ways to convey his sincerity and humanness to clients—even sometimes by blatantly violating his own principles of good counseling, as in the fourth interview with Herbert Bryan:

> S337. I used to have the idea that there was perhaps one significant event which I had repressed to the subconscious which I needed to call up from the subconscious for my therapy. But I see now that the—no matter what the origin is, these things after all operate under present circumstances, and that it's the present operational function which is—which does have the true significance.
>
> C337. I'm tempted to say—you're damn right. M-hm. I think so ...[96]

Initial Impact

The publication of *Counseling and Psychotherapy* received a mixed reception. On the one hand came increasing fame for its author. The term "Rogerian" came to describe, for many, a whole new orientation toward psychotherapy and counseling. He was elected to offices in several prestigious professional organizations, an increasing number of graduate students transferred from other professors to his sponsorship or came to Columbus to study with him, and he received numerous requests for speeches and workshops. The psychological establishment, on the other hand, mostly ignored the book. It was not even reviewed in any major journal of the psychological or psychiatric profession. Two reactions to the nondirective approach that Rogers often heard, and often from the same person, were, "It would be impossible to conduct psychotherapy in this way, and besides we're doing just this already."[97] The first part reflected the widely held belief that nondirective counseling was only surface therapy, too superficial to lead to any significant, long-term adjustment. The second part reflected the defensiveness which many therapists were then starting to feel about being directive, after Rogers had so vigorously associated directiveness with being authoritarian, outdated, and non-helpful. As one textbook described it, "Gradually psychologists began to realize that merely advising parents and children was not altogether effective. After Rogers introduced the concept and technique of client-centered counseling and demonstrated its effectiveness, direct advice giving became a bugaboo in many therapeutic circles."[98]

The reaction to this book would prove to be rather typical in Rogers' career. His work seemed to move individuals, rather than systems or establishments. Within a few years hundreds, even thousands of students would be flocking from around the country to attend his courses and take his ideas back home with them. But psychology departments, medical schools, and professional journals did their best to ignore or minimize his contribution. Arthur Combs, one of Rogers' first graduate students at Ohio State and later a leading psychologist-educator in his own right, recalled with some amazement the atmosphere in the established profession at that time.

> It is really very hard to believe the degree of rejection of Rogers and his concepts which dogged his steps in the early days. Here he was, advocating an approach to counseling and psychotherapy which was as American as apple pie, full of hope and belief in the democratic ideal. Here he was also, a product of American psychology operating at a period when American psychology was trying to be scientific with a capital S, and coming out foursquare for the necessity of applying research methods to psychotherapy practice to such an extent that during the '40s and '50s he and his students turned out more research on psychotherapy than had ever before existed. Despite all this, American psychologists by the thousands were completely enamored of psychoanalysis, a European product, contrary to most orthodox American psychology, based on the vaguest kinds of concepts and with almost a complete disdain for subjecting itself to the rigors of careful research. Looking at the degree of acceptance these points of view have now achieved, it is hard to believe that in those days humanists had practically to fight for their professional lives.[99]

As Rogers explained it at the time, "One might suppose that there would be a generally favorable reaction to this discovery [that the client could take charge of his own growth], since it amounts in effect to tapping great reservoirs of hitherto little-used energy. Quite the contrary is true, however, in professional groups. There is no other aspect of client-centered therapy which comes under such vigorous attack. It seems to be genuinely disturbing to many professional people to entertain the thought that this client upon whom they have been exercising their professional skill actually knows more about his inner psychological self than they can possibly know, and that he possesses constructive strengths which make the constructive push by the therapist seem puny indeed by comparison."[100]

Yet in spite of the resistance in the established psychological, psychoanalytical and psychiatric communities, Rogers' approach to counseling soon caught on. Writing on the history of psychotherapy, Vandenbos, Cummings and Deleon pointed out that "To the general public, psychotherapy was still a little known clinical activity in 1940. To the extent that it was known, psychotherapy was synonymous with psychoanalysis in the public mind. Between 1940 and 1959, the American public would begin to learn about (and use) psychotherapy."[101] A number of economic and environmental influences contributed to the growing "recognition of mental health and illness during the period from 1940–1959" and the growth of psychotherapy. These included the recognition of mental health needs resulting from World War II, the Veterans Administration's need for counselors and therapists, the expansion of health insurance as an employment benefit, and the establishment of the National Institute of Mental Health. "These events contributed to the expansion of training opportunities in psychotherapy, and they stimulated greater availability and use of psychotherapy by the general public." Thus, they wrote, "Given the context of the time, it was understandable that client-centered therapy as conceptualized by Carl Rogers ... became the dominant force in the university counseling centers ... it was not pathology-oriented and was suited to the intelligent, relatively normal problems of the college student. The basic concept was that an individual possesses a self-actualizing tendency that promotes health and growth. The psychotherapist facilitated the removal of emotional blocks or impediments to growth and promoted maturation, self-cure, and the assimilation of new experiences."

Beyond college counseling centers, Rogers' nondirective counseling informed and elevated the work of professional, semi-professional and paraprofessional counselors in a wide variety of settings, including school counselors, pastoral counselors, and mental health counselors and therapists in many helping professions. Until this time, "counseling" had many different meanings. That would continue, but with *Counseling and Psychotherapy*, counseling came to have a particular meaning which was common across its various settings and applications. Thus most introductory counseling textbooks today credit Carl Rogers with virtually founding the professional counseling movement in the early 1940s.[102] Gladding described how, "three major events in the 1940s radically shaped the practice of counseling: the theory of Carl Rogers, World War II, and government's involvement in counseling after the war."[103] Capuzzi and Gross wrote, "There seems little doubt that Carl R. Rogers, his ideas, and his disciples affected counseling from its core outward."[104]

Working with Graduate Students

The disciples—a term Rogers, then and later, would have hated—were just beginning. With his new book Rogers' stock among the graduate students at Ohio State rose even higher than before, with a corresponding loss of popularity among many of his colleagues. As Combs recalled, "Rogers' position on the campus was often one of being intensely admired, sought out and respected outside the Psychology Department, while in the Psychology Department he was often ignored, snubbed, or attacked in petty ways ... The students who were there at Ohio State at the time didn't help matters much ... I can remember we'd go around and talk about 'the Bible.' We thought this was pretty funny, you know, whenever we'd mention 'the Bible,' we'd raise our eyes to the sky and bow a few times. Well, the faculty didn't think that was particularly funny ... I'm sure he was cursed with his students."[105]

Rogers saw his graduate students quite differently. They provided his most stimulating experiences at the University—in the formal classroom, in the clinic, or in informal sessions and meetings. Several became his and Helen's lifelong friends. William Snyder remembered how "students were completely charmed and captivated by this man who was so warm and understanding and approachable, who had significant new, good ideas to share. Most of us saw him very much as an older brother, possibly a father surrogate … I asked to be reassigned from a previous advisor, whom I considered to be an old, decrepit mossback, compared to the young, vigorous, and really brilliant Carl. The fact that twenty-five or so of us asked to make such a transfer did not increase his popularity with the faculty. As a matter of fact Carl was assigned a stuffy little office, and originally you had to get into it by walking through another faculty member's office."[106] (He insisted on a private entrance, and got it.)[107]

Consistent with his nondirective approach to psychotherapy he was quite nondirective or student-centered in his teaching approach. "He believed in things like letting students grade themselves, if you bothered grading them at all," said Snyder.[108] As Father Charles Curran recalled, "He seemed to permeate the atmosphere around him with a genuine respect for graduate students as mature adults, equal to himself. He never assumed any prerogative of professional condescension or professorial eminence; yet at no time did he lose any position of dignity or authority. There always was about him a quiet dignity. And when he needed to assert his authority as a professor of a class or in the graduate school, he certainly seemed to me to do it with directness and unequivocal responsibility. At no point, however, did this clear image of himself assume tones of condescension or any indignity for the graduate student."[109]

On one occasion, for example, Curran and several other Catholic priests had quite a confrontation with Rogers on several issues. Since they knew of Helen's involvement in Planned Parenthood, and Carl's support for it, birth control was one of the liveliest topics discussed.[110] Curran described the scene:

I and some other graduate students associated with me decided to invite Carl to a private dinner and to confront him on some issues where we felt he was not consistent with his own ideas, and certainly in some ways not consistent with our thinking. At some point in the evening, the confrontation got quite hot, and very open things were said that, as I thought about it then and afterward, was a great act of trust on the part of this group of graduate students toward Carl. I knew of no professor then—and I've met few since that I believe could have taken as genuinely and as simply as Carl did the rough and somewhat impolite things that were said. And I remember afterwards thinking that he could show some kind of genuine resentment of this and even indicate it in some way by his manner toward us when we met again, or in his grading of us, in some form, in our graduate programs. The most remarkable thing about this to me is it seemed to me when Carl left, that he was pleased with the evening and in no way offended or even ruffled beyond the obvious effects of the immediate skirmishes that we had had, and that he left truly grateful, not as a full professor, but simply as a friend, for the dinner and the interesting company and the evening. And, again to my respect and admiration for him, at no point in our meetings later did any questions ever, even by remote suggestion, occur that he had been handled impolitely or roughly or in any kind of bad-mannered way. He seemed truly to understand our genuineness and openness in trusting him with our objections, our difficulties and even our feelings; and toward me personally, and I'm quite sure toward the others, he never showed the slightest negative response to what, in retrospect, could have been a somewhat impolite type of confrontation when he was the honored guest at a dinner."[111]

Within two years of his coming to Ohio State, twenty-five of the sixty or so graduate students working for advanced degrees in psychology were doing so under his supervision, and he had rejected several others for various reasons.[112] On one occasion, probably in 1942, Rogers invited all the graduate students who were working with him or who were interested in his work, about forty altogether, to his house and pointed out that probably, as a group, they would be having a significant impact on American psychology in the next twenty or thirty years.[113] In many cases this prediction proved to be true. Among others, Arthur Combs' work became very influential in the humanistic movements within psychology and education.[114] Victor Raimy, originally under Rogers' supervision and then on his own, contributed much to modern psychology's interest in the self concept.[115] Virginia Axline, who originally coauthored with Rogers a lengthy and moving case study of nondirective play therapy,[116] went on to advance the field of play therapy and popularize it in two well-known books, *Play Therapy* and *Dibs in Search of Self*.[117] (She wrote in the former book in 1947, "The principles of non-directive play therapy which are discussed in this book are based upon the non-directive counseling techniques which have been developed by Doctor Carl R. Rogers."[118]) Thomas Gordon, who worked with Rogers for several more years, developed parent, teacher, youth, and leadership "effectiveness training" models which had a great impact on parenting and the helping professions.[119] Nicholas Hobbs was president of the American Psychological Association and provost of George Peabody University. Others present went on to become psychology professors or run counseling programs at major universities.

Personal Life

Quite commonly—David remembered it as almost weekly—the Rogers would invite some of the graduate students to their home for informal professional meetings or for purely social occasions. David and Natalie both remembered fondly their ping-pong matches with Tom Gordon, Don Grummon, Nick Hobbs,

138

and the others, and David later felt that his own way of relating to his own students was greatly influenced by experiencing his father's rapport with his students.[120] He also remembered how "some of the conversations between my dad and those students—I was always permitted to sit in on them—began to give me a sense of his philosophy and his own professional concerns. It was here I began to realize that my father was a highly congruent man with a splendid value system. The kind of positive, unconditional regard he gave to others clearly extended to me and my sister. I don't believe I'm romanticizing this. I always felt that I could do or be whatever I wished to without losing his interest or affection. It was a precious gift he bestowed upon me."[121]

At home Helen always was Carl's partner in creating a warm and gracious setting that would facilitate comfortable interaction. Helen once wrote of herself, "I am essentially a home maker and have always felt that to make the wheels run smoothly and have an attractive home in which to bring our friends has contributed very substantially to the success and prominence to which Carl has risen."[122] Natalie agreed with this description—and added, "I feel certain that it was Helen's emotional support and extreme faith in her husband's ability that gave Carl the courage to stick his neck out professionally."[123] On the other hand, wrote Natalie, "This model played some havoc for me, when it came to my own marriage. I took on that same model without questioning whether it was right for me."[124]

Mother and daughter represented two different generations. With rare exceptions Helen did not seem to feel captive or resentful in a traditional woman's role. Friends of the Rogers always described her as a strong and forceful personality in her own right. Carl's student Bernard Steinzor's first impression was that she was "a very striking woman, taller than her husband and much more outgoing. One sensed she was a woman of great strength."[125] Throughout her life she pursued her independent interests in painting and in the Planned Parenthood movement. It was she who told David about venereal disease. There was "almost no discussion about sex with Dad, although he supplied me with numerous books." A naturally empathic person, Helen often served as combination mother and counselor to many of their friends—so successfully that Carl occasionally felt, "Oh, my God. She's better than I am!"[126] In later years, when I wrote to Helen and addressed the envelope to "Mrs. Helen Rogers" (this was just before "Ms." became popular), I was promptly rebuked and in friendly terms told, "By the way—I really am very proud of being Mrs. Carl R. Rogers—as my letterhead suggests, and while I love you to call me Helen, I also like my mail addressed as above—so I don't feel like a divorcee."[127] She was seventy then. (She did subscribe to *Ms.* magazine two years later.)

Natalie spent her years in Columbus attending the University's progressive laboratory school, one of the schools in the famous "Eight-Year Study."[128] Placed two grades in advance of her age level, at age twelve in the ninth grade, her 35-page report on "Progressive vs. Traditional Education in Elementary Schools" was a masterpiece of careful classroom observation and analysis. A typical paragraph read,

> Each family has its own problems and needs guidance from someone experienced in that field. Maybe John is an only child and has no chance to play with anyone so he becomes dependent upon his parents. Or Suzy is the youngest child in the family and is bossed so much she won't do anything for anyone else … These are just samples of some of the family problems where the nursery or elementary school can help.

It sounded so much like her father's writing style that I asked them if he had helped her; but both father and daughter remembered her doing it entirely on her own. Her teacher sent the paper to the principal with a covering note saying, "Natalie has put her very youthful finger on some things which many adults— even students of education—frequently overlook. I wonder whether many of our observers could give a better account of what they see in our classes and the others they watch. I think you'll agree with me that Natalie has had a rich learning experience in carrying forward the study of her problem. I think this is a good case in point of the unlimited opportunity inherent in the emphasis upon self-directed learning."[129]

Rogers never explicitly credited his family's experience with the Ohio State laboratory school as influencing his own views on self-directed learning; after all, he had studied progressive education with William Heard Kilpatrick and practiced it himself in his religious education work long before moving to Columbus. Still this first-hand experience with one of the study schools in the progressive education movement must have reinforced if not deepened his understanding of student-centered learning.

Since the Rogers family did not practice an organized religion, Natalie recalled, "I didn't have a Book to go by, so I spent a lot of time thinking about what was meaningful to me. I can remember going to bed at night and thinking a lot about that—religion and philosophy. I had to figure it all out for myself."[130] She felt they not only tolerated but also encouraged her independence. "I didn't feel I was bound to home. When I was thirteen, I went to a work camp in West Virginia for coal miners' children, sponsored by the Ethical Culture Society and the American Friends Service Committee, where we built the housing, fed the children, and so on." David felt one of the implicit messages in their family was "You're on this earth to be of service."[131] If so, Natalie was clearly getting the message. But when she wrote home and "asked to bring a poor little miner's kid home and adopt her, they were very sympathetic, but explained very firmly that it wouldn't work and it just couldn't be done." She did return to the camp for two more summers as a counselor, however.

In one of those summers, between her junior and senior year in high school,

Natalie wrote a letter to her father, addressed "Dear Pop," in which she described at length her working with a severely withdrawn girl who was assigned to her tent whose father was killed in a mine explosion a year and a half before. It was an extremely perceptive letter, and Natalie was clearly very creative in how she helped the girl come out of herself and become engaged with others. She added a postscript saying "When I get home you're going to have to teach me more about analysis—therapy etc. After talking to Norman I realize how interesting it is and how you never let me know part of your knowledge."[132]

Three days later he answered, in part, "Dear Nat, I don't know when I have enjoyed anything so much as I did your letter about Dixie. I surely think, and the family does too, that you have the makings of a swell psychologist or teacher or social worker. It sounds as though you have sure done a great job with her, and she sounds like an interesting child." He signed off, "Lots of love, Pop."[133]

Upon returning home she read *Counseling and Psychotherapy* and, like many readers, felt it spoke to her personally. She remembered reacting, "Hey, this is just the way I think," and being surprised her father thought that way too. Later in high school she visited Virginia Axline's classroom, was very impressed by her way of working with children, and decided that she would like to become a play therapist.[134]

David, too, thrived in the Ohio State Lab School. Although his mother and Aunt Meg often told him what a good student his father had been, school had meant little to David until Ohio. He had always put in the minimum of effort, although he continued to get good grades on the strength of his natural abilities. At the Lab School there were no grades and class attendance was optional, so he tested the limits of the system for the first three months. Then one day, as he recalled, while working on a project, he realized, "This is really fascinating." That was a turning point. "I feel I owe this school an enormous debt. It really turned me on toward learning—city planning, how it would be fun to be an architect, poetry, English lit., writing."

During a career week in his junior year he became interested in medicine and spent a period of time shadowing the doctor father of his girl friend, the woman he later married. Later he also credited his uncle Walter Rogers, M.D., as having influenced his choice of career.[135] Recognizing his potential, the school director encouraged him to work even harder, telling him that, when he went to college, he could not be both a good student and a playboy. Graduating from high school in 1942, David proceeded to try to prove him wrong. But after a year and a half at Ohio State (where there was no tuition fee because of his father's position), he realized he had no real direction. He decided to apply early to Harvard and Cornell Medical Schools and was accepted at both. Although David regarded his father as a sympathetic listener at the time, he did not discuss the decision with his parents, actually choosing Cornell because he liked the pictures in the catalog better. Later he discovered that Cornell Medical College was in New York City, not in Ithaca in the beautiful Chenango Valley, as he had thought from the pictures.[136]

During the Rogers' four years in Ohio the graduate students were consistently impressed with each member of the Rogers family and the relationships among them. Tom Gordon recalled how, "For me, Carl and Helen Rogers fulfilled the role of a second set of caring parents, as well as providing a model of what a marital relationship and parenting should be."[137] Charles Curran saw in Carl and Helen "a genuine openness and naturalness to their own children as well as to others."[138] He recalled that someone once asked Rogers if he used the nondirective counseling method with his children and that Rogers somewhat explosively answered, "Hell, no, I'm not a counselor to my children. I am their father." To Curran this remark seemed to characterize Rogers' relationship to his children. "Somewhat like the minister's children, we sometimes think of the psychologist's children as having some kind of special burden to bear and a certain kind of official good children's or successful children's role they have to carry out. I found none of this at all in my occasional visits to Rogers' home. On the contrary, it seemed a very ordinary, but rich and genuinely respectful relationship, as any sensitive, considerate father would have with his children. There were no tones, not even remotely, of the somewhat stiff quality that psychologists sometimes have with their children, in trying too hard to play the role of understanding parents."

Speaking of David and Natalie, Curran also recalled, "I admired them. I felt pleased, in the way an adult is, that he is around charming and likeable, alert children who respond openly to him ... They were both remarkably normal, in the best sense of that term, and each, in his or her own way, obviously already outstanding and unusual ... While he was not a hero to his children, he had their rich and deep respect."

Another graduate student recalled an event which, for him, illustrated the type of relationship Carl and Helen had with their children. As part of his supervised field work, William Snyder was administering intelligence tests to several of the more gifted students at the University School and interpreting the results to them. David Rogers, near the end of his high school career, was among those Snyder tested. The boy's scores were astoundingly high, and in interpreting the results to David, Snyder explained that the tests showed he had intellectual abilities which made him capable of doing anything he wanted to do, in terms of a career. David went home and told this to his parents and, very honestly, asked if they thought this were so. To Snyder, this event indicated how relaxed the Rogers were about bringing up their children. Many parents would have been continually reminding their children of how bright they were and how they should be using their abilities. The Rogers had the easy confidence that David and Natalie would come to recognize their own abilities and find their own interests without much pushing from their parents.[139]

This proved to be true. David received his medical degree, with highest honors, in 1948, at age twenty-two. Natalie entered Stevens College in Missouri, in 1944, just before her sixteenth birthday. Both went on to impressive careers.

On July 1, 1941, at Warwood, Walter and Julia Rogers celebrated their fiftieth wedding anniversary, receiving over 200 guests who came to offer their best wishes. All the children and grandchildren made an impressive picture for the family album: Lester, head of the Bates and Rogers Construction Corporation, with his wife Lucile and their four children; Margaret, a school teacher, unmarried and living with her parents; Ross' wife Jean and their two children (Ross had died in 1933); Carl, Helen, David and Natalie; Walter, an obstetrician-gynecologist in Pasadena, with his wife Elise and their two children; and John, also an officer in Bates and Rogers, with his wife Ruth and their daughter. While still not close to his parents emotionally, Rogers' relationship with them became more comfortable, less volatile, as he became more established in his career and more confident in his own independence. His father died January 3, 1944 in Rochester, Minnesota.

Professional Activities

Fortunately David and Natalie were developing their own interests in Columbus, for their father's growing professional stature meant more and more commitments which competed with his family time. Even before the publication of *Counseling and Psychotherapy* in 1942, Rogers had become prominent in many professional organizations. The publication of the book only increased the momentum of his already growing reputation. He remained involved in the American Orthopsychiatric Association, serving as vice-president of the national organization in 1942.[140] He also became deeply involved in the newly formed American Association for Applied Psychology, a group which splintered off from the American Psychological Association because of objections to the rather authoritarian structure of the parent organization and its relative lack of interest in clinical and applied psychology.[141] Rogers' rise in that organization is somewhat indicative of his growing professional stature in the early 1940s. In 1940 he was a member of the executive committee of the Clinical Section. In 1941 he became chairman of the Clinical Section, served on the Executive Committee of the Ohio branch and on the national Committee on Professional Training, and became an associate editor of the organization's *Journal of Consulting Psychology.* In 1942 he remained as chairman of the Clinical Section and also became a member of the national Board of Governors and associate editor of *Applied Psychology Monographs.* In 1943 he was elected President of the national organization, serving the 1944–45 term.

"Meanwhile," he later wrote, "Robert Yerkes was arguing that if the parent organization, the APA, could be reorganized so as to be democratic in its structure, all of psychology might again be brought together."[142] Serving on the Subcommittee on Survey and Planning in Psychology, with such distinguished figures as Robert Yerkes, Ernest Hilgard and Edwin G. Boring, all former presidents of the American Psychological Association, he expended much time and energy attempting to reunify the profession.

His rising stature was helped considerably by the many studies and articles bearing his name that were appearing in the professional journals. "At Ohio State University," he wrote in one article, "… we have phonographic and typescript accounts of nearly one hundred interviews."[143] He then went on to describe this valuable new tool, the electronically recorded interview. In another article on "The Development of Insight in a Counseling Relationship," he wrote, "In the counseling and research on counseling which is being carried forward at Ohio State, we are gradually accumulating more information about this important aspect of psychotherapy."[144] He had a way of creating an excitement about the work he and his students were doing, of calling attention to himself and his university, but in a way that was hard to call arrogant; since the tone was always tentative about what they were learning, forward-looking in terms of new questions they were investigating, and inviting in that he seemed always to hold out the offer to others to join them in the valuable work. All told, he had about twenty articles and studies published between 1940 and 1945.

In addition, his students' work at Ohio State was soon adding to his reputation and to the growing interest in nondirective therapy. By 1945 he was able to refer in his writings to eight theses and dissertations on the nondirective approach. The students themselves, adapting and expanding on their dissertations, had published about a dozen articles in the professional journals by 1945, all mentioning Rogers and the work going on in Columbus. This was only the beginning of Rogers' and his students' research efforts—a handful of studies compared to the deluge to come. Nevertheless it was highly noticeable, pioneering work in a field which had never before attempted serious and extensive, quantitative scientific research on a therapeutic approach. In the introduction to his article "Counseling," in the April 1945 *Review of Educational Research,* Rogers was able to write: "For the first time in the history of these reviews, there is sufficient research in the process of counseling to justify a separate chapter …"[145]

As he had in Rochester, he became quite involved in committee work and consulting in the Columbus community, giving speeches to groups like the Home Economics Institute, the Ohio Guidance Association, the State Welfare Conference, Columbus Psychological Society, various school faculties, parent and church groups, and many others. He conducted an extensive survey of "Mental Health Problems in the Columbus Public Schools," based on 1,500 school children studied in grades one through six, which led him to conclude that there were over 5,000 seriously maladjusted children in the Columbus schools.[146] He did a statewide survey on the problems of youth in wartime.[147] He served as consultant to several schools regarding their guidance programs and arranged for several of his graduate students to get part-time or full-time positions working as counselors in churches, schools, and youth groups in the community. In May of 1942 the *Columbus Citizen* ran a five-part newspaper series on Ohio State's Psychological Clinic, with Rogers featured prominently throughout the series. He sounded far from nondirective in these articles, when it came to advising parents.

Says Dr. Rogers, "Tell the children the truth, when they ask about the sirens and the blackout. Be entirely realistic about it … Say calmly and matter-of-factly, 'Why, yes—there is a possibility that German planes may come over Columbus some day. But it isn't a very big chance. And certainly, there's a very, very small chance that bombs will hit our house.'"[148]

If there is one particular factor in child training that Dr. Carl R. Rogers, clinic psychologist, is particularly emphatic about, it is this: Give your child a chance to become an independent, responsible person—a chance to grow … Managing an allowance is one of the best ways to learn responsibility," Dr. Rogers declares. "But let your child handle the money absolutely by himself. Don't dictate how it should be spent. If he wants to spend the whole quarter, or whatever it is, in one day, and be broke the rest of the week, let him do it! Let him take the consequences … As your children grow older, encourage them to plan their own parties, to choose their own clothes. What if they do make rather a mess of things once in a while! They'll learn many valuable lessons from their mistakes … A child must learn to take the risks of growth," says Dr. Rogers, "even though he gets some bumps in the process. It's the only way he can get the satisfaction of growing." [149]

Wartime Work

While Rogers' stature was growing nationally in the professional community, as well as locally and throughout Ohio, by an interesting series of events he gradually became deeply involved in the national wartime, and then the peacetime effort. The beginning of this involvement was described in the November 1942 *Psychological Bulletin*:

For a number of years the Division of Program Surveys, U.S. Bureau of Agricultural Economics, under the direction of Dr. Rensis Likert, has had a staff of interviewers conducting intensive interviews with farmers to explore all aspects of rural attitudes toward farm programs. With the coming of the war, this survey work was greatly expanded to cover urban as well as rural groups, and its scope broadened to cover topics of national significance in war time.

145

This rapid expansion meant multiplying the staff, and created a need for training new members in interviewing techniques. The Division became interested in the "non-directive" approach to treatment interviewing which is being developed by Dr. Carl R. Rogers and his students at Ohio State University, and in the phonographic training devices which have been used there. The "non-directive" approach, in which the interviewer is trained to develop techniques which release emotionalized attitudes without directing the client or influencing the expression of such feelings, seemed particularly applicable to the survey task of getting attitudes, and reasons or factors underlying those attitudes. Dr. Likert made arrangements for his interviewers to be given an intensive period of training at Columbus ... In all, forty-two interviewers were sent to Ohio State for this training, each group staying for one week ... According to those in charge of the surveys, the training program ... conducted by Dr. Rogers and Mr. Charles Cannell ... did much to improve the field work of these interviewers.[150]

In 1943 Nicholas Hobbs, former graduate student of Rogers and then a major in the Psychological Branch of the Air Force, asked Rogers to conduct a new survey, later called "Adjustment After Combat: A Study of Returned Combat Gunners and Their Utilization in the Flexible Gunnery Training Program."[151] In conducting the survey, Rogers and his staff interviewed 100 gunners who had been returned to the United States after serving their required number of combat missions overseas. Many of them had participated in air raids in which there were terrible losses, such as those over the Ploesti oil fields in Romania where sometimes as many as twenty-five percent of the planes were lost in a single mission. They were having a difficult time adjusting to army life back in the States. Aside from suffering varying degrees of battle fatigue and what today might be called post-traumatic stress disorder, the men also felt that their skills and knowledge were not being used. They had been in actual combat, in life or death situations where performance was all that counted. Now they were required to sit through gunnery classes conducted by young lieutenants who had never seen combat, forced to march up and down on parade grounds, shave every morning, shine their shoes, and otherwise play at military life. It was not long before they became disgruntled and then became discipline problems of major concern to their commanding officers. Rogers listened to these men, encouraged them to express their feelings, their frustrations, their fears and anxieties. Based on his findings, he made eighteen recommendations designed to help them adjust to their new situation and to use their resources more effectively so they would feel they were continuing to play a meaningful role in the war effort.

Again the government was pleased with Rogers' work. In distributing Rogers' ninety-page "restricted publication," the commanding officer of the base where the study was conducted wrote a covering letter in which he said, "The accompanying study of the adjustment of ex-combat gunners to their duties in

Training Command Schools is believed to be a very important contribution towards understanding gunners with combat experience and towards their fullest utilization in the gunnery training program. The efforts of Dr. Rogers and his assistants are greatly appreciated by all who have given thought to this problem."[152] The letter was more than perfunctory, as many of Rogers' recommendations were implemented.

As the war years continued, an increasing number of men and women entered the armed forces and faced the problems of adjusting to military life. Simultaneously more and more soldiers were returning from overseas and bringing back with them problems of adjustment to civilian life and stateside military life. As Rogers described them, "There is the homesick and lonely inductee; there is the service woman who is deeply upset because her engagement has been broken; there is the man who is concerned about his wife's behavior while he is far from home; there are the returned servicemen, often bitterly resentful in regard to civilian life and confused as to their own aims and purposes; there are the wounded and handicapped individuals who, in spite of good medical care, feel deeply insecure as they endeavor to face the world; there are the psychoneurotic individuals whose conflicts and instabilities bring them often to the civilian individual in whom they feel confidence."[153]

Once again Rogers was asked to help. He accepted the offer of a one-year appointment as Director of Counseling Services for the United Service Organization (USO), although he would not begin this assignment until the fall of 1944, as he was spending that summer as Visiting Professor at the University of Chicago, which was quite an honor for a new professor. Writing to a colleague about his USO responsibilities, he explained, "My function will be to train the professional staff workers (there are about 3,000 of them) in counseling techniques which will enable them to handle more skillfully the problems of personal adjustment which come to them. Consideration will also be given to the intelligent use of community resources in gaining additional help for the maladjusted serviceman. The USO is finding it necessary to modify and individualize its club program in localities where there are considerable numbers of handicapped men, wounded men, psycho-neurotics, and returned combat men. It would be part of my job function to help in adapting the USO program to the needs of these special groups."[154]

The short appointment meant a move back to New York City, where the USO headquarters were located. Carl and Helen rented an apartment at Twenty-third Street and Seventh Avenue and enjoyed the city where they had spent his graduate-school days two decades earlier. An added job benefit was that David was attending Cornell Medical College in New York City at the time. Unfortunately Carl's job did not give him all that much time in New York.

One of the basic models he set up for training the USO volunteers was a short intensive training course (today it might be called a workshop) of eight to twelve hours. In a twelve-hour course, typically, the first six hours would be spent in lectures and discussions. Topics covered were: "adjustment problems and motivations," "basic counseling principles," "applying basic principles in the casual contact," "the use of resources in dealing with individuals," and "a local program for dealing with individuals in the USO." Following this period of mostly didactic teaching, four hours would normally be spent in practice and demonstrations. The client portions of a phonographically recorded interview would be played or read, and the workers would write in the responses they would make and then discuss their various responses in light of the client-centered principles they had just been taught. Then, using volunteers from the group to role-play a serviceman and a worker, several interviews would be staged before the entire group, followed by a general discussion of the worker's responses. The final two hours would be devoted to dealing with the questions, concerns, weaknesses, and interests of the particular group of workers.[155]

Rogers repeated this course all over the country. By mid-1945 he also had conducted less intensive half-day or whole-day workshops for 655 workers and had met for shorter demonstrations and talks, all told, with 4,500 to 5,000 USO volunteers.[156] The repetition was too much for him. Rogers was a forward-looking person, always experimenting with new ideas, methods or applications. But in 1944–45, week after week, with group after group, he had to muster up his energy to repeat the same ideas over and over again in the same context, trying to be as enthusiastic each time as he was the first time, hearing and responding to the same questions. Although successful throughout the year, he came to hate his job—the repetition and the pace—and to look forward to the end of his tenure with the USO. Even the amusing skits the workers would perform at the party that usually followed each course tended to get repetitive, as time after time he watched them gleefully enact the scene of the USO volunteer who dutifully repeats the words of the serviceman who threatens suicide, goes over to the window, and finally jumps!

At least two of the workshop venues proved memorable. When he went to San Diego, California, Helen accompanied him and visited nearby La Jolla. They thought at the time that this would be a nice place to retire to.[157] (Although Rogers never actually retired, twenty years later they did move to La Jolla.) On another occasion an intensive course had been scheduled in advance at a downtown hotel in a southern city; but when Rogers arrived he found that an unforeseen problem had arisen. The hotel, in accepting the original reservations, had not realized that black people would also be attending the course. During this period of legalized segregation in the southern United States, it was against their policy to rent rooms or serve food to "colored." When Rogers stated very clearly that black people were fighting and dying for their country alongside white people, and if the hotel wasn't willing to let them room and eat alongside each other there would be no conference, the hotel relented.[158]

As always it came easily and naturally to Rogers to put his experience and insights down on paper. As a part of his job he wrote a series of brief articles or position papers that were distributed to all the USO branches and used in his training courses. In "A Counseling Viewpoint for the USO Worker," he summarized why the client-centered approach was especially useful in counseling servicemen. First, it works, it's effective. Second, it can be taught relatively easily, even to semi- and non-professionals. Third, it can be used safely, as compared with methods which intrude into the client's life or his unconscious mind. And "finally it may be stressed that it is based on a philosophy which is fully consistent with the highest development of democratic living ... a viewpoint built upon the assumption that the individual has worth and dignity, and has the capacity to choose and live a spontaneous, independent, self-directed life."[159]

Speaking to a wider audience, he wrote several articles on working with the returned servicemen, which were published not only in one of the major psychology journals ("Psychological Adjustments of Discharged Service Personnel" in *Psychological Bulletin*), but also in more popular magazines like the *National Parent-Teacher* ("When the Serviceman Returns to His Family") and the *Journal of Home Economics* ("Wartime Issues in Family Counseling").[160] Just after leaving the USO, he coauthored with John L. Wallen, a graduate student working with him at Ohio State University, another book, entitled *Counseling with Returned Servicemen*.[161] This little book, published the following year by McGraw-Hill, was actually a simplified version of *Counseling and Psychotherapy,* applied specifically to the returned serviceman. Given its particular timing and focus, the book had a relatively short life and narrow audience; but it remains a simply written and very concise summary of Rogers' views on counseling at the end of his stay at Ohio State.

Move to Chicago

When the Rogers left Columbus for their year in New York with the USO, it was a permanent farewell to the Ohio city. Ralph Tyler, who had invited Rogers to be Visiting Professor at the University of Chicago and who held several important posts at the university, was very impressed with Rogers' work. At the end of the summer he invited Rogers to move to the University of Chicago permanently and to set up a counseling center there. Since Rogers was so obviously isolated in his own department at Ohio State (he practically had to beg for increased secretarial help in the Psychological Clinic), he realized the move to the new setting would give him more freedom. Most importantly the new counseling center would be an ideal source of data for the major scientific research he was eager to begin on the process of therapy.

In what must have been a halfhearted attempt to persuade him to stay, Rogers' department chairman at Ohio State, Harold Burtt, told him, "Well, Carl, this nondirective thing you're pushing certainly won't last long; but if you stay here, you'll always have a home to come back to."[162] Neither this dubious support nor the $5,448 salary he was now receiving at Ohio State was enough to persuade him to remain. However, since he was already committed to a year of working with the USO, the move to Chicago had to be delayed. They sold their house, stored their furniture, and moved to New York. Because Carl had to be in New York to begin work, Helen stayed behind to take charge of the packing and moving. When this was completed, she drove alone to New York City.[163]

At first the thought of leaving Columbus and moving to Chicago had been very unpleasant and difficult for Helen. Hardest of all was leaving their new home, which they had planned and built to last their lifetime and into which she had put so much work. Now after three years they were selling it. As Helen later wrote, "The invitation to go to the University of Chicago was not an easy one for me to accept. I knew it meant greater freedom for Carl to explore new fields and to establish a Counseling Center of the sort that would develop and put into practice his ever-growing theories and convictions in his philosophy of therapy. I knew it was right to go. I also knew it meant leaving my beautiful rural home and finding a spot to live in the dirty, slummy area of the South Side of Chicago. Luckily, our children had departed for college ... So we decided that apartment living was wisest for us in the big city. This being 1945, at the end of the war, housing was almost impossible to find. But luck was with us and we found a large, airy apartment with a fine view of Lake Michigan and within walking distance of the Counseling Center. This made living in Chicago very acceptable to me."[164]

Fortunately they had the summer to make their move from New York and Columbus to Chicago. Again Helen had to handle most of it, while Carl spent two months recuperating from another operation. It seems the surgery at the Mayo Clinic in 1926 had done some damage and new adhesions were forming on his ulcer. The new operation at the Presbyterian Medical Center in Columbus was a success, for he never had any more problems in that area.[165] By August he was better again and ready to move on to a new chapter in his life, one that would result in a prodigious amount of innovative work and that would win him international recognition.

LEFT: *Carl, circa 1908.*

BOTTOM LEFT: *Julia Rogers and her five children in Oak Park.* Clockwise: *Lester, Carl, Walter, John, Margaret.*

BOTTOM RIGHT: *Carl, circa 1911.*

Warwood

Carl at the University of Wisconsin, 1920.

Walter and Julia Rogers at Warwood, circa 1916.

The delegation to China, 1922. Top row, fourth from right: *Carl.*
Fourth from left: *traveling companion Kenneth Latourette.* Seated,
center: *delegation leader Dr. John Mott.*

Carl and Helen, honeymoon, September 1924.

RIGHT: *Helen and Carl,*
summer 1929.

Natalie and David near Seneca
Lake, 1934.

Carl, December 1934.

Walter and Julia Rogers' Golden Wedding Anniversary, July 1, 1941. As identified in family album, seated l. to r.: Mrs. Walter C. Rogers; Mrs. John Rogers; Miss Margaret Rogers; Mrs. Walter A. Rogers; Walter A. Rogers; Carol Rogers; Mrs. Sherman Johnson, widow of Ross W. Rogers; Mrs. Carl R. Rogers. Standing: Lucile Rogers; Mrs. Lester C. Rogers; Lester C. Rogers, Jr.; Lester C. Rogers, Sr.; Dr. Carl R. Rogers; David Rogers; John W. Rogers; Dr. Walter C. Rogers; Barbara Rogers; Natalie Rogers; Nancy Rogers. Seated in front: Janet, Diane, Marcia, and Steve. (ORLIN KOHLI)

ABOVE: *First officers of the American Psychological Association, as reorganized in 1946: Helen Peak, Recording Secretary; Donald Marquis, President-elect; Carl R. Rogers, President; Dael Wolfle, Executive Secretary.*

ABOVE: *Rogers with a client at the University of Chicago, circa 1950.*

LEFT: *Portrait, 1952.* (LOUISE BARKER)

ABOVE: *Helen and Carl in Estes Park, Colorado, summer 1960.*

LEFT: *Rogers in Japan, 1961, with Tsutomo Endo and interpreter Logan Fox.*

BOTTOM: *"I want to speak to you as Carl Rogers, in 1969, not as a medieval symbol. So I hope I will not offend you if I remove these medieval trappings . . ."*

*Portrait of Carl Rogers
in the seventies: at home
in his garden, leading
a televised encounter
group, talking with
college students and
faculty.*

CHAPTER 6

The Chicago Years: Part One
1945–1951

Late in 1945 a graduate student in Massachusetts wrote to Rogers asking for his help on a paper she was writing on "Carl Ransom Rogers, 1902–." He sent her some autobiographical material, and she wrote a short, insightful analysis of his life and work, concluding with: "This fall, Rogers moved to the University of Chicago. I suppose this means that he's still going up. It will be interesting to see whether he has created his masterpiece, or whether he can keep hold of his original scientific, hardheaded approach, and apply it to new problems. I suppose he'll have to spend some time on validation of what has been done so far … Can it [his method] be applied further? To treatment of more serious cases, for instance? … If I have been right about the characteristic energy of Carl Rogers, I don't think that he'll stop now."[1]

She was right. The next twelve years at Chicago turned out to be the most prolific and productive period of Rogers' life. During this time he published one minor and two major books[2] and almost sixty articles and studies; he served as President of the American Psychological Association and as president or officer of many other prestigious groups; he won numerous awards and honors; and he saw the publication of approximately 250 articles and studies, not including his own, on the nondirective or client-centered approach.[3] It was for him also a time of continuing personal growth and adventure, as well as some personal turmoil.

For the first half of this twelve-year period, the creation of the Counseling Center, the refinement of his counseling approach, his evolving leadership style, and Rogers' personal development were the major themes. During the latter half of the period the theoretical and research dimensions of his work received the greater emphasis.

Getting Started

Rogers had come to Chicago with a mandate to set up the University's first Counseling Center. With him came many students from Ohio State who valued their continued contact with Rogers enough to compensate for the problems of moving from one university to another. Among those to make the move with him as a staff member was Virginia Axline, whose book *Play Therapy* was about to be published.[4] Next to Rogers she became the best-known figure in the Center.

While Rogers had been promised he could create a new counseling center, he did not realize that finding a suitable location would be problematic. After they looked at the choir loft and balcony of a nearby church and other unsuitable places, the Counseling Center was given the south and west sides of Lexington Hall, surrounding "a delightfully odoriferous campus bakery," and a budget to renovate the old building and reorganize the physical setting.[5] The space was cramped, the roof leaked, the setting never would achieve a bright or new look; nevertheless the Counseling Center staff and their families threw themselves into the renovation with enthusiasm. They created eleven small rooms for offices, counseling rooms, a play-therapy room, an observation room, and a meeting room.[6]

As one student, then staff member from that period, Bernard Steinzor, recalled, "The sense of being pioneers in a new adventure was very evident and very great ... Helen Rogers took much initiative with the wives in making curtains and selecting furniture ... while the men did more of the physical labor. It was a sense of establishing a Center out of a community of people engaged in a variety of actions."[7] Steinzor also remembered Rogers inviting the staff out to the Rogers family homestead near Glen Ellyn.

A few years later, in September 1949, the Counseling Center moved to a larger space in another building, a former nurse's dormitory at 5737 Drexel Avenue. There again the staff became the interior decorators. "We wanted to repaint it," Rogers recalled. "Well, that was a big deal: the university didn't have money for it; no, we couldn't get someone to do it; we couldn't hire anyone nonunion ... We were blocked."[8] So, as Manuel Vargas recalled, "We had a painting party; and I was very happy to see Carl come in with his blue jeans, as the rest of us did; and we all wielded paint and brush and scaffolding and ladders, and so forth, as we painted the walls of the three stories of the Counseling Center. There was a great deal of informality among us, so we were all able to enjoy this kind of experience together."[9]

In their self-renovated settings the staff of the Counseling Center plunged into their work with zest, building what was soon to become one of the best-known centers for psychotherapy and psychotherapeutic research in the country and in the world. From 4,000 therapeutic interviews held with clients the first year, the number grew to over 11,000 interviews several years later.[10] But, as

Rogers wrote in his first annual report on the Counseling Center's work, "The figures cannot begin to picture the variety of individuals who have come for help. College students of sixteen, men and women in their sixties, children four and five years of age brought by their parents, as well as all the intervening ages; students in law, theology, social work, psychology, education, medicine, as well as the College; lawyers, ministers, business executives, journalists, housewives, physicians; returned veterans and their wives; parents and their adolescent offspring—these are some of the groups. The problems presented have represented an equal variety. Personal and social inadequacies, marital problems, fear of academic failure, inability to function efficiently, sexual conflicts, vocational perplexity and confusion—a wide range of maladjustments ..."[11]

Rogers' own daily routine was similar to that which he had established at Ohio State. He walked to and from the Center each day, often returning home for lunch. Once at the Center he wore many hats—primarily counselor, researcher, teacher-supervisor, and administrator. As a member of the Department of Psychology he also taught graduate courses and served as advisor to graduate students working on their advanced degrees. It was a small department when he came, with only six faculty.[12]

Most important he was a counselor, a therapist. In the twelve years he was at Chicago, he maintained a steady number of clients—usually from seven to ten individuals, whom he saw for an average total of fifteen or more counseling hours per week.[13] In one of his annual reports he wrote, "The largest single block of my time goes to this activity. Most of my clients are students, many of them students-in-training in this field."

Throughout his career Rogers stressed the value of his direct experience in counseling. Again and again in his writings he emphasized the importance of his time spent with clients. "It is from this rich and varied and deep contact with individuals that most of my hypotheses for research and the concepts for theory arise."[14] "It is my laboratory."[15] "It is the laboratory which is most basic to my work, namely the laboratory of interpersonal relations."[16] Or as he stated with much more feeling in the preface to his next major book, *Client-Centered Therapy*, "This prefatory note cannot be concluded without a word of thanks to the people who have really written it, who have, in the most genuine sense been its major contributors—the clients with whom we have worked. To these men, women and children who have brought themselves and their struggles to us, who have with such natural grace permitted us to learn from them, who have laid bare for us the forces which operate in the mind and spirit of man—to them goes our deepest gratitude."[17]

In addition to his counseling, Rogers also taught graduate courses, led a practicum in counseling for advanced graduate students, and supervised the work of many of the younger staff members at the Counseling Center. In his first eight years at Chicago he chaired or served on the committees of thirty-one successful Ph.D. candidates and a large number of Masters students.[18] The contact with his students was, as it had been at Ohio State, very stimulating for him. The case conferences, the teamwork on research projects, the open-ended discussions, the criticisms of his methods and ideas, the chance to build on each other's thinking—all this gave Rogers the occasion to reevaluate constantly his own concepts and techniques and to continue growing.

And grow he did. Just at the time that "nondirective counseling" was gaining widespread national attention, and many professionals and students were coming to Chicago to study with him and learn the "Rogerian approach," the Rogerian approach was changing. At first glance the change was rather puzzling and seemingly contradictory: in his thinking and writing, Rogers began to de-emphasize the nondirective technique; while in his own clinical practice he became even more extremely nondirective than before.

From Nondirective to Client-Centered

As was typical with Rogers throughout his career, he did not change through thinking things over and deciding that another description of therapy would be more apt or logical. The impetus for change *always* resulted from his direct experiences in therapy and human interaction and from his desire to understand better the processes and phenomena involved. He was always an inductive scientist, rather than a deductive theorist—inclined to experience, observe, record, look for patterns, and only much later begin to build the explanations, hypotheses, and theories to account for the observed data. Years before, in seeing what the effects of the various therapies were on clients, he had developed his nondirective approach—not because it was philosophically more defensible or because it was supported by the literature, but because, based on his observations, he believed it was more effective. In the same way his thinking began to change when he came to Chicago. This time the changes came about not only as he observed *his* clients, but also as he watched other nondirective counselors.

At Ohio State, with the USO, and at Chicago, he had worked with hundreds of counselors-in-training—watching them struggle to learn "The Method," seeing the results as they applied the techniques of simple acceptance and reflection of feeling in their work with clients. What Rogers came to realize, time and time again, is vividly described by one of his students, a minister named Walter Yoder, who himself had labored to learn the method.

> Because the client-centered, nondirective counseling approach has been rather carefully defined and clearly illustrated, it gives the "Illusion of Simplicity." The technique seems deceptively easy to master. Then you begin to practice. A word wrong here and there. You don't quite reflect the feeling, but reflect content instead.

154

It is difficult to handle questions. You are tempted to interpret. Nothing seems so serious that further practice won't correct it. Perhaps you are having trouble playing two roles—that of minister and that of counselor. Bring up the question in class and the matter is solved again with a deceptive ease. But these apparently minor errors and a certain woodenness of response seem exceedingly persistent.

Only gradually does it dawn that if the technique is true it demands a feeling of warmth. You begin to feel that the attitude is the thing. Every little word is not so important if you have the correct accepting and permissive attitude toward the client. So you bear down on the permissiveness and acceptance. You will permiss and accept and reflect the client, if it kills you.

But you still have those troublesome questions from the client. He simply doesn't know the next step. He asks you to give him a hint, some possibilities; after all you are expected to know something, else why is he here? As a minister, you ought to have some convictions about what people should believe, how they should act. As a counselor, you should know something about removing this obstacle—you ought to have the equivalent of the surgeon's knife and use it. Then you begin to wonder. The technique is good, but … does it go far enough? does it really work on clients? Is it right to leave a person helpless, when you might show him the way out?

Here seems to me is the crucial point. "Narrow is the gate" and hard the path from here on. No one else can give satisfying answers and even the instructors seem frustrating because they appear not to be helpful in your specific case. For here is demanded of you what no other person can do or point out—and that is to rigorously scrutinize yourself and your attitudes toward others. Do you believe that all people truly have a creative potential in them? That each person is a unique individual and that he alone can work out his own individuality? Or do you really believe that some persons are of "negative value" and others are weak and must be led and taught by "wiser," "stronger" people?

You begin to see that there is nothing compartmentalized about this method of counseling. It is not just counseling, because it demands the most exhaustive, penetrating, and comprehensive consistency. In other methods you can shape tools, pick them up for use when you will. But when genuine acceptance and permissiveness are your tools it requires nothing less than the whole complete personality. And to grow oneself is the most demanding of all.[19]

In the latter half of the 1940s Rogers came to speak and write about this point with increasing frequency and conviction.[20] In his own words, "It is common to find client-centered therapy spoken of as a method or a technique. No doubt this is due in part to earlier presentations which tended to overstress technique. It may more accurately be said that the counselor who is effective in client-centered therapy holds a coherent and developing set of attitudes deeply imbedded in his personal organization, a system of attitudes which is implemented by techniques and methods consistent with it. It has been our experience that the counselor who tries to use a 'method' is doomed to be unsuccessful unless this method is genuinely in line with his own attitudes. On the other hand the counselor whose attitudes are of the type which facilitate therapy may be only partially successful, because his attitudes are inadequately implemented by appropriate methods and techniques."[21]

In a similar vein he wrote, "to create a psychological climate in which the client feels that kind of warmth, understanding and freedom from attack in which he may drop his defensiveness, and explore and reorganize his life style, is a far more subtle and delicate process than simply 'reflecting feeling.' It calls for a total sensitivity to the client in his own perspective and the communication of this kind of acceptance and understanding ... The overall tone of the counseling situation becomes the concern of the therapist rather than a specific kind of phrase of verbalization ... If the counselor's feelings convey an attitude of subtle approval or disapproval, direction or guidance, etc., then all the 'reflection of feeling' in the world would still fall short of implementing a deeply client-centered orientation."[22]

In his earlier writings the therapist's technique clearly received the major emphasis. Although the therapist's attitude always had been mentioned, it had received much less attention. Now the balance was reversed. "The primary point of importance is the attitude held by the counselor toward the worth and significance of the individual."[23] Not only was technique de-emphasized, but Rogers began to avoid even using the word, preferring to use the term "implementation" to connote the method by which a basic attitude is conveyed.

The therapeutic attitude itself stemmed from a basic *hypothesis* about human growth. Rogers had come to believe this hypothesis while working in Rochester and Columbus, but at Chicago he began to state it more explicitly and frequently as the starting point for his whole conception of therapy. It went:

> [T]he client-centered therapist operates primarily upon one central and basic hypothesis which has undergone relatively little change with the years. This hypothesis is that the client has within himself the capacity, latent if not evident, to understand those aspects of his life and of himself which are causing him pain, and the capacity and the tendency to reorganize himself and his relationship to life in the direction of self-actualization and maturity in such a way as to bring a greater degree of internal comfort. The function of the therapist is to create such a psychological atmosphere as will permit this capacity and this strength to become effective rather than latent or potential.[24]

How does the therapist create this psychological atmosphere? Primarily by conveying two attitudes to the client—*acceptance* and *understanding*. "It would seem that when the individual is deeply accepted as he is, when the private world of his own reality is genuinely understood and genuinely accepted by another, without evaluation, and when this understanding and acceptance is communicated to the individual, this optimum atmosphere exists."[25] In the late forties these two attitudes, successfully communicated to the client, became for Rogers the major ingredients in effective psychotherapy. Around the turn of the decade he began to use other terms in place of "understanding," but the essential concept remained the same.

In describing the first of these criteria, acceptance, Rogers would frequently write in this vein: "The therapeutic phenomenon seems most likely to occur when the therapist feels, very genuinely and deeply, an attitude of acceptance of and respect for the client as he is, with the potentialities inherent in his present state. This means a respect for the attitudes which the client now has and a continuing acceptance of the attitudes of the moment, whether they veer in the direction of despair, toward constructive courage, or toward a confused ambivalence. This acceptance is probably possible only for the therapist who has integrated into his own philosophy a deep conviction as to the right of the individual to self-direction and self-determination … It may help to discuss briefly the meaning of the term 'respect,' as we have been using it. In other orientations there is also respect for the client or patient, but this is usually respect for the person as unrevealed. It is a respect for something underneath, not respect for the person as he seems to himself at that moment. In client-centered therapy, however, the counselor attitude which we have found most fruitful is a complete acceptance of the person as he seems to himself at that moment. It is only as he is dissatisfied with this self that he explores further into his attitudes and feelings."[26]

Rogers himself seemed able to communicate this acceptance and respect. An excerpt from an interview—one which he frequently quoted—provides an extreme example. The counselor was Virginia Axline.

Miss Gil, a young woman who has, in a number of therapeutic interviews, been quite hopeless about herself, has spent the major part of an hour discussing her feelings of inadequacy and lack of personal worth. Part of the time she has been aimlessly using the finger paints. She had just finished expressing her feelings of wanting to get away from everyone—to have nothing to do with people. After a long pause comes the following:

S (Subject, or Client): I've never said this before to anyone—but I've thought for such a long time—This is a terrible thing to say, but if I could just—well *(short, bitter laugh; pause),* if I could just find some glorious cause that I could give my life for I would be happy. I cannot be the kind of a person I want to be. I guess maybe I haven't the guts—or the strength—to kill myself—and if someone else would relieve me of the responsibility—or I would be in an accident—I— I—just don't want to live.

AXLINE: At the present time things look so black to you that you can't see much point in living—

S: Yes—I wish I'd never started this therapy. I was happy when I was living in my dream world. There I could be the kind of person I wanted to be—But now— There is such a wide, wide gap—between my ideal—and what I am. I wish people hated me. I try to make them hate me. Because then I could turn away from them and could blame them but no—It is all in my hands—Here is my life—and I either accept the fact that I am absolutely worthless—or I fight whatever it is that holds me in this terrible conflict. And I suppose if I accepted the fact that I am worthless, then I could go away someplace—and get a little room someplace—get a mechanical job someplace—and retreat clear back to the security of my dream world where I could do things, have clever friends, be a pretty wonderful sort of person.

AXLINE: It's really a tough struggle—digging into this like you are—and at times the shelter of your dream world looks more attractive and comfortable.

S: Yes. *(A long pause. Complete change of voice.)* So I don't see why I should waste your time—coming in twice a week—I'm not worth it—What do you think?

AXLINE: It's up to you, Gil—It isn't wasting my time—I'd be glad to see you— whenever you come—but it's how you feel about it—if you don't want to come twice a week—or if you do want to come twice a week?—once a week?—It's up to you. *(Long pause.)*

S: You're not going to suggest that I come in oftener? You're not alarmed and think I ought to come in every day—until I get out of this?

AXLINE: I believe you are able to make your own decision. I'll see you whenever you want to come.

S: *(Note of awe in her voice.)* I don't believe you are alarmed about—I see—I may be afraid of myself—but you aren't afraid for me—*(She stands up—a strange look on her face.)*

AXLINE: You say you may be afraid of yourself—and are wondering why I don't seem to be afraid for you?

S: *(Another short laugh.)* You have more confidence in me than I have. *(She cleans up the finger paint mess and starts out of the room.)* I'll see you next week—*(that short laugh)* maybe. *(Her attitude seemed tense, depressed, bitter, completely beaten. She walked slowly away.)*[27]

"I learned courage from her," Rogers said of Axline.[28] Such a dramatic example of the therapist's complete acceptance of the client, *as she is,* calls to mind the minister's earlier questions of how far must one carry these therapeutic attitudes? The answer for Rogers goes back to the therapist's faith in the basic hypothesis, in the capacity of the client to choose wisely, given the proper psychological climate. In his words,

"Is the therapist willing to give the client full freedom as to outcomes? Is he genuinely willing for the client to organize and direct his life? Is he willing for him to choose goals that are social or antisocial, moral or immoral? If not, it seems doubtful that therapy will be a profound experience for the client. Even more difficult, is he willing for the client to choose regressing rather than growth or maturity? to choose neuroticism rather than mental health? to choose to reject help rather than accept it? to choose death rather than life? To me it appears that only as the therapist is completely willing that any outcome, any direction may be chosen—only then does he realize the vital strength of the capacity and potentiality of the individual for constructive action. It is as he is willing for death to be the choice, that life is chosen, for neuroticism to be the choice that a healthy normality is chosen. The more completely he acts upon his central hypothesis the more convincing is the evidence that the hypothesis is correct."[29]

Although it would be comfortable to turn the hypothesis into a "law," Rogers recognized that "it is actually a hypothesis in human relationships, and will always remain so. Even for the experienced counselor, who has observed in hundreds of cases the evidence which supports the hypothesis, it is still true that for the new client who comes in the door, the possibility of self-understanding and intelligent self-direction is still, for the client, a completely unproved hypothesis."[30]

What happens, then, when the client's words and actions cause the therapist to doubt the basic hypothesis and tempt her to intervene in the client's therapy in a more directive fashion? Here Rogers' extremism, courage of convictions, and scientific attitude are apparent. "If the counselor feels, in the middle of an interview, that this client may not have the capacity for recognizing himself, and shifts to the hypothesis that the counselor must bear a considerable responsibility for this reorganization, he confuses the client, and defeats himself. He has shut himself off from proving or disproving either hypothesis. It is this confused eclecticism, which has been prevalent in psychotherapy, which has blocked scientific progress in the field. Actually it is only by acting consistently upon a well-selected hypothesis, that its elements of truth and untruth can become known."[31]

More and more for Rogers, this acceptance of the client, as he is at the moment, became a *sine qua non,* a necessary condition for effective psychotherapy. But the acceptance alone, without the therapist's deep understanding of the client, would be of little value. Most of us have experienced the doting relative or the flattering acquaintance who seems so accepting and positive toward us; yet this attitude, while it may feel good to receive, has very little lasting or significant value. Consciously or unconsciously we recognize its superficiality. This would be especially true for the client in therapy. With all of his own self-doubts and self-rejection he would be likely to respond to acceptance-without-understanding by thinking, "If you really knew me as I know me, if you knew what I've done, if you knew the things I feel, I bet you wouldn't be so accepting then. You'd probably be shocked or offended, or you'd pity me, or you'd tell me I'm wrong or bad or abnormal." Only if the therapist really understands the client, as the client understands himself, can the therapist's acceptance of the client enable the client to be more accepting of himself. Only when the client feels deeply understood can he truly trust the therapist's acceptance.

Therefore Rogers emphasized the counselor's understanding of the client as a necessary corollary to her acceptance. By understanding, he meant "the therapist's willingness and sensitive ability to understand the client's thoughts, feelings, and struggles from the client's point of view. This ability to see completely through the client's eyes, to adopt his frame of reference, has seemed to be an important way of implementing the fundamental hypothesis and is the basis for the use of the term 'client-centered.' To receive completely what the client is trying to communicate of his feelings even when his communication is confused or incoherent or fragmentary—to be able to enter into the client's private world and see it from his point of view—this is what we mean by adopting the client's frame of reference."[32]

This notion of "adopting the client's frame of reference" replaced the earlier emphasis on "reflection of feelings." Quoting himself, Rogers wrote, "The present author, in a paper given in 1940 stated, 'As material is given by the client, it is the therapist's function to help him recognize and clarify the emotions which he feels …' This has been a useful concept, and it is partially descriptive of what occurs. It is, however, too intellectualistic, and if taken too literally, may focus the process on the counselor. It can mean that only the counselor knows what the feelings are, and if it acquires this meaning it becomes a subtle lack of respect for the client."[33]

On the contrary, the therapist's attempts to adopt the client's frame of reference must be done in the most tentative, interested, and accepting manner. Rogers began to use the word "empathy" to describe the process. By no means did he invent the word; it had been used in psychotherapy for many years. He simply appropriated it to convey his meaning and proceeded to popularize it widely. He began to use the term "understanding" less and "empathy" and "empathic" more.[34] He often emphasized that empathy meant seeing the world as if one were the client, but never so totally identifying with the client that the "as if" quality was lost.

The flavor of this "sensitive empathy," as Rogers often called it, is captured in a recorded interview with a "Mrs. Oak."

MRS. OAK: Uh, I caught myself thinking that—that—that during these uh, sessions, uh, I've been sort of singing a song. Now that sounds uh—uh, vague, and—and—and uh—uh, not actually singing … sort of a song without any music. A—a, uh, probably a kind of poem coming out. (M-hm.) and uh, I like the idea, I mean it's sort of come to me with—without anything built out of—

160

of anything. And in … following that, it came, it came this other kind of—of—of a uh, feeling. Well, I s—s—found myself sort o—of asking myself uh, is that the shape that cases take? (M-hm). A uh—uh, is it possible that I—I—I am just verbalizing and, and—and uh, at times kind of become intoxicated with my own—own, u—uh, verbalizations? (M-hm). And then uh, following this, came, well, am I just taking up your time? Uh … then a doubt, a doubt … (M-hm.) Then something else occurred to me. Uh, from whence it came I—I don't know, no actual logical kind of a sequence of the thinking. The thought struck me: We're [*two words missing*] uh, overwhelmed or uh, doubtful, or—or uh, we can show concern or, or an—a—any uh, interest when—when the, when blind people uh, learn to read with their fingers, uh, Braille. And I don't know, it—it may be just sort of—of … it's all mixed up … it may be that's something that I'm uh, uh, eg—experiencing.

ROGERS: M-hm. Let's see if I can get some of that "uh—uh," that sequence of feelings. First, sort of as though you're … and I gather that the first one is a fairly positive feeling … as though maybe you're kind of creating a poem here … uh, a song without music somehow but something that might be quite uh, quite creative, and then the—the feeling of a lot of skepticism about that. "Maybe I'm just saying words, uh, just being carried off by words that I, that I speak, and maybe it's all a lot of baloney, really." Uh … and then a feeling that uh … perhaps you're almost learning a—a new type of experiencing which would be just as radically new as for a blind person to try to make sense out of what he feels with his fingertips.

MRS. OAK: M-hm. M-hm.[35]

The ability to move from one's own frame of reference to the client's internal frame of reference was a very difficult one for students of counseling to learn. As Rogers described it, "This struggle to achieve the client's … own perceptual field and see with him as perceiver is rather closely analogous to some of the Gestalt phenomena. Just as by active concentration, one can suddenly see the diagram in the psychology text as representing a descending rather than an ascending stairway or can perceive two faces instead of a candlestick, so, by active effort, the counselor can put himself into the client's frame of reference. But just as in the case of visual perception the figure occasionally changes, so in the case of the counselor, he may at times find himself out of the client's frame of reference, and looking at the client as an external perceiver …"[36]

To give the reader a somewhat more real and vivid experience of the attitudinal set he was describing, Rogers suggested that the reader put himself in the place of the counselor, and consider the following material, which was taken from complete counselor notes of the beginning of an interview with a man in his thirties. "When the material has been completed," wrote Rogers, "sit back and consider the sorts of attitudes and thoughts which were in your mind as you read."

CLIENT: I don't feel very normal, but I want to feel that way ... I thought I'd have something to talk about—then it all goes around in circles. I was trying to think what I was going to say. Then coming here it doesn't work out ... I tell you, it seemed that it would be much easier before I came. I tell you, I just can't make a decision; I don't know what I want. I've tried to reason this thing out logically—tried to figure out which things are important to me. I thought that there are maybe two things a man might do; he might get married and raise a family. But if he was just a bachelor, just making a living—that isn't very good. I find myself and my thoughts getting back to the days when I was a kid and I cry very easily. The dam would break through. I've been in the Army four and a half years. I had no problems then, no hopes, no wishes. My only thought was to get out when peace would come. My problems, now that I'm out, are as ever. I tell you, they go back to a long time before I was in the Army ... I love children. When I was in the Philippines—I tell you, when I was young I swore I'd never forget my unhappy childhood—so when I saw these children in the Philippines, I treated them very nicely. I used to give them ice cream cones and movies. It was just a period—I'd reverted back—and that awakened some emotions in me I thought I had long buried. *(A pause. He seems very near tears.)*

Rogers pointed out that, after reading this material, such thoughts as the following could represent an external frame of reference of the counselor.

I wonder if I should help him get started talking.
Is this inability to get under way a type of dependence? Why this indecisiveness? What could be its cause?
What is meant by this focus on marriage and family? He seems to be a bachelor. I hadn't known that.
The crying, the 'dam,' sound as though there must be a great deal of repression.
He's a veteran. Could he have been a psychiatric case?
I feel sorry for anybody who spent four and one-half years in the service.
Some time we will probably need to dig into those early unhappy experiences.
What is this interest in children? Identification? Vague homosexuality?[37]

"Note that these are all attitudes which are basically sympathetic," Rogers wrote. "There is nothing 'wrong' with them. They are even attempts to 'understand,' in the sense of 'understanding about,' rather than 'understanding with.' The locus of perceiving is, however, outside the client ... By way of comparison, the thoughts which might go through your mind if you were quite successful in assuming the client's internal frame of reference would tend to be of this order.

You're wanting to struggle toward normality, aren't you? It's really hard for you to get started.
Decision-making just seems impossible to you.

You want marriage, but it doesn't seem to you to be much of a possibility.

You feel yourself brimming over with childish feelings.

To you the Army represented stagnation.

Being very nice to children has somehow had meaning for you. But it has been—and is—a disturbing experience for you. [38]

"If these thoughts are couched in a final and declarative form, then they shift over into becoming an evaluation from the counselor's perceptual vantage point. But to the extent that they are empathic attempts to understand, tentative in formulation, they represent the attitude we are trying to describe as adopting the client's frame of reference."[39]

Mistakenly many people thought, and still do think, of nondirective counseling as a rather passive approach—a "laissez-faire psychology," as one writer called it.[40] Actually, as the previous examples indicate, adopting the client's frame of reference demands the utmost in active listening, concentration, and communication on the part of the therapist. Partly for this reason Rogers, in the late forties, began to avoid the term "nondirective" and began to use the "client-centered" label almost exclusively. He also realized that nondirective was a "term of rebellion ... saying what we were against" and did not capture the essence of the approach, which was adopting the client's frame of reference.[41] It was to his ongoing chagrin that, for decades, many individuals in psychology and psychotherapy continued to talk of the "nondirective method" and thought of Rogers' contribution in terms of his thinking and practice in the early forties.

But now the irony. At the same time that Rogers' writings were becoming decreasingly nondirective in their reduced emphasis on technique in favor of the counselor attitudes of acceptance and empathic understanding, Rogers' own clinical practice and that of his colleagues at the Counseling Center were becoming *more* nondirective. A study by Seeman, analyzing cases handled in 1947–1948, used the same method for measuring counselor techniques as Snyder had used in his study of cases from 1940–1942. The later study showed that over the six-year period, the client-centered therapists had steadily increased the frequency of their nondirective, reflection-of-feeling responses to the point where these constituted eighty-five percent of the counselor's statements![42] This finding seemed to emphasize a point Rogers had made—that a counselor need not fully believe the "basic hypothesis" upon beginning her work, that by testing the hypothesis with clients, she might prove or disprove it to her own satisfaction. For the group around Rogers, at least, it was apparent that their experiences with therapy led them "to depend more fully on the basic hypothesis of the approach than was true a half dozen years ago. It seems that more and more the nondirective therapist has judged understanding and acceptance to be effective, and has come to concentrate his whole effort upon achieving a deep understanding of the private world of the client."[43]

For Eugene Gendlin, who worked with Rogers in Chicago and after, and made major contributions to the client-centered approach over many years, this radical nondirective, client-centered approach "put Rogers ahead of the country … In 1945, blacks, women, gay people and others found help at the Counseling Center because these therapists knew that *every* client had to teach them a new world … These therapists never forced a policy on a client. They would not coerce a woman to stay in a marriage, as psychoanalysts generally then did. Nor would they decide what another person's sexuality should be. To therapists trained by Rogers, it was obvious that *every* person is at the directing center of a life and that one can help people only by means of their own intricacy and their own steps."[44]

In 1951 Houghton Mifflin published Rogers' third major book, *Client-Centered Therapy,* in which Rogers set forth his and his colleagues' current thinking and practice.[45] The world of psychology and psychotherapy at large paid little attention to it, and like its predecessor it was not reviewed in the professional journals. On the other hand it received a warm reception from the growing number of individual counselors, psychologists, and helping professionals who were either involved or interested in the client-centered movement, and it became a best-seller in the field. For them the book was challenging and controversial. In it Rogers spoke very openly about the changes in his thinking and practice which had taken place over the last several years. The first chapter was titled "The Developing Character of Client-Centered Therapy." Whereas one chapter of *Counseling and Psychotherapy* had been titled "The Directive Versus the Non-Directive Approach," the comparable chapter in *Client-Centered Therapy* was called "The Attitude and Orientation of the Counselor." In it he wrote, "As I look back upon some of our earlier published cases—the case of Herbert Bryan in my book, or Snyder's case of Mr. M—I realize that we have gradually dropped the vestiges of subtle directiveness which are all too evident in those cases. We have come to recognize that if we can provide understanding of the way the client seems to himself at this moment, he can do the rest."[46]

In addition to describing the changes in his thinking and practice of therapy, Rogers devoted a major section of the book to applications of the client-centered approach to other fields. He wrote, "The individual who comes to rely upon this hypothesis in his therapeutic work finds almost inevitably that he is driven to experiment with it in other types of activity."[47] In this section, with the help of several colleagues, he began to explore the implications of client-centered therapy for a wide range of other helping functions. Elaine Dorfman, Nicholas Hobbs, and Thomas Gordon wrote chapters on "Play Therapy," "Group-Centered Psychotherapy" and "Group-Centered Leadership and Administration," respectively. Rogers wrote chapters on "Student-Centered Teaching" and "The Training of Counselors and Therapists." Although he had written a few articles touching on the applications of his approach to other fields,[48] this section of

Client-Centered Therapy was his first attempt to apply their insights and experiences to other fields in a consistent and organized manner. It signaled what would come in later years, when Rogers and his colleagues would continue to explore the implications of the "basic hypothesis" in various fields. The kernels for several of Rogers' later books are contained in these chapters.

Speaking Personally

Another change evident in *Client-Centered Therapy* was Rogers' developing personal style of communication. As a writer and a speaker he had always communicated his ideas in a clear, down-to-earth, non-esoteric manner, and in that sense he always came across as a genuine person. Having been trained in an academic setting, however, where it was proper to refer to oneself only in the third person, Rogers had followed the traditional mode for many years. "The author believes ...," "the present writer has found ...," "explored by this investigator," would be the normal way he would insert any self-reference. Gradually he came to feel that the pronoun "I" was legitimate, even preferable in many cases. And as he began to use the first person in his speeches and writings, he became even more real and personal to his audience. A passage from the preface to *Client-Centered Therapy* gives something of the flavor of his developing style.

> This book is about the highly personal experiences of each one of us. It is about a client in my office who sits there by the corner of the desk, struggling to be himself, yet deathly afraid of being himself—striving to see his experience as it is, wanting to *be* that experience, and yet deeply fearful of the prospect. The book is about me, as I sit there with that client, facing him, participating in that struggle as deeply and sensitively as I am able. It is about me as I try to perceive his experience, and the meaning and the feeling and the taste and the flavor that it has for him. It is about me as I bemoan my very human fallibility in understanding that client, and the occasional failures to see life as it appears to him, failures which fall like heavy objects across the intricate, delicate web of growth which is taking place. It is about me as I rejoice at the privilege of being a midwife to a new personality—as I stand by with awe at the emergence of a self, a person, as I see a birth process in which I have had an important and facilitating part ... The book is, I believe, about life, as life vividly reveals itself in the therapeutic process.[49]

The change in style may not seem very remarkable; but in the academic, and especially the scientific community, it was then (and to a large extent, would be now) considered an unusual, if not suspicious departure from the norm. One editor was sufficiently surprised by this that he included the following footnote on the first page of Rogers' article:

The editor raised a question with the author regarding the frequent use of the personal pronoun in the manuscript and received a reply which deserves quoting. "The fact that it is in quite personal form is not accidental nor intended to make it a letter. In recent years I have been experimenting with a more personal form of writing for I believe that putting an article in more personal form makes it communicate more directly and, even more important, keeps us from sounding like oracles. Instead of saying, 'This is so,' one is much more inclined to say 'I believe this is so.' I just wanted you to know the reason why it is expressed in a more personal way than is considered to be good scientific writing." This argument appeared particularly to fit the nature of the article in question and the original flavor of the writing is retained. —Ed.[50]

As did Hobbs, Dorfman, and Gordon in their chapters in *Client-Centered Therapy*, throughout the book Rogers also frequently used the pronoun "*we*." "We have learned ...," "As we look back ...," "It has been our experience ...," and so on. This was not the "regal we" in which the individual projects his own viewpoint onto those around him. Rogers was referring to a very specific "we"—his colleagues and students at the Counseling Center at Chicago.

The Counseling Center

It was at the Counseling Center that most of Rogers' work really took place. Aside from his fifteen or more hours per week of counseling, for Rogers and for most of the other people connected with the Center it was the interpersonal relationships among staff and students that constituted the greatest satisfaction of being there.

Rogers was not the Counseling Center's Director—he was its Executive Secretary. This was his decision, and it had a special significance for him. First, he was a counselor and scientist, not an administrator. He had no intention of diverting the major thrust of his life's work into details of maintaining a complex operation. Perhaps even more important, his faith in the individual's capacity to guide his or her own life was not confined to clients and students only. He had a similar belief about groups. From the beginning he encouraged the Counseling Center personnel to work together to define the purposes and procedures of the Center. One student from that period, Norman Brice, recalled, "I learned so much from just observing Carl ... One thing I learned was a way to administer a group of professionals by *trusting* them and by *delegating my authority to the entire group.* This I have done in the fifteen years I have had administrative responsibility for the counseling program at Chico State College."[51]

A description of the Counseling Center, prepared in 1953 by a "committee of the staff," explained that "over a period of seven years the Center organization has seemed to develop in one particular direction—toward flexibility, informality, and group-centeredness. This has been possible primarily because those who originally were given authority and leadership for the Center have been willing, perhaps even eager, to transfer their authority to the total group and to distribute their leadership among the members of the group."[52] After one of Rogers' several attempts to explain the Center's mode of operation to the Dean Robert Strozier, the latter said, "Well, I don't understand it, but I want you to know that if anything goes wrong over there I'm going to hold you responsible." After a moment's thought Rogers said, "That's O.K. with me, so long as you understand that I am *handling* that responsibility by giving it to us as a group."[53]

A staff member of the Center from 1947–1953, Julius Seeman, remembered how "Carl provided a genuine, thoroughgoing climate of democracy in Center government. There was diffusion of responsibility in both day-to-day administration and in basic policy making. Staff members could exert major influence on policies in terms of their ability to persuade or influence other staff members. A concomitant of this power diffusion was the fact that Carl did not offer strong emotional support or protection to staff members. They had to make it on the power of their ideas. Carl did not play papa. This is not to say that staff members never perceived him in that way or that they did not want that kind of support. It is simply that Carl didn't behave in those terms."[54]

This democratic structure applied not only to the permanent staff members but also to the students. Bernard Steinzor was a student at the Center in 1945, when everything was just getting underway. He remembered the "sense of collegiality and democratic working together. The development of policies, of fee schedules, of relationships to the Dean's Office, and all the other problems that come up in a counseling center attached to a university were all worked through in as democratic a way as can be hoped for."[55]

On one occasion the secretarial and professional staff spent endless hours deciding whether to fire a secretary. They had tried to help the person but it just hadn't worked out and so, after many meetings and discussions, they decided to terminate the staff member's employment. Later Rogers reflected, "Now that seems like a lot of time to spend on one individual, but that was one of the things I learned there: often basic attitudes and basic philosophy somehow get crystallized in an issue which in itself seems minor. And so you spend hours talking about something that in a good hierarchical organization would be settled in ten minutes, and here are twenty or thirty people working on it. But when that is resolved, then issues which would seem major, like approving a budget or adopting a major policy, can be settled in five minutes."[56]

As Rogers described it, in his Annual Report for 1950, "This working together has not been primarily in unity or smoothness. We have been annoyed with each other; as individuals we often feel frustrated that the others do not appreciate the truth we see; as individuals we develop differing ways of carrying on therapy and of viewing therapy, and we feel disappointed that the others do not see it our way; we wrestle, often painfully, with problems which could be 'solved' very neatly and easily by a more authoritative organization; but in all of this, our feelings and our desires and our struggles are out in the open, and from this freely expressed, individualistic 'chaos' comes a deeper, organic type of unity which is very precious to us. It makes the Center our Center. It makes it an exciting creative spot to work where no one can predict what 1951 will bring forth, except that it can be predicted that we will push further into the unknown than we have in 1950."[57]

There were several different categories of personnel at the Center— professional "staff members" who usually had joint appointments in the Department of Psychology and the Counseling Center, graduate students taking a practicum or internship, research fellows, post-doctoral fellows, visiting or temporary staff members, and secretarial staff. At first the only interns accepted at the Center were University of Chicago students. In 1950, Rogers' former student Nicholas Hobbs, then on the faculty at Teachers College, Columbia University, suggested that *his* student Armin Klein become an intern at the Counseling Center. This set a precedent of hosting interns from other institutions, which continued thereafter. Klein recalled how "I brought with me the subculture of my school, calling him Carl ... I was surprised to find that the Chicago interns were aghast that I should act so familiar with this austere, very reserved, and dignified man. It hadn't been done before by students at that level. Carl accepted it well, and the other interns began to risk it, all of us helping him with his long, slow process of loosening up, which continued in his reserved fashion the rest of his life."[58]

One student, Leonard Hersher, said of Rogers, "When it came to hiring people for the Counseling Center, he had the idea that one should hire a good person with potential rather than one who held certain skills. And that people should try different things. He seemed to have no objection if people hired as research workers or secretaries became therapists."[59] Rogers told the story of how "a repairman came one Saturday afternoon to mend some damaged equipment. He found a secretary typing away, and began asking her questions about the place. Her responses were all of this sort: 'Well, we see students and others who need help.' 'We do research.' 'We ...' Finally the repairman said disgustedly, 'What do you mean by this "we" stuff? Don't you work for somebody here?' After a thoughtful pause, the secretary said, 'No. This is our outfit.'"[60] Interestingly, after years of hard effort, this secretary, Charlotte Ellinwood, went on to receive a Ph.D. in Clinical Psychology from the University of Chicago, helped in part by a no-interest, unsecured loan from Rogers.[61]

The result of the flexibility of jobs was considerable overlap in the roles everyone played. Students and staff would both be carrying on therapeutic interviews with clients and, thus, to an extent, would be colleagues, as well as supervisor and supervisee. All groups might be engaged in research, so it would not be unusual to have several of the inexperienced students studying the transcripts of interviews conducted by the experienced staff members or post-doctoral fellows, analyzing their failures and successes in fostering therapeutic change. Since the staff meetings consisted of permanent staff members, temporary staff members, and graduate interns, running the Center on a democratic basis meant that no one person or group had complete control over the direction of the Center. This was what Rogers wanted. He believed that new knowledge in psychotherapy would best be produced if the Center personnel were free to explore their own hunches, to exercise their creativity, to set their own priorities, and to make mistakes.

Compared to other pioneers in the history of psychotherapy, Rogers had no desire to achieve unanimity of thought and practice among his followers. One student, Richard Reed, recalled "a seminar which met at the Rogers' apartment near the university. The class (about 20 graduate students) met from 7:30 p.m. until all hours. Rogers, with the others in the group, was a student too. Members of his staff, counselors (Bill Kell, Ollie Bown, etc.), came and read a paper to us. All of us commented on the paper when it was finished. Then we'd divide into groups of three or four and go into separate rooms where we discussed the 'meat' of the paper. After 30 or 45 minutes we would reassemble, make comments in the group again and have a supper. It was then—during these 'moments' in the seminar when I learned more definitely to assess the man's simplicity, brilliance, acceptance ... He always appeared to have time to listen to any of us. He never imposed his ideas. Always he joined us as ... a learner."[62]

Eugene Gendlin recalled how "Rogers published the transcripts of a case of his that was a failure. In the intern group he would play tapes of model interviews, but sometimes he would bring in a bad one, saying, 'I don't know what's going wrong here.' The students could hear a great deal going wrong, and it made them feel free to present their own bad interviews."[63]

Sometimes Rogers asked his classes, at the beginning of the course, if they would all be willing to accept a grade of B, so they wouldn't have to worry all through the quarter about how they might impress him to get a good grade. They would be freer to pursue their own goals.[64] Usually, though, he solved the grading problem by using a system of self-evaluation in which the students evaluated their own progress and helped determine their own grade.

"It was the most thrilling and exciting place to be," agreed Richard Farson, Rogers' research assistant in 1949 and colleague for many years. Yet, paradoxically, he saw another side to the Counseling Center's cohesion. "It had almost the feeling of a ... I shouldn't use the word *cult*, but that's what comes to my mind, in a sense ... the feeling that you were *right*. There was a righteousness about it—that we were on the right track and that Psychology generally wasn't. We not only knew what to do but we knew how to do it. We knew what needed fixing and we had the power to do that. We had such a belief in ourselves, such confidence. There were enemies on the outside. Psychiatry was an enemy. Psychoanalysis was an enemy. They treated Carl very badly, by and large, in those days. We had what these cultish groups have. You have an enemy outside that keeps you kind of bonded in our cause. That was thrilling but I think it was naïve. I don't fault Carl for this at all but I think it's just what happens when you get [righteous]. He was always trying to keep us focused on research and so forth. I don't think that was naïve on his part."[65]

Gerard Haigh agreed about the cultish atmosphere of the Counseling Center. "When I became a member of the staff, that became my professional family with Carl as our father and our guru ... We staffers felt that we were an elite and privileged group in being associated with him ... While we had many struggles with each other in our Carl-centered community, we shared Carl's vision, and this inspirited our life together. I'm sure we tended to be righteous. I know that we believed that our approach to therapy was the best but I think we also tended to believe that it was the only right one ... I guess we were True Believers and Carl was both our guru and a True Believer himself."[66]

One factor mitigating against any cult-like insularity was the interdisciplinary nature of the Center staff. Staff member Laura Rice recalled "the variety of disciplines, in addition to psychology, that were represented at the Chicago Counseling Center. Graduate students from the Religion and Personality Program at the Divinity School came for training in psychotherapy and counseling, and in the process opened up for the rest of us some of the important ideas current among theologians. There were students and faculty from the Committee on Human Development, with their emphasis on understanding the biological and social aspects of development. Others came from Education, Sociology, Anthropology, Philosophy, and Social Thought. This variety of backgrounds led to an openness in exploration, an absence of the kind of rigidity often found in groups whose backgrounds are too similar. Each of us had to take a close look at our own presuppositions; things that were taken for granted by one group were opened up for questioning by another."[67]

Rogers, moreover, hardly acted like a cult leader who insisted on obedience and unanimity. Jim Bebout remembered, "There was no such thing as working *under* Carl Rogers—it seemed a question of 'doing your own thing' alongside him and with his considered approval. I remember staff meetings at Chicago at which all hell was breaking loose (about firings, personal relationships, or salaries). As loud as the staff screamed at each other, with a corner of all eyes on Carl, it was none of his responsibility, and if he contributed anything to the melee, it would always be a personal reaction."[68]

One woman, Dr. Rosalind Dymond Cartwright, came to the Counseling Center in 1951 to serve as Research Coordinator. She remembered how "there were petty jealousies, troubles of all kinds at that time, but they weren't in Carl. And they infuriated him. I never saw him quite so angry as when an issue was brought up at staff meeting and people turned to him to see how he would vote, to follow his lead or his nod. He didn't want that kind of role, he didn't like that behavior on the part of other people. He wanted them to respect themselves sufficiently to speak for themselves without waiting for him."[69]

In one of his annual reports Rogers described this phenomenon more specifically. He wrote, "the young faculty members on the staff can satisfactorily become free and independent of my influence and my reputation ... Personally I find great satisfaction in the evidence that there is growing leadership among our staff members. People who are interested in psychotherapy and learning theory turn immediately to Butler, for example, rather than to me. People who are interested in groups—group therapy, group administration and so forth, turn at once to Gordon, recognizing the quality of thinking he has done in this field. People who wish to know about research methodology turn to Seeman, Grummon or others on the staff because they have established their own reputations in these areas. I feel that the *Center* is less and less a one man show and this pleases me very much."[70]

Above all, Rogers was a great listener. This was one of my own first impressions of him. In 1970 I had driven across the country to meet him and Helen at their home in La Jolla, California, to discuss the possibility of my writing his biography. When I arrived, Helen was occupied with a friend, so Rogers and I went into his study to talk for about forty-five minutes. When we came out to join Helen, he summarized our conversation for her by reviewing, without notes, all the major points I had made during those forty-five minutes. I remember my astonishment, thinking, "My God, this man *really* heard everything I said! What an incredible listener he is!" Then I laughed at myself for reacting this way, remembering why I had traveled across the country to meet him, realizing that I really need not have been surprised to discover his ability to listen.

My reaction then was typical of those who knew Rogers at most any point from the 1940s on. Since Rogers first popularized the concept of empathic listening, or "active listening," it has come to be a well-known practice in the helping professions.[71] But for people who experienced this type of attention from Rogers himself, it usually left an indelible impression. His colleague at Chicago, Rosalind Dymond Cartwright, described him as "the most acute listener I have ever known."[72] Norman Brice, a Counseling Center student, remembered that he had "accepted an offer to join the staff of Michigan State as a counselor. I came into Carl and asked him if he might be able to work me into one or more counseling interviews, since I had never experienced him directly as a therapist. He managed to work in four. At the end of the first session with Carl, I came out to Virginia Hallman, his secretary, and practically shouted, 'Now I know the secret ingredient!' She was kind of low-key and gave me a 'What's with you?' response. I told her I have never felt so deeply and fully understood and so completely respected in all my life, and that the effect on me was electrifying."[73]

Rogers' ability to listen empathically and his ability to encourage independent, creative work among his staff and students might be seen as two facets of one major quality: his great capacity to understand and accept another person as a separate individual, capable of self-direction and worthy of trust. I frequently have heard said of him: "Carl Rogers is the most Rogerian person I have ever met."

Hence in classes, too, it was natural for him to respond empathically to students' comments, trying to understand the meaning the comments had for them. Joan Chodorkoff, a former student who became a college professor herself, wrote, "The thing I remember most vividly that has stuck with me is my initial feeling that when Carl turned to a student who asked a question and responded, that there was something ungenuine or overdone or ritual about it. Until I asked my questions, and I got that being accepted feeling! It is genuine and a student does grow on it."[74] Richard Farson recalled how "he was the first person, the first faculty member I'd ever encountered who took me seriously. I think that's what everybody's experience was. He took you seriously. He thought what I had to say was worth listening to. Of course what happens then is that what you have to say gets better."[75]

The combination of Counseling Center structures that encouraged equality, freedom, and autonomy among staff and students, as well as Rogers' own personal presence as a trusting, accepting, understanding, concerned professor, seemed to have the effect of freeing students and staff to follow their own lights and to engage in highly productive and creative work. Gerard Haigh recalled, "There was an intense creative excitement at the Center. Carl and his graduate students saw ourselves as pioneers exploring the frontiers of psychotherapy and human relations. There seemed to be no limit to the applicability of client-centered principles. He supported us in reaching to the utmost limits of our own imagination as exemplified by a graduate seminar which Tom Gordon and I offered titled 'Implications in Client-Centered Therapy for Dyadic Relations, Family Relations, Industrial Relations, and International Relations'!"[76]

The equality and independence that students were encouraged to utilize carried over into the publishing area as well. Students did papers and reports, but instead of being told to write papers on subjects about which their teachers already knew, they were encouraged to develop new ideas and new research projects that would extend the limits of the entire group's knowledge. Again they were called upon to act not like "students," but as professionals. With this type of trust and expectation, they rose to the higher standards and produced a large number of valuable research studies and theoretical papers, many of which influenced Rogers' own thinking. He and the staff also initiated the "Discussion

Papers" designed to encourage dialogue among staff and students over new ideas and methods. Anyone in the Center could have a paper he or she was working on mimeographed and circulated among the staff and students. This stimulated provocative discussion and thinking, which resulted, eventually, in more cogent publications.

Rogers would quote or make reference to his students' and staffs' work in most of his articles. He built much of his own reputation by reporting and synthesizing the ideas of others. But it is significant that among the scores of former colleagues and students who shared with me their experiences with Rogers, not one said that Rogers had unfairly taken credit for someone else's work. On the contrary, several pointed out how fair he tried to be and how generously they had been treated.

Elaine Dorfman, who wrote the chapter on play therapy in Rogers' *Client-Centered Therapy,* remembered, "Late on the evening of 11.3.49, I was notified of my father's death in New York. Since it was necessary for family reasons to leave town at once, I phoned my friend Lynn Rudikoff, of the Counseling Center staff, asking her to tell Rogers the next morning that I was unsure about plans to return and write."[77] The next day Rogers wrote her the following letter:

Dear Elaine:

I was terribly sorry to hear this morning from Lynn that your father had passed away. I think I have some notion of the sorrow and strain and responsibilities that can be involved in such a situation. I just want you to know that we are all sorry to hear the news and hope that the situation will not make too many demands upon you.

I had already dictated a letter telling you of your appointment to our courtesy staff and I am going to enclose it with this one, though there is nothing in it that needs your attention until you return.

Lynn tells me that you sent a message that you would be unable to complete that chapter on play therapy. I am not quite sure how to interpret this, but I assume that you meant that you would be unable to complete it by the tentative deadline! I am not even sure that the other chapters will be completed by the first of January and in any event, as I think I mentioned to you, I want the book to be right, not just finished by some particular date. So, unless you have really concluded that you do not wish to write the chapter I would very much like to have you continue with that responsibility.

In this connection I have been thinking a little further about your statement that somewhat later in the year you would welcome some financial backing (I wonder if your father's death may even make this need more pressing). In any event I should think that in making a fairly modest estimate you should eventually get $1500 or so for the chapter you are writing, in royalties. (This is on the assumption that the new book will sell somewhat in the same fashion as the old.) I suspect that these royalties would mean more to you now than they would later and I would be very happy to give you an advance of $1,000 on expected royalties. This could be repaid to me as royalties come in. It could be made available to you now or at any time you would think advisable.

You do not need to give me an immediate response to these questions. I am going to send this to your home address because it seems to me that it might influence some of your plans for the current year ...
Sincerely,
Carl Rogers[78]

The letter truly astonished her. "First, I had no idea that my contribution would mean royalties to me. Second the *offer* to lend me $1,000, at that time an enormous sum, was completely unheard of (and still is, some 20 years later). It was a gesture of complete faith, since neither he nor I knew whether my as yet unwritten chapter would prove acceptable for his book ... On the topic of this same book, you may be interested to know that royalties to all four authors were shared pro rata. Likewise, we are all co-owners of the copyright, although it is by contract registered in Rogers' name. This egalitarian arrangement with two former students and one current student demonstrates, I think, Rogers' commitment to non-power relationships."[79]

A Character Sketch

The cooperative, egalitarian, accepting side of Carl Rogers was the side which most people knew, or assumed to be there from the tone of his writings. Another quality that was often recognized by those who knew him personally, but which often surprised those who knew him only through his writings, was his strength and "drive." Colleagues and friends described him as "a very hard driving, forceful individual"[80] and "driving, ambitious," and having a "realistic sense of his own personal importance in the contemporary world but nevertheless unassuming."[81] This theme comes up again and again. Fred Fiedler wrote, "Considering Rogers' concern with client-centered therapy, his permissiveness and non-directive methods, I found him to be a very hard-headed and disciplined person. He was certainly not 'cuddly.' I did not feel that anyone could put something over on him (and I don't believe that any of us tried—even if we had wanted to)."[82]

His college debating experience served him well. Charles Ferguson "saw and heard him on a panel in a crowded ballroom in The Palace Hotel at the APA meetings in San Francisco when his work and ideas were under attack by eminent men. He waited patiently and collectedly while his several critics turned their attack on him, and then he spoke coolly, clearly, persuasively and skewered the lot ... he was cool, collected, competitive; he was intellectually tough, he knew where he stood, he was well informed and he was extremely able."[83]

David Rogers also saw his father as competitive. He realized this when his father once asked him, "How did *you* get so competitive?" David thought this characteristic was particularly evident when his father and uncles got together. This and Ferguson's picture of Rogers as a cool competitor is borne out by several of the "battles" which Rogers fought at the University of Chicago. The first was over a rather trivial incident but illustrates Rogers' readiness to stand up for his rights, his delight in rhetorical battle, and his tendency toward witty sarcasm—usually wielded gently but sometimes with a real edge to it.

Before Rogers came to Chicago, Robert Hutchins, the acclaimed President of the University, had instituted the "4E policy." This policy meant that the faculty would receive a relatively high pay schedule, but in return they would relinquish all monies earned from speeches, consultation, and writing to the university. This was done to foster a sense of community among the faculty and to discourage them from spending the bulk of their time seeking to enhance their own reputation or finances away from the university. On one occasion the University disallowed certain expenses Rogers claimed for Helen's accompanying him on a consulting trip, citing a rule that a Mr. Colwell had formulated that spouses could not accompany faculty on trips shorter than forty-five days. In a letter to the Assistant Comptroller, Rogers summarized the situation and concluded:

> As I puzzle over this situation, I see that I have made three mistakes in regard to it.
>
> In the first place, I had assumed that the relationship between the University and a faculty member was one of mutual confidence, decency and fair play. I thought that I could trust the University to be fair and equitable, and thought that they would feel the same way about me. I see now how mistaken I was. Your implicit attitude in this seems to be based on the assumption that "He's probably a chiseler unless he can prove otherwise." I realize that I should have taken the same attitude toward the University, and will now try to do so.
>
> In the second place, I was evidently mistaken in thinking that I needed my wife with me. I have the greatest regard for Mr. Colwell as a scholar and administrator, but I had not realized that he knew when I needed my wife. I shall of course consult him before taking her on any other trip. Incidentally one of the big disappointments of this whole affair is your refusal to send me the fascinating rules governing such situations. I had looked forward to receiving this Kinsey Report in Reverse. I wanted to know the evidence on which it was based. Is forty-five days the average time that faculty members can go without their wives, or is Mr. Colwell the norm which we must all try to achieve? Also how are exceptions made? What sort of evidence must one submit? Must the evidence be made public? (It seemed to me that at the very least this set of rules would be good for a skit at the Faculty Revels.)

But this is a digression. The third mistake which I seem to have made was to have submitted fair expenses instead of actual expenses, with the evidence therefore … I shall now correct all three mistakes …

He went on to re-itemize his expenses, attach his receipts, and continue his letter:

I will appreciate it if you will please send me a check for $505.38 … I realize that it is considerably more than the money I earned, but I hereby give you full permission to take the additional amount from the $1,100 I turned in the previous month.

It seems to me that as it now stands, everyone will be happy. You should feel very satisfied that you have been able to impose the rule that I cannot take my wife. I will feel very happy to receive $200 more than I had expected as reimbursement. The University should be very satisfied since, to judge by their administration of the 4E contract, their purpose seems to be to make every faculty member detest it. In this they have your very efficient help.

I feel much better having gotten this off my chest. Now I suppose that I will have to give my time to worthwhile work until the next time when I try to turn money over to the University, when I am sure you can think up some new way of making the experience annoying.[84]

Another more serious example of Rogers-as-protagonist occurred in 1951, after the University of Chicago's Laboratory School had been studied by a committee of the University Council, chaired by the university's chancellor. The committee's report was very critical of the school, which was progressive in its educational philosophy. The report began by making it clear that "we are convinced that the chief end of education should be growth in knowledge and intellectual powers." Although the committee admitted that "as compared with the average achieved by students throughout the nation, the students in the Laboratory School are advanced by about three years in most basic intellectual skills" and "also compare favorably with other superior students who enter the College," still they felt that "dominant influences in the school clearly encourage concern for the 'happiness' and 'socialization' of the child as the ruling end of education. Consequently, 'democratic' rituals may be observed at the expense of disciplined work under legitimate authority."[85]

This report came during the period when Senator Joseph McCarthy's anti-Communist crusade was having a chilling effect on free speech and democratic practices around the country. When the committee's report came to Rogers' attention, he took the initiative of writing a letter to the members of the committee and to others involved in the matter. Part of his letter read:

176

I realize that basic philosophies differ. I think differences are best explored when attitudes are brought out clearly, and for this I commend your report. I share with you a feeling that many of the procedures in the Laboratory School are accurately labeled as democratic rituals. But I disagree, as deeply as it is possible for a person to disagree, with the point of view you take. You feel that the solution for this situation is discipline by authority—giving up the democratic attempt. I can think of no better way of undermining the already badly shaken democratic philosophy of this country than to move the elementary schools in the direction of a more authoritarian philosophy. My own experience in working with individuals and groups leads me to believe that the solution lies in a direction which is diametrically opposed to yours. I feel the solution is to work toward a real democracy in our schools, with each individual genuinely participating in responsible choices. I would replace "democratic rituals" with real democracy rather than with authoritarianism. I would aim for responsible self-discipline, not for discipline imposed by "legitimate authority."[86]

His opposition to McCarthy was apparent in at least two professional presentations in the following years.[87] Without mentioning the senator by name, there was little doubt about whom he was referring to in a talk on changing attitudes in oneself and others. After describing the totalitarian methods of Hitler, Mussolini, Stalin and Mao, he added, "I am sure all of us could cite examples from our own experience in our own country. A person with power can use psychological methods to change attitudes, whether it is an experimenter in a laboratory who controls certain electrical switches, or whether it is a dictator or a leader who controls press, and media, and organizational machinery."[88]

On another occasion his disagreement struck much closer to home. Throughout his career Rogers had frequent differences with the psychiatric profession, especially when they would take the position that psychologists are not qualified to carry on intensive psychotherapy. Years before, in Rochester, there had been the year-long battle over whether a psychiatrist or a psychologist would be appointed as the head of the Child Guidance Center which Rogers had initiated. As the psychology profession grew and as it developed a greater interest in the areas of counseling, psychotherapy and clinical psychology, this issue arose with increasing frequency in a variety of settings throughout the country. At Chicago it had been a source of friction from the start, with the University Medical School Department of Psychiatry at Billings Hospital taking a dim view of the activities of the large and prestigious Counseling Center, which handled 800–1,000 new clients a year. There had been several open conflicts between the "Rogers group" and the "Billings group" during the late forties and early fifties, but it became particularly bitter in the middle fifties.[89] Something of the flavor of the relationship between the two groups can be sensed from one small part of a twelve-page memorandum Rogers wrote to Lawrence Kimpton, Chancellor of the University of Chicago, in November 1956.

177

I would like you to know of some of the statements which are being made about me and the Counseling Center by members of the medical group at the University. I believe you would want this situation brought to your attention. Let me give an example.

Dr. Aldrich, of the Department of Psychiatry, in a conversation with me on October 24, said, "From where we sit you are practicing illegal medicine with patients for whom the medical group here is responsible. What you are doing is not only illegal but dangerous." He went on to say that in his opinion I was violating the code of ethics of the American Psychological Association regarding the obligation of psychologists to have adequate channels of medical assistance ...

These remarks by Dr. Aldrich are similar to ones we have heard previously from Billings. My reaction can be stated by one sentence. I am tired of being maligned and slandered by members of the Billings group who know almost nothing of our work ...

Dr. Aldrich's statements contrast so sharply with the statements and actions of physicians and scientists who do know something of our work, that I would like you to consider some of these contrasts.

1. Dr. Harold G. Wolff of Cornell Medical School is one of the world's leading authorities in psychosomatic medicine. He has been a serious student of my work, and knows it very well. A week ago he asked me if I would serve with him as a consultant to the Department of Defense on a top-secret matter having to do with mental health. He said, "I am asking the five top-ranking men in the country in this field to serve on this task. You are one of the five, and I hope you will serve."

Now I submit that I may be one of the top-ranking men in the country in the field of mental health, or I may be an unethical law-breaker in my work. I do not believe that *both* statements can be true.

2. Dr. Seymour Kety is a leading neurologist and director of research for the National Institute of Mental Health. Dr. Merton Gill is a leading psychoanalyst. Doctors Kety and Gill studied intensely the work and program of the Counseling Center for the Ford Foundation. The result of their study and that of their committee (which included Dr. John Romano, a leading psychiatrist) was that the Counseling Center was one of 20 organizations selected out of many hundreds of applications for support in the field of research in mental health. A five year grant of $350,000 was made.

I submit that we may be an outstanding organization in the field of mental health, or we may be a group working illegally, unethically and dangerously. I do not believe it possible that we are *both* ...[90]

These examples illustrate how Rogers often "fought by memo." Late in life he said of himself, "I can write a very strong memorandum—well organized, very persuasive and firm—no beating around the bush. It's only very rarely that I can confront people that way. I can do it more easily through a memorandum, and that, I realize, is a real weakness."[91] His memos, particularly the sarcastic ones, sometimes carried the day but rarely endeared him to administrators or colleagues who were their target. For better or worse, these examples show someone who is hardly the stereotype of the all-accepting therapist. His son David commented of his father; "He can be just tougher than hell."

Richard Farson agreed. "He was a tough guy. I can remember in one of the papers, one of the research projects I turned in for him when I was his research assistant. He wrote on the top, 'Definitely disappointed' which seemed so uncharacteristic, so different from anything that Carl stood for. How would he ever be evaluative with one of us, you know? He was right and I had to redo it, and it was a great learning experience for me, actually, to be caught up that way."[92]

Occasional private memos aside, he was typically gracious, cordial and politic in public. But even there, on rare occasions, his judgmental or sarcastic side came through—not toward individuals per se but toward ideas or tendencies with which he disagreed. The University of Chicago had a famous, interdisciplinary program in Human Development presided over by pioneering developmental psychologist Robert Havighurst. Rogers and his colleagues worked very cooperatively with Human Development, often sharing some of the same students; hence it was not surprising that he was asked to present a paper at the Second Human Development Banquet in 1951. In his talk Rogers minced no words about the state of human development research about human relationships. Not necessarily referring to the faculty present, but not excluding them either, Rogers commented:

> I believe that this briefly characterizes most of the studies which have to do with human relationships. I cannot say that I am greatly impressed with the results. The people who are doing such researches tend to develop an assurance which is awe-inspiring to behold. They have so much information, their methodology is so impeccable, their conclusions so certain, their understanding so shallow. They seem to be bright and shining—but very brittle. It seems impossible for investigators to regard human beings from an external point of view, and still to grant them the full respect which they deserve as persons. It seems also, when one studies their findings, that all their countings and measurings have missed the subtleties and depths of human relationships. And so, when I ask myself whether these will be the individuals of wisdom and creative insight who will contribute deeply to our understanding of the relations between man and man—understandings so desperately needed by the world—I confess that I find myself very skeptical."[93]

Summing up comments and anecdotes like these which illustrate Rogers' assertiveness and directness, Norman Brice wrote, "What has bothered me so through the years has been the misguided notions of some who have read bits and pieces of what he has written and have proceeded to miss the whole point of what he has to say. They so often regard Carl as a softie, a 'gentle Jesus' type of person, permissive to a fault and therefore weak and ineffectual. In contrast to this, I have never in all my life met such a strong man as Carl. He puts *first* in his writings about psychotherapy the concept of *congruence* and that means *being yourself.* Being yourself means that you express anger when you feel it or boredom when you feel it, and that you are an authentic person in your own right. So many people don't seem to get that message. Someone, somewhere who does understand Carl said of him that he has a 'whim of steel.' Carl is nobody's pushover. He is a very, very strong and controversial man."[94]

There seems to be a considerable discrepancy between Rogers' associates' view of him as both accepting *and* assertive and many readers' rather one-sided impression created by his writings. How was it that this man who behaved in a confident, direct, and self-assertive manner withheld from his writings the tone or examples or transcripts of interviews or whatever it would take to convey more of the person he was? In my opinion the answer to this lies in another set of Rogers' characteristics that were frequently mentioned by his students, associates, and friends—great warmth, giving, and caring combined, paradoxically, with an impression of distance and aloofness.

I have heard dozens of people describe him as "warm." It seems to be one of the first things mentioned by most people who knew him for any length of time. Arthur Combs wrote, "The love and the genuineness of the man has a way of getting through to almost everyone who sees him or hears him. He seems to be able to convey even to a very large audience the feeling that he is expressing himself honestly, genuinely and caringly to each person in the audience. The interesting thing is that he really does."[95]

Yet many other people, and often the same ones who described him as warm, also saw him as being occasionally or frequently aloof. Part of this impression, undoubtedly, was caused by Rogers' shyness, a boyhood quality he never quite got over. Many people expect a famous figure or a leader to be extroverted, socially self-assured, the life-of-the-party, and so on. Rogers fitted none of these stereotypes. He was always ill-at-ease at social gatherings. Even in later years when he became involved in the encounter group movement, he would often begin a group by expressing some of his own nervousness or feelings of unsureness about what would happen. "Most individuals who have attained some status," he wrote, "tend to dominate a situation—they are brilliant in conversation, tend to be the center of attention in any group, simply cannot be ignored. I, on the contrary, am absolutely at my worst if I am expected to be a 'leading figure' or an 'exciting person.' As my wife can testify, I simply 'clam up' and seem to be the dullest person around."[96]

At the University of Chicago he and Helen once got on an elevator heading to an upper floor where Rogers was to deliver a lecture to a large audience. Just before the door closed, a young couple entered. As the four of them ascended, the young woman asked her friend, "Have you ever met this guy Rogers?" "Oh, yes," he said impressively. "What's he like?" she asked. "Well, he's a very unprepossessing kind of person," began the young man, as the door opened and they all left the elevator.[97]

Beyond his natural reticence, which must have occasionally been mistaken for aloofness, there was still some validity to those impressions of Rogers as somewhat withdrawn. Although Arthur Combs saw Rogers as "a person of deep sensitivity and compassion," he noted "a kind of paradox which I think is common to men like him: He has the capacity for intense concentration and is capable of responding flat out to persons who have real need of him like clients and members of his encounter groups and the like. He is likely, however, to seem somewhat aloof to persons in more casual contacts. It is almost as though he did not quite know how to handle situations in which he could not operate with the kind of intense giving which he shows in his professional relationships."[98]

John Levy suggested that Rogers "is blocked here, not only by his shyness, but also very strongly by his intense integrity. Carl is very strongly committed to emotional honesty, and some of his reserve is a result of his fear of conveying an emotion which he does not feel, or communicating it more intensely than is real. He has a passionate commitment to honesty, in his relationships no less than his work ... He has a strong need for privacy and for his own living space. He has developed an ability to say 'No,' and he says it in a way which is unmistakable. He values himself quite highly (this does not negate his shyness) and has learned to protect himself from those who would take advantage of him. Sometimes this comes out harshly, and sometimes people are offended. He doesn't play social games very well, or professional games, and often seems more interested in being sure that his position and his attitude are understood accurately than he is in protecting people's feelings or in being diplomatic."[99]

Shy and private, by nature and by choice. Warm and caring or cold and aloof—according to the beholder. T.M. Tomlinson tried to put the pieces together. "What kind of person is Carl Rogers? For me he is a person of whom I can as easily say 'I hardly know him' as 'He is one of the most important people in my life.' People often say with dismay that Rogers is really a cold man whose personality and life style are at direct variance with his writings and professed beliefs. They are wrong of course, but only because they expect something different than they get ... I don't know where those expectations come from ... What Rogers gives personally is what he says, namely, acceptance. He isn't demonstrative about it and most people don't know it when it's happening; only later do they realize the nature of their experience with him. Rogers doesn't give love; he's fairly lovable but not very loving. That, I think, is what leads to the conclusion that he's cold, i.e., people approach him expecting to be loved immediately for what they are, whereas Carl simply accepts them for what they are without implications of love. It's an easy distinction to draw, but most people are hard put to do it and feel rejected because they are not embraced. At the same time, however, it is difficult to feel that one is inside Carl Rogers. There are no psychic veins and arteries which pump blood from him to us, thus there is little feeling of shared worlds. The worlds touch but they don't overlap except in rare circumstances. What this sums to is that Carl is very much like the rest of us, some things are public, some things are private, sometimes he's gentle, sometimes he's tough, etc., except that he has a vision of how it ought to be and, to the extent possible for him, he practices it, always hoping that others will benefit and even more, that others will push beyond his own limits of behavior and thought."[100]

Julius Seeman took Tomlinson's analysis one step further and related Rogers' remoteness to his theoretical development as well as his personal style. "I worked with Carl for six years and felt that I got to know him relatively well in a professional context. But there was always a certain reserve when it came to personal self-disclosure, and I learned virtually nothing about his personal life during those six years. In retrospect I see this attribute as quite compatible with his early theoretical position and its emphasis on autonomy. However, there was also another central theme which I saw in Carl's development, both personally and professionally, and it touched also on the issue of autonomy. I think that the history of Carl's development, personal and theoretical, could fit on a continuum from insulation to involvement. His early theory emphasized the permissiveness of the therapeutic climate, and said astonishingly little about a person-to-person relationship with the client. Even the concept of 'reflection' was an insulating one, picturing as it did the mirroring of the client's own self as given back by the therapist. This distancing climate, however, had by 1950 come to be questioned, and alternative formulations were in the air. The reexamination took two forms. A small group at the Counseling Center talked of a more involved relationship and considered 'caring' and 'love' as ways to describe the relationship. Another dimension emphasized the congruence of the therapist, and suggested that such congruence had to involve greater self-disclosure by the therapist ... It seemed to me that about this time Carl's therapy was reflecting some movement toward a more internal and involved style, though I still experienced an underlying reserve. It was to take years of steadily growing involvement before Carl's personal self came through in therapy."[101]

Seeman's description implies that Rogers, in the middle years of his stay at Chicago, was commencing another period of change. Several previous changes had already taken place in his therapeutic style. In the early and middle 1930s, from an interest in manipulating the external conditions of a child's environment, he became more interested in psychotherapy as the means for helping the individual. From the middle 1930s to the early 1940s, from the use of directive methods for psychotherapy, he came to rely on and develop nondirective methods. From the middle to late 1940s, from an emphasis on nondirective methods, he came to emphasize client-centered attitudes—acceptance and empathic understanding. The change now occurring was the insertion of "congruence" as the third major ingredient in the therapeutic relationship. The change did not come about all at once, but it turned out to be one of the most personally significant changes in his life.

Personal Crisis

In Walter and Julia Rogers' household, emotional displays were considered a sign of weakness; they interfered with good common sense and getting one's work done. Hence young Carl Rogers learned to keep his emotions to himself and even ignore them if he could. Perhaps it was the suppression of feelings in his own upbringing that later helped Rogers recognize the importance of the client's being aware and accepting of his feelings. Acceptance and empathy became the therapist's tools for helping the client to accept and understand his own feelings. Little or nothing was said of the *therapist's* feelings, other than she *should feel* accepting and understanding if she wants to be helpful. What of the therapist who doesn't feel accepting or understanding with a particular client or at a particular time? Rogers provided no transcripts or anecdotes to answer the question. Thus he provided a very unrealistic picture for readers of his books who had to assume that either Rogers and his group were "perfect"—always accepting, always understanding—or that this presentation of therapy was much oversimplified and unrealistic. Apparently, even though he had come to understand the importance of the *client's* feelings in the relationship, his own personal background still held him back from giving due attention to the therapist's feelings.

The turning point came during the years 1949–1951. This was a time when Rogers experienced "two years of intense personal distress" and almost had a serious psychological breakdown that could have required hospitalization. In his own words, pieced together from several published and unpublished accounts and documents, here is what occurred:[102]

"There was a deeply disturbed client (she would be regarded as schizophrenic) with whom I had worked fairly extensively at Ohio State, who later moved to the Chicago area and renewed her therapeutic contacts with me. I see now that I handled her badly, vacillating between being warm and real with her, and then being more 'professional' and aloof when the depth of her psychotic disturbance threatened me. She began to take up a bigger and bigger part of my therapy time …" "In the last six months I have seen her five times a week," he wrote in May 1949.[103]

"She would sometimes appear sitting on our doorstep. I felt trapped by this kind of dependence. She said she needed more warmth and more realness from me. I wanted her to like me though I didn't like her. This brought about the most intense hostility on her part (along with dependence and love), which completely pierced my defenses. I started to feel it was a real drain on me, yet I stubbornly felt that I should be able to help her and permitted the contacts to continue long after they had ceased to be therapeutic, and involved only suffering for me. I recognized that many of her insights were sounder than mine, and this destroyed my confidence in myself, and I got to the point where I could not separate my 'self' from hers. I literally lost the boundaries of myself. The situation is best summarized by one of her dreams in which a cat was clawing my guts out, but really did not wish to do so."

"It seems as tho [sic] for a time I became the one being worked on in the relationship. It was as tho [sic] I was in therapy with a very shrewd and highly interpretive therapist, the only difficulty being that the 'therapist' was psychotic, and because of her own needs had to try to destroy me."[104]

"The efforts of colleagues to help were of no avail, and I became convinced (and I think with some reason) that I was going insane. One night, we saw a movie with some very bizarre happenings on the film, and I thought quite seriously, 'Well, when I'm locked up and start to hallucinate and so on, they'll think it all comes from inside me and actually a lot of it will be what I saw in this movie.' I was sure it was going to happen. I was so raw emotionally that anything had a real impact. Yet I continued this relationship, destructive to me, because I recognized her desperately precarious situation, on the brink of a psychosis, and felt I *had* to be of help."[105]

In March and April Rogers entered therapy with one of his colleagues in the Counseling Center, Nathaniel Raskin. "[T]hat has perhaps helped a little but not enough," he wrote at the time.[106] Consequently, "Gradually I realized I was on the edge of a complete breakdown myself."

He wrote to a former colleague from Rochester, John Warkentin, M.D., now in Atlanta, telling him of his distress and asking, if it became necessary, whether he or Carl Whitaker would be willing to take him on as a patient on a moment's notice. Whitaker, Chair of the Department of Psychiatry at Emory University, was already establishing a reputation as an innovative psychiatrist. He and his colleagues, including Warkentin and Thomas Malone, often worked with psychotic and schizophrenic patients and were experimenting with the therapist using himself more fully in the relationship, entering into an experiential, emotional relationship with the client.[107] Rogers had been interested in their work and told Warkentin, "There are few people away from here in whom I have confidence, and you and Whitaker are tops in this few."[108] Warkentin wrote back immediately saying he had consulted with Whitaker, they were both available, and given Warkentin's prior relationship with Rogers, Whitaker would become Rogers' therapist if needed.

Then suddenly the feeling of desperation "became very urgent. I had to escape. I am everlastingly grateful to Dr. Louis Cholden, the promising young psychiatrist, who was working in the Counseling Center at that time, for his willingness to take over the client on an hour's notice. I invited him to lunch at the Faculty Club. I said I needed help and explained the situation. He said, 'All right, how about my seeing her next week?' I must have shown something then and he must have been fairly sharp, because he added, 'Or isn't that soon enough?' I said, 'Well, she's coming in this afternoon.' I was really in a panic state at that time.

"I pulled a desperate trick on her. Knowing that she wouldn't want to see anyone else of her own accord, I arranged to give some kind of signal to the secretary, when Dr. Cholden should come into the office. He came in, I said a few words to introduce them and quickly left. She, within moments, burst into a full blown psychosis, with many delusions and hallucinations. She started telling Cholden of how she was related to me in some way, there was some uncle in Wisconsin and so on." (Later she tried to gain entrance to Rogers' apartment and tried to hang a large sign out their window saying, "Come Home!")

"As for me, I went home and told Helen that I must get away, *at once*. We were on the road within an hour and stayed away two or three months on what we can now calmly refer to as our 'runaway trip.' Shortly after leaving, I wanted to buy a couple of cans of beer. I went into a store, got the beer, paid for it, came out and thought with amazement, 'My God, I was able to do that!' I was fairly far gone. Helen's quiet assurance that I would come out of this distress in time and her willingness to listen when I was able to talk of it were of great help."

They headed south, in the direction of Atlanta and therapy with Whitaker, but never actually got there. They meandered through the Great Smokey Mountains and spent a chilly month or so at the family's cabin on Seneca Lake. Eventually, Rogers began to feel he could return to Chicago.

"However, when we returned I was still rather deeply certain of my complete inadequacy as a therapist, my worthlessness as a person, and my lack of any future in the field of psychology or psychotherapy." "I felt my problems were so serious it would only be threatening to ask a staff member to help me with them. I am deeply grateful that one member of our group [Oliver Bown] simply told me that it was obvious I was in deep distress, that he was not afraid of me or my problem, and that he was offering me a therapeutic relationship … He said, 'I just want you to know that I can see you're in trouble. And I also want you to know I'm not afraid of you. If you'd like to talk to me, I'd be glad to do so.' … I accepted in desperation."

The therapy went on for over a year.[109] At times it felt like they were making progress; at other times Rogers would begin to feel a rising panic. At one such point he wrote to Carl Whitaker again, reminding him of the situation and renewing his request for help if needed. He used an analogy to describe his predicament to Whitaker. "It seems as tho [sic] she dynamited away at a very basic wall of my personality until she had driven a hole through at the bottom, and I had vivid experiencing of dimly understood forces in myself which were outside the wall. I still cannot say what the forces or experiences are except that they seem deeply turbulent and destructive, and that the term psychotic seems to fit them ... What I want to do, in terms of the analogy, is to take down the wall, get acquainted with these other parts of me which are not in my 'self,' and to build a much lower wall around a larger space which will include them within myself ... [Working with Oliver Bown and with Louis Cholden who can help with medications] I am moving ahead in the vacillating and painful but normal path which is therapy ... But the rub is that the wall has been deeply dynamited and is so shaky that I have a deep fear that instead of being able to take it down gradually, it may collapse into a heap of rubble at some unexpected moment. If it does, then I am really in trouble ... If I should go all to pieces in my attempt to get to the bottom of this thing, would you be able to take me on short notice, even in the psychiatric ward if need be? ... I suppose it is strange that I don't feel more sense of shame or stigma or something but I don't. I feel that it is possible for some devastating things to happen to atomic scientists just because they don't as yet know all that should be known about the field. I think we're dealing with equally potent material, and that sometimes, because it is a new field and we know so little about it, we may get burned too."[110]

Again, reassured by the help available in Atlanta if needed, he remained in Chicago and continued with his therapy, remaining remarkably productive in his work considering the circumstances.[111] Over the months, Rogers' therapy with Bown yielded increasing results, providing significant support, release, insight and, most importantly, self-acceptance. Although he never elaborated on it, apparently the darker "forces and experiences" he glimpsed beyond his known self diminished upon examination and/or were accepted and incorporated into his sense of self. Hence, "[I] gradually worked through to a point where I could value myself, even like myself, and was much less fearful of receiving or giving love. My own therapy with my clients has become consistently and increasingly free and spontaneous ever since that time."[112]

These last two sentences deserve a closer examination. Rogers seems to be identifying two problems he had, quite apart from the relationship with the disturbed woman. That he came to value and even like himself suggests that at some level he had not valued or liked himself. That he became much less fearful of receiving or giving love suggests that such a fear previously existed. Reflecting on this period shortly before he died, Rogers said, "I realize that probably my deepest problem was not being able to like or love myself."[113]

It is at first glance ironic that even Rogers should have had to deal with this problem. If there was any one issue common to the hundreds of clients he had helped over the years, it was that they did not accept themselves. The manifestations of this lack of self-acceptance were vastly different, but the root problem was still the same: At some level, different for different people, they believed they were not "okay"—not lovable, not capable, not good enough. In his own words, Rogers felt, "Nobody could love *me,* even though they might like what I did. I was an unlovable person. I really was inferior, but putting up a big front."

This feeling was buried quite deeply. It had been years since he had to continually work and produce to be deemed worthy in his parents' eyes; since he felt he had to excel to compete with his older brothers' accomplishments; since he last heard his mother suggest that anything he might accomplish would still be "as filthy rags in Thy sight, oh Lord"; since he had to keep his feelings submerged, because expressions of feelings, particularly negative ones, were not welcomed; since he had to endure his family's teasing which eroded his tender self-esteem. These cumulative experiences had been clouded over by time. Subsequent years of professional success and a growing personal confidence had been almost enough to render that underlying, childhood remnant of non-self-acceptance irrelevant. Perhaps he might have gone along and not been troubled by those early scars and lived his life out as a satisfied and famous man. On the other hand perhaps this unfinished business from childhood—all the teasing, all the not-so-complimentary nicknames, all the criticism for being too absentminded or too immersed in fantasy or not religious in the proper way, in short, just not good enough—perhaps this had created a wound that was near to the surface and, had the relationship with the disturbed woman client not developed, something else would have triggered the process of distress, then therapy.

We will never know how it might have happened, only what did happen. The personal stress precipitated by the prolonged and complicated therapy with his client led to his entering into therapy with one of his staff members. The therapy, which started out by exploring specific current problems, led gradually toward deeper unresolved problems of self-attitudes and self-acceptance. Of his therapy he commented, "I have often been grateful that by the time I was in dire need of personal help, I had trained therapists who were persons in their own right, not dependent upon me, yet able to offer me the kind of help I needed. I have since become rather keenly aware that the point of view I developed in therapy is the sort of help I myself would like, and this help was available when I needed it."[114]

He felt greatly helped by his therapy, writing in July of 1951, "I believe that during the past year the therapy I have conducted has been better than anything I have ever done before. I think that my counseling is showing increasing results from my own therapy undertaken two years ago when I was really personally disturbed by the deep hostility of a client. I think that I see in myself now more freedom in venturing into deep emotional relationships with clients, less rigidity, more ability to stand by them in their deepest emotional crises."[115]

CHAPTER 7

The Chicago Years: Part Two 1951–1957

Of the many people who were interviewed for this biography or who sent their recollections of Rogers from the early 1950s, none commented on seeing any major changes in his personal or professional style during or after his therapy. Many did not even know he was in therapy; although Gerald Haigh recalled, "Everyone was in counseling with someone else. Even Carl was in counseling with one of his own graduate students, which impressed us all."[1] In any case, Rogers' warmth, acceptance, and understanding were still apparent to all. And people would still see him as reserved and as sometimes aloof or distant, though perhaps not so frequently. The changes were more apparent in other ways. One was in his personal writing style, mentioned earlier. A second change toward a more spontaneous, personally revealing style came in Rogers' increasing stress on the therapist's *congruence* in therapy.

Congruence Continued

As suggested earlier by Jules Seeman, the congruent therapist was not Rogers' idea, but one which several members of the Counseling Center were exploring at the time. In fact several of his colleagues of that period pointed out that, except in the research area, Rogers was less of an innovator than he was a learner and a popularizer. Manual Vargas said of him: "He was able to learn and very sincerely was willing to listen to others and learn from their experiences. He was able to learn from the viewpoints of his students and it is this ability that helped him to be in the forefront of much of the thinking and the research in psychotherapy. And even now [1970s] he's still moving in the advance group. However, since he was primarily committed to research and the rational explication of psychotherapy, I do not see him as being an innovator and he was not that at the Counseling Center. It was others of us who were more willing to try out new reactions to our clients, and it was some of us who were more willing to work out our emotional reactions in the therapeutic relationship, as well as outside of it, and who were more willing to do a variety of new approaches—change the hours, extend the hours, be much more flexible than he seemed to be. But he was able to observe, to listen, to empathize, to learn from the rest of us."[2]

Rogers readily acknowledged that congruence was not his idea, stating in a 1958 forum, "I think I essentially picked up this idea from the Atlanta group that's working with Carl Whitaker."[3] While Rogers may not have introduced the concept of congruence, he certainly was the one who is most responsible for its widespread usage in psychotherapy and the other helping professions today. He also recalled coining the actual term, based on the geometric concept of congruent triangles.[4] Beginning in 1956, he began to use the term with increasing frequency.

In his first published use of the word Rogers stated,

> … it appears essential that the therapist be genuine, or whole, or congruent in the relationship. What this means is that it is important for the therapist to be what he is in his contact with the client. To the extent that he presents an outward facade of one attitude or feeling, while inwardly or at an unconscious level he experiences another feeling, the likelihood of successful therapy will be diminished. It is only as he is, in this relationship, a unified person, with his experienced feeling, his awareness of his feelings, and his expression of those feelings all congruent or similar, that he is most able to facilitate therapy. It is only as the therapist provides the genuine reality which is in him, that the other person can successfully seek the reality in himself. The therapist is nondefensive about the reality in himself, and this helps the client to become nondefensive.
>
> The following paragraphs describe some of the attitudes [acceptance and empathy] which, if genuinely held, seem most conducive to therapy, but it seems even more important to be genuine than to hold these attitudes. Thus, if the therapist is persistently bored in the interview, or feels a persistent disbelief in what the client is saying, it is better for him to voice these genuine feelings than to pretend to a more positive attitude which he does not have. This seems especially true if he is able to express his feelings as something pertaining to himself, not as an accusation toward the client. He may be able to say, "I feel bored in this interview," *not* "You are boring" or to say, "I find myself disbelieving what you say," not "You are untruthful." This is an area in which our point of view is changing, and this paragraph is written tentatively as an indication of the

direction of some of our more recent practice and thinking. It seems likely that the more deeply the counselor can be himself in the relationship, the more certainly will therapy take place.[5]

As Rogers further explored the concept of congruence, he modified this statement slightly. He pointed out that congruence does not mean the therapist interrupts the client to say, "I feel hungry," or "I wonder what my wife is doing right now," whenever these thoughts occur. Rather, it is when feelings in the therapist occur persistently and are relevant to the relationship that the therapist would do well to express them. Otherwise they will surely be communicated anyway and are likely to interfere with the therapist's ability to continue to accept and empathize with the client. In addition, when such a message is not communicated clearly it is likely to confuse the client, who has to guess what the therapist is feeling.

Uncharacteristically Rogers provided few examples in his writing of how a therapist might be congruent in therapy. Normally he tried to make his concepts come alive by providing excerpts from transcripts of real interviews. He did not do this with congruence. Apparently at the time he began to emphasize the therapist's congruence in the relationship, he was still finding this somewhat difficult himself. Or stated differently, although he was experiencing a growing congruence himself, the habit of many years of withholding his own feelings was still present, and this influenced his writing on the subject. One of the few fully articulated examples of his own congruence in therapy comes not from any article or book, but from the unpublished transcript of a discussion he had in 1958 with a group of psychologists and psychiatrists at the University of Rochester. After mentioning that the therapist's being congruent with his client "sounded like a wild and crazy idea when I first heard it," he gave an example from his own life.

I'm sure that one of the problems that troubled me for a long time and probably still does to some degree is that I don't like to have people cling. I can bear it to have people have lots of feelings toward me but if I sense something that seems like clinging, I tend to get a little uneasy. One very disturbed woman that I was working with kept asking for more frequent interviews. My feeling was "She's just grabbing more and more—there is no limit to this." I don't think I was too much aware of that but I'm sure that that was what I was feeling.

I would feel, "Oh—I suppose I should see her more—because she is in a pretty bad state." It is no doubt that it was a grudging agreement. Then I realized that my attitude changed so that now when she was coming in I would feel— "Oh, here she comes again!" which is not exactly the attitude I feel towards most clients. I felt, "I'm *not* a therapist for her any more. There aren't the attitudes that will help her" and I felt really very much troubled by it because I felt, "She has trouble enough of her own. I can't burden her with my problems." This didn't seem fair.

So it was a difficult internal struggle. I was surprised to find how deeply it troubled me to stop the flow of the interview at one point and say, "There's something I've got to talk over and that is that I'm just no longer feeling comfortable with these greater and greater demands on my time. I just feel as though you're pushing me to the wall. I can't stand it." She was quite jolted by the fact that *I had* interrupted her struggling with her own problems but she listened and said, "But I've always *said* I wanted more time if you felt you could give it to me." I said, "Yes, I realize you always have used those words but I guess I didn't feel you meant them." So we had a good discussion about the issues. The amazing thing to me was that that just dissolved my feeling that I was being pushed and pushed. As a matter of fact, shortly after that I did give her additional time and just didn't feel any strain about it. I was able to give it to her not *feeling* that she was demanding more and more.[6]

Another example of Rogers' congruence in therapy comes in a letter from one of his students at Chicago, who wrote, "A fellow graduate-student friend of mine was almost literally tossed out of psychotherapy with Rogers. Rogers had grown quite tired of the student's self-indulgence and refusal to accept mature responsibility, and Rogers told him so in no uncertain terms."[7]

Significantly both of these examples are unpublished. A dearth of examples of this nature has made "congruence" one of the most ambiguous and easily misunderstood of the concepts Rogers popularized. Ironically, Rogers said in the late 50s that one reason he didn't say more about congruence was that he was worried it could be too easily misunderstood and misused "and can kind of seem to be a license for just pouring out any of our feelings on the client. I always feel real tentative and dubious in talking about it for fear I won't communicate what I really mean."[8]

Another reason he may have been reluctant to elucidate the concept and practice of congruence, beyond that the therapist might use it inappropriately, was that congruence also made the therapist vulnerable. This is revealed in another comment he made in the University of Rochester discussion.

... where the therapist feels some persistent, non-therapeutic attitude—I believe there are really constructive possibilities in expressing those attitudes to the client. If you try this ... then you will find that, as Whitaker or Warkentin put it, in such situations the therapist really temporarily becomes the client. If I'm trying to explain to you that I really don't find it easy to accept these things that you say or I'm troubled by the fact that somehow I really don't *like* you and usually I *do* like people who come to me, that is by no means an easy thing to do. It's just as difficult for me to express that to a client as it is for the client to express to you these feelings that he's frightened of and doesn't like and so on. So that in a very real sense you temporarily reverse the role.[9]

191

This was risky territory for Rogers, in spite of his personal therapy and subsequent growth. So he wrote relatively little on the subject, essentially repeating a few key points about congruence but providing few examples and little depth of discussion. With acceptance and empathy being easier conditions for therapists to implement, congruence in the way Rogers meant it was less often understood and practiced than the other conditions. Thus at least sometimes, as Bernard Covner suggested, "the non-directive approach, in retrospect, served as a convenient cop-out for people lacking in wholesome self-assertiveness."[10]

Rogers hardly lacked self-assertiveness; yet there *was* some connection between his therapeutic approach and his personal evolution, particularly with respect to congruence. His initial nondirective approach allowed him to be both deeply engaged and somewhat insulated from his clients and from his own feelings. His own period of distress and therapy made him much more aware of his feelings and how he dealt with them. His desire to be more in touch with his feelings and express them when appropriate in his personal life made him receptive to his colleagues who were arguing for the importance of the therapist's congruence in therapy. Accepting this idea and popularizing it himself made Rogers that much more convinced of the importance of congruence in all relationships, including his own. Thus each aspect of his life, the professional and personal, reinforced the growing congruence in the other.

It is not surprising that his friends and colleagues did not see a dramatic change. The process unfolded over at least a seven-year period—from the start of his therapy to the advocacy of congruence in his writings. Then it continued to unfold. Clearly Rogers was still working on it in 1962, when he demonstrated the concept at a conference.

Carl played a tape recording of a session which I think was by Carl Whitaker and a man who was in some kind of psychotic state. After a particularly long, intellectualizing and affectless statement by the "patient," Whitaker's response was, "Oh, shit!" That broke through the intellectualizing and started a real person-to-person relationship between Whitaker and his patient. After the playing of the tape, Carl said something to the effect that he had great admiration for the ability of Whitaker to do some of the things he does, even though he himself (Carl) didn't feel he would be able to operate that way. Following this, there was a question and answer period. One fellow stood up ostensibly to ask a question, but prefaced it with a long intellectual lecturing discourse. People began squirming in their seats and, when he had finished, Carl had a kind of whimsical smile on his face and said, "After having just heard Whitaker's tape recording, my first impulse is to say, "Oh, shit!" He brought down the house. He followed that, however, with a very respecting and honest response to the fellow's question."[11]

When Rogers later became involved in encounter groups, he *did* start to use more concrete examples of congruence in his writings. This occurred as he was becoming increasingly congruent himself. In fact, it will become apparent that part of Rogers' motivation for entering the encounter group movement was a desire for greater spontaneity and expression of affect in his own life. It is enough to say, for now, that the period of the late forties to late fifties was one which legitimized and encouraged the expression of personal feelings, both for Rogers the person and Rogers the therapist.

Unconditional Positive Regard

Congruence was not the only concept Rogers borrowed from his colleagues and students. In the mid-fifties, influenced by a dissertation of one of his doctoral students, Stanley Standal,[12] Rogers substituted the phrase "unconditional positive regard" for what he had until then always called "acceptance." Again, he did not adopt the term all at once, but played with the concept for a few years, getting the feel of its meaning by using it in several articles in piecemeal form, as in 1956 when he wrote, "By acceptance is meant a warm regard for the client as a person of unconditional self-worth."[13]

Before long he adopted Standal's own term. Its meaning was not too different from what he had always meant by acceptance, but it seemed to capture that meaning better for him. Using it himself for the first time, he explained, "To the extent that the therapist finds himself experiencing a warm acceptance of each aspect of the client's experience as being a part of that client, he is experiencing unconditional positive regard. This concept has been developed by Standal ... It means that there are no *conditions* of acceptance, no feeling of 'I like you only if you are thus and so.' It means a 'prizing' of the person, as Dewey has used that term. It is at the opposite pole from a selective evaluating attitude—'You are bad in these ways, good in those.' It involves as much feeling of acceptance for the client's expression of negative, 'bad,' painful, defensive, abnormal feelings as for his expression of 'good,' positive, mature, confident, social feelings, as much acceptance of ways in which he is inconsistent as of ways in which he is consistent. It means a caring for the client, but not in a possessive way or in such a way as simply to satisfy the therapist's own needs. It means a caring for the client as a *separate* person, with permission to have his own feelings, his own experiences."[14]

With the incorporation of the term "unconditional positive regard," Rogers solidified his conception of the therapist's role. In a speech in 1946 he had said the counselor's role was "best described by the terms: "warmth, permissiveness, acceptance, understanding, and nondirectiveness."[15] At Chicago, little by little, he augmented, abridged, and modified this description. Warmth and acceptance became acceptance and liking. Acceptance and liking became "a warm regard for the client as a person of unconditional self-worth," which became unconditional positive regard. Understanding became empathy. "A nondefensive genuineness," later called congruence, was added to the list. Though permissiveness and nondirectiveness were maintained in practice as effective ways of implementing the key attitudes, they were dropped in theory. Years of experience, hundreds of clients, years of training new therapists, hundreds of staff meetings, classes, and informal sessions, voluminous readings, research findings, the reflection that results from writing—all these provided him with the data and the occasions to continue to modify his thinking, to achieve the formulation which best expressed for him what effective therapy is all about.

In 1949 he had written: "It no longer appears impossible that we may at some foreseeable date be able to make a statement of this sort, with objective evidence for it. 'If conditions a, b, and c are met, then a process of therapy is initiated which involves changes x, y, and z in the attitudes and personality of the individual.'"[16] In 1956 he made such a statement for the first time: "If the therapist provides a relationship, in which he is (a) genuine, internally consistent; (b) acceptant, prizing the client as a person of worth; (c) empathically understanding of the client's private world; then the client becomes (a) more realistic in his self-perceptions; (b) more confident and self-directing; (c) more positively valued by himself, (d) less likely to repress elements of his experience; (e) more mature, socialized, and adaptive in his behavior; (f) more like the healthy, integrated, well-functioning person in his personality structure."[17]

A year or so later he further developed his formulation of the *a, b,* and *c,* in one of his most important and influential essays, "The Necessary and Sufficient Conditions of Therapeutic Personality Change."[18]

Necessary and Sufficient Conditions

In his introduction, he explained how for years he had been trying to understand what the essential ingredients of therapy were: "As I have considered my own clinical experience and that of my colleagues, together with the pertinent research which is available, I have drawn out several conditions which seem to me to be *necessary* to initiate constructive personality change, and which, taken together, appear to be sufficient to inaugurate the process."[19]

The first two conditions he listed were described as preconditions to therapy. First, there must be some type of psychological contact between client and therapist; in other words there must be a relationship. Second, the client must be in a state of some psychological malaise, dissatisfaction, or in Rogers' terms "in a state of incongruence, being vulnerable or anxious." Then came the three conditions which he had been developing in recent years. "3. The therapist is congruent or integrated in the relationship. 4. The therapist experiences unconditional positive regard for the client. 5. The therapist experiences an empathic understanding of the client's internal frame of reference and endeavors to communicate this experience to the client." Then adding a sixth condition, lest it be taken for granted: "The communication to the client of the therapist's empathic understanding and unconditional positive regard is to a minimal degree achieved." "No other conditions are necessary," he wrote. "If these six conditions exist, and continue over a period of time, this is sufficient. The process of constructive personality change will follow."

Such an extreme and specific statement had many implications, and Rogers was quick to spell out many of them: "it is *not* stated that these conditions apply to one type of client, and other conditions are necessary to bring about psychotherapeutic change with other types of client … It is *not* stated that these six conditions are the essential conditions for client-centered therapy, and that other conditions are essential for other types of psychotherapy … It *is not* stated that psychotherapy is a special kind of relationship, different in kind from all others which occur in everyday life … It is *not* stated that special intellectual professional knowledge—psychological, psychiatric, medical, or religious—is required of the therapist … Intellectual training and the acquiring of information has, I believe, many valuable results—but becoming a therapist is not one of those results … It *is not* stated that it is necessary for psychotherapy that the therapist have an accurate psychological diagnosis of the client."[20]

This point in Rogers' evolution deserves a more careful examination in light of what we know of his career. Over many years the man had developed his ideas and methods and had formulated them into an approach which was called "nondirective therapy." All over the country, and in many parts of the world, counselors, therapists and other professionals were practicing his "method," many of them calling themselves "Rogerians." Then, during the late forties and early fifties, he began to change his thinking and to suggest that the methods are not nearly as important as the attitudes of the therapist. Then, in modifying these attitudes, he came to believe that, even more important than the therapist simply holding these attitudes, the attitudes must be lived and experienced by both therapist and client in a genuine, interpersonal *relationship*.

When one concentrates on the single steps in a long staircase, he or she may neglect to notice that whole floors are passing by. So it was with Rogers' changes during this decade. All the subtle modifications of terms and concepts and techniques could easily obscure the major changes in thinking and practice which had occurred. In the twelve years at Chicago he moved from the *method* to the *attitudes* to the *relationship* as the key ingredient in the therapeutic process. In so doing he diminished the importance of the very approach he had been building for the previous twenty years.

After all, if congruence and empathy and unconditional positive regard are the key aspects of the relationship, couldn't the Freudian, Jungian, Adlerian,

Sullivanian, Gestalt, or rational therapist (as cognitive or rational-emotive-behavioral therapists were then called),[21] or the practitioner of almost any other school of therapy form a relationship with her patients which has these three ingredients? True, they may be expressed differently. But isn't the psychoanalyst's emphasis on free association, to some extent, a desire to understand the client from his own frame of reference? And isn't the cognitive therapist's unshakable belief that the patient can learn to approach his problems in a rational, systematic manner also a form of unconditional positive regard? And isn't the Gestalt therapist's refusal to be manipulated by her patients a sign of congruence? Although Rogers did not go into detail on this point, he answered affirmatively. In fact he was quite fond of quoting several studies done by one of his students, Fred Fiedler, which showed how experienced therapists of *different* schools of thought were more similar in their actual practices than experienced and inexperienced therapists of the *same* school of thought.[22] Moreover, some of the qualities that the experienced therapists had in common were some of the very conditions Rogers was now calling necessary and sufficient for therapeutic change—namely, "the therapist's ability to understand, to communicate with, and to maintain rapport with the client."[23] These were landmark studies, beginning a tradition that would be followed by Rogers and his colleagues and later by the "common factors" and "therapeutic alliance" tracks in psychotherapy research. Rogers' essay on the "Necessary and Sufficient Conditions" has been credited with spurring on several decades of research on the characteristics of effective psychotherapy.[24]

Rogers always continued to prefer his own client-centered style as the best way he knew for him to enter into a therapeutic relationship with his clients. But he remained open to other therapeutic approaches which contained enough of the necessary conditions to be helpful to clients. Bernard Steinzor told of how, "Even though Rogers knew of my development away from a 'Rogerian,' he would still on occasion, when people asked him about possible counselors in New York, refer people to me. This kind of real tolerance of differences, despite Rogers' own emphasis on his own mode, is one of his really great qualities, and perhaps can even be considered one of the significant contributions he's made to the development of ways of thinking about psychotherapy. He has been mistakenly considered to be a rigid technician, whereas the spirit of his work has always been open to people developing their own style."[25]

Paul Bergman of the National Institute of Health wrote to Rogers in 1959, saying, "I was very touched by your willingness to participate in my plans. You have been very good to me for many years now. Even though I now propose formulations different from yours, I consider my having encountered you and your work one of the lucky and great events of my life."[26]

196

Research on Psychotherapy

For Rogers there was no contradiction between being open to other therapeutic approaches and postulating such an extreme view as the necessary and sufficient conditions for successful psychotherapy. Aside from acknowledging that practitioners of other approaches also could provide the core conditions of a therapeutic relationship, the necessary and sufficient conditions were and always remained for Rogers *a hypothesis.* The scientist had not become a polemicist. If he stated his views in extreme and specific terms, it was only because the more categorical he was, the more he and others would be able to support or reject the hypothesis through sound research. Therefore, when he wrote his article on the necessary and sufficient conditions of the therapeutic relationship, for each condition he tried to suggest an operational way of defining and measuring it.

In 1951 Rogers had written, "Like Maslow, the writer would confess that in the early portion of his professional life he held a theoretical view opposed at almost every point to the view he has gradually come to adopt as a result of clinical experience and clinically oriented research."[27] Even thereafter he continued to modify his views. How was it possible for Rogers—who might have become emotionally tied to any one of his various formulations—to keep changing his thinking, to use later writings to correct or modify earlier writings, to risk losing the large number of adherents to the nondirective and client-centered methods by outgrowing them? Many people as they grow older or as they achieve prominence in some field, cling to one set of ideas or practices, for in this unchanging position comes a type of security, a buffer against the confusion, complexity and changing conditions around them. It was not that Rogers did not need some kind of security too; he simply got that security from a different source. As he explained it, "adherents of any clinically effective procedure tend to become dogmatic. If client-centered counseling does not provide sufficient examples, psychoanalysis or Rorschach will be glad to oblige. As the clinician's emotional security becomes tied up with dogma, he also becomes defensive, unable to see new and contradictory evidence. But when research is persistently undertaken, the security which all of us must have tends to become lodged, not in dogma, but in the process by which truth is discovered, in scientific method."[28]

He really believed it, that "psychotherapy may become a science, applied with art, rather than an art which has made some pretense of being a science."[29] It was a quality that many of his students and colleagues remembered very vividly. Fred Fiedler recalled how, "My Ph.D. proposal was very controversial. It proposed that experts of different schools were more similar to each other than they were to non-experts of their own school. Rogers, probably in a rash moment, said that he wouldn't believe this study even if it came out the way I said it might. While this was not exactly a comforting comment from a member of your thesis committee, I nevertheless worked on the study and Rogers has since then quoted the study widely. In my opinion it testified to the flexibility of the man as well as to his willingness to adapt his own thinking to empirical data rather than the other way around."[30]

This willingness to adapt his thinking to empirical data is illustrated in Rogers' long monograph "A Theory of Therapy, Personality and Interpersonal Relationships, as Developed in the Client-Centered Framework." Having stated that the three major therapeutic conditions were sufficient to initiate therapy with any client population, he included a footnote saying, "This paragraph may have to be rewritten if a recent study by Kirtner is confirmed. Kirtner has found, in a group of 26 cases from the Counseling Center at the University of Chicago, that there are sharp differences in the client's mode of approach to the resolution of life difficulties and that these differences are related to success in therapy. Briefly, the client who sees his problem as involving his relationships, and who feels that he contributes to this problem and wants to change it, is likely to be successful. The client who externalizes his problem and feels little self-responsibility is much more likely to be a failure. Thus the implication is that different conditions of therapy may be necessary to make personality change possible in this latter group. If this is verified, then the theory will have to be revised accordingly."[31]

Eugene Gendlin recalled how, when the Kirtner study was completed, "most of the staff of the Counseling Center were outraged and sought to argue one loophole or another against the study. Only Rogers welcomed the findings and cited them in his next publication. Rogers sought to argue with all the rest, saying, 'Don't you see, facts are always friendly. This will lead us to some further step.' When the retort was, 'But perhaps thus-and-so would account for the findings differently,' Rogers would say, 'And perhaps you will be the person to find that in your next study.'"[32]

When Rogers first entertained the idea of undertaking research in psychotherapy there were no precedents for him to follow. The privacy of the psychoanalyst's or psychiatrist's office had always been sacrosanct. Recording or transcribing actual interviews was just about unheard of. One had only the psychotherapist's word as to whether a particular method was effective or not; and so many different therapists declared that their methods were effective. It was, indeed, to use Rogers' phrase, "an art which made a pretense of being a science." Which methods really worked and which were merely "placebos" that gave the patient the illusion that he was being helped? How was one psychotherapeutic approach similar to or different from another? Which approaches were more effective with what sorts of clients? What constitutes real therapeutic personality change or growth or health? What happens in "successful" psychotherapy? All these questions and others were wanting answers as the field of psychotherapy continued to grow and spread.

Then, in the early 1940s, Rogers, with the help of his student Bernard Covner and his client "Herbert Bryan," revolutionized the field of therapy by recording, transcribing and publishing for a wide audience a complete, verbatim series of psychotherapeutic interviews. Although, as pointed out earlier, others had begun recording therapy before him, after Rogers popularized the practice, he and others began to record interviews on a regular basis. These recordings and transcripts provided the raw data on which sound research could be conducted. Several of these recorded interviews were published in books and articles—by Rogers, William Snyder, and others.[33] Speaking in 1947 at a panel on research in psychotherapy, Rogers was able to say, "we have at the Counseling Center of the University of Chicago a half dozen unpublished complete cases with every interview recorded and transcribed, available to qualified research workers in the field."[34] Within a few years the number had grown to nearly thirty.[35] In addition they had scores of single interviews recorded and many of them transcribed—again, available for research and for the training of counselors. In 1956 Rogers wrote that among client-centered therapists, "thousands of therapeutic interviews had been electrically recorded and studied."[36]

With this data on which to work, the research studies followed almost immediately. Elias Porter's dissertation, which he completed at Ohio State in 1941 and which was published in 1943, was the first of the studies in the client-centered framework.[37] By 1950 Rogers could speak of some forty research studies that had been completed.[38] By 1952 the number had grown to sixty.[39] In 1957, when Desmond Cartwright's "Annotated Bibliography of Research and Theory Construction in Client-Centered Therapy" was published, Cartwright was able to describe 110 separate research studies. I found at least thirty others, most of them published, which could be added to Cartwright's pre-1957 list, bringing the total to 140 or more. Because Cartwright's listing did not include the applications of client-centered therapy to areas such as group therapy, play therapy, education, industry and group leadership, nor did my thirty additional studies include many of these areas, there is good reason to believe that if an accurate summary were ever made of all the research done on the client-centered approach from 1943 to 1957, the number of studies would be considerably higher, perhaps as many as 200 separate researches.

What, then, did all these researchers spend their time discovering? A close look at the work of Rogers and his colleagues and students over this fifteen-year period suggests to me three phases of the research that are worthy of discussion.

The first research phase was concentrated in the early forties through 1948, although it continued to a lesser extent into the fifties. Cartwright listed thirteen studies through 1948 that might be included in this phase. Almost all of them fit a pattern which I would term "exploratory and descriptive" in nature. For the most part these studies took the recordings or transcripts of interviews or cases and attempted to classify what happened during these therapies from various points of view. Porter, with his pioneering study, devised a system to measure the degree of directiveness or nondirectiveness a counselor employed.[40] The scale was then used to rate individual counselors. Curran carefully studied the changes in emotional expression and insight over one case.[41] Snyder categorized both counselor and client statements, so he could see what type of client responses followed particular counselor responses.[42] Raimy, in a study which was to have much significance in later years, measured the changes in self-references made by clients during the course of their therapy.[43] Occasionally the studies in this period would distinguish between cases which the counselor regarded as successful or unsuccessful, to see if what was being measured would turn out to be different in the two types of cases.

What these researches had in common was that they attempted to find out *what happened* in nondirective counseling. In *Counseling and Psychotherapy* Rogers had said that therapy was a fairly predictable process in which expression of feeling led to insight which led to positive actions by the client. He also said that the nondirective method encouraged insight. These earlier studies attempted to put his description to the test, to see if what he said happened in therapy really did happen with any predictable degree of reliability. In general the results supported Rogers' observations, as when Bergman showed that when clients asked for advice, structuring, or opinions from the therapist, if the therapist complied, the client tended to abandon self-exploration; but if the therapist reflected back the clients' feelings at the time, the result was further exploration and insight.[44] However, what the studies did not do to any great extent was to support the effectiveness of Rogers' overall method. If one found, for example, that acceptance by the therapist led to verbalized insights by the client, as Snyder's study did,[45] it might support Rogers' notion of what happened in therapy; but it did not show that this insight made any real difference in the client's life or that six months after therapy he was any different from when he began. Nor did it show that nondirective therapy was any more effective than any other approach.

Thus the research was exploratory only. It was a time of developing ways to measure some of the therapeutic phenomena or variables. It was a time of seeing whether, in fact, the therapeutic process was similar to what Rogers had been describing in his writings. The research raised many more questions than it answered; but this was not necessarily a weakness, in that early research in any field often tends to be more descriptive than prescriptive.

The second phase of the research (which ran simultaneously with the third) attempted to demonstrate how clients changed as a result of client-centered therapy. In this phase the investigators took some other already-proven tool in psychological research and applied that tool to determine the results of the client-centered method. Thus several studies used the Rorschach ink blots to see if, after client-centered therapy, diagnosticians would rate the client's Rorschachs as having shown improvement.[46] Several studies used other "projective techniques" to measure adjustment after therapy, including the Thematic Apperception Test (TAT), in which the client is shown a cartoon-type figure and asked to tell a story connected with the picture, thereby revealing many of his unresolved issues.[47] Bartlett, working in a Veterans Administration hospital, had clients' "training officers" rate their degree of improvement in adjustment six months or more after they began counseling.[48] Haimowitz investigated whether clients' attitudes toward minority groups changed as a result of therapy, the hypothesis being that as hostility toward oneself decreases in therapy and self-acceptance increases, one will grow more accepting of and less hostile toward other groups.[49] Other researchers used the lengthy Minnesota Multiphasic Personality Inventory (MMPI) to assess the results of client-centered therapy.[50] Still others used tests of anxiety, attitudes toward self and others, perceptual acuity, and even Galvanic Skin Response and heart rate.

These studies were attempting to use known methods of assessing psychological health to determine the kinds of outcomes client-centered therapy produced. The research was done in a more or less random fashion, with each researcher following her own hunch, using some measure she was probably familiar with, and finding a population to work with—whether it was patients in Veterans Administration hospitals, current cases in the Counseling Center, transcripts of previous interviews, or whoever else was available. In general the results were positive, showing favorable change after therapy. It was a very important phase of the research, because by using known measurements of proven reliability and validity, client-centered therapy was given an added legitimacy in the eyes of many psychologists—not to mention the added confidence given to client-centered therapists themselves. As these accepted instruments showed that clients had changed for the better during and after client-centered therapy, then it became increasingly difficult to dismiss the approach as ineffective or superficial.

As valuable as it was, however, this second phase of research had some serious flaws. First, the number of clients studied in most of the researches was very small, usually ranging from one to ten clients, with an occasional exception where the client population was larger. A small sample is usually characteristic of pilot studies and exploratory research and can yield many valuable results. But the expectation usually is that the researchers will repeat much of their work with larger populations in order to be sure that their results were not merely due to chance or reflected some unusual characteristics shared by the few clients or particular therapists. Thus, on a panel discussion on research in psychotherapy, a psychiatrist, Lawrence Kubie, criticized the lack of any larger studies and, probably referring to Rogers who was also on the panel, said, "Until these come into existence we will continue to have large numbers of publications with large claims based on a few cases, and books published which ought to be mere pamphlets or case reports—ballyhoo instead of science."[51]

A second problem with the research was that, in almost every case, there were no experimental controls provided. For scientific purposes it is really not possible to state that therapy is effective in bringing about this or that change, unless there is another group, a control group, which is very much like the group that receives therapy, and this comparison group receives no therapy or receives some other type of treatment. If the experimental group changes in a way the controls do not, then, since the only thing they received that the controls did not was the therapy, it can be maintained that changes in the clients were caused by the therapy. So, while many of these studies of the second type produced clear, positive results, a common reaction was still to question: How do you know *the therapy* produced these results? Maybe once people are motivated to change enough to want to go into therapy, then even if they don't receive therapy, they still improve anyway. Or maybe the test-taking is the catalyst that encourages the client to start thinking about his situation, which then leads to positive changes. Experimental controls would be needed to find out which variables were really responsible for any changes.

A third shortcoming in the research was that, in measuring the outcomes of client-centered therapy, none of the measurements really assessed what Rogers regarded as the key ingredient in the change process, namely, the client's attitudes toward himself. It was these changing self-attitudes, self-concept, self-acceptance or self-rejection, self-esteem and self-evaluation which seemed to Rogers and others to be the main factors in the behavioral changes that often occurred during and after therapy. But in trying to assess the results of therapy, Rogers had only tests and measurements derived from other orientations. The Rorschach or TAT tests, for example, had mostly a psychoanalytic background and interpretation. The scales of ethnocentrism and prejudice were developed by the social psychologist. The job supervisor's estimation of the client's progress was given in terms of employment, not psychological criteria. These were all very important tests, insofar as they enabled the client-centered group to show the psychoanalysts, the social psychologists and the employers that there were some significant results brought about by their therapeutic approach. But in all of these tests the clients were viewed from an outside perspective. There was still the disappointment that, as yet, there was no way to reveal the therapeutic process in scientific terms from the point of view of greatest interest to the Rogers group—from the viewpoint of the client himself.

It was these three problems that were addressed by the third phase of research undertaken by the staff and students of the Counseling Center. It began as Rogers' idea, although as usual it was modified by the input of his colleagues. As "principal investigator" on the original research proposal (with the help of James Miller, Psychology Department Chairman, who was increasingly supportive of Rogers' work), he was able to obtain a five-year grant of $172,000 from the Medical Division of the Rockefeller Foundation, enabling them to begin.[52] When this funding was ending, Rogers secured another $97,000 from the United States Public Health Service, $30,000 from the Grant Foundation, and $5,000 from another source.[53] Shortly thereafter the Ford Foundation awarded Rogers and the Counseling Center still another $350,000 over five more years.

Given the initial funding, the Counseling Center was able to set up a "program design," that is, "the planning of an integrated series of research activities, focused on a central problem and involving a number of scientists for several years."[54] The number of researchers working on the project ranged from fifteen to thirty over the several years it continued.[55] About ten persons stayed involved in the project from beginning to end, while the rest stayed for various lengths of time. These people came to be known as the "Research Group." Since its members overlapped with the "Rogers group"—a popular name for the Counseling Center staff and associates at Chicago—the terms were often used interchangeably.

The clients in the study were organized into two "blocks." Block I consisted of twenty-five clients (and the same number of controls) who came to the Counseling Center seeking help and who agreed to participate in several batteries of psychometric tests in conjunction with their therapy. The information collected became the data upon which the researchers conducted their different studies. Later, a second group of clients would constitute Block II, thus providing a whole new set of data upon which to base new studies.

Although Rogers was the principal investigator for the purposes of getting the grants, the research program was carried on in typical Counseling Center fashion. The leadership was "group-centered." Using the same body of data, each researcher explored the questions and hypotheses that were of interest to him or her. As to the nature of the research, several of the group wrote, "There are studies concerned with process and with outcomes. There are researches in which the object of the study will be the client's visual perception, his physiological reactions during the interviews, his verbal productions, his social attitudes, his concepts of himself, his values, his social behavior. Looked at from another point of view, there are represented in the program, studies of the client alone, of the therapist alone, and of the relationship between client and therapist."[56]

Because many of the members of the Counseling Center were graduate students, they participated in much of the research on the project—test administration, data analysis, counseling, generating hypotheses, and writing the actual reports. In the first three to four years of the project, nine doctoral dissertations and four Master's theses were completed, and an equal number were in process.[57]

The first problem of the previous research, the small number of clients, was to some extent corrected in the program design. With twenty-five clients in the first block and more in the second it was possible to have greater confidence in their conclusions than when one, five, or even ten clients constituted the entire population. Although the twenty-five clients in the first block would not be considered a particularly large number today, at the time it was an impressive, even historic advance in psychotherapy research of this type. The significant number of clients also had the advantage of allowing many different therapists to work with the clients. In this way the results would not merely reflect the unique style or talents of one particular therapist.

The second problem of the previous research, that of controls, also was confronted. How can you get a control group for an experiment in psychotherapy? The ideal solution that comes to mind is to randomly select only fifty percent of those who come seeking help, and tell the other half that you're sorry, there is no room for them, but would they mind taking this battery of tests periodically for the next couple of years, so you can see how they fare compared to the group that is getting therapy. While this might be desirable from a scientific viewpoint (assuming one could get the rejected clients to cooperate and that being rejected did not influence their trajectory), it is untenable from an ethical standpoint. How, then, does one manage to provide controls for one's experiment? The Research Group solved the problem in two ways, neither of which was perfect from a scientific point of view, but both of which were better than anything that had been done previously in research on psychotherapy.

The first method of controlling the experiment allowed for the possibility that it was not the therapy that produced the changes in clients, but perhaps other variables which might not at first be apparent. For example, maybe in simply having someone take the personality tests every few months, the very act of taking the tests and thinking about the items begins to initiate a personality change process in an individual. The only way to control for these extraneous variables would be to have another group of people who are not in therapy, but who are very similar to the people in therapy, and who take the same tests, and see what happens to them during this time period. Therefore the research design arranged to have each person in therapy "matched" with another person who took all the tests but did not receive therapy. This control group was composed of people who volunteered to serve as subjects for a "research on personality." They were paired with the therapy group on the basis of sex, student or non-student status, age, and socio-economic status. Clearly the matching was still far from exact; but it was hoped that combined with the second control method, most of the possible intervening variables could be accounted for, and they might say with reasonable certainty that, if any changes came about in the therapy group, the therapy was the cause of the change.

Of course, the major flaw in this type of matching was that the experimental group came to the Counseling Center in a state of incongruence, desirous of receiving help and wanting to change. The control group did not. To control for this important variable, therefore, the research design included a second method of control. What they did was to ask half of the experimental group, the therapy group, to *wait two months* before beginning their therapy. If it could be demonstrated that the "no-wait group" began to change in the beginning two months of their therapy, but that the "wait group" did not change during the waiting period, then it could be maintained that motivation for therapy and test-taking, by themselves, could not account for the changes, and that it was the actual therapy that produced the results. Again, the design was far from perfect—the therapy and wait list groups were still not completely equivalent.[58] Still, the design was the first large-scale, serious attempt to provide research controls for an experiment in psychotherapy.

Finally, the third problem of the previous research was tackled—the lack of any instrument to measure changes in the client's self-perceptions so that these could be correlated with therapist actions and client outcomes. Previous attempts had been crude and unscientific. Rogers had attempted to develop an instrument that included all the things a person could experience about himself, but grew frustrated with the long list that did not seem very useful. Then he heard from one of his students, Margaret Hartley, about a course she was taking with William Stephenson, a British-trained researcher then teaching at the University of Chicago. He had developed a measurement tool known as the "Q-technique."[59] "She began to describe it," Rogers recalled, "and it was like a conversion experience. I said, 'We can use this for measuring the self!'"[60] Now the Rogers group had a tool with which they could assess the results of counseling in the manner they had been hoping for.

The Q-technique that Rogers and his associates[61] adapted to fit the counseling process began with a "population of self-referent items" that were originally drawn from statements that real clients had made about themselves in counseling interviews. Some examples were: "I am a submissive person," "I am a hard worker," "I am really disturbed," "I am afraid of a full-fledged disagreement with a person," or "I am likeable." The client would be presented with 100 of these self-referent items on cards and be asked to sort the cards, usually into nine piles—the first pile being those self-descriptions which seemed most like him and the ninth pile being those which were most unlike him. Only a certain number of cards were allowed in each pile, so that the sorting approximated a bell-shaped curve and was, therefore, easier to work with for statistical purposes.

All the clients in the study were asked to do three different types of "Q-sorts" at different points during their therapy. The first was the Q-sort of items they regarded as most like themselves and most unlike themselves, that is, their "self-concept." The second was a sorting of items that were most like the person they would like to be or least like the person they would like to be—their "ideal concept." The third was a sorting of which items they thought best described the "ordinary person" and which items were least like the ordinary person. By administering these three Q-sorts at different testing points before, during, and after therapy, it was possible to assess how the client's attitudes toward himself changed, if he became more like the person he wanted to be, and how his attitude toward other people was affected by therapy. The results showed, among other things, that in client-centered therapy, clients' self-ideals over therapy were reduced to more achievable proportions and their self-concepts changed to become more like the self they wanted to be, the self-concepts changing even more than the ideal selves.

"Our work," wrote Rogers, "has been similar in intent to that of Piaget, for example, rather than to that of most American psychologists. Piaget's study of the stages in the development of intelligence and reasoning in the child, based on the analysis of the way these processes *seem to the child,* is a significant instance of this sort of approach."[62]

Having developed this final tool for their research, the group was able to proceed with their program design. The time and effort involved in gathering their data make it obvious why so few people had previously cared to undertake any extensive research on psychotherapy. Several test points were designated: just before therapy began (and before the waiting period began for the "wait group"), after therapy was completed, and after a follow-up period of six months to a year. At each of these test points, the client completed (1) an SIO (Self, Ideal, Ordinary) Q-sort; (2) a Thematic Apperception Test; (3) the Willoughby Emotional Maturity Scale; (4) the Self-Other Attitude Scale, designed to measure antidemocratic trends, ethnocentrism, political-economic conservatism, dependence upon experts, acceptance of the worth of others, and desire to change others; and (5) a role-playing situational test designed to determine how the client would react to others in certain critical impersonal situations.

In addition to these measurements which were always taken at the various test points, other data included: (6) a short personal history form filled out by the client at the beginning of the therapy; (7) a request for the names of two friends who knew the client well and whom he was willing to have contacted so that they might fill out the Emotional Maturity Scale on him over the course of the therapy; (8) recordings and transcripts of every counseling session (and these were *still* before tape recorders); (9) SIO Q-sorts after the seventh, twentieth and, if the therapy lasted that long, after each succeeding twentieth interview until the end of therapy; (10) a counselor sorting of the Q-items at the end of therapy based on how she thought the client would sort them (this was used to assess the counselor's empathy); (11) a counselor rating scale used to assess her picture of the outcomes of the therapy, the quality of the relationship between her and the client, and the nature of the therapeutic process just completed; (12) two follow-up interviews which were given after the follow-up tests were administered—one interview with the counselor and one with a test administrator who didn't know the client—both interviews being used to determine, in detail, the client's evaluation of his therapy and the results it did or did not produce; and (13) a follow-up questionnaire which was somewhat similar to the follow-up interviews.

If one wonders where those hundreds of thousands of dollars in grant money were spent, the listing above should be an indication. A single, forty-interview case required almost 700 hundred hours of time by the counselor, client, psychometrist, control subject, and transcribers to gather all the data necessary for the research (not counting the client's time in therapy).[63] Considering how these 700 hundred hours were repeated twenty-five times in Block I alone, it is staggering to contemplate the investment of time and energy in this project.

Having all that data certainly had its advantages, though. A team could spend their lifetimes analyzing the results. There were hundreds of interrelationships that could be explored. Did clients whose self-concepts became closer to their ideal concepts also show positive changes on the TAT tests? Clients who were shown by the Self-Other Scale to be more rigid and authoritarian— were they more likely or less likely to change as a result of client-centered therapy compared to clients who were less rigid? Did the clients of counselors who were more empathic show greater change? How did the "wait" therapy group compare to the "no-wait" therapy group, and how did each of these compare to their control groups? In cases that counselors regarded as "successful," were the "objective" tests also more likely to show positive change? Dozens of staff members and graduate students were able to use the group data to explore these and numerous other questions. The results were published in single studies and in combined efforts such as the June 1949 issue of the *Journal of Consulting Psychology*. At one time Rogers had been the associate editor of this journal, and president and multi-office-holder in the parent organization, the American Association for Applied Psychology. Consequently the journal was always a friendly forum for Rogers and his students. The June 1949 issue was devoted entirely to the studies which the Rogers group had been undertaking (most of them at their own expense, before the grant money was awarded). Seven research reports were included, and Rogers wrote what he called "A Nonobjective Introduction."

> The seven research studies in psychotherapy which follow this introduction are all based upon the same group of cases. They are, as research reports should be, cautious, objective, impersonal, formal, and always mindful of the standard error in drawing their conclusions. But this introduction to them is personal, incautious and speculative and the reader is hereby warned against it. It is written to indicate that the series of projects reported are more than a cold collection of tables, charts, and correlation coefficients—they constituted a discouraging, exciting, difficult and rewarding experience for all of us who participated.
>
> "The studies are based upon ten completely recorded and transcribed cases, with pre and post tests ..." How simple that statement looks in type! No one would suspect the profanity toward all recording devices which it conceals—the tapes that split, the wires that broke, the discs that were an inaudible jumble of squeaks and hisses. To say that this is a random selection of cases is inaccurate— to call it a selection by frustration would be more sound—consisting of all those

cases in which neither mechanical gremlins nor circumstances frustrated the completion of the case. The miracle is that it does seem to have a number of the characteristics of a random sample ...[64]

Five years later, in 1954, although the research program was still in progress, Rogers and his co-editor Rosalind Dymond [Cartwright] published an entire book on the Block I results.[65] *Psychotherapy and Personality Change* was published by the University of Chicago Press, making it the first of Rogers' major books that Houghton Mifflin did not publish since the three titles that began with *The Clinical Treatment of the Problem Child* in 1939. But Rogers felt it appropriate that the Press publish the book since the University had, in a sense, sponsored the research project through the offices of its Counseling Center. The University was glad to accept. It was a good decision. This highly technical, scholarly work remained in print for at least twenty-five years and six printings.[66]

The first section of the book consisted of an Introduction that described the project, its purposes, how it developed, its design and procedures. The second and major section was its "Findings," containing eleven studies derived from the First Block of clients. Then Rogers wrote two very lengthy analyses of individual cases—one a "success," the other a "failure"—showing how all the different research tools could be used to study the therapeutic process, in depth, with one client. He also wrote the conclusion.

Rogers' tone conveyed a feeling for the people behind the research. "In endeavoring to introduce the reader to the total investigation to be reported," he wrote, "there keeps coming to mind the oft-repeated statement of Robert Hutchins about the university of which he was chancellor: 'It isn't a good university; it's just the best that there is.' One can perceive in this epigram nothing but pride and confidence; on the other hand, one can perceive in it a deep disappointment in falling so far short of the aim. In very much the same ambivalent spirit I am tempted to say of what follows in this book, 'It isn't a good research in psychotherapy; it's just the best that there is.'"[67] To elaborate he proceeded with sections headed "We Point with Pride" and "We View with Disappointment" to indicate some of his and his colleagues' feelings about their work, mentioning with equal candor the study's strengths and its shortcomings.

By introducing the work of his colleagues and students in this manner, Rogers was putting himself in a position to be seen as the human figure and the moving force behind the scientific research. That he got most of the credit is interesting in light of the fact that he carried out almost none of the studies. Nor did he conduct any of the thirteen early studies included in the "exploratory phase" of research. This pattern continued into the later stages of the research. In Desmond Cartwright's bibliography of the 110 client-centered research studies mentioned earlier, Rogers was the author of only three.[68] It is ironic to think that Rogers wrote more research reports *before* he came to Chicago than he did once he arrived there; yet this Chicago period was by far the most prolific time for research on client-centered therapy. During his pre-Chicago years he had been developing his own skills in the research area. Once he came to Chicago it must have seemed more exciting to be the *facilitator* of many research studies than to be the author of only a few. And, as often happens when people are free to do their own work, the group-centered method of leadership turned out to be much more productive than would have been the case if Rogers had controlled or written most of the studies himself.

Still, indirectly, the credit for the voluminous amount of research done in these years belonged to Rogers. First, in almost every article he had ever written he had stressed the need for further research. In 1940, for example, he not only made this point, but foreshadowed much of the work he and his colleagues would later do. He wrote, "attention might be called to the research opportunities with which the therapeutic process bristles. There is the need of adequate records—stenographic, even phonographic—upon which comprehensive studies may be based. There is the question of accessibility for therapy. Can we draw a line between those who would profit, and those who might be better helped by other treatment procedures? There is the need for both imagination and research in the field of expression. Are the same basic feelings expressed in dreams, in play materials, in dramatic constructions, in verbalizations? There is need for much more study of the give and take of the interviewing process. How is expression encouraged, how may interpretations be made, how may the therapeutic process be accelerated through the interview? There is the need for translating individual therapy into group procedures, to make it more widely helpful. There is the need for much more refined analysis of complete records and formulated in terms of known psychological facts."[69] This was a typical example of how his writing opened doors of exploration through which he, his students, and his readers would later venture.

Because of his influence and example as a research-oriented practitioner, the Counseling Center at Chicago was set up and developed from the beginning with an eye toward research. The recording equipment, the permission to use the clients' time to fill out questionnaires and take tests for their studies, the added secretarial help for typing up transcripts, reports, and results—all these were present from the start. Then, because of the atmosphere Rogers created at the Counseling Center, many staff members and students were encouraged to initiate their own research projects and also learn from their colleagues in meetings and discussions. Here Rogers was able to be very influential—suggesting research ideas, helping others improve their research designs, and raising questions that stimulated the development of new studies. In addition, because he was the dissertation advisor to so many graduate students, he was able to work directly with and help students prepare and execute research studies in the client-centered method. Acknowledgements of his assistance can be found on numerous articles resulting from his students' dissertations—from Lipkin's formal "The Author is indebted to Dr. Carl R. Rogers for his help in planning and carrying through the project on which this article is based, for his criticism of the manuscript and for his writing the summarizing discussion,"[70] to Raskin's informal inscription "to Dr. Rogers ... who thunk it up ... Nat."[71]

Because Rogers wrote both widely and prolifically, and because wherever possible he would refer to the research that was going on at the University— often mentioning specific studies and authors by name—the atmosphere created within the Counseling Center was one of great excitement. Students and colleagues realized that if they produced a good research study, it was very likely that their names or results would be publicized in writing and before conventions across the country. This, and the growing number of people who were visiting the Center to study, observe, or participate in its work, helped to create a sense that what they were doing was terribly important. Gerald Haigh recalled how "Most of us went to Chicago to do counseling, not to do research. But when we got there we found that Carl was deeply committed to research. We rather quickly adopted that value. We found ourselves recording counseling sessions; studying interview typescripts; judging variables for each others' theses; writing and publishing studies; and glorying in the reputation Carl and our group were getting in professional circles. Senior psychologists were paying respectful attention to us even before we received our degrees. I remember the pride I felt at my first professional convention when Jerry Bruner introduced me to a fellow Harvard professor as 'one of Carl Rogers' fair-haired boys.'"[72] This kind of reinforcement was an impetus to further research and publication.

Finally, Rogers facilitated most of the research at Chicago through the more than half million dollars in foundation support he managed to obtain. So although he did not conduct and write up the results of many studies himself, when the influence of his attitudes and ideas, the atmosphere and norms and structures he created at the Center, and his roles of publicist and fund-raiser are all combined, it was appropriate that he received all the credit he did for the research from this period.

Professional Reputation

And receive credit he did. As early as 1950 the *Encyclopaedia Britannica* wrote, "These first efforts of Rogers to subject his methods of nondirective therapy to scientific test constituted a landmark for clinical psychology."[73] The *Library Journal* acknowledged that the research project reported in *Psychotherapy and Personality Change* was "the first thoroughly objective study of outcomes of psychotherapy in which adequate controls have been utilized."[74] The American Personnel and Guidance Association selected the book as the outstanding research work in the field. In the *Journal of Consulting Psychology* Hans Strupp wrote, "The research effort by Carl Rogers and his students to describe and elucidate the process of nondirective counseling has provided objective evidence in an area in which such evidence has been sorely lacking ... The result of this development is a reasonably well-documented body of knowledge concerning client-centered counseling but almost a total absence of empirical data on psychoanalytically oriented therapy."[75]

Placing the Rogers group's research efforts into historical perspective, Joseph Matarazzo wrote in 1965 that "his approach to the interview stimulated research more than the works of any single writer on the interview before or since," and that the Rogers and Dymond volume was "probably the single most important research publication on interviewing (as found in psychotherapy) of the decade."[76] C.H. Patterson wrote in 1966, "it must be noted that the client-centered approach has led to, and is supported by, a greater amount of research than any other approach to counseling or psychotherapy."[77] Hall and Lindzey, in their popular textbook *Theories of Personality*, paid similar tribute: "Rogers has been a pioneer investigator in the area of counseling and psychotherapy, and deserves a great deal of credit for stimulating and conducting research into the nature of the processes that occur during clinical treatment ... Largely through his efforts, we are beginning to learn something about the processes of psychotherapy."[78]

By no means were reactions to the client-centered research entirely positive. There were many psychologists and others who would have agreed with Allen Calvin's article "Some Misuses of the Experimental Method in Evaluating the Effects of Client-Centered Counseling,"[79] or with Eysenck's review of research in psychotherapy in which he said of the Rogers and Dymond book that "the faults of the experimental design are such, however, that on the grounds of merit alone it is doubtful whether it should have been included,"[80] or with Lloyd Humphreys of the National Science Foundation who thought Rogers had "a retrogressive influence on psychology, basic and applied ... He has treated the 'soft' side of psychology in a 'soft' manner when it needed tough mindedness."[81] As Rogers himself admitted in the Introduction to *Psychotherapy and Personality Change*, their research was far from perfect. But even those who were critical usually made a point to praise his dedication to the scientific method. One of his most bitter critics among clinical psychologists wrote to an editor at Houghton Mifflin in 1949: "Carl has always been willing to subject his ideas to experimental verification. One may question the superficial nature of much of the experimental design and the thinking back of it, but at least the man is willing to check his beliefs against empirical findings."[82] Criticisms of *Psychotherapy and Personality Change* tended to offer this same acknowledgment. As a reviewer in the *American Journal of Sociology* wrote: "[Although] I found myself irritated by the use of fluctuating criteria of significance, [and although] very few hypotheses in this volume were established on the secure probability level of .01 or less, [still] the

211

present volume … is valuable not only because of the manifest character of its method but also because its content is of great significance for clinical and social-psychological theory."[83]

The accolades outnumbered the criticisms by far. Respect and enthusiasm were the major reactions to the research generated by the Rogers group. So much was this the case that, in 1956, Rogers, along with two other prominent psychologists, Kenneth W. Spence and Wolfgang Kohler, was selected to receive the first Distinguished Scientific Contribution Awards ever to be presented by the American Psychological Association. As chairman Dr. Arthur Melton explained to the assembly representing a great number of the 15,000 members of the association then, "The awards have been created in an attempt to express the debt of many of us to the few of us who, in the course of a lifetime or a significant portion thereof, make distinguished contributions to the development of the science of psychology. Your Committee on Awards used two criteria in selecting the three persons to be so honored this year: (a) the contribution must have represented a major effort of the scientist's career and must have been made, or have come to its full development, in the past ten years; (b) the trio of contributions honored in any one year must reflect the broad scope of scientific psychology."

As stated in his citation, Rogers had been selected to receive the Award

for developing an original method to objectify the description and analysis of the psychotherapeutic process, for formulating a testable theory of psychotherapy and its effects on personality and behavior, and for extensive systematic research to exhibit the value of the method and explore and test the implications of the theory. His imagination, persistence, and flexible adaptation of scientific method in his attack on the formidable problems involved in the understanding and modification of the individual person have moved this area of psychological interest within the boundaries of scientific psychology.[84]

Twenty years later, looking back over his long career, Rogers wrote, "Never have I been so emotionally affected as I was by the scientific contribution award and its accompanying citation. When I was elected to an office it could have been partly due to my ambition, for I was ambitious to get ahead in my profession. But this award was to me, in some sense, the 'purest' recognition I had ever received. For years I had been struggling to objectify knowledge in a potential field of science that no one else seemed to be concerned about. It was not ambition nor hope of any reward that pushed me on. In the empirical research itself there was more than a little desire to prove something to others—clearly not a scientific goal. But in the basic phases of the work—the careful observation, the recorded interviews, the hunches as to hypotheses, the development of crude theories—I was as close to being a true scientist as I ever hope to be. But it was clear, I thought, that my colleagues and I were just about the only ones who knew or cared. So my voice choked, and the tears flowed, when I was called forth, at the 1956 APA convention, to receive, with Wolfgang Kohler and Kenneth Spence, the first of the awards for a *scientific* contribution to psychology. It was a vivid proof that psychologists were not only embarrassed by me, but were to some extent proud of me. It had a greater personal meaning than all the honors which have followed …"[85]

This honor, the American Psychological Association's highest award then, came near the end of Rogers' tenure at the University of Chicago. But his national prominence in the field of psychology had begun much earlier. It had started with the publication of *Counseling and Psychotherapy* in 1942 and, as described earlier, had continued with the publication of more articles, his participation on many committees of the American Psychological Association, the honor of being elected as the first President of the American Association for Applied Psychology, and his work attempting to bring the APA and AAAP back together again. So when he moved to Chicago in 1945, he was a well-known figure, with a growing stature in the psychological profession.

Nevertheless it did seem premature when he was elected president of the American Psychological Association in 1945 to serve the 1946–1947 term. About one fourth of the APA membership then indicated an interest in psychotherapy,[86] and certainly this minority were far from unanimous in their support of the "nondirective method." Furthermore, Rogers and his students and colleagues had barely begun their research efforts, so this could not account for his election by the research-oriented association. Rogers' own explanation for why he was elected, with many other prestigious psychologists to choose from, is simple. "There were two other more august figures in contention. They couldn't decide, so rather than offend one or the other, they chose me."[87] Shortly before he died, he gave a longer explanation of how he became president of APA.

There was a nomination for president and president-elect. I was nominated for president and I declined that. I thought, 'I don't deserve to be president of this new organization; Jack Hilgard has worked on it much harder than I have, and he deserves to be president.' And so I only accepted the nomination for president-elect. I thought I did deserve that. Then, to my astonishment, Garrison, a statistician from Columbia, was elected president—the first case in the APA, I think, where lobbying did the trick. The New York City group got behind Garrison and elected him. He didn't really deserve it, if I may say so. And Jack Hilgard, because he was nominated for both president and president-elect, whatever votes he received were split. So I'd done the smartest political thing I could have done by just having my name for president-elect. I was elected president-elect; by the next year I was president. [88]

Rogers' prestige in the APA continued to grow during and after his term as president. From 1946 through 1957, at nine of the twelve annual conventions, he presented one, two, or even three papers or presentations on each occasion. He continued to serve on several committees of the APA and was President of the Division of Clinical and Abnormal Psychology from 1949 to 1950. In 1950, just before the APA convention, he was selected as one of three outstanding practitioners to conduct a post-doctoral training institute at Penn State.

When the American Academy of Psychotherapists was formed in 1956, Rogers was elected its first president. Psychotherapist Vivian Guze recalled how her husband Henry Guze, Albert Ellis and Jules Barron "met in a hotel room and hammered out what they would do." They decided to form the Academy to bring together clinical psychologists, psychotherapists and psychiatrists—a goal Rogers had long shared. Because of his stature in the fields of psychology and psychotherapy, "They invited Carl Rogers to be the first president."[89] When Guze and Ellis asked Rogers if he would be willing to be nominated, he agreed.[90]

Meanwhile his prolific writing was appearing in a wide variety of professional journals. Besides those published by the usual psychological journals, his words saw print in publications as varied as: *Marriage and Family Living*,[91] *Teachers College Record*,[92] *Pastoral Psychology*,[93] *American Journal of Nursing*,[94] *Harvard Educational Review*,[95] *Educational and Psychological Measurement*,[96] *Annals of Allergy*,[97] *Scientific American*,[98] *Management Record*,[99] *ETC* (the journal of the Society for General Semantics)[100] and *Harvard Business Review*,[101] to name a few.

As this list of publications suggests, Rogers had a diverse appeal. He never let himself get tied down to one professional identity or clique within a profession. For years he moved back and forth primarily between psychology, social work, and, later, the education profession, and among many associations within these professions. "He travels fastest who travels alone" was a maxim Rogers applied to himself, confident that if his contribution had merit, it would attract the attention it deserved.[102]

His classes at Chicago reflected his growing reputation. Theron Alexander, later a professor at Temple University, was a student of Rogers then and recalled how "I took several courses under him and most of the time there were three or four hundred people in them that met in a large auditorium. People came from all over the world, and the University did not feel it could make any restrictions on who could come in. So they just kept getting a larger and larger auditorium until it accommodated the people ... He would start out to discuss some topic and maybe discuss it for ten or fifteen minutes and then open it up to discussion. People were very anxious to discuss and it was never a dragging discussion. Most of the time it was very interesting ... The people were so excited, either by great hostility for the ideas or enamored with the ideas; but there were enough who were either way to have arguments not only with Rogers but with each other across the auditorium ... In his heyday, he was probably the most talked about person in psychology. He thrived on controversy, even though he avowed strongly that he eschewed it. 'No student just goes to a professor for information.' He would like to say something like that to start a discussion. Actually, he was so controversial and so many people argued with him and got very upset with him that he must have enjoyed it or he wouldn't have engaged in so much of it."[103]

Through Rogers' and his students' efforts, the influence of the client-centered approach began to spread to other helping professions—education, social work, nursing, pastoral counseling, even management.[104] In the *Journal of Pastoral Care*, for example, the Very Rev. H. Ralph Higgins wrote:

> the modern clergyman will welcome a type of psychotherapy whose basic assumptions are compatible with a religious view of the nature and destiny of man, and whose techniques may be readily learned and effectively applied without the necessity of a medical background or a rigid psychological training ... In the newer techniques of client-centered therapy the clergyman has available a method which can prove of immense significance and genuine practical benefit in his work ... The Christian teaching that suffering can be turned to joy, sin forgiven, and redemption attained, greatly fortifies the attitude of the pastoral counselor in undertaking parishioner-centered therapy ... It may also be pointed out that just as Christianity is a way of life to be lived and not a proposition to be argued instead of lived, so client-centered therapy is a method of counseling which can be proved only as it is practiced in sincere obedience to its basic hypothesis. "By their fruits ye shall know them" applies equally to therapy and to the Christian life.[105]

Or, as the Assistant Executive Secretary of the American Nurses' Association, Evelyn B. Ferguson, wrote in their journal, "Dr. Rogers' general hypothesis that the relationship he describes 'offers exciting possibilities for the development of creative, adaptive, inner-directed persons' has great meaning for all—not only for nurse counselors, public health nurses, educators, and administrators, but also for any nurse who is interested in helping a person with a problem."[106]

His work even began to influence business and industry. Rogers had been associated with a more egalitarian management style as early as 1951, when Thomas Gordon's chapter on group-centered leadership in *Client-Centered Therapy* publicized Rogers' approach to delegating authority to the group. The next year Rogers' presentation on "Communication: Its Blocking and Facilitation" was published along with co-panelist E.J. Roethlisberger's presentation in the *Harvard Business Review* under the title of "Barriers and Gateways to Communication."[107] It was often reprinted, and 40 years later, when it was republished as an "HBR Classic," John Gabarro, Professor of Human Resource Management at Harvard Business School, described how

Reading "Barriers and Gateways" today, it is hard to understand the stir the article created when it was first published. But in 1952, Rogers's and Roethlisberger's ideas about the importance of listening were indeed radical. Not only did they stake out new territory that was anathema to the gray flannel ethic—namely, the idea that people's feelings mattered. But they also challenged the sanctity of hierarchical relationships by suggesting that managers take their subordinates' thoughts and feelings seriously. Today, however, these insights are so basic as to be obvious which shows how much impact their ideas have had and how far management communication has come.[108]

Even *Time* magazine, in 1957, acknowledged Rogers' stature in the psychology profession by devoting three columns to him and his work—complete with full photographic portrait and typical *Time* writing style:

> Among variegated practitioners of talk-it-out treatment for emotional problems, Chicago's Psychologist Carl Ransom Rogers, 55, has long been a maverick. He calls his method "client-centered therapy," tries manfully to define it: "We see therapy as an experience, not in intellectual terms. We treat the client as a person, not as an object to be manipulated or directed." Snorts a Chicago psychoanalyst of neo-Freudian persuasion: "Rogers' method is unsystematic, undisciplined and humanistic. Rogers doesn't analyze and doesn't diagnose. We have no common ground." To Rogers this is fine ...[109]

All this acclaim made the Chicago years a time when he was much in demand, receiving many invitations to give speeches and workshops to various professional groups. In his annual report for 1952–1953 he noted, with a little sarcasm at the end: "During the year I have been invited to speak to three important medical groups: at the opening of the Psychiatric Institute of the University of Maryland, where I gave a short paper; at the Forum of the Menninger Foundation at Topeka, where I was the speaker at the largest forum they have ever had; and at the Department of Medicine of the University of Illinois, where I spoke to their monthly seminar. These invitations may even foreshadow the day when our own medical school might be interested in what we are doing."[110]

In addition to the speeches and workshops, he accepted offers to serve for a quarter or semester as "Visiting Professor" at five universities: the University of California at Los Angeles (1947), Harvard (1948), Occidental College (1950), the University of California at Berkeley (1953), and the University of Wisconsin (1957). He also received an honorary doctoral degree from Lawrence College in Appleton, Wisconsin (1956); and his alma mater, Columbia University, presented him with its silver Nicholas Murray Butler Medal in 1955. The latter was awarded to him when he delivered an address at the inauguration of Dr. Hollis Caswell as the new President of Columbia's Teachers College.[111]

As Rogers' stature in the psychological and other helping professions grew, so did a mystique about him. Arthur Combs recalled a story that illustrates this. Before the APA convention in 1950 Rogers was leading a post-doctoral institute in which he counseled a very disturbed young man for two weeks, before the group of participants. The therapy, as several members of that group recalled years later, seemed extremely skillful, moving, and successful. Combs remembered how, after each therapy session, "Carl chaired a discussion of what had happened … During this time he did not particularly answer questions but acted in a sense like a counselor for the group. On the last day the group asked him to respond more directly to questions they had and he agreed. He is a real master at this sort of thing and can often answer a question with the kind of statement that has great impact. While he was doing this a storm came up and it became darker and darker in the lounge where this session was being held. Then, at one point when Rogers had just completed a beautiful answer to a student's question somebody, somewhere pulled the switch and all the lights came on in the room. For a moment there was a kind of stunned silence in the group, then someone was heard to exclaim, 'My God! Dr. Rogers! Do you walk on the water, too?'[112]

Others have commented on his ability to electrify a room, to energize a group with his sincerity and quiet charisma. This would be particularly apparent on panels whose participants were somewhat hostile to Rogers' ideas or methods. The result was usually a lively session that alternated between antagonism and camaraderie. The following excerpts from a 1952 panel discussion before the American Association of Marriage Counselors gives something of this flavor.[113] Rogers had given the major address.

CHAIRMAN LAIDLAW: Thank you so much. This has been, I know, a real treat to all of us to hear such an outline not only of a technic but of a philosophy of life, a philosophy that entails continual growth, and it is so unlike some of our scientific friends who make some outstanding mistakes in their early years, in their early writings, and then spend the rest of their lives defending them …

ROBERT HARPER: I think we can take a cue from Dr. Rogers in making ourselves, all of us, more flexible, more willing to learn about what we are doing. But it seems to me, Dr. Rogers, that you carried this point of striving to be flexible in one's rationality, to the extreme of rejecting rationality, very often, in the counseling process … I think this nebulous new discovery that neither you nor your client seemed very rationally to depict is essentially a religious experience and not a scientific contribution to the counseling field; that it is a religious experience, unchecked, unscientific, unvalidated, unreliable …

ROGERS: That is a very worthwhile comment. I think that you will probably get much more enjoyment and satisfaction out of the forthcoming issue of the *Psychological Service Center Journal*, which contains three long articles on our research, with control groups and careful measurement and reliability, and factor analyses of the Q sort, and so on … Let me come back, too, to your statement that I seem to be going off in mystical directions, and so on. Well, that doesn't frighten me as long as it is well rooted in solid experience. I think I can only try to interpret the experiences that I have in the way that seems most appropriate to them, and I wouldn't be honest if I said that the most appropriate way to interpret therapy is simply to feel here is a complex organism and you manipulate it this way and something constructive comes out of that manipulation …

ABRAHAM STONE: Now, I haven't the slightest doubt that Dr. Rogers in his work obtains excellent results because he has a quality of personality, an intensity of feeling and a spiritual temper which not many of us, unfortunately, possess. The majority of us, I fear, could not do as well in our work unless we had a more realistic, a more concrete and, shall I say, a more directive approach to some of the problems that come before us. (Applause.)

ROGERS: Thank you, Dr. Stone, especially for what I suppose was intended as a compliment, but I can assure you that at home I am not regarded as the spiritual type. (Laughter.) …

ALBERT ELLIS: I happen to be in a radically different position from that of Bob Harper. Having attacked Dr. Rogers in print several times, I can now afford to be kind to him; and to most of what Dr. Rogers said tonight I would agree, and would highly commend his manner of saying it. I would say that his errors, if you would call them such, were largely errors of omission, as Abe Stone would appraise them, rather than of commission …

Ellis went on to elaborate on Rogers' "errors of omission," describing a patient of his own who exhibited extreme paranoid thinking.

ELLIS: I consider it my duty as a therapist gradually to point this out to the patient; and, so far, I have apparently effectively been doing so, and have been showing him how he developed the rationale for Oneness and Goodness out of his sexual and other problems. However, if I were a philosopher myself, or if I were another kind of therapist—such as a Karen Horneyite or perhaps a Carl Rogersite—it would be the easiest thing in the world for me to accept sympathetically this paranoid thinking of my patient. If I did so, when we would finally come to the end of our therapeutic relationship, I would feel much elated about understanding and accepting his ideas, and he would feel wonderfully happy knowing I accepted him and his philosophy—and heaven knows where we would end up. I doubt whether, according to almost any criteria which we usually have of helping the patient—and that is frankly what I am in this profession for, to help the patient—I doubt if we would end up with anything like a so-called normal, or well adjusted, or effectively functioning human being … If I fully appreciated and accepted his paranoid thinking, and if we both ecstatically went off to end up in some religio-mystical state of paranoia à deux,

I am sure that his concept of himself, as objectively shown through the Q technic or any other technic, would definitely appear to be more favorable—and would, of course, agree with my own Q technic matchings of his therapeutic "progress." The question would still legitimately arise, however: Would the patient (or the therapist!) really then be improved? ...

ROGERS: I think that I should like to agree with Dr. Ellis that if he treated this patient of his in the way that he described, by accepting and agreeing with his philosophical notions, I am as sure as he is that such a procedure would work out badly. This is a good example of real failure in communication, obviously, because I really have not been talking about that at all ... I would agree also that if the way we are using the Q technic is simply to objectify a testimonial type of statement, I would see no point in it, either.

LENA LEVINE: In the first place, I want to express my gratitude at meeting the master. Until now the only persons I heard from were the disciples. If I may predict on the basis of the development of your thinking to May, 1952—although I don't know the rapidity of your growth, that in a few years you will have discovered the science of psychoanalysis which has a very, very excellent record, and that it will be the one to which you will find you were growing ... [She continued.]

ROGERS: Thank you for your first bit of information. (Laughter.) ...

And so it went. The panel members would begin by mentioning some widely acclaimed, positive quality of Rogers and exaggerate it or use it to criticize him, often in a condescending manner. Many apparently expected "the master" to be a pushover. While others might have risen to the bait and become somewhat aggressive, he invariably responded with equanimity—with humor and sincerity. Although he would usually respond to the substance of any criticism (which is omitted from these excerpts), the tone of his answer always contained enough agreement or humor or desire to understand the other's position that the response tended to minimize a potential argument. As a frustrated antagonist once exclaimed, "Damn it, you can't fight with Carl Rogers!"[114]

This, perhaps, explains the good personal feelings so many people had toward him, even those who disagreed with much of his thinking or practice. Milton Wexler recalled Rogers' "charm and sincerity ... I was always impressed ... with a very special quality which seemed so engaging that it lent added conviction and strength even to viewpoints with which I did not particularly agree."[115] William Archie, evaluating a grant proposal Rogers had submitted, wrote to psychologists across the country for their reactions to the proposal, and said, "not a single person to whom I wrote ... said an unkind word about Carl Rogers. Even when they obviously disagreed with his viewpoints as a professional psychologist, they all thought he was an honest man and said so."[116]

Personal Life

The Chicago years were very different for the Rogers from their previous times together. Both children were off pursuing their own education, careers and families, so Carl and Helen had their apartment at 5844 Stony Island Avenue all to themselves.

David was attending Cornell University Medical College when his parents moved to Chicago. A year later he married Cora Jane Baxter ("Corky") who was going into her last year at Wellesley College; both of them were twenty years old at the time.[117] When he entered medical school, "it was with the idea of going into … either surgery or psychiatry. Surgery because of the love I've always had for doing things with my hands, psychiatry because of the powerful influence of my father."[118] But medical school, some years at Johns Hopkins as an intern and assistant resident, and several more years in postgraduate training and research opened his eyes to other possibilities, and he eventually began specializing in research on infectious diseases. He returned to New York City to become Assistant, then Associate Professor of Medicine at Cornell and Chief of the Division of Infectious Diseases at the New York Hospital. He served in the U.S. Naval Reserve for ten years, including on the U.S.S. Leyte in the Mediterranean during the Korean War. Between 1951 and 1958 he had over twenty scientific papers on infectious diseases published in the professional journals.[119] In the years between 1950 and 1954 he and Corky had three children—Anne, Gregory ("Greg"), and Julia ("Julie").

Natalie, who was only fifteen when she graduated from high school, completed two years of undergraduate work at Stevens College in Missouri. Still planning on becoming a psychologist, she transferred to DePauw University in Illinois where she completed a Bachelor's degree in psychology. Since she was close to Chicago at DePauw, when she went home on school vacations she often became involved in the work of the Counseling Center. "I watched his counseling sessions through a one-way mirror and sat in on Center discussions."[120] Using the data from the Center she wrote and had published two research studies which her father often cited in his writings.[121] After DePauw she moved to New York City to work full-time with the United World Federalists, making speeches and organizing for world government. There she met and, in 1950, married Lawrence Fuchs, who was then working on his Ph.D. in political science at Harvard. When he became a faculty member at Brandeis University, they settled in the Boston area. Their three daughters, Janet, Frances ("Frannie"), and Naomi, were born during the years 1952 through 1957. When she was pregnant with Janet, on her twenty-third birthday, Natalie received these two notes from her parents:

> Dearest Nat-Larry—Happy birthday, Nat. We will be thinking of you and
> remembering what a happy day it was for us 23 years ago. And it makes it

doubly happy now to know you are going to be responsible for another birthday in March. Hope you have as nice a baby as we had. We have enjoyed both of your recent letters lately. They really mean very much to us and it's always a red letter day when I find mail from any of my four kids in the box ... We love you both very much, Mom

Dear Nat, I hope this reaches you on a very happy birthday. It seems a long time back that I was pacing up and down the house at 180 Eastland Ave., wondering whether Helen should go to the hospital right away or wait a while. For some reason that part of the experience stays with me quite vividly. And to think that a whole generation has whizzed by—a short one to be sure—and that now in a few months you'll be wondering whether or not it's time to go, and Larry will be doing the pacing! ... Dad[122]

Later Natalie wrote, "When I was in college I used to get birthday letters from my father telling me how much he loved me and what a happy but frightening day it was for him when I was born [with Helen's hemorrhaging]. He had come close to losing his sweetheart. After several such greetings I asked to be spared the gory details of my after-birth."[123]

Both David and Natalie felt they could talk to their father fairly openly during their earlier years; but, as this recollection suggests, it was during the Chicago years, as young adults, that they felt they achieved a truly comfortable and open relationship with him. "I felt I could start to talk to him openly in Chicago," said Natalie, who even used him as a therapist at times.[124] David said, "I felt Dad was terribly consistent in his several roles. I could sit down and talk to him as a therapist, even though he was my father. I knew he was my father but I also felt he was my friend."[125]

Thus, during the Rogers' early Chicago years, David and Natalie wrote to their parents about their love lives (including David asking his father, tongue-in-cheek, "Dear Pop ... What is the psychologists' viewpoint on the length of engagements?"), about Nat's struggling with some of her academic work, about David's disappointment and insecurity in his residency at New York Hospital, and other personal subjects.[126] A few years later, David closed a seven-page, typed letter to his father from New York Hospital saying, "If I can give my kids anything like the background I received in terms of security and fundamental know-thyself sort of dignity ... I'll feel very pleased with what the world has given me. You're a pretty terrific guy and I don't tell it to you half often enough, but I feel I've had an awful head start on most of the population ... with the ideas which seeped in from your fine and humble philosophy of life."[127] On another occasion, he explored his feeling upset with his parents about their apparently unsatisfactory reaction to his and Corky's request for help when Corky was sick. The insightful, honest and open communication, in which David took responsibility for his part in the situation, illustrated the openness in his relationship with his parents.

221

In turn, both parents wrote regularly to their children, Helen being "the [more] prolific one of the family as far as burning up the paper is concerned," as David put it in a letter at the time.[128]

With their children away from home, Carl and Helen had a freedom they had not experienced since their first year of marriage in New York City. They also had the financial means now with which to take advantage of that freedom. The University of Chicago assisted them by allowing faculty to take one of the four quarters away from the campus. Once Carl had become established at the Counseling Center, he and Helen made it their annual custom beginning in 1951 to spend the winter quarter in Mexico or the Caribbean, a two- to three-month getaway that typically started or ended with a visit to their children and growing number of grandchildren out East. Once headed south, they would be thankful to be away from the Chicago winters. For example, their vacation in 1952–53 included Christmas in Boston with Natalie, Larry and Janet; San Juan, St. Thomas, Martinique, St. Lucia, three weeks in Granada, Trinidad; and finally Florida where they visited Carl's mother and sister. In 1955–56, they spent three weeks in Bequia, a small island in the British West Indies, four weeks in St. Vincent, and visited Haiti and Trinidad.[129] Sometimes they invited their children and grandchildren to join them for a week or so, if they could get away.

As had been his custom as far back as 1922 when he traveled to the Orient, Carl often recorded his observations in letters to friends and family back home. He would occasionally have the letters duplicated at the Counseling Center and sent to more friends than he could possibly have written to personally. One such letter described a scene in a church in Tecalpulco, a small Indian village in Mexico, during a fiesta. It shows his keen eye for detail as well as his tendency to reflect upon his observations:

> While the dance goes on, another group catches our eye. Six people, an older man, and assorted women and girls are chanting. The man is the leader. He carries a candle and a cheap leaflet in his hand, on which are the words of the chant. As they sing they move slowly backward, a shuffle at a time, toward the church door, always facing the altar in front. The man's voice is cracked and frequently off key. The woman next to him peers out from under a black rebozo with a face like a dried apple. The others can't see the words too well, and fumble and halt in their singing. Yet as the droning chant is repeated over and over, in their slow retreat down the long nave, one cannot help but be impressed by this picture of simple reverence. No one told them to do this—this is their Lenten offering of hymn and supplication, and Nuestro Senor must see it, as do we, as an expression of more real worship than would be found in ten churches on city boulevards.[130]

But traveling about as tourists did not characterize the Rogers' winter vacations. Traveling typically by ship, they much preferred to find a quiet spot they enjoyed and to stay there for anywhere from two to eight weeks. There they could really rest and paint and write and engage in what came to be a favorite pastime of both Carl and Helen—snorkeling. Carl described their schedule in one of his letters, written from Bequia in 1956.

> Here is the way the day goes. We waken to the sound of the gentle surf, and the crowing of a rooster or two, and step out on our porch. The harbor is dotted with boats, mostly rowboats, filled with men who have been fishing since four or five o'clock. We stroll down to the beach to see what new shells have washed in ... As the sun comes over the ridge behind us, Carmen, the neat and smiling girl from the hotel, appears with a tray of breakfast. After breakfast, Helen paints, I daub, or we read or write letters or walk along the beach collecting shells, until we decide it is time for a swim. The water is a beautiful green, though because of a long spell of rough weather it is too cloudy for our masks and snorkels to be of maximum use. The water is warm, the sun is hot, and everything conspires to make us feel languorous. Lunch and dinner we eat at the hotel, but four-o'clock tea (at which we first turned up our noses) is brought to the cottage by Carmen. The food is excellent, and all in all we feel that we are not being overcharged when we pay $9.00 a day for the two of us, which includes all our meals (*and* afternoon tea!), our cottage, occasional use of a row boat, and a climate and view that seems as close to Paradise as mortals are permitted to come.[131]

Carl would bring some work along to Paradise and usually spend a few hours a day reading or writing. His writings began to range far afield from his clinical experience and research findings. These few months each year, away from the daily cares and routines of the Counseling Center, gave him the distance with which to view his own work and to see its implications in many areas. He began to read philosophy again, as he described in the introduction to an article he wrote entitled "Persons or Science: A Philosophical Question."

> I first became acquainted with the work of Søren Kierkegaard and that of Martin Buber at the insistence of some of the theological students at Chicago who were taking work with me ... Though Kierkegaard lived one hundred years ago, I cannot help but regard him as a sensitive and highly perceptive friend. I think this paper shows my indebtedness to him, mostly in the fact that reading his work loosened me up and made me more willing to trust and express my own experience ... Another helpful element in writing the paper was that I was far away from colleagues, wintering in Taxco, when I wrote the major portion of it. A year later, on the Caribbean island of Grenada, I completed the paper by writing the final section.[132]

Referring to the winter quarter of 1952, he wrote, "I made it my purpose during the Winter Quarter to get some perspective on my work and to extend my thinking into the theoretical and philosophical implications of what we are doing. I not only read, but really studied, some of the most significant recent books in psychology, such as Hebb's *Organization of Behavior* and Marx's collection of writings on Psychological Theory. I also read a couple of books on modern physics to try to learn more of the development of science and theory in a field other than my own. But much the most rewarding reading was in the field of philosophy. Kierkegaard was a most exciting discovery to me, and Buber very stimulating. Sartre and Whitehead each contributed something. Now that I have returned I am beginning to realize the impact that this reading, and the opportunity for leisurely thinking, has had on me. I know that it will sharply influence my work and my writing."[133]

His prediction was correct. Some of his best-known essays, many of which were later published in *On Becoming a Person* in 1961, were written during winter vacations or stemmed directly from the reading and thinking he was able to do in Mexico or the Caribbean. "Personal Thoughts on Teaching and Learning" (1957), "A Note on the Nature of Man" (1957), "Persons or Science: A Philosophical Question" (1955), and "A Therapist's View of the Good Life: The Fully Functioning Person" (1957) are examples of his thinking and writing during this period.

Remembering how Rogers "took time out for vacation and extensive travel" and how "he often brought back good ideas," Julius Seeman reflected that "Carl seemed to have the ability to work in a sustained way and to take distance from his work. I always felt him to be steadily productive without any indication that he was driven or compelled to produce."[134]

Consistent with this appraisal, professional work never characterized the major part of the Rogers' winter vacations. Excerpts from one particular letter of his, written from Bequia in 1956, gives an excellent picture of Carl and Helen's pleasure in snorkeling together and also shows how Carl's sense of adventure at age 54 had not diminished much from that of the young man of 22 who on the eve of his return from the Orient spent all night climbing Mt. Fujiyama.

Yesterday was a day of real adventure, and I guess I'll have to write about it to get it out of my system. It all begins with our snorkeling, which we find most fascinating. Every day that the water is clear we don our masks and snorkel tubes and investigate the nearby waters. We have a little private "aquarium" that we love—a big rock on the harbor floor, right out from the hotel, with a bevy of many-colored fish and two lobsters always around it. Then there are the coral heads quite far out that we swim to when feeling particularly bold, and other favorite spots. Helen and I discovered what we call our "prehistoric fish"—a strange creature with two fins forward which it uses like paws, turning over sea-urchins, and scraping for tid-bits along the bottom, and two enormous fins trailing backward which at times open out into great semicircular wings, tinged with translucent purple edging. And then Helen spotted a fish which we are now sure was a barracuda—and watched him while she called me. When I swam over and spotted him, he politely swam away …

They had met three young Americans and the next morning Carl went with them in a big rowboat, outfitted with sails, to do some snorkeling.

We sailed out into the large waves beyond the harbor and scudded down to the southern end of the island, which ends in a rocky narrow tip, with three great rocks or tiny islands on beyond … The water was blue black and very deep. The waves were enormous and they went surging in to the great rocks and up and up, bursting into spray—and then falling, draining, sucking away, down and down, until twenty feet of rocks and boulders were exposed which had been covered when the wave was at its height … By that time it looked too exciting to miss, and I thought of a scheme which was sufficiently safe to me. I donned my mask and snorkel and went overboard, having first fixed a trailing rope from the boat to hang on to. I was glad I had, because in the very rough sea, small amounts of water kept getting into my breathing tube and giving me trouble. But the sight was tremendous. You could see straight to the bottom in what they said was thirty to seventy feet of water, and a great fantastic landscape it was … [At a new location] I decided, though I was now somewhat cold, to go overboard for a few moments. I stayed for nearly an hour … And then as I turned my head I saw the shark. Four feet, six feet—I wouldn't know for sure, but the tail was unmistakable shark! He was heading away from me, down near the bottom, and because I was so close to the boat I didn't feel frightened.

By this time we knew we would already be late for lunch, so we piled aboard in a drizzle … the wind outside the cove was very strong. The mast was set, the various stays were pulled tight, the mainsail and jib unfurled and we turned out into the wind. Did it hit us, and did we move! … we set a northwest course (heading approximately for New York!) so that when we got far enough out into the ocean, we could come about into a northeasterly direction which would take us back into the harbor. It was a wild ride. The waves were larger and larger as we got further out to sea, and the wind was vicious, heeling us over in sudden puffs. I've never been in a boat that shipped so much water … Then all at once it happened. We were zooming along into the heavy sea, drenched with spray by every crest, with the sails as tight as drums, when a particularly angry gust hit us and crunch! the five inch mast snapped off like a broken match! … The moment the mast gave way the whole boat careened to the side we were sitting on and we might have capsized if we hadn't all jumped as one man to the middle of the boat … It was all so sudden I can't honestly say that I was upset, but I surely would have been if I had known that Helen had been watching our progress from the hotel, miles away, with our trusty binoculars. She knew it was rough, because at times our boat would disappear in the trough of the waves and only the top of the mast and sail would be visible—then it would come into view again on the crest of the next wave. But suddenly to her complete dismay the sail disappeared while we were in a trough, and when the boat appeared it had no mast! She was really frightened then, and went tearing down the shore until she found a sailboat just coming in and persuaded them to sail out to find us.[135]

They made it back safely. And although this day's adventure was considerably more dramatic than a typical day's itinerary, they always regarded the decade or so of yearly winter vacations as among their most memorable and pleasurable times together.

In addition to the long winter vacations, the Rogers occasionally spent summer weeks at their Seneca Lake cabin, sometimes inviting friends and colleagues from Chicago to join them.[136] An unexpected visit occurred in the spring of 1949 on their "runaway trip," described earlier. As Helen remembered it, "We finally came to roost at our hideaway on Seneca Lake and spent a month roughing it in our cabin in the cold temperatures of May in New York State. There were periods of real despair which we weathered together. It never occurred to me that he could not or would not recover. We roamed the hills and I taught him all I could about painting. We spent many hours enjoying and exploring and painting the countryside."[137] In his words, "throughout this whole period Helen was certain this state of mind would pass away, that I was not insane, and showed in every way how much she cared. Wow! That's the only way I can express my gratitude. That's what I mean when I say she has stood by me in critical periods."[138]

She had stood by him another time, earlier in their stay in Chicago. "During my forties," he wrote, "there was a period of nearly a year when I felt absolutely no sexual desire—for anyone. No medical cause was found. Helen was confident that my normal urges would return, and simply 'stood with me' in my predicament. It is easy to think up possible psychological causes, but none of them 'click' as far as I'm concerned. It remains a mystery to me. But her quiet continuing love meant a great deal to me, and probably was the best therapy I could have had. At any rate, I gradually became sexually normal once more."[139]

He was able to reciprocate this "standing by" during their years at Chicago. As he described this period, "Helen's mother suffered several strokes as she grew older. This had the unfortunate (but not rare) effect of markedly changing her personality. Where she had been a warm and kindly person with strong intellectual interests, she became a carping, suspicious, sometimes viciously hurtful person. This was terribly hard on her daughters, but particularly on Helen, who would feel terribly crushed and hurt by the psychological jabs which came from a mother with whom she had been very close. Her mother became impossible to live with, and could not live alone. Then came hard decisions—to take her from her apartment; to place her in a nursing home (the best of which is a forlorn place); to face the fact that she was no longer the person she had been. Helen felt terribly guilty about what she was doing to her mother, and her mother retained enough shrewdness to know how to heighten that guilt. Through six long and very trying years I believe I stood by Helen. She could not help but feel hurt, guilty, and upset by her twice-weekly visits to her mother. I could let her have those feelings, but also let her know that I thought the accusations false, the decisions sound, and that I believed she was doing the best anyone could in a most distressing and complex situation. I know that she was strengthened and helped by my 'standing by.' Our physician son also was of much help to her in understanding the physical and psychological deterioration which had taken place, and that her mother's complaints were not to be taken at face value."[140]

Carl's mother and his sister Margaret continued to live at Warwood after Walter Rogers' death in 1944. Walter left a substantial estate, from which Carl and his siblings received annual dividends and from which they were able to give generous gifts to their children.[141] Julia Rogers sold the family homestead in 1953, when she and Margaret moved to Daytona Beach, Florida. After Julia's death the following year, Margaret continued to live in Daytona Beach for her remaining years.

Aside from Carl and Helen's close relationship with brother Walter and Elise Rogers, Carl's relations with his other brothers and sister over these years remained cordial, yet distant. When the first copies of *Client-Centered Therapy* were printed near the end of 1950, he sent copies as Christmas presents to each of his siblings[142]—a practice he followed all his life when a new book of his was published. When the *Time Magazine* article about him appeared, Lester, John and Walt all sent their congratulations.[143] They clearly were proud of their brother.

The Rogers' personal life in Chicago was full and social. Helen was often involved in the Counseling Center in nonacademic ways, with many get-togethers at their apartment for meetings or for purely social occasions. These were times Helen enjoyed very much. She later wrote, "It was during this period in Chicago that it was brought home to me frequently that my husband was emerging as a very well-known and important person in his field of endeavor. At the most unexpected times—signing a charge-a-plate or giving my name and address for the sending of packages—the person would look at me and say, 'Are you THE Mrs. Carl Rogers?' It was a new and joyful experience to find my husband influencing so many people in so many different walks of life."[144] In addition to her homemaking, two major interests from earlier years still occupied her. She continued to paint and to be active in the Planned Parenthood movement.

During this period Carl developed more hobbies himself. He had always loved to work with his hands. Now he began to take an interest in painting.

According to several of their friends, he did *extremely* well. This seemed to threaten a private area of Helen's sense of competence, and partly for that reason and partly because he had so much else to do, he gave it up.[145] Another of his hobbies was making mobiles. Helen remembered, "We were intrigued with Alexander Calder's new idea of art in motion. Carl, coming from an engineering family, enjoyed the combined problem of balance and composition that you are faced with when making a mobile. I remember that once I had to be in the East for two weeks, when the second of our grandchildren was born. 'Grandma' was called to take care of little Anne, so I left Carl and our daughter, Natalie, to care for themselves. I returned to find they had been having a 'ball' making mobiles, experimenting with cardboard, balsa wood, copper, aluminum. I found a mobile hanging in every room of the house, including the bathrooms! This hobby has continued to be a great source of joy through the years and Carl has made some unusual and very artistic creations."[146]

This was not only his wife's opinion. Visitors at the Rogers' home in California often commented on the intriguing mobiles they saw and were amazed to find that Rogers was their creator. The same was true with his color photography, another hobby he loved, especially during their trips to Mexico and the Caribbean. He seemed to excel whether working with his head or his hands. Interestingly, when fifty past presidents of the American Psychological Association were rated on the Strong Vocational Interest Blank, Rogers tied for fifth place as an artist. (He also placed third for the forest service, fourth as a farmer and, ironically, sixth as a minister, and was down near the bottom of the list, that is, *least similar* to an office worker, purchasing agent, and accountant.[147] In this context it is not surprising that in later years his professional writings began to emphasize the trusting of one's own instincts and inner voice. That could be seen as the artist speaking to the scientist. The polarity between artist and scientist was an important tension within him, always moving him beyond previous formulations, whether his own or others'.

Actually all four of the Rogers had an artistic bent. Clearly influenced by their professional artist mother, and amateur artist father, the children had always engaged in art projects at home. As they grew older their interests and talents increased. Natalie became accomplished in painting and dance and integrated many expressive arts into her future career as a psychotherapist. David became an outstanding sculptor in wood, taking driftwood from the Seneca Lake shoreline, for example, and shaping and polishing it into beautiful human and animal figures, eventually showing them in exhibitions. Years later, after her parents and brother were gone, Natalie's home in Santa Cruz, California was a breathtaking sight, filled with Helen's paintings, Carl's mobiles and photography, David's sculptures, and her own artwork.

Developing Theory

As Rogers began to think more philosophically and widely about the implications of his work in psychotherapy, he also began to devote more time to thinking about and developing a theoretical foundation for his previous work. In part this came from a personal desire to understand more fully the phenomena he was observing in his work. Another motivation was the pressure from others who criticized him for not having a sound theory on which to build his therapeutic approach.

He did not originally feel the need for formalized theory. Partly this stemmed from his pragmatic nature. "I was a practical clinician and held an open scorn of all psychological theory, as my early students at Ohio State can testify."[148] Another part of his skepticism about theory was based on its role in the scientific process. As he wrote in 1951, "There is no need for theory until and unless there are phenomena to explain. Limiting our consideration to psychotherapy, there is no reason for a theory of therapy until there are observable changes which call for explanation. Then a unifying theory is of help in explaining what has happened, and in providing testable hypotheses about future experiences. Thus, in the field of therapy the first requisite is a skill which produces an effective result. Through observation of the process and the result, a parsimonious theory may be developed which is projected into new experiences in order to be tested as to its adequacy. The theory is revised and modified with the purpose—never fully attained—of providing a complete conceptual framework which can adequately contain all the observed phenomena. It is the phenomena which are basic, not the theory."[149]

As reluctant as he was to begin theorizing, he was equally reluctant to embrace the "self" or "self-concept" as the heart of his psychological theory. One of his students at Ohio State, Bill Kell, had conducted a study of juvenile delinquents in Columbus, using Rogers' component factor method from his Rochester years. Rogers thought that the component on family background would be the strongest predictor of the child's later success or failure. Kell thought that the social experience factor would be most predictive of outcomes. Both were surprised to see that the self-insight factor was the best predictor of future behavior, with an extremely high correlation between self-insight and favorable outcome.[150] Fresh from twelve years in a social work context in Rochester, Rogers could hardly believe the results and did nothing with them at the time. Two years later another student, Helen McNeil, replicated the study and found similar results: self-insight was the best predictor of future behavior.[151] Now Rogers began to accept the findings. He had recently written *Counseling and Psychotherapy*, in which he had recognized the importance of self-insight for the client's growth in therapy. Maybe the "self" somehow was at the heart of personality change. Still Rogers was reluctant to follow the implications of this idea too far and did not publish Kell, McNeil and his findings for several more years.[152] Possibly this was because the Kell and McNeil studies were mostly about self-*insight*, a familiar concept central to psychoanalysis, and in that sense, no great insight itself.

In Chicago, some of his students, particularly Victor Raimy and Arthur Combs, were thinking about the self in new ways and, as Rogers later acknowledged, influenced his thinking. In 1947, he told an audience, "We at Chicago are currently doing much thinking about the concept of self as the organizing and creative and adaptive core of personality."[153]

That year he first theorized publicly about the "self-concept" in his presidential address at the American Psychological Association's convention in Detroit. He later recalled, "I had stewed over it all year. I was by no means ready to call it finished when the time arrived. I think of it as psychologically unsophisticated, but the germ of a good idea."[154] At the same conference Victor Raimy and Arthur Combs were giving talks on the same subject, but Rogers' tentative formulation got the most attention—mostly negative. He recalled that "following the address … Chairman John Anderson and I went to the men's room which was crowded with psychologists, buzzing loudly with talk. When I entered, all conversation stopped. The silence was deafening. I felt I had interrupted many highly critical comments."[155]

His theory developed gradually over the following years[156] and achieved its two fullest descriptions in a chapter entitled "A Theory of Personality and Behavior" in *Client-Centered Therapy* in 1951 and in "A Theory of Therapy, Personality, and Interpersonal Relationships, as Developed in the Client-Centered Framework," written in 1957 and published in 1959 in Koch's massive series *Psychology: A Study of a Science*.[157]

Rogers' theory was a "phenomenological theory," that is, a theory which begins with the assumption that every individual perceives a separate world of phenomena all around him and also within himself. This "phenomenal field" governs his behavior. For example, the infant may be picked up by a friendly, caring person; but if the infant *perceives* the person as strange or frightening, he will behave accordingly, with fear, crying, pulling away—all to the adult's dismay. Thus, while many individuals' phenomenal fields may overlap as they perceive the same phenomena, it is also true that part of any individual's phenomenal field may *not* correspond to what others would agree is "reality." The extreme example is the person who is hallucinating. The hallucinations he sees are real for him in that they are part of his phenomenal field.

Rogers' theory was also a "self-theory," the *self* being one very important part of a person's phenomenal field. Here he followed a recent tradition in psychology, a relatively new school of thought, which regarded the *self* as the "organizing and creative and adaptive core of personality"[158] which was most influential in determining a person's behavior. For Rogers the self was "the organized, consistent conceptual gestalt [i.e., overall framework] composed of perceptions of the characteristics of the 'I' or 'me' and the perceptions of the relationships of the 'I' or 'me' to others and to various aspects of life, together with the values attached to these perceptions."[159] For example, a perception of the self might be "I am six-feet-two inches in height." A perception of the self in relation to others might be "I am tall." The value attached to this perception might be "I am too tall."

The concept of self grows out of the interaction between the child and his environment. Whether or not he comes to feel he is a lovable or capable person depends on the extent to which he is treated as a person worthy of love and respect by his parents, his friends, his teachers. Once this concept of self is formed it is difficult to change, and it governs a person's behavior. If a person thinks he is not very capable, he will, despite all the evidence of success to the contrary, continue to go into new situations feeling not very capable. Moreover, if he feels incapable, it is likely his behavior will reflect this. As the famous Coleman Report showed in 1966, the greatest factor affecting students' success in schools was their self-concept, particularly their sense of control over their own destiny.[160]

Not only is a person's self-concept difficult to change, the person also builds up "defenses" to maintain it. This often means denying or distorting new evidence which would tend to threaten the old self-concept. For example, the mother who views herself as a loving and responsible person, a "good mother," finds herself experiencing the beginnings of resentful and rejecting feelings to her third child, whom she really did not want to have. To admit these hostile feelings would threaten her image of herself as a caring and unselfish mother. Consequently she denies the negative feelings and instead finds reasons in the child's behavior to feel justified in finding fault with him. The child feels the rejection and behaves in a way that justifies her negative opinion of him. When he behaves more positively, she becomes suspicious of his motives and wonders what he wants from her. Their relationship deteriorates. Inside she feels a growing anger toward her child and toward herself, but cannot understand it. She begins to feel she is failing as a mother. This is diametrically opposed to her self-concept and causes her great unhappiness and anxiety. She is greatly confused about herself, her actions, and her feelings. She comes to therapy for help.

This example is typical of many individuals who come for therapy. They are feeling some anxiety or conflict because their previous self-concepts are being threatened by new feelings or facts which are not consistent with their view of themselves. When this "incongruence," as Rogers sometimes called it, is small, the person may experience only minor discomfort, and the process of dropping his defenses by admitting the new data to awareness and enlarging his self-concept may be a relatively easy one. This happens to all of us at times, outside of therapy. On the other hand, if the previous self-concept is very deeply imbedded in one's personality, and the new evidence to be incorporated seems to him so inconsistent with his concept of self that he can see no way that it *can* be incorporated, the effect can be one of enormous stress. In its most extreme form the stress may be

231

so hard to cope with that a psychotic break, such as schizophrenia or catatonia, is the only way the person finds for resolving the conflict.

In therapy, the goal is for the person to become more open to all of his inner and outer experience so that he can incorporate new evidence into his concept of self without undue stress. The mother may then acknowledge, "Yes, I basically am a loving and responsible mother, but I also felt and feel a lot of resentment toward my third child, and this has caused me to act in certain ways." This can only be done when the client can lower his defenses and experience his feelings and his relationships without distortion or denial. He is able to lower his defenses because of the therapeutic relationship, in which the therapist's congruence, empathy, and unconditional positive regard make the climate so safe that the client feels free to explore the most frightening, uncharted aspects of his experience. Gradually his self-concept changes, is enlarged by this newly discovered information. He no longer feels threat or anxiety, because he has become open to the feelings which were threatening his defenses. In the process he has not only learned to cope with the initial problems he had, but he develops a greater confidence in his organism. He learns that if he can be open to his experiences, admit his feelings, somehow he will be able to integrate these into his personality and make whatever decisions need to be made in a rational manner. Old defense patterns are no longer necessary. These have been replaced with the individual's feeling a greater trust in himself and greater confidence to deal with life as it is, people as they are, and himself as he really is.

Rogers presented his theory in *Client-Centered Therapy* as a series of nineteen propositions, with a discussion following each proposition. For example, some of the earlier propositions were stated as follows:

I) Every individual exists in a continually changing world of experience of which he is the center.

II) The organism reacts to the field as it is experienced and perceived. The perceptual field is, for the individual, "reality."

IV) The organism has one basic tendency and striving—to actualize, maintain and enhance the experiencing organism.

V) Behavior is basically the goal-directed attempt of the organism to satisfy its needs as experienced, in the field as perceived.

VIII) A portion of the perceptual field gradually becomes differentiated as the self.

IX) As a result of interaction with the environment, and particularly as a result of evaluational interaction with others, the structure of self is formed—an organized, fluid, but consistent conceptual pattern of perceptions of characteristics and relationships of the "I" or the "me," together with values attached to these concepts.[161]

In the fourth proposition, Rogers included the concept of the "actualizing tendency," which became central to his thinking over the years. As psychologists Laura Rice and Leslie Greenberg noted, "he adopted Goldstein's concept of an actualizing tendency in human beings … Kurt Goldstein was an eminent neuropsychologist at the Institute for Brain Damaged Soldiers in Germany who had become impressed by the capacity of soldiers with brain injuries to reorganize their own modes of functioning. Goldstein's observations that people reorganized in constructive ways confirmed Rogers' view of the basic human motivation toward growth and wholeness, the actualizing tendency, which became the one central motivations concept in his theoretical system."[162] Although Goldstein was the first to use the term and popularize the concept[163]—and Rogers cited him—Rogers built the concept into a broader theory of personality.

In the Koch volume, Rogers extended his self-theory to a still larger theoretical framework, including "A Theory of Therapy," "A Theory of the Fully Functioning Person," "A Theory of Interpersonal Relationships," and "Implications for Various Human Activities, such as Family Life, Education, Group Leadership and Group Conflict." All these theories included testable propositions which might lead to research that could confirm or alter the various theoretical formulations. Here he extended the "if–then" propositions of "The Necessary and Sufficient Conditions of Therapeutic Personality Change" to comparable propositions on how such conditions can unleash growth, learning, productivity and creativity in many walks of life. It was quite a *tour de force*. In effect, his formulation tied together the many strands of theory, research and practice of his career to date.

Few people read the longer exposition in Koch. Most formed their understanding of Rogers' self-theory from the substantial chapter in *Client-Centered Therapy* in which Rogers' described how the concept of self is formed, how it influences behavior, how problems arise, and how change occurs in the development of a healthier personality in therapy. As usual, little in Rogers' self-theory was invented by Rogers. He was the first to acknowledge his influences in the formation of his theory, namely: Goldstein, Angyal, Maslow, Mowrer, Kluckhohn, Lecky, Sullivan, Masserman, Murphy, Cameron, Murray, White, Snygg, Combs, and Burrow, as well as his colleagues and students at the Counseling Center.[164] Nevertheless, with all these other theorists to choose from, when Calvin Hall and Gardner Lindzey wrote their text on personality theories—which was for many years perhaps the most widely used text on the subject in graduate schools across the country—they chose Rogers' theory as the prototype for their chapter on self-theory, writing, "For our specimen theory we have selected Carl Rogers' formulation because it is the most fully developed statement of self-theory. Moreover, Rogers has buttressed his speculations with an imposing array of empirical supports … Rogers' theory of personality represents a synthesis of phenomenology as presented by Snygg and Combs, of holistic and organismic theory as developed in the writings of Goldstein, Maslow, and Angyal, of Sullivan's interpersonal theory, and of self-theory for which Rogers himself is largely responsible, although he acknowledges a debt to Raimy and Lecky."[165] Patterson wrote in 1966 that Rogers' theory "is one of the more detailed, integrated and consistent theories which currently exist."[166]

Psychologist Peter Merenda argued that Rogers was a student of Prescott Lecky at Columbia University and failed to acknowledge Lecky's theory of self-consistency as the basis for his self-theory.[167] Indeed, Rogers' self-theory had a number of striking and important similarities to Lecky's theory of self-consistency, first shared in Lecky's 1928–29 course at Columbia. However, Rogers had already moved to Rochester at that time and could not have taken this class; nor is there any record of his ever taking a class with Lecky or hearing him speak.[168] Lecky did not publish articles on his theory. His book *Self-Consistency* was published posthumously in 1945.[169] Rogers did credit Lecky's book in his 1947 Presidential Address to the American Psychological Association, explaining how as one of several sources for his thinking, "Lecky's posthumous book, small in size but large in the significance of its contribution, has brought a new light on the way in which the self operates, and the principle of consistency by which new experience is included in or excluded from the self. Much of his thinking runs parallel to our observations."[170] He credited Lecky twice in *Client-Centered Therapy* in 1951 writing, "Mead, Cooley, Angyal, Lecky, and others have helped to advance our knowledge of the development and functioning of the self."[171] And he credited him again in the longer theory presentation in the Koch volume in 1959, describing how "Lecky's little posthumous book reinforced" their own thinking about the self,[172] implying that Lecky's influence did not come until his own thinking was well along.

This was characteristic of Rogers. As he explained in his Presidential Address to the APA, the main source of his thinking was his and his colleagues' clinical experience. Their theoretical ideas emerged as they sought to understand and explain the observed phenomena. Toward this end, they would also draw on others' theories and explanations, accepting or rejecting elements as these did or did not clarify their own experience. When others' ideas proved useful, Rogers did his best to credit the sources he was aware of. As he told an interviewer, "I don't mind at all stealing ideas. I steal them from everybody, but if it comes to publication I give people credit … when I get down to writing something I do try to think 'Now, where do those ideas come from …?' But I'm sure I have at times slipped up on that."[173] One such time was in his APA address when he neglected to credit Victor Raimy for contributing significantly to his thinking about the self. He was terribly chagrined when he later recognized this omission; he said "I was just devastated by it," and he made up for it in many future publications.[174]

It is certainly *possible* that Rogers might have heard about Lecky's ideas years earlier, before his own theory evolved. However, he was quite capable of forgetting about ideas if they did not impact him at the time and then later coming up with a similar idea on his own without realizing he may have heard it before. Arthur Combs, one of Rogers' acknowledged sources for his self-theory, said this is to be expected in the development of knowledge. "Ideas are in the air; you don't always know where your ideas come from." At the time Rogers was beginning to write and speak about his self-theory, recalled Combs, there were four books about the self which came out about the same time, including Snygg and Comb's *Individual Behavior*. "I remember [Rogers'] Presidential Address ... where Don Snygg and I felt very grateful for the kind comments he was making about our work, and I've always felt this way."[175]

Rogers' contribution to psychological theory was not unlike his contribution to psychotherapeutic method. As we saw, he did not invent any of the particulars of nondirective or client-centered therapy, nor did he claim to. Yet he combined them in a consistent and extreme articulation and demonstration of this "newer direction" in psychotherapy. Because of his wisdom in synthesis, his skillful writing and his personal example, Rogers' revolutionized counseling and psychotherapy in his time. Similarly with his self-theory of personality development. He did not invent many, if any, of the constructs. But he developed the big picture. He combined the ideas that were "in the air," as Combs put it, and related the theory to research (in which Rogers really did break new ground) and to practice in psychotherapy, education and everyday life. The resultant theory was so encompassing and far-reaching and so clearly stated that it made its way into the textbooks and, to this day, self-theory is most associated with Rogers' name. In the end, his genius was less as an inventor than as a synthesizer, demonstrator and disseminator of innovative ideas. It is probably true that, in the end, others like Lecky did not get as much credit as they deserved; but this was less Rogers' doing than the way the history of ideas operates. Only a few leaders get top billing; others get footnotes. Compared to competing theories of the self, Rogers' personality theory apparently was judged to be the most comprehensive, useful, and accessible; hence it is the one that survives in textbooks today.

Ironically, possibly one reason for the popularity of Rogers' work and the effectiveness of his dissemination was that he did *not* spend a great deal of time on theory or tracing and crediting the sources of his thinking, even when he was aware of them. While Rogers was reasonably well-read (in response to participants' questions in a 1958 workshop he made knowledgeable comments about Piaget, Whitaker and Malone's *Roots of Psychotherapy*, John Rosen's direct therapy, "the Hollingshead and Redlich book," communications theory, Whitaker and Warkentin, Maslow, "George Kelly's book" and other such references),[176] still he was the first to admit that he was not a serious scholar and did not care to delve into the history of the ideas he was exploring.[177] "Reading, I fear," he wrote, "has most of its value for me in buttressing my views. I realize I am not a scholar, gaining my ideas from the writings of others."[178]

Nor was he much interested in theory. He told his students at Ohio State, "I have no use for psychological theory," although he later admitted, "I realized eventually that I had no use for psychological theory which was not my own."[179] If he happened to be aware of a source, he would cite it, but he did not go out of his way to even approximate a serious literature search to see who else might have addressed the same subject or who else might have anticipated his current ideas. Nor did he take the time to explicate how his ideas were similar to or different from others'. For example, in *Client-Centered Therapy* he used only a single sentence to acknowledge all the sources mentioned above, with one citation for each author, with little if any further discussion of what they contributed to his thinking. This was probably both a weakness and a strength. His own work may have been enriched and improved by knowing more about what other scholars and scientists had done before. He may have built stronger bridges to more colleagues in academia if he cited and discussed their work. On the other hand, if he dwelled too often on how others had approached the problems he cared about, or spent too much time focusing on theoretical issues that *others* cared about, Rogers might have lost some of his creative, innovative edge. And his own voice may have lost some of its uniqueness and quiet authority. For better and worse, this was his style and it remained consistent throughout his career.

Rogers' attitude toward theory development is well illustrated by an exchange he had with the renowned existential psychotherapist Rollo May. As two leaders in the growing "humanistic psychology" movement, they became friendly over the years and had many occasions for dialogue—on panels, at meetings and through their writings (see next chapter). Norman Brice recalled a conference panel in 1962 when, "Rollo said very seriously to Carl something to the effect that he found no 'ontology' in Carl's theory. He brought up the same question a couple of more times. After the third time, Carl turned toward Rollo with what seemed to me to be a combination of whimsy and exasperation and said, 'Rollo, if you want an ontology, *you* write one. I don't feel the need for it.'"[180]

Reluctant to begin theorizing in the first place, Rogers was still reluctant to place too great an emphasis on his own formulation. Commenting on the relation of theory to science, he wrote in 1959, "I believe that there is only one statement which can accurately apply to all theories—from the phlogiston theory to the theory of relativity, from the theory I will present to the one which I hope will replace it in a decade—and that is that at the time of its formulation every theory contains an unknown (and perhaps at that point an unknowable) amount of error and mistaken inference. The degree of error may be very great, as in the phlogiston theory, or small, as I imagine it may be in the theory of relativity, but unless we regard the discovery of truth as a closed and finished book, then there will be new discoveries which will contradict the best of theories which we can now construct." He continued:

To me this attitude is very important, for I am distressed at the manner in which small-caliber minds immediately accept a theory—almost any theory—as a dogma of truth. If theory could be seen for what it is—a fallible, changing attempt to construct a network of gossamer threads which will contain the solid facts— then a theory would serve as it should, as a stimulus to further creative thinking … I am sure that the stress I place on this grows in part out of my regret at the history of Freudian theory. For Freud, it seems quite clear that his highly creative theories were never more than that. He kept changing, altering, revising, giving new meaning to old terms—always with more respect for the facts he observed than for the theories he built. But at the hands of insecure disciples (so it seems to me), the gossamer threads became iron chains of dogma from which dynamic psychology is only recently beginning to free itself.[181]

For Rogers, then, the value of his theory was in its testable hypotheses about how individuals may be helped in therapy, education and other venues. His initial research led to the theory. His theory, in turn, would encourage his own and future generations to do more research on the self and on the conditions of unconditional positive regard, empathy and congruence as they might enhance growth in therapy and other contexts. As textbook authors Hall, Lindzey and Campbell wrote in 1998, "Whatever the future of Rogers' theory may be, it has served well the purpose of making the self an object of empirical investigation. Many psychologists have given theoretical status to the self, but it is to Rogers' credit that his formulations regarding the phenomenal self have led directly to the making of predictions and to investigative activities. Heuristically, his theory has been an extremely potent and pervasive force."[182]

Move to Wisconsin

While Rogers was writing his longest and fullest theoretical formulation for the Koch volume, a major change was in the offing. At the height of his career, at a time when the Counseling Center of the University of Chicago was regarded by many as the most innovative center in the country for research and practice in psychotherapy, Rogers surprised the world of psychology by leaving Chicago to move to the University of Wisconsin.

In the spring of 1957 he had been invited to spend one semester in the Department of Education at Wisconsin as the visiting "Knapp Honorary Professor." Virgil Herrick, a professor of education at Wisconsin, had been most responsible for bringing this about, and the Rogers and Herricks became close friends after that. The five months at Wisconsin were very enjoyable and productive for him. A Wisconsin student, Charles Truax, would never forget one seminar Rogers led. He told of how "I would challenge him … and Carl wouldn't operate that way ... I'd say, 'What is your evidence?' and he'd say, 'Well, you don't feel that what I am saying is of real meaning,' and I'd say, 'That's right, now defend yourself,' and we went back and forth like this a few times, and he'd respond in the therapist role by saying something like, 'The son-of-a-bitch won't fight back,' and I'd say, 'That's right!'"[183]

Rogers recalled, "I held a seminar for faculty members in which I was, I fear, rather rigidly 'student-centered.' I had not yet learned how to place full responsibility with the group and yet give freely of myself. Nevertheless, it was an exciting and unusual experience for most of the participants. I also held a large seminar for graduate students in counseling, psychology and education. This was highly successful and, judging from letters over the years, had a significant impact on the lives of the members. During this time, Helen and I had many warm personal and social contacts with faculty members in education, psychiatry, and with several of the psychologists."[184]

The guest professorship also gave him considerable free time for his own thinking, research, and writing. He spent many hours listening to recorded interviews trying to better understand the process of therapy. His later paper "A Process Conception of Psychotherapy" was a direct outgrowth of this time and proved to be an important development in his thinking.[185]

"Meanwhile Vergil Herrick was working devotedly and selflessly behind the scenes to bring me to Wisconsin. I had assured him that nothing could lure me from Chicago, and he had challenged me to write out the description of a position which would entice me. I wrote a description of an impossible position—appointments in both psychiatry and psychology, opportunity to train psychologists and psychiatrists, time for therapy and research with psychotic and normal individuals (the two extreme groups where I felt my experience was deficient), and other improbable requirements. To my amazement, he was able to bring this about, though the approval of ten separate committees, besides his persuasive talks with many individuals was necessary."[186]

Once Rogers had made the decision to move, while still in Wisconsin he wrote to the Counseling Center staff to explain his decision fully, "so that the period of rumors and uncertainty would be as brief as possible." His explanation to his friends and colleagues conveys the meaning of the move to him.

You will want to know why I have accepted this position. The biggest reason is the opportunity it gives for greater impact. What influence will I have at Chicago if I remain there? As I see it I will have a continuing influence on the profession of psychology, I will have some influence on the research we are doing, though the research leadership is rightly passing to the younger people. I will have some influence through the development of new ideas. If I come to Wisconsin, I will have all of those possibilities of exerting influence plus the opportunity to have an important impact on a whole new profession. Psychologists and psychiatrists will sit in the same seminar with me, and will participate in the same research projects with me. If psychologists and psychiatrists get a feeling for what the experience of therapy means, and at the same time a feeling for the research approach to these problems, I think this could set a very significant pattern of future development in the whole mental hygiene field. There will be eleven new psychiatric residents per year, each of them planning to stay for three years. Thus there will be an opportunity to be in contact with thirty-three young psychiatrists at any one time and an equal or greater number of psychologists. This represents a really outstanding challenge. If we can turn out here, psychologists and psychiatrists who are accustomed to working together, and with twin capacities for doing effective therapy and carrying on sound research, it could start a revolutionary trend in the whole mental health field. So this matter of potential impact is the big reason why I have decided to make a move.

Other elements of the picture are the opportunity to influence the University in more general ways. For instance, I will have an opportunity to influence the program in guidance and counseling in the School of Education which is most eager to see me stay on. My influence upon the University as a whole has in a sense already begun. Some of the most interested members in my seminar are the Associate Dean of the College of Letters and Science, the Dean of Women, a member of the Department of Psychiatry, the psychiatrist in charge of the Child Guidance Center, members of the faculty of the School of Social Work, of the Department of Speech, and Sociology, as well as Psychology and Education. The atmosphere has been in general very cordial toward my ideas.

Another factor which has influenced us is the opportunity to live in a beautiful spot. Helen has not been happy with the conditions in Chicago, and I share this feeling, though I am less troubled by it than she is. We certainly would not move solely to obtain better living surroundings, but when a rare professional opportunity comes up, combined with the chance to live in a nice home in a lovely city, the combination is irresistible.

There are some other reasons, but all of them I think are minor. One of them is that I have always felt that a person does what he can do in one institution in a period of some six to ten years. I have stayed twelve years. By moving now, to a new University, I'd have the opportunity to make a significant dent in a new situation during the ten or fifteen years before I retire. If I stay much longer at Chicago it is unlikely that there would be the opportunity to move, and it is also unlikely that I would be in the new place long enough to make my influence felt. So this opportunity seems to have come at an appropriate time.

He continued for another page, discussing some of the realities of the transition— the funding at Chicago for their research project, the doctoral committees he was sitting on, the future of the Counseling Center—and suggested how he would try to help facilitate the solutions to these various problems brought about by his departure. He signed his letter "with the warmest affection for all of you," but then felt the need to add a postscript, which perhaps explains as much about his move to Wisconsin as all the other reasons he provides.

P.S. As I think over what I have dictated, I realize that in one respect it does not quite express my feeling. Because I fear that my decision will cause temporary pain and upset, I have soft-pedaled my own feeling of enthusiasm. I tried once to tell staff in a memo—you may remember it—what a large streak of pioneering spirit there is in me. I really am kin to the old frontiersmen, and my feeling at the present time is that I can hardly wait to throw my pack on my back and leave the settlement behind. I itch to get going! In my feelings I am already in the excitement of meeting the new problems, new challenges, and the broad horizon of new opportunities I see here. The thought of new wilderness to explore, with all that I believe it will mean to me and to others in the way of significant learnings and fresh developments, is like wine in my blood. I feel ten years younger.

So if what I am saying in this memo seems to you as if I am talking to you from a distance, halfway up the ridge on the trail of a new adventure, you are right, for that is the way it is. What I hope you will realize is that this in no way alters my affection for you, but is simply my need to keep on going.[187]

CHAPTER 8

Freud, Skinner, Rogers, and Other Dialogues

"During the psychologically fertile years of the 1940s and 1950s," wrote textbook authors Moursund and Erskine, "new schools of thought were taking hold in the U.S. psychotherapeutic community. Two of these, as radically different from each other as they were from the ideas of the psychoanalysts, were to leave their own indelible marks on the psychotherapeutic landscape. Each has become a part of the thinking—the psychological worldview—of virtually every therapist in practice today. These two schools of thought were behavioristic learning theory on the one hand, and the client-centered therapy of Carl Rogers on the other."[1]

Actually Rogers was not alone in providing a counterpoint for psychoanalysis and behaviorism, two schools of psychology prototypically represented by the work of Sigmund Freud and B.F. Skinner. Abraham Maslow, in the 1950s, often spoke of a growing "third force" in psychology, which he said showed signs of becoming the most important emphasis in modern psychology.[2] The third force has been known variously as holistic, existential, humanistic, or more recently, positive psychology. While there have been a number of leading figures in this movement, Carl Rogers has been universally acknowledged as one of the pioneers or father figures of humanistic psychology and for decades was arguably its leading spokesperson. While Rogers and Freud never met, Rogers and Skinner met on several occasions, including an historic debate and a longer, but little-known dialogue.

The goal of this chapter is not to attempt a thorough analysis of the work of these three men or the schools of thought they helped foster, but rather to draw several comparisons that may help to better understand Carl Rogers' thought and historical contribution to psychology. Such a comparison will inevitably be incomplete and oversimplified, as it seeks to highlight differences between Rogers and Freud and between Rogers and Skinner. It will also be limited by the frames of reference in which each man lived and worked. It was difficult for them to step back from their life-long work and recognize points of commonality and possible ways their approaches might be integrated. At the end of the chapter, I will try to remedy this oversimplification somewhat by pointing out more recent work that has tried to bridge some of the dichotomies between the psychoanalytic, behavioral and humanistic orientations. Along the way, there are some interesting stories about Rogers' dialogues with B.F. Skinner and other leading intellectuals of the twentieth century and his (and tangentially Skinner's) association with the Central Intelligence Agency.

Freud, Rogers, and Human Nature

Sigmund Freud (1856–1939) is the universally acclaimed father of modern psychotherapy. As Armin Klein wrote, "Freud had initiated modern psychotherapy during the latter part of the [nineteenth] century in his context of the authoritarian culture of Victorian Europe, and the sub-culture of medicine. His great contribution to society was calling attention to unaware motivations and feelings and the way that they become hidden from awareness. He created a psychotherapy to help people learn more about themselves and their unaware motives. He developed these contributions within a biological and mechanical model. He saw difficulties in living as illnesses in their many described forms, or 'diagnoses.' He 'treated' these 'neuroses' as if there were tangible, consistent, and predictable patterns to unhappiness. By Rogers' time, psychotherapy was, then, prescriptive and administered externally from the knowledge of the therapist."[3]

Although Freud was born almost a half century before Carl Rogers, in an entirely different cultural context, in a sense they were almost contemporaries. Freud was living, writing, evolving, and promulgating his approach to psychoanalysis in the 1920s when Rogers was being introduced to psychotherapy and Freudian thinking in New York City. This was a time when psychoanalysis and its jargon were gaining widespread popularity in many Eastern American cities. Freud was similarly active throughout the 1930s, Rogers' years in Rochester, when the latter was experimenting with and developing his own ideas about psychotherapy. For Rogers then, Freud was not only a figure of *historical* importance, but an active, distant colleague whose influence permeated Rogers' academic and professional environment.

As described in some detail earlier, Rogers was not very taken with the Freudian approach, as his own training in psychological testing and measurement (not to mention his earlier scientific farming background) inclined him to be somewhat scornful of the intangible and unmeasurable concepts like id, ego, superego, Oedipus complex, and the like. He much preferred the more defined world of personality testing and tangible measures of adjustment to what seemed to him the almost mystical procedures of the psychoanalysts. This is not to say that he was entirely unchanged from his exposure to psychoanalytic theory and methods. Speaking of his early nondirective method that emphasized release, insight, and positive action, he wrote in 1946, "… In its concepts of repression and release, in its stress upon catharsis and insight, it has many roots in Freudian thinking."[4] But on the practical level Rogers was not much affected by his exposure to psychoanalysis and, instead, developed his own theories and methods out of his experience in working with clients in Rochester, Columbus, and Chicago. As his approach developed a coherence of its own, contrasts to the psychoanalytic approach became clearer. But at no time did he work out his thinking as a reaction to Freud, as an antithesis to the psychoanalytic thesis. It always grew out of its own soil of experience.

Aside from differences in method, one of the most apparent contrasts in the thinking of Rogers and Freud is in their basic evaluation of human nature. Freud was very clear on this point. The human being, at his core, is wild, unsocialized, selfish, and destructive. If a person's "id" were to govern his behavior, the results would be disastrous. Fortunately the "superego" develops to serve as a conscience for the individual, and the "ego" develops to negotiate the demands of the id and superego and to relate to the outside world in a realistic fashion. The healthy individual is a person who has managed to "sublimate" the libidinal energy of the id toward more socialized channels. Underneath, however, lurks the untamed beast, glimpses of which can be caught in dreams, fantasies, and free associations. "Our mind," wrote Freud, "is no peacefully self-contained unity. It is rather to be compared with a modern State in which a mob, eager for enjoyment and destruction, has to be held down forcibly by a prudent superior class."[5]

Rogers said it took years for him to get over both his religious and his Freudian training with their view of humans as being fundamentally evil.[6] He gradually adopted a more positive view, maintaining that at his core, the human being is basically socialized, constructive, and trustworthy. For this view he was greatly criticized by psychoanalysts and nonpsychoanalysts alike. It has been said that this opinion of human nature is unsound for it is based on Rogers' work with only mildly neurotic people, not those whose profound conflicts show the deeper, darker, demonic, side of human nature. He has been accused of being naïvely optimistic, underestimating human evil[7] and unable to fathom the concept of sin.[8] To this type of charge he once replied, "It disturbs me to be thought of as an optimist. My whole professional experience has been with the dark and often sordid side of life, and I know, better than most, the incredibly destructive behavior of which man is capable."[9] Although most of his psychotherapy was conducted in university clinics, this did not mean his work

243

with clients was confined simply to vocational counseling and mild problems of adjustment, as the following excerpts from an interview with a woman client illustrate.*

CLIENT: (... *begins to talk in hard flat voice, quite unlike her usual tone. Does not look at counselor. There was much repetition, but the following excerpts give the major thoughts.)* You feel I want to come, but I don't! I'm not coming any more. It doesn't do any good. I don't like you. I hate you! I wish you never were born.

ROGERS: You just hate me very bitterly.

CLIENT: I think I'll throw you in the lake. I'll cut you up! You think people like you, but they don't ... You think you can attract women but you can't ... I wish you were *dead.*

ROGERS: You detest me and you'd really like to get rid of me.

CLIENT: You think my father did bad things with me, but he didn't! You think he wasn't a good man, but he *was.* You think I want intercourse but I *don't.*

ROGERS: You feel I *absolutely misrepresent* all your thoughts.

CLIENT: ... You think you can get people to come in and tell you everything, and they'll think they're being helped, but they're *not!* You just like to make 'em suffer. You think you can hypnotize them, but *you can't! You* think you're good, but you ain't. I hate you. I *hate you!*

ROGERS: You feel I really like to make 'em suffer, but I *don't* help them.

CLIENT: You think I haven't been straight, but I have. I *hate you.* All I've had is pain, pain, pain. You think I can't direct my own life, but I can. You think I can't get well, but I can. You think I had hallucinations, but I didn't. I hate you. *(Long pause. Leans on desk in strained, exhausted pose.)* You think I'm crazy, but I'm not.

ROGERS: You're sure I think you're crazy.

CLIENT: *(Pause.)* I'm tired, and I just can't get loose! *(Despairing tone of voice, and tears. Pause.)* I had a hallucination and I've got to get it out! ... *(Goes on about her own deep conflicts, and tells of the hallucination she has experienced, with terrific tension in her voice, but with an attitude very different from that at the beginning of the interview.)*

(Later in interview)

CLIENT: I knew at the office I had to get rid of this somewhere. I felt I could

---

* [Rogers' footnote] Just as it is impossible to convey on paper the venom and hatred in the client's voice, so it is utterly impossible to convey the depth of empathy in the counselor's [Rogers'] responses. The counselor states, "I tried to enter into and to express in my voice the full degree of the soul-consuming anger which she was pouring out. The written words look incredibly pale, but in the situation they were full of the same feeling she was so coldly and deeply expressing."

come down and tell you. I knew you'd understand. I couldn't say I hated myself. That's true but I couldn't say it. So I just thought of all the ugly things I could say to you instead.

ROGERS: The things you felt about yourself you couldn't say, but you could say them to me.

CLIENT: I know we're getting to rock bottom …[10]

By the time he left Chicago, Rogers had been a psychotherapist for thirty years. Interviews of the type portrayed above, while not typical for him, occurred often enough over the years. He had many opportunities to observe and interact with the many levels of the human personality. And always he came back to a positive view of human nature. "Professional experience has forced upon me the realization that man, when you know him deeply, in his worst and most troubled states, is not evil or demonic."[11] Or, as he put it just before his death, "I feel that if people were evil, I would be shocked or horrified at what I found if I was able to get through to the core of that person. I have never had that experience—just the opposite. If I can get through to a person, even those whose behavior has a lot of destructive elements, I believe he or she would want to do the right thing."[12]

Was it that humankind was "basically good"? Although people often attribute such a viewpoint to Rogers, he never quite put it in those terms. He often explained his viewpoint through the use of metaphor or analogy with the world of plants and animals. In 1977 he wrote, "I remember that in my boyhood the potato bin in which we stored our winter supply of potatoes was in the basement, several feet below a small basement window. The conditions were unfavorable, but the potatoes would begin to sprout—pale white sprouts, so unlike the healthy green shoots they sent up when planted in the soil in the spring. But these sad, spindly sprouts would grow two or three feet in length as they reached toward the distant light of the window. They were, in their bizarre, futile growth, a sort of desperate expression of the directional tendency I have been describing. They would never become a plant, never mature, never fulfill their real potentiality. But under the most adverse circumstances they were striving to become. Life would not give up, even if it could not flourish. In dealing with clients whose lives have been terribly warped, in working with men and women on the back wards of state hospitals, I often think of those potato sprouts. So unfavorable have been the conditions in which these people have developed that their lives often seem abnormal, twisted, scarcely human. Yet the directional tendency in them is to be trusted. The clue to understanding their behavior is that they are striving, in the only way available to them, to move toward growth, toward becoming. To us the results may seem bizarre and futile, but they are life's desperate attempt to become itself. It is this potent tendency which is the underlying basis of client-centered therapy and all that has grown out of it."[13]

Many years earlier, in the fullest discussion he ever gave to the subject, an article called "A Note on the Nature of Man," he had approached the topic from a different angle.

Let me see if I can take the discussion of these points of view into a fresh area where perhaps we have somewhat fewer preconceived biases. Suppose we turn to the animal world and ask ourselves what is the basic nature of the lion, or the sheep, or the dog, or the mouse. To say that any one or all of these are basically hostile or antisocial or carnal seems to be ridiculous. To say that we view their nature as neutral means either that it is neutral in terms of some unspecified set of values, or that their natures are all alike, all putty waiting to receive a shape. This view seems to me equally ridiculous. I maintain that each has a basic nature, a common set of attributes generally characteristic of the species. Thus the sheep is by far the most gregarious or group-minded, the mouse the most generally timorous. No amount of training—therapeutic or otherwise—will make a lion out of a mouse, or vice versa, even though a wide degree of change is possible. There is a basic substratum of species characteristics which we will do well to accept.

We might take a closer look at some of those characteristics. Since the lion has the most pronounced reputation for being a "ravening beast" let us choose him. What are the characteristics of his common nature, his basic nature? He kills an antelope when he is hungry, but he does not go on a wild rampage of killing. He eats his fill after the killing, but there are no obese lions on the veldt. He is helpless and dependent in his puppyhood, but he does not cling to the dependent relationship. He becomes increasingly independent and autonomous. In the infant state he is completely selfish and self-centered, but as he matures he shows, in addition to such impulses, a reasonable degree of cooperativeness in the hunt. The lioness feeds, cares for, protects, and seems to enjoy her young. Lions satisfy their sexual needs, but this does not mean they go on wild and lustful orgies. His various tendencies and urges come to a continually changing balance in himself, and in that sense he is very satisfactorily self-controlled and self-regulated. He is in basic ways a constructive, a trustworthy member of the species *Felis leo*. His fundamental tendencies are in the direction of development, differentiation, independence, self-responsibility, cooperation, maturity. In general the expression of his basic nature makes for the continuation and enhancement of himself and his species.

With the appropriate variations, the same sort of statements could be made about the dog, the sheep, the mouse. To be sure each behaves in ways which from some specific point of view are destructive. We wince to see the lion kill the antelope; we are annoyed when the sheep eats our garden, we complain when the mouse eats the cheese we are saving for our picnic; I regard the dog as destructive when he bites me, a stranger; but surely none of these behaviors justifies us in thinking of any of these animals as basically evil. If I endeavored to explain to you that if the "lion-ness" of the lion were to be released, or the 'sheep-ness' of the sheep, that these animals would then be impelled by insatiable lusts, uncontrollable aggressions, wild and excessive sexual behaviors, and tendencies of innate destructiveness, you would quite properly laugh at me. Obviously, such a view is pure nonsense.

I would like now to consider again the nature of man in the light of this discussion of the nature of animals. I have come to know men most deeply in a relationship which is characterized by all that I can give of safety, absence of threat, and complete freedom to be and to choose. In such a relationship men express all kinds of bitter and murderous feelings, abnormal impulses, bizarre and anti-social desires. But as they live in such a relationship, expressing and being more of themselves, I find that man, like the lion, has a nature. My experience is that he is a basically trustworthy member of the human species, whose deepest characteristics tend toward development, differentiation, cooperative relationships; whose life tends fundamentally to move from dependence to independence; whose impulses tend naturally to harmonize into a complex and changing pattern of self-regulation; whose total character is such as to tend to preserve and enhance himself and his species, and perhaps to move it toward its further evolution. In my experience, to discover that an individual is truly and deeply a unique member of the human species is not a discovery to excite horror. Rather I am inclined to believe that fully to be a human being is to enter into the complex process of being one of the most widely sensitive, responsive, creative, and adaptive creatures on this planet.

So when a Freudian such as Karl Menninger tells me (as he has, in a discussion of this issue) that he perceives man as "innately evil" or more precisely, "innately destructive," I can only shake my head in wonderment. It leads me to all kinds of perplexing questions. How could it be that Menninger and I, working with such a similar purpose in such intimate relationships with individuals in distress, experience people so differently?[14]

Later in the same article he asked this last question again, thinking of Freud himself. Freud, too, was a keen observer of the therapeutic process and the human personality. How was it that the two of them ended with such different views of human nature? Rogers offered an interesting hypothesis—an untestable one, unfortunately—to answer the question: "It has been my experience that though clients can, to some degree, independently discover some of their denied or repressed feelings, they cannot on their own achieve full emotional acceptance of these feelings. It is only in a caring relationship that these 'awful' feelings are first fully accepted by the therapist and can then be accepted by the client. Freud in his self-analysis was deprived of this warmly acceptant relationship. Hence, though he might come to know and to some extent to understand the hidden and denied aspects of himself, I question whether he could ever come to accept them fully, to embrace them as a meaningful, acceptable, and constructive part of himself. More likely he continued to perceive them as unacceptable aspects of himself—enemies, whom knowing he could control—rather than as impulses which, when existing freely in balance with his other impulses, were constructive. At any rate I regard this as a hypothesis worthy of consideration."[15]

The client, in other words, internalizes the therapist's attitude toward him. If the therapist regards the client with unconditional positive regard, the client will develop that same attitude toward himself, valuing all parts of his inner experience, without labeling some impulses good and others bad. If the therapist regards the total organism of the client as trustworthy, the client, too, can develop this attitude toward himself. Freud, though he developed much self-understanding (the "empathy"), did not develop the sense of basic self-trust which Rogers described. Not having found it in himself, neither did he find it in his patients, and he therefore continued to hold the view that humans, in their most inner selves, are destructive and antisocial.

Ironically the two men were not so far apart. Although he did not use the terminology, Rogers would be the first to admit the presence of id-type and superego-type impulses in humans and the ego-type mechanism or function which weighed all of the person's impulses and arrived at the behavior meant to maximize all his needs, both selfish and social. Both Freud and Rogers saw the psychology of the person function in this similar way. The point of difference arose in the primacy Freud gave and the equality which Rogers gave to the id functions. For Freud the id was basic and terrible; for Rogers it existed simultaneously and equally with the superego and was not to be feared but accepted.

From this difference stemmed a difference in psychotherapeutic approach. The Freudian, who was accustomed to thinking of the darker reality behind the more superficial, civilized superstructure, would use interpretation of the patient's free association to attempt to discover and help the patient discover: What's behind this? What really happened? What are the real, deeper feelings he's not saying? Where did this all begin? What is the real meaning of this memory, or slip, or figure of speech, or behavior? One analyst might do this in an accepting way, so that the patient would come to feel a real safety to say whatever came into his mind, a freedom from evaluation, an atmosphere of trying to understand himself and his experiences. Another psychoanalyst might create an opposite tone of suspicion and mistrust which the client would come to feel toward himself. In the latter case, the result of years of analysis could be a person who is greatly self-conscious and continues to view his own words and deeds with suspicion and lack of acceptance. In the first case, an accepting, genuine, and empathic analyst might be building the same attitudinal ingredients into the relationship that Rogers advocated. As the previously mentioned Fiedler studies showed, the results achieved by the experienced Freudian and experienced Rogerian would often be surprisingly similar.[16]

While most of Rogers' statements about psychoanalytic thinking and practice were quite negative, his references to Freud personally were usually respectful and often seemed to indicate that Rogers identified with the earlier pioneer, as when he said, "I feel more and more sympathy with a statement that I understand Freud made—that he 'was not a Freudian himself.' I certainly feel and know very well that I'm not a non-directivist myself."[17]

Skinner

At the same time that Freudian thinking was becoming popular in many parts of the United States, another movement in psychology was emerging and taking hold. This movement took place, not in the doctor's office or the hospital, but mostly in the scientist's laboratory. It began with E.L. Thorndike, just before the turn of the century in the United States,[18] and with Pavlov in Russia in the early twentieth century.[19] Working with animals to discover the principles of human learning, both these men used the concepts of "stimulus" and "response" to understand how learning took place. Pavlov's famous experiments with dogs showed how, by pairing an unnatural or "conditioned" stimulus (like ringing a bell) with a natural or "unconditioned" stimulus (like a piece of meat), the dogs' natural, unconditioned response (salivation) could eventually be induced by ringing the bell, even when no meat was present. His approach came to be called "classical conditioning." Thorndike, Pavlov, and other, later scientists, were called "behaviorists," because their main interest was in the subject's behavior, as opposed to his (or its) feelings, goals, or motivations. In the early twentieth century John B. Watson became the leading figure in behavioral psychology in the United States.

B.F. Skinner, in the 1930s, began working in the behaviorist tradition.[20] His work was based on the observation that if a particular behavior or response was rewarded or "reinforced," it was more likely to occur again. It did not matter what stimulus produced the original response. Most of Skinner's experimental work was done with pigeons. By reinforcing with food certain behaviors of pigeons, Skinner was able to teach pigeons to dance, play ping-pong, and even keep guided missiles on their proper course. By varying the timing and consistency of the reinforcement, Skinner showed how the animals' learning could be either strengthened or "extinguished."[21]

This appealed to American psychology. Like the testing and measurement movement, Skinner's behaviorism was concrete. The results could be measured. The principles could be readily demonstrated in the laboratory. Moreover, Skinner's basic work could be understood easily by laypersons and academics alike. We have all been reinforced by parents or teachers for "good" behavior, or punished for the opposite (which Skinner did not recommend), and most of us have rewarded some pet for fetching or sitting or purring; so that we readily accept the validity of Skinner's learning principles. His school of "operant conditioning" soon became, and still is, the most widely taught learning theory in colleges across the country. In fact, largely because of Skinner's influence, by mid-century behaviorism came to dominate American psychology. As psychologist George A. Miller said of behaviorism,

> It was perceived as the point of origin for scientific psychology in the United States. The chairmen of all the important departments would tell you that they were behaviorists ... The power, the honors, the authority, the textbooks, the money, everything in psychology was owned by the behavioristic school ... those of us who wanted to be scientific psychologists couldn't really oppose it. You just wouldn't get a job."[22]

Like Rogers who, when he became confident in his understanding of the principles of effective psychotherapy, began to apply these insights to other related fields, Skinner also began to apply his principles of learning to spheres other than the laboratory. In a widely read novel, *Walden Two,* Skinner described his ideal society, built upon the principles of operant conditioning.[23] By rewarding certain behaviors, the architects of *Walden Two* were able to produce people who were happy, productive, secure, and able to deal with frustrations. Neither democracy nor capitalism was necessary in this utopia, yet the citizens felt free, they had as many if not more choices than they presently do in almost every facet of life, and all lived in material comfort and security. The book is fascinating in the way it takes one set of traditional Western values, that is, the use of technology and science in solving problems and in furthering "progress," and shows how these values render other traditional values—like democracy and capitalism—obsolete. Yet the motives of Frazier, the chief mover in the book, and Skinner, the author, are scientific, not political. Thirty years after publication *Walden Two* had sold well over a million copies,[24] and thirty years later it is still going strong—a testimony to its unique insight into a culture whose technological, democratic and traditional values are often in conflict.

Another area into which Skinner extended his influence was that of education.[25] "Programmed learning," various "teaching machines" and eventually computer learning programs were all direct outgrowths of Skinner's pioneering work. His impact even extended into the field of therapy. Although there are different types of "behavior therapy," some approaches are based on operant conditioning techniques.[26] In one study, for example, a behaviorist worked with three hospitalized, chronic, paranoid schizophrenic patients. She instructed all the hospital personnel who came into contact with the patients to ignore—that is, not reinforce—their bizarre or paranoid verbalizations. When working with them herself, she would, if they began to say bizarre things, turn the other way or change the subject. On the other hand, normal comments and behaviors were reacted to by therapist and hospital personnel with nods, pats on the shoulder, full attention, and the like. By not reinforcing abnormal behavior and reinforcing normal behavior, the normal behavior increased to the point where all three patients were able to leave the hospital in three months.[27] Behavior therapy spread very quickly, and the number of studies that support this approach, especially when later developed into "cognitive-behavior therapy," eventually surpassed the record previously held by the client-centered model.[28]

Of course Rogers didn't read Skinner in college, nor Skinner Rogers. The two men were contemporaries, with an age difference of only two years, Rogers the elder. They grew out of the same native soil, each steeped in the methods of scientific inquiry. Each liked to tinker with his hands; each had an artistic bent.[29] Each was a maverick in his field. They worked on different, though related problems—Skinner in learning principles, Rogers in psychotherapy—each building a school of thought from his own scientific endeavors. Skinner had an established and concrete behaviorist tradition upon which to build his work. Rogers, though he had predecessors, had a much less clearly defined tradition.

Gestalt and Humanistic Psychology

Although Rogers developed his client-centered theory and practice by borrowing pieces from various other approaches and adapting them based on his own clinical experience and research, he could have found a strong theoretical and experimental tradition for his work in Gestalt psychology, as developed by the German psychologists Max Wertheimer,[30] Wolfgang Kohler,[31] and Kurt Koffka,[32] before and after the First World War.

As Hall and Lindzey explained, "The chief tenet of Gestalt psychology is that the way in which an object is perceived is determined by the total context or configuration in which the object is embedded. Relationships among components of a perceptual field rather than the fixed characteristics of the individual components determine perception."[33] The significance of this movement for the development of psychology was that it was the first time that not only importance but *credence* was given to the individual's perception of reality. Freudians were certainly interested in the patient's inner world, but they viewed the patient's perception of reality as distorted and attempted to uncover the underlying truth. In a sense, they were outsiders looking into the person, trying to discover what was *really* there. The Gestalt psychologist—who worked primarily with monkeys and other laboratory animals and attempted to generalize their findings to human beings—could be described as trying to get inside the individual in order to look out, seeing the perceptual field as the animal or person himself saw it, and accepting that field as real to the subject and therefore sufficient.

The behaviorists, like the Freudians, viewed the individual from an external frame of reference, but unlike the Freudians, they showed little or no interest in the person's internal frame of reference, distorted or otherwise. Their interest was solely in behavior, and as they usually explained it, an animal learned to solve a problem by behaving randomly, until one of its random behaviors paid off with a reward, thus causing it to repeat the desired behaviors to receive another reinforcement. This change in the animal's behavior was synonymous with learning. Koffka, however, showed how a monkey could sit in his cage and look over sticks he had played with before, and get the "insight" to attach two sticks together to reach the banana which lay more than a stick's length out of reach. Putting the sticks together and reaching through the cage bars for the banana was not a random behavior but a clearly goal-oriented, reasoned, problem-solving attempt. Here was an approach to psychology which seemed very consistent with Rogers' evolving thinking, an approach that emphasized self-directed, problem-solving behavior to achieve one's goals and move toward self-actualization.

At the time that Rogers began developing his ideas, however, he was working with problem children in a clinic in Rochester. The theories and laboratory experiments of the Gestalt psychologists were foreign to the practical problems he encountered daily. Although he did acknowledge the influence of Gestalt psychology on his thinking,[34] this influence came much later, once he had developed the client-centered approach and sought a theoretical foundation for it.

Rogers was not alone in trying to build a psychology and psychotherapy based on different assumptions from the Freudians and behaviorists. A growing number of psychologists, therapists, and other helping professionals were working daily with thousands of clients, in clinics, schools, consulting rooms, minister's offices, homes, and agencies. Psychoanalysis was clearly inappropriate in most of these situations. The learning principles derived from studying rats and pigeons seemed equally irrelevant. Work in behavior therapy had barely begun. Psychological tests and diagnoses were only a small part of the answer for most of the problems encountered. Where were all these non-analytic, non-laboratory-oriented, non-medical professionals to turn?

Many turned to the American Association for Applied Psychology, the offshoot of the American Psychological Association that had been formed in the late thirties as an antidote to the laboratory-oriented parent organization. Their attitude toward the APA could be characterized as, "You're not asking the most important questions—questions about human growth and change and helping relationships." Many turned to Rogers' 1942 book *Counseling and Psychotherapy* as the most detailed, practical description and rationale for a new style of helping yet written. And many turned to Rogers' contemporaries who were moving in similar directions. The work of Rank, Taft, and Allen has been mentioned earlier as an influence on Rogers' development. More widely known as intellectual colleagues of Rogers were Kurt Goldstein, Abraham Maslow, Gordon Allport, and Rollo May.[35]

These individuals and others were building a body of theory, method, case studies, and research which gradually came to be known as "humanistic psychology." Because the words "humanist" and humanistic" are used in so many different contexts—from the classical humanism of ancient Greece and Rome to the humanist counterpoint to ecclesiastical domination in the Middle Ages to contemporary agnostic or secular humanism—humanistic psychology is a difficult term to define. The tendency of many proponents is to regard "humanistic" as standing for all good things one might be or do, which unfortunately suggests that other approaches, by contrast, are non-humanistic. Clearly any responsible therapist in the Freudian or behaviorist tradition is a caring person with humane goals for the client, and moral and ethical procedures for reaching these goals. On the other hand, detractors from humanistic psychology often take an opposite, yet comparable stance—associating "humanistic" with all that is negative, non-scientific, touchy-feely and superficial in psychology. In spite of these pitfalls in defining humanistic psychology, a definition is necessary to understand Carl Rogers' contributions to the development of psychology.

I would describe three characteristics of humanistic psychology. The first and second arguably are qualitative differences between the humanist and the traditional psychoanalytic and behaviorist schools. The third distinction is more a matter of emphasis rather than distinctiveness. Rogers' work exemplified all three characteristics.

First, humanistic psychologists have shown a decided interest in developing our understanding of psychological *health*, in working with so-called "normal" or even "above average" populations, in exploring the limits of human potential. Freud built his entire system on his experiences with disturbed patients and on his self-analysis. The goal of analysis was to alleviate the symptoms and enable the patient to sublimate his negative impulses into productive work and socially conventional behavior. Sublimation might even contribute to creativity and art in the exceptional individual, but this was not a developmental goal for the average person. Similarly, behavior therapists work specifically with that which is malfunctioning or producing anxiety in a person. Their concept of health, implicitly, is the absence of undesirable symptoms or behaviors. The humanists reversed this trend. Goldstein demonstrated how individuals with brain injury often find alternative pathways to accomplish cognitive functions. He was more interested in what his patients *could* do than what they couldn't and was the first to use the term "self-actualization" to describe the inexorable drive of individuals to realize their goals and potentials.[36] Maslow used this concept and posited a "hierarchy of human needs," showing how people begin with physiological and emotional needs which, if not met, cause illness but, if met, allow people to move on to meet their need for self-actualization, that is, for creativity, meaning, and "vocation" in life. He noted that self-actualizing people sometimes had "peak experiences"—moments of ecstasy, beauty, and understanding—and he spent many years studying the characteristics of peak experiences and of the self-actualizing person.[37] Rogers, in the late 1950s, began to write of the "fully functioning person" and attempted to describe what "the Good Life" would be for the psychologically healthy and self-actualizing person.[38]

Early work of this type provided a scholarly foundation for professionals moving in similar directions. The group dynamics work of the late forties and fifties, influenced by Gestalt-trained Kurt Lewin in social psychology,[39] further enriched the humanist movement in psychology, which expanded into the "human potential movement"—human relations and sensitivity training, encounter groups, body awareness, meditation, and so on—of the sixties and seventies, in which Rogers remained a leader. These approaches attempted to explore the limits of human potential, asking questions like: What are human beings capable of? How can normally functioning individuals most fully realize their capacities for creativity, relationships, spirituality and other human values? To what extent can daily living become a peak experience? To what extent can *social institutions* be re-created to provide maximum growth and health for their constituents? Whatever one's view of the benefits or excesses of the movement, this meaning of the term "humanistic" stands in marked contrast to other forces in psychology which have focused on helping people solve their problems so they can make an "adjustment" to living. The humanists have said, "We don't yet know what real living is!" Probably this aspect—the shift from a medical model focused on diagnosing and eliminating illness to a growth model focused on understanding and fostering human potential—most clearly distinguishes humanistic psychology from the psychoanalytic and behavioral traditions.

Second, humanistic psychology has had a major concern in discovering and working with that which is uniquely human about human beings.[40] As novelist Tom Robbins wrote, "What is it that separates human beings from the so-called lower animals? Well, as I see it, it's exactly one half-dozen significant things: Humor, Imagination, Eroticism … Spirituality, Rebelliousness, and Aesthetics, an appreciation of beauty for its own sake."[41] Among humanistic psychologists, the ability to make conscious choices would be added to the top of that list, as would values, goals, love and other emotions. For years the practice in psychology had been to study the learning process in laboratory animals and then extrapolate these understandings to human beings. Thus, when Thorndike demonstrated that rats learned certain tasks through repetition, many psychologists and educators eagerly used this to justify classroom learning by repetitive drill. The humanists believed that working with people, not animals, was the best way to build a body of data upon which a full and accurate understanding of human beings could emerge.

Like the behaviorists, the Freudian approach was built upon a model which was not unique to human beings—the medical model—which works as well for veterinarians and tree surgeons as it does for physicians. As suggested above, this model assumes that significant departures from normality equate to illness and that every illness, physical or mental, has a cause. If the expert can accurately diagnose the cause and, with the patient's cooperation, take appropriate remedial measures, the problem can be eliminated. In classical psychoanalysis, if the patient could be helped to understand the proper interpretation as to the source of his difficulties, the difficulties would go away. The patient didn't have to do anything, other than cooperate with the analyst. "I'm being analyzed" suggests a passive role. But this reduces the patient to an object, not the subject or the author of his own destiny. Just as things have been done to him that once *caused* his problems, so now things were being done to him that would remove his problems.

The humanists insisted that this explanation was not sufficient, that human beings *choose* and, in this way, are different from other creatures or natural objects upon which external forces operate. Surely the environment (culture, family, peers, etc.) provides many stimuli, hurts, pressures, rewards and other influences; but ultimately the person chooses his response. Humans both choose to give in to the social and emotional pressures which surround them and choose to behave differently or think differently about themselves, at least to some extent. Rollo May, for example, accepted the importance of the patient's understanding the sources of his problems but, like Rank, said that unless he acted upon this understanding with a willful act in the direction of health, he would not get better.[42] In this emphasis on free choice, humanistic psychology has also been known as existential psychology. The human being's ability to choose was an assertion virtually ignored by the Freudians, who stressed understanding, and denied by the behaviorists, who saw cause and effect, response and reward, as the entire explanation for animal or human behavior.

A final characteristic of humanistic psychology is its phenomenological emphasis, that is, an emphasis on the individual's perception of reality (phenomena) and of his relationship to that reality. This is not unique to humanistic psychology but a matter of emphasis. More than other orientations the humanists tend to show a greater interest in *the client's* or the individual's picture of his world or to attach a greater importance and validity to it. For Rogers, adopting the client's frame of reference in an empathic way was the client-centered therapists' primary approach. Victor Frankl's "logo-therapy" and Rollo May's "existential" psychology and psychotherapy emphasized the importance of each patient finding a subjective meaning for his existence.[43] "Values clarification" practitioners sought to help individuals develop and act upon their own personal value system.[44] Following in the progressive tradition, advocates of "open education" sought to capitalize on students' interests and goals as the motivational foundation for learning.[45] Other humanistic therapists, human relations trainers, and educators demonstrated their phenomenological orientation in other ways.

Such approaches take seriously and work with the client's conscious view of the world and his place in it. While the patient's inner world is of course essential in classical psychoanalysis, the Freudians attached less significance to the patient's conscious phenomenal field, often trying to bypass it through free associations and dreams or deal only with particular parts of it, such as the patient's attitudes toward the therapist and therapy (and even these attitudes are viewed primarily as a transference from earlier relationships). Similarly, the early behaviorists obviously had no interest in the inner world of the rats in their laboratory. Some behavior therapists tended to ignore the patient's inner world and confine their efforts to reinforcing or extinguishing particular behaviors. Other early behavioral therapists did attempt to change the client's perceptions (e.g., "I'm a failure" or "Everyone's against me") but focused on only certain aspects of the client's thinking and reinforced those, while inhibiting others. In short, the humanists have tended more than others to accept and work with the whole person the individual perceives himself to be.

This description of three distinguishing characteristics of the humanist psychology movement does not include the cultural and social context from which it emerged. As Armin Klein wrote,

> I see him [Rogers] in his context, as an American phenomenon, reflecting American values from the Midwestern farm culture in which he grew up and reflecting the American pragmatist philosopher-psychologists before him, especially William James and John Dewey. The values of self-reliance, respect for the uniqueness of the individual, and the struggle for the development of new visions of democracy expressed this influence at the beginning of this [20th] century. Rogers followed in the tradition of those great American philosopher-psychologists, and he became one of them in the course of his life ...[46]

Another aspect of the American context was its roots in Yankee ingenuity and reliance on technological progress. Rogers was acutely aware of the limitations of science and the progress it fostered. As he wrote in 1942, during the Second World War, "What a picture that is of our world situation! We have conquered space, and go from coast to coast in one daylight. We have defeated time, and the ironic result is that we can hear tomorrow's bombing of London tonight. We have learned in incredible fashion to control the physical universe. We can bend to our will and our purpose the strength of steel, the power of liquid oxygen, the penetrating force of radium and the infrared rays. We control with a flip of the switch complex resources which yesterday we could not even have dreamed about. We have achieved amazing technical control over the physical universe— yet we cannot live together."[47] At a time when the world was becoming increasingly impersonal and alienating, at a time when technology seemed to be spreading into almost every area of life and threatening humanity's control over its own destiny, and at a time when totalitarianism was sweeping over many parts of the globe and engaging in genocide at unprecedented levels, the humanists believed that their work had great potential for helping humanity survive and flourish. Looking back over his life's work, Rogers tried to describe its social significance. What he said of his own contribution could be generalized to include the whole humanist movement as a way of understanding its historical importance.

> ... it seems that without knowing it I had expressed an idea whose time had come ... to use a chemical analogy, as though a liquid solution had become supersaturated, so that the addition of one tiny crystal initiated the formation of crystals throughout the whole mass. What was that idea ... that crystal? It was the gradually formed and tested hypothesis that the individual has within himself vast resources for self-understanding, for altering his self-concept, his attitudes, and his self-directed behavior—and that these resources can be tapped if only a definable climate of facilitative psychological attitudes can be provided ... it was discovered that they had wide applicability ... Situations involving persons, change in the behavior of persons and the effects of different qualities of interpersonal relationships, exist in almost every human undertaking. Hence others began realizing that perhaps the testable hypothesis of this approach might have almost universal application, or might be retested or reformulated for use in an almost infinite variety of human situations.[48]

Because Rogers spend many decades doing just this—developing a theory of human development, applying it to a large variety of human situations, and testing his theory and method with extensive scientific research—Rogers became arguably the leading voice in the humanistic psychology movement. This movement gathered more and more followers through the 1940s, 1950s, and especially in the 1960s. In 1961 the Association of Humanistic Psychology and its *Journal of Humanistic Psychology* was formed, with Rogers as one of its founding sponsors. He had been approached about becoming president of the new group, but felt that after serving as president of the American Association for Applied Psychology, the American Psychological Association, and the American Academy of Psychotherapists, he had had enough of that kind of responsibility. "I simply felt I shouldn't be president of everything," he later explained.[49]

President or not, Rogers became and remains for many the father of humanistic psychology. As leading textbook authors Hall, Lindzey and Campbell wrote of Rogers in 1998,

> ... no one has been more influential in providing an intellectual tradition in which research on the self might flourish. His dictum that "the best vantage point for understanding behavior is from the internal frame of reference of the individual himself" has been a rallying point for many psychologists. His passionate regard for humanistic values in psychological research as presented in so many of his writings and in his famous debate with B.F. Skinner has helped to polarize the thinking of psychologists. His optimism, his implicit faith in the inherent goodness of humans and his steadfast belief that troubled people can be helped are attitudes that have attracted many people who consider behaviorism too cold and psychoanalysis too pessimistic. That there is a "third force" in psychology as viable as behaviorism and psychoanalysis [is] due in very large part to Carl Rogers.[50]

The Rogers–Skinner Debates

With the behaviorist and humanist movements in psychology developing simultaneously, it was inevitable that the leaders in both movements would eventually come to know of each other's work. Especially so, since Rogers and Skinner were tending to generalize the findings from their own laboratories to a wider variety of situations. Had they remained focused on the specific scientific problems presented by their separate work, they might never have clashed publicly. But as they began to write with conviction about such fields as child rearing, education, and society, the contrast between their viewpoints became increasingly evident. And when they finally spoke directly to one another on the issues of their disagreement, the "Rogers–Skinner debate" soon became the most widely popularized discussion of the differences between behaviorist and humanistic psychology.

Actually Rogers began the Rogers–Skinner debate much earlier than 1956, when the two men first spoke from the same platform. A decade earlier he had written, "The clinical experience could be summarized by saying that the behavior of the human organism may be determined by the influences to which it has been exposed; *but it may also be determined by the creative and integrative insight of the organism itself.*"[51] He did not want to deny Skinner's truth, but as his own italics indicate, he insisted that this was not the only truth. While Skinner devoted his life's work to the first half of the statement, Rogers devoted his to the second part. Yet Rogers was concerned with the implications of the different emphases. Referring to the first trend—understanding behavior as determined entirely by its antecedents—he wrote humorously, though pointedly: "If we are happy about

258

its application to students, then we will be happy when it is applied to us. But I doubt this. Do we really believe that we will be better, more effective faculty members when the dean has the complete record of our lives, our abilities, our personalities—the same type of record we are striving to build up in regard to students? When your request for curriculum changes, for better teaching facilities, your request for promotion, your difficulties with the Buildings and Grounds department, your tension with your wife, are all understood by a benevolent dean in the light of your test results and your Rorschach pattern, will you be more effective, will your university be a better place? Certainly much wiser guidance can be given you. You can be helped to see that promotion is hardly justified in view of your ability on the College Faculty aptitude test, which has enabled us to select such a homogeneous faculty. It can be gently hinted to you that the dissension in your home and your truculence in faculty meetings as well as your disputes with the janitor, grow out of your unresolved conflict in regard to authority, and that psychiatric guidance would assist you in all three respects. When you leave for another university, your cumulative record can be forwarded to your new dean, who can also evaluate you and your behavior in the light of all this knowledge."[52]

Of course, Skinner and the operant conditioners would not go in for all this personality testing either; but Rogers saw the attempt to control people with psychological information and the tendency to control them through the selective reinforcement of their behavior as part of the same basic direction. "It is the direction in which an increasing portion of the world is moving. Life seems too complex. We should surrender the responsibility for our lives into the hands of someone wiser—a dean, or a psychiatrist, or eventually of course, into the hands of the state."[53]

In another article, written only a few years after the fall of Hitler, Mussolini and Hirohito, and now moving into the Senator Joseph McCarthy period, he continued the argument, pointing out that, "This cultural direction would have much weight behind it. Man's need for dependence runs very deep. To leave individual guidance primarily in the hands of the master, the ruler, the priest, has a long history, and it would not be too surprising if it were followed by a tendency to leave the basic guidance of individual lives in the hands of the doctors of mental health. The wave of the future appears to contain in it a strong tendency toward admitting our own incapacity to deal with our problems in this complex world and laying our destiny in the hands of a few who seem stronger. If this is the direction which we are taking, then the major trend in clinical psychology and psychiatry is serving a useful purpose in laying an effective technological groundwork for eventual control by the state, or by a small group which regards itself as the state."[54]

Thus Rogers laid the groundwork for their debate before he ever mentioned Skinner by name. That first occurred in a 1949 article in the *Harvard Educational*

Review (the year after Skinner moved to Harvard), in which Rogers wrote, "… it is my concern that this major trend in clinical work [*counselor*-centered therapy] leads gradually and subtly to some loss of confidence in the ability of the self to evaluate, to a basic dependence growing out of that loss of self-confidence, to a lesser degree of personhood, to a subtle and sincerely well-meaning control of persons by a group which, without realizing it, has selected itself to exercise control … From the broader social point of view I have also come to view this development with concern. Does it not lead to a philosophy of social control by the few? Not many psychologists or psychiatrists have voiced the possibility. Skinner, a psychologist not himself in the clinical field, is one of the few to do so, and to advocate such control. In regard to 'extending the practices of an experimental science to the world at large,' he says, 'we can do this as soon as we wish to do it.'"[55]

It was at a symposium at the American Psychological Association's annual convention, on September 4, 1956, that Skinner and Rogers both spoke on "Some Issues Concerning the Control of Human Behavior." Two days earlier Rogers had received the Distinguished Scientific Contribution Award from the APA. Skinner's work also was very familiar to the APA members, and the hall was filled to overflowing. Each man had prepared a paper and had had a chance to read the other's paper before the convention and revise his own. The meeting followed one conventional debate format. Skinner read his paper first. Rogers then had a somewhat longer time in which to read his paper and react to what Skinner had said. Finally, Skinner had another, smaller amount of time for a final rebuttal.

They were excellent antagonists. Each was skillful with words, logical, humorous, widely read, an expert and leader in his own field, and deeply committed to his point of view. Even though they did little actual debating, the mere fact that the two of them would stand on the same platform to offer divergent positions on an issue that concerned a large part of the psychological community marked the occasion as an historic confrontation.

Rogers did not object so much to Skinner's desire to more effectively predict and control human behavior, but he argued that he and Skinner differed over the questions of: Who will be controlled? Who will exercise control? What type of control will be exercised? Most important of all, toward what end or what purpose, or in the pursuit of what value, will control be exercised?[56] On the last question, of ends and values, he characterized Skinner's utopia as a static one in which people were "happy and well-behaved"[57] and maintained that "at a deep philosophic level" *Walden Two* and *1984* were "indistinguishable." Rogers would have humans become "self-directing, self-actualizing, creative, and adaptive." Toward these ends and values he would enlist the help of science. Near his conclusion, he stated, "It is my hope that we have helped to clarify the range of choice which will lie before us and our children in regard to the behavioral sciences. We can choose to use our growing knowledge to enslave people in ways never dreamed of before, depersonalizing them, controlling them by means so carefully selected that they will perhaps never be aware of their loss of personhood. We can choose to utilize our scientific knowledge to make men happy, well-behaved, and productive, as Skinner earlier suggested. Or we can insure that each person learns all the syllabus which we select and set before him, as Skinner now suggests. Or at the other end of the spectrum of choice we can choose to use the behavioral sciences in ways which will free, not control; which will develop creativity, not contentment; which will facilitate each person in his self-directed process of becoming; which will aid individuals, groups, and even the concept of science to become self-transcending in freshly adaptive ways of meeting life and its problems."[58]

Skinner did not see his ideal society in static terms at all. After quoting many of his critics who had characterized *Walden Two* as combining the worst aspects of the Dark Ages and dictatorship, he responded by saying,

One would scarcely guess that the authors are talking about a world in which there is food, clothing, and shelter for all, where everyone chooses his own work and works on the average only 4 hours a day, where music and the arts flourish, where personal relationships develop under the most favorable circumstances, where education prepares every child for the social and intellectual life which lies before him, where—in short—people are truly happy, secure, creative, and forward-looking. What is wrong with it? Only one thing: someone "planned it that way." If these critics had come upon a society in some remote corner of the world which boasted similar advantages, they would undoubtedly have hailed it as providing a pattern we all might well follow—provided that it was clearly the result of a natural process of cultural evolution. Any evidence that intelligence had been used in arriving at this version of the good life would, in their eyes, be a serious flaw. No matter if the planner of *Walden Two* diverts none of the proceeds of the community to his own use, no matter if he has no current control or is, indeed, unknown to most of the other members of the community (he planned that, too), somewhere back of it all he occupies the position of prime mover. And this, to the child of the democratic tradition, spoils it all ...[59]

It saddens me to hear Rogers say that "at a deep philosophic level" *Walden Two* and George Orwell's *1984* "seem indistinguishable." They could scarcely be more unlike—at any level. The book *1984* is a picture of immediate aversive control for vicious selfish purposes. The founder of *Walden Two,* on the other hand, has built a community in which neither he nor any other person exerts any *current* control. His achievement lay in his original *plan,* and when he boasts of this ("It is enough to satisfy the thirstiest tyrant") we do not fear him but only pity him for his weakness.[60]

261

But for Rogers, "… in Skinner's presentation here and in his previous writings, there is a serious underestimation of the problem of power … To hope that the power which is being made available by the behavioral sciences will be exercised by the scientists, or by a benevolent group, seems to me a hope little supported by either recent or distant history. It seems far more likely that behavioral scientists, holding their present attitudes, will be in the position of the German rocket scientists specializing in guided missiles. First they worked devotedly for Hitler to destroy the U.S.S.R. and the United States. Now, depending on who captured them, they work devotedly for the U.S.S.R. in the interest of destroying the United States, or devotedly for the United States in the interest of destroying the U.S.S.R. If behavioral scientists are concerned solely with advancing their science, it seems most probable that they will serve the purposes of whatever individual or group has the power."[61]

Richard Evans wrote a short biography of B.F. Skinner and gave a copy of it to Carl Rogers. In the cover he wrote, "To Carl Rogers, without whom Fred Skinner would be at a loss for a protagonist–antagonist whom he really respects."[62] That respect grew not only out of the 1956 symposium, but out of two subsequent meetings they had early in the 1960s. The APA debate was published in *Science* magazine shortly after it took place and has received wide attention, with many requests to reprint it elsewhere.[63] The two subsequent meetings have received very little publicity and many interested people are not aware of their occurrence.

The December 1960 meeting was arranged by the American Academy of Arts and Sciences as one of a series of closed conferences on "Evolutionary Theory and Human Progress." On this occasion they invited twenty-nine outstanding figures in psychology and other disciplines to attend.[64] Skinner delivered one of the papers on "the design of cultures," and Rogers participated in the discussion. Rogers penned this note while Skinner spoke, "He avoids, like the plague, the dual questions of choice and values."[65] He then asked Skinner during the discussion period: "From what I understood Dr. Skinner to say, it is his understanding that though he might have thought he chose to come to this meeting, and might have thought he had a purpose in giving this speech, such thoughts are really illusory. He actually made certain marks on paper and emitted certain sounds here, simply because his genetic make-up and his past environment had operantly conditioned his behavior in such a way that it was rewarding to make these sounds, and that he as a person doesn't enter into this. In fact, if I get his thinking correctly, from his strictly scientific point of view, he as a person doesn't exist."[66]

In replying, Skinner said that he would not go into the question of whether he had any choice in the matter, but stated, "I do accept your characterization of my own presence here."[67] (Rogers later said that he admired Skinner's consistency.[68]) Later in the meeting, Rogers jokingly proposed that they get a person skilled in operant conditioning to shape the behavior of the individuals in that group, toward the direction of producing a blueprint for a model society. Of course, all irrelevant behaviors toward that end would have to be extinguished, including the humorous stories that had been told at the meeting and Maslow's going to sleep in a comfortable chair.[69] In spite of these brief exchanges, Rogers and Skinner's personal contact at this meeting was actually minimal, and not for another year and a half would they get a chance to engage in an extended discussion.

This came about in 1962 on June 11 and 12, when B.F. Skinner was in Wisconsin to receive an honorary degree from Ripon College. Faculty at the University of Minnesota's Duluth campus who were former students of Rogers at Chicago learned that Skinner would be in the neighborhood, as it were, and got the idea to invite Skinner and Rogers to come together for two days of meetings.[70] They felt that with the longer time to talk, with a smaller audience, and with an informal, spontaneous agenda, the two men would be much more likely to have a dialogue instead of a debate. Skinner accepted. Rogers was at the University of Wisconsin in Madison when he received the invitation. He wasn't enthusiastic about the idea, but he figured that Minneapolis was only about four hours away from Madison and that since Skinner had to travel all the way from Harvard, he would probably say no. When he found out that Skinner already *had* accepted and that the invitation had come not from the Minneapolis campus but from the Duluth Campus, still three hours farther north, he had no choice but to follow through on his commitment.[71]

The format allowed for fifteen minutes of opening remarks by each of the principals, a break, then an hour and fifteen minutes of discussion between them. That evening an invited panel would discuss the issues raised, and the audience would then break into small groups to continue the discussion themselves. The next morning Rogers and Skinner would have another hour and a quarter of discussion, a question-and-answer period with the audience for an hour, and then a final opportunity for brief closing remarks.[72] After the program chairman Gerald Gladstein introduced Rogers and Skinner, and pointed out that this would be a dialogue, with no debating or speechmaking, he called upon Rogers to begin with his short summary of the issues which separated the two of them. Rogers proceeded to give a fifteen-minute speech on the importance of the humanist movement in psychology, philosophy, religion, and politics. Next came Skinner's turn.

> Thank you very much, Dr. Gladstein … I always make the same mistake! When debating with Carl Rogers I always assume that he will make no effort to influence the audience. [Laughter from audience.] And then I have to follow him and speak as I am speaking now to a group of people who are very far from free to accept my views. [Laughter.]
>
> In fact, I was just reminded of a story that I once heard about Carl Rogers, and I'll tell it now hoping to confirm or have him deny it. I suppose it is

apocryphal; at least I'm sure it has grown in its dimensions. The story as I heard it is as follows: Carl Rogers was never much of a duck hunter, but he was persuaded upon one occasion to go duck hunting. He and some friends went into a blind and sat on a dreary, cold early dawn, and no ducks arrived, until the very end of the time when shooting was possible. Finally, one lone duck came in and his friends allowed him to shoot, and he did. At the same time, along the shore a few hundred yards away, another man shot at the same duck. The duck fell— plop. Dr. Rogers got out of the blind and started toward the duck. The other man got out of his blind and started toward the same duck. They arrived at the same moment. Dr. Rogers turned to him and said, 'You feel that this is your duck.' [Much laughter.] The reason I was reminded of that story was that the end of it is that Dr. Rogers brought the duck home. [Laughter.] I shall do my best to prevent a similar ... [Laughter].[73]

From that point on, the dialogue became friendly, often personal, filled with humor, and punctuated with laughter by both speakers and the audience. Rogers, of course, was compelled to reply to the duck hunting story, which had some basis in truth. He once *had* been duck hunting with his brother in Wyoming, *had* shot a duck which had fallen, and *did* wade out in the shallow lake only to find another duck hunter who also claimed the bird as his. (Later he wondered: "It's a story I thought only our two families knew. I don't know where the hell he picked that up.")[74] The only difference was in how the story ended. As he explained to the audience, "I'm sure I don't know how word of that got to Harvard; but there's a great deal of truth in that story, except for the punch line. Instead of saying, 'You feel that you shot the duck,' we resorted instead to a procedure very highly regarded in scientific circles—we flipped a coin, and that proved that I had shot the duck. [Much laughter.]"

The next morning the roles were reversed, with Skinner now using his opening remarks to give a long speech with an emphatic ending. This time it was Rogers' turn to comment, "Dr. Skinner told me he got up early this morning. I didn't know he got up *that* early. [Much laughter.]"

They covered a good deal of ground in their several hours together. Their topics included utopias, the role of the behavioral sciences, the nature of freedom, the importance of feelings and the subjective life, education, child rearing, the nature of verbal behavior, creativity, and science. Rogers was very pleased to hear some of the things Skinner had to say, for they seemed to speak directly to some of the points he had raised in their first debate and in the December 1960 meeting.

At one point, for example, Skinner said he was "very much concerned about the possible misuse of the behavioral technology." At another point he said he would choose creativity as one of the traits of citizens in his ideal society. Previously Rogers had criticized Skinner's utopia as characterized by only "static" values, that is, a "happy, productive, and well-behaved" citizenry. On the subject of feelings and subjective experience, Skinner spoke very eloquently of his own inner life—his love of music, his angry feelings which occasionally surprised and dismayed him—but denied that these emotions had any "causal efficacy" in influencing his behavior. His statements about feelings and subjective experience left Rogers somewhat uncertain as to where Skinner stood on that issue. Rogers quipped, "At one point yesterday, he said with real conviction, 'I believe …' I was so shaken by this, I've forgotten just what it was he believed. [Laughter.]"

One subject that came up frequently was the perennial dilemma between free will and determinism. To a questioner who asked, "Is a subjective feeling of freedom sufficient evidence that this freedom is real and that man is not subject to the control of his genetic and environmental conditions?", Rogers summed up his position by saying, "I think that that indicates some misunderstanding of the point of view I've presented, because as I've said, I feel in thorough agreement with Dr. Skinner—that, viewed from the external scientific, objective perspective, man is determined by his genetic and cultural influences. I've also said that, in an entirely different dimension, such things as freedom and choice are extremely real … I would remind you of the example I gave you of Victor Frankl in the concentration camp. It would be very interesting to try to tell him that the freedom of choice which remained to himself was completely unreal. He knew it was real, because he saw people who did not exercise that, who felt that they were completely controlled, die like flies. For the ones who had the best chance of survival were the ones who still retained the concept that 'I am a person. I choose.' And so for me, this is an entirely different dimension which is not easily reconcilable to the deterministic point of view. I look at it as being similar to the situation in physics, where you can prove that the wave theory of light is supported by evidence; so is the corpuscular theory. The two of them are contradictory. They're not at the present state of knowledge reconcilable; but I think one would only be narrowing his perception of physics to deny one of these and accept only the other. And it is in this same sense—that's why I keep using the term paradox—that I regard these two dimensions as *both* real, although they exist in a paradoxical relationship."

Sometimes their communication was not very effective, as when Rogers said of Skinner, "I'm not quite sure who it is he's talking to, but somehow he's not talking to *me*," and later Skinner spoke of how "you and I ought to be able to analyze verbal behavior better than that." On the other hand there were several times when real understanding did occur between the two, as when a questioner referred to an article Skinner had written and Rogers answered: "I welcome being reminded of that article of Dr. Skinner's in the *American Psychologist,* which was a very inspiring article on the processes of science as he had experienced them in his own career …[75] I hadn't quite thought of that in relation to this discussion. As I remember that article, Dr. Skinner there gives a very vivid picture of the scientific life as process, and this is exactly the kind of thing which I've been trying to describe as the 'Good Life' from any angle—that far from knowing where he was going to come out, he had to live in process and had to let learnings emerge as they emerged, and they shaped his behavior, and so on. Now, somehow this makes me feel a great deal better about Dr. Skinner [Laughter]—to realize that in his own life he values that emerging unpredictable process, and I guess what I've been trying to say about the kind of culture I would want to design and the kind of outcomes I see in therapy when therapy is successful, is it leads to exactly that kind of thing— that the individual becomes an ongoing process of life in which the outcome is not set. There are *not* static goals. You don't even know whether you will come out happy. You are living this on a day-by-day basis, endeavoring to be open to all your experience—this was another aspect of that article, of endeavoring to be open to all aspects of what had occurred in order to learn from them … On this we would really get together, because this sense of life as a process which can only be existentially lived if it is to be meaningful—that makes all kinds of sense—makes to me much more sense than saying, 'Here is where we should come out, and we must plan it that way.'"

To which Skinner replied: "This may be an historic moment. I think I have been changed by that argument. The point of that article was actually to criticize the codification of science by methodologists, statisticians, design of experiment people, who having very little experience with science as it is practiced, try to tell you how the scientist works. I think it's a great mistake to teach our young psychologists science in the form of statistics, because this has very little to do with actual scientific practice. However, I'm not going to concede everything, because I am interested in teaching scientific practice as such, and I should suppose that with skillful planning one could make sure that more people would be the product of lucky histories of this sort than is now the case. I'm sure I've had a great deal of luck which has not only directed me in profitable directions, but has kept me going by the very lucky schedule of reinforcement which I've experienced. But I think this ought to be viewed as a very important factor in building scientific dedication, and some of it can be arranged. Although I quite agree that you cannot foresee all of the courses it's going to take, and I'm now beginning to understand what you mean by 'becoming.'" [Applause.]

Some of Rogers' closing remarks aptly captured the tone and context of the memorable dialogue.

"I would like to say, I've acquired an increasing respect for Dr. Skinner, the person—his sincerity, gentleness, his wit, his wide scholarly interests, the honesty with which he is trying to face the implications of the directions in which the behavioral sciences are taking us. I certainly have learned deeply from him, both in the past and during these meetings. I have often felt and would like to say that I think he is the one person in the behavioral stream of psychology who has really had a highly significant impact on our society and our culture, and I respect his work.

"I think that there do remain some profound differences between us, though I think definitely less than when these discussions commenced. But I suspect that the deeper differences will not be reconciled by us. They will be reconciled by you [the audience] and by other people. One thing that I thought might come up for mention in this discussion, but it hasn't so far, is that—I don't know whether Dr. Skinner is aware of this—but a former student of his and a former student of mine are working together on developing a programmed instruction for the improvement of interpersonal relationships ... [Laughter.]

"There's one helpful, hopeful and ironic thing that I'd like to mention: For a man who believes that value and choice and purpose really retain very little of their ordinary meaning in a scientific world, there is just no question but what Dr. Skinner's work has stirred up, will continue to stir up, enormous controversy over choice, of values and purpose and the directions that we choose to go. And in this sense I feel he's really on my side because that's exactly what I would like to do, too. That's the way I see the purpose of this meeting, that we have tried to expose various points of view, various possible purposes, various values in regard to education, in regard to the design of a future culture—and that the choice of those values is something that we all will be working on over the years to come."

Rogers had the impression that all the sessions, which had been audiotaped, would be made available to the public, on tape or in printed form. On several occasions he indicated that "the only thing I've ever regretted about any of our meetings is that Skinner has never been willing to release the full transcript, nor even the full tape recordings, of our nine hours [sic] of encounter in Duluth in 1962."[76] They both did give permission to the American Academy of Psychotherapists to condense the entire dialogue into one tape and make this available to the public.[77] Skinner eventually agreed to the release of the entire dialogue, which was made available in recorded form in 1976 and in printed form in 1989.[78]

Of course the debate did not end in 1962, although Rogers and Skinner did not confront each other publicly after this. They did meet on several occasions at conferences and meetings and always maintained a friendly relationship. When Skinner was invited to Rogers' eightieth birthday celebration, he wrote, "Dear Carl: Sorry I can't be with you on October 9. We could exchange views on intellectual self-management in old age. You obviously have your own system, and it would be fun to see how we differ. I always thought we went on playing the same old tunes after our exchanges, but we did tune the fiddles a little more accurately. All best wishes, Fred."[79]

And so the so-called Rogers–Skinner debate continues to this day. In 1947 Rogers had written, "Significant problems of social philosophy are also involved in these diverging attitudes regarding therapy. If objective study supports the conclusion that dependence, guidance, and expert direction of the client's therapy and life are necessary ... then a social philosophy of expert control is clearly implied. If further research indicates that the client has at least the latent capacity to understand and guide himself, then a psychological basis for democracy would have been demonstrated. It is therefore an issue in which sound research is vital."[80]

These words suggest a faith that society and government will adopt the findings of the behavioral sciences, even to the point of changing political and social paradigms. Yet Rogers also recognized that government and industry readily co-opt science and scientists for their own ends. While policy makers and businesses often are guided by scientific evidence, they are just as prone to selectively choose the research on health, education and social policy that best supports their political, religious and social leanings and economic interests. Hence the Rogers–Skinner serial debate on the role of the behavioral sciences, education, freedom and control, and social and political values remains relevant today. Whether the future will be more congenial to Rogers' or Skinner's vision of science and society will be determined partly in laboratories and classrooms, but also in state and national legislatures and in world events.

Rogers and the CIA

As a result of his 1956 debate with B.F. Skinner, Carl Rogers became a prominent cautionary voice regarding the use of the behavioral sciences to manipulate and control human behavior. Yet, in what has to be one of the greatest ironies of Rogers' life, two months after the debate with Skinner, Rogers began working with the United States Central Intelligence Agency on a program of research on psychological methods to influence human behavior. Unknown to any of his colleagues at the time and for 20 years thereafter, it is a story that is still unknown to most of Rogers' followers and to the wider professional community.[81]

Frightened by Communist brainwashing techniques used before, during and after the Korean War, the Central Intelligence Agency (CIA) undertook an extensive research program in the 1950s to better understand how the human mind can be influenced and controlled, as well as resist such influence. Under the code name MKULTRA, Agency projects included studies of Communist defectors, strategies for interrogating prisoners, the use of prostitutes for entrapping potential sources who would then be subject to blackmail, the use of shock treatment and hypnosis for altering human memory, and numerous experiments on the use of marijuana, LSD and other mind-altering drugs for interrogation, persuasion and mind control.[82] In many of these experiments, the research methods involved extreme risks to the subjects who were often unwitting or unwilling participants, practices that violated commonly accepted ethical standards, even then, for the conduct of research using human subjects.

Harold Wolff, M.D. was a prominent neurologist working at Cornell Medical School and New York Hospital (at the same time David Rogers was there) and became a confidant of CIA director Allen Dulles when Wolff was treating Dulles' son for an injury sustained during the Korean War. Dulles commissioned Wolff and his Cornell colleague Lawrence Hinkle to conduct a major study of Communist brainwashing techniques that was completed, soon thereafter declassified, published in a professional journal, and "still remains one of the better accounts of the massive political re-education programs in China and the Soviet Union."[83] In 1955 Wolff formed the Society for the Investigation of Human Ecology, housed at Cornell, to conduct other CIA secretly funded research, including interviewing Chinese students living abroad and defectors from the Hungarian Revolution. The CIA soon recognized the value of the Society to serve as a "front organization" to fund other CIA research, including some of the less savory MKULTRA projects.[84] The Society then split off from Cornell. Wolff and Hinkle remained President and Vice-President, CIA-appointee James Monroe became the executive director; and a new board of directors was formed, including: Dr. Joseph Hinsey, head of the New York Hospital–Cornell Medical Center; John Whitehorn, chairman of the psychiatry department at Johns Hopkins University; former Assistant Secretary of State Adolf A. Berle; and the esteemed psychologist, Carl R. Rogers. Future board members would include: Leonard Carmichael, head of the Smithsonian Institution and former APA president; Barnaby Keeney, President of Brown University; and George A. Kelly, psychology professor at Ohio State University. Rogers remained on the board at least until 1961 when the Society changed its name to the Human Ecology Fund.[85] The Fund was finally disbanded in 1965.

Because much about the Society for the Investigation of Human Ecology was shrouded in secrecy, the nature and full extent of Rogers' involvement is not entirely certain. Nevertheless, a reasonably clear picture emerges from period documents, from later histories, and from interviews Rogers gave to Patricia Greenfield and John Marks after the CIA declassified many of its materials and released the participants from their confidentiality agreements.[86] The resulting information enables us to develop an understanding of how and why Rogers became involved, the nature of his own CIA-funded research, and less clearly, how much he knew about the other Society-funded studies.

In a memorandum dated November 1956 to Lawrence Kimpton, Chancellor of the University of Chicago, Rogers wrote, "Dr. Harold Wolff of Cornell Medical School is one of the world's leading authorities in psychosomatic medicine. He has been a serious student of my work and knows it very well. A week ago he asked me if I would serve with him as a consultant to the Department of Defense on a top-secret matter having to do with mental health. He said, 'I am asking the five top-ranking men in the country in this field to serve on this task. You are one of the five, and I hope you will serve.'"[87] Some twenty years later Rogers told an interviewer, "James Monroe came to me and told me that Dr. Harold Wolff, a neuropsychiatrist whom I had a lot of respect for, was heading up an organization to do research on personality and so on. Then he told me more and I realized that it had secret aspects to it."[88]

Rogers' main reason for agreeing to work with the government was loyalty—a willingness to serve his country. That Rogers was a critic of the McCarthy period hysteria during the Korean War did not alter the fact that he was a reasonably patriotic American, with family history dating to the early Colonial period, with a love for his native soil (literally and figuratively), with a son serving on active duty in the U.S. Naval Reserve during the Korean War, and with a track record of working with the military on various psychological projects, such as the study of returned aerial gunners during World War II and his year with the United Service Organization before moving to Chicago. Thus when asked to become a board member of the Society for the Investigation of Human Ecology, as he later explained, he had "no objection to helping the CIA."[89]

Years later, when CIA abuses in this period came to light and when many Americans' faith in their government's veracity and ethics was weakened, the CIA became a suspect arm of government in many quarters. But this was very different in the 1950s, when faith in America's prosperity and moral superiority was strong. As Rogers later explained his motives, "It was an organization that, as far as I knew at the time was doing legitimate things … It's impossible in the present-day climate of attitude toward intelligence activities to realize what it was like in the 1950s. It seemed as though Russia was a very potential enemy and as though the United States was very wise to get whatever information it could about things that the Russians might try to do, such as brainwashing or influencing people. So that it didn't seem at all dishonorable to me to be connected with an intelligence outfit at that time. I look at it quite differently now."[90] Or as he later told Marks, "We really did regard Russia as the enemy."[91]

This same sentiment was expressed by other Society grantees, such as Edgar Schein, a well-known social psychologist at MIT's Sloane School of Management, who was a consultant to the Society and was aware of its CIA connection. He recalled, "… we were not seeing the CIA in any unusual or villainous or different role from the Navy or the Army or any other piece of the U.S. government. It's only in today's context that this even becomes an issue … What people can't grasp is how much of a change there has been in the public attitude. The CIA was a hero, and the question of taking money from them wasn't by the remotest stretch of the imagination an issue."[92] Another prominent grantee, Charles Osgood, recalled, "there was none of the feeling then of the CIA that there is now, in terms of subversive activities."[93]

While patriotic inclination was probably the main reason Rogers agreed to join the board of the Society for the Investigation of Human Ecology, there was another reason for participating. It was made clear to Rogers that one benefit of working with the Society would be funding for some of his own research. Indeed, Rogers did receive two grants from the Society: $15,000 for a project on the psychological and physiological correlates of psychotherapy and $8,750 for the study of psychotherapy with schizophrenic patients.[94] Both of these grants were paltry sums, considerably smaller than the average grant of about $35,000 on MKULTRA projects or the largest grants which were as high as $400,000.[95] These two grants came after Rogers moved to the University of Wisconsin and was eager to obtain funding for his research there. The two small grants served as seed funding for larger grants that Rogers would soon obtain from other, more traditional sources. But Rogers had agreed to join the Society board when he was at the University of Chicago, where he had already established an excellent track record in obtaining huge grants, and before he knew he was moving to Wisconsin. So it is doubtful that the prospect of Society funding would have been his major motive at the time for joining its board of directors.

On the first grant, while colleagues worked on the physiological correlates of psychotherapy,[96] Rogers wrote a manual for studying process change in psychotherapy which was then used in his research project on psychotherapy with schizophrenic patients. The second grant supported the implementation of the psychotherapy with schizophrenia project.[97] This was the work he went to Wisconsin to do and is described in the following chapter. Rogers acknowledged the Society and other funding sources in two publications that stemmed from these projects,[98] but there is no indication that Rogers altered his research agenda to suit the CIA's needs. On the other hand, minutes from a CIA meeting at the time, which Rogers never saw, indicated that the Agency hoped it might learn something from Rogers' research with schizophrenic patients.[99] Perhaps their logic was: if one could find a way to get a person who was withdrawn or resistant or out of touch with reality and therefore not forthcoming with accurate information to open up and talk and share his or her true thoughts and feelings, such a method might just work with resistant prisoners, defectors or enemy agents.

According to Marks, this was standard Agency practice. In return for a small grant, they in effect would have a scientist on retainer, giving Agency staff access not only to the scientist's findings on the funded project but to the scientist's broad knowledge and network of associates. Other prominent scientists who served as consultants to the Society in this manner or who had basic research projects funded by the Society included psychologist and future APA president Charles Osgood, psychiatrist Martin Orne, social psychologist Edgar Schein, sociologist Jay Shulman, anthropologist Edward Hall, and not surprisingly, as a leading advocate of using psychological knowledge to influence human behavior, B.F. Skinner. Having luminaries like these on the payroll in turn gave the CIA access to other scientists. "You could walk into someone's office and say you were just talking to Skinner," said an MKULTRA veteran. "We didn't hesitate to do this."[100]

While Rogers' own research agenda and methods seem perfectly ethical and unaltered by his covert funding, there remains the question of what Rogers' knew of the other Society and MKULTRA projects. These research studies ranged from basic to applied, from topics not remotely connected to CIA interests to those directly commissioned by the Agency. Basic research projects included a sociological study of Levittown, Long Island, the foreign policy attitudes of people who did and did not own fallout shelters, and the effects of circumcision on Turkish boys.[101] These were "cover projects" that gave the society an air of scientific respectability and diversity. Their principal investigators were unaware of the actual source of their funding. Other Society projects were more directly connected to Agency concerns. Some might appear fairly innocent on the surface, such as an MKULTRA-sponsored series of annual conferences funded through the Josiah Macy Foundation, on "Problems of Consciousness" in which the likes of Margaret Mead and Jean Piaget participated with no clue as to the real funding source, while the CIA organizers took copious notes.[102] A less innocent Society project took place at Ionia State Hospital in Michigan. The focus of this project was to test the effects of LSD, marijuana, and hypnosis on sexual offenders, both with and without their knowledge. The Society reasoned that the resistance of sexual predators to admit their reasons for committing crimes could be likened to spies withholding secret information.

How much did Rogers know about all these activities? Lawrence Hinkle and John Marks, two key informants on this topic, suggested that Rogers and some of the other Society board members were "playing essentially figurehead roles," lending scientific credibility to the Society but mostly unaware of the details of its operations.[103] Hinkle said that he himself was often given papers to sign without understanding their implications, implying that Monroe and the other CIA-appointed staff were really in charge, and he and most of the board were kept in the dark about many of the projects.[104] We do know that Rogers, in his role as grantee, would occasionally be consulted on other projects. For example, Rogers recalled one meeting at which "He and other people in the field of personality and psychotherapy were given a lot of information about Soviet Premier Nikita Khrushchev. 'We were asked to figure out what we thought of him and what would be the best way of dealing with him. And that seemed to be an entirely principled and legitimate aspect. I don't think we contributed very much, but, anyway, we tried.'"[105]

In his role as board member, presumably Rogers would know even more about Society operations. One would think that as a board member he must have been informed of at least the titles of the various Society-funded research projects, so he must have known that, in addition to the more basic and benign research projects, there was experimentation with LSD, questioning techniques, and other less traditional and potentially problematic research topics. Perhaps board members were not given even this information and he agreed to simply support the work of the organization as a figurehead board member, trusting Harold Wolff as someone who would not fund illegal or unethical activities. Or perhaps he knew the general content of the research but not the details. For example, a proposal might request funding to study the effects of LSD on the self-disclosure or memory of college students, but it seems unlikely that the full board would be told that the college students were to be duped into the experiment and not informed that they would be receiving an experimental drug.

With project headquarters in New York and Rogers in Wisconsin, his contact with Society activities may have been minimal. On the other hand, fellow board member Adolf Berle knew enough of what was being proposed to have some reservations about joining the board and write in his diary, "I am frightened about this one. If the scientists do what they have laid out for themselves, men will become manageable ants. But I don't think it will happen."[106] Yet Berle was based in New York and, unlike Rogers, was a close friend of Harold Wolff and had originally put Wolff in touch with the CIA, so he may have had more knowledge of the Society's activities than Rogers did. Or maybe Berle's comment simply paralleled Rogers' own misgivings about the dangers of using science to control human behavior.

Lawrence Hinkle told John Marks, when reviewing drafts of the latter's book before publication, "I should like to put in a good word for the other scientists such as Dr. John Whitehorn and Dr. Carl Rogers ... In my opinion these were men of the highest integrity ... I think that they relied upon the 'bona fides' of Harold Wolff for guidance in these matters and that they were in fact unaware of much of what was going on with the Society and its affairs"[107]

In the end, we simply do not know how much Rogers knew about the more dubious projects of MKULTRA. Although there is no evidence that Rogers was involved directly in or even knew about any unethical research practices on the Society-funded projects, his very involvement with the CIA makes him suspect to some critics. Colin Ross, M.D., an expert in the field of multiple personalities and trauma, reflected just this negative perception of Rogers' involvement when he said sarcastically, "... yes this is Carl Rogers of Rogerian psychotherapy fame. He was actually a spook psychiatrist with top secret clearance who was on the Advisory Board of one of the funding fronts and received funding for psychotherapeutic research on schizophrenia. It's a very funny thing that Mr. Friendly Carl was in the network."[108] Another writer asserted that "Rogers' behavior does raise some doubts about whether or not his philosophy, methods and writings can be trusted as guidelines for others to follow."[109]

In a 1978 letter from Lawrence Hinkle to Rogers' son David, his former colleague with whom he had recently served on a high-level scientific committee, Hinkle wrote,

What you should know is that I find nothing in all this that reflects any discredit upon this University [Cornell] or upon men such as your father who agreed to participate with the "Society" in its early days. Quite to the contrary, as I think you will see, the University responded to a national request from people at high levels in our government and performed a very creditable service in producing a report under conditions that I would have to describe to you as about ten times more onerous and difficult as those that you and I recently had to deal with in the report that we evaluated for the Academy of Sciences. There were, I think, some misjudgments on the part of some people connected with this, and it is clear that some of the actors in this drama had personalities that were not easily malleable; but I think that everyone on the academic side, and most of those that I knew on the CIA side, acted according to his best judgment, in his own light and in light of the attitudes that were prevalent at the time.[110]

If Hinkle is correct, that given the attitudes and standards of the time Rogers' involvement with the CIA was honorable, by today's standards it might not be. We now understand how in the 1950s in America, behind the growing prosperity, behind the fascination with the new medium of television and its model American family of Ozzie and Harriet and quiz show hero Charles Van Doren, and behind glamorous Hollywood icons like Elvis Presley, James Dean, and Marilyn Monroe, there lurked another America of poverty, racial discrimination, quiz show scandals, and Tuskegee College experimentation in which scientists observed the course of untreated syphilis in unsuspecting African-Americans over a 40-year period.[111] We are no longer innocent. The law now holds boards of directors responsible for the actions of their organizations where due diligence might have alerted the directors to abuses and illegalities. So with hindsight, yes, Rogers should have asked, should have known, and should have refused to participate, even indirectly, in any unethical research practices.

Of course hindsight was not available to Rogers in the historical moment. And so, using Rogers' well-popularized practice of empathy, we are left wondering what *we* would have done if we were in his shoes at that time. From today's perspective we also can appreciate the historical ironies associated with Rogers' CIA involvement. One irony is that at a time when behaviorism dominated academic psychology, it was the CIA that became arguably the main supporter of research on human subjective phenomena—beliefs, perceptions, values, and inner states of consciousness. Another is the Rogers–Skinner juxtaposition. Although Rogers had commented on issues associated with the uses of science in society earlier in his career, it was only after the debate with Skinner in 1956 that Rogers became a leading voice in the behavioral sciences cautioning against the dangers of using science to control human behavior and in favor of using science to help free individuals to achieve their potential. Is it too much to speculate that his growing eloquence on this subject was enhanced by whatever secret knowledge he subsequently gained of the CIA's mind control and behavior control experiments? It would be ironic indeed if getting involved with the CIA helped propel Rogers in his opposition to the use of the behavior sciences by those in government or industry who would attempt to control and manipulate human behavior.

274

Other Dialogues

Carl Rogers' 1956 debate with B.F. Skinner began a series of dialogues with some of the world's leading intellectuals of the twentieth century. It seemed that as Rogers' stature in psychology grew, and as his writings began to touch on or influence philosophy, religion and other fields, individuals in those fields recognized points of convergence and divergence between Rogers and leading scholars in those fields and arranged occasions for them to meet. Hence over the following years, Rogers had public and recorded dialogues with Israeli philosopher of religion Martin Buber (1957), behavioral psychologist B.F. Skinner (the 1962 dialogue), German-American theologian and philosopher Paul Tillich (1965), British scientist and philosopher of science Michael Polanyi (1966) and American anthropologist, communications theorist, and developer of the double-bind theory of schizophrenia Gregory Bateson (1975). He also participated in a symposium on the American theologian and social activist Reinhold Niebuhr (1956) and a published correspondence with existential psychotherapist Rollo May (1959 and 1981–82). A more distinguished group of thinkers would be hard to imagine.

After Rogers' death, all these exchanges were compiled and published in a single volume, *Carl Rogers: Dialogues*.[112] As the introduction to that collection stated:

> To a degree, the dialogues and correspondence can be categorized by Rogers' interaction with the theologians (Buber, Tillich, Niebuhr), the psychologists (Skinner, Bateson, May), and the scientist (Polanyi). However, as the dialogues richly reveal, such a division would be misleading. All three theologians were vitally concerned with helping relationships, with succoring the psychologically and spiritually troubled, with the "I–Thou" encounter, with forgiveness and the state of grace as it may be experienced between the person and God or person to person. The three psychologists were concerned with the "nature of man," with helping their clients find meaning in life, with understanding the "good life" and with the question of free choice and free will versus determinism—all profound and perennial theological questions. And all seven of Rogers' counterparts cared deeply about science—how we know, the relation between knowledge and faith, and the role of values and beliefs in the pursuit of science … Ironically, Carl Rogers—the student minister turned agnostic, the psychologist, the scientist—became the fulcrum for a series of fascinating exchanges that sometimes touched lightly upon and at other times delved deeply into many of the most profound questions of religion, psychology, and philosophy.[113]

Of all these exchanges, the one that has received the most attention over the years is Rogers' dialogue with Jewish philosopher of religion and philosophical anthropologist Martin Buber. Communications professors Kenneth Cissna and Rob Anderson have described it as a meeting between the twentieth century's leading intellectual of dialogue, Buber, and the century's leading practitioner of dialogue, Rogers.[114] Consequently it has been the subject of numerous articles and books.[115]

Rogers and Buber discussed many issues: *Invitations and stories:* What kinds of invitation, self-disclosure and verbal and nonverbal cues encourage openness and communication? *Mutuality and therapy:* Is it possible for genuine dialogue or "moments of meeting" to occur between individuals who have different roles (such as patient and therapist), status, or power in the relationship? *Inner meeting and dialogue:* Can one have a dialogue with oneself? In what ways is "a person's relationship to himself" similar or different from interpersonal dialogue? *Human nature:* Is human nature positive (characterized by an "actualizing tendency" according to Rogers) or polar, equally prone to moving in a positive or negative direction (Buber)? *Acceptance and confirmation:* What role does acceptance and confirmation play in the interpersonal healing process in therapy and beyond? How does Rogers' notion of acceptance compare with Buber's concept of confirmation? *Within and between:* What is the difference between the separate "individual" and the "person" in relationship to others? Can one be that self "which one most deeply *is*" (Rogers) when not in dialogic relationship with others (Buber)? *The nature of empathy:* Is it possible to truly enter the feelings and worldview of another person without giving up one's sense of self (Rogers) or critical perspective (Buber)?[116]

The result, say Cissna and Anderson and moderator Maurice Friedman, was a genuine dialogue, a "moment of meeting" between the two men which changed them both.[117] Buber, who until then did not believe that dialogue in public was possible, and in fact, had to be convinced by Rogers to allow their dialogue to be audiotaped, became convinced that public dialogue was indeed possible. And Rogers, say these authors, came to understand and appreciate the "I–Thou" qualities of human relationships more fully. Indeed, less than a year after their meeting, Rogers wrote his well-known essay "The Characteristics of a Helping Relationship," in which he quotes Buber's remarks in the dialogue on the importance of "confirming the other" in relationship.[118]

However, how much Buber actually influenced Rogers is uncertain. Rogers knew of the other's work before their 1957 dialogue; his students at University of Chicago read Buber.[119] But how much Rogers' early reading of Buber *influenced* him versus *confirmed* his own experience remains to be demonstrated. Similarly, the case for the influence of the dialogue on Rogers' *subsequent* development is speculative. Certainly Rogers did give greater emphasis to interpersonal communication and relationships after 1957, but he was moving steadily in that direction anyway. There is no indication that the meeting with Buber changed this trajectory, but it very well may have accelerated or deepened it.

In any case, the moderator of the Buber–Rogers dialogue, Maurice Friedman, himself a respected scholar of philosophy and religion, wrote, "even after 30 years, the issues raised in their dialogue still seem to me momentous."[120] To some extent, the same could be said for Rogers' exchanges with the other scholars. For example, in their taped dialogue in 1965, Rogers and Paul Tillich spent their time comparing and contrasting Tillich's theological concepts—the essential nature of humans, the ground of being, forgiveness, grace, acceptance, freedom, the demonic, and so on—with concepts and experiences that Rogers drew from psychotherapy.[121] The issues of human nature and human potential, freedom and control, meaning and values, self and relationships, education and human development, growth and healing, and science and society raised by the comparison of Freud, Skinner, Rogers and humanistic psychology in this chapter are echoed, enriched and extended in Rogers' dialogues with Buber, Tillich and these other luminaries in science, philosophy and religion.

It might be added that in 1978 Rogers also had a dialogue with the famous British psychiatrist R.D. Laing. This was preceded the day before by an almost-violent encounter between Laing and his colleagues and Rogers and his colleagues. Laing had a clear need to get Rogers and his group to admit the darker side of human nature and became so frustrated with their "California nice-guy bullshit," as he called it, that he insulted them and went so far as to spit in one of their drinks to get a rise out of them.[122] Rogers was ready to pull out of the next day's public dialogue, but Laing reminded him of the thousand people who expected them to perform, so Rogers went through with the public meeting. To make matters worse, "Rogers had put up $2,000 to help book the London Hilton as a venue for the debate and Laing, who was broke, refused to repay the money."[123] The meeting with Laing was not one of Rogers' more pleasant memories.

Integration and New Developments

It would be remiss to close this selective comparison of Freud, Skinner and Rogers without questioning the dichotomy between behaviorism and humanism and between psychoanalysis and humanism that has been assumed throughout the discussion. It would be equally remiss not to acknowledge important recent advances in drug therapy, developmental psychology, cognitive behavioral therapy, psychiatry, psychoanalysis, positive psychology, brain science and other developments that bear upon the issues raised in the Rogers–Skinner debate but which are beyond the scope of this biography.

Rogers hinted about a possible reconciliation between behaviorism and humanism in his closing remarks with Skinner in 1962; but as Carl Pitts wrote in 1973, "There is an argument going on today in psychology which, like most arguments, dichotomizes into bipolar, antagonistic points what are assumed to be two different 'schools' of thought, humanism and behaviorism. Crudely put, the humanists seem to view the behaviorists as manipulative, depersonalizing, and controlling slaves to scientism, concerned with forcing men into submission, conformity, and docility. The behaviorists view humanists as soft-headed, nonscientific, vague, sentimental, and hopelessly caught up in nonoperational, meaningless values. The charges have been made public and the battle lines set, particularly since the now famous Rogers and Skinner debate."[124]

Rogers, in the symposium with Skinner and on other occasions, acknowledged that the client-centered therapist is engaged in the reinforcement and control of the client's behavior. To a group of graduate students at the University of Rochester, he said, "… if you think of therapy as operant conditioning and certainly there is enough evidence in that field to make us think very seriously about the meaning of that—then I've come to feel that perhaps my hypothesis would be that effective therapy consists in the reinforcing of all experienced feelings. So then when you have reinforced *all* the feelings of the individual, then he can *be* all of those and he can be himself."[125] To Skinner and the APA he said, "As therapists, we institute certain attitudinal conditions, and the client has relatively little voice in the establishment of these conditions. We predict that if these conditions are instituted, certain behavior consequences will ensue in the client. Up to this point this is largely external control, no different from what Skinner has described … But here any similarity ceases."[126]

The main difference, in his opinion, was that of ends. While the humanists were attempting to help clients become more self-directing, Rogers feared that behavior techniques would be used increasingly to externally control individuals' behavior. Commenting on a 1961 article by Rogers in which he had voiced this concern, Pitts wrote that "recent work in behavioral psychology … has not fulfilled the warning of 12 years ago. Behaviorists have been and are increasingly concerned about teaching self-direction."[127]

At the University of Minnesota, for example, Drs. Ann Duncan and Wells Hively taught behavior modification techniques to teenagers in therapy and their parents. The teenagers and parents set their own goals. One wanted to control his temper more effectively, another wanted to be more accepting of her child, a third wanted to pick at her face less often, a fourth wanted to lose weight, and so on. Each person was given a "wrist counter," an attractive leather bracelet with moveable beads. Once the participants clearly identified their desired behaviors (each time the mother gave a compliment, each time the girl resisted the desire to pick at her face, etc.), they began to count on their wrist counters how often the desired behavior occurred each day. They learned to chart and graph the data they were gathering about themselves. Their own satisfaction in noticing their own positive behavior was reinforcing, and the desired behaviors increased in frequency. In group sessions they reported on their progress, received further information and reinforcement from the group, discussed problems and identified new goals.[128] Had the term not already been appropriated by the humanists, these behavior therapists might well be called "facilitators."

Pitts gave other examples of behaviorists who were teaching their clients to be independent and self-directing. Rogers, responding to the Pitts article with appreciation, concluded by saying, "In my estimation, behaviorists have come a long way in admitting the human being with his capacity for choice and decision and subjective appraisal back into the realm of psychology. In other words, they are rapidly becoming humanistic in their approach, and now the only discussion is what methods can the individual choose to most effectively change his behavior."[129]

Continuing to observe this new trend in behaviorism, Rogers wrote in 1977, "In fairness to behaviorists it should be said that many of them have come to adopt a greatly changed view of the politics of relationships. In the commune Twin Oaks, patterned initially after Walden II, the residents often choose for themselves which behaviors they wish to change, and select the rewards which will be most reinforcing. Clearly this is completely opposed to the politics of the strict behaviorist, since it is self-initiated, self-evaluated change. It is not the environment shaping the individual's behavior, but the individual choosing to shape the environment for her own personal development."[130]

Rogers even went so far as to appreciate that there may be a short-term role for behavioral techniques as a preparation for a client-centered approach. Although he never wrote about this, he told a workshop group in 1975 how the Louisville, Kentucky public schools, with whom he was working, wanted to use student-centered learning in the classrooms but found the students unable to control themselves long enough for the teachers to develop a facilitative relationship with them. Hence "we began to use behavior mod methods to reward the children for sitting in their seats for 10 minutes at a time until their behavior was such that they could be reached through a more human approach."[131]

Similarly, the psychoanalytic and psychodynamic approaches to therapy have also undergone many changes and developments since Rogers used Freud and psychoanalysis as a foil for differentiating the client-centered and humanist models. He recognized this himself at the beginning of *Client-Centered Therapy* (1951) when he wrote, "Though it [client-centered therapy] has developed along somewhat different paths than the psychotherapeutic views of Horney or Sullivan, or Alexander and French, yet there are many threads of interconnection with these modern formulations of psychoanalytic thinking."[132] And even if Otto Rank was no longer welcomed among the psychoanalytic establishment, Rogers readily acknowledged that, "Especially are the roots of client-centered therapy to be found in the therapy of Rank, and the Philadelphia group which has integrated his views into their own."[133] Shortly before his death Rogers compared Heinz Kohut, "a major innovator in psychoanalysis, and Milton Erickson, an innovator who went far beyond hypnotherapy" to his own thinking, finding a number of points of convergence among them, as well as some significant differences.[134]

In more recent years, many cognitive behavioral therapists have come to recognize that, in addition to their particular techniques, the therapist's *empathy* is essential for effective therapy. Behavioral techniques alone are not sufficient.[135] As cognitive therapy pioneer Albert Ellis wrote in 1992, "As I unconditionally accept my clients *with* their poor and defensive behavior, the more they usually open up, become increasingly honest and authentic with themselves, as well as with me." In the same article he also affirmed the importance of congruence in psychotherapy, although he qualified his position by saying "I take the middle ground of being as honest *as feasible* instead of trying to be as honest *as possible*."[136] In fact, as the final chapter will demonstrate, the last two decades of research on "common factors" in effective psychotherapy and on the "therapeutic alliance" have shown that, whatever one's approach or techniques in therapy, the relationship between the therapist and the client remains arguably the most important factor in successful psychotherapy. Thus much of the world of psychotherapy has come to recognize that the client-centered, humanist model need not, indeed should not, be polarized from psychodynamic, behavioral, cognitive or other schools of psychotherapy.

Nor has humanistic psychology ceased its development with the passing of its pioneers in the late twentieth century. Building on the foundation that Maslow, Rogers, May and their colleagues established, under the new banner of "positive psychology" contemporary psychologists are continuing to explore the very questions that concerned the humanists: What is psychological health? What is happiness? How are they achieved? But more than most humanistic psychologists, Rogers being a notable exception, the positive psychologists are conducting and gathering considerable scientific research in the logical positivist tradition to develop a body of knowledge about human wellness—including positive emotion, strengths-based character, and healthy institutions.[137] In one book on *Positive Therapy*, "The authors openly attribute much of positive psychology to Rogers and his person-centered therapy."[138]

Meanwhile advances in drug therapy and neuroscience have challenged many professions and disciplines to rethink their assumptions. As we continue to learn more about the interface of biology and psychology and the relationship between biological, psychological, social and spiritual well-being, we will no doubt obtain further insight regarding the ideas of Freud, Skinner, and Rogers and the schools of thought to which they contributed. When leading brain scientists combine forces with the Dalai Llama to study the process of meditation and its psychological and physical health benefits, it is clear that new integrations of disciplines are emerging.[139] What these new developments will teach us about the human condition, human potential, education, and healing can only be imagined.

CHAPTER 9

The Wisconsin Years
1957–1963

Many people are familiar with Rogers' work as founder of client-centered therapy and researcher at the University of Chicago and are also familiar with his later role in the encounter group movement and education. But the seven-year interim in Wisconsin is a time of which little is known, even by Rogers' followers, and a time which Rogers himself often wished he could forget. He once called it "the most painful and anguished episode in my whole professional life."[1] His dream in moving to the University of Wisconsin was never fulfilled. The hope of having psychologists and psychiatrists working together on joint training and research projects never materialized to any significant degree. No great precedents were set in the education and training of psychologists and psychiatrists. His joint appointment in Psychology and Psychiatry enabled him to work in both realms, but helped little in bringing the two together. And crisis and conflict within his own team made the experience a difficult and disappointing period in his academic life.

Getting Started

When Rogers left Chicago, he told his colleagues that the "terrific sadness" that he would feel if he were really leaving them was somewhat softened, because their "bonds of common purpose and common understanding" would keep them in contact and because, "I think I, like each one of us, am able to create a climate, wherever I am, which will permit such a group to grow and flourish."[2]

281

But when he got to Wisconsin, he founding himself "really suffering for want of a support group," and as soon as he had research funds to support them, he hired Eugene Gendlin, Philippa Mathieu and some others from Chicago to join him.[3] He stayed in touch with other colleagues from the Counseling Center for years to come, but as we shall see, his hope of forging a new collective at Wisconsin comparable to the "Rogers group" in Chicago was not to be fulfilled.

Rogers spent a considerable portion of his time during the autumn of 1957 writing grant proposals to fund his research.[4] While his main goal in coming to Wisconsin was to do research on psychotherapy with schizophrenic and normal individuals, he also sought funding for two other projects upon his arrival. Rogers, Virgil Herrick from the School of Education, who had championed Rogers' move to Wisconsin, and John Rothney applied for and received a $275,000 grant from the National Institutes for Mental Health to support a program of teacher training to facilitate mental health.[5] Rogers' role in this project was "in a steering capacity," serving as chairman of the "Executive Committee." He never published anything from the five-year project or spoke of his experience on it. This suggests that he developed the project out of gratitude for Herrick's facilitating his move to Wisconsin, demonstrating his willingness to collaborate with colleagues across the university, but letting Herrick and Rothney effectively conduct the project while Rogers attended to his other research.

Rogers began another collaborative project with Robert Roessler, M.D., from the Department of Psychiatry, Norman Greenfield, Ph.D., and Chicago doctoral student Jerome Berlin to study the "correlation of psychological and physiological variables in personality and personality change." The physiology of personality and psychotherapeutic change was never of great interest to Rogers, so at first it seems surprising that this was a significant part of their project and that Rogers was senior author with Roessler and Greenfield of an unpublished manuscript titled "Psychosomatic Relationships in Adaptation," written to guide their research.[6] Again, perhaps including the physiological element in the research was a way of establishing positive relationships with colleagues in the Department of Psychiatry of which he was now a member. Indeed, using Rogers' contacts, the investigators got a $15,000 grant from the Society for the Investigation of Human Ecology (the CIA-front organization discussed in the previous chapter), followed by a grant of over $100,000 from the National Institute of Mental Health for three years of continuing support. Although Rogers wrote a one-page note describing how he happened to conduct a therapy session with a woman who was hooked up to various electrodes, and there is also a memo in his files describing his curiosity about how psychotherapy might be affected when patients had recently been given sodium amytal by hospital staff to calm them down,[7] there is no evidence that Rogers remained involved with the physiological side of the project. In fact, when Roessler and Greenfield organized a 1961 conference at Wisconsin on the physiological correlates of personality and edited a book of the proceedings, Rogers was never even mentioned.[8]

While his colleagues worked on the physiological aspects of the project, Rogers worked on the psychological correlates of psychotherapeutic personality change—a subject much closer to his heart—using some of the project funds to support himself and colleagues to develop a manual for measuring process change in psychotherapy.[9] This work was central to his main research interest in Wisconsin.

The Psychotherapy with Schizophrenia Research Project

Having spent his professional life working mostly with relatively mildly disturbed individuals, "neurotics" as they would often be classified, Rogers was eager to see if his hypotheses about the necessary and sufficient conditions of personality change worked also with seriously disturbed and with normal populations. His occasional experience with more seriously disturbed individuals told him it did. The joint appointment at Wisconsin gave him the opportunity to test this question through more careful research.

However, obtaining the substantial funding needed for the ambitious research project he intended was not easy. The University of Wisconsin had a million dollar Wisconsin Alumni Research Foundation to support internal research projects, typically in the physical sciences. They set a new precedent by supporting Rogers' social and behavioral science research with initial funding over a two-year period, allowing him to bring Gene Gendlin from Chicago to manage the project.[10] An $8,750 grant from the Society for the Investigation of Human Ecology provided outside, seed funding, and eventually Rogers received another $162,000 in outside funding to continue the research.[11] Thus working under the auspices of the Psychiatric Institute in the Department of Psychiatry of the University, Rogers established a pioneering research project on the treatment of schizophrenics and normals through the therapeutic relationship.

A group of forty-eight subjects, comprised of patients at the Mendota State Hospital and of normal, volunteer adults from the community, was selected for the study. Sixteen "more chronic" schizophrenics (those who had been hospitalized for more than eight months), sixteen "more acute" schizophrenics (those who had been hospitalized for less than eight months), and sixteen "normals" comprised the total of forty-eight. Each group of sixteen was composed of eight matched pairs, that is, individuals who were similar to each other on the basis of sex, age, socio-educational status and degree of psychological disturbance. By the flip of a coin, one member of each pair was selected for therapy. The other would serve as the "control." If the patients who received therapy changed during and after the therapy, and if their matched control did not change, then it could be said that the change was due to the therapy and not to some other factor. Eight therapists, Rogers one of them, worked with three clients each, insuring that any positive or negative results could not be attributed to the skill or lack thereof of only one or two therapists. The clients took a battery of research instruments at three- and six-month intervals. In addition, one independent interviewer, who had nothing else to do with the research, held a "sampling interview" with each of the forty-eight subjects early in the study and every three months thereafter.

Actually, Rogers and his colleagues were putting their theories to a hard test. This was not a simple case where half of the group received therapy and the other half did not. Every patient in Mendota State Hospital normally received a great deal of attention—recreational programs, group therapy, occupational therapy, and so on. The question really was: Would the group that received all the treatment offered by a modern, efficient hospital *plus* individual psychotherapy do any better than the group which received all the treatment offered by a modern, efficient hospital? If the experimental group did improve more than the controls, it would indicate that the individual therapy was powerful indeed. Another problem for the therapists in the research project was that establishing a therapeutic relationship with schizophrenic and normal individuals was a very different thing from conducting therapy with individuals who came voluntarily to a clinic seeking help. The normals in the study often felt that they did not need therapy, and although they had volunteered to participate in a psychological study and to spend time doing it, they were reluctant to go into their personal lives in great depth and tended to stay on a rather superficial level of discussion. The schizophrenic patients, on the other hand, were often extremely reluctant even to talk to the therapists. When they found out that the therapists could not get them discharged from the hospital, they were reluctant to spend time with a "talking doctor." They often felt they did not need help, or they were very fearful, withdrawn persons who cringed at any physical or emotional closeness the therapist offered. These and other problems made it very difficult for the therapists even to begin their therapeutic contacts with many of their prospective clients.

To make it more difficult, Rogers and most of his colleagues in the research had little or no experience working with such seriously disturbed individuals. They had hoped to have several therapists from the hospital staff and from other than a client-centered orientation participate in the research; but when these other therapists heard that every interview was to be recorded, they declined to participate in the study. Consequently, Rogers and the others had to develop their own methods of reaching the patients and, eventually, came up with several creative means of making contact, building trust, and offering and starting a therapeutic relationship with the schizophrenic subjects. Later Rogers recognized that "we would have done better ... had we spent a year or two working with schizophrenics without any attempt to do research and then start a research project."[12]

One thing Rogers and his colleagues soon learned was that they needed to be much more active in the interviews and to use their own feelings more to demonstrate their congruence, understanding, and caring. One of Rogers' patients, for example, "Jim Brown," was extremely withdrawn and uncommunicative. After Jim remained silent and withdrawn for thirteen minutes in one session, Rogers said to him, softly and very slowly, "I kind of feel like saying that 'If it would be of any help at all I'd like to come in.' On the other hand, if it's something you'd rather … if you just feel more like being within yourself, why that's ok, too … I guess another thing I'm saying, really, in saying that is, 'I do care. I'm not just sitting here like a stick.'" Then, after another minute, he added, "And I guess your silence is saying to me that either you don't want to or can't come out right now, and that's ok. So I won't pester you, but I just want you to know I'm here."[13]

At another time he said to Jim, who had just been rebuffed by another patient, "I guess some part of you just feels, 'Here I am hit with another blow, as if I hadn't had enough blows like this during my life when I feel that people don't like me. Here's someone I've begun to feel attached to and now *he* doesn't like me. And I'll say I don't care. I won't let it make any difference to me—But just the same the tears run down my cheeks.'"

The next time they met, the following exchange took place:

Jim: That's why I want to go, 'cause I don't care what happens.

Rogers: M-hm, m-hm. That's why you want to go, because you really don't care about yourself. You just don't care *what* happens. And I guess I'd just like to say—*I* care about you. And *I* care what happens. [Silence of 30 seconds.] [Jim bursts into tears and unintelligible sobs.]

Rogers: [tenderly] Somehow that just—makes all the feelings pour out. [Silence of 35 seconds.]

Rogers: And you just weep and weep and weep. And feel so badly. [Jim continues to sob, then blows nose and breathes in great gasps.]

Rogers: I do get some sense of how awful you feel inside—You just sob and sob. [He puts his head on desk, bursting out in great gulping, gasping sobs.]

Rogers: I guess all the pent-up feelings you've been feeling the last few days just—just come rolling out. [Silence of 32 seconds, while sobbing continues.]

Rogers: There some Kleenex there, if you'd like it—Hmm. [sympathetically] You just feel kind of torn to pieces inside. [Silence of 1 minute, 56 seconds.]

Jim: I wish I could die. [sobbing]

Rogers: You just wish you could die, don't you? M-hm. You just feel so awful, you wish you could perish. [Rogers laid his hand gently on Jim's arm during this period. Jim showed no definite response. However, the storm subsides somewhat. Very heavy breathing.][14]

In reflecting on the longer transcript of these interviews Rogers wrote:

> I felt a warm and spontaneous caring for him as a person, which found expression in several ways—but most deeply at the moment when he was despairing. I was continuously desirous of understanding his feelings, even though he gave very few clues. I believe that my erroneous guesses were unimportant as compared to my willingness to go with him in his feelings of worthlessness and despair when he was able to voice these. I think we were relating as two real and genuine persons. In the moments of real encounter the differences in education, in status, in degree of psychological disturbance, had no importance—we were two persons in a relationship.
>
> In this relationship there was a moment of real, and I believe irreversible change. Jim Brown, who sees himself as stubborn, bitter, mistreated, worthless, useless, hopeless, unloved, unlovable, experiences my caring. In that moment his defensive shell cracks wide open, and can never again be quite the same. When someone *cares* for him, and when he feels and experiences this caring, he becomes a softer person whose years of stored up hurt come pouring out in anguished sobs. He is not the shell of hardness and bitterness, the stranger to tenderness. He is a person hurt beyond words, and aching for the love and caring which alone can make him human. This is evident in his sobs. It is evident too in his returning to the office, partly for a cigarette, partly to say spontaneously that he will return.[15]

Jim made steady progress in his therapy with Rogers over many months. Charles Truax recalled how Jim "was about ready to be discharged from the hospital, and some aide on the ward said something about he wasn't going to get discharged or something like that, and he just blew his lid, flipped out, and got very upset. When Carl came out to the hospital and met him, he talked to him like a Dutch uncle. 'What do you mean getting upset? Who is he to listen to? To hell with him!' And so on. He was mad because he had put in a lot of time with this patient and here he was blowing it, stupidly. And I think he communicated very well to that man, 'I care. I care very much what happens to you.'"[16]

Jim eventually was discharged and continued to live an independent life outside the hospital. An audiotape of one of the therapy sessions with Rogers and Jim was later published under the title of "Mr. Vac."[17] Jim remained in contact with Rogers for years thereafter, calling him every few years, with a "Hi, Doc," to report proudly that he was doing well and never returned to the state hospital.[18]

As the exchange with Jim illustrates, Rogers' own therapeutic style developed during this period as he became increasingly congruent, forthcoming, and able to connect more deeply and personally to his clients. So did Rogers and his colleagues' scientific repertoire continue to develop. They created several new instruments to measure the process of therapy. Halkides developed scales with which outside judges, listening to audiotapes of therapy sessions, could rate the therapists on their demonstrated levels of the three conditions, and Barrett-Lennard created the widely used Relationship Inventory, used by clients themselves to rate their therapists on the core conditions.[19] In their dissertation studies, both researchers found that therapist congruence, empathy, and unconditional positive regard were, in fact, correlated with positive outcomes in therapy. Building on this work for the major new research program at Wisconsin, discrete scales for congruence, developed by Donald Kiesler, and for accurate empathy and unconditional positive regard, developed by Charles Truax, were employed.[20]

Another scale they used measured *the process of psychotherapy*. Over the years, Rogers had changed from describing therapy as a nondirective technique to a client-centered attitude to a person-to-person relationship. It was not enough for the client-centered therapist to have or demonstrate the helpful attitudes; the client had to perceive these attitudes, thus constituting a relationship. In this person-to-person relationship where the therapeutic conditions are present, Rogers said, a process of therapeutic personality change would be initiated. It was Rogers' former student and colleague Eugene Gendlin who began to explore and who helped Rogers to understand in greater depth the therapeutic process that the client undergoes. It centered around Gendlin's theory of experiencing.[21]

In Gendlin's view, the individual has within him a continually changing process of experiencing going on at all times. This experiencing includes the person's perceptions, his thoughts, his memories, his feelings, but also the meanings he attaches to all these in the present moment. Some of his experiencing, hunger for example, may be readily accessible to his awareness. Other parts of his experiencing, some feelings of fear perhaps, may be less accessible. The defensively organized person, to varying degrees, is not aware of his experiencing or constructs it in a rigid manner. He denies that he is angry when really he is. He might always experience people of another ethnic group in a rigid, stereotyped way. He might believe he is unlovable, when almost everyone who knows him well expresses their affection and caring for him. In the latter case he clings rigidly to one of his "personal constructs" ("I am unlovable"), thus denying a major part of his experiencing. In therapy the client becomes more aware of his inner experiencing, becomes less defensively organized as he admits more of his experiencing into his awareness, and develops more flexible and realistic constructs about the world and about himself. Since his experiencing is always changing, he lives flexibly, continually open to and consulting his experiencing as a guide to his behavior.

Rogers gave much thought to Gendlin's concept of experiencing. In 1957 when Rogers was at Wisconsin for the spring semester as visiting professor, he spent many long hours listening to tape recordings of interviews, trying to discover what patterns could be discerned in the client's changing manner of experiencing over the course of therapy. His address to the American Psychological Association in 1957, as the previous year's recipient of the Distinguished Scientific Contribution Award, described his emerging "process conception of psychotherapy."[22] In May of 1958, he discussed it with a group of psychologists in Rochester, New York. Reflecting on an audiotape of a counseling session he just played for the group, he said,

> I mostly want to call attention to this part we just played [where the client says] "I'm just a pleading little boy" and here again he used kinesthetic means. In trying to get at what he was feeling he put his hands in supplication. It is a good defined example of what I mean by the previously denied experience seeping through into awareness. He even uses that phrase "seeping through" before he quite gets to this point. Here it seems to me that he's really *experiencing* himself as pleading. In terms of the process levels, a person might talk about such experiences. He might describe them as having them in the past. He might exhibit them first of all. Probably this individual has exhibited them all his life. He might describe relevant material in the past or even describe some present feelings but it is this experiencing of it in the immediate moment of a relationship and experiencing it with some degree of acceptance that I've come to think of as the real moment of change in therapy.[23]

In this quotation Rogers referred to "the process levels," a new idea he was developing at the time which further operationalized the concept of experiencing and connected it to other indices of mental health.[24] Rogers formulated a seven-point scale to indicate where a person is in his manner of experiencing. On the lower ends of the scale, the individual's feelings and personal meanings are unrecognized and unexpressed; he is remote from or unaware of his inner experiencing; where there is incongruence between what the person is experiencing and what he is expressing, he is unaware of the incongruence; there is a lack of communication of self; experience is construed rigidly, and the person sees his construction not as his own perception or generalization but as fact; he does not recognize his problems or his responsibility in relation to his problems or there is no desire to change; he avoids close relationships as being dangerous.

For an example of someone at the extreme low end of this scale, one might picture a person with paranoid schizophrenia. He is sure "they" are out to get him. His failures are never his own; "they" are responsible. Sometimes he has these strange feelings inside him, but they are not "his own"; they are being sent into him through the people on the television. He does not want to get close to anyone on the ward or even the therapist, for such exposure would make him vulnerable and be very dangerous.

On the other end of the process scale, at stages six and seven, the individual fully experiences his feelings and personal meanings; he frequently tunes into his inner experiencing and uses it as a major referent to understand himself; any incongruence is temporary only because he is constantly referring to his inner experiencing; because he is so in touch with his inner experience his communication of self is rich and varied; his constructs and generalization about himself and his world are tentative, flexible, subject to change as new data emerge in his experiencing; he accepts responsibility for his problems; he relates to others openly and freely on the basis of his immediate experiencing.

In the process scale, Rogers was exemplifying the thrust of humanistic psychology by describing "mental health" in concrete terms, by moving from a conception of sickness or disturbance or maladjustment to its implied opposite— what he shortly came to call the "fully functioning person." This was the last major stage in his developing theory of personality change; his later years were spent exploring new applications of his theory and methods to other fields.

Rogers and his colleagues developed ways to measure the subtle differences among stages. The process scale could demonstrate at what point the client was when he entered therapy and where he was at any particular time during or after the therapy. In fact Rogers and his associates found this was possible even by taking only four-minute samples of the therapy dialogue and having these rated by independent judges. In the research on schizophrenics they went so far as to train undergraduates who had absolutely no relationship to the research project to rate these four-minute samples. Their reasoning was that if these novices who had practically no prior understanding of the process of therapy could be trained to identify accurately where individual clients were on the process continua (they could), and if these independent judges' ratings would correlate highly with one another (they did), then it could be demonstrated that this was a reliable way of measuring an individual's degree of psychological maturity.

Armed with these new tools for research on psychotherapy, plus many of those which had been longer established in the field, the Psychotherapy Research Group or the "Schiz Project," as it was often called, was able to proceed, gathering the data which would support or negate their hypotheses. Although there were several hypotheses stated by the research group, these narrowed down to the interrelationships among three major variables: *therapist conditions* (congruence, empathy, and unconditional positive regard), *process level and movement* (on the seven-stage process scale), and *outcomes* of therapy. The latter was determined on the basis of traditional psychological tests, evaluations by ward personnel, release from the hospital, and the like. Essentially the combined hypotheses were: the greater the therapist conditions in therapy, the greater would be the client's movement along the process scale, and the greater the movement on the process scale the greater would be the positive outcomes of therapy; and these differences would be greater in the therapy group than in the control group.

Were the hypotheses confirmed by the mountains of data gathered—the storeroom bulging with hundreds of taped interviews, the volumes of transcribed interviews, test results and analyses, the scores of research reports written? As early as 1958, when Rogers began to describe their research study at professional meetings, many segments of the psychotherapeutic community eagerly awaited the results. Their curiosity, however, was not to be satisfied fully for nine more years, in 1967, when *The Therapeutic Relationship and Its Impact: A Study of Psychotherapy with Schizophrenics,* "edited by Carl R. Rogers with the collaboration of Eugene T. Gendlin, Donald J. Kiesler and Charles B. Truax," was published by the University of Wisconsin Press. The long interim was a time of frequent stress, conflict, and crisis, at times so serious that the research project was almost terminated, numerous legal suits were threatened, and the book's publication was jeopardized.

The Conflict in Wisconsin

Some of the major protagonists in the long, agonizing story were presented by Rogers in his introduction to their 625-page volume: "Though the many individuals who shared in this enterprise are named in a separate section, I would like to mention several whose leadership was especially significant in making the program what it is. Dr. Eugene T. Gendlin initiated the program, with all of the detailed arrangements which that implies, and has contributed a basic theoretical formulation upon which a number of our process measures have been built. Dr. Charles B. Truax organized the initial data collection and analysis. The ratings on which his studies were based mysteriously disappeared and have not been recovered. This unfortunate fact made Dr. Truax's preliminary reports unusable in this book. Dr. Donald J. Kiesler gave leadership to the rerating and re-analysis of all the data, and has shown a high degree of determination, efficiency, and research competence in carrying through this task."[25]

In Rogers' own opinion, the problem began when he failed to take the time and care needed to allow the Psychotherapy Research Group to become a truly group-centered, self-directing group.[26] He had accomplished this at Chicago, but, being occupied with many other projects, long speaking trips and visiting professorships, he did not give group-centered team building the necessary attention at Wisconsin. The trouble surfaced during his long absence from Wisconsin in the summer of 1962 through the spring of 1963, when Rogers spent a year as a Fellow at the Center for Advanced Study in the Behavioral Sciences at Stanford. Rogers began to receive letters from many different members of the project that one person in the research group, Charles ("Charlie") Truax, was attempting to subvert the project toward his own ends. First they claimed that he had refused to give them access to the project data on which they could do their studies. Then it was said that someone had discovered in Truax's office a pile of manuscripts based on project data that contained Truax's individual copyright. Their conclusion was that he intended to use the entire project data to publish a work under his own name. To add insult to injury, they said, he even had used the title that everyone expected would appear on their joint publication.[27]

As it turned out, Truax was scheduled to be in California shortly, and Rogers arranged a meeting with him. He assured Rogers that the rumors were false, that several misunderstandings had contributed to them, and that it could all be worked out when Rogers returned to Madison. Meanwhile most of the Project staff in Madison was clamoring for his dismissal for unethical behavior. Rogers took the slower course of trying to go through channels to bring pressure to bear upon him to release the data that was in his control, which he had by now removed to his own home. When pressure by the University finally was put upon him to release the data, the boom fell. He called the police to declare that the project data had been stolen. The materials were never found, nor was any clear evidence uncovered as to what happened to it.

When Rogers heard the latest episode, he decided to act, but again chose a slower course than many of the Project staff were urging him to take. In a letter to Donald Kiesler and Philippa Mathieu he admitted, "Yes, I am probably slow in taking such actions. It takes a long time to convince me that a person is intentionally unethical, and intentionally destructive ..."[28]

Some may be inclined to react, "Aha, that's where his optimistic picture of human nature got him." A student close to Rogers at the time saw it somewhat differently. "Sure, Rogers' trusting nature gets him into trouble sometimes. But hundreds of times it's worked, and think of the added benefits he's gotten from all *those* relationships."[29]

At any rate, the time lapse had given Truax the chance to contact other forces in the University who disliked Rogers and to build his own support base. He also threatened the University with a lawsuit if they attempted to dismiss him from the project. The Rogers group could not muster the support it needed to take the action they wanted. Moreover, Rogers didn't want their scientific endeavor to be associated with scandal and controversy. He resigned himself to Truax's remaining with the project. Later he wrote that "one of my serious mistakes was not firing Charlie immediately. By the time that I was really convinced that he was a scoundrel and presented the case against him through the Psychiatric Institute and stated my determination to fire him, they not only would not concur in the action but would not even permit me to take the action, which was a very humiliating situation."[30]

Then began the long period of painstaking re-analysis of all the data upon which scores of studies had already been based. New judges had to be trained to listen to the recorded interviews, new data had to be obtained from the hundreds of test instruments the patients and therapists had taken, new statistical operations were required to analyze all this data. Donald Kiesler and Philippa Mathieu, with the help of Marjorie Klein, eventually completed the task and wrote up the results in several chapters in the "Schiz book."[31]

But this solution to the stolen data presented still a new set of problems. Having to redo a major part of the research created an entirely new staffing hierarchy in the leadership of the project. It also meant that the original contributions anticipated from the various project leaders would not be fulfilled and other individuals would be making contributions which were much greater than had been expected. Therefore the question of credit and authorship for the book increasingly became a major issue. Rogers, Gendlin, and Kiesler felt that Truax should no longer be one of the major editors. Rogers, however, believed that they were bound by a prior written agreement which said that Rogers, Gendlin, Kiesler, *and* Truax would be the editors, and that they would be likely to have a lawsuit on their hands if they attempted to do otherwise. This created bad feelings from Gendlin and Kiesler, who believed that Rogers should take a stand on having only three editors, lawsuit or not. To further complicate matters, Gendlin felt strongly that Philippa Mathieu should be added to the list of editors because of all the work she had done in redoing the data collection and analysis. Mathieu agreed, but did not feel strongly about this and never complained to Rogers; but Gendlin thought she was being taken advantage of. Kiesler, on the other hand, was equally adamant that Mathieu should *not* be an editor, that she was given ample credit throughout the book, and that four editors was one too many already, let alone adding a fifth. By this time Rogers had left Wisconsin and was living in California permanently, Kiesler had moved to the University of Iowa, Gendlin was at the University of Chicago, and the publisher, the University of Wisconsin Press, was in Madison. Resolving the problem through letters proved to be an impossible task. Letters would cross in the mail; misunderstandings occurred; a long silence by Gendlin was interpreted by Rogers as agreement, only to be followed months later by Gendlin's informing them that he was still not satisfied and they could not use his chapters in the book until he *was* satisfied. Instead of improving, the situation deteriorated. Dozens of letters and many angry words went back and forth.

In 1966, in August, Kiesler wrote to Rogers and Gendlin:

> Our basic problem, as I see it, is that good men sometimes castrate themselves by not acting at the proper time. I don't think Carl acted (he should have immediately fired Charlie, and denounced him to NIMH): Gene had a lawyer, but didn't use him. Now, Gene has to stand for something, so he is backing us toward the precipice. But his stand is at the wrong time and for the wrong reason. But it makes him feel better, because he knows he didn't act when he should have. [Then, after another two pages of analysis:] So my proposed strategy: If this letter leaves Gene unshaken then nothing will budge him. But neither will I budge, because my appropriate time to act is now. This is my moment—and unlike both of you I will not

compromise a position I feel is just. If I did, I would later, like Gene, have to do something impulsive to prove that I'm still in possession of integrity. And, like Gene, it would probably involve the wrong target and certainly the wrong time ... So I say, if Gene does not budge, then we're finished—unless you Carl, agree to remove his name and chapters from the book.[32]

The same month, on the very official-looking legal stationery of Kirkland, Ellis, Hodson, Chaffetz and Masters of Prudential Plaza in Chicago, Gendlin's lawyer wrote Rogers a strong letter indicating that "our client may be irreparably damaged (1) if the work is published without identification of Dr. Gendlin's role, or (2) if the work is published with an identification of Dr. Gendlin's role that has not been approved by him." But "in an effort to bring the current dispute to a quick and amicable settlement," the addition of Mathieu's name as editor, and a few related, minor changes, would suffice.[33]

Rogers immediately wrote Kiesler, asking for his reaction to Gendlin's lawyer, and Kiesler quickly replied,

> You're squirming, sliding, and slipping again ... your letter of August 29 is completely inappropriate ... I gave you my decision ... If the authorship is changed from its present format without my approval, then I'll have to get in this legal act ... I've completed my job for you, and in case you've forgotten, very efficiently and competently with much sweat ... Don't look to me for any more creative solutions. This is your baby. And realize that I want this book to come out since I think it's a good contribution. But I will not let it come out, *ever,* if you change your stand on the *four* major authors.[34]

This was one of the most "unsuccessful" episodes in Rogers' career. It took his colleague Eugene Gendlin years to forgive him.[35] Rogers' successes were so frequent and varied many view him as some kind of archetypal, benign father figure, all-knowing and wholly consistent. To view him at a time when he was most fallible presents a different perspective. His final letter in this exchange shows a very real human being, with strengths and weaknesses combined.

> Dear Gene and Don:
> ... Now that the deadlock between the two of you is absolute and complete, I will wait a while until I have cooled off and then I will make my decision as to what the spine, the cover, the title page, and the author list will be. I am in no hurry to make that decision but I will let you know when I do make it. I can assure you that I will try to take into account every factor and will make the fairest decision I can, but I will make it.
> I probably would be able to make the decision in such a way that I would then be sued by all of you—Gene, Don, and Charlie. This will give me all the

joys of triple litigation to which, of course, I look forward with enormous pleasure and anticipation. I can't quite wait to see the judge's face when he realizes that you have been irreparably damaged in your personal lives and professional careers by: having had included in the book all of the chapters which you have submitted for it and having been given full opportunity for editing those chapters in the way that you see fit; when your names are prominently displayed as major authors and full and explicit credit has been given you, not only on the author's page but in the acknowledgements and introduction; when the important parts you have played in the research have been fully explicated and commended. He may be a bit baffled to realize that the damage you have suffered is because the name of one person, whom we all sincerely agree should be given special credit, appears in type which is either too large or too small, which is either above or below a certain line, which either appears on one page or two or on the cover also. I am sure he will be sympathetic in realizing that this has cast a black shadow over your total career.

I am also sure that the judge can do nothing but rule in your favor when he realizes how righteous you both are. It makes me regret that one of the scales we never developed was one for self-righteousness. The correspondence we have had on this topic of authorship could then be submitted to a group of bright undergraduates for a "blind" rating as to who is the most righteous of the three—Charlie, Gene, or Don. I had always thought Charlie would win hands down, but I have had increasing doubts. I seem to be the only one who has made mistakes, but since those are glaringly evident to both of you I do not need to go into them.

I guess the above gets rid of some of the bitterness that I feel about all of this. I have tried to hold it back in recent months, hoping against hope that some amicable decision could be reached. I feel I have failed at this for the same reason that I have failed with Charlie. I really don't know how to deal with people who never in their lives have made a mistake, and whose every action and impulse has been perfectly right. It must be very pleasant to live in such a world. Some people feel that this is a very childish and immature world but, of course, you two know that it is not.

I also think of, and this is not intended as a criticism, but just as a fact of life, my enormous depression when I first read some of Don's chapters. They were so dull! Some people here who had been reading the manuscript with interest waded part way into Don's chapters and then quit in despair. I know Gene has never read them, because he made suggestions about Chapter 5, which were absolutely contradicted by Don's chapters. My own optimistic estimate is that out of every million people who might hear of the book, possibly 500 might buy it or start to read it, and five would complete the reading of Don's chapters. I hope I am wrong but only time can tell.

Well, I see the bitterness is still coming out. Let me try to express some of the other feelings which are mingled with it. I think back to the day when I felt so gleeful because Gene had agreed to come and initiate the project and I knew he had the skills and aptitudes which would make that possible where I did not. I felt then and feel now enormous gratitude that he was willing to undertake that task and for all that he has done since to carry the project through. I think of the great satisfaction I felt when Don agreed to take the responsibility for trying to redo the research which Charlie had made such a mess of, a mess which I handled rather poorly at 2,500 miles distance. In spite of what I have said above about the dullness, I do appreciate the incredible amount of effort which Don, Philippa, and Marge put into the production of those chapters and I sincerely hope that some readers will appreciate their dedicated thoroughness.

I guess that lets you know where I stand as of this moment. Sincerely, Carl.[36]

Rogers, recognizing the strength of his feelings and giving expression to them, drew an instant reaction from Kiesler, who wrote:

Dear Leader:

Congratulations! For the first time I've known you you've decided explicitly to make a decision despite the group! Usually, you've been able to seduce the group to your decision anyway. It's beautiful to see the group process in action—when the individual Experiencings are merged into one big, absolute Experiencing in the sky, with the great White Father presiding. Congratulations, again! For the first time you are being congruent in our interaction. That dull, righteous Kiesler! In the moment of truth, the great White Father is able to say to himself "Piss on Unconditional Positive Regard! That Kiesler is a pain in the ass!"

At last, you are talking like a Leader. And rightly so! It really is your baby, Carl. You have to resolve this mess all by yourself. I'm so excited by the newly emergent Rogers that I am willing to say: "OK, Carl. I'll go along with whatever you decide! I withdraw all threats of legal counteraction. You have my proxy!" I say this fully aware that it is likely you will now take the course of least resistance and simply do whatever Gene wants. But, that's up to you. I'll sit back and watch what ensues. I support your stand fully. It's the only way out of the predicament. But I wanted, for once, to hear you admit that that's what has to be done. Righteously and dully, Don …

P.S. Would you add a simple sentence in the Introduction asking the five people who read Kiesler's chapter to contact him so he can send "Thank you" cards?[37]

The "Schiz Project" Results

The actual solution seems anticlimactic compared to the agonizing three-and-a-half year process which preceded it. The editorship/authorship was listed as Rogers, Gendlin, Kiesler, and Truax, as originally agreed, and special credit and recognition were given to Philippa Mathieu in several ways and places throughout the book. No one sued anyone. Unfortunately the book's publication was anticlimactic also. If the psychological and psychiatric community had once been waiting expectantly for the results of the Psychotherapy Research Project, by now most people had forgotten about it. The book eventually sold out its first printing, and the publisher decided not to reprint it since the demand was so small.

The final anticlimax was the results of the research. These were mixed, with some of the hypotheses supported and some of them unsupported by the data, and with some new insights emerging that were not directly connected to the hypotheses.

On the whole there were no significant differences between the therapy group and the control group as to process movement in therapy, and only some small positive differences as to outcomes of therapy. This, of course, could be explained in several ways: The control group in the hospital was getting excellent therapeutic treatment also; the number of patients in the study was too small to show statistical significance, and some of the data could not be used. For example, the hospitalized patient who made the most progress had been released from the hospital and refused to take the final battery of tests, meaning his data could not be used. Rogers spoke with this man, his former client "Mr. Vac" (a.k.a. Jim Brown), and could have convinced him to take the tests. But, as Rogers remembered, "I didn't have the heart." The man told him, "I refused to take them. I'm free of that stuff. I don't want to be reminded of my experience in the hospital." Rogers recalled, "Well, that was a tragedy as far as the research was concerned but an enormous triumph as far as his development was concerned. If he had taken the test, I'm sure it would have changed the results of the research; there was a small enough number of clients in the research that one extreme success like that would have weighted the results."[38] This research was the major focus of Rogers' career at that point. Surely he could have rationalized how his client's participation would not be harmful to him but would help others. Instead he put what he perceived to be his client's interest above his own. Consequently Rogers and the others were disappointed not to see a greater difference between the therapy and control groups.

When the overall data were examined more closely, however, some positive and important findings were apparent. For the most part, high therapist conditions of congruence and empathy *did* correlate with successful outcomes of therapy. The results even showed that where these conditions were low, patients deteriorated—a new and sobering finding indeed. These results gave solid support to Rogers' basic theory. (They were confirmed by a follow-up study by Truax and Mitchell conducted nine years later.[39])

The results having to do with the scale of process in therapy were also mixed. The findings showed that therapist conditions did not correlate with movement along the process scale, but that movement along the process scale did correlate with successful outcomes in therapy. There was also a positive correlation between therapist conditions and process *level,* rather than movement. Although it could not be interpreted with certainty whether the therapist conditions allowed the client to begin therapy at a higher level of process or whether the clients who began at a higher process level tended to elicit higher conditions from their therapist, the concept of process level seemed to offer new possibilities for research.

In many ways the "Schiz book" was a significant contribution. Both the positive and negative findings added something to the body of knowledge about therapy with schizophrenics. But perhaps more importantly, the book suggested many new avenues of research. The explication of the research design, along with appendices which included several of the new scales developed by Truax, Kiesler, and others, would enable other researchers to build upon their techniques and findings. It was a real advance in psychotherapy process research. Excellent chapters by Gendlin on clinical techniques for working with schizophrenics and by Rogers on the significance of this research provided informative, non-esoteric reading. A daring example of openness in research was provided by the team asking an independent group of experts to listen to some of their session transcripts and contribute their observations to the published volume. The reactions of the "commentators"—Paul Bergman, O. Spurgeon English, William Lewis, Rollo May, Julius Seeman, and Carl Whitaker, half Ph.D.s, half M.D.s—raised provocative questions for the client-centered therapists, including their observation that the process seemed to discourage patients from expressing negative, hostile or aggressive feelings and that the therapists seemed to be controlling their own feelings as well.[40] The book deserved a serious and thoughtful discussion by the field.

But it didn't get one. The long delay in publication and the lack of consistent, dramatic results gave this book a very different reception from that which Rogers and Dymond's earlier research volume *Psychotherapy and Personality Change* had received in 1954. While the excitement over the earlier work was widespread, the "Schiz book" made a relatively small impression in the psychological–psychiatric community. To a large extent this explains why this period of Rogers' career is not very well known to the interested public. His major endeavor of the six-year period turned out to be a mixed success, fraught with major disappointments and conflicts. It reached publication years later than intended, and then, as he had predicted, was read by only a relative handful of individuals.

Relationships in Wisconsin

As usual, Rogers' relationships with his graduate students were very satisfying during his stay at Wisconsin. Gene Bleeker, a student and rater on the Schiz Project, recalled how Rogers was a "keen, keen listener. I have not met many people in my life that have the intensity of concentration that he does when he is focusing in on what someone else is trying to say. He listens in his total body, not just his ears, and his whole presence and being is focused in on me when I'm talking to him and that's communicated ... I just sense that here is an individual who is really striving to hear and to understand what I'm trying to say." [41]

Such impressions of Rogers' empathy, and of his positive regard and consideration, remained common among his students and others at Wisconsin. But, unlike previous periods in his life, now people also began to notice and be impressed by his congruence. Allen Bergin remembered a small, weekly postdoctoral seminar he participated in at the University of Wisconsin in 1960–61 that included ten psychiatric residents and two postdoctoral psychology fellows. "I tended to talk quite a bit and maybe show off my Stanford training a little. At one point, Carl essentially told me in very definite terms to 'be quiet.' I was shocked by such behavior coming from this father of nondirectivism. I was further amazed afterwards, as he was giving me a ride home, when he said: 'I'm sorry I had to tell you to shut up in there, but if you ever dominate the discussion like that again, I'll do it again.' I have never forgotten since then that having warmth and empathy does not mean being weak." [42]

Another student, Doug Schoeninger, invited Rogers to visit a seminar of students who were meeting at the Lutheran Center to discuss philosophy, science, religion, and values. Schoeninger hemmed and hawed and, in effect, said, "I want you to come but I really hesitate to ask you because I know you're busy." He remembered Rogers breaking in and saying, "Well, damn it. I can make up my own mind. If you want me to come, you ask me, and if I don't have the time, I'll tell you I don't have the time. Don't protect me." [43] Gene Bleeker also recalled Rogers' congruence. "He's obvious glad to see me and enjoys my presence, and when he doesn't, he lets me know *that*, in a non-cutting sort of way." [44]

His congruence was not as well received by some of his colleagues at Wisconsin. Although Rogers enjoyed positive relationships with some colleagues and administrators, once again his conflicts with other members of the faculty and University administration proved to be a source of tension and disappointment, just as at Ohio State and at the University of Chicago. Was this a coincidence, or was it a pattern that reveals another side of the personal and professional Carl Rogers?

A person with new ideas will always be threatening to some people, especially when the innovative person is attracting others to his position or, in a university, attracting doctoral students away from other professors. This explains much of the resistance Rogers and his work encountered throughout his career—Rogers' work truly *was* threatening to the status quo. The medical establishment bitterly opposed counselors and psychotherapists encroaching upon their territory. Many counselors and psychotherapists opposed nondirective and then client-centered counseling and psychotherapy. And, as Rogers began applying his ideas to other fields, individuals in education, management, the ministry and other areas would strenuously oppose his influence.

Nevertheless, the person with new ideas still has many options as to how he or she will behave within a given institution. In a university, some professors, particularly young ones, are intimidated by others in their department or by the administration, and give up some of their more controversial or non-conforming ideas or projects. Gradually they drift toward the norms within their group and refrain from making or suggesting changes which would be likely to incur disfavor from the rest of the group. Rogers clearly was not of this type. He always acted on his beliefs, often quite stubbornly and tenaciously. If anything, this quality intensified rather than mellowed with age. The greater his reputation, the more he could afford to go his own way, either because he had more power or, as at Chicago and Wisconsin, he was tolerated more readily. Settling for less than his bottom line was hardly his way.

Other innovative professors go about their business, influencing their classes, graduate students, and whichever colleagues are interested, but do not attempt to change things throughout the department or college or university. This was not Rogers' way either. Partly because he always rebelled against procedures that seemed ineffective and partly because he resented some of the things being done to his own graduate students, he would make it his business to try and change student selection procedures, curricula and course requirements, examination and grading systems, and practicum and supervision procedures.

Given the desire to change such departmental or university practices, others go through channels or use planned, strategic methods to reform their institutions. They proceed carefully, patiently, fully cognizant of where the power in the institution resides and what consequences each of their actions will have throughout the structure. Again, Rogers did not tend to operate in this manner. If he did, he probably would never have come to Wisconsin in the first place, realizing that just because several faculty and administrators were urging him to come and convinced others to go along, this did not mean he would automatically have the flexibility he wanted when he got there or that a majority of colleagues in the Psychology or Psychiatry Departments would be receptive to his ideas. He was a scientist and a therapist and, increasingly, a thinker and writer about many issues, including interpersonal communication. But he was not an organizational man or a politician. Wisconsin student and project member Doug Schoeninger thought Rogers had been naïve for not recognizing how Truax was forming alliances elsewhere in the University to isolate Rogers and his research project.[45]

(Years later, when Rogers was connected with the Center for Studies of the Person in California, he would proudly call CSP a "non-organization.")

It was not that Rogers was incapable of diplomatic, political behavior. He had demonstrated this in bringing together two major branches of the psychology profession in the 1940s, in the many offices he was elected to in the social work and psychology profession, and in initiating and heading a joint committee of the Wisconsin Psychiatric Association and the Wisconsin Psychological Association in 1959 that "gradually diffused an incipient legal and legislative battle which was splitting the two professions in that state."[46] For a time he tried to work through channels to bring about change in Wisconsin, as illustrated by an example he related many years later.

> … fairly early in the game, I felt that one thing I could contribute there would be to unify the training of psychiatrists, clinical psychologists and social workers. They all eventually did much the same thing in one aspect of their work. I received some approval from the chairman of the Department of Psychiatry and real approval from the chairman of the Social Work Department, who worked with me to create a plan for an extended first course of training in interviewing, counseling, and therapy, but, to put it in the most general terms, it would be first and foremost a course on how to deal with human beings in a helpful manner. We worked it out quite carefully and presented the plan to all three departments, but all three departments voted it down.[47]

At that point he gave up, at least on this initiative. At Ohio, Chicago and Wisconsin, it appeared he had neither the patience nor the inclination to continually attend to the institutional politics, to find the politically effective route, to follow all the steps necessary to effect long-term institutional change.

Rather Rogers' preferred style of organizational change was what I would call "direct communication," with his favorite tool being the letter or memorandum. We saw examples of this in his Chicago period. When he was displeased (or pleased) about something, he wrote a letter to the particular individual or group and said just what was on his mind. For example, a year-and-a-half after coming to Wisconsin, he wrote a four-page memorandum to the Psychology Faculty critiquing the program's first year of graduate training in psychology, particularly their first year "Proseminar" used in part to screen out weaker students, their emphasis on methodology over creativity, and the "rigidity of the department in applying rules and regulations at both the undergraduate and graduate levels."[48] He offered seven "tentative suggestions" for changes to the program.

Perhaps this direct style of communication reflected his growing desire to be congruent. Perhaps on a more fundamental level it reflected his life-long need to connect with people, to know and be known by others (although it may also have reflected his shyness that he would so often do it by letter rather than in person). His direct communication approach must have also demonstrated his belief in the importance and ultimate triumph of open, honest communication, the assumption or hope that others would at least be open to receive his forthright communication, that they would respond with honest communication of their own, and that together the parties would work the matter through to a successful conclusion. That it often did not work out that way in institutional, political settings seems not to have discouraged him from trying again.

So when little changed in the four years after he wrote the previous memorandum, he then wrote a longer memo, picking up the themes he had addressed earlier. This lengthy memorandum exemplifies his direct communication mode and gives a very good picture of the situation in which he saw himself in Madison, as of January 1, 1963.

MEMORANDUM
TO: The Executive Committee and the Faculty of the Department of Psychology, University of Wisconsin
FROM: Carl R. Rogers
RE: The possibility of dissociating myself from the Department

As a number of you know, I have become increasingly doubtful during the past couple of years that it would ever be possible for me to work out a suitable pattern for my own activities within the Department, in view of the Department's fixed policies and philosophy. For this reason, I am seriously considering separating myself from the Department. I would like the Executive Committee and the faculty to know this and to know something of my views before I make any definite decision.

I think that my past history shows that I can tolerate a large degree of difference between my own views and the views of the department or organization with which I work. I have gradually realized, however, that there is a limit in the degree to which differences can be tolerated. I would like to set down some of the aspects of the Department and its policies with which I feel myself in great and deep disagreement.

1. The Policy and Philosophy of Graduate Education

The Department is deeply dedicated to what seems to me to be a self-defeating philosophy and policy of graduate education. Most of you know my views on this, but I would like to give the picture of the situation as I see it, outlining very briefly the policies which are current.

a. We devote considerable time and energy to selecting the best possible graduate students out of the many who apply.

b. In a variety of ways we manage to create a climate which tends to keep them threatened from the day that they arrive. This climate, which tends to persist, is composed largely of ambiguous threats which cannot be clearly faced by the student.

c. We devise an examination system which for several years keeps students continually thinking of the possibility of failure rather than innovating ideas for their own research.

d. In the training of these graduate students, we spend an inordinate amount of time on the statistics and methodology of research and on inculcating a mindset of hypercritical attitudes, both of which constitute further insurance that no significantly original ideas will develop.

e. During their graduate years we threaten our students enough, fail them enough, discourage them enough, so that only about one out of five or six of these carefully selected students obtains a Ph.D. Not all of those who leave are flunked out. Some of them leave in protest against the sterility of the curriculum, others because they cannot stand the general Departmental climate, which they feel is characterized by such phrases as "the student be damned," "shape up or ship out," "education consists of threats and punishment."

f. We congratulate ourselves that, since only one out of five or six achieves a doctoral degree, this proves that we have high standards. By this same token, Harvard Medical School, which only fails 1% per year, is obviously a school of low standards.

g. We ignore the fact that our educational policies with our graduate students run directly counter to the best research on learning and creativity. We ignore the fact that our policies also run counter to the ideal program of graduate education proposed by a carefully selected committee of scholars, of which one of our own group (Harlow) was a member.

h. The few Ph.D.s we turn out are so orthodox and conventional that they are acceptable to any other equally orthodox department. We look upon this as further evidence that we are doing a good job.

i. We seem quite satisfied with our graduate program and, with few exceptions, have little desire to re-examine what we are doing. That students regard the program as punitive, as lacking in venturesome honesty and intellectual excitement, and deficient in good faculty–student relationships, gives us almost no concern. The fact that many other psychologists regard the Department as one of the most tradition-bound in the country is likewise of little or no concern. We are, it seems to me, very comfortably smug.

… I am also deeply impressed by the fact that the more small changes we painfully achieve, the more the situation remains fundamentally the same, because the attitudes seem to be unchanged. I want to speak of this a bit more fully …[49]

And he did, for three-and-a-half more single-spaced pages. Unfortunately Rogers' direct communications like this rarely elicited responses in kind, especially when written from a distance of over two thousand miles, from California. On another occasion, when he sent a memorandum to several members of the Psychiatry

Department, inviting them to meet to discuss policy matters, one department member replied, "I am not aware that the Department has empowered you to call committee meetings." At any rate his memoranda did serve to make his positions clear. When he saw that his latest attempts were having little or no impact, he wrote, on May 8, 1963, another memorandum, this time, "Re: My resignation from the Department."[50] Although he resigned from the Psychology Department, he continued to work with the Wisconsin Psychiatric Institute, at least for a while, pursuing his research interests there and helping young staff members plan research and obtain funding.[51]

Personal Life, Professional Travel

For all the negative experiences Rogers was having in connection with the research project and the University during his stay in Wisconsin, his extracurricular life was entirely different, with many professional successes and personal pleasures.

A major joy to the Rogers was their new home, of which Helen wrote: "When we moved to Madison, Wisconsin, in 1957, and found a beautiful home on Lake Monona I felt my 'cup runneth over.' This was surely a spot in which I could spend the rest of my days."[52] This was the lake to which Carl took Helen on picnics as university students some 35 years earlier. Now they had a spacious home, set on an acre of land with a large lawn running down to the lake. Although only about a five-minute drive from the University, it was a country setting. Here the Rogers did a considerable amount of entertaining. A former colleague of Rogers' from his Rochester years, Louise Johnson, remembered spending the weekend at the Rogers' home. "I was impressed with the telephone calls from former students and the dropping in for a social call by two former students who were passing through on vacation, one bringing his wife and children. From the conversations I could sense the warmth of the friendly relationship which existed between the man and those whose lives he had touched and the high regard and affection felt for him."[53]

Helen liked the life in Madison much more than in Chicago. She developed more of her own friends and found social norms much more relaxed and free of strict protocol. For both, their home on the lake was their favorite of all the houses and settings they had lived in, and for a while it seemed likely that this is where they would spend the rest of their lives. They liked it so much that when a developer threatened to buy some adjoining acres and squeeze as many houses as possible onto the land, Carl and Helen were so threatened that their quiet setting would become noisy and cluttered, that they bought the adjoining property themselves and resold it in larger lots, at some financial loss.[54]

Another of Carl and Helen's continuing pleasures was their winter vacations to warmer climes. In previous years they had often stopped at David's and Natalie's homes in New York and Boston on their way to or from their destination. Now they often invited David or Natalie's families to join *them* for part of their annual Caribbean vacations. They also visited David and Corky and the grandchildren at Seneca Lake, New York, at the cabin Carl had built a quarter century earlier, and visited Natalie and Larry and the grandchildren in Hawaii where they lived for two years when Larry was head of the Peace Corps in the Philippines. In 1961 they spent their Christmas in Nashville, where David was now Professor and Chairman of the Department of Medicine at Vanderbilt University Medical School and Physician-in-Chief at Vanderbilt University Hospital.

During his father's Wisconsin years, David had had another fifty or more scientific papers published in medical journals and had became a nationally recognized leader in the field of bacterial diseases, especially staphylococci. In 1961 he was voted one of the Ten Outstanding Young Men of the Year by the United States Junior Chamber of Commerce. About the same time, in the early years of the modern civil rights movement, he was taking considerable risks in promoting racial integration at Vanderbilt. David felt that he learned a lot from his father that helped him in his role as medical administrator and teacher. As he later told an interviewer, "Some of Dad's skills rubbed off … I sometimes play the counselor's role. I'm much more comfortable with the human side of medicine. As a teacher of medicine, I will show students that I care, that I'm vulnerable, that I don't know, that I'm congruent."[55]

In the late fifties and sixties, Natalie and Larry Fuchs were living in the Boston area where Larry was a faculty member at Brandeis University. Meeting Abraham Maslow at a social occasion in 1956, he suggested that Natalie enter their graduate psychology department. So with three young children, Natalie returned to her interest in psychology, working on her Masters degree one course at a time. She recalled how, "With Abe Maslow as my mentor and thesis advisor, my interest in combining my experience in client-centered therapy and creativity got the green light. Abe was particularly interested in the creative, self-actualizing person. He encouraged me to design a research project that would be fun and creative. He understood the importance of phenomenological research … I wrote my master's thesis, 'The Play Therapist's Approach to the Creative Art Experience,' using information and examples I gleaned during an outdoor class I set up for children, including my own, in our own back yard."[56]

Natalie remembered that when the family would get together, Carl and Helen would "focus more on the adults than on the kids. With the chaos and a lot going on at once, they get confused and don't know how to relate to it."[57] When they would be with one grandchild at a time, however, they were able to communicate and relate much more effectively. Carl also liked doing active sports and projects with his grandchildren. Living right on Lake Monona, the Rogers had a speedboat, and Carl liked to tow the grandchildren on water skis. Natalie's daughters remembered how he would take them snorkeling. They also remembered with delight the bar and refrigerator Rogers had in their basement, which the girls would play with, on, and around, whenever they came to visit.[58] In 1963, wrote Rogers, "We had a fine Thanksgiving family reunion with Dave and Corky, Nat and Larry, and our six active grandchildren. Because of the youngsters it was a very active weekend. We played touch football. There was a continuous ping-pong tournament going on in which fortunes waxed and waned. We went on a moderately successful search for Indian arrowheads. We enjoyed a delightful Thanksgiving and good conversation with all our family. My sister from Florida was also present and we enjoyed having her there."[59]

In addition to their usual winter vacations the Rogers spent a great deal of time away from home on various professional trips. A look at some of the major addresses and workshops he gave from January to August 1958 gives a good indication of the range of topics and travel resulting from his stature in the helping professions. In January he spoke to the Minnesota Counselors Association. In February he was a leader in a three-day conference for educators at Goddard College in Vermont[60] and a participant in a three-day symposium on psychotherapy with schizophrenics in Louisiana.[61] (Carl and Helen enjoyed Mardi Gras in New Orleans that year.) In March he spoke to the psychology staff at Manteno State Hospital in Illinois on research in psychotherapy. In April, in St. Louis, he lectured to the American Personnel and Guidance Association on "The Characteristics of a Helping Relationship"[62] and, in Washington, D.C., to the American Psychological Association on "Research in Psychotherapy."[63] In May, on the topic of psychotherapy, he conducted a two-day seminar for the Department of Psychology at the University of Rochester in New York and gave two lectures at the University of Chicago. In the summer he gave a four-week seminar at Brandeis University in Massachusetts (where they spent extended time with Natalie, Larry and the grandchildren), and in August was a co-leader of a five-day workshop on group leadership in Ojai Valley, California. This list does not include several minor addresses or any of the lectures or consulting he did during that period in his own state of Wisconsin or in the University community.[64]

Rogers' reputation was such that he received, in addition, a good many invitations for visiting professorships or other commitments that required a major period of time away from home. During his stay at Wisconsin he accepted two of these invitations.

The first spanned the summer of 1961, beginning with a two-week Pacific voyage to Hong Kong and Japan.[65] It resulted from the efforts of Logan Fox, a former student of Rogers' who was a professor at Ibaraki Christian College and had been instrumental in spreading client-centered therapy in Japan. Since 1955 Fox and several Japanese colleagues had been conducting workshops in client-centered therapy in several parts of that country. In a culture that had traditionally suppressed feelings in favor of outward form, Rogers' ideas and methods had been gaining surprising interest and acceptance. The incredible cultural revolution that Japan underwent after the war apparently had created enormous tensions, with many people caught in the transition between a traditional and modern culture and lifestyle. As one Japanese counselor summed up Rogers' importance to him, it was "to teach me the basic way of becoming to be democratic and not authoritative."[66] By 1961 Fox and his colleagues thought that the counseling movement in their country had a sufficient foundation that a visit from Rogers would be particularly timely and would spur on the client-centered movement considerably. After obtaining his agreement, they began setting up an extremely full schedule of speeches and workshops for Rogers, both to give him as much impact as possible and to raise the money for the trip.

With barely a few days' rest during the six-week visit, Rogers did everything from presenting forty-five-minute speeches to conducting five-day workshops with groups as varied as: 150 clinical psychologists and educators in Kyoto; a conference of school and college counselors in Kyoto; the Osaka Mental Health Association; the Japan Industrial Training Association in Tokyo; the Tokyo University Child Guidance Group; a conference of the Christian Education Association in Gotemba; a group of parole, probation, and institutional workers and psychiatrists sponsored by the Japanese Ministry of Justice; the Social Psychologists' Association in Tokyo; and other comparable groups. It was hard for Fox to say no to groups who wanted to hear Rogers. Consequently the pace was really too much for Carl and Helen and it took a great deal of the enjoyment out of the trip. On one occasion, when Rogers was complaining about having to give another presentation, he said to Fox, "Logan, the only thing that keeps me from complaining more is that you are working harder than I am."[67]

Fox served as Rogers' interpreter throughout the trip, and was often with Carl and Helen ten and twelve hours a day. There were two incidents that stood out most vividly in his mind which he described several years later in an introduction to the Japanese collection of Rogers' writings. "One experience drew me especially close to Rogers. For years I had idolized him and had tried so hard to be like him in my interpersonal relations. But I so often failed to be accepting of people and had often felt real guilt over my failures. But after about three days of the Kyoto workshop, one evening after a particularly trying day which had been dominated by some particularly irksome behavior from one of the leaders of the workshop, Rogers and I stood in the hotel lobby expressing our opinions about this man. I couldn't resist kidding Rogers about the unfriendly remarks we were both making, and said, 'But, Carl, we're not being very accepting of this man, are we?' He responded, 'What the hell, he's no client of mine.' And in that moment my god became human, years of guilty feelings dropped away, and I said to myself, 'It's going to be a good six weeks.'

"There was another memorable experience in Kyoto. Rogers had expressed an interest in Zen Buddhism, so a meeting with a well-known Zen Master

[Hisamatsu] was arranged. A small group was present for the occasion and interest ran high. Zen Masters are noted for their ability to get straight to the heart of any matter and Rogers was eager for a real person-to-person encounter. So he opened the discussion by saying, 'I have read the transcript of the discussion you had with Jung and I must say that I found myself disappointed, particularly with the rather abstract quality of the discussion.' At this the Master began an apology for the transcript, suggested that it was a poor translation, and stayed on the defensive for the rest of the discussion. We were never quite sure why it turned out as it did, but it certainly did not produce the kind of encounter we had hoped for."[68]

Helen had her own problems with their whirlwind tour of Japan. Traditionally women were subservient to men in the Orient. When Carl was occasionally invited to a dinner or reception, but she was not, this hurt her. Even more unpleasant were the Japanese reactions to her height. A tall, white-haired woman in a country of short, dark-haired people, she seemed to be an object of curiosity, comment, and even ridicule throughout the trip. People would stop, stare, point their fingers, make comments, giggle—all this right to her face. On one particularly painful occasion she had to wait forty-five minutes for a subway, and each time another train would empty its passengers on her platform all the passengers streaming out would see her, stop, and register their amazement. All she could do was stand there, hoping her train would come soon. Her impression and, to some extent, Carl's impression of Japan was colored negatively by these experiences. (He would return years later and have a much more positive impression.)

Nevertheless Rogers' influence in that country continued to spread, and within a few years, a Japanese publisher, Iwasaki Gakujyutsu Syuppansya (in English, Academic Press), brought out a seventeen-volume collection of Rogers' work, including numerous journal articles and unpublished writings that are relatively unknown in the United States.

The second occasion on which the Rogers spent an extended time away from Madison for professional reasons was during a nine-month period from August 1962 to June 1963, when Carl was a Fellow at the Center for Advanced Study in the Behavioral Sciences in Stanford, California. This privately funded group was well known for their practice of bringing together small groups of some of the best minds in the world and giving them a liberal living allowance and the freedom to spend a year doing anything they wished. The hope was that a cross-fertilization of ideas would take place that would enrich the work of each individual and the behavioral sciences as a whole. During Rogers' year in Stanford he came in contact with some outstanding individuals whose thinking he found stimulating and whose acquaintance he valued highly. Two, in particular, were Michael Polanyi and Erik Erikson.

Polanyi, the noted British philosopher of science,[69] was several years older than Rogers and seemed to have an encyclopedic knowledge of the history of philosophy and science and an ability to integrate his technical and philosophic knowledge in ways which greatly impressed Rogers, who later recalled, "I do stand somewhat in awe of a real scholar like that, even though on the other hand, I'm damned if I think that's the most productive approach to life. Michael is all intellect ... He devours ideas, and he's absolutely single track. If he was to talk to you, in three minutes he'd be around to your view of philosophy of science, and he'd be pumping you for whatever you might know ... or whatever his latest specific topic was ... But I do have a lot of respect for him. And I realize he sends us a Christmas card and I don't reciprocate. And I haven't sent him either of my last two books. I was thinking about this the other day. And it's because I think, 'Oh, hell, they're not scholarly enough for Michael to appreciate.' But I realize that why I was good for him was because I wasn't scholarly. I brought something else to it. He respected the fact that I brought to him practical experience in the world that sort of bolstered some of his views but was different from anything he could offer ... I really *should* send him copies of my books."[70]

He was right in his assessment of Polanyi's attitude toward him. When asked in 1971 for his personal reaction to and recollections of Rogers, he wrote of "... my internal struggle between my deep friendship curiously combined with a slight personal knowledge. The fact is I love Carl Rogers, but really know very little about his many years of decisively effective work. I love his temper[ment], so beneficent with the overhacked domain of modern mental efforts, but I really know only the way he thinks and helps by his purity. I think I disagree with its particulars, but this does not affect my joy of his person ... If you can find a place for a page, or half a page, which smilingly tells this affection for Rogers, I could try to say something of this kind. I would be embarrassed in trying this, but my affection for him might overcome this."[71]

Rogers, in turn, was very much influenced by Polanyi's thinking and, as a result, over the next several years, did much more thinking, speaking, and writing on the nature of science.

Erik Erikson was a noted psychoanalyst whose writings have been read widely by both professionals and laypersons.[72] Rogers felt "his very appearance is therapeutic ... He just does have an aura of being a good therapist. Both Helen and I liked him very much."[73] Erikson was also impressed by his contact with Rogers. After attending several sessions in which some of Rogers' tapes of therapy were played and discussed, Erikson commented, "Gosh, after listening to that, I feel like I'd like to go back to doing analyses." Rogers was quite certain the comment was meant favorably.[74] Rogers was also amazed to hear Erikson speaking very critically of the psychoanalytic establishment and told him these ideas were a breath of fresh air and he should publish his thoughts as they could be very influential in bringing about change. Erikson responded, "No, I couldn't. I grew up in Freud's household." Later Erikson sent Rogers a copy of his new book, which contained a chapter on "The First Psychoanalyst" and a handwritten note saying, "Carl: some reasons why. This is an address given at Freud's 100th birthday in the U of Heidelberg. Erik."[75]

Through contact with Erikson, Polanyi, historian of ideas Lancelot Whyte, future Nobel laureate physicist Richard Feynman, and other distinguished intellectuals and scientists, Rogers had a very stimulating year at the Center for Advanced Studies.[76]

On Becoming a Person

Another source of satisfaction for Rogers, which was some compensation for the unpleasant experiences at the University, was his writing. He continued to be prolific throughout the entire period, with many new articles appearing in journals or as book chapters each year. By far the most significant publication of this period came in 1961 with his seventh book, *On Becoming a Person*.

For several years he had contemplated pulling together many of his essays in book form. At one time this was to be a collection of essays on creativity. At another time he thought about a collection of more philosophical writings, applying insights from psychotherapy to many traditional philosophical questions. The book turned out to be both of these things and more. Over the years he had written a large number of essays both directly and indirectly related to psychotherapy. Collecting various articles, he found enough material for a substantial volume which included twenty-one essays—much more than the short collection of essays on creativity he had contemplated a few years earlier.

Rogers found the writing of *On Becoming a Person* to be easier and more enjoyable than any of his previous books. The volume practically wrote itself, taking about three weeks' work on Rogers' part, and this under the most ideal conditions. Since it was a collection of essays, it required little original writing. What was required was choosing the essays, organizing them under appropriate headings, writing introductions to them, and doing whatever rewriting was needed to eliminate much of the repetition. The bulk of this was done on a three-week retreat Carl and Helen took near Estes Park, Colorado, from August 19 to September 5, 1960. In a rustic cottage they rented, they enjoyed a simple life with few distractions. Deer grazed within sight of the front door. Rogers worked hard on the book every morning and some of the evenings; in the afternoons they explored the magnificent countryside and mountains. At the end of three weeks the book was just about completed. The idyllic setting and the ease of writing were always for him a most enjoyable memory.[77]

On Becoming a Person synthesized the work of the major part of Rogers' career thus far. It is not just a book on psychotherapy, although the first sections of the book are on that subject. It is a book on the process of becoming a person, a process which takes place not only in therapy, but potentially in every facet of daily living. Logan Fox once wrote of his studies with Rogers, "It had never been my intention to be a psychotherapist. I was a minister and a college teacher. But this was not unusual among those who were attracted to Rogers. In the group at Chicago there were ministers, teachers, social workers, writers, and many other specialists besides the clinical psychologists. And so as a disciple of Rogers in Japan, it was not my intention to launch a counseling movement. I was interested in applying his ideas in religion, in education, in school administration, and in the home. I think I was not unique in those interests. Somehow, each person who studied under Rogers became interested, not in becoming a professional counselor, but in trying to improve human relations wherever he might find himself."[78]

On Becoming a Person illustrates Fox's concept, applying client-centered therapeutic principles to many different types of human relationships. It represented the growing variety of Rogers' interests and of the areas in which his work was becoming influential. From the personal, introductory chapter to the long list of Rogers' publications (1931–1961) at the end, the book was a statement of the person and professional Carl Rogers had been becoming throughout his life.

The introductory chapter is a good illustration of this. Entitled "This is Me," the chapter is a composite of two talks he had given. One had been at the University of Wisconsin, the other in a lecture series at Brandeis in which Archibald MacLeish, Margaret Mead, Robert Frost, Eleanor Roosevelt, Norman Thomas, Walter White, and many other noted figures had been previous speakers. "The response to each of these talks," Rogers wrote, "has made me realize how hungry people are to know something of the person who is speaking to them or teaching them. Consequently, I have set this chapter first in the book in the hope that it will convey something of me, and thus give more context and meaning to the chapters which follow."[79]

This chapter was a continuation of his tendency of the previous years to become increasingly personal in his writing style. More and more often phrases like "It has been my experience that ..." and "From what I have seen ..." would appear in his writing. Beyond such phrases, he would elaborate on the same theme in many of his essays.

> I would like to make it very plain that these are learnings which have significance for me. I do not know whether they would hold meaning for you. I have no desire to present them as a guide for anyone else. Yet I have found that when another person has been willing to tell me something of his inner directions this has been of value to me, if only in sharpening my realization that my directions are different.[80]

> I have stated the preceding section as strongly as I am able because it represents a deep conviction growing out of many years of experience. I am quite aware, however, of the difference between conviction and truth. I do not ask anyone to agree with my experience, but only to consider whether the formulation given here agrees with his own experience.[81]

Out of my experience with my clients, and out of my own self-searching, I find myself arriving at views which would have been very foreign to me ten or fifteen years ago. So I trust you will look at these views with critical skepticism, and accept them only in so far as they ring true in your own experience.[82]

Under "experience" Rogers sometimes included his experience in research and at other times referred only to other life experiences. Not only did he follow this stylistic model more consistently, he even began to include in some of his writings paragraphs in which he would describe his own personal and professional background. In "This is Me" he shared his history at greater length than he had ever before done in writing. Of all his autobiographical writings, this first chapter of *On Becoming a Person* is perhaps the best known. It demonstrates his growing desire to be seen and known as an individual, to achieve a more personal encounter in his relationships, even with his readers.

He devoted the next two sections of the book to his ideas on therapy, giving many excerpts from therapeutic interviews to illustrate his points. One of his best-known essays was included here—"The Characteristics of a Helping Relationship." In one part of the essay he adapted the principles of client-centered therapy into a series of questions he would ask himself as a person in a helping relationship. As he elaborated on each question raised, he made it clear that he was not only speaking of the therapist-to-client relationship but of all helping relationships. This is one reason why the essay has been reprinted in the journals of so many professions.

1. Can I *be* in some way which will be perceived by the other person as trustworthy, as dependable or consistent in some deep sense? ... 2. Can I be expressive enough as a person that what I am will be communicated unambiguously? ... 3. Can I let myself experience positive attitudes toward this other person—attitudes of warmth, caring, liking, interest, respect? ... 4. Can I be strong enough as a person to be separate from the other? ... 5. Am I secure enough within myself to permit him his separateness? ... 6. Can I let myself enter fully into the world of his feelings and personal meanings and see these as he does? ... 7. Can I be acceptant of each facet of this other person which he presents to me? Can I receive him as he is? Can I communicate this attitude? Or can I only receive him conditionally, acceptant of some aspects of his feelings and silently or openly disapproving of other aspects? ... 8. Can I act with sufficient sensitivity in the relationship that my behavior will not be perceived as a threat? ... 9. Can I free him from the threat of external evaluation? ... 10. Can I meet this other individual as a person who is in process of *becoming* or will I be bound by his past and by my past?[83]

The Fully Functioning Person

Rogers was frequently asked what his picture of the healthy person was—the product of a lifetime of ideal helping relationships, or successful psychotherapy? This was a variation on one of the oldest philosophical questions humans have grappled with through recorded history: To what end does a person live? What is the purpose of life? What gives life meaning? In Part IV of *On Becoming a Person* he included two essays dealing with this question—"'To Be That Self Which One Truly Is': A Therapist's View of Personal Goals"[84] and "A Therapist's View of the Good Life: The Fully Functioning Person."[85] In these and other essays he described the optimum in human functioning as he had seen it evidenced in the growth of the individuals he encountered in therapy. For him this optimum in functioning was not a fixed state, with a fixed or ultimate set of values to which one aspired. Rather, "the good life is a process, not a state of being. It is a direction, not a destination. The direction which constitutes the good life is that which is selected by the total organism, when there is a psychological freedom to move in *any* direction."[86]

Where this psychological freedom does exist or where it increases in degree, Rogers saw certain common directions in people's style of living. First, the "more fully functioning person" is "open to his experience," that is, aware and acceptant of his feelings, perceptions, and thoughts. He has a "trust in his organism," a confidence that when he is open to *all* of his inner and outer experience and not blocking out certain parts of his experiencing, then his inner directions and promptings are a trustworthy guide to action. He has an "internal locus of evaluation"; that is, although he is aware of and sensitive to the "oughts" and "shoulds" and expectations of others, he trusts his own judgment as the most important guide to right and wrong, desirable and undesirable, in a given situation. There is an "increasingly existential living," in which "the self and personality emerge from experience, rather than experience being translated or twisted to fit preconceived self structure."[87] Such a person, said Rogers, seems to move away from facades and toward congruence in his daily living. There is an increase in spontaneity and creativity.

This line of thought was consistent with many humanistic psychologists' views of psychological growth and well-being. As usual, Rogers explained it more clearly and in greater detail. To those who said an openness to experience, a trust in one's organism, and an internal locus of evaluation would inevitably lead a person to run amuck, Rogers answered, "The person who is fully open to his experience would have access to all of the available data in the situation, on which to base his behavior; the social demands, his own complex and possibly conflicting needs, his memories of similar situations, his perception of the uniqueness of this situation, etc., etc. The data would be very complex indeed. But he could permit his total organism, his consciousness participating, to consider each stimulus, need, and demand, its relative intensity and importance, and out of this complex weighing and balancing, discover that course of action which would come close to satisfying all his needs in the situation. An analogy which might come close to a description would be to compare this person to a giant electronic computing machine [computers were new and gigantic then]. Since he is open to his experience, all of the data from his sense impressions, from his memory, from previous learning, from his visceral and internal states, is fed into the machine. The machine takes all of these multitudinous pulls and forces which are fed in as data, and quickly computes the course of action which would be the most economical vector of need satisfaction in this existential situation. This is the behavior of our hypothetical person.

"The defects which in most of us make this process untrustworthy are the inclusion of information which does *not* belong to this present situation, or the exclusion of information which does. It is when memories and previous learnings are fed into the computations as if they were *this* reality, and not memories and learnings, that erroneous behavioral answers arise. Or when certain threatening experiences are inhibited from awareness, and hence are withheld from the computation or fed into it in distorted form, this too produces error. But our hypothetical person would find his organism thoroughly trustworthy, because all of the available data would be used, and it would be present in accurate rather than distorted form. Hence his behavior would come as close as possible to satisfying all his needs—for enhancement, for affiliation with others, and the like."[88]

Surely the organism will make mistakes, whenever crucial data are missing, or when there is not enough time to compute all the data thoroughly; but if the individual remains open to his experience, then new data will come in, and new decisions can correct the old ones.

Rogers himself was a good example of such a fully functioning person—open to new data, altering his thinking based on his experiences, continually changing and growing, outgrowing himself into new ideas and professional emphases. To use an oft-quoted Rogers passage, "This whole train of experiencing, and the meanings that I have thus far discovered in it, seem to have launched me on a process which is both fascinating and at times a little frightening. *It seems to mean letting my experience carry me on, in a direction which appears to be forward, toward goals that I can but dimly define, as I try to understand at least the current meaning of that experience.* The sensation is that of floating with a complex stream of experience, with the fascinating possibility of trying to comprehend its ever changing complexity."[89]

Rogers' picture of the fully functioning person is in striking contrast to the typical Western notion of success in life, whether that is a home in the suburbs, a tenured position on a faculty, an idyllic farm in the country, or a secure retirement. It suggests that we never arrive at a final goal, that life is a continual state of change, that we remain open to our experiences and flow with them, that when we stop growing we commence dying. People may live happily ever after in fairy tales and Hollywood movies, but according to Rogers, fully functioning success is a continual process of growth and change.

On the other hand, as critics have pointed out, Rogers and other humanistic psychologists are typically Western in their individualistic emphasis.[90] Other cultures might place filial piety or obligations to the family or community or God *above* the individual's need for self-actualization. Rogers' fully functioning person would certainly attend to such obligations, but in the end would determine how much to fulfill others' expectations in light of one's own total value system. Hence ultimately the individual is in the center. In contrast, other systems put the needs of the family, the community, the church, or the state before the individual's needs. When carried too far, such subjugation of the individual becomes oppressive or totalitarian. However, critics argue, individual freedom when carried too far becomes unduly selfish, narcissistic and inimical to traditional values and community welfare.[91]

Closely tied to Rogers' concept of the fully functioning person was his view of the creative process, discussed in a chapter which appeared near the end of *On Becoming a Person.*[92] To Rogers, creativity was not a skill or personal quality which some people have and others do not, but a process which all people go through to one degree or another. One part of the creative process is an openness to experience. The artist is open to the sensory world around him and to the feelings and images within him. The creative scientist or inventor is a keen observer of the phenomena she is studying and, like the artist, is open to the unformed, the vague, the sometimes preposterous ideas, hunches and hypotheses which well up within her. Then there is a trusting of one's organism, a confidence that allows a person to follow a hunch, to try out an idea or solution, to create something new. Along with this self-trust is a locus of evaluation which is mostly within the person rather than without. This enables the artist to say, "I know that no one has ever painted this way before, but I think my approach has merit, and I will keep doing it this way," or the scientist to say, "I know this line of thinking goes against the present theories in my field, but I think this would be a valuable direction to pursue." Such qualities of personality—openness to experience, trust in oneself, an internal locus of evaluation—lead to creative living. Creative living leads to creative accomplishments, which may be anything from artistic and scientific contributions, to good storytelling, to a sense of design and decoration, to a better way to do a mundane task, to a new and different lifestyle. Just as psychological safety helps a person become more fully functioning, so does psychological safety nurture creativity. Psychological threat, on the other hand, nurtures rigidity of thought and psychological defensiveness. The fully functioning person, then, is creative. To the extent that each of us becomes more fully functioning, we also increase our capacity for creative living.

Persons or Science?

In the fifth section of *On Becoming a Person,* Rogers included three chapters on "Getting at the Facts: The Place of Research in Psychotherapy." Here he reviewed much of the research he and others had done in the field. In a chapter called "Persons or Science? A Philosophical Question,"[93] he also included a lengthy exploration of his personal struggle with two points of view about therapy and how this struggle had broader implications for psychology in general. One viewpoint was that therapy is an intensely personal experience, that it is lived fully and subjectively in a person-to-person encounter with the client, that the therapist is not a scientist applying this or that technique but a congruent human being endeavoring to enter into a deeply personal helping relationship with another human being. The second point of view was that of a scientist. Therapy must be studied rigorously with the tried and true methods of science. All vague concepts like congruence, unconditional positive regard, and empathy must be operationalized and measurable. An individual's subjective impressions may be anything from biased to psychotic; therefore objectivity and detachment are crucial to the scientist. To sum up the dilemma: the personal goal of the therapist is to live fully in the relationship; the scientist's goal is to remain detached and understand it.

Not only did he see this as a conflict he personally felt between two sides of himself, he also saw it as a tension between two points of view, in psychology— between those who were interested primarily in understanding the person as he experiences himself and the world subjectively and those who were interested only in the person's behavior, as viewed from the outside. Since science views its subject objectively, when people are the subject of science they therefore become objects. Rogers asked, "If we project ourselves into the future, and suppose that we had the answers to most of the questions which psychology investigates today, what then? Then we would find ourselves increasingly impelled to treat all others, and even ourselves, as objects. The knowledge of all human relationships would be so great that we would know it rather than live the relationships unreflectively. We see some foretaste of this in the attitude of sophisticated parents who know that affection 'is good for the child.' This knowledge frequently stands in the way of their being themselves, freely, unreflectively—affectionate or not."[94]

His way out of the dilemma was to go back to viewing the human purposes of scientific investigation. "Science," he wrote, "has its inception in a particular person who is pursuing aims, values, purposes, which have personal and subjective meaning for him."[95] These purposes may be a burning desire to discover truth, the hope of getting a degree or tenure, the wish to solve an important problem, or any number of other human goals. In pursuit of some particular solution to a problem, there is a *creative phase,* where the person thinks he has come up with an invention, a new technique, a newly observed relationship, a hypothesis which will move him closer to achieving the goal of his research. But is it true? Does the new invention really work, or what are its side effects? Is the newly observed relationship due only to chance, or is it a consistent relationship which will appear again and again under similar conditions? Does the new technique work only because of the person using it or the person receiving it or will it work for different clients and with different practitioners? "Experience has shown each one of us that it is very easy to deceive ourselves, to believe something which later experience shows is not so."[96] It is here that science comes in, not as an end in itself, a god to be worshipped above all other human endeavors, but as a tool—a tool which helps us check our observations and conclusions against a more objective reality to see just how good our solution, our invention, our technique, our generalization, our hypothesis really is.

For Rogers, then, both realities—the subjective and the objective—were crucially important. His goal, based on past experience, was to enter into a subjective human relationship with his clients. His belief, based on past experience, was that this would most likely lead to a therapeutic relationship and psychological growth. But how could he be sure? Maybe he was kidding himself, remembering only the successful cases upon which he built his generalizations. Scientific research allowed him to check himself, to discover blind spots, to improve and modify his techniques—in short, to achieve his goal more successfully. Without science he was akin to a faith healer. With science only, there could be no client-centered therapy. A warm human being was needed for that. The continuing struggle between the subjective and objective was, for him, a desirable tension, one which would keep him growing and changing. It was when he denied one side or the other that he was no longer the person or the effective therapist he wished to be.

The same held true for the tension between the subjective and the objective in the behavioral sciences. As long as science gave credence and importance to individuals' goals, feelings, values, and other inner experiences, objective scientists could help people. As long as the "experientialists" included a scientific method in their operations, they would remain professionals and not cultists. Both were necessary for the behavioral sciences to be of significant help to society and individuals. "'Science' will never depersonalize, or manipulate, or control individuals," he wrote. "It is only persons who can or will do that ... What I will do with the knowledge gained through scientific method—whether I will use it to understand, enhance, enrich, or use it to control, manipulate and destroy—is a matter of subjective choice dependent upon the values which have personal meaning for me. If, out of fright and defensiveness, I block out from my awareness large areas of experience—if I can see only those facts which support my present beliefs, and am blind to all others—if I can see only the objective aspects of life, and cannot perceive the subjective—if, in any way, I cut off my perception from the full range of its actual sensitivity—then I am likely to be socially destructive, whether I use as tool the knowledge and instruments of science, or the power and emotional strength of a subjective relationship."[97]

Having recently concluded his second and longer dialogue with B.F. Skinner, in *On Becoming a Person* Rogers pulled together his thoughts on the behavioral sciences to a greater degree than ever before. In addition to the three chapters in the research section he included two more at the end of the book on "The Behavioral Sciences and the Person."[98] After years of experience as a behavioral scientist he was becoming more and more interested in and concerned about the part the behavioral sciences would play in dealing with the world's human problems. A few years later Rogers' interest in the uses and methods of science would again occupy a good deal of thought and another volume.

Widening Applications

The sixth and largest section of his collection of essays applied the insights of client-centered therapy to several other areas of daily living. One was education. In a short essay, "Personal Thoughts on Teaching and Learning," he wrote an extreme statement of his educational views, including such italicized statements as: *"It seems to me that anything that can be taught to another is relatively inconsequential, and has little or no significant influence on behavior." "I have come to feel that the only learning which significantly influences behavior is self-appropriated learning." "I realize that I have lost interest in being a teacher."* [99]

In another, longer essay, "Significant Learning: In Therapy and in Education,"[100] he discussed how the principles governing a successful therapeutic relationship also apply to the teacher–student relationship in the classroom. Here he was generalizing on the basis of his own teaching and supervision experiences over the years. This was the beginning of a major interest for Rogers. Over the next few years he would continue to extend his thinking in this area and would become deeply involved in the subject of education.

In the several essays in this section Rogers made two major points: first, that the conditions of congruence, unconditional positive regard, and empathy not only foster growth and significant learning in therapy, but they do the same in every helping relationship; and second, that the benefits of living as a more fully functioning person—congruent, in process of becoming, trusting oneself, open to experience, and the like—can be seen in *all* human relationships. In education this is probably easier to recognize than in some other areas of application, for in education the teacher's role lends itself to adopting the therapist's conditions, and the student's role traditionally has been supposed to be that of openness, growth, becoming. But what about in the family, for example? Here, too, Rogers believed that the parents' congruence, unconditional positive regard, and empathy can be enormously growth-facilitating for the children. In

THE LIFE AND WORK OF CARL ROGERS

"The Implications of Client-Centered Therapy for Family Life" he illustrated how family relationships frequently change after one member had been involved in therapy and this one person's growth begins to influence the rest of the family. First, there tends to be more expression of feeling in the family, a richer emotional life. Relationships tend to move away from facades, pretense, and defensiveness; there is an improvement in two-way communication. "… the individual learns to recognize and express his feelings as his own feelings, not as a fact about another person. Thus, to say to one's spouse, 'What you are doing is all wrong,' is likely to lead only to debate. But to say 'I feel very much annoyed by what you're doing,' is to state one fact about the speaker's feelings, a fact which no one can deny."[101] With this type of communication developing, there tends to be a greater willingness for the individuals to be separate, to have feelings and values of their own, which can be respected or at least tolerated, even if these are different from the other's.

Not content to confine the application of his ideas to education and the family, Rogers argued that the same principles of helping relationships and psychologically healthy living could be used to improve communication between disputing groups and even nations. He included a presentation he first delivered in 1951[102] in which he had told an audience, "Some of you may be feeling that you listen well to people, and that you have never seen such results. The chances are very great indeed that your listening has not been of the type I have described. Fortunately I can suggest a little laboratory experiment which you can try to test the quality of your understanding. The next time you get into an argument with your wife, or your friend, or with a small group of friends, just stop the discussion for a moment and for an experiment, institute this rule. 'Each person can speak up for himself only *after* he has first restated the ideas and feelings of the previous speaker accurately, and to that speaker's satisfaction.' You see what this would mean. It would simply mean that before presenting your own point of view, it would be necessary for you to really achieve the other speaker's frame of reference—to understand his thoughts and feelings so well that you could summarize them for him. Sounds simple doesn't it? But if you try it you will discover it is one of the most difficult things you have ever tried to do. However, once you have been able to see the other's point of view, your own comments will have to be drastically revised. You will also find the emotion going out of the discussion, the differences being reduced, and those differences which remain being of a rational and understandable sort …

"I am indebted to Dr. S.I. Hayakawa, the semanticist, for pointing out that to carry on psychotherapy in this fashion is to take a very real risk, and that courage is required. If you really understand another person in this way, if you are willing to enter his private world and see the way life appears to him, without any attempt to make evaluative judgments, you run the risk of being changed yourself. You might see it his way, you might find yourself influenced in your attitudes or your personality. This risk of being changed is one of the most frightening prospects most of us can face. If I enter as fully as I am able, into the private world of a neurotic or psychotic individual, isn't there a risk that I might become lost in that world? Most of us are afraid to take that risk. Or if we had a Russian communist speaker here tonight, or Senator Joseph McCarthy, how many of us would dare to try to see the world from each of these points of view? The great majority of us could not listen, we would find ourselves compelled to evaluate, because listening would seem too dangerous. So the first requirement is courage, and we do not always have it."[103]

Many people have tried Rogers' laboratory experiment in listening. In fact, it became and remains a popular communication exercise used in numerous human relations training, professional, and educational settings. "Rogerian listening" and then "active listening" became widely used terms to describe empathic listening, in which the listener shares with the speaker his own understanding of the feelings and meanings the speaker has shared. Rogers and his doctoral student Richard Farson used the term "active listening" as early as 1957 in a publication they wrote for the Industrial Relations Center of the University of Chicago.[104] Rogers was asked to give a speech and write a booklet applying the work at the Counseling Center to the field of industrial relations. Farson recalled that Lee Mahood of the Industrial Relations Center suggested the term as a focus for their essay.[105] Thomas Gordon, Rogers' former student and then colleague, later popularized the term and practice of active listening in a series of popular books on parent, teacher and leader "effectiveness training."[106]

In attempting to apply his theories and methods to interpersonal and intergroup conflict resolution, Rogers was advocating more than good listening. Honest, open communication was another part of it. As he wrote in 1960, "Let us take a look, for example, at the conduct of our country, in its foreign affairs. By and large we find, if we listen to the statements of our leaders during the past several years, and read their documents, that our diplomacy is always based upon high moral purposes; that it is always consistent with the policies we have followed previously; that it involves no selfish desires; and that it has never been mistaken in its judgments and choices. I think perhaps you will agree with me that if we heard an individual speaking in these terms we would recognize at once that this must be a facade, that such statements could not possibly represent the real process going on within himself. Suppose we speculate for a moment as to how we, as a nation, might present ourselves in our foreign diplomacy if we were openly, knowingly, and acceptingly being what we truly are … What would be the results? To me, the results would be similar to the experiences of a client when he is more truly that which he is …

"We would be much more comfortable, because we would have nothing to hide. We could focus on the problem at hand, rather than spending our energies to prove that we are moral or consistent. We could use all of our creative imagination in solving the problem, rather than in defending ourselves. We could openly advance both our selfish interests, and our sympathetic concern for others, and let these conflicting desires find the balance which is acceptable to us as a people. We could freely change and grow in our leadership position, because we would not be bound by rigid concepts of what we have been, must be, ought to be. We would find that we were much less feared, because others would be less inclined to suspect what lies behind the facade. We would, by our own openness, tend to bring forth openness and realism on the part of others. We would tend to work out the solutions of world problems on the basis of the real issues involved, rather than in terms of the facades being worn by the negotiating parties.

"In short what I am suggesting by this fantasied example is that nations and organizations might discover, as have individuals, that it is a richly rewarding experience to be what one deeply is. I am suggesting that this view contains the seeds of a philosophical approach to all of life, that it is more than a trend observed in the experience of clients."[107]

Further Recognition

In his introduction to *On Becoming a Person* Rogers had written, "Stated in the simplest way, the purpose of this book is to share with you something of my experience—something of me. Here is what I have experienced in the jungles of modern life, in the largely unmapped territory of personal relationships. Here is what I have seen. Here is what I have come to believe. Here are some of the perplexities, questions, concerns and uncertainties which I face. I hope that out of this sharing you may find something which speaks to you."[108]

A great number of people did. As Brian Thorne wrote, "The book broke free from the professional world of psychology and showed that client-centered principles had application in almost every facet of day-to-day living."[109] As soon as the book was published, personal letters began coming to Rogers, forwarded by the publisher, in numbers much greater than any of his previous books had elicited. They were from professionals and laypeople alike. A young woman from Connecticut began her letter in a way which Rogers would see repeated hundreds of times: "Dear Carl, I do not want to write to you as Dr. Rogers, for although we have never met, I feel a personal closeness to you through reading many of your thoughts and feelings. At times, for me, it feels as if you are here with me or I am with you, helping me face the reality of life as a growing adult."[110]

A Wisconsin pastor wrote,

Dear Mr. Rogers:
When a recent blurb about your book came from the Pastoral Psychology Book Club, it seemed worth the investment and I sent for it. Your opening Part I on "This is Me" is one of the most appealing things that has yet come to my attention

from our many American psychologists. The all-present mood of acceptance has such a healing power about it that it has clung to me and I cannot, though I would not, rid myself of it. As the Quakers say, "The Lord willing, I hope to finish your book." In the meantime the breath of fresh air that it has thrown into my experience makes me your debtor. This is one of the few books which does not seem to scoop up the harsh judgments of the author to indicate the trash in all the rest of us. Spiritually, sir, you are a biped and I am glad to see you standing so tall—nor does it make the rest of us seem shorter; we're about ready to reach up there, too.[111]

A dramatic example of how the book seemed to touch people for different reasons, in many walks of life, is this excerpt of a letter from Seattle, Washington, written more than ten years after *On Becoming a Person* was published. Unsolicited letters like these continued to come to Rogers for the rest of his life, for many of those years at the rate of two or three per week.[112]

A teacher friend who was losing the struggle against alcoholism—(this was over a year ago)—accepted my suggestion that he read "On Becoming a Person." And since Rogers, he *has* become again, probably more so than before his booze era ... This really intelligent, good man appeared to be on the way out; and his wife and two sons are so wrapped up in him that their future seemed a useless prospect. Although you may not really need it, one more bouquet won't hurt: your thinking and its wording rang the right bell, and saved a whole family. We're truly glad you're here.[113]

Shortly before he died, Rogers recalled that he had once described himself metaphorically as "someone who was a shy person who'd written messages, sealed them in a bottle and tossed them into the ocean, and it was astonishing the number of shores on which they'd washed up. I feel that way about a lot of ... the personal writings I've done. I've been able to express myself more personally in writing than I used to be able to in speaking. I think now I can do it in speaking, too. At any rate, it became my own way of putting myself out where I was too shy to put myself out in ordinary social contacts, and people have responded to that very, very deeply. I still get letters—quite a few—from people who have just for the first time read *On Becoming a Person* and how much it has meant to them and how it's changed their lives."[114]

It was ironic. Houghton Mifflin had shown little enthusiasm for the book. Again their worry was, who would buy it? It was too technical and narrowly focused for the layperson, the teacher or the parent, they thought, and not technical or focused enough for the therapist, counselor, or researcher. Yet its sales were excellent from the start, and by 1971, ten years after publication, it had sold more copies than any of Rogers' other books, all of which had been available for many years more.[115] What the publisher had not counted on, but what Rogers had sensed, was that humanistic psychology had come into its own. In the forties and fifties, interest in this third force in psychology had been growing, but only among a small number of professionals in various fields. In the sixties, just as various other movements were gaining public attention—civil rights, peace, students, women—so was humanistic psychology making its force felt in professions from counseling and psychotherapy to education to social work to business. It was seen in the growing interest in sensitivity training and encounter groups; in the church's explosion into new styles of worship and dress; in the use of psychedelic and other consciousness expanding drugs. Sometimes it was difficult to tell where politics left off and psychology began. Was the spread of rural and urban communes in the sixties, for example, more of a political phenomenon or a social-psychological one? The point is that people in all walks of life were attempting to guide their lives toward goals of their own choosing, which was precisely the goal of most humanistic psychologists and the gist of most of their writings. To help individuals achieve their full potential, to become self-actualizing or fully functioning, to clarify their values, to relate more effectively to those around them—this was the language of humanistic psychology, and it meshed comfortably with the other political and social movements of the sixties. The idea whose time had come was accepted readily by thousands, possibly millions, of professionals, laypeople, and students. *On Becoming a Person* appeared exactly at the right time. Rogers, while long well known in the psychology profession and by many in other helping professions, was now catapulted into even greater fame among various professional communities and the interested public.

Yet in spite of the book's excellent sales, Rogers had publisher problems. Houghton Mifflin had been an appropriate publisher for his earlier books. Aimed at specialized professional readers, published as hard cover volumes, priced fairly expensively, the books sold well. The publisher and author were pleased. For a book of this type, five or ten thousand copies sold over the years was considered successful. With Rogers' books selling in the range of 100,000 copies each, Houghton Mifflin was both ecstatic and complacent. By the late fifties and early sixties, however, the publishing world had changed in two ways. First there was now a much wider audience of readers interested in psychology, sociology, and other areas in the behavioral sciences. A good writer like Erich Fromm, a social psychologist, could make the best-seller list and reach well over a hundred thousand readers in the very first year of publication.[116] In the new genre of "popular psychology," books like *Games People Play* could sell well over a million copies.[117] Second, the rise of the paperback book had revolutionized the publishing industry. A volume that previously would have cost $4.95 to $7.95, for example, could now be available in paperback from $0.95 to $1.95 (no longer, alas). There were smaller profits for the publisher and fewer royalties for the author on each book sold; but at such low prices, sales might increase five- or ten-fold, the net result being greater profits and royalties and five or ten times more people reading an author's work.

Rogers realized all this too late. Had he worked with another publisher on the book it might have done much better than it did, even though in traditional publishing terms it did very well. After a few years he began to have some sense of this and asked the publisher to put out a paperback edition of *On Becoming a Person* to make it more easily available to a wider audience. The publisher thought the book was doing well as it was and rejected the idea. This began a long and often angry correspondence between Rogers and Houghton Mifflin. He did everything he could to convince them to put out a paperbound volume. Rogers said the correspondence "shows me at my snottiest."[118] When they said, "Do you realize we'd have to sell three times as many copies in paperback as we now do in hardback," Rogers wrote back that he would guarantee they'd sell at least three times as many and would repay them the difference in profits if he was wrong. Still they said no. Finally they relented and published a Sentry paperback edition at a quality paperback price of $2.95. During the first year after publication it sold four times as many copies as the cloth edition had sold the year before. Sales have been excellent ever since, with over 600,000 copies in print by 1978 and certainly well over a million by 2006.[119]

Other honors continued to add to Rogers' esteem and reputation. Just at the beginning of his time in Wisconsin he was serving his two-year term (1956–58) as the first president of the American Academy of Psychotherapists. One of the things the AAP did was to begin building a catalogue of audiotaped therapeutic interviews, conducted by some of the leading figures in the different therapeutic schools. These were duplicated and sold to the members and to the general public. Rogers contributed the first tapes to this series, six of them—more than any other therapist in the collection.[120] It was through these AAP tapes that many people heard Rogers for the first time and gained some insight into the active and caring involvement of the client-centered therapist—a sense which is not conveyed as effectively in written transcripts. When AAP and others began to produce films and later videotapes of therapy, again Rogers was one of the first and most frequent therapists featured.[121]

One set of films from this period that added considerably to Rogers' reputation was the "Gloria" series. In 1965 Everett Shostrom produced three hour-long films, featuring Carl Rogers, Frederick ("Fritz") Perls and Albert Ellis, each explaining and then demonstrating for about a half hour his client-centered, Gestalt or rational-emotive therapy approach with the same client, Gloria.[122] Each therapist was a master of his craft and the contrast of their styles was vivid. Gloria was asked at the end of the full-day experience what her reactions were to the three therapists. At the time she said that if she were beginning therapy she would like to work with Rogers, but that in her present situation Perls' challenging approach might be best for her. Over the years, as she continued to reflect on her experience, she became increasingly angry with Perls for the way he had treated her and increasingly appreciative of Rogers, writing,

> During the Perls portion of the film I was aware of being my most defensive self, full of distrust, confusion, and suspicion of the therapist's approach and reaction (or more appropriately—nonreaction) to me. I was afraid of being attacked and resented the position I allowed myself to be in. What I needed most at that point in my life was permission to be me. Instead I found myself with Perls in a vicious circle of game playing, of having to respond on demand in a specific manner, of being trapped into gaining approval by first knowing and then giving an expected reply ...
>
> In contrast to being totally disassembled with Dr. Perls, my body felt perfectly grounded with Carl Rogers. I felt whole, intact, in other words, a person with Rogers. It wouldn't be fair to say that Rogers "gave" me anything. But something happened in those few short minutes which has stayed with me ever since. He simply helped me to recognize my own potential—my value as a human being. All the words couldn't possible express the importance of that to me.[123]

Gloria corresponded with Carl and Helen Rogers, about one or two letters a year, for the next fifteen years, until her death from lung cancer in 1979. Rogers said, "I was often touched by her letters ... I am awed by the fact that this fifteen-year association grew out of the quality of the relationship we formed in one thirty-minute period in which we truly met as persons. It is good to know that even one half-hour can make a difference in a life."[124] The *Three Approaches to Psychotherapy* series became one of the most written about and one of the best-selling set of training films and videos in counseling and psychotherapy ever produced.[125]

Rogers continued to serve during 1957 as a member of the Policy and Planning Board of the American Psychological Association, as a Consulting Editor to *Psychological Monographs,* and until he resigned in 1958, on the Editorial Advisory Board of the *Journal of Consulting Psychology.* Thereafter he quickly diminished his involvement with professional organizations, serving only again in 1960 as Chairman of the Nominations and Elections Committee of the AAP and in 1963 on a distinguished APA committee chaired by psychologist Kenneth Clark examining the academic preparation of psychology researchers and practitioners.[126] The latter committee recommended a two-track system for education in psychology—the traditional Ph.D. degree for training in research and the Psy.D. (Doctor of Psychology) degree for training practitioners, comparable to an M.D. for physicians.[127]

In 1961 Rogers was elected Fellow of the American Academy of Arts and Sciences, a group comparable to the French Academy but not nearly as well known or influential in the United States as its counterpart is in France. In

1962, after a committee of the American Personnel and Guidance Association reviewed fifty-six journals and several monographs and books published between September 1960 and August 1961, he was awarded that organization's "Certificate for Outstanding Research." Again in 1962 he was one of two individuals honored by the Division of Clinical Psychology of the American Psychological Association. In presenting to him the award for the Distinguished Contribution to the Science and Profession of Clinical Psychology, the chairperson read:

> Clinical Psychology has suffered a long time from anxiety neurosis reactive to the problems of psychotherapy; Dr. Carl Rogers has provided us with a defense mechanism against this anxiety. He, more than anyone else, initiated effective research in psychotherapy by opening the office to let us observe the therapist in action. Carl Rogers accustomed us to having complete records of what goes on. These records have become so common in research that we do not readily recall the times before Rogers when detailed study of the course of psychotherapy was nearly impossible. Methods from him and his students gave us our first objective studies of the progress and effectiveness of psychotherapy. Not least in this contribution was the first clear delineation of one way to do psychotherapy— client-centered therapy ...
>
> Dr. Rogers has become an international representative of American clinical psychology and in that role has contributed to the concept of scientific psychology as vigorous and healthy by his willingness to debate and experiment and change rather than rest upon authority and fixed opinion. We must, in justice to his contributions, emphasize the qualities of personality that have drawn to him hundreds of students, attracted not only by his achievements but by his persistent devotion to an ideal.
>
> If we cannot add much to his public honor, we do at least express our collective recognition of the value of his contributions to clinical psychology and of the scientific qualities that have influenced so many of us.[128]

Move to California

Brian Thorne wrote how Rogers "went to Wisconsin to make an impact, and he notably failed. He wrote a book and discovered that he was suddenly influential beyond his wildest dreams."[129] The net impact of his experiences in the early sixties was becoming increasingly clear to Rogers. His successes and the influence his work was having were earned outside the university—through his writing, speeches, workshops and professional activities. The university setting at Wisconsin had proved not only less productive than he had expected, but also produced a series of continual frustrations, offset by only occasional high points. So in the summer of 1963, at the age of sixty-one, he announced his decision to resign from the University of Wisconsin, and to move to California at the end of the year. As he explained the move:

"Quite unwittingly I had had a part in the formation of an adventurous new organization on the cutting edge of the behavioral sciences. Richard Farson, Thomas Gordon, and I had conducted a workshop in human relations in California in the summer of 1958. Dr. Paul Lloyd, a California Institute of Technology physicist who had become increasingly interested in the field of interpersonal relationships, was one of the participants. As a result of many discussions following that workshop, Farson and Lloyd founded the Western Behavioral Sciences Institute, a non-profit organization devoted to humanistically oriented research in interpersonal relationships, with a particular focus on the manner in which constructive change in interpersonal relationships comes about. At the time of its establishment in 1959, I accepted their invitation to serve on its board of directors. My motive was to encourage what seemed to me a pioneering venture in an area in which pioneering is often unwelcomed by established institutions.

"From the first, Farson, whom I had known for many years, urged me to come out as a Visiting Fellow, or to join the staff, or in any other way I chose to affiliate more closely than as a remote board member. I had never accepted any of these invitations, partly because of other obligations, partly because I felt that my contribution could certainly best be made through a university. While I was at the Center in Stanford in 1963, he repeated over the phone this invitation to join their staff. I gave my stock response, but later began to mull over the question. What was a university, at this stage of my career, offering me? I realized that in my research it offered no particular help; in anything educational, I was forced to fit my beliefs into a totally alien mold; in stimulation, there was little from my colleagues because we were so far apart in thinking and in goals. On the other hand, WBSI offered complete freedom with no bureaucratic entanglements; the stimulation of a thoroughly congenial interdisciplinary group; the opportunity to facilitate learning without becoming entrapped in the anti-educational jungle of credits, requirements, examinations, more examinations, and grudgingly granted degrees. As Helen and I talked it over, we were very reluctant to leave our Madison friends and our lovely home, but I recognized that professionally I could now leave university life without too much regret and that from a realistic point of view, I would have a much deeper membership in a 'community of scholars' at WBSI than at any university I knew. So we decided to make the move."[130]

Rogers had other offers at the time, including named chairs at Duke and Chicago. "He chose us," recalled Farson. "I thought, 'God, that's amazing.'"[131] But it wasn't really. Rogers had had enough of university life and wanted more freedom. As he explained to friends and colleagues, WBSI would give him complete "freedom from all routine responsibilities." It would allow him to "devote my energies to the understanding of, and resolution of, the problems and tensions of 'normal' human relationships" and to explore "the potency of intensive group experience for individual growth and change." It would allow him to demonstrate the potential of humanistic psychology in the same way that moving to the Counseling Center in Chicago had allowed him to demonstrate the client-centered approach to counseling and psychotherapy. Perhaps the model of professional education developed at WBSI—"a climate of freedom which will enhance creative interdisciplinary learning"—would help inspire "a better pattern of professional education" at universities. And finally, "… the new position offers a very generous increase in salary, ample secretarial and other assistance, good friends on the staff and Board, an easier climate for the older years we are entering."[132]

While there were many in the Department of Psychology (where he was still teaching an interdisciplinary seminar) and a few in Psychiatry who probably felt their lives would be considerably easier without Rogers, the sentiments of many other faculty and students throughout the University were well stated by University President Fred Harvey Harrington, who wrote to Rogers upon hearing of his resignation, "Although I understand your decision to leave Madison, it distresses me very deeply … In a very real sense your decision shows our failure to provide for you the opportunities and atmosphere you deserve. This is our fault, not yours; and I hope that in the years to come we will measure up better, and be able to keep men like you."[133] Nine years later Harrington recalled how Carl Rogers "was very important to us. He was one of those most responsible for the renaissance of the Sixties, which restored the University of Wisconsin to a position of national leadership in the social sciences. He was one of the first stars who came; and I can remember clearly how elated we all were. We were on the way; we were getting somewhere. And so we did; much followed that would not have happened if Carl and a few others had not come."[134]

To his colleagues in the Psychotherapy Research Group, just before his and Helen's departure from Madison, Rogers wrote, "One reason for writing this memo well in advance is that I want you to know that neither my wife nor I like farewell parties, going away gifts, or anything of that sort. We have had enough of those in our lifetime and we do not want any more. Consequently, I am seriously requesting that no plans of this sort be made." He also invited them all to stop by for individual farewells where they could talk personally. He said that he had packed and unpacked his books enough times in their many moves and had no desire to do so again. Therefore, aside from the relatively few books he would take with him, if they wished to look through his library and help themselves to any titles they wanted, they should feel free to do so. The rest would go to Goodwill Industries.

So, after a Thanksgiving reunion in Nashville with David and Corky, Natalie and Larry, all six grandchildren, and Carl's sister Margaret, the Rogers left

Wisconsin and the Midwest where they had lived most of their lives, and drove to California.[135] From New York City to Rochester, Rochester to Ohio, Ohio to Chicago, and Chicago to Wisconsin, each of his previous westward moves had taken him further into new territory in his profession. Where was there still to go? Even Rogers, in December 1963, would not have imagined how much more innovative work was still before him. But Abraham Maslow, who recently had been a Visiting Fellow at WBSI, had some inkling of the importance of the move, writing to Rogers,

> Dear Carl, I think you are doing the right thing. I discussed this possibility at great length with several of the institute people when I was there and we all agreed that this was best for you, for the institute, and for the world in general … Congratulations! Cordially, Abe.[136]

CHAPTER 10

The California Years
Part One:
Encounter Groups and Education
1964–1972

At Home

Helen Rogers doubted that they would ever find a home she could love as much as the Monona Lake house they were leaving. Once again, though, they found an ideal location. After a few weeks of looking they discovered their new home in La Jolla, California. They moved in late December 1963 and, as Helen described it, were settled in enough to host "our first party—for the Board and several of the staff of Western Behavioral Sciences Institute (WBSI). Imagine a party on the 29th of December with the doors into the patio wide open and guests not only circulating through the house but sitting outside under the full moon. We have to get adjusted to this La Jolla living."[1]

It did not prove difficult. La Jolla is a unique community in Southern California. Though technically a part of San Diego, it is separated from the city by a large hill, to the top of which tourists and residents often come to look down upon the lights of San Diego to the southeast and Mission Bay to the south. There, sheltered from the San Diego smog and the hot desert winds and cooled by the breezes from the Pacific, sits La Jolla, with its beautiful coastline and ocean view and its year-round temperate weather—rarely colder than forty-five Fahrenheit degrees on winter days nor warmer than eighty degrees in the summer.

Houses, mostly expensive ones, start across the oceanside boulevard and continue all the way up the hills which divide La Jolla from San Diego and from inland California. If one turns off Torrey Pines Road, La Jolla's main thoroughfare near the ocean, and starts up Hidden Valley Road, the road twists and turns higher and higher as one gets closer to the top of the hill. Near the top the view is magnificent, with many miles of coastline visible to the north, the blue Pacific on the western horizon, and to the east "ridge after mountain ridge stretching away into the distance, capped by the snow-covered tip of Mount San Gorgonio, ninety miles away."[2] Up there, on a little side road, at 2311 Via Siena, sat the Rogers' home, a modern dwelling, with floor-to-ceiling glass walls, looking out over the grand vista and also surrounding a bright inner courtyard. Birds used often to fly in through an open glass door, so Rogers eventually rigged up a net to catch them and release them outside.[3] One visitor, duly impressed both by the physical openness of the home and by the personal openness of the Rogers, commented, "At the end of the evening I distinctly recalled musing that if anyone could afford to live in a glass house it would be Carl."[4]

The house appeared large and expansive at first, but there were actually only five main rooms: a large living-dining area, kitchen, guest room-study (originally two rooms which they converted to one), and master bedroom. Across the courtyard was a simple studio-workshop which the Rogers had had constructed before they moved in as a room for Helen for her art projects and sewing.[5] Rogers made his office in the guest room-study. There he wrote in the morning and had his small collection of books and several files of articles, journals, and papers (he had another office at WBSI). In later years, when he needed more space and to get a bit farther from the phone, Rogers took over the studio, adding a desk and workbench. He would do his writing out there and work on his mobiles or fix things that needed repair.[6]

Occasionally in speeches or publications Rogers mentioned his hobbies—his mobiles, photography or gardening—sometimes comparing the growth-promoting conditions he provided for his plants and the therapeutic conditions which help clients grow. Such brief references barely suggested his real dedication to these pastimes—in fact, with respect to gardening, one would say his passion. In the interior courtyard, all around the exterior of the house, and in an enclosed ten-foot-square walled garden adjoining their bedroom, Rogers spent many hours a week, sometimes several hours a day, caring for his plants and flowers—seeding, watering, weeding, fertilizing, transplanting, pruning. Tuberous begonias were among his favorites, and when visitors set eyes upon these bright red, white, or flame-colored flowers, sometimes as large as eight inches across, they often exclaimed that they hardly could believe the flowers were real. Even the lemons that the Rogers squeezed for the drinks they enjoyed serving themselves and their guests came right off the little tree growing year round outside their kitchen window. His involvement in gardening can be appreciated from a letter he wrote to a South African friend: "I enjoyed very much hearing about your garden. I wish it were possible to send me some of the aloes. I grow several South African plants and have two succulent gardens. Aloes grow very well in this climate but I expect shipping them is out of the question … Gardening is like anything

330

else—one comes to specialize more and more in the rare things. I now have three bushes of the protea family growing ... They produce incredible blooms but are very difficult to grow. Mine are still thriving and I hope some day they may even have blooms ..."[7]

The Rogers quickly came to love their new home, with its airy expansiveness, simplicity, view, garden, and climate. When the owner of a vacant, sixty-seven acre property in the neighborhood applied to develop the land intensively, the Rogers opposed the development, attending the public hearing and writing a letter of opposition.[8] High above the ocean, then, the Rogers had the privacy and leisure to enjoy their time alone and with the friends who visited them. When they entertained, Carl typically would do the barbecuing, and afterward would clean up the patio and living room while Helen did the dishes. These were special times, both with the company and in their feeling like partners while tidying up after the others had left. The home and atmosphere they created were consistent with their picture of themselves. A friend wrote, after visiting them in California, "Dearest Helen and Carl, It almost seems as if the world's alright when we're with you." A colleague commented of Carl and Helen, "Why marriage is so powerful an institution I'll never know, except that there must have been a time when there were a lot of marriages like that."[9]

Aside from living in a beautiful setting, they were also near enough to the city and its resources for their work and avocations. For Helen, San Diego provided the opportunity to resume her work with Planned Parenthood. Madison was a small town that Helen had found cool to the family-planning concept. Here the climate seemed more receptive; in fact, at the time they arrived, a branch of Planned Parenthood was just getting started. It was difficult to raise the funds to get the program launched, and for a few years it was uncertain as to whether they would succeed. Then came the opportunity for some substantial federal funding if they could raise enough money locally to match a small part of the bigger grant. For many years Helen had intended to donate a significant sum to this cause when she died. She now concluded that as long as the money could be used effectively at this point, she might as well do it sooner than later.[10] Her $10,000 gift established the San Diego County Planned Parenthood firmly on its feet,[11] and she remained active in the branch for several years until health problems required her to stop.

Western Behavioral Sciences Institute

For Rogers it was less than a ten-minute drive down the hill and along Torrey Pines Road to number 1121, the offices of the Western Behavioral Sciences Institute (WBSI). The story of how he came to be making that ten-minute drive dated back six years, to 1958. As mentioned earlier, it was then that Rogers was invited by Thomas Gordon and Richard Farson to serve with them on the staff of an intensive workshop on group leadership, which they had organized in Ojai, California.[12] Both Gordon and Farson had been doctoral students of Rogers and were now working together in a private consulting firm, Gordon and Farson Associates.

One of the workshop participants was Dr. Paul Lloyd, a wealthy California Institute of Technology physicist. Lloyd had retired years before and was spending most of his time on his extensive ranch near Rancho Santa Fe, part of a family inheritance derived from the Ventura oil fields. He was extremely impressed with Rogers and Farson and much of the work going on in the behavioral sciences. "The Ojai conference was a hell of a good experience for me," he recalled. "Carl Rogers elevates the individual; he made me feel worthwhile. I looked up Dick when I got back to San Diego because I thought I might set up a foundation to provide scholarship funds for people who otherwise might not be able to attend such workshops."[13] But Farson had been trying unsuccessfully for some time to establish a university research center with a humanistic orientation. Instead of focusing on scholarships, he developed a proposal for establishing an independent institute which Lloyd agreed to fund. They and social psychologist Wayman ("Bud") Crow soon established WBSI. Starting then, and continuing over several years, Lloyd began selling off $760,000 worth of Rancho Santa Fe land, which enabled the Institute to get started and survive during difficult periods. Rogers was the first person after Lloyd to be invited to serve on the Board of Trustees. He accepted and continued on the board when he finally moved to California to become a "Resident Fellow" at WBSI.[14] Another board member was the famous semanticist and future Senator from California, S.I. Hayakawa, who had been a faculty member at Chicago simultaneously with Carl Rogers.[15]

The second most prominent WBSI fellow was Jack Gibb, a leader in human relations training and management consulting who "turned down the chairmanship of Columbia University's social psychology department and a professorship at Yale in favor of a permanent WBSI association in 1963," about the same time Rogers agreed to come.[16] Abraham Maslow, Charles Osgood, Theodore Newcomb and other famous psychologists came for a time as visiting fellows, before and during Rogers' tenure at WBSI.[17] Philosopher Abraham Kaplan was a visiting fellow when his picture appeared on the cover of *Time* magazine. Paul Tillich came for a WBSI conference; his Institute-sponsored dialogue with Rogers, discussed earlier, was his last public appearance.[18]

Rogers had told his friends in Wisconsin that one minor advantage of moving to WBSI was "a very generous increase in salary." This was initially $25,000 a year, a substantial salary for an academic in the 1960s.[19] A *San Diego Magazine* and *New York Times* article in 1967 popularized the notion that Rogers routinely donated his salary back to the non-profit organization, which was not the case, although his income-producing WBSI activities may have contributed as much to the institutional coffers as his salary. He also donated $27,000 which "kept several projects going" at WBSI.[20] His and Helen's income from salary, writing royalties, speeches, workshops, consulting, a part-time appointment at a nearby university, and investments provided a very comfortable living in those days, but not enough for them to be considered wealthy by U.S. standards at the time.[21]

His contributions to WBSI, then, were a good indication of how excited he was about the organization and its goals. Here was a group of men and women dedicated to furthering research about human learning and development and to applying that knowledge to improving human relations and solving social problems. Bud Crow and several other WBSI psychologists, for example, were working with the United States Joint Chiefs of Staff War Games agency, using 384 Navy recruits to simulate how tensions and problems can lead to war and how better communication could reduce tensions and lessen the probability of war. Farson and Lawrence Solomon, a California Western University psychologist, had a $23,000 grant from the office of Naval Research to study how to better predict leadership ability. They produced some interesting results showing how much leadership potential there is in the average person. This led to another project in which Solomon and Betty Berzon showed that leaderless groups could often be as effective as those with trained leaders. This, in turn, led to Berzon's getting a research grant from the San Diego Vocational Rehabilitation Administration to use the leaderless groups to help Department of Rehabilitation clients get back on their feet, helping one another to overcome the physical or emotional handicaps that interfered with their employment. Solomon had the largest WBSI grant, a study of the War on Poverty in San Diego County, funded by the U.S. Office of Economic Opportunity.[22] Staff members also developed simulation games for high school students to learn about national politics and international affairs.[23]

Much of the funding of WBSI projects came from government sources, where the "big money" was. Later this would create a problem for the Institute; but this was the type of work in which fifty or so active researchers on the staff of WBSI were engaged—trying to learn more about helping people by working with people, trying to change the traditional model of the detached researcher to one of the involved, committed researcher, learning from one's own experiences in the real world.

The Behavioral Sciences

It was this role for the behavioral sciences that truly excited Rogers. Although he had written about it several times before coming to California,[24] his most extensive contribution on the subject came during his tenure at WBSI, in collaboration with another staff member, William Coulson. For six months, beginning in 1966, Rogers, Coulson, and others at WBSI had been working on a program of investigating the philosophy of the behavioral sciences. Dissatisfied with the idea that the logical positivist tradition in science, with its objectification of the subject of study, was sufficient for the study of human beings, their program had four goals: "to examine the current assumptions on which the behavioral sciences are built, and the model of science currently held in this field; to consider the various points of view which bear on this problem, and the contributions each has made; to hold small conferences—in which the individuals would be from different sciences, and would hold different orientations in the philosophy of science; [and] to assist in formulating a philosophy of science and a model of science more appropriate for present-day behavioral sciences."[25]

When project members learned that Michael Polanyi, the British scientist and philosopher whose book *Personal Knowledge*[26] and other writings had contributed much to understanding the investigator's personal role in the pursuit of science, was in the United States as Senior Fellow at the Center for Advanced Studies at Wesleyan University, they invited him to come to WBSI for a small conference with a dozen or so people, mostly WBSI staff. He accepted, but soon one idea led to another and the conference got bigger and bigger. It was eventually held in cooperation with the Philosophy Department of the University of California at San Diego, where Dr. Polanyi delivered an all-university lecture, and with the Salk Institute, which contributed the physical site for the conference and whose Drs. Jacob Bronowski and Jonas Salk participated in the conference. Other philosophers and scientists from England, France, Israel, and the United States also participated.

The format generally consisted of a speech followed by discussion, the two major exceptions being Dr. Polanyi's all-university address and a televised dialogue between Rogers and Polanyi. Rogers and Polanyi's respect and affection for one another—stemming from their time together at the Center for Advanced Study at Stanford a few years earlier—failed to set the tone for the conference. Rather the conference was characterized by a decided lack of communication among the representatives of the various disciplines and even among those of the same disciplines. There was, in Rogers' words, "feeling and passion in the encounters which occurred so freely ... There was the very rationalistically minded member of the conference who came out repeatedly with such passionate statements as 'This is nonsense,' 'You are completely wrong.' There was the representative of the hard sciences who felt that the sciences of man should 'put off mathematics as long as possible, and put off philosophy indefinitely!' There was the prominent psychologist who, stung by sharp criticism of present-day psychology, made the remark (only partly facetious) that future conferences should be limited to only psychologists, who could consequently understand one another."[27]

Rogers, as much as anyone, was in the thick of the discussion, not only as a clarifier and facilitator, but usually as an opinionated participant, as the following exchange illustrates.

ROGERS: Now wait a minute. I take a strong dislike, I will admit, to the academic one-upmanship that seems to me to be your hallmark. I accept most of the criticisms which you just made of what I said—but they don't apply at all to the example that Farson gave ... [later] I want to ask you before you leave, something of where you stand. You always tear down other people, but what the hell do you stand for?

BAR-HILLEL: I'm not a sociologist or a psychologist. Why do I have to stand for anything ...? But I can say that *methodologically* many of the remarks that I heard today are methodologically quite wrong.

ROGERS: I'm sure that whatever anyone said would to you be quite wrong.

BAR-HILLEL: No, I disagree quite strongly. Many things which you said in your talk three days ago, I found perfectly acceptable. But today, this particular formulation and this pseudo-intrusion of responsibility and so on—these I regard as pseudo-formulations.

MORRISON: We want to know where you stand in philosophy. I would like to know very much.

BAR-HILLEL: I stand 12½ percent to the right of Carnap. What kind of a question is that: "Where do I stand in philosophy ...?" I'm a philosopher of science, a philosopher of language, a philosopher of mathematics, an analytic philosopher, an algebraic linguist. What other information ...[28]

If the previous example shows Rogers' impatience and sarcasm, which often arose when he was frustrated, a later excerpt from the discussion shows his tenacious, college debater's side.

ROGERS: Let me ask just one question. You must probably, in your own lifetime, have changed from some enthusiasms for operationism and logical positivism to enthusiasm for a different view. Is that a choice that you made? Or was that the result of scientific findings?

BAR-HILLEL: Of the scientific findings of other people, sure. It was a development introduced by the fact that we had, in addition, a better understanding of methodology of science.

ROGERS: So it was not a choice on your part. It was simply that the facts moved you in that direction.

BAR-HILLEL: Oh, but they moved me, they didn't move others. So obviously some choice elements were involved, because the same facts as I see them were available to everybody. And since not everybody went in this direction ...

ROGERS: This is what we're saying here, that the choice we make as to what science is and what science means and what the appropriate methods of science are, are choices that we make, and those choices make a sharp difference.

CROW: And they're not to be answered solely by scientific knowledge.

BAR-HILLEL: But the fact that so-and-so made this choice and so-and-so did not make this choice is a fact that has to be investigated, and can be investigated by science. That A did make this move and B did not, this is obviously part and parcel of purely scientific investigations … [Later] Very often—I am afraid I will again offend people—very often scientists when they philosophize (and they do it, for instance, today), very often they go quite wrong, and a good knowledge of a good methodology of science might help them not to philosophize wrongly. So the philosophy of science, the methodology of science, may help scientists not to philosophize in the wrong direction.

CROW: Is what Polanyi is saying—is that right or wrong? And is that a scientific question?

BAR-HILLEL: On Sunday I made my point very clear. I don't want to repeat it. I definitely think that Polanyi is wrong in most of what he said, as I understand it, but I don't want to repeat my arguments.

CROW: Is it on the basis of scientific evidence that he is wrong?

BAR-HILLEL: Of methodology of science. On the basis of methodology of science.

ROGERS: That's not science, that's a creed.

BAR-HILLEL: What kind of a dichotomy is this? Is science a creed?

ROGERS: Methodology of science is something that scientists themselves have dreamed up and believe in.

FAIRCHILD: It's an invention.

BAR-HILLEL: I don't believe in any methodology of science. I don't even understand this strange mode of speech—I'm not a fideist.

ROGERS: You just said your judgment about Polanyi's statement was based on methodology of science.

BAR-HILLEL: Yes, he's using the wrong methodology. What is so strange about it?

ROGERS: Well, you believed in one methodology.

BAR-HILLEL: What do you mean by "believe it"? What do you mean, I have to believe it?

POLANYI: No, you don't believe it, you know it.[29]

Coulson and Rogers edited the proceedings of the conference—four papers, many excerpts from the discussions, the televised Polanyi–Rogers dialogue—

added some introductory and summary comments, and through the Charles E. Merrill Publishing Company of Columbus, Ohio, had a small volume published entitled *Man and the Science of Man*.[30] Rogers hoped the book would demonstrate "the growth of a new view of behavioral science … a view so radically different from the current view that it will be shocking to many."[31] He did not want to minimize the enormous accomplishments of the traditional scientific methodology, but believed that "the whole enterprise of science can be seen as but one portion of a larger field of knowledge in which truth is pursued in many equally meaningful ways, science being one of those ways."[32]

Five years after publication the book had sold a grand total of 2,100 copies, by far the least successful book in Rogers' career.[33] The only review I could locate said, "*Man and the Science of Man* is an exciting and well-edited book. It brings forward one of the central problems in the social and behavioral sciences today. Perhaps it is because the book is exciting, that this reviewer also finds it somewhat disappointing. This book just touches the surface of one of the most important issues facing the social and behavioral sciences today. *Man and the Science of Man* appears to make a minimal contribution to the resolution of the conflict."[34]

Aside from the book just touching the surface of the subject, as the reviewer said, I would suggest another reason for the book's negligible impact. Throughout his career Rogers frequently was critical of previous conceptions, sometimes even his own. But always, in addition to his criticisms, he gave very concrete examples to show the alternative he was advocating. But here, in criticizing the traditional mode of scientific inquiry in the behavioral sciences, he provided practically no concrete alternatives or examples. Most of the discussion is quite intellectualized and abstract. One might have expected Rogers to find a way to include case studies of scientists who employed this new philosophy and methodology of the behavioral sciences. Or we might have expected a discussion of many research studies in the mode he was advocating. Such specific examples had always characterized his writing. Here they were lacking; though to be fair, it was a collaborative effort on Rogers' part, and the authors may have consciously chosen simply to report the conference, rather than write an extensive treatise themselves on the subject. Still, Rogers was stating that this new approach to science "would lead to choices of different problems as worthy of investigation; to hypotheses of a sharply different sort; to methods sharply different from those in use today."[35] From reading this volume alone, it is hard to tell just what problems, hypotheses, and methods those would be. Did they mean "qualitative research" methods, "ethnography," or "participatory action research," for example? One can't tell; the terms were never even mentioned.[36] Rogers wrote (honestly, but perhaps a little presumptuously about his own work), "I regard this as a prophetic book" which "gives us a glimpse of the science of man as it will be perceived in the future."[37] That may be; in a sense the book was prophetic. But although the discussion is quite stimulating, if the book was meant to be a signpost pointing toward the future, it was a signpost whose letters were hard to read, and the traveler would have much difficulty getting under way.

To be fair to Rogers and Coulson, the new paradigms in social science research at the time were just beginning to become more widely known and discussed. If Rogers was just learning about them himself at the time, he would continue learning over the coming years and, in 1985, would publish an article titled "Toward a More Human Science of the Person" in which he cited emerging scholars in qualitative research, heuristic research, human inquiry, and new approaches to evaluation, and provided many examples of these newer research models in practice.[38] Also to be fair to Rogers and Coulson, the book had another purpose. It was the first in a series called *Studies of the Person* which they would edit for the Charles E. Merrill Publishing Company. The series was designed to explore the many issues that would contribute to our understanding of the human being as the subject, not the object, of science. If the first book in the series lacked specific examples, the later volumes would attempt to fill the gap. Within a few years a dozen or so books—mostly in psychology and education—would be published by Merrill, many of these receiving much more attention than the keynote book of the series.

When the series began in 1968, Rogers thought he would enjoy his co-editor's role. It seemed a good way to relax, keep up with new ideas through reading manuscripts, and help sponsor younger men and women whose work deserved wider attention. As it turned out the role proved tedious.[39] Although he helped some good manuscripts reach publication, the pile of unread manuscripts in his study became less of a pleasurable prospect and more of an unwelcome intrusion which kept him from his own work. Allowing the publisher to continue using his name on the book covers ("Studies of the Person—A series originated by Carl R. Rogers and William R. Coulson"), Rogers resigned from the co-editorship in 1973. For several years thereafter the series continued under Coulson's direction.

Encounter Groups

While WBSI members worked on many different types of projects, the activity that undoubtedly got the most publicity was its use of "encounter groups." In this Rogers was the leading figure at WBSI, with Dr. Jack Gibb running a close second. For about a decade, starting in 1964, Rogers became intensely involved in the encounter-group "movement" and became known nationally as a leader in the field. The magazine *Psychology Today* called him the "grand master."[40] An article in the popular *Look* magazine referred to him as "an elder statesman of encounter groups."[41] Some people even believed that Rogers invented encounter groups, which is untrue, but suggests that a brief historical look might be in order.

In 1946 and 1947 the famous Gestalt psychologist Kurt Lewin and his colleagues were developing a type of leadership training that utilized the intensive small group as a vehicle for learning. They were discovering how, in the absence of a formal agenda, a group could study its own development—the communication patterns within the group, leadership issues, the development of group "norms," the reactions of members to one another—and how this type of learning could have great impact on the attitudes and leadership styles of group members.[42] After Lewin's death in 1947 his colleagues continued to develop this learning model. The initial purpose of the groups was to "train" individuals to be more effective leaders. This was done by helping them to better understand group dynamics and to be more "sensitive" to the reactions of others in the group, especially to how their own behavior affected other group members. Because of this emphasis on training and sensitivity to others, the small groups became widely known as T-Groups (T for training) and the overall approach as "human relations training" and "sensitivity training."

For many summers in Bethel, Maine, the initial group of investigators and their colleagues continued to hold workshops under their organizational name, the National Training Laboratories. Initially affiliated with the National Education Association, the group later changed its name to the NTL Institute for Applied Behavioral Science, with headquarters in Alexandria, Virginia. NTL, as it is popularly called, has been more responsible than any other organization for spreading human-relations training. As Rogers readily admitted, "NTL did the real pioneering in the encounter-group movement, and really have been the prime moving force in the whole thing."[43] For many years they had a network of certified "trainers"; they and their members sponsored a good deal of research in the group dynamics area; they further developed their training approaches into the areas of organizational and community development; they collaborated on a university graduate program in organizational development; and they performed contracted services for hundreds of large and small industrial, religious, and educational organizations.[44]

Also in 1946 and 1947, Rogers and his colleagues at the Counseling Center of the University of Chicago were themselves experimenting with the small, intensive group. This was different from group therapy, per se. Shortly after arriving in Chicago, Rogers tried that, too. He told a class, "People are doing group therapy. I've never done any, but if some of you would like to volunteer we could try some group therapy." About ten or twelve students did volunteer and he conducted nine group therapy sessions.[45] That experiment aside, Rogers had by then developed a teaching style which had much in common with the later encounter group. He didn't teach. He provided resources, but let the class decide what it wanted to do, attempting to clarify the thoughts and feelings of students as these emerged. In this leadership vacuum conflict was not uncommon, nor was closeness, as members finally began taking the responsibility for the group on their own shoulders and started sharing resources and helping one another. Thus, quite naturally, Rogers began developing his own style as group "facilitator," as he came to call it.

At the same time, he and his colleagues were confronted with a task which took them in a similar direction. The Veterans Administration asked the Counseling Center to run short training programs for personal counselors who could work with the many returning GIs who needed psychological help.[46] Realizing that this training required experiential learning, they wondered how they could provide a large number of people with actual experience in counseling in a short period of time. Their solution was to create small groups in which the Center staff members would serve as "counselors" to the whole group. It was hoped that this would help the members to "better understand themselves, to become aware of attitudes which might be self-defeating in the counseling relationship, and to relate to each other in ways that would be helpful and could carry over into their counseling work."[47] What they found was that the group members became extremely close, that members began counseling and helping one another, and that the experience seemed to have an enormous impact upon the participants.

The key difference between the NTL groups and the Chicago groups was that the former had as their major focus the professional training of leaders, with the personal growth of the participants being a secondary gain; while the latter had the personal growth of the participants as its major focus, with the expectation that this personal growth would enable the individuals to be more effective in their helping relationships. Rogers recalled, "It was probably in 1947 that Tom Gordon went to Bethel to visit the NTL lab there. I remember that he came back quite critical and sure that we were doing a better job. They were, at that time, very much focused on the skill training where our approach was much more closely allied to the therapeutic and the differences are quite sharp. I guess as a result of that we didn't pay much attention to NTL for some years."[48]

Still, Rogers did not attach much importance to their experience with intensive small groups at Chicago. He was just getting his major research under way at the time and had enough trouble designing the research to measure the process and outcomes of individual psychotherapy. Measuring the "group therapy" process seemed to him an insurmountable task.

A few years later, though, he had another experience along these lines, as he told an interviewer in 1967. "The next time I was involved in a group experience was in the autumn of 1950 when I conducted a postgraduate seminar type of therapy held just before the APA meetings. I remember that for one hour each day I counseled a client in front of a group of twelve. The discussion periods started off on a somewhat academic basis, but as we got into it, sharing more and more deeply of our personal experiences, our failures, and our difficulties, it became a moving personal experience. All of us left there feeling we had gained deeply. What amazed me was the long-lasting effect from the experience. It was then that I began to realize the potency of group experience."[49]

After that his classes and training workshops and an annual summer workshop at the Counseling Center given throughout the early and mid-fifties often took on the intensity of these prior experiences. But he wrote and said little on the subject, occupied as he was with his major research on individual psychotherapy. Then in the summer of 1958 he was invited by Gordon and Farson to be with them on the staff of the two-week workshop in Ojai, California (which indirectly led to the formation of WBSI). He recalled, "I suspect it was the first one in which I had participated in which it was clear that the main focus was on our interpersonal relationships and that this was a group of people who came for that purpose and not because they felt serious problems."[50]

In the sixties he began to do an increasing number of workshops of this type, with his focus shifting more toward the intensive group experience and away from a cognitive focus on a particular topic such as therapy or leadership. At the same time "sensitivity training," as it was being called more often, was gaining increasing popularity throughout the country. Esalen Institute, founded in 1962 and located on the Big Sur coastline in California, gained wide publicity for its work with groups, often geared more toward the personal growth of participants and including more nonverbal and sensory awareness activities than the NTL network tended to use. By now the "trainer," "group leader," or "facilitator" was becoming an accepted role in the helping professions, and many individuals were earning most or all of their livelihood by going from group to group helping people grow personally and/or learn new skills in group participation and leadership. It was a modern version of the traveling Chautauqua religious revival meetings, except the focus was on the horizontal not the vertical dimension, and the behavioral sciences not the scriptures was the gospel being experienced, not preached.

People often asked, "Well, what is it exactly that happens in an encounter group? What do people do?" This is difficult to answer, partly because it is a different experience than many people have had, and partly because there are many different types of groups, with various participant compositions and various styles of leadership. One description of Rogers', though, tried to encompass most of the groups he was a part of: "The basic encounter group is relatively unstructured, which provides a climate of maximum freedom for personal expression, exploration of feelings, and interpersonal communication. Emphasis is on interaction among the group members, in an atmosphere which encourages each to drop his defenses and facades and thus enables him to relate directly and openly to other members of the group. Individuals come to know themselves and each other more fully than is possible in the usual social or working relationships; the climate of openness, risk-taking and honesty generates trust which enables the participant to recognize and change self-defeating attitudes, to test out and adopt more innovative and constructive behaviors and subsequently relate more adequately and effectively to others in his everyday life situation."[51]

What attracted Carl Rogers to all this? When he left Wisconsin in 1963, he was a sixty-two-year-old man who had made an enormous contribution to his field and, following most conventional patterns, should be getting ready to settle into semiretirement to enjoy his autumn years working around his garden, keeping up on his profession through reading and occasionally writing an article, making a speech, or helping some younger colleague along. Moreover, here was a rather levelheaded individualist, a conservative when it came to fads and movements, a product of Midwestern reserve and inhibition, a husband for almost forty years, grandfather of six, wealthy enough not to need the money which attracted some to the group-work field—in short, here was one of the least likely candidates to start a whole new phase of his career by entering the young, energetic, and erratic "human-potential movement" which seemed to be growing so fast in popularity across the nation.

On the other hand, it was all very logical. Rogers' style from the beginning was that of a maverick and a pioneer. Whether moving from job to job or theory to theory, he had left comfortable places before. On leaving Chicago he had said he was eager to go to Wisconsin to work with "psychotics and normals," two populations he had had little contact with until then. For six years he worked with schizophrenics, but the research component which dealt with a normal population did not work out. Normals did not seem to want to enter into psychotherapy, so he was unable to test his general hypothesis that congruence, unconditional positive regard, and empathic understanding would help even normal individuals grow toward greater psychological maturity and openness. The small-group experience seemed an ideal occasion to extend the application of his theories and methods. Thousands of normal people were flocking to these groups. In fact, in most advertising it was stressed that the groups were not designed to be a substitute for therapy but were designed for well-functioning individuals who desired to increase their personal satisfaction and effectiveness in life. Here was the perfect occasion for Rogers to be Rogers—accepting and understanding—and to see how this would help normal people in their quest for growth.

Accepting and understanding, yes, but also *congruent*; and herein lies another reason for Rogers' entering the encounter-group field. As a former student wrote, "I'm not surprised he went into Encounter eventually. It could easily be a natural outgrowth from his original ideas of neurosis, but it might also reflect his own need to be closer, and to touch."[52] In earlier chapters we saw Rogers as a shy boy, sensitive, liking people, but awkward in social settings. When he was a young man, it was primarily through church-related work that he made contact with others his age. Previously quoted comments by his associates described a man who could appear both warm and aloof yet entered readily into deep emotional contact with people when he had the occasion, as in therapy. In his own professional approach he gradually recognized the importance of the congruent therapist, a whole person in the relationship. This recognition coincided with his own therapy, in which he came to trust his own feelings more and to value himself more. Even in his writing style he came to project himself and reach out to the reader in increasingly personal ways. The composite is a picture of a man striving in different ways throughout his life to share more of himself, to come into closer contact with people around him. Where the setting encouraged this, as in therapy, he was capable of extremely close relationships and delighted in them. But in most other situations it was rarely easy. There was always the reserve to overcome. As many colleagues have commented, he lacked a natural spontaneity, although he strove always to be genuine and usually inspired trust in those who knew him. Thus, for Rogers, encounter groups provided not only a realm of further professional interest, but a vehicle for his own personal growth, a chance to move along the same process continuum as his clients, toward a greater trust in and openness to his feelings and a greater willingness to risk himself in relationships.

One of the major reasons he put forward for the widespread growth of intensive groups was the loneliness people feel when cut off from each other or when they feel that the deepest parts of themselves are not acceptable to others. "I can speak very personally about this," he wrote, "because I feel that risk-taking is one of the many things I myself have learned from experience in encounter groups. Though I do not always live up to it, I have learned that there is basically nothing to be afraid of. When I present myself as *I am,* when I can come forth nondefensively, without armor, just me—when I can accept the fact that I have many deficiencies and faults, make many mistakes, and am often ignorant where I should be knowledgeable, often prejudiced when I should be open-minded, often have feelings which are not justified by the circumstances—then I can be much more real. And when I can come out wearing no armor, making no effort to be different from what I am, I learn much more—even from criticism and hostility—and am much more relaxed and get much closer to people. Besides, my willingness to be vulnerable brings forth so much more real feeling from other people in relation to me that it is very rewarding. So I enjoy life very much more when I am not defensive, not hiding behind a facade, but just trying to be and express the real me."[53]

For example, "I am often slow to sense and express my own anger. Consequently, I may only become aware of it and express it later. In a recent encounter group I was at different times very angry with two individuals. With one I was not conscious of it until the middle of the night and had to wait until the next morning to express it. With the other, I was able to realize and express it in the session in which it occurred. In both instances it led to real communication—to a strengthening of the relationship and gradually to the feeling of genuine liking for each other. But I am a slow learner in this area and consequently have a real appreciation of what others go through as they try to relax their defenses sufficiently to let immediate feelings of the moment seep through into awareness."[54]

The incident he was describing may have been this one, told in more detail by group member, corporate executive Bill Laughlin: "One of the participants had been cynical about life, had been withdrawn from the group for the entire week and was, in fact, a very unpleasant fellow. Carl was determined he was going to open this person up. He tried about every concept, every approach that he had … It simply didn't work. On the very last morning (we were to leave at noon) he came in completely haggard after a sleepless night. With tears in his eyes (I have often thought he was a tremendous actor) he told of how much empathy and love he had for this individual and how his complete inability to get through to him caused him to turn and toss all night. He told us of his immense anguish, and that he would never again be involved in a T-Group for executives because of his tremendous weaknesses and inability to cope with the situation. 'I'm just not any good at this kind of thing with the executives.' Of course, this set the whole group up to an immediate high. The result was vicious attacks on the withdrawn participant, which, to make a long story short, opened him up. By twelve o'clock, our departure time, Carl and the poor fellow were in each others arms weeping copiously. It was a peak experience for all—beautiful, satisfying and very helpful to the individual."[55]

Friends and family frequently commented on the changes they saw in him resulting from his encounter group experiences. Natalie said, "I've seen a tremendous change in him. I just can't get over it. He was very private through my high school days, and I grew up very private—not revealing myself at all, but I could help other people talk. He was that way; he could help other people open up about themselves but not say anything about himself. The group experiences he has had have changed him into being much more self-revealing, much more open about his needs for affection and being affectionate or demonstrative." For example, "being physical—the way he gives me a hug or a kiss or the way he will come sit down and put his arm around me, particularly if I may be in some emotional pain, or the way I see him in groups talk about himself or move—take himself out of a place and move toward somebody. I don't think it ever would have occurred to him to get up and move physically closer to somebody before he'd been in encounter groups, that that would matter, that that feels good to him as well as to the other person."[56] David thought his father was always able to be himself, even before his involvement with encounter groups, but his examples were all from the encounter group period. "He can tell somebody 'You bore me' in ways that aren't terribly offensive. When he's decided to go to bed, he'll leave or say 'I'm going to bed.' He's quite comfortable being himself. Once I called him and he said, 'It bothers me that you only call me when you want something.' He's totally consistent."[57]

Whatever his motives for becoming involved with encounter groups, he certainly became deeply involved. During the five-year period from 1964 through 1968 he served as facilitator in dozens of groups lasting from one day to eight days, not including the shorter groups and the brief demonstrations of encounter groups he did before live audiences. Each year NTL invited him to lead a group in their "Presidents Lab," a week-long training experience for the presidents and executive officers of large corporations. For three years he had an ongoing relationship with the California Institute of Technology, where he spent two days a month working with the "Honker Group" of faculty and administrators. Also over a two-year period, he and his colleagues conducted numerous groups for administrators, faculty, and students in the Immaculate Heart College and School System in Southern California. He had two-day to five-day experiences with the administrators and faculty of the six Claremont Colleges; with a number of trustees, administrators, faculty, and students of Columbia University just after that University's famous student uprising in the spring of 1968; with the faculty and students of thirteen junior colleges; with the counseling staff of several colleges; with business executives at various levels; with administrative, teaching, and supervisory nurses; with religious workers of many denominations; with inner-city, African-American and Hispanic "consumers" of health services and health agency "providers" of medical services; with mental health workers in all categories; with couples; with adolescents; with many teachers; and with many university classes taught in an encounter-group fashion.[58]

In all these groups Rogers' role was that of "facilitator." He preferred this term to "trainer," maintaining that he was not training anyone toward a specific goal, but facilitating or helping each individual achieve his or her own goals during the course of the group's life. As in individual therapy, the conditions of congruence, unconditional positive regard, and empathic understanding were the most essential ingredients in his facilitative role. One might wonder, how can a person be congruent if he is playing a role? For Rogers there was no conflict. He viewed himself in the group first and primarily as a person, a real person with many different goals—to grow himself, to learn more about groups, to achieve meaningful contact and communication with others, *and* to be helpful to others when he could. The facilitator was but one dimension of the person he was. If he tried to "act like a facilitator" in a group, that would undoubtedly be incongruent and group members would likely sense this before long. But simply *being facilitative* was a natural part of his personal behavior, one which he prized, one which he demonstrated frequently in or out of encounter groups.

Sitting in the circle of a dozen or so strangers, he would often begin a group by saying something like, "Well, here we are, I feel a little nervous right now. I don't know how this will turn out. It's really up to us to make of this group what we wish to. And I'm also a bit excited right now and eager to get to know you." And much to everyone's dismay, he might stop right there. Filling this unusual leadership vacuum would come several reactions: typical introductions that one of the members might initiate; small talk; one or two expressions of personal feelings— "I'm a bit confused at what's happening here," "I hope this group will help me to understand myself better," expressions that would often go unnoticed or be ignored, as the group would not yet be ready to move to more intimate communication; and talk about outside-the-group situations or past feelings they have had, as this, too, would be easier to discuss than what they are feeling or experiencing in the "here and now." Some members might even question the leaders' credentials or ability, as when a high school girl who had no idea who Rogers was, asked him, "I think this sounds like kind of a risky thing. What are your qualifications for doing this?"[59] Throughout all this Rogers probably would be relatively passive, chuckling along with a joke but not encouraging a partying atmosphere, nodding and letting people know he was hearing them, conveying an attitude which implied, "That's OK. I know you're a little nervous. It is an unusual situation, I admit. But I'm confident. You're doing fine. We're doing all right as a group. It will all work out." Throughout this "milling-around" period, however, Rogers would be conveying, nonverbally and verbally, a strong attitude of acceptance to the group members. As he once described it, "I wish very much to make the climate psychologically safe for the individual. I want him to feel from the first that if he risks saying something highly personal, or absurd, or hostile, or cynical, there will be at least one person in the circle who respects him enough to hear him clearly and listen to that statement as an authentic expression of himself."[60]

Somehow this attitude of acceptance would reach the participants, and they would experience the freedom to express more personally the feelings, thoughts, experiences, and hurts within them. This would not happen all at once, but gradually and tentatively. As people would begin to share more of themselves, Rogers would tend to become more active in his empathic responses. To a husband who had just uttered a very complicated and somewhat incoherent statement, Rogers would say, "And so, little by little, you have come to hold back things that previously you would have communicated to your wife? Is that it?"[61] To two individuals disagreeing with one another on the subject of marriage, he would say, "There is a real difference between the two of you, because you, Jerry, are saying, 'I like smoothness in a relationship. I like it to be nice and tranquil,' and Winnie is saying, 'To hell with that! I like communication.'"[62]

As these earlier expressions of feeling are understood and accepted, the level of group trust deepens, and people feel safe enough to share even more of themselves. In one of Rogers' groups, for example, there was a government executive, a man with high responsibility and excellent technical training as an engineer. Rogers recalled how "at the first meeting of the group he impressed me, and I think others, as being cold, aloof, somewhat bitter, resentful, cynical. When he spoke of how he ran his office he appeared to administer it 'by the book' without warmth or human feeling entering in. In one of the early sessions, when he spoke of his wife, a group member asked him, 'Do you love your wife?' He paused for a long time, and the questioner said, 'OK, that's answer enough.' The executive said, 'No, wait a minute! The reason I didn't respond was that I was wondering if I ever loved anyone. I don't think I have *ever* really *loved* anyone.' It seemed quite dramatically clear to those of us in the group that he had come to accept himself as an unloving person ... [B]efore the week was over he had thought through new ways of handling his growing son, on whom he had been placing extremely rigorous demands. He had also begun genuinely to appreciate his wife's love for him which he now felt he could in some measure reciprocate."[63]

These deeper expressions of feeling often involved members sharing their feelings toward one another, positive and negative. This often led to what Rogers called a "basic encounter," a moment of real and accepting contact between individuals, a meeting without facades, an "I–Thou" relationship. One woman described such an incident in a letter to Rogers, following their experience together in an encounter group. After describing herself as a "loud, prickly, hyperactive individual," whose marriage was in serious trouble and who had felt that life was just not worth living, she wrote, "I had really buried under a layer of concrete many feelings I was afraid people were going to laugh at or stomp on which, needless to say, was working all kinds of hell on my family and on me. I had been looking forward to the workshop with my last few crumbs of hope. It was really a needle of trust in a huge haystack of despair ... the real turning point for me was a simple gesture on your part of putting your arm around my shoulder one afternoon when I had made some crack about you not being a member of the group—that no one could cry on your shoulder. In my notes I had written the night before, 'There is no man in the world who loves me!' You seemed so genuinely concerned that day that I was overwhelmed ... I *received* the gesture as one of the first feelings of acceptance—of me, just the dumb way I am, prickles and all—that I had ever experienced. I have felt needed, loving, competent, furious, frantic, anything and everything but just plain *loved*. You can imagine the flood of gratitude, humility, release that swept over me. I wrote with considerable joy, 'I actually felt *loved*.' I doubt that I shall soon forget it."[64]

Rogers was certainly no stranger to the phenomenon of seeing people grow by experiencing previously denied or distorted feelings and incorporating these into an altered self-concept. What was new for Rogers was the extent to which he himself began operating in terms of his feelings. This had several dimensions.

First, he came to trust himself more than ever before. One particular occasion is a good illustration of this, when his head would have told him to do one thing, but his total inner experiencing told him something else. Sue was a high school girl, shy, serious, trusted by her peers. "The next day some very moving feelings were expressed, and the group paused for quite a time in silence. Sue finally broke into it with some highly intellectual questions—perfectly reasonable but somehow not at all appropriate to what was going on. I felt, at some intuitive

347

level, that she was not saying what she wanted to say, but she gave no clue as to what her real message might be. I found myself wanting to go over and sit next to her, but it seemed a crazy impulse, since she was not in any obvious way asking for help. The impulse was so strong, however, that I took the risk, crossed the room, and asked if I could sit by her on the couch, feeling that there was a large chance I would be rebuffed. She made room for me, and as soon as I sat down she leaped into my lap, threw her head over my shoulder, and burst into sobs. 'How long have you been crying?' I asked her. 'I haven't been crying,' she responded. 'No, I mean how long have you been crying inside?' 'Eight months.' I simply held her like a child until the sobbing gradually subsided. Little by little she was able to tell what was troubling her."[65]

His learning to trust his feelings more also applied to making physical contact with group members, as Natalie remarked. Achieving physical closeness with men and women other than Helen was a long way from his Midwestern upbringing, and he wrote, "I admire the younger people who are looser and freer in this respect."[66] Still he learned. "When a young woman was weeping because she had a dream that no one in the group loved her, I embraced her and kissed and comforted her. When a person is suffering, and I feel like going over and putting my arms around him, I do just that."[67]

His greater self-trust also involved being more aware of his fantasizing and a willingness to use his fantasies as an effective communication tool. He wrote, "For example, 'I suddenly had the fantasy that you are a princess, and that you would love it if we were all your subjects.' Or, 'I sense that you are the judge as well as the accused, and that you are saying sternly to yourself, "You are *guilty* on every count."' Or the intuition may be a bit more complex. While a responsible business executive is speaking, I may suddenly have the fantasy of the small boy he is carrying around within himself—the small boy that he was—shy, inadequate, fearful—a child he endeavors to deny, of whom he is ashamed. And I am wishing that he would love and cherish this youngster. So I may voice this fantasy—not as something true, but as a fantasy in me. Often this brings a surprising depth of reaction and profound insights."[68]

The previous examples show Rogers being increasingly expressive of the impulses, fantasies, metaphors, and dimly formed feelings he experienced. What about the more definite feelings to which he could clearly attach words, which were much more comprehensible to him and verbally communicable to others? Here, as in other cases, his learning came slowly. "In one particular group of educators there had been much superficial and intellectual talk, but gradually they moved to a deeper level. Then in an evening session the talk became more and more trivial. One person asked, 'Are we doing what we *want* to do?' And the answer was an almost unanimous 'No.' But within moments the talk again became social chatter about matters in which I had no interest. I was in a quandary. In order to allay a considerable early anxiety in the group, I had stressed in the first session that they could make of it exactly what they wished, and operationally they seemed to be saying very loudly, 'We want to spend expensive, hard-won weekend time talking of trivia.' Had I said in the first meeting, '*We* can make of this what we wish,' which would have been preferable and probably more honest, I would have felt free to say, 'I don't like what we are making of it.' But I was quite certain that in my attempt at reassurance I had said, 'You can make of it what you wish.' We always pay for our blunders. To express my feelings of boredom and annoyance seemed contradictory to the freedom I had given them.

"After wrestling within myself for a few moments, I decided that they had a perfect right to talk trivia, and I had a perfect right not to endure it. So I walked quietly out of the room and went to bed. After I left, and the next morning, the reactions were as varied as the participants. One felt rebuked and punished, another felt I had played a trick on them, a third felt ashamed of their time-wasting, others felt as disgusted as I at their trivial interchanges. I told them that, to the best of my awareness, I was simply trying to make my behavior match my contradictory feelings, but that they were entitled to their own perceptions. At any rate, after that the interactions were far more meaningful."[69]

Gradually, through many emotional experiences, he developed definite guidelines for how he wished to deal with his own feelings. "I endeavor to voice any *persisting* feelings which I am experiencing toward an individual or toward the group, in any significant or continuing relationship. Obviously such expressions will not come at the very beginning, since feelings are not yet persistent ones. I might, for example, take a dislike to someone's behavior during the first ten minutes the group is together, but would be unlikely to voice it at that time. If the feeling persists, however, I would express it.[70]

"I tend to confront individuals on specifics of their behavior. 'I don't like the way you chatter on. Seems to me you give each message three or four times. I wish you would stop when you've completed your message.'[71]

"… I like to confront another person only with feelings I am willing to claim as my own. These may at times be very strong. 'Never in my life have I been so pissed off at a group as I am at this one.' Or, to one man in the group, 'I woke up this morning feeling, I never want to see you again.'

"To attack a person's defenses seems to me judgmental. If one says, 'You're hiding a lot of hostility,' or 'You are being highly intellectual, probably because you are afraid of your own feelings,' I believe such judgments and diagnoses are the opposite of facilitative. If, however, what I perceive as the person's coldness frustrates me or his intellectualizing irritates me, or his brutality to another person angers me, then I would like to face him with the frustration or the irritation or the anger that exists in *me*. To me this is very important."[72]

Rogers tried to share his feelings not only during the group, but afterwards as well. Although it was not expected of him, he almost always followed up with some kind of group letter to the participants, as this excerpt from a long letter illustrates:

I am dictating this on Monday ... I am a little surprised at the sharpness of the memories that I have regarding each one of you ... I have various images of Dick but the one with the most meaning to me is when we were all moving about with our eyes closed and he twice pushed me vigorously out of his space and then our fingers touched and we tentatively explored the boundaries of the space between us and then with ever greater hesitancy he crooked the finger to indicate that he was inviting me—perhaps—into his life space ... When we came home, both Helen and I felt very much drained. We slept for 12 hours and now I ask myself sort of gently, not compulsively, "What meaning did it have for me?" ... Perhaps by the time this letter reaches you the experience will have cooled off and you may not be willing really to accept the final phrase of this letter but I want to state it as I feel it right now. With sincere love and affection for each of you—Carl.[73]

After one session of his ongoing group at the California Institute for Technology, he wrote the members a memo with a different tone than the previous one.

... I *was* angry. The thought flitted through my mind at one moment that it would feel good to just walk out of the group and out of Caltech forever. Why was I so angry ...?

As nearly as I can catch it, it just struck me, rather suddenly, with great force, that Caltech was a lousy place for infants ... human infants, infant ideas, infant interpersonal relationships, and infant science. It seems like a lousy place to *grow*.

Before I try to explain myself, let me remind you of what an infant is. An infant is an ungainly, poorly proportioned, messy, smelly being. He can't communicate well, can't understand well, is exceedingly imprecise and inaccurate in everything he fumblingly does. Besides this, he is demanding. The only things which draw us to him are his helpless fragility, which evokes a warm response in some of us, and his enormous potential, which evokes a favorable response in almost all of us.

Now what would (does) happen to an infant at Caltech? If anyone were fool enough to entrust a human infant to our care, the baby would be dissected within the hour to see what was making him tick. After all, that's the only scientific attitude ...[74]

This Carl Rogers is a far cry from the nondirective therapist who nods acceptingly as his client jumps out the window. While it was an exaggeration and distortion in the first place, the old characterization of Rogers is further outdated and inaccurate for not taking into account his significant movement toward a genuine person-to-person relationship, both in individual therapy and later in group work. It is interesting to speculate whether, if he went back to individual therapy after having worked with encounter groups, Rogers' style as a counselor–therapist would have been any different. Just before moving to Wisconsin, and while working with schizophrenics there, he recognized and wrote about the importance of the congruent therapist. But, as discussed earlier, his writing on the subject was rather vague, with an uncharacteristic dearth of illustrative examples. Working with encounter groups, he seemed to come to really understand and experience the meaning of congruence in a helping relationship. It seems to me inevitable that this experience would markedly affect his individual therapy if he had returned to that type of work. Such a change toward greater congruence would not be a contradiction of his previous practice, but a fuller, more sophisticated elaboration of a direction in which he had always been moving. Indeed, as we will see from demonstration therapy interviews he conducted in subsequent years, his individual therapy style did include more of his feelings and become more spontaneous and intuitive.

It is also interesting to note that the spontaneous use of his own feelings that he cultivated in encounter groups was a skill which Helen Rogers possessed all along. Many friends of theirs commented on this. As one said, "Helen is a very warm, supportive, direct, strong individual. When I talk with both of them, Helen is the one who's more apt to come out and 'give it to me,' if that's what I need—either really call my bluff or tell me exactly how she sees what's going on. And at times she's done this with such clarity and simplicity and directness, I've really been thankful to her."[75]

Still it was not surprising, with her husband becoming so involved with encounter groups, that she would try it herself. Her first experience, in 1964, was rather disastrous. She had considered using a different name in the group so she would not be associated with her famous husband and therefore could be treated just like any individual group member. But this went against her own sense of honesty; it didn't feel right to her to lie about her name. So during a round of introductions at the beginning of the group, she identified herself and asked everybody to please forget it and just treat her as "Helen." Unfortunately it didn't work. People couldn't seem to disassociate her from her husband, and she never really felt accepted for being herself. This left a sour taste in her mouth for encounter groups. The next year she tried it again and had a more positive experience.[76] But in the end she decided that encounter groups were not her cup of tea. She had mixed feelings about their value, sometimes appreciating Carl's work in this area, sometimes feeling skeptical about it and threatened by the intimacy he seemed to achieve with group members. Later Rogers posited that the problem Helen had relating to group members was more her doing than the others', recalling that "the people who were facilitating those groups ... wrote that she was absolutely incredible at shutting off expressions of feelings by others in the group. Carefully safe."[77] In any case, as she approached seventy, this just didn't seem to be the way she wished to spend her time.

Natalie Rogers also experienced her first encounter group around then, flying from San Diego to San Francisco with her father and his colleagues [CSP staff members] to a large event with many encounter groups that they were conducting with faculty of Sonoma State College.[78] The encounter group brought unresolved feelings and issues in Natalie and Larry's relationships to the surface. For a while she wondered, "Are workshops good? I still don't know … Is it worth it?"[79] (Later she became a workshop leader herself.) Larry also had mixed feelings at first, then concluded that the workshop was very helpful to their relationship.[80] For better or worse things were never the same, and for the next six years or so they struggled to save their marriage.

Compared to Helen's skepticism and Natalie and Larry's initial mixed reactions, Rogers' feelings about encounter groups were unequivocally bullish. He stayed involved in group work for many years, believing that the intensive group was "the most rapidly spreading social invention of the century, and probably the most potent."[81] In addition to leading many groups, he also tried to popularize them as much as he could. He made a series of twenty-six half-hour tapes for Instructional Dynamics Incorporated, in which he talked about all aspects of encounter groups, sometimes in dialogue with others who had expertise in particular applications of the intensive group.[82] He also used the mass media, particularly film and television. He was interviewed several times on educational television stations. On one occasion the TV camera focused on an encounter group for several minutes; then Rogers, who had been sitting in the circle with his back to the camera, turned out of the group, walked toward the camera and began sharing his thinking about encounter groups. Probably the most widely viewed television group was one led by Rogers and his colleague Tony Rose in 1970.[83] It was one of eight programs on the drug abuse problem, filmed at and produced by station WQED in Pittsburgh. In addition to Rogers and Rose there were eight participants, each with a different perspective on drugs: Randy, black, a former addict who had grown up among crime and drugs; Amy, white, a nineteen-year-old from a small private college; Joe, white, seventeen, curious about drugs; Paul, white, a middle-aged narcotics officer; Mac, a black woman who had lost a son to a heroin overdose and who ran a rehabilitation home in a black neighborhood in Pittsburgh; George, a white graduate student who said he was a revolutionary; Russ, white, a nineteen-year-old who was a heavy drug user; Diane, black, a middle-class graduate student whose brother was an addict.

The action on this film could hardly have been staged to produce more drama. On one morning, for example, Diane and George launched a strenuous attack on Rogers. Diane said, "I have seen a lot about Rogers in magazine articles and everywhere. He is a big name and shit! What has he given to us?" George accused Rogers of taking all the credit for the discoveries of others; then saying "This is stupid and superficial and I am going to go out into the real world," he walked out of the group. Amy began crying after witnessing such hostility. Tony, Rogers' co-facilitator, crossed the circle to hug and comfort her. After George left, Russ said, "My mother reached out but my dad has no compassion whatsoever. He never held me, nor cried with me." (By now Russ, Amy and Joe were crying.) "You need at least one person to hold you. I couldn't talk when George was here. He's like my dad—so sure he's right. I could never be violent. I know how it feels to get kicked and hit." Rogers put his arm around Russ's shoulder and told him he had heard very clearly his deep need for a father. Russ put his head on Rogers' shoulder and said, "If my father had held me for just one minute …" He sobbed as he said this, feeling it very deeply. A little later Randy said that he would rather die than go to prison again (he was scheduled to be sentenced a few days after the group. Later Rogers tried to intervene with the judge on his behalf),[84] and Russ said, "That's why kids take drugs—because they can die to get away from the horrors of life. We have to be ashamed of feelings in our culture. We can't express them." Later he said, "My grandmother gives me love. Sometimes we sit for hours and talk. She really listens to me. And now I have this group too. I talked with Amy till after 1:00 this morning. You know, I'm really afraid of girls and it was good to be able to talk with her without being afraid." Paul, the narcotics officer, was visibly moved. He showed an increasing understanding of Russ, Randy, and the others. When the group ended, he shook hands with some, hugged Amy very warmly and, wiping the tears from his eyes he said, "How am I going to make an arrest now?"

This and the other programs in the series won WQED-TV the prestigious Peabody Award for outstanding radio and television journalism.[85] Yet, as powerful a group as this one was, it did not receive the fame which another Rogers encounter group did. The sixteen-hour group, facilitated by Rogers and Richard Farson, was filmed over a weekend in March 1966 at the San Diego State College television studios.[86] It was edited into an hour-long, documentary film titled "Journey Into Self," produced and directed by Bill McGaw and distributed by WBSI. One particular sequence featured Jerry, a competent business executive. Rogers described how, "somewhat puzzled by the statements of others in the group, he said in an early session: 'I look at myself with some strangeness because I have no friends, for example, and I don't seem to require friends.' In a later session when he heard Beth, a married woman, talking of a remoteness she felt between herself and her husband and how much she craved a deeper and more communicative relationship, his face began to work and his jaw to quiver. Roz, another member of the group, seeing this, went over and put her arm around him and he broke into literally uncontrollable sobs. He had discovered a loneliness in himself of which he had been completely unaware and from which he had been well defended by an armor-plated shell of self-sufficiency."[87]

Stanley Kramer, the well-known Hollywood producer and director, took an interest in this film, even appearing in a brief introduction to it.[88] Between his help, and Rogers and Farson's appearing at several California theatres for the film's premier showings, the documentary received a considerable amount of attention. To the delight of Rogers, Farson, McGaw, and WBSI, "Journey Into

Self" was nominated in 1968 for an Academy Award in the Feature Length Documentary category and eventually won the prestigious "Oscar."[89]

On Encounter Groups

In addition to the tapes and films, Rogers' major means of explaining encounter groups to the general public was through his book *Carl Rogers On Encounter Groups*, published in 1970. While he was putting together the manuscript of this book, which included expansions of several former essays and speeches as well as some new material, an editor at Harper & Row Publishers named Donald Cutler showed up at Rogers' door to see if he was working on any books. When Cutler heard that Rogers was writing a book on encounter groups, he showed considerable interest and asked if he could take a copy back to New York with him to read and show the publisher. Rogers explained that he only had one copy and did not want to lend that out, but that after he had finished the draft he would send a copy to Cutler. Not to be put off, Cutler asked if he could borrow the manuscript and take it down to a drug store in La Jolla to duplicate on their copy machine. In a typically trusting manner, Rogers let him take the manuscript, and that began a relationship which proved to be gratifying to them both. Cutler obtained the contract with Harper & Row, one of the oldest and biggest publishing houses in the country. This was Rogers' first "trade book," aimed at a wide audience of general readers. To publicize the book, Harper & Row got Rogers an invitation to appear on Dick Cavett's nationally televised interview show. They were amazed when Rogers declined. "But one show will lead to another," they said incredulously. "That's what I'm afraid of," he answered, not relishing the idea of making frequent cross-country trips to sell books.[90] Still by January 1978, the book had sold 237,000 copies,[91] and helped associate the name of Rogers and encounter groups even more closely for professionals and laypeople alike.

In his first chapter he traced the history of the encounter-group movement. In the second he described the "process of the encounter group," outlining fifteen overlapping stages of development he saw most groups going through and giving specific examples of each to make the process vivid for the reader. In a unique third chapter, "Can I Be a Facilitative Person in a Group?", he described his own behavior and attitudes as a group facilitator and behaviors he regarded as non-facilitative. In a field where very few individuals were willing to risk describing what it was they did in leading intensive groups, where a mystique had grown up around the role of the charismatic or enigmatic group "trainer" or "facilitator," Rogers' chapter provided a real challenge and a reference point. He wrote, "I sincerely hope that this presentation will encourage others to speak for their own styles of group facilitation."[92]

In the fourth chapter, and in another chapter on research on encounter groups, he discussed the crucial question of what happens after the group is over. Is it only a weekend love affair which members go through with their groups, or are there lasting positive or negative behavior changes that show up in participants' relationships with their families, their friends, or at work? Here Rogers cited evidence both anecdotal and scientific. Some of Rogers' participants described enormous changes for themselves, when questioned weeks or months after the group. "I am more open, spontaneous. I express myself more freely. I am more sympathetic, empathic, and tolerant. I am more confident. I am more religious in my own way. My relations with my family, friends, and co-workers are more honest and I express my likes and dislikes and true feelings more openly. I admit ignorance more readily. I am more cheerful. I want to help others more."[93]

Other participants were more specific and less grandiose about the changes they observed.

"I was bothered about the squabbling between Marie and Alice. I was bothered about Marie's bedwetting. I was bothered that I couldn't give them a lot of affection. I was bothered because they never really talked to me. I was bothered by some of the hurtful things Pete and I could say to them. So, when I came floating home Sunday with this new real self, I was anticipating a response of sorts. What I didn't anticipate was the quickness and the intensity of the response." Shortly after she got home, it was bedtime for Marie, the ten-year-old daughter. Her mother asked Marie if she could scrub her. "Within the space of an hour we talked about menstruation, God, the Devil, Heaven, Hell, hating someone so much you wanted them dead, stealing candy from the kitchen, nightmares, monsters in the window. Of course we had talked about these things before, but never with such completeness. Alice, who is fifteen months older than Marie, came wandering into the bathroom and shared this experience with us. I ended up scrubbing her also. This surprised me—that she wanted me to bathe her—as her body is becoming adolescent and she is very self-conscious about this. Marie said, 'What did you do at that meeting—learn how to be nice to kids?' I said, 'No, I learned how to be myself, which is really pretty nice.'"[94]

Others described its effect on their work. Robert Edgar, Provost of Kresge College, a division of the University of California at Santa Cruz, wrote,

In some sense he [Rogers] was the founder of Kresge College. I first started on a personal growth journey and an educational journey as a consequence of the faculty seminar with him [run as an encounter group] where I first learned about student-centered learning. The concept excited me intellectually—I tried it in my classes immediately with disastrous results. I learned from this for the first time that the students were frightened of me and this then began a process of self-confrontation and change … This led me to take the job as Provost of a new

355

college at Santa Cruz which is now in existence. The underlying philosophy of the college is largely influenced by the contact that I've had with Carl Rogers. My ideas about education grew from his but are not his ... I can thank him for being the catalyst in my life and in the life of Kresge College. Up until that seminar at Caltech I never heard of him, I never heard of student-centered education ...[95]

Still other participants saw no behavior changes, only an image of what life might be. "The group experience is not a way of life but a reference point. My images of our group, even though I am unsure of some of their meanings, give me a comforting and useful perspective of my normal routine. They are like a mountain which I have climbed and enjoyed and to which I hope occasionally to return."[96]

Then, heavily quoting and drawing upon a book chapter written by his colleague Dr. Jack Gibb,[97] Rogers summarized the research evidence in support of the anecdotal assertions by participants. Gibb had "analyzed 106 studies, including 7 earlier reviews of such research. He had also examined 123 additional studies which did not measure up to his criteria for inclusion, as well as 24 recent doctoral dissertations from 13 universities."[98] His analysis indicated,

> The evidence is strong that intensive group training experiences have therapeutic effects ... Changes do occur in sensitivity, ability to manage feelings, directionality of motivation, attitudes toward the self, attitudes toward others, and interdependence ... The research evidence clearly indicates no basis for making any restrictions as to group membership ... Groups without leaders are effective as training media ... To be optimally effective the group training must be relevant to the organizational, family, and life environment of the person ... Effective consulting relationships on a continuing basis are at least as important as what occurs in the group sessions in determining impact upon the participants ... Training experiences to be optimally effective ... should be concentrated in uninterrupted and continuous sessions ... There is little basis for the widespread concern among lay groups about the traumatic effects of group training.[99]

Many professionals, as well as laypeople, have been concerned about the possible harmful effects of intensive groups. The research just cited was very important in addressing those concerns, but it should be noted—and Rogers would often brush over this point—that any group leader known to researchers like Gibb and others and willing to have his or her group observed, recorded, transcribed, or analyzed would most probably be a fairly responsible, fairly competent practitioner. As encounter groups and sensitivity training burgeoned and spread dramatically during the 1960s and early 70s, some less responsible and less competent individuals billed themselves as "trainers" or "facilitators" and ran groups. If an equal amount of research were done on these groups, it is likely

356

that the results would be less positive than the studies Gibb reviewed.

A responsible and competent group leader like Rogers, though, was caught in a difficult position on this issue of risk and damage in intensive groups. If he glossed over the problem and said there are no risks, he would lose credibility with laypeople and professionals alike. If he dwelt on the risks, he would scare people away from an experience he believed in strongly. And if he took the middle road of saying "choose your leader wisely," he would have to answer the question: Choose by what criteria? Unfortunately it is difficult to tell a good leader by his or her paper credentials. In individual therapy Rogers maintained that being a naturally accepting and understanding person was as good a qualification for becoming a counselor as having a formal credential. His belief was similar with respect to group work. In fact Chapter 9 of *On Encounter Groups* described the "La Jolla Program," a summer program designed to train professionals *and* laypeople to become facilitators. Caught in the dilemma of how to react publicly to charges of psychological damage in encounter groups, Rogers more often than not defended the intensive group, and mentioned only in passing the possible dangers resulting from unqualified leaders. Later on, as the encounter-group phenomenon continued to spread in popularity, he began more frequently to acknowledge the problem of the unqualified or harmful leader. A good example of his advocacy of encounter groups (and his readiness to debate a critic when he thought it was warranted) can be seen in a letter he wrote to the editor of *The New York Times Magazine,* after it had published a scathing attack on encounter groups, written by a psychiatrist.[100] Rogers wrote:

I read with interest the article by Dr. Maliver in your issue of January 3, 1971 ("Encounter Groupers Up Against the Wall"). There are many good things about the article and in many respects I find myself in agreement with Dr. Maliver. However, there is one omission in his analysis which is so glaring and so important that I think it needs to be corrected.

First I would like to stress some of my points of agreement. Like him, I deplore the growing commercialism of the whole encounter group movement. Like him, I believe that highly interventive, interpretive, and attacking methods in the group may cause personal damage and there is now research to back up this point. Like him, I deplore the games and gimmicks that have come to play such a large part in many groups and the manipulation which often accompanies their use. I too am concerned about the over rapid development of growth centers, the use of untested approaches like bioenergetics, Rolfing, and the like.

The enormous deficiency in the article is Dr. Maliver's seeming unawareness of a totally different approach to groups than the one he describes. It is quite true that on the one hand there is the manipulative, aggressive, interpretive, interventive leader, or "trainer," with a background usually in group dynamics, psychoanalysis, Gestalt therapy, bioenergetics and the like. On the other hand, there are an enormous number of groups conducted by facilitators who put their trust in the individual and in the group, who are genuinely trying to facilitate the emergence of insight and personal growth, who are nonmanipulative, who permit the natural group process to emerge. The facilitators of these groups usually have a background in client-centered or existential psychotherapy, student counseling, or forward-looking and innovative education. Such an approach does not tend to cause personal damage.

A number of years ago I made a survey of nearly 500 people who had been in groups I had conducted or had supervised. The follow-up was made a number of months after the group experience. Two out of nearly 500 said that they thought the experience had been more damaging than helpful. For all of the others it ranged from neutral or moderately helpful to the great majority who found it a highly positive and meaningful experience still affecting their behavior. Dr. Jack Gibb has made an excellent summary of well over 100 research studies on the outcomes of encounter groups and sensitivity training and discovers that the findings are generally positive. "… The evidence is strong that intensive group training experiences have therapeutic effects."

He also concludes that there is very little basis for the widespread concern among lay groups that group experiences are traumatic for individuals. The most careful study along this line was done by Batchelder and Hardy. Twelve hundred YMCA secretaries had been through encounter groups conducted by or supervised by Dr. Gibb, who belongs in the group entirely overlooked by Dr. Maliver and who places heavy emphasis on the development of trust within the group. Dr. Batchelder and Dr. Hardy decided to make a thorough investigation of this since here was a homogeneous group that could be reached. They collected the names of more than forty individuals who were reported to have been damaged by the group experience. When these individuals were contacted, all but four of them reported that this was a gross misunderstanding, that they had not been damaged, and that the group experience had been a profitable one. Four felt that the experience in the group had been negative for them when it occurred but by the time they were interviewed they had concluded that the experience had been positive. One man out of the twelve hundred felt that the experience was damaging at the time and still was hurtful to him. Nevertheless, he was working very effectively in his job.

This confirms absolutely my own experience in working with a staff of colleagues with the Immaculate Heart College, high school, and grammar schools in the Los Angeles area. We heard many reports that people had been damaged by their group experience and when tracked down these always melted into second- and third-hand rumors about nameless individuals. So I will stoutly maintain that when the facilitator of a group has a trustful belief in the capacity of the individual and of the group to develop a richer and more insightful life and better interpersonal communication, the risk to the individual is so slight as to be almost non-existent.

Another bit of evidence is contained in the work of the La Jolla Program, conducted each summer by a number of my colleagues. Over a four-year period they have helped build facilitative skills in more than 600 people involved with groups. In addition, weekend groups have been held for more than 8,000 individuals in order to give the 600 potential group leaders a chance to utilize themselves as facilitative persons. Out of these more than 8,500 individuals, four psychic breakdowns are known to have occurred. I and my colleagues regard this as unfortunate but probably no more than would occur statistically in any group of that size over the same period of time.

On the other hand, the kind of approach described by Dr. Maliver does produce "casualties." A recent study reported by Dr. Irving Yalom of some 210 students who had had encounter group experience showed a "nine percent casualty rate," but some of the casualties were minor. The outstanding finding is that when the group is led by an aggressive, charismatic, intrusive, challenging person, with a sense of mission and endeavoring to convey a feeling of confidence, the members of such groups show little lasting effect and a high casualty rate, quite contrary to the experience in the less structured groups where leaders endeavor to let the group process develop of its own accord.

I do not know whether Dr. Maliver purposely ignored this whole side of the encounter group movement or whether he is genuinely unaware of it. If the latter, he could certainly learn much about it by reading my book, *Carl Rogers On Encounter Groups*, Harper & Row, 1970—I feel he has done a disservice by giving a reasonably accurate but one-sided presentation.[101]

Another chapter in *On Encounter Groups* described "The Lonely Person—and His Experiences in Encounter Groups." Rogers spent one paragraph of this chapter discussing the "existential" aloneness which is a part of the human condition—the reality that all of us are alone, will die alone—and the need to come to grips with this reality instead of denying and trying to escape from it. Others in the humanistic psychology movement, like Victor Frankl, Rollo May, or James Bugental, wrote extensively on this topic,[102] but Rogers referred to it as "an important issue but one on which I shall not dwell."[103] In this connection he once told an interviewer that his friend Rollo May "told the story that I once questioned the existence of tragedy by saying that Romeo and Juliet might have been all right with just a little counseling. I probably did say that. I'm more optimistic than Rollo. He is an existentialist—so am I, but my philosophy has more room for hope."[104]

It was a different kind of loneliness Rogers was writing about. "I wish to speak more of the loneliness that exists when the person feels that he has no real contact with other persons. Many factors contribute—the general impersonality of our culture, its transient quality, its anomie—all elements of loneliness which grow more marked when we are crowded together. Then there is the fear, which resides in a great many people, of any close personal relationship … But I believe there is a still deeper and more common cause of loneliness. To put it briefly, a person is most lonely when he has dropped something of his outer shell or façade—the face with which he has been meeting the world—and feels sure that no one can understand, accept, or care for the part of his inner self that lies revealed."[105]

Again and again in the encounter groups he conducted, he noted how many individuals expressed that they had gotten closer to people in their group than they had felt to most of the people in their daily lives, even family. He noted also how much people seemed to value this contact, how validated and affirmed they seemed to feel by having others know them well, the good and the bad, and still accept them. He concluded, "It is, I believe, one of our most successful modern inventions for dealing with the feeling of unreality, of impersonality, and of distance and separation that exists in so many people in our culture. What the future of this trend will be I do not know. It may be taken over by faddists and manipulators. It may be superseded by something even more effective. At the present time it is the best instrument I know for healing the loneliness that prevails in so many human beings. It holds forth a real hope that isolation need not be the keynote of our individual lives."[106]

Other chapters of the book dealt with the subjective experience of change during and after an encounter group, as experienced by the participant; the applications of encounter groups to all kinds of individuals and institutions; and the training of group facilitators. In his closing chapter he gazed into his "cloudy crystal ball" and tried to see the future of the encounter group movement. When this was published he was sixty-eight years old and had devoted the previous six years to studying, experiencing, and, as it were, *co-leading* the encounter group movement.

"What are some of the directions it may take? In the first place, I must acknowledge that it may all too easily fall more into the hands of the exploiters, those who have come onto the group scene primarily for their own personal benefit, financial or psychological. The faddists, the cultists, the nudists, the manipulators, those whose needs are for power or recognition, may come to dominate the encounter group horizon. In this case I feel it is headed for a disaster. It will gradually be seen by the public for what it would then be; a somewhat fraudulent game operating not primarily for growth, health, and constructive change, but for the benefit of its leaders …

"To the extent that this development takes precedence, 'encounter group' may come to be a dirty word, just as 'progressive education' did years ago. It may be worth our while to look at the parallel. Because progressive education became ultrapopular and was carried on more and more by extremists and by those with little or no understanding of its basic principles, it became anathema to the public, and educators were careful to deny that their schools were examples of it. I know of no educator today who would state publicly that he stands for progressive education. Therefore it seems to have died out. Meanwhile, the roots of almost every innovative change in education in the last several decades can be traced back to the thinking of John Dewey and to the principles which were in fact the underlying guides for the best of progressive education.

"I can envision the same thing happening to encounter groups, sensitivity training, T-groups, and all the rest. They would become objects of condemnation and die out. Meanwhile, all the essential elements—the building of trust in small groups, the sharing of self, the feedback, the sense of community—would continue to find labels and guises by which they could operate to bring about the changes and communication we so desperately need."[107]

On the positive side, he wrote, encounter groups might grow and spread in their use and their applications. For the individual this could offer the prospect of a life in which continual growth and real closeness with others become the norm, not the exception. For the culture, this could mean a better approach to intergroup tensions and conflict, a creative means for organizational renewal and growth, a way to help citizens readjust to "future shock" and the rapid pace of technological change. For science, encounter groups could offer a new laboratory for the study of human growth, with the opportunity for each group member to become a self-scientist and to participate actively in the data gathering process. For philosophy, encounter groups might offer a new perspective on the Good Life and the purpose for living. In short, "These changes may occur in persons, in institutions, in our urban and cultural alienation, in racial tensions, in our international frictions, in our philosophies, our values, our image of man himself. It is a profoundly significant movement, and the course of its future will, for better or for worse, have a profound impact on all of us."[108]

To some extent his predictions have come true. Certainly such groups are not nearly as popular as they were in the 1960s and 70s. Encounter groups have not changed the world as Rogers hoped they would, and in that sense, his original faith in this small group technology now seems misplaced and naïve. Yet intensive small groups are still used regularly in various educational, training, recovery, and psychotherapeutic venues. To that extent, the intensive small group has become an accepted, if somewhat limited, practice in many educational, therapeutic and professional settings.

Center for Studies of the Person: The Split from WBSI

Rogers' most intense period of involvement in encounter groups spanned the years 1964 through 1969, although he continued to facilitate many groups over the following years. Near the end of this period came a series of what he called "events which have given me more agony than anything else I can recall in my professional life,"[109] even surpassing the unhappiness with his problems at

Wisconsin. These events led shortly to the factionalization of WBSI and the eventual resignation of Rogers and about twenty-five staff members who formed a new and separate organization.

When WBSI had been formed in 1959 there had been a commitment to have it be a uniquely democratic organization, with power in the hands of the staff and delegated upward to the administration and Board of Trustees as the need arose. It was understood that to satisfy the laws of the State of California, it was necessary to have a fictional autocracy, that is, a Chairman of the Board, a President, an Executive Director, and a set of administrative procedures; but in reality the non-profit organization would operate in a democratic fashion. Initially it worked this way to a large degree. Staff members initiated different projects, either alone or with other staff members. Decisions about how WBSI monies would be spent were made by the persons involved in the various projects. Individuals felt a great deal of autonomy to develop their own programs, seek funding, and carry out their ideas. Rogers was not the only one who returned some of his salary or consulting fees to the organization. The weekly staff newsletter was always an open forum.

Then, after a few years of successful operation, WBSI began experiencing some of the problems that success brings to any organization. As more government funding poured in, there were pressures for different accounting procedures and tighter controls over spending and record keeping. As Rogers and other staff members began gaining wide publicity for their work in encounter groups, some staff and Board members became uncomfortable about WBSI's image getting too closely tied to "sensitivity training" and the possible losses of funding that might result. The various projects or "Centers" no longer felt that they had complete autonomy, as they were asked to adjust their programs for the benefit of the entire organization. As these trends continued, there was much internal disagreement, negotiation, and problem-solving intended to keep the organization together and working toward its goals.

There were personal issues and power conflicts as well. While Richard Farson credits Rogers with putting WBSI "on the map," he also thought that Rogers' personal style of colleagueship and organizational naïveté contributed to WBSI's organizational problems and eventual division. On the personal level, Farson reflected,

> Carl had students. He didn't have colleagues as much … His students could grow into colleagues as I did. He loved us but we were always, I think, deferential … We had people like Abe Maslow and [Theodore] Newcomb and people like Paul Lloyd and Bud Crow, who were brilliant. They never really made it with Carl. That is, he didn't pay much attention to them. He didn't give Bud Crow the time of the day … So he wasn't really good at that sort of thing. He just didn't have colleagues. A guy like Rollo May just adored colleagues and loved

having that kind of interaction, you know, give and take with people who were
his peers. You go to his place for dinner and Bruno Bettleheim would be there or
some other major figure in the field. You would see that he liked colleagues and
not just students. Carl was vulnerable on that count, I think. I don't think he
ever really enjoyed the critical give and take of a university faculty or of a place
like WBSI, which had people who were intellectual peers ... That led to antipathy
... particularly between Bud Crow and Carl. It was not an antipathy that had
any outward motions, it was just a feeling, sort of a seething feeling in Bud, that
he was being [ignored]. Carl, he didn't even give it a thought. It never occurred
to him that it would be a problem.[110]

Farson also thought Rogers failed to appreciate the complexities of organizational
life. He recalled how, "We were always experimenting with how to organize
ourselves better. We prided ourselves on applying what we knew to our own
operation." So the seventy or more staff members of WBSI went through a day-
long simulation exercise to work on their organizational structure. At one point
the facilitator formed interest groups and asked all those devoted to Rogers to
form one group. After some time, that group sent a messenger back to the
simulation leaders saying, "'We're no longer in the simulation, we're going to do
this. We're going to do this.' Carl went along with that ... So we wound up
essentially doing that. We called that group the 'Center for Studies of the Person'
... They functioned as that group from then on in the organization of WBSI.
We didn't do a lot of the things very differently then, but we were organized a
little differently, and that [was] not a healthy organization for Carl because Carl
then was just surrounded by his devotees and not by the rest of us who were
critical, who could be critical.

"Then Carl came after me to give up my directorship of the institute. He
thought ... that Paul and Bud and I had too much power ... even though we
operated in the most democratic way. Carl could not see that strong membership
required strong leadership. He never could understand that. He was never good
at thinking paradoxically, never good at ... Asian thought; the co-existence of
opposites is part of their thinking. He was very linear. I've always thought that
Carl and Skinner were like two peas in a pod. They were so similar in every
respect, their history, their style, their writing ability, their single-minded devotion
to a single track of thought and so forth. Carl was very much that way, I think.
I was so vulnerable to whatever Carl wanted at the time, so grateful to him for
being at WBSI, for being with us. I went to Bud and Paul and I said, 'I think we
should give up our jobs.'

"I was stupid enough about organizations not to guard very carefully the
leadership we had. But Carl was even more naïve than I was on this ... I think
that was a reckless thing to do ... he was so committed to democratic
management, thinking that it had to be completely without hierarchy and so
forth. I regard that as the real weakness in Carl."

So Farson, Lloyd and Crow gave up their leadership positions, and a management committee of staff took over the leadership (although Farson continued to perform some administrative functions). As long as Richard Farson was director he had been able to keep the different groupings functioning in some harmony. After giving up this role, even more conflicts ensued. When Farson left to take another job in Los Angeles, Paul Lloyd was made director, supposedly temporarily, and the factional problems became even more serious. Still, Rogers thought they had found reasonable solutions to their problems at the June 1968 Board meeting. Apparently they had not. A month later he wrote a long and sad letter to the Trustees, expressing his dismay about the authoritarian, anti-democratic procedures that were being put in place by Lloyd, Crow and their allies. Rogers wrote,

> I felt that the most important decision of our Trustees' meeting was that the Centers were to be as autonomous as it is humanly possible to make them. This fact released untold energies in the Center for Studies of the Person, as we called our group. New projects, new ways of raising money, the idea of all of us turning in our fees so our full energies would go to the Center—dozens of new ideas were sprouting all over the place. It was an exciting period like the first days of WBSI ... Within a week I was more depressed than I have ever been before. [He was feeling so sick about it physically that he saw a doctor.] The reason was that although I deeply love WBSI and have worried about it during various previous crises, this was the first time that the dream had ever been strangled from within.[111]

He went on to describe how the leadership of WBSI had begun to implement a series of authoritarian, hierarchical measures, from censoring the weekly staff newsletter to hiring expensive cost accountants to instituting new bureaucratic procedures. "We will now be run by cost accountants just like any reactionary business firm," wrote Rogers, and with the kind of sarcasm and exaggeration that came out when he felt self-righteous, added, "these by-laws are the most Hitlerian I have ever seen. They make the Divine Right of Kings look like a weak-kneed sissified theory." He pointed out that it was legally possible in California for a corporation to conduct their affairs in a democratic fashion and related how, "When I met Jonas Salk the other day he told me of the tremendous progress they have made in democratizing the Salk Institute where now a group composed of the younger scientists, the Senior Fellows, and representatives from every group involved in the Institute, work with the President in an Operating Committee. Knowing the mess that they had been in a year ago, I congratulated Jonas very sincerely on the obvious progress they have made. His response was, 'But we learned it all from WBSI.'"

Rogers then suggested that he might be forced to resign from WBSI and requested thirty minutes at the next Board meeting to present his case and his suggestions for averting a crisis in the organization. These included:

> That we give consideration to every means by which we can honor Paul for all
> that he has done for WBSI—the giving of his fortune, the giving of his time, his
> energy, his interest, his affection. I would like to honor him in every way possible
> … That we retire Paul from the presidency which he neither sought nor desired
> and which now involves him in bitter controversy which he detests … I love
> Paul, and I know he loves WBSI, but in spite of his good will and his desire to be
> the best father possible I believe he is ruining the organization we all love. Hence,
> this letter … Sadly, Carl.[112]

A colleague of Rogers, reflecting on these events, said, "He will not accept being
a second-class citizen—not even a little bit … I think that he felt he wasn't being
appreciated. Other people felt like they weren't being appreciated and would
kind of go along with it. But he would not go along with it. In that situation, I
don't think of him as being warm and loving at all. I think that he was mad and
I think that was right. And he was hurt."[113]

That hurt is apparent. Along with his letter to the Board of Directors, Rogers
included another few pages that were in a very different style and written "when
I was in the depths of my despair."

> I want to tell you cats something about a flick I seen a while ago—*Camelot.*
> They tell me some of the eggheads thought it was strictly from Dullsville. But
> not me. I thought it was groovy. I dig all this stuff about knights in armor and a
> king who is scared of getting hitched to some broad he's never seen, and fellows
> and their chicks tumbling in the flowers and having some fun doin' it—and a
> lot of other stuff. But I'm not going to try to tell you the whole story—I'm not
> *that* square!
>
> But there's one bit—the last part of the flick—which stays with me and stays
> with me, and I *don't* know *why.* There's this screwy old dope Arthur, see, and he's
> just about to lose his last battle. Course there's a lot before that, because he was
> *really* nuts—an idealist I guess is what the squares would call him.
>
> Anyway, he's had this cockeyed idea that if a gang of guys were all sworn to be
> loyal to each other—like the Rangers or any other gang—and if they had a "common
> purpose" like "trying to make the world a better place to live"—yeah, that's how
> square he was, then they could trust each other and live together as friends. He
> didn't even want to be the boss, the top dog! He even built a round table, so that
> every guy was just as good as the next guy, see, and nobody even tried to tell
> anybody else what to do. If a knight wanted to rescue some dame in distress (how's
> that for kookiness!) or kill some friggin' dragon, O.K., he just went ahead and did
> it—maybe alone, or with some buddies. And the king's treasure belonged to
> everybody, see, and if you needed a new suit of armor you just looked in the

treasure house to see if there was enough, and if there was, you took some. Well, as I say, you can see that Arthur was strictly from the loony bin!

Crazy thing was, it *worked!* For a long time at least, 'bout ten years, I think. Then one day a cat came along who was smart, see? And he knew that the name of the game was *power,* not this crummy "cooperation" and "love" and "trust" and all that crap. So as soon as he sold this idea to some of the guys, the whole thing cracked up, as any dope would expect. So the knights got to fighting and killing each other, and mistreating the peasants. Arthur's best pal stole his chick. He was *so* badly clobbered he had to skip the country, and in this last scene he's sitting there in a darkening field, knowing that the other army, led by his best friends—well, his ex-pals really—were going to attack in the morning and he would certainly be defeated, and either get his head chopped off or he'd be stuck in the hoosegow—dungeon, they call it—for good and always. So he's not exactly feeling bright and cheery, see?

And then this squirt, this young kid, comes out of the darkness and starts to talk with him. And Arthur finds that for this kid the Round Table, and the stories about it, were just all he *lived* for! For him, Arthur and his knights were the greatest! He knew everything they'd done, the names of all the guys, and the adventures they'd had. He knew 'em like a kid knows the batting average of every Yankee on the squad. He was willing to do *anything* for Arthur, see, even *die* for him.

So Arthur—this gets to him, see—so he sends the kid away, and he sings a song to him telling him how to spread the news. Kinda touching, really, though 'course it didn't *really* get to me.

Crazy thing is that I've heard the song later, on records, and you know what—they've got it wrong! I didn't quite catch the lingo, but I *remember* it, and they got it wrong on every single record.

What Arthur really sang, sorta choked up and all, when he told the brat what to do, went like this—

> Ask every person if he's heard the story,
> And tell him loud and clear if he has not.
> Don't let the memory die
> That once—this ain't no lie
> For one brief shining moment
> There was *double you be* ess *eye!*

For some reason, I sorta got a lump in my throat, even though I don't dig the last line—some sorta code, maybe. But when I think of that song when I'm alone, sometimes—gosh you'll think I'm nuts—a tear or two runs down my cheek. I guess it's because Arthur—kook that he was—seemed so damned disappointed.[114]

The Board was not moved by such sentiment. From their point of view, the Center staff members were being unreasonable, pulling a power play, wanting things their own way or threatening to quit. They were not responsive to Rogers' ultimatum. So he did resign, and along with about twenty-five other staff members from WBSI, formed a new group, using their former name "Center for Studies of the Person"—or "CSP" for short.

Although Rogers' version of these events got the most attention at the time, and his role is the best known, he was not necessarily the prime mover in creating the new center or splitting off from WBSI. As Tom Gillette described it a few years later, "I would put Bill Coulson and Bruce [Meador] and myself in the front lines of leading us out of WBSI and into CSP. Carl was in the second line."[115] In this version Rogers was as much caught up in the group process, in the momentum toward separation, as leading it. On the other hand, if Rogers did not support and go along with the division of WBSI, it probably would not have happened, and in that sense he *was* ultimately responsible for what occurred.

Over the years the story of their departure has taken on mythic proportions, with Rogers relating in his oral history shortly before his death how, "A group of us left WBSI in the middle of one night. That's literally true. We weren't quite sure whether they would agree to our taking the property that we felt belonged to us: desks, typewriters, files and so on; and so Bill Coulson's idea ... was to rent a moving truck, and one evening we went into the WBSI, took out all our things, brought them to the new quarters, and the next morning we were established as the Center for Studies of the Person."[116]

Richard Farson who, in spite of this episode, remained friends with Rogers all his life, had a very different version of the story. He recalled,

> I think there is a whole myth about their sneaking in the middle of the night and stealing stuff. They seemed to be very proud and happy about that. The fact of the matter (I remember the discussion very well in the board meeting) is we just would give them what they needed to start their organization. We gave them some contracts [i.e., contracts obtained by Center staff but legally owned by WBSI] and we gave them some furniture and so forth ... They think that they stole some furniture but we gave it to them. The fact is that their organization was still WBSI ... Their letterhead [said] "a development of WBSI." They didn't have any corporate papers. They didn't have any 501(c)3 [tax-exempt status]. They didn't have what they needed, so we decided that we would sponsor that group. They didn't become autonomous until they were able to stand on their own. We tried to help them.[117]

Eventually Center for Studies of the Person did achieve its independent legal status and the break was complete. What was experienced at the time as a most painful episode by everyone involved turned out to be a freeing move which neither Rogers nor the many CSP staff members I talked to ever regretted.

Initially, CSP's goals sounded similar to those of WBSI; in organizational structure, the two groups were very different. Although CSP was legally organized as a corporation, the members proudly thought of themselves as a "non-organization" headed by a "non-director." That is, the director had no power to direct anyone, but was empowered to speak for the organization publicly and to raise support for its various projects. It was a revolving position, one which Rogers never held. Not too far from WBSI they rented office space at 1125 Torrey Pines Road in La Jolla. There was a reception and secretarial area, several small offices or consulting rooms, and a large meeting room, thickly carpeted and brightly colored. Each member contributed a small sum to pay the rent and office expenses. They would all get together for weekly staff meetings, at which both personal and professional agendas were likely to be raised.

From this base, members organized themselves into various "projects," many of them carryovers from WBSI, many of them new ones. By 1970, with the membership up to around forty-five, the following projects were listed in CSP's brochure: Educational Innovation Project (using encounter groups to change a large school system, headed by Doug Land and Carl Rogers); the Adolescent Drug Abuse Project; the La Jolla Program (for training group facilitators); the Conference Planning Service; the Research Design Center; the Project on Community; the Workshop Project; the Project for Developing Awareness through Interracial Encounters; the Institute for Drug Education; Psycreation (for developing humanizing products for the general public); the Collegiate Development Project; and the Entry Training Project (to facilitate the entry of unskilled people into the world of work).

Other than the secretarial staff, no one received a salary from CSP. Members were responsible for setting up and carrying out their own projects, and whether the funding came from granting institutions or in payment for services provided, each project had to support itself. Thus most of the members had other jobs or sources of income in addition to their work with CSP. In 1969, for example, twenty members were full-time or part-time teachers at nearby colleges or universities.[118] Membership was selective but fluid. By becoming involved with some Center members and working on their project, a person could participate in the life of the Center and gradually come to know many of the other members. If that person then desired to join, the members would vote on this. Any member could choose his or her own title, except for "director." Rogers called himself a "Resident Fellow," the same title he had held at WBSI.[119] Norman Chambers, who became a member in 1969, recalled how, "Carl did the egalitarian thing very very well. Carl shared requests [to do workshops] with all of us. That was constant and it was contagious. It was a group of colleagues who were equal in every sense of the word ... He was one member, not *the* member.[120]

Shortly after breaking from WBSI, Rogers gave a slightly different picture of his place in CSP, telling an interviewer, "... in previous years, I would have felt very responsible for that group, because, like it or not, I'm sort of the ideological head of the place, even though I am not the administrator. This time I really comfortably do *not* feel that responsibility. I feel that these are mature young people, and that they know what they're getting into, and if the whole thing fails, they will all land on their feet, so I can relax and enjoy them and feel this is a damn good experience while it lasts."[121] It lasted a long time, and Rogers became less the "ideological head" of the group over the years, as others matured professionally and intellectually; although he always occupied that role to some degree.

Because WBSI had been formed to do action research, help people and improve society, it was natural that, in its early phases, CSP would also see itself as a group designed to reach out to the world around them through many and diverse projects. As the early CSP projects that were continuations of those begun at WBSI ended, however, or as funding sources ceased funding, it became apparent that the basic "outreach" premise upon which WBSI had operated might not apply as consistently to the new organization. With most of the members involved in jobs and careers outside of CSP, and with their devoting a large portion of their time to teaching, counseling, group work, or research in the community, many members began having a different expectation as to what they wanted from CSP. Many, like Rogers, still wanted CSP to be a group of close colleagues and friends working together for a common cause, that of helping people and changing the world around them and, by setting an example, making a significant difference in the conduct of the behavioral sciences throughout the country. Many others wished CSP might be primarily a "support group," an association of like-minded people who could learn from each other, have fun together, and derive emotional and intellectual support from one another. They were already reaching out on their own jobs, helping others, and improving conditions around them. This second group wanted more personal benefits from CSP. Of course, few individuals were totally at one end of the continuum or the other. Rogers, for example, believed that by working together they would naturally develop close personal ties and there would still be time left over for comradeship and mutual support. Others responded that that was all right for him, because he didn't have a full-time job elsewhere. They had only several hours a week for CSP and had to choose whether they wanted to spend that time primarily on professional projects or on mutually supportive discussions and activities.

For many years there remained sometimes a mild, sometimes a forceful tension between these two viewpoints. Rogers and many members remained active in professional outreach projects, others less so. Virtually all the members spoke highly of the personal benefits they derived from their "non-organization." And there were enough in the active camp that during the 1970s to mid-80s CSP was a productive and creative milieu for the authorship of books and articles, for educational events and training programs at the Center, and for innovative projects and outreach to individuals and institutions around the world. Particularly in the

1970s it was a "Mecca" of sorts to which people would come for client-centered work—to meet Carl Rogers and his colleagues, take workshops, be visiting fellows, and experience CSP as an alternative organizational model. Someone once compared this period, perhaps a bit grandiosely, to Paris in the 1920s for all the current and future thinkers and leaders in psychology and social and intellectual change who gravitated to CSP and joined in its activities and values. It certainly remained the home of most of Rogers' professional activities *and* a cherished support group for the rest of his life.[122]

Personal Life

In moving to California, Carl and Helen had distanced themselves still farther geographically from their children and grandchildren. In other ways, however, they all grew closer during this period—partly because the grandchildren, as teenagers and young adults, were now able to have more mature relationships with their grandparents, partly because both David and Natalie had occasion to work with their father professionally, and partly because of personal turbulence in David and Natalie's lives. It was a difficult period, but it resulted in real communication that led to deeper and richer relationships between Carl and Helen and their children. Unfortunately, it also included conflict, separation and divorce—first for Natalie and Larry, then for David and Corky.

Carl and Helen tried to provide support for all *four* of their children, as Helen once put it.[123] Thus Carl carried out a frank and thoughtful correspondence with Natalie's husband Larry and provided telephone counseling on many occasions to David's wife Corky.[124] When the former couple separated and it appeared they would divorce, Rogers wrote Larry a long letter, describing how he understood each of their sides in the conflict and how each had tried to make the marriage work, without success. He concluded, "I think that what I am trying to say is that I love and care for each of you, not as perfect creatures, but as very fallible, imperfect persons. And as a very fallible, imperfect person I expect to go on valuing each of you, caring for each of you ... I don't *want* to take sides, (though I do feel very supportive toward Nat right now) & I deeply hope that you can end it without rancor, because I care very much for each of you and for your lovely girls ... Much love to you, Dad."[125]

Eventually, as the divorces became more bitter, Carl and Helen did end up taking their children's side. Feeling caught in the middle, and recognizing the potential of adversarial divorce litigation, Rogers eventually stopped answering Larry's letters, which biographer David Cohen used to damn the great communicator for refusing to communicate.[126] After their divorce, Larry remarried and Natalie learned how to be a single woman who greatly cherished her independent life and many diverse relationships. Her book *Emerging Woman*

(1980) tells her story, beginning with her early acculturation to male–female relationships in the Rogers' home, through her marriage, divorce and newly found and still developing identity.[127] Similarly Cohen painted a very negative portrait of Rogers conspiring with his son David to deprive Corky of her share of some of the marital assets, eventually leading to her suicide. However, from the family's viewpoint, Corky had had a long history of mental illness, alcohol and drug abuse, suicide threats and suicide attempts, and therefore it was only prudent to protect David and his children's financial interests.[128]

David's marital difficulties led to many self-doubts. Ironically, this was exacerbated by his idealizing his parents' marriage, feeling he could never live up to their example, not realizing that his parents were just beginning to have their own marital stresses that would grow even larger in the years ahead. Aside from his marriage, David struggled with other issues of personal and professional identity and life purposes. He also worked too hard and experienced continual stress. Desperate to make a change that might benefit his marriage and himself, he made "what, in retrospect, was probably a foolish decision."[129] He left Vanderbilt University in 1968 and moved to Baltimore, Maryland to assume one of the most prestigious positions in medicine in the country—Dean of Medicine of The Johns Hopkins University School of Medicine and Medical Director of the Johns Hopkins Hospital. Of course this did nothing to relieve the pressure, and soon the combined stresses of the move, his new position and "our tormented marriage" contributed to a life-threatening medical event that, although never clearly diagnosed, was probably a heart attack.[130] This served as a wake-up call that eventually led him to end the marriage and leave Johns Hopkins.

At one point in the late sixties, with both children going through marital difficulties, David's life in jeopardy, Helen and he experiencing new conflict in their own relationship (to be discussed in the next chapter), and WBSI going through its break-up which caused him such anguish, Rogers had a terrible year or two in which he began to suffer from health problems himself. He was anxious, his blood pressure rose, and he experienced heart palpitations, among other symptoms. Eventually, as the separation from WBSI ended and Center for Studies of the Person proved a satisfying new arrangement, as David recovered his health, and as his stress over his children's marriages lessened as those situations gradually resolved, Rogers' own good health and positive outlook returned. After his divorce in 1972, David entered a much happier, lifelong, second marriage to Barbara Louise ("Bobbie") Lehan.

David grew to appreciate his father more and more over these years, and vice versa. He confided his doubts and demons to his father and found a supportive counselor and friend. David commented, "He's one of the most fantastic human beings I've ever met. He's not afraid of new things. I learn something from him each time. There is almost nothing that frightens him in human experience."[131]

In addition to his administrative roles at Johns Hopkins, David continued his research and writing—publishing about forty more articles in the next ten years—and his work with the prestigious *Year Book of Medicine,* which he edited for at least two decades.[132] After three years at Johns Hopkins, about the time of his divorce and remarriage, he moved to Princeton, New Jersey, to become President of the Robert Wood Johnson Foundation, the second largest private foundation in the United States (after Ford), and the largest sponsoring medical research.[133] During this period father and son had a chance to work together on an interesting and important project.

Orienne Strode, who had been secretary and administrator at Center for Studies of the Person for several years, had been married to a physician and was alarmed at the inability of many doctors to handle the considerable stress associated with their work. She noted the strain on family relationships that doctors often experienced, the surprisingly high rate of drug addiction among doctors, and other signs of a real need for help in dealing with the pressures associated with long and erratic hours, dealing continually with disease and death, and carrying such a heavy responsibility. She began planning a project that would address the emotional needs of physicians. One weekend in 1971 when David Rogers happened to be visiting his parents in La Jolla, someone asked Strode how Carl and his son, two distinguished men in their fields, got along. That caused Strode to picture father and son together and suddenly an idea came to her: "That would be a great team if I could talk them into it. And so I went to Carl and Dave with the idea. And they offered not only their prestige and their support, but helped rewrite the brochure."[134] The brochure described the project's objectives.

> *Interpersonal*: to acquire new ways to relate more effectively with colleagues, office staff, patients, and family; to develop realistic patterns of change when change is indicated. *Professional*: to minimize the possibility of malpractice claims; to develop better listening skills; to become more aware of the power of one's personality as a therapeutic force; to learn how to continue caring for patients without taking total responsibility for them; to define personal and professional goals. *Personal*: to deal effectively with stress and fatigue in one's life and in the lives of patients; to incorporate continuing learning into personal development; to risk being one's self and to enjoy the attendant rewards; to examine one's personal and professional life and assess its satisfactions.[135]

On some level father and son must have recognized that these were personal learning goals they had been working on for years and could still benefit from. In any case, they designed a series of workshops for medical educators, believing that if they could influence the teachers of medicine, they would have the greatest long-range impact on the field. Helen Rogers was delighted with the prospect of her husband and son working together, and she and Carl donated $12,000 to get the project started. David signed the initial invitations and participated in the first two workshops. Carl led groups in the first four workshops and usually presented a paper or came for a dialogue with the participants in later workshops. Eventually the participants also included medical administrators, people from medical foundations, medical students, internists, residents, and spouses of the physicians.

Originally intended to provide a combination of personal growth and organizational development strategies, the workshops quickly came to utilize the encounter-group mode almost totally. This was what the physicians seemed to want and need—an opportunity to be themselves and to express and explore the many personal and human relations issues connected with their work. "Human Dimensions in Medical Education" became an ongoing project of Center for Studies of the Person, directed by Orienne Strode. By 1978, about one thousand medical educators—many of them in high positions of influence—had participated in workshops. Counting medical students, spouses and others, by 1980 the number had grown to "several thousand" past participants.[136] Aside from the national programs, which drew participants from all over, workshop alumni also invited project staff to conduct workshops and interventions in their own medical schools and hospitals. By the time the project ended in 1987 for lack of continuing funding, it had worked with about 13,000 individuals.[137] By then other influential medical educators who were inspired by their participation in a Human Dimensions workshop had begun publishing articles about the physician–patient relationship in medical journals and initiated other projects in medical education and administration, such as the Association for Physician and Patient which continues to promote many of the values of the Human Dimensions project today.[138]

All told, the project had a significant influence on the profession: directly, by helping thousands of physicians' enhance the human dimension of their relationship with patients, and indirectly, by influencing foundation officials, hospital administrators and physicians to become more open to other dimensions of holistic health care. Simultaneously, countervailing pressures in the health care industry were encouraging physicians to spend less time with patients, practice defensively, focus increasingly in specialized areas, and often rely more heavily on pharmaceuticals than prevention. In any case, the project certainly influenced the practice and priorities of David Rogers, whose professional writings began to reflect the human dimension of medicine. This is illustrated by three of his titles: "The Doctor Himself Must Become the Treatment," "Medicine and Change," and "Illness Must Be Understood Not in Scientific but in Human Terms."[139]

Natalie Rogers had been practicing psychology in the Boston area for close to a decade in a variety of work settings: a psychiatric hospital, children's hospital, community clinic, school for disturbed children, and in private practice.[140] Soon she would move to California where her career as an innovative psychotherapist in her own right would blossom. Just as her father was learning through encounter groups to express his own feelings more, Natalie was learning to do the same; although, as most of the family agree, she had always been their most volatile member to begin with. A letter she wrote to her parents in 1965, for example, about her daughter Frances, says a lot about Natalie, but also reveals much about the relationship, past and present, between Natalie and her parents.

> About Frannie: I give up on trying to communicate with you two about her, except to say that when I am a grandmother and see one of my grandchildren acting out in ways which seem to be saying, "I want attention and love, I feel unwanted," that I'll make a special effort to do the things for *that* child and take the time and mental effort to ask myself "Why does she behave that way? What am I doing to make her behave that way?"
>
> I feel that I have a right to point out to you, although this may be dirty words in your language, since I'm your daughter and have grown up under your parentage, that both as parents and grandparents, you *say* you want people (including children I surmise) to express their feelings; but you reward with love those who keep their angry feelings to themselves. I didn't hear either one of you say one word about Janet the night she got what *she* wanted by walking out of the house and hiding and not saying anything. I assume that all kids try very hard to get what they want when they want it. Janet told me she didn't want to go someplace and you insisted (you're right, I feel). And so she hid. This brings no wrath upon her, apparently. Fran, in the same situation would have argued til she was blue in the face. This brings your wrath. I fall into the same trap, sometimes, as a parent; but let's face it: when we do this, we're tacitly saying to children: the best way to get what you want is not by saying it, but by manipulating us some way, so as not to be troublesome.
>
> Well, I said I wouldn't communicate about Frannie, but I still am. Both of your comments about Frannie anger me beyond words. I guess it's that I'm so damn disappointed that a very mothering mother and great psychologist father would take such a simple way out as to say, "Look, this kid is selfish." I had hoped for more … If you've got to the end of this letter you're pretty good sports …[141]

The three of them argued about this issue for some time, but both Carl and Helen were glad that Natalie did confront them. On another occasion she wrote to her father, "Since I am in an angry mood and my therapist keeps telling me some of my anger at Larry is displaced anger at you I'll get it off my chest …"[142] Natalie's relationship with her parents became increasingly close in later years, in part because she was able to share such feelings more openly and they were able to reciprocate. Having said that, it was easier to hurt Helen's feelings through confrontation than Carl's, so the children occasionally would write to their father and ask him not to share the contents with their mother. When Helen occasionally got wind of this, she was doubly hurt, especially since her identity was built significantly around her role as mother and now that primary relationship was being threatened.

Just as the Rogers worked hard to maintain and deepen their relationship with their children through the sixties and beyond, so the relationship with their grandchildren became a source of increasing satisfaction to them, especially as the grandchildren became teenagers and young adults. Whenever the opportunity arose, the Rogers would make a real effort to have time alone with each of the six grandchildren, both Carl and Helen together and each one with each grandchild. Carl once described how "one of the most flattering things that has happened to me in this past year is to have my 18-year-old granddaughter—whom I don't see very often, so I couldn't expect her to trust me too much—come to me one evening and simply begin to talk. Soon she was talking about all the things that concern 18-year-olds—personal, interpersonal, sexual, philosophical. To find that she could talk so freely and honestly and openly with me, many, many years her senior, was an exceedingly flattering thing. I felt very much honored. When she asked me about some things she was uncertain about, and what she should do, I said, 'Don't expect me to give you any advice. You are already so much further beyond where I was at your age that I couldn't possibly offer any advice, but I will help you think about these things if that's what you would like to do'—and so we talked until far into the night."

Helen, too, felt close to her grandchildren and was able to understand and accept much about their behavior which others her age would not understand or accept. On one occasion in the early seventies she happened to make a passing reference in conversation to "one of my granddaughters and the boy she is living with." Although it would hardly be remarkable today, this so surprised me at the time, that a woman in her seventies could be so casual about this behavior in one of her grandchildren, not yet twenty, that a few years later I mentioned it to her. Her response was: "Hell, if we were born into their generation we would probably be doing the same thing. Besides, by now, five out of my six grandchildren are living with or have lived with someone, without being married. I'd better be able to accept it."[143]

Carl cherished his relationship with his grandchildren, saving virtually every letter, birthday card, and thank you card they sent for the many gifts the Rogers bestowed on them.[144] They called him "Granddaddy" and "Granddad" and eventually several began calling him "Carl" after participating in and even co-leading workshops with him. He regularly wrote reference letters for them—for college admissions, employment, or on one occasion to a draft board supporting the grandchild's request for conscientious objector status. In a letter to Anne and Julie, he wrote, "You will have to live a long, long time to know how I felt about being taken to the airport by two such lovely granddaughters simply because they *wanted* to take me. I appreciate it more than I can say." But, ever congruent,

375

he was equally prepared to challenge or confront them when he felt the need, adding, "I hope both of you will get over some of your competitiveness. It seems to be the curse of the Rogers family. I want you to know that I would love each of you just as much if you were "B" students or "C" students, or dropped out of school—just so you continue being yourselves. You are very precious people to me and I hope the school year starts out well for both of you … Grandaddy."[145] Similarly, he once wrote to his grandson, "Dear Greg, This is a letter I hate like hell to write but I love you and I've *got* to get things straightened out between us. It has to do with my growing concerns and doubts about you and the way you obtain and use money. Let me tell you how it has developed in me …."[146] A frank correspondence between both of them ensued.

The grandchildren, in turn, felt particularly appreciative about Carl and Helen's acceptance and interest in them. One, as a teenager, said, "He's a really nice man who you can talk to." Another said, "I've always felt like myself with him." Another talked of how she had invited Helen to the apartment where she and her boyfriend were living, and how they talked of many different topics, including Helen's growing up, her attitudes about sex, and her work in Planned Parenthood. The granddaughter cherished this time of getting to know her grandmother, woman to woman.[147] Greg wrote "Dear Granddaddy" a long letter in 1971, ending it, "Write me soon, you mean a lot to me & I want you to know that you're such a comfort because I know you'll always be there when I need you & for that I love you."[148]

One granddaughter remembered an incident when "I was talking with Granddaddy and Nana was there too. I was telling them about [a particular topic]. They were really receptive. There was no flak. There might have been a lot of things they objected to about the way I was living, but they didn't *at all.* It wasn't a personal threat to them in any way … I remember that whole scene and the genuine feeling about them I have. I have a calm feeling when I think of them." Years later, granddaughter Frances recalled doing projects such as making mobiles with her grandfather, saying he "wasn't particularly demonstrative, but extremely patient and permissive in allowing us to experiment."[149]

Another recalled a scene with her grandparents which she found particularly amusing. "From the other side of the wall, I overheard this snatch of conversation, and I didn't want to hear it, but … Nana was commenting. And they started getting into this argument about saying 'I think that ….' Like saying, 'I think that this painting is ugly' instead of just saying, 'This painting is ugly,' without prefacing it by 'I think.' Obviously Granddaddy was on the 'I think' side, Nana was on the 'non-I think' side. And they went on for an hour, until I was going bananas. He would say, 'You should say "I think" before making a statement of opinion, to qualify it.' And she disagreed with him. 'You shouldn't have to say that; it's obvious.' The point was not whether I agreed with one or the other—they both seemed to have their points—but that they spent an hour doing it.

Absurd. I'm sure they must have had this discussion many times."

Rogers' relations with his siblings was less consistently satisfying than with his children and grandchildren. Carl and Helen's friendship with Walter and Elise Rogers remained strong, and the couples found times for occasional visits, especially when Walter and Elise moved to Tucson, Arizona. They also visited sister Margaret in Florida and invited her to family get-togethers. With Lester and John the relationship was more distant, because of geography and divergent interests and politics. The two brothers continued to operate and expand their father's successful construction company for half a century. Lester became President in 1937. John took over in 1966 and was still in charge in the 1980s when company income averaged $100 million annually.[150] Yet although their careers and politics had moved in different directions, Lester and John's affection and pride in their brother's accomplishments are evident in their correspondence with him.[151] John consulted Carl on his wife's serious psychological difficulties, and Carl then corresponded with his sister-in-law's psychiatrist, for which John was most appreciative.[152] Carl, who continued to send his relatives copies of his new books, wrote Lester, "I appreciate your reaction to my book on encounter groups … I was interested that you thought this was the best book I have written" and said he would also send him a copy of *Freedom to Learn,* warning Lester that he might not like its contents.[153] Lester replied with good humor, "I shall be glad to receive 'Freedom to Learn.' The title, at least, conforms to my beliefs—but with your comment on the book, I think I shall take a blood pressure pill & read the book in a reclining position."[154] Later Lester wrote Carl that he actually liked the book. But then when Lester sent in his $15 renewal for CSP membership and included a jibe about the Center living off government welfare, which was seen by Carl's and CSP's secretaries, Carl was apparently terribly embarrassed and offended by what he called:

Your snide and sarcastic note … I am enclosing $15.00 in cash and asking to have your name taken off our mailing list. The reason for enclosing the cash is that you still can deduct your contribution … I think it should appeal to you to be able to take $15.00 of tax deduction which you don't really deserve. … this note of yours really turns me off. Please expect no more communications from me, no more material from the Center, no more attempts at communication whatsoever. I am sorry for this but it seems that communication is really impossible between us … I don't really understand what activates your hostility toward me, though I suspect it is partly jealousy or envy. I guess I will add to that a bit. [He then reported the impressive sales figures for five of his books.] I am sure that part of my motivation in citing these figures is to brag, but part of it is to say that a number of people seem to appreciate the point of view that we hold here. I am sorry that you do not … in the last year I have felt that I have really been unreasonable in not trying to communicate something of myself to the older brother whom I admired so much. This, however, marks the end. You will never receive material from the Center again and I can assure you you will receive nothing from me. You will not be bothered by a brother whom you believe to be on welfare ... Sometimes I feel that my bitterness about situations has increased, though my bitterness is about situations quite different from yours, but I regret for both of us if we become bitter old men. That seems like the worst fate that I can imagine. Affectionately, but finally, Carl.[155]

Lester replied by writing a letter to "My dear Carl" which, under the circumstances, was remarkably gracious, affirming and good humored. He repeatedly reminded and reassured Carl of his great pride in Carl's accomplishments and his previous expressions of appreciation for *On Encounter Groups* and *Freedom to Learn*. He apologized. "For whatever I said that hurt your feelings, I hasten to apologize because my only intention was to continue my subscription and to joke with my brother of whose reputation I am proud." With considerable insight he pointed out, "It is strange to me, that as an experienced and respected psychologist, who makes it a business to understand 'weird' people like me, you should feel that I am '*hostile*' when I differ with your viewpoint or try to ask questions that will enable me to understand it. As I read ... *Encounter Groups*, it seemed to me that you got some fairly rough stuff thrown at you, but always took it gracefully or forcefully as occasion demanded, but I didn't recall any case where you replied to what sometimes *really was* hostility, like you did to me. It is difficult for me to understand why *my* desire to communicate (and I do mean that!) should always be considered as *hostile* ... There's a TV ad where a tenor sends forth such strong vocal vibrations that he breaks a pane of glass with them! That always seems to occur when I send vibrations to you that don't quite jibe with yours, and it's truly a sad experience ... And here are your 15 bucks right back at you ... My deductions overrun, anyway—and besides, what I *want* is the stuff *from the Center*. I hope I'm never to old to learn—and if the only way you'll allow me to learn from *you* is to keep my own thoughts and unanswered questions "Top Secret"—I'll gladly do so rather than hurt your feelings so severely ...."[156]

What was going on here? In his public life, Rogers almost always reacted to criticism with graciousness and even humor. But as he got older he became more impatient with his critics and opponents, old and new. As colleague Betty Berzon commented in 1971, "He is given to a very sarcastic way of expressing himself when he's feeling hostile. He has an acerbic wit, a very sharp tongue that he seems to be doing less and less to curb in his later years. When he is resentful of something or he feels he has been wronged in some way, he is very strong in his attack on whomever he feels has wronged him."[157] This mostly seeped out in private, in the presence of trusted friends and colleagues, and it by no means characterized Rogers. He certainly never became anything like the bitter old man he referred to above. But uncharacteristic moments of sarcasm and non-acceptance occurred somewhat more often. Sometimes he was just being, well ... *human*, revealing as Logan Fox described earlier with relief, that Rogers was not an all-accepting saint.[158] But sometimes there *was* a bitterness or anger present that was not characteristic of Rogers. In the particular interaction with Lester, unresolved feelings from childhood clearly were evident, as the two brothers played out the old family drama of siblings teasing Carl with what they insisted was good-humored fun and Carl reacting or overreacting with hurt and anger. Possibly there was another factor operating, which I will discuss in the following chapter.

When the Rogers moved to California, continued ownership and use of the Seneca Lake vacation property in New York was no longer feasible, so they deeded it to David and Natalie. But Carl and Helen continued to travel regularly, sometimes to visit their growing family or take vacations, often in connection with invitations for Carl to deliver presentations or conduct workshops around the world. In the winter of 1965, for example, they took a two-month trip, mostly by ship, to Hawaii, the South Seas, New Zealand and Australia, including three weeks of lectures and workshops for psychologists and psychiatrists in Australia. In the spring of 1966, after a talk he gave at Harvard, they spent two months in Europe, including three weeks in Paris, then Belgium and Amsterdam, then two weeks of vacation driving around the French countryside, then some work in Lisbon, and two more weeks driving around Portugal.[159] They went to Mexico that winter and again for more than two months in 1970.

As usual Rogers wrote detailed letters describing their adventures; or more accurately, he now dictated them and mailed the tapes home, where they were transcribed, duplicated and mailed to family, friends and colleagues.[160] In one such letter he wrote from Tepoztlan, Morelos, Mexico, he described a comedy of errors in navigating the narrow streets, including "the screamingly funny moment when we found the awful cobblestone road to the Posada *choked* with cars, and a car descending straight down upon us in the very narrow central lane—and Helen made *him* back *up*hill, instead of us backing *down*! Whereupon I killed my engine, but *good*! But what a wife!"[161]

Teaching and Learning

During his time at WBSI and CSP, along with his major commitment to the encounter-group movement, Rogers spent an equivalent amount of attention applying his insights to the field of education. This was not something which began for him in the 1960s. Ever since his course at Teachers College with William Heard Kilpatrick forty years earlier, he had appreciated the basic premise of John Dewey's educational philosophy—that the primary avenue for education is and should be *experience*. His own experiences—boyhood agricultural experiments, the trip to China, his marriage to Helen, the self-initiated discussion group at Union Theological Seminary, his work in the Rochester clinic—had provided many of his most significant learnings. As a psychotherapist he came to believe that experiencing previously denied or distorted feelings and experiences and experiencing the therapist's deep acceptance and understanding change a person's self-concept, which in turn changes one's behavior.

Therefore, from the beginning of his teaching career at Ohio State, he endeavored to make education a process of experiential learning for his students. His practicum in counseling, one of the first, if not *the* first in America, was such an attempt to have students learn by doing. Not just talking about research but having his students actually do important research was another type of learning experience he provided. As his nondirective approach to counseling developed, he quite naturally began to use a comparable approach in conducting classes and workshops. One student, Samuel Tenenbaum, in a four-week summer course Rogers conducted in 1958 at Brandeis University as a visiting professor, gave a detailed account of Rogers' "nondirective teaching."

In a friendly, relaxed way, he sat down with the students (about 25 in number) around a large table and said it would be nice if we stated our purpose and introduced ourselves. There ensued a strained silence; no one spoke up. Finally, to break it, one student timidly raised his hand and spoke his piece. Another uncomfortable silence, and then another upraised hand. Thereafter, the hands rose more rapidly. At no time did the instructor urge any student to speak.

Afterwards, he informed the class that he had brought with him quantities of materials—reprints, brochures, articles, books; he handed out a bibliography of recommended reading. At no time did he indicate that he expected students to read or do anything else. As I recall, he made only one request. Would some student volunteer to set up this material in a special room which had been reserved for students of the course? Two students promptly volunteered. He also said he had with him recorded tapes of therapeutic sessions and also reels of motion pictures. This created a flurry of excitement and students asked whether they could be heard and seen and Dr. Rogers answered yes. The class then decided how it could be done best. Students volunteered to run tape recorders, find a movie projector; for the most part this too was student initiated and arranged.

Thereafter followed four hard, frustrating sessions. During this period, the class didn't seem to get anywhere. Students spoke at random, saying whatever came into their heads. It all seemed chaotic, aimless, a waste of time. A student would bring up some aspect of Rogers' philosophy; and the next student completely disregarded the first [and] would start fresh on something else altogether. At times there were some faint efforts at a cohesive discussion, but for the most part the classroom proceeding seemed to lack continuity and direction. The instructor received every contribution with attention and regard.

He did not find any student's contribution in order or out of order ... Dr. Rogers neither agreed or disagreed. It was not his habit to respond to students' contributions unless a remark was directed specifically to him; and even then he might choose not to answer. His main object, it seemed to me, was to follow students' contributions intelligently and sympathetically.

The class was not prepared for such a totally unstructured approach. They did not know how to proceed. In their perplexity and frustration, they demanded that the teacher play the role assigned to him by custom and tradition; that he set forth for us in authoritative language what was right and wrong, what was good and bad. Had they not come from far distances to learn from the oracle himself? Were they not fortunate? Were they not about to be initiated in the right rituals and practices by the great man himself, the founder of the movement that bears his name? The notebooks were poised for the climatic moment when the oracle would give forth, but mostly they remained untouched.

Queerly enough, from the onset, even in their anger, the members of the group felt joined together, and outside the classroom there was an excitement and a ferment, for even in their frustration, they had communicated as never before in any classroom. In the Rogers class, they had spoken their minds; the words did not come from a book, nor that of any other authority. The ideas, emotions and feelings came from themselves; and this was the releasing and the exciting process.

In this atmosphere of freedom, something for which they had not bargained and for which they were not prepared, the students spoke up as students seldom do. During this period, the instructor took many blows; and it seemed to me that many times he appeared to be shaken; and although he was the source of our irritation, we had, strange as it may seem, a great affection for him, for it did not seem right to be angry with a man who was so sympathetic, so sensitive to the feelings and ideas of others. We all felt that what was involved was some slight misunderstanding, which once understood and remedied would make everything right again. But our instructor, gentle enough on the surface, had a 'whim of steel.' He didn't seem to understand; and if he did, he was obstinate and obdurate; he refused to come around. Thus did this tug-of-war continue. We all looked to Rogers and Rogers looked to us ...

... they began to demand more insistently that Rogers assume the traditional role of a teacher. At this point, the blows were coming Rogers' way rather frequently and strongly and I thought I saw him bend somewhat before them. (Privately, he denied he was so affected.) During one session, a student made the suggestion that he lecture one hour and that we have a class discussion the next. This one suggestion seemed to fit into his plans. He said he had with him an unpublished paper. He warned us that it was available and we could read it by ourselves. But the student said it would not be the same. The person, the author, would be out of it, the stress, the inflection, the emotion, those nuances which

381

give value and meaning to words. Rogers then asked the students if that was what they wanted. They said yes. He read for over an hour. After the vivid and acrimonious exchanges to which we had become accustomed, this was certainly a letdown, dull and soporific to the extreme. This experience squelched all further demands for lecturing. In one of the moments when he apologized for this episode … he said: 'You asked me to lecture. It is true I am a resource, but what sense would there be in my lecturing? I have brought a great quantity of material, reprints of any number of lectures, articles, books, tape recordings, movies.'

By the fifth session, something definite had happened; there was no mistaking that. Students spoke to one another; they by-passed Rogers. Students asked to be heard and wanted to be heard, and what before was a halting, stammering, self-conscious group became an interactive group, a brand-new cohesive unit, carrying on in a unique way; and from them came discussion and thinking such as no other group but this could repeat or duplicate. The instructor also joined in, but his role, more important than any in the group, somehow became merged with the group; the group was important, the center, the base of operation, not the instructor.[162]

This description of what the students experienced sounds very much like the client who gradually comes to realize that the therapist is not going to solve his problem for him, that he has got to do the work himself—or the encounter group members who eventually recognize that the leader is not going to lead, that they have to take responsibility for the group themselves. But this was a college course. Was therapy or an intensive group experience all that resulted from this kind of "teaching"? Tenenbaum mentioned another student in this course who raised this very question. "'Should we be concerned,' he asked, 'only with the emotions? Has the intellect no play?' It was my turn to ask, 'Is there any student who has read as much or thought as much for any other course?' The answer was obvious. We had spent hours and hours reading; the room reserved for us had occupants until 10 o'clock at night, and then many left only because the university guards wanted to close the building. Students listened to recordings; they saw motion pictures; but best of all, they talked and talked and talked."[163]

The student, Dr. Samuel Tenenbaum, was no impressionable youth, but an educational scholar who had written a biography of William Heard Kilpatrick, Rogers' former professor at Columbia.[164] In fact, two sessions into Rogers' class Tenenbaum wrote Kilpatrick to tell him about this new professor he met whose ideas seemed so reminiscent of Kilpatrick's. "He impresses me most favorably as Stanley Hall did you … In so many ways he reminds me of you—sympathetic, sensitive, restrained in a gentlemanly way. His mind is first-rate and it is open to his students."[165] Tenenbaum summed up his experience with Rogers by saying, "If we accept Dewey's definition of education as the reconstruction of experience, what better way can a person learn than by becoming involved with his whole self, his very person, his root drives, emotions, attitudes and values? No series of facts or arguments, no matter how logically or brilliantly arranged, can even faintly compare with that sort of thing."[166]

As Rogers developed his style as a "nondirective teacher," he was also reading other writers (like Nathaniel Cantor, Earl Kelley, Donald Snygg, and Arthur Combs) whose educational views seemed consistent with his own.[167] Gradually he began to formulate his own educational philosophy, drawing upon these sources, but as usual, primarily upon his own experience. The basis of his philosophy could be summarized in one sentence, which he wrote in 1951: "We cannot teach another person directly, we can only facilitate his learning."[168] This appeared in the first lengthy exposition of his ideas on education—his chapter on "Student-Centered Teaching" in *Client-Centered Therapy*. Here he described how he and his colleagues' thinking on education had gone through a similar evolution as had their thinking on therapy. He had moved from being technically nondirective, or what he later called "rather rigidly 'student-centered,'"[169] practically refusing to share anything of himself directly with students, confining his role solely to that of the nondirective counselor, to being more flexible in his behavior and placing greater stress on the teacher's attitudes than on his techniques. As he wrote in 1951:

We may state briefly our present concept of the role of the leader in an educational situation when the aim is to center the process in the developing aims of the students … Initially the leader has much to do with setting the mood or climate of the group experience by his own basic philosophy of trust in the group, which is communicated in many subtle ways … The leader helps to elicit and clarify the purposes of the members of the class, accepting all aims … He relies upon the student desire to implement these purposes as the motivational force behind learning … He endeavors to organize and make easily available all resources which the students may wish to use for their own learning … He regards himself as a flexible resource to be utilized by the group in the ways which seem most meaningful to them, in so far as he can be comfortable in operating in these ways … In responding to expressions from the group, he accepts both the intellectual content and the emotionalized attitudes, endeavoring to give each aspect the approximate degree of emphasis which it has for the individual and the group … As the acceptant classroom climate becomes established, the leader is able to change his role and become a participant, a member of the group, expressing his views as those of one individual only … He remains alert to expressions indicative of deep feeling and when these are voiced, he endeavors to understand these from the speaker's point of view, and to communicate this type of understanding … Likewise when group interaction becomes charged with emotion, he tends to maintain a neutral and understanding role, in order to give acceptance to the varied feelings which exist … He recognizes that the extent to which he can behave in these differing fashions is limited by the genuineness of his own attitudes. To pretend an acceptant understanding of a viewpoint when he does not feel this acceptance, will not further, and will probably hinder, the dynamic process of the class.[170]

Though filled with pages of support, examples and elaboration, this chapter in *Client-Centered Therapy* was never very influential in the educational field because the book was read primarily by psychologists and therapists. It was another article, actually a speech, presented a year after the publication of *Client-Centered Therapy*, which became one of Rogers' best known, most widely quoted and reprinted treatises on education.[171] In April 1952 he had been invited to address a conference at the Harvard Business School, to present a demonstration of "student-centered teaching."[172] That winter, on their quarter vacation in Mexico, he read a good deal of the Danish philosopher Søren Kierkegaard and was impressed by that nineteenth-century man's "honest willingness to call a spade a spade."[173] He decided he would try to state in simple terms his convictions about the teaching–learning process and then invite the audience to react, "endeavoring to understand and accept the often very divergent reactions and feelings" of the group. He later wrote, "I may have been naïve, but I did not consider the material inflammatory." He simply figured it would provide a good discussion starter and, since this was a group of sophisticated educators interested in the discussion method, they would also keep in mind that the point of his presentation was to provide an example of student-centered teaching, not to make a definitive statement about education.

So Rogers came before the Harvard group, explained that he wished to "present some very brief remarks, in the hope that if they bring forth any reaction from you, I may get some new light on my own ideas," and proceeded to give one of the shortest speeches he ever made, barely over a thousand words, taking about five minutes to deliver. Essentially, the points he made were:

My experience has been that I cannot teach another person how to teach ... It seems to me that anything that can be taught to another is relatively inconsequential, and has little or no significant influence on behavior ... I realize increasingly that I am only interested in learnings which significantly influence behavior ... I have come to feel that the only learning which significantly influences behavior is self-discovered, self-appropriated learning ... Such self-discovered learning, truth that has been personally appropriated and assimilated in experience, cannot be directly communicated to another ... As a consequence of the above, I realize that I have lost interest in being a teacher ... When I try to teach, as I sometimes do ... It seems to cause the individual to distrust his own experience, and to stifle significant learning. Hence I have come to feel that the outcomes of teaching are either unimportant or hurtful ...

As a consequence, I realize that I am only interested in being a learner, preferably learning things that matter, that have some significant influence on my own behavior ... I find it very rewarding to learn, in groups, in relationships with one person as in therapy, or by myself ... I find that one of the best, but most difficult ways for me to learn is to drop my own defensiveness, at least temporarily, and to try to understand the way in which his experience seems and feels to the other person ... I find that another way of learning for me is to state my own uncertainties, to try to clarify my puzzlements, and thus get closer to the meaning that my experience actually seems to have ... It seems to mean letting my experience carry me on, in a direction which appears to be forward, toward goals that I can but dimly define, as I try to understand at least the current meaning of that experience ...

Then he took up the consequences and implications his views would have, if others shared his thinking.

[W]e would do away with teaching. People would get together if they wished to learn ... We would do away with examinations. They measure only the inconsequential type of learning ... we would do away with grades and credits for the same reason ... We would do away with degrees as a measure of competence partly for the same reason. Another reason is that a degree marks an end or a conclusion of something, and a learner is only interested in the continuing process of learning ... It would imply doing away with the exposition of conclusions, for we would realize that no one learns significantly from conclusions.

I think I had better stop there. I do not want to become too fantastic. I want to know primarily whether anything in my inward thinking as I have tried to describe it, speaks to anything in your experience of the classroom as you have lived it, and if so, what the meanings are that exist for you in your experience.[174]

He had hoped for some response from the audience, but was amazed with the tumultuous reception his remarks engendered. People reacted very strongly, mostly negatively. Surely he didn't mean what he said. He was exaggerating to get a reaction from them. What he was saying threatened every one of their jobs. Occasionally, a quiet voice would echo experiences similar to Rogers'. Whatever the speaker's attitude, Rogers tried to understand and accept it. He gave such responses as, "I guess you feel I am grossly unfair to the teaching profession and all that it stands for." Or, "If I understand you correctly, I guess you believe that my stance on teaching is absurd."[175] He refused to defend himself, occasionally reminding them that he was only describing his own experience, not asking them to agree. The discussion went on and on, with participants (they were no longer an audience) exploring more and more deeply their own thoughts and feelings about teaching, disagreeing with one another now as often as with the speaker. Ironically, they got so caught up in the content of the discussion that few of them seemed to realize that they were participating in a demonstration of student-centered teaching, which was the main point of the presentation. The next morning one conference member told Rogers, "You kept more people awake last night!"

His "Personal Thoughts on Teaching and Learning" did not reach publication for five more years. As he later wrote, "My views on psychotherapy had already made me a 'controversial figure' among psychologists and psychiatrists. I had no desire to add educators to the list."[176]

Until now Rogers' teaching philosophy emphasized two progressive education principles: *experiential learning,* and giving students considerable *choice or freedom* to work on problems that are meaningful to them. A third progressive education principle was also implicit in his approach: *social learning,* that is, having students learn important social skills by working together in groups. But Rogers had an additional insight of his own to add to these progressive learning concepts—*the relationship* between teacher and student. As early as 1946, in *Counseling with Returned Servicemen,* Rogers and Wallen had included this one sentence in passing: "Schools are beginning to take into account the fact that the nature of the interpersonal relations between teacher and pupils—and among pupils themselves—is usually more important than the technique or teaching or the textbooks in determining what the pupil learns."[177] Five years later, in his education chapter in *Client-Centered Therapy,* Rogers began to describe that relationship by explaining that the teacher's creating an accepting climate and trusting the students were helpful in freeing them to engage in independent, meaningful learning. Finally, in 1959, shortly after writing his landmark essay "The Necessary and Sufficient Conditions of Therapeutic Personality Change," Rogers expanded upon this theme in another well-known article comparing "Significant Learning: In Therapy and In Education."

In therapy he saw five conditions which led to significant learning—learning which makes a difference in the client's behavior, attitudes, or personality. First, he must perceive a problem he wants to work on; there must be a desire to change, to grow, to cope more effectively. Second through fourth, the therapist must provide the conditions of congruence, empathic understanding, and unconditional positive regard. Fifth, the client must perceive to some degree these conditions offered by the therapist. Speaking of education, Rogers identified a similar set of conditions. First, significant learning can be encouraged to the extent the student is working on problems and issues which are real and important to him. Second, significant learning can be facilitated to the extent the teacher is genuine and congruent, the extent "… he becomes a real person in the relationship with his students. He can be enthusiastic about subjects he likes, and bored by topics he does not like. He can be angry, but he can also be sensitive or sympathetic. Because he accepts his feelings as his feelings, he has no need to impose them on his students, or to insist that they feel the same way. He is a *person,* not a faceless embodiment of a curricular requirement, or a sterile pipe through which knowledge is passed from one generation to the next."[178]

Third and fourth are acceptance and understanding. The "teacher who can warmly accept, who can provide unconditional positive regard, and can empathize with the feelings of fear, anticipation, and discouragement which are involved in meeting new materials, will have done a great deal toward setting the conditions for learning." The accepting, trusting teacher creates a set of expectations that students tend to live up to, just as the nontrusting, suspicious teacher creates a self-fulfilling prophecy in which students produce all the evidence to justify the teacher's negative preconceptions. This trust, acceptance, and understanding are especially important when students are taking risks, exploring ideas and feelings which are new to them, attempting projects at which they are not sure they will succeed. To foster significant learning the teacher is greatly helped by a genuine belief in "the self-actualizing tendency in students. The hypothesis upon which he would build is that students who are in real contact with life problems wish to learn, want to grow, seek to find out, hope to master, desire to create."

Finally, and here the condition is somewhat different in education than in (client-centered) therapy, the teacher endeavors to provide resources to assist the students in their self-directed learning. These resources include not only the traditional resources of books, materials, audio-visuals and the like, but the teacher herself as a resource—a person who has had considerable experience with life and learning and who knows of other resources which could help the student.

As in his shorter presentation, he commented on his view of what education is not, and again he emphasized the importance of self-evaluation. "I believe that the testing of the student's achievements in order to see if he meets some criterion held by the teacher is directly contrary to the implications of therapy for significant learning. In therapy, the examinations are set by life. The client meets them, sometimes passing, sometimes failing. He finds that he can use the resources of the therapeutic relationship and his experience in it to organize himself so that he can meet life's tests more satisfyingly next time. I see this as the paradigm for education also."

All of Rogers' thinking on the subject of education reported thus far predates the 1960s and certainly predates 1964, the year with which this chapter begins to concern itself. It might seem more logical to have included this discussion in an earlier chapter. I have delayed it, however, for two reasons. First, education did not become a major focus or interest of Rogers until the 1960s. Although he wrote an occasional article or made an occasional speech on the subject, he really was most interested in psychotherapy during those years and, other than with respect to his own teaching, spent very little time thinking about education. The second reason is that, although he had developed most of his educational thinking before the 1960s, it was not until then that his ideas caught on. His first writings on therapy, in the early 1940s, had catapulted him into becoming a known and controversial figure among psychologists. Except among some school guidance counselors and school psychologists, he remained little known as an educator until relatively late in life.

The "progressive" movement in American education had, for the most part, dissipated by the end of the Second World War. During the fifties, when he was developing and occasionally writing about his views on teaching and learning, American education was responding to the Soviet Union's Sputnick, placing a renewed emphasis on mathematics and science. There was little time for such ideas as eliminating teaching, grading, degrees and the like. Then, in the sixties, two new influences became significant on the educational scene. First, through the efforts of groups like the National Training Laboratories, and personal growth centers like Esalen Institute, and books like Rogers' *On Becoming a Person* and Maslow's *Toward a Psychology of Being*,[179] by the early and mid-sixties the "human potential movement" began to be felt in many areas of American life. Businesspeople, religious leaders, school administrators, teachers, and others would attend workshops, encounter groups, human-relations laboratories and the like and come away feeling, "Why can't I bring this type of learning and growing experience back to my own system?" Many educators began thinking, "If only our students could experience learning which is as involving and exciting as what I have just gone through!" But how does one accomplish that, short of turning every classroom into an encounter group?

Another influence, occurring simultaneously with the human-potential phenomenon in the United States, provided a partial answer for this question. In 1967 the *New Republic* magazine published a series of three articles by Joseph Featherstone on the "primary schools in Britain."[180] These articles heralded the beginning of the widespread interest in the United States in what came to be known variously as "open education," "open classroom," "open schools," "free schools," "alternative schools," and other related practices.[181] What the British primary school was all about, though, was an attempt to build upon the natural desire of young children to explore their world, to act on their curiosity, and to grow. Its major vehicles were a classroom rich in learning materials—books, arts and crafts supplies, typewriters, Cuisenaire rods and balance scales (gamelike materials that help children learn mathematical and scientific concepts), and other learning resources—plus human beings (teachers, aides, older students) available to help the youngsters set goals and carry out learning activities. Much of the thinking behind the open classroom approach derived from the work of the Swiss developmental psychologist Jean Piaget, who helped demonstrate the importance of a child's active interaction with his environment as an aid to concept formation.[182] In the United States the learning approaches used in the British primary school were soon adapted and generalized to fit primary, elementary, junior high, senior high, and college learning situations. At these upper levels of education the concept of learning by doing and students' choosing their learning goals was particularly timely with so many students and teachers in the socially active 1960s rebelling against an educational system which they saw as too often "irrelevant."

Thus two new and important forces were being felt in American education— the advocates of some form of human relations training or, more broadly, humanistic psychology in the classroom and the advocates of open education. What these forces needed and welcomed was a person or group to pull together the different innovations that were being advocated, to describe these in an easily understood fashion, and to give a firm psychological foundation to the whole movement to "humanize" education. Rogers was such a person, and the Association for Supervision and Curriculum Development, under the influence of Arthur Combs and others, which drew heavily on the thinking of Rogers and other humanistic psychologists, became the educational group which was probably the most influential along these lines.[183]

Most of Rogers' educational ideas were already formed; now he had an audience to hear and read them and take them seriously: The most significant learning occurs when the content has meaning to the student. We must help students learn to set their own goals and achieve them. We must facilitate, not direct, the learning process. Education of this sort strengthens the student psychologically, enables him to deal more effectively with life, to continue to learn and solve his problems as he grows older. The primary goal of school should be to "grow persons," not merely teach subject matter. Education is not just a cognitive endeavor but a social and emotional learning process. These ideas, which were essentially a new iteration of most of the major concepts of the earlier progressive education movement, had seemed extreme or idealistic a decade before when Rogers introduced them. Now they were sought after and applauded by an increasing number of educators. Articles by Rogers began to appear in some of the largest or most influential educational journals, like the *Harvard Educational Review,* the *Yearbooks* of the Association for Supervision and Curriculum Development, the National Education Association's *Journal* with its more than one million readers, the influential *Educational Leadership,* and *Instructor* magazine reaching approximately 300,000 elementary school teachers.[184] He became more and more sought after as a speaker for educational audiences, large and small. During 1966, for example, he spoke to audiences of four thousand members at the American Personnel and Guidance Association, three thousand at the Association for Supervision and Curriculum Development, and two thousand at the California Guidance and Counseling Association, as well as many smaller audiences.[185]

While sharing his educational ideas with a wider audience, Rogers continued to practice and refine his style of student-centered teaching with his own on-going classes. For several years he held a part-time faculty appointment at United States International University in San Diego. He regularly taught courses and workshops there and worked with a considerable number of doctoral students. Several WBSI and CSP staff members did their doctoral work at USIU and completed their dissertations under Rogers' supervision.[186] One student was as impressed with Rogers' organization as he was with the freedom Rogers afforded students. "Although the students were free to do what they wanted to do, he was so well organized himself that that inspired them to be organized. And he seemed to really care whether or not they did their assignments. He communicated that it made a difference to him. He communicated this, first of all, by being prepared himself, by being on top of the situation. If he said he was going to read your paper, he'd read your paper. When he would come to class, he would have several things he *could* do. Like he would have maybe six questions [so] that, if the first one wasn't of interest … he'd go to another one … And he didn't have to get through all six of them. He would always have time for the students, for there to be dialogue, but he was always ready for several different eventualities."[187]

Freedom to Learn

The more Rogers taught, wrote and spoke about education, the more teachers wrote him letters or contacted him telling him of the experiments they were conducting in their classes that supported (or contradicted) his ideas. Gradually his thinking took on greater substance as he had more and more examples and research at his fingertips to support his generalizations. By the late 1960s he had enough published articles, unpublished speeches, and new ideas and examples about education that when his niece told him, "Your articles have so much significance for education, but there's no book of yours," he decided to pull together and add to his writing in a book on education.[188] It was published by Charles E. Merrill Publishers in 1969 under the title *Freedom to Learn: A View of What Education Might Become.*

The book was about significant, meaningful, experiential learning. He wrote in his introduction: "Let me define a bit more precisely the elements which are involved in such significant or experiential learning. *It has a quality of personal involvement*—the whole person in both his feeling and cognitive aspects being *in* the learning event. *It is self-initiated.* Even when the impetus or stimulus comes from the outside, the sense of discovery, of reaching out, of grasping and comprehending, comes from within. *It is pervasive.* It makes a difference in the behavior, the attitudes, perhaps even the personality of the learner. *It is evaluated by the learner.* He knows whether it is meeting his need, whether it leads toward what he *wants* to know, whether it illuminates the dark area of ignorance he is experiencing. The locus of evaluation, we might say, resides definitely in the learner. *Its essence is meaning.* When such learning takes place, the element of meaning to the learner is built into the whole experience …

"I believe that all teachers and educators prefer to facilitate this experiential and meaningful type of learning, rather than the nonsense syllable type. Yet in the vast majority of our schools, at all educational levels, we are locked into a traditional and conventional approach which makes significant learning improbable if not impossible. When we put together in one scheme such elements as a *prescribed curriculum, similar assignments for all students, lecturing* as almost the only mode of instruction, *standardized tests* by which all students are externally evaluated, and *instructor-chosen grades* as the measure of learning, then we can almost guarantee that meaningful learning will be at an absolute minimum ... But there *are* alternatives—alternative practical ways to handle a class or a course—alternative assumptions and hypotheses upon which education can be built—alternative goals and values for which educators and students can strive. I hope that these will become clear in the following chapters."[189]

The first three chapters attempted to illustrate these alternatives through highly specific and detailed descriptions of three teachers. The first was Barbara Shiel, a sixth-grade teacher, who gradually found ways to give her students freedom to learn things that were important to them, but who was also able to remain congruent herself, not allowing the students' freedom to go to extremes that violated her own sense of comfort and order. The next chapter showed Dr. Volney Faw, an undergraduate psychology professor who, in a very structured manner, with requirements and grading procedures all spelled out from the beginning, managed to provide students with an enormous number of choices for learning psychology in ways that would have meaning to them—for example, reading, writing a psychological autobiography, working with old people, taking psychological tests, receiving counseling, doing case studies, etc. The last example was "My Way of Facilitating a Class," in which Rogers described his own approach to setting requirements, establishing grades, and conducting a class or workshop. Much of the substance of *Freedom to Learn* appears in these three chapters, and I have heard many people comment that they wished he had pictured even more teachers, at all levels of education, at work with their students. It was in these chapters that all his theoretical writings on education really came alive. As in the past, Rogers' concrete examples and case studies made his ideas and theories understandable and accessible to practitioners.

In the two chapters of Part II he described in a bit more detail the role of the teacher who wants to encourage self-directed learning and specific methods for accomplishing this. He spent a good deal of time, of course, describing the conditions of congruence, empathy, and "prizing, acceptance and trust," the last being a more suitable description for teachers than "unconditional positive regard," although in most ways the concepts were the same. He also went into extra detail in his discussion of congruence. "Some teachers," he wrote, "raise the question, 'But what if I am *not* feeling empathic, do *not*, at this moment, prize or accept or like my students. What then?' My response is that realness is the most important of the attitudes mentioned, and it is not accidental that this attitude was described first."[190]

Miss Shiel, for example, wrote in her journal that her students were not cleaning up after using their art materials and that consequently the room was looking more and more chaotic. "I find it maddening to live with the mess—with a capital M! No one seems to care except me. Finally, one day I told the children ... that I am a neat orderly person by nature and that the mess was driving me to distraction. Did they have a solution? It was suggested there were some volunteers who could clean up ... I said it didn't seem fair to me to have the same people clean up all the time for others—but it would be solved for me. 'Well, some people like to clean,' they replied. So that's the way it is ... I used to get upset and feel guilty when I became angry. I finally realized the children could accept *my* feelings too. And it is important for them to know when they've 'pushed me.' I have my limits, too."[191]

Among the methods Rogers regarded as the most useful to the facilitator of learning, he listed and discussed: the provision of resources; the use of learning contracts; helping students learn how to conduct an inquiry and discover things themselves rather than giving them the predigested and pre-organized knowledge to merely memorize; the use of simulation activities to provide experiential learning; programmed instruction when this would help a student learn something he wanted to learn more efficiently (he even quoted Skinner, without sarcasm!); the basic encounter group; and self-evaluation.

The next section of the book was called "Some Assumptions." Here he included his short controversial piece "Personal Thoughts on Teaching and Learning," discussed earlier. Another short and cogent statement of his educational assumptions was "Regarding Learning and Its Facilitation." Then came "Current Assumptions in Graduate Education: A Passionate Statement." It is no coincidence that it was written in 1963, when he was so frustrated with the University of Wisconsin's graduate psychology program and other practices that he resigned and moved to California. The paper had been rejected by the APA's leading journal *The American Psychologist*; but it soon became what Rogers guessed was "one of the most widely read unpublished papers of the past decade."[192] In it he enumerated and discussed what he saw as the implicit assumptions that seemed to guide most graduate education.

1. The student cannot be trusted to pursue his own scientific and professional training.
2. Ability to pass examinations is the best criterion for student selection and for judging professional promise.
3. Evaluation is education; education is evaluation.
4. Presentation equals learning. What is presented in the lecture is what the student learns.
5. Knowledge is the accumulation of brick upon brick of content and information.
6. The truths of psychology are known.

7. Method is science.

8. Creative scientists develop from passive learners.

9. "Weeding out" a majority of the students is a satisfactory method of producing scientists and clinicians.

10. Students are best regarded as manipulable objects, not as persons.

In trying to illustrate each of these assumptions, he used some strong language ("it seems a scandalous waste of manpower ...," "It is incredible the way this preposterous assumption has become completely imbedded in graduate education in the United States," etc.)[193] and some vivid examples to prove his point. "If the day comes," he concluded, "when psychology wishes to make a thoughtful appraisal of its methods of professional preparation, it will, I believe, throw out most of its current assumptions and procedures."[194] He emphasized that, although his remarks were aimed in particular at graduate education in psychology, they could be applied readily to graduate, undergraduate, and pre-college education in most other areas as well. In his next chapter he proposed "A Revolutionary Program for Graduate Education," one designed to reverse the implicit assumptions he had just described. In another chapter he offered "Some Thoughts About Educational Administration."

The last major section of the book discussed "The Philosophical and Value Ramifications" of the earlier sections. Here he included speeches, articles, or revised presentations which had already appeared in print, although with slightly different titles: "A Modern Approach to the Valuing Process," "Freedom and Commitment," and "The Goal: The Fully Functioning Person."[195] All these chapters helped put the longer-range goals of humanistic education in a broader psychological and philosophical perspective and to deal with questions like: Toward what ends are these newer approaches to education more effective or desirable? What is the ultimate goal of education? What is the Good Life? A final section of the book described "A Plan for Self-Directed Change in an Educational System," which will be discussed below.

It was a powerful presentation. In one of the chapter summaries he wrote, "I'm sorry I can't be coolly scientific about this. The issue is too urgent. I can only be passionate in my statement that people count, that interpersonal relationships are important, that we know something about releasing human potential, that we could learn much more, and that unless we give strong positive attention to the human interpersonal side of our educational dilemma, our civilization is on its way down the drain. Better courses, better curricula, better coverage, better teaching machines, will never resolve our dilemma in a basic way. Only persons, acting like persons in their relationships with their students can even begin to make a dent on this most urgent problem of modern education."[196]

For once one of Rogers' books was reviewed in several journals. He may have wished otherwise. Of five reviews I located, four were mostly negative.[197]

The reviewers saw Rogers' educational thinking as superficial and adding little new to his earlier writings on the subject. Edgar Friedenberg wrote, "Like another American philosopher, Huckleberry Finn, Carl Rogers can get in almost anywhere because the draft of his vessel is so terribly shallow; it never gets hung up. It is almost eerie to read a discussion of basic existential issues affecting human life by a man who, despite an enormous range of honestly assimilated experience, seems to have no sense of tragedy, and not as much as one might expect of the complexity of human conflict."[198] R.S. Peters of the University of London's Institute of Education wrote, "What is surprising ... is that an author who strongly advocates openness to the experience of others should put together a collection of papers that are meant to be of general relevance to educational problems in such a seeming state of ignorance and innocence about educational theory and practice. Freedom is fine; and so is self-directed exploration. But there are other values, both in life and in education—truth, for instance, humility, and breadth of understanding ... But then, as one reads on, one begins to understand the free-floating character of the book, its lack of any proper historical, social, or philosophical dimensions. It is not really an attempt to think systematically about the actual problems of teaching and learning in a concrete historical context. It is Carl Rogers 'doing his thing' in the context of education."[199]

It was the same old story. Vocal critics in the academy—sometimes insightfully, sometimes unfairly—tended to ignore or minimize his contribution. Meanwhile thousands of individuals out in the field began buying and reading and showing their friends copies of his book. Of the entire "Studies of the Person" series which Charles Merrill published, *Freedom to Learn* was the best seller by far, with a sale of 300,000 copies by January 1978.[200]

What was it that students, teachers, and administrators all over the country saw in the book that the critics somehow missed or devalued? In the fall of 1970 all the students in three undergraduate classes I taught at Temple University read ten chapters of *Freedom to Learn*. Although, ironically, this was a class *requirement*, all but two of the students responded positively to what they read. One social work major wrote: "Never before have I regretted my choice of an academic major as when I read Carl Rogers' *Freedom to Learn*. Every concept was challenging, every chapter too short. When a person reads a book from the title to the last bibliography, the book must be powerful." One of my classes was composed entirely of black students, older people who had spent years working in community agencies and who were now returning to college to get a degree. One man wrote, "In reading Dr. Rogers' book, *Freedom to Learn,* I found myself automatically agreeing in such a manner that I felt I could have written parts of the book myself, that's how real it all seemed. In particular, Rogers' comments on the two types of learning, which are experiential and by rote, struck me as falling very close to my loosely formulated hypothesis explaining my eagerness to learn while I was 'out on the street' compared to my being almost turned off since entering college." A woman from this class wrote, "Let me begin by stating that I will treasure Rogers' 'Freedom in Learning,' [sic] and I sensed his ideas, his thoughts and his learning experiences reaching out and touching the very core of one's existence …."[201]

Many of the student papers echoed the sentiment that readers seemed to feel, again and again, in Rogers' later writings. "His way of coming across is honest and direct." "I felt as if he was talking to me and really trying to communicate." "His written words possessed character—it was as if I was being introduced not only to his theories, but to his personality as well. As I progressed through the book I became increasingly caught up in Rogers' enthusiasm and in his goals for education."[202]

These quotations illustrate how Rogers' ideas became a part of the thinking of thousands of people throughout the helping professions. His research was known less and less as the years went by. His elaborate theory of the self and personality change was never widely known, although it was often excerpted in psychology textbooks, to be memorized and forgotten by generations of students. Few people were or are familiar with the scope of his career or his changing theories. People would encounter Rogers at different stages of his career: child guidance, nondirective counseling, client-centered therapy, psychotherapy research, self-theory, becoming a person, the behavioral sciences, encounter groups, education. They would read a book or article on one of these subjects and find that it spoke to them personally and influenced their work or approach to life. Later they would read a new book by Rogers, or hear him speak on a new subject, or see a recent video, and would again be touched by his ideas or influenced by his example. This would continue to happen for years to come, as Rogers continued to extend his work into new aspects of human relationships, both personal and political.

Changing Educational Systems

With encounter groups and education being the main priorities in Rogers' career since moving to California, it is not surprising that he eventually would begin to combine these two areas of interest. He had worked with school personnel, especially counselors, for many years, providing experiential workshops in which they learned the skills and attitudes of the client-centered helper. In leading encounter groups, he worked with many individual teachers and administrators, among various other professionals in his groups. Individual participants would often say, "If only the other teachers in my school could have an experience like this." "If only my principal were here." It was natural that Rogers would soon become curious as to what would happen in such a case. What if an entire faculty or an entire school system *did* go through an encounter-group experience?

Would that have any effect on the teaching and learning that would go on in the schools? Would teachers more readily become facilitators of learning?

As he was by now receiving weekly, and by the turn of the decade sometimes daily invitations to address or visit school systems, it was easy for him to respond to an invitation by saying, "No, I would not come and give a speech or direct a workshop for your faculty; but my colleagues and I would come for a weekend of encounter groups with your teachers and administrators." He got quite a few takers. Rasa Gustaitis described one such experiment.

> Alma College, near Los Gatos, California, is one of the two top Jesuit training centers in the country. Its students, who have lived for a decade or longer under the Society's tutelage, are used to rigid discipline with much formality and severe restrictions on personal emotional life.
>
> A year ago last spring, Dr. Carl Rogers and nine of his associates from the Western Behavioral Sciences Institute, a small think tank in La Jolla, California, came to Alma to conduct a weekend of encounter groups. Nearly the entire community of more than three hundred voluntarily took part in these meetings, designed to encourage people to react freely to one another. Since then, life at Alma has changed.
>
> In the dining room, where faculty, students and lay brothers used to sit at separate tables, all now eat together. In some classrooms where dry lectures had been customary, small groups now engage in lively discussion. One professor scrapped the notes for an entire course soon after the weekend and asked his students to draw up personal study plans. A few students left the order for civil life. One, who was inspired to explore himself and the world beyond sanctioned boundaries, was dismissed.
>
> The Alma upheaval is not atypical of what happens to groups and institutions that come into contact with the mild-mannered, soft-spoken Dr. Rogers …[203]

Rogers was impressed by the kind of changes he saw occur in systems after they had experienced encounter groups. Experiences like that at Alma led him to think that if he could demonstrate the power of encounter groups to change a large school system, this "would have not only lasting impact on one school system but … would start a ferment which would spread throughout the country."[204] He began seeking funding for his idea, initially without any success. He also began describing his plan to various audiences, hoping to attract attention to it in the educational community and get a school system to volunteer. He even wrote an article called "A Plan for Self-Directed Change in an Educational System," which *Educational Leadership* published in 1967 and which became the final chapter in his book *Freedom to Learn*.[205] His plan called for working in a large school system, with numerous encounter groups composed first of administrators, then of teachers, then of students, then of parents, and then "vertical groups" representing a cross section of roles. Participation would be voluntary. A second stage of the plan called for training individuals within the school system to then become group facilitators themselves, to continue to carry on the intensive group experiences after the outside consultants had left the system. Rogers listed various outcomes he hypothesized would result from participation in encounter groups. These included more democratic, flexible leadership styles by administrators, more innovative teaching by teachers, more commitment and more taking of responsibility by students, and better communication throughout the school system.

Even before the *Educational Leadership* article appeared, Rogers was circulating a draft of it and letting it be known that he had such a plan, if only the school system would come forward. Several systems did indicate an interest in participating, and before long Rogers and his colleagues at WBSI had finalized arrangements with the Immaculate Heart system in the Los Angeles area, which included the Immaculate Heart College, several high schools, and many parochial elementary schools which the Order staffed and supervised. Meanwhile, after having failed to obtain funding from public sources, Rogers and WBSI finally were able to raise money from private sources. A $70,000 grant from the Mary Reynolds Babcock Foundation and a $30,000 personal gift from Charles Kettering II enabled the project to get underway. Interestingly, both Babcock and Kettering had previously participated in encounter groups. Kettering regarded Rogers as "an absolutely first-rate scholar, educator, humanitarian, and general all-round great human being."[206] A later grant from the Merrill Foundation and a gift from Everett Baggerly to the Immaculate Heart College helped the project continue.[207]

Representatives of the Immaculate Heart system and from WBSI met periodically throughout the project to plan next steps and evaluate results. Within ninety days from the start of the project during the fall of 1967, "forty-five administrators and faculty members of the College volunteered for the first encounter sessions. They were divided into four groups, met for one intensive weekend and then these same four groups met for a second weekend. Thirty-six high school administrators and faculty members from three high schools met in small groups for two weekends … Forty student leaders from a high school met in three groups for one weekend. When, a month or more later, they met for a second weekend their faculty (counted in the preceding paragraph) were now willing to meet in groups composed of both faculty and students, a mingling which they had at first avoided. They soon found themselves communicating across generations. One hundred and eighty teachers, administrative staff, and principals from twenty-two elementary schools have met in many small groups at different times for two weekend encounter groups, often separated by a month or more."[208]

The initial response was mostly positive, along the lines suggested in Rogers' plan. Communication seemed to improve among many individuals and in many schools, innovations in teaching and learning and administration began, and a great deal of excitement was generated. On the negative side, there were those in the system, mostly people who had not participated in the groups (but not entirely, for a small number of the groups seemed to have been ineffective and generated their share of "informed" critics), who were skeptical or critical of the program. Many did not fully understand the goals of the program, many others simply felt excluded, though not quite ready to volunteer for the next round of groups. The WBSI staff found that their initial conception of their role as simply group facilitators was inadequate. They had to become "consultants" in every sense of the word. They were called upon to counsel individuals who wanted help in pursuing issues which had arisen in the encounter groups. They were asked to address the entire college faculty on the subject of educational innovations, as well as an assembly of Immaculate Heart students and faculty, many of whom had little idea of what the project was doing and were therefore fearful and apprehensive. They were invited by faculty to attend many classes to provide experiences for these teachers' students. They received many new requests for weekend or evening encounter groups and wherever possible these were organized. They soon came to realize that they were not simply studying, as had been Rogers' initial intention, the effects of encounter groups on an educational system; rather, as he later wrote, they were "studying the impact of a dedicated group of individuals who are interested in persons, who want to communicate with persons, and who are interested in facilitating communication between persons, upon an educational system."[209]

By the start of 1968 two things were occurring simultaneously. While the project staff were being invited to lead groups and sessions for many different kinds of classes and groups within the College and the schools, some serious polarization was also taking place among many parts of the College and school community. This was especially true in the elementary schools, staffed partly by the Sisters of the Immaculate Heart Order. About a year *before* the project began, these Sisters had begun formulating "new and experimental ways of living, acting under the instructions of Vatican II, that religious orders should experiment with ways of living which were more relevant to modern life."[210] The Sisters' representative to "Chapter," their council, had come close to finishing their proclamation by the time they first participated in an encounter-group workshop. Although they were moving in this direction anyway, "… it appears that the workshop with the Chapter delegates may have helped them in some degree to have the courage to map out new ways of life … By early autumn the proclamation was made public. Among other things it indicated that the Sisters were free to wear habits or not as they desired, to choose the names that they preferred—either baptismal or religious, and in general freed them to live a much more independent life in the community, serving in the ways that they thought were most relevant and helpful."[211]

Enter Cardinal McIntyre and a group of conservative Catholics who were deeply opposed to the changes they saw occurring. Over the next year there was much bitter controversy, resulting finally in some forty to fifty of the Sisters who were teaching in parochial elementary schools having to leave and seek employment elsewhere. Referring to these events, Rogers and William Coulson wrote, "The year has been one of crisis and reappraisal for most of the members of the Order."[212]

Meanwhile, as the first year of the project drew to a close, there was increasing sentiment on the college campus to reject the help of the "La Jolla group," the outside consultants. Rogers saw in this phenomenon the healthy, adolescent phenomenon of "I want to do it myself." Others saw it due in part to the consultants not being willing to go far enough in entertaining alternatives to their original plan and therefore encouraging this resistance.[213] At any rate, the number of encounter groups held seemed to drop off sharply and there was almost a feeling of relief among many on campus that the year was drawing to a close. Simultaneously, however, the Administrative Council of the College, composed of the president and her top executives and deans, was meeting with Rogers and Sheldon Davis, an organizational consultant, in a "task-oriented group." More work-oriented than an encounter group, they listed problems they needed to deal with, including interpersonal problems among themselves, proceeded to deal with the problems one at a time, including these interpersonal ones—which at times led to tears—mapped out action plans where appropriate, and at subsequent meetings reported on the action steps taken. By all reports this was a highly successful experience, resulting in better communication, a democratization of the way the College budget was arrived at, an impetus for one of the vice-presidents to enter a training program in organizational development, and many other constructive and lasting changes.

From the beginning the project staff and Immaculate Heart had built into the project an ongoing evaluation by outside consultants who had no other direct connection with the project. Thus Drs. Morton Shaevitz and Donald Barr, both of the University of Michigan, made six extended visits to the College, spaced from one to four months apart and lasting over two years. They spent many hours talking with students, faculty, and administrators, gathering data to assess the extent to which changes had or had not taken place at the College. The description, so far, has drawn upon their evaluation[214] as well as on the perceptions of Rogers and his colleagues. Shaevitz and Barr described the beginning of the second year, the fall of 1968, as a period of "minimal activity." The formal activities of the outside consultants had ceased, although they were invited to conduct a workshop for the Library Science Department which "eventually developed an independent program, using encounter technology, which is now being introduced to librarians across the country." "A lot of latent anger toward the project staff" was still occurring, however. Shaevitz and Barr called the final stage of their observations, covering the spring of 1969, "Gone But Not Forgotten; Internalized But Not Recognized."

"The project was being talked about in the past tense," they wrote. "A number of staff and students still felt very positively about the project and about their own experiences in groups, but generally accepted the fact that a phase was over, and they were moving in other directions. These other directions seem to include a greater emphasis on task-oriented groups, planned all-community problem-solving approaches, and the utilization of consultants with more systems-oriented philosophies ... We believe the project intervention led directly to some of the new procedures being used in decision-making and in interpersonal relations at Immaculate Heart College." Still a year later, three years after the project had begun, Rogers would hear reports or receive letters like that written by a professor of education from the college. "We are working on a self-initiated and self-directed program in teacher education. We had a fantastically exciting weekend workshop here recently. Students, faculty, and administration, 75 in all, brainstormed in a most creative and productive way. One outcome is that the students will immerse themselves in schools all over the city observing classes, sitting in on faculty meetings, interviewing teachers, students and administrators. Our students will *then* describe what *they* need to know, to experience, to do, in order to teach. They will then gather faculty and other students around them to assist them in accomplishing their own goals."[215]

Rogers was very pleased with the results. As he wrote in 1970, "I believe that the material I have cited ... justifies the statement that in important ways we have achieved our initial objective, namely, that of initiating self-directed change in a large educational system. We have had no close working contact with the College or any other part of the system for more than two years. Yet, self-initiated, innovative changes in the direction of making the organization a more human and participative one are continuing at an exciting rate. To me it shows that if the top leadership is willing to be experimental, the encounter group and its offshoots of brief confrontation groups, task-oriented groups, and the like can be successful in helping individuals and institutions to become changing, self-renewing, and adaptive in their reactions to modern problems."[216]

Unfortunately, the story did not end there. The conflict between the order and the church, which had begun before the Rogers group arrived, continued to ferment. The Immaculate Heart Project no doubt supported and accelerated what was already occurring—the sisters asserting themselves and becoming increasingly independent, even if that meant placing themselves in opposition to church authority. This conflict continued after the Rogers group ceased their interventions in the Immaculate Heart system. Eventually the Vatican stepped in and supported the Cardinal in insisting that the nuns conform to more traditional church rules. The sisters refused to conform and, upon threat of dismissal, felt compelled to resign their teaching positions in the Los Angeles public schools. Eventually they separated from the official Catholic church, forming their own independent order, the Immaculate Heart Community, which continues to exist today.[217]

The Immaculate Heart College and high school continued to operate as innovative, self-directing institutions for many years. In fact, as late as 1975, eight years after the project began, Rogers would write his brother-in-law that, "I regard Immaculate Heart College as an outstanding example of the kind of education needed in the modern world." After describing its innovative programs and operating style, he concluded by saying, "My opinion of Immaculate Heart College is that it is very much alive, and that its administration, its faculty, and its students are well able to cope with the changing and difficult problems of the future. In my estimation this is the kind of college which deserves support."[218] Not enough people saw it that way. The major upheaval within the Immaculate Heart system caused its financial supporters to withdraw their support, and the college eventually closed its doors in 1980.

Was the polarization and conflict that led to the dissolution of the Immaculate Heart school system necessary? If we were to ask many professional, organizational consultants their opinion of Rogers' style of intervention in the Immaculate Heart system, we would probably hear significant criticism of the WBSI intervention strategy. By the time Rogers and his colleagues began the Immaculate Heart Project, the National Training Laboratories had been conducting human relations training groups for twenty years. By the late fifties and early sixties many of the NTL groups were realizing that there were definite limitations to the use of T-groups or sensitivity groups, that is, groups designed primarily to be good learning experiences for the participants. They came to believe that when working with an entire system in an ongoing relationship, a much more sophisticated approach was necessary, compared to simply offering encounter groups. This broader approach would include an array of alternatives for working with a system—intensive groups when appropriate, but also "process consultation,"[219] "third-party consultation,"[220] conflict resolution, simulation exercises, counseling, what would later be called "strategic planning," and many other helping approaches. This overall field of "organizational development," as it is generally known, had developed considerably by 1967, when the Immaculate Heart Project began.[221] Many of the people in this field, reading reports of how Rogers and his colleagues learned that they needed to do more than encounter groups with the Immaculate Heart system, would undoubtedly shake their heads at Rogers' naïveté. They would criticize him for remaining at the sensitivity training stage when an organizational development approach was more appropriate. Perhaps all that polarization was not necessary and the conflicts could have been resolved in a more productive way.

To some extent Rogers would admit this. In the early seventies he wrote to one of the Immaculate Heart leaders, "Like you I recognize how naïve we all were when we started the project—and by and large I'm glad of it. We weren't even adequately aware of all the intricacies of organizational development, or the problems of changing institutional systems. But I remember an incident in the task-oriented group of the Administrative Council, held I believe in 1968. President Helen Kelley was being quite critical of the project, and I felt that most of her criticisms were valid. I told her that if we were doing it all over we would certainly start much more slowly. Her response was immediate and surprising. 'Oh no! If you hadn't held all those encounter groups so quickly I don't believe we would have seen so much change!' So, as I say, I'm glad that we couldn't foresee all the consequences of some of our enthusiastic behavior."[222]

This assessment, however, came before the system dissolved. Rogers' critics, of course, had no doubt where the blame for that lay.[223] His colleague William Coulson came to regret his role in the Immaculate Heart and other projects and dedicated much of his life to telling the world about the errors of his and Rogers' ways in failing to respect the legitimate role of authority in education, parenting, the church and society.[224]

A few years later the public school system of Louisville, Kentucky, undertook a program, "Project Transition," similar if not bigger in size and scope than the Immaculate Heart project. The Louisville district had "the greatest number of low-income students … the highest number of underachievers … the most pupils dropping out of school … the most delinquency referrals … the highest student and teacher turnover" in the state. In fact it had the second largest dropout rate among large cities in the nation. There were about 60,000 children in the district, about 60 percent white and 40 percent black; 34.1 percent were from families with a $2,000 or smaller annual income or receiving welfare.[225]

Louisville's progressive School Board, composed of three white and two black members, hired a new school superintendent, Newman Walker, who was familiar with encounter groups and with other advances in the behavioral sciences and education. Walker hired Car Foster to head his Department of Organizational Development.

Unlike Rogers, Walker and Foster were successful in obtaining substantial funding from the Office of Education. With the funding, they were able to begin a massive change effort which, like the Immaculate Heart Project, emphasized human relations training for school personnel. In addition, however, the Louisville program included plans to reorganize many of the schools into smaller teacher–student teams using an open education model; the provision of funds and resources for teachers, administrators, or schools to support and encourage educational innovations on the grass-roots level; and other initiatives.[226]

The Louisville story is interesting not so much because Rogers had any direct influence in its inception or execution, but as an illustration of the indirect and symbolic role he came to play in educational systems and for individual educators throughout the country. The Louisville leadership acknowledged that their initiative was based on Rogers' premise that "significant learning rests upon certain attitudinal conditions which exist in the personal relationship between the facilitator and the learner."[227] In fact they purchased some five hundred copies of *Freedom to Learn* and distributed these widely among interested teachers and administrators in the district. But they conceived and began the project without any participation by Rogers. When he did become involved, the Louisville experience provides a good example of a new consulting style Rogers came to adopt and frequently employ in the late sixties and seventies. When operating in this mode, he came not so much as a speaker or workshop leader but as Carl Rogers—to spend some time, to talk with people, to share some of his ideas when appropriate, and to listen and learn. This is clearly indicated in Car Foster's recollections of Rogers' visits to Louisville.

> Upon his first visit here, I don't suppose that I have ever been quite as nervous about meeting a person and entertaining a person as I was with Carl Rogers. [He went on to talk about how often he had been disappointed in meeting famous people or writers and seeing how differently they acted from what they advocated in their writings.] I'm very happy to report that I didn't find him that way. He is the kind of person that lives his lifestyle pretty much according to the way in which he writes, and the belief seems to be very, very deep. He was one of the easiest persons to accommodate as a visitor and consultant within our system of anyone I've had here. I have entertained some one hundred sixty consultants and guests in this system in the past three years, and he is, by far, the easiest one that I have had to work with. We agreed at the beginning that whenever he wanted to work he worked, and whenever he wanted to retire he retired. I never had to worry about whether I was keeping him too long or whether he wanted to have dinner with someone that night or whatever. I asked him and he replied very forthrightly and honestly with me.
>
> There was a tremendous interest in people when they heard that Carl Rogers was coming, and my hardest task was keeping people away from him because he would be bombarded by dozens and dozens of people that wanted to sit in and talk with him by the hour had we allowed this to happen.
>
> We went into school systems, he talked with people. In general the entire system was open to him. In the first visit, we had a Board meeting scheduled one afternoon, and I had something else for him that I thought he might like to do. I gave him his option of that or going to a regularly scheduled Board meeting. He selected the Board meeting, reluctantly, but he said, "I think I need to see how they operate." This was a regular Board meeting and there wasn't anything planned, but something unusual did happen. That was some students brought a petition to the Board for the Board to consider some things; and in likestyle in terms of how our school board has been operating, they listened very attentively to the students, were very complimentary of their

403

work and proceeded to take some action on it, of doing some things to answer to student needs. I thought it was fairly routine, although I knew it was unusual for most school boards to do this. Carl Rogers was sitting there and hadn't said anything, but was listening very intently. He raised his hand and asked permission to speak to the board, and when I looked around I noticed there were actually tears in his eyes. He told them that he had witnessed something there that afternoon that he had never seen before in his life. That was a school board that was actually responsive to students and listening to what students said and taking some action on it. He said, truthfully, he didn't think that there was another school board in the United States that would measure up to this kind of commitment.

He spoke to several groups while he was here and appeared to thoroughly enjoy interacting with them. He visited with some schools and he asked that I take him to some of the better schools—that was where our projects were working—then he turned around and asked me to take him to some of our worst schools, and I accommodated him. I took him exactly where he wanted to go. I think he felt like we were really being honest with him and letting him see everything that was here. Later on he spoke of this and said he didn't think we had a lot to hide and that we had problems, we *knew* that we had problems and that we were trying honestly to face up to them.

On his second visit, he brought with him two other people from the Center for Studies of the Person, because he wanted other people ... to verify that we weren't overrating some of the things that we were doing ... During this time, he did not make very many public appearances. It was strictly as a consultant to us and to talk with us.

Most of the people within the system who still talk about his two visits here are amazed that a man of the stature and the caliber of Carl Rogers can say so often, "I really do not know about this. I have very little knowledge in this area." His admittance of where he has no expertise or where he does not know too much about the application of various procedures was of such a nature that, I think, people tended to believe even more strongly the other things that he did have to say.

Most of all Foster was impressed by what he saw as Rogers' "fantastic modesty in his effect upon people and even his symbolic importance to people of just being able to meet him and listen to him and talk with him ... I think he underrates his importance with other people, when he has such a tremendous influence on people's lives. Perhaps he may have to do this, because it would be a tremendous burden to know that you are this influential with so many people's lives."[228]

As indicated, Rogers was as impressed with the Louisville Schools as they were with him. In *On Encounter Groups*, he devoted four pages to describing "Project Transition," calling it "the boldest and most promising venture I know of in education systems at the present time."[229]

The project continued to operate successfully, achieving initial positive results; but then it got caught up in a bigger problem that eventually ended the experiment prematurely. A desegregation suit that had been working its way through the courts eventually led to a court-ordered busing plan that, in effect, merged the Louisville city schools with the surrounding suburban schools. The mostly-white suburban schools were suspicious or hostile to the innovations going on in Louisville. Superintendent Walker, caught in the middle of the conflict and essentially stripped of his power, left for another position. The promising Louisville experiment ended as the situation deteriorated into "anti-busing riots, violence, hatred."[230]

What, then, are we to make of the Immaculate Heart and Louisville experiments in self-directed change in large educational systems? Some years later, in a new edition of *Freedom to Learn*, titled *Freedom to Learn for the 80s*, Rogers candidly reported and reflected on these and several other similar experiences with self-directed change in schools and colleges (some of which he was directly involved in, some not). He called them "a pattern of failure," a phrase which Rogers' critics were quick to pick up on, suggesting that he was admitting he was wrong.[231] But Rogers did not see it that way exactly. Rather he continued to regard these experiments as validation for his basic hypothesis, that when individuals, or in this case individuals in systems, are given a supportive, facilitative climate that encourages them to set their own directions, then great positive energy and creativity is released and significant learning and growth take place. Rogers' belief in that proposition never wavered. However, he was sobered by the pattern of failure that consistently followed these successful experiments. He explained the eventual results by pointing to factors outside the experiments themselves—the furor going on in the Catholic Church, the politics of desegregation in Louisville, the threat innovation poses, the lack of a leadership pool to draw upon when innovators leave or retire, creeping bureaucracy in successful programs, and the lure of power in all systems.[232] All these reasons, while often valid, beg the question of whether self-directed change and innovation of the kind Rogers advocated in educational systems are, in fact, possible. Once the barriers to change are recognized, can perhaps more sophisticated organizational interventions be planned to introduce and sustain long-term innovation? In short, is it possible to significantly change large school systems? As Rogers turned his attention to still wider applications of his work, this was a question he left unanswered. Decades later educators and politicians continue to ask the same question.

Professional Honors

In almost every chapter of Rogers' adult life I have included a section on his growing reputation. This chapter is no exception. If one were to plot his rising esteem and influence on a graph, there would be a steeply rising curve covering the three periods of Rochester, Ohio, and Chicago, a leveling off during most of his years at Wisconsin, and then another rapidly rising curve to cover his early California years, possibly a steeper rise than at any previous point in his career.

The period began after publication of *On Becoming a Person* in 1961, when a larger audience than ever before could identify with Rogers' theories and methods, now expressed in a less technical form. Then, in addition to his psychological writing, which continued to appear in the journals of the psychology and psychotherapy professions, his educational thinking began reaching an ever-widening audience as many of his articles appeared in some of the most popular educational journals and magazines. So, too, did his articles start appearing in the new *Journal of Applied Behavioral Science*, published by the National Training Laboratories for human relations trainers and community and organizational development specialists.[233] Both the *Newsletter* and the *Journal of Humanistic Psychology* also publicized his thinking among the members and followers of the Association of Humanistic Psychology.[234] The new popular magazine *Psychology Today* recognized his stature and published an interview with him and three of his articles within a two-year span.[235] In addition CRM Books put out two large, attractive volumes meant to serve as interesting and contemporary textbooks for psychology courses. Although the authors were listed as "contributors" in the back of these volumes rather than next to their articles, Rogers wrote chapters for these books.[236] They sold very well and were read widely in psychology courses across the country. He even wrote a short article which was circulated in major newspapers across the country.[237] The *Minneapolis Star* called the piece "'Process' People Replacing Those with Timeless Goals," and the editor introduced it by saying, "This is the ninth of 20 essays by leading men in the world's academic community. Today's writer discusses many issues concerned with what we call 'the good life.'"

Aside from *On Becoming a Person*, Rogers wrote four other books during this period, which contributed substantially to his reputation. Of these, three have already been discussed—*Man and the Science of Man*, which sold hardly any copies at all, and *Freedom to Learn* and *On Encounter Groups*, both of which sold very well indeed. The fourth was *Person to Person: The Problem of Being Human*.[238] Barry Stevens, a woman who was born the same year as Rogers and who had experienced great emotional turmoil and many interesting life experiences, approached Rogers, whom she knew only a little, and proposed that they compose a book together. Rogers was first to admit, "It was entirely her idea. *Person to Person* is her book. The one thing I regret about the book is that she talked me into putting my name first on it, because she knew it would help to sell the book. And I shouldn't have let her do that, because it's a damn lie. It's her book, and I never feel good about seeming to author something that I really didn't."[239] On the other hand, he later wrote that, "When Barry Stevens learned that I was annoyed because my name was first on her book she was

LEFT AND BELOW: *Rogers at his desk and in the garden, La Jolla, California.*

ABOVE: *Carl and Helen Rogers' 50th anniversary, 1974.*
STANDING, FROM LEFT: *Julia Rogers, Janet Fuchs, David Rogers, Natalie Rogers, Gregory Rogers, Frances Fuchs, Naomi Fuchs, and Ann Rogers.* (Bobbie Rogers)

LEFT: *Rogers in his garden.*
(Jim Hedstrom)

BELOW: *Walking on hill outside his home,*
La Jolla, California.

BELOW:
Carl and
Natalie Rogers.

RIGHT: *Rogers and his colleagues, Center for Studies of the Person, c. 1969.*

LEFT: *Person-Centered Workshop Staff, Ashland, Oregon, 1976.*
STANDING FROM LEFT: *Carl Rogers, Joanne Justyn, John K. Wood, Jared Kass, Maureen Miller (O'Hara), Natalie Rogers, and Maria Bowen.*
KNEELING: *Dick and Marian Vittitow.*

BELOW: *Rogers facilitating a group at Esalen, Big Sur, California.*

THE EVOLUTION OF PSYCHOTHERAPY

Faculty

December 11-15, 1985

Phoenix, Arizona

Bruno Bettleheim, James Masterson, Jeffrey Zeig, Ronald Laing, Ernest Rossi, Erving Polster, Salvador Minuchin, Lewis Wolberg,
Rollo May, Arnold Lazarus, Judd Marmor, Aaron Beck, Carl Whitaker, Murray Bowen, Thomas Szasz, Paul Watzlawick, Jay Haley, Joseph Wolpe,
Albert Ellis, Mary Goulding, Robert Goulding, Zerka Moreno, Cloé Madanes, Virginia Satir, Miriam Polster, Carl Rogers

First 'Evolution
of Psychotherapy'
Conference,
Phoenix, Arizona,
December 1985.
(Courtesy:
Milton Erickson
Foundation)

International workshop, El Escorial, Spain, 1978.

Rogers visiting Freud's house, Vienna, 1981.
(Courtesy: Reinhold Stipsits)

Counseling a Japanese man, with translator.

Carl Rogers and Ruth Sanford (standing) in South Africa.

Central America conflict resolution workshop, Rust, Austria, November 1985.
FROM LEFT: *Unknown, Leopold Gratz, Austrian Foreign Minister; Carl Rogers;
Alberto Segrera, translator, Mexico; Karl Vak, President, Z Bank, Vienna.*
(Erich Janzso)

Counseling a woman in Soviet Union, with translator.

*Bringing the person-centered approach to the Soviet Union,
while Marx and Lenin look on, October 1986.*

Addressing theater audience at his 85th birthday celebration, December 1986.

indignant. She said my name should be first on the book because it would never have been written without me, that she would bring in a batch of her free-floating stream of consciousness material expecting me to be very harsh about it and I always encouraged her to do more. So, perhaps, I did have more to do with the book's creation than I give myself credit for."[240]

Anyway, Stevens took four essays previously written by Rogers[241] and three written by Rogers' former colleagues (Gendlin, Shlien, and Van Dusen)[242] and very skillfully wove her own experiences around these essays. Her free-flowing memories and associations came across with a great deal of power and often served as a vivid case study of what the professionals were talking about. The style of the book was so unusual, though, that she was unable to find a publisher. Some chapters were highly technical, others were more in a diary or train-of-thought style. Publishers wondered who would buy such a book. Finally, as a last resort, John Stevens, Barry Stevens' son, who was also interested in psychology, set up a publishing company just to publish his mother's book. This type of small, individual publishing venture is almost always doomed to failure; yet, for whatever reasons—Rogers' name on the cover probably being a primary one—the book was a great success. At one point it was selling about two thousand quality paperback copies a month, successful by any publishing standards. Stevens went on to publish another book by his mother and two by the Gestalt psychologist Fritz Perls. Eventually these books were doing so well on the market that Pocket Books, one of the biggest publishers of paperback books, bought the rights to some of them. *Person to Person* then reached an even wider audience, and Rogers' name became still better known by the layperson interested in psychology.

He also made an increasing number of personal appearances, often before large assemblies. In 1965 and 1966, for example, he spent 142 and 148 days, respectively, away from home.[243] This included vacation periods; but considerably more than half the time was spent conducting encounter groups, giving speeches and workshops, and consulting. From 1967 through 1970, partly because Helen's health was getting worse and she could not travel with him as much as before, he spent 112, 96, 83, and 70 days (and usually nights) away. Even this last figure, however, is substantial, and all that traveling over many years brought him into personal contact with tens of thousands of people across the country. Beyond his writings, the various films and tapes mentioned earlier—mostly on encounter groups and mental health—served to give Rogers a wider public viewing. An increasing number of people came to know him as a three-dimensional person, not the nondirective caricature often portrayed by psychology professors. This and his ever more personal writing style brought him much closer to thousands of people in psychology, education, and other helping professions and accounts for the kind of aura about him which Car Foster described in the previous section. His public dialogues with Buber, Tillich, Bateson and other intellectual leaders of the period, most available in published or recorded form, also contributed to his growing renown. So did the numerous audio cassette tapes and videotapes he made, including the twenty-six tapes on encounter groups and another ten-cassette series on the development of selfhood, youth, marriage, parenthood and mental health.[244]

All this contributed to an enormous volume of daily mail, which Rogers estimated as amounting to "150 to 250 letters per week, most of which are of the type which cannot be ignored, and 40 to 50 long distance calls per week of which the same can be said. Probably 80% of all my correspondence and calls are inviting me to engage in some activity."[245] Consequently around 1968 Rogers experimented with using a form letter to respond to all the requests he was receiving. Addressed to "Dear Person who has written me a letter," he explained how his mail had grown to "such momentous proportions" that he was caught between neglecting the writing and other work he wanted to do and killing himself by doing that *and* answering his mail.[246] The next eight paragraphs enumerated the reasons people typically wrote him and his response to those requests. "If your letter asked me to give a lecture or participate in some program, please know that I am fully obligated for the next year … If your letter wished to discuss some aspect of my thinking, I will enclose a pertinent reprint if one exists … If your letter was a request for personal help, I will write the name of someone in your vicinity whom I can recommend, providing I know such a person … If you wished to participate in a group with me …" And so on, elaborating briefly on each point. Naturally such an approach was less than satisfying for many recipients. David Cohen recalled how he and an instructor of his at Oxford received this form response from Rogers and found it "astonishingly cold and pompous" and "the very opposite of everything Rogers stood for."[247] Rogers submitted a foundation proposal for secretarial help and expenses, but it was not funded.[248] Eventually he hired a part-time secretary from his own funds to help with his correspondence, often dictating his responses.[249] This proved to be a more satisfactory solution, which he continued for the rest of his life; although periodically, keeping up with his mail felt oppressive over the years.

And, of course, there were more awards. In 1964 he was named "Humanist of the Year" by the American Humanist Association. "For Outstanding Contribution to the Understanding of World Affairs," he was made a Fellow of the Institute on World Affairs of San Diego State College. He received in 1967 the Distinguished Contribution Award of the American Pastoral Counselors Association, an ironic accolade for a man who had left the seminary a half-century before. He was awarded his second, third, and fourth honorary doctorate degrees from Gonzaga University in 1968, Santa Clara University in 1971, and the University of Cincinnati in 1974. He served on the editorial boards of the *Journal of Humanistic Psychology*, the *Review of Existential Psychology and Psychiatry*, and *Voices*, the journal of the American Academy of Psychotherapists. In 1968 he received the Professional Achievement Award from the American Board of Professional Psychology, the certifying board for the American Psychological Association. The citation read, in part, "… Carl Rogers, wise and gifted student of the human psyche, has helped to shape the theory and practice of human relations at home and abroad … As professor of Clinical Psychology, as psychotherapist, as author and consultant, and now in all these roles at the Western Behavioral Sciences Institute, you have shaped the scientific outlook of specialists in various fields from psychiatry and education to political science and industrial management. … Your brilliant formulation of the principles of non-directive therapy and your outstanding contributions to ways of dealing with interpersonal and intergroup tensions are counted as landmarks in the psychological sciences and are signalized by their humanitarian as well as professional outlook."[250]

Finally, in 1972, he received the first Distinguished Professional Contribution Award from the American Psychological Association, thereby becoming the first psychologist in history to receive both the APA's Distinguished Scientific Contribution Award and their Distinguished Professional Contribution Award. Again the citation explained the reason for this tribute.

> His commitment to the whole person has been an example which has guided the practice of psychology in the schools, in industry, and throughout the community. By devising, practicing, evaluating, and teaching a method of psychotherapy and counseling which reaches to the very roots of human potentiality and individuality, he has caused all psychotherapists to reexamine their procedures in a new light. Innovator in personality research, pioneer in the encounter movement, and respected gadfly of organized psychology, he has made a lasting impression on the profession of psychology.[251]

His former colleague from Chicago, Rosalind Dymond Cartwright, said of him, "Carl provided a role model for a couple of generations of therapists, clinical psychologists, counseling people and others … he is a living example of the theory. He is a man who has continued to grow, to discover himself, to test himself, to be genuine, to review his experiences, to learn from it, and to fight the good fight, which means to stand up and be counted, to stand for something, to live honestly, fully, in the best human sense."[252]

He had achieved almost every honor and award possible in his own profession and a good many in other professions as well. As the century entered the seventies, so was Carl Rogers approaching his seventies. Following conventional aging patterns then, surely it was time to slow down or retire.

CHAPTER 11

The California Years
Part Two:
Personal and Political Awakenings
1969–1987

"At ten o'clock on the morning of June 7, 1969," reads a Sonoma State College publication, "some 1,500 friends and relatives of the Class of 1969 gathered by the side of a beautiful little lake to share in the Eighth Annual Commencement exercises."[1] Carl Rogers was on the rostrum in cap and gown to deliver the commencement address. Stepping to the podium he began by explaining, "As an undergraduate I majored in medieval history. I have enormous respect for the scholars of the Middle Ages and their contributions to learning. But I want to speak to you as Carl Rogers, in 1969, not as a medieval symbol. So I hope I will not offend you if I remove these medieval trappings—this nonfunctional cap, this handsome but useless hood, and this robe, designed to keep one warm even in the rigors of a European winter."[2] Then he removed the garments and proceeded to address the graduating class on "The Person of Tomorrow."

This picture of sixty-seven-year-old Carl Rogers stepping out of the past to speak to young people and their parents about the future aptly characterizes Rogers' concerns in the latter years of his career. For Rogers was a pioneer. And where does a pioneer go once he has opened the field of psychotherapy to scientific investigation; formulated and popularized a new method of psychotherapy; established the facilitation of growth through therapeutic conditions as a leading school of thought throughout the helping professions; developed a major theory of personality and personality change; been a pioneer and leader of the humanistic psychology movement; been one of the most influential popularizers of the intensive group experience; provided educators with a psychological foundation for student-centered learning; and, by presenting a personal example of his theories

410

and methods, served as a model for thousands of people to emulate?

His concerns broaden, and he looks toward the future.

Youthful Relationships

In my first interview with Rogers he told me, "I hate old people who reminisce."[3] He has frequently made comments like, "We could count on the fingers of one hand the people our own age we really enjoy. The rest are all too stuffy."[4] When he worked on his "autobiography" in 1965 for a collection of autobiographical essays by well-known psychologists, he said it took him and Helen months to recover from spending that much time looking in the past.[5] Both the scientist and the artist in him needed new challenges and were not content with past accomplishments. His interest in the future went hand in hand with his association with young people. He had always valued his contact with graduate students, and this continued after he left the university setting. As he described it: "Probably the major factor in keeping me alive as a growing therapist is a continuing association with young people on a thoroughly equalitarian basis. I have always worked with young staff members; I have never found people my own age stimulating except for rare and fortunate exceptions. I find that younger people are full of new ideas, exploring the boundaries of our disciplines and raising questions about any sacred cows which I hold dear. This keeps me stimulated, moving, and I hope growing."[6]

In an earlier passage, Richard Farson pointed out the drawbacks to Rogers' surrounding himself almost exclusively with younger colleagues: the unequal power that existed in his collegial relationships; his younger colleagues' willingness sometimes to follow his lead rather than voice their misgivings; his missing out on more cogent and fundamental challenges to his theory and practice which older colleagues of stature might have provided. As Maria Bowen said, years later, "It was impossible to develop original ideas around him."[7] Yet, in spite of these drawbacks, his friends and colleagues at Center for the Studies of the Person continued to stimulate and challenge him in their own way. Here were forty or so people with whom he attended weekly meetings and social gatherings and with whom he often worked very closely, as on the Immaculate Heart Project. When CSP was formed in 1968 and still part of WBSI, most of them were in their twenties, thirties and forties. Many of them were involved in exciting projects in drug abuse education, black–white encounter groups, film making, inventing and marketing humanistic products, and dealing with all sorts of issues, problems and client populations. Both directly and indirectly Rogers was involved in all this and profited from it.

He also profited in a more personal way, as several of his CSP colleagues explained to me at one of their meetings. "He has a truly caring community around him," said one. "I think this has been a very good support group mechanism for him. It has allowed him to experience kinds of freedom—personal and cognitive—that he might not have had if it weren't for the existence of this organization."[8] Another member told of how Rogers' fame typically creates a distance between him and other people. "Rogers and I and some others had conducted a day-long workshop for school administrators in Reno, Nevada; he was talking and I was helping lead the small groups. We had a really good day and I was excited about it. We were eating dinner and I was saying something to him like, 'You know, I really think what you did today was great. I was really excited about it.' And he turned to me and he looked me in the eye and he said, 'You know I've heard enough of that bullshit not to want to hear any more of it today.' And I almost fell off the seat, I was so surprised. And then I thought to myself that he's really telling me where he is. I've heard him talk a number of times about how that putting him up on a pedestal and making him more special or talked about is really a problem he's had to face more and more."[9] In contrast, explained another member, "most people here feel free to tell him things, both positive and negative. I can remember at the annual meeting this year, there were a couple of times that people got mad at him and felt free about doing that. I think there are few places he can really go where he's treated pretty much like other people, where he's not put on a pedestal. In effect, if we think he's full of shit one of us will say that."[10]

Many of the CSP members impressed me as having an almost paternal or maternal attitude toward him. They were pleased about "how far he's come along in the last few years."[11] They were proud of his growth. And they were amused by his idiosyncrasies. One member recalled the first summer he met Rogers at the Center. "I was very excited about the fact that here I was and here he walked these halls and that kind of thing. And, as I was talking to someone, in walks this fellow. He's sort of balding with a few hairs on his head, in a sports shirt, with shorts on, none of which matched, black socks on and tennis shoes, with a heavy, heavy briefcase. And he sort of stumbled in and looked like he knew where he was going."[12] The other CSP members, hearing this story, nodded their heads and smiled, as if to say, "Yes, that's Carl."

Rogers' friends and colleagues at CSP appreciated him as much as he did them. In a group interview in 1975 they described his consideration ("he has always taken that extra bit of trouble to write the memo or the note or call you and tell you that you did a particularly good job on something"), his open-mindedness ("he continues to really change his mind"), his courage in getting involved with encounter groups ("When he could have continued being the grand old man of one thing, he moved into the forefront of another thing") and his "will power" ("If he was taking a wagon across the western United States, he'd be one of those who would make it." "Particularly if Helen went along," added one of the women members).[13]

His California colleagues, like his students at Chicago, often described Rogers' ability to listen and the respect, care and understanding he communicated. They also reiterated his faith in the individual, including "a touch of recklessness in the way he assigns responsibilities. Untested individuals are given important tasks and are seldom checked up on. There are exceptions, but this happens frequently enough to lend an air of confused excitement to his personal commitment to careful planning."[14] But, in addition, his colleagues communicated a sense of closeness that was not there as much before. As Tom Gillette wrote, "Although I couldn't see myself asking him to go down to TJ for a couple of pitchers at the Long Bar, I can pass a bottle around with him and others and we can all of us talk freely about such things as 'Extra Marital Sex I Have and Have Not Had.'"[15] That would have been unheard of before he came to California. The times had changed but so had Rogers. Beyond the professional benefits many of the younger CSP members derived from being associated with Rogers, they also valued their personal relationship with him. He seems, in these descriptions, more approachable, more self-disclosing, more fully a person. Even in his "stuffiness," as two colleagues pointed out, there is a passionate, feeling person clearly visible. ("He's kind of stuffy and straight, but he's also a little mad in the right direction." "The only thing he really flirts with is being stuffy. But he doesn't make it. His passion shines through."[16])

Not all colleagues found him universally accepting. One recalled, "There are lots of people here who he wants to change," and after naming several of them, said, "and he does things which are not warm and accepting. He'll say something, not very often, every once in a while, like, 'I wish you'd stop acting like a good old country boy.' He was saying that I use that style as a defense and don't take myself seriously."[17] In commenting on his relationships at CSP, Rogers told me about a number of his colleagues whom he thought had a "lack of self-discipline and organization" or were "looking inward too much."[18] Still he still accepted and appreciated them anyway.

In addition to his younger friends and colleagues at CSP, Rogers' work in encounter groups also brought him into close contact with young people from different walks of life. Out of all these experiences in unstructured interaction with young people, he developed a style of informal interaction with small groups which he utilized with increasing frequency. Instead of giving a speech or presentation, he found it more satisfying and enjoyable simply to sit down with a small group of about twenty to one hundred people and chat. Often a formal speech would be combined with a smaller, informal meeting. His eminent stature in the fields of psychology and education undoubtedly made this possible. If Carl Rogers told an inquirer, no, he would not give a presentation, but he would be glad to talk with them informally, there was little chance that they would miss that opportunity. And these informal contacts seemed to have as much impact on the group, if not more, than his formal presentations did. In one cross-cultural communication workshop, with ninety-eight students from the United States and around the world, the evaluations indicated that "the sessions with Carl Rogers were reported to be of great value for most of the participants. Students and educators reported that the interaction encouraged them to put their own thoughts and experiences into perspective. By either agreeing or disagreeing with the opinions of Dr. Rogers, many were helped to define and evaluate their own reactions and impressions. A final session with Carl Rogers interacting with the total community was mentioned as especially important by 90 of the participants."[19]

I saw this phenomenon operate when Rogers talked with a group of some fifty undergraduates at the Irvine campus of the University of California, and when he met with thirty-five teachers at the National Humanistic Education Center in New York State, and on several other occasions. Excitement, of course, existed before he even arrived. There would be no agenda, no presentation. Usually on a tight schedule, he would be ushered in by someone responsible for his visit, he would sit in a comfortable chair up front, he would be introduced, and taking a few minutes, he would tell a little bit about himself or perhaps tell of his current interests. He did not seem to assume that anyone knew who he was, but he seemed to enjoy being there. He would invite the group to make any comments or ask any questions which interested them. The kind of effect this tended to have is well illustrated by a letter written by a young man to a student of mine, who shared it with me.

> My Dearest Terrill,
> It's Saturday night; nine o'clock, and I decided to stay at home tonight and spend at least the first part of the evening with you. I feel like I'm on top of the world, and there's no particular reason except that I'm turned on to psychology and life ... I must confess that while things in general are turning me on, one experience in particular is responsible for my present mood. Today I spent six hours with Carl Rogers.

He goes on to explain how he managed to sit in with a group of twenty-five students at United States International University in La Jolla.

> The group was excellent both because Carl Rogers is brilliant and so were the students ... Anyway, it was not an encounter group in the typical sense of the word; it was more of a seminar about encounter groups. But the big story is Carl Rogers. He is magnificent!!! To look at him and talk to him you might think that he was the nice, old man next door—not the most influential figure in psychotherapy today. He is kind, sweet, gentle, honest, congruent, humble, sincere, attentive, endearing ... And at the same time when he opens his mouth and discusses anything about people, his subtle genius is almost obvious. And

yet, if I didn't know that he was Carl Rogers I may have walked away thinking that he was all of the above mentioned qualities but never realizing that he was either a psychologist or famous. To me, that is the highest mark of genius and greatness. I guess that in spite of the many superlatives I used, I still may have left out his greatest attribute: he is human through and through.

Maybe I could sum up my feelings in the simplest way possible: I think that I love him. Now, my only problem is how to explain why I feel this way after being with the man for only six hours in a large group. I guess what it is about him that makes him so instantly charming is that he represents the finest of human beings at a time in my life when the need for "real" people is so desperate. Here I am trying to understand myself and the world and as a result in an emotional state varying (from minute to minute) between ecstasy and dread-filled depression; I walk into this strange room and discover a man so deeply human that you want to cry for joy. Yes, Mrs. Robinson, there is a Colonel Sanders! He has the kind of overflowing warmth and compassion that makes you feel like going over to him, telling him all of your problems, and then lying on his lap ... He is the father that every child wishes he had. For me, he is the supreme hope for humanity ...

Rogers makes you feel important because he listens to you with a genuine concern. And more important, he does this in a completely natural way; no technique was perceptible to me. Like I said, you feel like you're talking to the guy next door, or better yet—to your best friend, as opposed to feeling like you're talking to an authority figure, a therapist, a teacher, a wise man, etc.[20]

Beyond this young man's superlatives, I think he shows real insight into why young people often responded to Carl Rogers so positively. Perhaps there was an additional explanation. Young people then were (and still are) often isolated from old people. And unlike many of today's seniors who remain active, travel widely, exercise regularly and use the latest technology, the old people whom young people of the 1970s did come in contact with were products of the Great Depression. The typical retirement age for those who could afford it was 65, and that was considered "old." Old people were more likely to live conservatively, stay at home, avoid risks and value stability. An older person with whom young people could identify was rare. Rogers was that sort of rare person, not only thinking about topics of interest to young people—relationships, change, learning, social issues—but thinking about them in "youthful," even radical ways. As a young person (then) who knew Carl Rogers, I felt more *hopeful* about my own old age. It was exciting to think that forty years later I might be as alert and vital as he was.

The Person of Tomorrow

As indicated above, the relationship was reciprocal. Young people "turned on" Rogers as much as he them. The more these contacts continued, the more enamored he became with what he called "The Person of Tomorrow"[21] and, later, "The Emerging Person."[22]

Amidst all the problems in his own country and throughout the world, Rogers saw this "emerging person" as a source of evolutionary–revolutionary change. He found emerging persons in many places. "I find them among corporation executives who have given up the gray-flannel rat race, the lure of high salaries and stock options, to live a simpler life in a new way. I find them among long-haired young men and women who are defying most of the values of today's culture to form a counter culture. I find them among priests and nuns and ministers who have left behind the dogmas of their institutions to live in a way that has more meaning. I find them among women who are vigorously rising above the limitations which society has placed on their personhood. I find them among blacks and Chicanos and other minority members who are pushing out from generations of passivity into an assertive, positive life. I find them among those who have experienced encounter groups, who are finding a place for feelings as well as thoughts in their lives. I find them among creative school dropouts who are thrusting into higher reaches than their sterile schooling permits. I realize too that I saw something of this person in my years as a psychotherapist, when clients were choosing a freer, richer, more self-directed kind of life for themselves."[23]

Read again the sentence above that described emerging women: "women who are vigorously rising above the limitations which society has placed on their personhood." Four years earlier, when Rogers had first written about his "person of tomorrow," he consistently referred to him as "he" and "the New Man."[24] Four years later he had dropped this terminology and was writing, "He (or she)— I wish someone would provide us with a bisexual set of pronouns …"[25] At seventy-one, he was struggling to wrench himself free from one of the basic language conventions he had lived with all his life. More important than the change in wording is that, in those four years, Rogers had been aware of and open to one of the most important liberation movements going on around him. It wasn't always easy. He recalled one workshop he co-led with Natalie Rogers, when he had been mentioning some of the group members' previous contributions by referring to "Some of the things that *he* said, and that *he* said and that *he* said," and "My daughter just flew up in a rage. She said: 'Where are the women? Why don't you mention any of the women who spoke up?' And that really hit me where I live. I thought for a while and then I said, 'Well, I guess my awareness hasn't extended to that point yet.' As I thought it over, a number of the women had said things that were just as valuable as the things that the men had said."[26]

As Natalie Rogers described it, "He learned a lot from the women that were around him. I mean, his writing changed. In his later years, those of us who were feminists—Betty Meador in her way as a Jungian feminist, and Maria [Bowen] and Maureen [O'Hara] and myself and Gay [Swenson] [helped him recognize] the fact that women really were [treated as] second-class citizens. He didn't really understand that. We really had to drive that home. He got it."[27] Hence he was able to grow with the culture—to understand its sexual politics, perceive its new directions, interpret the meanings, extrapolate the implications, and champion the underlying values. Over the coming years, as we will see, he continued to benefit from the intellectual, professional, political and spiritual interests and activities of the women who were his close associates at CSP. They contributed significantly to his remaining on the cutting edge of his field and to his on-going personal and intellectual growth.

What were the characteristics of this emerging man or woman whom Rogers perceived? First was a "desire for authenticity," a freedom from facades, an aversion to "hypocrisy, deceit, mixed messages ... doublethink and doubletalk." Second was a belief that "institutions exist for people," an opposition to "all highly structured, inflexible, bureaucratic institutions." Beyond these two major qualities, he noted: "the unimportance of material things"; "a nonmoralistic caring"; "the wish for intimacy"; "a skepticism about science"; a fascination with "the universe within" the person, from one's feelings to "esoteric and transcendental religious" experience; a desire to live "in balance with nature"; a person "in process," always changing; and finally, one who lives by "the authority within," having "a trust in his own experience and a profound distrust of all external authority."[28]

Acknowledging that few individuals possessed all these characteristics and that their proportion to the whole population was small, he still believed that the emerging person stood the chance to have a revolutionary impact upon society. Of course, wrote Rogers, there would be opposition by those whose position could be characterized by slogans such as: "The State above all ... Tradition above all ... The intellect above all ... Man should be shaped ... The status quo forever ... and Our truth is *the* truth."[29] These forces might slow down the "emerging evolution," Rogers thought, but would not likely be able to stop it—not when it was already being lived in the daily lives of so many people. And what if the emerging person gained influence and changed the culture? Rogers concluded his article:

This emerging person would not bring Utopia. He would make mistakes, be partially corrupted, go overboard in certain directions. But he would foster a culture which would emphasize certain trends, a culture which would be moving in these directions:

Toward the exploration of self, and the development of the richness of the total, individual, responsible human soma—mind and body.

Toward the prizing of the individual for what he is, regardless of sex, race, status, or material possessions.

> Toward human-sized groupings in our communities, our educational facilities, our productive units.
>
> Toward a close, respectful, balanced, reciprocal relationship to the natural world.
>
> Toward the perception of material goods as rewarding only when they enhance the quality of personal living.
>
> Toward a more even distribution of material goods.
>
> Toward a society with minimal structure—human needs taking priority over any tentative structure which develops.
>
> Toward leadership as a temporary, shifting function, based on competence for meeting a specific social need.
>
> Toward a more genuine and caring concern for those who need help.
>
> Toward a human conception of science—in its creative phase, the testing of its hypotheses, the valuing of the humanness of its applications.
>
> Toward creativity of all sorts—in thinking and exploring—in the areas of social relationships, the arts, social design, architecture, urban and regional planning, science.
>
> To me these are not frightening trends but exciting ones. In spite of the darkness of the present, our culture may be on the verge of a great evolutionary–revolutionary leap. I simply say with all my heart—Power to the emerging person and the revolution he carries within.[30]

In waxing so optimistically, was Rogers describing a temporary social phenomenon or fad, or was this truly a character portrait of the person of tomorrow? Was he blinded by the Aquarian age of the 1970s and the California counterculture that surrounded him? Or through the ephemera of the current decade did he discern a future that is still unfolding? Clearly he hoped it was the latter, and for several years he became something of a publicist for this emerging person. In 1981 he even presented a workshop with his daughter Natalie and granddaughter Frances Fuchs on "New World/New Person: A Three Generational View," exploring the changing conceptions of the good life across their generations.[31] As time wore on, in later writings he acknowledged that the younger generation sometimes carried its search for authenticity and new experience to excess; still he continued to champion the image of the emerging person. He extended his description of such a person to twelve characteristics: openness, desire for authenticity, skepticism regarding science and technology, desire for wholeness, the wish for intimacy, process persons, caring, attitude toward nature, anti-institutional, the authority within, the unimportance of materials things, and a yearning for the spiritual.[32] While acknowledging that few persons fit this general description and even fewer, if any, embodied all these characteristics, he maintained his hope that this was, indeed, the direction of tomorrow. He concluded his last book, *A Way of Being*, with the words: "This is the person-centered scenario of the future. We may choose it, but whether we choose it or not, it appears that to some degree it is inexorably moving to change our culture. And the changes will be in the direction of more humanness."[33]

Becoming Partners

Of all the aspects of the "person of tomorrow," the one which most fascinated Rogers was the attempt of younger people to develop intimate relationships and growth-producing living arrangements with what he called members "of the other (I refuse to say opposite) sex."[34] This led, in 1972, to the publication of his thirteenth book, *Becoming Partners: Marriage and Its Alternatives,* published by Delacorte Press, with Delta and Dell paperback editions.

He had not originally intended to publish a book on marriage. It actually began with an invitation by Scott, Foresman and Company to write a textbook for introductory psychology courses, written from a humanistic perspective. At first Rogers was not interested, feeling that even though it would be a worthwhile book and he could probably do it, it was not a book that really came from within himself. He didn't want to feel obligated to "cover" the field. It wouldn't be his book, coming from the deepest parts of himself and his experience. After much urging, however, he agreed to the assignment. His plan was to take some of the key issues of concern to young people and write about these from his own perspective, referring also to the work of others and suggesting further readings and activities for readers to pursue. The topics would be: finding oneself; relationships with others (parents, siblings, intimates); communal living; urban problems; minority groups; drugs; and so on. He would call it *Being Human.*[35]

He wrote six chapters, the first three entitled: "Can We Be Human in the Classroom?" "Who Am I? How Can I Find Myself?" and "Am I Alone?" The next three were on the subject of marriage: "Shall We Get Married?" and two chapters based on the unusual yet in many ways typical experiences of two married couples he interviewed. The chapters pleased him, especially the last three, but he was finding the going very tedious and slow. While writing usually came easily for him, it was now often painful and anxious work. At times he gave up on the book, only to resume it again for another few weeks and months before the discouragement returned. As he told an audience in 1971, "It has made me sharply aware of the fact that every previous book I have written has been written because I wanted to say something. I have not written for a particular audience, or to serve some significant purpose." And he quipped: "So—will Carl Rogers finish this book? Will he be able to meet its enormous challenges? Tune in next year to hear the latest installment of *Being Human.*"[36]

Not only did the chapters on marriage give him the most satisfaction, they seemed to excite the several people to whom he showed the early drafts of his completed chapters. Just at the time when he was beginning to conclude that he had the kernel of a small book on marriage aimed at a general audience, Donald Cutler, the Harper & Row editor who had helped *On Encounter Groups* reach publication and who was now a literary agent at the respected Sterling Lord Agency in New York City, also contacted Rogers to say he thought the marriage chapters he had read could, with some additional material, make "an attractive short book on the subject for trade publication."[37] Thereupon Rogers freed himself from his contract with Scott, Foresman, quickly completed the book with a great deal of enthusiasm, allowed Cutler to place it for him, and within a year *Becoming Partners: Marriage and Its Alternatives* was published.

In his introduction he explained how he hoped his book might be unique. "I know," he wrote, "that you can find out anything you want to know about the *externals* of marriage and partnership. You can find out the differences in male–female sexual needs and timing. You can read books on how to improve the sex act. You can study the history of marriage. You can find out what percentage of young people of college age are living together without marriage. You can read lists, compiled from questionnaires, of the major sources of satisfaction and dissatisfaction in married couples—and on and on and on. We are inundated by data. But rarely do we discover a true picture of what a partnership is like, as perceived and lived and experienced from the *inside*. That might be the new element I could add."[38]

His first chapter, one of those from "Being Human," was "Shall We Get Married?" In it he described the current trend toward greater freedom in sexual relationships, the lessening of possessiveness, the growing distrust of marriage as an institution, and the increasing sentiment that a relationship is "significant, and worth trying to preserve, only when it is an enhancing, growing experience for each person."[39] These observations, though timely and perhaps admirably contemporary for a man of seventy, were not original. The O'Neills' book *Open Marriage*, published before Rogers', had been a best-seller.[40] Rogers' particular contribution came with his ability to have people trust him with their intimate feelings and details of their relationships. Throughout the book he provided short vignettes and longer case studies telling of the experiences of many different couples in the words of the partners themselves. Some of these came to him through lengthy letters, but most came through tape-recorded interviews. One woman, for example, shared the story of how she happened to get married.

At the time it was the thing to do. "Here are all my friends getting married, what am I gonna do? I'm a senior in college, that's pretty old. I better start thinking about marriage. I don't know what else I can do. I can teach but that's not enough."

The person that I married was a very popular man and I was a very insecure person, *very* insecure; and I thought, well, golly, I'm going with this person and everybody likes *him,* so maybe if I marry him, everybody will like *me!* The man that I married, I didn't feel he really listened, but I did feel security. That, and not knowing what I'd do when I graduated—that's why I got married.

The reason why I got engaged was because a very good friend of mine had gotten engaged and she had a very pretty ring, and was making all these wedding plans. My friends were saying, "God, Joan, when are you and Max getting married? You've been going together for three years now. You better not let him get away. If you let *him* get away, you're stupid!" My mother said, "Oh, Joan, when are you going to find another person like Max? He's so outstanding and responsible and mature and secure." I felt, "This is the one I should marry because my close friends, my roommate, my mother all say it," and although I had these doubts going on inside me, I thought, "Well, you're so insecure and so stupid that you don't know your own feelings." I thought, "They know what's best for you and you don't so you had better follow their advice."

I had guts enough to tell Max why I was doing it and I said I was really kind of scared to get married and said, "I don't know if this is really right for me." And he said, "Don't worry. You'll learn to love me." I did learn to love him in a brotherly way, but it didn't go beyond that. When the wedding gifts were unwrapped and all the newness wore off, and the newness of having a baby wore off, then I really started feeling, "Oh you stupid idiot, you should have listened to yourself." Because I had been saying those things to me, but I just wouldn't listen because I thought I was too screwed up to know what was best for me. So I was right after all.[41]

Along with these case studies came Rogers' comments, scattered throughout the various couples' narratives. His sensitive empathy and years of experience helped him identify and elaborate on the major themes. In the case of Joan, for example, he wrote, "There are several elements which, for me, stand out in Joan's experience. First of all, it shows how prone we all are to yield to social pressures. A female college senior should be planning to get married, and socially that's *that.*

"The dangers of advice stand out so very clearly. Out of love and caring and concern her mother and her good friends all know what is best for her to do. How easy it is to direct the life of another and how very difficult it is to live your own!

"The fear of squarely facing one's own problems. Joan knew she was insecure. She knew she was frightened of the future. She realized she couldn't get to her own feelings. But instead of facing those inner problems squarely and directly, she did what so many of us do; she built the illusion that she could find the solution outside herself—in another.

"Finally, what impresses me is that Joan, as is true of so many others, experiences no trust in her own feelings, her own inner unique reactions. She is dimly aware of the doubts she has about the relationship, of the lack of a feeling of deep love, or her unreadiness to commit herself to this man. But these are only feelings. *Only feelings!* It is not until after marriage, and after having a child, that she realizes what reliable guides her gut reactions were, if she had only *trusted* them enough to *listen* to them."[42]

Besides Joan's experience and two others described in the first chapter, Rogers chose to include a nine-page section on "My Own Marriage." Here, with surprising candor, he told of his and Helen's earlier sexual problems during their first year of marriage, of the one-year period in his forties when he was inexplicably impotent but from which he recovered thanks in part to Helen's confidence and patience, of the way Helen helped him through his unhappy experience with the schizophrenic woman and their "runaway trip," how he helped her through her mother's terminal illness, and of several other incidents and themes in their marriage. In one tender paragraph, he shared how "in the middle of some event or scene Helen may say to me, 'Do you remember when we ...' and I say, 'Of course,' and we both laugh together because we know we are both thinking of the same experience. And while our sex life is not quite the same as in our twenties and thirties, our physical closeness, our 'snuggling,' and our sex relationships are somewhat like a chord which is not only beautiful in itself, but also for its many, many overtones which enrich it far beyond the simple chord."[43]

This section of the first chapter had an effect similar to his "This Is Me" introduction to *On Becoming a Person*. It turned the book into a personal as well as a public document. Describing his forty-seven years of marriage in such seemingly frank terms, he became more credible to the reader, became a living, interesting person, and the book communicated in a more personal way and with more impact.

The next several chapters described the experiences of several different couples. One couple had lived together several years before getting married. They were rather immature about relationships, and in fact got married as a result of an argument in which he told her to get out, she said no, he said, "Okay. Then do you want to get married?" and she said, "Okay." At various times in their recounting of their experiences, Rogers would interrupt to comment, as when he noted, "One fascinating bit of insight is Dick's dawning recognition that resolution of a conflict is not an instantaneous magic thing. He is beginning to realize that it may take "work and time" to achieve a better relationship, a more harmonious living together. Here is a man of twenty-four who has learned math and history and English literature and yet has scarcely a beginning knowledge of interpersonal relationships. How irrelevant can our education get?"[44]

Another couple, married over ten years, was attempting a marriage in which both partners were free to pursue their own interests and growth and experience other relationships, even sexual ones; yet in which they were making great efforts to keep their communication with each other open and honest, and to continue working on improving their own emotional and sexual relationship.

Psychologically they were much more mature than the previous couple, yet the outcome of their marriage was also in question. Commenting on their honest portrayal of all the emotions—fear, jealousy, joy, love, hate, excitement, and so on—that continually played a part in their marriage, Rogers wrote: "When I was a boy, I loved to read stories about the early frontiersmen in this country, the hunters, the moccasin-shod explorers who ventured into the 'trackless wilderness,' crossed the Allegheny mountains, risking their lives, facing danger openly, far out ahead of the cabin-dwellers who would follow. I get this same feeling of excitement when I read the honest statements of Roy and Sylvia about their marriage. They are just as truly pioneers, exploring the far reaches of the relationship between a man and a woman. The risks they take are just as real as those taken by Daniel Boone. They live with uncertainty and at times with fear and doubt. They too have a goal which is both vague and definite. Just as the frontiersman kept pushing on, endeavoring to open up unknown territory, so these two are exploring the terra incognita which lies ahead in a modern marriage. I do not know whether their efforts will lead to success—who could know?— but they have my deep respect as they open new trails through the wilderness of human relationships. They have broken many of the conventional rules of 'what marriage should be' and are striving, with real dedication to each other, to build a new model for a permanent man–woman relationship. It is built on continually growing self-knowledge, on a complete sharing of even the most painful and shameful personal feelings, on permission for each to grow and develop together or separately, on a commitment which is real but fluctuating, on a changing, flowing union which carries no guarantee except that of further change."[45]

One of the case studies in *Becoming Partners* was that of Natalie and Larry's marriage and divorce. Of course Rogers had extensive knowledge of this relationship and was able to describe its dynamics in detail and draw out of it lessons to be learned. Although Rogers disguised their names and identifying details, those who were close to Natalie and Larry might recognize the subjects.[46] Apparently Larry did not know this chapter was going to be included, because he wrote Rogers' shortly after publication saying how dismayed he was to have his privacy invaded without his knowledge or permission, especially now that he was remarried.[47] It appears that Rogers did not answer this or a second letter. Two months later Larry wrote Rogers that, "I was hurt about the material in the book. But I am over the latter and I know you only want to help people … I want you to know that I still love you as a person and I didn't mean my letter to cut off communication between us."[48] Since the letters in the Library of Congress on this subject may be an incomplete record of Rogers and Larry's communications on this topic, it is hard to know if this was an uncharacteristic ethical violation on Rogers' part or if he had good reason to think he had leave to use this material.[49]

Another chapter described the experience of one woman who went through two unsuccessful marriages before developing her own identity and personal strengths to the point where, coupled with a kind and secure partner, she was able to discover the type of intimacy for which she had been striving so long. A sixth chapter succeeded in getting the book banned in South Africa. It presented a very sensitive portrayal of a loving marriage between a black man and a white woman, as described by the man, who also described the breakup of his unsuccessful first marriage. Another chapter described a fifteen-year marriage in which the partners were experimenting with other relationships, attempting to grow as individuals while at the same time they were trying to grow together. In a chapter on "Communes as Experiments in Human and Sexual Relationships" he analyzed the interpersonal issues typically arising when individuals attempted to develop new forms of intimate relationships and lifestyles in various types of communal situations. For him the communal experience, though different in form from the nuclear family structure, illustrated the same themes as had the experiences of the other couples he had described. He wrote: "In every one of these situations something has been learned. There is pain, distress, shock, surprise, caring, loving, and despair. But none of these is final, nor are they *finished* experiences. They are part of a process of living, loving, learning—all of it open between them.

"I speak of this at such length because I think it is not sufficiently recognized that this is an almost completely new mode of life. The sharing of bad feelings as well as good, of pain as well as loving, of looking inward to discover what one is really experiencing, is very literally a new pathway. These young people have not seen it in their parents, their schools, their ancestors. They would not find it in Oriental cultures where 'saving face' is so important. They would not find it in European tradition in which, especially in matters of love, deceit is the rule.

"No, young people and others are today trying out a genuinely new way of living. To me it is refreshing and hopeful. But I am sure that I am not enough of a prophet to say that it will be the way of our culture tomorrow. All I can say is that this open sharing of *all* of one's self nearly always, in my experience, leads to personal growth. I can also add that I believe it is very rare that a person who knows this way of living prefers to go back to living with the facade, the armor, the self-deceiving and other-deceiving 'front' which characterizes the great majority of the people. So we cannot know what the future holds for Clyde and Libby and Myra except that each one is likely to grow as a person."[50]

In a final chapter, he summarized many of the themes that recurred in the experiences of the different couples he had introduced. He spoke of the dedication to a growing relationship, the risky communication of persisting feelings to one's partner, the abandonment of traditional role expectations and assumption of freely chosen roles, and the becoming of separate selves—all of which seemed to strengthen the relationships he had described. If these kinds of qualities and acts did, in fact, help relationships survive and flourish, what implications would this have? Here he wrote of what we as a society might do, if we believed these qualities were important. We would lend encouragement to the experimental attempts to build new forms of relationship. We would not allow the law to interfere; "any partnership pattern entered into by mutually consenting adults"[51] would be legal. We would change our educational systems into institutions which would help build the skills and attitudes for better human interaction and human communication. We would especially educate our children in the skills and attitudes necessary for effective partnerships. We would, as a matter of course, institute intensive group experiences for couples, especially before marriage. Families would learn to use "family group meetings" to work through problems and hurts. We would experiment with better ways of caring for our children, especially the children of divorce, where an archaic legal system introduces so much unnecessary hurt and conflict for the child and the parents.

Concluding the chapter and the book, he wrote, "I want to add that the concept of partnerships—married or not—as a vast and promising laboratory has been forced on me by my learnings from these couples. I did not start with this idea at all. I tried to choose reasonably representative people. They did not—and do not—seem to me to be unusual couples or unusual persons, except for their surprising willingness to tell of their life as it is. Only gradually did I see that here is an enormous, exploring experiment, going on all about us ... Unheralded and unsung, explorations, experiments, new ways of relating, new kinds of partnerships are being tried out, people are learning from mistakes and profiting from successes. They are inventing alternatives, new futures, for our most sharply failing institutions, marriage and the nuclear family."[52]

Given the popularity of the topic in the 1970s—the geometric rise in premarital sex and cohabitation, the interest in "open marriage," the growth of communes, and the like—the book sold well: 47,000 copies the first year, 125,000 by 1977.[53] Shortly after its publication, Rogers wrote a friend of how he went to Pullman, Washington, "where a committee of thirty undergraduate and graduate students persuaded me to come up and help them with a 'Workshop on Partnering.' Up in what seems to me like that god-forsaken country they managed to get an audience of 700 people and to run the whole show with an efficiency that any professional conference organizer would envy. It was really a very heartwarming experience and renews my ever-present faith in young people."[54]

Older and Growing

Late in 1970, about the time when he was beginning the textbook on psychology which eventually evolved into *Becoming Partners,* Rogers wrote an informal letter to circulate among his friends. Entitled "A Day In My Life," it read:

Many of you must wonder what an elderly man does with his time; how he manages to keep himself from being bored to death. I am listing below a few of

425

the things that happened on one day, November 5, 1970, a day when I had no appointments. I don't claim that it is a typical day but neither is it atypical.

5:00 A.M. Urgent phone call from a woman in northern California who had gotten to know me in a 1955 workshop, has heard me speak since, and must see me. She is coming to San Diego in two days. (In spite of my telling her I just did not have time, she *did* see me.)

The morning mail arrived at home and at the office I found the following items: A letter from an educator in Suva, Fiji Islands, wanting to know my latest writings on education. He had become interested through David Williams of New Zealand who was visiting Fiji and whom I had known in Chicago in the 1930s. But the Fiji Islands! My memories of Suva are of very black policemen in white shorts and women with turbans on their heads and one of the wildest outdoor markets I have ever seen. And they want to know Carl Rogers on education!

A letter—would I be interested in the presidency of a Mid-West college? A letter from a tough black man—a convicted drug pusher and stick-up man, now in jail awaiting sentence from his last trial—wanting copies of my books! He was a member of the Pittsburgh drug group which Tony Rose and I conducted, and is a lovely person in spite of his record.

A letter saying that a course is to be offered at the New School for Social Research in New York City entitled, "Carl Rogers, Psychologist and Educator" [taught by the author].

A fan letter regarding *Freedom to Learn.* A student had been in a course taught by someone infected by the book, who conducted his course like an encounter group. "The results were exactly the kind of experience you described in *Freedom to Learn.*"

Dictated replies to these and a dozen other letters.

Received a dust jacket of *Carl Rogers on Encounter Groups* from Harper & Row with a most laudatory comment about the book by Philip Slater.

Received a copy of *TIME Magazine* with my picture and a quotation or two, found in a mediocre article on the human potential movement.

A phone call regarding some changes they are making in the film, "A Conversation with Carl Rogers" which is soon to be distributed. Checked garden. Little watering needed. Snapdragons and pansies—recently transplanted—doing fine. New gorgeous flowers on my best camellia! Hanging begonia still blooming. All others gone. Acalypha cuttings (gorgeous red leaves) beginning to sprout, after dubious period. Attempt to grow moosehorn fern from spores appears failure. Can't win 'em all.

Saw Philip Slater, the author of *The Pursuit of Loneliness: American Society in Crisis,* being interviewed on the Keith Berwick show. Having never met him was fascinated to see him after his comment about my book.

11:00 P.M. Long distance phone call from a student at Plattsburgh, New York. That's 2:00 A.M. his time! He had just finished reading *On Becoming a Person*

426

and was very much excited by it. Wanted me to know that, and also wanted to know if there was some graduate school that shared my kind of ideas.

In between times, trying to get a little writing done on my new book, taking Helen out to an enjoyable movie and dinner, and calming down from the excitement. I wish I could cut off some of the stimuli.

As you can see, it is a very boring life.

When I first read this letter, I was struck by its similarity in tone to the letters which a twenty-year-old Carl Rogers wrote home from his travels to China, telling of how many pages of this or that book on the Orient he had read each day, how many miles he had traveled, how many students he had met with, and the like. Beyond the "objective report" of his activities one senses the pride he has in his accomplishments. I often sensed this pride in Rogers. His work was important to him and he liked to find that it was important to others. Because he wanted to make a difference, he was genuinely pleased to discover new examples of his impact. As modest as he may have been in his typical public demeanor, he was not without ego. Every six months, when the publishers sent royalty reports, he recorded the latest figures with running totals of each book's sales. He was clearly proud of his accomplishments.

Yet the pride stopped short of vanity, in the sense of pride as a momentary feeling attached to a particular accomplishment and vanity as a characteristic personality trait. Part of this may be explained by a genuinely humble feeling Rogers had about his place in the scheme of things. As he once wrote, "I have many fields of interest ... my professional work is not the be-all and end-all of my existence. Somehow I have an inwardly light touch in regard to my work. It is not all there is to life. Sometimes I am struck with the absurdity of my earnest effort to help a person, complete a research, write a paper. Placed in the perspective of billions of years of time, of millions of light years of interstellar space, of the trillions of one-celled organisms in the sea, of the life struggle of billions of people to achieve their goals, I cannot help but wonder what possible significance can be attached to the efforts of one person at one moment of time. I can only do my part as one infinitely small living unit in this vast ongoing universe. But such a perspective helps to keep me from feeling too self-important."[55]

Such a metaphysical perspective, however, is only one explanation for the humility which so often impressed people who met Rogers. To call undue attention to himself or his ideas would contradict his philosophy. He hated to be idealized. When asked to speak about himself in 1971, he told an audience, "It is embarrassing because it puts so much stress on what the Russians call 'the cult of the individual.'"[56] His whole professional life had been devoted to furthering the principle of *trust your own experience*. So he had little respect for would-be disciples. He said in 1971, "People are continually asking me or writing me to inquire if I have changed. Some of the letters are pathetic in their search for a guru. They say essentially, 'I hear you have entirely changed your thinking and your way of working. Please tell me it isn't so. To whom will I turn if you have changed?'"[57] As one colleague succinctly put it: "He hates 'Rogerians.'"[58] Affirming this point David Malcolm recalled how,

> Years ago, at a convention in San Francisco, I was riding in a crowded taxi with a talkative driver who noticed our convention name tags and remarked, "Say, I had a couple of your buddies in this cab this morning and one of them said to the other 'Are you a Rogerian' and the other said, 'No, I'm a Rotarian.'" A few weeks later I was moderator for a panel and, in a moment of whimsy, introduced Carl Rogers by telling this story and adding, "Now my first question to you, Dr. Rogers, is: Are you a Rotarian?" In a flash, Carl responded, "No, and I'm not the other, either!"[59]

Making a similar point, David Cain recalled attending a person-centered workshop with Rogers in 1977 and asking for a private meeting where he told Rogers, "'I sort of have embraced what you do, but I don't need you sitting on my shoulder observing and evaluating any more, so I have come here to let you know that I am flicking you off.' And he was certainly pleased with that. And I said, 'I feel like we are equals as therapists or people or professionals, not in terms of my accomplishments, but in terms of just being professionals and striving to improve ourselves and so on.' And he said, 'I feel like we are equals, too,' and he slapped his hands on his knees and he basically said, 'I think we are finished talking.' It was an important moment for me to just be affirmed by him and he was completely genuine in his affirmation."[60]

It would certainly have pleased Rogers to be knocked off Cain's shoulder. He once described how it made him "unhappy ... when people sort of mindlessly try to follow me or anybody else. One of my favorite Zen sayings is: 'When you meet the Buddha—kill the Buddha.' I think that's extremely good advice. When you find the guy who has all the answers, the person you ought to follow, the person that shows you the way to go, well ... I'd try and get rid of him psychologically. I hope you don't really kill him, but, at any rate, get rid of him psychologically."[61]

At the same time he didn't have a sense of personal self-importance. David Cain recalled a time, before he knew Rogers personally, when he saw Rogers speak to a large audience and afterwards found himself in the men's room, standing at the next urinal from Carl Rogers. "I looked to the right and I said, 'You, too?' And he said, 'Yeah, it is the great leveler, isn't it?'"[62]

In any case, Rogers' "Day in My Life" letter, in addition to illustrating the pride he took in his work, characterizes something of the flavor of this stage of his career during the early and mid-1970s. As the letter suggests, he slowed down a little, spending most of his time in La Jolla, enjoying the fruits of his more than four decades of productive work. On the other hand, he kept on working, forging ahead into new areas of thought and practice. Even at a somewhat slower pace he was still very productive.

As he began to slow down, he traveled less, participated in fewer encounter groups, and accepted speaking and workshop invitations less often. Several of his articles were of a retrospective bent, which had not been typical of him before this time. He continued to prize very highly his friends and colleagues at Center for Studies of the Person. He spent a good deal of time in his garden.

Describing his own aging process, in 1977, at seventy-five, he wrote, "I do feel physical deterioration. I notice it in many ways. Ten years ago I greatly enjoyed throwing a frisbee. Now my right shoulder is so painfully arthritic that this kind of activity is out of the question. In my garden I realize that a task which would have been easy five years ago, but difficult last year, now seems like too much, and I had better leave it for our once-a-week gardener. This slow deterioration, with various minor disorders of vision, heartbeat and the like, inform me that the physical portion of what I call 'me' is not going to last forever. Yet I still enjoy a four-mile walk on the beach. I can lift heavy objects, do all the shopping, cooking and dishwashing when my wife is ill, carry my own luggage without puffing."[63]

The years were not nearly as kind to Helen as they were to Carl. Although a successful operation completely cleared up a hiatic hernia and bleeding ulcer, her arthritis had become worse over the years and began to confine her to a wheelchair. She was experiencing a great deal of pain almost daily.[64] Carl took over the major part of her care and for a period of about two years did almost all the shopping, cooking, and cleaning for the two of them. Happily, a successful hip joint operation in 1973 worked wonders on her condition. She began to walk about more, swim almost daily at a local health club, and they even signed up for a thirty-five day Mediterranean cruise, on a freighter, for the winter of 1974. Unfortunately, after they came east in January the voyage was delayed, then canceled. Although they enjoyed their time with Natalie and David's families out East, they were both very disappointed to miss this chance to resume their beloved pastime of traveling.[65] Shortly thereafter Helen's arthritis worsened again, other ailments caused further problems, and she began to feel that she would never travel again.

They did travel to a resort in Carmel Valley, California where they greatly enjoyed their fiftieth wedding anniversary with all their children and grandchildren for several days and nights.[66] But respites like this were rare, and with the burden of Helen's care, as well as his professional responsibilities on his shoulders, Carl began to feel more distraught, harried, and depressed than he had in many years. In one workshop in 1974 he realized that he was losing his ability to care for others, so troubled was he by his own pressures and feelings. He felt as though he was being "nibbled to death by ducks" (a phrase used by one of the participants which Rogers felt perfectly described him).[67] When a workshop participant asked him, "Could you take a day off just because you wanted to?", it threw him into a confused state of mind. That night he dreamed "that I was arrested for no reason at all except that I was 'just enjoying myself'" and decided he needed to make a change.[68] In "the most irresponsible decision I have made in fifty years," he cancelled eighteen talks or meetings he was scheduled for in nine cities over thirty-two days (his colleagues attended armed with tapes and films of Rogers) and resolved, in spite of Helen's condition, to take some time for and by himself.[69] Shortly thereafter, after arranging for someone to stay with Helen, he went to a cottage on Stinson Beach in California for ten days alone. He went without any expectations of working. The time was just for him. He read, took long walks on the beach, and spent long hours thinking or simply being (he also placed a nightly telephone call to check on Helen). These were precious days to him. Although he took no more time like this, just for himself, for the next several years, he frequently referred back to those ten days as being so very important in helping him regain his balance and sense of well-being.

Back home he realized he would need help in caring for Helen, so they hired a young woman to work in that capacity. Unfortunately Helen's condition continued to deteriorate. She was unable to produce red blood cells and was growing increasingly weak. For a time in 1976 it seemed she was dying. Carl and Natalie Rogers, working together in one workshop, told the participants on the first night that they might be called away at any time. Letters to friends during this period often expressed the unhappiness he felt in seeing his lifelong partner grow old and weaker and experience such pain in the process.

Again he took over the household responsibilities.[70] Once again he began to feel the strain of it all, not only the chores but the confining relationship. He was feeling alive, vital, still growing in new directions, becoming an increasingly radical thinker in many ways. Helen, as her health deteriorated, was feeling increasingly conservative on various issues and emotionally dependent on Carl. Never one to handle dependency well to begin with, Carl was caught in the turmoil of many mixed emotions—love for Helen, resentment for what he felt as her "clinging" behavior, admiration for her courage in facing the physical pain she felt, frustration at feeling there was nothing he could do, depression at feeling that his life was being controlled and hemmed in. For a period he saw a therapist-friend to get some help in dealing with his confusion and discouragement. It was for him the most trying period of their fifty or more years of marriage. He felt a greater distance from Helen than he had ever felt before. And whenever he contemplated dealing with her directly about this, he would stop himself, feeling that this would be neither a thoughtful nor productive thing to do with a dying person. This contributed to his sense of helplessness even further. On one occasion when she had expressed that she really had nothing to live for except to live for him, he said, "Then I can understand why you want to die," and left the room in deep despair.[71]

But then, in the latter part of 1976, Helen's condition began to improve. Her system began making its own red blood cells again for the first time in two years.[72] Not only was there physical improvement, but psychologically she came alive again. She took up painting and crafts and began to initiate projects on her own. Having thought that she would never leave La Jolla again, she took a weekend trip to San Francisco to test her strength and, when she found that she was able to get along, she accompanied Carl for three weeks, in the summer of 1977, to the rustic Sagamore Conference Center in the Adirondack Mountains of New York State.[73]

Ironically, Helen's "rebirth" introduced new problems into the marriage. Once she resolved in her own mind that living her life for her husband was not a sufficient reason for living, and that she would have to find some additional purposes of her own, she began to experience some resentment toward him for having had the opportunity to live his own life as he chose, over all those years. The resentment was exacerbated by a new interest Carl was showing in other women for the first time in their long marriage (a topic to be discussed below). This led to further hurt and anger. As Helen voiced her angry feelings, it became clear to Carl that she could take some of his resentment as well. Consequently, there was more anger present in their relationship than ever before. To Carl this was a healthy sign. As they worked on their relationship, sometimes he felt they were moving closer to one another again, sometimes not. As he wrote in 1977 and shared with several groups in the next few years,

> She has met her pain and her restricted life with the utmost of courage ... She is making remarkable progress in fighting her way back, often by sheer force of will, to a more normal life, built around her own purposes. But it has not been easy. She first had to choose whether she wanted to live, whether there was any purpose in living. Then I have baffled and hurt her by the fact of my own independent life. While she was so ill, I felt heavily burdened by our close togetherness, heightened by her need for care. So I determined, for my own survival, to live a life of my own. She is often deeply hurt by this, and by the changing of my values. On her side, she is giving up the old model of being the supportive wife. This change brings her in touch with her anger at me and at society for giving her that socially approved role. On my part, I am angered at any move that would put us back in the old complete togetherness; I stubbornly resist anything that seems like control. So there are more tensions and difficulties in our relationship than ever before, more feelings that we are trying to work through, but there is also more honesty, as we strive to build new ways of being together.[74]

Rogers' brief summary of their "tensions and difficulties" only begins to suggest the years of anguish he and Helen lived through as they coped with her health problems and their struggles around closeness and separateness in their relationship. Rogers' personal papers and diaries from this period are filled with one entry after another in which he summarized his and Helen's conversations. Ever the excellent listener, he would fill pages with empathic summaries of Helen's feelings of resentment and despair. Helen: "Your love is so dutiful. You feel an obligation, so you'll take care of me til I die … I try so hard, & it's not worth it. I wish I could die tonight." "We don't have any relationship any more. You're just a stone image. You help so many other people—they think you're God—why can't you help me?" "[Helen] resents the fact that I'm such a sober person to live with—no lightness or humor, a lousy conversationalist."[75] Next to these synopses of Helen's feelings he would record his own feelings and reactions. "I feel confused & upset. I'm a bit scared by the *truth* of what she is saying." "I want to increase our companionship & to be more loving toward you … I will not be controlled by you. I'm probably hypersensitive about this, but I will not." "I wish I could learn to *play*, just for *fun*.…I've never been much good at that & I'm worse now … I need to appreciate and like myself more. Then I wouldn't be such a sober-sided, withdrawn guy."[76] This went on for years. It is painful to read, more so to imagine how painful it was to experience.

Working on one's relationship after fifty years of marriage is hardly the stereotype most of us have of the "golden years." Yet it was Carl and Helen Rogers' reality throughout many of their California years, particularly from the mid-1970s to Helen's death in 1979.

Because of Helen's health problems and his own slowing down of activities during part of the 1970s, Rogers conducted most of his professional work in these years out of his office at home in La Jolla, often inviting associates, interviewers, and students to his home instead of traveling to see them. His professional correspondence was voluminous. In Rogers' study one day, I began to comprehend the range of letters that he received by noticing a little stamp collection he was saving for a friend's son. In two or three months he had taken stamps off envelopes sent to him from: Ireland, Greece, Poland, India, United Arab Republic, Australia, Canada, Netherlands, Israel, England, Italy, Norway, Bahamas, Belgium, Japan, Argentina, Spain, Philippines, and Germany.

His "fan mail" continued as usual. A writer would say, "I just read your book and I must tell you …" and he would have to figure out which of his more popular books was being referred to—*On Becoming a Person, Person to Person, Freedom to Learn, On Encounter Groups,* or *Becoming Partners*. Reactions to *Becoming Partners* were typical, as in this Texas woman's letter in 1973.

Dear Dr. Rogers, I want to take a moment of your time to thank you for your writings. I first became acquainted with your books through a gift copy of *Becoming a Person*. I had just entered therapy at the age of 28 and my counselor hoped that the book would help me. It did—it was a turning point on my road

432

to indeed "becoming a person." A short time later, I became involved in encounter work—first as a participant, then as a facilitator—and your book on encounter groups was invaluable in helping me experience myself and other people. After a period of pain, I finally began to open myself up to others. Now, I have come upon *Becoming Partners* and, once more, I have learned from you and gained insight into my relationships with men. I want to thank you from the bottom of my heart for your influence on my life.[77]

Another reaction to the book came from Logan Fox, Rogers' old acquaintance and interpreter on their 1961 trip to Japan.

Carl, you never cease to amaze me. You are one of the stubbornest men I have known, refusing to retreat from your own interests and your own perceptions. Some of us zig-zag all over the place, crossing and recrossing your path, while you doggedly walk one of the straightest paths I know. Yet, at the same time, I have known no one who has kept growing as you have. I especially felt this after reading *Becoming Partners,* since that was a book I really didn't expect from you. But it was beautiful; so much like you, yet with a fresh and courageous handling of material that I guess was not easy for you (not that you are "square," but neither are you a "swinger") … again you serve to remind me of hungers in me to which I am not always faithful. I know you don't see yourself as anybody's conscience, but in so many ways you have been one to me. Except that I don't resent this conscience as I, at times, resent the rigid superego I inherited. Thank you, Carl, for being you … Affectionately, Logan.[78]

Letters often began with "I'm sure you must have heard this story many times before, but …" and would go on to tell Rogers how he had changed their lives. Many of these came from grateful clients of *other* client-centered therapists, thanking him for influencing their therapists and occasionally telling Rogers how, indirectly, he had not only changed their lives but *saved* them.

Sitting at his desk at home, Rogers dictated his answers to most letters. "Dear Nancy, Yes, I have heard the story before but rarely have I found it told in such a deeply personal, compelling and beautiful way. I was very moved by your letter. I guess all I can say is that I am really so delighted that you are finding yourself and liking yourself and realizing clearly what you had been through and the direction in which you are going …"[79] "Dear Cathy, Letters like yours are the real reward that I get from my work. I am happy to know if I've made a difference in your life. I am sure you must have faced many difficulties with your white/ black marriage and I can imagine some of the personal problems and conflicts that that's created for you … my book on 'Becoming Partners' was banned in South Africa and I'm sure it is because it includes an account of a black/white marriage …"[80]

Valerie Henderson, Rogers' secretary from 1973 on (who later became his colleague as well), would stop by the house, pick up the tape, take it home to transcribe and add whatever enclosures Rogers indicated, and a day or two later bring back the letters for his signature and pick up the next tape.[81]

Then there were the little battles or issues to clear up. As usual Rogers would enjoy waging war with his pen, as when he told an editor, "I think you better tell your legal hacks to get off my back and write a human document and not to think they can get away with murder because they sent me a check for $50."[82] Or when he responded to a psychology professor by writing, "I don't believe you will get the kind of person you want and I don't think you deserve him. Your department sounds incredibly smug. I think the sooner the undergraduates move out, the better off they will be. If I knew a good person who would fit the kind of post you mention, I certainly wouldn't recommend that he come to your place. Sorry."[83] Or when he resigned from his part-time professorship at the United States International University, in a letter to the Dean and President that Rogers circulated widely, so it received a good deal of national publicity within the psychological profession.[84] Referring to a new set of rules governing student conduct—including search of their cars and dormitories, a "loyalty oath" to the University's rules which students had to sign, and so on—Rogers wrote, in part:

> The most incredible portion of the statement is this. "… The University must reserve the right … to deny the re-enrollment of any student when such action is deemed to be in the best interest of the University or the student." I believe that historically this has been known as the Star Chamber procedure. I have never known such a procedure to be used except under dictatorships. As I read it very carefully, it means that at the end of a term a student simply disappears. Why? He does not know, nor do his fellow students. Who made the decision? "The University." What is the effect? Obviously the effect is to cause students to distrust each other, the faculty, and the administration. Who will be the next informer? No one knows. Since he has signed a statement saying he will support all university policies and regulations, each student must keep his dissenting thoughts to himself, lest he be seen as a "trouble-maker" and caused to disappear. This, to my mind, is dictatorship at its worst.[85]

And the little surprises. The invitations to address all sorts of groups and audiences around the world (which he would either decline or answer with "I never make any commitments over the phone. Write me a letter and I'll think about it").[86] The continual references to his work that would come to his attention. The dissertations based on his formulations, sent to him from time to time, from universities all over the world. A very popular book of poems and reflections, *Notes to Myself* by Hugh Prather, dedicated "to Carl Rogers (whose *On Becoming a Person* showed me where to look)."[87] New publications by former students and colleagues: *New Directions in Client-Centered Therapy, Innovations in Client-Centered Therapy,* and others.[88] Copies of new research studies on client-centered therapy sent to him from around the world. And three more honorary degrees: from the University of Hamburg, Germany; from Holland's Leiden University, celebrating its 400th anniversary (both institutions set precedents by sending representatives across the ocean to present the degrees to Rogers in special ceremonies held in La Jolla); and in 1978 from Northwestern University.[89]

Political Awakening

The picture of a less active Carl Rogers in the early and mid-1970s, enjoying the fruits of a rich career, is only half the picture. Throughout this period he continued to grow, continued to work, and continued to extend his thinking into new areas of human knowledge and concern. And in the second half of the seventies he picked up the pace again, commencing a remarkably active and productive final decade of his life. Professionally, the decade was devoted to exploring the social and political implications of his life's work in the client-centered mode.

Since his trip to China a half century earlier, Rogers had been interested in social issues, economic problems, and politics. But he chose to work in a scientific and helping profession where almost all his time was spent focused on individuals. Occasionally he recognized the profound political implications of his work, as in a 1952 article where he described the directions clients move in client-centered therapy.

> It is not toward the safety of conformity, it is not toward the disregarding of certain feelings and impulses in order to be more comfortable in their culture, it is not toward taking over the standards of some group. It is inevitably toward the difficult and rewarding task of accepting one's feelings, of choosing those values and those behaviors which make for long-term satisfaction; it is toward living independently in the group; it is toward self-government in its deepest personal terms, and its most profound psychological meanings. It is for this reason that any totalitarian regime would be well advised, as an early step in its program, to liquidate all those who have had any experience with client-centered therapy. Otherwise the vital experience of having discovered the possibility of self-direction within one's self would remain a stubborn and deeply resistant force opposing all attempts from the outside to control or direct thought and behavior.[90]

He wrote this during the Joseph McCarthy period, one of many indirect references he made in opposition to suppression of civil liberties and to the social conformity of the time. (Interestingly, he did not publish it at the time.) A few years later, he

435

expanded on this theme in his debate and dialogue with B.F. Skinner. But these insights or comments of a political nature were relatively rare diversions, not the real focus of his work in individual counseling and psychotherapy. He was "a revolutionary with a narrow focus," as he later described it.[91] During his career, that narrow focus had steadily broadened and continued to do so: from children and families to psychotherapy with individuals, to putting his toe into the waters of group leadership, philosophy, and education. When he left university life with its continual responsibility for major research projects, teaching and advising, however, he had more time to think about related areas of interest and made more significant contributions to the philosophy of science, education, and relationships, as his books *Man and the Science of Man*, *Freedom to Learn* and *Becoming Partners* illustrated. In addition, his work at WBSI and CSP, especially in encounter groups, brought him in much closer contact with groups and individuals who were very involved in dealing with all of society's problems. In the seventies, once his own work schedule began to slow down a bit, he had a little more time to think about these broader issues. Perhaps also he realized he was enough of an established figure, a man of stature and respect, that he could afford to speak out on social issues without damaging his career.

At any rate, he did begin to speak out. He criticized CBS television for firing the Smothers Brothers for their left-leaning political satire.[92] In 1970, as a member of the Committee for New Directions in California, he wrote a letter to hundreds of friends, colleagues and contacts urging them to support Jess Unruh in his campaign to defeat California's governor Ronald Reagan in his bid for re-election.[93] But partisan politics was not Rogers' métier. He was more likely to speak out on social issues than about campaigns or candidates. In one speech which he delivered on several occasions, and which was published in the *Journal of Humanistic Psychology* in 1972, he spoke of "Some Social Issues Which Concern Me."[94] In many of his articles and speeches during the seventies he continued to refer to one or more of the social problems he addressed in this speech. These included: overpopulation; decaying cities; the eroding institution of marriage; the problems our laws and customs create for children of separated parents; racism and minorities; our "dying educational institutions"; a growing police state; and "our obscene war" in Southeast Asia. (He didn't discuss the environment because he said that was one problem we were well aware of and showing some commitment to deal with it.) He minced no words.

> The Pentagon and CIA appear to be major forces in formulating our foreign policy. The CIA was training troops in Laos years ago, without knowledge of Congress or the people. Presidents seem unable to stand up to these great bureaucracies. For purposes of "national defense" we maintain more than one and one-half *million* troops in 119 foreign countries. Is this for defense? Military and totalitarian governments are being financially and militarily supported by

the United States, in numbers probably never equaled in the history of the world. Yet we proclaim ourselves as the backers of the free and democratic world.[95]

Why do we not stop this incredible slaughter and waste and destruction, this sordid, interminable, and expanding war? I believe it boils down to one central reason. As a country we cannot bear to say that we have made a horrible, massive *mistake.* We cannot bear, in short, to lose face. What a reason for continuing. The one thing we might learn from this incredible tragedy is to gain a clear view of the enemy. If we peer closely through the blood and death and awful ruin we can see the enemy clearly. He is us.[96]

I believe our culture is facing a life and death crisis on many fronts, and that I have an obligation as a citizen to speak out. I am frightened about our destiny as a people, as a nation. So I want to take as clear a stand as I can on a variety of issues, including our insane wars ... I recognize very well that I am no expert in most of the fields I shall mention, but I shall simply voice the attitudes and views of one deeply concerned person.[97]

In one talk in 1971 he referred to the war in Vietnam, saying, "Sometimes I think the words of one of America's favorite songs should be changed to read, 'God forgive America, our home-destroying home.'"[98] On another occasion he said that if we would apply our knowledge of the behavioral sciences to deal with problems in race relations in the United States, and if "we back that effort with a sum at least equivalent to the cost of all our B-52 bombers—then there might be a chance of preventing the bloody tragedy which faces us."[99]

Another facet of his interest in social issues came with a very unusual encounter group he led in 1972. Although he gradually tapered off doing encounter groups in the seventies, this one occurred when he and Bill McGaw collaborated on another encounter documentary, as they had on the Academy Award-winning *Journey Into Self.* Only this time the risks were more than psychological for the participants. It was initiated and organized by Pat Rice, a CSP member who had recently left the Jesuit order and who had been conducting encounter groups and workshops in Northern Ireland.[100] At considerable expense they brought across the Atlantic Ocean, to the studio of WQED in Pittsburgh, a group of Irish Catholics, Irish Protestants, and British—including an officer in the English army, a mother whose son had been shot by a British soldier, a probable member of the Irish Republican Army (because the IRA was illegal, he couldn't admit it), a clergyman, and others, to comprise a diverse group involved in "the troubles" in Northern Ireland.[101] Rogers and Rice facilitated the group. Although the depth of understanding and acceptance achieved by the participants on the film was not nearly as great as in a typical encounter group, nevertheless the group did move significantly, though reservedly, toward viewing one another as human beings without the stereotypes and enmity associated with religion and nationality.[102] Rogers invested some $22,000 of his own in the project. After the filming Rogers and McGaw tried unsuccessfully to raise an additional $50,000 necessary to distribute the film properly in the United States; consequently it was not viewed for some time publicly on Rogers' side of the ocean. However, it was shown in Northern Ireland in many colleges, youth groups, and religious communities. At one point some of the group members—in teams of two, a Catholic and a Protestant—risked their lives showing the film in movie theatres in Northern Ireland, after which they would lead a discussion with members of the audience. During this process four copies of the film were destroyed by paramilitary groups on both sides of the conflict.[103] It was later released as a video in 1973, under the title "The Steel Shutter." and distributed by Center for Studies of the Person."[104]

In many of the encounter groups Rogers led, members would often challenge both Rogers and the field of humanistic psychology in general as being irrelevant to the more important social and political issues of the day. Some political activists would (and still do) react to psychotherapy and encounter groups as being irrelevant or even "counterrevolutionary," insofar as they might distract people from solving important social issues and focus instead on "getting one's own head together" or establishing a few intimate relationships or realizing one's personal goals. These arguments all came up when Rogers and his team were asked by the National Health Council, which consisted of the American Medical Association, American Dental Association, nurses' organizations, insurance companies, hospitals and other "health providers," to facilitate a conference between themselves and a group of black residents of the inner city, Mexican-American farm workers, and other poor, grass-roots "health consumers." The conference was tense and volatile. The lower-class health consumers simply didn't play by the middle-class rules of professional conferences. Rogers and his colleagues facilitated twenty groups with twenty or more providers and consumers in each. In spite of the consumers' hostility and suspicions about the providers and the facilitators' motives, and in spite of the defensiveness and self-righteousness of the providers, real communication took place. But the consumers did not leave their politics at the door, nor did the facilitators ask them to. During the conference they drafted a series of resolutions about improving health care and demanded that these resolutions be discussed and voted upon at the last general session. As Rogers summarized it, "The conference then, after heated discussions, passed a long series of resolutions ... The conference ended with highly affirmative feelings, not only on the part of the 'consumers' but on the part of most of the establishment members as well. The surprising result was that in the ensuing year a very large number of these resolutions were carried out."[105]

Even with the occasional experience like this or the Northern Ireland encounter group, Rogers did not feel moved to think deeply about the connection between the client-centered approach and the world of politics and power. These were two encounter events among many good case studies to show that encounter

438

groups have all kinds of applications. His focus was on the encounter group method, not on the bigger social and political issues the method raised. Thus his speaking out on social issues and politics remained on the individual level, as a concerned citizen. He made no attempt to relate his life's work to these broader areas of concern, except to recognize that dictators and totalitarian leaders would not welcome a person-centered approach that supported individual self-direction. Even when he experimented with encounter groups to change whole educational systems, his focus was more on groups and educational administration and pedagogy than on thinking systematically about social and political change.

The turning point came in 1973, with three related incidents. First was his reading of Pat Rice's dissertation on the Northern Ireland encounter group. As Rogers learned more of the powerful aftermath of the group on the lives of its participants and many of its viewers, he wrote to Rice saying,

> To me it underscores one very positive point: we have a pilot model, on a very small scale, of how bitter conflicts might be moved toward resolution. The impact of even this one tiny venture has been significant. It stirs my imagination to think what might be possible were there a thousand human relations or communications groups meeting throughout Belfast. It makes me wish that governments could become aware of the human resources and skills that are now available to help in such bitter situations.[106]

About this time, Alan Nelson, a young psychologist and a colleague of Natalie Rogers, happened to ask Rogers about the politics of the client-centered approach to psychotherapy. Rogers answered that there were no politics in the approach, meaning that no partisan or liberal or conservative political agenda was involved. As Rogers describes it, Nelson responded "with a loud guffaw. When I asked my questioner to explain, he replied, 'I spent three years of graduate school learning to be an expert in clinical psychology. I learned to make accurate diagnostic judgments. I learned the various techniques of altering the subject's attitudes and behavior. I learned the subtle modes of manipulation, under the labels of interpretation and guidance. Then I began to read your material, which upset everything I had learned. You were saying that the power rests not in my mind but in his organism. You completely reversed the relationship of power and control which had been built up in me over three years. And then you say there is no politics in the client-centered approach!'"[107]

This clicked for Rogers. While humanistic psychology was proliferating in the sixties and now the seventies, so were many important political and social movements. The civil rights movement, the peace movement, the student movement, and now the women's movement were all speaking the common language of empowerment. They rejected the concept of top-down control, of artificial limitations placed on the ability of blacks, Vietnamese, students or women to achieve their full potential. They sought to return "power to the people," to enable them to make the decisions that affected their lives. Rogers realized that his life's work represented a psychological foundation for these political movements, and these movements suggested a political dimension to his work that he had never recognized. He wrote, "This was the beginning— perhaps a late beginning—of my education regarding the politics of interpersonal relationships. The more I thought and read, and the more I sensed the present-day concern with power and control, the more new facets I experienced in my relationships in therapy, in intensive groups, in families, and among friends. Gradually I realized my experience ran parallel to the old story of the uneducated man and his first exposure to a course in literature. 'You know,' he told his friends later, 'I've found out I've been speaking prose all my life and never knew it.' In similar vein I could now say 'I've been practicing and teaching politics all my professional life and never realized it fully until now.'"[108]

As Rogers reevaluated his life's work from a political perspective, the more he thought about it the more he began to see connections. Politics was more than "the methods or tactics involved in managing a state or government," as *Webster's Dictionary* defined it. When applied to human relationships, politics became, as Rogers defined it, "the process of gaining, using, sharing or relinquishing power, control, decision-making. It is the process of the highly complex interactions and effects of these elements as they exist in relationships between persons, between a person and a group, or between groups."[109]

He went on to describe how "this new construct has had a powerful influence on me ... It has caused me to take a fresh look at my professional life work. I've had a role in initiating the person-centered approach. This view developed first in counseling and psychotherapy, where it was known as client-centered, meaning a person seeking help was not treated as a dependent patient but as a responsible client. Extended to education, it was called student-centered teaching. As it has moved into a wide variety of fields, far from its point of origin—intensive groups, marriage, family relationships, administration, minority groups, interracial, intercultural, and even international relationships—it seems best to adopt as broad a term as possible: person-centered."[110]

What he saw in all these areas was the attempt to return the power, the control and the decision-making to the person and away from the authority or the institution or those with the most physical or economic power. All around him, for the previous decade or more, he had witnessed and supported various movements for human liberation—"power to the people," "participatory democracy," "the population with the problem has the best resources for solving the problem," "student rights," "Vietnam for the Vietnamese," "children's rights," "sisterhood is powerful," "patient's rights," and so on. These, he said, were the slogans of the decade, and they described on a political and social level what he had been saying all along for the helping professions. What he had been saying, essentially, was that, given a facilitative climate, the individual has the resources to solve his problems and guide his life far more effectively than any power or authority or expert can do for him. What would happen if this hypothesis were extended to all power relationships—if those in positions of power were to be personally congruent and genuine, if they were truly to trust those over whom they exercised control, if they were really to listen empathically to what those controlled were saying, and in the final analysis, if they were to relinquish that control in favor of more egalitarian human relationships?

At the same time that Rogers was becoming increasingly intrigued by this question, still another event occurred which moved him further in the same direction. This was a letter from his daughter. Natalie Rogers, recently divorced, was by now a skilled therapist and group leader in her own right, with a good deal of experience with alternative kinds of institutions in the Boston area that were experimenting with new forms of non-authoritarian power relationships. She told her father:

> I wanted to put on paper some of my feelings about my group and individual therapy work and the thoughts I so often have about you and client-centered therapy. I feel I should write this, because I keep asking you to do things with me and/or friends and colleagues of mine and it occurs to me you may think I am one of many others who might want to use your name, etc. I do want to use your drawing power but much more important than that is how important your philosophy of therapy is to me right now. As I see individual clients and we get into tight emotional spots, I am so very glad to have a theoretical framework from which I can take a thermometer reading and do what I believe is the right thing in a relationship to the client. That's not to say that I always live up to my standards ... but at least I know what I am trying to do, which gives me a solid feeling as a therapist. And when I ask for feedback from clients as to the most meaningful times we have together or moments of help for them, they inevitably come back with a statement about being really heard, or deeply understood. The most simple notion that to really understand someone emotionally helps them to come to relevant, personal, meaningful solutions or insights is an amazing one. Being a little older and a little "wiser" than I used to be can get in my way occasionally because I'm tempted to give advice. When such a feeling overcomes me, instead of giving the advice I try to share something of my experience with them and let them take it or leave it.
>
> All of this is to say that I not only love you as a father, but am more and more re-appreciating the philosophy you have formulated. It is also to say that I would like a few more occasions to work closely with you. Although we have been in a couple of things together, I don't think we've ever co-led any kind of group. I'd really be interested in thinking up something we'd like to do together. I'm also excited about the possibility of working something out that would interest you

with the Greenhouse people; because we are good people, working in a way that is struggling to be politically in touch yet humane—an almost impossible task. Much love, Nat.[111]

Rogers' response to Natalie's request to work together was, as she recalled, "Sure, what can you think of?"[112] Natalie thought about that question over the following year. In 1974 she moved to California, locating north of San Francisco, a day's drive from her parents. There she would develop her own private practice in psychotherapy, begin training others in client-centered therapy, and continue to develop her own approach of "client-centered expressive therapy," combining her interest in the visual arts, dance and movement, and other media with client-centered therapy. Shortly after moving to California, visiting her parents in La Jolla, she walked into her father's office and finally answered his question. She suggested doing a different kind of workshop together.

Person-Centered Workshops and Communities

Natalie's suggestion initiated a discussion which led Carl and Natalie Rogers, Alan Nelson, and two of Carl's colleagues from Center for Studies of the Person, Betty Meador and John K. Wood,[113] to offer two new workshops in 1974. These unusually long, three-week workshops, held at the University of California, San Diego and University of California, Santa Cruz, were not intended to have a particularly political focus, but rather to explore the implications of the client-centered approach for therapy, education, intensive groups, and other human relationships. What happened, however, was that the workshops became political events. Although a good deal of time was spent in ongoing encounter groups and special-interest groups, regularly scheduled "community meetings" were also held. In these meetings the staff and participants came to experience a closeness and sense of community that was as powerful as it was unique in their experience. The sixty-five or so "community members" often were able to operate with the same intensity and openness as that which is more typically experienced in a small encounter group. The group handled its community "business" in these large meetings, but also was able to deal with very personal issues in a supportive way. All this was not achieved at once, but as it evolved, Rogers and the staff re-experienced the potency of the client-centered philosophy. Here the same principles of congruence, positive regard (including caring and trust), and empathy were operating in a large and diverse community of people. Whereas before, Rogers had only speculated about the broader, social applications of the client-centered approach, now he and his colleagues were actually experiencing such an instance.[114]

The Santa Cruz workshop also had many "social radicals and revolutionaries," as Rogers recalled. "It was one of the things which got me focused more on politics.

It had a big influence on people like that, because I think the revolutionary people often are quite blind to the personal factors. The workshop helped to educate the squares like me and the fanatics like them."[115]

The staff's excitement about the process and the sense of community that they saw reoccur in both workshops in 1974 prompted them to schedule another workshop of the same type, at Mills College in California, in the summer of 1975.[116] Carl and Natalie Rogers and John K. Wood continued on the staff, and new staff members Joanne Justyn (who had been business manager the year before), Maureen Miller (O'Hara), Jared Kass, Maria Bowen, David Aspy, and Dick and Marian Vittitow joined their ranks. For the first time the phrase "Person-Centered" replaced "Client-Centered" in the workshop title, which also contained an explicitly socio-political theme: "A Person-Centered Approach: The Process of Individual Growth and Its Social Implications." Building on their experience of the previous summer, the staff decided to offer less structure and leave more of the decisions about the workshop to the entire group, which included 126 participants. With social justice in mind they allowed participants to set their own tuition fees commensurate with their income levels. Whereas in the previous workshops the staff had set up a regular schedule for community meetings and encounter groups, and time for special-interest groups, this summer they set the structure for the first few days only and, even then, left many hours of those days open for participants to spend as they wished. Other than some brief introductions the first evening, none of the community meetings were structured by the staff.

In the absence of any kind of typical, large-group leadership direction, the participants, whether they liked it or not, had to take charge of their own workshop experience. For many it was enormously frustrating. The staff, especially Rogers, received a great deal of resentment and anger for not fulfilling their role, for being "irresponsible," for being irrelevant to the pain and suffering experienced by people in many of the countries from which the participants came. "One young woman cried because of the great deal of personal sacrifice she and her sponsoring organization had made to send her to this workshop, and she wondered how she could return home and tell everyone that she really hadn't learned anything."[117] Some participants tried to give leadership to the group, suggesting schedules to follow, offering topics for group consideration, or stating needs they hoped the group would respond to. Sometimes these attempts at directing the community's progress were successful, other times not. Rogers was particularly impressed at how the community chose to reject a small group's beautifully worked out method for having large groups, small groups, interest groups and so on, in favor of using a more intuitive method of scheduling their time. They were saying, in effect, "Back home, we always live by schedules. We know how to do that. Why don't we see if we can be together, without a schedule, and still somehow meet the needs of individuals." Sure enough, at pivotal times, the whole community would somehow come together in the meeting room,

443

even though no one had formally announced the meeting. Midway into the sixteen-day experience the feeling of a supportive, egalitarian community was present and, with peaks and valleys, the workshop continued to be a powerful learning experience for staff and participants alike.

For Rogers, experimenting with a new workshop format like this was a bigger risk than he might have realized at first. At one point in the workshop, the morning after a very positive evening session, ironically he was feeling depressed. In the large group meeting he was overcome by his feelings and wept. Later he analyzed his reaction. "I cannot deny that I have had a definitely significant part in initiating the trend toward a person-centered approach to many facets of living. Many, many people are moving in this direction. That is satisfying, of course, but it also constitutes a great burden of responsibility. How do *I* know that this direction is sound? Every movement and trend in history has its flaws and contradictions which tend to bring about its downfall. What are the flaws that I am too stupid to see? To what degree am I *misleading* people through my ideas and my writings? There is absolutely no one to say, and I was feeling the burden of being out in front.

"Writing this later, I also see the reason why the down feelings hit me at just this time. The whole process of the community, as exemplified in the meeting the night before, was pushing me into unknown areas. I had helped start a trend that now had a life of its own and was taking me I knew not where. We were 'getting better at whatever the hell we're doing.' I explored this burdened feeling tearfully with the group—I weep easily—felt guilty at taking so much of their time (just like every other participant) and was temporarily relieved. It was only later in the day that I realized the burden had completely dropped away, and I again had the courage to move with the flow."[118]

By 1976, at Southern Oregon State College in Ashland, Oregon, with 130 participants, the workshop title had become "The Person-Centered Approach: Individual Change and Its Social Implications." In 1977, with 100 participants, the workshop was held on the East Coast, at the National Humanistic Education Center's Sagamore Conference Center in Raquette Lake, New York. In between the Oregon and New York workshops, Rogers and several of the staff also conducted one long and several shorter workshops in Brazil. These included three two-day workshops—in Recife, Sao Paulo, and Rio de Janeiro—attended by some 600 to 800 people each.

On each of these occasions, in Oregon, Brazil, and New York, the staff moved further and further in the direction of giving total responsibility for the workshop to the entire group. They set less and less structure; so that by the New York workshop in 1977 all they did was announce the first community meeting at which time they introduced themselves personally to the group. They did not even suggest the possibility that encounter groups or interest groups or community meetings might be a part of the workshop. All that eventually did occur, but it came from the members' initiation, not from the staff. At one point the chaos in the community seemed so great and group decisions so difficult to reach, that even Rogers doubted the wisdom of the staff's decision about trusting the community so totally with the direction of the workshop. "Either I had helped launch an incredibly stupid experiment doomed to failure, or I had helped to innovate a whole new way of permitting ... people to sense their own potentialities and to participate in forming their own learning experience."[119]

As it turned out, the results were always the same—even with 800 people in a foreign culture and speaking a language different from most of the staff's (in Brazil a translator sat in the group next to each staff member who did not speak Portuguese). The groups *did* find a direction. The participants learned to listen to one another. The workshops allowed diversity, yet experienced a powerful sense of community. And the experience seemed to have important political implications which were always close to the surface of the group's consciousness and were at times verbalized explicitly by community members.

In Brazil the political implications of the person-centered approach were particularly apparent. As Rogers said, "We were there at the right time, in the right country, with the right approach that they were very hungry for. I think it is because democracy there is a real issue and to talk about individual freedom, self-actualization, and that kind of thing, is just what people are dying to hear in a country that they fear may continue totalitarian. Secret police were in at least one of our meetings."[120] Issues of authority, decision-making processes, the use of power, balancing the needs of the individual and the group, dealing with members who were "different," and so on all were experienced by participants in very personal ways. Many connections were made between how the community resolved these issues in the workshop and how they are typically dealt with in the outside world.

Rogers came to believe more and more strongly in the importance of this new application of the person-centered approach. He and different configurations of colleagues continued to offer such workshops for several more years. Although each workshop was different, with different themes, different audiences and even different cultures, the experience of community building was replicated again and again. At the beginning of a workshop, one participant after another, without much initial success, would try to get the group to participate in a particular activity, urge the community to adopt a new focus or format, ask for help on personal or professional issues, and ask—in fact, frequently demand—that the staff, particularly Rogers, play a more active role. This period of jockeying about, attempting to establish group purposes, leadership and ways of working and being together would often go on for days. It produced enormous frustration, anger, and cognitive dissonance. "I came here to get something from Carl Rogers"; "People are getting hurt by others in this community and the staff is doing nothing to intervene"; "All my professional life I have believed in and used the client-centered approach. If this is what that means, then I think I have been making a great mistake." Yet the leadership vacuum also produced great excitement, meaningful encounters and deep personal learnings for many or most of the participants (as determined by participant self-reports in follow-up evaluations). Eventually, the large group found its collective voice and developed a way of working, which often involved establishing a time structure that included encounter groups, special interest groups, demonstrations and the like. As the group began to take more responsibility for its own direction, then Rogers and the staff felt comfortable sharing more of themselves as persons and professionals without having to worry that they would be taking the leadership back from the group.

Was all the *sturm und drang* worth it? Were all the hours and days of anguishing power struggles and soul searching necessary for participants to really understand the person-centered approach? The staff seemed to think so, believing that the political implications of the person-centered community experiences were critically important. Here were groups of sometimes several hundred individuals from different backgrounds, often different countries, demonstrating and experiencing the proposition that they could be trusted to organize their own living and learning structures. In one large group, an Israeli and a Palestinian participant had an incredibly powerful encounter, moving from deep anger and stereotyping to considerable understanding. In others there were similar, important rapprochements between blacks and whites, middle class and working class, different nationalities, and sub-groups of all sorts, including the ones who wanted to have free time in the early afternoon and the ones who wanted to have it in the late afternoon and who had been fighting for supremacy as though their lives depended on it. In all these situations, almost invariably, the community worked it out, and by working through their conflicts, without rules and structures imposed from above, they developed a real sense of community, humanity and affection which included a healthy respect for one another's differences. To Rogers and the staff, this was a powerful metaphor and model which needed to be demonstrated as widely as possible. Democracy, real democracy, works! For them, the open-ended, person-centered community became the epitome of learning structures and the logical extension of the person-centered approach.

Some of his colleagues saw the unfolding of the person-centered community in almost mystical terms. As Maureen (Miller) O'Hara wrote, "It is as if the group consciousness becomes tuned to the consciousness of the individuals who give it existence. At the same time, the individuals align themselves and their activities to the music of the whole … In these moments it does not matter whether one speaks of someone's individual reality or of the group's reality, because at these moments they are identical."[121] For Rogers, it was the practical and political implications of the person-centered community that were most important.

In addition to two more person-centered workshops offered by the same core group—at Nottingham University, England in 1978 and Princeton

University in 1979—dozens of person-centered workshops were conducted around the United States and abroad by Rogers, CSP colleagues, and other projects that had a relationship with Rogers and CSP, such as the Center for Interpersonal Growth in New York and the Center for Cross-Cultural Communication in Europe, which will be described later. Counselor educator Ruth Sanford was associated with the former Center. She recruited Rogers, four participants from the 1977 Sagamore workshop, and others to do a person-centered workshop the next year at the C.W. Post College Campus of Long Island University. They then joined with the newly formed Center for Interpersonal Growth, which continued to conduct person-centered workshops and other programs, with Rogers flying in to be on the staff each year from 1978–1984. He was listed as a "consultant" to the Center on their brochure.[122]

Yet for all their potency, the strictly community-centered, person-centered workshops did not catch on to any major degree. For one thing, they tended to be long, residential workshops, which logistically were difficult and expensive to organize or attend. Second, they were enormously risky. What workshop leader or sponsoring organization wants to continually risk a revolt of frustrated and angry participants, especially a large group of them? Even Rogers suffered from the risk level of person-centered workshops. During the 1977 Sagamore workshop, while the community remained in chaos and seemed as though it would never come together, he wrote in his journal, "Last night and this morning I hit the lowest point. Really wasn't sure we'd make it this time." The next afternoon was even worse: "Went to cottage, couple drinks, nap, then felt lower than I ever felt in workshop ... Perhaps the major hypothesis of my life will be disproven in this workshop." And two days later: "... more and more pain, frustration, confusion, doubt. Always feel my deepest convictions and hypothesis are on the line. Awful."[123] Rogers always felt vulnerable on this point. The person-centered hypothesis, that people could be trusted to take responsibility and thrive in a person-centered relationship, was always subject to be disproved with any new client, small group or, now, large workshop. Hence for Rogers, perhaps more than most workshop leaders, this was a highly risky undertaking in which he was tense and anxious for several days until the community finally began to come together.

Third, Rogers and his staff conducted virtually no research on the process or outcomes of the workshops. Years earlier Rogers would not dream of ending a group like this without a fairly careful questionnaire to the participants, or a follow-up questionnaire. Now he often seemed satisfied if several participants wrote him letters afterward saying how meaningful the experience was to them. David Cain, who attended the Sagamore workshop in 1977 and followed the approach over the years, recalled, "I honestly didn't believe that [the person-centered community workshops] allowed for people to have a voice of their own. Twenty percent of the people dominated eighty percent of the time, and a few voices were rarely if ever heard ... I felt the large group experience had too much power to be damaging, too much power for people to fight over air time. I thought in many ways it brought out the worst in people … All the maneuvering and all the days and hours it took just to get from large group to small group, and then people were accused of trying to number themselves off to get in Carl's small group … The community ended with closeness, discord, frustration and incompleteness."[124] How typical or accurate was this description?[125] No one knew; the data was not collected. Without more solid evidence regarding process and outcomes, it was unlikely this risky and volatile workshop format would catch on.

At the same time, while critical of the workshop format, Cain was "enormously impressed with Rogers' patience and presence. In a group of 100, the seventy-five-year-old man turned in the direction of each speaker and gave that person his complete attention the entire time that person spoke. And I realized that there was something extraordinary about Carl, and it was his capacity to focus and concentrate … far in excess of anybody that I had ever known or have ever known to this day. I just don't know how he could sit so patiently and genuinely attend to each person whether he spoke to that person or not, and ninety percent of the time he did not utter a word. But you were fully aware that when a person spoke, he may have had the divided attention of ninety-nine people but he had the full attention, each moment, of Carl Rogers."[126]

Maureen O'Hara also recognized that "The absence of a clear research agenda was a real problem for us. We had the experiences. We knew that something significant was happening but there was very little systematic attempt to codify what we were learning and to put it up against any kind of inquiry beyond living through the experience … I once said to him, 'Carl, you need to establish a research agenda around this work because otherwise it's just something that people will experience and will have whatever individual transformation they have, but it doesn't contribute to society's repertoire of tools and approaches.' His answer was really clear and it was the same one he gave to many people which was, 'No, no, no. I've done my work; if you want to see that done Maureen, you do it.'"[127] But no one did. Most of those around Rogers were even less inclined toward systematic empirical research than he was.

In addition, it always seemed to me that using the minimally structured person-centered community as the main format for a large-group workshop was a model that few facilitators could pull off. Not because they weren't skillful, but because they weren't Carl Rogers. For many or most participants in these workshops, a primary goal was to see, hear and experience Carl Rogers. That they did. They got to see him operate in the large-group meeting, as David Cain described; they sat a few feet away as he conducted a demonstration therapy session; they heard him speak of his latest interests and got to ask him questions; and maybe they got to be in his small encounter group or sit next to him at breakfast or dinner. Whatever they thought of the rest of the experience, encountering Rogers was inevitably a high point. Other workshop leaders, no matter how good they might be, did not have this advantage. Many participants would not give an "ordinary" workshop leader the benefit of the doubt before revolting or would not forgive the workshop leader for all the anguish of the experience. To Rogers, on the other hand—this seventy-five-year-old man, who was so sincere, so accepting, so impressive and inspiring—they *would* give the benefit of the doubt and stick with the experience. They would forgive him for whatever agony they endured and count themselves fortunate for having had the experience, even if they did not go on to utilize the large-group, person-centered workshop or community approach in their own work.

For all these reasons, after a number of years Rogers, the La Jolla group and the Long Island group all virtually abandoned the pure, person-centered community workshop model; although some of the CSP staffers in their own projects continued to use it on occasion, and various person-centered organizations continue to use the community-centered meeting format as an important part of their annual conferences and meetings.[128] Rogers, in spite of his infatuation with the approach, eventually recognized that this extreme model of group-centeredness was not necessarily the most productive way of conducting large workshops. As Valerie Henderson said, "Carl began to question its efficacy. It began to seem like a kind of tyranny [her word]. The absence of the structure became a structure in itself. It's still a problem—people thinking that the lack of structure is the only way to be person-centered. He wouldn't say that was the wrong way to go. But he had a lot of questions about it. It was experimental."[129]

So for Rogers, the unstructured person-centered community became one valuable model, but not the only one. There was a continuum of choices as to how much structure to introduce in a person-centered learning experience. Approaching his eighties, Rogers came to prefer a modus operandi that was a little less volatile and that allowed him to share more of himself with groups. He developed a way of working which served him well throughout the rest of his life. He still occasionally delivered formal presentations at conferences and sat on professional panels; but where possible, he much preferred a workshop format that was more typical of the initial person-centered workshops—an eclectic combination of presentations, demonstrations, whole-group interaction and, where feasible, small group encounters.

He typically conducted such workshops with one co-leader, although he occasionally joined the staff of a larger program someone else had organized. Whether the workshop topic was "An Introduction to the Person-Centered Approach," a favorite, or "Transitions" or "Education for the 80s and Beyond" or some other focus, the same basic elements tended to be present. Participants got to hear Rogers discussing the client-centered/person-centered approach to helping relationships; they watched him conduct a live, unrehearsed therapeutic interview with a member of the audience; they experienced a bit of student-centered teaching or an encounter group in the way Rogers and his co-leader facilitated the discussion period, they heard about and perhaps experienced something of Rogers' latest interests (increasingly his work in applying the person-centered approach to intergroup and international problems); and perhaps they experienced one or more person-centered community meetings. As leader, Rogers gently offered or suggested these options to the group, and the group readily agreed.

On Personal Power

As might be expected, Rogers did not wait long before communicating to others his deepening appreciation of the political and social implications of the person-centered approach. Early in 1977, at the height of his involvement in and excitement about the person-centered community workshops, Delacorte Press published Rogers' fourteenth book, entitled *Carl Rogers On Personal Power: Inner Strength and Its Revolutionary Impact.*[130]

In the first chapter of the book, "The Politics of the Helping Professions," he described the person-centered approach and the therapeutic setting out of which it originated. Although Rogers and his colleagues had been using the term "person-centered" in their workshop titles since 1975, it was in this chapter that he first explicitly used and explained the phrase that would come to characterize his life's work. From that time on, "person-centered" replaced "client-centered" as the umbrella term for his overall approach to helping and human relationships, and for many, "person-centered counseling" and "person-centered therapy" also became the terms of choice to describe this particular approach to counseling and psychotherapy.

Then he launched immediately into exploring the various applications of the person-centered approach, all evaluated from a political perspective. In each chapter, he used case studies—sometimes short examples, sometimes studies as long as thirty pages—to help his ideas come alive. One chapter described "the new family" and its attempts to move away from parent-centered power and put more control in the hands of the entire family, with many decisions reached through the honest sharing of feelings, good communication, and group consensus. Another two chapters explored "the revolution in marriage and partnership." Here Rogers interpreted the new interpersonal politics between men and women fostered by the women's liberation movement. What distinguished his discussion from that in *Becoming Partners* was his greater focus on issues related to power, control, and decision-making in intimate relationships. Other chapters explored the political implications of the person-centered approach when applied to education, administration, intercultural tensions, and working with oppressed groups. In the latter area he discussed at length the similarities he saw between his own work and that of Paulo Freire, whose book *Pedagogy of the Oppressed* described how Freire had sought to help illiterate Brazilian peasants find their own power and identity and take increased control over their lives.[131] He used a case study of his and his colleagues' work facilitating communication between black and Hispanic health "consumers" and government, industry and non-profit health care "providers" as an example of how a person-centered approach can empower the powerless and lead to productive change.

In the section on administration Rogers explored his ideas on leadership and management to a greater extent than he had previously. Since his years at Chicago, with Thomas Gordon's chapter on group-centered leadership in *Client-Centered Therapy* and Rogers' *Harvard Business Review* article on listening and communication, Rogers' name and some of his ideas were known to many in the field of management.[132] These works preceded Douglas McGregor's influential book on *The Human Side of Enterprise* which mirrored Rogers' evolving thinking about the benefits of a management style that relied on employee self-direction and integration of employee and company goals (McGregor's "Theory Y") versus more directive and controlling management based on authority ("Theory X").[133] McGregor, drawing on only management literature, did not cite Rogers, nor did Rogers later cite McGregor. It wasn't until his work with encounter groups in the sixties brought Rogers into frequent contact with managers and administrators that he further developed his thinking about organizational leadership. The crisis at WBSI, when it appeared that the organization was moving from a Theory Y to Theory X style of leadership and Rogers and his colleagues split off to form Center for Studies of the Person, stimulated Rogers to think even more about leadership and power. Shortly thereafter, working with a National Training Laboratories' "President's Lab" in 1969, Rogers lectured the top executives on the distinction between "influence and impact" versus "power and control." He also shared his own philosophy about leadership and power:

> I want very much to have influence and impact, but I have rarely desired to, nor known how to, exercise control or power. My *influence* has always been *increased* when I have given away my *power* or *authority*. By refusing to coerce or direct, I think I have stimulated learning, creativity, and self-direction. These are some of the products in which I am most interested. I have found my greatest reward in being able to say "I made it possible for this person to be and achieve something he could not have been nor achieved before." In short I gain a great deal of satisfaction in being a facilitator of becoming. By encouraging a person's ability to evaluate himself, I have stimulated autonomy, self-responsibility, and maturity. By freeing a person to "do his thing," I have enriched his life and learning, and my own as well …"[134]

A colleague at Center for Studies of the Person commented of Rogers, "It's a paradox. He's out there and he's powerful and he wants attention and he likes to be seen, but he somehow likes to be in the shadow, too, and not be held in

451

awe."[135] Rogers appreciated this paradox to some extent, often quoting Lao Tse's famous dictum: "With the best of leaders, When the work is done, The task is accomplished, The people all say 'We did it ourselves.'"[136]

So by the time *On Personal Power* was published, Rogers already had exercised considerable influence in the world of business and industry. Richard Farson wrote, "His ideas are the main ones used to support efforts toward democratic or participative management in industry. There has probably not been a single organizational development or management training program in twenty-five years which has not been built on his theoretical foundations."[137] With a little less hyperbole, Robert Kramer made a similar point, describing, "Carl Rogers, a pioneer in the applied behavioral sciences who did as much as anyone else to influence the current generation of thinking about people in organizations. Even though managers may not recognize Rogers by name, his spiritual presence hovers over the entire field of organizational behavior and development (OBD). Almost every introductory textbook in OBD heralds active listening or some variant of Rogers's nondirective, or client-centered, approach, as a prerequisite for employee empowerment, team building, or humanistic management."[138] In *On Personal Power*, Rogers pulled his ideas on organizational administration together. He described the benefits of distributing power to team members and employees and provided research, case study and anecdotal evidence from the literature, contemporary practice, and his own experience to support his person-centered approach to administration.

The next major section on the "person-centered approach in action" provided some lengthy case studies to help illustrate his thesis and widen it to other areas. In one chapter he described the 1975 Person-Centered Workshop, explaining in great detail how fees were set, how participants were selected, how room assignments were made and how each aspect of the workshop was handled so as to empower the participants. In another chapter he quoted Alan Nelson describing his experience as director of a children's camp in which he facilitated shared responsibility among the campers and how the "powerless" campers discovered their own power when the facilitative camp climate was interrupted after Nelson was fired. Another chapter described a couple trying to work out the issues of power and jealousy in their relationship.

The next section had a single chapter intended to offer a theoretical base for the person-centered approach. This was the "actualizing tendency," a concept which Rogers had used in *Client-Centered Therapy* in 1951 to explain the human being's tendency to actualize its potential.[139] In this chapter he discussed the concept in greater detail than ever before. In a long, poetic paragraph he described the tiny, palm-like plants he recently saw on the California coastline struggling to survive and grow under extremely adverse conditions. "Here," he wrote, "in this palm-like seaweed, was the tenacity of life, the forward thrust of life, the ability to push into an incredibly hostile environment and not only hold its own but to adapt, develop, become itself."[140] He suggested that this tendency in human beings "toward fulfillment, toward actualization, not only toward the maintenance but also toward the enhancement of the organism" was a trustworthy base to operate from politically. Although he did not explore the implications of the actualizing tendency for politics and power more specifically in this chapter, in the next and final section of the book he again described the "emerging person," his former "person of tomorrow," who would "spearhead the quiet revolution" which Rogers saw coming—indeed, which he saw occurring.[141] He called this person "a new political figure," and described how emerging persons, that is, individuals who are seeking to actualize themselves in the fullest sense, will be individuals who will resist rules for rules' sake, will resist social and political impediments to their reaching their potential (as in the women's movement), and will resist external attempts to control them. Rather they will demand authenticity in their leaders and work for freedom, civil liberties and self-determination in their organizational and governmental structures.

As an example of such a new political figure, Rogers described one of the political projects of California legislator John Vasconcellos, a man who played a very important role in Rogers' life and work in his later years.[142] Vasconcellos, who ended a 38-year career in the state legislature in 2004, was for many years arguably the second most powerful member of the California legislature, setting public policy for 25 million Californians. As chair of its Ways and Means Committee, he oversaw the sixth largest budget in the world. Trained to be a Catholic priest, Vasconcellos had moved into politics but early in his political life experienced great value conflicts, self-doubt and psychological distress. He credited client-centered therapist Leo Rock with literally saving his life. This led him to read widely and deeply in humanistic psychology and to take a series of weekend workshops at Esalen, in one of which he met Carl Rogers in 1970. Vasconcellos became Rogers' political coach and Rogers' became Vasconcellos' life coach.[143] They maintained a close personal and professional/political relationship for seventeen years until Rogers' death.

Vasconcellos often spoke of Rogers' profound effect on his life and career, especially how he attempted to apply various principles he learned from Rogers—particularly authenticity, listening and trust—in his political work, usually with excellent results. Personally he found Rogers to be an inspiring role model and a cherished friend. In a newsletter to his constituents, Vasconcellos said, "... much of my recent legislation (concerning peace, self-esteem, birthing, parenting, crisis control and conflict resolution) demonstrates Carl's influence on my professional and personal life."[144] Rogers, in turn, often mentioned Vasconcellos' innovative projects in his speeches and writings, such as Vasconcellos' legislation supporting self-esteem promotion in California's schools or, as in *On Personal Power*, his Self-Determination Network. Vasconcellos assisted Rogers on many projects, such as the Carl Rogers Peace Project to be described later; but more importantly he confirmed and extended Rogers' understanding of and belief in the explicitly political applications of the person-centered approach.

One of the first reviewers for *Carl Rogers On Personal Power* was David Rogers, who liked the book but thought his father's tone a bit too evangelistic. Rogers answered him, "I think it is quite possibly true that I am becoming more 'hard sell.' I don't particularly like that and am not quite sure why I do it. In talking it over with John Wood the other day, he said that perhaps it was because I was getting older and felt there was little time left to get a message across. That isn't a conscious motive, but it might have something to do with it … Anyway, your reactions are always thoughtful and useful to me. Please continue to send them and I'll continue to do the same in regard to things you send me."[145]

The reception for *Carl Rogers On Personal Power* beyond the family was typical of many of Rogers' books. Initially, to Rogers' puzzlement, it was "utterly ignored by reviewers in every newspaper and journal."[146] Eventually a few reviews appeared and these were mixed. The *Library Journal* found it "insightful and compassionate … Both the well-read humanist and the newcomer will find this book most interesting and thoroughly refreshing."[147] *Contemporary Psychology's* reviewer, on the other hand, thought the book did "not really break new theoretical ground," had an "inspirational rather than systematic mode of presentation" and was unrealistic insofar as "international disputes are regarded as resulting from misunderstandings and feuds, and therefore resolvable through interpersonal techniques aimed at increasing mutual appreciation of the persons involved." Since Rogers seemed to regard all social institutions as stifling, the reviewer asserted, "Politically speaking, the actualization position is clearly anarchistic."[148]

Although the book sold reasonably well—24,000 copies within six months of publication—it did not sell as well as his other recent works. Rogers was puzzled about this and speculated about what he regarded as its lukewarm reception. "1. Perhaps the book fails to get across the fact that what is being presented is a completely different philosophy of power which turns upside down all the major institutions of our culture. I thought I was saying this clearly but perhaps not. 2. Perhaps people feel there is nothing new in the book, since it covers fields I have covered before. Perhaps the shift to a new *perspective* on those fields is not noticeable enough. I think this is close to the attitude of the man who is writing my biography … 3. Perhaps the book is not understood because it is ahead of its time and basically too threatening."[149] Given these wonders, Rogers must have been pleased with the review that appeared a few months later in the respected journal *Teachers College Record*.[150] While still critical of some aspects of the book, the reviewers clearly appreciated what Rogers was trying to accomplish. They wrote:

Criticisms of humanistic psychology and education appear with increasing frequency. Marin repudiates the humanistic perspective as the "new narcissism," as a movement that encourages a selfish "turning inward," that "smothers social conscience." Schur condemns the human potential movement for being too "self-indulgent," preoccupied with "individual ecstasy" rather than being attentive to hard "political realities." Jacoby inveighs against humanistic psychology because it is "unintellectual," "repressive," and "conformist." Kozol criticizes humanistic open classrooms as designed to "quiet controversy, contain rebellion, and channel inquiry into accepted avenues of discreet moderation …"

... what makes the book especially important is Rogers's attempt to recast his seminal clinical contributions in a new, political mold, thereby responding at least inferentially to the political critiques of humanism. For the first time in print, Rogers has enlarged his system to include an explicit political, even activist dimension. Taken in its totality, the book is not so much a late-life summary of his main ideas as it is an impassioned reaffirmation of his person-centered philosophy set within a political context … this is Rogers's first major attempt in print to confront the charge that he is excessively naïve in his political views, that he is overly preoccupied with individual psyches in small group settings, and that he is oblivious to the exploitation of oppressed peoples around the world … In many ways, the book can be read as a moving vindication of humanistic theory and practice, even though this was not the author's intent in writing it."[151]

Having said that, the reviewers went on to say that Rogers *was* politically naïve in his "tenacious bias toward small-group dynamics as the best methodology of resolving *all* conflicts"; in his "unwavering, often unexamined, faith that the appropriation of individual psychological power will transfer *ipso facto* to a seizing of political power from the authoritarian professional and the dictatorial social or political leader"; and in how he "oversimplifies the concept of power" and fails "to differentiate between power as individual psychological capacity and power as collective activity toward social change." They thought that Rogers missed a key distinction between his own work and Paulo Freire's. "The major difference between the two men is that Rogers leaves the individual at the point of psychological empowerment; Freire helps the individual to translate psychological empowerment to concrete political activity that will ensure further personal liberation … Rogers concentrates on the personal *meaning* of power and reform; activists like Kozol and Freire are concerned with advancing the *political* content of power in order to galvanize collective action toward social change. Each approach is correct and necessary, although seriously incomplete without the other."[152]

It was not unusual for Rogers to be criticized for oversimplifying about organizational, political, and social change. I agreed with the reviewers who said that *On Personal Power* suffered from this shortcoming, for in departing further than ever from the "laboratories of interpersonal relations" he knew the best[153]—

therapy, education, and the intensive group—his writing, I think, sometimes lacked the broad and accurate perspective present in most of his other works. Yet I came to appreciate this book more over the years, as I better understood its importance in the trajectory of Rogers' life's work. In many ways, the book was Rogers' most complete statement of his philosophy. The person-centered approach was not simply an approach to therapy or teaching or group work or other particular relationships, but an approach to all human relationships, be they helping relationships, personal relationships or political relationships. While he may not have presented his ideas as effectively or persuasively as usual, nevertheless the ideas were important and carried his previous work to another level. The book put the client-centered/person-centered approach to helping and human relationships in a social and political context. This had always been present, beneath the surface, but was rarely made explicit in Rogers' previous writings and, even then, not fully explored. Now Rogers was thinking seriously about the implications of the person-centered approach for the social and political order. Thus the *Teachers College Record* review asserted, "*On Personal Power* is, in many ways, Rogers's most expansive and impressive work."[154]

As usual with Rogers, however, the strength of the book was not only in whatever theoretical viewpoint it might offer, but in the personal way Rogers reached the reader through examples, case studies, and his own personal and professional experiences. As one of the reviewers quoted above said, pejoratively, the book *was* inspirational. That was one reason people read Rogers—not only to gain professional ideas but to be encouraged to be hopeful and person-centered in their life and work. Therefore it was apt that the *Record* reviewers, after several pages of criticism in their balanced review, ended in their own personal and inspirational way.

> Our own attraction to Rogers's ideas is based on our first-hand contact with him; in many ways he has changed our lives significantly. Like thousands of human-service professionals throughout the world, we have read and learned from his writings on client-centered therapy and teaching as facilitation; we have ourselves led process groups for many years; and we are striving to become humanistic, person-oriented counselors and teachers. Obviously, something in this man's world view, in this man's helping style, has touched us and others deeply. We feel that in spite of its weaknesses, some of which it will be easy for critics to overdraw, Rogers's latest book clarifies once and for all for us why his system, and why the humanistic movement in general, has such widespread appeal. We quote Rogers: "I think the ideals of democracy are still pretty revolutionary. To me, a person-centered approach is the embodiment of these ideals in the immediacy of human relationships. It cannot be reduced to a strategy or a technique. It is an attitude embodying respect for the integrity and worth of persons; it is a way of seeing and relating to the world and others. It is a way of

being either lived in the present or denied, for person-centered politics is as immediate as people and relationships. A person-centered approach provides a perspective from which it can be clearly seen that democratic traditions and values are neither preserved nor fostered by authoritarian systems." Truly, Carl Rogers is still a teacher for our times.[155]

Decades later the counseling and psychotherapy professions would begin to focus on the role of the counselor and therapist in multi-cultural contexts and promote the roles of advocate, consultant and systems change agent as legitimate functions of the helping professional. Although Rogers would not necessarily agree with all aspects of this trend, particularly if it meant urging or coaching the client to take action or taking responsibility for the client, it can be argued that he anticipated by some years the field's recognition that one's approach to therapy and education has definite social and political implications, and that all helping and other relationships take place in a political and social context. It is ironic that the person-centered approach is sometimes criticized for being apolitical when Rogers was one of the first to spell out the politics of his approach.[156]

On Personal Power also anticipated Rogers' own future work. By focusing intensively on the social and political implications of the person-centered approach, Rogers became increasingly interested in exploring the implications of his widening theory for widening practice. Having begun with individual therapy and then moved to group work, education, and person-centered communities, he was now interested in applying the person-centered approach to even wider cultural and political contexts. Thus, as we shall see, he became increasingly involved in international, cross-cultural work and in international tension-reduction and peacemaking efforts.

Personal Relationships

In his essay "Growing Old: Or Older and Growing," seventy-five-year-old Carl Rogers described the previous ten years as "the most satisfying decade of my life."[157] This is a puzzling statement, given the tensions described earlier in his relationship with Helen and given other health problems that will be described later. Yet there were other factors that would have contributed to Rogers' satisfaction at this stage of his life. Certainly one factor was his considerable productivity, including five books, his leadership in the fields of encounter groups and education, and the beginnings of his work on the political implications of the person-centered approach. But much of his satisfaction derived from more personal reasons—close collegial relationships, a growing closeness to his children and grandchildren, and deepening friendships with men and women—in short, intimacy.

457

As we saw earlier, Carl and Helen's relationships with their children and grandchildren had become increasingly open and close, including cleaning up some old hurts and unfinished business from their earlier years as a family, supporting David and Natalie through difficulties in their marriages, and sharing in the grandchildren's growth and struggles over identity, sexuality and careers. Rogers wrote of the joy he and Helen felt over their children being "two of our best and closest friends, with whom we share our inner lives."[158]

He also wrote in the late 1970s, "In the past few years I have found myself opening up to much greater intimacy in relationships. I see this development as definitely the result of workshop experiences. I am more ready to touch and be touched, physically. I do more hugging and kissing of both men and women. I am more aware of the sensuous side of my life. I also realize how much I desire close psychological contact with others. I recognize how much I need to care deeply for another and to receive that kind of caring in return. I can say openly what I have always recognized dimly: that my deep involvement in psychotherapy was a cautious way of meeting this need for intimacy without risking too much of my person. Now I am more willing to be close in other relationships and to risk giving more of myself. I feel as though a whole new depth of capacity for intimacy has been discovered in me. It is a capacity which has brought me much hurt, and an even greater share of joy.

"How have these changes affected my behavior? I have developed deeper and more intimate relationships with men; I have been able to share without holding back, trusting the security of the friendship. Only during my college days—never before or after—did I have a group of really trusted, intimate men friends. So this is a new, tentative, adventurous development which seems very rewarding. I have also had much more intimate communication with women. There are now a number of women with whom I have platonic but psychologically intimate relationships which have tremendous meaning for me. With these close friends, men and women, I can share any aspect of my self—the painful, joyful, frightening, crazy, insecure, egotistical, self-deprecating feelings I have. I can share fantasies and dreams. Similarly, my friends share deeply with me. These experiences I find very enriching." [159]

All this was true—except for the word "platonic." Beginning in 1975, for the first time in fifty-one years of marriage, the seventy-three-year-old Rogers became interested in other women. Not that he didn't always appreciate beauty and enjoy the company of women, but all evidence suggests that he had been monogamous for over half a century. What changed? Why now?

First, it was the 1970s. Here was a decade in which young people, and some older ones, were rejecting traditional moral restrictions and, as Rogers eloquently described in his book *Becoming Partners*, experimenting with various forms of new relationships. Open marriage was being justified widely as an egalitarian route to growth and intimacy in human relationships. This was especially true in Rogers' California milieu. Sexual and relationship experimentation were in the air, and as *Becoming Partners* demonstrated, Rogers was open to it all, at least intellectually.

Second, for twelve years Rogers had been intensely involved with encounter groups—a highly charged, emotional setting pregnant with possibilities for sexual intimacy. As Rogers had written in 1969, "in mixed intensive workshops positive and warm, loving feelings frequently develop between members of the encounter group and, naturally enough, these feelings sometimes occur between men and women. Inevitably, some of these feelings have a sexual component and this can be a matter of great concern to the participants and—if the feelings are not worked through—a profound threat to their spouses."[160] This aspect of encounter groups was equally if not more true for the person-centered workshops Rogers was now engaged in, where the larger number of participants and facilitators and the longer time frames provided more opportunities for relationships to develop. While certainly no Hollywood idol, apparently many women seemed to find Rogers attractive. Perhaps it was the aura about him; perhaps they were seeking a father figure, or perhaps they just found him cuddlingly, endearingly attractive. His colleague Maureen O'Hara recalled how "women really did come on to him pretty blatantly" in workshop settings—women from their mid-thirties on.[161]

Third, his and Helen's own sexual relationship had virtually ended. In 1979, he wrote in his diary that he and Helen had had "nearly 10 years of no sex."[162] Yet his libido was still strong. He wanted to resume their sexual relationship, but she did not. He did not want to go outside his marriage, but his desires were frustrated within it. Even so, he might have waited until Helen died, a prospect that seemed relatively imminent as her health continued to fail. But there was one additional factor that gave Rogers a particular sense of urgency about experiencing other relationships. As he described it at age seventy-five, "The female form still seems to me one of the loveliest creations of the universe and I appreciate it greatly. I feel as sexy in my *interests* as I was at thirty-five, though I can't say the same about my ability to perform. I am delighted that I am still sexually alive, even though I can sympathize with the remark of Supreme Court Justice Oliver Wendell Holmes upon leaving a burlesque house at age eighty: 'Oh to be seventy again!'"[163]

This was an honest and endearing revelation, though not specific. In fact Rogers was experiencing what today would be termed erectile dysfunction—an increasing difficulty in getting and maintaining an erection and having an orgasm.[164] As he wrote in one diary entry, "I begin to think I have only a few more orgasms left in my life."[165] Medication for this condition, now commonplace, had not yet been discovered. From his view life was passing him by. He became increasingly desperate to experience an intimate, exciting sexual relationship before it was too late.

So here was a man who relished and extolled new experience, personal growth and change. All around him people were experimenting with new forms of relationships. They were open about their sexuality. The counter-culture even provided philosophical and psychological justification for such relationships. Opportunities readily presented themselves. Yet he felt trapped at home, taking care of Helen, with whom he no longer had a sexual relationship and with whom he experienced diminishing intimacy. He wanted to break free and experience an important part of life he felt he was missing out on. Moreover, he felt he did not have much time left.

Given all these factors, it is a wonder that Rogers did not become involved in one or more relationships outside his marriage sooner than he did. But as free-thinking as he was intellectually, and unencumbered by any formal religion, he was still a product of Midwestern conservatism. He had been sexually involved with only one woman his entire life. He did not want to hurt her or jeopardize his marriage. He was an ethical workshop leader who had always avoided inappropriate relationships with his clients. As a famous psychologist he was doubly aware of how participants tended to put him on a pedestal and would therefore be even more vulnerable to exploitation. Moreover he was still basically a shy person and would be reluctant to make an overture to a woman. And even if he worked up the courage he would be concerned about what effect such activity might have on his reputation if it became public. Finally, he was still something of a Puritan, highly self-disciplined and not inclined to simply have fun.

The irony is that when he finally allowed himself to cross the line, he fell in love with a participant at one of the person-centered workshops with whom he carried on an unconsummated love affair for four years. They barely did more than kiss. She was in her thirties, married, lived in another part of the country, and resisted his attempts to have the relationship move beyond an essentially platonic level. He was like a moon-struck adolescent. It is painful to read his letters to her, filled as they are with pleading, demeaning, and embarrassing requests for more than she is willing to give.[166] She sent mixed messages—sometimes setting limits and creating distance, sometimes being caring, invitational, flirting. Clearly she was gaining a great deal from the relationship—his interesting company, the excitement of associating with a man of his stature, his excellent counseling and emotional support, and some not insignificant financial assistance. If he exercised any good sense, he would have realized this was an unhealthy relationship and ended it himself. But what did he know? He was a world authority on communication, but it was like he was dating for the first time. As he told his young colleague Maureen Miller (O'Hara), who had studied human sexuality, "You know sometimes I feel like despite the difference in our ages, I'm kind of like your teenage brother, and I'm trying to figure how to do all this stuff, and I am about as savvy as the average teenager would be. So if you don't mind, I would like to bounce off some thoughts about what are some of the feelings and stuff that I have been having, as I don't know how to interpret some of this." Then he would tell O'Hara about how a woman had spoken to him and looked at him and ask if this meant the woman was making a pass at him.[167]

It was a whole new experience and not confined only to the unrequited relationship just described. Rogers did have a few, more or less single, satisfying, sexual experiences in the few years before Helen's death. Probably this contributed to his describing the decade as "the most satisfying in my life." But it was not without its turmoil and conflict for him and, of course, for Helen. He might have just acted on his desires, done so discreetly, and spared Helen the additional pain of knowing about his feelings and then his activities. But that would not have been Carl Rogers. His whole professional and personal life had been built increasingly around the values of congruence and open, honest communication. His recent *Becoming Partners* heralded the importance of open, honest communication in marriage, of the importance of partners' taking the scary risk of sharing their inner truth with one another. Would his not doing so with Helen be anything less than hypocrisy?

And so he shared with Helen his attraction to women and his dilemma about whether and how to act on it. "You can imagine what it was like for her," recalled Valerie Henderson. "'My life is getting smaller and smaller and the one man I really love just wants to go out farther and farther.' He didn't do it in reaction to her."[168] He did it to meet his own needs, but naturally it hurt her. This led to arguments, which often involved her attacking and criticizing him and him clamming up and withdrawing. He wanted to problem solve; she wanted his fidelity, period.

Not only did Rogers share his feelings with Helen, but on several occasions he discussed his dilemma with workshop groups with whom he had developed feelings of trust and closeness. The issue was hard enough for Helen, in failing health and often homebound, to deal with in private. It was still harder and more embarrassing to hear in public, as on probably at least two occasions he shared their situation with a group where she was present.[169] Naturally all this contributed significantly to their stormy relationship in their later years. Yet they kept working on the issue in their own way. At one point, getting with the program, she agreed with him that he should be free to pursue other relationships. But she did not really believe this and later retracted her permission. As close colleague Maureen O'Hara recalled,

> I think my own sense of it was that it hurt Helen very much and that he suffered a great deal because of that, that his regret about it had to do with not being able to convince Helen that it was possible for him to be in more than one intimate, emotional, or sexual connection without it diminishing or disrespecting her or that relationship. She wasn't in that world though. It was a complete and utter culture clash as far as I can see. He was living in this sexual revolution world and surrounded by people who were justifying very, very new kinds of behavior and

she was living in another world. She was also sick. She was also watching her beloved husband having a completely new life where she was in a place where she couldn't in any way enjoy that with him. So I think it was a really tragic part of the story ... I think in his own mind he was not disrespectful to Helen; I think he wanted to have a congruent, authentic relationship with her at the same time he wanted to experience these new opportunities that were available.[170]

The issue remained a continual source of emotional pain, Helen being continually re-hurt and angry and often critical and blaming of him, Rogers vacillating between understanding and accepting her feelings and being angry and resentful about her attempts to control him; between trying hard to support and care for her and feeling terrible and guilty that he was hurting her; and between curtailing his activities to be with her and insisting on living his own professional and personal life independent of her. In other ways—family occasions with children and grandchildren, entertaining friends, occasionally traveling together as when Helen accompanied him to the Sagamore workshop in 1977—their partnership remained intact and provided some satisfaction and companionship, but just as often it was a sad and difficult relationship for them both. She alternated between despair and determination to live her life as best she could. He continued to provide physical care for her, in person and through friends and professional aides, and to provide emotional care and support to the best of his ability under the circumstances.

Those are the facts. But how do we understand and perhaps judge this difficult but important period in the Rogers' marriage? In discussing this subject with those who lived through this period with Carl and Helen Rogers and especially with those hearing these details for the first time, I am struck with how people bring their own experiences and moral values to the story. It is difficult not to impose one's own attitudes about the marriage contract, the rights and responsibilities of partners, and the meaning of honesty in relationships to this situation. For me, the Rogers' predicament symbolizes at least two issues that were prominent in the 1970s but really are universal dilemmas in the human condition.

The first is the challenge of balancing freedom and responsibility. As discussed earlier, one of the main values of the humanistic psychology movement was and is self-actualization. Yet others would say that beyond self-actualization, individuals also have a responsibility, an obligation, a duty to others. Although Rogers avoided the terms responsibility, obligation and duty, he never saw a theoretical conflict between individual need satisfaction and responsible human relationships. For him, human nature was social; it was a human characteristic to want to be connected in trustworthy relationships with others. Therefore his "fully functioning person" would be motivated by *both* socially oriented goals and self-actualizing ones. In a sense they are one and the same; one actualizes oneself in relationships. But theory aside, in life there is a real tension between

462

meeting one's own needs and attending to the needs of others. This is a universal human dilemma. Some individuals and cultures lean toward putting the others' needs—the spouse, the family, the organization, the society—before one's own. Some individuals and sub-cultures lean toward self-satisfaction to the neglect or diminution of other commitments or obligations. We probably all have known people whom we would judge as having erred on one side or the other. Did Rogers err in his balancing act of trying to care for Helen's needs on the one hand and follow his professional and personal goals on the other?

Colleague Maureen O'Hara said, "I wouldn't call it selfishness, but I would say that he, in the choice between self-sacrifice on behalf of the relationship or self-expression on behalf of his own growth and his own self-realization, he chose his own self-realization. I wouldn't say it was an error. I would say that was a choice." Yet at the same time, O'Hara noted that "part of the problem with the person-centered philosophy as an ideology or as a moral position is it was much more focused on one's moral obligations to one's self than it was about one's moral obligations to other people and I think it is one of the weaknesses of the theory." She also said that "the people who were close to Helen were very concerned about how hurt she was and pretty angry at Carl for his behavior."[171] Rogers' colleague and Helen's friend Ann Dryfuss had commented some years earlier, "Helen has a kind of stableness and rootedness and gentle firmness, and these qualities have made it possible for Carl to continue on his own ventures and be the man he is. She's just such a good creature and has been so good to him ..."[172] Now that Helen was dying, these friends thought he owed her a similar loyalty. Now it was his turn to put more of his desires aside to properly care for her in her remaining years.

Natalie Rogers disagreed. She was close to both her father and mother during this period; she knew what they were going through, and she did not judge her father negatively for the choices he made. She believed her mother also had responsibility for the situation and the choices she was making and that her father did about the best he could to meet her mother's needs and continue on his own path.[173] Close associate Valerie Henderson had a similar evaluation. "He was still able to go out and be in the world and her life was getting narrower and narrower ... It is like you are drowning and the person who can't make it is pulling you down with them. I think that is what he felt about Helen. He just didn't want to die yet. Her need was for him to be there all the time and hold her and comfort her. It makes me sad but neither one was a villain."[174] In the end, our own values and experiences around fidelity probably will determine how we judge or accept Rogers' choices.

Once Rogers made the choice to engage in relationships outside his marriage however, there is almost universal agreement among those close to the Rogers at the time that he handled it badly. There is some difference of opinion as to whether he should have told Helen about his feelings and mentioned other relationships at all, or kept these things hidden from her so as to avoid hurting her unnecessarily. But there is complete agreement that talking about his dilemma or his behavior in public, even to the limited extent he did so, was unnecessarily hurtful, humiliating, and selfish to the extent that he was working out his own issue at her expense. As Valerie Henderson recalled, "After she died I told him at one time how angry I had been at him because I thought he had not been careful for Helen, and he agreed. He said, 'I don't think I did it well and I don't know how I could have done it.' I think that was part of it—it is like people who have a lot of feelings but they don't know how to express them, and when they do, they blurt it out or say something inappropriately. I think some of that was true for them."[175]

It was clear that Rogers did not intentionally try to hurt Helen. Whatever carelessness or ineptness in the content and timing of his communication probably occurred because he was terribly confused about his own feelings and was desperate for help. That said, what *should* Rogers have done about self-disclosure? If he could have done so carefully and skillfully, should he have discussed his dilemma with Helen or kept his private life to himself? Again Rogers' situation reflects both an issue characteristic of the 1970s and a timeless dilemma in all human relationships. Rogers, after all, was "the elder statesman of encounter groups."[176] And like most people who participated in encounter groups, let alone years of practicing therapy, the value of honesty, openness, and freedom from facades became increasingly important to him. Arguably this was a genuine contribution of the encounter movement and this period in popular psychology. Yet how far should open and honest communication be taken? Is honesty always the best policy? What things are better left unsaid? Is it okay to cry in the office? Is it right to tell someone your feelings if it will hurt theirs? Is deception sometimes justified? These are perennial questions that philosophers have discussed through the ages, that pop psychologists opine about regularly, and that every individual faces in his or her own relationships. So Rogers experimented. He tried to be consistent with some of his most important principles of human relationships. He tried to share his reality, be authentic, listen to and accept Helen's feelings, try to achieve solutions that would meet as many of both their needs as possible. Sometimes he got it wrong and hurt someone he loved. Sometimes he got angry. Sometimes he did not live up to his ideals. One could say some of his behavior illustrated the excesses of the encounter group movement and would not be wrong. One could also say that some of it represented the best of the movement and not be wrong either.

After the Sagamore workshop in the summer of 1977, Helen's health resumed its decline. Rogers wrote in a letter the next year, "Helen's health seems to be steadily sinking these past three years, which is very discouraging and troublesome. When I last saw you, I probably told you that she was no longer making her own red blood cells and had to have blood transfusions. This problem has continued.

She's had fourteen blood transfusions in the past seventeen months and a variety of other symptoms as well. The blood condition is not leukemia and not a malignancy, but it is certainly mysterious and debilitating."[177] A few months later he wrote that getting twenty hours a week of help with Helen's health care was a relief, but that doing everything around the house had been hard on him.[178] On January 19, 1979, Helen fell and broke her hip. Rogers was leading a workshop in Venezuela at the time, and David and Bobbie Rogers were staying with Helen. She was taken to the hospital, operated on, and remained in the hospital, in and out of intensive care, for the next nine weeks until her death on March 29. Family and friends were with her continually, with many intimate conversations about their relationships. Death and dying were discussed openly. Helen made it clear that she was not quite ready to die but would know when she was and would let them know.[179] During this period, "Helen had visions of an inspiring white light which came close, lifted her from the bed, and then deposited her back on the bed."[180]

"One day," Rogers wrote, "when she was very near death, I was in an internal frenzy which I could not understand at all. When I went to the hospital as usual to feed her her supper, I found myself pouring out to her how much I had loved her, how much she had meant in my life, how many positive initiatives she had contributed to our long partnership. I felt I had told her all these things before, but that night they had an intensity and sincerity they had not had before. I told her she should not feel obligated to live, that all was well with her family, and that she should feel free to live or die, as *she* wished. I also said I hoped the white light would come again that night."[181]

Apparently Carl's words gave Helen the reassurance she needed and released her of any obligation to continue living for others. That evening she called the nurses on her floor together, thanked them for all the care they had given her, and told them she was going to die. After that she took no food and very little liquid. The next morning she went into a coma, emerged from it briefly several times to speak with friends, lapsed back into the coma and died peacefully the next morning, with Natalie holding her hand and vividly experiencing her mother's spirit leaving her body.[182]

Helen Rogers' death in 1979 freed both partners—she from her physical suffering and loneliness, he from the tension between meeting his independent professional and personal needs while remaining committed to Helen and their relationship and tending to her physical care. As Valerie Henderson recalled, "I know that they definitely came together toward the end because he loved her. He really did."[183] Their parting had been caring and complete. Now he was "on his own" again, for the first time in 55 years. Never really having ceased, he threw himself back into work and life with gusto. He found that he not only still retained his great capacity for work, but discovered new wells of energy for relationships and even for play.

Loving and being loved were a major theme of Rogers' final years. After Helen died, he wrote an "addendum" to his earlier essay, "Growing Old: Or Older and Growing," in which he said, "As the year drew to a close, I was increasingly aware of my capacity for love, my sensuality, my sexuality. I have found myself fortunate in discovering and building relationships in which these needs can find expression. There has been pain and hurt, but also joy and depth."[184]

This brief description only hinted at the whole picture, intentionally and appropriately so. Now single again, Rogers had really joined the younger generation. At age seventy-eight, he developed intimate, loving, sexual relationships with three women and maintained all three relationships simultaneously for the next half dozen years. They were older, mature, professional women, from their late fifties to their seventies. One was a former school counselor, director of school guidance, and counselor educator. One had a Ph.D. in developmental psychology and had been a humanistic teacher educator at the university level for many years. One was an Alexander technique therapist. Two lived on the East Coast of the United States and one in England. One was married, and her husband knew and approved of her relationship with Rogers. The other two were divorced. At least two had children. Rogers made it clear that he was not considering marrying again or having an exclusive relationship, although in his private diaries he sometimes entertained the latter notion. They, in turn, were independent women who, in one case, would not consider leaving her husband, and in another would not want to leave her life and practice in England. So there was a common understanding. As he said to one of them, "I would hope that you would be able to accept and enjoy [the] relationship for exactly what it is."[185] While sometimes one of them might want more than he was able to give in terms of time together, each of the women understood and accepted the situation and cherished their relationship with Rogers, as he did with them, "each of whom I love in a different way."[186]

Finding time with each of them, around some of his road trips and on their periodic visits to La Jolla, was a bit of a juggling act. An entry in one of his diaries was entitled, "Keeping Relationships Straight."[187] One year, for example, all three partners came for visits of ten days or longer—all in a two-month period. Yet he managed to maintain each partnership as a discrete, discreet, and precious relationship. One partner often worked with Rogers, serving as co-facilitator or co-faculty at more than forty intensive groups, workshops and conferences sessions across the U.S. and around the world over nine years.[188] They kept their personal relationship confidential, and while many participants no doubt wondered whether they had more than a collegial relationship, they maintained their privacy. In a 1984 workshop, I asked Rogers a question that would have made it very easy for him to tell a bit more about their relationship, but he artfully dodged the query and added, with a twinkle in his eye, "Nice try, Howie."

Although, as quoted earlier, Rogers wrote at age seventy-five, "I feel as sexy in my *interests* as I was at thirty-five, though I can't say the same about my ability to perform," he was nonetheless surprised and delighted to discover that he was "a marvelous lover."[189] Somewhat like the gentle, patient gardener, who created the conditions for his plants to flourish and blossom, at least by his own account in his diaries, Rogers, through touching, kissing and other sensual and sexual contact, seemed to give great pleasure to his partners and, often without achieving orgasm himself, derive great pleasure, excitement and satisfaction in the physical closeness and especially the loving intimacy of the relationship.[190] He clearly was delighted with and proud of his sexual reawakening and facility, not only in the three relationships cited, but in a few other, brief and passionate liaisons.[191] He marveled over and relished how, in these relationships, he was loved for himself. The intimate human connection was as wonderful a part of the experience for him as the sexual. As he wrote in his diary after a week with one of his partners, "I was happy, spoiled, loved. I gave love in abundance, & it was rec'd joyfully, & I spoiled her, & we just were incredibly easy together. But bed—that was ecstasy!"[192] I shall spare the reader further details. Rather I would summarize by pointing out how the shy and lonely youngster in Rogers never failed to be amazed at the making of a new friend, the I–Thou meeting in therapy, the "basic encounter" in a small group, the large group community meeting experiencing one mind, and now, again for the first time in many years, the union of man and woman in emotional and sexual intimacy.

On a less intense level, Rogers also deepened many personal friendships in the years after Helen's death. Maureen O'Hara recalled, "I don't think Carl had people that he went to play with. They were all people that he went to work with."[193] That was accurate; virtually all of Rogers' friends were people he worked with to some degree. Nonetheless he valued his friendships and, after Helen's death, made a special effort to make time for friends and social occasions. He was frequently invited to CSP colleagues' homes for dinner and parties and was often touched by the warmth with which he was received. He and David Malcolm had lunch several times a year together. Rogers spoke of his personal relationships, but not to brag. Malcolm recalled, "I never remember his joking or saying anything salacious or exploitative. He was more interested in talking about what it's like to be *us,* that is, older men. I have a feeling I played a role … there wasn't any other man in his age group." When they parted, Rogers and he would say, "We should do this more often."[194]

In spite of their friendship, Malcolm sensed, "It was very lonely to be Carl Rogers. He had to be referee at the Center. He had so much to live up to. He wouldn't play favorites. He had a different road to walk. I felt, 'There is a very lonely man.'" In fact, when Malcolm won an award in 1986 (for which Rogers had written a long, careful and detailed letter of support), Rogers wrote him a congratulatory note, adding, "We are each loners, I think, but of different sorts."[195]

Still, Rogers made an effort to push beyond whatever shyness or tendency to being a loner or actual loneliness he felt and take some time, in the midst of his busy work schedule, to spend with friends.

He also played a good deal more than before. For example, around 1983 Rogers took a ten-day vacation with Reinhard Tausch and his twenty-year-old daughter Daniella on Sanibel Island, Florida.[196] Tausch voiced a desire to go on a catamaran, as he had never sailed before. That evening Rogers took out a pencil and paper and, recalling his sailing days on Seneca Lake, gave Tausch a lesson on how to sail. The next day they rented a catamaran and Rogers took Tausch and Daniella out into the Gulf of Mexico. Tausch was a little nervous but recalled that eighty-one-year-old Rogers was perfectly competent at the helm and they had a great time. On other days they and Rogers played Frisbee on the beach.

Once when I visited Rogers in La Jolla in the 1980s, presumably to interview him about his activities for an eventual new edition of his biography, he expressed how burdened and stressed he felt with his work schedule and how he hadn't taken a day off in many weeks. So I suggested we do just that—put aside our agenda and take time just to have fun together. Knowing his Calvinist work ethic, I doubted he would consider taking a weekday off just for fun; but much to my surprise he agreed, and we spent an enjoyable day visiting the relatively new San Diego Zoo's animal park out in the country.

Travel, always a great love of Rogers, was another way he took time to enjoy himself. This was facilitated by his increasingly active, international workshop schedule, to be described. Typically he added days or weeks onto each trip to sightsee and travel in the host and neighboring countries, often accompanied by one of his three partners.

He even stopped protesting about friends' making a fuss over his birthday. He wrote how "a large group of friends came to my home, bringing food, drink, songs, and surprises to celebrate my seventy-eighth birthday. It was a wild, wonderful, hilarious party—with love, caring, fellowship, and happiness—which I will never forget."[197]

His eightieth birthday party with his friends and colleagues was an even larger and more elaborate occasion, which he summarized in a thank you letter to his friends:

> It was a marvelous party—wild and wonderful—with so much love and warmth of spirit that I felt enveloped by it. I loved the conversation and the laughter and the champagne and the skits—both funny and corny. It was good to be laughed at and laughed with. And the presents—utterly uncalled for, but so ingenious. Maxine's symplic cactus, Maria's enormous birthday cake, Nel and Ed's *New York Times* of January 8, 1902 (!), the puzzle from Val & Lloyd (I never thought it would intrigue me, but it has!), Jim Hardy's intricate drawing, so full of obscure meanings, Doug's cartoon of my proboscis, the incredible TV interview with

Maureen & Pook talking to the man in the street ("Keep on writing those songs"), and champagne from Mary and from others, and Gay's little hand-published story, the rug from Betty, the flowering begonia, the table bouquet, and on and on and on … And to top it off, I've had loving messages by phone and cable from Natalie and David, from individuals and groups in Florida, New York, Arizona, Ohio, Texas, Washington State, Illinois, New Jersey, Sweden, Brazil, Germany, Mexico, Switzerland, South Africa, Japan, England, Italy, Norway, etc., etc. I feel I'm in a cocoon of caring.[198]

The next week, Rogers, his two children, six grandchildren, and now three great-grandchildren all returned to the Carmel Valley Inn for a four-day celebration of his eightieth birthday.[199]

Rogers' letters to his friends in the 1980s often included the line "I'm having a great time," or words to that effect. His work, his family, his love relationships, and his friendships were all giving him the deepest satisfaction. This did not simply occur on its own, as a reward for having lived a good life. He continued to work and stretch himself to make it happen. Whether conducting therapeutic interviews before audiences of hundreds of professionals around the world, or as we shall see, bringing hostile groups together to reduce international and inter-group tensions, or trying to maintain honest and intimate relationships in his personal life, he continued to challenge himself, to explore new personal and professional frontiers. By engaging so fully with others in his professional activities, he continued to develop new friendships and deepen old ones.

However, the satisfaction with life that Rogers communicated publicly and experienced privately was only part of the story. At the same time that he was experiencing the excitement of new relationships and new professional directions, he was struggling with demons that few people close to him were aware of.

Physical and Mental Health

In "Growing Old: Or Older and Growing," Rogers included an interesting self-observation. He wrote, "It is often said or assumed that the older years are years of calm and serenity. I have found this misleading. I believe I do have a longer perspective on events outside of myself, and hence am often more of an objective observer than I might have been earlier. Yet in contrast to this, events which touch *me* often evoke a stronger reaction than they would have years ago. When I am excited, I get very high. When I am concerned, I am more deeply disturbed. Hurts seem sharper, pain is more intense, tears come more easily, joy reaches higher peaks, even anger—which I have always had trouble with—is felt more keenly. I believe that emotionally I am more, not less, volatile than I used to be. The range from feeling depressed to feeling elated seems greater, and either state

469

is more easily triggered."[200] He wondered to what extent this greater volatility might be a function of growing older, or of his lifestyle, or of "the greater sensitivity acquired in encounter groups."

All these factors were probably true, but some of his emotional volatility probably had another cause which he chose not to write or speak about. Rogers had a serious problem with alcohol. In his later years, he recognized he had a problem. In his private journals he acknowledged that he drank too much for his own good, and at times he acknowledged it was a serious problem, although soon thereafter he would minimize it. To my knowledge, he never used the terms "alcoholism" or "addiction" to describe his situation.[201] And remarkably, very few people outside his immediate family knew he had a problem with alcohol, let alone recognized its seriousness.

It was not a problem that originated late in life, nor was it his alone. Throughout their years in Columbus, Chicago, Madison, and La Jolla, it was common knowledge that Carl and Helen Rogers were a congenial host and hostess at frequent gatherings at their home. They enjoyed having friends, colleagues and graduate students over and entertained on a regular basis. If it was a social occasion (as compared to a discussion group with students, for example), alcohol would be served, and Carl and Helen enjoyed their drinks along with their company. At such times Rogers would become more relaxed and convivial, but this could be said of many at the gathering. There was nothing out of the ordinary about it—no inappropriate behavior, no hint of a problem in Rogers' personal or professional life.

Yet, during Rogers' Chicago years, Richard Farson noticed how Carl and Helen, when packing for a trip, would routinely put a couple of bottles of liquor in their suitcases. This seemed a bit odd to him at the time, since one could always purchase a bottle at most of their destinations. But he didn't give it any more thought at the time. Nothing in Carl or Helen's behavior suggested there was any reason to.[202]

And so it went for many years. Probably their consumption of alcohol increased gradually. Initially it helped them relax in social settings. Then, Natalie Rogers observed, "he started out by drinking a glass of wine to enhance or free up his writing. It uninhibited his ability to let the words flow."[203] Later on, if he experienced anxiety a few drinks of vodka seemed to lessen it. If Helen experienced some physical pain, as she did increasingly, a few drinks seemed to alleviate that. If life's pressures were too stressful, drinking would help relieve the stress. If Carl had trouble sleeping, he would take a drink or two or three to help him get back to sleep. Later, as Helen experienced emotional pain around her declining health and sense of losing her husband, drinking provided temporary relief. Most of their drinking was done in private. To all the world nothing was amiss. They held their liquor well. He remained productive and effective in his work. Except for the occasional ulcer flare-up, Carl seemed a model of good health and successful aging.

It is not clear, then, when occasional social drinking became drinking too much, in the sense of not being good for one's general health, or when alcohol consumption crossed a line and became alcohol dependence. Certainly the problem had risen to that level by the late sixties, during the stressful period around the break-up of WBSI, David's heart attack and David and Natalie's separations.[204]

When I spent several days interviewing Rogers in March of 1971, at the end of our first day of work together and before dinner, he told me how he and Helen regularly enjoyed a few drinks before and around dinner, as it helped them relax, and invited me to join them. They continued being their lucid selves throughout the evening and on subsequent occasions, so like Farson in Chicago, I thought no more about it at the time. Thirty years later, reading Rogers' correspondence in the Library of Congress, I discovered that a few weeks before my visit, Rogers had written to their son David how Helen "has certainly aged a good deal in the past year or year and a half. I have too, but not so much. It is surprising how her energy level has gone down. She is just exhausted ... Arthritis not quite so severe ... a great deal of difficulty with her hiatic hernia ... We both drink a good deal, 8–10 drinks every 24 hours, very much spaced out through the day and night."[205]

In the mid-70s, as Helen's health continued to deteriorate, she drank more than was good for her. Valerie Henderson observed that both he and Helen drank a lot, long before she was housebound.[206] Carl was drinking close to a bottle of vodka a day. Natalie and David regularly wrote their father to share their concern about his drinking. David instructed him about the health consequences of too much alcohol. In Rogers' journals he acknowledged his problem to a degree, worrying about the weight he was gaining and saying he wanted to cut back on alcohol, get more exercise and eat more healthily. Encouraged by such sentiment, Natalie wrote in 1977, "You would do your body a real kind favor if you could stop drinking. And I see you actively working on that."[207] By the next year, after there was no improvement, her words were stronger and more confronting:

> I ... came to the kitchen to find you making your breakfast at 6:30, and you were smelling strongly of vodka. (Are you aware that your pores seem to be sweating vodka these days? I even smelled it on the beach with the breezes blowing, and I smell it when you drive me to the airport) ... I am seeing you gaining too much weight ... I see you depressed, with a thick foggy veil around you so that I can't get very close to you ... I see you beginning to shake (just as Mom did) and stagger even as we walk on the beach. I see you beginning to lie to me and to others, or kidding yourself and others about your intake ..."[208]

A few months later, David wrote his father that Natalie's concerns mirrored his own.

... she mentions, in her usual observant way, problems that I've noted that she puts in a different category. These include your weight gain, uncertain walking, the fact that you seem so hyped up—perspire profusely, your shakiness, that you often repeat stories or incidents or feelings [without] recognizing that you've told em before. In brief, that's her list. I guess I would add your persistent nasal stuffiness, groggy voice, bouts of heart irregularity, retinal (eye) problems just to complete the list of medical type problems which seem to be troubling you these days. It would be my guess ... that most of that array of problems stem from your Vodka intake. The thing which I would want you to think about the hardest is that the most troublesome symptoms—the "inner racehorse"—the feeling that you're going to jump out of your skin—the sweating—the feelings that a drink used to remedy (and still does)—are quite certainly *caused* by alcohol. You're a lively sensitive tense guy and there were many pressures. But I think you're now somewhat caught on an agonizing treadmill and that the very symptoms which make a drink a necessity to keep from going bananas, subsequently return in subtly worse form *because* of the funny things which go on as your blood alcohol level falls ... There are some more peripheral symptoms that I'm quite sure are alcohol induced. Your very tentative gait and floppy feet. I would guess you've got a little peripheral neuritis in your legs—the shakiness and loss of finer motor coordination and quite probably your feelings of excessive fatigue and ...[209]

And David, the renowned physician, went on for several more pages discussing his father's symptoms, their causes, and his recommendations for eliminating or, failing that, reducing his alcohol intake. Natalie and David's recitation of many of the classic signs of alcohol dependency leaves little doubt as to the seriousness of the problem. He, on the other hand, vacillated between recognizing the seriousness and minimizing it, as when he wrote in 1980, "Concerned about my drinking ... even though experience may show that drinking is not deleterious. (I have gone to sleep three nights with one glass of wine, one night with one drink. Have cut my drinking to about two drinks per day.)[210] Two months later he wrote,

Then last night I frightened myself as I have once before. I woke a little before 2 a.m. to find that I was setting my electric clock ahead (a moderately complicated thing to do). It must have been similar to sleepwalking , because I was more and more surprised at what I was doing, as I gradually became fully awake.

I'm sure it has to do with drinking, because after no hard liquor all day, just wine at a ... party and dinner, I drank *a lot* to get to sleep. It really doesn't help much with sleep, is very bad for me. I've been drinking less on my trip, but here at home it is easy to fall back into it.

I have had one other similar experience. I got up one morning and found that the single bed next to mine had been opened, as if for someone to sleep in.

I *knew* it was not that way when I went to bed. I finally came to the reluctant conclusion that I had done it in my sleep! Again, I had drunk 4 or 5 drinks to get to sleep.

 This is a frightening thing to contemplate. All I need is to start doing strange things in my sleep! It may well be that drinking could be a life and death matter in this respect ... Perhaps the blood cell difficulty is also due to drinking. I've got to take it *seriously*.[211]

Then he might proudly tell Valerie Henderson, "I have never had a hangover in my life," implying he could handle his problem.[212] His journal entries indicated how he worked at cutting back on his consumption, for a time dropping to one to two drinks a day. But even that affected him badly, particularly if he drank them at night.[213] Then his consumption would increase again. Sometimes he also took valium to help him sleep.[214]

 At least once he took his drinking problem seriously enough to try to quit altogether. In 1985, when he went into the hospital for a neck injury, resulting in his having to wear a brace for some weeks, he asked Maria Bowen and Valerie Henderson to go over to his house and clear out his liquor cabinet. Since he was somewhat detoxified from his hospital stay, he wanted to get off alcohol entirely. But his resolution was short-lived.[215] Rogers' difficulty with alcohol lasted all his life.[216]

 What is so astounding is that hardly anyone other than Natalie and David, Bowen, Henderson and possibly one or two other confidants knew of Rogers' problem. Alberto Segrera recalled picking Rogers up at the airport in Mexico and the first thing Rogers asked for was to be taken to buy bottles of Vodka.[217] But this was not typical of his colleagues. In interviews with many of his closest associates from the seventies and eighties—people who traveled and co-led workshops with him of a week or longer duration—when asked about Rogers and alcohol, no one recognized he had a problem, and no one could recall any time when he appeared less than fully functioning in professional settings. A few said they recalled occasional times when he might be a bit "high" on a social occasion or at dinner at the end of a work day, but a lot less than others around the table, and normal enough in their experience.[218] Maureen O'Hara's observations well captured what most people close to him saw:

My experience with Carl's drinking was that we would, after we'd done a piece of work, we would go and have a glass of wine or we'd go have a vodka or something ... or when I went over his house for an interview or a conversation, we would probably have lunch and then we'd probably have a gin and tonic. I have no personal experience with him having been drunk or saying that he had a drinking problem. I think he was a man of his generation, again, where the cocktail at five was what you do, but I never saw him drinking while he was working. I never saw him drunk with people that you would consider to be clients. I mean, I never saw him drunk in a workshop. I never saw him drunk actually. I saw him a little tipsy on more than one occasion but usually everybody else in the room was, too.

After Rogers' death some people, like Germain Lietaer in Belgium and Peter Schmid in Austria, heard rumors that Rogers had a drinking problem, but made it clear they never saw any evidence of it while he was alive.[219] Schmid said, "I realized that he liked to drink a lot and when he was in Austria in the evenings, I wouldn't say he was drunk, but he was quite … in Austria's language … he was 'illuminated' … He was in '82 in Hamburg one week in our home and university and I never saw him drinking in the day, but after we were going to sleep he drank something, and we spoke of this and he said it's so very hard for him to sleep … he had disturbance to sleep, but in the morning he was always very, very prepared and we were going to the university and there was no problem."[220] More typical was David Cain's comment that, "I don't know of anybody who ever saw him inebriated or inappropriate or drunk. I don't have any sense or gossip that Carl had a drinking problem of any sort whatsoever," or David Malcolm's, "I never had any inkling of it at all."[221]

What emerges, then, is a picture of a high-functioning, closet drinker, self-medicating with liquor to reduce anxiety, stress and intermittent depression. Rogers' journals make it clear he had difficulty sleeping and would spend many hours in the late night and early morning drinking, writing in his journals and working on his correspondence. He would say that alcohol enabled him to eventually get back to sleep; others told him—and sometimes he recognized—that it was the alcohol that was interfering with his normal sleep. And contributing to his weight and other health problems. He was seriously ill, but he would not admit it. Or if he did, he would soon retreat into rationalization that he was still functioning effectively, which was true.

Why the rationalization and denial? How is it that a man noted for his honesty failed to be honest with himself and others about this problem? Perhaps he feared the consequences for his reputation, wanting to avoid the stigma typically associated with alcohol abuse. In particular, critics are especially unkind to psychologists who are not the very models of mental health themselves. But if that was his major fear, he would not have left his correspondence and private journals for posterity to see. Perhaps the answer is no different than that for any person with substance dependency. An addiction is, after all, an addiction. There's no point searching for a rational reason for a person clinging to it.

Yet, having said that, the drinking probably also was useful in masking over other issues that were difficult to face. As he wrote in one diary entry, "I have been—and am—in a strange mood. The most obvious way to describe it is that I seem to be anxious and depressed when I am alone with myself."[222] Three weeks later he mused, "There is nothing, at the moment, nothing I'm vitally interested in—not my garden, not editing my new book, not the Learning Program, etc. And I am rather keenly aware that I am only what I *achieve* not what I *am*. What am I, inside? I'm a good lover (with no one to love). I am a tender, compassionate person. I'm strong and tough when there is a real *need* for that, but it's hard for me. I'm intelligent. I'm lovable. I'm open. Am I interesting and valuable to myself?"[223] And two weeks later: "Is it the fear of death which makes me anxious? Possibly. I'm not as much at peace with death as Helen was. I looked at the possibility that these symptoms might mean I'm dying *now*—that I don't have 7 years."[224] Around the same time he wrote, "I believe I am lovable, but do I love myself? That, is the unanswered question. Certainly I'm not getting fun out of life these days, and that seems very much too bad."[225]

Too bad, indeed. It is remarkable that Rogers' wrote this entry shortly after successive, multi-week, joyful visits with his three lovers. Previous journal entries had been filled with ecstatic reports of their loving and lovemaking. Yet, reading this last journal entry, it seems as if none of that ever happened. It is as though there are two Carl Rogers here. During the day and evenings, when in touch with people, he's fully engaged in his work and in his relationships. In his work, he is arguably more effective than ever—as therapist and group leader, inspirational speaker, lucid writer. In his relationships, he has many rich friendships with his colleagues and others—deep, intimate sharing, laughing, connecting. In his romantic relationships, he relishes in the intimacy, sensuality, sexuality and romance. With his children and grandchildren, again, gratifying personal, often intimate connections. It would seem he has everything. Yet when he is alone, another Carl Rogers emerges—brooding, troubled, anxious, sometimes depressed, occasionally bitter, and lonely. How can these rather dramatic mood swings be explained?

To some extent they probably were, as he described it earlier, a part of his aging process. He probably also missed Helen a great deal.[226] His new love relationships certainly enriched his life, but that was different from the life-long, daily connection and security he experienced with Helen, even when their relationship was stormy. As we shall see, his attempts to communicate with Helen after her death suggest a loneliness that other relationships could not entirely relieve. Some might say that part of temperament is genetic and that perhaps Rogers' highs and lows had a biological basis. In addition to these possible factors, Rogers' emotional volatility was certainly exacerbated by his considerable alcohol consumption. Drink affects different people differently, elevating or depressing their mood and variously affecting their behavior. While earlier in life getting a bit high may have enabled Rogers to relax and enjoy himself more, as it still did on social occasions, as time went on there seems little doubt that later in life alcohol had a depressing effect on him. So the profound discontent with himself and life that often revealed itself in his private, late night and early morning musings could certainly be attributed to his drinking and the anxiety and depression it contributed to. (I cannot help but speculate that at least some of the uncharacteristically bitter or hostile letters he occasionally wrote, like the one to his brother Lester discussed earlier, may have been written during these late-night episodes of drinking.)

But this is only a partial explanation, because drinking does not create emotional and psychological issues that are not already present to some degree. It may exacerbate them but it doesn't create them. So the discontent in Rogers' psyche or soul, as it were, was there already. His own account of the sources of his unhappiness (when his public autobiographical writings are combined with his private journal entries) is clear: the lack of unconditional love and acceptance in his childhood, the hurts inflicted by sibling rivalry, conditions of worth associated with achievement, and feelings of sinfulness engendered by family and religion. His siblings scoffed at the assertion that their parents were unloving or the family teasing extreme, but that did not alter Rogers' *feeling* of being unloved and unaccepted, left out, ridiculed. He wrote in his journal one night that he could not recall a single instance of parental overt affection or touching and asked his brother Walter if that was his experience. Walter agreed that that was how he remembered his mother but not his father.[227] Carl could not remember loving validation in words or touch from either of them. He wondered if that's why touching and caressing and physical contact with women now, even if it didn't involve orgasmic sex for him, was so important to him—as a loving affirmation he did not experience as a child.

Apparently Rogers' own therapy years earlier, while it certainly confronted these issues and seemed to provide a measure of new self-acceptance that allowed him to move on effectively in his professional life and relationships, did not touch or resolve some core self-concept issues or deep hurt or grief. Without the drinking, perhaps this layer of hurt or unfinished personality development would have remained dormant. If there were psychological scars that had never fully healed, perhaps they would have remained simply as scars, with little effect on the system's functioning. But Rogers' on-going drinking tore at the scars and reopened the old wounds. From one decade and year to the next, it is impossible to say to what extent Rogers' self-esteem issues, loneliness and health problems contributed to his drinking and to what extent the drinking contributed to these problems. Certainly the relationship was reciprocal.

And so, in a sense, there *were* two Carl Rogers. One was the Rogers most of the world knew through his various professional roles and his typical "way of being"—a man remarkably consistent with his professional values, philosophy, and person-centered approach to relationships. Hence the vast body of testimony describing Carl Rogers as an embodiment of the fully functioning person and professional he wrote about—a man, I would say, who modeled his teachings at least as congruently as any prominent psychologist in history. The other Carl Rogers was the one very few people (not even me during his lifetime) were privy to—a man who was not at peace with himself, who suffered from a drinking problem, who was surrounded by love but deeply lonely.

Yet Rogers was one person, not two. Like any of us, he contained conflicting and contradictory characteristics. Because his publicly known persona, both professional and personal, rose to the level of greatness, the contrast of that with his private, tormented side seems that much more dramatic, and for those who knew him or felt they knew him, that much sadder.

Spiritual Journey

In his later years, a nuance began to appear in Rogers' description of the therapeutic process. He began to speak of an intuitive, transcendental, even spiritual aspect of the client-centered relationship. Some authors and associates saw this as a significant new dimension of the person-centered approach, or even "the emergence of a deeply spiritual Rogers."[228] Some saw it as an interesting, but relatively unimportant episode in his professional trajectory of ever-widening applications of the person-centered approach. Still others saw it as an uncharacteristic and misguided detour into paranormal and psychic phenomena. My own view is that, while Rogers never returned to being "deeply spiritual" in his later years, this period in Rogers' intellectual, emotional and spiritual evolution was indeed significant—for him personally and for the person-centered approach.

As described earlier, in his encounter group experiences Rogers had come to trust his intuition more. If he had a strong urge to put his arm around someone, even though they appeared to be saying, "Keep away from me," he might do so. If he suddenly had a fantasy of a participant sitting on a throne wanting all the group members to be her subjects, he might voice that fantasy, not as the truth, but simply as his own fantasy. Very often these intuitive reactions turned out to unleash "a surprising depth of reaction and profound insights."[229] Hence he found himself trusting his intuition much more in small groups, in individual therapy, and in person-centered communities. His colleague Andre Auw noticed this change in Rogers' style. "He began to use metaphors … if a priest was saying I'm not sure if I'm ready to lead or not,' Rogers might say, 'I picture you're halfway up a hill. You can't go up and you can't go down. It's too scary.'"[230]

Trusting himself more than ever in therapy and group settings, operating on a less conscious, more intuitive level, he found himself often concentrating so fully on the other person, entering into the client's world with such deep empathy, that at times it felt as though he were hardly a separate person at all. Certainly on one level of consciousness he remained separate; that boundary was always important to him. But when he was most in tune with the other person, he, Rogers, no longer seemed to matter. He was not Carl Rogers, attempting to be empathic with the other person. He was *with* this other person.

It was as though they were so much on the same wavelength that they were no longer separate. He did not have to take a split second cognitively to frame his responses; his responses happened. But if he was not framing or willing these empathic responses, where were they coming from? It was as though the words were coming on their own, as though some unseen force was working through him, as though he were the willing conduit through which larger forces were working. In 1980, after a particularly powerful demonstration interview in CSP's La Jolla Program, he wrote in his diary, "I realize there was a spiritual quality to our relationship during that hour. We were so in tune with each other that somehow we were in tune with the universe. I feel very uncertain about any way of describing it but I was much moved by the interview and by the reactions it stirred in the group."[231]

Were he a more traditionally religious person, he might have credited some divine force or holy spirit for guiding his words. That was not Rogers' inclination; still he could not deny his feeling that something was happening here, at special moments in therapy and in intensive groups, which could not be fully explained by his previous formulations. So he tried using other words to describe it, recognizing that while congruence, empathy and unconditional positive regard "have been investigated and supported by research ... recently my view has broadened into a new area which cannot as yet be studied empirically."[232] In 1980, in a chapter in *A Way of Being* entitled "The Foundations of a Person-Centered Approach," and later in other writings, he suggested that there might be "one new characteristic" of a growth-promoting relationship. "When I am at my best, as a group facilitator or as a therapist," he wrote, "when I am closest to my inner, intuitive self, when I am somehow in touch with the unknown in me, when perhaps I am in a slightly altered state of consciousness [in the relationship], then whatever I do seems to be full of healing. Then, simply my *presence* is releasing and helpful to the other ... [At those moments] it seems that my inner spirit has reached out and touched the inner spirit of the other. Our relationship transcends itself and becomes a part of something larger. Profound growth and healing and energy are present."[233]

He quoted a participant in a recent workshop who said, "I found it to be a profound spiritual experience. I felt the oneness of spirit in the community. We breathed together, felt together, even spoke for one another. I felt the power of the 'life force' that infuses each of us—whatever that is. I felt its presence without the usual barricades of 'me-ness' and 'you-ness'—it was like a meditative experience when I feel myself as a center of consciousness. And yet with that extraordinary sense of oneness, the separateness of each person present has never been more clearly preserved." Rogers acknowledged, "[I realize that] this account partakes of the mystical. Our experiences ... it is clear, invoke the transcendent, the indescribable, the spiritual. I am compelled to believe that I, like many others, have underestimated the importance of this mystical, spiritual dimension."[234]

Intuitive ... altered state of consciousness ... inner spirit ... mystical ... transcendent ... spiritual? Was this Carl Rogers, the sober professional and rational scientist who had banished religion from his life over fifty years ago, speaking? Had he lost his objectivity? Or had he finally come to his senses? What was going on?

Much was going on in the last fifteen or more years of Rogers' life. All around him, especially in California, spiritual movements flourished. The West had rediscovered the East, and many Americans, reared on Christianity and Judaism, were dabbling in or seriously practicing Buddhism, Hinduism, Sufism and other so-called Eastern religions—or practices derived from those religions, like meditation and yoga. Both traditional Christianity and religious mysticism experienced renewals. Simultaneously, both counterculture and mainstream elements in the West became enamored with mind-altering drugs, primitive religion, and psychic phenomena. It was as though an entire culture embraced Hamlet's insight that "There are more things in heaven and earth, Horatio, than are dreamt of in our philosophy."[235]

During most of the 1970s Rogers remained aloof from these developments, except on an intellectual level. Through reading and close friends, he was exposed to anecdotes about paranormal events and learned about theories of a universe where time and space and mind and matter were not such discrete phenomena as Western philosophy and science had always assumed. A CSP colleague recalled how Rogers "really got excited about a film which showed the faith healers in the Philippines. He saw it at Sonoma State and he brought it here to show to us. He had a very open mind about it and wanted to check himself out in the presence of us."[236] When Rogers addressed the American Psychological Association in 1972, on the occasion of his receiving their Distinguished Professional Contribution Award, he spoke of a number of "challenges" to the psychology profession. Organized around a series of questions—Dare we develop a human science? Do we dare to be designers? Dare we do away with professionalism? Can we permit ourselves to be whole men and women?—he ended with the challenge he thought was "the most dreadfully threatening to psychologists ... Is this the only reality?"[237] After referencing William James' seminal work on the varieties of religious experience, he briefly discussed the thinking of psychologist Lawrence LeShan on paranormal phenomena, author/anthropologist Carlos Castaneda's experiences with a Yaqui Indian shaman in Mexico, and Ostrander and Schroeder's book on *Psychic Discoveries Behind the Iron Curtain*.[238] Although the veracity of Castaneda and some of the Soviet research was later questioned, Rogers continued to gather additional sources for this line of thinking and wrote further essays exploring the nature of "reality" and the universe.[239] Here he included the work of physicists Fritjof Capra and Ilya Prigogine who were taking Einstein's insight about the non-linearity of time and space to other dimensions, calling into question our traditional notions of reality.

As much as Rogers labored over these formulations, for most of the seventies such questions were primarily of intellectual interest. As he wrote in the 1972 essay, "I have never had a mystical experience, nor any type of experience of a paranormal reality, nor any drug-induced state that gave me a glimpse of a world different from our secure 'real' world."[240] Nor did he have any experience—or want to have any—of the more traditional spirituality of the Christian religion. Ever since he left off studying for the ministry in 1926, his rejection of organized religion or any spiritual orientation remained consistent for himself, although he had no difficulty with others holding such views. When his brother-in-law Herbert Ullmann (Helen's sister's husband) shared his Christian faith with Rogers in 1975 and his wish that Rogers had a faith like his that could comfort him as he approached death, and hoped that his sharing these thoughts would not alienate Rogers,[241] Rogers answered,

> You may be sure that in no way did it alienate me; in fact I feel much closer to you because of it. I think you revealed yourself more in this letter than in anything I have ever had from you in writing ... I am very happy that you have found, through the years, the convictions that you find it helpful and comforting to live by. In the same way my experience has led me to convictions that give my life meaning and permit me to face death with a calm feeling. I think the only thing I would fear and heartily dislike would be a long period of pain and illness before death ... I get a little feeling from your letter that you wish I shared those same beliefs and I appreciate that desire, but I guess I can't give a positive response ...[242]

All this began to change in the late seventies, as Rogers' intellectual interest in various dimensions of the new sciences, spirituality and psychic phenomena became more personal. A number of events occurred more or less simultaneously.

In January 1977, as described earlier, Rogers and his colleagues spent several weeks in Brazil conducting workshops. Team member Maria Villas-Boas Bowen, who grew up in Brazil, had maintained her native belief in spiritism. Through her contacts, Rogers, Bowen, John K. Wood, Maureen O'Hara and other team members were able to spend a week or so after the workshops visiting various Brazilian spiritualists, psychics, and clairvoyants. It was a paranormal tour-de-force, which Rogers documented in his private diary.[243] Rogers witnessed or heard about telepathy, precognition, reincarnation, poltergeists, clairvoyance, spiritual guides, and communication with the dead. He was fascinated but not convinced. Comments in his diary included, "All in all, interesting, but very general, not too convincing" and "We have heard a lot *about* psychic phenomenon. Have had no very convincing experience of it."[244] In one diary entry he described a long evening with several mediums. Two of them took on other personalities or incarnations or spiritual identities, and one of these spirits interacted with Rogers

480

and answered his questions. Rogers wrote, "... it was to me a fascinating demonstration of different personalities and the same person, and possibly of regression to former personalities. It was long-winded but seemed genuine. They might have been deceiving [them]selves but were not trying to deceive me. Several disappointments. They made *no* checkable statements and no predictions that could be checked. The guide's name doesn't match either of the two named previously. Then turning it into a sales pitch for spiritualism, after having gotten rid of John and Maureen, seemed tricky and suspicious. I'm glad I had the experience; it was very dramatic but certainly doesn't *prove* anything."[245] When informed that in a prior life he was an Egyptian, Rogers' only reflection was, "Shades of Nefertete!! [sic]"[246]

While still doubtful, after returning home he told several audiences, "Ten or fifteen years ago I felt quite certain that death was the total end of the person. I still regard that as the most likely prospect," although, he added, now he was open to the alternate possibility of the human spirit continuing after death.[247]

His next experiences occurred closer to home. Although Helen was even more skeptical than he was about the paranormal, as she grew increasingly infirm and closer to death, encouraged by her friends Maria Bowen, Gay Swenson (Barfield), Audrey McGaw and others, Helen became interested in psychic phenomena. Natalie Rogers was also serious about spirituality and influenced her mother to be more open to spiritual experience. Late in 1977, Luiz Gasparetto, a Brazilian medium who claimed to channel famous deceased artists, held a session at the Rogers' house. Gasparetto went into a trance and, in the dark, produced twenty large paintings in the style of Manet, Picasso, Utrillo, Toulouse-Lautrec and many others in little more than an hour. Helen, who was initially "probably the most skeptical of the 18 persons present" was "deeply impressed," both at the painter's skill and the apparent lack of any rational explanation other than psychic abilities.[248] Two days later, the medium met in a private session with Carl, Helen and Maria Bowen and channeled Lautrec and psychoanalyst Carl Jung who talked with them about life and death. Jung told Rogers that he worried too much about Helen and that after she died he would "be free enough to finish your mission in terms of humanity."[249]

About this time three of the Rogers' close friends and colleagues—Maria Bowen, Gay Swenson and Valerie Henderson—were seeing a well-known medium in the San Diego area, Adele Tinning, and encouraged Carl and Helen to visit her.[250] As Rogers described it,

> Helen was a great skeptic about psychic phenomena and immortality. Yet, upon invitation, she and I visited a thoroughly honest medium, who would take no money. There, Helen experienced, and I observed, a "contact" with her deceased sister, involving facts that the medium could not possibly have known. The messages were extraordinarily convincing, and all came through the tipping of a

481

sturdy table, tapping out letters. Later, when the medium came to our home and my own table tapped out messages in our living room, I could only be open to an incredible, and certainly nonfraudulent experience.[251]

Another contributing factor toward Rogers' growing interest in the mystical or spiritual realm was his deep involvement in person-centered group experiences in the late 1970s. He was always aware of how a group was more than the sum of its individual members, but earlier he would not have attributed this to any mystical or spiritual cause. As he told a group in 1958, when asked about his religious views, "If I have any religious point of view, it is that whatever is going on here at the best moments in our small groups, or at the best moments in our community groups, is some sort of a force in the universe that can be released. I think it is a force in us, not a force somewhere up there, not a force in the past." When asked, "Isn't that point of view a religious point?" he answered, "No, I don't like to call it religious because I would prefer to call it lawful. There is something lawful about the fact that a spirit of that kind exists and can be released. The only reason I don't like to call it religious is that term has so many connotations that, for me, I don't like. But nevertheless, I am quite aware of that fact that the issues that religious people are trying to deal with are also issues that I would like to be able to deal with. And in that sense, I feel close to it." Later he added, "I really don't think of myself as having a spiritual life. I think that my spirit is nourished by the deepest of human contacts. I always feel nourished when something really deep happens between me and another person in therapy, or in a group, or something like that. I feel just renewed by that, and that is terribly important to me. That's why it's a real need of mine to do something like this [be in a group or a learning community]. For example, I couldn't stay home and write all year. I have to touch base. I have to feel this all over again. I have to experience things again to somehow be confirmed in what I'm thinking."[252]

In the late seventies, however, he became open to the idea that what was happening between people in groups involved more than just the people. As Maureen O'Hara described it, "He was interested in the question of: is there a consciousness that transcends the individual? And I think a lot of that was fueled by the experiences in groups. He was doing a lot of groups at the end, not just the PCA [Person-Centered Approach] groups, but he was doing several groups a year. One of the things that I can attest to about my own experience is that, if you go through a lot of those groups, you are constantly being called into a more open consciousness. In a sense, you're called into experiences that are very close to mystical experiences … it is sort of a transcendental moment of understanding that it's all connected … There were times when we would come into a group and everybody had had the same dream—fifteen people in the group had had the same dream … We had experiences in Brazil that were just incredibly difficult to explain by just staying in the material realm … Those kind of experiences happen frequently in those groups. It's impossible if you go through that on a regular basis, as we were, not to break out of the sort of Western limited worldview that limits what is knowable to the concrete material world. I know that that was happening to Carl, too."[253]

Simultaneously, Rogers was becoming open to transcendent experience on a more personal level. In the years before Helen's death, when Rogers was feeling great stress and many conflicting emotions, he asked CSP member Andre Auw to be his therapist.[254] Although a former doctoral student of Rogers at USIU, Auw was closer to Rogers' own age than other CSP members and a former Catholic priest. Rogers often referred potential clients to him. Auw told Rogers, "I'm honored. But I need permission from you to do it my way." Rogers replied, "Oh, God, yes." Hence as part of the therapy, Auw had Rogers doing meditation and breathing exercises. He said that Rogers was very willing to engage in these activities and "willing to take a different perspective on his issues."[255] How transcendental Rogers' meditation actually was is not known, but presumably this experience, too, helped him become more open to a spiritual dimension.

All these events converged to launch Rogers on a ten-year period, from around 1977 to his death, that could rightly be described as a spiritual journey. New experiences around Helen's death in 1979 furthered his evolution. In the hospital Helen had a number of dreams and visions of her deceased family members that impressed Rogers with their vividness and realness, at least to Helen.[256] As reported earlier, she also had "visions of an inspiring white light which came close, lifted her from the bed, and deposited her back on the bed."[257] When Rogers told her how much he loved her and that he hoped the white light would come again for her that night, this seemed to release her and allowed her to die peacefully shortly after. The next evening, wrote Rogers, "… friends of mine who had a long-standing appointment with the medium previously mentioned [Adele] held a session with this woman. They were very soon in contact with Helen, who answered many questions: she had heard everything that was said while she was in a coma; she had experienced the white light and spirits coming for her; she was in contact with her family; she had the form of a young woman; her dying had been very peaceful and without pain."[258]

Summarizing these events around Helen's death, Rogers wrote, "All these experiences … have made me much more open to the possibility of the continuation of the individual human spirit, something I had never before believed possible. These experiences have left me very much interested in all types of paranormal phenomena. They have quite changed my understanding of the process of dying. I now consider it possible that each of us is a continuing spiritual essence lasting over time, and occasionally incarnated in a human body."[259]

Alberto Segrera thought that one of Rogers' motivations "for becoming interested in something more than the interpersonal" could be characterized as, "I don't think there's anything [to it], but I'm willing to do anything I can to contact Helen."[260] He wanted to know she was at peace. He wanted to know she accepted his new life without her. That is speculative, but what began as Rogers' interest in the survival of other people's consciousness after death, particularly Helen's, evolved, said Maureen O'Hara, into an interest in the survival of his own consciousness after death. While not an unusual interest for humans in general and eighty-year-olds in particular, this was new for Carl Rogers. The journey took two forms. One was a continuation of his exploration of psychic phenomena and non-traditional (at least from a Western, middle-class perspective) forms of healing and spirituality. The other was a search for a spiritual dimension of life that was independent of spiritism and psychic phenomena but also independent of organized religion.

In the first area, he occasionally visited or attended a session with a psychic. He saw the San Diego psychic Adele one or two more times. If another medium he knew of came to town or might be available in the area, he might see them or invite them to his home. When spiritualist-inclined visitors from Mexico visited one year, they held a Ouija board session with him.[261] From what I can tell, these experiences happened more frequently around Helen's death, then tapered off as other relationships and professional activities took more of his time and attention in his final years.

Sometimes he would invite other friends and colleagues along to share the experience and verify his own perceptions. Richard Farson recalled attending a "table tapping" session in which they would ask questions and then go through the alphabet and the table would "tap" (that is, move slightly) when they got to the right letter, eventually spelling out the name of the person who had a message for them. Thus Carl was able to ask Helen questions and receive answers.[262]

On another occasion Rogers attended a gathering and had a special audience with Swami Muktananda (1908–1982), a famous Hindu spiritual leader, one of whose many ashrams was in California.[263] The two-day event in December 1980 was organized by Association for Humanistic Psychology president and *Aquarian Conspiracy* author Marilyn Ferguson.[264] Rogers' diary entries describe how Muktananda told him that he, Rogers, was "a fully realized person" and talked with him about that. (Characteristically, Rogers thought, "To me that seems rather sad, because I would not want to be in a state of perfection where there was no further ... growth or challenge.")[265] Rogers raised a number of points of disagreement with the Swami, including telling him "that I was put off by the fact that people worshipped him ... He replied he worshipped the God in every person who was in the audience, therefore he did more worshipping of the inner cells in them than they worshipped him."[266] Rogers told him "that I seemed to be moving in a spiritual direction and that some people see me as spiritual, but that I'm not even sure of the meaning of the word." Muktananda replied, "You are very spiritual." Upon Rogers' request, Muktananda laid his hands on Rogers to transmit "shaktipat"—chakral energy, a form of spiritual initiation that Muktananda had given to "untold thousands of spiritual seekers."[267] "Certainly I received no power from him," wrote Rogers, "but it was very worthwhile experience." At the end of the event, when participants were taking their leave, Muktananda told Rogers, "You are a great soul" and gave him a gift of a small, white ivory elephant, which apparently had great meaning. "He reached out and embraced me, which I am told is *most* unusual. I was really touched." A week later he received a letter from an associate, Ann Dreyfuss, who told him that shortly after seeing Rogers the Swami stopped her "for a minute—very unusual—to tell her that he likes me; that I am a wise man, have *very* good understanding, have a good heart." She added, "Carl, he said this with *such* love and intensity." Apparently Muktananda's followers were amazed at how much "Baba" seemed to like Rogers, how much time he spent with him, and how he gave Rogers a gift. Rogers enjoyed the attention and validation and in turn liked Muktananda, but was a bit skeptical that the Swami might be flattering him to turn him into one of his devotees, as had happened with Joseph Chilton Pierce whom Rogers had met that weekend and whose *Crack in the Cosmic Egg* Rogers had recently read.

Muktananda wasn't the only one who thought Rogers had a highly evolved consciousness. Another medium, who received messages through guided typing on a typewriter informed Rogers, through a friend, that the "universe is being guided by a committee of 9 … [who] were trying to prepare the transformation of the world … There are several beings on the planet who are hugely evolved (not clear whether they are of the nine or guided by the nine) … These included Ram Dass, Patricia Sun, and Carl Rogers, 'though he doesn't know it yet.'"[268] Rogers felt overwhelmed by such messages. He sensed that maybe it was true that he had some special role to perform, but was unsatisfied with second- or third-hand revelations. He asked himself, "Why can't I have some inner experience, some meditative flash, some sign—psychic or otherwise, to let *me* know. Meanwhile I plug along as I've always done. If I'm a highly evolved person, I'm also a very primitive one. What the hell does it all mean? Jung tells me of my 'mission' and it seems to me that I've had other statements. But none of this happens in *me* so I'm mystified.

Although his psychic and spiritual explorations were clearly an important theme in Rogers' later years, particularly from 1977–1981, he was reluctant to write much about them. As a distinguished scientist and professional himself, he knew full well how traditional science and the professions view paranormal phenomena. Even when scientists or professionals themselves might be religious, it was customary not to mix religion with science or professional practice.[269] Whether or not psychic occurrences or life after death were "real," Rogers knew these subjects were landmines in the fields his work had influenced. He had no intention of undermining his past professional contributions or current international work by leaving himself, or Helen, open to ridicule. So, publicly, he shared only a few brief anecdotes about his own experiences, hinted that there might be more to come, and left it at that.

But unlike other private areas of Rogers' life that few people knew about, virtually all of Rogers' associates and friends who had contact with him in his later years knew of his interest in the paranormal. However, when asked whether Rogers truly believed in life after death, communication from the other world, or other paranormal experiences, or whether he was merely interested in and open to the possibility of these phenomena, his associates differed markedly in their answers. Richard Farson thought Rogers "bought it hook, line and sinker" and was appalled and saddened by his friend and mentor's gullibility. Maureen O'Hara thought he "got led down the garden path" by some around him who were inclined to spiritualism.[270] She wrote that, "Carl gradually read less and less from psychology and increasingly turned to writers such as Marilyn Ferguson, Fritjof Capra, Rupert Sheldrake, physicists such as David Bohm and Illyn Prigogine, and New Agers, many of whom frequently crossed the line between science and pseudoscience. Carl became increasingly involved with gurus, psychics, and physicists."[271]

Others thought Rogers remained the empiricist, open to the possibility of these phenomena but retaining his critical judgment. Valerie Henderson, who attended sessions with Rogers and the psychic Adele, said, "I don't think he was ever convinced." Lloyd Henderson agreed. So did Natalie Rogers who saw him as "skeptical but interested, really interested and open to having experience."[272] Reinhard Tausch saw Rogers as open to the possibility of life after death and psychic phenomena, but not convinced.[273] David Cain recalled that when Rogers was eighty-four or eighty-five, he told Cain about his experience with the painter who channeled Toulouse-Lautrec (described earlier) and another similar experience. Cain said, "Now I don't think Carl embraced that sort of thing by any means, but for some reason his mind opened more to those sorts of extraordinary, atypical, unexplainable experiences that he never entertained at earlier points in his life." Cain pointed out that Rogers tended to be very agreeable about other viewpoints, "but that didn't mean that he agreed with you or was changed by it." He recalled an anecdote from Rogers' Chicago years where Rogers was counseling a railroad worker. Rogers was so understanding and accepting that, after the interview, the man said, "That Dr. Rogers, he surely knows a lot about railroading."[274] His point was that Rogers' openness to the ideas around him did not mean he truly bought them.

Rogers continued to evaluate each psychic experience with a critical eye. For example, in a diary entry of January 6, 1980, he wrote, "... the Ouija board session was disappointing. It seems as though it was definitely Nella's unconscious," meaning it was the medium's unconscious speaking rather than an external spirit communicating through her. Yet, even if Rogers remained open-minded but unconvinced until the end, the very fact that he actively chose to participate in such experiences over many years suggests an interest, nay, a fascination with the subject that is noteworthy. It suggests to me that while his scientific mind could explain away a great number of his experiences with the paranormal, there were other experiences that he could not explain away. These experiences deeply impressed him and he sought other experiences to learn more. Particularly the possibility that Helen might be trying to communicate with him, that there was information from the other side that could bring him greater peace of mind, and that he and Helen might meet again in another life certainly appeared to have a hold on him.[275]

In addition to his paranormal explorations, which his friends and colleagues were well aware of, his spiritual journey also had a private side that few of his intimates knew of. One who did was Maria Bowen, who also served as a therapist to him in the 1980s. In one journal entry he wrote of "a particularly good session with Maria" in which they explored the "possibility of *surrender*—to a higher self, higher power or energy. The spiritual, which will not come from without, but from within." Feeling that he was finding his way back to his true self, he added, with totally uncharacteristic Christian imagery, "I found myself 'till I find my rest in Thee.'" Three days later, he wondered, "What would it mean to be more spiritual? To surrender more to the all-pervading spirit—within and without. To feel that I was in a caring universe, and that if I make a mistake, forget something (some detail in planning my trip) it won't be fatal. There is a caring spirit. I would not need to be in such total control … I would have more joy … Toward the end I laughed and said, 'By God, we're making progress!', and shed a few joyful tears." [276]

The next year he wrote, "I've had two unusual dream experiences, which had a different quality. I woke once with the 'realization' that for a moment I had been at one with the cosmos … I feel more at peace with myself this morning. I hope it lasts. Kinda let myself feel that I am part of the divine, that God is in me, is struggling in me to *be* in the world? Seems as though that is the direction that I'd like to take—being part of a struggling, imperfect God still creating his world. (Read an interesting book on the Gnostic gospels which portrayed Jesus as a mystic, who only symbolically and in visions appeared to his disciples after death, and who did not suffer at the crucifixion, because his spirit was already dancing on top of the Cross. Also loved mary m, and she was one of strongest of his disciples.)"[277]

Here we see Rogers struggling with his place in the cosmos, wanting very much to find a healing energy in the universe. Did he ever find it? Brian Thorne, in an eloquent exploration of Rogers' spiritual quest and its implications for the person-centered approach, described how Rogers' original religious fervor never entirely left him, that his belief in the trustworthy direction of human nature in a supportive environment was another form of faith, and that he pursued the understanding and dissemination of this faith system throughout his life with the passionate commitment that was as much a vocation as his original calling.[278]

487

Moreover, his ongoing intellectual search for a transcendent worldview that would comprehend the connection between atoms, micro-organisms, human beings as individuals and in relationships, and the universe was nothing less than a religious meditation on the nature of the universe.

Indeed, Rogers continued this meditation through the seventies and culminated in the period before Helen's death with his description of what he called the "formative tendency" in the universe. For years Rogers had made the *actualizing tendency*, the inexorable drive of individuals to strive to achieve their potential, a cornerstone of the person-centered approach. Now he saw that the actualizing tendency—the *individual* drive toward complexity, organization and becoming—mirrored a similar tendency in the universe. Acknowledging a debt to Nobel laureate biologist Albert Szent-Gyoergyi, historian of ideas Lancelot Whyte and others, Rogers wrote, "there appears to be a formative tendency in the universe, which can be observed at every level"—from the formation of molecules, to the formation of crystals, to the growth of cells, to human growth and development, to the formation of complex solar systems and galaxies. "This is an evolutionary tendency toward greater order, greater complexity, greater interrelatedness."[279] Rogers suggested this formative tendency was a counterpoint to the commonly accepted phenomenon of entropy, the universal tendency toward deterioration and disorder, which he acknowledged as operating as well. But once again, as with his description of the positive and trustworthy aspects of human nature, Rogers was the optimist. While others might emphasize entropy or chaos in the universe, Rogers saw a stronger force in the positive, creative movement in the universe, a vision of unfolding complexity and fulfillment of potential in all forms of life and in the universe itself.

Moreover, if there was this creative tendency at work in the universe, perhaps it was possible for people to know it or experience it personally, fully, and not just intellectually. Thus writers and scientists who were then experimenting with altered states of consciousness afforded us a glimpse at a different way of understanding or experiencing reality.[280] Rogers wrote that individuals who experienced altered states of consciousness described "this evolutionary flow ... as tending toward a transcending experience of unity. They picture the individual self as being dissolved in a whole area of higher values, especially beauty, harmony, and love. The person feels at one with the cosmos. Hard-headed research seems to be confirming the mystic's experience of union with the universal."[281] Thus, Rogers wrote, "I hypothesize that ... In humankind, this [formative] tendency exhibits itself as the individual moves from a single-cell origin to complex organic functioning, to knowing and sensing below the level of consciousness, to a conscious awareness of the organism and the external world, to a transcendent awareness of the harmony and unity of the cosmic system, including humankind."[282]

It is noteworthy that Rogers used the word "hypothesize" in his fullest description of the formative tendency. It suggests that while he worked out his worldview intellectually and had a number of personal experiences that were consistent with this view, he never had a classic "religious experience" of enlightenment, mystical union or being "born again" that resulted in a personal knowledge of the universe, a transcendent reality, or God. Even when he wrote to psychologist Allen Bergin in 1979, after having published his article on the formative tendency, that, "I do believe there is some kind of a transcendent organizing influence in the universe which operates in man as well. I lean toward the notion that perhaps this force is a struggling force and that we are a part of the struggle to make the universe a better place to live in … My present very tentative view is that perhaps there is an essential person which persists through time, or even through eternity," it was still "perhaps" and "a very tentative view." It was not a deeply held conviction, and certainly not what William James called a "noetic" experience, that is, an absolute knowledge that is all-encompassing and transcends cognitive understanding.[283] As Rogers' colleague Valerie Henderson put it, "At the end he wasn't willing to say there is a God or give a name to anything of the sort, but he said, 'there is a force in the universe. I can't describe it. I can't say I know what its properties are,' but he tended to think it was a positive force, like the formative tendency."[284]

One quality of the "emerging person" that Rogers wrote about was that of being a spiritual seeker. Rogers remained such a seeker himself until his death. He never reached the end of his spiritual journey, but the experiences and insights he had along the way arguably enriched him and his work significantly. His spiritual journey gave him hope, occasional peace of mind, or at least an understanding of what peace of mind might feel like if he could attain it. His spiritual journey which produced his insights about the formative tendency in the universe gave his entire system of thought and practice a deeper foundation in science and philosophy, if not also religion. For Maureen O'Hara, Rogers' spiritual journey was part and parcel of his life's work and who he was as a person.

I think Carl was what I would call a very spiritual person all his life. I think it's the kind of spirituality that scientists have, where you are in love with the universe, where everything is something that you could learn from, everything is meaning laden and everything is a sign that the universe is unfolding according to its intrinsic nature to become. I think everything that I have read of Carl from way back and my knowledge of him in the last 16, 17 years was that he was a man that was enthralled by creation and he could be as moved by a begonia or by a woman expressing her deepest fears in a group or by a conversation with a friend or with a large group or with some mysterious phenomena that he'd just heard about. So, in that sense he was … I call that spiritual. Anybody that is in the world in that way, as an appreciator of it all … that is to say that he was very much in touch with the divine. His belief in the formative tendency, if you

489

think about it, that's a metaphysics, that's a spiritual position. It doesn't fit the notion of random, meaningless universe. He buys the notion that the universe is meaningful and that it's moving toward greater complexity, towards greater realization, and he says that there is this specter in all things and all of nature and in human beings towards greater and greater complexity. So, in some ways, I don't want to overstate this, but in some ways his life is a meditation on that reality. I think that's the heart of all the great religions. But his form for it was not a religious form. It was more of a direct engagement with the mysteries than it was a religious observance. So, I don't think he was having an awakening at the end, I think he had always been awake. I think that's why people of the church have always seen his work as being core, around which they could build their own approach to counseling or pastoral care or ministering.[285]

Others would have to make the bridge from Rogers' philosophy to their own religious inclinations; he would not do it for them; although they often tried. Shortly before his death, Rogers told an interviewer how,

Another time, a group of young priests were trying to pin me to the wall, saying that I must be religious. I finally said to them and it is something I still stand by—"I am too religious to be religious"—and that has quite a lot of meaning for me. I have my own definition of spirituality. I would put it that the best of therapy sometimes leads to a dimension that is spiritual, rather than saying that the spiritual is having an impact on therapy. But it depends on your definition of spiritual. There are certainly times in therapy and in the experience I have had with groups where I feel that there is something going on that is larger than what is evident. I have described this in various ways. Sometimes I feel much as the physicists, who do not really split atoms; they simply align themselves up in accordance with the natural way in which the atoms split themselves. In the same way, I feel that sometimes in interpersonal relationships power and energy get released which transcends what we thought was involved.[286]

Yet he appreciated the irony that others often saw him in religious terms. He told Allen Bergin in 1979 how, "I had to smile the other day when talking to Mwalimu Amara. He is a splendid black man, a minister who worked for quite some time with Elisabeth Kübler-Ross, and who has a lot of psychic ability, as well as spiritual qualities. He told me that when he gets to feeling depressed, he reads some of 'the gospels by Rogers.' When the people around laughed at his remark, he said, 'Well, this guy has been writing religious stuff for many years and it's about time that he admits it.'"[287] Doug Land recalled how "On more than one occasion I suggested to him that he might be a closet Christian. He [Rogers] was amused by that and said, 'Well, that's your problem.' He saw the grace within each of us."[288]

Sometimes Rogers was less than amused at the attributions people made about his religious proclivities. Maureen O'Hara remembered, "In my last conversation with him, he still had a pretty skeptical take on the religious people that were trying to turn his work into a new justification for Christianity. He was not happy with that because he saw religions in those denominational and sectarian ways as being more responsible for divisiveness than for human connectedness."[289] This last recollection is significant, coming a few weeks before Rogers' death. It reminds us that, as vital as Rogers' spiritual journey was to him, particularly in the late 1970s and early 1980s, it was not the most important chapter of his final years. Rather it was his efforts regarding human connectedness and divisiveness that dominated the remainder of his professional life. As Brian Thorne said, Rogers did not take his spiritual exploration much further in his final years, and his attention to the topic was intermittent.[290] While he continued to be interested in the spiritual arena, it claimed only a small part of his remaining time and attention. His work in international conflict resolution and peacekeeping became his dominant interest.

CHAPTER 12

The California Years
Part Three:
Peacemaking
1977–1987

In spite of the time and energy absorbed around Helen's illness and dying, his own physical and mental health issues, his new personal relationships, and his spiritual journey, remarkably, after Helen's death Rogers embarked upon one of the most productive periods in his long life. A major part of this work was a series of workshops around the world focusing on the person-centered approach in general and its application to intercultural communication and conflict resolution in particular.

Cross-Cultural Work

It is hard to strictly delineate when Rogers' person-centered workshop period of the mid to late seventies changed to the cross-cultural workshop period of the late seventies through the eighties. The person-centered workshops he and his colleagues conducted led to a deeper understanding of his theory's social and political implications, implications he explored in his book *On Personal Power*. Having begun with individual therapy, then having moved to group work, education, other helping professions and now person-centered communities, he became interested in applying the person-centered approach to even wider cultural and political contexts. Thus he became increasingly involved in international cross-cultural work and, as we shall see later, in international tension-reduction and peacemaking. While he never could have predicted his life's work would follow this trajectory, looking back it was a logical progression—from individual therapy to ever-widening applications of the person-centered approach.

It happened rather quickly, considering that the first "person-centered workshop" took place in 1974. For one thing, people from all over the world attended the person-centered workshops, making cross-cultural communication a prominent theme throughout these experiences. Moreover the workshop title and theme, which was often a variant of "The Person-Centered Approach: Individual Change and *Its Social Implications*" (emphasis added), attracted many participants with a social and political agenda. Wishing to encourage this, since these workshops typically had more applicants than could be accommodated, the staff consciously selected participants to maximize diversity. Thus blacks and whites, Israeli Jews and Palestinians, Latin American social activists and Californian spiritual-seekers, men and women, and other representatives of different groups and cultures regularly met one another in these workshops. As trust built in the group and people took the risk of sharing their deeper feelings, inevitably conflicts between worldviews emerged and experiences in cross-cultural communication and conflict resolution occurred. Consistently the protagonists from different groups achieved a greater level of understanding and acceptance of one another—sometimes modest, sometimes great, often very dramatic.

International participants in these workshops would then invite Rogers and his colleagues to conduct workshops in their own countries. For example, Eduardo Bandeira and other Brazilians who participated in the 1976 workshop in Ashland, Oregon or other CSP programs that summer invited Rogers and his team to do a series of workshops in Brazil in 1977.[1] In 1978 Rogers wrote how in Mexico, "Natalie and I enjoyed working together on a workshop which emphasized dealing with oppressed people. It was organized by three Mexicans who had been to our workshop and the staff consisted of seven Mexicans and three from the U.S."[2] But the greatest explosion of activity around the person-centered approach and cross-cultural communication at this time took place in Europe.

Rogers and his work had been introduced to Europe as early as 1949 by Professor J.R. Nuttin of Catholic University in Leuven, Belgium.[3] As Brian Thorne documented in his brief history of the person-centered approach in Europe, in the fifties and sixties there was steadily growing activity and interest in the person-centered approach in many countries and occasional visits from Rogers during this period.[4] This gradual movement increased dramatically in the late seventies and early eighties, in part as a result of the efforts of Charles ("Chuck") Devonshire, Andre de Peretti, and Alberto Zucconi.

In the late sixties, Devonshire had been director of the Psychological Service Center of the College of San Mateo in California, when Rogers and fourteen members of WBSI conducted San Mateo's annual counseling institute, and Devonshire had co-facilitated a small group with Rogers. In 1972, Devonshire and CSP member Andre Auw designed and conducted a workshop explicitly on cross-cultural communication at San Mateo, "organized along the lines of similar programs at the Center for Studies of the Person ... and with the consultation of Dr. Carl R. Rogers."[5] Devonshire was so impressed by the learning experience that occurred when people from different cultures met in a person-centered workshop format that he formed the Cross-Cultural Communication Project which, in collaboration with CSP, began scheduling workshops in Europe the next year. His renamed Centre for Cross-Cultural Communication soon built an active program of person-centered, cross-cultural workshops in several countries. He also helped create separate Facilitator Development Institutes in some countries.[6] Rogers lent his support to many of these ventures, allowing his name to be used as a co-founder of the Institute and serving on the staff of some of the programs, along with other CSP members.

Meanwhile Andre de Peretti had been active for many years in promulgating the person-centered approach in France and beyond. In 1977 he and his family visited La Jolla, and a discussion began between Rogers and de Peretti about CSP and de Perretti planning a large international gathering using a balance of European and CSP staff as facilitators.[7] Eventually it was determined that Chuck Devonshire, with his excellent network of contacts throughout the continent, would be the European coordinator of the event, with Gay Swenson being the CSP coordinator. This resulted in a large, person-centered workshop being held in El Escorial, Spain in 1978. The 173 participants plus staff represented twenty-seven countries. This was the first time that a significant international gathering like this had taken place, and the Americans and Europeans alike were impressed with the critical mass of European and worldwide person-centered activity represented there. Valerie Henderson recalled how "hopeful and inspiring" it was to meet leaders of the person-centered approach from across Europe. The workshop was conducted mostly in the person-centered format that the CSP group had been using in recent years, although in addition to the unstructured community meetings, small encounter groups were planned in advance with facilitator teams made up of a CSP member and a European, male and female, co-facilitating each unstructured small group throughout the program. For example, Gay Swenson and Andre de Peretti co-facilitated one small group, Valerie Henderson and Brian Thorne facilitated another, and so on.[8] As will be described below, the workshop was volatile, exciting and ultimately very successful, doing much to increase the momentum of the person-centered approach in Europe and beyond.

After the El Escorial workshop, Alberto Zucconi of Italy and several CSP staff members wanted to build on the momentum by beginning an ongoing training program in the person-centered approach in Europe. Zucconi was a leading proponent of the person-centered approach in Italy and had been a staff member of the Living Now Program at CSP for several summers. Together Zucconi, Devonshire's Center for Cross-Cultural Communication, and CSP sponsored a new workshop in Italy for the following year, both to introduce the person-centered approach to more Europeans and to use it as an occasion to develop a European training program. Again a team of CSP and European leaders staffed the workshop which was held at Lake Albano, near Rome and which again had about 175 participants.[9] Out of that event, Zucconi and Devonshire, with Rogers' support, launched a project that became the Institute for the Person-Centered Approach, International. One of the Institute's main activities was its Learning Program—a three-year training program in client-centered therapy and the person-centered approach, admitting twenty participants per year. It included two intensive workshops of nine days each and regular weekend workshops throughout the three years.[10] Zucconi and Devonshire launched the program in 1980 in Italy, with Rogers joining them in June that year for an event in Rome.

By the early eighties, then, there was so much activity going on in Europe that it was hard to tell the players without a scorecard. In addition to the national associations and other developments described below, Devonshire's Center for Cross-Cultural Communication was offering workshops in at least ten European countries; Facilitator Development Institutes were operating with local leadership in Great Britain, Holland, West Germany, France, Italy, and Sweden; and on-going Learning Programs were operating in Rome, Lugano (Switzerland) and London.[11] And Rogers and his CSP colleagues were in the thick of it. Rogers' name appeared on many brochures as co-founder of the program or institute. Moreover, from their inception and into the new century, Rogers (during his lifetime), and other CSP colleagues were active participants in the Centre for Cross-Cultural Communication workshops and on-going Learning Programs organized by Devonshire and Zucconi. In addition, as the person-centered approach caught on in different countries in Europe, leaders in those countries invited Rogers and his colleagues to conduct workshops. Depending on the auspices and purpose, some of the workshops had an explicit cross-cultural communication theme, with a special effort made to recruit and select participants from different national, ethnic, religious and cultural backgrounds. Other workshops might focus on training therapists, facilitators and others in the person-centered approach. In either case, given the international settings and multinational composition of staff and participants, cross-cultural issues would inevitably arise.

The workshops typically had two cross-cultural aspects. First was cross-cultural communication and conflict resolution. As Maureen O'Hara wrote, "In his last years, Rogers and various colleagues ... took the client-centered message to over twenty countries, including: South Africa, where we facilitated encounters between blacks and whites; Latin America where North encountered South; Europe, where Eastern bloc Marxists met Western humanists; and Ireland, where Protestants met Catholics."[12] Second was the appropriateness and applicability of the person-centered approach to other cultures. Could this

American invention readily be exported to other countries and cultures? Was this primarily a white, Western, middle-class approach to helping relationships and personal growth, or was the person-centered approach equally relevant and applicable to people of color or poverty or settings where political and economic survival was more urgent than personal self-actualization? While both these themes were present in the earlier person-centered workshops in the United States, they were present more often, more explicitly and more prominently in the international and cross-cultural workshops of the late 1970s to 1980s.

Another difference between the two periods was that the cross-cultural workshops were typically more structured than the open-ended person-centered workshops of the 1970s. Schedules were planned in advance to include a combination of presentations, demonstrations, whole community meetings, small encounter groups, and sometimes sessions around particular topics of interest to participants. Workshops like these proved to be an ideal vehicle for Rogers to communicate his ideas, his work, his current interests, and himself—a lifelong need which, if anything, seemed to increase in his final years. It was as though he had a sense of urgency about sharing the person-centered philosophy with a world that appeared to be teetering between self-destruction and self-actualization. From 1977 to 1985, aside from dozens of workshops and presentations he gave in the United States, Rogers traveled to Brazil three times, Mexico five times, Spain twice, England three times, Venezuela, Italy twice, Poland, Finland, Austria four times, West Germany three times, South Africa, Kenya, Zimbabwe, Japan, Switzerland, Hungary and Ireland, to spread the person-centered approach (not to mention personal side trips to China, Sweden and elsewhere).[13] Many of these trips were several weeks in duration and involved two or more workshops in each country. In 1986, the year before he died, eighty-four-year-old Rogers and seventy-nine-year-old colleague Ruth Sanford undertook a four-week journey to South Africa, with person-centered workshops in Johannesburg and Capetown; a three-week trip to the Soviet Union, with two intensive workshops and several large, public meetings in Moscow and Tbilisi; and a return trip to Hungary involving a week-long workshop in Budapest.

Once it was decided that Carl Rogers would be coming to a country to co-facilitate a workshop, it was not long before his hosts or others invited him to meet or work with other groups in that country. For example, Peter Schmid recalled Rogers' ten-day visit to Austria in 1981.[14] It included a lecture to a large audience at the University of Vienna co-sponsored by Schmid's person-centered institute and the Institute for Psychotherapy of the Medical Faculty; a meeting with Rogers and twenty-five to thirty leading psychotherapists (mostly psychoanalysts), in which Rogers gave an introduction, did a short therapy demonstration with Alfred Pritz (who later became president of the World Association for Psychotherapy) and conducted an extended discussion;[15] a common meeting with both of the theological faculties of the University; and

496

the main workshop, which was conducted under the auspices of The Austria Program.[16] Rogers and CSP colleagues Doug Land and Valerie Henderson co-facilitated the workshop which included community meetings, small groups, a demonstration interview, theory discussions, and other sessions.

Schmid remembered Rogers as participating fully in all aspects of the meetings, discussions, workshops and other events. He was impressed with how consistent Rogers was with his writings. "I experienced Carl doing what he himself described always to do—not to attack, not to go against somebody else, what somebody else is feeling." Instead he was "a very modest analyst and only being friendly to people." Even when people were argumentative or asked highly theoretical questions, "He always responded with trying to best explain his ideas, so this was very impressive to everybody who was at that [small group meeting with leading psychotherapists]. So I cannot [understand] any descriptions that later he was more arrogant or that he didn't have to go into details. He always was very polite and patient in answering such questions."

Another example of Rogers' intense international workshop schedule was his six-week trip to Europe in September–October 1983.[17] It included presentations, meetings and workshops with social workers in London; participants in the London Learning Program; educators, psychologists and others in Geneva; participants in the Italian Learning Program and then all three European Learning Programs in Geneva; probation officers and a public talk in Bonn, Germany; nurses and physicians in Basel, Switzerland; and therapists and social workers in Stuttgart and Hamburg, Germany. One notable event, on the last night of his Geneva workshop, was when Rogers gave a talk to the *Club Diplomatique* whose members were the international diplomatic corps based in Geneva. About seventy-five diplomats and seventy-five workshop participants attended. As one workshop participant recalled, "It was offered, not required, but many diplomats came to hear Carl Rogers talk about a person-centered approach to conflict resolution."[18] All told, in addition to three press conferences, Rogers met with about 2,400 people in "twelve separate groups for periods ranging from four hours to four days," in which he conducted seven therapeutic interviews before different audiences.[19]

He learned how to pace himself, taking time to relax in each country before and after his workshops, visiting castles and sites of interest, taking a couple of hours to rest each afternoon when he was working, and even taking a ten-day vacation in the south of France with his partner from London. After the last workshop, in Hamburg, wrote Rogers, a small group remained and "This turned into a group of deep sharing, especially in regard to coping with death and grief. Both Reinhard [Tausch] and another man had lost their wives recently and I four years ago. We were able to share our feelings in a very supportive way." Valerie Henderson, his younger CSP associate, recalled, "When we would come back from a trip, I'd be exhausted while he'd bounce right back and be ready to start again."[20]

João Hipólito attended two of Rogers' European workshops and noticed how Rogers did not speak as much as people expected him to in the large group sessions. Yet he was still very active in his own way, listening extremely carefully to everything that was said so "he could understand what was going on and give really deep feeling of understanding and being with the person."[21] As Rogers told a group in South Africa some years later, "I've been interested in myself in recent years to realize that I think I say less in each group that I'm in. Someone spoke to me about the meetings here in Cape Town and said, 'You certainly keep a very low profile.' No, it isn't keeping a low profile; it's simply that I find that often if I am fully present, the group picks up facilitative ways of being themselves, and if I don't respond to this person somebody else responds better than I had in mind."[22] Hipólito thought it remarkable how in a demonstration interview, "Once he [Rogers] was working, it was as if the world didn't exist anymore. You could see him as if he was under a glass bowl, you see, and nothing passed through this wall, and his attention was exclusively on this meeting, this intervention." As usual people were very impressed with the effectiveness of Rogers' demonstration interviews, but Hipólito wondered whether it was a fair test. "I remember one of the persons that was interviewed came hundreds of miles to come to be interviewed by Rogers. Perhaps that gives some distortion on the interview. You see people came: it was not just that somebody was there and suddenly had a problem and Rogers took him and made an interview that was a demonstration and there was a cure." Rather Ruth Sanford pre-screened the interviewees and selected the person who was going to be interviewed by Rogers.

But Sanford's screening of interview candidates was cursory; she usually had only a brief time to select someone who seemed reasonably verbal, whose voice would project, whose presenting issue seemed amenable and appropriate for a demonstration interview, and who offered no "red flags" that might cause her to distrust the person's motives.[23] Screening or not, the risk Rogers was taking was obvious to everyone. What if the client did not open up and begin to explore her feelings? What if the encounter group or the person-centered community went nowhere or, worse yet, blew up in an expression of hostility that could not be mitigated or resolved? Rogers, on stage before a typically packed auditorium, appeared oblivious to such fears, as he attended with incredible focus, empathy and concern to the client and her deepening expressions of feeling; or as he sat with the audience patiently accepting their various expressions of frustration or confusion, believing they would eventually recognize and experience the potency of the person-centered approach to learning and building community.

Even when the workshops were conducted with language interpreters, as they often were, participants were invariably moved to see Rogers at work. His ability to establish an immediate rapport with his client in therapy, to engender enough trust for encounter group participants to share meaningful feelings, and to reach a large audience with his personal style of presenting and responding to them were all impressive at any stage in his career. For a man in his eighties, by now a legend in psychology, to have traveled across the world to be with them and to share so much of himself was an unforgettable experience for most. Interest in Rogers, client-centered therapy and the person-center approach continued to grow on five continents as a result of his globe-trotting endeavors.

Emerging Democracies

Many of Rogers' cross-cultural communication and person-centered approach workshops took place in countries behind the Iron Curtain or in newly emerging democracies. This led to interesting situations and demonstrated how a person-centered approach might appeal to individuals and groups working for self-realization and participatory democracy and, conversely, be a threat to authoritarian governments. If Rogers thought he was beginning to understand the political implications of the person-centered approach when he wrote *On Personal Power* in 1977, the next ten years of his life were even more of a laboratory for exploring the political and social import of his life's work.

Brazil was not a stable democracy in 1977 when Rogers and his colleagues convened three workshops in Recife, São Paulo, and Rio de Janeiro, attended by some 600–800 people each. Speaking publicly about individual freedom, self-actualization and self-determination was not typical in this society, and the secret police were present at least at one of the meetings. Even with the large groups and time delays of interpreting between Spanish and English, these workshops and others they conducted in Brazil had a great impact on the participants. They also impacted the larger society as "Media coverage was incredible. Newspaper coverage, the equivalent of *Time* magazine, *Life* magazine, published all kinds of material about what was going on."[24] At the end of his visit, Rogers wrote in his diary, "What has this whole trip meant to me? It has meant that a whole country (or so it seems) can be ready for a PCA explanation. It is astonishing to think they appreciate it because of their emotional nature, but perhaps even more because they are actually struggling to keep Democracy alive, where it is in real danger. I recognize now that media were in part genuinely interested, and in part using me to say the things they don't dare to say themselves. Anyway the time was certainly right."[25]

Valerie Henderson recalled how the 1978 workshop in Spain started out in Madrid at the Quixote Hotel which was then being retro-fitted to be the Russian Embassy.[26] Participants became suspicious that the rooms were "bugged," so after a few days, the whole workshop with 173 participants from twenty-seven nations plus staff moved from Madrid to El Escorial, to the Residencia San Jose. Germain Lietaer remembered how the workshop was "fairly wild," with much "contesting about social and political issues," such as the injustice of the workers in the hotel where they were staying earning such low wages. "These were issues which were discussed a lot … much more than psychotherapy, for instance."[27] Rogers found the ten-day workshop, utilizing two or three languages, to be "Very difficult, very struggling, finally very successful."[28] Henderson recalled how inspiring it was to be bringing the person-centered approach to a country still emerging from years of dictatorship under Generalissimo Franco.

Dee Aker was on the staff of the 1979 workshop in Poland. She recalled how, "Although banned in Poland, *Freedom to Learn* … had been read by everyone who came to work with him and his three colleagues …"[29] After Rogers gave formal lectures to the university medical school in Warsaw, they did a ten-day person-centered workshop in the countryside. Of the ninety participants, said Aker, "we knew at least ten were informants for the government. It was obvious who the informants were. People were so afraid to talk. All of Carl's books were underground."[30]

João Hipólito remembered attending the 1984 workshop in Szeged, Hungary along with 300 or more participants from many European counties, as well as North America, Japan and elsewhere. "It was to be filmed for a research proposal, but it was a Communist country and people were suspicious, worried … Those days were difficult days and there was a great discussion going on in the meeting to know if the group was agreed on the filming or not."[31]

Rogers was deeply impressed by the warm reception he and the person-centered approach received in these countries. As he noted after his 1977 Brazil trip, "I have signed perhaps 500 books in the three conferences, most of them newly purchased. I have been kissed, hugged, had my picture taken times without end. I can't go anywhere without being stopped, sometimes mobbed. The attitudes are so receptive and welcoming to me *and* my ideas it is overwhelming. Far more acceptance than in U.S."[32]

In the United States, people often take their democracy for granted. Not so in the countries behind the Iron Curtain and in other newly emerging democracies that Rogers visited in the late seventies and eighties. As the Japanese counselor, previously quoted, said in the 1960s, Rogers helped "to teach me the basic way of becoming to be democratic and not authoritative."[33] His life's work demonstrated how person-centered helping relationships can unleash healing, self-direction, and creativity in individuals and groups in all walks of life. As countries around the world strove to resolve inter-group tensions and practice self-government and self-determination, many recognized in Rogers' work not only useful methods for helping professionals, but a positive, person-centered, empowering, democratic philosophy consistent with their national aspirations.

South Africa

Rogers and Ruth Sanford's trips to South Africa represent a good case study of his cross-cultural work and the issues associated with the exportability of the person-centered approach to other cultures. They first worked in South Africa in 1982.[34] At that time the country was still in the grip of apartheid—a system of strict racial boundaries in which black South Africans were segregated into ghetto areas and were required to carry passes to travel; in which tens of thousands of black African men, for economic survival, had to leave their families to work in the mines for months on end; in which the security police operated with impunity against the black citizens; and in which many other injustices prevailed. Nelson Mandela, leader of the African National Congress, remained in prison after twenty years of incarceration. An international outcry against these abuses was taking hold. Some critics were supporting sanctions—a boycott of South Africa in terms of investment, tourism and commerce—while others urged constructive engagement to bring about change. As might be expected Rogers was in the constructive engagement camp. Len Holdstock, a South African white who had been a student of Rogers at Wisconsin and a Visiting Fellow at Center for Studies of the Person in the mid-seventies, invited Rogers to come and sponsored their visit.[35]

"Being able to welcome him and Ruth Sanford at the airport," wrote Holdstock, "with the drumming, the dancing and the ceremony conducted by the *izangoma* [native traditional healers], presented a most memorable occasion for them as well as for me."[36] Sanford recalled how Holdstock arranged workshops and presentations for them "at the University of the North, in Johannesburg and Cape Town, and at Stellenbosch University. We also worked in Zimbabwe and Kenya. Because Len had wide associations and deep sympathy with various traditional and tribal groups of the South African community, he opened the doors to Soweto, Cape Flats, Kwandebele, and other homelands … He made it possible for persons from all parts of South Africa to participate, particularly in the Johannesburg intensive workshop. We met in his home with *isangoma*, traditional religious leaders and healers, and learned of the native traditional forms of counseling which they call 'throwing the bones.' We were much impressed with the dedication and the respect for the individual with which these rituals were undertaken."[37]

At the universities they met with groups of faculty and students. In Cape Town and Johannesburg they met with large audiences of professionals, activists and interested public. As Sanford recalled, in one workshop they found themselves facing a crisis. It had been announced as a weekend workshop in the person-centered approach, yet they found themselves "on a raised platform in an amphitheater with an audience of six or seven hundred persons" who "for the most part … knew little or nothing of Carl's work."[38] Because he was experiencing vision problems at the time, Rogers couldn't lead off by reading a paper, and there was no opportunity for small groups. So they spoke to the audience about themselves, why they came to South Africa and the resources they brought with them. Then, making microphones available to the audience, invited the audience's participation and sharing of concerns and expectations. This led to a morning of "lively dialogue."

Later Rogers and Sanford facilitated a 90-minute, demonstration encounter group with eleven black and white participants. Some of the conversation might seem fairly tame today, but for some of participants it was the first time that they ever shared their real feelings with a person of the other race and the first time that blacks and whites shared a stage as equals. Near the beginning, one black member of the small group said, "For sure I feel good about being part of this kind of group. Being an African in South Africa with these artificial barriers keeping us apart. I feel out in the cold. I don't get to know people. They don't get to know me. I would like to be myself here and let you know how I feel. I hope you will do likewise." Rogers responded with typical empathy: "It must be quite an isolated feeling to feel that much of a barrier."[39] As trust built in the small group, participants shared more difficult feelings.

> Rhoda: Can I say something about that? I find it difficult to reach out to black people, and I think largely because I'm scared you're going to blame me and hit out at me, as a person, for where you're at. And, yeah, I'm *afraid*.
>
> Alan: I'm certainly not scared of personal contact and when I hear you talking I keep saying, "Not me. I'm not one of those whites." Yet we've got white skins, so we're part of it.
>
> Carl: One of the things that interests me is that when we talk in general, then the feelings are deeply opposed. That's when the feelings of bitterness and hatred come out. When we speak of person-to-person contacts, then the tone becomes quite different. The feeling is very different. That is a very significant aspect of our discussion.
>
> Rhoda: It is for me.
>
> John: And it's so sweet to feel it. Much can be done in one-to-one contact. I'm amazed. I can remember only twice it has happened to me that a white person I didn't know managed to see me as a human being.

It wasn't all easy reconciliation. When one white participant, Jeff, tended to minimize the problems around race, he got a strong reaction from John and many members of the audience.

> Jeff: You're having to work hard. Your feeling of inferiority, is that not within yourself? Not within me. I'm ready to accept you. Are you ready to accept that I can accept you?
>
> John: But you see the problem is real, that *you are white*. I might do the same job as you but because I am black I will not get the same salary you get, and you will get away with it. I would like you to *hear* that. That I am all the time being denied this God-given right. And this is saying to me, "You are not human."
>
> Jeff: John, we're back in generalities again. In many areas these differentiations

502

have been taken away, where you are being paid what I am being paid. (*Negative comments from the audience.*) No, I don't need to hear the voice from the audience. I can prove it by statistics.

Shirley: (*speaking for the first time*) Jeff. I would like to say something to you. I think that what John is saying is that he feels that he's not getting paid as much as a white man doing equivalent work. That's what you say, John, not in generalities. You are talking about *yourself.*

John: About myself, but even so about my other fellow blacks. It's a real problem for me.

Jeff: It's changing. You've got to admit it's changing. (*Again protests from the audience.*)

Rogers and Sanford, of course, had no idea how this would turn out. But the group continued to explore their feelings, both positive and negative, with Rogers particularly, playing the facilitative role, or as he would put it, being the facilitative person he was, conveying acceptance and understanding to each member and occasionally sharing his own feelings and perspective, as he did near the conclusion of the group.

Shirley: John, I've been sitting next to you all afternoon, and I sense in you a tremendous tension and almost frustration. I just wonder if there is something you'd like to ask of somebody here in their group? You seem to want something to grow out of this meeting.

John: Yes. I can say it this way, Shirley. Can you accept me to a point where I can accept that I'm accepted? (*Long silence.*)

Shirley: I think it might be too glib if I just said "Yes." But if I understand you correctly, I *can* accept you to a point where you can accept that you have been accepted. Yes.

John: Yes. Why...

Carl: I feel, John, that in her continued attempt to come back to you to help clarify what you want, she is *showing* her acceptance of you.

John: Okay. I accept that I am accepted. (*Laughter from the audience.*)

Carl: If this is the final meeting of this group, I want to say that I have learned a great deal. I feel there is some hope in the person-to-person acceptance that we have experienced and talked about. We haven't moved a great distance but it seems to me that if this kind of meeting could continue, it would hold hope.

After a few more people spoke, Rogers brought the group to a close and opened the conversation to members of the audience. This led to more of a community meeting-style encounter in which audience members continued the discussion begun in the demonstration group. Rogers also conducted a demonstration counseling session with a white South African, again leading to further discussion of process and content. Even stronger feelings were sometimes expressed, including suspicion of the person-to-person process that might been seen as an alternative to collective action to bring about change.

These examples give some sense of the other workshops, presentations and meetings during the 1982 South Africa visit. Four years later, upon invitation from earlier workshop participants, Rogers and Sanford returned to South Africa for about six weeks.[40] By this time tensions in the country were even higher than during their earlier visit, but so was hope for change. World economic sanctions were hurting the economy. Future Nobel Peace Prize winner Nelson Mandela was still a political prisoner, and there was widespread fear that a race war could erupt at any time, with blacks taking out their rage on the white population for generations of oppression, or the whites instituting even more repressive measures to hold on to power. Voices of reconciliation and peaceful solutions were struggling for acceptance.

It was in this historical moment that Rogers and Sanford again brought their person-centered approach to cross-cultural communication to South Africa. But this time they had a more sophisticated plan for training and dissemination. This was accomplished with the help and leadership of Shirley Shochot and a bi-racial committee of South Africans, most of whom participated in one of the 1982 workshops. In addition to large group presentations, demonstrations, and professional meetings, Rogers and Sanford would conduct two four-day training sessions, one in Cape Town and one in Johannesburg, each with forty persons representing the diversity of race, gender and politics in South Africa. These were "80 preselected Black and White helping professionals and others whose political roles extended from members of Parliament to revolutionary guerrillas."[41] At least one member of Parliament had never held a conversation with a black person before.[42] The goal of these sessions would be to have the participants experience the person-centered approach themselves *and* learn to be facilitators to help others develop better understanding and communication between the races in South Africa. The weekend following each training workshop, Rogers and Sanford conducted a large meeting open to the public. The large group then divided into smaller sub-groups of twelve to twenty diverse participants, each one led by a pair of the newly trained facilitators, each pair of facilitators including a man and woman of different races when possible. By this approach, about 1,000 South Africans experienced a person-centered approach to cross-cultural communication and tension reduction, while eighty developed skills in facilitating such dialogue. Rogers told a television interviewer at the time that, "His vision was that one day, every town, village, and district would have its own 'intergroup encounter centre' where interracial groups would be trained in the art of better communication in order to overcome prejudice, stereotyping, and hatred."[43]

In introducing themselves to the training group in Cape Town, Rogers and Sanford, as usual, told a bit about themselves and their hopes, and Rogers explained:

> I want to say another word or two about what we do or how we go about it. We're eager to set a psychological climate, and it's very strange the way that comes about. I realize it comes about mostly by our way of being. That's a strange thing to say but what we're talking about is not a technique. It's not a strategy. It's not a method. It's something that is based on a whole philosophy of being and it is that that we represent, I think, in the group. There are other aspects to it. When I'm in a group I really want to understand as sensitively and deeply as I can what is being expressed. I think one of the rarest experiences in the life of any one of us is to be deeply heard and understood and not judged—simply heard and accepted. That kind of nonjudgmental, empathic listening is something I endeavor to do when I'm in a group, and when I'm really sensitive and really understand deeply, it's a very powerful element. I feel that when I can unconditionally accept the other person, that helps. That helps the process. That unconditional acceptance is often misunderstood. It isn't something that I can feel or think anyone can feel all of the time for everyone, but when there are the moments in which I unconditionally accept you as a person, just as you are right now, that's a very healing, very releasing experience. And when I can be very genuine and real in everything that I'm doing, when I can be very present in the group, fully present, without façade, without any white coat, either real or imaginary, that seems to help to initiate the process. So those are some of the things I think that are important in setting a climate.[44]

As he told the participants, he did not have any particular solution to bring but rather a process for finding a solution. Much as he might have said about his approach to individual therapy, he told the group "I feel that often it is quite possible to deal with conflict without fully understanding the cause. Certainly here in South Africa the causes go back generations. I don't pretend to have a complete understanding of the causes but I can understand the present conflict and the present feelings, and it has been my experience that in dealing with the present conflict, it is possible to bring about a degree of reconciliation even though one doesn't pretend to fully understand all of the causes, because I think those are extremely complex."[45]

Multicultural Issues

Not surprisingly, and certainly not for the first time in South Africa or in his other international work, while many participants were waiting for just such an opportunity to communicate across boundaries and jumped right in, others were skeptical about such an approach succeeding, or angry at the presumption behind it. As one participant of color told them, "white people have used our therapy to tell me that they [hear] me and understand me and they damn well not going to do anything else about it … I've been discriminated against from birth in all spheres—education, politics, economics … It's unrealistic. I'm very pessimistic about it … Apartheid and [segregated] group areas has been very successful. I'm not sure that within my lifetime we are going to eradicate any of this."[46] In fact one black activist got so angry he walked out of a workshop and did not return for two days.

Inevitably in such an intense, politically charged situation, all the doubts and criticisms about the person-centered approach would be given voice. In South Africa and elsewhere, the person-centered approach would be called a white, middle-class, Western approach to therapy, education and human relationships, less applicable or inapplicable to other cultural, economic, and political contexts in the U.S. and around the world.

For the most part, multicultural critiques of the person-centered approach are based on the premise that the approach is essentially *individualistic*. It is said that the approach emphasizes self-actualization at the expense of an individual's duty to family, group or collective. In this sense, the person-centered approach could be seen as inimical to the filial piety of some traditional cultures, obedience to the church, loyalty to the state, or devotion to any object or cause beyond oneself. Not all cultures or groups value self-actualization as one of their highest values, nor do they necessarily value the overt expression of personal feelings. While the person-centered approach seems to place a premium on expression of feelings, other cultures and groups prefer more subtle or no expression of emotion in order to maintain social harmony.

Part of this critique gets to the very concept of self implied in Rogers' and other humanistic psychologists' writings.[47] Sampson distinguished between "self-contained" individualism and "ensembled" individualism. "Self-contained individualism is characterized by firmly drawn self–other boundaries. Personal control is emphasized and social responsibility takes the form of 'contractual exchange relationships involving reciprocity.'"[48] Thus engagement with others comes from free choice, because engagement gains the person either some tangible or potential benefits—from material gain to friendship to love to a better, fairer world which is also ultimately in one's own interest. "Embedded individualism, on the other hand, emphasizes more fluidly drawn self–nonself boundaries and field control. Relationships are noncontractual, mutually obligatory and communal, and as such operate by different rules than those which govern a more contractually oriented approach. Assistance is given and received without it being evaluated in material terms or in terms of an infringement on personal freedom." As South African psychologist Judora Spangenberg described it,

It should be kept in mind that the African culture has a strong community orientation. It is a deeply embedded value that individuals do not exist alone, but owe their existence to their ancestors, those unborn, the entire community, and all of nature. African Black people perceive themselves to be intimately connected to their ancestors. The welfare of the extended family as a whole is valued more highly than individual achievement, and the concept of sharing, or *ubuntu*, is important. *Ubuntu* forms an inherent part of rural African life and the traditional African worldview. Broodryk defined *ubuntu* as a communal way of life that deems society must be run for the sake of all, requiring cooperation, sharing, and charity.[49]

"Since its introduction, worldview has become one of the most referenced constructs in the multicultural counseling literature," and the argument that individuals will tend to reflect the individualistic or collectivist worldviews of their cultures is widely accepted.[50] Moreover, it is now widely accepted that the multiculturally competent counselor or therapist will seek to understand and work with the worldview of the client, rather than impose the worldview of the therapist.[51] Critics say that the person-centered approach reinforces an individualistic worldview and therefore is less applicable with clients or in cultures that have a collectivist worldview.

Following from this criticism is the charge that, being primarily individualistic rather than collectivist in its orientation, the person-centered approach fails to attend to the social context as both cause of and potential solution for personal difficulties. It fosters individual rather than contextual, collective or political solutions. In so doing it fails to utilize resources and support structures in the community that may be of help to clients. Moreover, some problems do not have individual solutions but can only be solved through social and political action.

Reflecting many of these criticisms in their widely read text on multicultural counseling, Sue and Sue dismiss the person-centered approach as largely inappropriate for multicultural settings.[52] Len Holdstock, who organized Rogers and Sanford's first trip to South Africa, agreed with some of these criticisms.[53] While still believing that the person-centered approach could be used with multicultural sensitivity, he criticized Rogers and Sandford for coming into the country without steeping themselves in the native healing traditions and then ignoring such traditions, expecting that this American invention would simply translate to South Africa and could not be improved by integrating it with native traditions. Holdstock was "sufficiently disillusioned with the traditional way of implementing the PCA in South Africa, not to participate in the second visit."[54] Swartz went so far as to call Rogers' visit a "safari," seeing it as a smokescreen for the more prevalent silence over apartheid, and arguing that dialogue was not going to solve South Africa's problems.[55] Dawes thought Rogers' cross-cultural encounter groups in South Africa were little more than "Band-Aids" on the festering wound of apartheid.[56]

Of course Rogers and others saw all this differently. As early as 1951, in *Client-Centered Therapy*, Rogers had written that, just as "The best vantage point for understanding behavior is from the internal frame of reference of the individual himself ... the only way to understand another culture is to assume the frame of reference of that culture."[57] In this insight, wrote Jeffrey Cornelius-White, Rogers anticipated the "postmodern paradigm shift similar to the relativistic and social constructivist assertions of multicultural counseling and psychotherapy."[58] Throughout his career Rogers said that the primary effort on the part of the person-centered therapist is to try to understand the client's frame of reference as the client understands it him or herself. When he was questioned a month before his death about his South African experience, Rogers acknowledged that "it is important to be as grounded as one can be in the culture, but to be prepared for the fact that it will probably be inadequate—that there will be some surprises."[59] Therefore, said Rogers, the therapist or group leader's "whole mind-set is a readiness to understand, to try to grasp what it is that has meaning for the person at this point. And that gets across to the group—that *desire to understand*" (emphasis in original). Rogers thus affirmed the basic tenet of multicultural counseling which says the counselor or therapist should be knowledgeable about other cultures and should seek to understand and honor the client's worldview. This was not a late-in-life insight. In 1951, in *Client-Centered Therapy*, Rogers had written,

> It is desirable that the student should have a broad experiential knowledge of the human being in his cultural setting. This may be given, to some extent, by reading or course work in cultural anthropology or sociology. Such knowledge needs to be supplemented by experiences of living with or dealing with individuals who have been the product of cultural influences very different from those which have molded the student. Such experiences and knowledge often seem necessary to make possible the deep understanding of another.[60]

Thus there is a reciprocal relationship between empathy and multicultural sensitivity. Empathy enhances the therapist's ability to be multiculturally sensitive, and multicultural sensitivity enhances the therapist's ability to be empathic.[61] Similarly, argued Cornelius-White, it is not only empathy, the desire to understand clients and group members, to indwell in their experience, that makes the person-centered approach applicable across cultures. He argued that the other two core conditions are equally important in multicultural contexts.[62]

Unconditional positive regard is, after all, an attitude of ultimate respect and prizing of the individual. For clients who have been oppressed, stereotyped, or devalued for much of their lives, the therapist's unconditional positive regard serves to contradict the previous messages of oppression. This was one of the things that meant the most to Daphne Koza, a student of psychology from Soweto, South Africa, when she first encountered Rogers' work. "I understood this man to be emphasizing the importance of listening, acceptance, and a nonjudgmental attitude in dealing with human beings. I knew that as a black person I had, over generations, *not been listened to* by the white minority government in South Africa. I had been rejected and *negatively judged* by them. My whole human dignity had been trampled on and I felt very angry and bitter." When she eventually met and worked with Rogers on his two visits to South Africa she was not disappointed. "He truly listened, was very accepting and nonjudgmental. He had such embracing warmth that one could not help but feel trusted and trusting in a relationship with him."[63]

The person-centered therapist, as per Rogers, accepts and prizes clients *as they are*. She does not seek to change the client's values or worldview. Eugene Gendlin pointed out that Rogers and his colleagues in Chicago led the country in demonstrating respect for clients of diverse backgrounds. (To expand on an earlier quotation) "In 1945, blacks, women, gay people and others found help at the Counseling Center because these therapists knew that *every* client had to teach them a new world. A black client might spend months teaching a therapist about black experience. However, another black client might say with relief after one hour, 'With you I can forget about race.' These therapists never forced a policy on a client. They would not coerce a woman to stay in a marriage, as psychoanalysts generally then did. Nor would they decide what another person's sexuality should be. To therapists trained by Rogers, it was obvious that *every* person is at the directing center of a life and that one can help people only by means of their own intricacy and their own steps."[64]

For Rogers this acceptance and prizing of clients as they are even extended to their manner of expressing themselves. When asked whether it would not be ethnocentric for a therapeutic approach to expect an American style of expression of feelings in another culture like South Africa, Rogers answered, "To the extent that it did, it wouldn't be in accord with person-centered theory. Because I would like to be able to accept what *is*. If the norm for this person is to grieve openly and loudly, okay. I'd like to be able to accept that. If, for this other person, grieving is something private that hardly shows on the surface at all, okay. I'd like to be able to accept that. I think the only problem I see is one of expectation. If you're going to expect a certain degree of affect—if you expect that of the process—then that can be artificial. If the degree of affect is what is comfortable, reasonable, or natural for this person, this group, or these people, then that's fine."[65]

Likewise the third core condition, congruence, is appropriate and arguably essential in multicultural contexts, especially if the therapist is of a different cultural, economic or other background than the client. All people, and therefore all therapists, have biases, prejudices and blind spots. All have worldviews that affect their counseling practice. Congruent therapists are more likely to be aware of their worldview and how it affects their counseling practice. Congruent therapists are also more likely to be aware of their own biases, fears and judgments of clients from different backgrounds and therefore more able to work on those attitudes and less likely to unconsciously act upon them. Again, this was a long-held view of Rogers, who wrote in 1942 in *Counseling and Psychotherapy*, that to be an effective counselor requires, among other things, "An understanding of the self ... Unless there is this considerable degree of insight, he will not be able to recognize the situations in which he is likely to be warped and biased by his own prejudices and emotions."[66] Looking at another meaning of congruence, with a client who is less familiar with the milieu of psychotherapy or mistrustful of a counselor of a different cultural background, being real or genuine is more likely to engender trust in the client than being perceived as playing a distant professional role.

By relying on the therapeutic relationship itself, characterized by the three core conditions, person-centered counselors and therapists tend to avoid directive techniques. While it has been suggested that some cultural groups benefit from more direction from their therapist, others have suggested that the relative *non*directiveness of the person-centered approach makes it particularly conducive to multicultural counseling contexts. As South African psychologist Judora Spangenberg wrote, "In person-centered counseling, the absence of overt techniques, in contrast with more directive counseling approaches, is an asset in a cross-cultural context, because techniques themselves may represent a form of cultural insensitivity and oppression."[67]

To argue that Rogers' core conditions and avoidance of directive techniques make the person-centered approach *inherently appropriate* for multicultural applications, however, does not resolve all the problems or concerns associated with the multicultural applications of the approach. To start with, the person-centered approach *is,* as its critics charge, highly individualistic. I don't believe that Rogers ever acknowledged this—at least in those terms. For one thing, in person-centered counseling and facilitation, *the process itself*—by validating the individual and his or her own feelings, thoughts and perceptions—strongly supports personal autonomy. Consider a client from a culture that is strongly matriarchal or patriarchal or authoritarian who comes to a person-centered counselor. Throughout the client's life, he or she has been told, "What *you* think doesn't matter. *Your* feelings are not important. You will follow your family or your group's way. That is your duty; you do not have a choice." Now, without the person-centered counselor ever having to say it explicitly, a different message comes across. "What *you* think *does* matter. I am interested in *your* feelings. What is the path *you* want to follow? How you live your life is *your* choice." The counselor need not say a word against the values or norms of the family or traditional culture; nonetheless, the process of person-centered therapy itself inculcates the values of personal autonomy and individualism. By so doing, it clashes with traditional or totalitarian cultures.

Rogers *did* acknowledge this as far as authoritarian governments, leaders, and educators were concerned. In fact he was proud that the person-centered approach supported democratic values, independence, and creativity. He also acknowledged the potential for the person-centered approach to conflict with the hierarchical authority of the Catholic church, writing, "our experience has led us to be willing to place the locus of evaluation and choice completely in the individual. This seems deeply opposed to any concept of an external or dogmatic authority as the locus of evaluation."[68] Just as Martin Luther put personal experience of God before ecclesiastical authority, Rogers always trusted the individual's own experience as the highest authority. He never said look to others or to the group for direction. He said listen to others, be aware of social expectations, but in the end judge for yourself and make your own choice. That is *not* a collectivist position. He described his "emerging person" or "person of tomorrow" as someone who believes in "The authority within. These persons have a trust in their own experience and a profound distrust of external authority." For that reason, they would not be valued by those who would put "Tradition above all."[69]

However, to my knowledge, Rogers never made the intellectual leap to recognize the general principle that, in supporting individual autonomy as it does, the person-centered approach might be in inherent conflict with *all* traditional cultures and, in that sense, impose its own set of values. Perhaps to Rogers this would not seem like an imposition since, in his experience, clients and group members choose to come or choose to continue with person-centered therapists and group leaders. If they did not find it helpful, they would not continue. However, this begs the question, since a person might find something helpful without realizing some of the consequences of that help—in this case the reinforcing of Western individualistic values. (And in other settings, seeing a therapist or being in a student-centered classroom might not involve an entirely free choice.)

Acknowledging the strong individualistic value orientation of the person-centered approach, however, does not necessarily mean that it is *exclusively* individualistic. From the start, Rogers' self theory emphasized that, "*As a result of interaction with the environment, and particularly as a result of evaluational interaction with others, the structure of self is formed*" (original emphasis).[70] Not only is the self formed in relationship to others, similarly it is the *relationship* that is necessary for growth and change in counseling and psychotherapy. And, as any client-centered therapist will attest, a great deal of time in therapy is spent exploring the client's relationships with others. Moreover, Rogers' work in encounter groups and person-centered communities certainly moved the approach beyond an individualistic orientation.

Nevertheless, to the extent that the person-centered approach *is* clearly individualistic in its orientation, this does not necessarily make it inappropriate or less applicable to cultures who do not share this orientation. That is because cultures and individuals are rarely, if ever, all one way or the other—individualistic or collectivist. Cultures, classes, religious groups and other communities typically have some characteristics that are traditionally collective and others that are individualistic and modern. Likewise individuals, whether from primarily individualistic or collectivist cultures, hold both individualistic *and* collectivist values and preferences. Societies and the individuals within them are, in fact, often *highly conflicted* over changing values and customs.[71] If I may be permitted a short editorial, this is an important reality that scholars and researchers who identify and study typologies, classifications and paradigms often overlook. People do not necessarily subscribe to only one worldview or value system: middle-class values or lower-class values, religious or secular, traditional or modern, individualistic or collectivist, Eastern or Western, black or white. Although one worldview or set of values may be dominant in a person or culture, there are often other, contrasting views and values that are important parts of their identities, that have meaning to them. Thus when generalizations categorizing traditional and Western cultures as collectivist or individualistic were put to the test, Oyserman, Coon and Kemmelmeier, in several meta-analyses involving from thirty-five to fifty studies, found that many widely accepted generalizations about different cultural groups did not hold up.[72] For example, in national comparisons, while it was true that European-Americans were more individualistic and less collectivist in their value orientations than most traditional cultures, there were many exceptions to this rule. For example, "Truly startling findings emerged for Korea and Japan: Americans were significantly higher in collectivism than Japanese were, and were not significantly different in collectivism from Koreans."[73] There were similar, both predictable and surprising findings in the United States comparisons. While Latino-Americans were no different on individualism and higher on collectivism than European-Americans, African-Americans turned out to be *higher* on individualism and no different on collectivism than European-Americans. Summarizing the Oysterman et al. meta-analyses, Williams wrote, "[W]orldview is not accurately predicted by race, ethnicity or national group ... the inconsistency with which the endorsement of individualism and collectivism follows hypothesized patterns is evidence for the need to be extremely aware of one's own biases when seeking to determine a client's worldview."[74]

These data are entirely consistent with a person-centered viewpoint. People are too complex to be viewed primarily in categories. To assume that everyone from a culture shares a set of attributes is a different kind of imposition and stereotyping. "In this regard, the concept of a typical African personality is strongly criticized by Sodi, who contended that the notion of an 'African personality' not only robs individual black South Africans of the possibility of individual expression but also carries the potential to perpetuate the racist assumption that 'all Africans are alike.'"[75] Thus when asked by an interviewer about his work in South Africa facilitating conflict between antagonists in another culture, Rogers said, "I'll make a paradoxical statement. I think one should try to prepare and also be very naïve." In that way the facilitator will not be misled by his own preconceptions about any cultural group and can capitalize on opportunities which an "expert" mediator might dismiss as having been tried and failed before. He added, "To rephrase the old saying: as wise a serpent, as naïve as a child."[76]

From a person-centered perspective, then, while people's cultural influences—including gender, race, ethnicity, religion, nationality, class, and other important characteristics—may be very important in forming their identities, persons are more than the sum total of these influences. They must be *treated* as individuals (pun intended). Cornelius-White pointed out that, just as some researchers argue that one should use different treatments for different diagnoses, the argument that one should use different methods for different cultures or ethnicities is problematic from a person-centered view. Ironically, "Despite repeated reviews of the literature, from meta-analytic, qualitative and effectiveness methodologies showing evidence to the contrary, Sue and Sue's promotion of treatment specificity [differential treatment for different ethnic groups] seems to indicate an attachment to the medical model with its reductionistic values of the dominant culture."[77] Instead, person-centered counseling and psychotherapy "aims to understand a person's entire experience with the emphasis on the client's own unique experience." In other words, each client internalizes cultural influences in different ways and struggles with and balances different identities in different ways. A person-centered approach can be useful in helping clients understand and sort out these multicultural issues, as well as other issues of the human condition.

Still the multicultural literature has provided valuable cautions, insights and recommendations as to how the person-centered approach, or any approach, might be more effectively implemented in different cultural contexts. Among other dispositions and strategies, counselors and therapists wishing to practice with multicultural competence should: be knowledgeable about their clients' cultural influences; be respectful of clients' worldviews; find out from the client what his or her desired goals of counseling are, explain how counseling works, and negotiate a common purpose; understand, respect and work with the client's understanding about healing; be willing to discuss and even initiate discussion about differences in the counselor and client's backgrounds; and be willing, within the limits of their own congruence and abilities, to utilize the client's resources and cultural traditions insofar as these are meaningful to the client.[78] Like any counselor, a person-centered practitioner who is unaware of these multicultural issues, ignores them, or implements these measures less than competently will be less effective in multicultural contexts. But when incorporated into a person-centered practice, these multicultural competencies enhance still further those aspects of the person-centered approach that make it particularly appropriate for multicultural applications.

Because many person-centered practitioners have been able to apply the person-centered approach in multiculturally sensitive ways, there are numerous case studies of the person-centered approach apparently succeeding with members of minority groups and in different cultures. In South Africa, Spangenberg described how by understanding and honoring the worldview of the client, by "not focusing on the client exclusively but of making the client as well as his or her relationships with family members, community, and culture the focus of the counseling relationship," by exploring in counseling "the ways in which interpersonal relationships with members of the nuclear and extended family can enhance the client's psychological well-being," and by accepting and respecting the practice of traditional healers whom the client might be seeing also, the person-centered approach was, indeed, a culturally appropriate approach for that country.[79] Baggerly and Parker described how child-centered group play therapy with elementary school age African-American boys "honors the African worldview [of *Nguzo Saba*] and facilitates self-confidence."[80] Cornelius-White showed how a person-centered approach helped address student–teacher power imbalance and was effective in enhancing multicultural sensitivity in a diverse group of counseling students.[81] Many more such examples could be given, but case studies of two individuals very close to Rogers may be a useful way of ending this discussion and relating it back to Rogers' own experience.

As of this writing, Norman Chambers has been a member of Center for Studies of the Person for some thirty-five years. He worked with Rogers on many projects over those years, right up to the week before Rogers died.[82] Chambers, who is African-American, was a leader in the 1970s in CSP's Multicultural Leadership Training Program—a seventeen-day program in which Rogers would often conduct sessions. He was a faculty member in the African Studies Program at San Diego State University for at least twenty-five years and has had a private counseling practice in San Diego, with Robert Lee, called the Multicultural Counseling and Consulting Center. His practice is essentially person-centered. When I presented the critique of the person-centered approach as not being sensitive to multicultural issues, Chambers said, "It's a fair concern … some people will feel no approach works for them if it wasn't developed specifically for them." As for the particular criticisms, he was not so sure. He said Rogers was very helpful to him in sorting out his own racial issues. "Carl said, 'If you're coming from center—from being centered, from closer to center—you'll be more effective … It made sense to me intellectually, but then I began to experience it." When asked if the person-centered approach needed to be adapted for different ethnic groups, Chambers answered, "The [core] conditions used differently? Yes and no. Mutual adaptation occurs when you're in any union with anybody. Part of my core says I'm going to be where they are and I am."

Marvalene Styles Hughes met Carl Rogers when she was director of the Counseling Center and other student service programs at San Diego State University.[83] As an African-American woman who grew up in Alabama in the era of segregation, she had experienced many blows to her self-esteem and, while having overcome significant obstacles to advance in her career thus far, she was filled with many doubts and insecurities about herself and her future. Although Rogers had long ago stopped seeing individual clients, he agreed to become Hughes' counselor. They saw one another about two times a month from around 1983–1986.[84] At Rogers' suggestion to protect her privacy, they kept their counseling relationship confidential because she was associated with many of Rogers' colleagues at Center for Studies of the Person. They also violated many of the traditional rules about professional boundaries, with Rogers' visiting her home and family and their becoming friends and colleagues. Hughes wrote and spoke of how Rogers' empathy, positive regard and congruence helped her find her deeper core of confidence in herself as a woman, an African-American, and an individual. He simply did not accept the limitations which she was inclined to place upon herself. She said, "I credit my relationship with him for helping me to know and appreciate who I am. He was the man who discovered me as a cocoon and nurtured that cocoon through its natural maturation until it became a butterfly ... I found faith in myself to pursue what otherwise would have appeared to be an impossible dream."[85] That impossible dream was her becoming the first black woman president of an American university, and she credited Rogers with being the Don Quixote who made it possible. She likened herself to the scullery maid Eldonza who, from viewing herself as "unworthy of kindness and gentleness," was transformed through the power of Don Quixote's affirmation to "the embodiment of perfect beauty and grace ... Dulcinea." Like Don Quixote, said Hughes, Rogers saw her "as if she already were what she potentially could be."

When Hughes left San Diego State to become Associate Vice-President at Arizona State University, she recalled Rogers saying to her, in essence, "You are now your own leader and your own therapist." Thus with Rogers "on my shoulder," as she put it, she continued in her career path, becoming president of the American College Personnel Association while at Arizona State, moving on to vice-presidencies at the Universities of Toledo and Minnesota, and then president of the University of California at Stanislaus in 1994. She also became the national president of the Association of the Women Presidents of the American Association of State Colleges and Universities. And demonstrating that there is nothing inconsistent between the person-centered approach and social action, after the fall of the Taliban in Afghanistan, which had terribly oppressed women, she led a highly public effort in support of education for women in Afghanistan;

she worked with the government of Ethiopia to build the first university for women in that country, and she worked with others to found a university and school for Palestinians in the West Bank in Jordan.

Of these efforts, she said, "Those are the kinds of projects that draw upon the theory and practice that Carl taught us. I honestly believe that it would not be possible for me to think as broadly were it not for what he valued and what he taught." Like Don Quixote, Rogers "would tell us to honor *our* passion and honor *our* vision of what can and should be versus what *is* at the moment." As with Norm Chambers, Hughes' experience with person-centered therapy enabled her to be "more effective" in the world. There is no evidence that person-centered practitioners or their clients are any less active socially and politically than their counterparts in other approaches. Certainly Rogers and many of his colleagues were very involved in the social and political causes of their day, both professionally and personally. Rogers, as we will see, utilizing the person-centered approach, became increasingly active in such activities in his later years.

Perhaps I have gone on too long on this topic. After all, this is a biography, not an essay on multiculturalism and the person-centered approach. Yet, the issue is so central to both Rogers' life's work and to the fields of counseling and psychotherapy today that I have regarded it as a worthy topic to explore in some depth; although I do not pretend to have done so thoroughly. Moreover, while I believe that the multicultural criticisms of Rogers and the person-centered approach have been important and helpful in encouraging person-centered practitioners to confront multicultural issues, to recognize their own cultural biases, and to implement the approach in increasingly more appropriate and effective ways across cultural boundaries, I am inclined to agree with Cornelius-White's statement that such criticisms are "often based upon misrepresentations, reflect inadequate reasoning, and are unappreciative of the meaningful contributions of person-centered therapy to the field of multiculturalism."[86] It seemed to me useful to discuss these criticisms in the context of Rogers' entire life and work.

Soviet Union

Rogers' last international, cross-cultural experience took place in the autumn of 1986 when he and Ruth Sanford spent almost four weeks in the Soviet Union.[87] As in South Africa, they came at a pivotal time in the history of the country. There were enormous political, economic and social tensions, which would lead to the breakup of the Soviet Union in 1991. But before that, under President Vladimir Gorbachev the Soviet Union was experiencing a greater openness than at any previous time in its modern history. As part of Gorbachev's program of "glasnost," visits from foreign professionals, artists and others were encouraged. The Association for Humanistic Psychology, for example, under the leadership of Francis ("Fran") Macy and Jack Hassard, had been conducting visits of North

American psychologists and educators since 1983.[88] Other professional associations made similar visits. While the ostensible goal was mutual professional development, such exchanges had a wider impact on intercultural understanding and bridge-building between previously hostile countries. It was hoped that the informal and friendly relationships that developed on the person-to-person level and at the level of professional associations would filter up to the governmental level. Thus the efforts of these non-governmental organizations and individuals were often referred to as "citizen diplomacy" or "two-track diplomacy." This approach was particularly appropriate in the Soviet Union, where various professional "institutes" associated with universities would also have ties to the government.

In the spring of 1985 Ruth Sanford and her husband Niel were planning just such a visit to the Soviet Union as part of a group of therapists and rehabilitation counselors under the title of Citizen Ambassadors.[89] She asked Rogers if he would like her to make inquiries about their working in the Soviet Union and he responded with enthusiasm. Knowing that Fran Macy, with his previous experience and contacts in the Soviet Union and his ability to speak Russian, would be the person to help arrange such a visit, she was delighted on their fall visit to run into him in Moscow and to begin their planning. A year later, she, Rogers and Macy left for the Soviet Union.

Their Soviet sponsor was Dr. Alexei Matyushkin, Director of the prestigious Institute of General and Pedagogical (Educational) Psychology. He arranged several large group presentations to professionals in Moscow (Russian Republic) and Tbilisi (Georgian Republic), as well as two four-day workshops with groups of forty-five and forty, respectively. The focus was to be mainly on education and the development of critical thinking and creativity in Soviet children. When Rogers asked Matyushkin whether they really wanted to raise independent and creative children, whether that wouldn't be dangerous, Matyushkin asked, "Why? How could it be dangerous?" Rogers responded, "Because when people get a sense of their own empowerment, they may not work in the same way that they are expected to in a country accustomed to strong direction and leadership." Matyushkin responded thoughtfully, "Yes, but it would be *more* dangerous not to."[90]

Although the focus was supposed to be on education, most of the participants turned out to be therapists and psychologists, so the focus shifted more to the person-centered approach in general, with applications to therapy, education and other relationships. In both the large groups and small workshops, Rogers conducted demonstration counseling sessions with volunteers selected by Sanford. The participants were as prepared as any new group Rogers had ever worked with, since Matyushkin had circulated copies of Rogers' articles, many translated into Russian and Georgian, which the participants had read and discussed in seminars beforehand.

The intensive four-day workshop in Moscow began in chaos. As usual Rogers and Sanford introduced themselves and shared their expectations that "it was now *our* group, not Carl and Ruth's group. Hopefully we would be able to integrate the cognitive and the experiential, the personal and the professional."[91] Instead the group spent the first day arguing bitterly about who should be allowed to attend, since ten or more "gate crashers" had more or less forced their way into the group, originally intended to be limited to thirty participants. Accusations of unfair dealings and attacks against other participants were so strong that the facilitators barely had a chance to be heard, let alone convey empathy and acceptance. Rogers thought, "Rarely, if ever, have I heard such personal vituperation, such vicious hostility directed personally toward present members of the group."[92] Although Sanford thought the original number should be maintained while Rogers felt more flexible about it, they both did their best to hear and accept the members' expressions and refused to make the decision for the group, in spite of many attempts to get them to do so. Rather they patiently expressed their confidence in the group's ability to decide how it wanted to spend its time. However, they did ask for five minutes of silence at the end of the day for the participants to reflect on their experience.

The next morning the tone was markedly different, as people had decided on their own that this was not a good use of their time. They shifted to more personal sharing of problems, including many expressions of sadness and despair about marital and family problems they were experiencing. While there was some attempt to listen to one another, again Rogers was amazed how the responses to personal expressions of feelings and problems "were almost invariably probing interrogations, dogmatic and judgmental interpretations, intellectual analyses, critical evaluations, or personal attacks ... I became so appalled by the way in which these persons—mostly therapists—were dealing with one another in an apparent attempt to be helpful, that I finally exploded with my feelings. I said that when a person expresses something personal, he or she is exposed and vulnerable, and that it is a very risky experience. I felt that in such situations they were much more sensitive to attack than when they were buttoned up in their usual defenses. Yet it was just when individuals exposed themselves in this way that the group was most savage in its interpretations, probings, and negative judgments. I felt *horrified* by what was going on and said so. My outburst was greeted with a long silence, but later it was clear that it had a powerful impact."[93]

When the one classroom teacher in the group who was also a principal asked to be interviewed by Rogers in front of the group, he hoped that would help turn things around. Instead, this woman, who turned out to run an usually progressive school, launched into a diatribe against psychologists who visited her school and then a litany of complaints about the children who did not know how to handle the freedom they were given. Rogers wrote, "The whole situation was amusing because from time to time I tried to shut off the flow of the torrent and was completely unsuccessful. She was going to be heard and she was!"[94] Apparently the participants listened carefully and learned something about working with gifted children, but when they voiced any appreciation of her, she deflected it. It was hardly a typical demonstration interview for Rogers.

On the third day, sensing the group was ready for something different, Rogers and Sanford proposed an experience in empathy. They divided the group into triads in which one participant would be client, one counselor, and one observer. The client would work on a real problem in his or life, the counselor would practice empathy, and the third member would observe the process. After fifteen minutes they would switch roles and the same for a third round, giving each participant a chance to play each role. Structuring an activity like this was not typical of Rogers and was probably more of Sanford's initiation. In any case, Rogers reported, the experience "seemed a very valuable and sobering lesson for all concerned, a recognition that though they had read about listening, talked about it, taught about it, they had actually never *done it*!"[95] Gradually over the course of the third and fourth day, people discussed professional and personal issues more deeply, listened more carefully, accepted one another more fully, and came to understand the person-centered approach experientially.

Whereas the Moscow workshop got to experience Rogers' congruence when he confronted them about the way they treated one another, Sanford confronted the Tbilisi workshop on the way they were treating *her*. She had noticed that questions were being directed to Rogers and not to her and she began to feel like she was withdrawing.

> The following morning, I told the group how I had been feeling. I didn't know what it signified, I said, but I felt very much a part of the group at all times except when theoretical or philosophical questions came up. I wondered whether it was because Carl was a renowned psychologist, a person of prominence, or whether it was because he was a man. In Georgia perhaps the man was looked to for the intellectual, the factual, and the theoretical, rather than the woman. Whatever it was, I would be interested in knowing. I did not want anyone to make an apology, but I said, "It took me until late in life to appreciate my brain, that I have a brain, and I don't want to give that up. So, I feel now that I have been honest with you about my feeling. Now I can become more wholeheartedly a member of the group."[96]

This led to an intense discussion of man–woman relationships. At the end the director of the local institute that had sponsored the workshop said he had not realized how he had unconsciously held a double standard regarding men and women and had not appreciated the women on his staff. Henceforth he intended to be more appreciative of their accomplishments. At the banquet at the end of the workshop, when his wife was present, the director reiterated his commitment publicly and said "That includes my wife."[97] At the parties concluding each of the small-group workshops there was great warmth and camaraderie and many toasts and expressions of how much participants had gained from their experience.

All told, about 2,000 Soviet professionals participated in the large and small workshops Rogers and Sanford conducted. These were among the first intensive, experiential workshops that had been offered in the Soviet Union, as previous visitors had mostly participated in seminars and presentations. It was also one of the first times that a psychologist did a live demonstration of his approach before a Soviet audience.[98] Although participants tended to avoid talking of politics or male–female roles (the Sanford-initiated discussion was an exception), Rogers was struck how the issues raised throughout their visit "were very similar to those that are raised in similar groups in the United States, in Brazil, in Mexico, in Japan, in Poland, in Hungary, in Italy, in the United Kingdom. It is astonishing how much there is in common. Certainly one of the elements found in every culture we have dealt with—and here I would especially include South Africa with the others—is the hunger for deeper and more personal communication and the desire to be accepted as a real person, problems and all, a unique individual with worth and significance."[99]

What impact did their visit have? One data point occurred two days after the Moscow workshop when Rogers was asked to present his summary of the workshop to a prestigious Scientific Council that made recommendations about funding and policy in Soviet psychology and education. Rogers suggested that the workshop participants would be in a better position than himself to evaluate the workshop and suggested that they be invited to address the Council. Thirty of the forty-five participants volunteered to speak to the Council. Remarkably, the auditorium was filled with over 300 others who wanted to hear about the workshop. Because of time limitations only nine of the participants got to speak. They were chosen randomly by Dr. Matyushkin who, demonstrating a learning from the workshop, alternated between men and women. The translation was recorded. Excerpts from two of the comments give a sense of how this sample of participants viewed their experience.

> I am a psychologist, not a psychotherapist. I have known Rogers' theory but this was a process in which *we* were personally involved. I didn't realize how it applied. I want to give several impressions. First was the effectiveness of this approach. It was a kind of process in which we all learned. Second, this process was moving, without a motor. Nobody had to lead it or guide it. It was a self-evolving process. It was like the Chekhov story where they were expectantly awaiting the piano player and the piano started playing itself. Third, I was impressed by the manner of Carl and Ruth. At first I felt they were passive. Then I realized it was the silence of understanding. Fourth, I want to mention the penetration of this process into my inner world. At first I was an observer, but then the approach

disappeared altogether. I was not simply surrounded by this process, I was absorbed into it! It was a revelation to me. We started moving. I wasn't simply seeing people I had known for years, but their feelings. My fifth realization was my inability to control the flow of feelings, the flow of the process. My feelings tried to put on the clothes of my words. Sometimes people exploded; some even cried. It was a reconstruction of the system of perception. Finally, I want to remark on the high skill of Carl and Ruth, of their silences, their voices, their glances. It was always some response, and they were responded to. It was a great phenomenon, a great experience.[100]

As Rogers summarized the next speaker's comments,

A professor said, "I want to speak as a scientist." He told of being impressed with the theory and principles underlying the person-centered approach. "The laws of human communication, discovered in America, were surprisingly functional in our situation." A bit later he made another point. "We are tempted to think that this is something that pertains only to Rogers, but this is not true. We, too, can concentrate for forty-five minutes, and can be effective in creating a therapeutic climate, recognizing negative feelings as well as positive." He emphasized that he was speaking of "our *clients*—not our *patients*!" He also said that he "would like to mention the great contribution of these two people to the increase of mutual understanding between our two countries. It is good to know that across the ocean there are human beings who have a warm feeling for us."[101]

"To hear them tell others of the personal and professional changes resulting from the workshop was for me a magnificent reward," wrote Rogers. "The impact we had on Soviet Psychologists was profound."[102] This was not only Rogers' opinion. The Association for Humanistic Psychology's Tom Greening, who was intimately familiar with the history of American psychologists visiting the Soviet Union, wrote, "This trip may go down in history as one of the milestones of humanistic psychology's contributions to citizen diplomacy."[103] Shortly after Rogers and Sanford left the Soviet Union, Fran Macy reported, "the national television program carried a one-hour special on them. They were shown presenting to large audiences in Moscow and being interviewed by two of the senior Soviet psychologists, Dr. Alexei Matyushkin ... and Professor A.A. Bodalev, then Dean of the Department of Psychology at Moscow State University. Many of my friends saw this program and said that it faithfully conveyed the person-centered approach and the Americans who were there to explain it and display it."[104]

The following month, "the most widely read popular Soviet magazine, *Ogonyok* (Number 47, 1986), devoted almost an entire page to 'Moscow Interviews with Carl Rogers: The Family and I.' It featured a large picture of Carl with the caption: 'Not long ago there took place the first visit to our country of the psychologist Carl Rogers, one of the founders of the Association for Humanistic Psychology in the USA.' The reporter described Carl's demonstration interview with an Estonian woman about problems among her mother, her daughter, and herself. This was conducted in English before an audience of 300. 'But these two did not hear or see anyone. They saw and heard only each other ... Utmost frankness, this is the chief condition for the scientific interview of Professor Rogers ... The professor vividly demonstrated to us what it means to be able to listen to one another and how important it is to be heard,' the reporter concluded."

Macy reported how "I also learned that the Academy of Pedagogical Sciences and the U.S.S.R. Ministry of Education will publish in Russian Carl's last book, *Freedom to Learn for the 80s*, which I had presented to them a year earlier," and he recounted several examples of how some of the Soviet professionals had changed their practices after their workshop with Rogers. This was corroborated repeatedly in the following years. Moscow university professor Julia Gippenreiter wrote, "Before Carl Rogers came, psychology as a field drew little interest because we focused on things like measuring eye movement, or some other such irrelevant research. When we heard that Carl Rogers was coming, we couldn't actually believe it. When he did arrive we fought to get into his workshops and swarmed to his lectures. Having experienced the Person-Centered Approach from this genuine and rather humble man changed my focus in psychology, as it did many others. I am now teaching teachers how to relate to their pupils and am using the principles of facilitation in my University classes."[105] In an article entitled "My Encounter with Carl Rodgers [sic]: A Retrospective View from the Ukraine," Alexander Bondarenko, a professor, psychotherapist, and author of three books on counseling, described the profound impact of Rogers' visit on his work and life.[106] Jack Hassard, who directed the Association for Humanistic Psychology's Soviet Exchange Project for at least seven years beginning in 1987, wrote how, "The Rogers visit has had a profound impact on the way some Soviets work among themselves. For example, Alexander Orlov, laboratory director in the Institute for General and Educational Psychology, has applied Rogers' concept of facilitation to the way he works with his colleagues ... One day, while we were walking together in Leningrad, he told me how important Rogers' group sessions had been, and he urged me to encourage another institute in Leningrad, which did not participate in the Rogers sessions ..."[107]

Natalie Rogers, who made four trips to work in the Soviet Union after her father's death, said, "I have since been told many times by Russians that my father's trip to the U.S.S.R. changed the face of psychology there."[108] Certainly Rogers and Sanford's trip was one among many that contributed to opening the Soviet Union to humanistic psychology. Nonetheless, Rogers' assessment that their visit had a profound impact seems born out by considerable testimony.

Development of the Person-Centered Approach

As Rogers crisscrossed the globe promulgating cross-cultural communication and the person-centered approach, the approach itself was evolving and developing around the world. These developments were most apparent in the rapid spread of the person-centered approach in Europe, in the maturing of different branches or approaches within the person-centered movement, and in the growth of professional organizations dedicated to the person-centered approach. (Another development, which will be discussed in the final chapter, was the on-going research on and related to the person-centered approach.) In some ways Rogers facilitated all these developments in his final years. In some ways he obstructed them.

The European Movement

Rogers' many trips to Europe in the late seventies and eighties gave impetus to a person-centered movement that had been growing in Europe for many years.[109] As suggested above, many European professionals had studied, practiced and taught client-centered counseling and psychotherapy for years, and in a few countries, associations and institutes had formed to promote the approach and train new therapists. Now, with Rogers and his colleagues introducing their theory and practice directly to thousands of professionals in many counties, a critical mass developed that soon snowballed across Europe.

Ironically, the Europeans succeeded by not following the example of Rogers and the Americans. As Dave Mearns, for years the leading figure in the person-centered movement in Scotland, and others pointed out, once Rogers left the University of Wisconsin, disillusioned with academia, he no longer pursued an academic research agenda.[110] Instead, he pretty much "did his own thing," in the language of the seventies. Indeed he could afford to. Mearns, who spent some time in California, described how during those years the enchantment with humanistic psychology was so great that, for example, "One thousand people queued up on a Friday evening at the campus of the University of California, San Diego to be enrolled into 70 weekend encounter groups facilitated by members of the La Jolla Program" (of Center for Studies of the Person).[111] Mearns explained,

> Carl Rogers was tired by the resistance he had encountered with the University sector and, instead, had taken his work to the people. With the incredible level of public appeal he encountered, it would have been difficult to make a different decision. However, "public appeal" has a transient quality and when it passed it found person-centered therapy with relatively few roots within the establishment institutions. Indeed, there was something of a resentment felt towards person-centered therapy by workers in the mental health and University sectors. This

was a justifiable resentment because we had, effectively, bypassed our clinical and academic colleagues, finding our validation less in terms of clinical audit and continuing scientific enquiry and more through the aforementioned public appeal. We even lost our ability to self-monitor and embrace critique. Critics became "non-believers" who could be ignored, or even vilified ... With the loss of ephemeral public appeal and our clinical and academic basis forsaken, rapid was the decline of person-centered therapy in the USA."[112]

Mearns argued that for "psychotheoretical systems" to become established and successful, they must patiently and strategically work to develop training programs, be integrated into university settings, work with and create professional associations, meet the needs of "purchasers" (government funding agencies and insurers, as well as clients), and develop an effective research program. Rogers did these things quite successfully for much of his career. He conducted groundbreaking research, funded by foundations and government, which was published widely in professional journals. He trained dozens of doctoral students in research and practice and helped them obtain positions in prestigious institutions around the country. Researchers and practitioners around the world came to study with him. He fought successfully for the right of psychologists to practice psychotherapy. He held leadership positions in the major professional associations. In short, he worked *within* existing organizations, as well as beyond them, and his influence was enormous.

When he left Wisconsin for California he all but abandoned this approach. He preferred to work independently with individuals, groups and organizations, but always as an outsider who came and left, not as an organizer building lasting institutions, programs and associations, or as a leader of such organizations, or as a principal investigator on research projects. His new approach to facilitating change certainly had its benefits—it allowed him to conduct and write about important experiments in small group work, education, community building, cross-cultural communication and conflict resolution—experiences that enabled him to deepen and expand his theory and practice and set an example for other individuals to follow. But while he was doing this, interest in the person-centered approach in the United States was starting to fade as the counter-cultural sixties and seventies gave way to the more conservative eighties and nineties; as the psychotherapy world became increasingly enamored with cognitive and behavioral therapies and evidence-based practice; and as the generation of Rogers-trained professionals in existing institutions began to retire without leaving a new generation behind.

Not so in Europe. Even before Rogers took the continent by storm in his final years, a number of individuals were establishing themselves in university settings and hospitals where they developed training and research programs in client-centered therapy. Reinhard Tausch and Jobst Finke in Germany, Germain

Lietaer in Belgium, Peter Schmid in Austria and others gradually built programs that combined research, training, practice and licensure.

When Reinhard Tausch first visited Rogers in 1961 in Wisconsin, he was interested in Rogers' work at Mendota State Hospital.[113] He made many subsequent visits to La Jolla where he learned of further developments in the person-centered approach. Later Tausch became a full professor of clinical and educational psychology at University of Hamburg and director of the University's Psychological Institute #3 for Person-Centered Therapy and Behavior Therapy. As the name suggests, he was not a purist insisting that the therapist be exclusively client-centered. Rather Tausch and his colleagues used both the client-centered approach and behavioral methods like desensitization to reduce patient symptoms of anxiety and other phobias.[114] Rogers toured Tausch's clinic in Hamburg and encouraged him to continue this eclectic approach. Along with their practice, Tausch, his colleagues and his students conducted extensive research on their work in individual and group psychotherapy and counseling, demonstrating results that satisfied patient, institutional and funding priorities (the "purchasers"). Hence his university-based institute became a viable, established, and leading center for psychotherapy training. Tausch's books on psychotherapy and "person-centered behavior in the classroom" sold an impressive 82,000 and 160,000 copies, respectively.[115]

Another German professor was the University of Essen's Jobst Finke. A physician and psychiatrist, he was Assistant Medical Director of the Clinic for Psychiatry and Psychotherapy in the University Clinic and in charge of postgraduate education. His numerous publications included empirical studies. Just before Rogers' death Finke became the first President of the ÄGG, the Medical Society for Client-Centered Psychotherapy, helping to achieve the bridge between clinical psychology and psychiatry that Rogers had been unable to accomplish in Wisconsin.[116] His younger colleague Ludwig Teusch, also a physician and psychotherapist, is now the Medical Director of the Clinic for Psychiatry and carrying on the tradition, demonstrating through their research, for example, how client-centered therapy alone is as efficacious as a combination of client-centered therapy and behavior therapy in helping patients with panic attacks, agoraphobia, and depression.[117]

Similarly, Germain Lietaer established a leading program at the University of Leuven in Belgium, conducting research on client-centered and experiential psychotherapy and training psychotherapists. Like Reinhard Tausch, Lietaer spent time in California learning about the person-centered approach experientially. There Lietaer was appalled at what he described as the "anti-intellectual, anti-research" atmosphere at Center for Studies of the Person; nevertheless he profited from the experience personally and was much impressed with Rogers whose behavior he found to be entirely consistent with his theory.[118]

Peter Schmid in Austria provides another good example of how the person-centered approach developed in Europe. As an assistant professor at the University of Graz, he founded the Institute for Person-Centered Studies in Vienna in 1969.[119] It was designed to give training courses and to do research—"not empirical research but philosophical and theoretical research," as Schmid explained. Unlike some European leaders in the person-centered approach, Schmid began this work before ever meeting Carl Rogers. But then in 1979 he, too, went to California to participate in the La Jolla Program, where he came to appreciate the experiential aspects of the person-centered approach more than through readings and recordings. He invited Rogers to visit Austria in 1981 and again in 1984, trips described above. Rogers' visits lent further impetus to the person-centered movement in Austria, and Schmid's institute flourished. In 2003, they had about thirty staff members and about one hundred trainees. "We are legalized by the government in order to train these therapists," Schmid explained.

Other European professionals followed the path of Tausch, Lietaer, and Schmid. Indeed, they had no choice. Unlike America a generation earlier, in Europe the universities and institutes were the only game in town. Individuals were not willing or able to afford to attend independent training programs simply for personal growth or to enhance their skills. Instead, aspiring professionals needed to obtain a recognized credential to practice their profession. Although, as Mearns said, "Rogers and his colleagues at the height of popularity of humanistic psychology were not particularly inclined to tackle the issues involved in certification, accreditations and regulation," their European counterparts recognized they must work with universities, university-connected institutes, and sanctioned professional associations to develop programs that would meet professional and governmental accreditation standards and therefore be able to train the next generation of person-centered practitioners.[120]

Valerie Henderson recalled how "Chuck Devonshire was enormously influential in helping the person-centered approach spread around Europe by organizing not only cross-cultural workshops but helping different institutes set up training programs. For example, there were three-year training programs in England where people would get their license as a person-centered therapist."[121] In Italy the Istituto Dell'Approccio Centrato Sulla Persona (Institute for the Person-Centered Approach), founded by Devonshire and Alberto Zucconi, was an official training center for the World Health Organization and its training programs were recognized by the Ministry of Education, universities, and regional accreditation bodies.[122] This was a typical pattern in Europe where, unlike the United States, it is common to have institutes that are associated with universities and that prepare professionals for accreditation and licensure. In the United States, the university programs themselves typically prepare professionals and provide the training that makes graduates eligible for licensure. With tenure and academic freedom for faculty, it is difficult to get a substantial number of faculty members committed to train students in a single paradigm. A semi-independent institute is more likely to establish itself around a particular model of counseling or therapy and to select a staff or faculty committed to that approach. In the United States, barely a handful of such institutes or programs existed that provided concerted training in person-centered counseling or psychotherapy, such as the Illinois School of Professional Psychology in Chicago and Saybrook Graduate . School in San Francisco.[123] Institutes that did both training and significant research were virtually non-existent. In Europe it was standard practice.

As a result of these efforts across Europe, and as the result of the formation of person-centered professional associations (which will be discussed subsequently), the person-centered approach became one of the most established and widespread approaches to counseling and psychotherapy on that continent. Ironically, in Austria, the birthplace of psychoanalysis, the person-centered approach is one of the leading therapeutic schools, more popular than psychoanalysis itself.[124] The same is true in Great Britain. In 1997 a survey was conducted of the British Association for Counselling and Psychotherapy's over 19,000 members. It was sent to 2,500 randomly selected members and had a 44% response rate. When asked, "Which of the following best describe your preferred models of psychological functioning?" (respondents could check more than one model), the responses that were checked by more than 10% of the members were: Person-centred 50.8%; Integrative 30.2%; Psychodynamic: Object relations 25.7%; Eclectic 19.3%; Transactional analysis 16.3%; Gestalt 14.2%; Psychodynamic: Freudian 13.5%; Psychodynamic: Jungian 12.8%; Cognitive-Behavioural 12.7%; Psychodynamic: Kleinian 12.3%; Cognitive 11%.[125]

In 2001 another survey was sent to *all* 19,400 members and had a response rate of 20%. It asked a question which helped understand the large number of British professionals who seemed to identify with person-centred counselling and psychotherapy.[126] When asked, "Within which of the core theoretical model(s) of counselling/psychotherapy were you trained?" (and here respondents could check only one response), the five leading responses were: Person-centred 35.6%; Psychodynamic 25.4%; Integrative 12.6%; Humanistic 5.4%; Other 5.2%. Clearly the person-centred approach has become institutionalized in the United Kingdom.

I must admit that all this came as a surprise to me. Before beginning my research on this edition of Rogers' biography, I had assumed that the declining interest I observed in Rogers and the person-centered approach in the United States was similar in the rest of the world. When my doctoral student April Jourdan and I discovered that in Europe, with a combined population much larger than the United States, the person-centered approach was one of the leading schools of counseling and psychotherapy, it was a revelation to this provincial writer.

Many of these developments occurred after Rogers' death in 1987. But they certainly began in Rogers' lifetime and were spurred on by the interest his many workshops, demonstrations, and presentations in Europe generated for the person-centered approach. Rogers himself could not help being impressed with the results. As early as 1979, he wrote a memo to colleagues describing how Alberto Zucconi and Chuck Devonshire were developing a person-centered training program in Europe (the Learning Programs, described earlier) and suggested they get together to develop such a program themselves.[127] But although Rogers and his colleagues did begin a "Learning Program" at CSP, it did not last. He predicted it would take "a three to five year commitment to the organization, promotion, and stable development of such a program."[128] Neither he nor his colleagues had the attention or resources to sustain such a commitment.[129] In Europe they had been doing it for years.

New Approaches

Since the 1960s and 70s, there have been several offshoots of the client-centered approach. Two of the major ones, known as the "focusing" and "process-experiential" approaches, remain closely aligned with or, as many would say, part of the person-centered movement. These approaches were initiated by Rogers' students and colleagues and grew independently of Rogers for two or three decades while he was alive and continued to develop thereafter. To understand Rogers' life's work, it is necessary to understand these two parallel approaches. A third major offshoot of the client-centered approach was "person-centered expressive therapy," developed by Natalie Rogers. As it developed somewhat later than the focusing and process-experiential approaches, it is discussed in the following chapter.

"Focusing" is based on the work of Eugene Gendlin who was Rogers' student at Chicago and then an important member of the staff of the Counseling Center there. Later he moved to Wisconsin to work with Rogers on the psychotherapy with schizophrenia research project; then he moved back to the University of Chicago where he was a professor of psychology for many years. He was a founder and longtime editor of the influential journal *Psychotherapy: Theory, Research, Practice, Training* and recipient of the APA clinical division's Distinguished Professional Psychologist award.[130]

From the late 1950s to early 1960s he and Rogers built off one another's ideas about the client's process of change in psychotherapy. As described earlier, Gendlin's insights about how clients can learn to refer to their own inner experiencing were incorporated in Rogers' developing theories and in the process scale for client change that they developed in Wisconsin.[131] After Rogers moved to California, Gendlin continued to develop his approach to helping clients learn to "focus" on their inner experiencing, on their felt bodily sense of feeling and meaning. This, of course, was always central to client-centered therapy and, for that matter, to almost all therapies. But Gendlin's approach, while still based in the core conditions of the therapy relationship, asked the client to attend more intentionally to what the client was experiencing at the moment. For example, psychotherapist Neil Friedman provided these comments on and excerpts from one of his therapy sessions with Gendlin:

Now, after some careful listening, he adds a focusing instruction onto this open-ended listening response.

Gene: Can you touch that feeling?

Neil: (eyes closed, pause) Confused. I am really confused.

Focusing has started to clarify the feeling.

Gene: Yeah, stay there …

Gendlin's intention is to keep me focusing.

Neil: I'm afraid their feeling about me will change … That feels heavy.

Gene: So there's some feeling there … some heavy certainty … that their feeling about you won't last.

Gendlin's listening response is right on target.

Neil: Yes! I want it too much …

Gene: Anything I want *that badly* …

Neil: No. Not anything. Just *this* kind of thing.

Gene: Oh! (genuine surprise) It is just *this* that won't work. Some sureness there … what is that sureness?[132]

Thus the combination of the therapist's empathic responses, questions and focusing instructions helps the client focus on his inner experiencing or felt sense in a particular way. While this approach is more directive than classical client-centered therapy, focusing advocates believe it is a more efficient and useful way to help clients further the goals of therapy.

Gendlin wrote about the focusing approach in the sixties and seventies.[133] His 1978 book *Focusing* was the first full description of his thinking to date and the most public statement that he had been moving in a different direction than Rogers. Gendlin also had some lingering anger at and disenchantment with Rogers from the conflict around publication of their 1967 volume on the schizophrenic project research. As a result of both factors—different directions and a strained relationship—the two men went their own ways for some years. There was no open conflict or rift, no ideological battle; each man simply pursued his own agenda. Rogers was not offended that one of his students and colleagues was taking a divergent tact; he had no desire to argue that Gendlin was wrong; in fact, he was open to the possibility that Gendlin might be on to something useful—there might be more effective variations of client-centered therapy. He just wished that Gendlin would do some scientific research to investigate this. Reinhard Tausch specifically recalled Rogers telling Tausch in La Jolla, "I told so … often to Gene, 'Gene please make empirical proofs of focusing …'"[134]

But Gendlin did not pursue that kind of research agenda, although he certainly had the skills to do so.[135] Also a philosopher, Gendlin pursued more of a theoretical research agenda with regard to focusing and experiencing, and he also pursued the development of focusing in practice. He founded the Focusing Institute, which developed branches around the world, and thereby established an independent movement within the person-centered tradition. Indeed, the focusing movement continued to acknowledge its client-centered identity. For example, in 2004, the Focusing Institute's website included an essay by Wiltschko in which he stated explicitly, "Focusing Therapy is a form of client-centered therapy, is part of the person-centered approach."[136]

Rogers and Gendlin, while never colleagues again, were cordial when their paths crossed. Rogers, particularly in his later years, would often explicitly credit Gendlin for the concept of experiencing, for example, "In formulating my current description, I have drawn on the concept of 'experiencing' as formulated by Gendlin (1962). This concept has enriched my thinking in various ways …"[137] In his last book in 1980 Rogers described some of Gendlin and Hendrick's recent work, and in a 1984 chapter on client-centered psychotherapy, he and Sanford referred to Gendlin's work on focusing.[138] Rogers and his colleagues invited (and paid) Gendlin to come to CSP to participate in their programs one year. Gendlin sent Rogers a warm message for his 80th birthday and wrote a laudatory eulogy at the time of Rogers' death; and when Rogers' oral history was published in 2002 on the one hundredth anniversary of Rogers' birth, Gendlin's tribute served as the Foreword.[139]

Another variation on client-centered therapy was initiated by Laura Rice, a student of Rogers and his colleagues at Chicago. She developed the idea of differential processing within the client-centered framework, believing that therapists might respond differently to different kinds of client statements, rather than always use the same kind of empathic response. She told an anecdote of how Rogers disapproved when she asked a fellow supervisee at Chicago what his intention was in making a certain statement to a client. Rogers thought the counselor should have only one intention—to empathically understand the client.[140] Undaunted, under Jack Butler's supervision, Rice developed scales to measure the client's vocal quality, believing that as a therapist could learn to recognize a client's expressive style, she could adjust her responses to convey a more evocative empathy.[141] "This expanded the view of empathy from understanding alone to include the major additional functions of evocation and exploration."[142] Rogers himself used empathy for more than simple understanding, as Leslie Greenberg demonstrated in his analysis of Rogers' interview with "Jim Brown," one of the schizophrenic patients in Wisconsin, discussed earlier.

> Near the beginning of these sessions, when Jim states that he "ain't no good to nobody, never was, and never will be," Rogers first responds with empathic understanding of this feeling: "Feeling that now, humm? That you're just no good to yourself, no good to anybody." This focus on feeling is accompanied by the very real prizing of the client in the statement, "Those really are lousy feelings." Jim begins to weep quietly but claims not to care. Even only reading the transcript,

one can feel Jim's hurt defiance. Rogers then responds strong and with a particular focus: "You tell yourself you don't care at all, but somehow I guess some part of you cares because some part of you weeps over it," and following a silence says, "I guess some part of you just feels, 'Here I am hit with another blow, as if I hadn't had enough blows.'"[143]

Greenberg comments: "With these responses Rogers senses deeply beyond what the client has said. This is not simple reflection. Rogers essentially picks up on a duality in the client's experience, a split between organismic experience and the self-concept, or between the real self and false self ..."

Rice's work took Rogers' interest in the process of therapy in general and client-centered therapy in particular to another level. At York University in Toronto, Canada she and her students continued studying how therapists could tailor their responses to different "markers" in the client's expression to evoke deeper exploration of feeling. "She was exploring the evocative use of empathy and Rice and Wexler's 1974 book [*Innovations in Client-Centered Therapy*] was an important book which had the information processing perspective."[144]

Rice's student Leslie Greenberg brought some new elements to Rice's research on the process of therapy. Influenced by the task analysis work and cognitive information processing perspective of French psychologist Pascual-Leone, who was a student of Jean Piaget and was on the faculty of York then, Greenberg brought further methodological skills to analyze the relationship between client markers and therapist responses. But, in addition to being a client-centered psychotherapist, Greenberg was also trained in Gestalt psychotherapy. He believed that the process of client-centered therapy could be advanced by the therapist's judiciously using Gestalt techniques when the client exhibited particular markers. For example, when a client expressed conflicting feelings on a subject, the therapist might ask the client to sit alternately in two chairs, voicing one set of feelings from one chair and addressing the opposite set of feelings from the other chair. This technique often helps bring a client's unrecognized, unexamined or conflicting feelings into greater awareness and clarity. While a traditional client-centered therapist would avoid such an intervention as being too directive, Greenberg believed that a therapist could invite, rather than direct, a client to become the personae in the empty chairs and could follow up with empathic responses to what the client said in a way that would be very much in keeping with the spirit of client-centered therapy. As Greenberg explained, "it wasn't either Gestalt therapy or client-centered therapy, it was a therapy with a client-centered relationship in which there were particular markers and then you use particular interventions."[145]

This was hardly the first time someone had suggested combining client-centered therapy with other theories or techniques from other schools. In fact, when Greenberg was asked whether, if he had been trained in another school of therapy other than Gestalt, he might have introduced a different blend of process-experiential therapy, he agreed he very well might have.[146] In any case, what was different about Greenberg's combination of Gestalt techniques with client-centered therapy was that he and Rice did extensive research on the process. Rice and Greenberg used their "process-experiential" approach to therapy to study the relationship between the client markers and the therapist interventions. They continued to collaborate as Greenberg moved to the University of British Columbia and then back to York again. Their edited book *Patterns of Change: Intensive Analysis of Psychotherapy Process*, published in 1984, described their and other colleagues' work over the past fifteen years.[147] It included contributions of Robert Elliott who had become an important member of their team.

Advocates of process-experiential therapy would argue that their approach remains essentially person-centered. As Robert Elliott wrote, "Working effectively with clients requires adapting the therapist's approach to the client's general presenting problems, the within-session task, and the client's immediate experience in the moment,"[148] all arguably client-centered characteristics. "Davis found that more than three-quarters of PE [process-experiential] therapists' responses were either empathic understanding (57%) or empathic exploration (19%), and that process-directing responses occurred about at a rate of 8%."[149] Clearly, the process-experiential therapists were operating in a predominantly client-centered manner.

Yet, although the proponents saw their work as basically client-centered, for years the process-experiential approach proceeded to develop separately and independently from the rest of the client-centered/person-centered movement. "Laura didn't join with the client-centered movement. She felt alienated from it basically," said Greenberg.[150] Rather they and their colleagues' reference group was the Society for Psychotherapy Researchers, formed in 1967, in which Rice and another Rogers' student, Godfrey Barrett-Lennard, took leadership roles.[151] Rogers, exhausted from the trials of the Wisconsin research project and its subsequent publication, and immersed in his new life and work in California, had little interest in these new developments.[152]

Only in his eighties did Rogers begin to recognize the potential significance of the process-experiential approach for the person-centered movement. As colleagues around the world whom he respected seemed to be paying attention to the developments in Canada, he too began to pay attention. And, in fact, it was entirely consistent with Rogers' "Necessary and Sufficient Conditions" hypothesis that he do so. In his famous essay, he was quite clear that client-centered therapy in its most nondirective form did not have a monopoly on empathy, positive regard and congruence.[153] If process-experiential therapists could demonstrate, as they appeared to be doing, that their particular approach to the therapeutic relationship could provide a sufficient dose of the core conditions to facilitate therapeutic change, he should have no reason to be defensive about it. Hence, as Greenberg recalled, in the 1980s he belatedly acknowledged Laura

Rice's research contributions to the client-centered approach.[154] However, it does not appear that he ever referred to or cited their work in his writings.

So during Rogers' lifetime the different schools of client-centered therapy remained separate. Rogers and his colleagues in California and a group around Chicago and others remained purely client-centered. Gendlin was developing and disseminating his focusing approach. Rice, Greenberg and Elliott were developing their process-experiential approach.[155] Most of the world interested in the person-centered approach followed Rogers' evolving career, while simultaneously, off the popular radar, the other branches were developing their theory, research and practice. It was not until after Rogers' death that the other schools became more widely known and a serious dialogue began among the different schools of client-centered therapy.

Organizations

Throughout his career so far, Rogers had resisted forming client-centered or person-centered organizations and certainly opposed any groups or organizations carrying his name. The example of Freud and his disciples fighting and splitting over differences in theory was too clearly in his mind. He wanted to avoid any type of organization that might rigidify his ideas or lead to political infighting. Part of this was a certain modesty about himself and his work. His close associate Valerie Henderson recalled how "Someone asked him one time, 'What do you think people will be thinking about you and your approach in 100 years?' He said, 'I don't care.'"[156] As described earlier, he hated "Rogerians."[157] Indeed, his whole philosophy encouraged individuals to realize *their own* potential, and he worried that any movement associated with him might cause people to focus on him and his ideas rather than themselves and their own development. Richard Farson recalled how,

> Once during the ferment of the 1960s, Carl was invited to address an audience of about a thousand people in San Francisco, a recognized hotbed of psychological revolution. The welcome for Carl was so enthusiastic as to be almost wild. These people had come to be led on a crusade. But instead of exploiting that mood of bright-eyed allegiance, Carl instead gave a sober talk dealing mainly with research findings and scholarly analyses. The speech had a distinctly calming effect on the audience, somewhat disappointing to those who had wanted Carl to give them marching orders. Afterward I queried Carl about why he had chosen to speak so scientifically to a group so charged for action. "They were primed for demagoguery," he said. "I thought I'd better give them what they should hear." This incident confirmed once again Carl's continuing commitment to discourage the development of a purely personal following. As a result, through the power of his ideas, he became one of the great leaders of psychology with a huge following of people most of whom do not know that it is he they are following."[158]

This abhorrence of hero worship, combined with his growing awareness of the politics of the person-centered approach, and his prior experiences with organizational politics all combined to leave him very suspicious of organizations per se. In a person-centered approach workshop in the mid-1970s he went so far as to say, "I feel that all institutions would be better off if they voluntarily disbanded at the end of 10 years and reorganized."[159] Hence for years he resisted any attempts to form an organization around himself or his work. As he explained in 1978, "It is not accidental that there has never been any 'school' of client-centered therapy. I have been approached many times by people who wanted me to start an institute or a society—something comparable to the psychoanalytic institutes. I felt that they showed that institutionalizing a point of view in therapy made it rigidly dogmatic and I resolutely refused to sponsor any such organization."[160] Again Valerie Henderson: "I don't remember him ever feeling otherwise. He did not want there to be a Carl Rogers' Institute. He didn't want anything that stopped the process of paying attention to what worked and what didn't help. That was the point for him. Pay attention to what you are experiencing, see what the results or consequences are and learn from it. Don't just think 'I have to do it this way because someone said so.'"[161]

Not surprisingly, this attitude of Rogers frustrated those who saw value in forming associations and institutes to study and disseminate the person-centered approach. João Hipólito recalled how Carlos Cardierr had organized a training program in Portugal and was organizing a society in the late seventies or early eighties.

> But when he wrote to Carl Rogers, Carl was very suspicious and he sent quite a hard letter saying that he was against training programs, against societies ... He didn't understand why we wanted to read the things about psychoanalysis or other things ... He forbad the use of his name for that society ... [it would make it seem] like he was dead, you know ... So it meant that the first society was called the Society of Anthropos Analysis [analysis of man] ... and he said he would send a collaborator to visit us and see ... Finally when John Wood [from CSP] came to Portugal ... he worked with us in our training programs and John Shlien, Nat Raskin came, Fred Zimring came. Barbara Brodley came, too. Brian Thorne, [Jerold] Bozarth came, too. And Barrett-Lennard. So we had a lot of [help, but] we never had agreement of Carl Rogers ...[162]

Peter Schmid said Rogers supported individuals developing the person-centered approach further, building on it, modifying and extending it based on their own experience; but he opposed groups forming, worried it would create Rogers clones. He even had a problem with the almost-8,000-member German association whose originally behavioral-oriented membership, under Reinhard Tausch's leadership, now accepted a strong person-centered component.[163]

In spite of Rogers' opposition, as Brian Thorne pointed out, "they did it anyway in Europe."[164] "We had made organizations against the will of our founding father," said Germain Lietaer. "In the Netherlands there was a society from 1970, here in Flanders from 1974, in Germany 1970." Lietaer recalled how, "When I came back [from California and] got together with our colleagues here, we founded an association of client-centered therapists. And Rogers was against, he was always [against it] ... I mean he was afraid that it would lead to dogmatists ... But what did we see? That the ... most dogmatic ones are the people of Chicago, you know [the ones who insist there is only one person-centered approach] ... so I think he was not right in being against organizations ... that being a big fault, I think ... I mean a big mistake from his point of view ... This having no organization also meant not having journals, not having communication channels ..."[165]

Yet as he got older, particularly in his late seventies and eighties, Rogers did become more interested in and concerned about how history would view him and his work. Valerie Henderson recognized that he had contradictory feelings about his legacy. On the one hand, "He said, 'I've done what I've done. I think it matters and what happens with it.'" On the other hand, "I really do think that he put his work out there for people to use it as they would; but if someone wrote an article dismissing it then he would really come back," that is, react to them.[166] While years earlier Rogers had told me "I hate old people who reminisce," now he wrote, "I have somehow gradually gotten over my strong dislike for looking back ..."[167] Consequently he began granting authors many more interview requests than he had ever done before. Maureen O'Hara recalled how,

> He wanted something to be left behind. I mean on a personal level. We talked a lot about this, that he was looking for a legacy, but he didn't want it to ... how do I want to say this? He always refused to be the pope of a new church or like a Freud with all his disciples who would be around him and then would fight about the orthodoxy of the [theory or method]. He didn't want that. But by the same token, towards the end of his life, he really was distressed at how, in what disarray the person-centered community seemed to be. With a lot of subgroups all over the place but not a coherent body of theory and practice that was going to continue into the next generations in any kind of organized way. He sort of was ambivalent. On the one hand he didn't want to be the guru, but on the other hand he really encouraged anybody that wanted to try to organize something that could continue on at a level of excellence.[168]

Actually, the success of the person-centered institutes and training programs in Europe freed Rogers from some of his concerns about establishing a person-centered institute himself. As he wrote in 1980, "The idea of such an institute has always been rejected by me, on the basis that its most likely outcome would be to develop dogma, narrowness, an orthodoxy focused on the one-to-one relationship. The situation has now changed. The person-centered approach has broadened to the point where its influence is felt in education, medicine and nursing, business, community development, philosophy, marriage and family life, communication and conflict resolution between and among cultures and other areas. It has spread geographically, with workshops in a dozen countries, from Japan to Poland. Programs of training have been established in Mexico City, Rome, Recife (Brazil), and other such programs are under consideration. The persons who are now leading this approach are extremely diverse and independent, and the establishment of an orthodoxy would appear impossible."[169]

In Rogers' later years, then, several programs, institutes or projects within Center for Studies of the Person were formed that more explicitly tried to further the person-centered approach, and some of them even bore Rogers' name. One umbrella entity was called "Carl Rogers and Associates: Person-Centered Programs," formed in 1980.[170] It only lasted for two years, but some of the sub-projects it spawned lasted for many years.[171] One of the sub-projects was the "Ongoing Learning Program" which offered a series of workshops on different aspects of the person-centered approach each season.[172] Another program of Carl Rogers and Associates was "The Carl Rogers Institute of Psychotherapy, Training, and Supervision." This was begun in the early eighties by Norman Chambers with seed money from Rogers. At first Rogers was reluctant to use his name in the title, but Chambers, who was African-American, explained, "Carl Rogers hadn't been introduced to the Latin, Black and Asian community. I wanted him to be seen immediately," and the name would help accomplish that.[173] The project provided intensive and long-term training in the person-centered approach and included the components of cognitive learnings, building clinical skills, supervision for licensure, personal growth and renewal, and social, ethnic and cultural awareness. A special feature of the institute was "to provide instruction and training designed to maximize the effectiveness of practitioners when working with persons from culturally diverse populations."[174] Training and supervision took place both at CSP and Chambers and Robert Lee's Multicultural Counseling and Consulting Center in San Diego. This project was never envisioned to be *the* Institute in the U.S. but some people saw it that way, which caused some resentment.[175]

In 1984 Maureen O'Hara, John K. Wood, Pat Rice, Rogers and possibly others created the Carl Rogers Institute for Advanced Studies. For two summers they operated a program for experienced facilitators to examine questions like the formation of group consciousness in contrast to focusing on individual growth. "It was more like a seminar," O'Hara explained. "We weren't training people but we were having an experience together which we were then reflecting on. What we tried to do was to put an intellectual reflection dimension into the work ... It took place in an experiential group. But we also had readings, and people came in to give presentations. I think Dick Farson came to one of them.

Carl did, gave some seminars … It didn't take us anywhere. For me the disappointment was we seemed to have learned what there was to learn and we couldn't push it into another phase or another chapter in that format, so at that point I think we just decided it wasn't worth doing it anymore."[176]

Another program Rogers encouraged was a workshop/institute called "Living Now." Gay Swenson had been hurt, angry and disappointed that she was not included on the staff of another CSP project, so he said to her, "Well, start your own program and I'll support you, too."[177] She did just that, offering annual summer workshops on various topics regarding human potential, helping relationships and social issues, held at University of California at San Diego since 1976 and continuing for twenty-two years under Swenson and others' direction.[178] True to his word, Rogers participated in the program every year until his death, even returning early from a conference in Hungary in 1986 to fulfill his commitment to Swenson.[179] Nel Kandel also operated the Carl Rogers Media and Resource Center at CSP, making Rogers' many films and videos on therapy, education and conflict resolution available for purchase and rental.[180] Still another project he lent his name to was the Carl Rogers Institute for Peace, which will be discussed below. All these projects and programs were under the CSP umbrella.

Reflecting on all these developments, O'Hara said, "I think he recognized that your work doesn't go on after you if it's not grounded in something just beyond your own personal presence. So … he encouraged the cross-cultural work with Chuck Devonshire, and he encouraged the multicultural work at CSP. And our Institute for Advanced Studies, and the Peace Project that Gay Swenson organized. And the Living Now program." The problem was,

> Carl underestimated the importance for people of working closely with him and therefore the political eddies around him as he moved from project to project, group to group. So, for example, when we were doing the Person-Centered Approach workshops, the team of people that were working on those had a really privileged relationship with him and it was glorious to be that close intellectually and psychologically with someone who was as wise and as creative and as bold as he was. So there was a real sense of being onto a really special project and it was very precious to all of us. The La Jolla Program had felt exactly that same way, when he participated with the La Jolla Program for all the same reasons. The cross-cultural folks around Devonshire had the same feeling. So Carl would go from group to group. Each of these groups would really treasure their relationship with Carl, really deeply treasure it; but [we and he] didn't have much of a sense of how to work with the other groups that Carl was also a part of. So instead of those groups being a collaboration of people who were pooling their learnings, they were more competitive about which is the true new idea … The expectation was that you weren't into anything that was collective. So instead

of having, creating, what in some disciplines might be thought of as a school of client-centered therapy with lots of different people adding to the collective learning and doing that deliberately the way scientists do, for example, it ended up with people developing their individual takes on things and being rather competitive with each other about whose version of all this is the real thing.[181]

While experimenting at Center for Studies of the Person with various institutes and programs that might promulgate the person-centered approach and create something of a legacy, Rogers also, finally, began to be open to the formation of wider associations that might insure the continuation of the person-centered approach in the future. No doubt by now he had observed the success of the European associations and institutes in helping the person-centered approach achieve a growing level of acceptance and legitimacy. So when Alberto Segrera of Mexico organized an International Forum on the Person-Centered Approach in June 1982 in Oaxtepec, Mexico, Rogers was supportive.[182] Segrera sent direct invitations to people around the world who were involved in the person-centered approach. Everyone was asked to bring a paper which was put into a volume for the participants; but in typical person-centered fashion the actual program was put together at the conference by the participants.[183] One planned event at the week-long forum was a public presentation that Rogers and Sanford made to 1,600–1,700 people in the municipal auditorium.[184] While there had been an even larger international representation at earlier person-centered workshops, like those at El Escorial, Spain and Lake Albano, Italy in 1978 and 1979, they were essentially large workshops. Mexico was the first full-fledged *forum* of the international community associated with the person-centered approach, especially as it pertained to counseling and psychotherapy. If the earlier workshops were intended to help participants experience and learn about the person-centered approach, the forum provided an opportunity to not only do that but to also step back and reflect upon and consider the future of the person-centered approach. As might be expected, the topic of forming an international organization came up and was hotly debated. While some were in favor, some spoke passionately against it and nothing was decided.[185]

The next year psychologist David Cain, a counselor at California Polytechnic State University who was associated with Center for Studies of the Person, decided to take matters into his own hands and formed the Person-Centered Therapy Network for people interested in the person-centered approach in counseling and psychotherapy. The following year he started publishing a newsletter for the Network. The same year, 1984, the Second International Forum took place in Norwich, England, again encouraged by Segrera, with the local sponsorship and organization of Brian Thorne and associates. At the Forum, Segrera, Cain and others talked about forming an association and decided to move forward. When they approached Rogers, he said, "Yes. I don't trust organizations as they exist now, but I think it's worth trying to see if we can create a different kind of organization."[186] Cain recalled how he had said to Rogers,

> "I think we ought to expand [beyond the Person-Centered Therapy Network]
> ... I think this is the time to expand this beyond therapy and open up to education
> and any other endeavor that could be embraced by the person-centered approach."
> He was fully supportive of that, of course. We were talking about a name, and I
> proposed the Association for the Development of the Person-Centered Approach,
> and Carl immediately focused on the word "development." He said he liked that
> ... because with his open mind and genuine humility, I think Carl felt there was
> of course more to discover, more to learn, further to go, and I think he also
> wanted to see his ideas carried forward.[187]

The first official annual meeting of the association was held in Chicago in September 1986. Rogers and Sanford attended this meeting at the International House at the University of Chicago, where they talked about their recent trip to South Africa.[188] About the same time, said Cain,

> I had decided we needed a journal, and I had decided not to ask anybody's
> permission ... because to ask anybody's permission was to open up an endless
> debate about who, how, why, when, where, and who the hell are you to do this,
> and blah, blah, blah, blah. And I had been aware that Carl had resisted formal
> organization and formal journals, and the whole bit ... So I just did it. I did go
> to Carl and I proposed it to him, not for permission, but I said, "This is what
> I'm intending to do and I would like your support and involvement," and he
> said "Yep, I don't know how involved I'll be, but you have my support." And he
> was involved for the year that he was alive during the publication.

Thus the *Person-Centered Review* was begun under Cain's editorship, independent of the Association for the Development of the Person-Centered Approach (ADPCA), with Rogers writing an article or column in each quarterly issue.[189] Jerold Bozarth, Arthur Combs, Julius Seeman and Brian Thorne were Associate Editors for the entire life of the journal which operated from 1986–1990, when Cain ceased publication due to an insufficient number of subscribers.[190] That Rogers would give this level of support to the new journal when he was so busy with his international work and other commitments indicates again the concern Rogers had in his final years about establishing the person-centered approach as a lasting school of thought and practice. His allowing his name to be used on Center for Studies of the Person projects, his support of the new person-centered organization, and his involvement with the new person-centered journal all testified to his interest in continuing the work and his own legacy.

The Peace Project

If Rogers was now somewhat evangelizing for the person-centered approach—conducting person-centered workshops around the world and beginning to support national and international person-centered organizations—it was not for the person-centered approach alone. He was genuinely concerned with the future of the planet. The older he was, and the more experience he had in facilitating communication and community among diverse groups, the more committed he became to reducing inter-group and international tensions and achieving world peace. His presentations and workshops, while still highlighting his theories and work in enhancing mental health, learning and individual development, always returned to the importance of applying person-centered approaches to the larger issues of resolving inter-group and international conflict.

To some extent he always had been interested in the applications of his work to conflict resolution, even on an international scale. He first speculated about "The Implications of Non-Directive Therapy for the Handling of Social Conflicts" in a speech in 1946.[191] Possibly inspired by that line of thought, around 1950, Tom Gordon, S.I. Hayakawa and Gerald Haigh led a seminar at Chicago on the implications of client-centered therapy for interpersonal, industrial, and international relations.[192] Rogers built on this theme in a 1951 presentation on "Communication: Its Blocking and Facilitation," suggesting how communication could be improved between antagonistic groups or even nations.[193] In a 1960 essay, "A Therapist's View of Personal Goals," he illustrated at some length how valuable it might be if nations as well as individuals would drop their facades and communicate who they truly were.[194] But although Rogers recognized the potential of the client-centered approach to reduce inter-group tensions, he had little experience in actually testing this proposition during his university years. When he left Wisconsin to join the Western Behavioral Sciences Institute (WBSI), Rogers said in a press conference that he chose to come to La Jolla because, among other reasons, working with WBSI would give him the freedom to pursue investigations of the tensions which affect the relationships of normal people. "The most crucial problem in the world today," he said, "is the solution of tensions between nations, racial groups, industrial groups as well as those between family members and individuals."[195]

At WBSI and then at CSP Rogers had many opportunities to test his belief that inter-group tensions could be lessened in a facilitative climate of genuineness, understanding, prizing and trust. In encounter groups—especially in ones like the Irish Catholic/Protestant group, the health consumer/health provider groups, and the drug group, all described earlier—and later in person-centered workshops, he often experienced this personally, as he saw how individuals and sub-groups gradually relaxed their defenses and allowed themselves to really listen to others whose views they previously distrusted or abhorred. As they listened, they began to move beyond their stereotypes and preconceptions and achieve a gradual recognition of their common humanity and common goals. Rogers was much impressed with the potential of honest, person-to-person communication to reduce interpersonal and inter-group tensions. After the Camp David accords of 1978, Rogers often wrote and spoke of the role President Carter played in facilitating communication between Menachim Begin and Anwar Sadat, leading to an historic peace treaty between Israel and Egypt.[196] It seemed that Carter provided the understanding of each position and acceptance of each protagonist that enabled Begin and Sadat to relax some of their defenses and eventually recognize the genuine desire of each for peace. An important breakthrough in the retreat came about when, ready to leave without an agreement, Begin began talking to Carter about his grandchildren and was inspired to try again to reach an agreement so that his grandchildren would not experience the world of conflict the Palestinians and Jews had known all their lives.

As Rogers became increasingly involved in cross-cultural communications workshops in the late seventies and early eighties, the usefulness of facilitating person-to-person encounters among individuals and groups in conflict became even more apparent to him. As he described the 1978 workshop in Spain, there were "Marxists and corporation managers; priests and non-believers; Americans and anti-Americans; feuding groups within Spain; and on and on. The workshop ended with a deep feeling of community. Mutual understanding and respect largely replaced the hostilities. 'Conflicts' had become understandable and respected 'differences' … There have been similar workshops, involving different types of factional differences, in Italy, Poland, Brazil, Japan, Mexico, France, the Philippines, and the U.S."[197]

Yet as energized as he was by the power of the person-centered approach to be helpful in reducing tensions among conflicting parties, he was also sobered by the conflicts he saw around the world. In South Africa it was not clear whether the country would disintegrate into a race war. The guerilla war in Nicaragua threatened to expand into a regional war throughout Central America. In Europe it was uncertain whether the so-called Cold War could be kept in a state of "detente" or whether it would erupt in national or regional conflict or even international nuclear war. In demonstration interviews Rogers conducted on his autumn 1983 European tour, he was deeply impressed and saddened by the somber feeling hanging over his clients. He was particularly touched by a counseling interview he conducted with a German woman who felt such despair about living under the threat of bombs and missiles the superpowers had pointed at her country and each other, that even though she wanted to have children, she could not picture bringing a baby into this world.[198]

Therefore, gratified as he was by the warm reception he and the person-centered approach were receiving around the world, Rogers was not at all complacent about the future. Rather he felt an increasing need to utilize his

541

knowledge and experience in the cause of world peace. A turning point came in October 1982, at a large public event that Gay Swenson organized to celebrate his 80th birthday earlier that year. It featured Rogers and New Age author Marilyn Ferguson and was called "Two Humanists, Two Generations: A Day to Honor the Planet, Its People and Our Preservation." Fresh from his recent experience facilitating communication among blacks and whites in South Africa, Rogers told the audience that he wished that nations would "export facilitators to each other rather than bombs." When asked that evening about his hopes and plans for the years ahead, Rogers told the group that "he hoped to devote whatever years of life might remain to him to the cause of world peace."[199] Valerie Henderson said, "I think that he felt that this is where his whole life's work was heading, what it really was about—that he wanted it to have some effect internationally. He was going to South Africa and Russia and other places and seeing a real need for *countries* to come together in the ways that he thought individuals could if given the right opportunity."[200]

Gay Swenson (later Barfield), Rogers' close colleague and good friend at Center for Studies of the Person, and other colleagues encouraged him to acknowledge the role that peace played in his work and see that this was a critical time in the world for him to apply his work to the cause of peace. As Swenson told him, "In my view, your work has always been about peace, Carl, at every level, internally, interpersonally and internationally," and she suggested to him that they form a project with other CSP colleagues to focus on conflict resolution and peacemaking.[201] This suggestion resulted three years later in an historic gathering in Rust, Austria. Barfield later said that the Rust workshop in November 1985 was the "capstone" project in Carl Rogers' life.[202] Thomas Greening called Rogers' peace project the "culmination" of his career.[203] I agree; therefore, I will tell the story in some detail; although it could well merit an entire volume itself.[204]

The Rust Workshop

Shortly after the 80th birthday celebration, in December 1982, Swenson initiated a meeting between Rogers, State Assemblyman John Vasconcellos and herself to see how they might turn Rogers' concept of exporting facilitators instead of bombs into an actual project.[205] This led to other meetings, contacts, introductions and conversations over the following months, which eventually led Swenson, through Vasconcellos' initiation, to contact Robert Muller, Assistant Secretary General of the United Nations. At this point, they had no specific plans, rather they were interested in "having state, federal and international statespersons meet with us to see how the person-centered approach could be useful in conflict resolution processes."[206] Swenson, Rogers, Vasconcellos, John K. Wood, Harold Bloomfield and Dorothy Lyddon met with Muller in August 1983, when he was in California for a conference. They had invited the long-serving Senator Alan Cranston from California to join them—thereby achieving state, national and international representation—but he was unable to attend.[207] Muller was supportive of their concept and, in turn, referred them to Rodrigo Carazo Odio, the former President of Costa Rica and President of the United Nations University for Peace in Costa Rica, founded three years earlier.[208] The following month Swenson met with Carazo when he was in California.[209] Rogers could not attend the meeting, because he was in Switzerland at the time, talking to the diplomatic corps in Geneva, in conjunction with a cross-cultural communications workshop. While Swenson reported to Rogers and their colleagues about the meeting with Carazo, Rogers reported on his presentation to the diplomatic corps.

> In my talk I stressed the experiences we have had in dealing with groups containing bitterly antagonistic factions … I described the group from Belfast which we held several years ago, and the conference of bitterly antagonistic "health consumers" and "health providers" held by the National Health Conference. I spoke of the progress which had been made toward reconciliation in both of these groups and some of the facilitative conditions which seems to promote such reconciliation. Then I analyzed the Camp David experience with Carter, Sadat and Begin, showing that there were many similarities between that experience and our own experience in these groups. I suggested some steps that might be taken to bring together diplomats and political leaders with people like ourselves in order that we might mutually learn from each other better ways of initiating dialogue between conflicting groups and facilitating a reduction of such tensions.[210]

While Rogers and Swenson explored many other ideas and possible collaborations, they continued to pursue the conversation with President Carazo and Murray Silberman, Director of Planning for the University for Peace. Gradually it emerged that Central America might indeed offer an opportunity to utilize the person-centered approach to reduce tensions and facilitate communication among political leaders in an international conflict situation.

In fact, officials in Costa Rica and at the University for Peace had been vitally interested in finding a solution to the armed conflict that had been going on in neighboring Nicaragua for many years and which threatened to engulf all of Central America.[211] In 1979, the Sandinista liberation movement had concluded a successful revolution in Nicaragua against the Samoza dictatorship which had been supported by an oligarchy of wealthy landowners. In turn, a new National Resistance movement (the "contras") was formed in opposition to the Sandinista government and began a guerilla war against it. Although the Sandinistas established their legitimacy in 1984 with 67% of the vote in a reasonably democratic election, the Reagan administration in the United States feared that the leftist Nicaraguan government might become a beachhead for Soviet and Cuban influence in the region and that the Sandinistas, beginning to operate in other countries, would destabilize Central American democracies. So the U.S. supported the contras and did their best to undermine the Nicaraguan government—imposing an economic embargo on the country, militarizing neighboring Honduras, and (unknown until the Iran–Contra scandal broke in 1986) providing illegal support to the contras. Thus the war went on for years, with thousands of deaths, and threatened to spill over into neighboring countries, destabilizing the area and threatening global stability by further drawing in the superpowers.

In the midst of this conflict, a number of Latin American nations were attempting to restore peace to Nicaragua and the region by bringing the parties together to try to work out a peace agreement. Their so-called "Contadora Process" (named for the island off the coast of Panama where the first meeting had taken place in 1983) developed a plan that "provided for democratic and representative government, honest elections, national reconciliation, a prohibition of foreign military bases and support for irregular armed forces in other countries, a reduction in armaments, and a withdrawal of foreign military advisors."[212] The Contadora Process had so far been unsuccessful, in part, because of the Reagan administration's unwillingness to accept a negotiated settlement that left the Sandinistas in power. Communication had broken down and the mood in Central America was somber.

It was in this historical context that Rogers and his colleagues offered their services as facilitators of a workshop for reducing tensions among conflicting parties in an international conflict. Carazo and the University for Peace saw the Californians' offer as an opportunity to get the parties in the Central American conflict talking again and offered to help convene such a gathering.[213] The idea was to enable those with leading roles in the conflict, such as leaders of opposing factions, governmental officials and heads of non-governmental organizations, to achieve a level of communication and trust that had theretofore been absent. Once the communication and trust were built, then the protagonists themselves, through their own diplomatic channels, could work toward realistic solutions to their conflict. Rogers and his colleagues' previous work in tension reduction had been essentially with laypersons; now they intended to work with leaders and their representatives who had the power or influence to bring about real change.

When it began to seem that a feasible project was in sight, in January 1984 Swenson and Rogers formalized their endeavor by forming the Institute for Person-Centered Approaches to Peace. Initially Rogers didn't want his name used in the title, because the intention was to focus on the person-centered process, not himself; but when it became clear that the initial name was vague to many people and cumbersome, and that Rogers' name had considerable publicity value, on his suggestion they changed the name to the Carl Rogers Institute for Peace.[214] From its inception however, most people referred to the project by its informal name: the "Carl Rogers Peace Project" or, simply, "the Peace Project."

Rogers kicked off the project with a personal donation of $8,000. From the start Rogers and Swenson were the co-directors. (Originally Swenson was to be the sole director, but they were convinced that for credibility in dealing with high-status world figures, Rogers should also be a director.)[215] To help them conceptualize a vision and plans for the new project, John Vasconcellos "organized and convened a weekend retreat at Dorothy Lyddon's Seven Springs Ranch in Cupertino in northern California. Twenty persons came together to discuss new patterns of politics and peacemaking, including whether humanistic psychologists collectively should take a public stand for a particular presidential candidate in the upcoming national election."[216]

From then on the major focus of the Peace Project was to organize an international gathering focused on the problems in Central America. As Maria Bowen explained, "Although it was not clear to us what specific outcomes the University for Peace group expected, the Carl Rogers Peace Project honored their wish to make the Central America Challenge the workshop theme. Conversely, although the University for Peace group members were not familiar with the Person-Centered Approach to group facilitation, they were willing to go through its process."[217] Naturally such a project would be of interest to the U.S. government who, until then, had done their best to undermine the Contadora peace process. At one point, when invitations were being sent out across the world, the Peace Project staff became suspicious that the government was tapping their phones and were quite alarmed and outraged about it. Rogers characteristically saw the positive side of the situation, commenting, "Well, that's not all bad. Maybe if they'll listen, they'll learn something."[218] Government spying aside, the whole venture was a risk, since it was entirely uncertain whether the funding could be obtained to host such a gathering, whether the parties involved would accept the invitation and, if both those challenges were met, whether such an event would actually be successful.

The funding challenge alone was considerable, since among other expenses, the organizers wanted to offer free transportation and accommodations to the participants. When John K. Wood left the project to move to Brazil, David Malcolm, a professor of education at San Diego State University, joined the planning team with the responsibility for grant writing.[219] In March of 1984 a number of public and private fundraising events with President Carazo were held in La Jolla for the University for Peace. Actor Dennis Weaver was an early supporter of the project, as was actor Robert Young.[220] Still there was not nearly enough funding to organize the event, even when the facilitators agreed to serve without pay. Fortuitously, a former student of David Malcolm had married a Viennese tour guide, Eduard Schmiege, who happened to know Karl Vak, the president of the Austrian Society for Foreign Politics and International Relations and head of the largest bank in Austria, the "Z-Bank." When Rogers was in Vienna in 1984 to participate in Malcolm's San Diego State summer overseas program, Schmiege introduced Rogers and Malcolm to Vak who, after some further communications, offered to pay for the accommodations for the workshop if it were held at one of the bank's properties, the Seehotel in Rust, Austria.[221] While it was beneficial to be in a retreat setting, far from the tension and violence of Nicaragua, ironically the Austrian location also added substantially to the transportation costs.

The decision to hold the meeting in Austria was made in January 1985 and tentative invitation lists were developed for the November event. In February and March the first round of invitations was sent to prospective participants to attend the workshop on "The Central American Challenge." Fundraising continued right up to the event. A $25,000 grant from the Carnegie Corporation was confirmed in June. Fundraising events at Rancho Santa Fe and Santa Clara were held in September.[222] A $30,000 anonymous gift to the Peace Project was received as late as October.[223]

As difficult as the fundraising was, the task of getting participants for the event proved even more frustrating. President Monge of Costa Rica and President Carazo and Murray Silberman from the University of Peace issued dozens of invitations to various Central and Latin American leaders,[224] as well as leaders from other countries; while Rogers and Swenson, with the help of California legislative leader John Vasconcellos, worked on gaining participants from the U.S. and elsewhere. Murray Silberman urged the Peace Project staff to downplay the workshop *process* goals in their invitations or subsequent communications, as participants would be motivated to come to *solve the problem*, not reduce tensions or increase communication per se. Heated letters flew back and forth between La Jolla, Costa Rica and Vienna on this issue.[225] Invitations were still going out in the fall when they consulted with John Marks of Search for Common Ground in Washington, DC to help insure there was a balance of conservative and liberal representatives. Marks played a very important role in gaining a wider range of participants than would otherwise have been achieved.[226] Still there were many disappointments—with invitations being declined, invitations being accepted, confirmed participants later withdrawing, in some cases at the last minute, and participants of lesser stature being substituted for the original invitee. However, eventually over forty individuals agreed to participate and actually attended the workshop.[227]

Participants could be categorized in three groups. First were the parties to the conflict, sometimes called the "delegates." These were the people who were directly involved in the conflict, indirectly involved as Latin American neighbors, or potentially able to influence the events in Central America. Second were individuals with expertise or experience in conflict resolution, peace or social activism. The idea was to "not just have the top-down leaders again determining world events without some interchange or dialogue with people that they might not be engaged with typically ... it was the more power-shifting, egalitarian representation of multiple voices who have interests in different ways in world peace."[228] Rogers provided the following description of these two groups, to which I have added additional, bracketed information to amplify on their backgrounds.

... there were fifty participants in the workshop (although four could attend only one or two sessions). There were three ex-presidents of Central American countries [Costa Rica, Honduras, Venezuela], the current vice-president of Costa Rica, three from ministries of foreign affairs [Austria, El Salvador, Sweden], seven ambassadors [Austria, Costa Rica, Columbia, Mexico, Nicaragua, Venezuela, U.S. (former)], seven legislators [three from Austria, Sweden, John Vasconcellos from the U.S., Venezuela, former president Mexican Chamber of Deputies]; four lesser or retired government officials [including a former U.S. senator (Democrat) and an aide to a U.S. senator (Republican)];

there were eight from academia, mostly professors [Costa Rica, Hungary, Poland; Switzerland, U.S., and several from University for Peace]; there were eight participants from institutes, foundations, and other organizations, several of them concerned with communication and cooperation [including U.N. Industrial Development Organization, the conservative Institute for Contemporary Studies; Choosing Our Future, the West German Green Party; North American Congress on Latin America, a Reagan appointee to the U.S. Institute for Peace, and actor Dennis Weaver who helped organize food distribution projects in poor communities]; there were five invited primarily because they were peace activists [Palestinian Center for the Study of Nonviolence in Israel, John Marks from Search for Common Ground, Physicians for Social Responsibility, a peace newsletter editor from the U.S., and an Gandhian activist from India];

there were two who were invited primarily because of books they had written [including William Ury whose book *Getting to YES* was widely used in business, industry and government as a conflict resolution method[229]] (although many others had also written books); there were two officials from the bank that subsidized the gathering in Austria [including Karl Vak] ... The seventeen nations from which the participants came are the following: Costa Rica, Honduras, El Salvador, Nicaragua, Columbia, Venezuela, Mexico, Chile, Austria, the United States, West Germany, Sweden, India, Poland, Hungary, the Philippines, and Switzerland, and two Palestinians living in Jerusalem."[230]

As diverse a group as this was there were two notable omissions. High officials in the U.S. State Department accepted invitations but then withdrew without explanation—an indication of the U.S. administration's hostility at the time toward the Central American peace process.[231] Thus, there was "no official U.S. government representation," although among the Republicans or conservatives represented, "there were a couple of people who had quasi-official standing with our government."[232] These included a speech writer for President Reagan. Another limitation was that, although there was a Sandanista present, there were no *contras* at the workshop, as such activity was illegal.

The third group of participants was the facilitators. As Marvalene Hughes recalled, "We didn't know who was going because we didn't know if the budget would afford to send a lot of us. In the classic person-centered kind of way, we made decisions about who should go."[233] Joining Rogers, Swenson and Malcolm were CSP colleagues Maria Bowen, Valerie Henderson, Norm Chambers, and Doug Land and other colleagues: Marvalene Styles (Hughes), university administrator; Lawrence Solomon, faculty member of the California School of Professional Psychology and specialist in tension reduction and organizational development; and Alberto Zucconi, Italy's leader in the person-centered approach who had co-organized numerous cross-cultural communication workshops around Europe.[234] The team's diversity was important, with equal numbers of women and men, Chambers and Styles being African-American, Bowen being Latino-American, and Zucconi being from Italy. Still, as Zucconi later recalled, some people looked skeptically at the facilitation team, saying "We're not experts." To this Rogers replied, "That's just the point. There are many experts, and look where it's gone."[235] Since Swenson would be busy as a facilitator, Dee Aker joined David Malcolm as administrative staff for the event. Alberto Segrera and Sylvia Dubovoy, person-centered leaders from Mexico, and Maria Bustamante, person-centered psychologist from Venezuela, served as translators.

The workshop was held from November 1–5, 1985 under the sponsorship of the University of Peace and the Center for Studies of the Person, with Carl Rogers and President Carazo as co-directors. Ironically, for a while it was uncertain if Rogers was going to be able to make the meeting. In late summer he broke his neck. Yet three weeks later, wearing a neck brace, he spoke to 300 people at a fundraising event for the Peace Project.[236] It was still another matter to travel across the world and lead an intense four-day event with world dignitaries about a life-and-death struggle. However, he insisted he was going, even if he had to wear a cervical collar and travel in a wheelchair for part of the journey, both of which he did.[237]

Rust was a quaint village on the Austria–Hungary border, complete with storks on the rooftops. The idea was to get away from all the publicity, cameras and influences that might pressure participants to remain in their typical roles, voice only their official positions, and be unwilling to take the risks associated with more genuine communication. For the same reason, the organizers tried to have the conference last a week or so, to give the participants enough time to achieve a real encounter, establish trust, and begin to work on solutions to the Central American conflict. But because of limited funding and, even more, the unwillingness of the participants to commit to a longer time frame, the meeting would last only four days. From the facilitators' point of view and experience this was a woefully short time; but from the participants' view it was an unprecedented commitment of valuable time for such an experimental, unofficial gathering.

Most of the meeting followed the format of a person-centered workshop, modified somewhat for the occasion. It was decided beforehand that whole group community meetings would take place each morning from 10 A.M. to 1 P.M., and smaller groups would be held in the afternoons from 3 to 5:30 P.M., with the participants divided into four sections, each facilitated by two staff members, one male and one female.[238] Still recovering from his neck injury, Rogers rested in the afternoons and did not facilitate a small group. Rogers would give a presentation the first evening and Carazo the next evening, followed by questions and discussion. English was the official language of the workshop, although Spanish was used more often. The staff decided to have the translation be sequential rather than simultaneous, so the listeners could better focus on the speaker's non-verbal and emotional expression as well as their words.[239] This slowed down the pace but allowed more time for listening.

Thus on the first morning of the workshop, participants sat in two concentric circles, mostly in clusters of allied viewpoints, as Rogers, in his cervical collar, began the proceedings. He introduced their host Karl Vak and co-leader Rodrigo Carazo who both welcomed the group and expressed their hopes for peace. After further acknowledgements and introductions, Rogers expressed his hopes for the workshop and described how a person-centered approach to communication might lead to greater trust and eventually to realistic solutions to the Central American conflict. In typical person-centered fashion he emphasized that this would be "*our* conference, which we would create together."[240]

People listened to the eighty-three-year-old psychologist with respect; then after a brief break, shortly after the session resumed the unofficial representative of the Reagan administration went on the offensive, attacking the Sandinistas for restricting freedoms and saying that the solution to the problem in Nicaragua was simple: just drop a bomb on the capitol Managua (which was controlled by the Sandinistas). A Nicaraguan government representative responded in kind, recounting what he described as the United States' long history of supporting "banana republics" in Latin America where the U.S. was more concerned about maintaining its own interests than the welfare of the Latin American people. This was followed by several other speeches expressing various viewpoints, little direct dialogue, and an interruption when the Austrian foreign minister Leopold Gratz entered the room with news cameras flashing, welcomed the participants, and expressed his hopes for a successful conference. Thus the workshop began— in typical, unpredictable, volatile, person-centered fashion!

Marvalene Hughes said, "The severity of the differences in Rust forced confrontation, interaction, and created a really vibrant dynamic."[241] Rogers and his colleagues reflected and accepted the feelings and viewpoints of the various protagonists. For example, "Early in the gathering, a lengthy and impassioned concern is accurately heard by Carl; he gently reminds the speaker that four days yet remain to hear the history of years of pain in an embattled Central American country … A Gandhian and a militant engage, escalate their differences; both are heard empathically and fairly, and the process moves on, avoiding right and wrong."[242] Some participants spoke with such continuous intensity that it was difficult to interrupt, let alone express an empathic response.

Part of the problem was different expectations among the workshop participants. The Latin American delegates, invited by the University for Peace, expected a more content-oriented conference, with participants giving speeches on their positions, which would hopefully lead to better mutual understanding of one another's viewpoints. The other delegates, invited by CSP, understood that this would be a workshop utilizing the person-centered approach to explore the different political perspectives and, therefore, there would be a significant focus on group and interpersonal processes.[243] Carazo and Silberman had told the CSP people to downplay the group process aspect in their invitations and orientation materials. The Peace Project staff resisted this suggestion and sent out full information about the group process to be employed. However, because of the many cancellations and replacements of participants at the last moment, many did not have this understanding in mind. The lack of a common "contract" among the participants and facilitators meant the facilitators were caught between wanting to do their usual job of intervening around interpersonal issues, including pointing out the consequences of long speeches on the group process, and recognizing that this would be viewed as disrespectful and inappropriate by the Latin Americans for whom the content of their presentations was of life-and-death importance. Thus the facilitators were much less active than they normally might have been. Swenson thought that "the staff's talents were highly unrecognized and underused, particularly in the general meetings rather than small groups. The staff too readily concurred during an early joint meeting with the United Nations University for Peace to remain low profile, to keep out of the way, to let the politicians talk to each other."[244]

To compound the problem, as might have been expected given cultural norms, the Latin American men dominated the conversation and sometimes ignored the women or treated their comments with condescension. Maria Bowen felt particularly frustrated in this situation. She normally would have challenged such behavior but in this context did not feel it was appropriate to challenge their cultural norms. On the one occasion when she did confront a group member, she was put down by another participant for treating that illustrious politician so disrespectfully. As she later pointed out, the norms among many participants in this theme-oriented, invitational, cross-cultural workshop, with a socio-political rather than personal growth agenda, with ex-presidents of countries and other senior officials who were not used to being treated on a familiar basis, presented real challenges to the facilitators.[245] Or as Gay Swenson wrote, "A difficult challenge in such a gathering relates to the issue of deference and respect for authority figures" versus "the maintenance of equality among all persons present regardless of culture, role, sex, influence, and so on."[246]

For the first two days the pattern of speech-making, minimal listening, and little expression of personal feelings continued, particularly in the large group, and a number of the participants felt increasingly impatient about the lack of progress. As usually occurs in person-centered workshops, some participants made suggestions for structuring the process: "role-play the different positions on the Contra/Contadora issues with a neutral third party facilitating; have Rogers conduct an interview to demonstrate person-centered conflict resolution techniques; have major adversaries dialog directly." Although, to the frustration of some, these things did not necessarily occur when suggested, "Many of these events occurred naturally, in either large or small group meetings, or outside the scheduled times, facilitated by staff and/or participants."[247]

Some dialogue began to occur in the small groups the second afternoon and thereafter. Gay Swenson noted in her journal how in her small group,

> I feel I did very good facilitating between U.S. _____ [names omitted to maintain anonymity] and the Central American in trying to get him to *hear* instead of *to convince*. Also we all dealt so beautifully and carefully with _____'s feedback to _____ re his "cold steely style—not person, of always being so very right." It was beautiful to see him become less defensive and to hear the load he carried in Washington as a legislative assistant who "couldn't be wrong, can't make mistakes." … Atmosphere of real trust finally and real dialog. Particularly moving to hear the _____ Ambassador _____ speak with both personal authenticity and passion …"[248]

Maria Bowen also noted that, compared to the whole group sessions, "In the smaller groups, there was less urgency, more time and space for talking to each other. Dialogues happened more easily, and the more intimate atmosphere freed people to be more personal. These ways of operating were then transferred to the larger group."[249] Also in small groups some of the participants shared their experiences in mediation and dealing with social problems. Marvalene (Styles) Hughes thought Dennis Weaver "was very effective … he had a lot of social service projects going and he talked about the importance of the projects that he had organized and how that could apply to the world as a whole."[250]

At that point President Carazo's evening presentation, in which he described the work of the University of Peace, seemed to focus the discussion on key issues of concern to the participants. After the session ended, the Central and Latin American group remained in the lobby and talked and argued late into the night, as did many of the other participants in a second group. Within these separate

551

groups communication was more direct and emotional than before and, although unplanned, seemed to be productive in terms of the workshop goals.

The next morning the atmosphere in the whole group was very different. There was more listening and more expression of personal feeling and emotion about the issues being discussed, along with political viewpoints. Although one participant protested that such "therapy" was not needed, people were willing to engage one another on a more personal level. The topic of sexism even came up for vigorous discussion. Although there were still sharp disagreements among members and strong negative emotions sometimes expressed, as one member put it, "the arguments made it clear to him that some people may be misguided, but that no one in the group was malevolent."[251] Demonizing "the other" was giving way to recognition of common human concerns, feelings and goals. Rogers wrote, "The outstanding thing ... was that people were listening to one another; they were responding to one another; there was real dialogue going on; the group process was clearly at work. Personally, as I rested after the morning session, I felt very relaxed and truly joyful. I knew now that whatever the conclusion of the workshop might be, it would be constructive. The process we had hoped to help initiate was under way. This was born out by the reports that came from the small groups that afternoon."[252]

As often occurs in residential workshops, when participants have the opportunity to continue to interact over meals and in hallways and hotel rooms, it was outside the official sessions that some of the most valuable communication took place. "Negotiations were going on constantly: in small groups, in the lobby, in bedrooms, in the dining room, at parties ... Politicians from the same country, who had not talked to each other for years, would try to work out their long-time differences."[253] On the third evening of the workshop, the participants were invited to a "*Heurigen*" at a nearby inn, an Austrian tradition celebrating the harvesting of the grapes and the tasting of the first spring wine. Aided by the considerable amount of alcohol consumed, more personal communication took place and many relationships were deepened. A U.S. citizen and a Nicaraguan agreed to present a proposal to officials they knew in their respective governments for peaceful co-existence between the two countries. As it happened, the Reagan speech writer sat across the table from one of the Sandinistas.[254] For a while the conversation was tense and angry. One even called the other a "son of a bitch." One of the translators began to cry and asked Alberto Segrera to take over the translation. Then the Sandinista reminded the U.S. representative of what he had said at the opening session. As he reached in his pocket at least one observer worried that he might pull out a gun. But he took out his wallet and showed the U.S. representative a photograph of his son. He pointed out that if, indeed, bombs were dropped on Managua his son would be killed. Did the other man really want that? "Oh, you have a son? I have a son, too." Here was his photograph. No, he didn't want the other's son to be hurt. And so they began to talk on a different level, recognizing their common goals and hopes that transcended political affiliation, achieving a human encounter that is difficult not to be changed by. By the end of the meeting, the two men were making plans to have their children exchange visits to their respective homes to get to know one another's countries and people better.[255]

The *Heurigen* also produced at least one insulting exchange in the informal setting, but on the whole, it was a meaningful aid to the workshop goal of facilitating a positive encounter among the participants. It also provided an indication of the respect the entire gathering had for Rogers who, at first, was not inclined to attend the evening event because he was tired. John Vasconcellos persuaded him that he should attend at least briefly. When Rogers walked in, everybody stopped their conversations, stood, and broke into applause.[256]

The final day of the workshop was supposed to consist of a morning whole community meeting, afternoon small groups, a 6:00 P.M. press conference in Vienna—a concession to those with a diplomatic agenda and to the Austria Bank who wanted a little publicity for their contribution—and a final, evening whole group meeting. When they were informed that morning that the press conference would have to be moved earlier in the afternoon, it temporarily disrupted the morning session. Nevertheless, the group adjusted to the new plan and then discussed and disputed the Contadora Process which was based on having the Central American parties work out their own solutions without the outside interference of the U.S. and European and other nations. Gay Swenson thought that by the fourth day the Contadora Process had become "the workshop theme, and a symbol of the search for national self-respect and personal empowerment. It is seen as holding hope for self-determination, nonintervention, and peaceful solutions of the enormous political, economic, and social challenges they and we all face together."[257]

In the midst of the heated discussion on the Contadora Process, the participant from Chile reminded people of the spirit of togetherness and optimism of the *Heurigen*, and that shifted the conversation for the rest of the morning to the value of the workshop experience for them, personally and politically. One speaker after another affirmed the importance of the experience. A Central American government official told how he initially doubted the unstructured agenda and disorderly process but came to feel that the method produced valuable outcomes. A member of the West German Parliament said she learned a great deal and hoped to use a similar process at home. A Palestinian said he was jealous and asked the organizers to arrange an experience like this for the Palestine Liberation Organization and the Israelis. Many other similar comments affirmed the value of the experience to the participants and their hopes and plans for the future.

This sentiment carried over into the press conference, introduced by Austria's Foreign Affairs Minister Gratz, where Rogers, Carazo and eight other participants—from Costa Rica, Honduras, El Salvador, Nicaragua, Venezuela, Sweden, the United States and Austria—spoke positively of the workshop experience and its hoped-for outcomes. The foreign ministry official from Sweden said she would recommend that the United Nations Commission on Building of Trust adopt the person-centered approach for its annual meeting in Stockholm and invite the CSP staff to facilitate the event. The U.S. and Nicaraguan participant who had formed a relationship in spite of their initial hostility described how that bond had developed and how they planned to meet again in Paris to make plans that they would convey to their respective governments.[258]

At the final evening session there were more words of praise for the workshop and two resolutions were passed around for participants to sign if they wished. One, which had been drafted by Rodrigo Carazo and others was a statement in support of the Contadora Process to be presented at an upcoming meeting in Luxembourg between the Contadora group and the European Common Market countries. A majority of the participants signed the statement.[259] The other was a declaration drafted by John Vasconcellos in support of the person-centered approach as a method for tension reduction and conflict resolution in this workshop and potentially in other international crisis situations.[260] Carazo and Rogers were given gifts by the participants. One of the Palestinians presented Rogers with a beautiful blue and silver vase made by Palestinian and Jewish co-workers in an Israeli factory "as a symbol of what is possible."[261]

Vasconcellos summarized the experience of Rust in a short poem:

We arrived
amidst a heavy fog, which gradually
lifted to become
sunny by the conclusion of our workshop;
on Hallowe'en yielding to the day of all saints;
in a town whose steeples house the nests of storks,
we hopefully midwifed the birth of more faith and
hope for, and a process leading toward,
peace![262]

Rogers' summary was more prosaic:

It seems clear that for most of the participants this had been a very meaningful and useful experience. We know of at least one person who felt very negatively about the workshop. I am sure there must be others. We are trying hard to collect all the data that would give the complete picture. but essentially, substantial progress was made in meeting the purposes that brought the workshop into being. Tensions were reduced. Lines of communication were opened. There was an experience of peace."[263]

Maria Bowen said the participant with negative feelings that Rogers referred to "objected mainly to the impression some of the participants gave of having more power to influence their government than they actually had, thus raising false hopes."[264] Lawrence Solomon, who analyzed the data from the participants' questionnaires that were completed at the end of the workshop, generally confirmed Rogers' impressions that the large majority of delegates had a positive experience; although he pointed out that because of their different expectations about the conference's purpose and process, "the Latins were consistently less positive about the experience than were the non-Latins. All the ratings are at the positive end of the scale, but there is a consistent relative difference between the two groups."[265] He recommended that if such an event were held again, future workshops should do a better job of developing participants' expectations beforehand.[266]

After Rust

Back home Rogers and the others gave newspaper interviews and shared their experience in presentations with many live audiences and in articles for journals and magazines. Rogers remained realistic about the net effect of the Rust workshop and his other work for conflict resolution and world peace. "I do not believe I deceive myself as to the significance of these efforts," he wrote. "Certainly we had no obvious influence on the total situation in any of these countries. But I derive much satisfaction from knowing that, on a small scale, we were able to demonstrate in each of these tension-filled groups, that meaningful dialogue could be established, that conflicts could be reduced, that a more realistic mutual understanding could emerge. We worked only on a test-tube scale, but we showed what was possible. Now the question is whether there is the social will to multiply these efforts."[267]

At this point the Peace Project's own long-term vision included: "applying person-centered principles to existing and potential crisis situations in a search for reconciliation" and "applying training and education programs with present and future international policy makers and world leaders on dispute resolution."[268] Carazo met privately with Rogers at his home in La Jolla to debrief the Rust gathering and discuss the future.[269] Almost immediately, planning for a follow-up meeting to Rust began. Again there was the challenge of obtaining funding for such a gathering. Television writer and producer Norman Lear offered the project $50,000 to facilitate a meeting between liberal and conservative journalists and media people, but Rogers declined, wanting to focus on his major priority, world peace.[270] However, Rogers, busy with many other commitments, including his 1986 trips to South Africa, the Soviet Union, and Hungary, had limited time and energy to devote to fundraising. Gay Swenson took the major responsibility for keeping the Peace Project alive and overseeing the fundraising events.[271]

When Rogers was in the Soviet Union, Swenson represented the Peace Project at an invitational meeting co-chaired by former Presidents Ford and Carter at the Carter Center on "Reinforcing Democracy in the Americas." This was the first conference held at the recently dedicated Carter Center whose work would eventually win President Carter the Nobel Peace Prize in 2002.[272] Swenson recalled how, "there were 300 or 400 people there, but when I introduced myself, he [Carter] said something lovely about Carl ... [Apparently] he had seen at least some of the films [of Rogers] and articles and things like that ... he said he had great respect for Carl Rogers and he hoped one day they could meet."[273]

Rogers' international work that year—in South Africa, Hungary and the Soviet Union—was entirely consistent with the mission of the Peace Project. It was mostly arbitrary as to which of his activities fell under which sponsorship: the Carl Rogers Peace Project, the Institute for Cross-Cultural Communications, Rogers as private consultant, or the various local sponsors of Rogers and Sanford's international workshops. Whoever the sponsor, Rogers' work for cross-cultural understanding and conflict resolution was all of a piece. Yet later in 1986 he wrote that he wanted all his peace activities in the Soviet Union, South Africa, Central America and elsewhere "to be brought together under the umbrella of the Peace Project ... my primary objective is to continue the activities of the Carl Rogers Peace Project ... My work in the direction of peace has been the central theme of my life for a number of years now and it will continue and the Peace Project is the major expression of that desire."[274]

By early 1987, when Rogers died, it was still not clear how the Peace Project would find the funding to survive and whether there would be a follow-up to the Rust gathering. He might have thought their effort with Central America was a worthy experiment which showed *the potential* of the person-centered approach for inter-group conflict resolution and international peacemaking. Had he lived a bit longer, as we will see, he would have learned that President Rodrigo Carazo later credited the Rust workshop with actually *being* the turning point for peace in Central America.[275]

Although the eventual outcome of the Rust workshop was still unknown, Rogers' lifetime of work dedicated to fostering human understanding—and particularly his more recent work in reducing tensions in inter-group, cross-cultural, and international conflict situations—gained increasing notice. In 1986 his supporters began the process of having him nominated for the Nobel Peace Prize. The Peace Prize is awarded annually to the person who "shall have done the most or the best work for fraternity between nations, for the abolition or reduction of standing armies and for the holding of peace conferences."[276] To be considered for this honor, the most prestigious of its kind in the world, a candidate must be nominated by an *invited* government official, non-governmental organization, or other individuals or organizations in particular categories.[277] Nomination letters include a packet of supporting materials. An average of 140 individuals or organizations have been nominated for the Peace Prize in recent years, but as this number has grown over time, there would likely have been a somewhat smaller number of nominees in 1987, possibly about one hundred.[278] To be nominated, then, is a far cry from actually being chosen to receive the award. Nevertheless, with some two hundred countries in the world from which nominations may be submitted, simply to be nominated is a distinct honor.

Rogers' nomination was initiated by John Vasconcellos and submitted by California Representative Jim Bates, the United States Congressman from Rogers' district in La Jolla. Gay Swenson helped Bates and Vasconcellos on the nomination and put the packet of supporting materials together.[279] While Rogers knew that a nomination for the prize was being discussed, he was not kept apprised of the details.[280] Hence he never knew that he actually was nominated for the Nobel Prize. Congressman Bates' formal nomination letter was written on January 30, 1987.[281] A copy of the letter arrived at Rogers' office on February 4, the day Rogers died.[282]

Because one cannot be selected posthumously for the Nobel Prize (unless the award has already been announced), Rogers' nomination could not be considered. Therefore it is not known just how serious a contender he was that year. The individual who did win the Nobel Peace Prize in 1987 was the sitting president of Costa Rica, Oscar Arias Sanchez, whose leadership in the peace process managed to forge a treaty that was signed by all the Central American presidents that year (see next chapter). In my opinion, even if Rogers had lived Arias would have been the more likely prize winner in 1987. In Arias' Nobel acceptance speech in Oslo, he spoke pointedly,

> ... to all members of the international community, and particularly to those both in the East and the West, with far greater power and resources than my small nation could ever hope to possess. I say to them, with the utmost urgency: Let Central Americans decide the future of Central America. Leave the interpretation and implementation of our peace plan to us. Support the efforts for peace instead of the forces of war in our region. Send our people plowshares instead of swords, pruning hooks instead of spears. If they, for their own purposes, cannot refrain from amassing the weapons of war, then, in the name of God, at least they should leave us in peace.[283]

As the *New York Times* reported, "The Nobel committee made no secret of the fact that it made the award in part to endorse the region's attempt to supersede East–West rivalry in the area by engineering its own peace plan."[284] Nobel historians Levinovitz and Ringertz agreed, writing, "The committee clearly hoped that the prize itself would provide an added impetus for peace."[285]

However, if Rogers had lived on, he could have been re-nominated for the Peace Prize in future years and could have won the Prize in a subsequent year, especially if his international peacemaking activities continued. He certainly had won the respect of many international figures who might have supported his nomination, such as U.S. President Jimmy Carter and Nobel laureate Oscar Arias who paid this tribute to Rogers, read at a symposium commemorating the 100th anniversary of Rogers' birth:

> Carl Rogers, a thinker and mover who has inspired generations in the United States and around the world. Carl Rogers was a man who firmly believed in the human capacity for good, and it is this quality of his that I most admire. Whether in the field of psychotherapy, education, or peace-making, it is vital to focus on the potential for progress rather than on problems and hindrances. Of course it is important to be realistic about the obstacles we face in any endeavor, but the heart of Carl's message, as I understand it, was never to let the obstacles cause us to lose sight of every human being's innate potential for problem-solving, and never lose hope in the continued evolution of individuals and of humanity as a whole. We are all, in some way, striving to improve ourselves, and his art and his passion was uncovering that striving and facilitating its full power to produce positive change.
>
> As a politician and peacemaker, I find Carl Rogers' optimism refreshing and inspiring. There are far too many voices crying out the defects, dangers, and roadblocks to human progress. The fact is that progress only happens when someone recognizes that it *can* happen, and then works to make it a reality. Cynics sneeringly call such people dreamers with their heads in the clouds. I say that the world needs all the dreamers it can get, and we are lucky to have had among us one of the best in Carl Rogers.[286]

A Way of Being

Rogers' international work in cross-cultural communication and conflict resolution, and the Peace Project in particular, were significant endeavors in their own right, but even more remarkable for someone to undertake in his late seventies to mid-eighties. And this work was only a part of Rogers' productive and adventurous final years.

Of course he continued to write. From the time he began his first diary after high school graduation, recording his experiences and learnings was about as automatic as breathing to Rogers. From the 1930s on, sharing his experiences and insights with a professional and later also a public audience was a continual activity for him. Thus in 1980 his fifteenth book, *A Way of Being*, was published. It was a collection of essays touching on the various subjects which had interested him in recent years. Most of the chapters had been printed as articles or delivered as presentations previously. It was somewhat modeled after *On Becoming a Person*, so it was not difficult to convince his earlier publisher Houghton Mifflin, for whom the former collection had sold so well, to publish the new volume.

Characteristically the first section included a series of personal essays about Rogers' life and career. "Experiences in Communication" was a somewhat personalized version of his famous "Characteristics of a Helping Relationship," describing the kind of communication he had come to value throughout his life. "My Philosophy of Interpersonal Relationships and How It Grew" retold highlights from his earlier "Autobiography" and "This Is Me" chapters,[287] with a particular emphasis on how his personal and professional experiences helped form his theory and practice. If there was any doubt before, he stated as clearly as ever: "As I look back, I realize that my interest in interviewing and in therapy certainly grew in part out of my early loneliness."[288] In the third essay, "In Retrospect: 46 Years," Rogers expressed his surprise over "the astonishing impact" his work had had and explored some of the struggles in his career, possible explanations, and wonders associated with that impact. The contents of the next essay, "Growing Old: Or Older and Growing," in which he discussed his health, state of mind, personal relationships, thoughts regarding death, and Helen's death, are described in earlier sections of this biography. Finally, "Do We Need A Reality?" described how there are many ways to understand reality, culturally and personally, and discussed how, therefore, it was important that individuals and groups learn to accept and live with one another's realities.

Three briefer sections of the book contained three essays on education, a new iteration of his "person of tomorrow" concept, and an updated bibliography of his writing. But the major section of *A Way of Being* explored various aspects of the person-centered approach to helping relationships. "The Foundations of a Person-Centered Approach" described his thinking about the actualizing tendency in individuals and the formative tendency in the universe, again described earlier in this biography. In "Empathic: An Unappreciated Way of Being," he took one of the important concepts of psychotherapy, which he had been instrumental in popularizing, and re-examined it in terms of his latest thinking and experience and recent research findings. "Ellen West and Loneliness" was a touching re-evaluation of a famous, psychoanalytic case study in which Rogers explored the estrangement from self and others in modern life and how empathy and acceptance can potentially bridge that isolation and make life worth living. It was a powerful indictment of the objective, medical model of mental illness that, in this case according to Rogers, resulted in the needless and tragic suicide of Ellen West.

In "Building Person-Centered Communities," Rogers described the person-centered community as both a professional experiment in workshop design *and* a potential challenge and opportunity for a culture that seems "to have made a fetish out of complete individual self-sufficiency, of not needing help, of being completely private except in a very few selected relationships."[289] In "Six Vignettes," he presented stories of clients' experiences in individual therapy, small groups or workshop communities that illustrated and personalized different aspects of the person-centered approach.

Finally, Rogers included a presentation he made at age seventy to a large audience of the American Psychological Association on "Some New Challenges to the Helping Professions." In it he challenged the field of psychology to develop a human science; to use their knowledge not just to repair the old but to design new educational institutions, cities, homes, workplaces and cultures; to do away with the rigid bureaucracy of professionalism; to become whole men and women in their professional lives, and to recognize that there is more than one reality. Each of these challenges, he said, "represents a possible move toward the enhancement, the deepening, the enrichment of our profession. Each one, in a word, represents for psychology a step toward self-actualization. If my perceptions have been even approximately correct, then the final question I would leave with you is 'Do we dare?'"[290] Here was Carl Rogers, challenging to its very roots the profession in which he had worked so successfully for half a century. It was fitting that Rogers delivered this tour de force on the occasion of his receiving the APA's first Distinguished Professional Contribution Award in which he was honored, in part, for being the "respected gadfly of organized psychology."[291]

After *A Way of Being* was completed, Rogers turned his writing attention to a new edition of *Freedom to Learn*. That 1969 publication had sold so well over its first decade that the publisher asked Rogers to prepare a new edition. (This is a standard practice to prevent students from buying used copies from which the publisher and author derive no income.) By then Rogers' attention had turned to other matters, so he was responsive when educator and author Hal Lyon suggested that he and Rogers co-author a book aimed more specifically at teachers in training.[292] It was to be titled "On Becoming a Teacher." Rogers was unhappy with Lyon's draft and invited other educators to add sections and comments to the text to enhance the work.[293] Then he invited educational researchers David Aspy and Flora Roebuck to re-edit the whole volume. Still uncomfortable with the result, he invited a few others to read and comment on the manuscript.[294] The feedback he received confirmed his misgivings about the book which, while containing much of value, had lost some of his voice and diluted his particular message. In the end, he did a new revision himself, resulting in Rogers' *Freedom to Learn for the 80s*, which was published in 1983. Although he included passages written by many other contributors, it was clearly Carl Rogers' voice that resonated throughout the work.[295]

The book was oriented more toward school teachers and teachers in training than the first edition had been. About half the chapters from the earlier edition were maintained. Rogers added new case studies of teachers and dropped several chapters having to do with graduate education, administration, and changing educational systems. A new chapter called "Researching Person-Centered Issues in Education" was added in which Rogers described, often in their own words, the work of David Aspy and Flora Roebuck in the United States and Reinhard and Anne-Marie Tausch in Germany. Throughout the 1970s these researchers and their colleagues had conducted extensive empirical research on teacher–student interaction and educational outcomes. Rogers described these studies as "among the largest and most exhaustive ever carried out in the field of education."[296] One project, for example, studied over 600 teachers and 10,000 students.[297] The results consistently showed that when teachers provided Rogers' core conditions of empathy, positive regard and congruence, students had higher academic achievement, better school attendance, less disruptive behavior, and higher independence and initiative, among other outcomes. Although Rogers himself was no longer involved in research, he often cited the Aspy, Roebuck and Tausch research programs to support the validity of his overall hypothesis that the core conditions lead to positive growth, learning and change in therapy, education and other settings.

Apparently *Freedom to Learn for the 80s* continued to sell well enough, even after Rogers' death in 1987, for the publisher to request a third edition. Natalie Rogers arranged for humanistic educator H. Jerome Freiberg to write this edition, which was published in 1994 as *Freedom to Learn: Third Edition* by Rogers and Freiberg.[298]

In addition to the two books, Rogers continued to write articles through the 80s. He did a number of reports on his international, cross-cultural communication and peacekeeping work. He also coauthored with colleagues several chapters on client-centered therapy for different textbooks. Typically he asked his coauthor to do the first draft which he would then edit. His 1985 article "Toward a More Human Science of the Person" was discussed in Chapter 10. Beyond these, most of his later writings tended to be retrospective pieces, relatively short comments and brief reflections on various topics. His output was still impressive, especially for someone in his eighties, but somewhat less prolific than at previous points in his career.

One reason that Rogers was doing a bit less writing in his final years was that he was having difficulty with his eyesight. This was one of many health problems that beset him in his late seventies and eighties. In 1977 he had a low white blood cell count, probably caused by medications. When the medication was adjusted the blood count improved. He had a slight heart attack in August of 1979 and was in the hospital for two weeks. Shortly thereafter he went to Poland for lectures and a ten-day workshop.[299] Later in the year he noted in his diary, "Had a fairly bad heart flip today" and "I was half sick with this damned sinusitis."[300] In October 1980 he noted, "I can sense my cataract slowly worsen. The one good physical thing is that I seem to have calmed down. My heart is less irregular and I don't feel as restless, I think."[301] He still got anxious about missing airplanes which, given all the traveling he was doing, was an ongoing irritant to his health. We may recall David Rogers' long list of problems and symptoms that he thought were associated with his father's drinking—the heart flutter, unsteadiness, weight gain, perspiration, difficulty sleeping, and others. Late in 1982 Rogers fainted and was taken to the hospital. After spending Christmas with Natalie, his grandchildren and great-grandchildren, Natalie wrote him that she was pleased that they had talked about his "will, money matters, disposition of your papers, etc. And I appreciate the way you are taking care of many details in advance of your eventual going."[302] This recitation of health problems, some ongoing, some intermittent, would lead one to think that Rogers was quite frail in his eighties. Yet, in spite of all his problems, Rogers managed to feel pretty strong most of the time and continued his active professional and personal life.

By 1981 his vision was growing steadily worse and by 1982 he was diagnosed with macular degeneration in both eyes.[303] He used a "Visualtek" reading machine to magnify the text, but it made reading awkward so he read less often.[304] In 1984, at the time the Peace Project was officially getting underway, he told the group at Dorothy Lyddon's ranch that his eyesight was failing and he didn't know how much longer he would be able to make a contribution to the world.[305] Then, as Valerie Henderson, who worked with him daily, recalled, "Someone sent him a regimen of vitamins that he tried and he swore that his eyesight improved. There were times when he didn't think he needed the machine anymore. It was amazing." The doctors said such improvement was not possible— macular degeneration is irreversible—but his vision did seem to improve somewhat. Still Henderson told him he shouldn't be driving anymore; "But he said, 'Well, I only go down to the village,' as if children don't run out in front of you in the village. I remember taking him for his driver's test [in 1986] and how he really sweated that."[306]

His fall in August 1985, in the lead-up to the Rust workshop, put him back in the hospital with a broken neck and a neck brace for two to three months. Later that year, he had pneumonia.[307] It was clear that he *was* in a vulnerable state. Valerie Henderson said he cherished his independence and loved living alone in his house.[308] But by January of 1987, after his eighty-fifth birthday, he rented the studio room in his home to a young woman, just to have someone on the premises who might help out and be available in case of an emergency.[309] Before that, as Henderson recalled, "he would take a nap in his bedroom ... and he'd take the phone off the hook in the kitchen, and I said to him, 'I wish you would take the phone of the hook in the bedroom. What if you had a fibrillation or something and needed the phone and you couldn't get out to the kitchen.' He said, 'Well, if that happens, I don't want to call anybody.' It was like, 'I would rather just go.'" Henderson saw this as a time in Rogers' life when he was still eager to try new things, personally and professionally, but when he was no longer able to do this, he wanted to go quickly. "It was like, 'Let me taste whatever I can taste new ... yet don't make it so that I can't function.' I really think that was huge for him."[310]

In spite of all these health issues, Rogers did continued to taste much that was new and fulfilling for the rest of his life. Aside from his active and adventurous work life, he spent rich times with his family and friends. His eightieth birthday party with his closer group of friends and colleagues was described in the last chapter. But even at the public event celebrating that birthday (the evening with Marilyn Ferguson attended by 500 people, when he and Ruth Sanford talked of their recent trip to South Africa), he was surrounded by friends and admirers. Many well-known psychologists and others like California Governor Jerry Brown surprised him with birthday wishes, in person or by letter.[311] The audience was then asked to write on balloons in pen their hope for the planet and for people and then release the balloons in the air. Then Maria Bowen brought in a birthday cake for him that said on it "Around the World in 80 Years."[312]

As described, Rogers continued to travel around the world for the *next five* years, with an average of three international trips each year, many of them several weeks or longer in duration. Combining pleasure with business, on a European workshop tour he took a barge trip on the English canals with his friend from England. On another European trip, before he began a month of workshops, they took a ten-day vacation in the south of France. When he returned to the Sagamore Conference Center in the Adirondack Mountains in 1984, he and his partner visited the Seneca Lake property in New York, which was still owned and used by his son David and his family.[313] Beyond his romantic relationships, other friendships with women were particularly important to him. As Gay (Swenson) Barfield recalled, "We spent a lot of different times together as kind of an extended family—on holidays, at Maria Bowen's, often for Easter and Christmas."[314]

Working together virtually daily on the Peace Project, Barfield was often impressed with how what Rogers wrote about in his books was his natural way of being. Once when Rogers was out of the country conducting a workshop in Brazil, she was house-sitting for him. One evening she went over to Maria Bowen's home and Rogers' house was burglarized. "The place was sort of a mess, and the television was gone and the VCR was gone." They got the message to him in Brazil and he said he'd take care of it when he came home in a couple of days. "I remember opening up the door, the front door, and saying, 'Oh, Carl, I just feel so awful; I was responsible.' And instead of him coming in and saying, 'Well now, what's missing? What did the police say?' he just looked at me and said, 'That must have been *so hard* for you, Gay, to be house-sitting and have that happen while I was away. You must feel so terrible.' Those are my words, but it was so perfect ..."[315]

Barfield also recalled how Rogers would continue to be surprised by his own popularity, as when his presence was acknowledged at the California Democratic convention in 1984 and he received a standing ovation from the 3,000 attendees. Two other examples of his popularity came in surveys of influential psychotherapists, both published in 1982. Smith's survey of the Clinical Psychology and Counseling Psychology divisions of the American Psychological Association found that Rogers was rated first among the "psychotherapists whom they consider to be most influential today."[316] A second study looked at 14,000 citations in three leading counseling and psychotherapy journals to determine the most frequently cited authors and works in the field. Rogers headed the list of major contributors of works published before 1957.[317] However, the flip side of these surveys was that when the researchers inquired about which books and authors were "perceived to be the most representative of the present zeitgeist in counseling and psychotherapy" and which works *since 1957* were most frequently cited, Rogers was ranked ninth in the first survey and below tenth in the second. Consistent with these trends, royalty sales on his books were falling in the 1980s, although they still helped support him. As he told an interviewer in 1983, "I haven't had any kind of salary for 18 years but the royalties on my books have provided a nice income. I never dreamt that my books would support me. I guess I used to think my support would come from investments. I used to think I was smart on the Stock Market. I became disillusioned completely by that."[318] While he could have been earning large speaking and consulting fees, instead Rogers worked gratis for causes he believed in or turned his fees over to the Peace Project or other CSP projects. Having given many generous gifts to his children and grandchildren, now without substantial investments or a pension other than Social Security, and with royalties starting to decline, Rogers still lived comfortably but was by no means wealthy by American standards.

Whenever the opportunity presented itself Rogers enjoyed visits to or from his children, grandchildren, and great-grandchildren. He also often worked with Natalie on workshops. After one conference they attended together he wrote, "Natalie and I did a joint session on personal power. It went very well, her talk being better, and better received than mine. I was proud of her."[319] Natalie had created and directed the Person-Centered Expressive Therapy Institute to further the approach she developed for integrating client-centered therapy with the expressive arts. Sometimes she invited him to participate in a program organized by her Institute. She recalled how, "When I asked people to get up and move, he would do it. He would join in. He was a good sport, and you know he was so inhibited about dancing and movement, because that wasn't allowed in his family; so he got some fun out of it."[320] On other occasions, Rogers invited Natalie to join him on a workshop *he* was leading. She worked with him in Mexico and Italy in 1978 and 1979.[321] In 1983 father and daughter traveled to Japan to lead workshops and, while there, visited Kyoto and the Inland Sea.

When asked by a reporter, "What brings Carl Rogers pleasure at age 84?" he answered, "My love relationships, the opportunity to try out a dream that everyone said was utterly impossible, and satisfaction in watching my big moose horn fern grow."[322] Above all it was the "dream," his work in utilizing the person-centered approach for international tension reduction and peacemaking, that most occupied Rogers' time and energy in his final few years. In 1984 he had told Alberto Zucconi, "The problem of preventing a nuclear holocaust has top priority in my mind, my heart and my work. That's why I'm doing what I'm doing, and I expect to continue for as long as I am able."[323] Snapshots from Rogers' eighty-fifth year or so illustrate both how he made peacemaking the primary commitment of his final years and how he remained remarkably active and vibrant in the last year of his life.

In December 1985, Rogers attended the first of an ongoing series of conferences on "The Evolution of Psychotherapy" in Phoenix, Arizona. Twenty-seven leading therapists attended and gave presentations. A reporter wrote how "Carl Rogers, who has influenced more therapists in this country than Freud, got a standing ovation from 4,000 people before he even said a word. It was, as organizer Jeffrey Zeig said, the Woodstock of psychotherapy."[324] Another described how "He wears a string tie, a benign and earnest expression. He's bald as a hoot-owl, and shows much vigor for one so far along in age. He smiles fetchingly at the audience after the wild applause, and says, 'I was really touched by that.' He then adds: 'It's always best to have it beforehand, anyway.'" In front of this vast audience and his peers, he then conducted a demonstration counseling interview with a member of the audience.[325]

In January and February 1986 Rogers and Ruth Sanford made their second extended trip to South Africa, described earlier. Preparations for trips like these took a great deal of time, including numerous communications about logistics, research on the countries and conflicts they would encounter, and planning for the various events. Their success in developing a cadre of trainers to foster interracial dialogue led them to be invited back for another two months the following year "to extend the network of persons involved there in dialogue across ancient acrimonies."[326]

At home he worked with colleagues on the Peace Project to plan and fundraise for a follow-up event on Central America and extend the work of the Peace Project to other areas and activities.

In July, Rogers and Sanford were in Budapest, Hungary working with some 300 people for a two-week period. As a result, plans were made for them to return to Europe the following year for a series of activities in Italy and Greece with the Center on Cross-Cultural Communication and Person-Centered Institutes of Europe directed by Chuck Devonshire and Alberto Zucconi.[327]

He returned from Europe in time to participate in the Living Now and La Jolla Programs of Center for Studies of the Person, where he spoke of his work for peace.[328] As Swenson wrote to the Peace Project's International Advisory Board in October, "Domestically, Carl has been equally active in speaking about the Peace Project work these last months, appearing on panels and speaking alone, doing videotapes and interviews … each with an emphasis on peace and conflict, whether between individuals, in the workplace or politically and globally. Carl continues to be surprised and appreciative of the standing ovations at Conventions such as "The Evolution of Psychotherapy" in Phoenix, The Association for

Humanistic Psychology in San Diego, and the American Association of Counseling and Development in Los Angeles, among others."[329]

In September and October, Rogers and Sanford first went to Chicago for the initial meeting of the Association for the Development of the Person-Centered Approach, where they spoke of their work in South Africa. Then they flew to the Soviet Union and over the next four weeks worked with some 2,000 professionals at their workshops and presentations in Moscow and Tbilisi. Again they were invited to return and made plans to do so the following year.

Back in California, in what would prove to be a fortuitous occasion, Rogers and Swenson attended a dinner for twenty invited guests by the President of the University of California, San Diego to honor Rev. Theodore Hesburgh, who was retiring from thirty-five years as President of the University of Notre Dame. Hesburgh was a prominent activist for peace and justice who had supported the Rust workshop although he was unable to attend.[330] Also present at the dinner was Joan Kroc, widow of McDonalds founder Ray Kroc.[331] As we will see, she would play an important future role in the continuation of the Carl Rogers Peace Project and world peace in general.

In November Rogers and Swenson attended John Vasconcellos' "Toward a Healthier State" symposium, held at the University of California, Irvine, which focused on "leadership development, peace, violence prevention, and healthy economic, environmental and public policies for California."[332] As Rogers was doing continually that year, they reported on the Rust workshop and on his and Sanford's work in the Soviet Union and South Africa. Again he received a standing ovation from the audience of 500.

The same month Carl, Natalie, and Natalie's daughter Frances Fuchs, who was also a psychotherapist, did a public presentation on "Fostering Creativity: A Three-Generational View." "Father/grandfather, mother/daughter, daughter/granddaughter talked about our current interests and discussed the creative process with each other."[333] Rogers' current interest, of course, was his conflict resolution and peacemaking work.

In addition to all these activities Rogers continued writing throughout 1986. He completed reports and articles on his trips to South Africa and the Soviet Union, several pieces for the *Person-Centered Review*, and other articles.[334] In December and January, he was writing seven articles or chapters and formulating a book on person-centered approaches to peace.[335]

He also spent a great deal of time keeping up with his mail which, according to his secretary and colleague Valerie Henderson, kept increasing through his final years.[336] And throughout the year, he participated in a series of oral history interviews conducted by David Russell of the Library at the University of California, Santa Barbara. John Vasconcellos had come up with the idea to form a national archive on humanistic psychology and obtained funding from the California legislature to house the archives at UCSB.[337] Russell conducted an extensive oral history with Rogers, consisting of about a dozen taped interviews from December 1985 to December 1986. The result was a rich collage of memories and reflections on Rogers' long life and career. (Unfortunately, the oral history would not be edited and published for sixteen years.[338])

Reflecting on his active life, professionally and personally, in a short article called "On Reaching 85," after mentioning his various international activities Rogers wrote, "From a personal point of view, I look with surprised satisfaction on the fact that I have been able to participate in dealing with such crucial conflicts. I could never have dreamed of such events at age 65! I also feel grateful to the multitude of persons who have made these ventures possible. In each case I have been on the visible tip of the iceberg, while the unsung efforts of countless individuals have made the events possible ... I hope it is clear that my life at 85 is better than anything I could have planned, dreamed of, or expected."[339] He concluded a letter that year by writing, "I wish you well in all that you are doing and hope you are finding life satisfying. I certainly am."[340]

With Rogers' eighty-fifth birthday approaching on January 8, Gay Swenson and Dee Aker organized a combination birthday celebration for him and fundraiser for the Carl Rogers Peace Project.[341] Contributions began at $125 per person. It was not a public event per se; rather invitations were sent to a few hundred people in California, the United States and around the world whom Rogers had worked with or had a special relationship with over the years. Over 150 friends, colleagues and associates attended and many others sent birthday greetings and contributions.[342] The event was held at the San Diego Repertory Theatre at the Lyceum in Horton Plaza, San Diego on Monday, December 22, 1986.

As the invitation described, the evening began at 5:30 with an "Update with Carl, after his recent return from the Soviet Union and prior to his departure for South Africa." Rogers arrived in a black limousine, escorted by Dee Aker and Gay Swenson, and entered under the theatre marquee announcing, 'Happy Birthday Carl Rogers." Looking dapper in a gray pinstriped suit, red-black plaid vest, and string tie with turquoise stone at the collar, Rogers sat on the theater stage and shared some of his recent experiences in citizen diplomacy in South Africa and the Soviet Union. Speaking for about a half hour without notes, his narration was clear, organized, informative, gripping, and passionate. In characteristic fashion he described the experiences of several of the workshop participants, recalling the details of their stories and struggles with understanding and precision. He made their human dramas come alive and related these to the political and social context of their countries and the potency of the person-centered approach for touching their lives and work. It would have been an impressive presentation under any circumstances. For the audience, seeing Rogers at age eighty-five, so cognitively sharp, intellectually stimulating, socially committed, and actively involved in promulgating the person-centered approach and world peace, it was an inspiring performance.

After a light buffet dinner, there was a performance of "Master Harold ... and the boys" by South African playwright Athol Fugard. This compelling play about race relations in South Africa happened to be playing in San Diego at the time and Swenson was able to reserve the small theater for the event. The theme of the play was particularly appropriate as Rogers and Sanford had worked in South Africa earlier in the year and were scheduled to return again in April.

At 9:00 p.m. came the "Birthday Celebration, Toasts, Entertainment and Bon Voyage—Champagne and Desserts." Of course there was a cake, with "Happy 85th Carl," and candles and the singing of "Happy Birthday." Then the toasts began. Proclamations honoring Rogers from Mayor Maureen O'Connor of San Diego and the California State Legislature were read. Many of those present shared their affection and respect and related telling or humorous anecdotes from their relationship with Rogers. A selection of birthday greetings and tributes were read from invitees who were unable to attend: Jonas Salk, Theodore Hesburgh, Elizabeth Kübler-Ross, Ken Blanchard, Fritjof Capra, Ram Dass, Tom Gordon, Rollo May, Norman Lear, Dennis Weaver, Virginia Satir, colleagues from Europe, Japan, South Africa, and many others. The message that seemed to mean the most to him was introduced and read by Gay Swenson who told how, "A couple of weeks ago, I was at the event with [Presidents] Ford and Carter, and I said to President Carter that I hoped someday that he would meet Dr. Rogers, because I thought they had a lot in common, and he said, 'Well, thank you very much. I take that as a personal compliment *to myself.*' And I didn't know this, but then this came in the mail ...

To Carl Rogers
Congratulations and sincere best wishes on your 85th birthday celebration. It is wonderful that so many of your friends and supporters could be with you tonight.

Your work as a peacemaker is internationally known and highly regarded. As you embark on still another mission—this one to South Africa—please know that you are in our thoughts.

God speed your journey. The world could use more global citizens like you.
With Warm Regards,
Jimmy Carter[343]

As these words from the former U.S. president and future Nobel Peace Prize winner were read, Rogers was clearly moved and shook his head from side to side with a combination of wonder and humility. Throughout the toasts and tributes, a guitarist played in the background, and the assembly sang "Let Peace Prevail" and other songs to guitar accompaniment. Finally Rogers asked to speak. He slowly rose and unsteadily walked the few steps to take the microphone; yet his voice was strong and his face was aglow with pleasure and emotion as he basked unashamedly in the many expressions of affection and esteem he had received. Wiping a tear from his eye, he said, "There is no possible way I could respond to all this. I just want to say: I feel *very much loved*. Thank you, thank you, thank you."

Rogers' actual 85th birthday came on January 8, and during that month he remained active, writing, giving interviews, planning their upcoming South Africa trip with Ruth Sanford, and working on the Peace Project. "At our last staff meeting with Carl," wrote Gay Swenson, "on January 15 at his home ... we committed ourselves to specific goals, as follows: supporting Carl's return to South Africa; a second Central America meeting (Rust II); outreach to create a meeting of Soviet and American leaders, development of a brochure for the project; further videos, articles and a book on person-centered approaches to peace; a 3-year theory development/research program."[344]

In the last week of January 1987 Rogers had a mini-stroke.[345] For a brief time, he couldn't remember the year, the date or his age. When he regained awareness he wasn't sure how long he had been disoriented. The doctor said there must have been a short time in which blood failed to get to his brain. But he recovered right away, and after a long work session, Rogers suggested to his companion that they go to Las Vegas for a couple of nights, just for the fun of it. He had never been there; in fact, he had shunned that kind of glitz all his life. But, now, he thought it might be fun to see what it was all about. As he told a friend at the time, "I've been to every other country in the world. I thought I ought to see this country, too."[346] So they went. They visited the night clubs, danced, gambled a bit, and had a grand time. When they returned to La Jolla on Friday, January 30, Gay Swenson brought over the film of his eighty-fifth birthday party which had just been completed, along with a set of all the birthday letters sent to him—many more than had been read at the party. "And so that night they watched the film of his birthday, and he got to see all the accolades from all over the world."[347] Later he and his friend put on an LP record album and danced and sang show tunes together.[348]

In the early morning hours of Saturday he fell on the way to the bathroom.[349] His friend and the young woman who was living in the studio heard noises and went to his room where they found him sitting on the bed. He was rushed to the Scripps Memorial Hospital with a broken hip. That afternoon he had hip surgery and came through the operation fine. He talked with his son David by phone both before and after the operation. Valerie Henderson visited and talked with him and heard from his orthopedic surgeon that Rogers had said, "Well, I am never going to go through that again," which she understood to mean that he did not want to live like that, in a cycle of increasing medical crises and interventions and that he was preparing to die.[350] Henderson reached Natalie Rogers who was giving a workshop in Mexico and was scheduled to go on to Acapulco for a vacation when the workshop was over. Henderson delivered Rogers' message that he "insists that Natalie goes on to Acapulco for her vacation."[351] After all, he'd transferred out of the ICU to a regular room; Ruth Sanford was with him the whole time; Valerie Henderson, Gay Swenson and Nel Kandel were also there; there was no need for her to change her plans. Natalie said to herself, "Nonsense, when the workshop is over, I'm going to La Jolla."

However, weakened from the operation, a few hours later Rogers suffered a cardiac arrest. The emergency team resuscitated him, but he immediately went into a coma from which he never recovered. The next morning, Sunday, David Rogers called Natalie, told her the news, and said he was flying to La Jolla. Natalie told her colleague Sylvia Dubovoy that she could not finish the workshop and flew to La Jolla immediately herself. Granddaughters Naomi and Frances Fuchs arrived on Monday. That day they gave the physician Rogers' "living will" and an advance directive written for him by an attorney emphasizing that he did not want heroic measures to keep him alive. David, the renowned physician, after studying all the medical charts and monitors, knew their father was brain dead and would remain in a permanently vegetative state, which was contrary to his wishes. Some of Rogers' life support systems were removed then, and David met with the chief of staff and the hospital ethics committee to ask that Rogers' wishes be carried out fully.

For the next three days, as he lay in a coma, family, friends and colleagues of Carl Rogers visited him in the hospital to say their farewells and share their love and gratitude with him. Every member of Center for Studies of the Person came.[352] David Cain picked up Tom Gordon and they drove down to say goodbye. The two women from Rancho Sante Fe who had helped organize a fund-raiser for the Peace Project paid their respects. Marvalene Hughes flew in from Arizona. Natalie and David, Maria Bowen, Valerie Henderson, Gay Swenson and Ruth Sanford were there most of the time. Natalie monitored the visitation process, as more and more people arrived wanting to share a few final moments with Rogers. Gay recalled how the visitors "would come in and visit and talk on both sides of the bed … It was so clear that his energy was really in the room. There were people there sometimes who had difficulty with each other, who were doing a lot better with each other as they talked on both sides of the bed with Carl …"[353]

Natalie remembered how, "Frances, Naomi and I spent time alone with Dad. We stood at his bedside holding each other's hand, including his hands in the circle. As we meditated, breathing slowly, lovingly, imagining light and peace, he calmed down. His agitated breathing seemed to quiet down to join ours."

On Wednesday Valerie Henderson brought over the letter that had just arrived from Congressmen Bates' office nominating Rogers for the Nobel Peace Prize. "We read the announcement to Carl as he lay in a coma and dying on February 4, 1987. It is my belief that he heard us," wrote Gay Swenson.[354] When just about all the visitors had come, Henderson told him, "It's okay now, Carl, everybody has been here" and Natalie said he could go any time he wanted to. "His hands gripped ours so tight that I thought my hand was going to break and it just gave me chills," recalled Henderson.

But there was at least one more visitor. Swenson had called John Vasconcellos who arrived that afternoon.[355] His final moments with Rogers give a good sense of the many leave-takings during those last days. Natalie greeted Vasconcellos warmly and they embraced. Then he broke into tears and Natalie consoled him and told him it was okay to cry. "She told me they had just told Carl that he had contributed enough to life and that he was free to go when he was ready."[356] Natalie asked him if he would like some time alone with Carl. "John sat down beside Carl, stroking his arm, breathing as deeply as he knew how, trying to discover something deep within himself to call his friend back to life. He thanked Carl for all he had given him, and for providing his first therapist, Leo Rock, with the capacity to touch John's shattered life and lead him back to wholeness. He thanked Carl for helping him discover his own capacity for knowing himself, for growing healthy, and for leading his own life."[357] He thanked Carl for other gifts, personal and political, and bid his friend goodbye.

Rogers often said he did not fear death, but did fear a long, undignified dying. Following his wishes and with the consent of the hospital ethics board, that evening all artificial life support systems were removed and Rogers died, with family and loved ones around him. Valerie Henderson said, "It was so beautiful how he was surrounded by people he loved and worked with, touching him on his forehead and on his shoulders and holding his hand. I was holding his feet and everybody was talking to him saying these wonderful things … then he just opened his eyes and took a deep breath and grabbed Natalie and my [Valerie's] hand and he gently passed."[358]

A prediction he had reaffirmed ten years earlier had come true. In "Growing Old: Or Older and Growing" he wrote, "As a boy, I was rather sickly, and my parents have told me that it was predicted I would die young. This prediction has been proven completely wrong in one sense, but has come profoundly true in another sense. I think it is correct that I will never live to be old. So now I agree with the prediction: I believe that I will die *young*."[359]

CHAPTER 13

Epilogue:
Rogers' Legacy
1987–

As might be expected, Rogers' death was followed by many tributes and recognitions. Center for Studies of the Person organized a memorial service for him on February 21, 1987 at the Sherwood Auditorium of the La Jolla Museum. About 500 people attended from California and around the country and world. Many family members and colleagues delivered eulogies—Natalie Rogers for herself and David Rogers, Frances Fuchs for the six grandchildren who were all present, Maria Bowen, Richard Farson, Valerie Henderson, Doug Land, Gay Swenson, John Vasconcellos, Gay Williams, and others. Natalie concluded her comments by saying, "The world has lost a great humanitarian, and we've lost a great father and grandfather and great-grandfather."[1] John Vasconcellos said,

> In a physical sense, Carl Rogers has left us. That's the sad news. The joyous—and hopeful news—is that Carl Rogers has left many of us more intact, in a phrase, more having 'become persons'—more whole and healthy, more faithful and trusting, more able to lead our lives affectively and effectively. We are living examples of his vision: that we human beings are innately inclined toward becoming constructive, life-affirming, responsible, and trustworthy."[2]

Excerpts from the video of Rogers' eighty-fifth birthday party were shown, including the tribute from President Carter, ending: "God speed your journey. The world can use more global citizens like you." And when Rogers in the video stood up to say, "*I feel very much loved*. Thank you, thank you, thank you," it was as though he was present and had heard it all.

The invitation announced that in lieu of flowers, "In celebration of Carl's life and work, the family has set up the Carl Rogers Memorial Fund for Peace and Human Development to be administered by Natalie and David Rogers …"[3] Natalie and David turned over the administration of the fund to Center for Studies of the Person. Half the proceeds went to the Carl Rogers Peace Project and half to other CSP projects of interest to Rogers.[4] A second memorial service on the East Coast was held on March 29 at Hofstra University on Long Island.[5] Many professional journals published special tributes or devoted entire issues to articles, reminiscences and eulogies about Rogers.

David Malcolm wrote just after Rogers died, "The death of Dr. Rogers presents a real challenge to all those of us who work with the Person-Centered Approach to find out to what extent we may have depended upon his charisma in the past and to learn how we are going to progress in the future without it."[6] As this chapter will illustrate, Rogers' work did indeed progress after his death, significantly so.

Following Rogers

Certainly the immediate tasks, programs, and projects he was working on took place and continued. Valerie Henderson was paid for a year to deal with his correspondence, collect his papers and send them to the Library of Congress.[7] Ruth Sanford went to South Africa in April as planned to work with "The Carl Rogers Program" directed by Shirley Chochot, who wrote after Rogers' death, "I am in awe of just how many other individuals and organizations the Program has influenced in its short life."[8] The network of facilitators they initiated in that country continued to grow, and professionals across South Africa who were influenced by the person-centered approach were available to be of help when the dismantling of apartheid began in the early nineties and the task of reconciliation began.[9] Over a decade after Rogers died, a gathering was held in South Africa in 1998 "to honor his [Rogers'] courageous and precedent-setting inter-racial dialogue work there with his colleague Ruth Sanford in the early 1980s, a most risky and tumultuous moment in South Africa's evolution. Now 92 years old and nearly blind, Ruth Sanford traveled to South Africa to accept accolades for both Carl and herself from a grateful group of multi-ethnic professionals and lay persons attending the International Person-Centered Forum in Johannesburg."

Other CSP colleagues went to Europe in 1987 to facilitate the cross-cultural communication and person-centered approach workshops that Rogers and they had been scheduled to conduct. As Gay Swenson reported at the time, "Other international events which were planned with Carl will go forward in his name and with other staff persons. In Rome, Greece, Costa Rica, France and Switzerland, through the spring and summer, various members of our staff will lead these workshops—Chuck Devonshire, Valerie Henderson, Alberto Zucconi, Marvalene Hughes, Natalie Rogers and myself. I am sure to have left out significant others."[10]

Many of these international workshop programs continued for years. So did Rogers' work in the Soviet Union. As Swenson reported in 1991, seven colleagues from Center for Studies of the Person "have offered trainings to hundreds of educators and other professionals in the Soviet Union this past year. In fact, they were there immediately after the attempted coup for three weeks of training workshops."[11] As we will see, Natalie Rogers became an active workshop leader in the Soviet Union and Russia.

Aside from particular workshops, CSP members continued to operate their various projects after Rogers' death, including several that he had helped to initiate. The La Jolla Program and the Living Now program were two projects that continued into the twenty-first century. Over the years, however, many of the Center projects became less active or ended, and the Center became primarily a support group for its members. It still existed as of this writing in 2007.

The Peace Project Continued

One CSP project that continued for almost ten years after Rogers' death was the Carl Rogers Peace Project. Because it was such an important initiative in Rogers' life—described earlier as the capstone of his career—it is fitting to narrate how the project evolved after his death and how the Rust workshop may be viewed by history.

Gay Swenson continued to direct the Carl Rogers Institute for Peace, with Valerie Henderson, Doug Land and David Malcolm as active, part-time, paid consultants to the project and other volunteer staff members continuing to meet periodically together to envision future directions. But without Rogers the project had lost its major inspiration. Finding funding for another meeting on "The Central America Challenge Phase II: Differing Perspectives—Common Future" was more difficult than ever.[12] Three grant proposals totaling three million dollars were being reviewed by major foundations and funding sources when Rogers died.[13] None was funded. One night in August 1987, with $1,000 left in the project bank account and no immediate prospects for further significant funding, as Gay Swenson later recalled,

> I went to bed and I said tearfully, "I've done everything possible, Carl ..." (I spoke to Carl in my head) "I've done everything I can to keep this going forward. We've done everything we can and we just can't do any more. There are no funds left and there's no way to carry this forward. But we *did* do that in Vienna [Rust], Carl, so that will long be remembered for what you wanted to happen, what *we* wanted to happen. And at that moment I sort of surrendered and let go. And the next morning, literally, in the office the next morning the phone rang,

and I answered it, and a woman's voice said, "Hello, Gay, I don't know if you remember me; this is Joan Kroc." And I said, "Oh, yes, of course!" She said, "You know, I know it must be so hard for you right now." And she said, "Today is my birthday ... and I want to give a little gift for my birthday to women who are working for peace ... I know it's not very much, but I know when Carl died it must have been very hard on you and your going forward, and I know what that's like when my husband died." And she said, "So are you sitting down?" And I said "Yes." And she said, "It isn't much, but it's $100,000."[14]

The gift was intended to help the Peace Project continue its work and serve as a catalyst for further funding. It enabled Swenson and the staff to move forward and organize the second meeting on Central America which took place in Heredia, Costa Rica from December 1–5, 1988.[15]

By 1988, the peace process in Central America had moved forward considerably.[16] The warring parties had met in Esquipulas, Guatemala and drafted a revised Contadora Plan treaty. The United States administration publicly supported this treaty, then worked behind the scenes to defeat it. Costa Rica's president Oscar Arias drafted still a new peace proposal. After the Iran–Contra affair became public and new U.S. efforts to sabotage the Arias plan became evident, all five presidents of Central America were so offended that they all signed the Arias Peace Plan in 1987. "With provisions designed to promote national reconciliation, cessation of hostilities, democratization, free elections, cessation of assistance to irregular forces, the nonuse of national territory for irregular forces attacking other states, international and internal verification, the 1987 peace accord caught the Reagan administration temporarily off balance, won worldwide acclaim, and earned Oscar Arias the Nobel Peace Prize."[17] Signing the peace plan was one thing, but implementing it was another, since the U.S. continued to undermine the treaty and the Nicaraguan government. This was the situation that existed when the follow-up conference to the Rust meeting took place in December 1988, co-sponsored by the Carl Rogers Institute for Peace, the United Nations University for Peace, and the University of Costa Rica.

Given his central role in the peace process, President Arias was fully supportive of the gathering. At the beginning of the workshop he invited all the participants to his home at the Presidential Palace. There, in his elegant living room, around the family Christmas tree, he reminded them of Rogers' important contribution to their process, spoke of him with great respect, and said "in the spirit of Carl Rogers" he would welcome an open-ended question and answer dialogue with the participants.[18] The opening session was inspirational for many participants and, in part, began to assuage the disappointment over the last-minute changes in attendance.

Until a few days before the meeting there was solid confirmation of attendance by many Latin American, high government officials, including former presidents, and contra and Sandanista representatives; but urgent, last-minute meetings on the peace process and other events throughout the region caused last-minute cancellations.[19] There were also cancellations from Washington following the November election, as the transition team for President-elect George Bush (the first) was preoccupied with making its appointments. In spite of their best efforts, the staff could not get any conservative attendees who would represent the U.S. administration's position. Hence the fifty or so participants were primarily university faculty involved with peace issues, non-governmental organizations concerned with peace, relatively few ambassadors and lower level government officials, and the workshop staff.[20] Initial disappointment over the cancellations aside, the group composition turned out to have some benefits. Although there were no dramatic clashes between seriously opposing viewpoints, the absence of high-level officials and diametrically antagonistic views enabled the participants to communicate much more equally and amicably, to listen more deeply, and to forge alliances more readily than they might otherwise have.[21]

The gathering took place outside of San Jose, the capital city. Once again the conference seemed helpful to the participants. As one of them wrote in a peace newsletter afterward, they "had the opportunity to relate to one another on a purely human level and to agree or disagree about deeply felt issues from that perspective. And once again I was reminded that there is nothing more powerful or more meaningful than one human being touching another."[22] In that atmosphere, the participants discussed problems in implementing the peace treaty in Central America and ideas for moving the peace process forward there and around the world. There were no breakthroughs or formal proposals or major plans to come out of the meeting, but it was another useful occasion for those with differing viewpoints to communicate productively and lay the groundwork for future cooperation and initiatives. Over the next two years talks continued on many levels of diplomacy, a new election was held, and peace was finally achieved in Nicaragua.[23]

In the face of all these events, it seemed to me at first that the contribution of the Rust workshop and the follow-up meeting to achieving peace in Central America was very modest. Therefore I was surprised at the Carl Rogers Symposium in 2002, commemorating the 100th anniversary of his birth, when Gay (Swenson) Barfield read the following communication from former President Rodrigo Carazo of Costa Rica in tribute to Rogers:

> Previous efforts for achieving peace in Central America, which were plenty, culminated in the Austria meeting. For the first time, representatives from all governments, groups in conflict and political parties from Central America met to talk about peace.
>
> The political and military difficulties were so strong that it was completely unthinkable that any kind of meeting could take place in Central America. All

the parties refused to meet at a place where journalists could reach them ... The conflict-resolution intellectual work done under the direction of Carl Rogers was also looking for a safe place for the event. It was finally coordinated that it should be celebrated in Rust (Austria) for four days. Carl made it possible.

There, for the first time, I repeat, representatives from all groups in conflict met and the first steps in reaching peace in Central America were taken. This was the real beginning of many things toward peace.

There is a picture of Carl Rogers in the central building of the University for Peace. Carl Rogers is in our memory and the Master in our heart.[24]

I wondered whether Carazo was simply being gracious and exaggerating the importance of Rust in order to send a laudatory comment for this occasion, not realizing that Carazo actually had written these comments two years earlier for Barfield to read at the groundbreaking event for the Joan Kroc Institute for Peace and Justice at the University of San Diego. Later I asked Dee Aker how the Rust workshop could have been so important in the peace process. Aker, who had coordinated many of the logistics for the Rust workshop and, along with Gay Swenson, was instrumental in the follow-up meeting in Costa Rica, had gone on to become the Deputy Director of the Joan Kroc Institute for Peace and Justice. She explained that the Rust workshop had, indeed, been the turning point in the Central American peace process. It was not that it or the follow-up conference produced any solutions. Rather it got the stalled Contadora Process going again. It gave the participants hope that communication and progress were possible. The participants then spoke to their contacts, higher up in the Sandanista and *contra* structure and in other world governments. These more influential people were persuaded to be open to and support further discussions and negotiations. And thus the process moved forward and eventually agreements were reached and peace was achieved.

So it was not that the Rust workshop led to the Costa Rica workshop and the Costa Rica workshop led to peace, but that the Rust workshop led to *many* further steps of which the Costa Rica workshop was just one, and *all* those further steps led to peace.[25] It was, as Rogers had said, not a case where the person-centered facilitators came with solutions. Those would come from the participants themselves, once greater communication and trust were established. Rogers and his colleagues brought *a process*, based on a theory about persons and their tendency to behave in increasingly less self-destructive and more self-actualizing ways when provided with relationships and environments characterized by trust, understanding and authenticity. If we take President Carazo at his word, Rogers and his colleagues initiated the process that unleashed the potential of the participants themselves to achieve peace.

After the Costa Rica workshop, because of the difficulty of finding funding for its more ambitious international goals, the focus of the Carl Rogers Institute for Peace turned to more regional projects in conflict resolution and urban diversity. Gay Swenson received a human relations award from San Diego County in 1992 for her work through the Peace Project in improving dialogue in local communities about the volatile border immigration issues."[26] She continued to operate the project, in increasingly smaller arenas, until it ended in 1996.

Aside from the Peace Project's direct accomplishments, there is no telling of the *indirect* influence that it and Rogers' personal example had on others. For example, inspired by Rogers' peacemaking activities, in 1990 Thomas Gordon organized his international Effectiveness Training network to conduct a one-day, international, conflict resolution event in which they trained 15,000 people in twenty-one countries in conflict resolution skills in one twenty-four-hour period.[27] John Vasconcellos' peace initiatives in the California state legislature were inspired and influenced by Rogers; Vasconcellos often credited him for this.[28] Vasconcellos also credited Rogers for influencing his "Politics of Trust" network, which has "peace" and "collaboration" as two of its major principles.[29] Steve Olwean, former president of Association for Humanistic Psychology, inspired by Rogers' example, as well as other influences, led numerous peace initiatives around the world. Vasconcellos, Gay Swenson Barfield, Marvalene Styles Hughes, Dee Aker and other colleagues and associates of Rogers, as well as many who read of Rogers' peacekeeping work, continued to carry his influence forward in different ways for many years.

Joan Kroc attended two or more events associated with the Peace Project where she would have heard Rogers speak of his work for peace and was impressed enough to make the $100,000 gift after his death.[30] Later she donated $6 million to Notre Dame for Theodore Hesburgh to establish the Kroc Institute for International Peace Studies and $25 million to the University of San Diego to found the Joan Kroc Institute for Peace and Justice. She gave another $50 million to the latter institute when she died, the largest such donation for world peace in history.[31] Certainly she had many influences, especially Father Hesburgh and her Catholic tradition. Still it is interesting to speculate how her contact with Rogers may have contributed to and influenced her own commitment to support the cause of peace. No doubt Rogers' influence in the Kroc Institute lived on through Dee Aker, staff coordinator and facilitator of the Rust and Costa Rica workshops, who was hired as the Kroc Institute's first Deputy Director as an outgrowth of her work on the Peace Project. As of this writing, she is Acting Director. Both Presidents Carazo and Arias accepted invitations from Aker to appear at the Joan Kroc Institute in the twenty-first century, indirectly continuing the legacy of the Carl Rogers Peace Project where the original connection between Rogers, Carazo and Arias had been made.

Other Developments
Rogers' two children also carried on in their father's tradition, indirectly and directly. After fifteen years heading the Robert Wood Johnson Foundation, in

1987 David returned to academic medicine at his Alma Mater, the Cornell Medical Center-New York Hospital. He became deeply involved in the AIDS epidemic, serving as chair of the New York City Mayor's Task Force on AIDS, chair of the New York State AIDS Advisory Council and, appointed by President George H.W. Bush, co-chair and vice-president of the National Commission on AIDS, serving alongside Secretary of Health and Human Services Louis Sullivan, Secretary of Defense (and future Vice-President) Dick Cheney, basketball star Magic Johnson and others. As spokesperson for the Commission he was a frequent critic of the administration's lack of leadership and effectiveness in the AIDS crisis.[32] He died in 1994 from colon cancer, at age 68. In his obituary he was described as "the articulate conscience of the profession over the last 30 years" and, reminiscent of his father, "He was forthright and passionate in his advocacy of his principles, often discomforting his audience, and he felt that one had to irritate complacent people in positions of authority ..."[33]

Natalie Rogers became a leader in the person-centered movement in her own right. She continued to promulgate her person-centered expressive therapy approach through the Person-Centered Expressive Therapy Institute, the many workshops she led, her book *The Creative Connection: Expressive Art as Healing,* and other writings.[34] The Person-Centered Expressive Therapy Institute, which she had founded in California in 1984, continued until 2006, with Institute staff conducting six-week, 400-hour training programs attended by participants from around the world. Satellite programs were developed in England, Argentina and Japan.[35] Unlike other person-centered orientations, the person-centered expressive therapy approach explicitly sought to integrate mind, body, emotion and spirit. The foundations of her work were the philosophy and methods of person-centered therapy expanded to use non-verbal forms of creative expression including movement, art, music, and journaling. In this sense, the work expanded and embodied her father's work on creativity as well as therapy.

When she was invited to the Soviet Union to continue her father's work after his death, she said she would be glad to come but would have to work in her own way. Her hosts agreed. She was warmly received and invited to return to lead workshops in the Soviet Union and then Russia, making four trips between 1989 and 1995.[36] In the United States and beyond, her work became increasingly known and acknowledged as a major approach within the field of art therapy and within person-centered therapy.[37] Like her father, throughout her seventies she traveled frequently around the world disseminating the person-centered approach.[38]

Ironically, Carl Rogers continued to "publish" after his death, with three new books in which he was the primary author and two major audio-visual productions that featured his life and work. Shortly before he died, Rogers asked me to collaborate with him on pulling together a collection of his articles into a reader that would include the major themes of his long career.[39] By the time my affirmative response reached him, he had died. Natalie and David Rogers supported the project's going forward, requesting that Valerie Henderson, Rogers' long-time colleague and secretary, work with me on the book. In reviewing the many possible selections, we soon recognized the potential for two volumes, rather than one, and Rogers' publisher Houghton Mifflin agreed. Hence *The Carl Rogers Reader* and *Carl Rogers: Dialogues* were both published in 1989.[40] The first volume included 33 articles from 1942 to 1987, organized around the themes of: personal essays, the therapeutic relationship, the person in process, theory and research, a human science, education, the helping professions, philosophy, and social and political applications. The second volume, as described earlier in Chapter 8, contained Rogers' dialogues and written exchanges with some of the leading intellectual figures of the twentieth century: Martin Buber, Paul Tillich, B.F. Skinner, Gregory Bateson, Michael Polanyi, Rollo May, and Reinhold Niebuhr. While *Dialogues* is currently out of print, the *Reader* continues in print in the United States, United Kingdom, and in several foreign translations.

The centennial of Rogers' birth in 2002 marked a renewed interest in Rogers and the person-centered approach worldwide. Many journals ran tributes, articles and recollections about Rogers. Several celebrations and commemorations were held around the world. Initiated by Natalie Rogers, she and Rogers' former colleagues organized "The Carl R. Rogers Symposium 2002: His Life—Our Work—A Global Vision," held in La Jolla that summer.[41] Some 350 attendees from twenty-three nations celebrated Rogers' life and contributions and, in a variety of plenary sessions, panels, presentations, and workshops, discussed and demonstrated how to carry the work forward in the world.[42] Natalie Rogers worked tirelessly to insure that two new resources were ready for the Symposium.

One was David Russell's lengthy oral history of Rogers, recorded in the year before his death. Published by Penmarin Books in California, *Carl Rogers: The Quiet Revolutionary: An Oral History* contained the Russell–Rogers interviews, as well as introductions by Eugene Gendlin, Brian Thorne and David Russell, scholarly endnotes by Jan Francis, and an extensive bibliography on Rogers and the person-centered approach compiled from many sources.[43] While covering some familiar territory, it also added new understandings about Rogers' personal and professional history and current work. It was a vivid picture of Rogers in his final year, demonstrating his energy and commitment to international conflict reduction, his intellectual clarity, and his human foibles.[44]

A second resource, developed and designed for Natalie Rogers by her daughter Janet Fuchs and Fuchs' partner Deb Huston, was "Carl Rogers: A Daughter's Tribute."[45] This CD-Rom production contains chronological excerpts from Rogers' books that illustrate the development of his theories, practice and personal reflections. It includes an extensive bibliography, photographs spanning his lifetime, video footage of counseling sessions and encounter groups, sections of his *China Diary,* and courtship/love letters to Helen. It was clearly a work of love that produced an excellent resource collection on Rogers' life and work.

Another resource that grew out of that symposium was a new video/DVD presentation on "Carl Rogers and the Person-Centered Approach." Containing narration, photographs, and audio and video excerpts of Rogers at work, this was the first major video production that traced the full trajectory of Rogers' life and work.[46] Early versions were shown at the La Jolla Symposium and at another Carl Rogers centennial event in 2002. This was the Carl Rogers Symposium held at the World Conference on Psychotherapy in Vienna. Many keynote and other sessions were offered on Rogers and the person-centered approach, some of a historical nature, but most on new theory, new research and new applications of the person-centered approach. Both of the Carl Rogers Symposia in 2002, along with other commemorative events and new publications and resources for educators and practitioners, demonstrated the vitality of the person-centered approach. They commemorated Rogers' historical influence while contributing to the renaissance in the person-centered movement that began after Rogers' death.

Historical Influence

The historical influence that Carl Rogers had on the field of clinical psychology, psychotherapy and counseling is reasonably clear. Rogers and his colleagues were the first to record, transcribe and publish complete cases of psychotherapy.[47] Using these recordings, Rogers conducted and sponsored more scientific research on psychotherapy than had ever been undertaken before and initiated process research in psychotherapy.[48] Rogers developed the "nondirective," then "client-centered" approach to counseling and psychotherapy, which became mainstays of therapists' repertoires.[49] In so doing he popularized the term "client" as the recipient of therapy in non-medical settings, virtually founded the professional counseling movement, and made professional counseling accessible to diverse helping professions.[50] For these accomplishments, he was the first psychologist or psychotherapist ever to receive the American Psychological Association's highest scientific and professional honors: its Distinguished Scientific Contribution Award and its Distinguished Professional Contribution Award, among many other honors.[51]

Rogers' "self theory"[52] became a prominent theory of personality which is still included in most personality texts today.[53] He served as President of the American Association of Applied Psychology, the American Academy of Psychotherapists, the American Psychological Association, and the APA Division of Clinical Psychology, among other offices. He was a founder and leading spokesperson for the humanistic psychology movement and for encounter groups.[54] He helped rekindle the progressive education tradition through his writings on education.[55] His many books, including *On Becoming a Person,* helped bring the tenets of the client-centered/person-centered approach and humanistic psychology to ever-wider audiences.[56] He demonstrated that a person-centered approach to conflict resolution had potential to reduce tensions and contribute to peacekeeping efforts in inter-group, cross-cultural, and international settings.[57] By his personal example, he served as a role model for two or three generations of helping professionals.

What is less certain is what role Rogers' work will play in the ongoing development of psychology, psychotherapy and beyond. Is Rogers' presence as strong as ever, or has it faded as research on other approaches has proliferated, new knowledge about therapy has emerged, protocols for research funding have changed, and other models, trends and pop psychology movements have developed? Without the living example of Carl Rogers—teaching, writing, and demonstrating his theories and methods around the world—have other researchers and practitioners continued to carry out and develop the client-centered/person-centered approach? Will current and future trends in research and practice render Rogers' contributions to that of historic, foundational interest only, or will Rogers' contributions remain valid, relevant and active through the twenty-first century?

The remainder of this chapter, written some twenty years after Rogers' death, examines four trends through which the status of Rogers' work may be ascertained—the number of publications on the client-centered/person-centered approach, the extent of person-centered organizations and training institutes around the world, the role of client-centered principles in the last several decades of research on psychotherapy process and outcomes, and the competing paradigms within the person-centered movement.

Some readers may wish to stop at this point. The biography of Carl Rogers— the story of his *life*—is concluded. The study of Rogers' *work* continues. In fact, one cannot fully appreciate the scope and influence of his work without understanding the new developments in the person-centered approach that occurred after Rogers' death.

Expanding Publications

One measure of prevalence is the number of publications appearing on a particular person or approach. By one count—in the PsychINFO database—from 1946 to 1986, not counting Rogers' own writings, 84 books, 64 book chapters and 456 articles, a total of 604 publications, appeared on Carl Rogers or the client-centered/person-centered approach.[58] In comparison, from January 1987 to September 2004, 141 books, 174 book chapters, and 462 journal articles appeared, for a total of 777 publications.[59] Therefore, not counting his own writings, more books, chapters and articles were written on Carl Rogers and the client-centered/person-centered approach in the seventeen years *after* his death than were written in the forty years before. If most of these publications simply made reference to Rogers' or the client-centered approach's historical role, this might not be significant; but, in fact, our scanning of these publications indicates that the vast majority encompassed new research, new theory, and new applications.[60]

These numbers are by no means a complete count of the person-centered literature. First, they are based on one particular source, reflecting only the journals reviewed for that database. Second, they reflect primarily the psychology field. As Rogers' work has permeated many different professions—social work, education, pastoral counseling, group leadership, and others—databases for other fields would reveal many more publications. Third, this count is limited to publications in English and therefore excludes the significant number of foreign language publications on the person-centered approach, particularly those in Europe where person-centered counseling and psychotherapy is a leading approach. In Japan alone, there were 165 articles on the person-centered *group* approach from 1970–1986.[61] Fourth, the citations included above reflect primarily a narrow construction of the client-centered or person-centered approach. A thorough bibliography including the two offshoots or variations of person-centered therapy—the focusing and process-experiential approaches—would yield many more titles and present a more accurate reflection of the current influence of the person-centered approach. Indeed, Lietaer identified 477 *books* on client-centered/experiential psychotherapy from 1939–2000, many in languages other than English, about twice as many titles as reported above.[62] And Peter Schmid lists over 6,800 books, chapters and articles on his "Person-Centered and Experiential Bibliography Online: 1940–2000."[63] To compare apples to apples, I would estimate that about a third to a half of these go beyond person-centered and experiential psychotherapy and extend into humanistic psychology and other related areas. Nevertheless, clearly there is a vast literature on Rogers and the person-centered approach.

However, using the same PsycINFO database for comparison, there is a significantly *larger* literature on Freud or psychoanalysis, Aaron Beck or cognitive therapy, B.F. Skinner or behavioral therapy, and cognitive behavioral therapy.[64] On the other hand, there were more references to Rogers or the client-centered/person-centered approach than there were to Frederick Perls or Gestalt therapy, Albert Ellis or rational emotive therapy, multicultural counseling, Alfred Adler or Adlerian therapy, psychodynamic therapy, William Glasser or reality therapy, Victor Frankl or existential therapy, and eclectic approach or integrative therapy.[65]

These numbers reflect a phenomenon observed during Rogers' lifetime. While his work was widely used in counseling, psychotherapy and other fields, academicians (who write most of the books and articles in the PsychINFO and similar databases) tended to ignore or downplay his work or take it for granted because some of his historic contributions became so incorporated into practice that they are now relegated to common sense. Clearly, as in Rogers' day, academic psychology still favors behavioral and cognitive orientations. Nevertheless, the person-centered approach, while by no means a leading topic of scholarship in psychotherapy and psychology, is alive and well. As the data above suggest, it is arguably the leading approach among the so-called "humanistic psychotherapies."[66] There is a steady stream of publications on theory, research and practice in this area. There is even a company devoted to publishing and distributing books, journals and audio-visual resources on the person-centered approach. PCCS Books, begun in England by Pete Sanders and Maggie Taylor-Sanders in 1993, has helped further the spread of the person-centered approach throughout the United Kingdom, Europe and beyond.[67]

Proliferating Organizations

Another measure of status is the number of professional organizations and journals utilizing the ideas of Carl Rogers and the client-centered/person-centered approach. By 2004 there were approximately 200 organizations and training centers located around the world dedicated to researching and applying the principles developed by Rogers.[68] For example, there is the Asociación para el estudio y desarrollo del Enfoque Centrado en la Persona in Argentina, PCA Institut Praha in the Czech Republic, Instituto dell'Approccio Centrato sulla Persona in Italy, and the Association for the Person-Centered Approach in South Africa. Many countries have more than one client-centered/person-centered organization.

Some of these organizations are fairly small, such as the Association for the Development of the Person-Centered Approach, the primary person-centered group in the United States (although it has international participation), with fewer than 200 members.[69] Others are quite large and active, such as the GwG in Germany (Gesellschaft für wissenschaftliche Gesprächspsychotherapie, often known in English as the German Association for Person-Centered Psychotherapy)[70] with over 4,300 members, the British Association for the Person-Centred Approach in England and the Association Francophone de Psycho-thérapie Centrée-sur-la-Personne et Expérientielle in Belgium, each with over 1,000 members. As these examples suggest, Europe is currently the most active center for research, training and practice in the person-centered approach, and the person-centered approach is one of the leading therapeutic approaches on that continent.[71]

Furthermore, there are Focusing Institutes located around the world.[72] As the experiential focusing approach developed by Eugene T. Gendlin is closely aligned to the person-centered tradition, these institutes could rightly be added to the list of organizations promoting the client-centered/person-centered approach.

In addition to the various associations and training institutes in various countries, there are umbrella organizations that connect the individual organizations and provide a means for communicating ideas among client-centered, person-centered and experiential theoreticians and practitioners. The Europeans had wanted to start an international person-centered organization for many years. Germain Lietaer recalled how before Rogers' death, "Almost behind the street we were talking ... about making an international organization ... but that was a taboo topic almost ... which we finally talked about with him, but he was not in favor of it ... He said we do not need it and so on, and the people of the United States dare not go against that ... We in Europe [said], "Well, he don't like it, but we will do it."[73] Although they did not form an international organization when Rogers was still alive, as we saw earlier, they did form person-centered associations in a number of individual European countries.

When the Association for the Development of the Person-Centered Approach (ADPCA) was finally formed in the U.S. shortly before Rogers' death, it was intended to be an international organization. It certainly had representation from many countries, especially at first. Meanwhile the International Forum on the Person-Centered Approach, first organized by Alberto Segrera and then coordinated by a local host or organizational sponsor in each location, continued to be held every three years independent of any association.[74]

But most of the members of the ADPCA were Americans and most tended to favor the traditional person-centered orientation.[75] "The truth is that it was more of a national organization with a few international members," explained Jerold Bozarth.[76] As Lietaer recalled, "After Carl Rogers' death, folks in Europe felt the need to get together. They [ADPCA] felt they were already international and so we didn't need another organization. We felt first that they were not truly international and second, that we wanted to focus on psychotherapy and counseling and not a broader area as in education and so on and that we wanted to go broader than just classical client-centered therapy." Lietaer said the European countries had been working on their own, in different languages. They needed to talk. They also needed to talk across different orientations—pure client-centered, focusing, process-experiential, diagnostic (those who took diagnoses seriously or saw the need to tailor research or practice to specific diagnoses—anathema to Rogers and traditional client-centered practitioners).

So Lietaer organized a new international conference that was held in Leuven, Belgium in 1988. "I mean the title of the conference was 'Client-Centered and Experiential' and that was already a big thing for some people," that the process-experiential approach would be given equal standing. There were "230 participants from all over the world, 50 maybe from the German speaking countries, 70 from United States, 50 maybe from Belgium itself, and then from all other countries ... We had several [keynote] speakers ... Reinhard Tausch of Germany, [Eugene] Gendlin, Laura Rice, and [Leslie] Greenberg." Rice and

Greenberg's keynote on "Fundamental Dimensions in Experiential Therapy: New Directions in Research" and Gendlin's on "The Small Steps of the Therapy Process: How They Come and How to Help Them Come" introduced their work of the past fifteen and thirty years, respectively, to the wider person-centered community.[77] The conference was mostly academic in focus, rather than operating like a person-centered community. The proceedings were published in a volume called *Client-Centered and Experiential Psychotherapy in the Nineties*.[78]

After that, International Conferences on Client-Centered and Experiential Psychotherapy were held every three years.[79] But there was still no truly international association. That began to change in 1996 after the first World Conference on Psychotherapy in Vienna. Many of the person-centered and experiential therapists who attended that conference were disappointed at "the lack of significant keynote contributions from the person-centered perspective at the World Congress and a recognition that much needs to be done if we are not only to take our rightful position on the international stage but also to make readily accessible to our colleagues from other orientations those aspects of our theory and practice which are only now beginning to be recognized and valued, without acknowledgement of their origin, as a result of developments and advances in other approaches to psychotherapy."[80] Consequently, thirty person-centered and experiential theorists and practitioners got together in the town of Bad Hall, Austria and drafted a letter to person-centered and experiential organizations, networks and individuals around the world proposing that an international organization be formed at the upcoming Fourth International Conference on Client-Centered and Experiential Psychotherapy. "This will be the tenth year since Carl Rogers' death," it concluded, "and an appropriate time to take a major step to ensure the continuing vitality and influence of the distinctive approach to psychotherapy to which we are committed in our various ways."[81] Thus the World Association for Person-Centered and Experiential Psychotherapy and Counseling (WAPCEPC) was formed during the International Conference in Portugal in 1997. As stated on the World Association's website,

> The aim is to provide a world-wide forum for those professionals who have a commitment to the primary importance in therapy of the relationship between therapist and client, an essential trust in the experiential world of the client and its centrality for the therapeutic endeavor, a belief in the efficacy of the conditions and attitudes conducive to therapeutic movement first postulated by Carl Rogers and a commitment to their active implementation within the therapeutic relationship, a commitment to an understanding of both clients and therapists as persons who are at one and the same time individuals and in relationship with others and with their environment, an openness to the elaboration and development of person-centered and experiential theory in the light of current and future practice and research.[82]

586

The Network of the European Associations for Person-Centered Counseling and Psychotherapy was also formed in 1997, subscribing to the same set of objectives. Since 1997 the renamed "World Conference for Person-Centered and Experiential Psychotherapy and Counseling" has been held on a triennial and now biennial basis.[83]

The influence of all the national and international organizations extends through their professional journals, which reach a wider audience than their membership and training programs. Schmid listed more than fifty person-centered or experiential periodicals and journals with primary contributions from client-centered/person-centered theorists, researchers and practitioners.[84] The list includes journals from Portugal, Germany, France, Great Britain, Mexico, Japan, Ireland, the Netherlands, Belgium, Canada, and the United States. There are regional journals as well, such as *Person*, published in German by the German, Austrian and Swiss associations. In 1992, two years after the *Person-Centered Review* ceased publication in the U.S., the ADPCA's *Person-Centered Journal* began.[85] On the international level, a new journal, *Person-Centered and Experiential Psychotherapies*, was created in 2001 by the World Association for Person-Centered and Experiential Psychotherapy and Counseling. Although the journal is published in English, it includes research contributions from non-English speaking countries, abstracts in German, Spanish, French, Portuguese and Japanese, and is available on the PsychoINFO database.

Membership of ADPCA and the World Association has been quite small— only a few hundred in each. Rather, most of the action is in the person-centered organizations of individual countries where membership and activity are often robust. ADPCA and the World Association have served more of a leadership role in the person-centered world, offering intellectual leadership through their journals (for example, the World Association's journal is now distributed also to the members of the Austrian, Belgian, British, Dutch, and Portuguese person-centered associations)[86] and providing learning, motivation and inspiration for those who attend ADPCA and World Association conferences and bring back energy and ideas to their home countries, associations and institutions.

Stepping back from all these details, it is clear that *all this activity is far more than that which occurred during Carl Rogers' lifetime*. Rogers, for the most part, discouraged institutes and organizations which bore his name or promulgated the client-centered approach. He was worried they would foster a personality cult or rigid orthodoxy. Rogers' death freed up a great deal of energy and initiative by person-centered theorists, researchers, and practitioners around the world, making the person-centered approach more of a broad-based, international movement than it ever was during his lifetime.

It was ironic. Rogers did not want to foster disciples. Yet by resisting organizations for so many years, with their conferences and journals and identity struggles, he discouraged opportunities for ideas to be exchanged and debated among the national and international leaders of the person-centered approach and, in this sense, stifled its growth. With the exception of Natalie Rogers who developed her own variation of the approach, those who stayed closest to Rogers remained tied to his formulations and had limited effectiveness in developing and spreading the person-centered approach or gaining its acceptance in academic and research circles, in spite of the growing body of research supporting it in North America and abroad. Worried about stifling individual development, they rarely formed institutes or training programs in the person-centered approach. Meanwhile in Europe, where there was widespread acceptance of both classical client-centered therapy *and* the person-centered experiential approaches of Gendlin and Rice and Greenberg, they went forward in a flexible and eclectic way—forming their various associations and institutes, creating training programs, conducting research, making the person-centered approach a mainstream school of thought and practice taught in universities and institutes and recognized by governments for licensing and funding.

Evolving Research

In 1957, "Rogers set forth a hypothesis that evoked more than 3 decades of research."[87] That hypothesis, essentially, was that when a therapist demonstrates the core conditions of unconditional positive regard, empathic understanding and congruence, and the client perceives these at least to a minimal degree, then psychotherapeutic personality change and its positive correlates are inevitable. Moreover, Rogers argued that these conditions of effective therapy operated independently of the therapeutic approach being employed. He wrote, "the techniques of the various therapies are relatively unimportant except to the extent that they serve as channels for fulfilling one of the conditions."[88]

How has Rogers' theory of therapy and the research that supports it held up over the years? Rogers himself stopped conducting research on individual psychotherapy after leaving Wisconsin in 1963 and after publication of *The Therapeutic Relationship and Its Impact: A Study of Psychotherapy with Schizophrenics* in 1967.[89] But others carried on the work. Research over the next quarter century involved many studies that supported the efficacy of the core conditions. In 1971 Truax and Mitchell reported on the results of 14 studies that involved 992 participants. Across these studies, there were 66 statistically significant correlations between positive outcome and the core conditions, versus one statistically significant negative correlation. The authors summarized,

> These studies taken together suggest that therapists or counselors who are accurately empathic, nonpossessively warm in attitude, and genuine, are indeed effective. Also, these findings seem to hold with a wide variety of therapists and

counselors, regardless of their training or theoretic orientation, and with a wide variety of clients or patients, including college underachievers, juvenile delinquents, hospitalized schizophrenics, college counselees, mild to severe outpatient neurotics, and the mixed variety of hospitalized patients. Further, the evidence suggests that these findings hold in a variety of therapeutic contexts and in both individual and group psychotherapy or counseling.[90]

In 1977 Gurman concluded that "there exists substantial, if not overwhelming, evidence in support of the hypothesized relationship between patient-perceived therapeutic conditions and outcome in individual psychotherapy counseling."[91] In 1986 Orlinsky and Howard's extensive review of process-outcome studies concluded that, regarding empathic resonance, mutual affirmation, therapist role-investment (which included the patient perceiving the therapist as genuine), and the overall quality of the relationship, "generally between 50 and 80 percent of the substantial number of findings in this area were significantly positive, indicating that these dimensions were very consistently related to patient outcome. This was especially true when process measures were based on patients' observations of the therapeutic relationship."[92]

In contrast to the growing evidence testifying to the efficacy of the core conditions in promoting therapeutic improvement (and conversely, low therapist conditions causing deterioration in clients), some studies showed no particular benefits resulting from one or another of the core conditions. Hence a number of research reviews of studies in the seventies and early eighties reported equivocal findings as to the efficacy or effectiveness of the core conditions.[93] Many reviewers then and since have pointed out that these studies and reviews were flawed in at least three respects.[94]

First, the studies often employed therapists who exhibited minimal levels of the core conditions. That is, many studies were comparing no facilitative conditions to minimal facilitative conditions. Patterson argued that, considering that so many studies on the core conditions found positive outcomes when therapists' levels of the conditions were minimal and when sample sizes were small only goes to demonstrate how effective the core conditions are when therapists are trained to provide high levels of positive regard, empathy and congruence.[95] When such bias is controlled for, Stubbs and Bozarth "did not find one direct study that supported the assertion that the conditions are not sufficient."[96]

Second, those who interpret studies that show no positive effect when therapists demonstrate one of the core conditions as evidence that that condition is unimportant misunderstand Rogers' hypothesis. For example, while therapist empathy in and of itself may not be a necessary condition of effective therapy,[97] what does seem important is that clients perceive their therapist to be empathic.[98] This, in fact, was Rogers' 1957 hypothesis—the client *must perceive* the therapist's empathy, unconditional positive regard and congruence. Studies that use only outside observer or therapist ratings to measure the core conditions fall short of testing Rogers' hypothesis, even though a large number have produced positive findings. The truer test of Rogers' hypothesis is achieved when the core conditions are rated by the client, and such studies have produced the most consistently positive findings.

Finally, that some studies, albeit a minority, show empathy by itself does not produce positive change does not mean empathy is not effective. It just means that, by itself, empathy is not sufficient. The same for unconditional positive regard and congruence. Rogers did not suggest that *each* condition was sufficient, but that *all* were sufficient. When all three conditions are present and the client perceives them, he said, positive change will occur. That single core conditions, by themselves, have so often been shown to correlate with positive therapeutic outcomes (see below) is all the more impressive, since even Rogers did not hypothesize that would be so.

Later Studies and Reviews

In spite of some equivocal reviews in the 70s, most research in the 1980s and 90s continued to support the importance of the core conditions. Reviewing twelve studies, Sexton and Whiston wrote in 1994, "This research seems to support previous findings regarding the importance of empathy in the counseling relationship."[99] Orlinsky, Grawe and Parks reported similar positive results in ten different studies from this period.[100] In 2002, Bohart, Elliott, Greenberg and Watson conducted possibly the largest meta-analysis of research on empathy, including forty-seven studies from 1961–2000, involving 3,026 clients, with 190 separate empathy-outcome associations studied.[101] They found a weighted, unbiased effect size of .32, which is considered a medium effect size. In the context of psychotherapy outcome research, this would be considered a meaningful correlation between empathy and positive therapeutic outcomes. Following in Laura Rice's tradition, as described earlier, while recognizing the importance of empathy, many researchers have suggested that empathy is a more complex concept than Rogers and others have recognized. They have argued that more research is needed to understand therapeutic empathy—its different forms and its most effective applications with different clients, in different therapeutic contexts, and at different stages of the therapy relationship.

As with empathy, of twenty-four relatively recent studies addressing therapists' "affirmation" of clients (a concept which includes acceptance, nonpossessive warmth and positive regard), a large majority of the studies showed a positive correlation between affirmation and outcomes, compared to some neutral and only one negative finding.[102] Orlinsky, Grawe and Parks "summarized the results of 154 findings ... drawn from a total of 76 studies. They found that 56% of the findings were positive, and that, again, the findings based on the patients' ... sense of the therapist's positive regard yielded even a higher rate of positive therapeutic outcomes, 65%."[103] Stated differently, there were 87 findings with a statistically significant positive relationship between therapist affirmation and positive outcomes, 63 findings that showed no relationship, and only 4 that showed a negative relationship.

Furthermore, most recent studies done following the "working alliance" model (discussed below), rather than the client-centered model, found similar findings. In sixteen studies, about half of the associations between therapist's warmth/positive regard and outcomes are positive, about half show no difference, and none are negative. However, again, "as noted by previous reviewers, when the patient rates both the therapist's positive regard and treatment outcome, a positive association between these and other variables is especially likely."[104] Farber and Lane concluded,

> The therapist's ability to provide positive regard seems to be significantly associated with therapeutic success—at least when we take the patient's perspective on therapeutic outcome. However, virtually all the significant findings bear relatively modest effect sizes, suggestive of the fact that, like the therapeutic alliance, it is a significant but not exhaustive part of the process-outcome equation. Extrapolating somewhat from the data, we conclude that therapists' provision of positive regard is strongly indicated in clinical practice.[105]

Research on congruence has been more ambiguous, with many studies showing a positive correlation with positive outcomes, many showing no correlation, and some showing a negative correlation.[106] As I suggested earlier, congruence was the least clearly explained of Rogers' core conditions; hence it may be the most difficult of the core conditions for therapists to get right. The research indicates, for example, that while certain amounts and types of self-disclosure by the therapist may be helpful, too much or inappropriate self-disclosure can be harmful.[107] Sachse and Elliott suggested that more research is needed to learn about how congruence can be employed most helpfully in counseling and psychotherapy.[108]

Research in Europe

As research on client-centered therapy in the U.S. diminished in Rogers' later years, when his professional attention turned elsewhere, research on person-centered and experiential psychotherapies increased significantly in Europe.[109] Reinhard Tausch and his students and colleagues in Germany engaged in a major program of psychotherapy research.[110] For example, in one large study involving 80 client-centered therapists and 149 clients and their waiting-list control clients, it was found that significant improvement in clients took place when therapists demonstrated two of the three core conditions.[111] (Again, this recalls Rogers' 1957 hypothesis that single conditions are not sufficient, but that all—or as this study demonstrated, at least two—of the core conditions are necessary for change.)

591

Studies in Belgium and the Netherlands by Lietaer and his colleagues produced similar findings.[112] Summarizing this period of research, Bozarth, Zimring and Tausch wrote, "The studies by Tausch and his colleagues as well as others in Europe are quite positive. Positive findings are consistent in the areas of individual psychotherapy ...; group psychotherapy; and groups with cancer patients, prisoners, judges, teachers, and geriatric individuals. The findings extend to encounter groups, education, and daily life activities."[113]

Speaking more broadly, Stubbs and Bozarth wrote in 1994, "Over four decades, the major thread in psychotherapy efficacy research is the presence of the therapist attitudes hypothesized by Rogers."[114]

A New Generation of Research

In spite of all the research support for empathy, positive regard and congruence, even some strong advocates of client-centered/experiential therapy have conceded or concluded that the core conditions may be neither necessary nor sufficient.[115] Germain Lietaer has pointed out that certainly there has been at least one case where a client perceived the therapist as empathic, accepting, and real, yet did not improve. This shows that the conditions are not sufficient for all clients. Similarly there have been individual patients who improved even though the therapist lacked one or more of the core conditions. Hence one cannot maintain that all the core conditions are necessary.[116] As Gelso and Carter stated, "the conditions originally specified by Rogers are neither necessary nor sufficient, although it seems clear that such conditions are facilitative" or as Lietaer said, "crucial."[117] As I would put it, while neither necessary nor sufficient for all clients, the core conditions are helpful to extremely helpful with virtually all clients.

Indeed, the direction of much of the latest research on psychotherapy outcomes is consistent with this view. This newer research has gradually come to recognize or acknowledge, first, that the success of psychotherapy is only partly determined by the psychotherapy itself, that is, by the therapist's approach, skill, attitudes and relationship with the client. For example, based on Lambert, Shapiro and Bergin's review of the voluminous research on psychotherapy outcomes, Lambert concluded that whatever positive change occurs during psychotherapy can be attributed approximately 45% to the psychotherapy (a combination of the therapy relationship and the therapist's techniques), 15% to the placebo effect (the client's expectation that this process will be good for him or her), and 40% to extra-therapeutic variables like the social and family support systems in the client's life, the client's ego strength, and fortuitous events.[118]

Another recognition of the newest generation of psychotherapy research, albeit a controversial one, is that the success of psychotherapy is not due primarily to the particular therapeutic approach—whether it be cognitive-behavioral, client-centered, psychoanalytic, or any other. Rather, these approaches are roughly equivalent in their effectiveness.[119] Some research has supported the superiority of certain approaches for certain client problems, such as cognitive-behavior therapy for the treatment of depression; however, many researchers have argued persuasively that, in addition to other limitations, these studies do not take therapist "allegiance" into account.[120] They suggest, for example, that the cognitive-behavioral therapists in these studies (and the researchers) had a level of training and commitment to CBT that was greater than the training and commitment of the therapists in the comparison groups and that when these differences in therapist allegiance are controlled for, the differences in treatment approaches all but disappear.

Common Factors and Core Conditions

Hence much of the latest research on psychotherapy outcomes has demonstrated that, rather than particular approaches, it is certain "common factors" in the therapy relationship that account for therapeutic change.[121] As Sexton and her colleagues explained, "Our major theoretical schools, although effective, seem no better than one another. Instead, it seems that there is some set of common elements and process underlying successful therapy."[122] Although Rogers was not the first person to suggest that common factors in the therapy relationship account for its benefits (Rosenzweig first introduced the idea in 1936),[123] he was the first to spell out this relationship in detail and conduct extensive scientific research on it. Years later, citing Hubble, Duncan and Miller's book on common factors research, *The Heart and Soul of Change*, Bozarth, Zimring and Tausch would write that "the pervasive conclusion of decades of therapy research [is] that outcome is related to common factors rather than particular therapies."[124]

The common factors in effective psychotherapy have been characterized many different ways. Lambert and Bergin catalogued *support factors, learning factors*, and *action factors*.[125] Among the support factors are therapist warmth, respect, empathy, acceptance and genuineness, positive relationship, and trust. New studies conducted by non-client-centered therapists continue to support the importance of these support factors.

For example, one of largest and best experimental studies conducted in the United States, funded by the National Institute of Mental Health, compared three treatment approaches for depression—administration of the drug imipramine; cognitive-behavioral therapy (CBT); interpersonal therapy; and "ward management" which was meant to serve as a placebo treatment.[126] What distinguished this study was that it involved many therapists and many patients who were randomly assigned to the various treatment groups.

> The patients were selected in terms of specifically defined criteria; three large medical centers were used in order to provide adequate samples of patients; manuals were available for each of the forms of psychotherapy being evaluated; the therapists were experienced clinical psychologists and psychiatrists who

received specialized training in one of the psychotherapies being evaluated; a variety of well-known standardized evaluative procedures were used; and competent statistical consultants participated in the project.[127]

As it turned out, there were no significant differences among the three therapeutic treatments on patient outcomes. *However*, across all groups, the therapist's empathy, positive regard and congruence at the end of the second session were significantly correlated with outcomes. As the authors wrote, "Higher levels of an experienced therapeutic relationship [that is, as experienced by the patient] were significantly related to better outcome, especially with the measures of change in general clinical and social functioning."[128] Bozarth, Zimring and Tausch wrote that the single best predictor of success at the end of therapy was the patients' perception of the therapist's empathy at the end of the second session.[129]

The Therapeutic Alliance and Core Conditions

In spite of the significant empirical support for Rogers' core conditions, other researchers have proposed other models as providing a more satisfactory explanation of the common factors that account for therapeutic progress. One of these is the therapeutic alliance or working alliance model, which originated in the psychoanalytic literature.[130] As Sexton et al. wrote in 1997, "The working alliance, social influence and interactional models of the counseling relationship have received considerable research attention and garnered strong empirical support. The strength of the evidence for these models far exceeds that demonstrated by the prevalent Rogerian model."[131] Although they present little evidence to support this claim with respect to the latter two models, research reviews and meta-analyses on the therapeutic alliance have helped establish this model as a popular new explanation for effective therapeutic relationships.[132] Orlinsky, Grawe and Parks wrote in 1994, "The strongest evidence linking process to outcome concerns the therapeutic bond or alliance, reflecting more than 1,000 process-outcome findings."[133]

Whether this *far exceeds* the core conditions model is debatable. Lambert wrote just two years earlier that, "Research on the therapeutic alliance has, as yet, far less research than that generated by client-centered theory"[134] (although subsequent research on the alliance has been profuse). In any case, as others have pointed out, "The results of the meta-analysis indicate that the overall relation of therapeutic alliance with outcome is moderate."[135] "Moderate" in this sense refers to effect size, or just how large the relationship is between the therapeutic alliance and the client outcomes. Statistically speaking, the same could be said of empathy.[136] As Bohart and colleagues wrote, "The effect size [for empathy] is on the same order of magnitude as (or slightly larger than) previous analyses of the relationship between therapeutic alliance and outcome."[137] While there is still some debate over the relative strength of the core conditions and therapeutic alliance models, nevertheless, there is little debate that recent, process-outcome research in psychotherapy has focused primarily on the common factors in the therapeutic or working alliance.

Ironically, as Lambert and Bergin wrote in 1994, "There is more disagreement about the therapeutic alliance construct than there was with the client-centered conditions."[138] Descriptions of the therapeutic alliance include the therapist's *engagement* (efforts to promote the process, active interventions, and showing interest) and the therapist's *collaboration* (taking a mutual, invitational, negotiating stance).[139] Another description of the working alliance includes "client–counselor agreement on goals, agreement on therapeutic tasks, and the emotional bond between client and counselor."[140] The therapeutic alliance is influenced by other common factors.[141] These include: the client's belief about the effectiveness of therapy and the client's hope and expectation about getting better;[142] whether the therapist's behavior fits the client's expectations; whether the client and therapist can establish a contract—a mutual understanding of how they will work together, how long it will take, how much it will cost, what kind of material will be explored and how they will do this. All these common factors in the therapeutic alliance affect the therapeutic outcome. Summarizing many different conceptions of the alliance concept, Gaston identified four broad dimensions: "the therapeutic alliance, or patient's affective relationship to the therapist ... the working alliance, or patient's capacity to purposefully work in therapy ... the therapist's empathic understanding and involvement ... [and] the patient–therapist agreement on the goals and tasks of treatment."[143]

As Gaston's description makes explicit, and as many scholars have pointed out, the Rogerian and therapeutic alliance explanations are not mutually exclusive.[144] Orlinsky et al. wrote in 1994, "Theoretical interest in the therapeutic alliance ... has continued the movement launched by Carl Rogers's (1957) conception of the therapeutic relationship ..."[145] Wampold wrote in 2001, "Empathy and the formation of the working alliance, for example, are intricately and inextricably connected."[146] For a striking example of this, we can look to Burns and Nolen-Hoeksema's study on the role of empathy as one component of the therapeutic alliance when using cognitive behavioral therapy for the treatment of depression. They reported:

> The patients of therapists who were the warmest and most empathic improved significantly more than the patients of therapists with the lowest empathy ratings, when controlling for initial depression severity, homework compliance, and other factors. This indicates that even in a highly technical form of therapy such as CBT, the quality of the therapeutic relationship has a substantial impact on the degree of clinical recovery. This is the first report we are aware of that has documented the causal effect of therapeutic empathy on recovery when controlling for the simultaneous causal effect of depression on therapeutic empathy.[147]

The results of their study were so robust that, thereafter, all patients at the medical center where the research was conducted were required to complete a "therapeutic empathy form" after each interview, so that therapists would get timely feedback if their patients perceived a lack of empathy on their part. "Thus, difficulties in the therapeutic alliance can be more rapidly identified and addressed."[148]

Indeed, it is the therapist's empathy, acceptance and genuineness that allow many clients to feel safe enough to enter into a real relationship with the therapist and be willing to develop an implicit or explicit agreement, understanding, or "contract" to engage in therapy. One client-centered therapist, Leslie McCulloch, explained how she was able to establish meaningful counseling relationships with male prisoners with diagnoses of Anti-Social Personality Disorder (ASPD).[149] Prison psychologists had given up on them; they were reluctant or refused to accompany McCulloch on her clinical rounds through the cellblock. On her first visit to the cells, prisoners exposed themselves, urinated, spat toward her and voiced obscenities. On subsequent visits, many inmates stopped these behaviors, began speaking with her, and agreed to participate in counseling sessions. Her fellow psychologists could not understand how she had accomplished this, but her explanation was simple:

> I treated them like human beings. I showed concern and interest while accepting their anger without judging it. I expressed my own limits by telling them that I was distracted by their behavior, that I wanted to give them my full attention, and that I found it difficult to do so when I was distracted. I told them that I valued speaking with them and hoped we would talk when they were not doing these other things.[150]

In this case, the therapist's empathy, unconditional positive regard and congruence made a therapeutic alliance possible. The process is similar in less dramatic cases. The core conditions both facilitate the therapeutic alliance and play an integral part in the therapeutic process. Rogers' core conditions may or may not be necessary or sufficient for effective psychotherapy (the debate is ongoing in the person-centered community), but whether considered among the common factors of effective therapy or a means to achieve a therapeutic alliance, the value of empathy, unconditional positive regard and congruence has been supported by the latest generation of psychotherapy process-outcome research. As Lambert concluded:

> Among the common factors most frequently studied have been those identified by the client-centered school as "necessary and sufficient conditions" for patient personal change: accurate empathy, positive regard, nonpossessive warmth, and congruence or genuineness. Virtually all schools of therapy accept the notion that these or related therapist relationship variables are important for significant progress in psychotherapy and, in fact, fundamental in the formation of a working alliance.[151]

The Therapeutic Relationship and Empirically Supported Treatments

This is not just the conclusion of a few individual scholars or of researchers with a client-centered leaning. At the end of the twentieth century, the Division of Psychotherapy (Division 29) of the American Psychological Association created a distinguished panel to summarize the research on effective therapy relationships.[152] This task force (of whose ten steering committee members none was particularly identified with the client-centered approach) was in part a response to the growing movement, especially in the United States, toward "empirically supported treatments." Federal funding of research on psychotherapy was moving strongly toward identifying those treatment approaches that were shown empirically to be effective, particularly with patients with specific diagnoses—anxiety, depression, drug abuse, and the like. Concerned that this movement essentially ignored thirty or more years of research that demonstrated that treatment approaches made relatively little difference compared to the therapeutic relationship itself, the task force was charged with summarizing the scientific research on the therapy relationship.[153]

Published in a massive volume called *Psychotherapy Relationships That Work* and summarized in their professional journal,[154] the task force's six main conclusions were:

> The therapy relationship makes substantial and consistent contributions to psychotherapy outcome independent of the specific type of treatment.

> Practice and treatment guidelines should explicitly address therapist behaviors and qualities that promote a facilitative therapy relationship.

> Efforts to promulgate practice guidelines or evidence-based lists of effective psychotherapy without including the therapy relationship are seriously incomplete and potentially misleading on both clinical and empirical grounds.

> The therapy relationship acts in concert with discrete interventions, patient characteristics, and clinical qualities in determining treatment effectiveness. A comprehensive understanding of effective (and ineffective) psychotherapy will consider all of these determinants and their optimal combinations.

> Adapting or tailoring the therapy relationship to specific patient needs and characteristics (in addition to diagnosis) enhances the effectiveness of treatment.

> The following list embodies the Task Force conclusions regarding the empirical evidence on General Elements of the Therapy Relationship primarily provided by the psychotherapist.[155]

Evaluating the strength of the various findings, the task force listed qualities and aspects of the therapy relationship according to whether they were: *demonstrably effective* across therapies; *promising and probably effective* across therapies; demonstrably or probably effective with particular types of clients, or not yet shown by research to be effective. The three aspects of the individual therapy relationship shown to be clearly demonstrated by the research were (not in order of importance): the therapeutic alliance, empathy, and goal consensus and collaboration. Aspects of the therapy relationship judged to be promising and probably effective were: positive regard, congruence/genuineness, feedback, repair of alliance ruptures, self-disclosure, management of countertransference, and quality of relational interpretations. The task force leader, referring to the recent Bill Clinton presidential campaign slogan, "It's the economy stupid," quipped that their findings could be summarized by the slogan, "It's the relationship, stupid!"[156]

In fact, said Robert Elliott, the evidence for the importance of the therapeutic relationship as posited by Rogers and others is now so strong that in his, Greenberg and Lietaer's chapter in the fifth edition of Lambert, Bergin and Garfield's prestigeous *Handbook of Psychotherapy and Behavior Change*, "we say it's now unethical … it's no longer scientifically justified not to offer training in experiential humanistic therapies in doctoral and internship training programs," since those therapies have demonstrated how to form a therapeutic relationship with clients.[157]

The Move toward Eclecticism and Integration

Consistent with this large body of research, most therapists in the United States have been moving away from a strict allegiance to specific therapeutic approaches or schools of thought.[158] Surveys of therapists over the past thirty years have demonstrated a growing proportion of practitioners who identify themselves as "eclectic" or "integrative," to the point where "the vast majority of therapists have become eclectic in orientation."[159] In many of these surveys, while a very small percentage of practitioners identify themselves as being primarily person-centered, a significant proportion of counselors, psychotherapists and social workers (typically 25–50%) identify "Rogerian," person-centered, experiential and humanistic methods as being a significant part of their integrative approach. Many more therapists, while not identifying themselves as primarily or partially person-centered, nevertheless incorporate Rogers' core conditions as important ingredients in their work. This was born out by a survey in 2006 of about 2,600 therapists who subscribe to the magazine *Psychotherapy Networker*. While 31% said they utilized a "Rogerian/client-centered/humanistic" approach, when asked "Over the last 25 years, which figures have most influenced your practice?" twenty years after his death, "the single most influential psychotherapist—by a landslide—was Carl Rogers."[160]

Competing Paradigms

After Rogers' death, the major offshoots of client-centered therapy continued to develop and expand. Natalie Rogers' person-centered expressive therapy was described above. Eugene Gendlin's Focusing Institutes have been established throughout Europe and in India, Israel, Japan, Taiwan, Thailand, New Zealand, Australia, Canada, and the United States, greatly expanding the numbers of professionals and laypersons involved in the focusing approach.[161] Focusing advocates can now point to a growing number of empirical research studies that have begun to establish the effectiveness of the approach.[162] Gendlin developed a manual for the focusing approach which is useful for both training and research purposes, as many research protocols today require manualized treatment.[163] Primarily situated outside university settings, it remains to be seen whether the focusing movement will survive Eugene Gendlin, Mary Hendricks and others who continued to promulgate the focusing approach into the twenty-first century.

The process-experiential approach has also flourished, continuing to refine its practice and expand its research base. Interviewed in 2003, Leslie Greenberg and Robert Elliott reflected on the development of the process-experiential movement after Rogers' death.[164] In 1993, their and Laura Rice's book *Facilitating Emotional Change* described the latest refinements in their practice.[165] Robert Elliott, from the University of Toledo, had brought a perspective on training to the work and helped the group develop clearer and more effective procedures for training therapists in the process-experiential approach. This, in turn, helped the researchers specify more clearly the elements of process-experiential therapy, particularly the six major therapist "tasks" in their emotion-focused, experiential model, which are:

> 1. Empathic attunement: Enter and track the client's immediate and evolving experiencing ... 2. Therapeutic bond: Express empathy and genuine prizing ... 3. Task collaboration: Facilitate mutual involvement in goals and tasks of therapy ... 4. Experiential processing: Facilitate optimal client experiential processing (modes of engagement) ... 5. Task completion: Facilitate client completion of key therapeutic tasks ... 6. Growth/choice: Foster client growth and self-determination.[166]

Elliott also brought the skills of meta-analysis to the team, resulting in a number of meta-analyses on the outcomes of client-centered and experiential psychotherapy.[167] Indeed, research has been a major focus in the process-experiential school. In the early nineties Rice and Greenberg received National Institute of Mental Health funding and did a clinical trial comparing client-centered and process experiential therapy for the treatment of depression—the so-called "York 1" study.[168] While clients receiving traditional client-centered therapy fared well, it appeared that those receiving process-experiential therapy fared even better, although the differences did not hold in the follow-up evaluation. A second study ("York 2"), combined with York 1, added enough statistical power to the data analysis to show that the added benefits of process-experiential therapy did last over time.[169] Hence Greenberg argued that process-experiential therapy is a superior approach to client-centered therapy alone. When confronted with the problem of *allegiance*—how a researcher's allegiance to a particular method often unconsciously biases the results in that direction—Greenberg said it was not an issue because he, as one of the main therapists in the study, is a good therapist in both modes and tried to do his very best with clients whether he was doing pure client-centered or process-experiential therapy.

His colleague Elliott did not accept that argument. By definition researchers are often unaware of how their biases influence the outcomes. Hence Elliott said, "I'm really not convinced that process-experiential is better than person-centered/client-centered." Rather, each appeals to different therapists for different reasons, and the therapist should pick the mode he or she is most comfortable with. Some therapists are comfortable with simply *being*, that is embodying the core conditions in the therapeutic relationship. Others, in addition to being empathic, prizing and congruent, feel best when they are *doing*, that is, implementing some of the process-experiential tasks.[170] "We think that doing these additional things adds something to it," said Greenberg. "In my view these more active interventions open people up a lot more quickly to get to deeper material which then you utilize the empathic process to help. It forms an amalgam in which the use of the process experiential method sort of opens things up and gets deeper much quicker. That's what I believe happens."

For this reason Elliott believes the process-experiential approach is useful "to appeal to cognitive-behavioral or psychodynamic people who can't buy the idea of exclusive client-centeredness, but feel the need to *do* something. They like the systematic nature of process-experiential. It kind of packages it and makes it look like something that's more familiar. So this is a good way to bridge the gap between person-centered and other approaches."

The approach continues to evolve. Elliott adopted the term "process guiding" to describe the therapist's role. Greenberg said now they were recognizing the importance of developing a collaborative focus—the focus being the client's identified problems, the ones the client is concerned about, as well as a focus on process goals for the client. "I've moved to a co-constructive view that we're both there, and we are co-creating and it's not that I am just following and you are determining as the client … so it's a much more dialogical view than Rogers proposed theoretically. And that's how I would see the resolution … in dialogue. I can offer and you can refuse. Then I respect your refusal or I engage with your refusal, but it's much more dialogical."

Elliott also described how "we've gone on training students and extending the therapy to other populations, learning more about the training process, learning more about applying the therapy to other kinds of client populations, like PTSD, for example, childhood trauma, abuse in particular … and some of us are beginning to work on other serious client problems, such as borderline personality, schizophrenia, panic." Germain Lietaer observed that this is a necessary trend for the person-centered movement. "If [we] want to have a place in clinical psychology and in psychiatry, I think we will have to write about how to do client-centered therapy with specific problems. So I think that's a turn some people will have to make … process differentiation … And we are doing that already but some are against it …"[171]

As Lietaer's comment implies, not everyone in the person-centered movement has welcomed the developments in process-experiential and focusing therapy with open arms. As we saw, for about two decades these two variations on client-centered therapy developed independently from Rogers and his colleagues' person-centered approach. It was at the first international conference on counseling and psychotherapy in Leuven, Belgium in 1990, organized by Lietaer, that the various schools really confronted one another for the first time. When Greenberg and Rice delivered one of the keynote addresses at the conference in Leuven, some of the reactions to their comments were extremely critical.[172] Barbara Brodley argued their approach wasn't client-centered at all—how could it be, if the therapist was directing the client toward the therapist's process goals for the client? John Shlien said if they wanted to do Gestalt therapy, that was fine; just don't call it client-centered therapy.[173] Tension between the branches of client-centered therapy has remained strong ever since, and not surprisingly, the development of the person-centered approach in counseling and psychotherapy has followed different trajectories in different countries. In Europe, for example, Peter Schmid saw a complex picture of the movements across that continent, with some countries following a more purist, client-centered model, others following the process-experiential version, and others finding their own way.

So I think that there's a strong connection to let's say genuine person-centered ideas in Britain … And on the other end of the thing, there is the Netherlands and the Flemish part of Belgium where there is a shift from Rogerian thinking, and for these people Les Greenberg was as least as important as Carl Rogers was. And, on the other hand, in Italy people are very much connected with California. In Austria we have a connection to the Center for the Study of the Person—they are where our Institute for Person-Centered Studies comes from. From the very beginning our main personal, intellectual connection was Doug Land [Rogers' CSP colleague], and we had a completely different way of developing the person-centered approach which we think is much more interested with Rogers' thinking than for instance the Germans who very much tried to find it on an academic level where their connection to behavior therapy came from. Then there are the Eastern European countries, Middle Eastern countries, former communist countries who besides Eastern Germany, they also had a strong connection to behavior therapy. But the Slavic countries and Hungary—they really started when they had the visit from Rogers. Rogers was in Hungary, Poland, Russia, you know, and they had a very different and slight independent approach from Western Europe. They had not very much literature from Western Europe. So they're much more connected to America than they were to Western European countries. And in France the person-centered approach is already beginning at the moment ... Spain has almost nothing. Portugal is like Italy, a strong connection to California.[174]

Robert Elliott summed it up more succinctly, saying that Holland, Germany and Belgium are oriented toward process-experiential, while the United States, England, and Austria are more traditionally person-centered. Gay Barfield saw France as having a longer and deeper tradition in the person-centered approach, with books by French practitioners like Andre de Peretti, Max Pages and Miguel de la Puente, and the person-centered approach being an officially acknowledged provider of mental health services.[175] Different observers might assess the trends differently, but it is clear that at least in North America and Europe there is a lively tension between the different, major schools of the person-centered approach.

The Future of the Person-Centered Approach

In attempting to assess the current status of Carl Rogers' contributions to counseling and psychotherapy, four indicators of prevalence have been examined. The number of publications on Rogers and the client-centered/person-centered approach has increased substantially since Rogers' death. Person-centered associations, organizations, and training institutes have proliferated around the world. Research on psychotherapy process and outcomes has validated the importance of empathy, unconditional positive regard and probably congruence—Rogers' core conditions for an effective therapeutic relationship. Various approaches within the person-centered movement are flourishing.

By all these indicators, the person-centered approach, which holds the therapeutic relationship as central to effective counseling and psychotherapy and healing in its own right, is alive and well. While relatively few therapists describe themselves as primarily client-centered in their orientation, client-centered principles permeate the practice of many, if not most therapists. Other schools of psychotherapy increasingly are recognizing the importance of the therapeutic relationship as a means to, if not a core aspect of, therapeutic change. The latest generation of research on psychotherapy process and outcomes—whether couched in terms of the core conditions, common factors or the therapeutic/working alliance—has validated many of Carl Rogers' original insights about the importance and nature of an effective therapeutic relationship. In short, the client-centered/person-centered approach appears to be experiencing something of a revival, both in professional activity and academic respectability.

Yet the history of the person-centered approach is still very much unfolding. There is no question that it will continue to exist for the foreseeable future. Not only is it a vibrant and arguably growing movement in psychotherapy and beyond, but as Margaret Warner argued, it is part of human nature to want "to make sense from the inside. Life must make subjective personal sense ..." Thus there will always be a place for the person-centered approach.[176]

While that may be so, what place or how large a place the person-centered approach plays in the field of psychotherapy and beyond will, I believe, be determined by how four major issues or questions are addressed: What does it mean to be "person-centered"? How big should the umbrella covering person-centered orientations be? Who will carry on the research and training in future generations? Will person-centered therapists accommodate the needs of government regulators, funding sources, and insurance companies?

As we have seen, there remain significant disagreements as to what constitutes a person-centered approach to counseling and psychotherapy, education, and other endeavors. For every person who would say that to be a person-centered therapist in the tradition of Carl Rogers one must avoid all forms of directiveness or therapeutic "activities," another would say that the person-centered therapist can combine the core conditions of empathy, positive regard and congruence with other techniques and orientations. As the Austrian psychotherapist and author Gerhard Stumm pointed out, the person-centered approach is often combined with other approaches such as Reinhard Tausch's use of relaxation techniques, Garry Prouty's "pre-therapy" interventions, Natalie Rogers' person-centered expressive therapy, or the use of Gestalt techniques in process-experiential therapy. Stumm said, "You can put the parts together like a good bouquet of flowers. If done well, it looks beautiful."[177] Others would say, whether or not it looks beautiful, it isn't client-centered therapy.

Similarly in education, to what extent can a teacher remain person-centered and still provide information, skill development, requirements, evaluation and other forms of structure for students? Thomas Gordon's Teacher Effectiveness Training model arguably taught a million or more teachers the skills of "I messages, active listening and no-lose conflict resolution"—skills that were highly consistent with the core conditions.[178] (Gordon's *Parent Effectiveness Training*, *Teacher Effectiveness Training* and other books sold five million copies worldwide!)[179] Robert Carkhuff's Human Technology, which included his Helping Model and Training Technology, was also a demonstrably effective method for teaching human relations and counseling skills to counselors, teachers, and parents.[180] Rogers was most skeptical of such efforts, fearing they reduced the person-centered approach to techniques rather than a way of being. He did not cite Gordon's or Carkhuff's highly influential work as contributing to the person-centered approach. Yet as evidence for the effectiveness of the person-centered approach in education, Rogers regularly cited and lauded Aspy and Roebuck's research which demonstrated the effectiveness of skill training, including Carkhuff's approach.[181] In that sense, Rogers was ambivalent himself as to what constituted a person-centered approach in that field. Surely in the different editions of *Freedom to Learn*, his case studies suggested that a person-centered approach could include a wide variety of teaching techniques, including some traditional ones. So what exactly does it mean to be person-centered in education?

The same dilemma presents itself in large group facilitation. At the Carl Rogers Symposium in California in 2002, the organizers planned one evening using the "open space technology" model. The idea was that participants would post topics of interest on newsprint; other participants would sign up for those topics; and then everyone would move to rooms or areas where each group would pursue its area of interest. For many participants this was too much imposed structure for a person-centered community. They argued that, instead, the whole group should experience a non-structured, person-centered community meeting in which any organizational structure would grow naturally out of the group process. A large minority withdrew from the open space plan and held their own person-centered community meeting (which, ironically, was entirely consistent with the open space model). There we were: over two hundred person-centered experts and practitioners that evening, with a significant disagreement over what it meant to be person-centered in a large group.[182]

What, then, *does* it mean to be person-centered? If person-centered therapists might be seen doing many different types of therapy, what if anything do they have in common? Germain Lietaer distinguished between "first order" and "second order" aspects of the therapist's role. First order characteristics are the main aspects of the approach's identity. These characteristics all involve the therapist's focus on the experiencing self, that is: moment-to-moment empathy, a high level of personal presence, an egalitarian dialogical stance, and a belief in the crucial importance of the Rogerian therapist conditions. Second order features are characteristic of but less central and not necessarily unique to the person-centered approach. These include: a conception of persons as self-actualizing, having a margin of freedom, basically social, and tending to balance autonomy and belonging, and a conception of the person-centered relationship as being holistic rather than symptom driven, and focused on positive growth.[183] For Lietaer, then, it is the *experiential* elements that are more central to person-centered experiential approach than the person-centered aspects. Peter Schmid would reverse that ordering, believing that its conception of the human person is the starting point for defining the person-centered approach. He says that "the distinguishing characteristics of a *person*-centered approach can be stated in the following three short sentences: 1. Client and therapist spring from a fundamental 'We.' 2. The client comes first. 3. The therapist is present."[184] These two examples alone illustrate how defining what it means to be person-centered is a significant challenge to counseling and psychotherapy and other fields.

The prior question leads to another: how large should the umbrella be that encompasses person-centered approaches? Just how many "united colors," to use Lietaer's phrase, can fit within the rainbow? The question can be framed as earlier, conceptualizing person-centered therapy as either traditional client-centered therapy or expanding its meaning to allow focusing therapy, process-experiential therapy, or other integrative therapies under the person-centered tent. Thus there are those who would stick to the label of person-centered therapy, while others prefer "person-centered experiential" therapy, while others would follow the title of world journal, *Person-Centered and Experiential Psychotherapies*. Less important than agreeing on a single label is the question of whether and how these different sub-orientations of the person-centered approach can work together—not only the client-centered, focusing, and process experiential schools, but other approaches like those of Natalie Rogers, Garry Prouty, Rainer Sachse's "clarification-orientated psychotherapy," and other current and yet-to-be-invented variations on client-centered therapy.[185] The future of the person-centered approach will be determined, in part, by whether the various orientations can develop a synergy that multiplies their individual efforts—as Margaret Warner put it, "one nation, many tribes"[186]—or whether, as in Rogers' lifetime, they go their more or less separate ways.

Others like Germain Lietaer have gone a step further. He argued that other humanistic, experiential psychotherapies, such as the existential, Gestalt, interpersonal, and psychodrama approaches, share important characteristics with person-centered therapy and are clearly distinguishable from psychodynamic and cognitive-behavior therapies. He and others have suggested that it might be wise for a number of the humanistic experiential schools that have legitimacy and research evidence to support their effectiveness to join together under the *experiential* or *humanistic* label. Only in such a confederation will they achieve the size and influence to counter the power of the psychodynamic and cognitive-behavioral schools.[187] If the third force in psychology is to be a real *force*, this argument goes, the umbrella must widen beyond the explicitly person-centered approaches. Looking ahead, then, it is unclear whether the client-centered/person-centered approach will remain a separate and distinct orientation in psychotherapy, or whether its expansion to the person-centered-experiential approach, as advocated by many leading person-centered scholars and researchers today, will become the accepted, wider orientation, *or* whether the person-centered-experiential movement will be subsumed under the more general heading of humanistic psychotherapies as others advocate.

Whatever schools are to be included under the person-centered umbrella, who will carry on the tradition of research and training? Rogers' students in the

U.S. (and many of *their* students) are now deceased or retired or close to retirement. The same could be said of many of the leaders in the person-centered movement around the world—Dave Mearns in Scotland, Brian Thorne in Great Britain, Reinhard Tausch in Germany, Germain Lietaer in Belgium, Minoru Hatase and Haruko Tsuge in Japan, Godfrey Barrett-Lennard in Australia and many others. This list will only grow longer. Is there another generation and another beyond that to assume the leadership in research and training that keeps a movement alive and well?

In the process-experiential branch of the person-centered approach the current answer seems to be affirmative. Robert Elliott, when interviewed in 2003 was fifty-three years old. He pointed out that Leslie Greenberg, a few years older, and he were still going strong and that there were a good number of younger people who were carrying on the tradition of research and training in this approach.[188] He pointed to the new book by himself, Jeanne Watson, Rhonda Goldman and Leslie Greenberg, *Learning Emotion-Focused Therapy: The Process-Experiential Approach to Change*, as an example.[189] Within the other schools of the person-centered approach and within each country that the person-centered approach has a significant presence, the same question pertains. As much as any other factor, having strong leadership in universities, training institutes and leading professional associations will determine the future of the person-centered approach. Will a new generation of such leadership be in place and ready to accept the challenge?

Finally, the ability of proponents to fulfill the expectations of government regulators, funders, and insurance providers will determine the future of the person-centered approach. The German experience provides a good example of this. At one point there were 7,500 members in GwG, the German Association for Person-Centered Psychotherapy.[190] Then the government took the association's ability to certify its members away, and membership dropped precipitously to 4,000. Around 2002, government certification was restored, in large part because the association was able to present a strong research case to support person-centered practice. The free fall of membership stopped and has even begun to grow slowly again, with about 4,500 members in 2003. At present, the association is now fighting for insurance reimbursement. If achieved, they expect their numbers to grow still further. German associations work a bit differently than those in the United States; but the point is essentially the same everywhere. Well-organized training programs, training manuals, evidence on general effectiveness, evidence of efficacy with specific diagnoses, and other trappings of established practice are often and, arguably, increasingly required for government agencies and insurance companies to license, fund and reimburse client-centered therapists. The situation is often similar in education, where evidence of successful outcomes, including higher test scores, is needed to convince administrators and government regulators to support or fund particular practices. If person-centered therapists, educators and other helping professionals need or want credibility among the powers that be, as Robert Elliott put it, they will have to "render unto Caesar" that which the regulators require.[191]

It may be decades before these questions are resolved. At least until then, the person-centered approach is still evolving. It is a vibrant international movement with burgeoning publications, organizations, research, theories, orientations, applications, and adherents. It has significant challenges to face if its renaissance is to continue, but clearly, it has survived its founder.

Yet, I suspect, Carl Rogers *personally* always will remain the foundation of the person-centered, humanistic, and positive psychology movements. Over a sixty-year career, through his live example, tapes and videos, and prolific writings, he became the archetypal father figure of humanistic psychology and the symbol of person-centeredness for several generations of helping professionals. Even as we understand the more complex personality that was Carl Rogers, he still exemplified the core conditions of congruence, positive regard and empathy and the fully functioning person. Even as new research and the hindsight of history may reveal limitations in his own formulation of the person-centered approach, some of the basic tenets he postulated and his personal example will likely endure as the foundation and inspiration for future generations of persons and professionals of many diverse orientations.

The extent to which the person-centered approach will permeate the psychological and helping professions of the future will be influenced, in part, by how much society values the outcomes that a person-centered approach to education and human development produces. In that light, it is uncertain how far societies will accept and encourage Rogers' "person of tomorrow." While Rogers may have personified the fully functioning person he espoused, it remains to be seen whether his vision of unfolding human potential becomes an increasingly accepted social ideal or a historical aberration. Will qualities of openness, authenticity and change be increasingly valued, at least by those who have the luxury of choice? Will men and women increasingly rely on "a trust in their inner experiencing" and "the authority within," or will political, economic, social and environmental upheavals and insecurity cause nations to gravitate toward increasingly authoritarian and fundamentalist forms of leadership? Will the behavioral sciences be used, as Rogers often put it, to empower or enslave humankind? Will individuals inexorably strive for self-determination and individuality—or willingly "escape from freedom"?[192] Whatever the outcomes, Rogers clearly outlined the issues and choices and, through his life and work, presented one vivid model for *becoming* a person.

ENDNOTES

Abbreviations

CR   Carl Rogers
HR   Helen Rogers
DR   David Rogers
NR   Natalie Rogers
LOC   Library of Congress
UCSB   University of California, Santa Barbara
   /CR   Carl Rogers Collection
   /R-K   Rogers-Kirschenbaum Collection
   /B   Barfield Collection

Preface

1. CR, letter to author, June 20, 1986. He also shared these sentiments with me verbally.
2. The LOC papers have no restrictions on access. Some of his notebooks at UCSB are restricted to the public, but following Rogers' instructions, were made available to me.
3. Natalie Rogers, author interview, March 27, 2003.
4. Cohen, 1997.
5. CR, letter to author, January 3, 1987.
6. CR, *A Way of Being*, 1980b: 80.

Chapter 1

1. Genealogical information from author interviews with Margaret Rogers, October 1972; transcript of interview between Wesley Westman and CR, September 15, 1962, unpublished, UCSB/R-K; and *The Rogers Family: Dates and Stories as Compiled by Margaret G. Rogers: 1st installment, 1981, 2nd installment, 1982, 3rd installment, 1983*, unpublished. LOC, Box 4, Folder 10.
2. Margaret Rogers, *This I Remember*, unpublished family reminiscences, n.d. LOC 4/10.
3. James S. Cushing, *Genealogy of the Cushing Family* (1st ed.). Montreal: Perrault Printing Co., 1877, privately printed. LOC 4/10.
4. Ibid.
5. *The Wisconsin Alumni Magazine, 23*, 7 (May, 1922): 232.
6. CR, 1967a, says two years. Margaret Rogers' "Julia Margaret Cushing Rogers—My Mother," essay attached to Cushing *Genealogy*, says "Mother left college after her Junior year to be married."
7. From a clipping in Margaret Rogers' scrapbook-album.
8. Address from Margaret Rogers, *This I Remember*, op. cit. (n. 2).
9. Philadelphia: Charles Foster, 1873.

10. Unless otherwise noted, sources for the remainder of the chapter are CR's autobiographical essay (1967a), author interviews with CR, March, 1971, especially tape 7, and the Westman interview, op. cit. (n. 1).

11. Leicester Hemingway, *My Brother Ernest Hemingway* (p. 21) (Sarasota, FL: Pineapple Press, 1996).

12. Michael Reynolds, High Culture and Low: Oak Park Before the Great War, in James Nagel (Ed.), *Ernest Hemingway: The Oak Park Legacy* (p. 26) (Tuscaloosa, University of Alabama Press, 1996).

13. Tom McNamee, Oak Park Maps Out Proud Literary Tradition, *Chicago Sun–Times*, October 17, 1983: 16. LOC 4/10.

14. Descriptions of the Oak Park home and Glen Ellyn farm are enhanced from viewing photographs in the family albums, in Natalie Rogers' possession in 2002.

15. CR to Valerie Henderson. Henderson, author interview, 2003.

16. HR, 1965.

17. Unless otherwise noted, recollections attributed to Margaret Rogers come from author interviews with Margaret Rogers, October, 1972.

18. Rogers & Russell, 2002: 24.

19. *Sinking* in Westman, p. 2 and author interviews. Neither CR nor the author could find any reference information for this title. Perhaps it was E.M.H. Edwards, *Commander William Barker Cushing of the United States Navy* (New York: F. Tennyson Neely, 1898) or Theron Wilber Haight, *Three Wisconsin Cushings: A Sketch of the Lives of Howard B., Alonzo H. and William B. Cushing, Children of a Pioneer Family of Waukesha County* (Wisconsin History Commission, April, 1910), the latter of which Walter Rogers had in his library in 1972. There is also a later biography of Cushing: R.J. Roske & C. Van Doren, *Lincoln's Commando: The Biography of Commander W.B. Cushing, U.S.N.* (New York: Harper & Bros, 1957).

20. Westman interview: 11.

21. Rogers & Russell, 2002: 25–26.

22. All recollections attributed to John Rogers come from John Rogers' correspondence with author, February 25, 1975.

23. Westman interview: 11.

24. CR, 1967a.

25. All recollections attributed to Walter Rogers come from author interview with Walter Rogers, 1975.

26. Author interview, March 1971, tape 7; see also Rogers & Russell, 2002: 39.

27. See anecdote in Chapter 10 where Carl virtually severed relations with his brother over a sarcastic jibe.

28. L.E. Grimes, Hemingway's Religious Odyssey: The Oak Park Years, in Nagel, op. cit.: 38 (n. 12).

29. Both quotations from Rogers & Russell, 2002: 24.

30. Grimes, op. cit. (n. 28).

31. Buggies and electric car, Walter Rogers interview.

32. First and third parts of quotation, CR, 1967a: 344; paraphrased quotation, CR, 1972b, in CR, 1980b: 28.

33. Rogers & Russell, 2002: 28.

34. Walter Cushing Rogers, letter to his daughter Margaret Rogers Lovallo, September 1974. LOC 1/4.

35. Margaret Rogers, *This I Remember*, op. cit. (n. 2).

36. HR, 1965: 94.

37. CR, letter to author, April 12, 1972.

38. CR, 1967a: 345.

39. Virgil E. Tipton, John Rogers of Bates and Rogers—A Legend in His Own Time. *The Builder*, Summer 1985 (pub. of the Associated General Contractors of Illinois): 12–15. LOC 1/1. Bates had dropped out of the business a few years after it began, so it was essentially Rogers' company.

40. Walter Rogers interview.

41. Walter Cushing Rogers to Margaret Rogers Lovallo, op. cit. (n. 34).

42. CR, 1961a: 6.

43. Many images of the farm from photographs in family albums in possession of Natalie Rogers in 2002.

44. Margaret Rogers, *This I Remember*, op. cit. (n. 2).

45. Although his class once came to the farm for a picnic. Rogers & Russell, 2002: 34.

46. CR, 1967a: 348.

47. Walter Rogers interview; Ross died in his thirties, Westman interview: 3.

48. John Rogers correspondence.

49. Rogers & Russell, 2002: 27.

50. Tasks described in CR, 1967a: 347.

51. March 24, 1920 entry in Rogers' unpublished diary with a gray cover, hereinafter referred to as the "Gray Diary." UCSB/R-K.

52. CR, 1967a: 346–347; also described in Westman interview: 11–13. In Rogers & Russell, 2002: 35, he describes his first experience of the moths as "an awesome thing. I suppose it was kind of a religious experience" and says he read a book by the French entomologist Fabre.

53. CR, 1967a: 347.

54. John Rogers correspondence.

55. Rogers & Hart, 1970: 506. This was a 1966 interview.

56. Rogers & Russell, 2002: 37.

57. CR, letter to author, April 12, 1972.

58. Rogers & Russell, 2002: 32.

59. "Camp Grant Cantonment," *Twenty-Fifth Milestone*, n.d. Booklet describing the history of Bates and Rogers Company. LOC 4/1.

60. Rogers & Russell, 2002: 41.

61. CR, 1967a: 348.

62. Rogers & Hart, 1970: 502.

63. Information from oratorical contest program in family album in possession of Natalie Rogers, 2002.

64. N.d. This unpublished diary had a brown felt cover and hereinafter is referred to as the "Brown Diary."

65. Walter Cushing Rogers to Margaret Rogers Lovallo, op. cit. (n. 34).

66. Brown Diary, July 9, 1919.

67. Brown Diary, August 13, 1919.

68. Quotations from Rogers & Russell, 2002: 45, 44, 40, respectively.

69. Ibid.: 45.

70. Brown Diary, September 3, 1919.

Chapter 2

1. "The freshman class of 1919 had approximately 2,376 students out of a total enrollment of 7,294; because of the war there were far fewer upper classmen." David Null, University of Wisconsin-Madison Archivist, personal email communication to Stephen Demanchick, September 16, 2005.

2. CR, 1967a: 348–349.
3. CR, 1961a: 6–7.
4. CR, 1967a: 349. CR reflects more on Humphrey in Rogers & Russell, 2002: 54.
5. Gray Diary, February 6, 1920.
6. CR, 1967a: 349.
7. Brown Diary, October. 5, 1919.
8. Brown Diary, November 13, 1919.
9. B. Thorne, Biographical Introduction, in Rogers & Russell, 2002: 4.
10. Gray Diary, "Plans for 1920," undated.
11. Gray Diary, Dec. 30, 1919–January 4, 1920.
12. Brown Diary, June 26, 1921.
13. Brown Diary, June 26, 1921.
14. CR, author interview, March, 1971, tape 3.
15. Rogers & Russell, 2002: 51–52.
16. The "Campus Notes" section of the *Wisconsin Alumni Magazine, 23*, 4 (February 1922): 133, announced that Rogers and Helen Kasbeer had been chosen "as two of the four undergraduate delegates-at-large from the United States," so apparently graduate students and/or other youth were also represented among the 10 delegates.
17. Sowers correspondence, October. 30, 1972; see also D. Davis & M. Duclos, *A Teacher for All Seasons: A Biography of Ray V. Sowers* (DeLand, FL: Dept. of Education, Stetson University, 1971).
18. Gray Diary, January 8, 1922.
19. CR, July 10, 1922 entry in an unpublished journal of observations and reflections on his trip to the Orient, hereinafter known as the "China Diary." Rogers archive, UCSB.
20. China Diary, February 15, 1922.
21. Rogers & Russell, 2002: 56.
22. China Diary, February 27, 1922.
23. China Diary, n.d. and February 16 and 24, 1922, respectively.
24. CR, "A Day in My Life." Mimeographed letter describing November 5, 1970. Unpublished.
25. China Diary, February 25, 1922.
26. China Diary, February 26, 1922.
27. China Diary, July 12, 1922.
28. Walter Rogers interview.
29. Gray Diary, November 13, 1922.
30. CR, 1967a: 351.
31. CR, 1922: 1–2. CR also wrote a shorter piece for the *Wisconsin Alumni Magazine, 24*, 2 (December, 1922), entitled "Wisconsin in China," in which he described how he met several Wisconsin alumni doing important work in China, such as John Childs, 1911, and Ray Sweetman, 1913. "John Childs is doing a wonderful piece of work in Peking. It is regarded by nearly everyone as the finest piece of student Christian work done in China. He has succeeded in uniting all the churches and the Y.M.C.A. and under their combined auspices forming the Peking Student Union, which is composed of and managed by the students of Peking" (p. 45).
32. China Diary, April 10, 1922.
33. China Diary, n.d.
34. See Jan Francis' biographical sketch in Rogers & Russell, 2002: 311.
35. China Diary, April 15, May 17, March 12, May 11, March 26, 1922, respectively.
36. China Diary, May 17 and March 27, 1922, respectively.
37. China Diary, June 20, 1922.
38. China Diary, April 26, 1922.

39. China Diary, July 17, 1922.
40. Gray Diary, July 12, 1922.
41. Rogers & Russell, 2002: 60.
42. CR, 1936a: 8.
43. Gray Diary, July 12, 1922.
44. China Diary, July 10, 1922.
45. Gray Diary, July 12, 1922.
46. China Diary, June 13, 1922.
47. China Diary, March 27, 1922.
48. Ironically, more than 80 years later there is still debate about the multicultural sensitivity and applicability of Rogers' person-centered approach. See discussion in Chapter 13.
49. Rogers & Russell, 2002: 70.
50. China Diary, "Meridian Day, 1922."
51. CR, 1967a: 352.
52. Walter Rogers interview.
53. CR, letter to author, March 26, 1976. $85 also in CR, "Some Autobiographical Omissions," which contains anecdotes not included in CR, 1967a.
54. CR, 1967a: 352.
55. CR, 1967a: 352.
56. Walter Rogers interview.
57. Ibid.
58. Rogers & Russell, 2002: 73.
59. CR, "The Soul of a Troubadour: A Psychological Study of St. Francis of Assisi," undated: 4–5. This and other college papers in UCSB/R-K.
60. CR, "The Development of Luther's Idea of Authority in Religion, 1518–1519," January 15, 1923: 17–18.
61. Rogers & Russell, 2002: 76.
62. Ibid.: 74.
63. Rogers, 1967a: 351.
64. The 1925 yearbook (which then covered seniors from the previous graduating class) listed the following activities and honors for Rogers: "Alpha Kappa Lambda—Sophomore High Honors—Phi Kappa Phi—Phi Beta Kappa—Y.M.C.A. Cabinet 3, Vice-President 3; Secretary Sophomore Commissioners—Intercollegiate Debate 3."
65. Sowers correspondence, October 30, 1972.
66. CR, Some Autobiographical Omissions: 5–6; also author interview, tape 36. UCSB/R-K papers.
67. CR, 1972a: 21.
68. Rogers & Russell, 2002: 77.
69. CR, 1967a: 349.
70. CR, 1972a: 21–22.
71. Rogers & Russell, 2002: 78. Also photograph in family album in Natalie Rogers' possession, 2002.
72. Brown Diary, June 19, 1921.
73. Gray Diary, November 15, 1921.
74. Gray Diary, December 7, 1922.
75. Gray Diary, January 8, 1922.
76. CR, taped response to author, dictated October 31, 1971, tape 2.
77. HR, letter to author, November 29, 1971.
78. Gray Diary, July 12, 1922.
79. Gray Diary, November 13, 1922.

80. Ibid.

81. CR, 1972a: 22.

82. HR, letter to author, January 17, 1972. Love letters in UCSB archive.

83. Gray Diary, February 26, 1922.

84. Gray Diary, September 17, 1922.

85. HR, letter to author, January 17, 1972.

86. CR, letter to author, March 26, 1976. CR corrects previous references to a Model T in Rogers & Russell, 2002: 82.

Chapter 3

1. CR, 1967a: 353.

2. CR, 1972a: 22.

3. CR, letter to author, March 15, 1977.

4. Ibid.

5. HR, 1965: 95.

6. CR, 1967a: 353.

7. Both quotations, CR, 1967a: 353. Wedding gift from author interview, January 25, 1975, tape 12.

8. Westman interview: 31.

9. CR, 1967a: 354.

10. Ibid.

11. CR, 1967a: 353.

12. Ibid.

13. CR, Second Paper for Systematic Theology 1, n.d.: 3.

14. CR, A Comparison of Certain Christian Leaders, for Church History 9, n.d.: 10–11. Both papers in UCSB/R-K.

15. CR, 1967a: 354.

16. E.g., G. Watson, *Social Psychology: Issues and Insights* (Philadelphia: J.B. Lippincott, 1966). Watson was also human relations trainer with the National Training Laboratories and a founder of Union Graduate School and the Union for Experimenting Colleges and Universities. See P. Flint obituary, "Dr. Goodwin Watson; Taught at Columbia," *New York Times*, January 5, 1977. See also Rogers & Russell, 2002: 315.

17. Rogers & Russell, 2002: 89. Here CR said the course was named "Ways of Working with Young People."

18. CR, Three Stories of Creation, July 19, 1925. This and ten other sermons in UCSB/R-K.

19. CR, sermon delivered in East Dorset, Vermont. Untitled, n.d.: 2.

20. CR, Some Autobiographical Omissions: 7. UCSB/R-K.

21. Rogers & Russell, 2002: 81.

22. A Brief History of Columbia, <www.tc.columbia.edu/aboutc>, retrieved November 3, 2004.

23. Rogers & Hart, 1970: 503.

24. Cremin, 1961: 220.

25. CR, 1967a: 355.

26. CR, "The Problem of Worship in Modern Religious Education," a term paper probably written in the fall semester of his second year at Union. This and other papers and examinations at Union in UCSB/R-K.

27. CR, Examination written for Religious Education 22, May 7, 1926.

28. Ibid.

29. Newcomb correspondence, 1972.

30. CR, Examination written for Religious Education 22, op. cit. (n. 27).

31. CR, 1967a: 354–355.

32. CR, note on author's manuscript, n.d.

33. CR, Some Autobiographical Omissions: 8; also in Westman interview: 36–37.

34. Ibid.: 8–9.

35. This would have been G.V.T. Hamilton, *A Research in Marriage* (New York: Lear, 1929).

36. CR, 1972a: 23–24.

37. HR, 1965: 95.

38. CR, author interview, 1971.

39. Quotations from CR, 1967a: 356; thumb sucking from Rogers & Russell, 2002: 83.

40. Quotation and next two anecdotes from CR, letter to author, March 15, 1977.

41. Louis Cohen, The Academic Department, in Freedheim, 1992: 743. Cohen cites Fernberger (1932), but Fernberger's graph (p. 5) shows a 1926 membership of about 500 and Fernberger does not discuss members' degrees. Fernberger shows that in 1930 there were 530 members (Ph.D. and two publications beyond dissertation required) and 571 associate members ("interested in the advancement of Psychology as a science"), and indicates that Columbia presented more papers at APA conventions than any other university.

42. Watson correspondence, 1972.

43. CR, 1967a: 355–356.

44. Ibid.: 355.

45. Author interview, March 1971.

46. CR, 1967a: 356; Rogers & Hart, 1970: 503.

47. Watson correspondence, 1972.

48. CR, 1967a: 356.

49. CR, 1969a: 192.

50. June 1. Important Events in the Life of Carl Rogers. In Thorne, 2003: 123.

51. CR, 1967a: 356.

52. Ibid.

53. Newcomb correspondence, 1971.

54. CR, 1967a: 356.

55. The Rorschach was a projective personality test interpreting subjects' descriptions of ten inkblot images. See D. Levy, The Use of Play Technic as Experimental Procedure, *American Journal of Orthopsychiatry, 3* (July 1933).

56. CR, 1967a: 357; Rogers & Hart, 1970: 503.

57. CR, 1931a: 4 and 26.

58. Cremin, 1961.

59. CR, 1967a: 357.

60. Rogers & Russell, 2002: 102. Rogers was referring to research which would have operationalized the concepts and systematically and statistically measured the variables of treatment and their outcomes.

61. Previous three examples from "Experience" section of an application Rogers later wrote for a position in Washington, DC, n.d., c. 1934. The test names are taken directly from a psychological examination Rogers administered to a child on November 11, 1929, after moving to Rochester. It is assumed that he had used most of these tests in his training at the Institute for Child Guidance.

62. CR, 1967: 357.

63. See, e.g., Ansbacher, 1990, and Watts, 1998. The former quotes Rogers as saying, "I was shocked by Dr. Adler's very direct and deceptively simple manner of immediately relating to the child and the parent. It took me some time to realize how much I had learned from him." He said this over 50 years later, never having mentioned any influence of Adler or his

ideas in between; while simultaneously he was often very explicit about many other influences, including Rank. Perhaps some unconscious memory trace of Adler later influenced Rogers, but I consider it more plausible to attribute this statement to Rogers' tendency, late in life, to be flattered when his work was compared to other great figures in psychology and to graciously try to build bridges between their work and his. In his oral history, shortly before his death, when Rogers was asked about Adler, he gave no indication there was any influence. Rogers & Russell, 2002: 104–105.

64. CR, author interview, tape 1.
65. CR, 1967a: 7.
66. CR, 1931a.
67. Rogers & Russell, 2002: 100.
68. CR, 1931a: 14.
69. Snodgrass, 1984: 332.
70. CR, 1961a. See Healy, 1915; Healy & Bonner, 1926.
71. Rogers & Russell, 2002: 101.
72. CR, 1931a: 64–65.
73. C. Johnson, Y.M.C.A. Press, personal communication, March 3, 1972. Attempts in 2002 failed to locate the successor of Y.M.C.A. Press to see if the test is still in print. Probably it is not.
74. New York: John Wiley & Sons: 124–125.
75. Westman interview: 33.
76. CR, Some Autobiographical Omissions: 9.
77. Population, retrieved from <www.census.gov/population/documentation/twps0027/tab16.txt>, November 3, 2004.
78. HR, 1965: 95; Rogers & Russell, 2002: 107–108.
79. CR, Some Autobiographical Omissions: 9–10.
80. CR, author interview, January 25, 1972, tape 12.

Chapter 4

1. Louis Cohen, The Academic Department, in Freedheim (1992): 743. Cohen was citing statistics from Fernberger, 1932.
2. Cremin, 1961; J. Marmor, The Evolution of an Analytic Psychotherapist: A Sixty-Year Search for Conceptual Clarity in the Tower of Babel, in J.K. Zeig (Ed.), *The Evolution of Psychotherapy: The Third Conference* (pp. 23–33) (New York: Brunner/Mazel, 1997); Vandenbos et al., 1992: 67.
3. E.A. Ferguson, *Social Work: An Introduction.* (2nd ed.) (Philadelphia: Lippincott, 1969).
4. Vandenbos et al., 1992: 73.
5. L.G. Lowrey & G. Smith, *The Institute for Child Guidance: 1927–1933* (p. 3) (New York: Commonwealth Fund, 1933), cited in Vandenbos et al., 1992: 72; see also Snodgrass, 1984.
6. N. Ridenour, *Mental Health in the United States: A Fifty-Year History* (p. 38) (Cambridge, MA: Harvard University Press for the Commonwealth Fund, 1961), cited in Vandenbos et al., 1992: 72.
7. *The Rochester Society for the Prevention of Cruelty to Children—A Children's Bureau for Monroe County, January 1, 1933 – December 31, 1933.* Annual Report, 44 pp. Further information in CR, "The 'Problem Children' of a Community. Thesis submitted as part of Examination for Senior Social Economist, Children's Bureau, Department of Labor, Washington, D.C.," n.d., c. 1934.
8. *From Our Files, Annual Report for the Year 1937*, Child Study Department, Rochester Society

for the Prevention of Cruelty to Children: 5.

9. CR, 1933: 27–28.
10. Ibid.: 32.
11. CR, 1939a: 3.
12. CR, 1967a: 358.
13. CR, 1972b, in CR, 1980a: 35.
14. Bennett & Rogers, 1941.
15. Healy, 1915.
16. Bennett & Rogers, 1941.
17. CR, 1939a: 60.
18. Rogers & Russell, 2002: 114.
19. CR, 1939a: 367–368.
20. CR, 1967a: 381; see also Rogers & Hart, 1970: 504.
21. Research program, CR, 1937b; other clinics, CR, 1939a: 148–150.
22. CR, 1933: 24.
23. Ibid.: 28–29.
24. Ibid.: 29.
25. Ibid.: 32–33.
26. Ibid.: 25.
27. Ibid.: 32.
28. CR, 1939a: 74.
29. CR, 1931: 535.
30. CR, 1939a: 5.
31. Ibid.: 274.
32. Ibid.: 175.
33. CR, 1937b.
34. CR, 1939a: 280.
35. Ibid.: 279.
36. Ibid.: 322.
37. In Rogers' early writings almost all the case studies presented are case studies of boys. This has several possible explanations. All of Rogers' camp and group experiences had been in boys' camps and groups. The excellent foster home Rogers wrote about most frequently was a foster home for boys. Boys far outnumbered girls in referrals to the Rochester S.P.C.C. Although these factors partially explain the imbalance, Rogers did have considerable experience working with girls, too. So one is left wondering. Interestingly, once he began to work primarily with adults, this phenomenon disappeared, and case studies of women appear in his writings as frequently as or more frequently than studies of men.
38. CR, 1937a: 238.
39. CR, 1939a: 291–292.
40. Ibid.: 296.
41. Ibid.: 185–186.
42. Ibid.: 298.
43. S.W. Hartwell, *Fifty-Five Bad Boys* (pp. 19, 21) (New York: Alfred Knopf, 1931). Cited in CR, 1939a: 299.
44. CR, 1939a: 301.
45. CR, 1967a; CR, author interview, tape 3, 1971.
46. CR, author interview, tape 3, 1971.
47. CR, 1939a: 301.
48. Johnson correspondence, 1972.
49. CR, 1939a: 300.

50. Ibid.
51. Ibid.
52. Ibid.: 303.
53. Ibid.: 310.
54. Author interview, March 1971, tape 3.
55. CR, 1939a: 320–321.
56. The student was Virginia Axline. See Chapter 5.
57. CR, 1946c.
58. CR, 1939a: 333.
58. Ibid.
60. CR, 1939a: 338.
61. Hall & Lindzey, 1957.
62. CR, 1939a: 334.
63. CR, 1937a: 235.
64. Ibid.
65. CR, 1967a.
66. CR, 1939a: 332.
67. Rochester S.P.C.C. Annual Report, 1933, op. cit.: 18 (n. 7).
68. *From Our Files*, 1937: 19.
69. *At Work with Children and Their Problems: Annual Report of the Child Study Department of the S.P.C.C., 1932–1933*: 4, 6.
70. CR, 1967a: 359.
71. CR, author interview, 1971, tape 4.
72. CR, 1939a: 322–323.
73. Ibid.: 324.
74. Rogers & Russell, 2002: 108.
75. E.g., Healy, 1915 and Healy & Bonner, 1926.
76. Actually sexuality was the area about which Healy differed most with Freud. "He had reservations about the sexual emphasis in Freudian theories." Snodgrass, 1984: 335. In his recollection, Rogers may have overemphasized the prominence Healy gave to sexual conflict as a causal factor in delinquency.
77. CR, 1961a: 10.
78. Ibid.: 10–11.
79. Ibid.: 11–12.
80. S. Freud, Further Recommendations in the Technique of Psychoanalysis. Chap. XXXI in *Collected Papers*. London: Hogarth Press, 1924. Quoted in Raskin, 1948: 94.
81. Raskin, 1948: 95.
82. CR, 1967a; Rogers & Hart, 1970; Rogers & Russell, 2002: 111–14.
83. Kramer, 1995b.
84. R. Kramer (ed.), *Otto Rank: A Psychology of Difference: The American Lectures* (p. xv) (Princeton, NJ: Princeton University Press, 1996).
85. CR, 1967a: 360.
86. Raskin, 1948: 95–96.
87. Rank, 1945. Cited in Raskin, 1948: 96.
88. Ibid.: 97.
89. Rogers recalled 2 days. Rogers & Hart, 1970; Rogers & Russell, 2002: 112–13. Kramer, 1995a: 55, said it was 3 days. Perhaps Rank's public lecture was on one day and his seminar lasted 2 days.
90. Rogers & Russell, 2002: 113.
91. He possibly first acknowledged her in a 1983 interview, Rogers & Haigh, 1983: 7. He also

mentioned her, probably in 1986, in an interview with Michelle Baldwin. Rogers & Baldwin, 1987: 49.

92. Rogers & Hart, 1970: 515.

93. CR, 1939a: 200.

94. Taft, 1933: 12, 14 and 17.

95. C.A. Gould, Case Illustrating the Use of Direct Personal or Psychological Treatment. *Visiting Teacher Bulletin, 12* (1937). Cited in CR, 1939a: 342.

96. CR, 1939a: 197–198.

97. Rogers & Hart, 1970: 517.

98. "First *major* book," because Teachers College published their students' dissertations as books at that time, although they did not receive wide circulation.

99. Editor's Introduction, CR, 1939a: v. Carmichael was also the series editor at Houghton Mifflin when *Counseling and Psychotherapy* (CR, 1942a) was published and, at that time, was described in the front of the book as "Secretary, Smithsonian Institution; Formerly President, Tufts College, and Director, Tufts Research Laboratory of Sensory Psychology and Physiology."

100. Rogers & Russell, 2002: 111.

101. CR, 1939a: 281.

102. CR, 1939a: 282–283.

103. CR, 1939a: 283–284.

104. CR, 1939a: 284.

105. Taft, 1933: v, in CR, 1937b: 57.

106. CR, 1937a.

107. See, e.g., CR, "Evaluation of the Work of the Rochester Girls Service League and Big Sister Council," December 1937; CR, "The Disciplinary Program at the [Lancaster] Boys' Industrial School," n.d.; and CR, the "Experience" section of his application for the position of Senior Social Economist with the Federal government, undated: 21. All in UCSB/R-K.

108. CR, 1967a: 360; Goodwin Watson is named in Rogers & Russell, 2002: 118.

109. CR, 1937b, 1937a, and 1939b, respectively.

110. CR, 1936.

111. "Experience" section of application, op. cit. (n. 106).

112. CR, 1967a: 360–361.

113. CR, 1961a: 12.

114. University *Bulletins,* 1928–1940, reviewed in Rare Books Division, Rush Rees Library, University of Rochester.

115. CR, 1967a: 360.

116. CR, 1967a: 343.

117. Natalie Rogers, 1980: 169; "The History of Blood Transfusion Medicine," retrieved from <www.bloodbook.com/trans-history.html> on October 20, 2005.

118. CR, 1942d: 14

119. CR, 1972a: 29.

120. NR, in Suhd, 1995: 187.

121. This and subsequent quotations, unless otherwise noted, are from author interview with Natalie Rogers, 1974.

122. DR, in Suhd, 1995: 276.

123. This and subsequent quotations, unless otherwise noted, are from author interview with David Rogers, 1975.

124. Walter Rogers interview, 1975.

125. NR, in Suhd, 1995: 184–5.

126. First and third sentences from DR interview; second sentence from DR, in Suhd: 277.

127. LOC, Box 4, Folders 8 and 9.

128. Walter Rogers interview, 1975.

129. This and next sentence, NR interview, 2003.

130. Letter from "Helen and Carl" to the Seemans, Newcombs, Montgomerys, Smiths, Neiderhausers, Vic Obenhaus and Fred Schumaker, October 27, 1931. UCSB/R-K

131. Seneca Lake materials in LOC, Box 4, Folder 15; Rogers & Russell, 2002: 121.

132. HR, 1965: 95.

133. CR and NR, author interview. NR was visiting. Summer 1970 or March 1971.

134. Natalie Rogers Fuchs, "Sex-Role Expectations: A Personal Statement," undated, unpublished paper. A similar version appears in NR, 1980: 13–16.

135. HR, author interview, March 1971, tape 5.

136. Quotation and cabin details in Rogers & Russell, 2002: 109, 121.

137. LOC 1/2, letters dated October 17, 1934; November 16, 1935; November 26, 1935; April 5, 1939.

138. Covner correspondence, 1971.

139. Snyder tape, 1971.

140. CR, 1967a: 361.

141. Rogers & Hart, 1970: 515–516.

142. CR 1967a: 361.

143. Both quotations, Rogers & Hart, 1970: 516.

144. Guidance Head Quits to Take Teacher Post: Psychology Chair to be Filled by Dr. Rogers, *Democrat and Chronicle*, October 29, 1939. UCSB/R-K and LOC 32/1.

145. HR, 1965: 96.

Chapter 5

1. David Rogers interview.

2. HR, letter to author, August 13, 1972.

3. Ibid.

4. CR, Semi-annual reports to Dean Klein and Dr. Burtt, June 12, 1940 and February 7, 1941. UCSB/R-K.

5. CR, Year 1942, Report to Dean Klein and Dr. Burtt. UCSB/R-K.

6. T. Gordon, in Suhd, 1995: 312–313.

7. CR, 1967a: 362; see also L. Schmidt & S. Chock, Counseling Psychology at Ohio State University: The First 50 Years, *Journal of Counseling and Development, 68* (January–February, 1990): 276–277.

8. Rogers & Russell, 2002: 128.

9. CR, 1967a: 362. Years later he said that Hedda Bolgar, who was a well-known psychologist then, was the one who told him that. Rogers & Haigh, 1983: 8.

10. William Snyder tape, 1971. Snyder pronounced the name "Burt[t]" and Rogers sent annual reports to "Dr. Burtt" (n. 4). Rogers incorrectly recalled "Berg" (see n. 162).

11. CR, 1940.

12. The panel presentations were reprinted in Watson, 1940. Thirty-eight years later, when Robert Sollod sent Rogers a copy of the Watson article, Rogers wrote, "I had completely forgotten it and I found that Goodwin did state a lot of the principles which were later incorporated into my thinking." Letter to author, October 9, 1978. Therefore Sollod argues that Watson had considerable influence on Rogers' nondirective method. (See R. Sollod, Carl Rogers and the Origins of Client-Centered Therapy, *Professional Psychology, 9*, 1 (1978), 93–104.) However, this influence should not be exaggerated: first because, 38 years later,

Rogers had forgotten that he had stated many of these principles in *his own* 1940 article, which he would have drafted before the panel presentation; second because other panelists made similar points as Watson did; and third, because Rogers cited the 1940 panel discussion in his forthcoming 1942 book, acknowledging its influence at the time.

13. CR, 1964b: 7.

14. Quoted in Cohen, 1997: 97, who also mentioned Hilgard and Buhler's appearances.

15. T. Sarbin correspondence, April 22, 1972; E.G. Williamson & J.K. Darley's *Student Personnel Work* (New York: McGraw-Hill, 1937) was a leading textbook at the time. See also Vandenbos et al., 1992: 71.

16. The presentation was later published as a chapter in CR, 1942a. Quotation: 19.

17. T.R. Sarbin, The Case Record in Psychological Counseling, *Journal of Applied Psychology, 24* (1940): 195. Cited in CR, 1942a: 24.

18. Rogers & Russell, 2002: 134–135. In fact, Sarbin became a leader, arguably the founder, of the narrative movement in psychology and psychotherapy which became popular around the turn of the 21st century. See T. Sarbin (Ed.), *Narrative Psychology: The Storied Nature of Human Conduct* (New York: Praeger, 1986).

19. Sarbin correspondence.

20. CR, 1942a: 28–30.

21. CR, 1964b: 8.

22. Sarbin correspondence.

23. CR, 1964b: 7.

24. B. Thorne, Biographical Introduction, Rogers & Russell, 2002: 11.

25. CR, 1964b: 8.

26. CR, 1961a: 14, 1967a: 361–362.

27. Snyder tape.

28. F.H. Allen, *Psychotherapy with Children* (New York: W.W. Norton and Company, 1942).

29. CR, letter to author, April 22, 1971, cited 110,000 sales to date. The manuscript remained in publication for most of the 20th century.

30. CR, 1942a: vii.

31. Taft, 1933.

32. Kramer, 1995a: 80.

33. New York: D. Appleton-Century Company.

34. CR, 1944d: 392, 1945b.

35. CR, 1942a: 253–254.

36. Initially Rogers tended to include a hyphen, but later tended to spell "nondirective" without the hyphen.

37. F. Allen, paper presented at the tenth anniversary of the Philadelphia Child Guidance Clinic, April 16, 1935. Quoted in CR, 1939a: 198–199.

38. CR, 1940, 1942a, 1943.

39. CR, 1943: 288–289.

40. CR, 1942a: 135–136.

41. Carl Rogers and Mike, audiotape. Volume 7C. Orlando, FL: American Association of Psychotherapists, c. 1965.

42. Axline & Rogers, 1945: 120–121.

43. Ibid.: 121.

44. CR, 1942a: 230.

45. CR, 1942a: 174.

46. CR, 1942a: 40.

47. CR, 1942a: 41.

48. CR, 1942a: 195–196.

49. CR, 1942a: 211.

50. CR, 1942a: 217–218.

51. CR, 1942a: 227–228.

52. CR, 1942a: 21–22.

53. Rogers' student William Snyder made a similar observation in 1945, writing, "while there are several people who have described systems of relationship therapy, and these various systems differ in the degree of non-directiveness which they advocate, it can probably be said that Rogers' point of view represents the most extreme development in the direction of the principles described." Snyder, 1945: 194.

54. Taft, 1933: 45. Also cited in Raskin, 1948.

55. Ibid.: 155.

56. Ibid.: 144.

57. CR, 1942a: 152–153.

58. CR, 1942a: 173.

59. CR, 1942a: 40.

60. CR, 1942a: 205.

61. CR, 1942a: 196.

62. CR, 1942a: 186–187.

63. CR, 1943: 284–285.

64. CR, 1942a: 209.

65. CR, 1942a: 208.

66. CR, 1942a: 210.

67. CR, 1946c: 417.

68. See, for example, E.H. Porter, *The Development and Evaluation of a Measure of Counseling Interview Procedures.* Unpublished doctoral dissertation, Ohio State University, 1941. Rogers was an active dissertation committee member while Frank Robinson was the dissertation "adviser"; A.E. Royer, *An Analysis of Counseling Procedures in a Non-Directive Approach.* Unpublished doctoral dissertation, Ohio State University, 1942; Snyder, 1945.

69. CR, 1942a: 123.

70. CR, 1942a: 122.

71. CR, 1942e: 431.

72. Snyder, 1945.

73. Lietaer, author interview, 2003.

74. Taft, 1933.

75. Letter from Earl F. Zinn to Granville Fisher, May 22, 1958, in J.E. Dittes, Appendix A: Previous Studies Bearing on Content Analysis of Psychotherapy, in J. Dollard & F. Auld, Jr., *Scoring Human Motives: A Manual* (pp. 325–351) (New Haven: Yale University Press, 1959). Rogers wrote it was the Yale Institute of Human Relations that had recorded the psychoanalysis, CR, 1948b: 96. Lasswell and Symonds information also in Dittes.

76 CR, 1939a: 280.

77. CR, Author interviews, tape 4; Dictaphone in letter from Bernard Covner to Frank Auld, Jr., November 18, 1957, in Dittes, op. cit.: 349 (n. 75).

78. Covner to Auld, ibid.

79. Schmidt & Chock, op. cit.: 277 (n. 7).

80. Covner to Auld, op. cit. (n. 77).

81. Covner correspondence, 1971.

82. Rogers & Russell, 2002: 132–133. See also Rogers & Haigh, 1983: 7, where Rogers said, "Our first recordings were done secretly."

83. CR, 1942e: 430.

84. Ibid.: 432.

85. CR, 1942a: 265–285.

86. CR, 1942a: 431.

87. Combs, in Suhd, 1995: 159.

88. Hall, 1967a: 66.

89. CR, 1942a: 104.

90. Arthur Combs, author interview, 1972.

91. Ibid.

92. CR, 1942a: 88, 254 and 255, respectively.

93. CR, 1942a: 92.

94. Carl Rogers & Mike, op. cit. (n. 41).

95. CR, from The Case of Mary Jane Tilden: Counseled by Carl R. Rogers, in Snyder, 1947: 128–203.

96. CR, 1942a: 359.

97. CR, 1964b: 8.

98. J. Palmer, *The Psychological Assessment of Children* (p. 396) (New York: Wiley, 1970).

99. Arthur Combs correspondence.

100. CR, 1946c: 419.

101. Quotations in this paragraph from Vandenbos et al., 1992: 74, 75 and 71, respectively.

102. See, for example, Capuzzi & Gross, 2001; Gibson & Mitchell, 1999; Gladding, 2000; and Nugent, 2000.

103. Gladding, 2000: 11.

104. Capuzzi & Gross, 2001: 13.

105. Combs interview.

106. William Snyder correspondence; it was Frances Maxfield's office that he had to walk through. Rogers & Russell, 2002: 126.

107. Combs interview.

108. Rogers discusses his self-grading practice in Rogers & Russell, 2002: 127–128.

109. Charles Curran tape, 1971.

110. HR, letter to author, August 13, 1972.

111. Curran tape.

112. CR, Report to Dean Klein & Dr. Burtt, Re: statement of professional service, 1941. UCSB/ R-K.

113. Bill Kell correspondence, 1971.

114. E.g., Snygg & Combs, 1949, 1959; Combs, 1962; A. Combs, D. Avila, & W. Purkey, *Helping Relationships: Basic Concepts for the Helping Professions* (Boston: Allyn and Bacon, 1971).

115. V.C. Raimy, 1944, 1948; *The Self Concept as a Factor in Counseling and Personality Organization* (Columbus, OH: Ohio State University Press, 1971, an edited version of his 1944 dissertation); *Misunderstandings of the Self* (San Francisco: Jossey-Bass, 1975).

116. Axline & Rogers, 1945.

117. Axline, 1947, V.M. Axline, *Dibs in Search of Self* (Boston: Houghton Mifflin, 1964).

118. Axline, 1947: 25–26.

119. E.g., Thomas Gordon, *Parent Effectiveness Training* (New York: Peter Wyden, 1970); T. Gordon & N. Burch, *Teacher Effectiveness Training* (New York: Wyden, 1974).

120. DR interview, 1975.

121. DR, in Suhd, 1995: 277.

122. HR, 1965: 96.

123. NR, in Suhd, 1995: 177.

124. NR interview, 1974. See also NR, 1980.

125. Steinzor tape, 1971.

126. CR, 1972a: 28.

127. HR, letter to author, November 29, 1971.

128. This landmark study of 1,500 students in 30 progressive schools, which culminated in the publication of D. Chamberlain, E. Chamberlain, N. Drought and W. Scott, *Adventures in American Education: Did They Succeed in College?* (New York: Harper & Brothers, 1942), demonstrated that the students did as well as or better than their matched pairs from traditional schools on virtually every measure of academic achievement, leadership and adjustment in college.

129. The paper, dated June 2, 1942, with comment by teacher (a Mr. or Ms. Eberhardt), was among CR's paper in the 1970s, when the author viewed them, and is probably now in the CR papers, LOC. See also Natalie's recollection in Suhd, 1995: 182.

130. NR quotations in this section from author interview, 1974.

131. DR quotations in this section from author interview, 1975

132. NR to CR, July 20, 1943. LOC 1/3.

133. CR to NR, July 23, 1943. LOC 1/3.

134. NR interview, 1974.

135. In a 1971 letter to Merlin K. DuVal, n.d., David mentions how he was influenced by uncle Walter to go into medicine and how he later took a tour of duty on the medical ship HOPE when Walter was serving as Chief of Staff aboard the HOPE. LOC 2/6.

136. Author interview, 1975. Twenty years later, David told a slightly different version of how he selected colleges in Suhd, 1995: 282.

137. In Suhd, 1995: 314.

138. This and following quotations from Charles Curran tape.

139. William Snyder tape. Ironically, Snyder did not know how Rogers in Rochester, as described in the previous chapter, had made certain his children were tested annually for intelligence and carefully recorded their scores.

140. An article in the *New York Times,* February 23, 1941: 14, summarized highlights of the American Orthopsychiatric Association's annual meeting and reported on the newly elected officers.

141. "In 1939, the American Psychological Association (APA) had 2,527 members. The vast majority of psychologists in the 1930s were in academic settings, and they did not identify themselves as psychotherapists or clinical psychologists." Vandenbos, et al., 1992: 74.

142. CR, 1967a: 362.

143. CR, 1942e: 429.

144. CR, 1944b: 331.

145. CR, 1945a: 155.

146. CR, 1942b, 1942c.

147. CR, "The Problems of Youth in Ohio in Wartime," unpublished, n.d., UCSB/CR.

148. M.J. Burton, "Don't 'Hush' Your Youngsters About War," *Columbus Citizen,* May 17, 1942.

149. M.J. Burton, "'Good' Children Have Troubles, Too," *Columbus Citizen*, May 21, 1942.

150. Psychology and the War: Notes, *Psychological Bulletin, 39* (1942): 794.

151. CR, 1944a.

152. Letter from Richard R. Waugh, Lt. Col., Air Corps, from Headquarters, Army Air Forces Instructors School (Flexible Gunnery) Buckingham Air Field, Ft. Meyers, Florida, to: All Concerned, Subject: Dr. Carl Rogers' Study, Adjustment After Combat, 16 April, 1944.

153. CR, 1945b: 1.

154. CR to Dr. Ernest Burgess, Department of Sociology, University of Chicago, October 4, 1944.

155. CR, *Understanding and Dealing with the Individual: Orientation Course.* New York: United Services Organization, 1944. Unpublished. LOC.

156. CR, *Report of the Director of Counseling Services*, June 29, 1945. Unpublished. LOC.

157. Rogers & Russell, 2002: 141.
158. CR, author interview, March 1971.
159. CR, 1945b: 7–8. UCSB/R-K.
160. CR, 1944c, 1945f, and 1944d, respectively.
161. Rogers & Wallen, 1946.
162. William Snyder tape; CR told a similar version, but incorrectly recalled the name as "Berg" in Rogers & Russell, 2002: 143.
163. HR, letter to author, August 12, 1972.
164. HR, 1965: 96.
165. HR, letter to author, August 12, 1972.

Chapter 6

1. N. Mercer, Carl Ransom Rogers: 1902–. N.d. UCSB/R-K.
2. Respectively, Rogers & Wallen, 1946; CR, 1951a; Rogers & Dymond, 1954.
3. This figure is derived by adding forty-five non-research oriented articles to the total number of research oriented articles mentioned below in this chapter. The figure of forty-five represents articles which I have found. It, too, may fall short of the actual total.
4. Axline, 1947.
5. CR, "Remarks At The Dedication of the New Psychology Building, University of Chicago," January 7, 1966: 2. Unpublished. UCSB/R-K.
6. CR, *Report of the Counseling Center, October 1, 1945 to August 1, 1946.* Undated. All the Conference Center reports referred to here are unpublished and among the UCSB/R-K papers; see also Rogers & Russell, 2002: 144 and 148.
7. Steinzor tape, May 9, 1971.
8. Rogers & Russell, 2002: 148.
9. Vargas tape, November. 12, 1971.
10. CR, Appendix I: The Counseling Center: Origin and Development, undated report from 1952, 1953, or 1954.
11. CR, Report of the Counseling Center, 1945–46, op. cit.: 3 (n. 6).
12. Leon Thurstone, Andrew Brown, and Forrest Kingsbury were the main figures, according to Rogers, "Remarks at the Dedication of the New Psychology Building," 1966, op. cit. (n. 5).
13. Based on CR, annual reports dated March 1951; April 14, 1952; June 8, 1953; September 13, 1954; and April 3, 1956.
14. CR, Annual Report, March, 1951: 2.
15. CR, Annual Report, April 3, 1956: 5.
16. CR, Annual Report, September 13, 1954: 2.
17. CR, 1951a: xii.
18. CR, Annual Report, June 8, 1953.
19. Quoted in CR, 1946c: 420.
20. CR, 1946c, 1949a, 1950b.
21. CR, 1949a: 82.
22. CR, 1950a: 27.
23. CR, 1949a: 82.
24. CR, 1950b: 443.
25. CR, 1949c: 14.
26. CR, 1950b: 443–444.
27. CR, 1951a: 46–47.
28. CR, notes attached to his letter to author, September 10, 1973. UCSB/R-K.

29. CR, 1949a: 94.
30. Ibid.: 84.
31. Ibid.: 85.
32. CR, 1950b: 444.
33. CR, 1951a: 27.
34. Since *empathic* was not widely used among the public at the time, several proofreaders and typesetters assumed there was a mistake and re-spelled the word "emphatic." Rogers never used the word "empathetic" which subsequently came into popular use.
35. Rogers & Dymond, 1954: 313.
36. CR, 1949a: 87.
37. CR, 1949a: 87–88, 1951a: 32–33.
38. CR, 1951a: 33–34.
39. CR, 1949a: 87–90.
40. R.W. Dettering, Philosophic Idealism in Rogerian Psychology. *Educational Theory*, 5, 4 (1955): 212.
41. Rogers & Russell, 2002: 253.
42. Seeman, 1949; Snyder, 1945.
43. CR, 1949a: 87.
44. Gendlin, Foreword in Rogers & Russell, 2002: xiii–xiv.
45. CR, 1951a. The full title—*Client-Centered Therapy: Its Current Practice, Implications and Theory*—was rarely used.
46. CR, 1951a: 30; this passage also appeared in CR, 1946c: 420–421.
47. CR, 1951a: 384.
48. CR, 1947a, 1948b, 1952b.
49. CR, 1951a: x–xi.
50. CR, 1957b: 199.
51. Brice correspondence, April 13, 1972.
52. The Functions of the Counseling Center—A Current Concept, prepared by a Committee of the Staff, January, 1953. UCSB/R-K.
53. Original source missing; however, CR told a similar version and named Strozier in Rogers & Russell, 2002: 145.
54. Seeman correspondence, April 19, 1972.
55. Steinzor tape. Apparently graduate students who were "interns" partipated in staff meetings, whereas regular graduate students did not. Rogers & Russell, 2002: 148.
56. Rogers & Russell, 2002: 147.
57. CR, The University of Chicago Counseling Center, Annual Report, 1950, March, 1951.
58. Armin Klein, 2000: 67.
59. Hersher correspondence, May 18, 1971.
60. Author interview, 1971.
61. Loan information from Memorandum of Agreement between Charlotte Ellinwood and Carl R. Rogers, December 15, 1950. LOC 32/2; K. Moon, Introduction to Charlotte Ellinwood's "Some Observations from Work with Parents in a Child Therapy Program," *Person-Centered Journal, 12*, 1&2 (2005): 31–32.
62. Richard Reed correspondence, November 10, 1971.
63. Gendlin, Foreword, Rogers & Russell, 2002: xiv.
64. Joan Chodorkoff correspondence, June 5, 1971.
65. Farson interview, 2003.
66. Haigh, 1988: 17, 18 and 20.
67. L. Rice, Preface, in Wexler & Rice, 1974: viii.
68. Bebout correspondence, June 15, 1971.

69. Cartwright tape, May 4, 1971.

70. CR, annual report, March 1951: 3–4.

71. For more on "active listening," see Chapter 9, section on "Widening Applications."

72. Cartwright tape.

73. Brice correspondence.

74. Chodorkoff correspondence.

75. Richard Farson interview, 2003.

76. Haigh, 1988: 18. In his 85th birthday note to CR, Haigh said that a "Don Hayakawa" also led this workshop. (Note to "Dear Carl," n.d., in "85th Greetings" folder UCSB/B.) In Suhd, 1995: 320, Tom Gordon recalled doing a similar workshop with the famous semanticist S.I. Hayakawa. Gordon thought the title was something like "Client-Centered Therapy Beyond the Clinic." Hayakawa was visiting lecturer at Chicago from 1950–55. He later credited Rogers as one of his influences in the Preface to his famous *Language in Thought and Action* (New York: Harcourt Brace, 1949). Rogers published two articles in *ETC: A Review of General Semantics* around this time and cited Hayakawa in his writing. Later Rogers' and Hayakawa's paths intersected at WBSI. The relationship and mutual influence of Rogers and the semanticist and future senator from California deserves more exploration.

77. E. Dorfman correspondence, October 7, 1971.

78. CR to Elaine Dorfman, November 4, 1949. Included in Dorfman correspondence.

79. Thomas Gordon recalled another example of Rogers' generosity. In a tribute after Rogers' death he wrote that he would never forget "the time he and Helen handed me a check as a gift so I could pay the attorney who helped me keep my adopted daughter Judy." T. Gordon, Tributes and Memories, *Person-Centered Review, 2*, 3 (August 1987): 398.

80. J.C. Nunnally correspondence, June 9, 1971.

81. Haigh correspondence.

82. Fiedler correspondence, May 28, 1971.

83. Ferguson correspondence, December 20, 1971.

84. CR, Memorandum to Arthur Lincicome, Assistant Comptroller, November 2, 1950. In folder "Battles at U of Chi," UCSB/R-K.

85. Report of the Subcommittee on the Laboratory School, submitted by Frank H. Knight, et al., distributed February 23, 1951. In folder "Battles at U of Chi," UCSB/R-K.

86. CR, Memorandum to Messrs. F.H. Knight, et al., March 5, 1951. In folder "Battles at U of Chi," UCSB/R-K.

87. CR, The Place of Psychotherapy in Modern Life, April 1952, 18 pages, unpublished, and What We Know about Changing Attitudes in Individuals, presentation at Arrowhead Springs, San Bernadino, CA, January 27–30, 1954. 18 pages, unpublished. Both in UCSB/R-K.

88. "What We Know…," ibid.: 5.

89. See folders "Rel. w. Medical School" and "'Battles' at U. of Chi," UCSB/R-K.

90. CR, letter to Chancellor Kimpton, titled "Relationship with the Department of Psychiatry and the School of Medicine," November 7, 1956. Unpublished. In folder "Battles at U of Chi," UCSB/R-K.

91. CR, Rogers & Russell, 2002: 161.

92. Farson interview.

93. CR, A New Emphasis in the Study of Human Relationships, unpublished paper given at Second Human Development Banquet, January 20, 1951. UCSB/R-K.

94. Brice correspondence.

95. Combs interview.

96. CR, 1967a: 380.

97. Related by Carl and Helen Rogers to author, March 1971.

98. Combs correspondence.

99. John Levy correspondence, June 25, 1971.

100. Tomlinson correspondence.

101. Seeman correspondence. Raskin, 1978, describes Oliver Bown and Eugene Streich as two of the colleagues who were exploring the greater awareness and use of the therapist's own emotions in the therapy relationship.

102. Unless otherwise cited, sources are CR, 1967a: 366–367 and CR, interviews with author, tape 12, January 25, 1975, and tape 6, March 1971.

103. CR to John Warkentin, May 10, 1949. LOC 32/2.

104. CR to Carl Whitaker, November 6, 1949. LOC 32/2.

105. I wonder if another reason Rogers felt he "had to" be of help was that, as he sometimes said, each new client for him offered the possibility of proving or disproving his theory of therapy. If he "failed" with a client, *this* client, it threatened the validity of his theory in his own eyes.

106. CR to Warkentin, op. cit. (n. 103).

107. John Neill, Biographical Introduction to the Work of Carl Whitaker, MD, in J. Neill & D. Kniskern, *From Psyche to System: The Evolving Therapy of Carl Whitaker* (New York: Guilford Press, 1982).

108. CR to Warkentin, op. cit. (n. 103); Warkentin's reply on May 11. LOC 32/2. Interestingly, later Rogers, Warkentin and Whitaker became the first, second and fifth presidents of the American Academy of Psychotherapists. D. Arbuckle, "Whither Goest this Academy?," *Voices, 30*, 1 (Spring 1994): 73–76.

109. That is my estimate based on the interviews and documents.

110. CR to Whitaker, op. cit. (n. 104).

111. For example, *Client-Centered Therapy* was published at the time, which would have required final writing, editing, reviewing proofs, etc. throughout 1949–50. Not to mention coordinating research, sponsoring dissertations, teaching, and conducting therapy.

112 CR, 1967a: 367.

113. Rogers & Russell, 2002: 164–165.

114. Brian Thorne suggested that perhaps Rogers "was led to create client-centered therapy because he himself needed the kind of healing it offered." Rogers & Russell, 2002: 13.

115. CR, Annual Report report, July 23, 1951.

Chapter 7

1. Haigh, 1988: 18.

2. Vargas tape.

3. Discussion of Client-Centered Psychotherapy with Dr. Carl Rogers, May, 1958: 26. Psychology Department, University of Rochester. 49 pp, unpublished. UCSB/R-K.

4. CR, personal communication to author, September 10, 1973.

5. CR, 1956a: 199–200.

6. Discussion of Client-Centered Psychotherapy, 1958: 27, op. cit. (n. 3).

7. Nunnally correspondence.

8. Discussion of Client-Centered Therapy, 1958: 25, op. cit. (n. 3).

9. Ibid.

10. Covner correspondence.

11. Brice correspondence, 1971.

12. Standal, 1954.

13. CR, 1956a: 200.

14. CR, 1957a: 98.

15. CR, 1952c.

16. CR, 1949b: 152.

17. CR, 1956c: 318.

18. CR, 1957a.

19. Quotations in this and next paragraph from CR, 1957a: 95–96.

20. Ibid.: 100–101.

21. At the time Rogers wrote this essay, rational therapy was still on its way to becoming rational-emotive and then rational-emotive-behavior therapy (REBT), and other forms of cognitive behavioral therapy were still over a decade away. See, for example, A. Ellis, *Reason and Emotion in Psychotherapy* (New York: Stuart, 1962); W. Dryden & A. Ellis, Rational Emotive Behavior Therapy, in Dobson, 2001: 295–348; and K. Dobson & D. Dozois, Historical and Philosophical Bases of the Cognitive-Behavioral Therapies, in Dobson, 2001: 3–39.

22. F. Fiedler, 1950; Factor Analysis of Psychoanalytic, Nondirective and Adlerian Therapeutic Relationships, *Journal of Consulting Psychology, 15,* (1951): 32–38; Quantitative Studies on the Role of Therapists' Feelings Toward Their Patients. In O.H. Mowrer (Ed.), *Psychotherapy: Theory and Research* (New York: Ronald Press, 1953).

23. CR, 1951a: 55.

24. See last chapter of this volume for a fuller discussion of this point. See also Bozarth, Zimring & Tausch, 2001: 153; Kirschenbaum & Jourdan 2005; and Stubbs & Bozarth, 1994: 109.

25. Steinzor tape.

26. Paul Bergman to CR, February 22, 1959. UCSB/R-K.

27. CR, 1951a: 482.

28. CR, 1949b: 152.

29. CR, 1946b: 588.

30. Fiedler correspondence, May 28, 1971.

31. CR, 1959c: 214. Rogers' "Theory of Therapy, etc." will be discussed later in the chapter. The study was W.L. Kirtner, *Success and Failure in Client-Centered Therapy as a Function of Personality Variables* (Unpublished Master's thesis, University of Chicago, 1955).

32. Gendlin correspondence, August 20, 1974; also described in E.T. Gendlin, Forward, in Rogers & Russell, 2002: xviii.

33. Rogers, 1942a; C.A. Curran, *Personality Factors in Counseling* (New York: Grune and Stratton, 1945); Snyder, 1947.

34. CR, 1948b: 96.

35. CR, 1951a: 13.

36. CR, 1956a: 207.

37. Porter, 1941; E.H. Porter, The Development and Evaluation of a Measure of Counseling Interview Procedures. *Educational and Psychological Measurement, 3* (1943): 105–126, 215–238.

38. CR, 1950b: 442.

39. CR, 1952a: 66.

40. Porter, 1943, op. cit. (n. 37).

41. Curran, 1945, op. cit. (n. 33).

42. Snyder, 1945. Jules Seeman replicated the study, see Seeman, 1949.

43. Raimy, 1948.

44. D.V. Bergman, Counseling Method and Client Responses, *Journal of Consulting Psychology, 15* (1951): 216–224.

45. Snyder, 1945.

46. G.A. Muench, An Evaluation of Non-Directive Psychotherapy by Means of the Rorschach and Other Tests, *Applied Psychology Monographs, 13* (1947); A.C. Carr, An Evaluation of Nine Non-Directive Therapy Cases by Means of the Rorschach, *Journal of Consulting Psychology, 13,* (1949): 196–205; A.K. Jonietz, *A Study of Changes in Perception in Relation to*

Psychotherapy (Unpublished doctoral dissertation, University of Chicago, 1950).

47. R.F. Dymond, Adjustment Changes over Therapy from Thematic Apperception Test Ratings (pp. 109–120). In Rogers & Dymond, 1954; D.L. Grummon & E.S. John, Changes over Client-Centered Therapy Evaluated on Psychoanalytically Based Thematic Apperception Test Scales (pp. 121–144). In Rogers & Dymond, 1954; S. Lipkin, Clients' Feelings and Attitudes in Relation to the Outcome of Client-Centered Therapy, *Psychological Monographs*, 68, Whole No. 372 (1954).

48. M.R. Bartlett & Staff, *Data on the Personal Adjustment Counseling Program for Veterans* (Washington, DC: Personal Adjustment Division, Adjustment and Guidance Service, Office of Vocational Rehabilitation and Education, 1949).

49. M.L. Haimowitz, *Ethnic Hostility—Displacement and Psychotherapy* (Unpublished doctoral dissertation, University of Chicago, 1950).

50. J.J. Gallagher, MMPI Changes Concomitant with Client-Centered Therapy, *Journal of Consulting Psychology, 17* (1953): 334–338; L. Hersher, *Openness to Experience and Client-Centered Theory* (Unpublished doctoral dissertation, University of Chicago, 1956).

51. In Brenman roundtable, 1948: 94.

52. In the Rogers and Haigh (1983) interview, Rogers says Miller helped him get a Rockefeller grant of $50,000 shortly after Miller became chair. It is unclear if this was the first part of the $172,000 grant, if it preceded that grant, or if Rogers' recollection of the amount was wrong.

53. CR, annual report, September 13, 1954.

54. D. Marquis, Research Planning at the Frontiers of Science, *American Psychologist, 3* (1948): 432; cited in Rogers & Dymond, 1954: 17.

55. Rogers & Dymond, 1954: 17.

56. T. Gordon, D.L. Grummon, C.R. Rogers & J. Seeman, Developing a Program of Research in Psychotherapy, in Rogers & Dymond, 1954: 22.

57. Ibid.: 17.

58. A client was placed in the wait control group "only if it seemed that waiting was not likely to cause him serious discomfort or harm." D. Grummon, Design, Procedures, and Subjects for the First Block, in Rogers & Dymond, 1954: 46; M.J. Lambert and A.E. Bergin make the same point in Achievements and Limitations of Psychotherapy Research, chapter in Freedheim, 1992: 362.

59. W. Stephenson, *The Study of Behavior: Q-technique and Its Methodology* (Chicago: University Press, 1953).

60. Rogers & Russell, 2002: 249.

61. M.W. Hartley, *A Q-Technique Study of Changes in the Self-Concept during Psychotherapy*. Unpublished doctoral dissertation, University of Chicago, 1951; J.M. Butler & G.V. Haigh, Changes in the Relation Between Self-Concepts and Ideal Concepts Consequent upon Client-Centered Counseling. In Rogers & Dymond, 1954.

62. CR, An Overview of the Research and Some of the Questions for the Future. In Rogers & Dymond, 1954: 429.

63. Gordon, et al., op. cit.: 17. (n. 56).

64. CR, 1949b: 149.

65. In the Rogers and Haigh (1983) interview, Rogers explained, "I began to learn something about politics of authorship, too. Roz Dymond and I did all the editing of that. It certainly didn't occur to me that therefore it would become known as Rogers and Dymond. She had not done any more of the research than the others and there were some hard feelings when the book was published—it should have been a multiple authorship rather than simply two names" (p. 9).

66. The sixth printing was in 1969. It was still in print in 1979.

67. Rogers & Dymond, 1954: 5.

68. Cartwright, 1957.

69. CR, 1940: 164.

70. S. Lipkin, The Client Evaluates Nondirective Psychotherapy. *Journal of Consulting Psychology, 12* (1948): 137.

71. In N.J. Raskin, An Analysis of Six Parallel Studies of the Therapeutic Process, *Journal of Consulting Psychology, 13*, 3 (1949): 206. Raskin inscription observed by author in Rogers' office, March 1971.

72. Haigh, 1988: 19. Actually some of the Rogers group were women, which first initials in citations tended to obscure.

73. Helen Peak, "Psychology" entry, 1950 Britannica Book of the Year: 571 (Chicago: Encyclopedia Britannica, 1950).

74. *The Library Journal, 79* (September 15, 1954): 1590, n.a.

75. Strupp, 1955: 1.

76. J.D. Matarazzo, The Interview. In B.B. Wolman (Ed.), *Handbook of Clinical Psychology* (New York: McGraw-Hill, 1965): 408 and 418.

77. C.H. Patterson, *Theories of Counseling and Psychotherapy* (New York: Harper & Row, 1966): 437.

78. Hall & Lindzey, 1957: 489.

79. In *Journal of Counseling Psychology, 1* (1954): 249–255.

80. H. Eysenck, The Effects of Psychotherapy. In H.J. Eysenck (Ed.), *Handbook of Abnormal Psychology: An Experimental Approach* (New York: Basic Books, 1961): 707.

81. Humphreys correspondence, June, 1971.

82. Quoted in C. Harrison, Carl Rogers and His Work, 1949. Unpublished. UCSB/R-K.

83. E. Freidson, Review of C.R. Rogers & R.F. Dymond (Eds.), *Psychotherapy and Personality Change. American Journal of Sociology, 6* (1955): 185 and 186.

84. American Psychological Association, *American Psychologist, 12* (3) March 1957: 128. Previous quotation: 125.

85. CR, 1973b, in Evans, 1975: 127–128.

86. CR, 1953a.

87. CR, author interview, March 1971.

88. Rogers & Russell, 2002: 138.

89. Other AAP founders were Carl Whitaker, Tom Malone and John Warkentin. George Dolger, Vivian Guze, Howard Halpern and Rollo May were also involved from the beginning. This and quotation, Vivian Guze interview, November 2004.

90. Rogers & Haigh, 1983: 12–13.

91. CR, 1945c, 1952d.

92. CR, 1956c.

93. CR, 1950a, 1951c, 1952c.

94. CR, 1956b.

95. CR, 1949c.

96. CR, 1946a, 1948c.

97. CR, 1950d.

98. CR, 1952a.

99. CR, 1953b.

100. CR, 1954.

101. CR, 1952b.

102. CR, 1967a: 376.

103. Theron Alexander, author interview, May, 1971. See also T. Alexander, *Psychotherapy in Our Society* (Englewood Cliffs, NJ: Prentice-Hall, 1963).

104. Matarazzo, 1965: 425, op. cit. (n. 76).

105. H. Higgins, Client-Centered Psychotherapy and Christian Doctrine, *Journal of Pastoral Care*, *3*, 1 (1954): 2, 5 and 11.

106. E.B. Ferguson, A Nurse-Counselor Comments, *American Journal of Nursing*, *56* (August 1956): 995.

107. Rogers, 1952b. The original panel presentation was at Northwestern University in 1951 and was published in the conference proceedings. In the *HBR* version, the editors changed the title and paired Rogers' presentation with Roethlisberger's. Thus sometimes this publication is listed as a co-authored article, although each author's contribution is actually separate and distinct.

108. In *Harvard Business Review*, November–December, 1991: 108.

109. Person to Person, *Time: The Weekly News Magazine*, July 1, 1957: 36, n.a. Rogers later told an interviewer that he liked the article's title and thought that "person to person therapy" was a better name for his approach than "client-centered therapy." That was before he began using the term "person-centered." Rogers & Frick, 1971: 103.

110. CR, annual report, June 8, 1953.

111. CR, 1956c.

112. Combs correspondence.

113. CR, 1952d.

114. CR attributed this quote to Bill Huntley in author interview, March 1971, tape 6.

115. Wexler correspondence, November 18, 1971.

116. Archie correspondence, May 6, 1971.

117. Miss Cora Jane Baxter is Bride of David Elliott Rogers, *The Columbus Citizen*, August 16, 1946. LOC 1/1.

118. DR, in Suhd, 1995: 283–284.

119. Curriculum Vitae, David E. Rogers, M.D., dated 12/74. UCSB/R-K.

120. NR, in Suhd, 1995: 189.

121. NR, Changes in Self-Concept in the Case of Mrs. Ett, *Personal Counselor*, *2* (1947): 278–291; Measuring Psychological Tensions in Nondirective Counseling, *Personal Counselor*, *3* (1948): 237–264.

122. CR to NR Fuchs, October 7, 1951; HR to NR Fuchs and Larry Fuchs, October 7, 1951.

123. NR, 1980: 169.

124. NR interview, 1971.

125. This and next paragraph, David Rogers interview, 1975.

126. "Dear Pop," LOC 1/5; other letters in this paragraph, LOC 1/6.

127. Letter dated July 29, 1951. LOC.

128. LOC 1/4.

129. LOC 4/11.

130. CR, A Mexican Evening, letter "To some friends," March 1, 1952, 6 pp. LOC 1/7.

131. CR, Dittoed letter, January 17, 1956, from Sunny Caribee Hotel, Bequia, St. Vincent's, B.W.I. In "Caribbean & Mexican Letters 1952–1966" file, UCSB/R-K; also in LOC 1/9.

132. CR, 1961a: 199–200.

133. CR, Report of Three Quarters Work, July 1951 through March 1952, April 14, 1952. UCSB/R-K.

134. Julius Seeman correspondence.

135. CR, Dittoed letter, dated February 5, 1956, from Bequia, British West Indies. UCSB/R-K; also LOC, 1/9.

136. Tom Gordon recalled his and his wife's visits fondly. Art Combs also recalled how he and Don Snygg visited for a day in 1947. Both recollections in their respective chapters in Suhd, 1995.

137. HR, 1965: 97.

138. CR, 1972a: 26.

139. Ibid: 25.

140. Ibid: 26–27.

141. Estate finances in LOC 1/8. DR's letter of July 29, 1951 thanks his father for the "overwhelming check … one whale of a check—and I'm a little concerned about whether you can really afford dumping such a large amount in one sum in my lap."

142. Their thank you notes in LOC 1/6.

143. LOC 1/9.

144. HR, 1965: 96.

145. CR, author interview, March 1971.

146. HR, 1965: 97.

147. D. Campbell, The Vocational Interests of American Psychological Association Presidents, *American Psychologist, 20*, 8 (1965): 636–644.

148. CR, 1959c: 249.

149. CR, 1951a: 16.

150. The correlation was .84. Rogers tells this story in CR, 1986e.

151. Although the correlation was not as strong as in Kell's study. Ibid.

152. Rogers, Kell, & McNeil, 1948.

153. In Brenman, 1948: 99.

154. CR, letter to author, June 4, 1973.

155. CR, 1967a: 366; similarly described in CR, op. cit. (n. 154) in which CR wryly described the experience as "Very ego-building!"

156. Rogers, Kell, & McNeil, 1948; CR, 1950c, 1951b.

157. CR, 1951a, CR, 1959c.

158. CR, 1948b: 99.

159. CR, 1959c: 200.

160. J.S. Coleman, E. Campbell, C. Hobson, J. McPartland, A. Mood, F. Weinfeld, & R. York, *Equality of Educational Opportunity* (Washington, DC: U.S. Government Printing Office, 1966): 22.

161. CR, 1951a: 483, 484, 487–491, 491–492, 497 and 498 respectively.

162. L. Rice & L. Greenberg, Humanistic Approaches to Psychotherapy, in Freedheim, 1992: 201.

163. Goldstein, 1940.

164. He listed them in this order in CR, 1951a: 481. He specifically cited: Goldstein, 1940; A. Angyal, *Foundations for a Science of Personality* (New York: Commonwealth Fund, 1941); Maslow, 1943a, 1943b; O.H. Mowrer & C. Kluckhohn, A Dynamic Theory of Personality. In J. McV. Hunt (Ed.), *Personality and the Behavior Disorders. Vol. 1* (New York: Ronald Press, 1944); Lecky, 1945; H.S. Sullivan, *Conceptions of Modern Psychiatry* (Washington, DC: W.A. White Foundation, 1945); J.H. Masserman, *Principles of Dynamic Psychiatry* (New York: Saunders, 1946); G. Murphy, *Personality: A Biosocial Approach to Origins and Structures* (New York: Harper & Bros, 1947); N. Cameron, *The Psychology of Behavior Disorders* (New York: Houghton Mifflin, 1947); C. Kluckhohn & H.A. Murray (Eds.), *Personality in Nature, Society and Culture.* (New York: Alfred Knopf, 1948); R.W. White, *The Abnormal Personality* (New York: Ronald Press, 1948); Snygg & Combs, 1949; T. Burrow, *The Neurosis of Man* (New York: Harcourt Brace, 1949).

165. Hall & Lindzey, 1957: 469 and 478. Rogers theory was still featured in their fourth edition, Hall, Lindzey & Campbell, 1998.

166. C.H. Patterson, *Theories of Counseling and Psychotherapy* (New York: Harper and Row, 1966): 437.

167. P. Merenda, Psychology of the Scientist: XXXVIII. Walter Vernon Clarke, 1905–1978,

Perceptual and Motor Skills, 47 (1978): 140–142; letters from Merenda to author, February 23, 2004 and March (undated), 2004. See also H. Ansbacher, Prescott Lecky's Concept of Resistance and His Personality, *Journal of Clinical Psychology, 37*, 4 (1981): 791–795, and M. Stevens, Prescott Lecky: Pioneer in Consistency Theory and Cognitive Therapy, *Journal of Clinical Psychology, 48*, 6 (1992): 807–811.

168. Lecky did not speak widely. Possibly Rogers met him at Columbia on one of Rogers' several return visits there, but Raimy and Combs told Merenda that Rogers never mentioned any affiliation with Lecky to them, so this is unlikely. Merenda letter, February 23, 2004, op. cit. (n. 167).

169. Lecky, 1945. A second edition in 1951 was edited and interpreted by F. Thorne.

170. CR, 1947b: 366.

171. CR, 1951a: 497.

172. CR, 1959c: 202.

173. E.g., his many citations in CR, 1951a, 1959c. Quotation from author interview, March 1971, tape #6.

174. Ibid.

175. Combs tape. Combs thought the address was in 1949 when Snygg and his book was published, but it was in 1947.

176. Discussion of Client-Centered Psychotherapy, 1958, op. cit. (n. 3)

177. Rogers told a group in 1975, "I don't regard myself as a scholar. I think there is a certain amount of truth to the notion that those who read don't write, and those who write don't read." Kim Francis, *Two Hours with Carl Rogers*, unpublished manuscript, n.d.: 53–54, UCSB/R-K; see also Rogers' comments on his own scholarship in Chapter 9 vis-à-vis Michael Polanyi.

178. CR, 1980b: 63.

179. Rogers & Russell, 2002: 246–247.

180. Brice correspondence, 1971. Brice paraphrased Rogers' comment from memory a decade later. If May had a greater interest in *theory* than Rogers, he acknowledged Rogers' strength in *practice*. When people asked him what existential psychotherapists actually do, he sometimes told them, "Well, examine the work of Carl Rogers and his associates and you will get a pretty good idea of what existential psychotherapy is." Quotation from early draft of CR, 1964b, written when Rogers was still at WBSI, i.e., before 1969. UCSB/R-K.

181. CR, 1959c: 190–191.

182. Hall, Lindzey & Campbell, 1998: 489.

183. Truax tape.

184 CR, 1967a: 368.

185. CR, 1958c.

186. CR, 1967a: 369. Rogers recalled "about twenty-three different committees" in Rogers & Russell, 2002, but his earlier, written recollection is more credible than the later (1986) interview.

187. CR, Memo to "All Staff Members, Counseling Center," May 15, 1957. UCSB/R-K.

Chapter 8

1. J.P. Moursund & R.G. Erskine, *Integrative Psychotherapy: The Art and Science of Relationship*. Thompson/Brooks Cole, 2004: 4.

2. A.H. Maslow, Toward a Psychology of Health. Paper presented at Cooper Union, New York City, October, 18, 1954. In C. Moustakas (Ed.), *The Self* (New York: Harper & Bros., 1956); What Psychology Can Learn from the Existentialists. Paper presented at the American

Psychological Association, 1959. In R. May, 1961.

3. A. Klein, 2000: 61–62.

4. CR, 1946c: 415.

5. S. Freud, My Contact with Josef Popper-Lunkeus, in *Character and Culture*, from Collier Books edition of the *Collected Papers of Sigmund Freud*, translated by J. Strachey (New York: Crowell-Collier, 1963); originally published: 1932: 303. Cited in CR, 1977: 16.

6. Author interview, March 1971.

7. See, for example, exchange between Rollo May and Carl Rogers in Kirschenbaum & Henderson, 1989a: 229–255.

8. Russell Becker, letter to CR, October 22, 1963, UCSB/R-K; W.L. Hiemstra, Carl Rogers' Philosophy of Man, *Journal of Pastoral Care, 18*, 1 (1964): 32–36. Cohen, 1997, repeatedly criticizes Rogers on this point.

9. CR, 1958b: 27.

10. CR, 1951a: 211–213.

11. CR, 1958b: 27.

12. Rogers & Baldwin, 1987: 49–50.

13. CR, 1977: 8.

14. CR, 1957b: 200–201.

15. Ibid.: 202.

16. See Chapter 7, n. 22 and 30.

17. Discussion of Client-Centered Psychotherapy, 1958: 45, op. cit. (Chapter 7, n. 3).

18. E.L. Thorndike, Animal Intelligence: An Experimental Study of the Associative Processes in Animals. *Psychological Review, Monograph Supplement, 2*, 8 (1898).

19. I.P. Pavlov, *Conditioned Reflexes* (London: Oxford University Press, 1927).

20. B.F. Skinner, *The Behavior of Organisms: An Experimental Analysis* (New York: Appleton-Century-Crofts, 1938).

21. B.F. Skinner, *Science and Human Behavior* (New York: Macmillan, 1953).

22. Quoted in B.J. Baars, *The Cognitive Revolution in Psychology* (p. 203) (New York: Guilford Press, 1986).

23. B.F. Skinner, *Walden Two* (New York: Macmillan, 1948).

24. Letter from L.D. Clepper, Jr., marketing manager for Macmillan Publishing Company to author, September 30, 1974.

25. B.F. Skinner, *The Technology of Teaching* (New York: Appleton-Century-Crofts, 1968).

26. For example, Wolpe distinguished between systematic desensitization, assertiveness training, operant conditioning and other behavior therapy approaches. J. Wolpe, *The Practice of Behavior Therapy* (3rd ed.) (New York: Pergamon Press, 1982).

27. T. Kennedy, Treatment of Chronic Schizophrenia by Behavior Therapy: Case Reports, *Behavior Research and Therapy, 2* (1964): 1–7.

28. See, for example, Review of the Evidence, in Richard Sharf, *Theories of Psychotherapy and Counseling* (3rd ed.) (p. 307) (Pacific Grove, CA: Brooks Cole, 2004); P.M. Emmelkamp, Behavior Therapy with Adults (pp. 379–427) and S.D. Hollon & A.T. Beck, Cognitive and Cognitive-Behavioral Therapies (pp. 428–466), both in Bergin & Garfield, 1994.

29. See B.J. Baars, The Double Life of B.F. Skinner, *Journal of Consciousness Studies, 10*, 1 (2003): 5–25.

30. M. Wertheimer, Untersuchungen zur Lehre von der Gestalt, II, *Psychol. Forsch, 4* (1923): 301–350. Translated and condensed as Laws of Organization in Perceptual Forms, in W.D. Ellis (Ed.), *A Sourcebook of Gestalt Psychology* (New York: Harcourt, Brace and World, 1938); *Productive Thinking* (New York: Harper and Row, 1945).

31. W. Kohler, *The Mentality of Apes*. Translated by E. Winter (New York: Harcourt, Brace & World, 1925); *Gestalt Psychology.* (New York: Liveright, 1929).

32. K. Koffka, *The Growth of Mind*. Translated by R.M. Ogden (London: Kegan Paul, Trench, Trubner & Co. Ltd., 1924); *Principles of Gestalt Psychology* (New York: Harcourt, Brace & World, 1935).

33. Hall & Lindzey, 1957: 206.

34. CR, 1951a: 4.

35. G.W. Allport, *Personality: A Psychological Interpretation* (New York: Holt, 1937); Goldstein, Maslow, May and others are discussed and cited below.

36. Goldstein, 1940; see also I.S. Freiman, Kurt Goldstein—An Appreciation, *American Journal of Psychotherapy, 8* (1953): 3–10, and F.A. Quadfasel, Aspects of the Life and Work of Kurt Goldstein, *Cortex: A Journal Devoted to the Study of the Nervous System and Behavior, 4* (1968): 113–124.

37. Maslow, 1943a, 1943b, 1959 op. cit. (n. 2), 1962.

38. CR, 1957d.

39. K. Lewin, *A Dynamic Theory of Personality* (New York: McGraw, 1935); *Resolving social conflicts*. In G.W. Lewin (Ed.), *Selected Papers on Group Dynamics* (New York: Harper, 1948).

40. This is captured in H. Jackins' title, *The Human Side of Human Beings* (Seattle: Rational Island Publishing, 1965).

41. T. Robbins, *Fierce Invalids Home from Hot Climates* (p. 101) (New York: Bantam, 2000).

42. R. May, Lectures at the New School for Social Research, New York City, Spring, 1965. Unpublished.

43. Frankl, 1963; May, 1961.

44. E.g., S. Simon, L. Howe & H. Kirschenbaum, *Values Clarification: A Handbook of Practical Strategies for Teachers and Students* (New York: Hart 1972/1979) and *Values Clarification: Your Self-Directed Workbook* (New York: Warner Books, 1995); H. Kirschenbaum, *Values Clarification Counseling*, in preparation.

45. E.g., M. Silberman, J. Allender, & J. Yanoff, *The Psychology of Open Teaching and Learning: An Inquiry Approach* (Boston: Little, Brown, 1972); E. Nyquist & G. Hawes, *Open Education: A Sourcebook for Parents and Teachers* (New York: Bantam, 1972).

46. Klein, 2000: 61.

47. CR, 1942d: 17.

48. CR, 1973b: 124–125.

49. CR, letter to author, October 25, 1973.

50. Hall, Lindzey, & Campbell, 1998: 487.

51. CR, 1946c: 422.

52. CR, 1948c: 3–4 in manuscript copy. UCSB/R-K.

53. Ibid.: 4.

54. CR, 1949c: 17.

55. CR, 1949c: 13.

56. Rogers & Skinner, 1956: 1060.

57. Ibid.: 1061.

58. Ibid.: 1064.

59. Ibid.: 1059–1060.

60. Ibid.: 1065.

61. Ibid.: 1061.

62. R. Evans, *B. F. Skinner: The Man and His Ideas* (New York: E. P. Dutton, 1968); inscription viewed by author, 1971.

63. Rogers & Skinner, 1956.

64. The particular theme of this conference was "Evolution and the Individual." Others present included Erik Erikson, Harry Harlow, Donald Marquis, Abraham Maslow, philosopher Ernest Nagel, and law professor Harold Lasswell. From official list of participants, UCSB/R-K.

65. CR, letter to author, October 25, 1973.

66. Ibid.; Rogers also repeated these excerpts from the 1960 meeting during their June, 1962 dialogue. See complete transcript of 1962 dialogue in Kirschenbaum & Henderson, 1989a.

67. Ibid.

68. E.g., Rogers & Hart, 1970.

69. CR, letter to author, October 25, 1973.

70. Drs. Moy Fook Gum and Gerald Gladstein were two of the faculty, and Gladstein moderated the dialogue. CR, letter to author, October 25, 1973; G. Gladstein, letter to author, June 25, 1988.

71. CR, author interview, March, 1971.

72. From conference program, titled "Education and the Control of Human Behavior: A Dialogue." UCSB/R-K.

73. Quotations from author's mid-1970s transcription of selected portions of original audio tapes. Subsequent quotations are from Virginia Conard's transcript of full dialogue, proofread by author, in Kirschenbaum & Henderson, 1989a: 82–152.

74. CR, author interview, March, 1971, tape 6.

75. The article was B.F. Skinner, A Case History in Scientific Method. *American Psychologist, 11*, 5 (1956): 221–233.

76. Rogers & Hart, 1970: 522.

77. Tape No. 10. Rogers–Skinner Dialogue, American Academy of Psychotherapists Tape Library.

78. Carl R. Rogers & B.F. Skinner, "A Dialogue on Education and the Control of Human Behavior." A 6-cassette Album edited by Gerald A. Gladstein (New York: Jeffrey Norton Publishers, 1976); transcribed and printed in H. Kirschenbaum & V. Henderson, 1989a.

79. Letter, September 8, 1982. UCSB/B. More on the context of the birthday celebration in Chapter 12.

80. CR, 1947a: 116.

81. The most complete version of these events is told in Demanchick & Kirschenbaum, *Journal of Humanistic Psychology*, in press.

82. Unless otherwise indicated, information in this section comes from Marks, 1979 and Ross, 2000. John Marks was the individual most responsible for exposing the CIA abuses of this period.

83. H. Wolff & L. Hinkle, Communist Interrogation and Indoctrination of "Enemies of the State"—An analysis of methods used by the Communist State Police, *AMA Archives of Neurology and Psychiatry, 76* (August 1956). Quote in Marks, 1979: 128.

84. Lawrence Hinkle confirmed these events in letters to John Marks, n.d. (1978) and to Dr. David E. Rogers, October 18, 1978. Letters in LOC 3/ 4.

85. Ross, 2000; Marks, 1979.

86. The interviews are reported in Greenfield, 1977 and Marks, 1979. Rogers never denied their contents and later hired Marks to work on the Carl Rogers Peace Project meeting in Rust, Austria, further affirming Marks' credibility as a source.

87. CR, Relationship with the Department of Psychiatry and the School of Medicine, Memorandum to Lawrence Kimpton, November 7, 1956. UCSB/R-K.

88. Greenfield, 1977: 10.

89. Marks, 1979: 168.

90. Greenfield, 1977: 10.

91. Marks, 1979: 168.

92. Greenfield, 1977: 10.

93. Marks, 1979: 169.

94. CR, University of Wisconsin "Professional Activities" reports for 1957, 1958 and 1959. UCSB/R-K; Ross, 2000.

95. Average calculated in Demanchick & Kirschenbaum, in press, from Ross's 2000 listing of 149 MKULTRA "subprojects."

96. Later published in R. Roessler & N. Greenfield (Eds.), *Physiological Correlates of Psychological Disorder* (Madison, WI: University of Wisconsin Press, 1962).

97. CR, "Professional Activities" reports, op. cit. (n. 94).

98. CR, 1962c; Rogers, Gendlin, Kiesler & Truax, 1967.

99. Greenfield, 1977: 10, cites a CIA memo from January 1960 to that effect.

100. Quoted in Marks, 1979: 171.

101. Marks, 1979; Ross, 2000.

102. Marks, 1979: 69.

103. Hinkle, letter to David Rogers, op. cit. (n. 84); Marks, 1979: 156.

104. Marks, 1979: 154.

105. Greenfield, 1977: 10.

106. Marks, 1979: 156.

107. Hinkle, letter to John Marks, op. cit. (n. 84).

108. C. Ross, *The CIA and military mind control research: Building the Manchurian candidate: Part One*. 1997: 4. Retrieved October 1, 2005 from <http://www.mindcontrolforums.com/radio/ckln01.htm>.

109. F. Rudmin, Carl Rogers worked for the CIA. *Peace Research, 31,* 4 (1999): 77.

110. Hinkle to DR, op. cit. (n. 84).

111. M. Harrington, *The Other America: Poverty in the United States* (New York: Macmillan, 1962); J.H. Jones, *Bad Blood: The Tuskegee Syphilis Experiment: New and Expanded Edition* (New York: The Free Press, 1993).

112. Kirschenbaum & Henderson, 1989a.

113. Ibid: 6–7.

114. Cissna & Anderson, 2002; see also H. Kirschenbaum & S. Demanchick, Much Ado about Dialogue. Review of Cissna & Anderson (2002). *Contemporary Psychology: APA Review of Books, 49,* 4 (2004): 422–424.

115. Cissna & Anderson, 2002 provide a full bibliography of publications on the dialogue.

116. The category titles are Cissna and Anderson's, ibid. The descriptors are from Kirschenbaum & Demanchick's review, op. cit. (n. 114).

117. Cissna & Anderson, 2002; M. Friedman, Reflections on the Buber–Rogers Dialogue, *Journal of Humanistic Psychology, 34,* 1 (1994): 47.

118. CR, 1958a; also CR, 1961a: 55.

119. Cissna & Anderson, 2002.

120. Friedman, op. cit.: 47 (n. 117).

121. Rogers & Tillich, 1966. Reprinted in Kirschenbaum & Henderson, 1989a. For a time the recorded dialogue was available as one of five tapes in *Carl Rogers on Tape*, Human Development Institute, Atlanta, Georgia.

122. Maureen O'Hara wrote an excellent, personal account of the encounter in her auto-biographical chapter in Suhd, 1995: 118–127.

123. Cohen, 1997: 15.

124. Pitts, 1973: 75.

125. Discussion of Client-Centered Psychotherapy, 1958: 38, op. cit. (Chapter 7, n. 3).

126. Rogers & Skinner, 1956: 1063.

127. Pitts, 1973: 75.

128. Duncan and Hively, personal communication with author, 1972; see also A. Duncan, Self-Application of Behavior Modification Techniques by Teenagers. *Research Training Paper No. 11.* Kansas City: Bureau of Child Research Laboratory, University of Kansas Medical Center, 1968.

129. CR, 1973a: 84.

130. CR, 1977: 19.

131. Kim Francis, *Two Hours with Carl Rogers*, unpublished manuscript. UCSB/R-K. It was surprising that Rogers used the word "we," as he was more of a consultant to the Louisville schools than a part of the planning or implementation team. He would have observed the behavior modification rather than participated in it.

132. CR, 1951a: 4.

133. Ibid. Ranks' banishment from the psychoanalytic establishment is discussed in Kramer, 1995a.

134. CR, 1986c: 125.

135. Several studies on this point are reported in Chapter 13.

136. A. Ellis, Ethics and the Therapist's Honesty. *Voices: The Art and Science of Psychotherapy, 28*, 3 (1992): 33 and 34. Original emphases.

137. E.g., M. Seligman & M. Csikszentmihalyi, Positive Psychology: An introduction, *American Psychologist, 55*, 1 (1990): 5–14; M. Seligman, T. Steen, N. Park & C. Peterson, Positive Psychology Progress: Empirical validation of interventions, *American Psychologist, 60*, 5 (July–August 2005): 410–421; Positive Psychology Center website <www.ppc.sas.upenn.edu>.

138. T. Peterson, review of S. Joseph & P.A. Linley, *Positive Therapy: A Meta-Theory for Positive Psychological Practice* (London and New York: Routledge Taylor & Francis Group, 2006). Reviewed in *Counseling Today*, February, 2007: 20.

139. Daniel Goleman, *Destructive Emotions: A Scientific Dialogue with the Dalai Llama* (New York: Bantam, 2004).

Chapter 9

1. CR, 1967a: 371. Although he would use comparable language to describe a later episode—the break-up of WBSI.

2. CR, Memo to Staff, *The Center Bulletin*, August 27, 1957. UCSB/R-K.

3. Rogers & Russell, 2002: 174.

4. CR, Professional Activities report for 1957. UCSB/R-K.

5. CR, Professional Activities reports for 1957, 1958 and 1959. UCSB/R-K.

6. CR, Professional Activities reports for 1958, ibid.

7. CR, "The Case of P.S.—A Young Woman: Comments," n.d., and "Some Questions about Sodium Amytal and Therapy (A Tentative Note)," 1959. Both UCSB/R-K. In the latter, Rogers wrote that he learned it would be wrong to encourage patients to reveal too much under sodium amytal, because they might regret or feel guilty about it later. His interest was more in the patient's welfare than in what the researchers (or CIA interrogators) might learn by this method.

8. See J. Berlin, *Some Autonomic Correlates of Therapeutic Conditions in Interpersonal Relationships* (Unpublished Ph.D. dissertation, University of Chicago, 1960); E.T. Gendlin & J. Berlin, Galvanic Skin Response Correlates of Different Modes of Experiencing, *Journal of Clinical Psychology, 17*, (1961): 73–77; and R. Roessler & N. Greenfield (Eds.), *Physiological Correlates of Psychological Disorder* (Madison: University of Wisconsin Press, 1962).

9. C.R. Rogers, A Tentative Scale for the Measurement of Process in Psychotherapy. In E. Rubinstein & M.B. Parloff (Eds.), *Research in Psychotherapy: Proceedings of a Conference* (pp. 96–107, April 12–15, 1958) (Washington, DC: APA, 1958); also Walker, Rablen & Rogers, 1960.

10. Fred Harvey Harrington correspondence. See also CR, Professional Activity reports for 1957 and 1958. UCSB/R-K.

11. A note in Rogers' handwriting (UCSB/R-K), says he received a total of $561,035 in outside funding. Subtracting the four known grants described above, leaves a balance of approximately $162,000.

12. Rogers & Russell, 2002: 175.

13. CR, A silent young man, in Rogers, Gendlin, Kiesler & Truax, 1967: 403.

14. Ibid.: 404 and 409.

15. Ibid.: 413.

16. Charles Truax tape, May 6, 1971. Truax did not name the patient; I surmise it was Jim.

17. See discussion of American Academy of Psychotherapist tape series below.

18. CR, letter to C.H. ("Mr. Vac"), September 12, 1970; CR, letter to author, March 23, 1971. Both in UCSB/R-K. "Hi, Doc" from CR, 1973b.

19. Halkides, 1958; Barrett-Lennard, 1959, 1962; Rogers, 1957a.

20. D.J. Kiesler, A Scale for the Rating of Congruence (pp. 581–584); C.B. Truax, A Scale for the Rating of Accurate Empathy (pp. 555–568); C.B. Truax, A Tentative Scale for the Rating of Unconditional Positive Regard (pp. 569–579). Each was a chapter in Rogers, Gendlin, Kiesler & Truax, 1967.

21. E.T. Gendlin & F. Zimring, The Qualities or Dimensions of Experiencing and Their Change, *Counseling Center Discussion Papers,* University of Chicago Library, *1,* 3 (1955); Gendlin, 1957, 1958, 1962.

22. CR, 1958c.

23. Discussion of Client-Centered Therapy, 1958: 18, op. cit. (Chapter 7 n. 3).

24. CR, 1957a; Walker, Rablen, & Rogers, 1960.

25. CR, Introduction, in Rogers, Gendlin, Kiesler & Truax, 1967: xviii.

26. CR, author interview, March, 1971, tape 5.

27. These and subsequent events were corroborated by several independent sources, including Allen Bergin interview and letters in LOC 32/8; Gene Bleeker interview, 1971; Eugene Gendlin correspondence; Donald Kiesler correspondence; CR, author interview, tape 5, and CR, 1967a. Donald Kiesler also sent me copies of dozens of letters from this period. I had written to Truax for general information on Rogers, but also specifically asked for his perspective on "the troubles at Wisconsin." Although Truax sent a lengthy tape, with a great deal of information about his relationship with Rogers over the years, there was a conspicuous fifteen minute or so gap in the tape just when he would have been discussing this period. I intended to write him again, but later learned from several sources that he had committed suicide, following what appeared to be a long history of psychological difficulties. Rogers wrote his widow, Janie Truax, a condolence letter to which she sent a very appreciative answer on July 18, 1974, and he in turn sent a kind and gracious answer on July 26, 1974. LOC 33/4.

28. CR to Donald Kiesler and Philippa Mathieu, March 13, 1963. Later Rogers recalled, "I understand Truax so much better now that I've watched Nixon. Maybe there *is* such a thing as a psychopath!" Letter to author, January 23, 1974.

29. Doug Shoeninger, reporting a statement attributed to William Fey, a colleague in the Department of Psychiatry. Author interview, March, 1971.

30. CR to Donald J. Kiesler, August 13, 1966. All letters cited here to or from Donald Kiesler are in the UCSB/R-K collection.

31. Rogers, Gendlin, Kiesler & Truax, 1967.

32. Kiesler to CR and Gendlin, August 10, 1966.

33. H.G. Krane, letter to CR, August 26, 1966.

34. Kiesler to CR, September 2, 1966.

35. Letter from "Gene" to "Carl," August 21, 1970. LOC 32/11.

36. CR to Kiesler and Gendlin, September 8, 1966.

37. D.J. Kiesler, September 19, 1966.
38. Rogers & Russell, 2002: 176.
39. Truax & Mitchell, 1971. However, as these results were so much more positive than those which the other researchers found, there are those who question, usually off the record, whether Truax's subsequent findings can be fully trusted.
40. Chapters were Truax and Commentators, The Client-Centered Process as Viewed by Other Therapists (pp. 419–506) and Rogers and Commentators, A Dialogue Between Therapists (pp. 507–520) in Rogers, Gendlin, Kiesler & Truax, 1967. Issues discussed in Raskin, 1978.
41. Gene Bleeker tape, 1971.
42. Bergin to Gay Swenson, November 12, 1986. In "85th Greetings" folder, UCSB/B. Also told by Bergin in author interview, 2003.
43. Schoeninger, author interview, 1971.
44. Bleeker tape.
45. Schoeninger interview.
46. Memo to Psychiatrists and Psychologists in Wisconsin, from Carl Rogers (listed first), Robert Roessler, Edwin Peterson, David Grant and Leland Reeck, April 1959, and minutes from "Joint Meeting of Committees of the Wisconsin Psychiatric Association and the Wisconsin Psychological Association on Relations Between the Professions," September 26, 1959. UCSB/R-K. Quote from CR, 1973b, in CR, 1980b: 55.
47. Rogers & Russell, 2002: 178.
48. CR, Memo to Psychology Faculty, Re: Program of First Graduate Year in Psychology, January 1959. UCSB/R-K.
49. CR, Memorandum dated January 28, 1963. LOC.
50. CR, dittoed letter. UCSB/R-K.
51. Described in CR to Donald Kiesler, April 8, 1963.
52. HR, 1965: 97.
53. Johnson correspondence.
54. T.M. Tomlinson correspondence; see also reference to "our 6-acre tract" in letter to Dave and Corky Rogers and Natalie and Larry Fuchs, March 31, 1960. LOC 1/11.
55. Author interview, 1975.
56. NR, in Suhd, 1995: 194. Citation: Natalie Rogers Fuchs, [Title], Brandeis University, Department of Psychology, 1960.
57. NR, author interview, 1974.
58. Author interviews with Janet, Frances and Naomi Fuchs, 1974.
59. CR, Memorandum to Staff, Psychotherapy Research Group, December 9, 1963. UCSB/R-K.
60. Presentation based on CR, 1957c.
61. CR, 1961c.
62. CR, 1958a.
63. CR, 1959b.
64. Data in this paragraph from Professional Activities—Professor Carl R. Rogers, Departments of Psychology and Psychiatry, Calendar Year 1958. UCSB/R-K.
65. Described in CR, Jottings from an Oriental Journey, June 27, 1961. Unpublished. UCSB/R-K. Itinerary of the Japan trip in LOC 4/12.
66. Minoru Hatase correspondence, October 28, 1972. Hatase translated several of Rogers' books into Japanese.
67. Fox, 1967: 14.
68. Ibid.: 11
69. E.g., Polanyi, 1964.
70. Author interview, March 1971.

71. Polanyi correspondence, 1971.

72. E.g., E.H. Erikson, *Young Man Luther* (New York: W.W. Norton, 1958); *Childhood and Society* (2nd ed.) (New York: Norton, 1963); *Identity: Youth and Crisis* (New York: Norton, 1968).

73. CR, 1967a: 372.

74. CR, Discussion with workshop participants at the National Humanistic Education Center, Upper Jay, New York, August 30, 1973.

75. "Freud's household" in letter from CR to Joseph Chassell, September 28, 1972. UCSB/R-K. Inscription observed by author in Rogers' study. The book must have been E. Erikson, *Insight and Responsibility* (New York: Norton, 1964). The chapter first appeared in *Yale Review* (Autumn 1956).

76. CR, 1967a: 372.

77. CR, author interview, March 1971, tape 5.

78. Fox, 1967: 6.

79. CR, 1961a: 3–4.

80. Ibid.: 16.

81. Ibid.: 106.

82. Ibid.: 166.

83. CR, 1958a; reprinted in CR, 1961a. Quotation: 50–55.

84. CR, 1960.

85. CR, 1957d.

86. CR, 1961a: 186–187.

87. Ibid.: 189.

88. Ibid.: 190.

89. Ibid.: 277. Original emphasis.

90. E.g. P. Cushman, 1990; Sampson, 1988.

91. This issue will be discussed at considerably greater length in Chapter 12, under the heading of Multicultural Issues.

92. CR, 1954.

93. CR, 1955.

94. CR, 1961a: 213.

95. CR, 1961a: 216.

96. CR, 1961a: 217.

97. CR, 1961a: 221 and 223.

98. Including CR, 1961b.

99. CR, 1957c. Reprinted in CR, 1961a. Quotation: 276.

100. CR, 1959a.

101. CR, 1961a: 318–319.

102. CR, 1952b.

103. CR, 1961a: 332–333.

104. Rogers & Farson, 1957.

105. Farson interview, 2003. Farson recalled how he wrote the first draft, Rogers made some changes and gave the speech, and Rogers gave him $300 of the $400 received for the chapter— the equivalent of a month-and-a half salary at the time for the delighted Farson.

106. Gordon, 1970, 1974; T. Gordon, *L.E.T.: Leader Effectiveness Training* (New York: Peter Wyden, 1980).

107. CR, 1960, in 1961a: 178–180.

108. CR, 1961a: xi.

109. Thorne, 2002a: 16.

110. J. David, letter dated March 11, 1973. UCSB/R-K.

111. R. Bond, letter dated January 24, 1963. UCSB/R-K.

112. CR, letter to author, January 23, 1974.

113. D. Lamont, letter dated November 23, 1973. UCSB/R-K.

114. Rogers & Russell, 2002: 186.

115. In a letter dated October 5, 1971, Rogers told his brother Lester that *Counseling and Psychotherapy* (1942a) had sold 83,000 copies; *Client-Centered Therapy* (1951a) had sold 112,000; and *On Becoming a Person* (1961a) had sold 180,000. By 1977, those figures had grown to 106,000, 173,000 and 565,000, respectively. 1971 letter and CR's 1977 calculation in UCSB/R-K.

116. E. Fromm, *Escape from Freedom* (New York: Rinehart & Co., 1941); *The Sane Society* (New York: Holt, Rinehart & Winston, 1955); *The Art of Loving* (New York: Harper and Row, 1956).

117. E. Berne, *Games People Play* (New York: Grove Press, 1967).

118. CR, author interview, March 1971, tape 3.

119. Details of this dispute come from a whole sheaf of correspondence with Houghton Mifflin, in Rogers' files, subsequently donated to LOC. Accurate sales figures for this and Rogers' other Houghton Mifflin titles were unavailable from the publisher in 2006. Brandy Vickers, HM, personal communication, November 15, 2006.

120. Tapes include Loretta, Mr. Vac, Miss Mun, Mr. Lin, Mike, Mrs. P.S. American Academy of Psychotherapists Tape Library. His interviews with Loretta were taped at the first summer workshop of the AAP in Madison, Wisconsin. Albert Ellis was also taped at the time. Vivian Guze interview.

121. For a listing of audiotaped and videotaped therapy sessions and interviews in which Rogers is featured, see the films available from <www.centerfortheperson.com>, and from Peter Schmid's website: <http://members.nusurf.at/pfs/bibliocrr.htm#films> and also <htm#video>, retrieved April 10, 2006.

122. The filming took place in 1964. Information for this section comes from: Gloria, Comment on Interview with Perls. Appendix (pp. 140–141) to R. Dolliver, E. Williams & D. Gold, The Art of Gestalt Therapy Or: What Are You Doing with Your Feet Now? *Psychotherapy: Theory, Research and Practice, 17,* 2 (1980):136–142; Rogers, letter to author, May 26, 1971; Rogers, 1984; S. Wickman, communication to the counselor education listserve (<CESNET-L@ LISTSERVE.KENT.EDU>), May 6, 2005: S. Wickman & C. Campbell, An Analysis of how Carl Rogers Enacted Client-Centered Conversation with Gloria, *Journal of Counseling and Development, 81* (2003):178–183; See also S. Weinrach, Ellis and Gloria: Positive or Negative Model (including a comment by Ellis), *Psychotherapy, 23,* 4, (Winter 1986): 642–648.

123. Gloria, 1980: 141, op. cit. (n. 122).

124. Rogers, 1984: 425.

125. A. Glauser & J. Bozarth, Person-Centered Counseling: The Culture Within, *Journal of Counseling and Development, 79* (2001): 142–147; *Three Approaches to Psychotherapy* is available from Psychological and Educational Films, 3334 E. Coast Hwy. #252, Corona Del Mar, CA 92625, <www.psychedfilms.com>.

126. Other members included Jerome Bruner, James Bugental, Kenneth Spence, Charles Osgood and other leaders in the profession. "Members: Committee on the Professional and Scientific Aims of Psychology," n.d. UCSB/R-K.

127. See D.R. Peterson, The Doctor of Psychology Degree, in Freedheim, 1992: 829–849.

128. APA, Division of Clinical Psychology, *Newsletter* (Fall 1962): 2.

129. Thorne, 2002a: 16.

130. Rogers, 1967a: 372–373.

131. Farson interview, 2003. Farson recalled Duke and Chicago. A May 23, 1961 letter from CR

to Walter Rogers tells how Duke University has "been after me very strongly to accept the distinguished professorship there with a quite surprisingly large salary and many good opportunities." LOC 1/12. Duke and Chicago also mentioned in Hall, 1967b: 51.
132. "Dear Friends" and "Statement by Carl R. Rogers," mimeographed letter and dittoed memorandum, both 1963, n.d. UCSB/R-K. "Statement" also in LOC 32/6.
133. Letter dated July 26, 1963.
134. Harrington correspondence, March 9, 1972.
135. Letter to "Dear Friends" from "Helen and Carl," December 31, 1963. UCSB/R-K.
136. Letter dated July 25, 1963. LOC 32/6.

Chapter 10

1. Letter to "Dear Friends," signed "Helen and Carl," December 31, 1963. UCSB/R-K.
2. Ibid.
3. Personal communication, July 6, 1971.
4. Ernest Poser correspondence, 1971.
5. Letter to "Dear Friends," op. cit. (n. 1); NR, email communication, November 22, 2006.
6. Description of the Rogers' home and their sentiments about it, from author's several visits in the 1970s.
7. CR, letter to Len Holdstock, September 12, 1973. UCSB/R-K.
8. CR, letter to City Planning Commission, June 11, 1970. The density of the development was later reduced.
9. Center for Studies of the Person, group interview, March 1971.
10 HR, author interview, March, 1971.
11. Helen Rogers Gives $10,200 to Local Planned Parenthood, Planned Parenthood Association of San Diego County, *Newsletter, 2*, 4 (Winter 1967–68). UCSB/R-K.
12. Rogers described it as a workshop on "human relations" and "group leadership." Farson remembered the title as "Developing the Therapeutic Relationship." Richard Farson interview, March 22, 2003.
13. Hall, 1967b: 51.
14. Details on the founding of WBSI from Farson interview, 2003; Hall, 1967b; Rogers, 1967a: 373.
15. Tom Gordon recalled organizing a seminar with Hayakawa on a topic like "Applications of Client-Centered Theory Outside the Clinic." In Suhd, 1995: 320. Haigh, 1988, recalled the title as "Implications in Client-Centered Therapy for Dyadic Relations, Family Relations, Industrial Relations, and International Relations."
16. Hall, 1967b: 53.
17. These and other visiting fellows from Hall, 1967b; Farson interview, 2003.
18. Kirschenbaum & Henderson, 1989a: 65.
19. Hall, *San Diego Magazine*, 1967b: 51; a *New York Times* article (June 14, 1967) by Richard Reeves, in a series on think tanks, said Rogers earned $25,000 and Farson $19,000; Farson recalled that at one point Rogers' salary was $30,000, while his own as executive director was half that, Farson interview; both articles said Gibb also turned his $25,000 salary back to WBSI.
20. Financial information from CR, "Some financial facts for Howie K," 4-page memo in CR's hand, December 5, 1974. UCSB/R-K.
21. Their adjusted gross income averaged $53,730 from 1964–1974. Still they felt wealthy enough, and possibly confident enough of future royalties, to donate $129,500 in tax deductible gifts and give $82,000 to their children, grandchildren and a niece during that period. After

donations and taxes, that left them an average of $23,365 per year to live on during that decade. Ibid. More will be said of the university position later.

22. Examples from Hall, 1967b.

23. Reeves, 1967, op. cit. (n. 19).

24. CR, 1955, 1961b.

25. Coulson & Rogers, 1968: 5.

26. Polanyi, 1964.

27. CR, Introduction, in Coulson & Rogers, 1968: 4.

28. Coulson & Rogers, 1968: 177, 184–185.

29. Ibid.: 185–188.

30. Coulson & Rogers, 1968.

31. CR, Introduction, ibid.: 8.

32. Ibid.

33. CR, letter to author, March 22, 1974.

34. Lynn Davie, Man and the Science of Man [book review], *Adult Leadership, 19*, 5 (November, 1970): 169.

35. Coulson & Rogers, 1968: 5.

36. These terms were all in use at the time, some just beginning to catch on. See, for example, U. Flick, *An Introduction to Qualitative Research* (London: Sage, 1970).

37. Coulson & Rogers, 1968: 8.

38. CR, 1985.

39. CR, letter to Andre Keogh, July 6, 1972. UCSB/R-K.

40. Editor's note accompanying CR, 1969b: 27.

41. Poppy, 1968: 69.

42. L. Bradford, J. Gibb & K. Benne (Eds.), *T-Group Theory and Laboratory Method: Innovations in Re-Education* (New York: John Wiley & Sons, 1964).

43. Hall, 1967a: 63.

44. "Our History," retrieved April 8, 2005 from <www.ntl.org/about-history.html>, n.a.

45. Rogers & Russell, 2002: 191. Hadassah Peres did her Masters thesis on the group, later published as An Investigation of Nondirective Group Therapy, *Journal of Consulting Psychology, 11*, 4 (July–August 1947): 159–172.

46. CR, The origin and scope of the trend toward "groups," in 1970a: 1–14.

47. CR, 1970a: 3.

48. CR, letter to author, June 1, 1974.

49. Hall, 1967a: 63.

50. CR, letter to author, June 1, 1974.

51. CR, from an advertising flyer for Carl Rogers and Richard Farson's filmed encounter group "Journey Into Self," 1968.

52. L. Hersher correspondence, 1971.

53. CR, 1970a: 113–114.

54. Ibid.: 65.

55. Laughlin correspondence, May 11, 1971. Laughlin was then Chairman of the Board of the immensely successful Saga Foods Corporation.

56. Natalie Rogers, author interview, 1973.

57. David Rogers, author interview, 1975.

58. CR, 1970a: 73.

59. Ibid.: 65.

60. Ibid.: 47.

61. Ibid.: 51.

62. Ibid.: 52.

63. Ibid.: 25.
64. Ibid.: 34.
65. Ibid.: 112.
66. Ibid.: 59.
67. Ibid.: 59.
68. Ibid.: 53.
69. Ibid.: 49–50.
70. Ibid.: 52–53.
71. Ibid.: 54–55.
72. Ibid.: 55.
73. CR, letter to "Dear Group Members," April 20, 1965, 3 pp. UCSB/R-K.
74. CR, Personal and Confidential Memo to: The Honker Group, May 12, 1965, 3 pp. UCSB/R-K.
75. Betty Meador interview, 1971.
76. Natalie wrote her parents, "I will be anxious to hear more about Mom's workshop experience—the good one," June 15, 1965. LOC 1/13.
77. Rogers & Russell, 2002: 213–214.
78. NR, email communication, November 22, 2006.
79. NR, letter to "Dear Dad," n.d., "approx. 5/12/65" written in CR's hand. LOC 1/13.
80. Larry Fuchs, letter to "Dear Mom and Dad," August 27, 1964. LOC 1/12.
81. CR, 1970a: 1.
82. CR, "How to Use Encounter Group Concepts." A series of 26 cassette tapes (Chicago: Instructional Dynamics, Inc., 1969).
83. The encounter group video, directed by Bill McGaw, was titled "Because That's My Way." See also, CR, "The Drug Scene—Divergent Perspectives," unpublished summary and impressions of the group, n.d., 21 pp. UCSB/R-K.
84. CR, letter to Mr. Stuart Savage, November 11, 1970. UCSB/R-K.
85. They received the 1971 award. <www.peabody.uga.edu>.
86. Information from WBSI Weekly Bulletin, March 28, 1966, in CR's file "TV Group 3/66." UCSB/R-K.
87. CR, 1970a: 109.
88. Kramer's film "2001: A Space Odyssey" received many Academy Award nominations the same year that "Journey Into Self" was released.
89. Another film was first given the Oscar, but it was later found to have been ineligible, and "Journey Into Self" was given the award in a private ceremony on May 7, 1969. CR, letter to author, July, 1974. See also R. Shale (Ed.), *Academy Awards* (New York: Frederick Ungar Publishing Co., 1978): 498. Also <www.awardsdatabase.oscars.org>, retrieved March 19, 2004.
90. CR, author interview, March 1971.
91. CR, letter to author, February 15, 1978.
92. CR, 1970a: 68.
93. Ibid., 1970a: 37.
94. Ibid., 1970a: 79.
95. Edgar correspondence, 1971.
96. CR, 1970a: 38.
97. J.R. Gibb, The Effects of Human Relations Training. In A. Bergin and S. Garfield (Eds.), *Handbook of Psychotherapy and Behavior Change* (New York: John Wiley & Sons, 1970): 2114–2176.
98. CR, 1970a: 117.
99. Ibid.: 118–120.

100. E. Maliver, Encounter Groupers Up Against the Wall, *New York Times Magazine* (January 3, 1971): 4–5, 37–41, 43.

101. CR, January 18, 1971. It is not clear if Rogers' letter was ever published. My *New York Times* search did not locate it.

102. J.T. Bugental, *The Search for Authenticity* (New York: Holt, Rinehart and Winston, 1965); Frankl, 1963; May, 1961.

103. CR, 1970a: 107.

104. Hall, 1967a: 62.

105. CR, 1970a: 107.

106. Ibid.: 117. He would return to this theme in his chapter on "Ellen West—And Loneliness" in CR, 1980a.

107. Ibid.: 158–159.

108. Ibid.: 168.

109. CR, Memo to the Trustees Who Were Present at the June 25–26, 1968 Meeting, July 30, 1968. Rogers wrote on this document, "I think this was never sent." UCSB/R-K. But it was, as trustee Bill Laughlin, president of Saga Foods Corporation sent me his copy. The events caused Rogers to feel ill enough to see a doctor. CSP group interview, 1975.

110. Farson reflections from author interview, 2003.

111. CR, Memo to the Trustees, op. cit. (n. 109).

112. This and previous excerpt, ibid.

113. CSP group interview, 1975.

114. Probably written on July 18, 1968. Unpublished. UCSB/R-K.

115. Tom Gillette, CSP group interview.

116. Rogers & Russell, 2002: 198.

117. Farson interview.

118. Center for Studies of the Person, 1969 brochure.

119. Information on CSP from interviews with members, including CR; Center brochures and documents, including "A View of CSP by One of Its Members, Carl Rogers," unpublished, n.d., 4 pp. All in UCSB/R-K; and personal observations.

120. Norman Chambers interview, 2003.

121. Rogers & Frick, 1971: 113–114.

122. The Paris analogy was not hers but passed on by Gay Barfield, email communication, November 11, 2006.

123. "Any of my four kids." HR to "Dearest Nat-Larry," October 7, 1951. Whole letter in Chapter 7.

124. For example, Corky wrote to "Dearest Pop" on February 19, 1961, expressing deep appreciation for the letter he wrote her "during my Calif. hospital sojourn 7 years ago." LOC 1/12.

125. CR, letter to "Dear Larry," March 8, 1969. LOC 2/8.

126. Cohen, 1997: 19.

127. NR, 1980.

128. NR interview, 2003. The letter that Cohen made much of was Rogers' advice to David to establish temporary residence in California. Cohen neglected to quote the part of the letter where Rogers wrote how in California, "All property is community property, & is split down the middle. Spouse and children are awarded payments according to their needs & the income available. No punitive aspect to it." This compared to New Jersey law where Corky presumably would have automatically been awarded the marital home. CR to David Rogers, August 13, 1970. LOC. See also DR, in Suhd, 1995: 279.

129. Ibid.: 279.

130. Ibid.

131. DR interview, 1975.

132. Beginning in 1966. Email communication, Tim Maxwell, Developmental Editor for the *Year Book*, at Elsevier Publications, September 22, 2005.

133. M.A. Farber, $1-Billion Legacy Makes Foundation the 2nd Biggest, *New York Times*, December 6, 1971. LOC 2/6; Nice Problem: Giving Away $45 Million, *Los Angeles Times*, April 8, 1973, 10–11. LOC 1/1.

134. Information on this project from author interviews with Orienne Strode, 1975 and 2006; Strode's comments in CSP group interview, 1975; author interview with CR and HR, January 25, 1975, tape 21; author interview with David Rogers, 1975; project brochures— all in UCSB/R-K.

135. "Human Dimensions in Medical Practice," brochure advertising the September 1980 and March 1981 workshop. Punctuation adjusted from brochure to text format.

136. Ibid.

137. Estimate by William Mahoney, M.D., cited in letter to author from Orienne Strode, February 9, 2006.

138. Founders were Dennis Novack, Mack Lipkin and William Clark, then at Brown, NYU, and Harvard, respectively. <www.physicianandpatient.org>. Another project, now approaching two decades in longevity, is the "Doctor as Teacher" program at University of California at San Diego, initiated by Ellen Beck, M.D.

139. DR, The Doctor Himself Must Become the Treatment, *The Pharos of Alpha Omega Alpha*, *37*, 4 (1974): 124–129; Medicine and Change, *Johns Hopkins Medical Journal, 153*, 8 (1973): 170–175; Illness Must Be Understood not in Scientific but in Human Terms, *American Medical News, 17*, 3 (September 3, 1974): 20.

140. NR, in Suhd, 1995: 196.

141. Letter from Natalie to "Dear Mom," September 13, 1965, shown to author by N. Rogers during 1975 interview. Also in LOC 1/13.

142. NR to CR, May 3, 1968. LOC 2/3.

143. Personal communication, n.d.

144. Most of the correspondence with grandchildren is in LOC, Box 2, in several folders.

145. Letter September 11, 1968. LOC.

146. Letter October 19, 1972. LOC 2/7.

147. These quotations and anecdotes from author interview with Naomi, Frances and Janet Fuchs, 1974.

148. Letter, October 6, 1971. LOC.

149. Remarks at CR's memorial service, February 21, 1987.

150. Virgil E. Tipton, John Rogers of Bates and Rogers—A Legend in His Own Time, *The Builder* (publ. of the Associated General Contractors of Illinois) (Summer 1985): 12–15. LOC 1/1.

151. See especially letters in LOC 1/11.

152. LOC, 1/ 10 and 11.

153. Letter July 22, 1971. LOC.

154. Letter July 29, 1971. LOC.

155. Letter October 5, 1971. LOC.

156. Letter October 15, 1971. It is not clear if Rogers responded, but when Lester died the following year, Rogers sent gracious remarks to be read at Lester's memorial service. Remarks in CR's handwriting. LOC 2/7. I am not sure if Rogers had a serious schedule conflict or if he simply chose not to attend the service.

157. Betty Berzon tape, June 1971.

158. See Chapter 9.

159. April 9–June 8, 1966. Itinerary in LOC 4/13.

160. Letters dated December 30, 1964, January 30, 1965, February 12, 1965, February 18,

1965. UCSB/R-K. See also LOC 12/1.

161. April 3, 1970: 2. LOC.

162. Tenenbaum, 1959, in CR, 1961a: 300–304.

163. Ibid.: 306–307.

164. S. Tenenbaum, *William Heard Kilpatrick: Trail Blazer in Education* (New York: Harper, 1951).

165. Tenenbaum, course paper titled "Course: The Process of Personality Change: A reaction by a mature post-doctoral student," 1958. Unpublished draft of his *Educational Leadership* article, op. cit. (n. 162). UCSB/R-K.

166. Tenenbaum, 1959, op. cit.: 306 (n. 162).

167. N. Cantor, *The Dynamics of Learning* (Buffalo: Foster & Stewart, 1946); E.C. Kelley, *Education for What Is Real* (New York: Harper & Bros., 1947); Snygg & Combs, 1949.

168. CR, 1951a: 389.

169. CR, 1967a: 368.

170. CR, 1951a: 401–403.

171. CR, 1957c.

172. This part of The Conference on Human Relations and The Case Discussion Method of Instruction had as its theme "Some Classroom Approaches to Influencing Human Behavior." Conference program. UCSB/R-K.

173. This, next two quotations, and aftermath of the talk, from CR, 1961a: 273–274.

174. Ibid.: 275–278.

175. CR, Recollections of Harvard Business School Meeting, 1952, April 3, 1972, memorandum prepared for author.

176. CR, 1961a: 275.

177. Rogers & Wallen, 1946: 94.

178. CR, 1959a, reprinted in CR, 1961a. Quotations here and below from 1961a: 287–290.

179. CR, 1961a; Maslow, 1962.

180. J. Featherstone, Schools for Children: What's Happening in British Classrooms. *New Republic*, August 19, 1967; How Children Learn, *NR*, September 2, 1967; Teaching Children How to Think, *NR*, September 9, 1967.

181. See, for example, A.S. Neill, *Summerhill: A Radical Approach to Child Rearing* (New York: Hart, 1960); E. Nyquist & G. Hawes, *Open Education: A Sourcebook for Parents and Teachers* (New York: Bantam, 1972); M.D. Fantini, *Alternative Education: A Source Book for Parents, Teachers, Students and Administrators* (Garden City, NY: Anchor Books, 1976); M. Silberman, J. Allender, & J. Yanoff, *The Psychology of Open Teaching and Learning* (Boston: Little Brown, 1972).

182. J. Piaget, *The Origin of Intelligence in Children* (New York: International Universities Press, 1952); *The Construction of Reality and the Child* (New York: Basic Books, 1954).

183. See, for example, the ASCD yearbooks: Combs, 1962; and R. Leeper (Ed.), *Humanizing Education: 1967 Yearbook* (Washington, DC: Association for Supervision and Curriculum Development, National Education Association).

184. CR, 1962a; 1962d and 1967b; 1963b; 1962d (again), 1967c and 1971a; 1971c, respectively.

185. CR, Report to Board of Trustees, WBSI, n.d. UCSB/R-K.

186. E.g., William Connolly, *Participation in a Communication Training Laboratory and Actualizing Changes in Church Leaders*, 1970; Frank Green, *The Effects of a Task-Encounter Workshop on the Administrative Staff of a Public School System*, 1970; Betty De Shong Meador, *An Analysis of Process Movement in a Basic Encounter Group*, 1969; Anna Harelson & Robert Harelson, *A Study of Actualizing Marital Relationships with an Emphasis on a Power-Strength Concept*, 1970. Not all were WBSI/CSP staff members.

187. Bruce Meador, CSP group interview.

188. Rogers & Russell, 2002: 209.
189. CR, 1969a: 5.
190. Ibid.: 112–113.
191. Ibid.: 108.
192. Ibid.: 169.
193. Ibid.: 174, both.
194. Ibid.: 185–186.
195. CR, 1964c, 1964a, 1963a.
196. CR, 1969a: 125.
197. E.Z. Friedenberg, Review of C.R. Rogers, *Freedom to Learn, Journal of Higher Education, 42* (1971): 238–242; J.P. Miller, Review of C.R. Rogers, *Freedom to Learn, School Review* (August, 1970): 591–596; R.S. Peters, Review of C.R. Rogers, *Freedom to Learn, Interchange, 1, 4* (1970): 111–114; S. Tenenbaum, Response to Dr. Mary Alice White's Review of C.R. Rogers, *Freedom to Learn, Contemporary Psychology, 15* (1970): 589; M.A. White, No Remembrance of Things Past. Review of C.R. Rogers, *Freedom to Learn, Contemporary Psychology, 15* (1970): 175–176.
198. Friedenberg, op. cit. (n. 197): 242.
199. Peters, op. cit. (n. 197): 111.
200. CR, letter to author, February 15, 1978.
201. D. Goodman, Standing Naked in the Wind, December 1970; G. Parker, no title, December 9, 1970; L.K. Francis, no title, December 1970, respectively. These and others student papers in UCSB/R-K.
202. R. Brown, student paper, December 8, 1970.
203. Rasa Gustaitis, "Rogers," a manuscript submitted to the *New York Times Magazine*, August, 1968. Unpublished. UCSB/R-K.
204. CR, Some possible remarks to members of the site visit of mental health B study section, Division of Research Grants, NIH, on September 29, 1966. UCSB/R-K.
205. CR, 1967c, CR, 1969a: 302–323.
206. Kettering correspondence, May 10, 1971.
207. The beginning and early stages of the project are described in CR, 1969a, and augmented by Rogers and Coulson's 1968 report and the Shaevitz and Barr 1970 report cited below.
208. CR, 1969a: 328.
209. Ibid.: 340.
210. CR & W.R. Coulson, Interim Report on the Educational Innovation Project. La Jolla, CA: WBSI, April, 1968. Unpublished. UCSB/R-K.
211. Ibid.: 36.
212. Ibid.: 37.
213. M.H. Shaevitz & D.J. Barr, Encounter Groups in a Small College: A Case Study. Mimeographed manuscript, April, 1970. Unpublished. UCSB/R-K.
214. Ibid.
215. CR, Addendum to the Epilogue: 1970: 15. Unpublished, UCSB/R-K.
216. Ibid.: 16.
217. <www.immaculateheartcommunity.org>, viewed March 2006.
218. CR to Herbert Ullmann, October 9, 1975. LOC 33/6.
219. E.H. Schein, *Process Consultation* (Reading, MA: Addison-Wesley, 1969).
220. R.E. Walton, *Interpersonal Peacemaking: Confrontation and Third-Party Consultation* (Reading, MA: Addison-Wesley, 1969).
221. E.g., W. Bennis, *Organizational Development* (Reading, MS: Addison-Wesley, 1969); W. Bennis, K. Benne, & R. Chin, *The Planning of Change* (New York: Holt, Rinehart & Winston, 1961); R. Lippitt, J. Watson, & B. Westley, *The Dynamics of Planned Change* (New York:

Harcourt, Brace & World, 1958).

222. CR, letter to Bonnie McWinney, quoted in B. McWhinney, Several Years Later—"Dear Carl," *Education, 95*, 2 (Winter 1974): 195.

223. See E. Michael Jones, *Libido Dominandi: Sexual Liberation and Political Control*. South Bend, IN: St. Augustine's Press, 2000) for a damning assessment of Rogers and humanistic psychology in general, and the Immaculate Heart Project in particular.

224. J. DeWyze, An Encounter with Bill Coulson. *Reader: San Diego's Weekly, 16*, 33 (1987): 1 ff. W. Coulson, Memorandum to Federal Drug Education Curriculum Panel, April 23, 1988. UCSB/R-K.

225. CR, 1970a: 144–145. Second in nation from Dickenson, Foster, Walker & Yeager, 1970: 111.

226. Dickenson, et al., ibid.

227. CR, 1969a: 106, quoted in Dickenson, et al., 1970: 114. They added that "it also stems more broadly from the whole Third Force Movement (Maslow, 1962)."

228. Car Foster tape, 1972.

229. CR, 1970a: 147–148.

230. CR, 1983: 232.

231. CR, 1983: 227; DeWyze, 1987, op. cit. (n. 224); W. Coulson, Interview on San Antonio, Texas's WOAI radio station, February 21, 1989; W. Coulson, Founder of 'Value-Free' Education Says He Owes Parents an Apology. *AFA Journal* (April 1989): 20–21. For a critique of Coulson's assertions about Rogers' recanting his philosophy, see H. Kirschenbaum, Denigrating Carl Rogers: William Coulson's Last Crusade, *Journal of Counseling and Development, 69*, 5 (1991): 411–413.

232. CR, 1983: 245–250.

233. CR, 1965a, 1968a, 1969c.

234. CR, 1970d, 1963d, 1965b, 1972d, and others.

235. Hall, 1967a; CR, 1968c, 1969b, 1969d.

236. CR, 1969d, 1970c.

237. CR, 1973c.

238. Rogers & Stevens, 1967.

239. CR, author interview, March, 1971, tape 3.

240. CR, letter to author, June 4, 1974.

241. CR, 1964c, 1963c, 1962a, 1962b.

242. E.T. Gendlin, Subverbal Communication and Therapist Expressivity: Trends in Client-Centered Therapy with Schizophrenics, *Journal of Existential Psychiatry, 4*, 14 (1963); J.M. Shlien, A Client-Centered Approach to Schizophrenia: First Approximation. In A. Burton (Ed.), *Psychotherapy of the Psychoses* (New York: Basic Books, 1961): 285–317; W. Van Dusen, The Natural Depth of Man, previously unpublished.

243. Figures derived from perusing Rogers' calendars, 1965 through 1970.

244. CR, "Mental Health Info-Pak Cassette Series." Chicago: Instructional Dynamics, 1970 or 1971.

245. CR, Proposal to the Laughlin Foundation: 3, undated, but accompanying cover letter from CR to William Laughlin is dated April 27, 1969. UCSB/R-K.

246. A copy of the letter, on WBSI letterhead, is in LOC 32/9. "1968?" is written on it.

247. Cohen: 17.

248. Proposal to the Laughlin Foundation, op. cit. (n. 245).

249. Phyllis Wetlaufer was Rogers' secretary for many of his early California years.

250. From untitled page in CR's files. UCSB/R-K. Probably part of a WBSI staff bulletin.

251. American Psychological Association, 1973.

252. Cartwright tape, May 4, 1971.

Chapter 11

1. N. Nichols, Introduction, *The Person of Tomorrow: Eighth Annual Commencement Exercises.* (Sonoma, CA: Sonoma State College, 1969): 1.
2. CR, 1969e.
3. CR, author interview, July, 1970.
4. CR, author interview, 1971.
5. Autobiography, CR, 1967a; comment, CR, author interview, March 1971.
6. CR, from a typed sheet in his files, entitled "Grass Roots Contacts." UCSB/R-K.
7. Remarks at Rogers' memorial service, February 21, 1987.
8. Tom Gillette.
9. Steve Doyne.
10. CSP group interview, speaker uncertain.
11. Ibid.
12. Steve Doyne.
13. CSP group interview, 1975. Quotations from Betty Meador; unidentified; unidentified; Earl Burrows; Orienne Strode.
14. Bruce Meador in Tom Gillette, Bruce Meador and Betty Meador, On Carl Rogers, *Voices* (Spring 1971): 69–70.
15. Ibid.: 69.
16. Quotations by Gillette and Meador, ibid: 69, 70.
17. CSP group interview, op. cit. (n. 13).
18. Author interview, March 1971.
19. C.M. Devonshire & A. Auw, A Cross-Cultural Communication Workshop. Unpublished paper, February 1973. UCSB/R-K.
20. Anonymous letter, October 17, 1970.
21. CR, 1969e.
22. CR, 1975. He used the former phrase again in a chapter titled "The World of Tomorrow— The Person of Tomorrow" in *A Way of Being,* CR, 1980b.
23. CR, 1975: 155.
24. CR, 1969e.
25. CR 1975: 155.
26. Rogers & Ryback, 1989: 28.
27. NR interview, 2003.
28. CR, 1975: 161–167.
29. Ibid.: 170–172.
30. Ibid.: 174–175.
31. February 28, 1981, sponsored by The Sonoma Institute. Flyer in Natalie Rogers folder, UCSB/R-K.
32. CR, The World of Tomorrow and the Person of Tomorrow, chapter in CR, 1980b: 339–356.
33. CR, 1980b: 356.
34. CR, 1971b: 21. UCSB/R-K. At that time Rogers and most other commentators on changing relationships gave little or no attention to same-sex relationships.
35. Described in CR, 1971b.
36. Ibid.: 23.
37. Cutler's letter quoted in CR, letter to Marguerite Clark, editor at Scott, Foresman & Company, October 18, 1971. UCSB/R-K.
38. CR, 1972a: 2.
39. Ibid.: 10.
40. N. O'Neill & G. O'Neill, *Open Marriage* (Philadelphia: Lippincott, 1971).

41. CR, 1972a: 12–13.
42. Ibid.: 13.
43. Ibid.: 29.
44. Ibid.: 42.
45. Ibid: 65–66.
46. The details were disguised sufficiently that I did not recognize who the subjects were until that was pointed out to me.
47. Letter to "Dear Carl," February 4, 1973. LOC 2/8.
48. Letter April 15, 1973. LOC 2/8.
49. When Natalie Rogers was asked in 2003 about the incident, she had completely forgotten that this case study was included in the book and could shed no light on the issue of permission. Author interview.
50. CR, 1972a: 150–151.
51. Ibid.: 214.
52. Ibid.: 220 and 212.
53. CR, letter to author, March 22, 1974; List of publication sales compiled by CR, n.d. UCSB/R-K.
54. CR to Art and Jane Shedlin, May 23, 1973. LOC 33/33.
55. CR, 1967a: 382.
56. CR, 1971b: 1.
57. Ibid.: 24.
58. Maria Bowen, CSP group interview, 1975.
59. D. Malcolm, Carl R. Rogers, *Person-Centered Review*, 2, 3 (August 1987): 411–412. Also told in Malcolm interview, 2003.
60. Cain interview.
61. Rogers & Ryback, 1989. Reprinted in Cain, 2002: 31. He used the same quotation in *On Personal Power*, 1977: 184.
62. Cain interview.
63. CR, 1980b: 71.
64. CR, letter to Mr. and Mrs. Arthur J. Shedlin, May 23, 1973. LOC 33/33.
65. CR, letter to author, March 22, 1974.
66. August 25–28, 1974. Carl and Helen paid $3,773 for the travel and lodging expenses for the whole family and gave $18,000 in stocks and other gifts to the grandchildren. Note by CR, titled "Cost of Golden Wedding," September 1, 1974, LOC; Invitation with details, June 15, 1974. LOC 11/3. Summary of weekend in CR, letter to Margaret Rogers, September 4, 1974. LOC 2/9.
67. "Nibbled to death" and Stinson Beach story from CR, author interview, Tape 21, January 25, 1975.
68. CR, letter to Rita Sperry, August 21, 1974. LOC 33/4.
69. Canceling commitments, CR, letter to Art and Jane Shedlin, September 26, 1974. LOC 33/4.
70. CR, letter to author, June 7, 1976.
71. Possibly from one of many drafts of Growing Old: Or Older and Growing.
72. CR, letter to author, August 11, 1976.
73. Critical biographer David Cohen (1997) made much of Rogers selfishly and unfeelingly not taking Helen with him to the Sagamore workshop in spite of her heartfelt pleas to accompany him, saying Rogers "always felt guilty about it" (p. 216). But Cohen got it wrong. Helen *did* accompany Carl to Sagamore. As co-director of the Sagamore Conference Center at the time, I can vouch that Helen was present; the Rogers had dinner at our home; I auctioned off a painting Helen made that week as part of a fundraiser, and it was an excellent time for her.
74. CR, Growing Old: Or Older and Growing. In CR, *A Way of Being*, 1980b: 85–86. He wrote

it around 1976, and read it to a number of workshop groups, but did not publish it until after Helen's death.

75. CR, personal notes, December 31, 1976, January 1, 1977, March 2, 1977, respectively. LOC 4/7.

76. CR, personal notes, December 31, 1976, April 25, 1977, August 1977, respectively. LOC 4/7.

77. Letter from Ms. Mickey McClure, May 22, 1973. UCSB/R-K.

78. Logan Fox, letter to CR, Oct. 29, 1973. UCSB/R-K.

79. CR, letter to Nancy Hawkey, November 18, 1974. LOC 33/4.

80. CR, letter to Cathy Wilson, December 22, 1975. LOC 33/6.

81. She worked for him and with him from February 1973 until his death. Henderson interview, 2003.

82. CR, letter to R. Roe, October 21, 1970. UCSB/R-K.

83. CR, letter to Professor Ulric Neisser, undated; but Neisser's request to Rogers, asking if Rogers had anyone to recommend for a faculty position, was dated March 2, 1971.

84. For example, it was published as Carl Rogers Resigns from USIU, *AHP Newsletter, 7*, 1 (1970): 1–7.

85. CR, letter to Dr. W. Ray Rucker [Dean] and Dr. William Rust [President], United States International University, June 22, 1970. UCSB/R-K.

86. HR, author interview, tape 5, March 1971. She added, "I hear him say this so often."

87. H. Prather, *Notes to Myself: My Struggle to Become a Person*. (Lafayette, CA: Real People Press, 1970).

88. Hart & Tomlinson, 1970; Wexler & Rice, 1974.

89. Hamburg and Leiden degrees described in undated news releases from CSP. UCSB/R-K.

90. CR, The Place of Psychotherapy in Modern Life, unpublished manuscript, 1952: 17–18. UCSB/R-K.

91. CR, 1972d: 45.

92. Rogers told Frank Stanton, Chairman of the Board of CBS, whom he apparently knew, possibly from a CEO workshop, "I often speak to large audiences, and I plan to use CBS as an example of what's wrong with our culture." Letter to "Dear Frank," April 1969. UCSB/R-K.

93. Mail-merged sample letter, n.d, probably October 1970. LOC, 32/11. Other committee members included former Governor Edmund Brown, Senator Alan Cranston, and well-known Hollywood celebrities like Bill Cosby, Milton Berle, Henry Fonda, Gene Kelly, Burt Lancaster, Jack Lemon, and Shirley MacLaine. List in CR's files. UCSB/R-K.

94. CR, 1972d.

95. Ibid.: 55–56.

96. Ibid.: 57

97. Ibid.: 45.

98. CR, 1971b.

99. CR, 1968a: 279.

100. Pat Rice described the whole experience in *The Steel Shutter*, unpublished doctoral dissertation, International College, 1978.

101. Rogers also described it in a letter to Art and Jane Shedlin, May 23, 1973. LOC 33/33.

102. Actually, as Rogers revealed in 1984 when it was safer to do so, there *were* some moving moments of reconciliation in the group, as when Becky, a Catholic, said of Dennis, a Protestant, "I think he fully understands me as a person," and Dennis answered, "I do, there is no question about that …" and Becky said, "And for that reason I am very grateful and I think I have found a friend." But it was determined that to show such reconciliation at the time would put the lives of the participants at risk if the film were shown in Northern

Ireland, so they were edited out. Rogers & Ryback, 1984: 5.

103. Interview with CR by Alberto Zucconi, "Rogers Peace Trains," in Association for Humanistic Psychology *Newsletter*, reprinted from APA *Monitor*, November, 1984.

104. The video was still available from CSP in 2006 at <www.centerfortheperson.org>.

105. CR, 1977: 112.

106. CR, Memo to Pat Rice, January 20, 1973, re Your Dissertation, "The Steel Shutter." UCSB/ R-K.

107. CR, 1977: 3

108. Ibid.: 3–4.

109. Ibid.: 5.

110. Ibid.

111. NR to CR, May 14, 1973. UCSB/R-K. "The Greenhouse people" refers to a group Natalie was part of in Boston.

112. Quotation from Natalie's remarks at CR's memorial service, February 21, 1987. In Suhd, 1995: 199, she wrote that she asked him the next year, in 1974, if he would like to work together with her, and he replied, "Sure, I would. What should we do?"

113. There was actually a John K. Wood and a John T. Wood who were both staff members of CSP at the same time; hence an initial is usually used.

114. There were many sources for evolution of the person-centered workshops, including but not limited to interviews with Rogers and workshop staff members, Rogers (1977) account of the 1975 workshop, Kim Francis' account of the 1975 workshop (see n. 116), and my own participant-observations of the 1977 and 1984 Sagamore workshops.

115. CR, author interview, January 25, 1975, tape 21.

116. Rogers described the workshop in "A Person-Centered Workshop: Its Planning and Fruition," in Chapter 8 in CR, 1977: 143–185. One participant, Kim Francis, a professor at Brooklyn College, wrote a manuscript, *Two Hours with Carl Rogers*, n.d., describing the workshop and including the transcript of a two-hour conversation Rogers held with the group. UCSB/R-K.

117. Francis, *Two Hours with Carl Rogers,* ibid.: 7

118. CR, 1977: 176–177.

119. CR, 1980a: 75.

120. CR, letter to author, March 15, 1977.

121. O'Hara chapter in Suhd, 1995: 134–135.

122. Center history described by Ruth Sanford in Suhd, 1995, brochure in UCSB/R-K, and website in 2001. The Center modeled itself after CSP, serving as an umbrella for the various projects of its small number of members.

123. June 27, 28 and 30 entries, Restricted Sagamore diary, UCSB/CR: 2/2.

124. Cain interview.

125. I heard two anecdotal reports of how when Rogers and his colleagues conducted a person-centered community meeting at the APA convention in San Francisco in 1977 half of the audience of about 1,000 left in bafflement or disgust.

126. Cain interview.

127. O'Hara interview.

128. E.g., the Association for the Development of the Person-Centered Approach, American Academy of Psychotherapists and the British Association for the Person-Centred Approach continue to use the person-centered community meeting format.

129. Henderson interview, 1991.

130. Again, as with *Carl Rogers On Encounter Groups*, he acceded to the publisher's desire to include his name in the title, heretofore uncharacteristic examples of calling attention to himself.

131. P. Freire, *Pedagogy of the Oppressed* (New York: Herder & Herder, 1970).

132. Gordon in CR, 1951a: 320–383; CR, 1952b.

133. *The Human Side of Enterprise* (New York: McGraw-Hill, 1960). Rogers went even further than McGregor toward group-centered leadership.

134. "Some notes by Carl Rogers … My personal preferences, convictions and experiences, which focus on the left end of the leadership continuum." Unpublished paper, 2 pp, Palm Beach, April 1969. UCSB/R-K.

135. CSP group interview, 1975.

136. Diane Dreher, 1995, in her biography of John Vasconcellos, said Rogers carried this quotation in his wallet. In a diary entry, he noted how at the end of the Sagamore PCA workshop, "I read Lao Tse on leadership" [to the group]. July 9, 1977. Sagamore diary, op. cit. (n. 123).

137. Farson, 1975: xl.

138. Kramer, 1995b: 197.

139. See earlier discussion in Chapter 7, including how Rogers built on Goldstein, Angyal, Maslow and others' ideas regarding this concept.

140. CR, 1977: 238. Next quotation: 243.

141. Ibid.: 255.

142. Information for this paragraph comes from author interview with Vasconcellos, 2003, Vasconcellos's panel presentation and session at the Carl Rogers Symposium, La Jolla, CA, July 2002; his Eulogy at Rogers' memorial service, reprinted in *Person-Centered Review, 2*, 3 (August 1987): 353–361; Diane Dreher's biography of Vasconcellos in Suhd, 1995: 339–372; and R. Trainor, The Strange and Most True Adventures of Don Vasco de Santa Clara, *California Magazine* (October, 1987), among other sources.

143. Vasconcellos used "mentor" in Eulogy, but in author interview said, "it was more of a coach than a mentor, I think, to be accurate." At the CR Symposium he said, "I was his political coach; he was my personal coach."

144. J. Vasconcellos, *Capitol Report*, December, 1985.

145. CR to DR, April 18, 1977. LOC 3/3.

146. CR, letter to Ellis Amburn, Editor-in-Chief, Delacorte Press, July 23, 1977. UCSB/R-K.

147. R. Halgin, *Library Journal*, April 1, 1977: 818.

148. S. Maddi, Rogers as Revolutionary, *Contemporary Psychology, 23*, 5 (1978): 300–301.

149. Sales figure and quotation from Rogers' letter to Ellis Amburn, op. cit. (n. 146). Rogers sent a copy of this letter with a "Memo to some friends," asking for their frank opinions of *On Personal Power*. "I want straight feedback," he wrote. UCSB/R-K.

150. R. Nash & R. Griffin, Carl Rogers: Still a Teacher for Our Times, *Teachers College Record, 79*, 2 (December 1977): 279–289.

151. Ibid.: 280 and 279.

152. Ibid.: 282, 284, 286, 285, 286, 288, respectively.

153. In CR, 1949a: 82, he had described therapy as his "laboratory of interpersonal relations."

154. Nash & Griffin, op. cit.: 279 (n. 150).

155. Ibid.: 288. To my knowledge, the writers were not students or colleagues of Rogers in the traditional sense, but might have attended a workshop with Rogers, seen him do a demonstration and/or read his writings.

156. Political and multicultural issues associated with the person-centered approach will be discussed further in Chapter 12.

157. CR, 1980a: 89. The essay title was suggested to him by Gay Swenson who thought his original title of "Growing Old" hardly did his subject justice. She had used it in her dissertation to describe women in the second half of life. G. Barfield, email communication, November 11, 2006.

158. CR, 1980a: 86.

159. Ibid.: 83–84.

160. CR, 1969b: 61.

161. O'Hara interview, 2003. His diary entries contain several incidents of women making overtures to him and report how, while he accepted their feelings, he declined their invitations.

162. CR, November 9, 1979. Restricted diary, UCSB/CR.

163. CR, 1980b: 71. In this 1980 chapter, he added to his earlier 1977 version, "Yes, or sixty-five, or sixty!"

164. He clearly writes of this in his restricted diaries, UCSB, e.g. entries of November 14 and November 24, 1979. It was also confirmed in a not-for-attribution interview with a close friend and confidant of Rogers.

165. Ibid., November 24, 1979.

166. Their correspondence is in LOC 40/4.

167. O'Hara interview.

168. Henderson interview, 2003.

169. In author interviews, Charlie O'Leary, Norm Chambers and Valerie Henderson recalled being present on such an occasion, but it is not clear if these were different or the same occasions or if there were others.

170. O'Hara interview.

171. Ibid.

172. Ann Dryfuss tape, 1971.

173. Natalie Rogers interview, 2003.

174. Henderson interview.

175. Ibid.

176. Poppy, 1968: 69.

177. CR, letter to author, March 11, 1978.

178. CR, letter to author, June 7, 1978. Helen's fall in letter from CR to author, February 16, 1979.

179. These events are described in CR, Maria Bowen, Natalie Rogers and others in Living the Process of Dying: Psychological and Personal Events Relating to Helen's Death on March 29, 1979, unpublished manuscript, 37 pp. UCSB/R-K; also more briefly in CR, 1980b: 90–91, and NR interview, 2003.

180. CR, 1980b: 90. Described more fully in Living the Process of Dying, op. cit. (n. 179).

181. CR, 1980b: 91.

182. Natalie, Maria Bowen and Audrey McGaw were in the room; others were in the hall. Rogers stepped out of the room two or three minutes before Helen died.

183. Henderson interview.

184. CR, 1980b: 95.

185. R. Sanford, in Suhd, 1995: 374.

186. Diary entry headed, "Keeping Relationships Straight," May 27, 1982. Restricted diary, UCSB/CR.

187. Ibid.

188. R. Sanford, in Suhd, 1995: 419.

189. CR, November 9, 1979. Restricted diary, UCSB/CR.

190. I include this detail because it's just the sort of revelation Rogers would include in a posthumous autobiography. I think he would have wanted us to know that old people, even without all the sexual vigor of youth, can experience sexual pleasure and personal intimacy if they will risk themselves in relationship, communicate with their partner, and care for, nurture and pleasure one another in ways that work for them.

191. He never did consummate the relationship with his 1975 infatuation, and they eventually ended it late in 1979. LOC 40/4.

192. Diary entry, January 3, 1980.

193. O'Hara interview.

194. David Malcolm interview.

195. CR's letter of recommendation for the Association for Counselor Education and Supervision's Distinguished Professional Contribution Award, November 22, 1985. Malcolm showed me the letter and Rogers' undated (c. April) 1986 note, Malcolm interview. This contradiction—that Rogers could connect deeply with people but still feel like a loner—will be explored further below.

196. Described in Tausch interview, 2003. Rogers combined this with visiting his sister in Orlando.

197. CR, "Growing Old …," 1980a: 95.

198. CR, "A Message from Carl, To: all who helped me celebrate my 80th …" January 10, 1982. LOC 4/2. The party was organized by the women members of CSP. G. Barfield, email communication, November 11, 2006. He had another, more public birthday event later in the year, which will be described in the following chapter.

199. Ibid. Plans for the January 15–19, 1982 event described in a letter from David Rogers to "The Rogers Clan," July 10, 1981. LOC 4/2.

200. CR, 1980b: 82. First presented in 1977.

201. Some would call that denial; others would say it was consistent with his long-term opposition to oversimplified and misleading diagnostic labels.

202. Richard Farson interview, 2003.

203. NR, email communication, November 27, 2006.

204. Although there is a good deal of documentation of the Rogers' drinking patterns in the 1970s and his in the 1980s, as will be shown, there is little earlier documentation. Therefore some of the description of the earlier years in this paragraph is speculative, yet consistent with their later history and characteristic of the trajectory of alcohol abuse in general.

205. Letter February 12, 1971. LOC.

206. Henderson interview, 2003.

207. Letter April 23, 1977. LOC 3/3.

208. Letter, February 7, 1978. LOC.

209. DR, letter to "Dear Dad," June 5, 1978. LOC and UCSB/R-K.

210. Dreams Diary, May 16, 1980. Restricted diary, UCSB/CR: 2/8.

211. Ibid., July 8, 1980.

212. Henderson interview, 2003.

213. Ibid., entries of July 28, August 24 and September 5, 1980.

214. Dreams Diary, op. cit. (n. 210), April 30, 1980.

215. Lloyd and Valerie Henderson and Natalie Rogers interviews.

216. Natalie Rogers interview.

217. Segrera interview, 2002. Segrera said Rogers' problem was worse when he got off an airplane.

218. Natalie recalled one or two occasions when she thought he was affected by alcohol when working, but she, who knew of Rogers' problem, was the only one who said this. Author interview, 2003. Possibly others had knowledge but chose not to share it with me, but judging from their affect when I asked and from other private details they were willing to disclose, I do not believe that was the case.

219. Lietaer interview, 2003.

220. Peter Schmid interview, 2003.

221. Cain and Malcolm interviews, 2003.

222. Dreams Diary, op. cit. (n. 210), April 19, 1980.

223. Ibid., May 5, 1980.

224. Ibid., May 16, 1980.

225. Ibid., April 30, 1980.

226. Valerie Henderson thought he did. Henderson interview.

227. Ibid., written in Tucson, AZ airport, November 26, 1979.

228. Kramer, 1995a: 55.

229. CR, 1970a: 53.

230. Andre Auw interview, 2002.

231. Dreams Diary, September 5, 1980.

232. CR, 1986a, in Kirschenbaum & Henderson, 1989b: 137.

233. CR, 1980b: 129; the phrase "one new characteristic" and the words in brackets appear in the 1986a version.

234. Ibid.: 129–130.

235. William Shakespeare, *Hamlet: Prince of Denmark*, Act I, Scene V.

236. Unidentified speaker, CSP group interview, 1975.

237. CR, 1972c: 253.

238. James, *The Varieties of Religious Experience* (London: Longmans, Green, 1928); LeShan, *Toward a General Theory of The Paranormal* (New York: Parapsychology Foundation, 1969); Castaneda, *The Teachings of Don Juan: A Yaqui Way of Knowing* (New York: Ballentine, 1968) and *A Separate Reality* (New York: Simon & Schuster, 1971); S. Ostrander & L. Schroeder, *Psychic Discoveries Behind the Iron Curtain* (New York: Bantam, 1971).

239. CR, 1978a, 1978b, 1979a.

240. CR, 1972c: 253.

241. Letter, October 1, 1975. LOC 33/6.

242. Letter, October 9, 1975. LOC 33/6.

243. "Brazil," Box 2, Folios 1 and 4, UCSB/CR. Restricted.

244. Ibid., Folio 4, February 4 entry.

245. Ibid.

246. Ibid., January 30, 1977.

247. CR, 1980b: 87. He also cited current authors Raymond Moody, *Life After Life* (New York: Bantam, 1975), Elisabeth Kübler-Ross, and Arthur Koestler who wrote of life-after-death experiences.

248. These events took place on November 8 & 10, 1977 and are described in CR et al., "Living the Process of Dying," op. cit. (n. 179). Some parts of the manuscript are included in Rogers' 1979 update to his "Growing Old" essay (CR, 1980a). The painter channeling is also mentioned in Henderson, Farson and Cain interviews, 2003. Farson skeptically wondered why the painters couldn't paint as well in 1977 as when they were living.

249. Ibid.: 3. Jung also mentioned in Rogers' Dreams Diary, December 3, 1979 and in Henderson interview, 2003.

250. Gay Barfield, electronic communication, September 30, 2006.

251. CR, 1980a: 90. The two meetings were on January 17 and December 17, 1978.

252. Discussion of Client-Centered Psychotherapy, 1958: 47–48, 60, op. cit. Chapter 7 (n. 3).

253. O'Hara interview, 2003.

254. Auw interview, 2002. Decades after the fact, Auw could not recall the exact years, but thought it was both before and after Helen's death.

255. Ibid.

256. CR, 1980b: 90.

257. Ibid.

258. Ibid.: 91. Also described in "Living the Process of Dying," op. cit. (n. 179).

259. Ibid.: 91–92

260. Segrera interview, 2002.

261. Dreams Diary, January 5 and 6, 1981

262. Rogers recorded one such session in his Dreams Diary entry of February 18, 1980.

263. He had been practicing in the West since 1970. His main ashram was in South Fallsburg, NY.
264. M. Ferguson, *The Aquarian Conspiracy: Personal and Social Transformation in the 1980s* (Los Angeles: J. P. Tarcher, 1980).
265. A separate notebook, titled "Muktananda" are among Rogers restricted papers at UCSB. Information and quotations are from entries dated December 13 and 14, 1980.
266. Gay Barfield recalled Rogers also saying that he was put off by all of the Swami's "followers," and "Muktananda humorously responded that he heard Carl himself had lots of 'followers' around the world." Email communication, September 30, 2006.
267. From website of the SYDA Foundation, <www.siddhayoga.org>.
268. Dreams Diary, December 3, 1979.
269. This is a viewpoint which may be changing. For example, a recent convention of the American Counseling Association was filled with sessions on the relationship between counseling and spirituality.
270. O'Hara interview.
271. In Suhd, 1995: 140.
272. NR interview, 2003.
273. Tausch interview, 2003.
274. Cain interview, 2003.
275. "Would meet again" from Brian Thorne interview.
276. Diary entries, May 16 and 19, 1980.
277. January 27, 1981.
278. Thorne, 2002b. NR also told me how she was interested in how Rogers' "faith changed—faith in some higher power to faith in the human being, as a psychologist, such tremendous faith in the positive good of the human being." Author interview, 2003.
279. Quotations from CR, 1980b: 124 and 133, respectively.
280. He gave as examples John Lilly, *The Center of the Cyclone* (New York: Bantam, 1973) and S. Grof & J. Grof, *The Human Encounter with Death* (New York: Dutton, 1977).
281. CR, 1980b: 128.
282. Ibid.: 133.
283. CR to A. Bergin, November 23, 1979. UCSB/R-K; James, *The Varieties of Religious Experience*, op. cit. (n. 238).
284. Henderson interview.
285. O'Hara interview.
286. Rogers & Baldwin, 1987: 50.
287. CR to A. Bergin, November 23, 1979.
288. Anecdote related at Rogers' memorial service, February 21, 1987.
289. She said this conversation was around Christmas 1986.
290. Thorne interview.

Chapter 12

1. CR, letter to author, March 15, 1977.
2. CR, letter to author, January 25, 1978. The workshop was probably in December 1977.
3. Thorne, 1998.
4. Ibid.
5. C. Devonshire & A. Auw, *A Cross-Cultural Communication Workshop*, February, 1973. Unpublished paper. UCSB/R-K.
6. E.g., Chuck Devonshire, David Mearns, Elke Lambers and Brian Thorne founded the Facilitator

Development Institute (British Centre) in 1975 which offered residential summer workshops on the person-centered approach for helping professionals. They were later joined by a fifth colleague, William Hallidie Smith. Thorne, 1998; Elke Lambers electronic communication to Maggie Taylor-Sanders, June 22, 2007.

7. Background on El Escorial and Lake Albano, Gay Barfield, email communication, November 26, 2006. I have omitted details regarding the politics of staffing and leadership of these and the resulting programs.

8. Other staff included Rogers, Maria Bowen, Doug Land, Pat Rice, Audrey McGaw, John T. Wood from CSP and Reinhard Tausch, Alberto Zucconi and others from Europe. Valerie Henderson and Gay Barfield, personal communications, November 29, 2006.

9. Staff included Rogers, Swenson, Henderson, Natalie Rogers, John K. Wood and Maureen Miller from CSP, Chuck Devonshire, and Europeans Patricia Moselli, Luciano Marchino and Alberto Zucconi who was Program Director. From program brochure: A Process of Exploring Personal and Social Power, June 22–July 1, 1979. Workshop languages were English and Italian.

10. Details from Henderson interview, 1991.

11. Summary based on review of many brochures of the period. UCSB/R-K.

12. O'Hara chapter in Suhd, 1995: 132.

13. Figures derived from perusing Rogers' calendars for this period, loaned to author by Valerie Henderson in 1993.

14. Schmid, author interview, 2003.

15. Ironically, while psychoanalysts in the U.S. thought little of Rogers, psychoanalysts in Freud's home country were most impressed with him. Schmid interview.

16. The Austria Program was an annual training program in the person-centered approach, still operating in its twenty-sixth year in 2004. Peter Schmid interview.

17. Described in CR, letter to "Dear Family and Friends," October 25, 1983. 9 pp. UCSB/R-K.

18. João Hipólito from Portugal, author interview, 2003. After the workshop, participants talked with the diplomats over dinner, followed by a question-and-answer session with Rogers, John K. Wood and Maria Bowen. They and Chuck Devonshire, and Alberto Zucconi worked with him on different occasions during the trip. CR, October 25, 1983 letter, op. cit.(n. 17).

19. Ibid.

20. Henderson interview, December 14, 1991.

21. Hipólito interview.

22. "Carl Rogers and Ruth Sanford 'In Conversation' at UCT Capetown, February 12, 1986." Unpublished transcript. 33 pp. UCSB/R-K.

23. Author's observation. Rogers and Sanford never explained their criteria, to my knowledge.

24. CR, letter to author, March 15, 1977.

25. Brazil diary, February 9, 1977. UCSB/CR: 2/1.

26. Henderson interview, 2003. Number of participants and nations from CR, "Steps Toward Peace 1948–1986: Tension Reduction in Theory and Practice." Unpublished paper to accompany grant applications, 1986: 3.

27. Lietaer interview, 2003.

28. CR, letter to author, April 6, 1978. Several informants mentioned how the entire workshop was filmed by Bill McGaw, but because funds were never raised to edit the production, as they had done on previous films like "Journey Into Self," the raw footage remained in McGaw's garage for decades.

29. D. Aker, 'Let's Not Kill the Dog This Time': Thoughts about Community and the Challenge of Inclusion, *Women's Times*, March 1993: 26.

30. Aker interview, 2003.

31. Hipólito interview.

32. Brazil diary, February 25, 1977.

33. Minoru Hatase correspondence, 1972.

34. Sources for the 1982 trip include: CR and Ruth Sanford, Journey to the Heart of South Africa, unpublished manuscript, 1983; Sanford's chapter in Suhd, 1995; R. Sanford, The Beginning of a Dialogue in South Africa, *Counseling Psychologist, 12*, 3 (1984): 3–14; CR, The Dilemmas of a South African White (1986b); Ruth Sanford, author interview, 1991; and others cited.

35. Some background information in Holdstock, 1990, 2005.

36. Holdstock, 2005: 125.

37. Sanford in Suhd, 1995: 421.

38. Ibid.: 375.

39. These excerpts and those that follow from Sanford, The Beginning of a Dialogue in South Africa, op. cit.: 4, 8, 8 and 11, respectively, (n. 34).

40. Sources for the 1986 trip include: CR and Ruth Sanford (1987), Reflections on Our South African Experience; "Carl Rogers and Ruth Sanford 'In Conversation' at UCT Capetown," op. cit. (n. 22); Ruth Sanford's chapter in Suhd, 1995; Hill-Hain & Rogers, 1988; Ruth Sanford, author interview, and others cited. The first source said the trip was seven weeks; the last source said it was "about five weeks": 422.

41. Hill-Hain & Rogers, 1988: 63. Alicia Hill-Hain was a graduate student of John Whiteley's at the University of California at Irvine who studied Rogers and Sanford's 1986 intervention in South Africa.

42. Ibid.: 67.

43. J. Spangenberg, The Cross-Cultural Relevance of Person-Centered Counseling in Post-apartheid South Africa, *Journal of Counseling and Development, 81* (winter 2003): 49.

44. "Carl Rogers and Ruth Sanford 'In Conversation'," op. cit.: 5–6, (n. 22). Rogers seems to be speaking extemporaneously.

45. Ibid.: 21.

46. Ibid.: 25.

47. E.g., P. Cushman (1990), Why the Self is Empty: Toward a Historically Situated Psychology. *American Psychologist, 45*: 599–611.

48. Holdstock, 1990: 113, summarizing and quoting Sampson, 1988: 20; also following quotation.

49. Spangenberg, op. cit.: 50 (n. 43). Her citations not included.

50. B. Williams, The Worldview Dimensions of Individualism and Collectivism: Implications for Counseling, *Journal of Counseling and Development, 81* (summer 2003): 370.

51. D. Sue, R. Carter, J. Casas, N. Fouad, A. Ivey, M. Jensen, et al., *Multicultural Counseling Competencies: Individual and Organizational Development* (Thousand Oaks, CA: Sage, 1998).

52. D. W. Sue & D. Sue, *Counseling the Culturally Diverse: Theory and Practice: 4th edition* (New York: John Wiley & Sons, 2003).

53. Holdstock, 1990, 2005.

54. Holdstock, 1990: 111.

55. L. Swartz, Carl Rogers in South Africa: The Issue of Silence, *Psychology in Society, 5* (1986): 139–143. Summarized by Holdstock, 1990.

56. A. Dawes, Politics and Mental Health: The Position of Clinical Psychology in South Africa, *South African Journal of Psychology, 15* (1985): 55–61.

57. CR, 1951a: 494.

58. J. Cornelius-White, "Teaching" Person-Centered Multicultural Counseling: Collaborative Endeavors to Transcend Resistance and Increase Awareness, *Journal of Humanistic Counseling, Education and Development, 44*, 2 (2005): 225–240. In the original, Cornelius-White used "MCT" for multicultural counseling and psychotherapy."

59. This and next quotation, Hill-Hain & Rogers, 1988: 63.

60. CR, 1951a: 437.

61. This was demonstrated explicitly in a study reported by M. Arzaga, S. Bauman, M. Waldo & L. Castellanos, Multicultural Sensitivity and Interpersonal Skills Training for Preservice Teachers, *Journal of Humanistic Counseling, Education and Development, 44*, 2 (Fall 2005): 198–208.

62. Cornelius-White, 2003. This is the most thorough discussion I have seen on the multicultural critique of the person-centered approach.

63. D. Koza, Tribute to Dr. Carl Rogers, *Person-Centered Review, 2*, 3 (August 1987): 330, 332–333. Original emphases.

64. Gendlin, Foreword in Rogers & Russell, 2002: xiii–xiv.

65. Hill-Hain & Rogers, 1988: 65.

66. CR, 1942a: 255.

67. Op. cit.: 51 (n. 43). For this insight Spangenberg cited C. Usher, Recognizing Cultural Bias in Counseling Theory and Practice: The Case of Rogers, *Journal of Multicultural Counseling and Development, 17* (1989): 62–71.

68. CR, letter to William M. Schenk, May 8, 1953. UCSB/R-K.

69. Both quotations, CR, 1980b: 351, 353.

70. CR, 1951a: 498.

71. See, e.g., S. Simon, L. Howe, & H. Kirschenbaum, *Values Clarification: A Handbook of Practical Strategies for Teachers and Students* (New York: Hart, 1971; Sunderland, MA: Values Press, 1978); Simon, Howe & Kirschenbaum, *Values Clarification: A Practical, Action-Directed Workbook* (New York: Warner Books, 1995).

72. D. Oyserman, H. Coon, & M. Kemmelmeier, Rethinking Individualism and Collectivism: Evaluation of Theoretical Assumptions and Meta-Analyses, *Psychological Bulletin, 128* (2002): 3–72.

73. Ibid.: 18, quoted in Williams, op. cit.: 371 (n. 50).

74. Williams, ibid.: 372.

75. Spangenberg, op. cit.: 52 (n. 43), summarizing T. Sodi, *In Search of the Essence of the African Personality*, paper presented at Second Annual Congress of the Psychological Association of South Africa, September 1996.

76. Hill-Hain & Rogers, 1988: 63–64.

77. This and next quotation, Cornelius-White, 2003, op. cit. (n. 62). His citations not included.

78. Sue & Sue, op. cit. (n. 52); Sue, Carter, Casas, Fouad, Ivey, Jensen, et al., op. cit. (n. 51).

79. Spangenberg, op. cit.: 50 (n. 43).

80. "Child-Centered Group Play Therapy with African American Boys at the Elementary School Level," *Journal of Counseling and Development, 83*, 387–396.

81. J. H. D. Cornelius-White, Teaching Person-Centered Multicultural Counseling: Collaborative Endeavors to Transcend Resistance and Increase Awareness, *Journal of Humanistic Counseling, Education and Development, 44*, 2 (Fall 2005): 225–239.

82. That week Rogers asked Chambers to his home to help craft a letter in response to a critic of the Carl Rogers Peace Project. Information in this paragraph from author interview, 2003.

83. Career Services Center, Student Employment, etc. Information in this paragraph from author interview, 2003 and M. Hughes, *Carl Rogers: Why Me?*, an address given at Carl Rogers Symposium, La Jolla, CA, July 2003. UCSB/R-K.

84. Hughes recalled it was two to three years during this period.

85. All quotations from *Carl Rogers: Why Me?*, op. cit. (n. 83).

86. Cornelius-White, 2003: 3. In the original Cornelius-White used "PCT" for "person-centered therapy."

87. Sources for the Soviet Union trip are: CR, 1987a, Inside the World of the Soviet Professional; Ruth Sanford's chapter in Suhd, 1995; Ruth Sanford interview, plus other cited sources.

88. Michael Murphy and others associated with Esalen Institute visited even earlier. See J. Hassard, The AHP Soviet Exchange Project: 1983–1990 and Beyond, *Journal of Humanistic Psychology, 30,* 3 (Summer 1990): 6–51.

89. Sanford in Suhd, 1995: 426.

90. Ibid.: 428. John Vasconcellos' version, in 1987: 359, was, "Isn't it somewhat dangerous to be doing that in a collectivist society?" "Yes, but not as dangerous as not doing it."

91. CR, 1987a: 484.

92. Ibid.

93. Ibid.: 486.

94. Ibid.: 487.

95. Ibid.: 488.

96. Sanford in Suhd, 1995: 430.

97. Ibid.: 430–431.

98. CR, 1987a: 499–500. In 1983 "Ilana Rubenfeld conducted the first AHP demonstration for Soviets in Moscow and then in Tbilisi." Hassard, The AHP Soviet Exchange Project, op. cit.: 15 (n. 88).

99. Ibid.: 493.

100. Ibid.: 496.

101. Ibid.: 497.

102. CR, 1987b: 151.

103. Greening, Commentary by the Editor, *Journal of Humanistic Psychology* [USSR citizen diplomacy issue], *27,* 3 (Summer 1987): 133.

104. This and next two quotations in F. Macy, The Legacy of Carl Rogers in the U.S.S.R., *Journal of Humanistic Psychology, 27,* 3 (Summer 1987): 305–306.

105. Quoted by Natalie Rogers in Suhd, 1995: 212–213.

106. In *Journal of Humanistic Psychology, 39,* 1 (Winter 1999): 8–14.

107. J. Hassard, op. cit.: 29 (n. 88).

108. NR in Suhd, 1995: 212.

109. Again, see Thorne, 1998, for a fuller history of the European experience.

110. D. Mearns, "The Humanistic Agenda: Articulation." Draft of manuscript submitted to *Journal of Humanistic Psychology,* n.d., 22 pp. UCSB/R-K.

111. Ibid.: 1.

112. Ibid.: 1–2. For the sentence ending with "vilified," he cited W. Coulson, "Reclaiming Client-Centered Counseling from the Person-Centered Movement." Comptche, CA: Center for Enterprising Families, 1987.

113. Information from Tausch interview, 2003, unless otherwise noted.

114. Tausch made it clear that they used one and then the other, never combining the two.

115. I believe these were R. Tausch & A.M. Tausch, *Gesprachs Psychotherapie: Einfulsam, Hilfreiche Gruppen—und Einzelgesprache in Psychotherapie und Alltaglichem Laben* (Gottingen: Hogrefe, 1960; Reinbek: Rowohlt, 1990), and R. Tausch, *Lebenseheitte: Vingang mit Belastenden Gefuhlen* (Reinbek: Rowohlt, 1989). Both were still in print as of 2003. Tausch interview.

116. He was president of the ÄGG from 1986–1999. "Contributors" biography in *Person-Centered and Experiential Psychotherapies,* 2002, *1,* 1&2: 156. Conversation with author at Third World Congress of Psychotherapy, Vienna, July 2002.

117. L. Teusch, *Person-Centred Research in Psychiatry,* presentation at Third World Congress for Psychotherapy, July 16, 2002.

118. Lietaer interview, 2003.

119. Under another name. Peter Schmid interview, 2003.

120. Mearns, op. cit.: 12 (n. 110).

121. Henderson interview, 2003. Brian Thorne, 1998, concurred and provided further examples.

122. 2001 poster for the IACP, which "to date has trained about 40,000 professionals." UCSB/R-K. Rogers is also listed as a founder in honor of his early support and participation, but Devonshire and Zucconi were the prime movers.

123. The Illinois School is now a branch of Argosy University. Many people thought the University of Georgia was such a place, but Jerald Bozarth wrote that actually he was the only faculty member who was explicitly person-centered. Email communication, November 21, 2006.

124. Author interviews with Peter Schmid, 2003, and Gerhard Stumm, 2002. See also A. Pritz, Austria, chapter in A. Pritz (Ed.), *Globalized Psychotherapy* (Vienna: Facultas Universitatsuerlag, 2002): 31, with chart showing that client-centered/person-centered is second only to systems/family therapy in Austria.

125. Email summary of survey results from Angela Couchman, Research and Development Officer, British Association for Counselling and Psychotherapy to Sheila Haugh, September 20, 2002, forwarded to author, September 25, 2002.

126. The British spelling of "person-centred," "counselling" and "behavioural" is maintained in these paragraphs.

127. CR, Memo from Carl Rogers, September 13, 1979, with accompanying letter describing the European program. UCSB/R-K.

128. Ibid. Program Coordinators on the 1981 brochure for the Ongoing Learning Program of Carl Rogers and Associates were listed as Valerie Henderson, Nathaniel Raskin, Carl Rogers and Lawrence Solomon. UCSB/R-K.

129. In his diary Rogers wrote, "It's very hard to face the humiliation of giving up on the Learning Program. I feel like such a fool—starting it with a big bang and 6 months later giving it up. Yet that *is* what I would like to do—without any doubt." April 3, 1980, Dreams Diary, UCSB/CR 2/8.

130. Footnote in Rogers & Russell, 2002: xi. That is the journal's current name.

131. Gendlin, 1957, 1958, 1962.

132. N. Friedman, Eugene Gendlin's Theory and Practice of Psychotherapy: A Personal Account, *Person-Centered and Experiential Psychotherapies, 2,* 1 (2003): 33–34.

133. E.g., Gendlin, The Experiential Response, in Hammer (ed.), *The Use of Interpretation in Treatment* (New York: Grune & Stratton, 1968); Focusing, *Psychotherapy: Theory, Research and Practice, 6,* 1 (1969).

134. Tausch interview. Tausch's language is maintained.

135. Some research studies on the outcomes of focusing-oriented therapy occurred after Rogers' death. See Chapter 13.

136. J. Wiltschko, *Focusing Therapy: Some Fragments in which the Whole Can Become Visible,* 1994: 2. Retrieved September 8, 2004, from <www.focusing.org/wiltschko.htm>.

137. E.g., CR, 1980b: 141.

138. CR, 1980b: 145; Rogers & Sanford, 1984.

139. Birthday telegram, October 6, 1982, in "Wires and Letters to be Read 1982" folder, UCSB/B; Foreword, Rogers & Russell, 2002: xi–xxi.

140. Leslie Greenberg interview, 2003.

141. See, for example, L. Rice, The Evocative Function of the Therapist, in Wexler & Rice, 1974: 289–311.

142. L. Greenberg, Remembering Laura Rice, Ph.D. In WAPCEPC newsletter, *2,* 4 (2005): 6. Also in *Person-Centered and Experiential Psychotherapies, 4,* 2 (summer 2005): 131–132.

143. L. Greenberg, The Case of Jim Brown: Commentary 2. In B. Farber, D. Brink & P. Raskin (eds.), *The Psychotherapy of Carl Rogers: Cases and Commentary* (New York: Guilford, 1996): 253, as is next quotation.

144. Wexler & Rice, 1974. Quotation from Greenberg interview. Robert Elliott presented a similar picture of this history in author interview, 2003.

145. Greenberg interview.
146. Ibid.
147. Rice & Greenberg, 1984.
148. R. Elliott, *Learning Emotion-Focused Therapy: The Process-Experiential Approach to Change*. American Psychological Association, November, 2003. Retrieved from The Process-Experiential Therapy Website, <http://www.process-experiential.org>, September 8, 2004: 2.
149. K.L. Davis, The Role of the Therapist Actions in Process-Experiential Therapy. (Doctoral dissertation, University of Toledo, 1994). *Dissertation Abstracts International*, 56, 519B (1995). Reported in Elliott & Greenberg, 2001: 290.
150. Greenberg interview. He also said Rice didn't think Rogers liked her because of differences in temperament.
151. Their journal is the *Journal for Psychotherapy Research*.
152. Although he may have attended the first meeting. Greenberg, interview.
153. CR, 1957a.
154. Greenberg, Remembering Laura Rice, op. cit. (n. 142).
155. Ibid.
156. Henderson interview.
157. "He hates Rogerians." Maria Bowen in CSP group interview, 1975.
158. Richard Farson, n.d. Note read at, given to and/or sent to Rogers for his 80th birthday celebration. LOC 4/2. Farson might actually have been referring to Rogers' comments to 3,000 at UC, Berkley in 1977, when the Association for Humanistic Psychology honored Rogers' 75th birthday. G. Swenson, letter to Cathy Book, bureau Chief of *Time Magazine*, May 2, 1999, in which Swenson nominated Rogers for the magazine's upcoming issue on 100 outstanding figures of the 20th century. UCSB/R-K.
159. Kim Francis, *Two Hours with Carl Rogers*, 1975, op. cit.: 46(Chapter 11, n. 116).
160. CR, letter to Robert Sollod, July 10, 1978. UCSB/R-K.
161. Henderson interview.
162. Hipólito interview. In 2002, Hipólito was President of this Association and Professor and Director of the Dept. of Psychology of the Universidade Autónoma de Lisboa.
163. Schmid interview.
164. Thorne interview.
165. Lietaer interview.
166. Henderson interview.
167. CR, letter to author, April 29, 1986. UCSB/R-K.
168. O'Hara interview.
169. "A Memo from Carl" on Carl Rogers and Associates letterhead, n.d. (1980). UCSB/R-K.
170. The "associates" were: Maria Bowen, Norman Chambers, Valerie Henderson, Nel Kandel, Nathaniel Raskin, Nancy Rice, Patrick Rice, David Ryback, Lawrence Solomon, Gay Swenson, Mary Ann Tucker, John K. Wood. Ibid.
171. Transition from C.R. & A. to independent CSP projects described in *Journey*, 1, 1 (November 1981): 5, a short-lived publication at CSP by John K. Wood.
172. The 1981 brochure listed these workshop topics in the spring and in the summer: History, Theory and Basic Concepts of the Person-Centered Approach; Development of Facilitative Skills; Exploration of Personal Issues; Implications and Applications of the PCA; Unanswered Questions: Intuition/Spirituality, Research and Concepts of Science in the PCA.
173. Chambers interview.
174. Quotation and program information from Institute brochure, n.d. (about 1981).
175. It remained vibrant for some years but after Rogers' death it became less active. Chambers interview.

176. Ibid. Wood's moving to Brazil was probably also a factor in the project's ending.

177. G. Barfield electronic communication, November 11, 2006.

178. Original directors were Swenson, Andre Auw and John K. Wood, with Nel Kandel as accountant. Later Swenson and Kandel were co-directors for many years. Staff included: "Arlene Wiltberger, Norman Chambers, Alberto Zucconi, Charlie O'Leary, with additions, depending on size, of Maureen O'Hara and many other CSPers over the years." Ibid.

179. Barfield interview, December 3, 2003. He did miss attending one year, but sent a taped presentation instead.

180. It began as a Carl Rogers and Associates project and then became an independent CSP project when C.R. & A. ended. Many of these tapes were made at the Living Now sessions. Barfield email, op. cit. (n. 178).

181. O'Hara interview.

182. Segrera recalled the dates were June 27 to about July 4. Alberto Segrera interview, 2002.

183. Armin Klein interview.

184. Sanford memoir in Suhd, 1995: 424.

185. Armin Klein/Grace Chickadonz interview, 2006.

186. Segrera interview.

187. This and next quotation, Cain interview.

188. Sanford memoir, Suhd, 1995: 431.

189. Titles were: The Dilemmas of a South African White; Rogers, Kohut, and Erickson: A Personal Perspective on Some Similarities and Differences; The Development of the Person-Centered Approach; Reflection of Feelings; Client-Centered? Person-Centered?; and On Reaching 85. From Volume 1, Number 1, 1986 through Volume 2, Number 2, 1987, respectively. The last two were published posthumously.

190. Just above 600. D. Cain, The Uncertain Future of Client-Centered Counseling, *Journal of Humanistic Education and Development*, *31* (March 1993): 133.

191. Presented at a seminar of the Bureau of Intercultural Education, New York City, February 18, 1946. Expanded to *Dealing With Social Tensions*, CR, 1948a; then adapted to Dealing With Interpersonal Conflict in *Pastoral Psychology*, CR, 1952c.

192. See details in endnote 76 in Chapter 6.

193. Published the next year in CR, 1952b.

194. CR, 1960. This and the previous pieces were included as or in Chapters 17 and 8 in *On Becoming a Person*, CR, 1961a.

195. B. Evans, Famous Psychologist to Join La Jolla Institute's Staff, *The San Diego Union*, September 5, 1963: a27. LOC 1/1.

196. E.g., CR, 1982 and CR & Ryback, 1984. According to a reporter, Rogers wrote Carter in mid-1982, suggested that Carter "consider forming an international mediating center," and asked for more information on the process of the Sadat–Begin mediation. An aide suggested he read about Camp David in Carter's soon-to-be-published memoir. Leigh Fenly, *San Diego Union*, October 12, 1982: D-1.

197. CR, Steps Toward Peace 1948–1986: Tension Reduction in Theory and Practice, unpublished paper to accompany grant proposals for second Central American meeting, 1986: 3. UCSB/B and UCSB/R-K.

198. CR, letter to "Dear Family and Friends," October 25, 1983, UCSB/R-K. See also Barfield interview.

199. First quotation, Swenson, The Rust Workshop: 311 (see below). Second quotation, D. Malcolm, Carl R. Rogers, *Person-Centered Review*, *2*, 3 (August 1987): 410. Nel Kandel, Gay Swenson and Antonio dos Santos coordinated the event; Swenson was moderator. Invitation, UCSB/ Barfield.

200. Henderson interview.

201. G. Barfield, email communication, September 30, 2006.

202. Barfield remarks at Carl Rogers Symposium, La Jolla, California, July 2002. Rust is pronounced "Roost." When mentioning Swenson in the 1980s I use her name then— Swenson. When mentioning her more recently, as in author interviews, I use her current name, Barfield.

203. T. Greening, Carl Rogers: 1902–1987, *Journal of Humanistic Psychology, 27*, 2 (Spring 1987): 134–140. As long-time editor of this journal, Greening had published many of Rogers' articles over the years.

204. I am indebted to Gay (Swenson) Barfield for many hours of interviews and for sending me two boxes of materials on the Peace Project, now or soon to be at the UCSB archive. Other accounts of the Rust workshop that contributed to this section are interviews with Rust workshop staff members Dee Aker, Norm Chambers, Valerie Henderson, Marvalene Hughes, and David Malcolm and Rust participant John Vasconcellos; CR, The Rust Workshop (1986d); Diane Dreher's (1995) essay on John Vasconcellos; and several accounts in a special issue of the *Journal of Humanistic Psychology* (*27*, 3, Summer 1987), including: Gay Swenson, When Personal and Political Processes Meet: The Rust Workshop (pp. 309–332), Maria V-B. Bowen, Special Characteristics of the Rust Workshop and their Influence on My Facilitation Process (pp. 348–363), and Lawrence Solomon, International Tension Reduction Through the Person-Centered Approach (pp. 337–347).

205. Meeting, December 12, 1982. Information in this paragraph from a memo from Swenson to Rogers, titled "Summary and Update Memo re Peace Project Proposal," October 8, 1983. UCSB/ Barfield; also Barfield interview.

206. Swenson, Summary and Update Memo, ibid. The abbreviation "pca" was used in the original.

207. He was attending the 20th anniversary commemoration of the 1963 March on Washington. Before entering politics Cranston had been president of the United World Federalists, a peace organization that Natalie Rogers had worked for years earlier.

208. The University for Peace was mandated as a "treaty organization" in the revised U.N. Charter. While separate from the U.N., the U.N. Secretary General serves as its Honorary President. <www.UPeace.org>, retrieved July 7, 2006.

209. He was meeting at UC Berkeley with Willis Harmon, Director of the Institute for Noetic Sciences, who agreed to allow Swenson to participate in the meeting.

210. CR, Letter to "Dear Family and Friends," op. cit.: 4 (n. 17, 198).

211. This and next paragraph based on: R. Fagen, *Forging Peace: The Challenge of Central America* (Basil Blackwell: A PACCA Book, 1987): 38–43; J. Booth & T. Walker, *Understanding Central America: Second Edition* (Boulder, CO: Westview Press, 1993): 159–167; and P. Ardon, *Post-War Reconstruction in Central America: Lessons from El Salvador, Guatemala and Nicaragua*. An Oxfam Working Paper (Great Britain: Oxfam, 1999). All three sources spell "contras" with a lower case "c."

212. Booth & Walker, ibid.: 163.

213. Dee Aker interview, 2003.

214. Name and donation information from Barfield interview and review of period documents. They actually used whichever title seemed to be most effective in each situation. On December 18, 1985, CR wrote the CSP Board saying the "Institute for Person-Centered Approaches to Peace" was too long and they wanted to change the official name to "The Carl Rogers Institute for Peace" using "Person-Centered Approaches to the Practice of Peace" as a further descriptor. Letter in Barfield papers. During the entire time, the "Peace Project" remained the most frequently used, informal name for the project.

215. Donation and titles, Barfield interview.

216. "They included Carl Rogers and his friend Ora Brink; Gay Swenson and John [K.] Wood of CSP; Michael Murphy, founder of Esalen; Jim Hickman and Dulce Murphy of the Esalen/

USSR Program; therapists George and Judith Brown from Santa Barbara, Willis Harmon, director of the Institute for Noetic Sciences; and Mitch Saunders, future director of California Leadership." Text and this quotation, Dreher, 1995: 357.

217. Bowen, op. cit.: 349 (n. 204) .

218. Gay Barfield comments at Carl Rogers Symposium, op. cit. (n. 202), and in Barfield interview.

219. He worked one day per week with the project for several years. Malcolm interview.

220. Weaver starred in the TV series "McCloud." Young had starred in the TV series "Father Knows Best" and "Marcus Welby, M.D."

221. Vak meeting, Malcolm interview, 2003. The bank's full name was Zentralparkasse und Kommerzialbank of Vienna. Information on Vak and bank in L. Solomon, op. cit. (n. 204).

222. The honorary committee for the Santa Clara fundraiser included prominent psychologists, educators, authors, actors and others, i.e.: Warren Bennis, Harold Bloomfield, Marilyn Ferguson, Hazel Henderson, Rev. Theodore Hesburgh, Gerald Jampolsky, Clark Moustakas, Robert Muller, Michael Murphy, Ruth Miriam, Jonas Salk, Virginia Satir, John Vasconcellos, Dennis Weaver, and Elizabeth and Robert Young. Gay Barfield interview, reading from a list.

223. The gift was not from Rogers, but from "a well known, popular writer of humanistic, pop psychology and organizational development … and to this day he's still writing." Barfield interview.

224. Monge invitations in "The Urgency of the Situation," n.a., n.d. probably June 1985, in folder "Peace Proj. 1985 files, corres, etc.," UCSB/ Barfield.

225. E.g. "Regarding Carl's letter to participants, he [Murray Silberman] insists vehemently, saying that RCO [Rodrigo Carazo Odio] is adamantly opposed to any letters coming from Carl or us describing the process, etc. He, they, are afraid that they would lose their participants. I pointed out that we do not want people thinking they are coming to something different than it is." Swenson memo to Peace Project Staff, August 28, 1985. Folder on "Peace Project 1985 files, corres, etc.," UCSB/B.

226. Marks also attended and played an active role at the conference. Search for Common Ground, then a relatively new organization, went on after Rust to become an influential and respected organization working for peaceful dialogue around the world.

227. Participants' accounts vary as to calling the event a workshop, conference, meeting or gathering. As the event did have all those characteristics, in each instance I have used the source's term or the one that seemed most appropriate to the context.

228. Barfield interview.

229. R. Fisher & W. Ury, *Getting to YES: Negotiating Agreement Without Giving In* (Boston: Houghton Mifflin, 1981). Ury was also associated with the Harvard Nuclear Negotiation Project.

230. CR, 1986d: 25–26. L. Solomon's summary of participants differs somewhat from Rogers. Rogers' listing *almost* matches the detailed records in the Barfield papers, UCSB, so I have amplified on his description, using information from the Barfield files. In the spirit of the conference, I have protected the anonymity of the participants while providing more information than has heretofore been shared publicly. I have mentioned a few names where they themselves were public about their participation.

231. Barfield interview.

232. L. Solomon, op. cit.: 338–339 (n. 204).

233. Hughes interview, 2003. Maureen O'Hara and Nel Kandel, who appear in a photograph of a planning meeting, did not get to go.

234. Styles and Solomon were originally going to attend as researchers only; but when the number of small groups expanded from three to four because more delegates agreed to attend the workshop, they were asked to also serve as small group facilitators. Bowen, op. cit.; Solomon, op. cit.; (both n. 204). Vasconcellos also participated in one or more staff meetings at Rust,

although he was technically a participant. Vasconcellos interview.

235. A. Zucconi, panel presentation at Carl Rogers Symposium, July 2002. Later on the team recognized the value of being familiar with the geography, issues and customs of the region.

236. Dreher, 1995: 357.

237. His friend Deborah ("Ora") Brink accompanied him as an aide to provide care and assistance as needed.

238. Session times in Solomon, op. cit. (n. 204). Project staff divided the participants so as to achieve maximum diversity in each group. President Carazo modified the group composition to put people he thought should be talking to one another in the same group.

239. Solomon, op. cit. (n. 204).

240. CR, 1986d: 28.

241. Hughes interview.

242. Swenson, op. cit.: 317 (n. 204).

243. Solomon, op. cit. (n.204), discusses this dilemma and its consequences more fully.

244. Swenson, op. cit.: 326 (n.204). The abbreviation UNUP was used in the original.

245. Bowen, op. cit. (n. 204).

246. Swenson, op. cit.: 321 (n. 204).

247. This and previous quote, Swenson, op. cit.: 324 (n. 204).

248. Names appear in original. G. Swenson, *Notes from Journal*, unpublished: 15 of 29 pp in UCSB/B.

249. Bowen, op. cit.: 363 (n. 204).

250. Hughes interview.

251. CR, 1986d: 32.

252. Ibid.

253. Bowen, op. cit.: 353 (n. 204).

254. The fullest version of this story I heard was Alberto Segrera and Alberto Zucconi's presentation to the Carl Rogers Symposium, in La Jolla, July 2002. Audio tape of session in UCSB/R-K. The incident was also mentioned in a number of author interviews.

255. Across several interviews and accounts, the story differed as to whether the children were teenagers or younger and whether the exchange actually took place. In Alberto Zucconi's presentation (ibid.), it did. Other interviewees, including Gay Barfield, thought the exchange was discussed but did not take place.

256. Vasconcellos, 1987: 357.

257. Swenson, op. cit.: 318 (n. 204).

258. They actually did communicate over the following year and talked to their governments about a process for building trust and working toward peace. Correspondence in UCSB\Barfield.

259. Bowen, op. cit.: 353 (n. 204).

260. Dreher, 1995: 358, wrote, "On the final day, Carl was moved to tears when all but one participant signed a joint testimonial." Presumably this was Vasconcellos' resolution, as Bowen said it was a "majority" that signed the Contadora resolution.

261. Barfield interview.

262. Quoted in Swenson, op. cit.: 331 (n. 204).

263. CR, 1986d: 39.

264. Bowen, op. cit.: 354 (n. 204).

265. Solomon, op. cit.: 345 (n. 204).

266. Ibid.; See also L. Solomon, Carl Rogers's Efforts for World Peace, *Person-Centered Review, 5*, 1 (1990): 39–56. Again, the problem was more complicated than that, because voluminous materials *had been* sent to participants beforehand to prepare them; but many didn't read the materials or they were not passed on to the substitute attendees. Barfield interview.

267. Rogers, 1987b: 151–52.
268. Swenson, op. cit.: 331 (n. 204).
269. Barfield interview.
270. Ibid.
271. David Malcolm and Sharon Bowman worked closely with her as well.
272. The Center was founded in 1982; the building dedication was October 1, 1986, and the conference was November 16–18, 1986. <www.cartercenter.org/about/history>.
273. Barfield interview. More of President Carter's remarks are reported later in the chapter.
274. CR, memo to Gay Swenson, "Re: Priorities," September 19, 1986. UCSB/B.
275. Quotation and details in next chapter.
276. A. Levinovitz & N. Ringertz (Eds.), *The Nobel Prize: The First Hundred Years* (London: Imperial College Press, 2001): 164.
277. Hence there are no frivolous nominations. Unless otherwise noted, information from <http://nobelprize.org/nominations/peace>.
278. Exact information for 1987 is not available, because information on nominations is sealed for 50 years.
279. Valerie Henderson interview; Barfield interview.
280. Henderson interview.
281. D. Malcolm, op. cit.: 411 (n. 199).
282. Valerie Henderson interview. Henderson, as Rogers' secretary and colleague, opened the letter. Letter arrival also in G. Swenson, letter to Peace Project Advisory committee, Project Donors, Supporters and Staff, August 1987.
283. From full text of Arias' speech, *New York Times*, December 11, 1987: A3.
284. F. Clines, 'Leave Us in Peace,' Costa Rican Pleads, *New York Times*, December 11, 1987: A3.
285. Levinovitz & Ringertz, op. cit.: 179 (n. 276).
286. Honoring 100 Year of Carl Rogers, Message to the Participants, From Dr. Oscar Arias, July 11, 2002. As read by Gay Swenson to whom President Arias had sent the letter to be read at the Carl Rogers Symposium, La Jolla, CA, July 2002. Forwarded by Gay Barfield by email communication to author, August 7, 2002. UCSB/R-K. Dee Aker said that at a meeting she later attended with President Carter and President Carazo that Carter credited Rogers with deepening all their understanding of the concept of trust. Aker interview.
287. CR 1967a; 1961a.
288. CR, 1980b: 34.
289. Ibid.: 198.
290. Ibid.: 258.
291. APA, 1973. Award discussed and citation quoted fully in Chapter 10.
292. Lyon had written a volume, *Happy to Be Here* (1970), in Rogers and Coulson's Studies of the Person series for Charles E. Merrill Publishers.
293. These included Reinhard and Anne-Marie Tausch, David Aspy and Flora Roebuck, and Jerome Freiberg.
294. I was one of the reviewers and was also invited to write the foreword. See letter to author from Marianne Taflinger, editor at Charles Merrill, July 9, 1980; CR, letter to author September 4, 1980; and CR, memoranda to Marianne Taflinger, Hal Lyon, Flora Roebuck and Howie Kirschenbaum (both) and Dave Aspy and Jerry Freiberg (latter), November 4, 1980 and November 25, 1980. These and the unpublished manuscript in UCSB/R-K.
295. Contributors, as listed on the title page, were Julie Allender, David Aspy, John Barkham, Kyle Blanchfield, Jerome Freiberg, Jeanne Ginsberg, Hugh Gunnison, Peter Ladd, Herbert Levitan, Barbara Shiel McElveny, "Winnie Moore," Flora Roebuck, William Romey, Ruth Sanford, Gay Swenson, Anne-Marie Tausch, Reinhard Tausch, and Alvin White.
296. CR, 1983: 197.

297. Aspy & Roebuck, 1977.

298. As of 2003 Freiberg was working on a fourth edition. J. Freiberg, personal communication, 2003.

299. Dee Aker interview. Because of his recent heart problem she accompanied him as his aide.

300. Dreams Diary, entry from Tucson airport, November 26, 1979. UCSB/CR.

301. Dreams Diary, October 13, 1980.

302. NR to CR, January 5, 1983. LOC 3/9.

303. CR, letter to Greg Rogers, November 9, 1982. LOC 3/8.

304. Henderson interview. See also CR, I Can't Read! *Visualtek News*, Summer 1983.

305. J. Vanconcellos, 1987.

306. Henderson interview.

307. J. Vanconcellos, 1987.

308. Henderson interview, 1991.

309. Natalie Rogers interview, 2003.

310. Henderson interview.

311. In "Wires and Letters To Be Read, Carl's birthday, 1982" folder, UCSB/ Barfield.

312. Barfield interview.

313. These trips were in 1980, 1983, and 1984. The Seneca Lake property remained in the family for at least another generation.

314. Barfield interview.

315. Ibid. She recounted this story with amusement, recognizing that it sounded like a parody of himself, but he was completely sincere.

316. D. Smith, Trends in Counseling and Psychotherapy, *American Psychologist, 37,* 7 (July 1982): 802–809. Quote on p. 807. 800 surveys were mailed; the usable response rate was over 50%. Weighted scores for the top five therapists were: Rogers–363, Ellis–229, Freud–117, Wolpe–87, Lazarus–84.

317. M. Heesacker, P. Heppner & M.E. Rogers [no relation], Classics and Emerging Classics in Counseling Psychology, *Journal of Counseling Psychology, 29,* 4 (July 1982): 400–405. The other two journals studied were *The Counseling Psychologist* and *Personnel and Guidance Journal* (currently the *Journal of Counseling and Development*).

318. Rogers & Haigh, 1983: 10.

319. April 26, 1980 entry from Atlanta. Dreams Diary, UCSB/CR.

320. NR interview.

321. Ibid.

322. E. Fine & J. Josephson, World Peace Parley Is Rogers' Dream Come True, *San Diego Union*, October 30, 1985, V-5.

323. Filmed dialogue between Rogers and Zucconi. Now at UCSB archive. Quote from summary in *APA Monitor*, November 1984.

324. Ann Japenga, Some of the Great Minds on the Mind Assemble for Conference, *Los Angeles Times*, December 18, 1985, V-4.

325. L. Milam, The Lourdes of Arizona: Psychotherapy's reigning wizards gather in Phoenix, *Networker*, September–October 1986: 52. Of course Rogers would say that more was going on than simply insight.

326. G. Swenson, letter to International Advisory Board Members, Institute for Person-Centered Approaches to Peace (Carl Rogers Peace Project), Re: Update of Activities since June 1986 Report, October 1986. UCSB/ Barfield.

327. Ibid.

328. Ibid.

329. Ibid. The latter organization is now the American Counseling Association.

330. See biography on <www.nd.edu/aboutnd/about/history/hesburgh>. Hesburgh support for

Rust in UCSB/ Barfield papers.

331. Barfield interview, November 12, 2003.

332. Ibid.

333. NR, in Suhd, 1995: 212. This was a reprise of the workshop they conducted five years earlier on "New World/New Person: A Three-Generational View" (see Chapter 11), a session they did at Natalie's Person-Centered Expressive Therapy Institute in 1984, and possibly other occasions.

334. For the most complete bibliography of Rogers' writings, see Schmid, 2005.

335. Henderson interview.

336. Ibid.

337. D. Russell, The UCSB Humanistic Psychology Archive, *Journal of Humanistic Psychology, 30*, 4 (Fall 1990): 57–61.

338. Rogers & Russell, 2002. See Chapter 13.

339. CR, 1987b: 150.

340. CR, letter to author, June 20, 1986.

341. Unless otherwise noted, information on this event comes from the two-hour videotape of the occasion distributed at the time by Center for Studies of the Person, interviews with organizers Gay Barfield and Dee Aker and other attendees, the invitation/brochure titled "In Celebration!," and materials in the "85 Greetings" folder in the UCSB/B papers.

342. As recollections of the number of attendees differed in author interviews, I used the number given in the newspaper account of the event: J. Hughes, Rogers celebrates 85th birthday; notables salute psychology's star, *San Diego Tribune*, December 23, 1986: B3. Attendance was not intended to exceed 200, as that was the theater's capacity.

343. On Carter Center letterhead, November 6, 1987.

344. G. Swenson, letter to Peace Project Advisory Committee, Project Donors, Supporters and Staff, August 1987.

345. NR interview.

346. Barfield interview.

347. Ibid. Barfield often commented that "in that film he got to hear his own eulogy while still alive." Email communication, November 11, 2006.

348. Ruth Sanford interview, 1991; Barfield interview.

349. Following details from Natalie Rogers interview, 2003. Corroboration in other interviews and documents, e.g. letter to "Dear Colleagues," on CSP letterhead, February 5, 1987, informing of Rogers' death.

350. Henderson interviews, 1991 and 2003. In 1991 interview, the quotation was "I'll never go through that again."

351. NR interview.

352. Barfield interview. Examples from many of the author interviews.

353. Barfield interview.

354. Letter to Cathy Book, *Time Magazine*, op. cit. (n. 158).

355. Barfield interview. Remaining details from Vasconcellos interview; J. Vasconcellos, Eulogy, 1987; and Dreher, 1995.

356. Vasconcellos, 1987: 360.

357. Dreher, 1995: 359.

358. Henderson interview.

359. CR, 1980a: 89. Emphasis his.

Chapter 13

1. Author's notes from the event.
2. J. Vasconcellos, 1987: 353.
3. From the announcement for the memorial service. UCSB/R-K.
4. About $25,000 was raised. The allocation of contributions turned out to be confusing for many donors and controversial among some of Rogers' colleagues who had different opinions as to how the funds should be used and what Rogers would have wanted. UCSB/B.
5. The actual sponsor listed on the invitation was "Hofstra University Counselor Education Alumni Association and other friends and colleagues of Carl Rogers."
6. D. Malcolm, copy of letter "To the Editor," sent to *Los Angeles Times*, San Diego County Edition, February 6, 1987.
7. Henderson interview, 2003. Other papers from CSP and the family were sent to the Donaldson Library at University of California at Santa Barbara.
8. S. Shochot, Tributes and Memories, *Person-Centered Review, 2,* 3 (August 1987): 428.
9. Nelson Mandela was released from prison in 1990 and elected State President of South Africa in 1994. He and the former President F.W. de Klerk championed reconciliation.
10. Gay Swenson, letter to International Advisory Board, Rust Participants and Staff, Project Donors and Supporters, Late February 1987. UCSB/B.
11. Annual Report to Donors and Friends, Carl Rogers Institute for Peace, 1991, n.d. UCSB/B.
12. "Six Month Report" from Gay Leah Swenson "To: Donors, Advisory Committee and Supporters," August 1988, accompanied by a proposal to the University of Costa Rica to collaborate on a gathering with the title as cited. UCSB/R-K.
13. Barfield comments at CR Symposium, La Jolla, CA, July 2002.
14. Kroc gave other similar gifts that day. Barfield interview.
15. G. Barfield, letter to President Oscar Arias, July 2, 2002, forwarded via email communication to author, August 7, 2002. UCSB/R-K.
16. See references on Central America and Nicaragua in Chapter 12, op. cit (n. 211).
17. J. Booth & T. Walker, *Understanding Central America* 2nd ed. (Boulder, CO: Westview Press, 1993): 164.
18. Barfield letter to Arias, op. cit. (n. 15).
19. Ironically, while the group in Costa Rica was meeting on the peace process, the five Central American foreign ministers were meeting in Mexico, on the occasion of the Mexican president's inauguration, to discussing how to re-invigorate the Arias Peace Plan.
20. Only a few of the invited participants had attended the Rust workshop, but almost all the Rust facilitators and staff were present again. Attendance information from G. Swenson, *First Notes—Costa Rica Meeting—December 1–5, 1988,* an unpublished 8-page summary of the event and from my review of the attendee lists from both workshops. UCSB/B.
21. Information on the meeting from Swenson, *First Notes,* ibid.
22. Ann Lencioni, A Costa Rica Experience, *On Beyond War, 46* (February 1989): 12. 25,000 copies were mailed worldwide. Carl Rogers Institute for Peace "End of Fiscal Year Report: 1988–89." UCSB/B.
23. Ironically, with the U.S. continuing to intervene in support of the *contras* and destabilizing the Nicaraguan economy and political process, the Sandanistas were voted out of office in 1990. They accepted the results; the U.S. more or less got its way; fighting stopped; peace was restored; and the long and difficult task of reconciliation and reconstruction began. More ironically, as of this writing in 2007, the Sandinista leader from the 1980s, Daniel Ortega, was just re-elected leader of Nicaragua, much to the dismay of the current U.S. administration under President George Bush (the second).
24. R. Carazo, *Under Carl Rogers, Central American Peace Talks Began at Rust.* Email communication

from Barfield to author, August 7, 2002. Correspondence in Rust Workshop file, UCSB/R-K.

25. Aker interview.

26. UCSB/B.

27. Gordon in Suhd, 1995: 332.

28. E.g., Vasconcellos, 1987; Dreher, 1995.

29. *The Politics of Trust*, The John Vasconcellos Legacy Project, Santa Clara, CA, n.a., n.d., c. 2002; Vasconcellos (1987) eulogized Rogers as "the pioneer of trust."

30. Donor and attendee lists, UCSB/B.

31. Aker interview.

32. See *New York Times* articles, e.g., July 31, 1989: A.9; December 7, 1989: A.26; April 29, 1990: A.1.

33. L. Altman, Dr. Dave E. Rogers, 68, Leading Medical Educator, Dies, *New York Times*, December 6, 1994: D.23.

34. NR, 1993.

35. NR, personal communication, January 24, 2007.

36. "Person-Centered Expressive Therapy Workshops in Russia." One page listing, n.a., n.d. Natalie Rogers folder, UCSB/R-K.

37. E.g., see chapter on "Person-Centered Expressive Arts Therapy" in Judith Rubin, *Approaches to Art Therapy: Second Edition* (New York: Brunner-Routledge, 2001): 163–177.

38. She was still active as of this writing in 2006.

39. CR, letter to author, January 3, 1987. UCSB/R-K.

40. Kirschenbaum & Henderson, 1989b, 1989a.

41. Hosted by Saybrook Graduate School, July 24–28, 2002. Steering committee was: Tom Greening, Valerie Henderson, Bob Lucas, Maureen O'Hara, Steve Olwean, Natalie Rogers, John Vasconcellos, Robert Schley.

42. NR, conference review in Association for Humanistic Psychology's *Perspective* (August/ September 2002): 12–13. Plenary and keynote sessions were offered by Saybrook Graduate School President Maureen O'Hara, Natalie Rogers, John Vasconcellos, educator Jerome Freiberg, Rogers' biographer Howard Kirschenbaum, Rogers' associate and college president Marvalene Hughes, Ohio Congressman and progressive presidential candidate Dennis Kucinich, and Peter Yarrow of Peter, Paul and Mary.

43. Rogers & Russell, 2002.

44. See reviews: D. Cain, review in *Contemporary Psychology: APA Review of Books*, 2003; H. Kirschenbaum, Encountering Carl Rogers—Fifteen Years After His Death, *Person-Centered and Experiential Psychotherapies, 2,* 1 (Spring 2003), 57–66.

45. Fuchs and Huston's production company was Mindgarden Media. Available from <nrogers.com> and PCCS Books in the UK.

46. Now being used in over 700 colleges, universities and training institutes worldwide. Written and narrated by Howard Kirschenbaum. Published 2003; distributed by Values Associates in the U.S. <www.HowardKirschenbaum.com> and PCCS Books in the UK <www.pccs-books.co.uk>.

47. CR, 1942a.

48. E.g., CR, 1949b; Rogers & Dymond, 1954; Rogers, Gendlin, Kiesler & Truax, 1967.

49. CR, 1942a, 1951a.

50. Capuzzi & Gross, 2001; Gibson & Mitchell, 1999; Gladding, 2000; Nugent, 2000.

51. APA, 1957, 1973.

52. CR, 1951a, 1959c.

53. E.g., S. Cloninger, *Theories of Personality: Understanding Persons* (Upper Saddle River, NJ: Pearson/Prentice Hall, 2003); J. Feist & G.J. Feist, *Theories of Personality: Fifth Edition* (Boston: McGraw-Hill, 2001); Hall, Lindzey & Campbell, 1998; C. Monte & R. Sollod,

Beneath the Mask: An Introduction to Theories of Personality: Seventh Edition (Hoboken, NJ: Wiley, 2002); R. Ryckman, *Theories of Personality: Third Edition* (Belmont, CA: Wadsworth, 2004).

54. E.g., Rogers & Skinner, 1956; CR, 1970a.
55. CR, 1969a, 1983; Rogers & Freiberg, 1994.
56. CR, 1961a, 1969a, 1977, 1980b.
57. CR, 1977; Kirschenbaum & Henderson, 1989b.
58. Statistics in this section were compiled by April Jourdan in Kirschenbaum & Jourdan, 2005.
59. Based on bibliographies in Russell (2002) and the PsychINFO database, January 25, 2002 and September 6, 2004, Psychological Abstracts Information Services. Not counting Rogers' own 16 books and over 200 professional articles. Reported in Kirschenbaum & Jourdan, 2005.
60. Ibid.
61. CR, 1987b: 150.
62. Lietaer, 2002a.
63. <www.pfs-online.at/rogers.htm>, retrieved November 27, 2006.
64. Kirschenbaum & Jourdan, 2005.
65. Ibid. In descending order of frequency. Descriptors are sometimes controlled by PsychINFO. For example, when one types "behavior therapy," PsychINFO tells the user to use the "behavioral therapy" descriptor. To derive the number for cognitive therapy, we had to ask for "cognitive therapy, not behavior and not behavioral." We recognize that more than one person's name is associated with any particular approach, but used one name so as to render a fair comparison.
66. Cain & Seeman, 2002.
67. See PCCS Books' website <www.pccs-books.co.uk>.
68. Based on research by author, April Jourdan, and Peter Schmid's website <www.pfs-online.org>, accessed in September 2004, which has a complete listing of organizations and training institutes around the world.
69. Yoko Allen, ADPCA membership secretary, email communication to members, November 12, 2006.
70. Literally "society for scientific talking therapy" or "conversation therapy." Peter Schmid, email communication, December 5, 2006.
71. Author interviews with Sara Boyle, João Hipólito, Margarethe Letzel, Germain Lietaer, Dave Mearns, Pete Sanders, Peter Schmid, Gerhard Stumm, Reinhard Tausch, Ludwig Teusch, Brian Thorne, Alberto Zucconi, and others.
72. Focusing Institute. Home page. Retrieved November 22, 2003, from <http://www.focusing.org>.
73. Lietaer quotations in this section from author interview, 2003.
74. After Rogers' death in California (1987), Brazil (1989) and every three years thereafter in the Netherlands, Greece, South Africa, Japan, Argentina, and Spain. Segrera remained active behind the scenes, helping to identify local hosts in each location and supporting them through the process of organizing and running the Forum.
75. E.g., a 2004 journal issue showed all the editors and four of the five members of the board of directors to be U.S. residents. *The Person-Centered Journal*, 2004, *11*, 1&2.
76. J. Bozarth, electronic communication, November 21, 2006.
77. In Lietaer, Rombauts & Van Balen, 1990: 397–414 and 205–224, respectively.
78. Lietaer, Rombauts & Van Balen, 1990.
79. Scotland, 1991; Austria, 1994; Portugal, 1997.
80. The Bad Hall Letter, July 1996. Germain Lietaer, Belgium; Maureen O'Hara, USA; Bernie Neville, Australia; Peter Schmid, Austria; Brian Thorne, United Kingdom; and Margaret

Warner, USA, lead signatories, and signed by all 30 participants. Website of the World Association for Person-Centered and Experiential Psychotherapy and Counseling. Retrieved August 25, 2006 from <http://www.pce-world.org/idxhistory/htm>.

81. Ibid.

82. World Association website, op. cit. (n. 80).

83. Chicago, USA, 2000; Egmond aan Zee, Nederlands, 2003; Potsdam, Germany, 2006. Future conferences are expected to be every two years, including Norwich, UK, 2008 and Italy, 2010.

84. <ww.pfs-online.org>, accessed in September 2004.

85. First organized by Jerold Bozarth and Fred Zimring and edited by Bozarth until 1996, it is still published today with one or two issues per year. Bozarth email, 2006, op. cit. (n. 76).

86. *"PCEP* to go to BAPCA Members," Journal News section, WAPCEPC *Newsletter, 2,* 4 (Spring 2005): 4; Maggie Taylor-Sanders, note on manuscripts, via email communication, January 9, 2007. As mentioned above, ADPCA membership recently shrank to under 200.

87. Bozarth, Zimring & Tausch, 2001:153.

88. Rogers, 1957a: 102.

89. Rogers, Gendlin, Kiesler & Truax, 1967.

90. Truax & Mitchell, 1971: 310.

91. A. Gurman, The Patient's Perception of the Therapeutic Relationship. In A. Gurman & A. Razin (Eds.), *Effective Psychotherapy: A Handbook of Research* (New York: Pergamon, 1977): 523.

92. Orlinsky & Howard, Process and Outcome in Psychotherapy: 365. In Garfield & Bergin, 1986: 311–381.

93. E.g., A. Bergin & R. Suinn, Individual Psychotherapy and Behavior Therapy. In M. Rosenzweig & L. Porter (Eds.), *Annual Review of Psychology, 26* (1975): 509–556; K. Mitchell, J. Bozarth, & C. Krauft, A Reappraisal of the Therapeutic Effectiveness of Accurate Empathy, Nonpossessive Warmth, and Genuineness. In Gurman & A. Razin, 1977, op cit.: 482–502 (n. 91); M. Parloff, I. Waskow & B. Wolfe, Research on Therapist Variables in Relation to Process and Outcomes. In S. Garfield & A. Bergin (Eds.), *Handbook of Psychotherapy and Behavior Change: Second Edition* (New York: John Wiley, 1978): 233–282.

94. Then: Mitchell, et al., ibid. Since: Patterson, 1984; Stubbs & Bozarth, 1994, cited in Bozarth, Zimring & Tausch, 2001: 166; R. Elliott, The Effectiveness of Humanistic Psychotherapies: A Meta-Analysis. In Cain & Seeman, 2001: 57–81.

95. Patterson, 1984.

96. Stubbs & Bozarth, 1994. Cited in Bozarth, Zimring & Tausch, 2001: 166.

97. Bergin & Suinn, 1975, op. cit. (n. 93); M. Lambert & A. Bergin, The Effectiveness of Psychotherapy. In Bergin & Garfield, 1994: 143–189.

98. Barrett-Lennard, 1962; P. Martin & A. Sterne, Post-Hospital Adjustment as Related to Therapists' In-Therapy Behavior, *Psychotherapy: Theory, Research and Practice, 13,* 3 (1976): 267–273.

99. T. Sexton & S. Whiston, The Status of the Counseling Relationship: An Empirical Review, Theoretical Implications, and Research Directions, *The Counseling Psychologist, 22,* 1 (1994): 6–78. Quote on p. 15.

100. Orlinsky, Grawe & Parks, 1994. Only one study overlapped with Sexton and Whiston's sample.

101. Bohart, Elliott, Greenberg & Watson, Empathy. In Norcross, 2002: 89–108.

102. Orlinsky, Grawe & Parks, 1994.

103. These included studies in Orlinsky and Howard's review in Garfield & Bergin, 1986: 311–381; quotation from p. 184 in B. Farber & J. Lane, Positive Regard. In Norcross, 2002: 175–194.

104. Farber & Lane, ibid.: 185.

105. Ibid: 191.

106. M. Klein, G. Kolden, J. Michels, & S. Chisholm-Stockard, Congruence. In Norcross, 2002: 195–215; R. Sachse & R. Elliott, Process-Outcome Research on Humanistic Therapy Variables. In Cain & Seeman, 2001: 83–115.

107. Orlinsky, Grawe & Parks, 1994.

108. Sachse & Elliott, op. cit. (n. 106).

109 G. Lietaer, The Client-Centered Approach after the Wisconsin Project: A Personal View on Its Evolution. In Lietaer, Rombauts, & Van Balen, 1990: 19–45.

110. See Bozarth, Zimring & Tausch, 2001, for a summary of this research program.

111. J. Rudolf, I. Langer, & R. Tausch, An Investigation of the Psychological Effects and Conditions of Person-Centered Individual Psychotherapy, *Zeitschrift fur Klinische Psychologie: Forschung und Praxis, 9* (1980): 23–33.

112. E.g. Lietaer, Rombauts & Van Balen, 1990; G. Lietaer, P. van Praag, & J. Swildens, *Client-Centered Psychotherapie in Beweging* [Client-Centered Psychotherapy in Action] (Leuven, Belgium: Acco, 1984); R. Van Balen, M. Leijssen, & G Lietaer, *Droom en werkelijkheid in Client-Centered Psychotherapie.* [Dream and reality in Client-Centred Psychotherapy] (Leuven, Belgium: Acco, 1986).

113. Bozarth, Zimring & Tausch, 2001: 162.

114. Stubbs & Bozarth, 1994: 109.

115. R. Tausch, The Supplementation of Client-Centered Communication Therapy with Other Validated Therapeutic Methods: A Client-Centered Necessity. In Lietaer, Rombauts & Van Balen, 1990: 447–455.

116. G. Lietaer, Remarks at Carl Rogers Symposium, Third World Congress on Psychotherapy, Vienna, Austria, July 15, 2002. Confirmed in author interview, 2003.

117. C. Gelso & J. Carter, The Relationship in Counseling and Psychotherapy: Components, Consequences, and Theoretical Antecedents, *Counseling Psychologist, 13,* 2 (1985): 220; Lietaer, 2002b.

118. M. Lambert, D. Shapiro & A. Bergin, The Effectiveness of Psychotherapy. In Garfield & Bergin, 1986: 157–212; Lambert, 1992; See also Hubble, Duncan & Miller, 1999, and Wampold, 2001.

119. R. Elliott, 1997; L. Luborsky, B. Singer, & L. Luborsky, Comparative Studies of Psychotherapies: Is It True That "Everyone Has Won and All Must Have Prizes?" *Archives of General Psychiatry, 32* (1975): 995–1008; M. Smith & G. Glass, Meta-Analyses of Psychotherapy Outcome Studies, *American Psychologist, 32* (1977): 752–760; M. Smith, G. Glass, & T. Miller, *The Benefits of Psychotherapy* (Baltimore: Johns Hopkins University, 1980); B. Wampold, G. Mondin, M. Moody, F. Stich, K. Benson, & H. Ahn, A Meta-Analysis of Outcome Studies Comparing Bona Fide Psychotherapies: Empirically "All Must Have Prizes." *Psychological Bulletin, 122,* 3 (1997): 203–215.

120. E.g., Elliott, 2001, op. cit. (n. 94); ; L. Luborsky, L. Diguer, D. Seligman, R. Rosenthal, E. Krause, S. Johnson, G. Halperin, M. Bishop, J. Berman, & E. Schweizer, The Researcher's Own Therapy Allegiances: A "Wild Card" in Comparisons of Treatment Efficacy, *Clinical Psychology: Science and Practice, 6,* 1 (1999): 95–106; L. Robinson, J. Berman, & R. Neimeyer, Psychotherapy for the Treatment of Depression: A Comprehensive Review of Controlled Outcome Research. *Psychological Bulletin, 108,* 1 (1990): 30–49; Wampold, 2001.

121. M. Goldfried, Toward the Delineation of Therapeutic Change Principles, *American Psychologist, 35,* 11 (1980): 991–999; J. Frank, Therapeutic Components Shared By All Psychotherapies. In J. Harvey & M. Parks (Eds.), *The Master Lecture Series. Vol. 1. Psychotherapy Research and Behavior Change* (Washington, DC: APA, 1982): 73–122; L. Grencavage & J. Norcross, Where Are the Commonalities Among the Therapeutic Common Factors?

Professional Psychology: Research and Practice, 21, 5 (1990): 372–378; Lambert, 1992.

122. T. Sexton, S. Whiston, J. Bleuer, & G. Walz, *Integrating Outcome Research into Counseling Practice and Training* (Alexandria, VA: American Counseling Assocation, 1997): 56.

123. S. Rosenzweig, Some Implicit Common Factors in Diverse Methods of Psychotherapy, *American Journal of Orthopsychiatry, 6,* 3 (1936): 412–415. See also discussion in Chapter 5.

124. Hubble, Duncan & Miller, 1999; Bozarth, Zimring & Tausch, 2001: 150.

125. Lambert & Bergin, 1994.

126. S. Blatt, D. Zuroff, D. Quinlan, & P. Pilkonis, Interpersonal Factors in Brief Treatment of Depression: Further Analyses of the National Institute of Mental Health Treatment Of Depression Collaborative Research Program, *Journal of Consulting and Clinical Psychology, 64,* 1 (1996): 162–171.

127. S. Garfield, Chapter 6. Research on Client Variables in Psychotherapy. In Bergin & Garfield, 1994: 220.

128. Blatt, et al.: 166, op. cit. (n. 126).

129. Bozarth, Zimring & Tausch, 2001.

130. E. Bordin, The Generalizability of the Psychoanalytic Concept of the Working Alliance, *Psychotherapy: Research and Practice, 16,* 3 (1979): 252–260; K. Menninger, *Theory of Psychoanalytic Technique* (New York: Basic Books, 1958).

131. Sexton, Whiston, Bleuer & Walz: op. cit.: 78 (n. 122).

132. E.g., L. Gaston, The Concept of the Alliance and Its Role in Psychotherapy: Theoretical and Empirical Considerations, *Psychotherapy, 27,* 2 (1990): 143–153; A. Horvath & D. Symonds, Relation Between Working Alliance and Outcome in Psychotherapy: A Meta-Analysis, *Journal of Counseling Psychology, 38,* 2 (1991): 139–149; L. Luborsky, P. Crits-Christoph, J. Mintz, & A. Auerbach, *Who Will Benefit from Psychotherapy? Predicting Therapeutic Outcomes* (New York: Basic Books, 1988); D. Martin, J. Garske & M. Davis, Relation of the Therapeutic Alliance with Outcome and Other Variables: A Meta-Analytic Review, *Journal of Consulting and Clinical Psychology, 68,* 3 (2000): 438–450; Orlinsky, Grawe & Parks, 1994.

133. Ibid.: 360.

134. Lambert, 1992: 108.

135. Martin, Garske & Davis, op. cit. (n. 132).

136. See Farber & Lane, op. cit. (n. 103).

137. Bohart, Elliott, Greenberg & Watson, in Norcross, 2002: 96.

138. Lambert & Bergin, 1994: 165.

139. Sachse & Elliott, op. cit. (n. 106).

140. Sexton, Whiston, Bleuer & Walz, op. cit.: 78 (n. 122).

141. Grencavage & Norcross, op. cit. (n. 121); Wampold, 2001: 150.

142. J. Frank, *Persuasion and Healing* (Baltimore: Johns Hopkins Press, 1961).

143. Gaston, 1990: op. cit.: 145 (n. 132).

144. E.g., C. Feller & R. Cattone, The Importance of Empathy in the Therapeutic Alliance, *Journal of Humanistic Counseling, Education and Development, 42,* 1 (2003): 53–61.

145. Orlinsky, Grawe & Parks, 1994: 308.

146. Wampold, 2001: 211.

147. D. Burns & S. Nolen-Hoeksema, Therapeutic Empathy and Recovery from Depression in Cognitive-Behavioral Therapy: A Structural Equation Model, *Journal of Consulting and Clinical Psychology, 60,* 3 (1992): 441–449. Quote: 447.

148. Ibid.: 445

149. L. McCulloch, (2000). A Person-Centered Approach to Anti-Social Personality Disorder. Unpublished doctoral dissertation, University of Rochester, Rochester, NY, 2000. *Dissertation Abstracts International, 61,* 09A, 3475; L. McCulloch, *The Person-Centered Approach in Crisis*

and Calm. Panel presentation at Thirteenth Annual Counselor's Renewal Conference, University of Rochester, Rochester, NY, January 22, 2003.

150. McCulloch, 2003, ibid.

151. Lambert, 1992: 104.

152. Norcross, 2001.

153. See also J. Bozarth, Empirically Supported Treatments: Epitome of the "Specificity Myth." In J. Watson, N. Goldman & M. Warner, 2002: 168–181; J. Bozarth, Research on Psychotherapy Outcome and the Person-Centered Approach, in *Person-Centered Therapy: A Revolutionary Paradigm* (Ross-on-Wye, UK: PCCS Books, 1998): 163–173.

154. Norcross, 2002, 2001.

155. Empirically supported therapy relationships: Conclusions and recommendations of the Division 29 Task Force. (n.d.): 2. Retrieved October 28, 2003 from <http://academic.uofs/faculty/Norcross/empir.htm> (website of committee chair John Norcross).

156. Norcross, 2001: 347. Rumor had it that Norcross sported a bumper sticker with this slogan.

157. Robert Elliott interview, referring to Greenberg, Elliott, & Lietaer, Experiential Humanistic Therapies. In M. Lambert, A. Bergin & S. Garfield (Eds.), *Handbook of Psychotherapy and Behavior Change* (New York: John Wiley, 2005): 493–538.

158. Lambert & Bergin, 1994; J. Norcross & M. Goldfried (Eds.), *Handbook of Psychotherapy Integration* (New York: Basic Books, 1992).

159. S. Garfield & R. Kurtz, A Study of Eclectic Views, *Journal of Consulting and Clinical Psychology, 45*, (1977): 78–83; D. Smith, Trends in Counseling and Psychotherapy, *American Psychologist, 37*, 7 (July 1982): 802–809; J. Norcross & J. Prochaska, A Study of Eclectic (and Integrative) Views Revisited, *Professional Psychology: Research and Practice, 19*, 2 (1988): 170–174; J. Jensen, A. Bergin & D. Greaves, The Meaning of Eclecticism: New Survey and Analysis of Components, *Professional Psychology: Research and Practice, 21* (1990): 124–130; J. Norcross & C. Newman, Psychotherapy Integration: Setting the Context. In Norcross & Goldfried: op. cit.: 3–45 (n. 158); Quote from Lambert & Bergin, 1994: 181.

160. N.a., The Top 10: The Most Influential Psychotherapists of the Past Quarter-Century. *Psychotherapy Networker*, March/April 2007. The 2,598 respondents were almost all social workers, professional counselors, and psychologists.

161. Focusing Institute. Home page. Retrieved November 22, 2003, from <http://www.focusing.org>.

162. See M. Hendricks, Focusing-Oriented/Experiential Psychotherapy. In Cain & Seeman, 2001: 221–251.

163. Gendlin, 1996.

164. Separate interviews with author. Quotations come from these interviews, unless otherwise noted.

165. Greenberg, Rice & Elliott, 1993.

166. Elliott & Greenberg, 2001: 282–283.

167. E.g., R. Elliott, 1997; L. Greenberg, R. Elliott, & G. Lietaer, Research on Experiential Psychotherapies. In Bergin & Garfield, 1994: 509–539; R. Elliott, Research on the Effectiveness of Humanistic Therapies: A Meta-Analysis. In Cain & Seeman, 2001: 57–81.

168. L. Greenberg, R. Elliott & G. Lietaer, Research on Humanistic and Experiential Psychotherapies. In Bergin and Garfield, 1994: 509–539.

169. R. Goldman, L. Greenberg & L. Angus, Initial Results from the York II Comparative Study on Experiential Psychotherapy of Depression. Paper presented at meeting of the Society for Psychotherapy Research, Braga, Portugal, June 1999.

170. For more on *being* and *doing*, see for example, L. Greenberg, Being and Doing: Person-Centeredness, Process Guidance and Differential Treatment, *Person-Centered and Experiential Psychotherapies, 3*, 1 (2004): 52–64.

171. Lietaer interview.

172. Conference papers were published in Lietaer, Rombauts & Van Balen, 1990.

173. Ibid.

174. Schmid interview.

175. Barfield, email communication, November 26, 2007. See Max Pages, *L'orientation non-directive en psychotherapie et en psychologie social* (Paris: Dunod, 1965); A. de Peretti, *Liberté et relations humaines ou l'inspiration non-directive* (Paris: Epi, 1966); M. de la Puente, *Carl R. Rogers: De a psychotherapie a l'enseignement* (Paris: Epi, 1970).

176. Remarks at Carl Rogers Symposium, La Jolla, July 2002.

177. Presentation at the Carl Rogers Symposium at the World Congress on Psychotherapy in Vienna, July 2002.

178. T. Gordon, *Teacher Effectiveness Training* (New York: Peter Wyden, 1974).

179. Gordon, *TET*, 1974; *PET*, 1970. *PET* sold 3.5 million of the total. Reported in T. Gordon, chapter in Suhd, 1995: 333–334.

180. E.g., R. Carkhuff, *Interpersonal Skills and Human Productivity* (Amherst, MA: HRD Press, 1983); *Helping and Human Relations* (Amherst, MA: HRD Press, 1984); E. Baumgarten & T. Roffers, Implementing and Expanding on Carkhuff's Training Technology, *Journal of Counseling and Development, 81*, 3 (Summer 2003): 285–291.

181. E.g., Aspy and Roebuck mention how they use Carkhuff's technology in CR, *Freedom to Learn for the 80s*, 1983: 200.

182. Author's observation.

183. G. Lietaer, remarks at the Carl Rogers Symposium, Third World Congress on Psychotherapy, July 2002. See also Lietaer, 2002b.

184. P. Schmid, The Characteristics of a Person-Centered Approach to Therapy and Counseling; Criteria for Identity and Coherence, *Person-Centered and Experiential Psychotherapies, 2*, 2 (Summer 2003): 104–120.

185. R. Sachse, From Client-Centered to Clarification-Oriented Psychotherapy, *Person-Centered and Experiential Psychotherapies, 3*, 1 (Spring 2004): 19–35. Natalie Rogers and Prouty discussed earlier. Exploring additional approaches and variations is beyond the scope of this work. For further discussion see: G. Lietaer, The Client-Centered/Experiential Paradigm in Psychotherapy: Development and Identity. In Watson, Goldman & Warner, 2002: 1–15.

186. M. Warner, Person-Centered Psychotherapy: One Nation, Many Tribes, *Person-Centered Journal, 7*, 1 (2000), 28–39.

187. See L. Greenberg, J. Watson & G. Lietaer (Eds.), *Handbook of Experiential Psychotherapy* (New York: Guilford Press, 1998); also Cain & Seeman, 2001.

188. Elliott interview, 2003.

189. Washington, DC: American Psychological Association, 2004.

190. More on name, op. cit. (n. 70).

191. R. Elliott, Render Unto Caesar: Quantitative and Qualitative Knowing in Research on Humanistic Therapies, *Person-Centered and Experiential Psychotherapies, 1*, 1 &2 (2002): 102–117.

192. E. Fromm, *Escape from Freedom* (New York: Holt, Rinehart & Winston, 1941.)

SOURCES AND
ACKNOWLEDGEMENTS

Sources

There is a vast amount of literature on Carl Rogers and his work available through normal library research methods, literature which has been drawn upon heavily in this volume and which is cited in the Endnotes and References. In addition, there are various special collections, primary sources, and other material that have been particularly helpful in this project and which may be helpful to others in the future. They are described below.

Rogers' Papers

The Library of Congress, Manuscripts Division, holds the largest collections of Carl Rogers' papers. He saved copies of much or most of his professional and personal correspondence throughout his life, as well as notes of conversations, financial papers, children's school work, and other documents. These papers were donated to the Library of Congress in 1977, 1982 and 1988. References to documents in this collection—in Box 2, Folder 3, for example—are cited as "LOC 2/3."

The Davidson Library at the University of California, Santa Barbara also houses a major collection of Carl Rogers papers and counseling tapes, encompassing the former "Carl Rogers Memorial Library" of Center for Studies of the Person and Natalie Rogers' donations of many of her father's papers. They are housed as the Carl R. Rogers Collection, HPA Mss 32, Department of Special Collections. These materials are cited in the endnotes as "UCSB/CR." Some files have restricted access.

In the 1970s, Carl Rogers loaned the author many of his papers with the understanding that these would be given to the Library of Congress when the biographical work was completed. Later he altered these instructions and requested that they be donated to the University of California at Santa Barbara. These letters, diaries, manuscripts, audiotapes, and other documents, along with the author's research materials, described below, are included in the "Rogers–Kirschenbaum Collection" in the Department of Special Collections, at the Davidson Library of the University of California, Santa Barbara. Items from this collection are cited in the Endnotes as "UCSB/R-K."

The extensive collection of tapes, transcripts and notes from the author's interviews; tapes and correspondence from Rogers' associates; and the numerous published and unpublished documents on Rogers' life and work collected by the author between 1970 and 2006 are or will eventually be housed in the Rogers–Kirschenbaum Collection, Department of Special Collections, at the Davidson Library, University of California, Santa Barbara (where the author's own papers will also reside in a separate collection). Items from this collection are cited in the Endnotes as "UCSB/R-K."

The collection of materials relating to the Carl Rogers Peace Project that was loaned to the author by Gay (Swenson) Barfield will be housed in the Barfield Collection in the Department of Special Collections, Davidson Library, University of California, Santa Barbara. Items from this collection are cited in the Endnotes as "UCSB/Barfield."

Rogers' Publications and Audio-Visual Materials

As would be expected, extensive use was made of Rogers' own published writings and the many audio and video presentations available of Rogers doing individual counseling and psychotherapy, leading groups, and giving presentations and interviews. When specifically referred to in the biography (and by no means all of them were), these sources are cited in the Endnotes and References.

For the most complete bibliography of Rogers' publications in English (and German translations), see Peter Schmid (2005), *The Carl Rogers Bibliography of English and German Sources* in the References. For links to several other outstanding bibliographies and listings of Rogers' publications and audio and video tapes and of others' publications on Rogers and person-centered/experiential psychotherapy, in many languages, see the World Association for Person-Centered and Experiential Psychotherapy and Counseling's website, <www.pce-world.org>. For the most complete listing of Rogers' recorded psychotherapy and counseling sessions and publications about them, see Germain Lietaer and Barbara Brodley's 2003 compilation: "Carl Rogers in the Therapy Room," also listed in the References. In the U.S., <www.carlrogers.info> provides access and links to many resources and archives, including Natalie Rogers' website, <www.nrogers.com>.

Autobiographical Writings

Included in Rogers' writings are about a dozen autobiographical essays from 1961–1987, most of them published, which provide detail and perspective on his life and work. These are cited in the Endnotes and References as appropriate. Those used most extensively are: "This Is Me," a chapter in *On Becoming a Person* (CR, 1961a); "Autobiography," a lengthy chapter in Boring and Lindzey's *History of Psychology in Autobiography* (CR, 1967a); "Some Autobiographical Omissions," including "several sections of more personal than professional interest," spanning the years 1920–28, which Rogers omitted from his "Autobiography"; "My Own Marriage," a chapter in *Becoming Partners: Marriage and Its Alternatives* (CR, 1972a); "Growing Old: Or Older and Growing," a chapter in *A Way of Being* (CR, 1980a); and "Living the Process of Dying," an unpublished compilation of Rogers and others' notes regarding the events around Helen Rogers' death. Another helpful, personal essay was Helen Rogers' "A Wife's Eye View of Carl Rogers," published in the journal *Voices* (HR, 1965).

Oral Histories

There are many published and unpublished interviews—in print, audio or video—in which Rogers reflected on his life and work. The following have been utilized the most frequently:

Author interviews and correspondence. The author conducted extensive interviews with Rogers—briefly in 1970, extensively in 1971, again formally in 1975, and in many informal conversations during meals, car rides and other occasions—and observed him in workshops and other professional and social settings for a total of about six weeks between 1971 and 1987. Rogers and the author also kept up a steady correspondence between 1971 and Rogers' death in 1987. This correspondence included Rogers' answers to author queries, corrections of factual errors in author's drafts of *On Becoming Carl Rogers* (1979), and unsolicited information and writings sent for the author's attention. Interview tapes and transcripts, notes, and correspondence are housed in the Rogers–Kirschenbaum Collection at the University of California at Santa Barbara (cited as UCSB/R-K).

David Russell interviews. A major oral history was compiled from thirteen interviews with Rogers in the year or so before he died. (See Chapter 12.) It was later published as Rogers and Russell, *Carl Rogers: The Quiet Revolutionary: An Oral History* (2002). It includes additional biographical information by several contributors. (See Chapter 13.)

Additional interviews drawn upon include the: Wes Westman interview, August 23, 1964, unpublished, in UCSB/R-K; Joseph Hart interview, August 5, 1966, published in Rogers and

Hart (1970); Gerald Haigh interview (CR & Haigh, 1983); Alicia Hill-Hain interview in January 1987 (Hill-Hain & Rogers, 1988) about South Africa and multi-cultural issues, and others.

Author Interviews
The author conducted many interviews with Rogers' relatives and current or former friends, colleagues and students. The 1970s interviews were all in person. The 1991 and 2002–6 interviews were mostly in person, while some were phone interviews which lasted from 45 minutes to over 6 hours. These interviews are referred to in Endnotes as, for example, "Aker interview, 2003," or the next time as simply "Aker interview." All interview tapes, transcripts and notes are deposited in the Rogers–Kirschenbaum Collection at UCSB. Interviewees and years (and countries of non-U.S. informants) were:

Dee Aker, 2003; Theron Alexander, 1971; Andre Auw, 2002, Gay (Swenson) Barfield, 2003; Allen Bergin, 2003; Maria Bowen, 1971; Sara Boyle (Scotland), July 2002; David Cain, 1991, 2003; Center for Studies of the Person, group interview, 1975, with: Maria Bowen, Earl Burrows, Gay Williams Dean, Steve Doyne, Jack Gibb, Tom Gillette, Len Holdstock, Doug Land, Bob Lee, Betty Meador, Bruce Meador, Pat Rice, Tony Rose, Orienne Strode, Lou Thayer (visiting), Ferdinand van der Veen, Terry Van Orshoven, John K. Wood (in quoting from this interview, sometimes the speaker was not identifiable on the tape or from author's notes); Norman Chambers, 2003; Arthur Combs, 1972; Robert Elliott, 2003; Richard Farson, 2003; Jerome Freiberg, 2002; Janet Fuchs, Frances Fuchs, and Naomi Fuchs, group interview, 1974; Leslie Greenberg (Canada), 2003; Vivian Guze and Gerald Bauman, joint interview, 2004; Valerie Henderson, 1991, 2003; João Hipólito (Portugal), 2003; Armin Klein and Grace Chickadonz, 2006; Margarethe Letzel (Switzerland), 2002; Germain Lietaer (Belgium), 2003; David Malcolm, 2003; Dave Mearns (Scotland), 2002; Betty Meador, 1971; David Meador, 1971; Maureen O'Hara, 1991, 2003; Charles O'Leary, 2002; David Rogers, 1975; Greg Rogers, 1975; Helen Rogers, 1971, plus many informal conversations; Margaret Rogers, 1972; Natalie Rogers, 1971, 1974, 2003; Walter Rogers, 1975; Pete Sanders (England), 2002; Ruth Sanford, 1991; Peter Schmid (Austria), 2003; Doug Schoeninger, 1971; Alberto Segrera (Mexico), 2002; Orienne Strode, 1971, 2006; Gerhard Stumm (Austria), 2002; Reinhard Tausch (Germany), 2003; Ludwig Teusch (Germany), 2002; Brian Thorne (England), 2002; John Vasconcellos, 2003; John K. Wood, 1991; Alberto Zucconi (Italy), 2002.

Author Solicited Tapes, Letters, Recollections, Etc.
The following sources are primarily letters and audiotapes—many of them quite lengthy—containing relatives', friends', colleagues' and students' recollections of and experiences with Carl Rogers, covering primarily the period from 1930 to 1972. Unless noted as "tape" below, the communication was in written form. These sources will be referred to in Endnotes as, for example, "Archie correspondence, 1971" or "Foster tape, 1972."

William Archie, 1971; Bill Barber, 1971; Jim Bebout, 1971; Daniel Bergman, 1971; Betty Berzon, tape, 1971; Gene Bleeker, tape, 1971; Leif Braaten (Norway), 1972; Norman Brice, 1972; Earl Burrows, 1971; Rosalynd Dymond Cartwright, tape, 1971; Joan Chodorkoff, 1971; Arthur Combs, 1971; George Corwin, 1972; Bernard Covner, 1971; Charles Curran, tape, 1971; Charles ("Chuck") Devonshire, 1971; James Dillon, 1971; Elaine Dorfman, 1971; Ann Dryfuss, tape, 1971; Robert Edgar, 1971; Alice Elliott, 1971, Richard Evans, 1971; Fred E. Fiedler, 1971; Charles Ferguson, 1971; Car Foster, tape, 1972; Logan Fox (Japan), 1971; Eugene Gendlin, 1972; Gerard Haigh, 1971; Fred Harvey Harrington, 1972; Minoru Hatase (Japan), 1972; Helen (Mrs. Virgil) Herrick, 1971; Leonard Hersher, 1971; Lloyd Humphreys, 1971; Louise Johnson, 1972; Bill Kell, 1971; Sister Helen Kelley, 1971; Charles F. Kettering, 1971; Donald Kiesler, 1972; W. Price Laughlin, 1971; John Levy, 1971; Margaret Milligan, 1971; Gardner Murphy, 1971; Theodore Newcomb, 1971; J.C. Nunnally, 1971; P. Pentony, 1972; Michael Polanyi, 1971; Harry Porter, 1982; Ernest Poser, 1971; Richard Reed, 1971; Gordon

Riley, 1972; John W. Rogers, 1975; Theodore Sarbin, 1972; Jules Seeman, 1972; Morton Shaevitz, tape, 1971; John Shlien, 1991; Ray Sowers, 1972; William Snyder, tape, 1971; Bernard Steinzor, tape, 1971; John Stevens, 1971; Samuel Tenenbaum, tape, 1972; Hobart Thomas, 1971; T.M. Tomlinson, 1971; Donald Tritt, tape, 1971; Charles Truax, tape, 1971; Eleanor Elliott Ullmann (CR's sister-in-law), 1971; Manuel Vargas, tape, 1971; Antoine J. Vossen, 1972; Goodwin Watson, 1972; Milton Wexler, 1971.

Memoirs

A number of memoirs have been useful sources, especially those included in Melvin Suhd's (1995) collection on *Positive Regard: Carl Rogers and Other Notables He Influenced*, which included contributions by Arthur Combs, Thomas Gordon, Maureen O'Hara, David Rogers, Natalie Rogers, Ruth Sanford, Haruko Tsuge and Akira Takeuchi, and Diane Dreher about John Vasconcellos. Other memoirs by Logan Fox (1967), Nathaniel Raskin (1978), Armin Klein (2000) and Eugene Gendlin (Foreword, Rogers & Russell, 2002) are listed in the References. A few examples were also used from the large collection of memories of and tributes to Rogers that were included in a special issue of *Person-Centered Review* (*Vol. 2*, No. 3, August 1987) after his death.

Acknowledgements

To all the individuals above who so graciously gave of their time and energy through interviews, correspondence and tapes—and often finding and sending accompanying documents—I express my deepest appreciation. It is these personal accounts of life and work with Carl Rogers that have made this work come alive for me over the years and, I hope, will do the same for readers.

To the many other men and women who have assisted in this project, I offer my sincere gratitude. That help came in a myriad of ways: sending information, documents or useful leads; providing research or editorial assistance; networking; providing feedback on early drafts, or offering other material assistance along the way. These individuals are listed below, to the best of my recollection. To those whom I have unintentionally omitted, I offer my apologies and equal appreciation.

Yoko Allen for ADPCA information; Ellis Amburn, formerly of Delacorte Press; Morey L. Appell; Chris Argyris; Marijke Baljon, Holland; Jerold Bozarth; Kenneth Cissna for information and scholarship on the Rogers–Buber dialogue; Virginia Conard, for transcribing the Rogers dialogues; Jeffrey Cornelius-White, for papers on multiculturalism; Donald Cutler, my former literary agent; Avo Debeer and Claude Missiaen, Belgium; Martin Duberman; Matt Duncan; Françoise Ducroux-Biass (France); John Eberhart; Daniel Eckstein; Ivan Ellingham (England); Cathy Ercolamento for secretarial assistance and all-around support; Kim Francis for manuscript including CR interview at Mill Valley PCA workshop; Janet Fuchs and Mindgarden Media for assistance with photographs; David Gartrell of the University of California at Santa Barbara Library; Gerald Gladstein for information on the 1962 Rogers–Skinner dialogue; Leslie Goldman, for photographs and poems on Rogers; Shirley Graham, interview transcription; Norbert Groddeck (Germany); Ruth Hapgood, editor at Houghton Mifflin; B. Joan E. Haines; Sheila Haugh (England), for information on the British Association for Counselling and Psychotherapy; David Herman; Lloyd Henderson, for assistance during the Valerie Henderson interview; Chris Jerome; C. Johnson, YMCA Press; H. Johnson; Rachel Jordan; Nel Kandel, former director, Carl Rogers Library at CSP, Donald Kiesler for voluminous documents on the problems in Wisconsin; Armin Klein, for the transcript of the 1958 University of Rochester dialogue with Rogers; Marvin Krantz of the Library of Congress Manuscripts Division; Elke Lambers (Scotland); Daniel Linnenberg on alcohol dependency; John Marks on the CIA story; Nancy Martin and Kathy McGowan, University of Rochester Library; Tim Maxwell, Elsevier Publications; Peter Merenda, for the Preston Lecky connection; Richard B. Moreland; Grigoris Mouladoudis (Greece); David Null,

University of Wisconsin-Madison Archivist; Pat Rice, for "Steel Shutter" dissertation; Person-centered support group members Grace Chickadonz, Jeffrey and Nancy Cochoran, Armin Klein and Leslie McCulloch, for feedback and suggestions; Anthony Rose, CSP; David Russell, University of California at Santa Barbara Library; Jordan M. Scher; Morley Segal; Janice Shapiro, research assistance; Jean Shaw, AAP historian; Sharon Shostrom, Psychological and Educational Films, on the "Gloria" series; Sidney B. Simon, all-around cheerleader, friend, colleague and sender of "piddly," some of it about Rogers; Robert Sollod; Rocky Stensrud, for his friendship, support and editorial assistance on the first edition; Sterling Lord Literistic; Chuck Stewart; Reinhold Stipsits (Austria); William Stillwell; Hans Strupp; Allan Turner (UK); Brandy Vickers, Houghton Mifflin; Paulus Wacker (Germany); Richard Watts, for the Alfred Adler connection; John Whiteley; Carol Wolter-Gustafson re International Forums/ADPCA meetings; Anne Wunderle (Switzerland); Jeffrey Zeig, for 1986 photograph of psychotherapy leaders; *and,* finally, to the student whose name I have long since forgotten, when I was a doctoral assistant and instructor at Temple University in 1970, looking for a dissertation topic, who gave me Carl Rogers' phone number.

To the *many* authors and people whose lives and work have touched Carl Rogers' life and work but whom I have not quoted, cited, acknowledged or mentioned in this volume, I offer my sincere apologies. The volume of material was simply too enormous to have incorporated and discussed all the topics, critiques, tributes, insights, examples and anecdotes in the literature, or all the individuals who worked with Rogers or made contributions to the person-centered approach. Where I have erred in overdoing certain topics or individual contributions while slighting or neglecting others, I must take responsibility. I would have liked to do more with the connection of Rogers' work to developments in narrative therapy, motivational interviewing, appreciative inquiry, feminist epistemology and critique, postmodernism, developmental and positive psychology, and more. Time and space ran out. Life must go on.

My special thanks to:

Rodney Napier, Larry Kraft and Leland Howe, who supervised my 1975 dissertation, *Carl Rogers: A Case Study of a Psychologist and Educator*, on which the first edition of the biography was based. Their faith that I could pull off a non-traditional dissertation, their ongoing contribution of helpful ideas, and their editorial assistance on early drafts of the original edition, contributed substantially to the original and final product.

Natalie Rogers and Gay Barfield for reading drafts of the final chapters and offering their corrections, feedback and suggestions. Any remaining errors or omissions are my responsibility, not theirs. Special thanks also to Natalie for permission to use many of the photographs in this work and to Gay for the Rust and 85th birthday photographs. Their support for all facets of this work has been steadfast and is much appreciated.

April Jourdan, Ph.D., my former student and doctoral assistant at the University of Rochester who began the painstaking process of retrieving and correcting citations and references for the earlier edition; finding new sources; and researching the current status of Rogers' publications and worldwide person-centered organizations.

Stephen Demanchick, Ph.D., my student and, for four years, doctoral assistant at the University of Rochester. Without his most competent and creative research skills in finding new sources, tracking down missing and incomplete citations, researching everything from the Buber–Rogers dialogue to the Central Intelligence Agency in the 1950s to the Contadora Peace Process in Central America, and offering his insight and support in ways too numerous to mention, this work would be much the poorer, or not at all.

Pete Sanders and Maggie Taylor-Sanders of PCCS Books for their initial faith in this project, their patience and flexibility, and their support throughout the publication process. Sandy Green for her excellent editorial contributions.

Finally, my special and enduring thanks to my wife, Mary Rapp, for her patience and support over many, many years of this project. I'm glad she got to meet Carl Rogers, once upon a time.

REFERENCES

The references cited in this section include: (a) Rogers' published writings referred to in the text (there were many others not referred to), (b) sources that focus on and are particularly important to Rogers' life and work, and (c) to save space, other published sources referred to *more than once* in the text, typically in different chapters. The even larger number of references cited in the Endnotes include: (d) references to Rogers' and others' non-published documents, and (e) background and related published references referred to *only once* in the text or referred to more than once in proximity in the same chapter (where "ibid." and "op. cit." are used).

Allen, F. (1942). *Psychotherapy with children.* New York: W.W. Norton.

American Psychological Association. (1957). The American Psychological Association Distinguished Scientific Contribution Awards for 1956. *American Psychologist, 12,* 125–133.

American Psychological Association. (1973). Distinguished Professional Contribution Award for 1972. *American Psychologist, 28,* 1, 71.

Ansbacher, H. (1990). Alfred Adler's influence on the three leading cofounders of humanistic psychology. *Journal of Humanistic Psychology, 30,* 45–53.

Aspy, D., & Roebuck, F. (1977). *Kids don't learn from people they don't like.* Amherst, MA: Human Resource Development Press.

Axline, V.M. (1947). *Play therapy.* Boston: Houghton Mifflin.

Axline, V.M., & Rogers, C.R. (1945). A teacher-therapist deals with a handicapped child. *Journal of Abnormal and Social Psychology, 40,* 119–142.

Barrett-Lennard, G.T. (1959). *Dimensions of the client's experience of his therapist associated with personality change.* Unpublished doctoral dissertation, University of Chicago.

Barrett-Lennard, G.T. (1962). Dimensions of therapist response as causal factors in therapeutic change. *Psychological Monographs, 76* (43, Whole No. 562).

Bennett, C.C., & Rogers, C.R. (1941). Predicting the outcomes of treatment. *American Journal of Orthopsychiatry, 11,* 210–221.

Bergin, A.E., & Garfield, S.L. (Eds.). (1994). *Handbook of psychotherapy and behavior change* (4th ed.). New York: John Wiley & Sons.

Bozarth, J.D., Zimring, F.M., & Tausch, R. (2001). Client-centered therapy: The evolution of a revolution. In D.J. Cain & J. Seeman (Eds.), *Humanistic psychotherapies: Handbook of research and practice* (pp. 147–188). Washington, DC: American Psychological Association.

Brenman, M. (1948). Research in psychotherapy: Round table. *American Journal of Orthopsychiatry, 18,* 92–118.

Buber, M., & Rogers, C.R. (1960). Dialogue. *Psychologia, 3,* 208–221. Reprinted in Kirschenbaum & Henderson, 1989a, (pp. 41–63).

Cain, D. (Ed.). (2002). *Classics in the person-centered approach.* Ross-on-Wye, UK: PCCS Books.

Cain, D.J. & Seeman, J. (Eds.). (2001). *Humanistic psychotherapies: Handbook of research and practice.* Washington, DC: American Psychological Association.

Capuzzi, D., & Gross, D.R. (2001). *Introduction to the counseling profession.* (3rd ed.). Needham Heights, MA: Allyn & Bacon.

Cartwright, D.S. (1957). Annotated bibliography of research and theory construction in client-centered therapy. *Journal of Counseling Psychology, 4,* 82–100.

Cissna, K., & Anderson, R. (2002). *Moments of meeting: Buber, Rogers, and the potential for public dialogue.* Albany, NY: State University of New York Press.

Cohen, D. (1997). *Carl Rogers: A critical biography.* London: Constable.

Combs, A. (Ed.). (1962). *Perceiving, behaving, becoming.* Washington, DC: Association for Supervision and Curriculum Development, National Education Association.

Cornelius-White, J.H.D. (2003). Person-centered multicultural counseling: Rebutted critiques and revisited goals. *Person-Centred Practice, 11,* 1, 3–11.

Coulson, W.R., & Rogers, C.R. (1968). *Man and the science of man.* Columbus, OH: Charles E. Merrill.

Cremin, L.A. (1961). *The transformation of the school.* New York: Alfred A. Knopf.

Cushman, P. (1990). Why the self is empty: Toward a historically situated psychology. *American Psychologist, 45,* 5, 599–611.

Demanchick, S., & Kirschenbaum, H. (In press.). Carl Rogers and the CIA. *Journal of Humanistic Psychology.*

Dickenson, W., Foster, C., Walker, N., & Yeager, F. (1970). A humanistic program for change in a large city school system. *Journal of Humanistic Psychology, 10,* 2, 111–120.

Dobson, K.S. (Ed.). (2001). *Handbook of cognitive-behavioral therapies* (2nd ed.). New York: Guilford Press.

Dreher, D. (1995). Toward a person-centered politics: John Vasconcellos. In M. Suhd (Ed.), *Positive regard: Carl Rogers and other notables he influenced* (pp. 339–367). Palo Alto, CA: Science and Behavior Books.

Elliott, R. (1996). Are client-centered/experiential therapies effective? A meta-analysis of outcome research. In U. Esser, H. Pabst, & G-W. Speierer (Eds.), *The power of the person-centered approach: New challenges—perspectives—answers* (pp. 125–137). Koln, Germany: GwG-Verlag.

Elliott, R., & Greenberg, L. (2001). Process-experiential psychotherapy. In D.J. Cain & J. Seeman (Eds.), *Humanistic psychotherapies: Handbook of research and practice* (pp. 279–306). Washington, DC: American Psychological Association.

Evans, R. (1975). *Carl Rogers: The man and his ideas.* New York: E.P. Dutton.

Farson, R. (1975). Carl Rogers: Quiet revolutionary. In R. Evans, *Carl Rogers: The man and his ideas* (pp. xxviii–xliii). New York: E.P. Dutton.

Fernberger, S.W. (1932). The American Psychological Association: A historical summary: 1892–1930. *Psychological Bulletin, 29,* 1–89.

Fiedler, F.E. (1950). A comparison of therapeutic relationships in psychoanalytic, nondirective and Adlerian therapy. *Journal of Consulting Psychology, 14,* 436–445.

Fox, L. (1967). Dr. Rogers and I. In *The complete works of Dr. Rogers. Vol. 18. Client-centered therapy in Japan.* Tokyo: Iwasaki Gakujyutsu Syuppansya.

Frankl, V.E. (1963). *Man's search for meaning: An introduction to logotherapy.* New York: Washington Square Press. (Originally published: Boston: Beacon Press, 1962).

Freedheim, D.K. (1992). *History of psychotherapy: A century of change.* Washington, DC: American Psychological Association.

Garfield, S.L., & Bergin, A.E. (Eds.). (1986). *Handbook of psychotherapy and behavior change* (3rd ed.). New York: Wiley.

Gendlin, E.T. (1957). A process concept of relationship. *Counseling Center Discussion Papers, 3* 2. (University of Chicago Library.)

Gendlin, E.T. (1958) *The function of experiencing in symbolization.* Unpublished doctoral dissertation, University of Chicago.

Gendlin, E.T. (1962). *Experiencing and the creation of meaning.* New York: The Free Press of Glencoe.

Gendlin, E.T. (1978). *Focusing.* New York: Everest House. (2nd ed. New York: Bantam, 1982.)

Gendlin, E.T. (1996). *Focusing-oriented psychotherapy: A manual of the experiential method.* New York: Guilford Press.

Gibson, R.L., & Mitchell, M.H. (1999). *Introduction to counseling and guidance* (5th ed.). Upper Saddle River, NJ: Prentice Hall.

Gladding, S.T. (2000). *Counseling: A comprehensive profession.* Upper Saddle River, NJ: Merrill/ Prentice Hall.

Goldstein, K. (1940). *Human nature in the light of psychopathology.* Cambridge, MA: Harvard University Press.

Gordon, T. (1951). Group-centered leadership and administration. In C.R. Rogers, (1951a), *Client-centered therapy: Its current practice, implications, and theory* (pp. 320–383). Boston: Houghton Mifflin.

Gordon, T. (1970). *P.E.T.: Parent effectiveness training.* New York: Peter Wyden.

Gordon, T. (1974). *T.E.T.: Teacher effectiveness training.* New York: Peter Wyden.

Greenberg, L., Rice, L., & Elliott, R. (1993). *Facilitating emotional change: The moment-by-moment process.* New York: Guilford.

Greenfield, P. (1977). CIA's behavior caper. *APA Monitor, 8, 12,* 10–11.

Haigh, G. (1988). A tribute to Carl. *Voices: The Art and Science of Psychotherapy, 23,* 4, 17–20.

Halkides, G. (1958). *An experimental study of four conditions necessary for therapeutic change.* Unpublished doctoral dissertation, University of Chicago.

Hall, C., & Lindzey, G. (1957). *Theories of personality.* New York: Wiley.

Hall, C., Lindzey, G., & Campbell, J. (1998). *Theories of personality* (4th ed.). New York: Wiley.

Hall, M.H. (1967a). A conversation with Carl Rogers: Speaks out on groups and the lack of human science. *Psychology Today, 1,* 12, 19–21, 62–66.

Hall, M.H. (1967b, April). The WBSI story. *San Diego and Point Magazine, 19,* 6, 45–54, 91–92.

Hart, J.T., & Tomlinson, T. M. (Eds.). (1970). *New directions in client-centered therapy.* Boston: Houghton Mifflin.

Healy, W. (1915). *The individual delinquent: A textbook of diagnosis and prognosis for all concerned in understanding offenders.* Boston: Little, Brown.

Healy, W., & Bonner, A. (1926). *Delinquents and criminals, their making and unmaking: Studies in two American cities.* New York: Macmillan.

Hill-Hain, A., & Rogers, C.R. (1988). A dialogue with Carl Rogers: Cross- cultural challenges of facilitating person-centered groups in South Africa. *Journal for Specialists in Group Work, 13,* 62–69.

Holdstock, L. (1990). Can client-centered therapy transcend its monocultural roots? In G. Lietaer, J. Rombauts & R. Van Balen (Eds.), *Client-centered and experiential psychotherapy in the nineties* (pp. 109–121). Leuven, Belgium: Leuven University Press.

Holdstock, L. (2005). In its awakening "cultural" awareness the person-centered approach needs to consider more than just racism. *Person-Centered and Experiential Psychotherapies, 4,* 124–130.

Hubble, M.A., Duncan, B.L. & Miller, S.D. (1999). *The heart and soul of change: What works in therapy.* Washington, DC: American Psychological Association.

Kirschenbaum, H. (1979). *On becoming Carl Rogers.* New York: Delacorte/Delta.

Kirschenbaum, H., & Henderson, V. (Eds.). (1989a). *Carl Rogers: Dialogues*. Boston: Houghton Mifflin.

Kirschenbaum, H., & Henderson, V. (Eds.). (1989b). *The Carl Rogers Reader*. Boston: Houghton Mifflin.

Kirschenbaum, H., & Jourdan, A. (2005). The current status of Carl Rogers and the person-centered approach. *Psychotherapy: Theory, Research, Practice, Training, 42*, 1, 37–51.

Klein, A. (2000). From where my songs have come. *Songs of living* (pp. 61–73). Rochester, NY: Author.

Kramer, R. (1995a). The birth of client-centered therapy: Carl Rogers, Otto Rank, and "the beyond." *Journal of Humanistic Psychology, 35*, 4, 54–110.

Kramer, R. (1995b). Carl Rogers meets Otto Rank. In Thierrry C. Pauchant & Associates, *In search of meaning: Managing for the health of our organizations, our communities, and the natural world* (pp. 197–223). San Francisco: Jossey-Bass.

Lambert, M.J. (1992). Psychotherapy outcome research: Implications for integrative and eclectic therapists. In J.C. Norcross & M.R. Goldfried (Eds.), *Handbook of psychotherapy integration* (pp. 94–129). New York: Basic Books.

Lambert, M.J., & Bergin, A.E. (1994). The effectiveness of psychotherapy. In A.E. Bergin and S.L. Garfield (Eds.), *Handbook of psychotherapy and behavior change* (4th ed., pp. 143–189). New York: John Wiley & Sons.

Lecky, P. (1945). *Self-consistency: A theory of personality*. New York: Island Press.

Lietaer, G. (2002a). *Client-centered/experiential psychotherapy and counseling bibliographical survey 1997–1999: With a special section on books 1939–2000*. Booklet distributed at the Fifth International Conference on Client-Centered and Experiential Psychotherapy. Retrieved January 17, 2005 from <www.pce-world.org>.

Lietaer, G. (2002b). The united colors of person-centered and experiential psychotherapies. *Person-Centered and Experiential Psychotherapies, 1*, 4–13.

Lietaer, G., & Brodley, B. (2003). Carl Rogers in the therapy room: A listing of session transcripts and a survey of publications referring to Rogers' sessions. *Person-Centered and Experiential Psychotherapies, 2*, 274–291. [Transcripts currently available to researchers and others from Barbara Brodley at <btb@dls.net>.]

Lietaer, G., Rombauts, J., & Van Balen, R. (Eds.). (1990). *Client-centered and experiential psychotherapy in the nineties*. Leuven, Belgium: Leuven University Press.

Marks, J. (1979). *Search for the "Manchurian Candidate": The CIA and mind control*. New York: W.W. Norton & Company.

Maslow, A.H. (1943a). Dynamics of personality organization. *Psychological Review, 50*, 514–539, 541–558.

Maslow, A.H. (1943b). A theory of human motivation. *Psychological Review, 50*, 370–396.

Maslow, A.H. (1962). *Toward a psychology of being*. New York: Van Nostrand.

May, R. (Ed.). (1961). *Existential psychology*. New York: Random House.

Norcross, J.C. (2001). Purposes, processes and products of the task force on empirically supported therapy relationships. *Psychotherapy, 38*, 4, 345–356.

Norcross, J.C. (2002). *Psychotherapy relationships that work: Therapist contributions and responsiveness to patients*. New York: Oxford University Press.

Nugent, F.A. (2000). *Introduction to the profession of counseling* (3rd ed.). Upper Saddle River, NJ: Merrill.

Orlinsky, D.E., Grawe, K., & Parks, B.K. (1994). Process and outcome in psychotherapy: Noch einmal. In A.E. Bergin & S.L. Garfield (Eds.), *Handbook of psychotherapy and behavior change* (4th ed., pp. 270–376). New York: John Wiley & Sons.

Patterson, C.H. (1984). Empathy, warmth, and genuineness in psychotherapy: A review of reviews. *Psychotherapy, 21*, 4, 431–438.

Pitts, C. (1973). Twelve years later: A reply to Carl Rogers. *Journal of Humanistic Psychology, 13*, 75–81.

Polanyi, M. (1964). *Personal knowledge*. New York: Harper & Row.

Poppy, J. (1968, July 9). It's ok to cry in the office. *Look*, 64–76.

Porter, E.H. (1941). *The development and evaluation of a measure of counseling interview procedures*. Unpublished doctoral dissertation, Ohio State University.

Raimy, V.C. (1944). *The self-concept as a factor in counseling and personality organization*. Unpublished doctoral dissertation, Ohio State University.

Raimy, V.C. (1948). Self-reference in counseling interviews. *Journal of Consulting Psychology, 12*, 153–163.

Rank, O. (1945). *Will therapy, and truth and reality*. New York: Alfred Knopf. Cited in Raskin, 1948.

Raskin, N.J. (1948). The development of nondirective therapy. *Journal of Consulting Psychology, 12*, 92–110.

Raskin, N.J. (1978). Becoming–A therapist, a person, a partner, a parent, a … *Psychotherapy: Theory, Research and Practice, 15*, 4, 362–370. Also in N.J. Raskin (2004) *Contributions to client-centered therapy and the person-centered approach* (pp. 104–117). Ross-on-Wye: PCCS Books.

Rice, L.N., & Greenberg, L.S. (Eds.). (1984). *Patterns of change: Intensive analysis of psychotherapy process*. New York: Guilford.

Rogers, C.R. (1922, June). An experiment in Christian internationalism. *The Intercollegian*, 1–2.

Rogers, C.R. (1931a). *Measuring personality adjustment in children nine to thirteen years of age*. New York: Teachers College.

Rogers, C.R. (1931b). *A test of personality adjustment*. New York: Association Press. (Revised as: Personal adjustment inventory, 1961.)

Rogers, C.R. (1933). A good foster home: Its achievements and limitations. *Mental Hygiene, 17*, 21–40.

Rogers, C.R. (1936). Social workers and legislation. *Quarterly Bulletin—New York State Conference on Social Work , 7*, 3, 5–9.

Rogers, C.R. (1937a). The clinical psychologist's approach to personality problems. *The Family, 18*, 233–243.

Rogers, C.R. (1937b). Three surveys of treatment measures used with children. *American Journal of Orthopsychiatry, 7*, 48–57.

Rogers, C.R. (1939a). *The clinical treatment of the problem child*. Boston: Houghton Mifflin.

Rogers, C.R. (1939b). Needed emphasis in the training of clinical psychologists. *Journal of Consulting Psychology, 3*, 141–143.

Rogers, C.R. (1940). The process of therapy. *Journal of Consulting Psychology, 4*, 5, 161–164.

Rogers, C.R. (1942a). *Counseling and psychotherapy: Newer concepts in practice*. Boston: Houghton Mifflin.

Rogers, C.R. (1942b). The criteria used in a study of mental-health problems. *Educational Research Bulletin, 21*, 2, 29–40.

Rogers, C.R. (1942c). Mental health findings in three elementary schools. *Educational Research Bulletin, 21*, 69–79, 86.

Rogers, C.R. (1942d). The psychologist's contributions to parent, child and community problems. *Journal of Consulting Psychology, 6*, 8–18.

Rogers, C.R. (1942e). The use of electronically recorded interviews in improving psychotherapeutic techniques. *American Journal of Orthopsychiatry, 12,* 3, 429–434.

Rogers, C.R. (1943). Therapy in guidance clinics. *Journal of Abnormal and Social Psychology, 38,* 284–289.

Rogers, C.R. (1944a) *Adjustment after combat: A study of returned combat gunners and their utilization in the flexible gunnery training program* (restricted publication). Fort Myers, FL: Army Air Forces Instructors School Flexible Gunnery.

Rogers, C.R. (1944b). The development of insight in a counseling relationship. *Journal of Consulting Psychology, 8,* 6, 331–341.

Rogers, C.R. (1944c). Psychological adjustments of discharged service personnel. *Psychological Bulletin, 41,* 689–696.

Rogers, C.R. (1944d). Wartime issues in family counseling. *Journal of Home Economics, 36,* 7, 390–393.

Rogers, C.R. (1945a). Counseling. *Review of Educational Research, 15,* 155–163.

Rogers, C.R. (1945b). A counseling viewpoint for the USO worker. USO [United Services Organizations] *Program Services Bulletin.*

Rogers, C.R. (1945c). Current trends in counseling: A symposium. *Marriage and Family Living, 7,* 4, 82–84.

Rogers, C.R. (1945d). The function of the USO volunteer in individual contacts. *USO Program Services Bulletin.*

Rogers, C.R. (1945e). The non-directive method as a technique for social research. *American Journal of Sociology, 50,* 279–283.

Rogers, C.R. (1945f, March). When the serviceman returns to his family. *National Parent Teacher,* 8–10.

Rogers, C.R. (1946a). Psychometric tests and client-centered counseling. *Educational Psychological Measurement, 6,* 139–144.

Rogers, C.R. (1946b). Research in nondirective therapy and its implications. *American Journal of Orthopsychiatry, 16,* 581–588.

Rogers, C.R. (1946c). Significant aspects of client-centered therapy. *American Psychologist, 1,* 10, 415–422.

Rogers, C.R. (1947a). Current trends in psychotherapy. In W. Dennis (Ed.), *Current trends in psychology* (pp. 109–137). Pittsburgh: University of Pittsburgh Press.

Rogers, C.R. (1947b). Some observations on the organization of personality. *American Psychologist, 2,* 9, 358–368.

Rogers, C.R. (1948a). *Dealing with social tensions: A presentation of client-centered counseling as a means of handling interpersonal conflicts.* New York: Hinds, Hayden and Eldredge. 30 pp.

Rogers, C.R. (1948b). Research in psychotherapy: Round table. *American Journal of Orthopsychiatry, 18,* 96–100.

Rogers, C.R. (1948c). Some implications of client-centered counseling for college personnel work. *Educational and Psychological Measurement, 8,* 540–549.

Rogers, C.R. (1949a). The attitude and orientation of the counselor in client-centered therapy. *Journal of Consulting Psychology, 13,* 82–94.

Rogers, C.R. (1949b). A coordinated research in psychotherapy. A non-objective introduction. *Journal of Consulting Psychology, 13,* 149–153.

Rogers, C.R. (1949c). Divergent trends in methods of improving adjustment. *Harvard Education Review, 18,* 209–219. Reprinted in *Pastoral Psychology,* November, 1950, (pp. 11–18.)

Rogers, C.R. (1950a). A basic orientation for counseling. *Pastoral Psychology, 1,* 1, 26–34.

Rogers, C.R. (1950b). A current formulation of client-centered therapy. *The Social Service Review, 24*, 442–450.

Rogers, C.R. (1950c). The significance of the self-regarding attitudes and perceptions. In M. L. Reymert (Ed.), *Feelings and emotions* (pp. 374–382). New York: McGraw-Hill.

Rogers, C.R. (1950d). What is to be our basic professional relationship? *Annals of Allergy, 8*, 234–239, 286.

Rogers, C.R. (1951a). *Client-centered therapy: Its current practice, implications, and theory.* Boston: Houghton Mifflin.

Rogers, C.R. (1951b). Perceptual reorganization in client-centered therapy. In R.R. Blake & G.V. Ramsey (Eds.), *Perception: An approach to personality* (pp. 307–327). New York: Ronald Press.

Rogers, C.R. (1951c). Through the eyes of a client. *Pastoral Psychology, 2*, 16, 32–40; 17, 45–50; 18, 26–32.

Rogers, C.R. (1952a). "Client-centered" psychotherapy. *Scientific American, 87*, 5, 66–74.

Rogers, C.R. (1952b). Communication: Its blocking and its facilitation. *Northwestern University Information, 20*, 9–15. Reprinted in *Harvard Business Review*, 1952, *30*, 4, 46–50; in *ETC: A Review of General Semantics*, 1952, *9*, 83–88, and others.

Rogers, C.R. (1952c). Dealing with interpersonal conflict. *Pastoral Psychology, 3*, 28, 14–20; 29, 37–44. (Adaptation of CR, 1948a.)

Rogers, C.R. (1952d). A personal formulation of client-centered therapy. [Paper followed by panel discussion.] *Marriage and Family Living, 14*, 341–361.

Rogers, C.R. (1953a). The interest in the practice of psychotherapy. *American Psychologist, 8*, 48–50.

Rogers, C.R. (1953b). Removing the obstacles to good employee communications. *Management Record, 15,* 1, 9–11, 32–40.

Rogers, C.R. (1954). Towards a theory of creativity. *ETC: A Review of General Semantics, 11*, 249–260.

Rogers, C.R. (1955). Persons or science? A philosophical question. *American Psychologist, 10*, 267–278.

Rogers, C.R. (1956a). Client-centered therapy. A current view. In F. Fromm-Reichmann & J. Moreno (Eds.), *Progress in psychotherapy* (pp. 199–209). New York: Grune & Stratton.

Rogers, C.R. (1956b). A counseling approach to human problems. *The American Journal of Nursing, 56*, 994–997.

Rogers, C.R. (1956c). Implications of advances in the prediction and control of behavior. *Teachers College Record, 57*, 316–322.

Rogers, C.R. (1956d) Review of Reinhold Niebuhr's, "The self and the dramas of history." *Chicago Theological Seminary Register*, 1956, *46*, 13–14. (Reprinted in *Pastoral Psychology, 9*, 85, 15–17.)

Rogers, C.R. (1957a). The necessary and sufficient conditions of therapeutic personality change. *Journal of Consulting Psychology, 21*, 95–103.

Rogers, C.R. (1957b). A note on the "nature of man." *Journal of Counseling Psychology, 4*, 199–203.

Rogers, C.R. (1957c). Personal thoughts on teaching and learning. *Merrill Palmer Quarterly, 3*, 241–243.

Rogers, C.R. (1957d). A therapist's view of the good life. *The Humanist, 17*, 291–300.

Rogers, C.R. (1958a). The characteristics of a helping relationship. *Personnel and Guidance Journal, 37*, 6–16.

Rogers, C.R. (1958b). Concluding comment. *Pastoral Psychology, 9*, 85, 25–28.

693

Rogers, C.R. (1958c). A process conception of psychotherapy. *American Psychologist, 13*, 142–149.

Rogers, C.R. (1959a). Significant learning. In therapy and in education. *Educational Leadership, 16*, 232–242.

Rogers, C.R. (1959b). A tentative scale for the measurement of process in psychotherapy. In E. Rubinstein & M.B. Parloff (Eds.), *Research in psychotherapy* (pp. 96–107). Washington, DC: American Psychological Association.

Rogers, C.R. (1959c). A theory of therapy, personality, and interpersonal relationships, as developed in the client-centered framework. In S. Koch (Ed.), *Psychology: A study of a science. Vol. III: Formulations of the person and the social context* (pp. 184–256). New York: McGraw-Hill.

Rogers, C.R. (1960). A therapist's view of personal goals. *Pendle Hill Pamphlet No. 108.* Pendle Hill, PA: Pendle Hill Publications.

Rogers, C.R. (1961a). *On becoming a person: A therapist's view of psychotherapy.* Boston: Houghton Mifflin.

Rogers, C.R. (1961b). The place of the person in the new world of behavioral sciences. *Personnel and Guidance Journal, 39*, 442–451.

Rogers, C.R. (1961c). A theory of psychotherapy with schizophrenics and a proposal for its empirical investigation. In J.G. Dawson & N.P. Dellis (Eds.), *Psychotherapy with schizophrenics* (pp. 3–19). Baton Rouge, LA: Louisiana State University Press.

Rogers, C.R. (1962a). The interpersonal relationship: The core of guidance. *Harvard Educational Review, 32*, 4, 416–429.

Rogers, C.R. (1962b, Summer). Some learnings from a study of psychotherapy with schizophrenics. *Pennsylvania Psychiatric Quarterly*, 3–15.

Rogers, C.R. (1962c). A study of psychotherapeutic change in schizophrenics and normals: The design and instrumentation. *Psychiatric Research Reports, 15*, 51–60.

Rogers, C.R. (1962d). Toward becoming a fully functioning person. In A.W. Combs (Ed.), *Perceiving, behaving, becoming: A new focus for education: 1962 yearbook* (pp. 21–33). Washington, DC: Association for Supervision and Curriculum Development, National Education Association.

Rogers, C.R. (1963a). The concept of the fully functioning person. *Psychotherapy: Theory, Research, and Practice, 1*, 1, 17–26.

Rogers, C.R. (1963b, March). Learning to be free. *National Education Association Journal, 52*, 3, 28–30.

Rogers, C.R. (1963c). Learning to be free. (Expanded version of 1963b.) In S.M. Farber & R.H. Wilson (Eds.), *Man and civilization: Conflict and creativity: Part two: Control of the mind* (pp. 268–288). New York: McGraw-Hill.

Rogers, C.R. (1963d). Toward a science of the person. *Journal of Humanistic Psychology, 3*, 72–92.

Rogers, C.R. (1964a). Freedom and commitment. *The Humanist, 24, 2*, 37–40.

Rogers, C.R. (1964b, September). *Remarks on the future of client-centered therapy.* Presented at a symposium on the future of client-centered therapy, American Psychological Association. In D.A Wexler & L.N. Rice (Eds.), (1974), *Innovations in client-centered therapy* (pp. 7–13). New York: John Wiley & Sons.

Rogers, C.R. (1964c). Toward a modern approach to values. The valuing process in the mature person. *Journal of Abnormal and Social Psychology, 68*, 160–167.

Rogers, C.R. (1965a). Dealing with psychological tensions. *Journal of Applied Behavioral Science, 1*, 6–24.

Rogers, C.R. (1965b). Some questions and challenges facing a humanistic psychology. *Journal of Humanistic Psychology*, 5, 1–5.

Rogers, C.R. (1967a). Autobiography. In E.G. Boring & G. Lindzey (Eds.), *A history of psychology in autobiography: Volume V* (pp. 343–384). New York: Appleton-Century-Crofts.

Rogers, C.R. (1967b). The interpersonal relationship in the facilitation of learning. In R. Leeper (Ed.), *Humanizing education: The person in process: 1967 Yearbook* (pp. 1–18). Washington, DC: Association for Supervision and Curriculum Development, National Education Association.

Rogers, C.R. (1967c). A plan for self-directed change in an educational system. *Educational Leadership*, 24, 717–731.

Rogers, C.R. (1968a). Interpersonal relationships: USA 2000. *Journal of Applied Behavioral Science*, 4, 265–280.

Rogers, C.R. (1968b). A practical plan for educational revolution. In R.R. Goulet (Ed.), *Educational change: The reality and the promise.* (pp. 120–135). New York: Citation Press.

Rogers, C.R. (1968c). Review of J. Kavanaugh's book, "A modern priest looks at his outdated church." *Psychology Today*, 2, 13.

Rogers, C.R. (1969a*). Freedom to learn. A view of what education might become.* Columbus: Charles Merrill.

Rogers, C.R. (1969b, December). The group comes of age. *Psychology Today*, 3, 27–31, 58–61.

Rogers, C.R. (1969c).The increasing involvement of the psychologist in social problems. Some comments, positive and negative. *Journal of Applied Behavioral Science*, 5, 3–7.

Rogers, C.R. (1969d). The intensive group experience. *Psychology today: An introduction.* Del Mar, CA: CRM Books.

Rogers, C.R. (1969e). The person of tomorrow. In *Eighth annual commencement exercises.* Sonoma, CA: Sonoma State College. Adapted for Rogers, 1980b.

Rogers, C.R. (1970a). *Carl Rogers on encounter groups.* New York: Harper and Row.

Rogers, C.R. (1970b). Foreword. In J.T. Hart & T.M. Tomlinson (Eds.), *New directions in client-centered therapy* (pp. vii–x). Boston: Houghton Mifflin.

Rogers, C.R. (1970c). Continuing growth versus maladjustment. In *Developmental psychology* (pp. 483–495). Del Mar, CA: CRM Books.

Rogers, C.R. (1970d). Some observations on education and a letter of resignation to U.S. International University. *Association of Humanistic Psychology Newsletter*, 7, 1, 1, 4, 6, 7.

Rogers, C.R. (1971a). Can schools grow persons? *Educational Leadership*, 28, 215–217.

Rogers, C.R. (1971b). *Carl Rogers–1971.* Paper presented at Center for Studies of the Person Lecture Series, February 5, 1971. Unpublished.

Rogers, C.R. (1971c). Forget you are a teacher: Carl Rogers tells why. *Instructor* (August/September), 65–66.

Rogers, C.R. (1972a). *Becoming partners: Marriage and its alternatives.* New York: Delacorte.

Rogers, C.R. (1972b). *My philosophy of interpersonal relationships and how it grew.* Paper presented at the Tenth Annual Meeting of the Association of Humanistic Psychology, Honolulu, August 31, 1972. In Rogers, 1980b, (pp. 27–45).

Rogers, C.R. (1972c). *Some new challenges.* Paper presented to the Annual Meeting of the American Psychological Association, Honolulu, Hawaii, September 2, 1972. *American Psychologist*, 1973, 28, 5, 379–387. Reprinted in Kirschenbaum & Henderson, 1989b, (pp. 235–259).

Rogers, C.R. (1972d). Some social issues which concern me. *Journal of Humanistic Psychology*, 12, 2, 45–60.

Rogers, C.R. Comment. (1973a). *Journal of Humanistic Psychology, 13*, 83–84.

Rogers, C.R. (1973b). *In retrospect: 46 years.* Paper presented at the meeting of the American Psychological Association, Montreal, August 28; reprinted in *American Psychologist, 29*, 2, 115–123; in Evans, 1975, (pp. 119–146); and in Rogers, 1980b, (pp. 46–69).

Rogers, C.R. (1973c). "Process" people replacing those with timeless goals. *Minneapolis Star,* November *26*, 9A.

Rogers, C.R. (1975). The emerging person: A new revolution. In R. Evans, *Carl Rogers: The man and his ideas* (pp. 148–175). New York: E.P. Dutton.

Rogers, C.R. (1977). *Carl Rogers on personal power.* New York: Delacorte.

Rogers, C.R. (1978a). Do we need a reality? *Dawnpoint, 1*, 2, 6–9. (Written in 1974.)

Rogers, C.R. (1978b). The formative tendency. *Journal of Humanistic Psychology, 18* (Winter), 23–26. Included in Rogers, 1980b.

Rogers, C.R. (1979a). Foundations of the person-centered approach. *Education, 100*, 2, 98–107. Included in Rogers, 1980b.

Rogers, C.R. (1979b). Groups in two cultures. *Personnel and Guidance Journal, 38*, 1, 11–15.

Rogers, C.R. (1980a). Growing old: Or older and growing. In Rogers, 1980b, (pp. 70–95). Also in Kirschenbaum & Henderson, 1989b, (pp. 37–56).

Rogers, C.R. (1980b). *A way of being.* Boston: Houghton Mifflin.

Rogers, C.R. (1982). A psychologist looks at nuclear war: Its threat, its possible prevention. *Journal of Humanistic Psychology, 22*, 4, 9–20.

Rogers, C.R. (1983). *Freedom to learn for the 80s.* Columbus, OH: Charles Merrill.

Rogers, C.R. (1984). Gloria—A historical note. In R.F. Levant & J. Shlien (Eds.), *Client-centered therapy and the person-centered approach: New directions in theory, research, and practice* (pp. 423–425). New York: Praeger.

Rogers, C.R. (1985). Toward a more human science of the person. *Journal of Humanistic Psychology, 25*, 4, 7–24.

Rogers, C.R. (1986a). A client-centered/person-centered approach to therapy. In I. Kutash & A. Wolf (Eds.), *Psychotherapist's casebook* (pp. 197–208). San Francisco: Jossey-Bass. Also in Kirschenbaum & Henderson, 1989b, (pp. 135–152).

Rogers, C.R. (1986b). The dilemmas of a South African white. *Person-Centered Review, 1*, 15–35.

Rogers, C.R. (1986c). Rogers, Kohut, and Erickson: A personal perspective on some similarities and differences. *Person-Centered Review, 1*, 2, 125–140.

Rogers, C.R. (1986d, summer). The Rust workshop: A personal overview. *Journal of Humanistic Psychology, 26*, 3, 23–45. Also in Kirschenbaum & Henderson, 1989b, (pp. 457–477).

Rogers, C.R. (1986e). What I learned from two research studies. In Kirschenbaum & Henderson, 1989b, (pp. 203–211). Also in Rogers & Russell, 2002, (pp. 262–270).

Rogers, C.R. (1987a). Inside the world of the Soviet professional. *Journal of Humanistic Psychology, 27*, 3, 277–304. Also in Kirschenbaum & Henderson, 1989b, (pp. 478–501).

Rogers, C.R. (1987b). On reaching 85. *Person-Centered Review, 2*, 2, 150–152. Also in Kirschenbaum & Henderson, 1989b (pp. 56–58).

Rogers, C.R., & Baldwin, M. (1987). Interview with Carl Rogers on the use of the self in therapy. In M. Baldwin & V. Satir (Eds.), *The use of self in therapy* (pp. 45–52). New York: Haworth Press.

Rogers, C.R., & Dymond, R. (Eds.). (1954). *Psychotherapy and personality change.* Chicago: University of Chicago Press.

Rogers, C.R., & Farson, R.E. (1957). *Active listening.* Chicago: University of Chicago/Industrial Relations Center.

Rogers, C.R., & Freiberg, H.J. (1994). *Freedom to Learn* (3rd ed.). New York: Merrill/Macmillan.

Rogers, C.R., & Frick, W.B. (1971). Interview with Dr. Carl Rogers. In W.B. Frick (Ed.), *Humanistic psychology: Interviews with Maslow, Murphy and Rogers* (pp. 86–115). Columbus, OH: Charles Merrill.

Rogers, C.R., Gendlin, E.T., Kiesler, D.J., & Truax, C.B. (Eds.). (1967). *The therapeutic relationship and its impact: A study of psychotherapy with schizophrenics.* Madison: The University of Wisconsin Press.

Rogers, C.R., & Haigh, G. (1983). I walk softly through life [interview]. *Voices, 18,* 4, 6–14.

Rogers, C.R., & Hart, J.T. (1970). Looking back and ahead: A conversation with Carl Rogers. [1966 interview]. In J.T. Hart & T.M. Tomlinson (Eds.), *New directions in client-centered therapy* (pp. 502–534). Boston: Houghton Mifflin.

Rogers, C.R., Kell, B.L., & McNeil, H. (1948). The role of self-understanding in the prediction of behavior. *Journal of Consulting Psychology, 12,* 3, 174–186.

Rogers, C.R., & Rappaport, M.E. (1931). We pay for the Smiths. *Survey Graphic, 19,* 508–509, 527, 533, 535.

Rogers, C.R., & Russell, D. (2002). *Carl Rogers: The quiet revolutionary: An oral history.* Roseville, CA: Penmarin Books.

Rogers, C.R., & Ryback, D. (1984). One alternative to nuclear planetary suicide. *Counseling Psychologist, 12,* 2, 3–12.

Rogers, C.R., & Ryback. D. (1989). An interview with Carl Rogers. *Person-Centered Review, 4,* 1, 99–112; also in Cain, 2002, (pp. 26–33).

Rogers, C.R., & Sanford, R. (1984). Client-centered psychotherapy. In H.I. Kaplan & B.J. Sadock (Eds.), *Comprehensive textbook of psychiatry IV, Vol. 2* (4th ed., pp. 1374–1388). Baltimore: Williams and Wilkins.

Rogers, C.R., & Sanford, R. (1987). Reflections on our South African experience: January–February, 1986, *Counseling and Values, 32,* 1, 17–20.

Rogers, C.R., & Skinner, B. F. (1956). Some issues concerning the control of human behavior. A symposium. *Science, 124* (3231), 1057–1066.

Rogers, C.R. & Stevens, B. (1967). *Person to person: The problem of being human.* Lafayette, CA: Real People Press.

Rogers, C.R., & Tillich, P. (1966). *Dialogue. Parts 1 and 2.* San Diego College Pamphlet. Reprinted in Kirschenbaum & Henderson, 1989a, (pp. 66–78).

Rogers, C.R., & Wallen, J.L. (1946). *Counseling with returned servicemen.* New York: McGraw-Hill.

Rogers, H. (1965). A wife's eye view of Carl Rogers. *Voices, 1,* 1, 93–98.

Rogers, N. (1980). *Emerging woman: A decade of midlife transitions.* Point Reyes, CA: Personal Press. Also published (1995) Ross-on-Wye: PCCS Books.

Rogers, N. (1993). *The creative connection: Expressive arts as healing.* Palo Alto, CA: Science and Behavior Books. Also published (2000) Ross-on-Wye: PCCS Books.

Ross, C.A. (2000). *Bluebird: Deliberate creation of multiple personality by psychiatrists.* Richardson, TX: Manitou Communications, Inc.

Sampson, E. (1988). The debate on individualism: Indigenous psychologies of the individual and their role in personal and social functioning. *American Psychologist, 43,* 15–22.

Schmid, P. (2005). The Carl Rogers bibliography of English and German sources. *Person-Centered and Experiential Psychotherapies, 4,* 3&4, 153–265.

Seeman, J. (1949) A study of the process of non-directive therapy. *Journal of Consulting Psychology 13,* 157–168.

Snodgrass, J. (1984). William Healy (1869–1963): Pioneer child psychologist and criminologist. *Journal of the History of the Behavioral Sciences, 20,* 332–339.

Snyder, W.U. (1945). An investigation of the nature of non-directive psychotherapy. *Journal of General Psychology*, *33*, 193–223.

Snyder, W.U. (1947). *A casebook of nondirective counseling*. New York: Houghton Mifflin.

Snygg, D., & Combs, A.W. (1949). *Individual behavior*. New York: Harper.

Snygg, D., & Combs, A.W. (1959). *Individual behavior: A perceptual approach to behavior*. New York: Harper and Row.

Standal, S.W. (1954). *The need for positive regard: A contribution to client-centered theory*. Unpublished doctoral dissertation, University of Chicago.

Strupp, H. (1955). An objective comparison of Rogerian and psychoanalytic techniques. *Journal of Consulting Psychology*, *19*, 1, 1–7.

Stubbs, J., & Bozarth, J. (1994). The dodo bird revisited: A qualitative study of psychotherapy efficacy research. *Journal of Applied and Preventative Psychology*, *3*, 2, 109–120.

Suhd, M. (Ed.) (1995). *Positive regard: Carl Rogers and other notables he influenced*. Palo Alto, CA: Science and Behavior Books.

Taft, J. (1933). *The dynamics of therapy in a controlled relationship*. New York: Macmillan.

Tenenbaum, S. (1959). Student-centered teaching as experienced by a participant. *Educational Leadership*, *16*, 2. Republished as Carl R. Rogers and non-directive teaching. In Rogers, 1961a, (pp. 299–310).

Thorne, B. (1998). The person-centred approach in Europe: Its history and current significance. In B. Thorne & E. Lambers (Eds.), *Person-centred therapy: A European perspective* (pp. 1–22). London: Sage.

Thorne, B. (2002a). Biographical introduction. In C.R. Rogers & D. Russell, *Carl Rogers: The quiet revolutionary: An oral history* (pp. 1–19). Roseville, CA: Penmarin Books.

Thorne, B. (2002b). *The mystical power of person-centered therapy: Hope beyond despair*. London: Whurr Publishers.

Thorne, B. (2003). *Carl Rogers* (2nd ed.). London: Sage.

Truax, C.B., & Mitchell, K.M. (1971). Research on certain therapist interpersonal skills in relation to process and outcome. In A.E. Bergin & S.L. Garfield (Eds.), *Handbook of psychotherapy and behavior change* (pp. 299–344). New York: Wiley.

Vandenbos, G., Cummings, N., & Deleon, P. (1992). A century of psychotherapy: Economic and environmental influences. In D.K. Freedheim (Ed.), *History of psychotherapy: A century of change* (pp. 65–102). Washington, DC: American Psychological Association.

Vasconcellos, J. (1987). Carl Rogers eulogy, February 21, 1987. Reprinted in *Person-Centered Review*, *2*, 3, 353–361.

Walker, A.M., Rablen, R.A., & Rogers, C.R. (1960). Development of a scale to measure process changes in psychotherapy. *Journal of Clinical Psychology*, *16*, 79–85.

Wampold, B. (2001). *The great psychotherapy debate: Models, methods and findings*. Mahwah, NJ: Lawrence Erlbaum Associates.

Watson, G. (1940). Areas of agreement in psychotherapy, *Journal of Orthopsychiatry*, *10*, 4, 698–710.

Watson, J., Goldman, R., & Warner, M. (Eds.). (2002*). Client-centered and experiential psychotherapy in the 21st century: Advances in theory, research and practice*. Ross-on-Wye, UK: PCCS Books.

Watts, R. (1998). The remarkable parallel between Rogers's core conditions and Adler's social interest. *Journal of Individual Psychology*, *54*, 1, 4–9.

Wexler, D.A., & Rice, L.N. (Eds.). (1974). *Innovations in client-centered therapy*. New York: John Wiley & Sons.

KEY DATES

1902	January 8. Carl Ransom Rogers born, Oak Park, Illinois
1919	September. Begins University of Wisconsin, Madison
1922	February–August. "China Trip"
1924	June. Receives B.A. in History
	August 28. Marries Helen Elliott
	September. Begins Union Theological Seminary
1926	March 17. David Rogers born
	Transfers to Psychology, Teachers College, Columbia University
1927	June. Receives M.A. degree in Psychology
1927–28	Internship at Institute for Child Guidance
1928	Moves to Rochester, New York
	Begins as child psychologist, Rochester Society for the Prevention of Cruelty to Children
	October 9. Natalie Rogers born
1929	Appointed Director of Child Study Department
1931	Completes Ph.D. degree
	"Personal Adjustment Inventory" published
1938	Appointed head of Rochester Guidance Center
1939	*The Clinical Treatment of the Problem Child*
1940	January. Begins at Ohio State University
	December 11. Client-centered therapy "born," Minneapolis, Minnesota
1942	*Counseling and Psychotherapy*
1944–45	Working with the United Service Organization
1945	Fall. Begins at University of Chicago
1951	*Client-Centered Therapy*
1954	*Psychotherapy and Personality Change*
1956	September 4. First Rogers–Skinner debate
1957	Fall. Begins at University of Wisconsin
	"The Necessary and Sufficient Conditions of Therapeutic Personality Change"
1961	*On Becoming a Person*
1964	January. Begins at Western Behavioral Sciences Institute (WBSI)
1967	*The Therapeutic Relationship and Its Impact: A Study of Psychotherapy with Schizophrenics*
1968	"Journey Into Self" wins Academy Award ("Oscar")
1969	Center for Studies of the Person (CSP) splits from WBSI
	Freedom to Learn
1970	*Carl Rogers on Encounter Groups*
1972	*Becoming Partners: Marriage and Its Alternatives*
1977	*Carl Rogers On Personal Power*
1979	March 29. Helen Rogers dies
1980	*A Way of Being*
1983	*Freedom to Learn for the 80s*
1985	November. Rust Workshop, Austria
1987	February 4. Carl Rogers dies, La Jolla, California

INDEX OF NAMES, PLACES
AND ORGANIZATIONS*

---

*This index contains names from the entire book (excluding the References) and places and organizations from all but the References and the Endnotes. Names in quotation marks are typically pseudonyms for clients and patients.

701